Developmental Social Psychology

From Infancy to Old Age

Kevin Durkin

BLACKWELL
Publishers

First published 1995
Reprinted 1996 (twice), 1997 (twice), 1998

Blackwell Publishers Inc.
350 Main Street
Malden, Massachusetts 02148, USA

Blackwell Publishers Ltd
108 Cowley Road
Oxford OX4 1JF, UK

Library of Congress Cataloging in Publication Data
Durkin, Kevin
Developmental social psychology: from infancy to old age/ Kevin Durkin.
p.   cm.
Includes bibliographical references and index.
ISBN 0–631–14828–0 (acid-free paper) — ISBN 0–631–14829–9 (pbk: acid-free paper)
1. Social psychology. 2. Developmental psychology. I. Title
HM251.D83   1995   94–47664
302–dc20   CIP

British Library Cataloguing in Publication Data
A CIP catalogue record for this book is available from the British Library

Commissioning Editor: Alison Mudditt
Copy Editor: Sue Ashton
Production Controller: Lisa Eaton

Typeset in Garamond 10.5/12pt
by CentraCet Ltd, Cambridge
Printed and bound in Great Britain
by T. J. International Limited, Padstow, Cornwall

This book is printed on acid-free paper

Short Contents

Contents

Figures

Tables

Boxes

Preface

*It is hard to imagine an academic division of labour that is more formidable,
and at the same time more artificial, than the division between social and
developmental psychology*
                    (Lapsley and Quintana, "Integrative themes," 1985, p. 153)

I try sometimes to amuse my advanced undergraduate students by reminding them of their naive beliefs as First Years that psychology was going to be about "people." Some two or three years of disciplinary socialization have usually convinced them that psychology is, at its very best, about *aspects* of people.

Oddly enough, jokes about studying people do not set senior undergraduates rolling in the aisles. If anything, a grey pallor spreads across some faces at the hint that anything so tangled might come up in the exam. Let's face it: the last thing you would want or properly expect to encounter toward the end of a psychology degree would be a question about *people* – at least, not whole people, stuck together like some First Year's fantasy.

Before proceeding any further, let me hasten to disappoint readers who are beginning to suspect that they have run across, and would prefer to run over, a holistic, touchy-feely sort of evangelist who advocates that the best thing for the Psych Department would be to sit around holding hands in a circle, caring and sharing and ascending through ever happier strata of personal fulfillment. We can do that on Sundays (or thereabouts, depending on cultural factors), but the working week is still best devoted to theory and data.

In raising the specter of people, it is not being proposed here that current research in mainstream psychology is misplaced and misdirected. There are good reasons for studying people in bits. There is so much to be learned about each aspect (social behavior, motivation, mental processes, perception, development, motor skills, abnormalities, creativity, memory, language – the list goes on) that, to be manageable and nontrivial, research simply has to be compartmentalized. The rigorous investigation of complex phenomena demands highly focused specialists. The exponential growth of psychology during the twentieth century reflects the many achievements of researchers who were able to define precise, workable topics and design specific procedures for investigating them. The continuing successes of their endeavors means that anyone working or studying in psychology these days is aware that the field is enormous and the number of specialisms and subspecialisms is increasing relentlessly. Ever finer domains of knowledge are generated, with esoteric conceptual apparatuses and bodies of literature, any one of which alone could take years of labor to master – and just as you think you are getting there, some new direction, some new way of looking at things, will invariably emerge.

Enriching and demanding as the knowledge explosion is, it is difficult to shake off a nagging suspicion that somehow the bits have got to hang together. Presumably, people themselves manage this integration, and psychologists have at least occasionally to face the question: should we think about what each other is doing? The assumption here is that exciting work is progressing in many areas of the discipline and that new insights, new directions and, occasionally, even new solutions to old problems might be attained through mutual attention and joint efforts. This book attempts a preliminary step toward reviving the mutual interest of just two bits of psychology, two bits that would seem on the face of it to be quite close neighbors, and once were: social psychology and developmental psychology.

Drawing social and developmental psychology together is scarcely the most radical of ventures but, as Lapsley and Quintana forewarn above, it is an intimidating task. While it once seemed obvious that people's social behavior is connected to their development (past and future), the proposition now sounds like a venturesome leap across historically constituted boundaries. Yet ironically, at least some social psychologists once took pride in their discipline's unique position "that in a time of intellectual specialization and of social and political disintegration, it promises a view of man as an actor in historic crises, and of man as a whole entity" (Gerth and Wright Mills, 1954, p. xviii). Many contemporary social psychologists would blush at such a bold idea, but it is not obvious that the subdiscipline as a whole has profited sufficiently through lowering its sights while raising its methods. Many developmental psychologists would be content to assign these problems to other colleagues, but it is not obvious that this subdiscipline can sustain indefinitely the metaphor of the developing person as a bundle of capacities and processes that emerge with only minimal accommodations to the surrounding human context.

This is scarcely the first call to the reintegration of the efforts of social and developmental psychologists. Three collections of review chapters published in the early 1980s drew together a rich body of empirical work and forward-looking theoretical formulations (Brehm et al., 1981; Flavell and Ross, 1981; Higgins et al., 1983). Since then there has been an impressive chorus of calls for greater interchange and many examples of progress (e.g., Carugati and Gilly, 1993; Collins and Gunnar,

1990; Costanzo, 1992; Doise, 1989; Hartup, 1991; Monteil, 1993; Moscovici, 1990; Pratt and Norris, 1994; Ruble, 1994; Sigel, 1985, and others to be encountered later). At the same time, to access and evaluate much of the theoretical and empirical content of this groundswell depends on a grasp of material from two still largely independent fields. These are typically presented to students in separate packages – understandably given their respective magnitudes, but disappointingly given their potential mutual relevance.

It is not so much a matter of principle as a matter of practicality that psychologists of different specialisms rarely speak to each other, but nevertheless they are evolving their own vocabularies and even different dialects. This makes it particularly difficult for the student to integrate material from different courses. I hope that this book will assist the student interested in both developmental and social psychology, encourage her or him to seek further integration, and to approach each subdiscipline with an eye to its relevance to the superordinate goal, namely the scientific study of people as they live, develop, and change in the real world.

Acknowledgments

A few distal debts first. Some former teachers and supervisors may not recognize their influences over the genesis of this text, but they are there, and I would like to take the opportunity to say thanks. In particular, thanks to Jim Johnson for encouraging interests in language, and to Con Lodziak for alerting me to the excitement of social psychology and much more. Thanks to David Bruce for invaluable guidance over the years, hard to summarize in the space available. In addition, some former colleagues certainly ought to see their influence: I doubt I would have ever meandered into developmental social psychology without the guidance of Derek Rutter and Geoffrey Stephenson, from each of whom I learned a great deal and who both encouraged and facilitated an early optimism that this was a topic worth pursuing, or developing socially, as it were.

On to the proximal. I am very grateful to the following friends and colleagues who provided thoughtful critiques of draft material: Annemaree Carroll, Ron Davidson, John Hattie, Steve Houghton, Jason Low, Chris Pratt, Paul Sparks, Yasmin Turbett and Clive Wynne. Just mentioning their names scarcely seems to do justice to their efforts in ploughing through early versions, suggesting relevant literature, and supplying other materials – but mentioned each is, with many thanks. Even bigger debt is owed to Drew Nesdale who, as one of the few true-blue developmental social psychologists, provided extensive comments on large chunks of the text and has been a source of ideas, encouragement, and uniquely Drewish perspectives throughout my time in Western Australia.

At Blackwell, the early encouragement of Philip Carpenter ensured that this project began, and the extraordinary patience and goodwill of Alison Mudditt ensured that it concluded. It has been a pleasure, for me, to work with them and my only regret is that I have violated the reciprocity principle every time a deadline approached. An anonymous reviewer worked painstakingly through a first draft with careful attention to detail, a masterly sense of overview, and a generous fund of suggestions for further readings. Many thanks to Brigitte Lee and the production staff at Blackwell. And special thanks to Sue Ashton for exceptional copy-editing skills, perceptive commentary and good humor via the faxes.

I am grateful to various friends and their children, as well as to various friends and their parents, for joining the text as photographic subjects. Thanks to Herb Jurkewitz for photographic assistance and advice, and to the children and staffs of the Child Study Centre, the Child Care Centre and the After School Centre, all of The University of Western Australia, for carrying on as normal and allowing me to capture some of it on film.

Finally, my major debts are to my wife, Parvin, a truly wonderful invention.

Chapter 1

Introduction

It is as if social psychology and developmental psychology were concerned with the same thing, the former in space and the latter in time, the first by way of the exterior and the second by way of the interior.
(Moscovici, "Social psychology," 1990, p. 169)

But unless boundaries are permeable, they retard rather than sustain the growth of new knowledge.
(Hartup, "Social development and social psychology," 1991, p. 23)

In this introductory chapter, we consider first what developmental social psychology is, asking why we need it and how we might set about building it. We step aside briefly to consider what is meant by the term "social," a label whose connotations among psychologists range from the pejorative to the panacea. Then, we consider another key concept, socialization, again one which means different things to different investigators, but one which can readily be demonstrated to relate to much more complex processes than the "shaping" or "molding" processes associated with it in everyday language. Some of the challenges to explaining development are outlined in a review of four major theoretical traditions which influence much contemporary research. These, in turn, are cognitive developmental theory (we concentrate chiefly on Piaget), social learning theory, evolutionary theories (especially ethology and sociobiology), and ecological theory. Finally, we consider the relationship between developmental social psychology and the real world, and the relevance of research conducted in different societies and cultures.

What is Developmental Social Psychology?

Before we approach the task of defining developmental social psychology, a few words about its parents are in order. Both social psychology and developmental psychology prove resistant to firm definition. We could make a start with social psychology by describing it as a subdiscipline of psychology concerned with the scientific study of human social behavior. Beyond this, scope for differences in emphasis and for downright disagreement creeps in. Most contemporary social psychologists would endorse Allport's description of the subdiscipline as "an attempt to understand . . . how the thought, feeling, and behavior of the individual are influenced by the actual, imagined, or implied presence of others" (1968, p. 3). But an influential minority would accept Tajfel's (1981) insistence that the individual cannot be the only target of social psychology, and that an at least equally important level of analysis should be the inter-individual, socially shared organization of understanding within which social influence becomes possible.

This is a long-running debate, to some extent exemplifying the differences between North American and European social psychology. We will not resolve the matter here, but it is important to note it since we will draw upon work from both traditions, and it should become clear that a developmental social psychology has much to contribute to the understanding of the nature and origins of both social influence and social construction. (A fact not lost, incidentally, on either Allport, whose theories of individual differences in personality admitted at least some contribution to earlier experiences, or Tajfel, whose influential 1981 book bears the marked influences of Piagetian and Brunerian developmental psychology.)

Turning to developmental psychology, we find initial unanimity over the basic concerns of the scientist in this area: the developmentalist aims to describe and explain the changes over time in human behavior and capacities. (Although some develop-mentalists study nonhumans, their metatheoretical goals usually include a contribution to the understanding of humans.) However, there is considerable dispute over what is meant by *development*. For some, development entails qualitative, largely self-directed, reorganizations of knowledge and abilities; for others, it is principally a maturational process whereby endogenous properties unfold according to innate preprogramming; for others, it is largely a matter of the accumulation of learning from experience. Developmentalists vary, too, in terms of their willingness to embrace individual differences (cf. Bronfenbrenner, 1988; Kochanska, 1993; Plomin, 1987; Scarr, 1992), some treating them as little more than background "noise" that probably reflects variations in stage attainment or minimal fluctuations upon nature's design, others as conclusive evidence of the impact of the environment, others as the outcome of complex genotype–environment interactions, and still others as the outcome of even more complex genotype–culture–environment interactions. Again, we cannot settle these and related disputes at the outset, but they bear importantly on the emergence of a developmental social psychology, and we will encounter examples of variants of these positions at many places in this text.

The best we can do for the moment is to take from these comments a couple of secure tautologies: social psychology is concerned with the social (however defined), and developmental psychology is concerned with development (however defined). Why and how should we put the two together?

Developmental Social Psychology: Why?

The *why* question is the easier one to answer. We have already touched upon it, in admitting the possibility that human beings themselves integrate social existence and developmental change. It is elementary yet widely overlooked by social psychologists that the phenomena they study do not arise out of nowhere, forming miraculously just before their subjects come to university (more on undergraduate subjects in a moment). For the developmentalist, it is axiomatic that "unless we understand the source, we will misunderstand the outcome" (Nelson, 1981a, p. 98).

Let us consider just one example, from a topic dear to the hearts of experimental social psychologists: how people generate explanations of performance. Darley and Goethals (1980) comment that lay psychological analyses of performance (attribution theories) tend to place a great deal of emphasis on the concept of ability (see chapter 9), and that the paradigmatic cases of ability seem to be those involving physical performance, such as running or weight-lifting. The notion of a fixed upper limit associates readily with these examples of human abilities, but we appear then to transfer the same notion to other domains, such as intellectual performance. We think of people as having fixed amounts of intelligence, an endowment of IQ which they carry around with them (cf. Mugny and Carugati, 1985). Why should we show this physicalistic bias?

A plausible reason is that physical tasks have developmental priority. They are prominent among the early challenges facing the child and they involve overt behaviors with observable outcomes, which render them interpretable to the young observer (Dweck and Nicholls, cited in Darley and Goethals, 1980). Related reasons are that social feedback to the developing person about his or her abilities may be expressed in correspondingly concrete terms, because the adult infers that this level of explanation will be most accessible, and that adults often have the power to influence the child's circumstances so that the upper limit description becomes a self-fulfilling prophecy. The point is that the underlying metaphors we apply as adults striving to understand others' behavior may be influenced by what we could grasp when we first began to make interpersonal appraisals and by our parents' intuitive conceptions of how they could help us.

But the relevance of a developmental approach to social psychology extends still further, beyond charting the origins of social processes and capacities. Although the fact was disregarded by developmentalists themselves for a long time, it gradually became apparent through the work of lifespan psychologists that while there is life there is development (Baltes, 1983; Filipp and Olbrich, 1986). That is, the preserve of the developmentalist is not some period prior to the point at which the social psychologist takes over. Instead, developmental change is one of life's few constants (Blank, 1982; Bornstein, 1989b; Goodnow, 1988b; Jessor and Jessor, 1977; Lerner and Busch-Rossnagel, 1981). Yet if this is conceded, the implications for a *non*developmental social psychology are decidedly uncomfortable.

Jessor and Jessor (1977) comment that though change is inevitable, it would be difficult to find much recognition of the fact in contemporary behavioral science. Fiske and Taylor (1991) reach a similar conclusion in their hefty review of research in social cognition. In fact, in social psychology the chances of even stumbling across change are largely restricted to short-term reactions to laboratory manipulations conducted upon an unusual group of beings, *college-age students*. The college-age student is the paramount object of study in social psychology. Between two-thirds and four-fifths of the subjects of experiments reported in the prestigious journals of this subdiscipline fall into this social category (Blank, 1982; Sears, 1986). Clearly, social psychologists believe that there is much to be found out about college students, and social psychologists devote their considerable methodological skills to dissecting the intellectual and behavioral propensities of these interesting entities. Yet, as Blank (1982) and Sears (1986) demonstrate, one could easily develop a persuasive argument that there is much that is exceptional about college-age students.

The trouble with students

Blank (1982) and Sears (1986) point out that, among other characteristics, students are self-selected to be more achievement-oriented, they tend to be more egocentric than older adults, their cognitive performance is above-average, their social attitudes are not yet crystallized, and they are more compliant. (Who else would allocate several hours a week to being experimented upon? Who else would put up with our lectures?) Students spend much of their time in environments which promote rationalistic approaches to problems. In fact, there is evidence that becoming a tertiary student can affect (improve) your formal reasoning capacity, and that this is especially the case with psychology students and others exposed to probabilistic statistics and multifactorial explanations (see Lehman et al., 1988; these investigators also provide reassuring confirmation that only chemists withstand these aspects of the intellectual provocations of university life.)

It could be alleged that students read a lot. They tend to come from particular socioeconomic strata with higher-level occupational aspirations. Students are also in a transition phase of their own lives, and in many cases entry into adult life and full personal autonomy still lie ahead. On this basis, Sears calls you, dear readers, a bunch of "lone, bland, compliant wimps who specialize in paper-and-pencil tests" (1986, p. 527).

But the problem is even greater than this unhappy description suggests. Since North American universities are especially productive in social psychology, it is not surprising to find that the great majority of research papers concern not just undergraduate wimps, but *American* undergraduate wimps (Sears, 1986). This holds for the leading American research outlets, but Sears went to the trouble of checking on American researchers' publications in international journals, too. He found that even here they tended to restrict their subject selection to (American) undergraduates (rather than American adults, or people in different societies). Some of my best friends are or once were American undergraduates, but on the basis of careful inspection I feel drawn reluctantly to agree with Blank's conclusion that "In many ways they are uniquely unsuitable populations from which to derive general laws" (1982, p. 18). In fact, having met and taught students around the world, I believe we can venture a generalization beyond even America and conclude that universities everywhere are packed with distinctly unsuitable populations.

This does not mean that all experiments conducted with students as subjects are irrelevant or meaningless: students constitute an interesting level of human life, suitable for some purposes and problematic for others (though see Blank, 1982, for a more pessimistic conclusion). It does mean that student-sample research needs to be placed in context, as contributions to the broader study of social behavior and social reasoning rather than the ultimate test of the validity of theories. We nerds who teach and test you wimps are reluctantly facing up to the fact that, although you turn up reliably each year in compliant heaps of half-baked experimental fodder, you may not be giving us the full story of human social reasoning and behavior. (But please do keep turning up.)

The trouble with change

Another reason why change may be less prominent on the social psychologist's agenda is that when attention does extend beyond the college student and beyond the laboratory, the effects of change can be so radical that they terminate what is being investigated. Take, for example, the study of relationships, another principal focus of social psychologists and one where data certainly are collected in diverse environments off-campus (cf. Buunk, 1996; Duck, 1992; Fletcher and Fincham, 1991; Gottman, 1994). Maccoby and Martin (1983, p. 2) point out that in an adult–adult relationship, dramatic changes on the part of one member may lead to a reassessment and even abandonment ("He is no longer the person I married, and I'm out of here"), while in a parent–child relationship dramatic change is endemic and calls for continuous adjustment by both parties. Hence, developmentalists place change high among their concerns, while social psychologists sometimes regret it as a source of subject attrition. However, social psychologists have recently become increasingly interested in change in the course of relationships, and this itself is part of a broader shift toward a collaboration with developmentalists (see Hartup, 1991).

Limits to the scientific study of the intellectual development of the hermit

If social psychologists could profit from a developmental perspective, the reciprocal benefit is possible, too. While understanding the relationship between source and outcome is crucial, it is sometimes overlooked that unless we take into account the social context, we will misunderstand the process. Developmentalists vary in terms of their willingness to admit a social dimension to their work. Unfortunately, much of developmental psychology does rest on the assumption that the most interesting things to be discovered about the developing subject are best identified by removing him or her from everyday contexts and conducting tests of individual performance. But metaphors of the child as a hermit, or as a mini-scientist with his or her own laboratory, fly in the face of daily developmental reality (Bruner and Bornstein, 1989). It does not take a great deal of investigation to discover that their subjects do not grow up in solitary cells, and that whoever else is around, and whatever context they do develop in, have fundamental implications for the nature of development. We will see many illustrations of this point throughout this text.

In sum, the answer to the question of why we need a developmental social psychology is threefold. First, social processes have developmental histories. All of the phenomena studied by social psychologists come about as the results of development, and we can aspire toward a fuller understanding by investigating that development. Second, social processes occur in developmental courses: unlike snapshots of undergraduates, "lives in progress are moving targets" (Cairns, et al. 1989b, p. 294). A developmental aspect to social psychology is a prerequisite to both descriptive and explanatory adequacy. To the extent that social psychology ignores this, it risks becoming a science of proximal effects (Costanzo, 1992), studying what is happening now, and what impinges upon people only in their immediate circumstances, with scant regard to their goals and futures. Third, developmental progress is intimately related to social context: to the stimuli, prompts, guidance, examples, expectations, constraints, choices and impositions provided by other people and the social structures they maintain.

Developmental Social Psychology: How?

All of this rhetoric brings us to the *how* question, and here the answer becomes more difficult. Clearly, like all children, developmental social psychology will inherit characteristics from each parent. But it will also make its own discoveries, grow up in a unique environment, and learn from others outside the home. How can we set about nurturing its ontogenesis? There are at least three strategies that could be adopted;

each has been, and each makes an important contribution to the work we will be considering through this book.

Strategy 1: a developmental slant on social psychology

One strategy is to take some or all of the central topics of social psychology (attribution theory, social comparison, social influence, person perception, intergroup relations and so on), and ask: how could each of these develop? This is a perfectly legitimate question, and raising it has indeed given a major impetus to research progress. We will see in later chapters many examples of insightful research ventures based in this approach, and there is wide scope for valuable future contributions. A particular benefit of this strategy is that it broadens the outlook of developmental psychology, and guides developmentalists to new perspectives on their traditional concerns. During the past decade or so, work along these lines has been quite fundamental to the emergence of an identifiable new synthesis, the beginnings of a developmental social psychology.

However, I suggest that it does not, or should not, suffice *alone* as a definition of developmental social psychology because it sets the parameters too narrowly. That is, it assumes that social psychologists have already determined what are the important topics, and runs the risk of accepting meekly that the task of developmental social psychologists is to tag on to the accepted wisdom an account of how children pick up the pieces.

There are several problems with such a starting point. First, the idea that social psychologists have asked all the questions worth asking and delineated all the topics worth investigating is a presumption that would cause any self-respecting developmentalist to suffer severe assimilative dysfunction. Social psychologists themselves readily acknowledge limitations to the predominant "middle-range theory" (Merton, 1957; Tajfel, 1981) character of the discipline which results in a state of affairs where "the topics in social psychology read more like a Sears and Roebuck catalogue than like a novel. They provide a listing of items of possible interest to the reader rather than a story with a plot, development of characters, and so on" (Kelley, 1983, p. 8). Social psychology is an exciting and wide-ranging field, but it is itself still developing; it lacks unifying grand theories, and even its catalogue listings suffer some alarming gaps, perhaps because bits of people are dispatched to other specialisms. To take just one example, if we left it to social psychologists to chart what is important, we would still be debating whether language fits into the processes of social interaction – try, for example, to find half a dozen social psychology textbooks with a chapter on language. A measure of caution is due in following the lead of those who fail to notice what is just below their nose, ringing in their ears and pouring forth from their pens.

Second, to define the scope of a developmental social psychology in terms of what is already being studied in adults runs the risk of committing what has been referred to variously as "adult egocentrism" (Zaitsev, 1992) and "the myth of the adult ideal" (Kassin and Pryor, 1985). That is, we could assume that the main focus of a developmental social psychology should be the uncovering of deficiencies in the child (and, perhaps, the decline of the older adult). It is indisputable that measuring the child in relation to adult standards will often lead to the unsurprising outcome that children tend to get better at a lot of things as they get older. However, this directs our investigation toward inherent cognitive deficits rather than specific socialization experiences (Chandler, 1982; Higgins and Parsons, 1983; Kassin and Pryor, 1985). Equally importantly, Kassin and Pryor point out that it fosters a delusion in our investigations of adults, namely that they function as paradigmatic logical information processors – an image that has grown in popularity as a function of the cognitive revolution but which has been tempered increasingly by the rediscovery that people have feelings, habits, heuristics and biases and that they perform differently in different contexts. Social psychologists wonder where these features come from; developmental psychologists have a pretty good idea.

Finally, another risk of this strategy is that it creates a fraction of a fraction, leading to an ever more narrowly defined research area. Neisser remarked in a related context some time ago that the last thing social psychology needs is the creation of an ever more ingrown social psychology (1980, p. 603). A study group on developmental approaches to mainstream social psychological topics is a very worthwhile endeavor, but it is one which accepts others' listings of topics and hence is less ambitious in the generation of new questions and new directions.

Strategy 2: a social slant on developmental psychology

An alternative approach might be to take developmental psychology as our base, and ask: what are the social dimensions of the phenomena developmentalists study? Again, this would be a worthwhile question, and it is one that is raised from time to time among developmentalists. However, the same problems recur: developmentalists have their own catalogue, and the social section suffers from a lot of gaps as a result of the distance from social psychology.

A crucial problem is that there is not *a* developmental theory (i.e., a dominant paradigm that most people working in the field accept) that can be taken for granted and improved with an infusion of social psychology. Some years ago many, though by no means all, developmentalists might have pointed to Piagetian theory as a major framework that seemed to deliver much in terms of an explanation of the structures and overall course of child development. Piagetian theory remains a vital source of influence and inspiration but, as you learned in First Year and as we will see in later chapters, many of its basic descriptive assumptions have been seriously challenged, and fewer and fewer developmentalists subscribe now to this or other "hard" stage theories. Indeed, one of the recurrent causes of dissatisfaction with Piagetian and similar stage theories has been their limited success in accounting for the interactions of the developing person with the social context, and the variability in developmental courses and outcomes.

Furthermore, it is not clear that a "social slant" deriving from social psychology would always be as social as is required. Developmental research often points to the importance of social phenomena that are actually treated as peripheral by mainstream social psychologists. A striking example is work on social processes in the construction of knowledge. This has been a recurrent concern of developmentalists through the work of Baldwin, Wallon and Vygotsky and others, yet the individualistic bias of much experimental social psychology has largely precluded attention to the ways in which joint understanding is attained.

Strategy 3: define the topics of social development, and study them

A third approach is to determine certain topics that self-evidently are prominent in social development, and take them as the focus of study. Examples include parent–child attachment, family influences, peer relations. This strategy is highly desirable because it keeps both of the major scientific criteria (description and explanation) to the forefront. Through the twentieth century there has been a strong tradition of social developmental research organized around topics such as these. Clearly, this work provides one of the vital tributaries of developmental social psychology. Its chief limitation for present purposes is that although its academic origins are quite diverse (Schneider et al., 1989), it has tended historically to locate itself as a subfield of developmental psychology and thus has had relatively modest contact with the theoretical and conceptual offerings of social psychology. Indeed, even within developmental psychology, social development has traditionally been regarded as a separate compartment, largely isolated from what has been the dominant mainstream, namely the study of cognitive development (cf. Shantz, 1983, p. 495).

One more strategy

Strategy 4, of course, is to tick the "all of the above" box. Each of the strategies just summarized leads to interesting and important research questions, and a developmental social psychology has little to gain by discarding any of them. Indeed, they are sketched here as indications of the variety of approaches through which we could promote a developmental social psychology, not as a set of choices from which we must determine the most desirable. Henceforth, this book will draw from each, reflecting the healthy heterogeneity that characterizes this growing field. Quite simply, this reflects the assumption that there is more to be gained from the dialectics and cross-fertilization of juxtaposition than from burying forever beneath convenient subdisciplinary boundaries.

In later chapters, then, we will encounter examples of each strategy. The reader may care to reflect from time to time on how a given researcher has conceptualized a given problem, and whether a shift in strategy would lead to a useful alternative way of looking at the issue to hand. However, to settle the definitional matter for the present, developmental social psychology is taken here to refer to the areas of intersection between social and developmental psychology, acknowledging that different contributors would place different stress on each of the adjectives in our awkwardly compounded title. I am sorry if, after all this prelude, the definition does not sound more exciting, but I hope that the content will be.

It should be added that many of the investigators whose work is drawn upon in this text would not necessarily call themselves developmental social psychologists, but this scarcely matters. The fact is that their work contributes to the overall task of the hybrid, which is to explain how human beings develop in social contexts and how social contexts are affected by human development. Pursuing these multi-layered questions is not facilitated by an exclusive definition or by a reluctance to consider diverse perspectives.

Two Key Concepts: Social and Socialization

Two terms which we will encounter repeatedly are "social" and "socialization." Many, especially those who prefer not to study them, take the meanings of these terms to be obvious, but this gives rise to widespread misunderstanding in neighboring areas of psychological literature. It is useful to note briefly some of the considerations involved in each, because explaining what is involved in social life and development, and in socialization, are critical long-term goals of developmental social psychology, rather than self-evident processes that we can already take for granted.

Social

The term "social" is used in different ways – we have already seen that even social psychologists dispute its potential meanings. More interestingly, among psychologists, it elicits different affective reactions. Naturally enough, it is regarded as a positive by those who embrace it and whose work is concerned with what they define as social phenomena. However, it is viewed with some suspicion by many whose theoretical and research interests derive from other approaches to development (which have been very productive through the middle of the twentieth century) focused on processes presumed to be *internal* to the developing child, namely the emergence of his or her cognitive capacities. We will consider this emphasis shortly, but for the moment it is worthwhile to take note that preoccupation with individual cognition – especially object-centered cognition – has led some traditional developmentalists to misleading assumptions about what is involved in social processes.

For example, in an otherwise theoretically sophisticated and informative book on the origins of face recognition, Johnson and Morton (1991) distinguish different types of approach to the study of development. In their terms, these include the *cognitivist* (emphasizing the information-processing capacities and limitations of the young), the *ethologist* (emphasizing the evolutionary adaptiveness of behavior) and the *neuroscientist* (emphasizing the development of the brain). For Johnson and Morton, these are the good guys. In addition, Johnson and Morton mention a fourth approach, which they call the *"social perspective."* This is the bad guy. According to these authors' interpretation, the social perspective "focuses on the identification of aspects of the social environment that influence the developing young ... but this is often to the neglect of the physiological and psychological changes which undoubtedly occur *within the young organism*" (p. 1; italic added). Notwithstanding the fact that faces (the main focus of these researchers' work) tend to be found positioned outwards on the upper frontal region of social beings and serve a number of important interpersonal functions for them, Johnson and Morton never mention the social perspective again.

No doubt sufficiently diligent literature searches could uncover someone, somewhere, who advocated a social perspective as caricatured in this passage, but it would be extremely difficult to find a contemporary social developmentalist, or a social psychologist more generally, who espoused such an impoverished view of human social and developmental processes as that which Johnson and Morton attribute to them. (Johnson and Morton do not cite any examples, and I find it equally hard to identify any.) What we will find as we venture further into developmental social psychology is that a social perspective necessarily entails attention to the biological and the cognitive, and a great deal more besides.

It is possible that Johnson and Morton had in mind someone like Watson who once proclaimed:

> Give me a dozen healthy infants, well-formed, and my own specified world to bring them up in and I'll guarantee to take any one at random and train him to become any type of specialist I might select — doctor, lawyer, artist, merchant-chief, and, yes, even beggar-man and thief, regardless of his talents, penchants, tendencies, abilities, vocations, and race of his ancestors. (1924, p. 82)

Watson was making a stimulating polemical point, but it remains the case that medical and law schools still find themselves obliged to rely on a complex interaction of ability, interests, socioeconomic background, political prejudice, chance and the right accent to sift through aspirant new professionals. The behaviorist's faith that "training" alone determines a person's development has been tempered over the decades as the complexities of the social world have become more apparent.

What is fundamentally at error in the biological-cognitivist's caricature of the "social perspective" is that it posits *unidirectional* influences. The core notion is that society "does something" to the child. This is not really a social process at all, because all the action is one-way. For reasons that will become clearer as we proceed, social developmentalists have long rejected this view, stressing that children are not simply the targets of outside forces but are actively involved in their interpersonal worlds, seeking information, eliciting reactions, processing their experiences, predicting outcomes, and both collaborating and conflicting with others as they come to understand and participate in the social world (Bandura, 1986; Corsaro, 1993; Dunn, 1988a, b; Maccoby and Martin, 1983; Schaffer, 1984a, 1992; Youniss, 1992). For these reasons, cognitive and biological perspectives are each quite essential to a social account of human development.

One reason why the social perspective cannot afford to overlook the psychological processes that occur within the organism is that the representational task in the social domain is considerably more demanding than that faced by the version of the information-processing child who never meets people. To borrow just one metaphor from a more persuasive account of a social perspective, Strayer et al. (1989) suggest a comparison between the representational challenge to a chess Grand Master facing simultaneous multiple opponents and the representational challenge to a preschooler facing day-to-day life in the kindergarten. The Grand Master has the easier task because the rules are fixed, the possible moves agreed in advance, and all interactions are one-to-one; social life is rarely so straightforward.

It is also important to avoid confusing *social influence* with *compliance* (Emler and Dickinson, 1993, p. 186). Social influence, Emler and Dickinson suggest (after Moscovici), involves complex processes of interpersonal and cultural negotiations, and these are demonstrably widespread in human existence from childhood onwards. In contrast, compliance is a behavioral acknowledgment of superior forces, and need not necessarily imply any underlying change or development in the actor. There is no doubt that in extreme circumstances (such as fulfilling First Year laboratory course requirements) some humans are obliged to comply to others' directives, but accounts of this pragmatic response should not necessarily serve as a model for the essential processes of social development. Only in misrepresentations of social perspectives is this presumed.

What, then, is involved in *social* life? Another view of social processes – and one which does find greater favor among some developmentalists – is that "social" means something akin to "harmony." We will encounter in later chapters important research which points to the joint, collaborative activity of partners (parent–child, teacher–child, child–child) in achieving cognitive advancement. One interpretation of this work could indeed be that social activity is a happily shared venture in which initially discrepant perspectives converge. There is much evidence that this is part of the story.

However, there is also scope for divergence, and divergence and conflict may be vital strands of social interchange and social development. Rather than a bed of harmony, there are respects in which "social life is a battlefield, in which diverse and contradictory influences permanently confront each other and where there is no such thing as a stable equilibrium of forces" (Codol, 1984, p. 316). Codol's summary, intended as a description of adult social life, could equally well serve as a motto for the developmental social psychologist. It captures an essential feature of the nature of social relations at any one point in time, and it emphasizes the ineluctable characteristic that was stressed earlier: change. As will be seen in later chapters, this does not mean that conflict is invariably a negative or destructive phenomenon – to the contrary, we will consider in later chapters arguments that not only are conflicts inevitable in development but also that some conflicts can enhance the nature and course of cognitive development, language development, and social relationships.

In short, "social" means different things to different psychologists, but it is straightforwardly a mistake to confuse it with unidirectional influence and, arguably, an oversimplification to equate it with harmony. It is also an oversimplification to suppose that the biological and the social are separate and that it is possible to study one without the other (see Bateson, 1987; Oyama, 1986).

Socialization

Socialization is the process whereby people acquire the rules of behavior and the systems of beliefs and attitudes that equip a person to function effectively as a member of a society. At a general level, developmental social psychology is the scientific study of socialization. Although socialization is a process experienced by most, it is observed directly by none: we can watch how some parties (e.g., parents, teachers) attempt to socialize others (e.g., children) but the ways in which these regulatory actions are incorporated into a developing person's social understanding and behavioral repertoire can only be inferred. Similarly, the activities of those who attempt to do the socializing are themselves multidimensional; their goals, strategies and reasoning are complex, and their consequences for development are difficult to unravel (Goodnow and Collins, 1990; Siegel et al., 1992). Socialization is often referred to as a given — as a straightforward process which is already understood — but in fact it remains a fundamental challenge to developmental social psychological theory.

It is interesting to consider that influential social psychologists once regarded socialization as "the central theme of social psychology" (Sherif, 1948, p. 1). Wundt (1900–1920) believed that adult social reasoning and behavior had to be understood as the outcome of lengthy developmental processes. Newcomb and Hartley (1947), charged by the American Society for the Study of Social Issues with the responsibility of compiling a text representative of the major themes of social psychology, produced a collection which not only allocated a large section to socialization but also included many other chapters drawing on research with young subjects: in those days, it seemed perfectly natural to integrate the study of social behavior with the study of social development. Lewin (1952), who regarded the segmentation of social and developmental aspects of behavior as an "utterly fruitless" exercise in pedantic classification, used issues in socialization to illustrate what he held as major concerns for his field-theoretic approach to social psychology. Brown (1965, p. 193) pointed to socialization as "the meeting ground of social science, of general psychology, and of the psychology of personality. It may reasonably be designated the central topic of social psychology." Yet as social psychology expanded and fractionated, socialization became less central and the topic slid naturally off toward the developmentalists — not all of whom turned out to be interested, for reasons indicated above.

Rather than dismiss the study of socialization as peripheral to the more fundamental problem of illuminating the psychological processes within the organism, it is useful to reflect briefly on the scale of matters to be dealt with in becoming socialized. There are two primary subgoals of socialization, namely *individuation* (determining one's own personal uniqueness) and *social connection* (discovering how to relate to, learn from, and function with other people; Costanzo, 1992; Shantz and Hobart, 1989). The rules of behavior and the value systems of a society cover an enormous range of phenomena, from the daily domestic practices of an individual's family and personal network, through the public expectations of the community concerning the behaviors appropriate to age, class, gender, and other social categories, to the understanding of societal structures and elaboration of moral systems. Learning to operate effectively in respect of each of these involves not only building a massive information base but also changing one's personal responsibilities and capacities for action (for example, shifting through childhood from dependency to autonomy). Furthermore, many parties and institutions may be involved – including parents, siblings, peers, church, school, mass media – and the contributions of any one may complement or conflict with the contributions of others. To reiterate an earlier point, socialization, although typically studied in the young, never ceases, since progress through life involves learning new roles, entering new relationships or institutions, adjusting to new developments in one's community and myriad other accommodations to a continually changing social environment. These are not just external events that happen to people, but ongoing involvements that are at the core of being human. Furthermore, they are not one-way processes, but involve influences acting in each direction (Bell, 1968). Hence, the study of socialization is multifaceted, and part of the reason why there is a proliferation of theories of socialization is that there is so much to account for. An overarching task of developmental social psychology is to explain how socialization comes about.

Theoretical Backgrounds to Developmental Social Psychology

Developmental psychology has many theories, social psychology has still more. As already noted, social psychological theories tend to be of the middle range, concerned with some specific topic or process, such as social comparison, attribution, and so on. These theories do generate important research questions, and we will consider them in later chapters. Developmental psychology produces "grander" theories, in the sense that they attempt to embrace and explain more phenomena and to provide more general, unifying accounts of human development. In this section, we will consider four of the most influential developmental theories: Piaget's cognitive developmental theory, social learning theory, evolutionary theories (ethology and sociobiology), and ecological theory. Social development and socialization are by no means the exclusive or even the central concerns of each of these theories, but each has important implications for how we conceive of these processes. As we address specific topics in the course of this book, applications, extensions, and variants of these theories will recur and it is useful to have some familiarity with their basic concerns and claims. An overview of each theory follows, with a note of some of the major criticisms that have been raised of it, and then a brief summary of each theory's implications for the study of social development and socialization.

Cognitive Developmental Theory

Contemporary developmental psychology is pervasively influenced by Piaget's theory of genetic epistemology, a theory which attempts to explain the origins and development of knowledge from infancy through to the higher levels of adult scientific thought (see Piaget, 1972, 1973a). Piaget's theory is wide ranging, reflecting his own theoretical influences from the fields of biology, philosophy, physics, mathematics, logic, and various psychological traditions, including psychoanalysis and Gestaltism. From the 1920s to the time of his death in 1980, Piaget led a major school of research, applying and testing his model in relation to many aspects of child reasoning. The enduring product is a body of ideas, insights, and techniques that provide a continuing source of inspiration and controversy to subsequent generations of developmentalists.

The sheer scale and diversity of Piaget's writings is worth stressing, if only to advise the reader that the overview which follows is necessarily incomplete. Some familiarity with Piagetian theory will be assumed at various places in this book, and the following is intended as a reminder of the principal tenets rather than a comprehensive introduction (see Flavell, 1963). Still more to the point, it is worth bearing in mind that Piaget himself entertained such a broad theoretical framework that it is somewhat risky to accuse him of overlooking anything. Thus, while it will be seen later that Piagetian cognitive developmentalism has fostered an image of the child as a kind of independent, mini-scientist engaged in an individualistic confrontation with the mysteries of the spatiotemporal environment, Piaget himself actually accorded social factors a prominent status in the explanation of the genesis of knowledge. Indeed, Piaget maintained that social psychology comes into all of the general problems to do with psychology, and argued strongly in favor of the study of the structures and processes of social coordination (cf. Piaget, 1973a, p. 26ff), insisting that inter-individual exchanges were a prerequisite to the formation of a "decentered epistemological subject" (Piaget, 1970, p. 361). Contemporary Piagetians vary in terms of how much note they take of this feature of the theory, but some have argued that the Piagetian framework has a great deal to offer to social psychology (cf. Doise, 1989).

The beginnings of knowledge

For Piaget, the beginnings of knowledge can be traced to action. The child enters the world with a limited set of reflexive, sensorimotor capacities which form the basis for its discoveries about its surroundings and its relationship to them. Through acting upon the world (initially, in a very primitive mode of touching, grasping, looking, listening) infants gain limited but functional bodies of information and schemes for further action. Thus, from the beginning the child is *adapting* to the world as it finds it and *organizing* its own elementary structures of knowledge. For example, the infant discovers that it can grasp things, and it applies this simple manual capacity repeatedly; the infant discovers that sucking elicits milk, and it begins to open its mouth or engage in sucking motions on the approach of the nipple (Piaget, 1936). Pick up a 2-month-old and you will find, whatever your gender, that it will turn optimistically toward your bosom. Presumably, the infant does not have a conscious theory of how to get fed, but it does have an active scheme for directing its feeding apparatus.

From these kinds of schemes, the infant's experiences become increasingly predictable and certain regularities become discernible in the environment. If the reach-out-and-touch action results in an interesting outcome (perhaps a mobile above one's crib moves and tinkles), then repeating the action should result in a repetition of the outcome. Babies make these discoveries within the first few months of life, and so become able to exert increasing amounts of control over their surroundings. In due course, they become aware that objects tend to continue to exist, that they can be retrieved if they fall out of sight or uncovered if placed under a cloth. They notice similarities and differences among objects, and experiment with the use of different objects in different functions. Eventually, toward the end of the second year, they begin playfully to make objects symbolize other objects – a bowl becomes a hat, a spoon serves as a makeshift "telephone" to gabble into like other people do, and so on.

Notice the constructive nature of the infant's discoveries. A scheme is established and repeated until it is familiar. Then, this body of knowledge is assumed as the child goes on to find out more, including more complex possibilities and combinations. This results in more advanced schemes which in turn serve as the base for further explorations. Two central points of Piagetian theory are illustrated here: (a) the child seeks actively to build its own "theory" of knowledge rather than merely absorb lessons from more skilled people; and (b), what the child can learn is constrained by what it already knows – the scheme for how to video-record a TV broadcast is not going to emerge in an infant who is still working on how to control the mobile above his or her crib.

Mechanisms of development

In Piaget's view, the child's cognitive development is very similar to that of organic growth (cf. Gold, 1987; Piaget, 1970). Both are characterized by *organization*, whereby the available information is structured into coherent systems, and *adaptation*, whereby the developing organism adjusts to the prevailing conditions in the environment. Two complementary processes are continuously involved in the course of development, *assimilation* and *accommodation*. Assimilation describes the integration of new information or experiences into existing organization; accommodation describes the modifications of existing structures to deal with new discoveries. Piaget maintains that "there is no accommodation without assimilation" (1970, p. 8).

Piagetian stages

The kinds of action that we have considered so far have in common that they are all organized around the infant's sensorimotor capacities. There is a qualitative similarity among them, an elementary way of dealing with the world that is based essentially on what can be handled, watched, and heard. In Piaget's view, this characteristic unifies early intelligent action: he refers to the period from birth to around the age of 2 years as the *sensorimotor stage*. The stage is not a static period, and throughout the child is working actively to discover more about the world and her or his effects upon it. Eventually, however, the infant's expanding repertoire and its new discoveries lead to a new level of understanding. The ability to symbolize is the forerunner of important new capacities: the child will shortly be able to conceive of a world beyond the here-and-now of its earlier physical experiences, a world in which it is possible to have a much greater influence over events and activities. In other words, there is something of a revolution in the child's thought, a break-through into a more sophisticated way of dealing with oneself and one's environment. This transformation is not instantaneous, but it is radical and, according to Piaget, consists of a shift into a new stage of cognitive development: the *preoperational* stage.

The stage concept is one of Piaget's best-known (though most controversial) contributions to developmental psychology. A stage is conceived of as a develop-mental period during which the child's thought is organized at a particular level. The child's responses to a variety of tasks will be characterized by broadly similar mental strategies. We have already seen that during the sensorimotor stage, the infant's activities are organized around physical and sensory activity. Although there are certainly developments within a stage (the sensorimotor period is sub-divided by Piaget, 1936, into six substages), at any one point the child's per-formance in one domain should be broadly consistent with her or his performance in another.

Further illustrations of this underlying unity can be obtained when we consider the *preoperational stage*. In this stage, which extends from approximately 2 to 7 years, the child is developing capacities to represent the world. We have already touched on the emergence of symbolic capacities, and a particularly important one is the development of language, which advances rapidly during this period. According to Piaget, language is one manifestation of representational capacity. Others, which also develop during the preoperational stage, include pretend play, imagination, and pictorial representa-tion (Piaget and Inhelder, 1966). But the preoperational child's thought is also subject to certain pervasive limitations. Two of the most studied are egocentrism and inability to conserve.

Egocentrism   Egocentrism refers to what Piaget saw as the preoperational child's inability to take the perspective of others. Remember that the child thus far has been conceived of as striving to master a complex and often mysterious environment, and to discover her or his own capacities. As symbolism emerges, it is organized around the child's own construction of the world, and at this stage the child finds it difficult to conceive of the possibility of other perspectives. To take some standard examples, the egocentric child fails initially to understand that certain relationships are reciprocal. For example, a 4-year-old girl with a sister might confirm that she has a sister. But does her sister have a sister? The 4-year-old might well say no, because having exhausted her data base on sisters in the family she cannot consider how things look from her female sibling's position. If the 4-year-old is asked next to reflect on the movements of the moon, she might explain that the moon follows her wherever she goes: this is obvious, because if you walk a distance and then look up again, it is still exactly the same distance from you. These areas of knowledge – sibling relations and the physical structures of the universe – seem quite remote, but the child's underlying cognitive organization is reflected in similar (egocentric) ways in her reasoning about each. Piaget and his colleagues provided many other examples in many other domains (Piaget, 1929).

Conservation   The preoperational child's alleged inability to conserve is demonstrated in Piaget's classic conservation of liquid task, and many variants. The child is shown two beakers of equal size, containing identical amounts of liquid. The child agrees the contents are equivalent. Then, the contents of one beaker are poured into another of a different shape, say taller and thinner than the originals. The child is asked whether the contents of the old beaker and the new are the same amount. Preoperational children typically insist that they are not – asserting, for example, that there is more in the tall one because the liquid is higher there. Similar results are obtained with transformations of amount (e.g., reshaping one of two balls of plasticine), length (e.g., moving one of two identical sticks so that the ends are no longer aligned), or number (e.g., taking two equal rows of coins and spreading one out); in each case, the preoperational child is likely to report that the amount, length or number has changed. In other words, the same stage of reasoning is reflected in several different tasks.

According to Piaget, underlying both egocentrism and failure to conserve is a mental tendency toward *centration*. Centration refers to a focus on only one aspect of a phenomenon. The child concentrates on her relationship to her sister, but finds it difficult to consider the reciprocal aspect of the link; faced with a transformed volume of liquid, she notices the increase in height, but overlooks the corresponding reduction in width.

Moving on to the next stage, *concrete operations* (from approximately 7 to 11–12 years), we find that the child is now able to handle many of the problems that were beyond the preschooler. The concrete operational child can conserve, and can conceive of the reverse of transformations (e.g., he or she can imagine the liquid from the tall, thin beaker being poured back into its former container and returning to the same level). The child's thinking during this stage is more logical and more flexible; he or she can classify sets of stimuli and can order them (for example, from smallest to largest). However, these new mental operations tend to be limited to stimuli that are either directly available or easily represented. Hence, the child can think about problems involving concrete objects but finds abstract representations such as algebra or symbolic logic too difficult.

The final stage of Piaget's model is entered (by those who reach it) during early adolescence. This is the period of *formal operations*, during which the child develops new abilities in abstract reasoning. At this stage, the young person can formulate hypotheses, conceiving of possible states and outcomes without requiring a concrete representation. The formal operational thinker can work systematically through a series of factors and combinations of factors to achieve an understanding of a particular problem. If this sounds like the activities of a scientist, it is no coincidence. Piaget sees the formal operational stage as the culmination of a long process through which the child has been observing, manipulating, theorizing, testing, and revising understanding in ways directly analogous to the development of scientific enterprise (cf. Piaget, 1972).

Given the logical sequence of the stage structures and the fact that each higher stage develops from its predecessors, it follows that Piaget regards the sequence as invariant. That is, each individual must proceed through them in the above order, although it is accepted that the pace of development and the ultimate level attained may vary as a function of environmental stimulus and other opportunities.

Criticisms of Piagetian theory

There are many criticisms of Piagetian theory and much evidence to contradict Piagetian accounts of what children can and cannot do at different ages. Although Piagetian theory remains influential in developmental research, the main thrusts of subsequent work have tended to undermine the notion of hard stages and to contradict Piaget's rather negative characterizations of infants' and preschoolers' competencies (for a variety of critiques see Bryant, 1974; Donaldson, 1978; Gelman and Gallistel, 1978; Wood, 1988; for a discussion of other stage theories, see Thomas, 1992). We will return to some of the specific issues elsewhere in the book, but for the moment three main issues should be noted. These concern the lopsidedness of applications of the theory, Piaget's ambivalence about the role of social factors in development and Piaget's neglect of the child's emotions.

Lopsidedness   Chandler (1977, 1982) has pointed to an irony in much Piagetian work that, despite the supposed interweaving of assimilative and accommodative processes in the construction of all knowledge, in practice Piaget and his followers emphasize the child's stage as the essential determinant of how she or he will approach a given task and the resultant knowledge. The standard approach for a Piagetian is to take a problem and attempt to uncover qualitative differences in how children of different stages tackle or explain it. This has its appeal, and alerts us to the possibility of important changes in how children reason, but it neglects the other side of the relationship — that is, the *content* of what the child is acquiring. It supposes that all meaningful variation lies within the child. In contrast to theories which represent the child as the passive victim of external forces, it is almost as if the *environment* is passive and there to be assimilated (Chandler, 1982; see also Hurrelmann, 1988). In short, "by this lopsided standard, people are seen to be lost in a subjective world of their own making" (Chandler, 1982, p. 226).

When we look more closely at social development, and in particular at the relationship between the child's reasoning about the social world and her or his social experiences, the liabilities of lopsidedness become clearer. For example, Higgins and Parsons (1983), while not denying that cognitive development may well involve qualitative changes, stress that many societies organize the child's life in a series of broadly arranged, age-segregated "social life phases", each bringing its own formal institutional structure and behavioral expectations. Hence, it is possible that at least some of the changes that develop-mentalists tend to explain in terms of progress in the child's cognitive capacities are actually reflections of advances or changes in the child's circumstances (see also Light, 1993).

The role of social factors in development   As indicated above, Piaget was too broad a thinker (and too frequently the recipient of critical feedback) to overlook something as pervasive as social factors in child development. Certainly, in one major work which continues to remain a valuable source to more socially oriented developmentalists, he did stress the importance of peer interactions as a mechanism of discovery (Piaget, 1932; see chapter 14). But this theme did not endure as a principal focus of Piaget's work, still less of the research of Piagetians more generally. Similarly, while Piaget saw a powerful relationship between intellectual advance and social context, much of his description of formal operational reasoning is focused on abstract logical achievements in terms of combinatorial logic. One of the defining characteristics of formal operational thought is the ability to conceive of different possibilities. Piaget and Inhelder (1966, p. 149) emphasize the source of these possibilities:

> In reality, the role of social factors (in the twofold sense of socialization and cultural transmission) is far more important and is favored more than was suspected by the intellectual transformations we have been discussing ... the world of value also can remain bound by concrete and perceptible reality, or it can encompass many interpersonal and social possibilities.

Nevertheless, in practice, most of Piaget's own research was devoted to topics seemingly at some remove from the social domain (such as the child's understanding of space, time, physics, probability). Assuming that these topics are asocial is itself something of a delusion, as Piaget's own comments above indicate and as became clearer when cross-cultural psychologists attempted to replicate the supposed universals of Piagetian theory in different environments (cf. Cole et al., 1971; Greenfield, 1976; Jahoda, 1986). More to the point, Piaget's methodologies – clinical interviews and experiments – focused on the reasoning of the individual child.

The neglect of emotions   Piaget studied so much that it may appear mean-spirited to object that he did not find a few extra years to squeeze in feelings. In fact, he did touch on affect in several works (e.g., 1936, 1973b; Piaget and Inhelder, 1966). Nevertheless, the enthusiasm which he inspired for the study of cognitive development led effectively to the neglect of emotions (Cicchetti and Pogge-Hesse, 1981; Cowan, 1978). Yet performances on Piagetian cognitive tasks – and, more importantly, actions in everyday life – are closely linked to emotional responses. Examples include pleasure at mastery, frustration at failure, boredom with familiar or undemanding stimuli, and anxiety in the face of uncertainty (Cicchetti and Pogge-Hesse, 1981; Cowan, 1978). This suggests, at the very least, that the two systems are unlikely to be independent. Piaget acknowledged this, but emotions remained peripheral to his theory and to later Piagetian research (see Cowan, 1978, for a discussion of the potential). Certainly, in much of Piaget's major work, one of the principal sources of emotional excitation was largely disregarded: interactions with other people.

   Note that this problem is by no means unique to Piagetian developmental psychology, but cuts across much work in cognitive development. In North American developmental psychology in recent years, cognitive developmentalists have been greatly influenced by information-processing models of cognition, in which the metaphor of the child as a mini-scientist is married with that of the child as computer. This approach, too, runs into similar difficulties. As one leading information-processing researcher puts it, the developing person is too often conceived of as "a cold, calculating chunk of hardware" (Dodge, 1991, p. 159), and this may not be the optimal metaphor upon which to base accounts of social development. It is striking that much recent work in information-processing accounts of child development has converged on the conclusion that the computer accounts for only so much, and that there is an urgent need to understand factors such as affect, mood, social context, and sociocultural variability (see Dodge, 1991, on emotions; Martin, 1991, on sex-role development; Stewart and Pascual-Leone, 1992, on moral development). While differing from Piaget over some of the details, information-processing theories share the premise of the individual as a solitary scientist – and run into similar problems.

In sum, Piaget's work makes many contributions to the study of child development, and has laid down paths that many other researchers have demonstrated to be worth following. But not all details of his accounts of development have withstood empirical challenge, and there are areas of neglect. The neglect is most marked in respect of social factors in development.

Social Learning Theory

Social learning theory derived initially from learning theory, the behaviorist school which was dominant in North American psychology through the first half of the twentieth century. Although in important respects social learning theory goes beyond earlier learning theories, it has in common with them a fundamental assumption that environmental contingencies play an important role in guiding behavior: "From the social learning perspective, human nature is characterized as a vast potentiality that can be fashioned by social influences into a variety of forms" (Bandura, 1973, p. 113). Or (for readers who like to spot the differences and accommodations to critics): "from the social cognitive perspective, human nature is characterized by a vast potentiality that can be fashioned by direct and observational experience into a variety of forms within biological limits" (Bandura, 1986, p. 21).

The early learning theorists were interested in child learning as one example of the processes of conditioning through stimulus–response associations (Watson, 1928), and later leaders in this field held that desirable behaviors could be encouraged by rewarding them when they occurred (Skinner, 1953). Although these models are important in the history of psychology, and still have enormous direct and indirect impact upon educational systems and parenting beliefs, their relevance to developmentalists was largely superseded by the advent of social learning theory, especially the version introduced by Bandura and Walters (1963), and subsequently elaborated, expanded, and revised by Bandura (1973, 1977) and Mischel (1973, 1979), and then re-named by Bandura (1986) as social cognitive theory.

Bandura and Walters (1963) felt that most extant research in learning theory was limited as a basis for explaining social behavior and personality development, for a number of reasons. First, most of the work had been conducted either on animals or on individual subjects in one-person situations. Generalizations from the pigeon in its Skinner box to the human in her or his social environment were supportable only by very generous assumptions. Second, the early learning theories could not account for the production of meaningful behaviors that had not been previously reinforced. Third, it is readily demonstrable that, even when attractive reinforcement is available, a subject cannot produce a behavior that she or he has never encountered before. Fourth, if (as Skinner and others maintained) novel behaviors were the outcome of successive approximations to desired behavioral patterns by operant conditioning, then human learning would be necessarily a very slow affair, since parents would have to wait a long time until a desirable behavior occurred spontaneously that they could then begin to work on. Fifth, children sometimes avoid a particular behavior, irrespective of their own reinforcement history for that behavior, if they see someone else receive punishment for it.

A more parsimonious mechanism to account for these facts about learning is *observation*. Observation speeds up considerably the process of discovery, and helps to explain how children can sometimes produce (imitate) behaviors for which they have never been reinforced, as well as avoid those which they have seen get others into trouble. Thus, Bandura and Walters introduced what has remained one of the most widely studied mechanisms in the field of social development, namely *observational learning*. It should be stressed that this was a continuation of the learning theory tradition rather than a radical break with it. Bandura and Walters maintained the importance of rewarding consequences: "Indeed, social behavior patterns are most rapidly acquired through the combined influence of models and differential reinforcement" (Bandura and Walters, 1963, p. 5).

In subsequent work, Bandura responded increasingly to the cognitive revolution that began in psychology in the 1960s, and focused attention particularly on the information-processing activities which are held to mediate the relationship between modeled events and matching performances by the learner. In due course, partly to clarify the distinctions between this cognitively oriented theory and early learning theories, Bandura (1986) relabeled the theory as *social cognitive theory*. Unfortunately, this new label, while good for the theory, is disastrous for the textbook writer, since there are at least two other meanings of the term "social cognition" enjoying widespread application in developmental and social psychology (we turn to these in chapters 9–11). Furthermore, much of the important empirical work accumulated in the social learning tradition has continued to retain the old label. Hence, for the sake of simplicity, in most parts of this book I will retain the old label (social learning theory) except when referring to distinctive features of the more recent formulations.

Learning from models

Bandura and colleagues point out that the child has access to an abundance of information via models (parents, siblings, teachers, media personalities, neighbors, and so on). But this does not mean that a child imitates all and sundry, buffeted randomly from behavior to behavior as she watches first her mother, next her father, and later the TV weather forecaster or the milk delivery person. Social learning theorists propose that children pay greater attention to some models than others, and that a number of factors influence what they will do on the basis of what they learn. Importantly, observing and learning a behavior does not necessarily mean that one will enact it oneself, and a behavior could be learned but not performed until a later time.

Vicarious consequences

One of the most useful things that models can do for us is provide illustrations of the consequences of *their* actions. If we see that groveling to the boss enhances a colleague's career progress, we learn an important fact about reward contingencies in the workplace; if we see our older brother scolded for swearing in front of Aunt Matilda, we learn about potential hazards in the interpersonal environment. In the first case, we experience vicarious reinforcement, in the second vicarious punishment. Bandura and Rosenthal (1966) demonstrated that classical conditioning effects (aversive reactions to a stimulus associated with negative consequences) can be induced by observing someone else experience an unpleasant outcome as a result of a hitherto innocuous action. Clearly, models can furnish us with a good deal of useful information.

The acquisition–performance distinction

Watching what is going on around us is one thing, actually enacting the observed behavior is another. As indicated, social learning theory does not hold that the latter invariably ensues. There is abundant evidence that it does not: life would be greatly simplified if all we had to do to meet our own needs was to watch the powerful and attractive reach high office, inherit wealth, or win Wimbledon – and then do the same. Bandura (1977), drawing on the information-processing paradigms dominant in North American psychology, proposed that the relationship between a modeled event and the matching pattern of behavior is mediated by four levels of process: attention, retention, production, and motivation.

Attention The onlooker's scrutiny of the potential model may be influenced by several factors, including the *distinctiveness* of the model and his or her attractiveness and power. For example, we may find the hero of the movie more attention-worthy than the villain or a bit player. Whether the behavior has *functional value* for the onlooker may also influence attention – how you handle your boss may be of little interest to me if I am unemployed. Other considerations include the *arousal* of the observer, his or her *expectations* about the model, and his or her own *past reinforcements*.

Retention Not all modeled events are equally comprehensible; if we find something difficult to understand, we are less likely to encode, retain, and reproduce it. Whether or not we use memory strategies (organization, rehearsal) has consequences for what we retain.

Production   Even if we attend to and retain a modeled performance, we may lack the skills necessary for its reproduction. This is why a Wimbledon championship is not on the agenda for most of us, and more generally why many actions produced by older individuals are not immediately replicable by many children.

Motivation   The key motivational processes, according to Bandura, are reinforcements, which may be direct external consequences, vicarious reinforcement, or self-reinforcement.

Notice that these processes can be applied by any (human) learner in almost any learning situation. The outcomes will be influenced by individual competence and age-related abilities but the potential for acquiring new information and enacting new performances is not dependent upon being at a certain stage of development. In other words, one of the distinctive features of social learning theory is that it predicts the lifelong ability of the individual to learn (Hurrelmann, 1988).

Reciprocal determinism

Although social learning theory is often interpreted and applied as a "shaping theory" (see Maccoby and Martin, 1983), Bandura himself has long stressed that the theory does *not* represent the person as the helpless victim of environmental influences. Nor does he favor the thesis that something in the person and something in the environment simply "add up" to determine behavior. In Bandura's view, it is an oversimplification to depict "individual" and "environmental" factors as independent influences: "Contrary to this assumption, the environment is only a potentiality, not a fixed property that inevitably impinges upon individuals and to which their behavior eventually adapts. Behavior partly creates the environment and the resultant environment, in turn, influences the behavior" (1973, p. 43).

The process through which this comes about is described by social learning theorists as *reciprocal determinism* (Bandura, 1977, 1986). An individual's characteristics (personality, beliefs, cognitive abilities) will influence his or her selections in the social environment: who to play with, what to do, what to avoid. These selections in turn influence the opportunities that he or she finds to develop skills and to learn about the consequences of particular attributes and behaviors. An aggressive child, for example, might find that she gains control over peers. This may be rewarding, and encourage her to maintain this form of behavior. In turn, the social environment will adapt to characteristics of the child. In the case of this aggressive individual, some peers may reduce interactions with her while others will be interested in aligning with her, controlling her, or defeating her. People are both products and producers of their environment (Bandura, 1986).

The self and social learning

Another important emphasis in Bandura's work is the role that the self plays in the regulation and evaluation of behavior. Two particular aspects of the self have been the focus of much work in social learning/ social cognitive theory: self-monitoring and self-efficacy.

Self-monitoring As a result of modeling and reinforcement, the self incorporates societal standards and monitors whether own behaviors are in line with adopted standards. In this way, behavior is regulated even in the absence of external reinforcement: "There is no more devastating punishment than self-contempt" (Bandura, 1971, p. 28).

Self-efficacy Self-efficacy refers to the individual's belief that he or she can exercise some control over events that influence his or her life (Bandura, 1986). Self-efficacy is intimately connected to motivation, since people's judgments of their own capabilities are likely to affect their expectations about their future behavior. Perceptions of self-efficacy influence how one responds to perceptions of a discrepancy between one's own behavior and that of a model. If you feel that the model's actions are within your range then you may attempt to emulate, but if you have a low sense of self-efficacy in respect of the modeled skill, then you may demur. These expectations, one's sense of self-efficacy, do not arise out of nowhere but reflect the individual's prior history of attainment and reinforcement. They have implications for future attainments, since a high sense of self-efficacy is likely to promote further efforts and experimentation, while low self-efficacy could result in avoidance of opportunities and challenges. A great deal of research has supported the relevance of self-efficacy as a dimension of personal mastery and goal-setting throughout the lifespan (Berry and West, 1993).

Criticisms of social learning theory

Social learning theory has many points of overlap with mainstream social psychology, especially in the North American tradition, which emphasizes external influences upon individual behavior. It takes the "exterior" and examines its implications for childhood (and other) learning. However, it has some limitations in terms of what it has to say about the "interior". Although current versions place great emphasis on internal cognitive processes, the theory is often criticised for failing to take note of cognitive *development* (Grusec, 1992; Grusec and Lytton, 1988; Maccoby and Martin, 1983; Perry and Bussey, 1984). Bandura (1986) certainly assumes changes in information-processing capacities with maturation and experience, but resists the notion of general structural reorganizations as a response to conflicts between developing understanding and empirical discoveries, as proposed by Piagetian and other cognitive developmental psychologists.

Another objection is that notions of reward, reinforcement, and punishment, although central, are not very clearly defined (Hogan and Emler, 1978). Hogan and Emler comment that the implicit definition is circular: something is reinforcing if a subject finds it reinforcing. Others have complained that Bandura's acknowledgment of biological factors is little more than lip-service, and too much emphasis remains on situational variables (Scarr, 1992; Wallace, 1993). Social learning theorists tend to be dismissive of the notion of personality as a major feature of social behavior, and do not address in detail the nature and origins of human emotions (Wallace, 1993).

Finally, despite its title, social learning theory is curiously limited in its conception of social context and social influences. The principal mechanisms of the social environment are taken to be modeling and reinforcement but, apart from this, little attention is paid to the ways in which other people help us to construct and enter the social world, how we acquire shared representations of interpersonal and societal phenomena, and how social arrangements make possible some developmental routes and inhibit others.

Evolutionary Theories: Ethology and Sociobiology

Studying the histories, successes and failures of various forms of life, Darwin (1859) came to the conclusion that evolutionary selection ensures that species are organized around two priorities: survival and reproduction. Those who do survive and prosper will pass on to their descendants the genetic characteristics that led to their own success; those who are less adaptive meet a different fate.

Darwin's theory has proven a useful basis for the explanation of many aspects of evolution. Although much work in evolutionary biology has been concerned with nonhuman species, scientists have also attempted to explore the implications of the theory for the study of humans. Two, related, manifestations of the theory have attracted considerable support as accounts of the bases of human social organization. These are ethology and sociobiology. Although neither theory is a psychological theory (that is, they are not concerned with human mental processes), they do raise interesting issues for the study of social development, and have been very influential in respect of both theoretical and methodological concerns in this field.

Ethology

Ethology is the study of animal behavior, with particular reference to behavior in natural environments (Eibl-Eibesfeldt, 1989; Hinde, 1982, 1992). Much ethological work is concerned with nonhumans, but humans are an interesting subset of the primates, and many ethologists have attempted to apply their methods and theories to the study of this species. Modern versions owe much to the work of Lorenz (1935, 1963) and Tinbergen (1953, 1973), European naturalists who emphasized the role of biological factors in the causes of behavior, and Bowlby (1969) who developed a highly influential account of mother–child attachment based on ethological theory and evidence of cross-species similarities in adult–young bonding. Leading contemporary ethologists include Eibl-Eibesfeldt (1989) and Hinde (1988, 1992), both of whom have elaborated the implications of ethological theory and methods for the social sciences.

Ethologists maintain that the behavior of members of a species is based at least in part on an inherited repertoire of capacities and responses. Ethologists are skeptical of the view – assumed by many psychologists and other social scientists – that behavior can be understood principally in terms of skills and information learned by each individual in the course of his or her development.

Consider some of the kinds of phenomena that ethologists study, and it is easy to see why they attribute much of the causation of behavior to nature. For example, many species appear to be preprogrammed to react to specific threatening stimuli (such as the color of the breast of some male birds, the angle of approach of certain predator fish, the baring of teeth by another canine); these kinds of signals often inspire fight or flight. In the terms of the early ethologists, fight or flight reactions are examples of *Erbkoordinationen* or *fixed action patterns* (FAPs), triggered by particular stimuli and designed to ensure the survival of the actor. Other preprogrammed behaviors serve to facilitate reproduction (such as birds' songs, preening or postures that signal sexual interest) and others to maximize the survival prospects of the young (such as building nests, rolling back into the nest any eggs displaced to the edge, attacking or diverting creatures that approach the young; see Hinde, 1982).

As we will see in later chapters, humans display some behavioral tendencies that are very similar to those that ethologists find in the wilds of nature. We are alert to threat signals from members of our own species and others, we engage in courtship rituals, we protect our young who are endowed with certain properties that serve to evoke our affection (cute faces; cf. Lorenz, 1943) and solicit interventions (crying; cf. Bowlby, 1969). Much of our day-to-day behavior is organized around basic concerns similar to those of the species we regard as lower. We give priority to our requirements for resources, such as foodstuffs and protection against the elements, and we do not take kindly to anyone who gets in the way of our access to these necessities; we strive to establish comfortable nests in the best positions we can get, and furnish them with materials we find in forests or on the backs of other animals. We may be a good deal more sophisticated than the humble chaffinch or the crested newt in our means of fulfilling our biological needs, but it is irrefutable that such needs are there, and that much of human social life is organized around them.

We should note certain particular strengths of the ethological approach. Hinde (1988) maintains that one of the distinctive features of ethology is in the *orienting attitude* it fosters toward the scientific study of humans. Ethologists insist that the first step of a rigorous scientific investigation must be to *describe* the phenomena of interest. Very few scientists, psychologists included, would disagree with this axiom, but not so many honour it in practice. Hinde comments that experimentally oriented psychologists may have been too eager to follow the scientific model of physicists, setting up highly contrived tests of abstract theories in laboratory contexts, instead of examining carefully exactly how humans behave and develop in their natural habitats. One of the major contributions of ethology to the study of social development has been via painstaking observational investigations of children's and parents' behaviors in authentic environments, such as homes, playgrounds, and schools. Still more importantly, the orienting attitude of the ethologist leads him or her, following Tinbergen, to ask of any behavioral phenomenon under investigation: what were the causes? How did it develop? What is its function? How did it evolve?

For the ethologist, then, attention ranges from immediate causation through to the evolutionary derivation of physical and behavioral capacities. One merit of this perspective is that it places human behavior in a broader setting than the history of a single hypothetical individual, the decontextualized "subject" of much psychological research.

Sociobiology

Sociobiology is a particularly controversial offspring of ethology. Sociobiologists share ethologists' interests in the application of Darwinian evolutionary theory to the social behavior of animals, including humans (Barash, 1982; Smith, 1987; Trivers, 1985; Wilson, 1975, 1978). The boundaries between the two approaches are not very distinct, and both maintain that a species' social behavior is organized to maximize its survival fitness. However, sociobiologists draw more extensively upon population genetics and some have tended to make bolder – more deterministic – theoretical statements about the implications of genetic survival for group and societal organization.

In its earliest and most polemical formulations (e.g., Wilson, 1975) sociobiology was promulgated as a biological explanation of social behavior which could dispense with most of (what the hard-nosed biologists regarded as) the fanciful conceptual fictions of the social sciences. Instead, everything could be explained by genetic endowment:

> Pavlov was simply wrong when he postulated that "any natural phenomenon chosen at will may be converted into conditioned stimuli." Only small parts of the brain represent a *tabula rasa*; this is true even for human beings. The remainder is more like an exposed negative, waiting to be dipped into developer fluid. (Wilson, 1975, p. 156)

As will be seen in chapter 13, based on revised accounts of the links between genes and fitness, sociobiologists have been able to formulate interesting solutions to longstanding paradoxes such as altruistic and self-sacrificial behavior. Another and especially controversial proposal is that of *parental investment theory*, the notion that an individual's behavior toward partner and offspring is governed by the costs and benefits of investment (Kenrick, 1994; Trivers 1985). This theory bears on some of the central relationships of interest to developmental social psychologists – namely those between men and women, parents and children – and we return to it in later chapters.

Early relations between psychology and sociobiology were not especially friendly. As a new beast eager to stake out its territory in a competitive environment, sociobiology was fond of taking agonistic postures and issuing threatening war cries (see Wilson, 1975, 1978). In turn, the very mention of biology is something of a red rag to many social psychologists, and biologically based theories are sometimes dismissed as flippantly as bio-cognitivists discard social perspectives. More recently, sociobiologists have moderated many of their more extreme deterministic claims, and psychologists have begun to take seriously the implications of a sociobiological perspective (Archer, 1996). Interesting prospects for some degree of synthesis are on the horizon (Buss, 1992; Crawford et al., 1987; Jackson, 1992; Kenrick, 1994;

MacDonald, 1988a, d; Smith, 1990; Vine, 1983). M. S. Smith (1987) shows that biological and psychological approaches to development are not necessarily incompatible, although they may often focus on different levels of analysis. Developmentalists, for example, have come slowly to acknowledge that development proceeds through the lifespan rather than just the first two decades; sociobiologists contend that humans as a species have been developing for thousands of years, and that what has been going on through this period might well bear on the status of human capacities as we currently find them.

At present, attempts to relate sociobiology to psychology are concentrated chiefly on enriching the theoretical framework of a model that has proven useful in the study of lower species but faces conceptual hurdles when directed toward us. But these interpretations have shifted the theory a long way from Wilson's early thesis that the "genes hold culture on a leash", and at the same time have raised very clearly issues that psychologists in general, and developmental social psychologists in particular, can scarcely afford to ignore.

Criticisms of biologically based theories of social behavior

We will meet a number of counter-arguments to specific proposals in later chapters, but three main critical objections may be noted for the present. These concern the issues of testability, biological determinism (i.e., the implication that biology is destiny, and that humans have no free will or self-determination), and the lack of a developmental perspective.

One of the major limitations of evolutionary theories is that in place of predictions, they offer retrospectives. That is, they provide accounts of how species adapted and then rest on the rather circular logic that we know these were the most adaptive strategies because they worked. Hence, the falsifiability of ethology/ sociobiology is often questioned (see Thomas, 1992): since we cannot manipulate or re-run evolution, how can we test their claims?

E. O. Wilson (1975), as a leading spokesman for the first wave of sociobiology, was dismissive of notions such as free will, emotional loyalties and culture, and, as we will see in chapter 5, sociobiologists and other evolutionists have been prone to extreme views of sex differences in behavior and achievement. It has been argued (e.g., Valsiner, 1989b) that many sociobiologists tend to confuse societal motivations (such as the need to reproduce) with individual reasoning, ignoring the mediating variable of culture. However, most contemporary ethologists and sociobiologists with interest in humans acknowledge the distinctiveness of this species in terms of its capacities to reflect consciously on its behaviors and social structures and to take deliberate steps to adjust them (cf. Barash, 1982; Hinde, 1988; Trivers, 1985).

Criticism of the lack of a developmental perspective is justifiable to a point, but this reflects areas of neglect and mutual suspicion rather than an inevitable schism. For example, Strayer et al. (1989) develop a cogent argument that evolutionary theories can explain not only humans' advanced cognitive abilities as an outcome of selective pressures, but also the emergence of social practices which facilitate development and adaptation to specific local conditions.

There are at least two ways of looking at biology. One is as the source of fixed limits; the other is as the source of immense potential. Many biological accounts, including some applications of ethology and sociobiology to the study of humans, have emphasized the former, deterministic, interpretation and sometimes these theories have been exploited to provide scientific justifications for inequities in societies (such as racial and sexual inequalities). But the rather circular reasoning which underpins these applications need not be embraced in order to acknowledge that human beings are biological organisms with finely adapted capacities and skills which have evolved over a long time and which permit us to tackle our environment in uniquely effective ways. It has to be said that much remains to be done to bring about a synthesis of evolutionary theories and developmental theories but, as sociobiologists have adapted beyond the teeth-baring epoch of their early work, the scope for fruitful interchange is becoming greater.

An Ecological Theory of Human Development

We have now considered broad theoretical perspectives which address, variously, issues of intra-organismic change, the influence of experiences and observational opportunities, and the impact of evolution. None of these approaches has a great deal to say about the contemporaneous social system within which new members of society are developing. Bronfenbrenner's (1979; Bronfenbrenner and Crouter, 1983) ecological approach provides a much more comprehensive attempt to explain the ways in which interactions among social structures affect the content and course of human development.

Bronfenbrenner represents the ecological environment as an interrelated series of environmental structures, each nested in the next "like a set of Russian dolls" (1979, p. 3). He proposes that the basic unit is the dyad, the parent–child relationship. The dyad itself is intimately related to the larger interpersonal structures, especially the nuclear family but also the other prominent social structures of everyday life, which may include the extended family, neighbors, friends, and others with whom the dyad interacts on a face-to-face basis. These complex interrelationships form a *microsystem*, a pattern of activities, roles, and interpersonal relations which are experienced by the developing person in a particular setting with particular physical and material characteristics (p. 22).

Microsystems are themselves nested within *mesosystems*. A mesosystem consists of the interrelations among two or more settings in which the developing person participates, such as home, school, and neighborhood. These in turn are nested within an *exosystem*. The exosystem consists of social settings which do not themselves directly involve the developing person as an active participant, but do provide contexts which affect the mesosystem and microsystem. Components of the exosystem, for example, include the extended family, parents' workplaces, the mass media, community services, and the educational system; the availability and quality of each of these may have implications for how a given family and its microsystems are organized. Finally, the outer shell of the series is the *macrosystem*, the belief systems and ideologies of the culture, which constitutes a pervasive set of values around which societal life is organized.

The ramifications of the structure at the outer level are readily demonstrated. For example, suppose the macrosystem is that of an advanced industrial society, placing the production of wealth at the top of its priorities. This has obvious consequences for how workplaces are structured and for the society's requirements of its educational system. As a result, adults attend the workplace for a certain proportion of their time and compete for advancement and rewards, while children attend the school for a certain number of years in order to acquire the skills to participate in the workplace. The exosystem takes on a particular shape to meet the society's broader economic and ideological priorities. Suppose that within the exosystem the available workplaces have no provision for child care and no part-time employment for males (reflecting other ideological assumptions about the optimal division of labor). In this context, a two-parent family might be obliged to organize its division of labor such that the father takes a full-time job and the mother undertakes principal caregiving responsibilities. Thus, the most basic of units – in this case, mother and child – wherein the developing person begins his or her discoveries about life is circumscribed by values and arrangements prevailing at seemingly remote levels.

Most readers of this book will live in societies that have a macrosystem similar to the above. But part of the force of Bronfenbrenner's model is to remind us that we should not assume the universality of our own macrosystem nor the developmental contexts and experiences it affords. Even among Western societies, Bronfenbrenner emphasizes, ostensibly the same "blueprint" could take on subtly different meanings in different nations (e.g., Bo, 1994; Cotterell, 1994). And if we look more widely, we find very different systems of social organization with very different consequences for development (see, for example, Tietjen, 1994). A still more important contribution of Bronfenbrenner's perspective is that it elevates developmental social psychological theory from the level of linear effects assumed in much of behavioral science (i.e., the idea of direct cause–effect relations among social variables) to a broader conception of the interrelations among systems (see Minuchin and Shapiro, 1983, for a fuller discussion of the implications for scientific paradigms).

Criticisms of ecological theory

One of the attractions in principle of Bronfenbrenner's model is that it offers a potential bridge between developmental psychology and social psychology. The problem is that the factors he highlights – the nature of social systems, the mutual consequences of different levels of societal organization – are actually neglected by much of contemporary social psychology. This is scarcely Bronfenbrenner's fault, but it points to an obstacle to integrating the theoretical perspective with what is actually available in social psychology.

It has been objected that the theory does not lead to very precise and testable predictions (Thomas, 1992) though, again, this may reflect the difficulties of fitting the theory in with existing developmental research, much of which has neglected contextual variables as depicted by Bronfenbrenner. Certainly, Bronfenbrenner (1979) articulates a long list of clear hypotheses about the relationship between development and social ecology, at least some of which have been supported by Bronfenbrenner's own research and others offer rich prospects for future researchers. Thomas (1992) holds that, none the less, the theory is imprecise about the relations among microsystems (e.g., how does involvement in family relate to involvement with peers?), about the implications of the diversity of social roles that an individual may have (e.g., son, older brother, friend, student) and the relative strength of system components (e.g., the effects of parents versus schooling versus media exposure versus peer pressure).

As Collins and Gunnar (1990) comment, Bronfenbrenner's emphasis on the impact of economic conditions on human development raises particularly urgent themes for applied research in contemporary societies which are developing large underclasses of people cut off from mainstream employment and living conditions. Perhaps the fairest conclusion at present is to agree with Thomas (1992) that not as much empirical work has yet emerged to test and develop this theory as has been the case with others, but it remains a very important reference point for developmental social psychologists because it attempts to deal head on with something that is addressed rather more indirectly by other theories: namely, the real world.

Implications for the Study of Socialization and Social Development

We have considered four quite different approaches to the study of human development. This by no means exhausts the theoretical perspectives that bear on different topics in developmental social psychology, but it provides a preliminary overview of the wide range of considerations that are relevant. We leave specific illustrations to later chapters, but let us return to a key concept, socialization, and note how each approach would represent it.

The central premiss of Piagetian theory in this respect is that the child is engaged in *self-socialization* (Ruble, 1987, 1994). Piaget sees the child as embarking upon an active search for information that will guide his or her social behavior. Mastering this information proceeds through a series of qualitative reorganizations, and an individual's intellectual status at any one point governs how he or she deals with new information or problems. Social learning theories place greater emphasis on the influence of environmental variabilities, but (especially in Bandura's social cognitive formulation) also regard as crucial the cognitive processes which guide how the learner attends to, retains, and retrieves information from his or her social experiences. In social learning theory, development is continuous rather than stage-like. Ethological, sociobiological, and related theories highlight genetic imperatives and heritability, but most accounts admit important contributions due to local conditions (MacDonald, 1988a). Bronfenbrenner's ecological theory also gives priority to the environment (though not denying that biology is implicated), and heightens sensitivity to the dynamics of intersecting social systems.

There are, then, considerable overlaps among the major theoretical approaches sketched here, as well as important differences. An emphasis on biological endowment is shared by both the ethological/sociobiological tradition and the Piagetian; stress on cognition as a mediator of behavior is common to Piagetian theory, ecological theory, and later models of social learning theory; each theory acknowledges some influence due to environmental factors. *All* of the theories acknowledge that human behavior and development entail biological and learned patterns as well as cognitive activity. There are differences among them in terms of the relative weights attached to different factors, but most stress that biology and learning cannot be separated neatly.

This is the point at which most of the major theories are beginning to converge. It would be difficult to find a theory which did not admit at least some level of interactionism in this sense. What remains problematic is to explain exactly how the interactions proceed. On the one hand, different theorists have come, grudgingly or otherwise, to acknowledge the relevance of factors other than those which they give priority; this reflects increasing theoretical maturity (and the benefits of social interaction among those with conflicting perspectives). On the other hand, these varying accommodations make each theory a little less distinctive and a little less falsifiable. And, furthermore, there is still a great deal left unexplained and under-investigated.

One way to perpetuate this state of affairs would be to haul up the factional drawbridges and concentrate on refinements to each theory within the safety of each subdiscipline. Another would be to confront the intersections, not only of the theories introduced here, but of other productive frameworks for the study of human social behavior and its development. This is essentially why we need a developmental social psychology. In the chapters which follow, the issues introduced here will recur many times. In many instances, proponents of the different theoretical perspectives offer competing explanations; elsewhere they focus on different levels of analysis; in some cases, research into certain topics has been dominated by one perspective and proponents of the others have tended to stand at a safe distance. Out of these efforts, and through increasing connections with mainstream social psychology, a develop-mental social psychology is emerging.

Developmental Social Psychology and the Real World

One of the distinctive features of developmental social psychology is that it bears on real-world issues and problems. Where possible, in this text I draw upon events and relationships in everyday life to illustrate the processes and phenomena that scientists are studying. Referring to the real world every now and again serves as a constraint upon a science that aims to explain the development and behavior of human beings, so much so that it may appear self-evident to the newcomer that the developmental social psychologist ought to take note of what is going on outside the laboratory. Self-evident perhaps, but surprisingly often disregarded in the parent subdisciplines. In a book entitled the *Social Psychology of Everyday Life*, Argyle (1992a) remarks that electing to write about this broad topic (everyday life), seemingly very much the preserve of social psychology, actually necessitates filling in the gaps that the field frequently overlooks.

Argyle would have a good deal more gap-filling to undertake were he a developmental psychologist. In this context, the focus of enquiry has often been conceived of in splendid isolation not only from the real world but even from any other human contact. As we have seen and will see again, many developmentalists have adopted models of the child as an isolate, functioning as a mini-scientist working all alone in the societal laboratory, as a biologically preprogrammed organism with most of its major behaviors ordained by nature, or as an information-processing calculator who quietly remits data from mental store to mental store. These metaphors have served useful short-term purposes, but time and time again careful study of human development has led to the conclusion that it takes place in real worlds, involving real people in interaction.

Developmental Social Psychology and Culture

As soon as we begin to contemplate the real world, of course, it is inescapable that there are many different versions of it. For the cultural psychologist, "reality" is the outcome of the ways in which members of a culture represent and share their collective understandings and values (Shweder, 1991). Actions or events that are ostensibly the same on the surface may have quite different meanings within different cultural contexts. For example, as simple an action as spanking may be regarded as a quite trivial child management technique in one culture, and a brutal form of abuse in another (Walters and Grusec, 1977); a day out at Disneyland is a socially approved reward in Anaheim, a vulgar descent into the cultural wilderness outside Paris.

Attention to culture is also important because it reminds us that a historical perspective on human nature is not the exclusive preserve of the ethologist or sociobiologist. Culturally oriented developmentalists also emphasize the importance of evolved patterns of behavior and ways of reasoning. Cross-cultural developmentalists, such as Cole (1992), argue that biology and the environment do not interact directly, but that their interaction is mediated by culture, which is constructed dynamically over a long time. Cole maintains that the fact that we evolve cultures is itself an important biological characteristic of our species, and the types of cultures we construct reflect our properties and our adaptations to specific environments: "the form of our nurturing is our nature" (p. 8). In a similar vein, LeVine (1989) points out that even biological givens, such as the capacity to acquire language, take on meaning only when they intersect with actual human contexts.

Unfortunately, developmental social psychology is hampered in its inclusion of culture by the lack of an agreed definition. The natural tendency to seek help from specialist neighbors is unlikely to attract a straightforward reply (Cole, 1992; Triandis, 1994). Cole (1992) estimates that definitions of culture among anthropologists run into several hundred. Cole's own concept of culture, which derives from Vygotskyan theory (discussed in chapter 11), is that human beings live in environments that have been transformed by the discoveries and artifacts of past generations, and that these artifacts serve to coordinate human beings' social organization as well as their relationship to the physical world.

This book does not aim to provide a wholly cross-cultural approach to developmental social psychology, not least because much of the leading work we draw upon here is restricted to just a handful of cultures with much in common, especially North American and European. But in the study of social development, social reasoning, and social behavior it is important to keep in mind that different cultures afford not only different things to learn but different ways to do the learning. Cross-cultural comparisons provide valuable natural laboratories, varying factors that experimenters cannot normally manipulate within a culture for ethical and practical reasons (Hopkins, 1989; Rogoff and Morelli, 1989), and they promote caution in the rush to deduce universals from data collected only from selected or convenient communities within the First World (Greenfield, 1994; Jahoda, 1986; Triandis, 1994).

Developmental Social Psychology and Methodologies

Many methods are exploited by the psychologists whose work we will consider in this volume. There is no revolutionary new developmental social psychological method. Although developmentalists have become keenly aware that the experiment is itself a form of social interaction (Bronfenbrenner, 1979; Davis, 1991; Garton, 1992; Light, 1986), it remains one of the most prominent and most effective tools of the discipline, and we will encounter innumerable examples of ingenious, rigorously designed, and meticulously controlled applications of this approach, both in laboratories and in the field. But there are other valuable techniques, too, including clinical interviews, observational studies and case reports. Developmental social psychologists employ cross-sectional and longitudinal designs. At various points in the text we will take note of findings from neighboring disciplines, including anthropology, sociology, and linguistics, where still different methods are exploited. Because this book is aimed at advanced undergraduates, it is assumed that the reader already has some familiarity with the strengths and weaknesses of different research methods, and for the moment the purpose of these comments is to remind you that each makes its contribution and each has its limitations (see, for example, Manstead and Semin, 1996; and Sabini, 1995, on methods in social psychology; Bremner, 1994; Shaffer, 1993; and Smith and Cowie, 1992, on methods in developmental psychology).

Choice of topics

Any textbook has to be selective, and not all topics or all research that could be treated under the heading of developmental social psychology have been included. My choice of topics has been guided by the four strategies for a developmental social psychology outlined above, and by what is available (and missing) in the literature. Some topics to be discussed in later chapters could be found in most developmental psychology textbooks (morality, language), and others in most social psychology textbooks (attribution theory, social comparison, nonverbal communication), and several in both (sex roles, prosocial behavior, aggression). What is remarkable about some of the latter is that, as indicated above, the vocabulary and dialect of each subdiscipline has evolved a body of literature that is almost – not completely, but almost – independent of its neighbor. I am not confident that I have overcome all of the translation problems, but I hope to be able to convey to the reader from time to time something of the differences and overlaps in the ways social and developmental psychologists have approached topics of mutual concern.

No topic in the book has been treated exhaustively, and one of my most difficult tasks was in deciding what to leave out. To assist the reader reluctant to become the sort of compliant wimp who accepts uncritically everything that she or he reads in a textbook, suggestions for *further reading* are given at the end of each chapter which will provide starting points for pursuing specific topics in greater depth. Obviously, the best source of material beyond the textbook is the scientific literature itself. Much of this research can be found by consulting the relevant periodicals, and the chapters that follow aim to provide guidance into the primary literature where the student can then make her or his own assessments.

Although a broadly topic-based approach has been adopted, it should be mentioned that many of the topics will re-emerge in other chapters. The reader may well spot many cross-connections that I have failed to make. If this happens from time to time, perhaps it is because you are beginning to put people together again.

Further reading

Bandura, A. (1986) *Social Foundations of Thought and Action: a social cognitive theory*. Englewood Cliffs, NJ: Prentice Hall.

The major statement of Bandura's theory, drawing together the conceptual basis, a mass of empirical research, and many provocative speculations in an impressive exposition.

Bronfenbrenner, U. (1979) *The Ecology of Human Development: experiments by nature and design*. Cambridge, Mass.: Harvard University Press.

This book is important as an introduction to Bronfenbrenner's own ecological theory, but also as a statement of many issues concerning levels of analysis in developmental psychology and the intersection of development and environment that any adequate developmental theory must address.

Chapman, M. (1988) *Constructive Evolution: origins and development of Piaget's thought*. Cambridge: Cambridge University Press.

An insightful account of the philosophical and biological underpinnings of Piaget's theory, with discussions of current extensions and reinterpretations.

Grusec, J. E. and Lytton, H. (1988) *Social Development: history, theory, and research*. New York: Springer-Verlag.

An advanced level textbook providing a valuable account of the historical and theoretical foundations of much contemporary work on social development, and detailed reviews of many key topics.

Hurrelmann, K. (1988) *Social Structure and Personality Development: the individual as a productive processor of reality*. Cambridge: Cambridge University Press.

A succinct but wide-ranging overview of socialization theories, including the psychological approaches discussed here and several sociological perspectives. Hurrelmann develops his own concept of socialization, relating personality, the family, and societal conditions.

MacDonald, K. B. (1988) *Social and Personality Development: an evolutionary synthesis*. New York: Plenum.

A stimulating discussion of the philosophical and empirical underpinnings of developmental psychology, with reviews of the ways in which cognitive developmental and social learning perspectives might be integrated within an evolutionary theory.

Excellent reviews of the major theories of developmental psychology can be found in:

Miller, P. H. (1993) *Theories in Developmental Psychology*, 3rd edn. Oxford: Freeman.

Thomas, R. M. (1992) *Comparing Theories of Child Development*, 3rd edn. Belmont, Calif. Wadsworth.

Chapter 2

Social Life and Infancy

*The development of the child's relationship to other
human beings involves some of the most difficult and
fundamental problems of child psychology.*
  (Buhler, From Birth to Maturity, *1937, p. 53)*

We saw in chapter 1 that it is common in the social sciences for "biological" and "social" accounts of human characteristics to be seen as opposing theoretical positions. At the most superficial level, biologically oriented theorists are understood to explain behavior in terms of innate preprogramming, while socially oriented theorists are sometimes taken to explain behavior exclusively in terms of the consequences of external, environmental forces that shape the infinitely malleable human subject. Yet if we begin at the beginning, and consider the early social life of the human infant, then it becomes immediately apparent that such a stark division between biological and social factors is misplaced and misleading.

In this chapter, we will consider properties that the infant brings with him or her – in the sense that they are present at birth or emerge shortly thereafter – and the ways in which the social environment accommodates to these. It will be clear that the biological endowments of the new member of the species are fundamental to the ways in which he or she becomes involved with other people. The responses and initiatives of those other people are vital too, not least because the infant's survival depends upon them but also because they provide the contexts within which the child learns to exploit, regulate, and extend his or her behavioral potential: the greater part of the infant's waking hours are spent in the company of other people (Sherrod, 1991). In short, we will see that from the beginnings of social life, the biological and the social are inseparable – indeed, in many respects, they are indistinguishable.

We will begin by examining how the infant is equipped to react to the world he or she enters. The infant has reflexive, sensory, perceptual and affective capabilities, all of which are apparent very early in life and all of which have important consequences for social development. They will be reviewed here in terms of signaling capacities, exploratory processes, and social interaction. Among the consequences of these developing abilities is the emergence of a feature of social life that is so commonplace among adults that we often overlook its significance: that is, the infant begins to display social *selectivity*, a form of interpersonal differentiation that is fundamental to much of human social organization (Buhler, 1930; Perez, 1878; Schaffer, 1971).

The infant does not have access to the principal means of human communication, language, yet is likely to have a variety of needs and interests to transmit to others. Infants feel pain, hunger, discomfort, frustration, pleasure, satisfaction, and a variety of other emotions, and are often highly motivated to express these states. They depend, for example, on others to feed them and minister to other immediate physical needs. The young human is dependent for survival upon the actions of others for a substantially greater stretch of the lifespan than any other species. This would be biologically disastrous were it not for a complementary disposition of others to ensure that the newcomer's needs are met. In respect of each of the capacities discussed, we will consider how parents are affected by what the child is doing. Not surprisingly, we will see that, typically, they are affected quite a lot. If we did not care for the young in these ways, society would fail to reproduce itself. Hence, there is a variety of evolutionary, affective, and rational reasons why people value and care for newborns. The biological dependence of the neonate places him or her in a social context in which others are correspondingly equipped and motivated to attend to him or her.

Nature gives the child some valuable assets in this respect. First of all, the baby

Figure 2.1   Infant crying: this behavior often ensures that others provide assistance, food, or comfort.

looks pleasant; that is, he or she is cute and cuddly. Of course, beauty is in the eye of the beholder, and there is evidence that the typical features of babies – such as a head-to-body ratio which is greater than that of the mature human, and disproportionately large eyes – are arousing to adults (Hess, 1970; Hildebrandt and Fitzgerald, 1979; Lorenz, 1943). Second, the child has the means of making overt signals to others. Chief among these are the elementary techniques of crying and smiling. These familiar capacities of infants turn out to have great potency, and each has attracted a great deal of research attention.

Signaling Capacities

Crying

A cry is one of the first signs we look for in the newborn as preliminary assurance that he or she is alive and well. Crying is virtually universal in infants (figure 2.1), especially during the first few months (St James-Roberts and Halil, 1991). It is not a learned behavior (although the infant soon learns to use it). Ethologists regard crying as an evolved pattern of defensive behavior, and point out that it is often accompanied by fixed action patterns such as the raising of one hand to the head, as though to protect oneself from blows. This can be observed even in very young children who have not suffered any threat of attack (Eibl-Eibesfeldt, 1989).

Types of cries

Analysis of the nature of cries reveals that they are a much more structured, informative and, in due course, manipulative feature of the infant than casual encounters might lead us to expect. In a seminal study, Wolff (1969) observed a group of infants for the first few months of their lives, spending many hours each week in their homes identifying the causes of crying, the different patterns of crying in different circumstances, the responses of the babies' mothers, and the effects of different types of interventions.

Wolff identified three main patterns of crying: the basic cry, the angry cry, and the pain cry.

The basic cry   This cry is often associated with, but not exclusive to, hunger. Wolff reported that it is a rhythmic cry, consisting of the cry proper (with a mean duration of 0.6 seconds), followed by a brief silence (0.2 seconds), a short inspiratory whistle (0.1–0.2 seconds), and then another brief rest period before the next cry proper begins. Wolff found this pattern of cry as early as half an hour after birth.

The angry (or "mad") cry   This cry is a variation of the basic pattern, but with shorter pauses between the cries due to the excess air forced through the vocal cords.

The pain cry   This cry (which Wolff recorded when nurses pricked the babies' heels to collect blood samples) is distinguished by a sudden onset of loud crying, a long initial cry, and an extended period of breath holding after the long cry.

Spectrographic illustrations of the three cry types are presented in figure 2.2. If you have access to a recently born infant, you might find it interesting to place a recorder in her or his room for a while, and compare the structure of the cries she or he emits with those depicted below. As Wolff points out, not all cries can be classified exactly under this framework and there are many intermediate or transitional forms, but you are likely to obtain good examples of the main types.

Wolff tested the causes of crying in various natural experiments, and found that although hunger and discomfort were indeed common motivators, during the early months several other events would prompt crying, including the departure from the room of a familiar person. Several investigators have demonstrated that very young infants who are in an initially calm state will cry in response to the recorded cries of another infant (Martin and Clark, 1982; Murphy, 1936; Sagi and Hoffman, 1976; Simner, 1971), a social dimension of crying which is of especial significance to the parents of twins and larger sets.

Adults' responses to infant cries

We are all aware of the force of infants' cries. Through crying, infants can tell us that they are around and that they want something, and most of them do so frequently. Very few adults can resist taking some action to appease or silence a crying baby. Some can be moved to extreme actions. In Cannock, England, in 1993 a mother

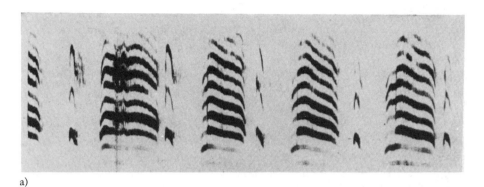

a)

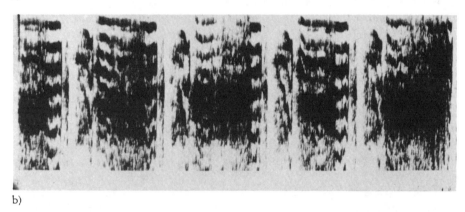

b)

c)

Figure 2.2 Spectrograms of infant cries. (A) Sequence of "basic" cries in a 4-day-old healthy full-term male infant. Fundamental frequency, 350–450 cycles per second. (For this and subsequent figures, spectrograms were written at twice the normal speed. Vertical axis: frequency range from 0–7,000 cycles per second; horizontal axis: time, 4.8 seconds of recorded vocalization.) (B) Sequence of "mad" (angry) cries in a normal full-term 4-day-old female after crying for 10 minutes and becoming increasingly excited. The black, fuzzy background reflects turbulence produced by excess air forced through the vocal cords. (C) Initial vocal response to pain, followed by a 7-second period of silence in expiration. (*Source*: Wolff, 1969)

was taken to court and cautioned to keep her especially persistent crying 8-month-old quiet (or else pay a large fine) as a result of neighborly dissatisfaction with the sounds her daughter emitted. The prevalence of crying in infant social relations is one of the starkest demonstrations of a point made in chapter 1, namely that social life is not invariably harmonious (see also Bradley, 1989; van de Rijt-Plooj and Plooj, 1993). At the extreme, persistent crying can initiate child abuse (Frodi, 1985; Kempe and Kempe, 1978).

Wolff (1969) noted that parents' responses to cries were variable, and tended to reflect personal style (resulting perhaps from previous childrearing experience or beliefs about child behavior). Some mothers respond to a basic cry by attempting to feed, others check the diaper first. However, one of the cry types elicited consistent reactions: the pain cry. Upon hearing this, mothers invariably rushed into the baby's room looking worried. It seems that people find this cry particularly compelling.

Subsequent research, taking physiological measures, such as heart rate or skin conductance, or ratings of the urgency of the cry, confirms that a crying baby has an arousing effect upon most parents (Boukydis and Burgess, 1982; Frodi et al., 1978; Lester, 1985) and on most non-parents, too (Freudenberg et al., 1978; Gustafson and Harris, 1990; Murray, 1985; Zeskind, 1980). Zeskind and his collaborators (Zeskind, 1987; Zeskind and Collins, 1987; Zeskind et al. 1985) have demonstrated that adults are sensitive to the contours of infant cries. For example, high-pitched cries are rated as more urgent; even non-parents listening to pain cries tend to show heart-rate accelerations. On the other hand, the latter segment of the pain cry is perceived as less arousing. Zeskind and colleagues speculate that there may be a biologically given synchrony between infant and adult, such that variations in infant arousal elicit commensurate responses in caregivers. Vuorenkoski et al. (1969) found that hearing recorded infant cries can lead to an increase in the mother's breast temperature, with the maximal skin temperature attained just a few minutes before feeding. Wasz-Hockert et al. (1985, p. 87) comment, "The cries prepare the breasts, in a sense, for feeding."

Crying and learning

From the beginning, the most useful counters to crying are provided by people. For example, Wolff (1969) found that as early as the second month infants would cry when a person they are looking at left the room, and cease crying upon her or his return. Because people, especially parents, are likely to respond to infant cries the infant is provided with many opportunities to discover a contingency relationship between one of its behaviors and events in the environment around it. Just how quickly the caregiver responds appears to influence the frequency of crying. Hubbard and van IJzendoorn (1991), in a longitudinal study of infants through the first nine months, found that if mothers delayed responses then the number of crying bouts reduced. The authors suggest that very prompt responses can overstimulate the child and hinder the development of autonomy (i.e., the child rarely gets a chance to come to terms with her or his discomfort independently). Although early cries are presumably spontaneous, children appear to become able to use them increasingly purposefully toward the latter part of the first year of life as they discover their effects upon others (Bell and Harper, 1977; Schaffer, 1971).

If we examine the kinds of things that adults do to appease crying infants – behaviors such as feeding, rocking, stroking, singing – we find that they have dual effects upon the child. On the one hand, they alleviate some excessive internal stimulation (hunger or discomfort), but on the other they afford the opportunity to experience new external stimulation (Schaffer, 1977). As a crying child calms down, she opens her eyes, becomes more alert, and monitors her surroundings (Korner and Grobstein, 1966; Korner and Thoman, 1970). In this way, the interpersonal response to the biological reflex provides a context for perceptual cognitive exploration.

Interpreting cries

Although caregivers' responses to cries are an integral aspect of early social interaction, we should not assume that parents are "puppets on a string, responding without a second thought to a particular type of cry" (Bell and Harper, 1977, p. 131), or that all parents behave in the same fashion at all times. Parents are concerned not only with the child's immediate wellbeing but also with their own adequacy as caregivers, and persistent crying can lead variously to anger and fatigue in caregivers (Dragonas, 1987) (and next-door neighbors).

Parents try consciously to interpret the meanings of the cries with which they are confronted. In addition to the standard causes of hunger, wind, pain, and cleansing needs, parents attribute cries to psychological motivations. Dunn (1977) found that parents explained infants' cries as reflecting characteristics such as "boredom," "temper," "naughtiness," and "crankiness," and interpreted individual differences in crying behavior (for example, among siblings) as manifestations of underlying personality differences. Bril et al. (1989) report that in some African societies parents perceive sex differences in infants' cries: girls cry four times while boys (being tougher) cry only three times. Hence, the infant's signals are given not only practical interpretations that result in physical responses but also psychological readings, which contribute to the family's emerging profile of his or her personality and future social behavior.

Parents also have ideologies of childrearing that influence how they interpret or respond to the child's behaviors (Parke, 1994; Parke and Tinsely, 1987). These can be informal ideologies, such as the traditional sets of beliefs passed from generation to generation among families within a particular culture, or they can be based on more explicit theories of child development, disseminated by popular books or parents' and women's magazines. Crying is a focus of conflicting advice as to whether, when, and how one should attend to it (Dunn, 1977; Newson and Newson, 1963). Hence, parents' interpretations and reactions to crying are informed both by physiology and culture. If we consider different cultures, we find variations in everyday practices.

Cultural factors in responsiveness to infant cries

It is hard to remain unaware of an infant's cry, and most adults react to it in some way. Whether this leads to direct attention to the baby, and what kind of attention, are subject to cultural variations. Within contemporary Western cultures, maternal responses to basic cries are variable and some will ignore them, at least temporarily (Hubbard and van IJzendoorn, 1991; Wolff, 1969). Konner (1972) reports that among the Zhun/twasi people of north-western Botswana mothers would never ignore infant cries. The reason appears to be not so much a discrepancy in the inherent nurturance of women in these different societies as the fact that the Zhun/twasi infants are always in the same room as the rest of the family, while Western homes at least afford separating walls. The Botswanans may not take recourse to the legal interventions open to the British families who prosecuted the parent of their relentless little neighbor, but the Zhun/twasi treatment of infant cries presents a clear illustration of the intersection of family microsystem and ecological context (cf. Bronfenbrenner, 1979; see chapter 1).

The Zhun/twasi mothers almost always responded to a crying infant by trying to breastfeed it. In some English homes, however, mothers who breastfed their infants at a fixed schedule became at a loss to explain crying between feeds and concluded that their milk supply was inadequate, often citing this inadequacy as the reason for giving up breastfeeding, although in fact the children of successful breastfeeders cried just as frequently (Dunn, 1977).

Marked evidence of cultural differences and cultural shifts in interpretations of infant cries is provided by studies of immigrant communities. For example, Frankel and Roer-Bornstein (1982) interviewed grandmother (aged 65–95 years) and grand-daughter (aged 20–30 years) samples of Kurdish and Yemenite women in Israel. The older women had borne most of their children in their home country, but had lived in Israel for some 30 years at the time of the study. Although all the women saw crying as often reflecting the baby's physical needs, the older women were significantly more likely to refer to mystical causes, such as the "evil eye" than were granddaughters. The younger generations were more likely to seek medical provisions or advice to deal with persistent crying, reflecting a rejection of the spiritual ideologies of their parents.

Another vivid if anecdotal example of how developments in a society's scientific and industrial knowledge base may permeate down to the most elementary processes of the parent–child microsystem is provided by Pollock (1983), who describes a nineteenth-century British father's solution to the aggravations of a crying dependent. He soaked a handkerchief in chloroform and plonked it on his son's face for a few minutes. Although the indisputable efficacy of this particular treatment has not led to the predicted boom in chloroform retail, it is certainly the case that the varieties of responses to cries – historically, across and within cultures – confirms that a variety of physiological, interpersonal, and social ecological factors influence infants' experiences.

Figure 2.3   Infant smiling: this behavior can elicit positive vocalizations and repetitions of desirable behavior in others.

Smiling

The smile is another commonplace but complex and powerful signaling mechanism that emerges in early infancy (figure 2.3). Known to social psychologists as the 'bilateral extension of the lateral aspects of the lip region' (Birdwhistell, 1971, p. 33), this nonverbal expression has the notable consequences that it enhances the appearance of the baby to onlookers, and that it serves to make interactions with the baby more rewarding. Physiological measures indicate that infants' smiles invoke physical arousal in the adult onlooker (Donovan and Leavitt, 1985). Social interactional analyses reveal that infant smiles are associated with chains of mutual activity between child and caregiver (Kaye, 1982). Caregivers are delighted by infant smiles, and the appearance of the first face-to-face smile is often greeted as a breakthrough in parent–infant relations (Emde et al, 1976; Newson and Newson, 1963; Robson, 1967).

Are infants' smiles social?

There is controversy as to whether early smiles are social. Spitz and Wolf (1946) noted that smiles could be elicited in 2-month-olds by the presence of another person, and concluded that even at this early stage the smile had a psychological and social meaning for the infant. Others have argued that the smile is an initially asocial response which becomes social during the first few months of life. Bilateral extensions of the outer lip regions have been observed in neonates (Leboyer, 1975) and even before birth (Prechtl, 1984). Smiles can be elicited in young infants by a variety of external causes, including the sounds of a bell or whistle (Wolff, 1963), changes in brightness or other contrasts or movements in the visual environment (Ambrose, 1961), and reappearance of familiar animate or inanimate objects (Piaget, 1936). Infants will sometimes smile in their sleep, spontaneously or in response to light touching or blowing on the skin (Emde et al., 1976; Freedman, 1965; Gerwirtz, 1965; Wolff, 1963). Several investigators have reported that infants break into smiles at the discovery of contingency relationships between their behavior and environmental events, such as learning to control a mobile (Sullivan and Lewis, 1988; Uzgiris and Hunt, 1970; Watson, 1972, 1985). One of the most charming illustrations of the relationship between smiling and understanding is that of Bigelow et al. (1990), who had infants watch faces of older children and adults appear at windows of different heights, such that in one condition a 5-year-old's face would pop up at the height of an adult: 12-month-olds viewing this incongruity were observed to chuckle.

There is little doubt that infants will smile independently of social interaction (as, of course, will older children and adults). Even so, to describe early smiling as asocial disregards the importance of the smile to the persons with whom the baby interacts and the fact that "nonsocial" stimuli, such as tickles, light blowing on the skin, and visual incongruities, are very often provided or set up by other people. Watson (1985) argues that infants become interested in (and pleased by) contingencies because they are becoming familiar with the predictability of events in the social world.

It was mentioned earlier that parents find infants' smiles appealing, but there is also evidence that the reciprocal interest occurs: infants prefer smiling faces. Kuchuk et al. (1986) presented 3-month-old infants with photographs of adult women, such that the women's expressions ranged from unsmiling through increasingly intense smiles. The babies' visual preferences increased directly with intensity of smile. Kuchuk et al. (1986) also collected measures of maternal caregiving styles at home, and found a relationship between the mother's use of smiling and encouragement of attention to her and the child's discrimination among smiling faces in the laboratory task. A plausible conclusion is that the infants were becoming aware of the salience of the smile in social interaction.

The other side of smiling, of course, is that we expect it to be reciprocated. Tronick et al. (1979) found that infants interacting with mothers who (at the experimenters' request) maintained a still face would initially try to get the interaction going with a smile of greeting, and when that did not work began to "sober up", and sometimes averted their gaze.

Even if the infant's early smile may not always be socially prompted or directed, it is very often incorporated into its social interactions as a result of the responses of social partners. As already mentioned, it makes interaction with the baby more enjoyable. In this sense, it is certainly of social import because it is part of the processes of a relationship. Trevarthen (1982) maintains that it is simply missing the point to regard the smile as a physiological response or as an outcome of some information-processing activity. The *meaning* of the smile is the crucial psychological variable, and this is wholly dependent upon social context: "Only the mind of another person can be affected by a smile. To smile, effectively, an infant must understand other persons". (1982: p. 78)

The nature of the smile develops during the early months, and infants do come to orient smiles to others in more structured and predictable ways. As early as the third week, Wolff (1963) observed that a specifically human stimulus – the voice – begins to elicit a smile more consistently than other stimulus configurations. He found that by about the fifteenth day of life, most of the North American infants he was studying responded to a high-pitched voice with a clear-cut, broad smile. Wolff reports another development in smiling in the fourth week. He points out that, although babies can pursue visual objects with coordinated eye and hand movements from within 18 hours of birth, there is a dramatic change within the month:

> Until now, however, when I was looking at the child who was in turn looking at me, I had the impression that the baby was looking through me and focusing somewhere at the back of my head. At three and a half weeks approximately, the subjective impression is that a radical change in the focus has occurred, and that the baby now seems to focus on the observer's eyes as if there were true eye-to-eye contact. (Wolff, 1963: p. 122).

True eye-to-eye contact is often a marker of intimacy and reciprocity in human inter-actions (Argyle and Dean, 1965; Rutter, 1984) and Wolff conveys here the emotional impact that eye-contact with an infant can have upon an adult. In general, this develop-ment is likely to lead to an intensification and expansion of parent–child interactions. Once again, there are individual differences in exactly when this milestone is reached, reflecting genetic, maturational, and environmental variables (Freedman and Keller, 1963; Kagan, 1974; Landau, 1977), but over the next couple of months the frequency of this elementary means of making contact increases markedly.

During the first year, children's use of smiling becomes increasingly organized. Smiles tend to occur in clusters, followed by pauses, and then more smiles (Fogel, 1982). Smiles serve an increasing range of purposes, including recognition, mastery, pleasure, surprise, and they are closely related to ongoing social activity. By the second year, the social context is an important determinant of whether and how much the child smiles. Jones and Raag (1989) had 17-month-olds engage individually in a nonsocial activity (toy play) while their mother sat nearby. The children broke spontaneously into smiles every now and then, in response to enjoyable features of the play. At such moments, they glanced at the mother. Mothers were instructed either to smile back or to be inattentive. When mothers were inattentive, the frequency of smiles-plus-glances declined dramatically. In a second experiment, a female stranger was included; her task was to provide a smiling response while the mother remained seemingly indifferent or preoccupied. The babies soon redirected their smiles-plus-glances to the person who was responding. It appears that by the age of 18 months at least, infants like to share their smiles. Jones and Raag (1989) speculate that smile production from its very beginnings may be dependent upon a social recipient.

Cultural factors in orientations to infant smiles

Although there are broad similarities in the early chronology of smiling, there are differences among caregiving contexts in terms of the reactions these early expressions elicit and the kinds of interventions perceived as appropriate in order to bring them forth. Broch (1990) reports that among the Bonerate villagers of Miang Tuu in Indonesia it is common for adults to fiddle with the genitals of a distressed baby in order to make it smile; this caregiving technique is not widely practiced in European and North American societies.

In Uganda, adults and siblings expend a great deal of effort talking and smiling to infants, attempting to prompt smiles in return (Super and Harkness, 1982). Super and Harkness (1982) point out that there are powerful motivators for this style of interaction in the local community, where upwards social mobility can be attained through the effective deployment of personal skills, unlike many traditional and contemporary societies where social standing can be determined on the basis of sex, age, or lineage. While in this context playful gregarious smiling is highly functional, in other systems children are expected to be quieter and well behaved. Super and Harkness point to Japan as an example of the latter, and note that Japanese mothers tend to favor quiet, controlled babies, and direct their caregiving strategies toward soothing and lulling their infants. A modest smile of contentment is promoted here, rather than expressions of uproarious enjoyment.

Evidence gathered in different contexts in Israel (such as home, kibbutz, residential institution, day nursery) indicates that the overall rate of smiling may vary from setting to setting. Gerwirtz (1965) found that children in the first two contexts were showing greater readiness to smile earlier than agemates in the institutional environments. Frankel and Roer-Bornstein's (1982) study of Kurdish and Yemenite mothers in Israel also found differences between communities (Yemenites believed that smiles appeared earlier than did Kurds). Even so, the evidence from each of these studies points to a dramatic surge in frequency of smiling in most infants at around the third to fourth month. One outcome is that parents in most cultures report that they now perceive the child as "more human" or "like a real person", in contrast to their earlier perceptions of the infants as "doll-like" (Emde et al., 1976, on American parents), as smiling in response to "the angels" rather than people (Frankel and Roer-Bornstein, 1982, on Kurdish and Yemenite mothers), or as "monkeys" (Super and Harkness, 1982, on Kipsigis mothers in rural Kenya).

Summary

The infant is equipped by nature with two potent signaling capacities: the cry and the smile. These are important attributes for both informational and emotional reasons. The cry conveys the message "come and sort this out," while the smile relays "that's good; do it again." The infant is biologically equipped to signal its states in patterned ways which mature members of the species can interpret reasonably well – and the mature members of the species are biologically predisposed to react to the stimuli the infant provides. Biologically given reflexes which can occur for a variety of reasons are given meaning by the caregivers, and affect the caregivers' behavior. The parameters of the caregivers' behavior are themselves influenced by the cultural ecology in which they live. The outcome is that infants' expressive behaviors develop in interaction with others who expect them to progress in particular ways, and who strive, perhaps unwittingly, to guide their offspring in those ways.

Exploring and Discriminating

In order to find our way in unfamiliar terrain, we have to explore. Much of the infant's environment is unfamiliar at first, and he or she begins to explore it. In early infancy, the means of exploration are limited in comparison to the standards of adults or older children. The infant cannot propel itself independently and cannot consult others verbally. But even the youngest infant does have some useful mechanisms provided by nature. These are its sensory capacities. We will review some of the evidence relating to two of the most important senses for human social interaction: vision and hearing.

Visual Exploration

The neonate's visual system is considerably poorer than that of adults (Aslin, 1987; Bremner, 1994; Mehler and Dupoux, 1994; Slater, 1989). Visual acuity is weak, and the ability to follow moving stimuli, although present, is slow and jerky. However, even from the first few days infants have visual abilities and preferences which enable them to discriminate among certain shapes, to recognize movements, to differentiate colors, to perceive distance, depth and dimensions and to scan objects' properties (Bremner, 1994; Meltzoff and Moore, 1992; Slater, 1989). During the first six months, these abilities develop extensively.

One question which has interested researchers of infant vision for some time is whether this ability is preadapted for social stimuli. That is, are infants constructed so that they find people visually interesting? It should be recognized that no one has proposed that infant visual capacities are *only* socially adapted. Clearly, it would be a rather perverse evolutionary outcome if the sense of sight functioned at first exclusively in response to social stimuli. But it is possible that infants are designed so that they find particular stimuli attractive, and the prime candidate considered by investigators interested in this possibility is the human face.

Infant attention to the face

The face is one of the most informative features of a human being, marking each individual's uniqueness and containing the principal means of expression. It can reveal what is currently holding the interest of its owner (e.g., what he or she is looking at). By a happy arrangement, it is intimately connected to the ears, the apparatus toward which we generally address vocal information. All in all, there are several reasons why the face is established early in life as the chief focus of much of our social intercourse.

There is no doubt that during the first few months of life, infants do become

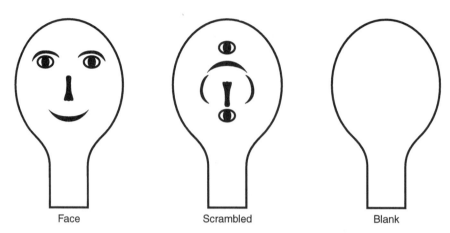

Figure 2.4   Stimulus shapes shown to neonates: regular face preferred.
(*Source*: Johnson and Morton, 1991)

interested in faces. One indication of this is that they smile at them (Spitz and Wolf, 1946). Ahrens (1954) demonstrated that as infants develop, it takes different amounts of visual facial information to sustain their interest. In his studies, at 6 weeks, a crude two-dot representation of the eyes was the most effective. Infants were likely to look and smile at this stimulus but were obviously engaged by more detailed representations. During the next several weeks the eye-like pattern remained effective, but realistic as opposed to schematic representations became more successful in eliciting interest. By 5 or 6 months, Ahrens found that a good three-dimensional representation of the face was necessary.

Investigating related issues, Fantz (1961, 1963) inspired a line of research into infant perception which continues today. Fantz's methodology exploited the visual fixation time of the infant in response to various stimuli. Presumably, if an infant attends for longer to one stimulus rather than others, then he or she has discriminated among the stimuli – and finds something more attention worthy. That something appeared to be the face.

Fantz compared fixation times of infants for a range of stimuli, including facial representations, simple patterns, asymmetrical forms, and blank white or colored surfaces. Interest was greater in the more complex, patterned stimuli, and chief among these was the schematic representation of a face. Fantz also reported that for infants from 1 to 6 months fixation times were greater for conventionally organized faces, rather than facial shapes within which the components had been jumbled.

One of the most interesting findings is that even newborns show a preference for representations of the normal face over a scrambled face or a similarly shaped but blank outline (Goren et al., 1975; Johnson et al., 1991). Extending Goren et al.'s initial work, Johnson et al. showed neonates (within the first hour after birth) stimuli such as those in Figure 2.4, and waited until the subject fixated on the image. Then, the experimenter moved the shape slowly along an arc, and recorded the baby's visual tracking. A reliable preference for the regular "face" was obtained, and the least favored stimulus was the blank.

The suggestion that infants come into the world prewired to orient toward faces of conspecifics (other members of the same species) is persuasive. However, an alternative explanation could be that the infant is predisposed to attend to high contrast symmetrical features, among which the face happens to be just one convenient example. The obvious test is to examine infants' preferences for symmetrical patterns versus face-like representations. The available evidence indicates that the face is preferred (Johnson and Morton, 1991; but see Slater, 1989, for an alternative viewpoint).

Johnson and Morton (1991) argue that neonates do have a primal mechanism which orients them toward faces when they appear in their visual environment. In their view, this is a reflexive, sensorimotor action, rather than a meaningful one, and it serves to "kick start" an attentional process: "there is nothing social or intentional in the new-born's preferential orienting toward faces" (1991: 141). Once the system is operating, the infant has to acquire and retain specific information about particular faces that it encounters. Obviously, these latter discoveries depend upon experience and learning, though it is plausible that the learning processes are constrained by neural organization.

However, to conclude that there is nothing social in this preferential orientation overlooks the fact that being social is not something that one does alone. As with crying and smiling, the infant's biologically given interest in faces is likely to be met by an enthusiastic audience, and to be incorporated into social life by other possessors of more mature neural organizations. Papousek and Papousek (1987) point out that all parents, even those who are aware of the limited visual capacities of the neonate, strive to ensure face-to-face, eye-to-eye contact with the baby from their first interchanges. Meltzoff and Moore (1993) argue that one of the reasons why faces are so interesting to babies is that they exhibit properties which correspond to the infant's own feelings. That is, the baby knows what it *feels like* to have a face, and he or she recognizes correspondences between these feelings and the facial properties and actions of others. Hence, the baby attends to faces as a means of identifying and learning about particular people; for their part, the other people in the infant's life are generally keen to make sure that they are identified and do become significant to the new member of the family.

Discrimination among faces

While faces are good for interacting with, they are also an exceptionally useful means of telling people apart. As highly experienced examiners of faces, adults take this for granted, but the differences among faces are actually rather subtle. Misfortune aside, all faces have a similar topography and key components: eyes, nose, mouth, and so on in roughly the same places. What hope has the infant, who is just beginning to attend to faces, of distinguishing one from another?

The social importance of such discriminations is obvious. Recognizing the differences among faces is helpful to working out constancies and recurrences in the social environment. Without this ability, each encounter with any person must be experienced as a novel social event. It would be impossible to build up a relationship with another individual if you failed to recognize that person on each reappearance. Not surprisingly, the central question for researchers here has become: how quickly does the child come to recognize its mother? Once again, the answer is: pretty quickly.

In a clever experiment, Carpenter (1975) set infants in an apparatus where they watched a hole at which a face would appear, while a voice was piped in via speakers. In this way, Carpenter was able to vary the combinations of stimuli available to the infant. For example, she could present different combinations of the mother's face, mother's voice, female stranger's face and female stranger's voice. Think about it for a moment: how would you react to finding your nearest-and-dearest's voice coming out of a complete stranger's face?

Using fixation times as the response measure, Carpenter found that infants as young as two weeks looked longest when presented with their own mother's face plus voice, followed by a condition in which they were exposed to their mother's silent face only. Perhaps most interesting were infants' reactions to the mismatch conditions where a familiar face was presented with an unfamiliar voice, or vice versa. In these circumstances, Carpenter reported that the babies found the presentation distressing, and responded by averting their gaze, and occasionally bursting into tears.

Unfortunately, Carpenter's experiment is limited by the fact that only one stranger was used, and raters were not blind to the condition (Bremner, 1994). However, several improvements and variations of this design have been undertaken in subsequent work (Bushnell, 1982; Bushnell et al., 1989; Field et al., 1982; Maurer and Salapatek, 1976) and, although there is still debate about exactly which features infants exploit in discrimination (Bremner, 1994; Slater, 1989), the evidence points consistently to the conclusion that infants can discriminate between their mother and other female strangers at a very early age – perhaps as early as 2 days (Bushnell et al., 1989; Field et al., 1982; Johnson and Morton, 1991).

Discrimination among others

Infants encounter many other people beside their mothers. Much of the research above has focused on maternal recognition for the obvious reasons that mothers are more often the primary caregiver and mothers are more often available to take part in research projects than fathers. Interesting questions remain about when infants recognize their fathers, and how this varies as a function of family organization. Similarly, it would be valuable to know more about when and how infants discriminate among siblings and peers. These topics are important, because distinguishing among people and the development of preferences, are prerequisites to social life. Research on these topics is scant, but several investigators have addressed issues concerning infants' discrimination among strangers. Barrera and Maurer (1981b), for example, found that infants aged 3 months can discriminate among photographs of adults hitherto unknown to them. This was the case both when the strangers looked quite different from each other and when they were chosen for similar facial features. (We consider other aspects of infants' reactions to strangers in chapter 3.)

The beginnings of physical attractiveness bias

One way in which people's faces vary is that some are more attractive than others. Furthermore, we tend to agree upon the relative physical attractiveness of a given set of faces (Jackson, 1992). Social psychologists have found that people who are perceived as physically attractive tend to be rated more favorably on other measures, including personality and competence (Berscheid, 1986; Jackson, 1992; McArthur, 1982). From a developmental perspective, one question of interest is how early in life children begin to discriminate among people on the basis of facial attractiveness. Samuels and Ewy (1985) addressed this question by measuring infants' (aged 3 and 6 months) attention to slides of pairs of adult males and females who were classified on the basis of the judgments of a large panel of adult raters as "attractive" or "unattractive." For each of the pairs of faces, the attractive member received more attention, usually substantially more. Other researchers have demonstrated that by 12 months, infants show a preference, when interacting with strangers, for attractive over unattractive faces, and they will play longer with dolls that have attractive rather than unattractive faces (Langlois et al., 1990).

These results are puzzling for a number of reasons. On the one hand, infancy is rather early in life to have picked up sociocultural biases about what constitute good looks. On the other hand, as Samuels and Ewy (1985) point out, there is no obvious evolutionary reason why infants should be predisposed to prefer facially attractive individuals – caregiving skill and motivation are as far as we know unrelated to attractiveness.

There is also evidence to suggest that a similar process can operate in the opposite direction. That is, adults' interactions with babies may be affected by individual differences in infant attractiveness. Stephan and Langlois (1984) found among black, white and Mexican American adults evidence of strong "beauty is good" stereotype effects: infants rated as attractive were perceived as smart, likable, and good, while less attractive babies were expected to cause their parents problems. Barden et al. (1989) found that mothers interacting with facially deformed infants were consistently less nurturant toward their child than mothers with nondeformed infants. Still more importantly, the mothers were unaware of the fact, reporting that they loved their babies and believed their caregiving to be unaffected by the child's disabilities. In short, from very early in social life, attractiveness seems to have some consequences for both what we perceive and how we are perceived. Needless to say, this is not the last time that physical attractiveness will be found to have social correlates and consequences, and we return to this topic in later chapters.

Auditory Attention and Discrimination

Yet another means of monitoring the environment is available to infants: they can listen to it. The auditory system operates from before birth, and heart-rate measures indicate that the fetus is sensitive to sounds outside the womb (see Aslin, 1987). Although the exact capabilities of neonates' hearing systems are not fully understood, there is evidence that newborns can hear reasonably well (Aslin, 1987; Bremner, 1994; Mehler and Dupoux, 1994). Neonates appear able to organize aspects of their own behavior around auditory information: they will turn their heads in the direction of sounds (Field et al., 1980; Muir and Field, 1979). Similar questions arise here to those we considered earlier in relation to visual perception. Are infants particularly interested in human sounds (voices), and do they discriminate among them?

Attending to the human voice

Even quite young infants demonstrate a preference for the human voice over other sounds, such as a bell (Eisenberg, 1976) or white noise (Colombo and Bundy, 1981). However, although infants can hear, they are less sensitive to lower frequency sounds than are older children and adults (Aslin, 1987; Mehler and Dupoux, 1994). Adults speaking to infants adapt their speech in a number of ways, but one of the most distinctive and most reliable is that they raise the pitch and introduce greater melodic contour than is found in adult–adult speech (Fernald, 1989; Fernald and Simon, 1984; Papousek et al., 1985; Shute and Wheldall, 1995). Several studies have found that infants prefer to listen to this form of adapted speech, sometimes referred to as "babytalk" (Fernald, 1985; Fernald and Kuhl, 1985; Mehler et al., 1978; Pegg et al., 1992; Werker et al., 1994). Note that one type of adult is biologically equipped to provide higher pitched sounds with greater ease.

Differentiating among speakers

There is evidence that infants prefer to listen to their mother's voice rather than that of a female stranger (DeCasper and Fifer, 1980; Field, 1985; Mehler et al., 1978). For example, Mehler et al. (1978) constructed an apparatus that enabled babies (aged 1 month) to control their own access to audio recordings by altering their sucking rate. If they sucked faster, they heard more of the voice more swiftly. Two orders of presentation were employed. After hearing a female stranger's voice a few times, some infants received their own mother's voice: these children accelerated their sucking. Other babies heard their mother's voice a few times, and then the female stranger's: these children decreased their sucking rate. The counterbalancing of order of presentation means that it is difficult to explain the results in terms of the novelty of the second voice, since in one condition the voice change seems to be associated with a desire to hear more, while in the other it brings about a reduction in pace. The critical factor appears to be familiarity: babies demonstrate a preference for their own mother's voice.

DeCasper and Fifer (1980) found evidence of this preference at only three days, an age at which babies would have had only around 12 hours' postnatal contact with their mothers (although, as the researchers point out, considerably longer prenatal exposure). Field (1985), working with babies with a mean age of just 45 hours and only about four hours' postnatal experience with their mothers, also found evidence of a preference for mother's face and mother's voice.

Differentiating among speech sounds

One of the most remarkable of infants' early perceptual capacities is their ability to discriminate among speech sounds (Aslin, 1987; Mehler and Dupoux, 1994). The first evidence of this capacity was provided by Eimas et al. (1971). These investigators habituated 1- and 4-month-old infants to a syllable (*pa*) by playing it repetitively at fixed intervals. Once the baby's response had stabilized, a new stimulus (*ba*) was introduced. Although the structural difference between the two sounds *pa* and *ba* is minimal, it does reflect an important categorical distinction in English (and other languages); choice of "p" versus "b" makes quite a difference to the meaning of __*at*, __*ark*, __*it*, __*ush*, __*ull* and so on. While 1- and 4-month-olds are not sensitive to the semantic differences among these words, they are sensitive to phonological contrasts. Eimas et al. (1971) found that children's attention picked up at the introduction of the slightly different sound. Even the younger infants seemed to detect that something had changed in the sound signal. A host of further experiments extended these findings, confirming that infants are sensitive to at least 50 different speech contrasts (see Aslin, 1987; Burnham et al., 1991; Mehler and Dupoux, 1994).

Other work has shown that infants can remember discriminations and can even discriminate much larger chunks of organized sound. Swain et al. (1993) habituated newborns to a word, and tested their preference for the old versus a new word some 24 hours later. They found that even with this delay, neonates still showed a preference for the novel stimulus. Still more intriguing, DeCasper and Spence (1986) had pregnant women read nursery rhymes twice daily during the final weeks of pregnancy. Subsequently, their newborn infants were provided with pacifiers that were equipped so that they could control the availability of a passage of speech. The babies – just 2 or 3 days old – showed a reliable preference for the familiar passage.

Clearly, these kinds of findings may have important implications for our understanding of how children acquire language, and most of the research is conducted with this in mind. We return to that question in chapter 6. For the moment it should be clear that sensitivity to the subtle variations among the vocal productions of other human beings is likely to be a useful asset to someone who will be spending a lot of time in the company of human beings.

Summary

The infant is equipped with sensory capacities which enable him or her to explore and learn about his or her social and physical surroundings. We have considered two of the most important here, vision and hearing (though there are others, including touch, taste, and smell, and the infant is able to interrelate information from these senses; see Bremner, 1994; Rose and Ruff, 1987). There is persuasive evidence that the infant orients vision and hearing toward other people, who have properties that coincide with the kinds of stimulus structure it finds most interesting. There is still more persuasive evidence that other people orient their behavior to exploit the infant's limited sensory capacities, and to promote the likelihood of face-to-face interaction. From very early in life, children discriminate among the people they encounter and develop preferences for particular individuals.

Infant Capacities and the Beginnings of Social Interaction

It is clear that the infant is much more than the squirming lump of flesh that was once supposed by the early behaviorists (cf. Watson, 1928). It has also been stressed above that the infant's caregivers are closely implicated in his or her experiences. Not only do they provide many of the most attention-attracting stimuli but they are in turn very attentive to any actions the infant cares to attempt. In normal caregiving contexts, they are prone to endow the infant's behaviors with social meaning. They strive to fit the newcomer into joint activities. We consider next some of the processes that are engaged as caregiver and child interact.

The Beginnings of Coordinated Activity

One of the most vital interactions that the infant has with other people is that of feeding. Although this appears on first sight to be straightforwardly a biological dependence, on closer inspection this basic imperative turns out to have important social correlates.

Kaye (1982; Kaye and Wells, 1980) found that mothers and babies develop mutual responsiveness around the burst–pause temporal structure of the infant's feeding. Mothers attempt to intervene by jiggling either the infant (if breastfeeding) or the bottle, and they report feeling that this will "wake" up the baby. Kaye and Wells (1980) found that jiggling itself actually reduced the likelihood of resumption of sucking, but that jiggling and stopping did tend to be closely followed by the next burst. The investigators experimented with the effects of varying the duration of a jiggle on the likelihood of restarting the sucking reflex, and discovered that short (1–2 seconds) jiggles seemed to do the trick most effectively.

This should mean that, if mothers are sensitive to the effects of their jiggles, they should shorten them as they gain increasing experience of their infant. This was what Kaye and Wells (1980) found. Observing mothers with their babies over the first two weeks, they noted that the length of jiggles dropped from an average of 3.1 seconds to 1.8 seconds. This suggests strongly that both participants are having an effect on the other from very early in the child's life: the baby's pause stimulates the mother to jiggle, and the end of the jiggle encourages the baby to suck again. What is particularly interesting about all of this, Kaye (1982) points out, is that there is no obvious functional explanation for the mother's interventions, since the baby is designed to keep sucking intermittently anyway and the mother (or the milk bottle) is designed to keep providing sustenance. Kaye argues that the only discernible benefits are to ensure that the mother takes an active role in the feeding and to provide her with behaviors from the child around which she can begin to provide some kind of order. In this earliest of social interactions, parent and child begin to do something which is not found in other species' feeding behavior (Kaye, 1982) but which is integral to many aspects of human communication: they begin to take turns.

Visual and Vocal Interaction

As noted above, the most valuable of human sensory systems, vision and hearing, are endowed in such a way that their optimal utility is assured when they are oriented toward the object of attention – in short, if you are interested in something, it helps if you turn your face toward it. As we have already seen, this leads naturally to an everyday parent–infant arrangement whereby the participants are often face to face. This is a familiar enough mode of interaction for the adult, of course, and it is one over which infants have only modest choice, in that their relatively restricted mobility means that they are picked up and held so as to present their faces toward their caregivers. Parents elect for this arrangement frequently, and they draw their baby back into it periodically if he or she diverts attention elsewhere (Papousek and Papousek, 1987; Schaffer, 1977, 1989a; Stern, 1985).

Once in the face-to-face position, the partners are not tied into an inflexible visual fix upon each other, but both adjust their behaviors in subtle and dynamic ways as the interaction proceeds. In one of the earliest descriptions of the flow of the mutual behaviors, Stern (1971) found that mothers and their 3-month-olds moved their heads in time with one another, almost as though they were engaged in a dance. Like most skilled dancers, they coordinated their movements and reacted to each other's actions. Many other studies, using microanalytic techniques, confirmed that parent–infant face-to-face interaction involves high levels of reciprocity in facial displays and bodily movements (see contributions to Schaffer, 1977, and figure 2.5).

The mother's behavior within the dance is markedly different from the behavior of adults interacting with other adults. She tends to exaggerate some of her acts – for example, by displaying a mock surprise face, consisting of raised eyebrows, wide eyes and open mouth – and she repeats much of what she says and does. Stern et al. (1977) found that approximately half of what the baby sees and hears in these interactions is part of a repeating sequence, in which both content and timing of the vocalizations or movements, and the pauses between them, are re-run immediately. Vocal repetition is particularly interesting because, after all, the 3-month-old does not understand a word the mother says. Perhaps the mother needs to endow the interaction with the means of expression most commonly used in human communications, or perhaps she

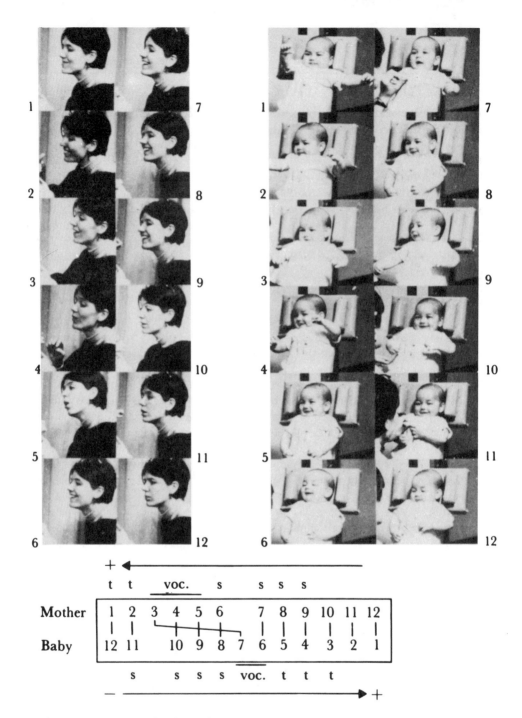

Figure 2.5 Mother–infant face to face. These photographs depict a 2-minute exchange between a mother and her son, aged 11 weeks. Independent ratings of the intensity of each participant's communicative displays (where 1 = highest, most assertive initiative, 12 = lowest degree of intimidation or initiative) reveal a near-perfect reciprocal relationship (t = teasing smile; voc = vocalization; s = intimated or amused smile).
(*Source*: Trevarthen, 1979)

believes that the exposure to repetitive words and phrases will help bring about the beginnings of the child's own language; either way, the adult often works hard to treat even the very young baby *as though* he or she were a genuine conversational partner.

Vocal matching

Infants emit a variety of vocal noises, such as coos, grunts, cries, laughs, gurgles and burps, often as a function of their physical state and activity involvement (Oller, in press; Smith et al., 1989; Stark, 1989). These vocal activities are also integrated into social interchanges between infant and parent (Beebe et al., 1985; Schaffer, 1989a; Tronick et al., 1979; Uzgiris, 1989). In the early months, high proportions of vocalizations of infant and caregiver are simultaneous (Papousek and Papousek, 1987). The Papouseks report that "coactional duetting" (vocal matching of pitch and prosodic contours) is particularly likely at times of emotional arousal, such as the expressions of pleasure or distress.

The content of vocalizations also provides evidence of mutual interest and influence. Papousek and Papousek (1989) found a high incidence of vocal matching in the utterances of two-, three- and five-month-olds with their mothers. Vocal matching refers to the perceptual similarity between adjacent maternal and infant utterances: one person makes a particular sound, and the other repeats it. Matching provides a means of affirming that some experience has been shared (Uzgiris, 1989). The Papouseks (1989) found that these were occurring at rates of 18–30 matches per 3 minutes of mother–infant interaction. At 2 months, around 41 percent of infants' vocalizations were imitated by the mother; by 5 months, the figure was over 58 percent. Furthermore, with the increasing age of the child, the mother's match became more complex (i.e., she imitated more than one feature of the infant's utterance at a time). Note that we are talking here about *mothers' imitations of babies*, not the reverse (see also Camaioni, 1993; Kugiumutzakis, 1993). Matching often occurred in runs of several turns, and the Papouseks stress that it is difficult to disentangle who is imitating whom in these contexts, but they observed a number of occasions in which 3- and 5-month-olds appeared to be striving to approximate the mother's sounds, often demonstrating pleasure when they came close.

Asymmetries in parent–infant interactions

Although parent–infant interactions are characterized by joint activity and mutual effects, there are important differences between the contributions of the mature and immature partners. Uzgiris (1989) shows that during the first year of life there is an asymmetry in mother–infant imitations such that, throughout, the mother is more likely to match an act of the child. However, in the latter part of the year, reciprocity increases and the infant increasingly attempts to match the mother's acts.

A striking contrast between the two members of the dyad is that one is prepared to maintain much more visual attention to the other. Especially in the first few months, the mother looks extensively at the baby during interactions, whereas the baby often

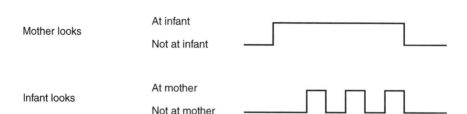

Figure 2.6   Maternal framing of infant's gaze: the mother's gaze begins before the infant's and continues until after the infant ceases to gaze.
(*Source*: Messer and Vietze, 1984)

looks elsewhere. Obviously, from the infant's perspective there are a lot of new things to look at, while from the mother's perspective there is one particularly fascinating being to focus upon. The mother's enduring attention seems to provide a "frame" (Fogel, 1977; Kaye and Fogel, 1980) for the baby's visual activity by continuously monitoring his or her face and providing a context within which the baby can look around while supported by an attentive partner (see figure 2.6). Once these circumstances are assured, other "individual" activity within the frame has potential social significance (Fogel, 1977, p. 147). The partners can play around, exploring together interesting aspects of their environment and generally increasing their shared activity.

In a large longitudinal study of mothers and infants when the children were aged 10, 26 and 54 weeks, Messer and Vietze (1984) found that patterns of looking were asymmetrical at each age point: mothers always looked more at the child than the reverse. Mothers' looks were longer, lasting on average over one minute while infant looks averaged around 10–20 seconds. Over the child's first year there were changes in how looks were used and paced. In particular, Messer and Vietze (1984) found that between 10 and 26 weeks there was a substantial increase in the frequency of maternal frames. Although the frequency of frames doubled, their duration halved. This reflected the faster pace of infant gaze, and the researchers conclude that the mothers and the infants may have been increasing the tempo of social gaze together jointly. During the next six months, the changes were less dramatic but nevertheless indicated a continuous progress toward equality within the dyad. By 54 weeks, each partner appeared to initiate or terminate looks independently of the gaze state of the other – maternal framing was no longer essential to ensure that the child's looks were bound to be met. Messer and Vietze point out that gaze itself probably becomes less salient during the period 6–12 months because during this period other communicative channels are emerging.

Turn-taking and vocal interaction

It is obvious to adults that when we interact verbally it is more effective if we take turns, so that one party speaks while the other listens. In the course of normal conversation, at many points we exchange roles, taking turns as speakers. Studies of adult conversations show that we are very good at this, achieving split second exchanges with remarkably little disruption (Rutter, 1984). When do infants and their caregivers begin to achieve vocal turn-taking?

Schaffer et al. (1977) studied interactions between mothers and their 1- or 2-year-old children and found that even with the younger subjects, vocal exchanges were very smooth. There were many exchanges in the course of normal playful interactions, and most of them were achieved without overlap; if overlaps did occur, they were usually very brief and did not appear to disturb the flow of the interaction. Most speaker-switches were achieved rapidly, with pauses of generally less than one second. Simultaneous vocalizations were usually explicable in terms of social motives and coordination (such as the mother exclaiming to control the child's actions, or joint laughter) rather than conversational incompetency.

Who calls the tune?

Much of the smoothness of conversational interaction that we assume in adult interactions is present, then, in the vocal interchanges of 1-year-olds and their parents. But to whom do we attribute credit for the efficiency of these interactions? Schaffer's view is that these kinds of finding "tell us nothing about the 'abilities' of infants to take turns" (1989a, p. 196). Instead, Schaffer argues that it is more likely that conversational smoothness is achieved as an outcome of the mother's action in skillfully inserting her contributions in the pauses between bursts of vocalizations produced by the infant. The mother, on this account, is allowing the infant to set the pace, but by near continuous monitoring and a very generous accommodation to her less-skilled partner, she transforms the encounter into what Schaffer calls a "pseudo-dialogue."

In cross-sectional and longitudinal studies of mother–infant turn-taking from 9 months to 3 years, Rutter and Durkin (1987) found evidence consistent with Schaffer's account. Up to 24 months, most of the interruptions came from the infants, and mothers appeared to tailor their behavior around the child's vocalizations. From about 18 months, there were marked changes in the children's use of gaze. From this time, they became much more likely to look at the mother at the end of their own utterances. This "terminal look" has been identified in studies of adult–adult interaction as one of the most effective cues that the floor is about to be offered to a listener (Beattie, 1983; Rutter, 1984). Its appearance in mother–infant interaction indicates an increasingly active contribution by the 18-month-old. Even earlier, the infants showed increased visual attention to the mothers when they were talking – again, a characteristic of adult–adult interactions, and one which Rutter and Durkin found clearly established by at least 12 months.

Other researchers have argued that the development of reciprocity and the finely timed turn-taking of vocal and physical activity during even the first few months of life indicate that at some level *each* participant is attuned to the temporal structure of the other's behavior (see Beebe et al., 1985). Trevarthen (1977, 1979, 1982; Trevarthen and Hubley, 1978) has proposed that babies are social from the beginnings of life, and that this is genetically endowed:

the human brain has systems which integrate interpersonal and practical aims together from the first few months after birth . . . Infants actively use human companions to gain knowledge from the time their minds recognize objects of knowledge, even before they can effectively manipulate things. (Trevarthen, 1982, p. 77).

On the basis of detailed frame-by-frame analyses of videotaped mother–infant interaction, Trevarthen (1977) produced evidence which he argues demonstrates that the infant is "calling the tune", controlling the pace and intensity of the interaction by displaying bursts of activity (vocalizing, wriggling, and gesticulating) and then, between bursts, looking attentively at the mother. The mother, for her part, tends to follow the infant. Trevarthen observed that, typically, she responds to excited expressions and hand-waving by smiling, shaking her head or speaking with her head held back. Frequently, the mother imitates the child's actions and expressions.

Subjectivity and intersubjectivity

This pattern of interaction was found among 2-month-olds and their parents, suggesting that even at this early age the infant has some rudimentary notion of its own capacities for action (a sense of subjectivity) and, still more intriguing, some awareness of the interrelationships between its own behavior and that of another (which Trevarthen calls *primary intersubjectivity*). Trevarthen and others (Braten, 1992; Hundeide, 1993) argue that intersubjectivity organizes infant social behavior from very early in life. During the next few months, the infant's cognitive development and interpersonal experiences lead to a greatly increased understanding of the world of people and objects, of the distinctions between people and objects, and of the means of communicating interests and desires to other people. By around 8 or 9 months, these developments result in the achievement of *secondary intersubjectivity* (Trevarthen and Hubley, 1978): a recognition that the world can be shared with others, and that objects can be the focus of joint activity. Trevarthen (1982) holds that during this phase, a new kind of interest develops in what others know about objects or what they can do with them.

Imitation, Joint Attention, and the Development of Routines

In the course of these early interactions, parents and children do more than learn to coordinate their behaviors. They begin also to share an understanding of the child's interests and capabilities, and to collaborate to develop the child's range of skills and information. Various processes are involved, but prominent among them are imitation and joint attention.

Imitation in early parent–infant interaction

Imitation occurs in parent–child interactions from shortly after birth. In lay theories, imitation is the sincerest form of flattery: the imitator manifests his or her desire to become like the imitated. Most developmental theories acknowledge imitation as at least an important component of how children learn. Imitation has particular significance as a medium of social transmission. Meltzoff (1985) notes that it provides a powerful and efficient means by which skills, rules, and social customs can be transferred from one generation to the next. Some theories of social development (including early versions of social learning theory) accord imitation a prominent role, not least because they assume that infants come into the world with little or no knowledge and have to acquire it through copying the more experienced.

Meltzoff (1985; Meltzoff and Gopnik, 1993) raises serious problems for learning–based accounts, and argues instead that the imitative behaviors of infants point to much more complex endowment. He stresses that imitation is a "double-edged" activity, with both social and cognitive dimensions. In order to imitate, the infant has to perceive the act to be copied, represent the act mentally, translate the act into analogous acts of his or her own (realizing that in some sense the other person is "like me"), and then organize his or her motor behavior to correspond with the content and sequence of the other person's act. Meltzoff's own research (to which we return in chapter 8) indicates some impressive capabilities of very young infants in this regard. In fact, Meltzoff maintains that infants have an innate psychological capacity to relate their actions to those of others, and that the infant is socially attuned from birth.

In their studies of vocal matching, Papousek and Papousek (1989) report infants' overt delight in the outcomes of their efforts to copy the behavior of their mothers. Another interesting feature of the interactions described so far is that adults imitate infants, too (cf. Papousek and Papousek, 1989; Trevarthen, 1977). Perhaps this indicates that the source of imitation is others' activity. Might it be that children first learn about the possibility of linking adult behaviors to their own through adults' frequent modeling of such associations? Meltzoff (1985) argues that this interpretation disregards the reasons why infants find parental imitations interesting in the first place. He proposes that parental imitation has a special status in the infant's world *because* infants are already capable of recognizing the correspondence between their own and adults' actions. Imitative runs of vocal and other actions provide both partners with an extended opportunity to relate their behavior in form and time, thus sharing in a reciprocal, communicative exchange. In such contexts, the infant begins to recognize that these people are "like me" (Meltzoff, 1985, p. 29). Consistent with this view, Field et al. (1985a) found that 3-month-old infants vocalized and smiled more frequently when their mothers imitated their actions. The traditional assumption that imitation is the means whereby the outside gets in – the child absorbs the surroundings – overlooks the complexity of the actions of the imitator.

Figure 2.7 Joint attention.

Joint attention

So far, we have considered parent–infant interaction with a focus on the mutual interest and responsivity of the participants. However, infants are also interested in other aspects of their surroundings, and as their own cognitive and manipulative abilities develop they direct increasing amounts of attention to the world of objects (Bornstein and Tamis-Lemonda, 1990; Collis, 1977; Schaffer, 1989a, 1992; Trevarthen, 1979, 1982). Schaffer and Trevarthen point to the age of 5 months as the approximate time around which the shift toward external interests begins. Once again, the child tends to set the pace by selecting some things for attention and not others, and the parent tends to respond. As already mentioned, parents interacting with babies are often willing to devote almost continuous visual attention to the child's behavior and interests (figure 2.7).

Collis and Schaffer (1975) observed mother–infant pairs in an unfamiliar room, with four prominently placed toys, known to be visually appealing to very young children. They found that if one member of the dyad was looking at a toy, the other one was, too. But when the researchers investigated the sequence of gaze patterns they found that it was usually the infant who looked first, and then the mother followed his or her gaze. Collis (1977) replicated this finding with a different sample, and found that infants begin to show a reciprocal interest in the direction of the mother's gaze only toward the end of the first year.

Collis and Schaffer (1975) label the process whereby two (or more) individuals come to focus on some common object "visual coorientation." Its developmental significance is that it incorporates the infant's environmental explorations in a social context, as Schaffer puts it "and so converts an *infant–object* situation into an *infant–object–mother* situation" (1989a, p. 197). Yoder and Munson (in press) found that mothers were more likely to respond to infant behaviors that contained evidence of coordinated attention. Joint attention provides opportunities to learn how to do things. Von Hofsten and Siddiqui (1993) demonstrated that infants (aged 6 and 12 months) can learn how to explore and manipulate objects through watching their mothers tackle the objects first.

The development of routines

As parents and infants develop their mutual patterns of interaction and as they share attention to objects, some of their activities recur. The baby discovers that a ball can roll from one place to another; her father stops its journey and rolls it back to her; she sends it off again, and he returns – before long, father and daughter have a routine with this particular toy. Another, and very popular, type of routine that parents and young children like to play is *peekaboo*, in which the adult repeatedly hides his or her face and upon reappearing exclaims "Peekaboo!" Enthralling activity to the participants, but on the face of it rather trivial behavior.

However, these repetitive types of parent–infant exchange appear both to serve important purposes and to reflect important underlying developments in the child. Bruner (1983a) argues that through participation in everyday, playful activities the infant learns more about the structures and demands of social interaction, preparing and rehearsing skills that will ultimately become essential to successful interchanges, such as conversation. Particularly interesting is Bruner's (1978) finding of a shift in responsibility for initiating give-and-take type games. In a longitudinal case study, he found that during the first few months of life, the parent typically starts the game up and leads the child through. But at around the age of 10 months, roles are suddenly reversed, and the child initiates 60 percent of the time, with the parent's initiations dropping to around 40 percent. Gradually, over the next few months, relative contributions are adjusted and the participants move toward more equal roles.

Cultural Variations in Parent–Infant Interaction

Most of the work on mother–infant interaction discussed so far has been conducted in Europe or the United States, either in laboratories or domestic settings. Extending this research to other cultures has provided some evidence of universalities, and some qualifications. For example, Keller et al. (1988) found that the patterns of eye-contact and joint dialogues found in Western (German and Greek) parents and infants were broadly similar to those of non-Western peoples (Yanomani Indians and Trobriand

Islanders). However, Schieffelin (1990) reports that the kinds of reciprocity and mutual attention that are favored by Western caregivers and their infants are much less common among the Kaluli of Papua New Guinea. Mothers in this society do spend a great deal of time with their infants and are attentive to them, but regard the preverbal child as having "no understanding" and rarely "converse" with them; they avoid eye-contact, and are more likely to position the infant to face outwards rather than *en face*.

Even among middle-class mothers in relatively similar Western societies, there appear to be substantial variations in patterns of interactions. Bornstein et al. (1991a) compared mother–infant–interactions in French and American dyads, and found some similarities (both encouraged infant attention to the environment and visual/tactile exploration) as well as some notable differences (American mothers appeared more didactic and more concerned to stimulate development). The investigators comment that the inter-country difference appeared to bear out Piaget's celebrated comments on the "American question," referring to the contrast between the Genevan conception of intelligence as constructive activity and what Piaget saw as the empiricist orientation across the Atlantic: how can you measure it and how can you get more of it?

Comparisons between French mothers and their counterparts from other societies, however, would suggest that the American question is not entirely irrelevant in the heart of Europe. Rabain-Jamin (1989) compared the interactional styles of native French mothers and West African mothers (immigrants to Paris) engaged in object play at home with their 10- and 15-month-old infants. She found marked differences in the use of verbal and nonverbal input, with French mothers both verbalizing to the child and coordinating verbal and nonverbal references more frequently. Rabain-Jamin (1989) argues that some African cultures place less weight than European cultures on the spoken word as a means of organizing interpersonal activity. African mothers were more likely to draw their infant's attention to a toy by drumming on it with their fingers than by calling the child's name and talking about the object. One African mother explained: "We give toys [to children] to play with. You give them toys to teach, for the future. We feel that children learn better when they are older" (Rabain-Jamin, 1989, p. 303).

Each orientation may be adaptive in its ecological context (Bronfenbrenner, 1979). The French mothers could reasonably anticipate a lengthy formal education ahead for their children, highly dependent upon the kinds of verbal skills, analytical strategies, and spatiotemporal awareness that parents can begin to introduce in everyday play activities. Mothers in traditional African societies could well expect their children to be immersed soon enough in the practical demands of domestic and community activities, where one learns through participation rather than preparation. Difficulties are threatened, of course, when the hitherto distinct cultures are juxtaposed.

In some Western societies, an important theme in the ideology of childrearing is the encouragement of autonomy, exploration, achievement, mastery, and verbal independence, whereas in some Asian cultures there is a greater emphasis on interdependence, social harmony, the strength of the parent–child bond, and group identity (Befu, 1986; Bornstein et al., 1990; Tobin et al., 1989). Bornstein et al.

(1990) studied mother–infant interactions in samples of Japanese and American subjects. The babies were 5 months old, around the age when their cognitive development and manipulative skills would predict increasing involvement with the physical environment (Schaffer, 1989a). The findings showed that, in both contexts, the relative amounts of infants' attention to their physical surroundings or their mother was consistent with maternal encouragement. However, there was a clear inter-cultural difference in maternal strategy for organizing babies' looking. When Japanese infants looked at their physical surroundings, their mothers tended to encourage them to attend to the mothers themselves; but when the infants looked at the mothers, the mothers guided their attention to the environment. Among the American dyads, the mothers encouraged their visual attention irrespective of whether the babies looked at the mother or the environment.

Why would mothers in one culture attempt to change their babies' focus of attention, while mothers in another zoom in with them and try to support their interest? The Japanese mothers seem to insinuate themselves into the infant's orientation, while the Americans prefer to underwrite the child's own discoveries. Bornstein et al. (1990) conclude that this reflects differences in the overarching cultural goals of the mothers, with Americans emphasizing the emergence of exploratory activity and initiative in contrast to a Japanese emphasis on guiding children's activities in the interpersonal realm. The authors go on to indicate the possible longer-term implications of contrasting styles of interaction, raising the "American question" again and noting that from the earliest days of schooling, Japanese children appear to perform considerably better than their US counterparts. Overall, these cross-cultural comparisons reveal similarities and differences. In each context, the parents' contributions to the development of interaction patterns is important; but how parents gear their involvements vary, seemingly as a function of higher-level goals and values in the relevant culture.

Summary

Caregivers and infants begin to coordinate their actions from the beginnings of life, and parents exploit the child's interest in facial stimuli (as well as their own fascination with the newcomer's facial behaviors) by orienting him or her to maximize visual contact. Infants appear to enjoy vocal interchanges long before they can speak, and strive to match their output to the sounds around them. There are asymmetries in the contributions of parent and child to early interactions, and there is disagreement among researchers as to the relative amounts of influence over the structure and progress of early dialogues. There is agreement that early dialogues are finely timed and exhibit characteristics that are basic to successful verbal interactions among adults. Infants generally enter a social world in which other people are very interested in them, although there are inter-cultural differences in the ways this interest is manifest and in the balance of activities encouraged by parents.

Individual Differences in Infants and their Caregivers

Some aspects of early human development are virtually universal. All nonhandi-capped children are equipped with similar sensory capacities and all share some degree of interest in the physical and social stimuli they encounter; similarly, most caregivers have at least some interest in their babies. Nevertheless, there is considerable range in the ways individuals participate in the social world. Some differences are associated with cultural beliefs about appropriate modes of interpersonal behavior, as we have just seen, but there may be others that arise from the constellation of behavioral propensities that the child manifests. For example, we have already noted that some children cry more or less than others, that some are perceived by their caregivers as having congenial personality characteristics, while others are regarded as "cranky" or "fussy." Indeed, most parents will report that from very early on they can detect personality differences among their children, and it does seem very plausible that an individual's personality will affect her or his social involvement.

This appealing commonsense idea brings us directly into a zone of conceptual and empirical crossfire between social and personality psychologists. First, there is a conceptual problem that, while everyone has some idea of what personality is, no one can define it precisely (Allport, 1937/ 1961). An authoritative textbook concedes that the term simply "defies scientific definition" (Wallace, 1993, p. 4). This does not mean that approximations to definition are unhelpful, but it does mean that we are dealing with an abstract and elusive phenomenon (or, more likely, system of phenomena). Following Allport, most psychologists would include reference to the characteristic behavioral, attitudinal, emotional and cognitive patterns that distinguish one individual from another – but this covers a great deal. Allport stressed also that personality is a *dynamic organization* (1937/ 1961). This highlights the possibility that a personality is continuously open to change – for example, as a consequence of adaptation to new experiences.

Second, even if we could agree upon a definition, there is long-running dispute about the extent to which identification of an individual's personality can reliably predict her or his behavior (Bem and Allen, 1974; Furnham and Argyle, 1981; Hartshorne and May, 1928; Mischel, 1968, 1977). In an influential critique of the predictive value of personality trait measurements, Mischel (1968, p. 146) pointed to a variety of evidence that the same person can behave quite differently in different situations. Mischel concluded that "the concept of personality traits as broad response dispositions is . . . untenable."

We will not pursue this debate here (see McClelland, 1992, for a response from the personality camp), but will try to show how recent work in developmental social psychology contributes new perspectives and new data – and more controversy! To do so, we need to consider the revival of interest in temperamental differences among infants.

Temperament in Infants

If we concede that personality includes values, beliefs, attitudes to social objects and events, and a self-concept that incorporates one's interpreted experiences, then it is clear that infants are somewhat limited in these regards. To speak of an infant's "personality" may be heartwarming to parents (and potentially significant for their relationship), but imprecise to the scientist. However, it may be more viable to attempt to identify constitutional differences in behavioral responses to the environment. For example, observation of a randomly selected group of infants will soon convince you that some are more active than others, some seem stable emotionally while others are more volatile, and there are inter-individual variations in approachability and adaptability. These differences – the infant's temperament – are sometimes regarded as reflecting the "raw material" (Allport, 1937/ 1961, p. 33) that the child brings into the social world and as "the minority of personality traits that have an inherited basis" (Buss, 1992, p. 73).

The concept of temperament, too, is subject to definitional uncertainty (Garrison and Earls, 1987; Goldsmith et al., 1987). Even so, most investigators use the term to refer to consistencies in the ways a given individual reacts to environmental experiences (Buss and Plomin, 1984; Rothbart et al., 1994; Thomas and Chess, 1989). Different investigators propose different accounts of the components of temperament, but a useful working summary of four major dimensions is provided by McCall (in Goldsmith et al., 1987). These are *activity* (the tempo and vigor of an individual's behavior), *reactivity* (the patterns of approach or withdrawal from stimulation), *emotionality* (the tendency to become aroused and upset), and *sociability* (the extent to which the individual seeks or spurns the company of others).

One of the best known studies of temperament is that of Thomas and Chess (1977, 1989). These researchers obtained detailed maternal reports on 138 American infants every three months during the children's first two years, and followed the same individuals at less frequent intervals through to adulthood (in the New York Longitudinal Study). Several dimensions of temperament were measured, and on this basis the investigators distinguished three broad clusters of temperamental characteristics in infants. This led to a classification of three temperamental types which has been widely used:

1 "Easy" infants (40 percent of the sample): these children generally adapt well to novel experiences, tend to be cheerful and easily pacified when distressed.
2 "Slow to warm up" infants (10 percent of the sample): these children tend to adapt slowly to novel experiences, are prone to crying and fussing, and are somewhat irregular in their daily routines.
3 "Difficult" infants (15 percent of the sample): these children tend to withdraw in the face of novel experiences, are generally negative in their moods and more intense in their reactions, and are irregular in their sleeping and eating habits.

Although there is dispute over the conceptual basis and factorial structure of the Thomas and Chess framework, the scheme has been widely used in this field. Whichever theoretical framework we accept, it should already be clear that the various dimensions of interest to temperament researchers cover features of infant behavior that we have seen earlier in this chapter to be integral to the beginnings of social life. A predisposition toward high or low activity levels, a willingness or reluctance to respond to novel experiences, or a particular degree of sociability could have fundamental implications for how an infant relates to other people (Hartup and van Lieshout, 1995). The work of temperament theorists raises the question: are there inherited and enduring individual differences among infants in these respects?

Heritability of temperament

In respect of heritability, twin studies provide some of the most interesting findings, and these are reasonably consistent in showing higher correlations between the temperamental characteristics of monozygotic twins than between those of fraternal twins (Goldsmith, 1989; Plomin, 1987; Plomin et al., 1988). Correlations between non-twin siblings tend to be quite low, though positive (Plomin et al., 1988). Unfortunately, these results do not establish firmly the contributions of inheritance, since it is possible that identical twins experience very similar environments, and it is possible that non-twin siblings experience different environments within the family (see chapter 4).

Other evidence which might be interpreted as demonstrating the heritability of temperament comes from comparisons of infants from different cultures. Chinese infants growing up in America (Freedman and Freedman, 1969) in China (Kagan et al. 1994) and Taipei (Prior et al., 1986, 1989) tend to be rated as less active and more withdrawn than Caucasian children. Among Australian children, significantly more infants of Lebanese or Greek backgrounds are categorized as "difficult" according to the Thomas and Chess criteria (Prior et al., 1987, 1989). While provocative, these findings are open to different interpretations. We have already seen that there are cultural differences in how parents orient to their babies. There are also methodological and translation challenges to studies which attempt to gauge parental interpretations of infant behavior using the same instrument in different cultures. And it should be noted there is considerable within-culture variability in temperamental characteristics and classification (Kohnstamm et al., 1989).

Stability of temperament

In respect of the stability of temperamental characteristics, the evidence is mixed. Kagan and his colleagues found that children identified as inhibited and fearful at 14 months continued to manifest correlates of social anxiety (such as accelerated heart rates in novel social situations) through their second, third, fourth and eighth years (Kagan, 1989; Kagan et al., 1988). On this basis, Kagan argues that some people have a shy or anxious temperament "because that is how their central nervous system is constructed" (1989, p. 141). Other studies, too, have found that dimensions of temperament tend to be relatively stable through the early years (Asendorpf, 1992; Bornstein et al., 1991a; Prior, 1992; Thomas and Chess, 1977, 1989). However, some researchers have found only low correlations between measures of temperament during the first and second years (Peters-Martin and Wachs, 1984; Rothbart, 1986, 1989).

The problem is a complicated one, since the forms of expressive behavior measured in assessments of temperament are themselves subject to both maturational changes (see contributors to Goldsmith et al., 1987) and shifting environmental demands (Garrison and Earls, 1987). For example, we saw earlier that there are developments in the qualities of infants' smiles in the first two or three months of life, such that adults now feel a sense of genuine social contact. There are maturational changes, too, in terms of responses to potential stressors (such as physical discomfort or novel events). Hence, it is difficult to disentangle temperamental factors from newly emerging competencies or other aspects of self-organization. At the same time, the developmental tasks facing the child are changing (e.g., caregivers' expectations about the child's role in feeding and cleansing, or mixing with others, are subject to change with the child's age). Overall, some developments in behavioral characteristics may be precipitated by biology, others by experience, and many by the interaction of these processes. For these reasons, careful longitudinal studies are essential (Rothbart, 1986, 1989).

Temperament in the family

We cannot quite get rid of parents, though. For one thing, there is a measurement problem (Garrison and Earls, 1987): most of the studies investigating the implications of infant temperament for social relations and social development have relied on parental reports of the babies' behavior. As Kagan (1989) comments, if you ask parents about their children's behavior you will tend to arrive at a set of dimensions which reflect parental concerns (such as fussiness, ease of management, fearfulness, sleep patterns). Studies which have compared temperament ratings of the same children by different adults (parents versus teachers) find weak or zero relationships (Eisenberg et al., 1993; Goldsmith et al., 1991; Stocker and Dunn, 1990), a pattern of results very similar to that found in studies of cross-situational behavioral consistency among older children and adults (cf. Mischel, 1968).

As has already been firmly established in the earlier parts of this chapter, parents interact closely with their infants from the outset. Hence, it is possible that parental styles and expectations may affect infant responsivity. Is this infant "difficult" or are her parents too intrusive in their caregiving activities? Is this infant "easy" or is his mother especially attuned to his every need and whim, always pre-empting complaints with sensitive attentions? If temperament is an important determinant of an individual's social behavior then it follows that the temperaments of those with whom he or she interacts may also be important (Buss, 1992). This raises issues of the "goodness-of-fit" of infant and parent temperaments (Lerner et al., 1989; Thomas and Chess, 1989). Suppose an infant is indeed relatively "difficult" in temperament: will her subsequent development be affected by the behavior of her parent(s)? Research by

Thomas and Chess (1989) indicates that the goodness-of-fit makes a considerable difference to the development and adjustment of infant temperament.

For these reasons, most researchers tend to take interactionist positions. "Temperamental factors impose a slight initial bias for certain moods and behavioral profiles to which the social environment reacts" (Kagan, 1989, p. 12). Debate continues over how substantial the initial bias is and how it affects and is affected by social experience.

Summary

There are individual differences among infants. To the people who interact with infants, and to some theorists, these differences reflect personality structure – or, at least, its beginnings. A major focus in this area of infancy research is the temperament of the child, behavioral consistencies that are thought to have a strong genetic component. Although there is some evidence of heritability and stability, the implications of temperament for subsequent development are controversial. It is difficult to distentangle effects due to the infant's temperament from effects due to the perceptions of her or his caregivers, or from the nature of their relationship. Most theorists acknowledge some degree of interaction between temperament and experience.

Conclusions

Rapid developments in infancy research have radically changed developmentalists' understanding of what the child brings into the world. We have seen in this chapter that the infant has sensory and reflexive capacities which enable it to explore actively. We have seen also that infants' visual and auditory capacities are not simply useful devices for inspecting the complex physical world they have just entered. They are the means of making contact with other humans, and sources of information for caregivers. From the earliest, seemingly most biologically compelled, interactions around feeding, infants and their caregivers begin to demonstrate mutual influences. It is clear that what nature has provided is crucial to the beginnings of social life, but it is also clear that social life transforms capacities into meaningful participation. In the next chapter, we examine how social participation leads to the formation of relationships, and how the central relationships influence subsequent development.

Further reading

Fogel, A. (1993) *Developing through Relationships: origins of communication, self, and culture.* New York: Harvester Wheatsheaf.

A thoughtful elaboration of the implications of work on mutual regulation in social interactions from infancy onwards, arguing that the human mind and the sense of self develop out of the processes of communication and relationship formation.

Granrud, C. (ed.) (1993) *Visual Perception and Cognition in Infancy*. Hillsdale, N. J.: Erlbaum.

Experimental research into infants' visual capacities and their integration with early cognitive developments.

Johnson, M. H. and Morton, J. (1991) *Biology and Cognitive Development: the case of face recognition*. Oxford: Blackwell.

A well-written and stimulating account of the relationship between biology and cognition in the development of face recognition in humans and other species. Perhaps a little thin on social perspectives.

Kohnstamm, G. A., Bates, J. E. and Rothbart, M.K. (eds) (1989) *Temperament in Childhood*. Chichester: Wiley.

Thirty-four chapters by leading temperament researchers from around the world. This volume discusses conceptual, empirical and applied issues in temperament research and provides several valuable cross-cultural perspectives.

Lester, B. M. and Boukydis, C. F. Z. (eds) (1985) *Infant Crying: theoretical and research perspectives*. New York: Plenum Press.

The nature and consequences of infant cries are discussed thoroughly in this collection of essays, ranging through physiological, acoustic, social, clinical, developmental, and comparative issues.

Lewis, M. and Feinman, S. (1991) *Social Influences and Socialization in Infancy*. New York: Plenum.

The editors propose that a social psychological perspective is relevant to the entirety of infant behavior and development, and contributing authors illustrate with reference to a wide range of sources and processes of influence.

Osofsky, J. (ed.) (1987) *Handbook of Infant Development, 2nd. edn*. New York: Wiley.

Twenty-seven chapters providing almost 1,400 pages of high-level reviews of research into many aspects of infant development. An essential sourcebook for advanced study in this field.

Schaffer, H. R. (ed.) (1977) *Studies in Mother–Infant Interaction*. London: Academic Press.

A book which drew together much of the early work on mother–child interaction and provided a stimulus for the rapid growth of this field. It remains a rich source of descriptions and interpretations of the details of the first social relationship.

Chapter 3

Attachment to Others

Till very recently I used to fly home to my mother when I got sick. In the full flush of temperature I'd make it to the airport and to the front door where a near collapse brought buckets of sympathy and love. It was worth the ticket.

I have finally weaned off such childish behaviour. I have spent the last week alone at home with the 'flu. A bit of nursing from the CPO (current permanent other) after work plus elaborate coughing over the phone to mum has had to suffice.

Lying here during the day I am forced to wonder how many other grown-up people out there — company executives, lawyers, bricklayers — are lying in bed alone at this very moment, their noses blocked with 'flu, their partners at work, thinking the same illogical thought: "I want my mummy!"

(Ostrow, The Weekend Australian, *1993*)

Ruth Ostrow is one of Australia's leading newspaper columnists. Her weekly article in the nation's quality newspaper is a source of provocative commentary on human affairs and the trials of modern urban life. Ostrow is highly regarded as a media personality and by her own account she lives an independent, jet-setting sort of existence based in the metropolis of Sydney. Her work takes her all over the world. She is thirtysomething. But Ostrow acknowledges here a longstanding emotional dependency which she freely admits is incongruous with other aspects of her personality and lifestyle.

Many can identify with Ostrow's account. Perhaps, if you are a student, you know the feeling. I used to teach in a British university, where part of my responsibilities included a personal tutor role (a kind of surrogate mummy who keeps files). In the British tertiary system, most students attend a university away from their home town. And so, in their late teens, lots of young adults find themselves in a strange environment, surrounded by strange people speaking of strange things, and separated from all that is familiar. This is a high stress experience in anyone's terms. The outcome is a good deal of "I want my mummy!", and each year it would fall to me and a couple of the bigger guys from Student Retention Services to restrain at least one victim of separation distress from packing it all in and catching the next train home. We can but speculate about the proportion of first-year students who cry themselves to sleep at night missing their mummy but I know people, now in high places, whose degrees were saved only by express courier delivery of the remains of their teddy bears, a last tenuous, cuddly link with the security of the maternal home.

All of which serves to remind us of two important things about mothers. First, they are a source of support and a buffer against stress. Second, the ties we form to them are enduring, in both directions: "a call for help even after 40 years will bring a mother to her child and evoke attachment behaviors equal in strength to those in the first year of life" (Klaus and Kennell, 1983, p. 2). Kropotkin (1939) tells us that colonialists in need of adult female slaves used to first steal their infants, knowing that this was the most effective way to ensnare the mother.

This powerful relationship brings us to one of the central concepts of developmental social psychology: attachment. An attachment is "an affectional tie that one person or animal forms between himself and another specific one – a tie that binds them together in space and endures over time" (Ainsworth and Bell, 1970, p. 50). Attachment as a relationship is supported by attachment behaviors designed to maintain the link. An attachment behavior is "any form of behavior that results in a person attaining or maintaining proximity to some other clearly identified individual who is conceived as better able to cope with the world. It is most obvious whenever the person is frightened, fatigued, or sick, and is assuaged by comforting and caregiving" (Bowlby, 1988, p. 27). In the infant or toddler, attachment behaviors include watching and clinging to the caregiver, crying for her or his attention, smiling at her or his reappearance (figure 3.1); in the adult, they include catching a train or plane home, or accumulating a hefty long-distance 'phone bill.

Attachment in early childhood is important because it is the starting point of our connections to others. Without these connections, we really would be no more than a hapless little data-cruncher, the imaginary information-processing child who is

Figure 3.1 An attachment behavior.

concerned only with the acquisition of knowledge and who gets its satisfactions by perpetually reorganizing information within itself. The significance of attachments tells us that there is something more to social development than transforming input. According to attachment theorists such as Bowlby (1988), emotionally mediated communication remains a principal feature of intimate relationships throughout life.

In this chapter, following an outline of the chronology of the early stages of attachment, we consider possible explanations of the phenomenon, drawing on some of the theoretical traditions introduced in chapter 1. Most research on attachment has been influenced particularly by ethological theory, especially via the writings of the British psychiatrist, John Bowlby (1969, 1973, 1980, 1988), and later the research of the American social developmentalist, Mary Ainsworth (1969; Ainsworth and Bowlby, 1991; Ainsworth et al., 1978). We will concentrate primarily on work arising from – or challenging – the ethological perspective. Among the most controversial issues arising from Bowlby's early work is the proposition that attachment is *monotropic*, focused on one person, and that that person is ideally the natural mother. We will consider various types of evidence bearing on this claim. Another thesis derived from ethological theory is that the mother herself is biologically preprogrammed to stick around the infant and ensure that she is there, ready for the attachment to come about; we will consider studies designed to test this claim. One of the most influential ideas arising from Ainsworth's research is the proposition that there are different types of attachment relationships that infants form to their caregivers, and an outline of the main types will be provided. We consider the possible antecedents of these relationships and the possible consequences.

The Emergence of Attachment

Detailed observational studies of the development of attachments between infants and primary caregivers have enabled researchers to outline a series of broad stages through which most children appear to progress (Bowlby, 1969; Schaffer and Emerson, 1964). Schaffer and Emerson's (1964) study is one of the most extensive, involving monthly observations of 60 Scottish babies during the first year, and then again at 18 months. Their methods, conducted in home visits, included monitoring the baby's reaction to various events and separations, such as the mother leaving the baby with other people or alone in a room, leaving the baby outside the house, putting it to bed, exposure to strangers, and so on. The form, intensity, and duration of the infant's protests were measured. The researchers also investigated the baby's reactions to the departures of various individuals. Did he or she react more intensely if the mother left or if a casual visitor left? On this basis, Schaffer and Emerson (1964) outlined three stages in the development of primary attachments:

1 *The asocial stage* (0–6 weeks): during this stage, the infant emits signals, such as crying and smiling, but these do not appear to be directed particularly to humans and are not specific to individuals.
2 *The stage of indiscriminate attachment* (6 weeks to 7 months): the infant now will cry for attention from anyone, whether familiar or stranger (1964. p. 22), and can be appeased by attention from anyone when distressed.
3 *The stage of specific attachments* (7–11 months): attachment behaviors are organized more selectively during this stage and are elicited by particular individuals. For many children, there appears to be an initial attachment to one individual, but some children form "multiple" attachments, to several figures. In Schaffer and Emerson's investigation, a majority progressed from a single to multiple attachments in a fairly brief period.

The attachment figure in Schaffer and Emerson's study was most often the mother, and the mother was most likely to become the "principal object" – the person who was associated with the most intense attachment behaviors. Even so, there were considerable individual variations among the sample, and some children became attached initially to other members of the household (fathers, siblings, grandparents). This substantial early study, then, did not offer a great deal of support for the thesis of monotropy.

Wariness of Strangers

Around the time the child is beginning to demonstrate clear preferences for specific individuals, he or she also manifests another and often quite vigorous social response: anxiety in the presence of unfamiliar persons (Bohlin and Hagekull, 1993; Emde et al., 1976; Schaffer and Emerson, 1964; Sroufe, 1977). If you pick up a 2-month-old, it is unlikely that you will invoke a markedly different initial reaction to that obtained by his or her principal caregiver. But try the same behavior with a 10- to 12-month-old, and you will begin to appreciate the active contributions the infant can make to his or her social situation. The child will stare cautiously, withdraw from you, look toward a familiar caregiver if one is present, and quite possibly begin to whimper, cry, or even scream the place down. The two developments, attachment to caregivers and wariness of strangers, develop during the latter part of the first year and seem to be intimately related processes.

We turn to theoretical explanations of these developments in a moment. It should be noted that many other investigators have examined aspects of the emergence of attachment and wariness of strangers, and this is one of the rare areas in the study of social behavior where there is broad agreement at least on the descriptive account: vulnerability to separation from the principal caregiver and wariness of strangers become particularly marked during the final quarter of the first year (Schaffer, 1990).

Theories of Attachment

There is little doubt that attachments occur, and that they are prominent features of many children's social involvements. But why should this be the case? It would be a lot more convenient and better for the economy if babies came in Huxley-like factory batches, to be raised in homogeneous, clinical conditions where they could be trained for their future functions.

Several theoretical frameworks have been advanced to explain attachment. The most prominent have been psychoanalytic theory, learning theory, and ethological theory. As already indicated, by far the most influential theory has been that based on the ethological approach, led by Bowlby, Ainsworth and others (references in the literature and later in this chapter to "attachment theory" normally mean the Bowlby–Ainsworth perspective). Theorists in this tradition, as we will see, incorporate some concepts and themes from the other approaches and from cognitive developmental theories. Hence, it will be useful to note the gist of the psychoanalytic and learning theories of attachment.

Psychoanalytic Theory

According to Freud's theory, human development proceeds through a series of psychosexual stages, the first of which is the oral stage, which lasts approximately one year from birth. During this period, Freud believed the child to be centred on oral experiences, one of his or her earliest and most basic sources of pleasure. In most circumstances, the natural provider of this pleasure is the mother and, because she satisfies the infant's needs for food, sucking, and nurturance, the infant invests libidinal energy in her; she becomes the primary love object in the baby's life (Miller, 1993). For this reason, Freud regarded the mother's status as "unique, without parallel, established unalterably for a whole lifetime as the first and strongest love-object and as the prototype of all later love-relations" (Freud, 1964, p. 188).

In Erikson's (1950, 1968) stage theory, the first year is concerned with the establishment of basic trust, and again the mother is attributed a key role in this achievement because she can minister to the infant's needs, providing a dependable source of nutrition and comfort. Oral experiences (sucking, biting, teething, and weaning) are seen by Erikson as the prototypes of taking and giving.

In both of the major psychoanalytic theories, then, the role of feeding is given prominence in the explanation of attachment. In each case the early relationship is seen as the foundation to subsequent progress. Although some of the psychosexual emphases of the Freudian approach tend to be peripheral to contemporary thinking about attachment, this perspective has had strong influence over the field in the priority it accords to the emotional relationship with the mother, the importance it attributes to the role of feeding and the assumed impact of early experience upon development.

Learning Theories

Learning theorists also maintain that feeding is a principal determinant of attach-ment. In fact, learning theorists acknowledge a conceptual debt to the psychoanalytic tradition in this respect (cf. Sears, 1965) but have a different theoretical framework and regard themselves as more rigorous in empirical matters. Learning theorists in general maintain that much of the parent–child relationship depends on their experiences of each other rather than the forces of instinct (Hay and Vespo, 1988).

Early learning theory

One early account proposed by some learning theorists has strong intuitive appeal. This is the *secondary drive hypothesis* of Dollard and Miller (1950). Primary drives are those which stem from a species' essential physiological requirements, such as hunger, thirst, bodily comfort. The human infant is dependent upon others to gratify these needs, and thus comes to associate others with relief from unpleasant sensations or tensions. The mother, Dollard and Miller (1950) point out, is associated with the primary reward of feeding on over 2,000 occasions in the child's first year – pretty good reason to begin to like someone. In learning theory terms, the mother attains the status of a positive reinforcer.

Learning accounts have also been put forward to explain why *mothers* become attached to their infants. For example, it has been suggested that (a) cessation of crying or onset of smiling are positive reinforcers to the mother, and thus promote the repetition of specific nurturant behaviors; (b) that the mother can be rewarded more subtly by the numerous signs of infant wellbeing and development; and (c) some stimuli associated with children may have acquired reinforcing value for females as a result of sex-typing during their own development (Gerwirtz, 1961).

One problem with early learning theory is the evidence from studies such as Schaffer and Emerson's (1964) that infants can become attached to people who are not responsible for essential caregiving and feeding. Indeed, many children become attached to parents who neglect or abuse them (Schaffer, 1971).

Social learning theory

A revised learning theory of attachment has been developed by Hay (1985; Hay and Vespo, 1988). Hay's account draws on social learning theory (introduced in chapter 1) and also incorporates the kinds of findings concerning infants' biological predispositions to attend to social stimuli discussed in chapter 2. However, she adds the proposal that the formation of the mother–child relationship involves purposeful social activities on the part of the adult. Attachment, on this view, does not just "happen" naturally, but comes about as parents "deliberately teach their children to love them and to understand human relationships" (Hay and Vespo, 1988, p. 82). Among other processes parents might adapt to bring this about are modeling (after all, they *show* the child affection extensively), social facilitation (they watch and assist much that the infant does), and direct instruction (they guide the child to reciprocate attention, they teach him or her to cuddle and kiss them).

Learning about one another is clearly an important part of the attachment process, and the learning theory framework has influenced the field more generally by creating a focus on the effects of the *experiences* of parent–child interaction. However, a remaining problem for the social learning account, acknowledged by Hay and Vespo (1988), is that it does not offer a very strong explanation of one of the most striking features of attachments, namely the emotional intensity that they involve.

Ethological Theory

We saw in chapter 1 that ethologists are concerned to explain the biological and evolutionary bases of social behavior. In one of his best-known studies, Lorenz (1935) described how the infants of some bird species, if exposed to a moving object during an early critical period, would attach themselves to it and follow it about wherever it moved. Lorenz called this phenomenon *imprinting*. It occurs most commonly between the young and its parent, but Lorenz showed that if another object is presented during

Figure 3.2   Konrad Lorenz with goslings.
(*Source: Time/Life*)

the critical period, then the infants will imprint upon it. In a celebrated photograph, Lorenz is shown with a string of geese (see figure 3.2) for whom a chance encounter during the critical period for imprinting seems to have led them seriously astray. The phenomenon of imprinting poses another problem for learning theory: the imprinting infant attaches itself instinctively to the mother-figure or substitute *prior* to any learning and independently of nutritional rewards.

Although much of the ethologists' work was concerned with nonhuman species, their approach has obvious implications for the study of humans who, after all, are also products of evolutionary adaptation. Like other species, humans need to ensure that their behavior is organized to promote survival and reproduction.

Such a conclusion was reached by Bowlby (1953, 1969), originally a psychoanalytically trained psychiatrist, who undertook a major study for the World Health Organization in the 1940s of the effects of mother–child separation in early childhood. In consultations with child-care workers in France, The Netherlands, Sweden, Switzerland, the UK, and the US, he found a widespread conviction of the importance for the healthy development of the young child of "a warm, intimate, and continuous relationship with his mother (or permanent mother-substitute – one person who steadily "mothers" him) in which both find satisfaction and enjoyment" (Bowlby, 1953, p. 11). Observational and clinical evidence indicated that the absence or serious disruption of the attachment relationship led to severe distress in the infant and sometimes to enduring behavioral–emotional problems. Bowlby became convinced that an attachment between caregiver and child was fundamental to normal development and he drew on Lorenz and others' ethological studies of attachment behavior in subhumans to develop an account of the place of attachment in nature, including human nature (see especially Bowlby, 1969, ch. 11).

Bowlby points to the ubiquity of proximity-maintaining behavior in the young of numerous species. He emphasizes the directed nature of attachment behaviors: the fact that they are focused on a specific individual, usually the mother. The parent and the young behave toward each other in ways very different from the ways in which they behave toward all others: "Individual recognition and highly differentiated behavior are, then, the rule in the parent–young relations of birds and mammals" (1969, p. 226). Attachment behaviors in humans, Bowlby holds, are manifestations of the same goals of survival as other animals, and operate in similar ways. Much of the evidence reviewed in chapter 2, concerning infant signaling and early social interactions, is consistent with Bowlby's thesis that human infants are endowed with means of communicating their needs and ensuring the proximity of caregivers.

Ethology and wariness of strangers

We saw above that as the child's attachment to particular individuals becomes manifest her or his discomfort in the presence of strangers also becomes apparent. The reasons why this latter development is so intriguing become obvious if you continue the mental experiment we began earlier, and imagine how you would approach an infant. Most likely, you would move carefully, lean toward the child, display a smile, perhaps wiggling a few fingers and uttering vocalizations from the coochy-coo area of your lexicon. You mean no harm. And most of the baby's experiences with strangers will have been of this order – people are usually affectionate toward infants. So, the infant has no obvious learning experiences which alert him or her to danger.

Why, then, does stranger wariness arise in most infants during the first or second year? One possibility, proposed by Bowlby, is that it is a rudimentary survival mechanism, built-in by nature. The developing child experiences conflicting motivations, such as the desire to be with the caregiver, interest in exploring the environment, and discomfort with the unfamiliar. In Bowlby's view, nature has organized a system of balances and checks to help ensure that the infant adjusts successfully to these tensions. One system says, in effect, "hang on here, this is warm and safe;" another says "that looks interesting, time for a wander;" and yet another says "it's a battlefield out there" (for a more formal account, see Bretherton, 1987). In the unpredictable, hazardous environments that our ancestors had to cope with, babies who yelled out at the sight of something or someone unfamiliar heading toward them would stand a better chance of recruiting protection. The emergence of some kind of fear system would thus be an adaptive counterbalance to the attachment system which, if unconstrained, could lead to the infant running happily into any predator's jaws. Hence, Bowlby (1969, 1988) argues that attachment behavior and wariness of strangers are organized by a homeostatic control system within the central nervous system (analogous to physiological control systems that regulate body temperature or blood pressure).

These balances and checks are useful enough, but how would one know when to call up the situationally appropriate system? Why does the infant not embrace the stranger with delight, and repel the caregiver with a display of rampant fear? Clearly, the infant must be aware of variability in the social environment. Consistent with cognitive developmental accounts, Bowlby proposes that the child in the latter part of the first year has learned to discriminate among people, and has developed object permanency (the knowledge that an object can continue to exist when no longer visible), thus making it possible to compare the stranger with representations of familiar caregivers. These cognitive developments alone seem insufficient to account fully for the emergence of attachment. In Bowlby's view, what transpires in the latter part of the first year is that as the infant develops internalized "working models" of the salient aspects of her or his world (including self and attachment figure), these representations are constrained and coordinated by the homeostatic control systems. Cognition is part of the story, but emotional organization influences how information is interpreted and dealt with (see Bretherton, 1987, 1992, for fuller discussions).

The ethological theory appears superior to social learning theory in terms of its ability to account for the affective features of attachment. None the less, the ontogenetic relationship between emotion and cognition remains puzzling (Cicchetti, 1990). For instance, we saw in chapter 2 that there is evidence that infants make social discriminations somewhat earlier than 9 months (and there is evidence to challenge the traditional Piagetian assumption that object permanency is not attained until late in the first year; cf. Harris, 1989b). It is not entirely clear why the development of marked affective expressions should occur only late in the first year. On the other hand, when more subtle physiological measures are employed (such as forehead skin surface temperature as an indicator of stress), then evidence of positive reactions toward the mother and negative affect in the presence of a stranger may be detected as early as 2–4 months (Mizukami et al., 1990).

Intensity of the stranger's approach

A further question remains. If the infant is developing individual preferences and wariness of strangers, surely he or she would soon reach the point where a trip to the supermarket would be a nightmare? Every passer-by is another unfamiliar stimulus object, every photo on a news-stand a representation of a potential predator. But in fact, while you may occasionally overhear a baby crying in the shopping mall, infants are rarely reduced to hysteria by the succession of anonymous faces they encounter as they are drawn gratuitously into the consumer society or go to the park.

An important factor seems to be the intensity of the intrusion. It has been found that the vigor of the infant's reaction can be exacerbated by having the stranger loom over the infant (Weinraub and Putney, 1978), but moderated by slowing down the approach of the stranger (Decarie, 1974; Trause, 1977) or by allowing the child scope to control what the stranger is doing (Mangelsdorf, 1992). If the stranger sits still and the baby is free to move around, then the child adapts to her or his presence more readily and may even make positive moves toward the stranger (Bretherton and Ainsworth, 1974). Place yourself in the baby's position and you can see that it is plausible that having a stranger some twelve times your size bear down upon you, gurgling and cooing from a great height, could instigate a degree of discomfort. In fact, Kaltenbach et al. (1980), in a laboratory study, found that *mothers* showed even greater signs of discomfort (e.g., gaze aversion) at the approach of strangers than did the babies. Again, sensitivity to what the stranger is doing could be explained as a preprogrammed defence mechanism. In the course of evolution, it is reasonable to suppose that the more energetic the approach, the greater the risk that some threat is entailed.

The ethological approach has been enormously influential in this area of developmental social psychology, and has introduced pivotal concepts and empirical techniques that have in turn generated large amounts of illuminating research, some of which we consider shortly. This framework sustains the Freudian emphasis on the emotional import of the attachment relationship but locates this in a broader account of the species' evolution and perpetuation. It allows for specific learning experiences but stresses the inherent homeostatic constraints on their effects. It incorporates elements of cognitive developmental theory but suggests why early discriminatory abilities and object permanency could be useful in the first place. Finally, it also highlights the importance of emotional security as a basis from which cognitive development can proceed.

Ethology, sociobiology, and the parents

Much of attachment work is concerned with the implications of the relationship for the wellbeing of the child. However, the ethological account, and subsequent, sociobiological theory, also generate interesting claims about the place of parents. For example, Bowlby (1988) maintains that parenting behavior itself has strong biological roots, and that is why such strong emotions are associated with it (although he adds that the particular form of parenting that individuals develop depends also upon experiences and cultural expectations).

Sociobiologists offer a related explanation in terms of *parental investment theory* (see chapter 1). Parental investment theory postulates that the cost of reproduction is greater to the female (Kenrick, 1994; Low, 1989). The female has only one egg per cycle, and can produce only a very small number of children at a time. When she does have a child the extent of the mother's commitment is already high (months of pregnancy, the discomfort of birth, the demands of a hungry infant and so on). Hence, rather than waste all of this effort, she is oriented naturally to take every care of the baby. As a result, she spends a lot of time with the child and becomes attached to it. Consistent with this theory, mothers tend to undertake primary child-care responsibilities even in unconventional domestic arrangements, such as alternative lifestyles and communal living in the US (Eiduson et al., 1982) and The Netherlands (de Kanter, 1988). What could be more natural?

A sensitive period for parenting?

Some researchers influenced by the ethological–sociobiological tradition have argued that nature does a little more to ensure that all works out satisfactorily during the period of the newcomer's greatest dependency, the early months of life. Noting that approximately 90 percent of human history was spent in hunting and gathering societies where separate responsibilities for hunting and child care were allocated along strict gender lines, Porter and Laney (1980) conclude that their mammalian heritage leaves human females "intrinsically better prepared than males for childrearing and attachment to their offspring" (p. 45).

According to this view, nature renders the mother susceptible to the formation of a bond with the infant, by increasing shortly after birth the presence of certain hormones which affect the mother's emotional state. For example, breastfeeding is known to increase the production of oxytocin (which has a calming effect) and prolactin (which is associated with positive feelings; Klaus and Kennell, 1983). Klaus and Kennell argue that these factors contribute to the establishment of a bond between mother and infant. Furthermore, they argue that since these processes are at their most intense shortly after birth, all possible practical arrangements should be effected to support the emergence of the bond. Think back to Lorenz's mother goose: if she wandered off at the critical moment, her goslings could imprint themselves on any old boot that happened to wander by. To avoid these unrewarding affinities, it would be biologically advantageous to have mothers themselves preprogrammed to stay close to their infants during the early period of dependency and attachment formation.

Testing the mother–infant bond

Klaus and Kennell (1976) conducted a very interesting experiment to test their hypothesis that close contact would be to the advantage of both mother and child. They argued that skin-to-skin contact with the baby was highly desirable at this time because it promoted the all-important bond, without which there was greater risk of inadequate parenting and even child neglect or abuse. It is certainly plausible that physical contact between parent and child is conducive to the beginnings of social relationships. Touch is an arousing mode of communication among humans, and one of the most elementary ways of expressing the closeness of a relationship (Argyle, 1988a). However, in the 1970s Klaus and Kennell's argument was a bold one because it contradicted the established practices of Western childbirth whereby infants are taken away from their mothers to be cleansed and inspected.

Klaus and Kennell tested their hypothesis by comparing the behavior of two groups of young mothers. One group was allocated to a "routine" condition, where mothers saw their baby only briefly upon delivery, were then separated from them for several hours, and then had regular feeding sessions every few hours. The second group, "extended contact", spent 1 hour of skin-to-skin contact with the infant within the first 3 hours after birth, and 5 extra hours for the next 3 days.

One month later, the researchers compared the two groups' interactions with their infants, and found differences which seemed to indicate that a stronger bond had been formed by mothers in the "extended contact" condition. These mothers displayed more soothing behavior when the infant was upset by medical examinations, they tended to maximize physical proximity to their babies, and maintained more face-to-face contact. One year later, mothers in the "extended contact" group still displayed more soothing and nurturant behavior, were more helpful to the doctors in a medical examination, and more likely to report that they disliked separation from their babies. Obviously, mothers in the "routine" condition would by this stage have had a lot of contact with their babies, too, but the signs were that their bonds were less powerful. The major difference, according to Klaus and Kennell, is the *timing* of that contact, and it appeared that the sensitive period is the first few hours after birth.

In a separate replication study involving 42 middle-class Swedish mothers (22 in an "extra contact" group, 20 in a "routine" group) the extra contact subjects revealed more holding and *en face* orientation at 36 hours postpartum (de Chateau, 1987). At 3 months, the extra contact infants smiled and laughed more, while infants in the routine group cried more. At one year, mothers in the extra contact group were less likely to have returned to work, even though there were no differences between the economic circumstances and opportunities of the two groups.

Klaus and Kennell's (1976) findings attracted a great deal of attention in the mass media and in scientific circles. It is generally recognized that Klaus and Kennell made a major contribution toward humanizing hospital practices by encouraging the provision of optimal circumstances for mothers to experience the pleasures and reassurance of early contact with their newborn. On the other hand, many hospitals took the point to heart to the extent that arrangements to establish bonding became as institutionalized as previous routines. Svejda et al. (1982, p. 92) cite one maternity ward instruction which read "do not remove the baby to the nursery until bonding has taken place." The idea filtered through to neighboring professions, and bonding became highly sought after. Schaffer (1990) remarks that social workers and health visitors sometimes conduct family assessments with the item "Has bonding occurred? (Tick one box, Yes or No)" included on their checksheets.

Problems for the bonding hypothesis

Despite the seeming naturalness of the hypothesis and the promising early evidence, a surge of research and debate around the issues raised soon began to cast doubt on the notion of a sensitive period for the formation of a bond. Bornstein (1989) points out that what we know of sensitive periods in general should lead us to be skeptical of the Klaus and Kennell claims, since most of the evidence for sensitive periods in humans locates them early in development (e.g., in infancy or childhood rather than the 20s to 40s). There are good evolutionary reasons why this might be the case, as sensitive periods are usually associated with the development of essential adaptive abilities.

Several replications and extensions failed to provide strong supporting evidence for the original study. Some investigators found differences between routine and extended groups in the first few days, but they were not sustained at 8–10 days (Grossman et al., 1981), at 1 month or later (Carlsson et al., 1979). Similarly, Hwang (1987a) found short-term effects associated with Caesarean delivery, which involves some initial *reduction* in maternal care (largely due to the fatigue of the mother) but the effects had disappeared at 3 months.

Another problem is that the outcome of any intervention experiment can be subject to the "Hawthorne effect" (cf. Lamb et al., 1985; Manstead and Semin, 1996): that being the focus of attention – almost any attention – can boost morale and influence behavior. The mothers in the Klaus and Kennell study were disadvantaged, inner-city Americans, and most were unmarried teenagers. It could be that participation in a project where they were being given special attention compensated for some of the difficulties that these young parents may have experienced. The subjects in de Chateau's (1987) Swedish study were from more affluent backgrounds, but it remains conceivable that they were excited by playing their part in a prestigious study of the benefits of maternal contact. Perhaps some had even heard or read about the issue in books or magazines for new parents; everybody is aware that mother's milk is best, and the idea of skin-to-skin contact seems to fit quite (naturally) with the same theme.

Other problems come to light when we take into account that pregnancy and birth in humans are not simply biological occurrences, but major life-events which are anticipated and evaluated. The social cognitions of the parents – the meanings they impose upon the event, the explanations they formulate for their emotions, and their expectations of the relationship with the child – may well have substantial influence over the development of the central relationship (Williams et al., 1987). K. E. Grossman et al. (1981) report that 34 percent of their (West German) sample who revealed that the pregnancy had been unplanned showed significantly less tender touch behavior than mothers who had planned the pregnancy. It seems that the desirability and convenience of the birth can affect the mother's experience. Further, other people's labels and attributions affect how we interpret emotional arousal (Leyens, 1996; Schacter and Singer, 1962). Shaffer (1993) suggests that the intense emotions associated with childbirth could be reinterpreted according to whether the mother has the opportunity to experience the delights of holding and manipulating the baby for the first time (thus attributing the arousal to positive associations of the circumstances) or whether the mother is left alone, with only her sensations of exhaustion or relief to focus her attributions upon. On this account, the opportunity for contact could indeed be important, but not because of the hormonal imperative so much as the social-cognitive adjustment to the life-event.

Perhaps the greatest weakness of the notion of a sensitive period for bonding is that it fails to take into account the dynamic and bi-directional nature of social relationships (cf. Svejda et al., 1982; Williams et al., 1987) Svejda et al. (1982) criticize the implication of some views of bonding that what is at issue here is the all-or-nothing phenomenon of one person "getting stuck" to another, and stress that relationships are processes which develop and change over time. Had the bonding theorists complemented their ethological expertise with some social psychology, they might have anticipated that "Once contact has been made, the fate of the relationship – its likelihood of formation and survival – depends on the level of outcomes the two persons experience" (Thibaut and Kelley, 1959, p. 64). Importantly, relationships involve input from *both* participants.

As a result of this debate, the notion of a sensitive period for maternal bonding is not widely accepted. It is widely accepted that the early relationship between a parent and child is an important one, and it is at least agreed that in many households, for whatever reasons, the mother is most often the principal attachment figure. We turn to the oft-neglected father later.

Summary

Clear signs of social selectivity are apparent in the normal infant during the latter part of the first year. Infants show a preference for the company of specific persons (usually the primary caregivers), and gradually come to display wariness of strangers. Several theories have been proposed to account for the establishment of attachments between child and caregiver, but by far the most influential has been the ethological theory of John Bowlby. Other elaborations of ethological/sociobiological perspectives in this area have been focused on the mother, and the controversial hypothesis that mother–infant bonding is facilitated by early physical contact. Support for the contact hypothesis has not proven robust, but support for the broader claims of ethologists concerning the emotional salience of the early relationship is more readily obtained. This does not confirm that only an ethological explanation can account for attachment, but it remains the case that this theoretical perspective has so far proven the most fruitful in this area. Let us now consider more carefully the nature of the attachment relationship – or relationships – for it turns out that there is a variety of possible forms.

Measuring and Categorizing Attachment

Investigators of attachment soon discovered that there are considerable individual differences in the nature of the relationship and the intensity of infant protests at separation (Ainsworth, 1967; Schaffer and Emerson, 1964). In order to gain a fuller picture of the nature of attachment, Ainsworth and her colleagues (Ainsworth et al., 1971; Ainsworth and Wittig, 1969) proposed that a single measure, such as separation distress, was an insufficient basis. They devised a simple experimental procedure, known as the Strange Situation, which allows for the collection of multiple measures in the course of a standard series of events. This procedure has the attractions that it generates a good deal of information about the current qualities of the relationship under study, it offers clues to the history of the relationship and it provides a basis for predictions about aspects of the child's subsequent development. It is also easy to replicate. These are grounds for regarding it as "the most powerful and useful procedure ever available for the study of socioemotional development in infancy" (Lamb et al. 1985, p. 3). The availability of such a tool has itself prompted a massive expansion in attachment research (van IJzendoorn and Tavecchio, 1987; Kagan, 1987). It is employed widely in this field, and it will be useful to know how it is conducted.

The Strange Situation

The standard Strange Situation procedure is conducted as follows.

Episode 1   The infant and caregiver are placed in an observational room by the experimenter, who then leaves.

Episode 2   The caregiver is inactive, and the baby is free to explore.

Episode 3   An unfamiliar adult enters the room; the stranger is initially silent, after one minute she begins to converse with the caregiver, and after another minute she approaches the baby; the caregiver leaves.

Episode 4   The stranger and the baby are left alone together.

Episode 5   The caregiver returns and the stranger leaves. The caregiver tries to resettle the baby. The caregiver leaves.

Episode 6   The baby is left alone in the room.

Episode 7   The stranger returns to the room, and begins to interact.

Episode 8   The caregiver returns again, and the stranger leaves.

Notice that at least three sources of potential distress are implicated in the Strange Situation (figure 3.3). The child is placed in an *unfamiliar physical environment*, there is *separation from the caregiver*, and there is *contact with a stranger*. Different combinations of these factors are tested, and the procedure is designed to become increasingly stressful (culminating in the kinds of intrusive actions by the stranger that we saw above are highly associated with infant discomfort). Importantly, the procedure allows for collection of several measures: the child's willingness to explore in unfamiliar

Figure 3.3   The Strange Situation.

spaces in the company of different people or alone, the child's reaction to separation from different individuals, the child's reaction to the presence of, and interaction with, a stranger, and finally the child's reaction to reunions.

Types of Attachment

Ainsworth and her co-workers studied the responses of large numbers of infants to the Strange Situation, and were able to classify three types of attachment, reflecting systematic differences in the security of the relationship. Ainsworth and colleagues' typology has provided a basis for a large amount of important research on the development of early relationships. The three attachment types originally identified are:

Type A: Avoidant   During Episode 2, the pre-separation phase of the Strange Situation, these children are relatively indifferent to the mother's location in the room and appear emotionless and superficial in their play with the toys. When the mother leaves, they do not manifest particular distress. When the mother returns, they do not strive to achieve contact, and show some signs of avoiding it; for example, they avert gaze or turn away.

Type B: Securely attached   During Episode 2, these children play happily with the toys and explore the new environment confidently. They do not manifest strong distress during Episodes 3 and 4, when the mother leaves them with the stranger. They greet the mother positively upon her return. They are likely to show distress when the mother leaves for a second time (Episode 6), and they reduce play and exploration at this point. Upon the mother's second return they go to her for comfort, they calm down relatively quickly and can then resume play.

Type C: Resistant   These children are most likely to become upset during Episode 2, and tend not to explore at this stage. Their orientation toward their mother is ambivalent; they show considerable distress upon her departures, yet prove very difficult to comfort upon her return; they rush to her, yet refuse to be consoled and struggle to be put down. They show anger and reject toys. They do not interact very much with the stranger and interactions with the mother include a lot of brief glances.

Most of the research on attachment types is based on this typology (including sub-types of each). However, subsequent research by Main and her colleagues has indicated that a fourth type may be distinguishable.

Type D: Disorganized and disoriented.   Main and Solomon (1986) found that a small proportion of babies lacked a coherent strategy for handling the stresses of the Strange Situation. Instead, their behavior appeared to be very poorly organized, involving idiosyncratic, almost self-contradictory combinations of proximity seeking and avoid-ance, seemingly incomplete movements and, sometimes, direction of wariness toward the parent rather than the stranger. Main and Solomon concluded that a new category was required to classify this minority of infants, and they proposed Type D, disorganized and disoriented.

The significance of attachment type

Three points should be stressed about the measurement and classification of attachment. First, these descriptions show clearly why single measures, such as strength of separation protest, are inadequate. A particular behavior needs to be understood in relation to its context (Sroufe, 1985). For example, a Type C infant may provide strong cries at separation, seemingly indicating strong attachment. Yet the same child may squirm or kick to be released from her mother's arms upon reunion, behaviors which viewed in isolation would appear to reflect the absence of attachment. We need to characterize the organization and quality of the overall relationship, and Ainsworth and colleague's typology is a major advance in this respect.

Second, it turns out that the most frequent type of attachment, observed in several studies, is Type B (securely attached). In work with large samples of US children, Ainsworth et al. (1978) found that about 70 percent of children form attachments of this quality. Of the remainder, approximately 20 percent fell into Type A, and 10 per cent in Type C. Obviously, distinguishing different types of a vital social relationship raises important questions about antecedents and consequences of the variations, and it will be seen shortly that much attachment research has been focused on these issues.

Third, although attachments clearly involve (at least) two parties, note that attachment type has become subtly associated with the *child*, who is referred to as a Type A or Type B, individual. Lewis (1990) objects that it is not clear why this should be so, since the higher-level understanding of the relationship originates in the adult rather than the prelinguistic infant.

How Strange is the Strange Situation?

Although the Strange Situation is now a well-established and widely used research procedure, we should note that it is not without its critics. Bronfenbrenner (1979) argues that the Strange Situation provides one illustration of a general problem in laboratory-based developmental research, namely that the setting itself furnishes an ecological context which may affect the very behavior under investigation. He points out that researchers who have compared infants' responses in standard laboratory and home-based versions of the procedures have found that attachment behaviors tend to be markedly stronger in the laboratory (Brookhart and Hock, 1976; Ross et al., 1975). Is it justifiable to extrapolate generalizations about social development from behavior in exceptional settings?

Attachment theorists would respond that the proof of the pudding is in the eating. If behavior in the Strange Situation can provide a reliable basis for predictions about other aspects of the child's development, then it is clearly a useful instrument. Lots of studies using the Strange Situation *have* demonstrated predictive strength (see below). However, the point remains that the meaning of the Strange Situation is interwoven with the social structures and processes of the infant's and parent's lives. We will see the relevance of this theme at several points.

Attachment and Development

If we can classify attachments reliably then we have a basis for further research into the correlates and consequences of the different types. Support for the reliability and validity of the typology has been provided in a number of studies (Sroufe, 1985), and infants' classifications have proven to remain consistent over periods of several months (Antonucci and Levitt, 1984; Waters, 1978), although this depends in part upon the general stability of the family unit (Schaffer and Emerson, 1964; Vaughn et al., 1979).

Does the Quality of Attachment Matter?

If we consider the different responses of infants to the Strange Situation, then it is immediately apparent that one group is most likely to find the opportunity for novel stimulation enjoyable, and responds by exploring the new toys and interacting with the new person. The Type B, securely attached, child seems to use the assurance of the relationship as a base from which to investigate and experiment. If there is a threat, the child knows that she or he can return to a reliable, supportive caregiver. This child enjoys periodic interaction with the caregiver, but the very security of this relationship affords scope for independent activity and discovery, both cognitive and interpersonal.

In marked contrast, the Types A, C and D children suffer insecurities or conflicts which disturb or inhibit their experiences. The Type A child will explore and interact, but can be so distressed by separation that she or he curtails these activities and the opportunity to share them. The Type C child is wary of exploring at all and the Type D child is quite uncertain what to do – scarcely comfortable bases for learning more about the world and one's ability to act upon it.

This suggests that Type B children may be relatively advantaged in terms of fundamental aspects of social and cognitive development. A good deal of empirical evidence supports this conclusion. Cassidy (1986), for example, found that Type B children were generally superior to their less securely attached peers in terms of negotiating the physical environment, a finding which supports the inference that these infants profit from a secure base by greater readiness to explore, and hence greater competence in exploration. Main (1983) used the Strange Situation paradigm to classify a sample of infants aged 12 months, and then tested the children at 20 months on the Bayley Scale of Infant Development, and at 21 months in a play session with an adult stranger and a set of unfamiliar toys. The Type B children scored higher on the Bayley Scale, engaged in more protracted and directed play, and interacted positively with the stranger. The Type A (avoidant) children minimized interaction with the stranger and would not enter into joint play; they did show normal levels of exploratory play. The Type C (resistant) infants were less involved in play, were more restless and showed less enjoyment.

Other studies have found similar advantages to Type B infants in terms of dimensions of their toy play (Lutkenhaus et al., 1985; Matas et al., 1978; Roggman et al., 1987; Wartner et al., 1994), autonomy, interpersonal competence and eagerness to learn during the toddler, preschool, and early school years (Booth et al., 1991; Sroufe et al., 1983; Suess et al., 1992; Waters et al., 1979; Youngblade and Belsky, 1992; and see chapter 4), and responsivity to unfamiliar adults in the school environment (Turner, 1993). Marcus (1991) reports that the same kinds of patterns obtain for children in foster care: those with secure attachments to their new caregivers turn out to be better adjusted and better performing in the early years of school.

There are some inconsistencies and failures to replicate in the literature (see Lamb and Nash, 1989; Lamb et al., 1985; Maslin-Cole et al., 1993; Riksen-Walraven et al., 1993), but it is generally agreed that the quality of attachment is an identifiable aspect of parent–child relations and one which provides a basis for predicting other aspects of the relationship and the child's development. Something "reliable and meaningful" seems to be being assessed by the Strange Situation procedure (Cassidy, 1994; Sroufe, 1985). Variations in the quality of attachment are associated with variations in the extent to which the child participates in important social and cognitive activities over the next few years. Attachment seems to have foundation-laying significance. Or does it? We return to this issue shortly, but first we need to consider the explanations of these variations in attachment types.

Antecedents of Attachment Types

Why do some parents and infants achieve secure attachments while others do not? Why are some insecurely attached infants avoidant while others are resistant? Answers to these questions are important for theoretical reasons, helping to explain individual differences in human development, but also for practical reasons, providing a basis for intervention to facilitate or improve parent–child relationships. Two main possibilities have attracted researchers' attention: the quality of caregiving, and the temperament of the infant.

The quality of caregiving

Ainsworth has maintained from her earliest work that the quality of attachment an infant has with his or her mother reflects the kinds of interaction that they have experienced during the child's first year, and that "whatever contribution the infant himself may have made to this interaction, his mother's contribution is significant" (Ainsworth et al., 1974, p. 106). Note that this emphasis admits an experiential variable to attachment theory – if Ainsworth is correct, then there is more to human attachment than honoring biological dictates.

Ainsworth et al. (1971) reported that mothers who scored high on a measure of sensitivity to the infant were much more likely to produce securely attached 1-year-olds, while insensitive mothers without exception produced insecurely attached infants. Further, specific patterns of maternal insensitivity were associated with the different patterns of insecurity in the infant. Mothers of avoidant infants tend to be impatient with the baby and unresponsive to its signals; mothers of resistant infants tend to be inconsistent in their caregiving, fluctuating in their enthusiasm for interaction and sometimes misreading the infant's cues. More generally, Schaffer and Emerson's (1964) study showed that one of the critical determinants of the child's attachment to other members of the family was the responsivity of the individual to the child: fathers or grandparents who played with the infant were more likely to become attachment figures than were relatively distant members of the household.

Several other studies have attempted to test the central hypothesis that sensitive caregiving produces securely attached infants (e.g., Egeland and Farber, 1984; Goldberg and Easterbrooks, 1984; Isabella, 1993; Isabella et al., 1989; Kiser et al., 1986; Moran et al., 1992; Rosen and Rothbaum, 1993; Sagi et al., 1985). In general, these studies have supported the broad claim that characteristics of the caregiving environment, particularly maternal sensitivity and the harmony of the customary interaction style, are associated with attachment type in the direction that Ainsworth claims.

Furthermore, when unfavorable contexts are studied – such as highly stressed, abusive, or neglectful families – negative outcomes tend to be revealed. Parenting stress and parental depression have been found to be associated with the development of insecure attachment in the child (Jarvis and Creasey, 1991; Radke-Yarrow et al., 1985). Carlson et al. (1989) found, in a sample of maltreated infants, that approximately 80 percent fell into the Type D (disorganized/disoriented) category. It is plausible that the highly conflictual interpersonal environment of the abusive home could jeopardize the organization of an attachment system. The child may seek proximity to the caregiver for all the normal reasons, yet suffer rejection or mishandling, which may result in even greater needs for reassurance, accompanied by distrust of an unpredictable attachment figure.

An alternative possibility is that the child him or herself has sufficiently serious behavioral problems that it is difficult for the parent to nurture a secure attachment. Overall, the evidence does not support this interpretation. Van IJzendoorn et al. (1992) conducted a meta-analysis of 34 clinical studies which examined the relationship between either maternal problems (such as depression, mental illness) or child problems (such as a handicap) and attachment. The results were clear that in the presence of a maternal problem there is a much greater chance of the child forming an insecure attachment, while among groups where the children have problems the distribution of attachment types was similar to the norms described above. Furthermore, although it has been found that when children are removed from abusive or neglectful home environments a substantial proportion go on to develop insecure avoidant attachments to their new foster parent, a minority establishes secure, Type B, relationships – and their caregivers tend to score highly on measures of sensitivity (Howes and Segal, 1993).

Lamb et al. (1985) remark that the various studies of antecedents have not produced a consistent or easily interpretable pattern of detailed results enabling us to specify exactly what features of parental behavior are of formative importance. They emphasize that we should not ignore the influence of other factors, such as the quality of the marital relationship, the degree of stress in the home, and cross-cultural differences in childrearing style (see below). At present, the evidence certainly points to a relationship between caregiving and attachment, but the dynamics require further explanation.

Temperament

Infants vary in a number of their behavioral characteristics (chapter 2). Individual differences in activity level, regularity, distractibility, responsiveness are apparent at a very early age. Some theorists have proposed, in contrast to the claims about the formative influence of caregiving style, that it is these infant characteristics that determine how the attachment takes shape. For example, Kagan (1987, 1989) has argued that inborn individual differences in the tendency to become distressed at separation may predict attachment type. Rieser-Danner et al. (1987) found that 46 percent of the variance in attachment classification was accounted for by individual differences in temperament ratings (of the infant by the mother).

The issue of temperament poses an important challenge to the Ainsworth position, because it could mean that the Strange Situation is measuring not the quality of a relationship but the nature of the child's endogenous characteristics. This undermines attempts to build a theoretical model of the development of relationships and their consequences by asserting that the real basis for prediction lies in measurements of the individual child, and in the continuity of intra-organismic properties. Not surprisingly, this proposal has led to lively debate between attachment theorists and temperament theorists. Some temperament theorists are skeptical of claims that behavior in the Strange Situation can really tell us so much about an individual's prospects (Kagan, 1987), while attachment theorists retort that the temperament hypothesis is "without basis" (Sroufe, 1985).

In defense of the orthodox attachment theory, it has been pointed out that when researchers have gauged the quality of an infant's attachments to both mother and father, they are often different: an infant might be securely attached to one, insecurely attached to the other (see below for a fuller discussion on attachment to fathers). If attachment quality reflected infant temperament, then presumably the child should form equally secure relationships with both of her or his principal caregivers. It has also been noted that parents' reports of infant temperament are not reliably associated with attachment type (Bates et al., 1985; Belsky et al., 1984; Weber et al., 1986). Studies which have compared the predictive power of maternal caregiving styles and infants' temperamental characteristics have found that the former is the best predictor (Belsky et al., 1984; Crockenberg and McCluskey, 1986; Goldberg et al., 1986).

However, Belsky and Rovine (1987) showed in a large longitudinal study that children who fell into certain subtypes associated with distress in the Strange Situation displayed as newborns significantly more behavioral instability (tremors, startles) than did children who fell into the nondistressed subtypes. This is consistent with the temperament hypothesis. Another longitudinal study of maternal and infant behavior by Lewis and Feiring (1989) found that it was the *child*'s early orientations that proved the better predictor of the subsequent relationship; children who at 3 months old showed a preference for playing with toys rather than people were more likely to be classified as avoidant at one year.

In the midst of this toing and froing, Belsky and Rovine (1987) have proposed a *rapprochement* of the traditional Bowlby–Ainsworth attachment theory and the temperament hypothesis. They suggest that children of different temperamental characteristics do present different challenges to their caregivers, but in turn the ways in which those caregivers respond to the infant's behavioral dispositions may determine the kind of attachment relationship within which she or he expresses these. A longitudinal study of 24 German mother–child pairs by Spangler (1990) provides evidence consistent with this bi-directional proposal. Spangler found that maternal responsiveness to the infant during the second year predicted the child's social competence at the end of the second year. However, mothers' responsiveness was itself associated with their perceptions of the child's temperament. Mothers who perceived their infant as difficult became less responsive to her or him by 24 months.

Continuing research and discussion may well focus on the interaction of temperament and caregiving, but for the present we should note once more the conceptual difficulties involved in attempting to attribute a developmental outcome to environmental *or* biological factors. Sroufe (1985) comments that experience transforms endogenous characteristics and it is naive to imagine that we can distinguish sharply between the influence of inherited child attributes and maternal caregiving orientations.

Does Quality of Attachment Really Predict Subsequent Development?

Let us return now to the associations between type of attachment and the subsequent development of the child. Attachment theorists such as Bowlby and Ainsworth regard the formation and qualities of the first relationship as crucial: providing the secure base from which the infant proceeds to explore and learn (or the insecure context from which the infant struggles anxiously). The secure base hypothesis is tempting. It fits well with all the evidence above of relative advantages to Type B infants, and it fits with a longstanding tradition of theoretical and popular speculations about the formative consequences of early experiences for later development. However, there is a problem which undermines the confidence with which we can arrive at such a conclusion.

The problem is that in looking at the relationship between parent–child interaction at Time 1 and the child's performance at Time 2, we are in danger of neglecting the relationship between parent–child interaction at Time 2 and performance at Time 2. We neglect also the relationship between parent–child interaction at Time 1 and parent–child interaction at Time 2. In short, there may well be continuities in the quality of a parent–child relationship throughout our study. This means that we cannot be sure what accounts for the associations we obtain: "the locus of stability in such predictive relationships could be in the caretaking environment, rather than in the child" (Lamb et al., 1985, p. 170). Indeed, on a strong version of this criticism the whole notion of a Type A (B, C, or D) "child" is quite misleading (Lewis, 1990).

Lamb et al. (1985) point out that much research in this area actually selects subjects demonstrated to have consistent attachment relationships, thus confounding initial attachment with continuing circumstances. Also, when children are studied in less stable domestic environments (Erickson et al., 1985; Vaughn et al., 1979) the predictive associations are less likely to be obtained.

For the present, it is reasonable to conclude that attachments are important, but not because they signify the setting of an unbreakable mold that is invariably favorable to Type B children and bad news for the rest. Attachments are important because they herald the beginnings of interpersonal contexts from within which the child will develop his or her interactions with the broader world. Some of these contexts are indeed more favorable than others and because in most cases children remain with the same caregivers there is a strong likelihood that there will be some continuities in the positive and negative qualities of the relationship. These in turn may continue to be associated with other aspects of the child's development. But there are possibilities of change in the relationship – for example, as a function of changes in the level of stress in the family – and there is the possibility of corresponding changes in the child.

Attachment in Older Children

The Strange Situation was devised for use with parents and infants, and the majority of attachment research has been concerned with developments during infancy and/or their predictive implications for the child's future development. Much less attention has been focused on the nature and measurement of attachment in older children, though we noted earlier that one of the important features of attachments is that they are enduring, even lifelong. However, some researchers have developed techniques for measuring attachment in older children, including separation–reunion experiences (Cassidy, 1988) and story completion tasks (in which the child is told part of a story about some domestic accident or stress, and required to tell what happens next; Bretherton et al., 1990). Again, these measures of attachment tend to be predictive of other social responses, with a clear advantage to children classified as secure. Importantly, attachment classifications made in infancy have been found to predict attachment classifications of the same children at the age of 6 with a high degree of consistency (Main and Cassidy, 1988).

Summary

Mary Ainsworth led a major development in attachment theory with the proposal of different types of attachment relationships and with the development of a standard, easily replicated technique for measuring these types. Attachment theorists, using this instrument, have found provocative evidence of associations between attachment type and a host of other social and cognitive developmental measures. The theoretical and practical significance of these findings led to a concern with the antecedents of the types. Ainsworth and her collaborators have argued that a crucial factor is sensitivity of caregiving. Temperament theorists, in contrast, have argued that individual differences in personality and manageability precede the development of a social relationship. The possibility of complex interactions between caregiving style and child characteristics remains a focus of research and debate. One other unresolved issue concerns whether features of a child's current behavior are best explained in terms of antecedent relationships or ongoing relationships.

Maternal Absence and Paternal Presence

Variations in the quality of parenting may be associated with variability in early development, but nature and society themselves ensure that there will be variations. What happens, for example, if there is no parent around at all? Or if one is removed? Many children are separated from their primary caregiver for short periods (for example, due to the hospitalization of the mother or the child) and a minority may be separated permanently by neglect, abandonment, or death of a parent. As we saw, Bowlby's early work was concerned with precisely these kinds of problems, and led him to the conclusion that disruption of the mother–child relationship could lead to serious negative consequences for the child. Most of the research has concentrated on *maternal* deprivation, partly in response to Bowlby's monotropic assertions, and partly because it remains the case in most cultures that mothers take the principal role in early caregiving. But fathers do crop up in children's lives, too, and researchers eventually began to wonder what significance they might have. We consider first the absence of mothers, and second the presence of fathers.

Maternal Absence

The relevant research is extensive (see Rutter, 1981; Schaffer, 1990), but the main points can be summarized with respect to short-term and long-term effects.

Short-term effects

It is not difficult to demonstrate that temporary separation from the mother is usually traumatic for most children aged over 9 months or so (Bowlby, 1973; Robertson and Robertson, 1971, 1989; Schaffer, 1990). Children respond to the separation initially with intense *protest*, followed by a period of *despair*. In due course, despair gives way to *detachment*, a phase during which the child appears less distressed and less interested in the attachment figure, even if she reappears. Hospital staff, very familiar with the practicalities of this sequence, used to interpret the detachment phase as a sign of recovery, but Bowlby and the Robertsons concluded otherwise, arguing that it is a form of resigned defensiveness and continuing stress for the child. Evidence that it is not a final phase of adjustment is provided by the re-establishment of the attachment if the mother remains present for a while, and by the reappearance of anxiety if she is removed again.

The impact of the removal of the key attachment figure may be mitigated or exacerbated by other aspects of the social context. The intensity of short-term distress and its consequences can be modified by the presence of other attachment figures (such as the father and siblings) and by maintaining continuity in other features of everyday life; the negative consequences can be worsened by additional deprivations and changes, such as are likely when the child is institutionalized (Schaffer, 1990). Nevertheless, there is little dispute that the short-term consequences of separation are usually very distressing to the child.

Long-term effects

Schaffer (1990) points out that the long-term effects of separation are difficult to investigate for practical reasons (involving many years of investigation with subjects scattered through many locations) and because of the number of potential confounding variables (such as the reasons for the separation, individual differences in resilience, the adjustment of the family as a whole, the quality of any substitute caregiving the child may receive, or the nature of any institution in which she or he may be placed).

Even so, the evidence available generally supports the conclusion that the long-term effects of short separations are rarely disastrous (Bowlby, 1973; Rutter, 1981; Schaffer, 1990).

But what of longer, or permanent, separations? Early evidence, based on children in orphanages, indicated that these could have very damaging effects upon the social, cognitive, and linguistic development of children and adolescents (Goldfarb, 1947; Spitz, 1949). However, these findings were based on children separated from their parents *and* placed in institutions, making it difficult to resolve whether it was the absence of one variable or the presence of another that led to deleterious outcomes. At the time of these studies, orphanages were not fun places, and the children were deprived of a great deal of social and intellectual stimulation.

Subsequent research in more humane institutions suggests that the nature of the environment certainly has a major impact. Tizard and Rees (1974, 1975) found that children reared in a residential nursery in London, where staff took pains to provide a friendly and intellectually stimulating environment, tended to perform reasonably well on measures of cognitive and linguistic development, although they were socially insecure. In this case, the staff were friendly but transient, and the institution had a high turnover of personnel with the result that children had difficulty in forming stable relationships with caregivers. In contrast, Dontas et al. (1985) studied infants in a Greek orphanage where one caregiver was allotted principal responsibility for each child and where the number of other caregivers was limited. These infants formed attachments to their institutional caregivers on pretty much the normal schedule, and their developmental progress was not markedly impaired by their unusual circumstances, unless the institutional caregiver herself left her post.

One of the most ambitious studies of the long-term effects of institutionalization is that of Dowdney et al. (1985) and Rutter and Quinton (1984), who compared a group of 89 women in their 20s, who had been institutionalized for several years during childhood, with a group of women of the same age and from the same locality in inner London, who had not been institutionalized. By young adulthood, the ex-care women were much more likely to have suffered personality disorders and broken relationships, and to have acquired criminal records. The ex-care women were much more likely to be rated as poor on measures of parental style. However, even among the women with this disadvantageous early background there was heterogeneity in psychosocial adjustment and quality of caregiving provided to own children. In particular, other social involvements seemed to make a considerable difference to outcome: ex-care women who reported positive school experiences, and ex-care women with harmonious marriages, were more positively oriented toward adult life and their own parenting responsibilities. The study confirms that institutionalization puts an individual at risk, but also that it does not necessarily eradicate all prospects of wellbeing in adulthood.

The Father and Attachment

Children also have fathers!
(Rutter, Maternal Deprivation
Reassessed, *1981, p. 127)*

In his early work, Bowlby stressed the importance of the mother to the mental health of the child. He did see a place for valuable contributions from fathers, but these were held to be rather indirect:

> Nevertheless, as the illegitimate child knows, fathers have their uses even in infancy. Not only do they provide for their wives to enable them to devote themselves unrestrictedly to the care of the infant and toddler, but, by providing love and companionship, they support the mother emotionally and help her maintain that harmonious contented mood in the atmosphere of which the infant thrives. (Bowlby, 1953, p. 13)

Beyond this, fathers were not of great interest to attachment researchers, nor to investigators of infant social development more generally, until Lamb et al. (1985) encouraged renewed attention to the "forgotten contributors to child development." This neglect was despite the evidence of Schaffer and Emerson's (1964) study that, while the mother was often the principal attachment figure, many infants formed attachments to other members of the household and sometimes the initial attachment was to the father (figure 3.4). Schaffer and Emerson remarked that the traditional image of family structure was no longer accurate, and elsewhere in Britain at around the same time other researchers of family life had found evidence of increasing domestic participation by fathers, concluding that "the modern father's place is in the home" (Newson and Newson, 1963, p. 147). One problem – perhaps intensified by the prominence of the Strange Situation as a methodological paradigm – is that the modern father remains difficult to get into the laboratory (e.g., if studies are conducted during work hours).

Even so, research which circumvented this obstacle during the 1970s confirmed earlier evidence that the forgotten contributor could indeed be an attachment figure, eliciting attachment behaviors (such as proximity seeking) similar to those oriented toward the mother, though not always as frequently (Kotelchuk, 1976; Lamb, 1977; Lytton, 1980). Some studies did find that while infants often show no consistent preference for either parent in situations which are familiar or unthreatening, when they are placed in a stressful situation they are more likely to seek comfort from the mother (Cohen and Campos, 1974; Lamb, 1976). In times of crisis, the "I want my mummy" reaction seems to prevail. However, these findings were obtained from children whose principal caregiver was the mother. Furthermore, given a choice between the father and an unfamiliar adult as sources of reassurance, infants head for dad.

One of the most interesting consequences of bringing the father into attachment research has been the discovery mentioned above that infants do not invariably form

Figure 3.4 Children also have fathers – and become attached to them.

attachments of identical type to each parent. In several studies using the Strange Situation, various patterns have emerged and the interpretation is controversial (see Fox et al., 1991). Some children are securely attached to both parents, but some are securely attached to one and insecurely attached to the other, and some children are insecurely attached to both (Grossman et al., 1981; Lamb et al., 1982; Main and Weston, 1981; Sagi et al., 1985; Suess et al., 1992). Fox et al. (1991), following a meta-analysis, conclude that concordance (identical attachment type to both parents) is the norm, but there are certainly exceptions. Main and Weston (1981) found that the nature of both of the child's parental attachments was associated with how they responded to a novel social situation (interacting with a clown). Children who reacted most positively where those with secure attachments to *both* mother and father; children with a secure attachment to one parent and an insecure attachment to the other were intermediate; and children with two insecure attachments were least responsive and most disturbed by the encounter.

Summary

There is little doubt that adverse early experiences associated with maternal deprivation are associated with greater incidences of problems in subsequent development. However, much depends on whether the deprivation is continuous, on whether it occurs in the context of other stressors and whether these are sustained, on what kinds of alternative care the individual receives, and on the nature of other relationships that she or he has the opportunity to form. In general, research on infants' relationships with fathers (who live at home) usually finds that attachments are indeed formed. It is rare for the attachment to the father to be stronger than that to the mother (Lytton, 1980), but this conclusion may reflect the practicalities of family organization rather than any universal barrier to infant–father attachment.

Culture and Attachment

From the beginnings of his survey of children's responses to separation, Bowlby (1953) had been struck by the consistency with which the consequences of maternal deprivation were reported in a variety of countries. In her early work with the Ganda people of Uganda, Ainsworth (1967) found patterns of infant distress on separation from the mother that were decidedly similar to those found in American children. It cannot be doubted that children growing up in substantially different societies become attached to their principal caregiver and that they react unhappily to separations from her or him.

Given the simple elegance of the Strange Situation as a means of classifying infant attachments, it is of obvious interest to determine whether the same types of relationship arise universally. In particular, researchers have been interested in whether the distributions of types are similar in other cultures to those obtained in the US by Ainsworth et al. (1978).

Many studies using the Strange Situation have been conducted around the world. Van IJzendoorn and Kroonenberg (1988) conducted a meta-analysis of these in which they examined inter- and intra-cultural similarities. Based on a total of 32 samples, involving almost 2,000 infants, three findings stand out. First, there are marked *intra*-cultural differences in the distributions of the types. For example, in three separate West German studies very different distributions of different types were obtained, and one of two Japanese studies yielded a complete absence of Type As but a high proportion of Type Cs, while the other obtained a more Ainsworth-like distribution. Overall, van IJzendoorn and Kroonenberg found that intra-cultural differences were 1.5 times as large as inter-cultural differences.

Second, the aggregated total pattern was actually very close to the Ainsworth "standard", as was the aggregated US pattern. However, even within the US there is considerable sample-to-sample variability. Third, there seems to be a pattern of cross-cultural differences. While Type Bs are the most common type, Type As are relatively more common in Western European countries, while Type Cs are relatively more frequent in Israel and Japan. What interpretation can we make of this variability? Sagi and Lewkowicz (1987) point out that the meaning of the Strange Situation may vary for the participants from context to context, and that there may be procedural variations among different studies.

Culture and the Strange Situation methodology

With respect to the meaning of the situation, it could well be that the nature of the parent–child relationship varies in different societies, for a host of reasons, and this could be reflected in the ways in which both parent and child approach the experiment. For instance, Japanese and kibbutzim children were found to respond to the Strange Situation with intensified distress, while many of the German infants showed very little. Further, the causes of the Japanese and Israeli children's distress appeared to be different. For the former, the separation episodes were stressful, presumably reflecting the fact that Japanese children are rarely separated from their mothers (Lamb et al., 1985); for the latter, the entrance of the stranger was the main problem, perhaps because kibbutzim children live in small, closed groups in which they are rarely exposed to strangers (Lamb et al., 1985). Conversely, some behaviors characteristic of Type Bs appear to German parents to be the hallmarks of "spoiled" babies (Sagi and Lewkowicz, 1987). In another demonstration of cultural differences in social perceptions, Harwood and Miller (1991) compared Anglo-American and Puerto Rican mothers' reactions to observations of infants displaying Types A, B, or C attachment behaviors. They found that the former perceived autonomous reactions more favorably, and the latter favored signs of obedience and relatedness. The Strange Situation may be not only strange but different, according to the backgrounds, assumptions, and expectations of the participants.

With respect to procedural variations, although the methodology is simple and well laid out to facilitate replication, in fact different researchers do find that they have to adapt it to local conditions. Thus, a Japanese investigator found that mothers were so uneasy about leaving their infant alone in the experimental room that she chose to omit this stage of the procedure altogether (Takahashi, 1986), a well-motivated amendment on ethical grounds, but an obvious problem when it comes to comparing across studies. Other minor differences (e.g., size and decoration of the room, kinds of toys available) are inevitable, and may affect subtly the ways in which the participants experience the procedure.

Although there is debate about the usefulness and limits of the Strange Situation (Lamb et al., 1985), it can also be argued that the differences among cultures simply underscore its value and, more importantly, the universal relevance of the attachment construct (see van IJzendoorn, 1990). For example, the explanations of inter-cultural variability above may add further weight to the thesis that there is a relationship between caregiving style and attachment formation: as different cultures practice different styles, variations in attachment types may follow. Recent research indicates that even subcultural differences in caregiving arrangements, such as Israeli family homes versus kibbutzim, may be associated with differences in attachment patterns (secure attachments were less frequent in kibbutzim-raised children; Sagi et al., 1994).

Summary

Cross-cultural work complicates our understanding of the processes of attachment – in useful ways. Research indicates that there are variations in the distributions of attachment types both within and between different societies. The available evidence reminds us of the need to avoid ethnocentrism, especially the assumption that data obtained in North American or European research are normative baselines; even within these societies there may be differences among samples. It reminds us that social events, including experimental research, are not simply manipulations that can be expected to have comparable consequences in all circumstances, but occurrences of diverse meanings for different people. It may mean, as suggested by LeVine (1989), that attachment theorists will be forced to make a retreat on their earlier claims of universality, or it may mean, as concluded by Bretherton (1992), that attachment theorists will have to expand the scope of their work to incorporate ecological variations.

Conclusions

In this chapter we have considered two of the most important features of human social relationships, the fact that they entail selective preferences for some individuals over others and the fact that these preferences are interwoven with strong emotions. There is theoretical dispute over the origins of attachment, but there is little disagreement that attachments are formed and that they matter greatly to the participants. Exactly how attachments contribute to subsequent development remains controversial. On the one hand, there is extensive evidence from attachment researchers that a particular type of attachment is associated with positive social, cognitive, and linguistic outcomes. On the other hand, critics point out that the attachment may provide not only a secure initial base, but also a *continuing* secure framework. Research examining the possible contributions of infant temperament has reasserted, at the very least, that relationships are two-way processes.

One other, more general, theme which becomes apparent is that attachment matters also to persons outside the relationship. That is, societies have their ideologies and values which influence what kind of domestic arrangements are regarded as most desirable, and even what kinds of emphases should be pursued in social developmental research. Bowlby's pioneering work was initiated in times of widespread social readjustment in the West following the Second World War, when the restitution of the family and the availability of male labor were widely held to be crucial to the rebuilding process. Female labor had actually kept the factories of Europe and North America ticking over quite successfully during the war, but there were a lot of returning soldiers for whom jobs had to be found, and it was time for a baby boom. Through contemporary eyes (in societies shifting toward technological industries that can draw equally well upon female and male skills), some of Bowlby's early assumptions and conclusions, especially about the role of mothers, may appear unduly conservative. Certainly, there is evidence that fathers can be attachment figures, even principal attachment figures.

As we saw at the beginning of the chapter, attachments are not exclusively phenomena of infancy. What happens in the early phases of social life may well have implications for subsequent development, and in the course of development new attachments may be formed. In later chapters, other developments associated with attachment will be considered. We turn next to the social context within which attachments are formed and from which entry into the broader community is launched: the family.

Further reading

Birns, B. and Hay, D. F. (eds) (1988) *The Different Faces of Motherhood.* New York: Plenum.

This collection examines attachments (and other aspects of parenting) from mothers' perspectives, including several critiques of traditional theories and the bias toward "blaming the mother" for difficulties in social development.

Bowlby, J. (1988) *A Secure Base: parent–child attachment and healthy human development.* New York: Basic Books.

Other texts by Bowlby cited in this chapter provide more detailed accounts of his work, but this book provides a lucid starting point, summarizing the implications of his views on the relationship between emotional ties and the child's mental health.

Bradley, B. S. (1989) *Visions of Infancy: a critical introduction to child psychology.* Cambridge: Polity Press.

The author points out that attachment theorists emphasize the desirability of positive affect in parent–child relations, yet neglect the prevalence of negative emotions. Why, for example, does the infant *cry* to bring about proximity? Bradley proposes an interesting alternative to the Bowlby–Ainsworth attachment theory.

Bretherton, I. (1992) The origins of attachment theory: John Bowlby and Mary Ainsworth. *Developmental Psychology*, 28, 759–75.

Bretherton recounts the history of attachment theory, providing not only an illuminating academic overview of the influences upon this tradition but also an account of the intertwining of professional careers and the genealogy of ideas and research.

Eyer, D. E. (1992) *Mother-Infant Bonding: a scientific fiction.* New Haven, Conn.: Yale University Press.

A lively critique of bonding theories and research, arguing that one of the reasons the idea took hold among maternity hospitals was that the medics knew their services were losing appeal to the woman-in-the-street, and they had to do something to boost business.

Isabella, R. A. (1993) Origins of attachment: maternal interactive behavior across the first year. *Child Development*, 64, 605–21.

This paper provides a useful review of the literature as well as a further longitudinal study supporting the hypothesis of a consistent relationship between caregiving style and type of attachment.

Schaffer, H. R. (1990) *Making Decisions about Children: psychological questions and answers.* Oxford: Blackwell.

Most of the issues discussed in this chapter bear very directly on crucial decisions made by parents, child-care professionals, and lawyers. Schaffer demonstrates how the implications of rigorous research in this difficult terrain can be drawn out and translated into practical choices.

Chapter 4

From Family to Peers

Your relatives can hurt you more than anybody because you love them the most.
> *(38-year-old American cable-layer, quoted in Komarovsky, Blue-collar Marriage, 1987)*

A couple in Moscow in 1992 advertised in a local newspaper their recently delivered, full-term and healthy baby; they wished to swap him for a larger apartment. It is not known whether they really intended to complete the exchange or whether their goal was to make an attention-grabbing public statement about the housing crisis in the city. The interest of the incident is that the proposal scandalized everyone else. Indeed, it diverted our attention briefly from the tribulations of the British Royal Family, the world's regular source of engrossing domestic drama.

We seem to be deeply interested in families. Our media are full of news items about unusual ones. Baby-bartering Muscovites are bad enough, but then there is the middle-class American couple who left the children to fend for themselves in chilly Chicago while Mom and Pop took a Christmas break down Mexico way, earning universal tabloid opprobrium and the title "the most hated parents in America." (Incidentally, it is now known that they watched *Home Alone II* on the flight south, a factor which I am sure you will agree raises the vexed "correlation–cause" question about media influences on parental behavior.) We do like to see happy families occasionally, and that seems to be what TV advertisements are for: they are replete with cosy households, which always consist of mom, pop, and two kids, and who are rendered even happier by the purchase and reheating of frozen food. But in between the ads, we prefer a good measure of homespun ghastliness, watching soaps about conflict-ridden families, such as the *Ewings* and the *Carringtons*, or sitcoms about monster moms, such as *Roseanne* and *Mrs Bundy*.

Psychologists are very interested in families, too. Social developmentalists place the family at the very top of the list of socialization contexts, clinical psychologists look to the family as the first stop in charting the origins of individual pathologies, and even social psychologists (whose concern for real-world social processes is sometimes in doubt) have become interested in recent years in the dynamics of families and the social-cognitive dimensions of domestic relations (see Argyle, 1992a). Neighboring disciplines such as ethology/sociobiology, sociology, and anthropology all concur on the centrality of the family as a principal social unit.

One of the reasons why the family is regarded as so important is because it provides the structural link between the developing individual and the outside world. For better or worse, the family is regarded as the preparation ground for entry into the larger social environment. Hence, although different societies endorse different types of family arrangements, most have a collective interest in promoting the family as a basis for social stability. In his acceptance speech at the 1992 Democratic convention, US Presidential candidate Bill Clinton used the word "family" 17 times, surpassing the previous American record for political veneration of this noun held by Vice President Dan Quayle since a 1988 acceptance speech in which he scored 11 uses (Krauthammer, 1992). Societies' leaders and the mass media dwell on problems, irregularities, and idealizations of family relationships as part of a continuing public discourse about what we are, what we would like to be, and what we fear becoming.

We are also interested in peers and friendships. Again, lay attitudes toward peers betray some ambiguity. On the one hand, it is readily established that peers are important features of the social context for most of us throughout life, and indications that a child has difficulties in peer relations are often taken as signs of developmental problems. On the other hand, the popular media warn regularly of the dangers of peer pressures on the young, and of the deleterious consequences that might result. Peer relations are sometimes thought of as the antithesis of family relations: an uncontrollable external milieu in which children are subjected to the arbitrary influences of irresponsible agemates. In fact, as we will see, entry into peer relations depends very much on parental decisions and family processes (and peers themselves tend to come from families).

In terms of a useful metaphor provided by Hartup (1989b), we are concerned here with both *vertical* and *horizontal* relationships, and aspects of their interactions. A vertical relationship is one formed between individuals of different abilities and status, such as parent and child. In a vertical relationship, roles and behavior are asymmetrical; the parent has greater knowledge and power than the child and assumes a controlling role to which the child is expected to defer. In a horizontal relationship, such as obtains between peers, the participants have (broadly) comparable social power. Roles and behavior here tend toward a more egalitarian and reciprocal balance. Although, as Hartup points out, vertical and horizontal relationships serve different functions in the child's development, their origins and functions are none the less closely interwoven. As we have already seen in our review of parent–child attachment, vertical relationships can provide a protective base within which the child can acquire initial social skills. Horizontal relationships afford contexts within which children can try out and elaborate these skills and learn of the complexities of cooperation and competition.

In this chapter, then, we consider the child's entry into the broader social world, starting with the family and working outwards, through babysitting and daycare to peer relations in the preschool and early school years. The chapter will not exhaust the relevance of family and peer relationships for developmental social psychology, since these social variables recur in respect of most of the topics we address. However, the purpose of the chapter is to introduce some fundamental themes in the study of the family and social development and to consider how the starting point of the family may influence early interactions around and beyond the home.

There are six main sections to this chapter. First, because most of the work on families is undertaken by developmentalists, we consider why the family might be of interest to social psychologists, who have tended to neglect it. In the second section, we address a still more basic question of why a small family unit (a couple) should seek to enlarge (by having children), asking: what do parents want from children? Different parental values and needs are associated with variations in childrearing styles, and evidence is reviewed which indicates that childrearing styles are in turn associated with variations in children's social behavior. Another basic dimension of family relations is introduced in the third section, where sibling relationships are examined. In the next three sections, we examine children's experiences of social relationship beyond the family, including other adults and peers; it is stressed that these involvements are not independent of or antithetical to family relationships. We consider how new relationships with peers afford opportunities for the practice of emerging skills and the acquisition of new ones. Individual differences in peer relations are discussed, with particular focus on the topic of social competence.

Throughout, key questions recur. Is the family all-important? What can we conclude about the continuities and differences between children's family relationships and their peer relations? To what extent do individuals choose or influence their own social worlds?

Social Psychology, Developmental Psychology, and the Family as a Group

One of the traditional concerns of social psychology is the group. Among other things, social psychologists are interested in how groups are formed, how they cohere (Hogg, 1992), how they influence the cognitions and opinions of their members (Moscovici 1985; Turner, 1991), how they contribute to the self-definition of individual members (Turner et al., 1987), and how they relate to other groups (Brown, 1996; Hogg and Abrams, 1988; Tajfel, 1981).

For the social psychologist, the family is one group among many (cf. Hogg, 1992, p. 2). But the family is the first and usually the most enduring social group that an individual joins (Sherif, 1984) and the most profound context of social influence (Costanzo, 1992). In most communities the family is the building-block group within which identity is formulated and around which relations to the social structure are negotiated. Experience of the family group may well have implications not only for how an individual adapts to later groups, but for the very nature of group identity. Consider this succinct description of the affective and cognitive concomitants of group membership. "In a group you can experience a unique sense of belonging and identity, accompanied by powerful positive feelings towards your fellow members. There is a unity of purpose, uniformity of conduct and attitude, and a shared sense of invulnerability" (Hogg, 1992, p. ix).

For social psychologists in the Tajfel "minimal groups" tradition it is axiomatic that mere membership – simply being labeled as a member of a group – can instigate these feelings. In a minimal group experiment, subjects are allocated arbitrarily to a laboratory-formed group which is then engineered into some competition with another, equally arbitrary, group. Typically, group members display a bias towards their own group (for example, in reward allocation; see Tajfel, 1981). The developmentalist does not dispute the importance of groups, but asks: where do these feelings come from? Why is group affinity so readily grasped? Does the fact that we can substitute the word "family" in the above passage tell us something about the generality of group processes or something about the ontogenetic precedence of the family? Schiffmann and Wicklund (1992) challenge the minimal group paradigm, objecting that prominent failings of the theory are the assumptions of no psychological variables in the subjects prior to group assignment and that the person will adopt any social identity. These assumptions might be less firmly entrenched if social psychologists were willing to contemplate the developmental contexts of group membership, starting with the first group.

It is notable that in Tajfel's seminal (1981) text, *Human Groups and Social Categories*, there is scarcely a mention of the family – except one, to which he alludes at the very beginning. Reasonably enough, this is his own family, which was largely destroyed by the Nazis during the Second World War. From this background, Tajfel describes his personal route into social psychology in the aftermath of the war, and explains his interest in intergroup relations in the light of his experiences working with Jewish survivors. It is easy to see how a person's involvement in the mass misery of those times could guide attention to the larger social structures and the social psychological processes that underpin them (Tajfel had much to say about stereotypes, prejudice, attitude change, and conflict). But perhaps something of the developmental context was lost in Tajfel's personal and intellectual response to that traumatic era. And since his writings have gained influence during the decades of segmentation of psychology, perhaps it is not surprising that the absence of the first group has scarcely been noticed by his followers.

This contrasts with the privileged status of the family among other groups. For example, data collected in West Germany before reunification suggest that family ties may outweigh other intergroup biases, even though the latter are often quite powerful. Davey (1987) reports that among young people 74 percent of those with relatives in the East were in favor of reunification, while among those without relatives "over there" only 54 percent were in favor.

The first group is a special one, not least because it is very hard to get out of it. Family relationships are biological in origin and socially obligatory, whereas the relationships studied by social psychologists are more often voluntary associations (Maccoby and Martin, 1983). Turning again to our TV sets for the exceptions that prove the rule, we are startled by the case of the 12-year-old boy in Florida who in 1992 made legal history, and even got into *60 Minutes*, by "divorcing" from his parents, whose caregiving he had found less than satisfactory. The boy had the opportunity to be adopted by wealthier, more stable and, in his view, more loving parents in another family – and off he went. In mundane reality, not only do few of us have this opportunity to acquire a better class of family but few would take it, because the unique sense of belonging and identity within our first group, the powerful positive feelings towards our fellow members, the unity of purpose, uniformity of conduct and attitude, and shared sense of invulnerability (Hogg, 1992) are not easily discarded.

As elsewhere, it should be stressed here that a degree of common interest between social and developmental psychologists should be of mutual benefit. Developmentalists certainly pay more attention to the family, but could learn from social psychologists of the importance of group processes. For example, one limitation of much of the attachment research that we considered in the previous chapter is that it focuses almost exclusively on *dyadic* relationships (especially, the mother–child relationship). There are good reasons for examining attachments as part of a system of family relationships (Donley, 1993; Kreppner, 1987; Schaffer, 1984b). Donley (1993) develops the argument that the child's attachment is not simply to specific individuals but to the family as an emotional unit. Similarly, social psychologists emphasize intergroup relations as crucial dynamics of social organization but there is scant developmental work on inter-family relations. Arguably a major dimension of social development – how your family sees things relative to the rest – is at present little studied.

Summary

One of the major focuses of contemporary social psychology is the study of group processes, including how groups are formed, how they operate, how they influence their members, and how they relate to other groups. One of the major focuses of developmental psychology is the family, the first and most enduring group that individuals enter. Many of the processes that experimental social psychologists study in the laboratory have their origins in the family. These are some of the reasons why the family is a particularly important unit for developmental social psychology, though it has to be acknowledged that much of the work unifying the two disciplines (our parents) around this topic has yet to be undertaken.

Parental Values and Childrearing Styles

Let us begin with one of the still widely favored starting points in families, the husband and wife. It soon becomes clear that the family choices and plans of any couple are circumscribed by larger social structures. Subsequently, we examine how parental values are manifest in childrearing styles.

Beginnings of the Family Group: Parental Needs and Societal Structures

Parents have needs and goals relating to their children. These reflect both what they want *from* their children, and what they want *for* them (Goodnow and Collins, 1990). Consider some of the findings from an extensive cross-cultural survey, the Value of Children Study, conducted by Hoffman (1987) and her collaborators. In each of the countries of Indonesia, Korea, the Philippines, Singapore, Taiwan, Thailand, Turkey, and the United States, between 1,000 and 3,000 married women under the age of 40, and at least a quarter of their husbands, were interviewed and asked about the advantages of parenthood, their requirements of their children, and their aspirations for the kinds of people the children would become. Marked differences in parental values were found from society to society, and within most societies there was a difference between urban and rural respondents.

When asked "what qualities would you most like to see in your children?", 78 percent of urban Indonesian respondents placed obedience at the top of their priorities, while only 11.6 percent of urban Koreans and 14.5 percent of urban Americans endorsed this item. Sixty percent of urban Koreans wished their child to become

Table 4.1 Mothers' accounts of the advantages of having children, by nation

	Turkey	Indonesia (Javanese)	Indonesia (Sundanese)	Philippines	Thailand	Korea	Taiwan	Singapore	USA
Economic utility	54.0	94.1	79.6	71.3	74.6	35.7	44.4	46.8	6.0
Primary ties and affection	34.3	14.0	34.7	46.1	12.9	36.8	44.8	58.6	66.1
Stimulation and fun	21.7	12.8	38.2	58.2	9.2	46.8	68.6	70.9	60.0
Expansion of self	10.4	28.6	41.5	8.9	4.7	23.7	38.1	21.2	35.3
Adult status and social identity	13.8	2.1	4.7	5.9	2.0	5.8	8.3	9.1	21.9
Achievement	4.6	7.8	7.7	3.4	1.8	30.1	2.8	3.0	11.1
Morality	6.7	0.5	0.4	1.9	1.9	2.3	0.4	0.2	0.8
Power	1.8	0.1	0.2	2.0	0.1	1.2	0.1	0.2	2.2
n	1539	984	965	1567	2288	1433	2103	904	1259

Source: Hoffman, 1987

independent and self-reliant; 2.4 percent of rural Indonesians and 4.1 percent of rural Turks shared this aspiration for their offspring. In general, people in predominantly rural countries, where subsistence resources were scarce, placed greater emphasis upon obedience and family solidarity; people in more affluent societies tended to favor autonomy and the development of personal virtues.

The findings also indicated that, across societies, the father's occupational status was associated with variations in childrearing values. In families where the father was engaged in professional or managerial employment, independence was sought in the children; in families where the father worked in the manual or service sectors, obedience tended to be preferred. Among the starkest demonstrations of cross-cultural variability in orientations toward children are the data in table 4.1, based on mothers' accounts of the advantages of having children (fathers' accounts were broadly similar; see Hoffman, 1987). Note the enormous differences in stress on economic utility between the US and all other countries, but especially the poorer Asian societies. Note also the attractions of "primary ties and affection" to citizens of the wealthier nations (America and Singapore).

It seems that how couples approach the creation and administration of their family group is closely tied to the nature of their social system, and their status and aspirations within it, as Bronfenbrenner's (1979) ecological theory would predict. Burns et al. (1984) and Nestemann and Niepel (1994) provide further evidence that *within* a society material standing and social status are associated with differences in parental values. For example, Burns et al. (1984) found that parents in more affluent neighborhoods placed greater weight on children's sociability than did parents in higher-risk, inner-city slum neighborhoods.

A good illustration of the influences of the exosystem upon the quality of childrearing is provided by Cotterell's (1986) study of families living in small mining and rural towns in inland Australia. In these communities, protracted periods of working in the bush or sessions on night shift in the pits mean that some of the fathers are away from home during the hours of childrearing. Investigating childrearing attitudes and behavior, Cotterell found that mothers with absentee husbands scored lower on measures of the provision of play and cognitive stimulation to their children. These cannot always be kept prominent among the priorities of a woman left to run the home on her own. If the mother had informational support from her social network, then she was more likely to provide greater levels of play, stimulation, warmth, and teaching to her children, but the mothers with absentee husbands tended to have smaller networks to draw upon, possibly because their heavier domestic load and lower availability of partner meant that they were less able to integrate into the local communities.

Orientations toward Childrearing

Parents have different views about the values of children, and they have different orientations toward childrearing. Since the middle of the twentieth century, a major thrust of research into social development and family processes has been directed toward characterizing the main types of parenting styles and investigating their consequences for child development. Although a variety of models has been generated, they tend to converge on two dimensions: emotional responsiveness and control/demandingness (Baumrind, 1989; Maccoby and Martin, 1983). In brief, parents' *emotional* orientation toward their offspring can range from warm and responsive to cold and rejecting; parents' *control* orientation can range from authoritarian power assertion to indifference and neglect.

One of the most influential models has been that of Baumrind (1967, 1971, 1989). Based on observational and interview studies, Baumrind identified three different patterns of parenting style: *authoritarian, authoritative,* and *permissive.* This typology (deriving from earlier social psychological work on variations in social climates; cf. Lewin et al., 1939) provides an important framework for much research and theory concerning the relationship between social context and social development. It is worth becoming familiar with the main characteristics of each pattern.

Authoritarian   In terms of emotional orientation, authoritarian parents tend to score low on measures of warmth and responsiveness, and are cold and punitive toward the child when she or he transgresses. On the control/demand dimension, they score high: they are strict, assert their power freely, expect obedience, and attempt to instil respect for authority. Because they are relatively intolerant of "childishness", they set high maturity demands. As communicators with their children, they tend to lack clarity, relying on orders rather than reasoning. An authoritarian parent is likely to tell her offspring: "No, you can't go to the video arcade because I bloody well said so. And stop swearing."

Authoritative   These parents are toward the warm and responsive end of the emotional continuum. They are affectionate, more supportive of the child's autonomy and interests, and they take note of the child's point of view. Authoritative parents also score high on control/demand and maturity expectations, but their emphasis is on fostering a sense of independent responsibility in the child. They differ from authoritarian parents in their modes of establishing standards and discipline. In particular, when providing directives or constraints they explain to the child the need for the particular regulation: "No, you can't go to the video arcade because the place is swarming with drug dealers and child molesters and it's not safe for people your age. I would be very worried about you."

Permissive Permissive parents vary on the emotional continuum: some are warm and indulgent, others are cooler, more remote, and lack interest in the child. They have in common a high level of tolerance of the child's impulses and activities. Permissive parents score low on control/demand: "Yeah, sure, go wherever you like, take some money out of your mum's bag."

Parental Style and Child Characteristics

In her 1967 study, Baumrind examined the relationship between parental style and the behavior of preschool children. She found that the children of authoritative parents were rated as more mature, more independent, more friendly, more active, and more achievement-oriented. The children of authoritarian parents were intermediate on these measures; they were rated as less happy, less trusting, and more withdrawn. Finally, the least competent children tended to be those of permissive parents; these children revealed the lowest levels of self-reliance and self-control.

Subsequent research has largely borne out these patterns. Baumrind (1989) reports that the relationships between parental style and child characteristics in her preschool sample remained strong when the subjects were re-tested in middle childhood. The children of *authoritative* parents tend to score higher on measures of self-esteem (Coopersmith, 1967; Loeb et al., 1980) and academic performance (Dornbusch et al., 1987; Steinberg et al., 1989). Authoritative childrearing styles are associated with more positive adjustment to family trauma, such as divorce or remarriage (Hetherington and Clingempeel, 1992). The children of *authoritarian* parents tend to score lower on measures of self-esteem (Coopersmith, 1967), have poorer peer relations (Putallaz, 1987), and in some circumstances have been found to display high levels of interpersonal aggression (see Maccoby and Martin, 1983). The children of *permissive* parents are more likely to show difficulties in adjusting to school, also tend to score higher than average on measures of aggressiveness, and in adolescence are more likely to be involved in delinquent and other problematic behavior (Lamborn et al., 1991; Pulkkinen, 1982).

Two questions stand out. Why do authoritative patterns bring about such favorable outcomes? Why is it that not every parent adopts this highly recommended mode of childrearing?

Possible benefits of authoritative parenting

Several reasons can be advanced to explain the benefits of authoritative parenting. First, the arrangement is an emotionally secure one. The parent establishes a firm, stable milieu within which the child receives the message that she or he is valued as a person and has individual rights. This may well be favorable to the development of self-esteem and a sense of autonomy. Second, the parent provides clear articulation of reasons and responsibilities. This could promote awareness of the feelings of others, understanding of moral and social standards, and aspirations toward shared goals (such as academic attainment). Third, the parent models and facilitates modes of interaction which involve give-and-take and attempts at mutual comprehension. This could nurture skills in interpersonal relations, which could in turn contribute to socially sensitive interactions with peers, resulting in better adjusted and more popular children.

Why are there non-authoritative parents?

Given these possible virtues of authoritative parenting it is natural to ask: why, then, can't everyone be like the Cosbies? The *Cosby Show* is very relevant, because it is a widely disseminated public statement of what is entailed in being a good guy on the domestic front. It is not alone: Baumrind's original subjects probably watched the *Dick Van Dyck Show*, where Dick and Mary exuded parental warmth and prosocial demandingness. For caregivers who lack a TV set, newspaper columns, magazine articles, and tips-for-parents books are readily available to convey much the same message in straightforward, practical terms. Look at the noticeboard the next time you visit your general practitioner. Most likely, you will see posters from parents' associations advising that "A child needs love. A child needs respect. A child needs choice. A child needs responsibility." You will not find the Authoritarian Aunties' proclamation "A child needs a good hiding" (and the Permissive Parents never got around to producing any poster at all). In short, the extolling of authoritative parenting is not restricted to esoteric academic publications but is part of the ideology of Western caregiving and the popular media: it is the socially desirable option. Research indicates that parents are influenced by scientific theories of child development as presented via the popular media (Burman, 1994; Young, 1991).

The return of the exosystem

One reason why not everyone incorporates the message may be that not all share the domestic comforts that upper middle-class professionals like the Cosbies take for granted. According to Bronfenbrenner (1979), the structures and processes within the microsystem of the family are influenced by higher-level systems, such as the exosystem (including the parents' workplaces) and the macrosystem (the broader ideological values of the society). In a study of 152 white American families, Bronfenbrenner et al. (1984) studied the relationship between mothers' work situations and their perceptions of their 3-year-old children. They found that among the poorer mothers, children were perceived as less attractive and less enjoyable. One such mother explained:

> We don't have any kind of life. When you work, you're constantly racing around back and forth. There's never any relaxation. Work, come home and work, go to bed . . . There's no way you can cram seven days of housework into less than two days . . . Seems like I'm always running around on my lunch hour. There's so little time. (Bronfenbrenner et al., 1984, p. 1367)

Stressful events at the points of intersection with the exosystem are likely to be more frequent in poorer families. In these family contexts, television viewing may be more a matter of transient relief from everyday burdens than an opportunity to reflect on idealizations of the parental role; posters at the doctor's may be less salient than the worry of how the bill is to be met.

Even in less financially pressured environments, there is a continuity from work life to home life. Hoffman (1987, p. 139) quotes an American father: "I work all day and the man's always telling me what to do. And everyone's always telling me what to do. But when I go home, I'm the one telling what to do. And those kids better mind or they know what for." Similarly, an American mother comments: "I'm in control there. I run the show – more or less. My husband's not around a lot and so it's pretty much my show" (Hoffman, 1987, p. 139). These remarks also suggest that members of different social classes have different conceptions of their place in society, which may influence the expectations they convey to their children. For example, a well-paid successful professional with a great deal of autonomy in her work might anticipate similar career paths for her children, and an authoritative style of parenting may be the "natural" way of encouraging the competencies, attitudes, and aspirations that are associated with advancement in the educational system. On the other hand, a lower-paid manual worker whose duties are largely directed from above (doing what "the man" tells him) may envisage his children fitting into the system at the same or slightly higher level, and thus feel that the young need to become accustomed to taking orders and showing respect for authority. Hoffman's (1987) data from the Value of Children Study, above, are consistent with this account.

The meaning and correlates of parental control may also be very different in different social systems. Chao (1994) points out that while autocratic, controlling styles of parenting are associated with problematic outcomes for many Western youths, in traditional Chinese communities high levels of parental control are associated with educational attainment. Chao warns that it may be ethnocentric to equate the latter type of parenting, within a Chinese community, with authoritarianism.

Marital discord

As stressed above, the family is a system, and processes or problems in one part of the system may well have repercussions elsewhere (Russell and Russell, 1994). Katz and Gottman (1991) found that unhappily married couples were prone to display indifferent, uninvolved parenting styles when interacting with their 4- and 5-year-old children, and the children in turn showed signs of stress on physiological measures as well as lower levels of peer interaction.

Parental personality

Another factor may be parental personality. After all, not everyone is equally comfortable with democracy or with autocracy. This is a particularly interesting issue because of the question of where the parent's personality comes from. Social psychologists are very familiar with the concept of the authoritarian personality (Adorno et al., 1950), an individual with a cluster of anti-democratic traits, strong convictions about the need for law and order, and a high degree of prejudice against members of outgroups. These people also crop up in our media families from time to time, as *Archie Bunker* or *Alf Garnett*. On the basis of clinical interviews, Adorno et al. (1950) argued that the origins of the authoritarian personality could be traced back to the kind of upbringing such individuals had experienced. Specifically, they reasoned that harsh parenting styles engender unconscious hostilities toward the parents which the child diverts toward more vulnerable targets, such as weaker individuals or members of minority groups. It is interesting to note that eminent dictators often turn out to have authoritarian fathers. Stalin, for example, was the son of a domineering, drunken, and violent peasant and Hitler's father, a senior civil servant, was a strong disciplinarian (Bullock, 1993).

These two case studies alone may not convince you (you probably know that Madonna's father was very strict, too). But there is more extensive quantitative evidence. Mussen and his co-workers (1987; Mussen and Haan, 1982) examined longitudinally the sociopolitical attitudes of a group of Americans and found that, from early adolescence to middle adulthood, liberals and conservatives had very different personality structures. Relatively liberal people were more questioning of authority, more independent, more concerned with "subjective matters and philosophical issues"; relatively conservative people were lacking in independence, relatively insecure, more conventional in their thinking, submissive to authority, uncomfortable with uncertainty, and high in need of reassurance. In both groups, these characteristics were consistent over a 35-year period.

Let us look back and look forward. Mussen's descriptions of the liberal individuals echo Baumrind's accounts of the children of authoritative parents. Mussen's conservative subjects display very similar attributes to the insecure and distrustful offspring of Baumrind's authoritarian parents. We lack data on the childrearing patterns of the parents of Mussen's subjects, but a plausible inference is that they are likely to have been similar to those identified by Baumrind. Byrne (1965) found that university students who scored high on Adorno et al.'s (1950) California F (for Fascist) Scale tended to have parents who scored high on it, too. Looking forward, we can reasonably speculate that personality characteristics that are relatively stable over 35 years will be manifest in these individuals' own parenting styles, so that they, in turn, will favor authoritative or authoritarian households respectively. Hence, it is plausible that there is at least some degree of intergenerational transmission of childrearing style and the attitudinal correlates of that style.

The child's personality

However, as already encountered in chapters 2 and 3, social relations between parent and child reflect the characteristics and behaviors of *each* party. Could the child's personality influence the kind of parenting that she or he evokes? Several researchers have argued that this is very likely. Temperament researchers propose that individual differences in temperament influence how individuals perceive and respond to their environments and "must necessarily have consequences for learning, child-rearing practices, and the effective socialization of children" (Rothbart et al., 1994, p. 36).

This conclusion is supported by the findings of Eisenberg and Fabes (1994) that the socialization practices of mothers of 4- and 6-year-olds were related to their children's perceived temperament. If a mother saw her child as having a difficult temperament (high in emotional intensity and negative affect) then she tended to react in ways that would relieve her own distress, provoked by the challenges of managing the child: typically, this kind of temperament invited more punitive (authoritarian) reactions. If the child was perceived as able to self-regulate, then mothers reported higher levels of supportive and constructive socialization reactions (authoritative patterns). It may be that different children are constitutionally predisposed to manifest particular patterns of behavior, and these manifestations evoke different types of responses.

A more general argument to this effect has been advanced by Scarr (1992), who holds: "Clearly, there are family differences: it is not clear that most of those differences are environmental" (p. 10). She proposes first that the shared genetic material of parent and child mean that they will have at least some personal characteristics in common as they set about constructing their microsystem, their home life. Second, as we have seen, people evoke from others responses that reflect their own characteristics and behaviors. Third, people actively seek out environments that enable them to fulfil their interests and meet their personality characteristics. The bright child looks for intellectual stimulation, the shy child avoids crowds, the physically gifted individual veers towards sports (Jackson, 1994; Rubin and Asendorpf, 1993; Scarr, 1992; Scarr and McCartney, 1983). In this way, maintains Scarr, *people create their own environments*.

Analogous arguments have been raised in challenge to Baumrind's account of parenting effects. Lewis (1981) argues that measures of "authoritative" parental control may actually be measures of the child's willingness to obey. Lewis argues that where Baumrind sees one of the hallmarks of the authoritative parent as a "respect for the child's decision", if we look at things from the child's point of view, then quite a different process may be envisaged. It could be that the child reasons: "My parents withdraw their demands after I convince them with my arguments" (1981, p. 561).

Summary

Reproduction is a biological fact, but it is clear from work reviewed here that parents bring strong values to their role. Cross-cultural research is particularly helpful in illuminating the diversity of parental needs and expectations, and much of the variety appears to be reflective of broader organization and goals in different societies' macrosystems. The family's place in relation to the exosystem (e.g., the work roles of the parents) have fundamental consequences for the parents' place in relation to the child (e.g., how much they see of each other, the authority structure of the home). Baumrind's and others' work establishes clearly that there are individual differences in childrearing patterns, and that these are associated with individual differences in sociability, social behavior, and attainment. Other researchers stress that there are also individual differences in children, detectable from early infancy, and these may evoke different types of parental behavior.

Change and Development within the Family: the Impact of Siblings

The family itself is a constantly evolving unit (Donley, 1993; Dunn, 1988a; Kreppner, 1992; Russell and Russell, 1994), linked with the past (the patterns of domestic organization that the parents experienced) and the future (preparing the children for their own roles as citizens and parents). Kreppner (1992) points out that reorganizations come about in the family as a result of developmental changes in the child(ren), such as learning to walk, talk, moving into social relations beyond the household, entering puberty, and so on. Change is rarely isolated to one individual within the family. For example, a natural research focus when the child reaches the age of school entry is the child: how he or she reacts to the transition. However, Anderson (1985) found that parents, too, experience substantial role stress around this period, partly because they feel that their adequacy as parents is being put to public test. This in turn affects how they behave towards the child. Another important context of change within the family is the arrival and development of siblings.

Siblings and the Complexity of Early Relations

Relations among siblings complicate the picture of the early social world. They fall somewhere in between vertical and horizontal relationships. Social power among siblings tends to be age-related in most cultures, such that younger children defer to their older brothers and sisters, and older children assume some protective and tutorial roles with respect to the younger members of their family. Overall, adapting Hartup's (1989b) metaphor, we could conceive of sibling relationships as *diagonal*: there are status and knowledge differences but there are also similarities (e.g. siblings may have in common that they are non-adults) and there is scope for more egalitarian social interchange than may be possible with adults.

One of the first points we should establish when considering sibling relationships is that they are not simply additive experiences that happen to accumulate within a given household. A child's relationship with her or his siblings is intimately connected to her or his relationship with her or his parents, to the parents' relationships with each other and to the parents' relationship with the siblings (Boer et al., 1992; Buhrmester, 1992; Dunn, 1988a, 1992; Kreppner, 1987; Sroufe and Fleeson, 1986).

The arrival of a sibling typically has immediate impact upon the mother–firstborn relationship because the mother's involvement in caregiving is disrupted by the birth itself, and because she has henceforth to distribute her caregiving to include the newcomer. One consequence is often that families reorganize their division of labor. In Western households, for instance, the father may increase his involvement in caregiving (Stewart et al., 1987) (though this is not inevitable; see Vergeer, 1987) and his relationship with the firstborn may alter (Kreppner et al., 1982; Lamb, 1977).

The firstborn's behavior often changes after the arrival of a sibling (Dunn, 1992; Gottlieb and Mendelson, 1990; Howe and Ross, 1990). Not surprisingly, given the disruption of so many aspects of familiar routines and relationships, distress is common, and many confrontations occur between parents and firstborn (Dunn et al., 1981; Stewart et al., 1987). Interestingly, when asked what they dislike about the new baby, preschoolers frequently mention "crying" (Stewart et al., 1987). This may seem ironic, given the value that crying has had in the firstborn's own infancy (see chapter 2) but, of course, cries have the double demerit from the preschooler's perspective of being inherently unpleasant stimuli *and* serving as a reliable means of diverting parental attention back to the baby.

Dunn and Kendrick's (1982) research indicates that what happens when another child joins the family may vary greatly according to the nature of the earlier parent–child relationship. For example, they found that if the mother–firstborn relationship was a very close one, the first child could be hostile to the new member of the family and show a marked drop in the quality and frequency of interaction with the mother. One year later, the mutual relations between the siblings were hostile. On the other hand, in families where the firstborn and mother had a confrontation-laden relationship, children tended to be especially friendly toward their new siblings. Also, in families where the mother suffered a period of depression after the sibling birth, the relationship between the siblings was often particularly warm. Over time, children appear to monitor their sibling's treatment and interaction with the caregiver, and the quality of the sibling relationship varies accordingly (Dunn, 1988b). Among the positive consequences are that parents report that children show signs of becoming more "grown up" and independent (Dunn et al., 1981), taking pride in their new status as a "big brother or sister" (Stewart et al., 1987).

Siblings and temperament

Research into early temperament and its correlates provides further illustration of the interdependencies and complex mutual effects among siblings and other family members. For example, we saw in chapter 2 that one problem in measuring the dimensions and stability of infant and temperament is that, since parents are often the sources of ratings, the focus and durability of any measures may be affected by the parents' own concerns and perceptions. The position may be all the more complex if the child has siblings. One interesting study (Schacter and Stone, 1985) found that many parents manifest a contrast effect, especially in perceptions of their firstborn and his or her immediately following sibling, such that if one child is perceived as "difficult" then the next is likely to be perceived as "easier" (or vice versa). Whether or not these perceptions are accurate, the findings suggest that within-family processes influence the mother's definition and possibly, in due course, the child's self-definition (e.g. how do you grow up if you are told regularly that "You are much more of a handful than Melissa was"?).

The temperament of *each* child may have some implications for the nature of sibling relationships (Brody et al., 1987; Munn and Dunn, 1989). For example, Munn and Dunn (1989) found that among sibling pairs studied when the younger child was 24 months old, difficult characteristics in the older child (negative moods, non-adaptable, non-distractable) were associated with less frequent joint pretend play between the children. High levels of "threshold" (sensitivity to noise, pain and social disapproval) in the younger child were associated with higher levels of joint pretend when the child was 36 months old. A plausible interpretation of these findings is that, when children are quite young, the temperament(s) of their older siblings may influence the extent and nature of their joint play (to simplify, if you've got a miserable older brother, joint pretend play may not be available or much fun), whereas as children get a little older those who are sensitive to others' interests or behavior may be better able to entice them into pretend play. Once again, a crucial aspect of development appears to be the goodness-of-fit between the temperaments of the different parties (Munn and Dunn, 1989; see chapter 2).

Siblings and Attachments

Within these shifts, the quality of the firstborn's attachment to each parent may change. Vergeer (1987) tested the attachment of 1-year-olds to their mother and father respectively in five Dutch families 6 weeks before and 6 weeks after the arrival of a new baby. She found that the relationship with either parent could change, though the father–child relationship was most variable. Teti and Ablard (1989) found that Type B (securely attached) infants developed more positive relationships with their siblings, and that the optimal arrangement seems to be that in which both children had a secure attachment to their mother. Dunn (1992) comments that Teti and Ablard's (1989) findings do not rule out alternative explanations: for instance, it is possible that the siblings' respective temperaments affect the quality of each relationship.

Siblings as attachment figures

Siblings themselves can be attachment figures (Bank, 1992; Schaffer and Emerson, 1964). As such, they serve similar functions to those associated with primary caregivers; as sources of comfort in the face of distress, and as bases from which to explore. Dunn and Kendrick (1982) found that parents of 8-month-olds (i.e., around the time when attachment are forming; see chapter 3) describe strong emotional orientations on the part of the baby toward the older child: "She thinks he's marvellous. Hero-worships him. If he plays with her foot, she kills herself laughing. She doesn't cry until he goes out of the room" (Dunn and Kendrick, 1982, p. 93).

To test whether sibling relationships do bear the hallmarks of attachment, Stewart (1983) conducted a study using a procedure similar to the Strange Situation with infants aged 10–20 months, their preschool siblings, and their mothers. He found that when the infant began to cry at the departure of the mother, the preschooler would often attempt to comfort and to reassure him or her that the mother would be returning. Distressed infants were calmed by this sibling nurturance, to the extent that they would return to play activities. Some of the infants, after monitoring the stranger warily for a while, would move so that their sibling could serve as a barrier between them and the adult, and then resumed play within this refuge. In other words, Stewart found among siblings the familiar proximity-seeking and secure-base phenomena that are characteristic of the more extensively researched parent–child attachments.

Siblings as caregivers

Historically, it has been common among immigrant families for older children to become surrogate parents because the mother would have demanding low-status employment (Hareven, 1989). Weisner and Gallimore (1977) reviewed the child-care practices of 186 societies and found that in 57 percent of them older children (who were often siblings) were the principal caregivers for infants and young children. In such contexts, siblings may function as much more than substitute food providers: they also serve as "culture brokers" (Ervin-Tripp, 1989) introducing their younger brothers and sisters to the shared understandings, the work and community practices of their society (figure 4.1).

The presence and roles of siblings are determined largely by the domestic structures sanctioned in particular communities. In some polygynous societies (i.e., where a man may take several wives) children may acquire quite large numbers of siblings. Valsiner (1989a) shows that the changing scale of the sibling context in monogamous and polygynous families can have dramatic effects upon the sheer number of the developing child's daily social contacts. If each wife produces a few more children, the polygynous domestic arrangement can be quite populous relative to Western experiences. Even this kind of calculation may be an underestimate of the incidence of child relatives in polygynous and other traditional collectivist societies, because the greater interdependence of families is likely to mean that other child kin are prominent in everyday lives. Tietjen (1989) asked Swedish children and children from a village-dwelling people in Papua New Guinea how many child relatives they knew; on average, Swedish children named 0.81, while the Maisin children named 10.80.

Sibling relationships are likely to be quite diverse in these communities. Again, although the greater numerousness is of interest and will obviously have consequences for the amount of social play the children experience (Tietjen, 1989), the network of relations among the family as a whole is affected by new additions and affiliations.

Figure 4.1   Many children spend a great deal of time in the company of siblings.

For example, Valsiner (1989a) notes that caregiving by older siblings is typically under adults' delegation, and the adults have different statuses according to their chronological position (first wives usually have greater status). Sometimes, wives use their power as adults over the children of their rival co-wives to express their feelings. A child may find that she or he is a scapegoat because of tensions in relationships elsewhere in the family. This in turn may affect relations with siblings, who may side variously with one parent or another, or affiliate with the victim. Similar patterns may well be familiar to Western readers acquainted with one procedure of domestic enlargement more common in our cultures, namely the blending of families as a result of divorce and remarriage. Families certainly do not become simpler as they become larger.

It is important to recognize that sibling caretaking does not provide identical or equivalent care to that provided by a parent (Boer, 1990; Bryant, 1992, 1994). In an American study, Bryant (1992) found that primary caregiver mothers and fathers provided greater support and more coping strategies than did primary caregiver siblings.

Siblings and the Ambivalence of Relationships

Siblings afford children with many opportunities and causes to explore emotions and behaviors that may have been rare or even absent before:

Young siblings fight with one another. They provoke and irritate one another with devastating lack of inhibition. They amuse and excite one another and engage in uproarious games together. They comfort and care for one another. No psychologist is needed to point out the passion, fury and jealousy, the range of emotion from gentle sympathy to wild aggression, that is expressed so uninhibitedly by siblings in their first three years. (Dunn and Kendrick, 1982, p. 84)

Ethologists and sociobiologists argue that relations with siblings stand a good chance of becoming ambivalent because two conflicting motives are inherent in the relationship (Hinde, 1988; MacDonald, 1988d; Smith, 1987; Trivers, 1985). On the one hand, siblings share genetic material, and the pursuit of inclusive fitness promotes looking after one's kin. On the other hand, siblings pose a competitive threat to access to (resource-controlling) parents. It is a harsh fact of life that one might maximize one's own inclusive fitness at the expense of one's siblings. Worse still, so might they.

However, it could be argued equally plausibly that the dynamics of actual social experiences are at least as important as surreptitious genetic dispositions. As stressed above, sibling relationships are formed within the context of broader family processes. Siblings furnish early notice that people are complex, and that our relations with others are multidimensional (Hartup and van Lieshout, 1995; Shantz and Hobart, 1989). As noted in chapter 1, social development involves two primary life-goals, individuation from others and becoming connected to others. These seemingly conflicting goals may help explain the occurrence and intensity of many sibling conflicts. On the one hand, each individual strives to assert her or his space and autonomy; on the other hand, the very fact of focused dispute entails an implicit recognition that the other person is significant.

The reality of human affairs is such that the individuals with whom we interact rarely have just one characteristic or elicit just one evaluation or emotion from us. Siblings love and hate, play and fight, nurture and hurt. One of Dunn and Kendrick's (1982) young subjects captured the incipient duality of interpersonal relations when he declared "I like my sister" – but recommended that she be returned to hospital.

Summary

Families are not static social entities. Each individual is developing and changing, and the arrival of new members incurs adjustments throughout the relationship system. The social world of the young child is complicated by the inclusion of a baby in the family partly in terms of its own emotional adjustment to the newcomer, but also by the behaviors and emotions that the newcomer manifests. These are dynamic processes which unfold in different ways according to the firstborn's responses and the circumstances in which both children receive care. The arrival of a sibling can arouse emotional reactions at the threat of being supplanted from a close relationship, or it can redirect a hitherto unsatisfied need for affection/affiliation toward a new party. Siblings provide some of the earliest indicators that social life can be a battlefield.

Beyond the Family

In most communities, children soon come into contact with adults other than their mother and father. Clarke-Stewart (1987) points out that even within Western societies, the range of early child-care arrangements is very large, involving different combinations of people (relatives, neighbors, family friends, child-care professionals), locations (own home, someone else's home, informal community arrangements, organized day-care centers), and other children (present/absent, same/different age group, few/many). If we broaden this to account for different sociocultural or historical contexts, the picture becomes still more varied, with nannies, servants, wet nurses, au pairs, lodgers, and other members of the community involved to different extents in children's daily lives (Hareven, 1989).

It was seen in chapter 3 that the initial reaction of infants to unfamiliar adults is often wariness and sometimes fear. This does not mean that young children are incapable of forming relationships with adults other than their parents. Laboratory studies have found that initially wary infants will often warm to an adult stranger within the course of a single session or over several sessions (Bretherton, 1978; Bretherton et al., 1981b; Smith et al., 1981). These processes are not random but reflect characteristics and actions of both infant and adult, as well as the social relations among adults. For example, an interesting observational study by Levitt et al. (1993) found that infants were least likely to avoid other adults to whom their mother felt strongly attached, but did avoid persons not placed on the mother's list of close network members.

Awareness of the diversity and importance of the social ecologies of development has prompted a growth of research interest recently in children's social networks and support systems (Belle, 1989; Clarke-Stewart, 1987; Ladd, 1983; Levitt et al., 1993; Nestemann and Hurrelmann, 1994; Tietjen, 1985). These studies find that the social networks of parents and their children overlap. The interdependencies become clear as we consider aspects of the child's relationships with other adults in two contexts, the home and day-care/nursery settings.

Other Caregivers in the Home Environment

Despite the widespread use of childminders in many contemporary societies (Clarke-Stewart, 1987; Smith and Turner, 1981), relatively little research has been conducted into the ways children adjust to them. Important exceptions include Kermoian and Leiderman's (1986) comparison of infant's attachments to mother and child caregivers among the Gusii people of Kenya, and Smith and Noble's (1987) study of British children's reactions to a series of visits from babysitters.

Childrearing among the Gusii is organized in ways which provide an interesting natural manipulation of caregiving activities. In this society, mothers use other (younger) caregivers extensively, and they divide roles in a distinctive way. The natural mother takes care of virtually all of the baby's physical needs (breastfeeding, cleaning), while the other caregiver provides constant companionship and play stimulation. By these arrangements, the Gusii conveniently separate caregiving functions – provision of physical care and cognitive/social stimulation – that are confounded in most circumstances where attachment has been evaluated. Kermoian and Leiderman (1986) reasoned that if both of these kinds of activities are necessary for the establishment of a secure attachment, then Gusii infants should be less likely to form such a relationship; on the other hand, if one service was more important than the other, then the infants should be more likely to develop secure attachments to the adult who provides it.

In fact, using a modification of the Strange Situation, Kermoian and Leiderman found that the proportions of children forming secure attachments to mother or caregivers was 61 percent and 54 percent, respectively, roughly the same proportion as found in samples of Western children (see chapter 3). As in other studies, these relationships were statistically independent; that is, a child might form a secure attachment to one caregiver and an insecure attachment to the other, indicating that infant temperament alone was unlikely to account for attachment type. The researchers conclude that the kinds of interactions provided by each caregiver – whether related to physical needs or social activities – are sufficient for the establishment of a secure attachment. Once again, the evidence reveals that infants can develop strong relationships with adults other than the natural mother and can form multiple attachments.

In Western societies it is common for infants to begin life predominantly in the care of parents and to experience other caregivers later. In a British study, Smith and Noble (1987) investigated infants' responses to adult female strangers who served as sitters, visiting their homes several times over a period of weeks or months. The infants were about 15 months old at the beginning of the project. The visits lasted for 3 hours, and the mother was present for the first 30 minutes.

The children's responses to the sitters proved generally to be positive. The infants tended to greet their sitter in a mildly friendly way and, although they sometimes cried at the departure of their mother, usually settled down quickly and were willing to interact with the sitter in the mother's absence. Within a few sessions, the sitters were able to initiate vigorous play with the babies, and responses were often positive, rarely negative. The babies' moods in the sitters' company appeared to be neutral or moderately positive most of the time. There were individual differences among the babies in terms of how well they responded to the new caregiver, and these were related to a variety of factors, including attachment type, infant temperament, previous separation experience, and the frequency of the visits. Overall, the authors conclude that the prognosis for babysitting is reasonably good: infants will accept the new adult and will relate to her, although they continue to display much more positive orientation towards the primary caregiver.

Day Care

In most industrialized societies in recent decades, the increased participation of women in the workforce and the rise of single parenthood has meant that substantial proportions of young children now spend parts of their week in day care. Such arrangements have myriad consequences for the child's social world. She or he is subject to repeated separations from, and reunions with, the principal caregiver(s). She or he is confronted with new adults. Unlike parents in the home, these new adults have responsibilities toward numerous children, and have to share attention among them – a task which they may perform with varying degrees of competence and sensitivity to individual differences. There are also peers in the child's world on a greater scale than ever before (figure 4.2).

The topic of day care and its effects is highly controversial because it has implications both for the roles of women and the healthy development of the young. In the early 1950s, strong opinions were voiced by authoritative sources convinced that child development, maternal wellbeing, and human progress in general depended on the uninterrupted provision of care by the mother. The use of day nurseries and crèches was decried as leading to long-term damage to the emotional health of future generations. Bowlby (1953, p. 16) recommended that:

> we must recognize that leaving any child of under three years of age is a major operation only to be undertaken for good and sufficient reasons, and, when undertaken, to be planned with great care. On no account should the child be placed with people he doesn't know.

Notwithstanding this warning, on various accounts, young children have been placed with people they do not know more and more frequently. As a result, large amounts of applied research funding have been directed toward finding out whether this practice has any effects, deleterious or otherwise. One of the principal findings had been that being placed with someone the child does not know does not appear immediately to be the disaster that was once feared. Although teachers behave differently from mothers, and although their attentions have to be distributed among many classmates, children can relate comfortably to them and in some cases become attached to them (Howes and Hamilton, 1992; Ragozin, 1980; Rubenstein and Howes, 1979). Familiar caregivers are not forgotten as a result of these new relationships: mothers remain the preferred attachment figure in times of distress (Kagan et al., 1978; Ragozin, 1980).

Other findings concerning the correlates of day care do appear to give cause for some concern. Several studies have found that disproportionate numbers of infants in day care are likely to be classified as insecurely attached when tested in the Strange Situation (Barglow et al., 1987; Belsky and Rovine, 1988; Chase-Lansdale and Owen, 1987; but see Clarke-Stewart, 1989, and Roggman et al., 1994, for fuller reviews). This is particularly so of infants who were placed in day care below 12 months, that is, during the period when initial attachments are forming. Other studies have found

a)

b)

Figure 4.2   Broadening social networks: activities with other adults and peers in (A) a day care center and (B) preschool.

that preschoolers who have been in day care since infancy are more prone to aggressiveness, negative social adjustment, hyperactivity, and anxiety (Bates et al., 1994; Haskins, 1985; McCartney et al., 1982).

Does this mean that fears of early opponents of day care are justified, and that the best place for mother and child is the home? Before considering possible explanations of insecure attachments and aggressiveness, we should note that there is also evidence of benefits to the child placed in day care, and some of this evidence seems to contradict the above. For example, large-scale investigations have found that day care is associated with superior measures of social competence and cognitive ability (Andersson, 1989; Clarke-Stewart, 1987; Clarke-Stewart and Fein, 1983). Andersson (1992) followed up Swedish children at the ages of 8 and 13 and found evidence that those who had entered day care before the age of 12 months were performing better in school and attained higher scores on measures of adjustment and social competence.

Interpreting the "effects" of day care

Clarke-Stewart (1989) argues that some of the findings above may not be as contradictory as they first appear, and that we should not leap to the conclusion that day care is inherently bad for children's social and emotional development. It is possible, for example, that ratings of some preschoolers as more aggressive may reflect the fact that their day-care experiences have encouraged them to become more independent, and more determined to get their own way. This may not always be as "nice" as the behavior of some other children, but it does not necessarily indicate enduring maladjustment. Parents who place their child in day care may themselves value independence in their offspring, and this may be reflected in their parenting styles.

It is also possible that children who are aggressive or otherwise difficult to handle are more likely to be placed in day care, because their parents need a break. Evidence of insecure attachments to mothers may not be due to the day-care experience itself but to a variety of domestic factors which lead the parent to place the child in day care. Clarke-Stewart (1987) points out that mothers who particularly like babies may be more inclined to stay at home while those who do not, go to work. This does not mean that all working mothers dislike babies, but that some mothers may opt for work because their interactions with the baby are less than satisfactory, as found by Hock et al. (1985). It may be that the meaning of the Strange Situation differs for infants who are used to regular departures and reappearances of their mothers who work out of home; as a result they may be less responsive to her removal from the laboratory and less effusive on her return (Clarke-Stewart, 1989; Ruble and Thompson, 1992).

It is also the case that external work plus parenting plus housework is tiring and stressful for the mother, and may well reduce her physical and psychological availability to the infant: "in other words, [it] is not that 40 hours of day care is hard on infants but that 40 hours of work is hard on mothers" (Clarke-Stewart, 1989, p. 270). The very stresses which lead some parents to place their child in day care may in turn be associated with how the child relates to his or her new circumstances, so that negative adjustments to day care may reflect negative circumstances in the home (cf. Goosens, 1987; Howes and Olenick, 1986; Vaughn et al., 1980) rather than the pernicious effects of leaving the child with strangers.

A crucial issue is the quality of the day care available, in terms of the ratio of staff to children, the professional skills and warmth of the staff, staff turnover, staff–parent communication, and educational materials provided. Research demonstrates consistently that high quality is associated with more favorable outcomes (Andersson, 1989; Howes, 1990; Kontos et al., 1994; Phillips et al., 1987; Vandell et al., 1988).

Overall, the question of whether day care is maligned or malignant (Clarke-Stewart, 1989) is likely to continue to attract controversy in public debate and research contexts. It is reasonable to conclude on present evidence that the extent of insecurity and aggression found in some day-care children does not fall outside the normal range of variability on these patterns. It is also very clear that an adequate explanation of the differences found in some (but not all) studies will have to be a multivariate one: it is an oversimplification to assert that day care is invariably bad or good for children.

Summary

Most children interact with people from outside their immediate nuclear family from quite early in life. How they respond reflects aspects of their existing relationships, their developmental status, and how their caregivers themselves react to the other individuals. Rather than disrupting existing attachments, experiences of other adults sometimes afford opportunities to form new ones. The effects of children's first institutional social contexts – day-care environments – are controversial but early warnings from some ethologically influenced observers have not been vindicated; many factors influence how a child adjusts to day care, but the experience is not universally disastrous and good-quality care may provide social and cognitive benefits.

Peer Relations: Entry and Functions

Parents (and sometimes siblings) figure prominently in children's early social lives but they are not the only people with whom infants interact. As will already be clear, there is diversity in the kinds of social circumstances children experience, both within and between cultures, but the starting point of peer relations is typically the family (Delgado-Gaitan, 1994; Godde and Engfer, 1994). In some cultures, this is organized quite systematically. For example, Hays (1988) describes an African community in which the elders assign children "best friends," thereby initiating a relationship that is considered as important in the community as a sibling relationship.

Other cultures may be less deliberate, but none the less parents arrange (and limit) the opportunities for infants and preschoolers to meet and play together (Rubin et al., 1989). Parents decide whether and where to place the child in day care, and what kind of educational context and activities they wish their offspring to engage in, and the kinds of friends they would wish them to have (Hartup, 1983; Parke and

Bhavnagri, 1989; Stipek et al., 1992a). Parke and Bhavnagri comment that in these ways parents (predominantly mothers) mediate between the family and the community, selecting the interpersonal environments they see as desirable for their young. Fogel et al. (1987) found that preschoolers were much more likely to interact with unfamiliar children if their mothers encouraged them to do so. Parents also provide models of social skills and interactions with the community, and we will see shortly that there is suggestive evidence that these characteristics are associated with child popularity and social behavior.

Although it is widely acknowledged that there are continuities between family and home, there is a diversity of opinion among social developmentalists as to the nature of the relationship. One position is that parallel processes occur in each context, and that what is needed is a unified theory of relationship formation (Hay, 1985; Nash, 1988). Such a theory has the potential attractions of greater parsimony. Otherwise, we might need a separate theory for each of the different categories of person with whom the child interacts: parent, sibling, peer, stranger, etc. (cf. Nash, 1988). Proponents of this position argue that there is little evidence that interaction skills emerge first with their mothers and only later with peers.

Another possibility is that the child experiences and learns different things from different people in his or her social network (Feiring and Lewis, 1989). According to this perspective the mother–child relationship is not the primary determinant of all others but is one (albeit often prominent) relationship among several, and these may well occur simultaneously, meeting different needs and posing different demands. Mueller (1989) has argued that children require different skills to interact with their peers from those involved with mothers (for example, different means of controlling others' behavior), and that these develop independently.

Most of the empirical research on early peer interactions has been conducted with Western children and we will focus primarily on that work here. The contributions of peers to social and intellectual development have attracted widespread and increasing attention from developmentalists, and we will be returning to issues relating to peers at many places later in the book. The term *peers* refers to persons with whom the child is on a "roughly equal footing" in social status and cognitive abilities (Foot et al., 1990). Often, this amounts to agemates, but children do share social activities with children of different ages (Ellis et al., 1981), and mixed-age peer relations are more common in some cultures than others (Whiting and Whiting, 1975). We should note also that "peers" overlaps with, but is not identical to, "friends": interactions with peers who are not friends may be important in some circumstances, and the formation of friendship is itself a developmental advance within the child's social relations. An overview of some of the major characteristics of peer relations during each of infancy, the preschool years, and the school years follows, and then we will examine particular aspects of peer relations, including emotions, conflicts, and the selection of friends. (Concepts of friendship are discussed in chapter 9.)

Infant Sociability

Infants show responsiveness to the presence and behavior of a peer from very early in life. Vandell and Mueller (1980) review several studies of infants' interest in peers which indicate the following broad pattern of development during the first year. By about 2 months, infants look at a peer. By 3 or 4 months, they will touch and explore another infant manually. By 6 months, they will smile and vocalize toward a peer. Over the next few months, as their ambulatory abilities increase, they will crawl towards and follow each other. By one year, varied social behaviors are employed in peer interactions, including laughter, gesture, and imitation.

Many of these behaviors are one-way, and simply documenting their frequency does not in itself show that reciprocal social interaction is taking place, or that relationships are forming. Vandell and Mueller (1980) point out that to make these claims we would need evidence of the mutual interest of the behaviors. If Child A directs a behavior to Child B, then to describe the interaction as *social* we would require evidence that Child B is responding. In fact, this does appear to be the case: Vandell and Mueller report that if a social response were to occur in infant–infant interactions, it was usually within 1.8 seconds of the initiator's behavior, while breaks between the children's respective behaviors when they were not interacting were closer to 30 seconds. Other research has shown that infants (aged 6 months) are more likely to cease an interaction when a peer is unresponsive (Hay et al., 1983). By this age, rates of touching each other begin to synchronize and interacting peers' moods begin to converge (Nash, 1988).

During the second half of the first year, peer interactions become increasingly rich as they exploit the expanding range of cognitive and communicative abilities the infant has available. Children become able to coordinate behaviors such as looking, smiling, vocalizing, and gesturing toward a peer (Bronson, 1981; Vandell et al., 1980), and are able to focus attention jointly on mutually interesting playthings (Bakeman and Adamson, 1984). Again, children are using with peers skills that are present in parent–infant interactions (see chapter 2). However, as mentioned above, it is not clear that skills are necessarily first learned with parents and then transferred to the peer context. If interactions with both are examined at the same age points, behaviors such as coordinating attention, expressing affect, and communicative acts are found to be used with each type of partner (Adamson and Bakeman, 1985; Bakeman and Adamson, 1984, 1986). Note that these parallel processes could be due either to the fact that similar demands are required in any interaction, or that some general property of sociability is emerging in the child.

In the second year, there are elements of both cooperation and conflict in infant peer relations (Nash, 1988; Shantz and Hobart, 1989). Children of this age can play together harmoniously in activities and games which require exchanges and turn-taking (Eckerman and Whatley, 1977; Goldman and Ross, 1978), and they engage in conversation-like sequences of vocalizations and imitations (Eckerman et al., 1975, 1989; Nadel-Brulfert et al., 1983). In these ways, children develop means of relating their behavior to responses from the other. Eckerman and Stein (1990) found that "imitation begets imitation" such that when another person imitated a toddler's play actions the child was much more likely to continue the actions and to contribute toward maintaining the shared focus. Through the practice of these skills young children begin to coordinate their behaviors in increasingly social peer interchanges (Eckerman, 1993; Nadel and Peze, 1993).

Although similar behaviors may occur in interactions with parents and peers, several studies have found that infants use their skills differentially according to social partner (Lewis et al., 1975; Vandell, 1980; Vandell and Wilson, 1987). This is consistent with the thesis, above, that the child is learning different things in different social contexts. However, whether this indicates that distinct interactional systems are developing or whether it demonstrates context-appropriate adaptions of a general sociability dimension remains uncertain (Lamb and Nash, 1989; Mueller, 1989; Vandell, 1980).

One thing which is clear is that young children *enjoy* peer relations. Even at 3 months, infants display more vocalizing, reaching, and squirming in response to a peer than to their own mirror image (Field, 1979). At 9 months, newly acquainted peers show more interest in each other than in their mothers or toys, and if they meet on future occasions they become more involved in each other and develop more complex play (Becker, 1977). Given the presence of both their mother and a peer, 10-month-olds look more frequently at the peer; slightly older children "converse" with and imitate the peer more than their mother (Rubenstein and Howes, 1976).

Peer Interactions among Preschoolers

During the preschool period, children's interactions with peers increase in frequency and develop in quality. From 12 months on, children become increasingly keen to interact with their peers (Ellis et al., 1981; Holmberg, 1980) and are provided with more opportunities to do so. Over the next few years, children begin to meet new peers in the neighborhood. This provides another example of the intersection of the community environment and child development (Bronfenbrenner, 1979; Parke, 1994). Neighborhoods vary considerably in terms of the numbers of children available, safety, accessibility to public resources, and to each others' homes; some evidence indicates that children from neighborhoods that afford more extensive peer interactions tend to develop more advanced social skills (Bryant, 1985).

Commonly, in Western societies, the main source of peer contact results from placement in day-care and preschool centres. Involvement in these contexts exposes the young child to a number of new personal and interpersonal challenges. The child's day is structured in a new way in a new location, new authority figures are introduced with novel relationships to many unfamiliar children (in contrast to domestic relations with parent and siblings), and the child is expected to regulate his or her emotions according to the requirements of an institution (Corsaro, 1993; Katz and Gottman 1991; Maccoby, 1980). A lot of research into preschoolers' social development has been conducted in nursery and playground settings, often using observational and ethological techniques (Blurton Jones, 1972; Ladd et al., 1988; Montagner et al., 1984;

Box 4.1   Parten's categories of play behavior

Unoccupied behavior

The child is not playing but may pay fleeting attention to activities proceeding around him or her.

Solitary play

The child plays alone, paying little or no attention to other children and their activities.

Onlooking behavior

The child watches other children playing. He or she may speak to the others, but does not join in. This category reveals interest in others and their activities, but limited participation.

Parallel play

The child plays with other children, and they engage in similar activities. Organization is minimal, and each child acts as he or she wishes rather than directing activities toward some joint goal.

Cooperative play

The child plays as part of a group, and roles or tasks are shared out in complementary ways. The group (or more dominant members) creates a sense of exclusivity.

Source: Parten, 1932

Parten, 1932; Promnitz, 1992; P. K. Smith, 1978; Strayer, 1980). Parten's (1932) early accounts introduced a framework for the study of preschoolers' play that has influenced much of the subsequent work in this field. She discerned six categories of behavior that preschool children manifested in their play environments. These categories, listed in Box 4.1, represent a scale of social participation, ranging from uninvolved through to genuine collaboration.

Studying 2–5-year-olds, Parten found that the frequency of relatively uninvolved behaviors toward peers declined with age, while the incidence of social activity (particularly associative and cooperative play) increased with age. The most frequent type of behavior at all ages in her sample was parallel play. Subsequent work indicates that preschoolers distribute their time approximately equally among solitary, parallel, and group (including both associative and cooperative) play (P. K. Smith, 1978). Bakeman and Brownlee (1980) suggest that the use of parallel play is often strategic: children would like the company of others but lack the social skills to break into an ongoing group activity, and so they hang around the edges. The researchers tested this by comparing the probability that, given that the child was in one state of play, he or she would shortly move to a different type. They found that parallel play was often succeeded by group play, and much less often succeeded by solitary play, supporting their view that parallel play is a warm-up/preparatory stage.

Peer Interactions among School-aged Children

The peer interactions of school-aged children are more complex, more selective, and subjectively more salient to the participants (Erwin, 1993). School attendance itself ensures that children spend greater amounts of time in peer company and goals of peer groups now become important features of social life (Hartup, 1983). Children from the primary years on have increasingly sophisticated understanding of other people, of relationships and interpersonal expectations and, in turn, their widening social experiences provide them with more reasons to develop these social-cognitive skills (see chapter 9). They also have more advanced linguistic abilities, which broaden the scope for conversation, negotiation – and sometimes conflict. Although school-aged children's peer-related activities are diverse, Zarbatany et al. (1990) found that conversing was at the top of pre-adolescent children's lists of things they do with their friends. Familiarity with the agemate becomes increasingly important during the school years: while toddlers and preschoolers will often play with any peer who happens to be physically present, school-aged children generally like to appraise new peers before joining in with them (Dodge, 1983; Erwin, 1993; Ladd and Price, 1987). In short, peer relations are heightened during the school years, but they also become more discriminating. Peer relations become particularly salient during adolescence, and we return to that topic in chapter 15.

Emotions, Attachments, and Conflicts in Peer Relations

As with most social relations, peer relations involve the emotions (Hartup, 1983). One of the clearest manifestations of this is in young children's attachments to peers; another is in the nature and role of conflicts.

Attachments to peers

From infancy, children show preferences among their peers and reveal distress at the loss of a close associate (Lewis et al., 1975; Vandell and Mueller, 1980). Preschoolers form affiliative relations to peers, and seek proximity to specific individuals (Strayer, 1980). During the preschool years, negative reactions to losing friends can be extreme (Rubin, 1980). Ladd and Price (1987) found that friendships formed during the preschool years often served as a "secure base" for children during the transition to school: children liked school more and were less anxious in the presence of familiar classmates.

Early peer relationships can be attachments in the sense that they are enduring over time, but their status among a child's various attachment relations is not established. In general, we could expect them to be different in character from the relationship between a child and her or his principal caregiver because the latter will often provide nurturance, knowledge, and communicative skills to levels that peers cannot attain. On the other hand, some researchers have found that close peer friendships among young children can occasionally compensate for deficiencies in the principal attachment to a parent (Dontas et al., 1985; Youngblade and Belsky, 1992). Obviously, ethical considerations rule out studies in which investigators might control timing, quality, and amount of exposure to parents versus peers; we could scarcely raise a sample of children in a peer-only condition to determine whether they form attachments.

Occasionally, however, real-world tragedies do bring about exactly these circumstances. One well-known case study was conducted with six German-Jewish infants who lost their parents in Hitler's gas chambers in the Second World War. At the age of 6–12 months, the children were placed in the camp's Ward for Motherless Children, where limited staff and facilities meant that they had only minimal interactions with adults and little in the way of playthings. The children's principal source of continuing social contact and stimulation was each other.

The camp was liberated some 2 years later and the children were then raised in a home in England, where they came to the attention of the psychoanalyst Anna Freud. Her report on this experiment in group upbringing reveals that the children formed strong attachments:

> The children's positive feelings were centred exclusively in their own group. It was evident that they cared greatly for each other and not at all for anybody or anything else. They had no other wish than to be together and became upset when they were separated from each other, even for short moments. No child would consent to remain upstairs while the others were downstairs, or vice versa, and no child would be taken on a walk or errand without the others. If anything of the kind happened, the single child would constantly ask for the other children while the group would fret for the missing child. (Freud and Dann, 1951, p. 131).

Their relationship showed a warmth and spontaneity far beyond that observed in ordinary relations between young peers, and it was notable that they were very egalitarian in their mutual relations (in contrast to vertical adult–child attachments). The children were initially hostile toward adults, and were difficult to manage but not to the extent that they were regarded as deficient or psychotic. Gradually, they came to form more positive relationships with their adult caregivers.

Overall, the history of these severely disadvantaged children points to the remarkable adaptability and resilience of infants' social propensities. As younger victims of the same kinds of events that guided Tajfel's intellectual development (see

p. 115), they remind us again of the close interrelationship of family and group processes.

Conflicts in peer relations

Preschoolers have limited understanding of emotions and of others' experiences of emotions (Harris, 1989a; see chapter 9) and are emotionally labile themselves with the result that they can become "flooded" by emotional states that dominate temporarily their attention and behavior (Parker and Gottman, 1989). This can lead to dramatic short-term fluctuations and eruptions in the course of peer interactions. On balance, preschoolers' interactions are more friendly than unfriendly (Hay, 1985), but conflicts are common in children's peer relations from this period on (Berndt, 1981; Erwin, 1993; Hartup and van Lieshout, 1995; Parker and Gottman, 1989; Shantz and Hobart, 1989).

Conflicts are not necessarily terminal to the relationship, and children do not regard conflict as incompatible with friendship (Aboud, 1989; Berndt and Perry, 1986; Erwin, 1993; Oswald et al., 1994; Shantz and Hobart, 1989). Because cooperative play occupies an increasingly central place in social relations, preschoolers tend to regulate their squabbles so that they do not undermine the broader purposes of working together (Dunn, 1993; Parker and Gottman, 1989).

In this respect, peer social relations appear to evoke certain types of behavior more frequently than do family contexts (Corsaro, 1993; Dunn, 1993; Pepler et al., 1982). For example, Dunn (1993) examined the use of reasoned argument by 3-year-olds at home (with mother and siblings) and by the same children when alone with a close friend. On the basis of much of the evidence reviewed above indicating continuities from family to external social life, we might predict that the proportions of reasoned and unreasoned argument at home should be positively correlated with the use of reasoning in peer–peer play. Surprisingly, Dunn found little evidence of such a carry-over. In particular, when a conflict came up at home, the children tended to engage in high levels of unreasoned protest (74 percent with siblings, 65 percent with mothers), but were less likely to use this means of assertion with peers (at 49 percent). Conciliatory, reasoned argument was more common in peer conflicts (at 22 percent) than in domestic strife (9 percent). It seems that we learn early in life that politeness is (sometimes) called for when dealing with peers. With reference to older children, Shantz and Hobart (1989) argue that conflicts are vital to social development because they enable peers to exchange their different perspectives, goals, and desires and then to work jointly to resolve them and arrive at some form of mutual accommodation. Consistent with this position, it has been found that, during middle childhood, conflicts are actually more common between friends than nonfriends (Hartup et al., 1993; Rizzo, 1989).

Peer Group Formation

From very early in their out-of-home lives, children enter into collectives of agemates (Hartup, 1983; Youniss, 1994). Some of these associations are short lived, but others are more enduring. Children's peer groups exhibit the characteristics and functions of adult social groups. As we saw earlier, for adults, group membership offers psychological distinctiveness, social identity, a sense of belonging, and mutual support (Hogg, 1992; Hogg and Abrams, 1988; Turner et al., 1987). Freud and Dann's (1951) case study, above, provides an extreme example of how important the group can become to toddlers. Even in minimal group experiments, young children soon come to display a bias toward their own group (Yee and Brown, 1992).

From/the beginnings of school life, children's spontaneous groups tend to be segregated by sex (Archer, 1992; Daniels-Beirness, 1989; Godde and Engfer, 1994; Maccoby and Jacklin, 1987; Whiting and Edwards, 1988). Girls' groups tend to be small — usually two or three participants — while boys' are larger, often involving three or more, sometimes moving in swarms around their play areas. Girls' friendships tend to be more exclusive; once dyadic, reciprocated friendships are set up they are less welcoming of newcomers. In contrast, boys' group friendships tend to be more accommodating.

As mentioned earlier, peer groups are not necessarily antithetical to family groups, and in some cases there is distinct evidence of continuity. Stevenson (1991) reports, for example, that the children of Japanese employees of car manufacturing firms who are temporarily resident in the US discriminate among each other sometimes on the basis of their fathers' companies. Each group has its own identity, and on occasions this affiliation is so salient that the Mazda kids would regard it as quite undesirable to associate with the Honda riff-raff, and vice versa. These biases are by no means peculiar to future executives in the automobile industry. The same processes can be observed in many locations where there is a Catholic school in the neighborhood of a Protestant one, when Ossies and Wessies get together (see chapter 10) or when different language communities live near to each other. Children's early groups reflect social opportunities framed by their family backgrounds (e.g., the neighborhood, social class, ethnicity, language) and similarity is a strong factor in peer preferences (Doyle, 1982; Ennew, 1994; Erwin, 1993; Hartup, 1983, 1992).

Peer groups have many functions, including contributions to the development of social identity, the sharing of norms of social behavior, the practice of social skills, and the establishment of social structures (Erwin, 1993; Hartup, 1983). Boys' groups tend to become organized into hierarchies very quickly (Daniels-Beirness, 1989; Maccoby and Jacklin, 1987; Sherif and Sherif, 1956). Hierarchies have at least two benefits: one is that decisions and directions can be achieved readily when someone is "in charge", and the second is that social relations and statuses are established (Hartup, 1983; Savin-Williams, 1980; Sherif and Sherif, 1956). Hierarchies are less pronounced among girls' groups, possibly because the smaller, dyadic focus of girls' social relations renders larger superordinate structures less relevant (Savin-Williams, 1980). The question of why boys' and girls' groups take such different forms is subject to controversy. Sociobiologists argue that boys are rehearsing the dynamics of dominance and achievement that will be fundamental to their adult lives, while girls are practicing behaviors that have evolved as conducive to reproductive success, such as cooperation with other females (Low, 1989).

One of the most vivid demonstrations of peer group processes among (male) school-aged children is the Sherif's classic Robber's Cave experiment (Sherif and Sherif, 1956), a fascinating social psychological study to which we will return in later chapters. Robber's Cave is a State Park about 150 miles from the city of Oklahoma. In 1954, the Sherifs and colleagues took 22 boys aged 11 to set up camp there. The boys came from white, middle-class Protestant homes and were matched as far as possible on size, athletic ability, and other skills. They were previously unacquainted.

The experimenters divided the boys randomly into two groups, and delivered them separately to the camp. At first, each group was unaware that there was another group around. Within days, each group had developed a definite structure, with stable statuses and organized rules to ensure they met their interdependent goals (such as preparing food, conveying canoes to water, sorting out play areas). Each group adopted a name ("Rattlers" and "Eagles"), and the boys put the group names on flags and T-shirts. In other words, peer interaction led swiftly to a sense of social identity, to positive feelings toward one's group, to relatively stable interpersonal statuses, and to organized collective activity. Group processes that in earlier childhood originate in or are mediated by family status now emerge readily when the children are left virtually to their own devices. We leave the Rattlers and the Eagles there for the moment, but bear in mind earlier forebodings: social life is a battlefield.

The Significance of Children's Friendships

Although we have considered peer relations in general, we have touched at several places on the salience of *friendships* among children. From early childhood on, behavior toward friends is differentiated from behavior toward other peers: more time is spent with friends, the relationships are more reciprocal, more pleasurable, and increasingly psychologically intimate (Hartup, 1983, 1992; Howes, 1989). Let us look now a little more closely at how friendships emerge, and what they entail.

As already mentioned, even quite young children begin to demonstrate social selectivity. By the preschool years, children develop positive peer relationships in which they seek each other's proximity, talk more to each other, exchange mutual glances, smile and laugh together more than with nonfriends: some children become virtually inseparable (Baudonnière, 1987, 1988). Clearly, these are among the criteria of friendship that we can also observe among older children and adults (Argyle, 1989; Duck, 1992; Patterson, 1988; Solano, 1986). Although preschoolers' conceptual understanding of what a friend is may not be as elaborate as those of older individuals (see chapter 9), the affective importance of friendship is already established. Werebe and Baudonnière (1988) found that pairs of "inseparables" when placed in laboratory play sessions with other same-sex peers oriented their verbal and nonverbal behaviors all the more intensely toward each other, making it very difficult for a third party to break in.

Why do young children value their friendships so strongly? Research indicates that friendships serve a number of important and developmental functions. Asher and Parker (1989, p. 6) identify seven main functions:

1 Fostering the growth of social competence.
2 Serving as sources of ego support.
3 Providing emotional security in novel or potentially threatening situations.
4 Serving as sources of intimacy and affection.
5 Providing guidance and assistance.
6 Providing a sense of reliable alliance.
7 Providing companionship and stimulation.

Illustrations of these functions will be provided in this and later chapters, but it is already clear that friendships are of considerable significance to the child. It is not surprising, in the context of the gradual emergence from family life into the demands and uncertainties of the broader social world, that the security, companionship, and guidance of friends holds high value for most children.

Summary

Children are interested in other children from infancy. During infancy and the preschool years, peer relations progress from simple visual attention and object sharing to complex patterns of interchange, which reveal strong positive affect as well as conflict and negotiation. Group formation is spontaneous and ubiquitous in preschoolers and older children, though there are gender differences in the size and activities of peer groups. Selectivity is characteristic of children's relations from quite early, and the formation of friendships serve a number of important social developmental functions.

Peer Relations: Individual Differences

Peer relations in general and friendships in particular are important, then, to the progress of social development. However, there are considerable individual differences in terms of how children relate to their peers. A moment's recollection reminds us all that during our schooldays, some children were very popular, some were regarded as OK, some were disliked, and still others were on the periphery, not especially liked or disliked but largely ignored.

Of course, any one person's intuitions or perceptions about others' social acceptance may be inaccurate. In order to attain more valid classifications, researchers have developed systematic methodologies. One method is the observational study of spontaneous peer relations. As indicated, researchers using observational techniques do find variations in peer acceptance in most children's groups (Montagner et al., 1984; Promnitz, 1992). Other methods include sociometric techniques such as peer nomination or peer rating (Asher and Coie, 1990; Coie et al., 1982; Miller and Gentry, 1980; Moreno, 1934). Peer nomination involves each child in a social group (e.g., a classroom) identifying those peers in the group whom he or she most likes or dislikes ("Who would you most like to play with?" "Who would you least like to sit next to?"); children can be differentiated in terms of the number and balance of positive and negative nominations they receive.

Although indicative of important differences in peer status, limitations of this method include the possibility that a liked peer might be momentarily forgotten at the point of testing, thus distorting results, and that it is uninformative about children who fall in the middle range of nominations (Miller and Gentry, 1980). For these reasons, many researchers prefer peer rating, which involves each child assessing every other child in the relevant group on some scale of likeability (often with reference to more than one social situation); a child's mean rating by his or her peers is taken as a measure of popularity. There are interesting ethical issues surrounding these techniques (how comfortable would *you* feel participating as subject and object in a sociometric exercise among your peer group?), but they tend to yield reliable and valid measures of popularity. They correlate reasonably well with observational data of actual peer interactions and preferences (Bukowski and Hoza, 1989).

Using these kinds of methods, different researchers employ slightly different classification schemes to describe children's social acceptance, but most tend to distinguish four or five types, similar to those identified by Coie et al. (1982):

1 *Popular children*, whom many of their peers nominate or rate favorably.
2 *Rejected children*, who are widely disliked.
3 *Controversial children*, who are regarded very favorably by some peers, but seen as disruptive by others.
4 *Neglected isolated children*, who are rarely nominated.
5 *Average children*, who are generally accepted and do not receive extreme scores on peers' ratings.

Individual classifications, although not absolutely irrevocable, tend to be fairly stable through childhood (Asher et al., 1990; Coie and Dodge, 1983; Erwin, 1993; Rubin and Daniels-Bierness, 1983).

Given the salience of peer relations and the functions of friendship outlined above, it is immediately obvious that there are potential liabilities to children who are unsuccessful in making and sustaining friendships. Research confirms that there is a strong likelihood that individuals who are rejected or unpopular at an early age will continue to experience negative social relations (Newcomb and Bukowski, 1984), miss out on the benefits of peer friendships (Asher and Coie, 1990) and be at greater risk of suffering in adulthood a host of developmental and psychosocial problems, including alcoholism, social anxiety, depression, delinquency, educational failure, and psychotism (Asher and Coie, 1990; Duck, 1992; Ladd, 1990; Rubin and Mills, 1988).

Correlates of Peer Acceptance

It comes as no surprise to any of us who have participated in the social world that some people are liked more than others. But *why* should this be the case? A number of important theoretical and applied questions which arise here have attracted a good deal of research among social developmentalists. Are there measurable characteristics that can enable us to predict a person's social acceptability? Why should selectivity and biases emerge so early in life? Is it possible to intervene to improve the skills and prospects of children who experience difficulties in peer relations?

Several factors can be identified as associated with children's social acceptance. These include relatively surface characteristics, such as physical appearance or even personal name, and external influences, such as teachers' attitudes. We will consider each in turn. Then, we turn to more psychological properties, such as interpersonal behavior and social understanding, usually grouped together under the heading "social competence."

Physical attractiveness

We have already seen preliminary evidence of appearance biases in human infants in chapter 2; preference for facially attractive individuals become still clearer during childhood. In a laboratory study, Dion (1973) found that preschoolers anticipated that attractive peers would make better friends, and in a field setting Dion and Berscheid (1974) obtained evidence that attractive children were more frequently nominated as "best friends." Langlois and Stephan (1981) summarize evidence to indicate that the physical attractiveness bias may interact with sex, such that attractive boys are sometimes viewed negatively by their peers, possibly because "prettiness" is stereotyped as feminine and is therefore less of an asset in young male peer cultures. Overall, though, the evidence suggests that being physically attractive is advantageous, and may become associated with more positive social behaviors during the preschool years. Coie et al. (1982) found that children's ratings of peers' physical attractiveness were correlated positively with liking, and negatively with disliking. This finding could be explained in either direction (e.g., people who are physically unattractive are disliked, or people who are disliked are perceived as physically unattractive). However, Langlois and Downs (1979) paired attractive and unattractive 3- and 5-year-old agemates in a laboratory study and found that, while there were no differences at age 3, by age 5 unattractive children were actually exhibiting more unattractive social behavior (more aggression).

Personal name

If facial appearance biases seem superficial and ill founded, the possibility that the mere sound of a child's name could influence her or his peers' attitudes seems an especially shallow basis for interpersonal judgment. But again the evidence suggests that this does occur. McDavid and Harari (1966) found that children with first names rated as attractive tended to be more popular than their peers with unattractive or odd names.

What's in a name? It could be that certain names are positively associated with high status figures; possibly unconscious stereotypes work to the advantage of individuals with liked names. It could be that the choice of an unappealing name reflects a more general parenting deficit (Hartup, 1983). You might think twice before landing your newborn with a name like Adolf, Spangberta, or Firklebugg, but if you were undeterred by the possible handicap that could result then it is reasonable to assume that your perspective-taking skills are not good, and this might spill over into all other aspects of your caregiving style. Levine and Willis (1994) found that parents who do give their children unusual names rarely anticipate others' reactions. Another possibility is that being the butt of continual teasing encourages the development of aggressive behavior – an old Johnny Cash song maintains that calling a son Sue is a good way to ensure that he learns to fight.

Sue fought his battles, though, in America and presumably while wandering the mid-West some decades ago. Perhaps McDavid and Harari's (1966) subjects also reflect the values of cultures since transformed. It may be that Western cultures have become more tolerant in the wake of patterns of migration and more pluralistic media representations which have exposed children to a greater diversity of personal names. We do not know if the same biases are evoked in other cultures.

Teacher influence

How a child stands in the eyes of her or his teacher may also affect her or his peer standing. Miller and Gentry (1980) review several studies which indicate that the congruence between a child's characteristics and the values endorsed by the class teacher may influence peer acceptability, though in complex ways. Drawing on social psychological accounts of normative influences, these authors suggest that teachers' influence may be strongest prior to the emergence of peer group norms. Thus, being treated by the teacher as a good example could be advantageous to the kindergartener (whose peers are still coming to terms with the new institution), but socially disastrous to the adolescent (whose peers may expect ingroup solidarity rather than identification with the establishment). Miller and Gentry (1980) add the important comment that peer acceptability in school (the setting where most studies tend to be conducted) may not be an accurate guide to peer relations outside the school.

Social Competence

This brings us to one of the most important, yet also one of the most elusive and dangerous concepts in developmental social psychology: social competence. Acquiring social competence is self-evidently important. Humans are a definitively social species and much of our evolutionary success and future prospects depend upon our collective efforts; for any individual, successful relations with her or his fellows is a crucial outcome of social development and adaptation. Few would dispute Asher and Parker's

(1989) summary above that social competence is an integral component of friendships – it is required to make friendships in the first place, and it is facilitated and developed in the course of being friends.

But exactly what social competence consists of is very difficult to determine. Virtually every account of the development of social competence begins by acknowledging problems and diversity of definitions (e.g., van Aken, 1994; Attili, 1989; Dodge et al., 1986; Hubbard and Coie, 1994; Oppenheimer, 1989; Rohrle and Sommer, 1994). The concept is elusive because it refers to an array of outcomes and skills, which are culturally relative and situationally dependent, not to a simple set of behaviors or attributes that can be identified on a standard checklist. Within any community, the requirements of social competence vary with gender and age (Attili, 1989; Daniels-Beirness, 1989; Ledingham, 1989).

In one sense, just about everything to be discussed in this book is related to the development of social competence: socially competent individuals are expected to be able to communicate effectively, to understand the self and others, to acquire a gender role, to observe the moral order of their community, to regulate their emotions, to adapt their behavior in response to age-related norms and so on. In short, they need to be able to use their knowledge and skills in ways which take account of their relations with others and which promote positive aspects to those relations (see contributors to Asher and Coie, 1990; Schneider et al. 1989). Dodge et al. (1986) suggest that, rather than ask what social competence is, we should investigate how the various aspects of social functioning relate to effective behavior.

While all aspects of behavior may be implicated in social competence, it is none the less viable to focus on specific behaviors that appear to correlate with social standing. Numerous studies of children's peer acceptance have attempted to identify behaviors that differentiate popular from unpopular children, and some consistent results have emerged. For example, in order to investigate the behavioral correlates of the five classifications listed above, Coie and Dodge (1988) screened a large sample of 6–9-year-old boys attending schools in North Carolina and obtained peers' and teachers' ratings, as well as collecting observational data on the boys' classroom behavior. The results indicated that popular children tended to be more prosocial, good at sports, and funny; rejected and controversial boys were the most aggressive and disruptive. Neglected boys tended to be rated by their peers as much lower on *all* measures (aggression, prosocial, sports, funny, unhappy). This would suggest that neglected children do not register much of an impression on any dimension, perhaps because they are less active altogether; however, on teacher ratings, the boys were rated as lower only on aggression, which suggests that their unfavorable peer status renders their behavior less visible to their peers.

It is often difficult to disentangle cause and effect in these kinds of studies. Do children become popular/rejected/neglected because of their social behaviors – or do they develop the social behaviors that match their designation by peers? If a child is seen as a disruptive troublecauser, her peers are going to avoid her, and so she may have to become more disruptive and troublecausing to gain some attention or to get her way. Ladd et al. (1988) investigated this issue by following a sample of 3- and 4-year-old preschoolers across a school year, assessing their social behavior and peer status at three times. Relatively stable individual differences in cooperativeness were identified, and these predicted a significant proportion of the variance in later measures of peer acceptance. Early arguing behaviors were less stable over time, but still predicted social acceptance at later time points. These findings indicate that children who are initially seen as cooperative tend to be liked, while children who are seen as argumentative tend to be rejected – even if they change their behavior later.

Several other studies add to the picture sketched here. Popular children tend to be good social problem-solvers, effective negotiators, supportive of others (Erwin, 1993; Mendelson et al., 1994; Putallaz and Gottman, 1981). Rejected children are more antagonistic and critical of peers, are more prone to hyperactivity, spend more time playing away from other children, and report stronger feelings of loneliness (Asher et al., 1990; Ladd and Price, 1987; Shantz, 1986). Neglected children engage in more cognitively immature play and engage in higher proportions of egocentric speech (Rubin, 1982a, b). These types of children also show marked differences in how they deal with the everyday but critical task of group entry (that is, joining a group of peers who are already engaged in some activity). Popular children approach confidently, and ask if they might join in, striking up conversations with the others; rejected children hover on the edges or embark on disruptive ploys, forcing their way in or grabbing materials; neglected children tend simply to stay away (Dodge et al. 1986).

The Origins of Social Competence

Notwithstanding the definitional problems noted above, it is obviously of scientific and practical interest to attempt to explain variations in social competence within a community. There are a number of possibilities, and each has attracted a good deal of research attention. They include some familiar variables: cognitive factors, family relations, and temperament.

Cognitive factors

One of the most influential recent models of the underpinnings of social competence has been that of Dodge et al. (1986; Dodge and Price, 1994). These investigators proposed an information-processing account of children's responses to social situations according to which social competence involves the successful application of five sequential steps. The steps are:

1   attending to and encoding the presented social cues;
2   interpreting the cues;
3   searching for a response;
4   evaluating the efficacy and likely consequences of the response;
5   enacting the response.

These processes are assumed to occur rapidly and often at a nonconcious level. Importantly, deficiencies at any one step can result in less than optimal social behavior. If (Step 1) a child fails to notice a social cue (a friendly gesture, another child's irritation) then he or she is unlikely to undertake any further steps, and may fail to adapt to the situation altogether. If the child does notice the cue but (Step 2) interprets it inaccurately (a friendly gesture is read as an insult or threat), serious mismatches may ensue. If these processes have been performed successfully but (Step 3) the child lacks a repertoire of suitable responses (e.g., does not know what to do when a peer is friendly), then his or her reaction may appear inept or hostile. At Step 4 it is vital to judge the appropriate intensity of one's response (should I wave back, or rush over and hug her?). Finally, successful implementation of Step 5 may call for verbal or motor skills (e.g., it may not be enough to reply to a friendly greeting with a flat "hello").

Dodge et al. (1986) had kindergarten and early school-aged children view videotapes of child actors at play, and tested their accounts or reactions at points corresponding to the above steps. On a later occasion, the same children were required to join two peers, who were already engaged in a building game. Children who performed successfully at the various stages on the first test were found more likely to perform successfully in the subsequent group entry task. In a second study using similar procedures, the investigators found that aggressive children displayed significantly higher levels of processing deficits at each step. Nonaggressive and aggressive children had quite different strategies when it came to the group entry task. The former asked if they could join in, and engaged in sociable chat. A more typical behavior of the aggressive children was to hover around the table and stare at the game; when asked what he was doing, one boy said "just watching . . ." It appears from this study that children do vary in their abilities to process social information, and that those who lack proficiency at this level seem most prone to unsuccessful or aggressive interactions in actual play.

This model provides an elegant account of the dynamics of the actual processes that occur during a social interaction. However, among the remaining questions is: why do individual differences in processing ability occur in the first place?

Family relations

Most of the major theories that we considered in chapter 1 predict some continuity between parent–child relationships and the quality of peer relationships (cf. Rubin et al., 1989, 1990). Social learning theorists see parental input as influental via mechanisms of observational learning and reinforcement. Ethological theories, such as attachment theory, maintain that maternal responsiveness influences the kind of attachment relationship the child has, and hence his or her security in exploring new social environments. From a cognitive developmental perspective, the kinds of intellectual stimulation and information provided in the child's early social experiences should influence the development of skills in understanding other people; furthermore, the kinds of ideas and beliefs that the parents hold about the nature of child development should influence their strategies in child management (and hence the child's developmental experiences). Bronfenbrenner's ecological theory predicts that the broader systems will affect the ways in which children experience relationships, first with their parents and then with others outside the home.

A great deal of research does support the common prediction here of links between family experiences and peer relations (e.g., Barth and Parke, 1993; Denham, 1993; Denham et al., 1991; Hinde and Tamplin, 1983; Rubin et al., 1990). A powerful illustration of how parents might "pave the way" into peer relations is provided by Russell and Finnie (1990). Observing Australian preschool children and their mothers in situations where the child had to join unfamiliar peers, these investigators found differences in maternal strategies associated with children's popularity. Mothers of popular children suggested strategies that helped the child to join in the current activity, while mothers of neglected children were more likely to guide the children to focus on the materials to hand. These starting points could be very influential upon the development of a social interaction. More generally, there is extensive evidence of relationships between family processes and children's prosocial behavior, and between family processes and the development of aggression (see chapters 12 and 13), two dimensions of social behavior that researchers have found predict social acceptance in the peer community.

Not surprisingly, attachment theorists have been especially prominent in investigations of the links between parent–child relations and peer relations. As we saw in chapter 3, for attachment theorists the parent–child attachment is seen as a critical determinant of subsequent development. Bowlby states the position clearly:

> Again and again we see details in the behaviour of a toddler, or in what he says, that are plainly straight replicas of how that toddler has himself been treated. Indeed the tendency to treat others in the same way that we ourselves have been treated is deep in human nature. (1988, p. 91)

Several researchers have produced evidence which is consistent with this hypothesis. Waters et al. (1979) found differences between Type Bs (securely attached) and non-Bs (insecurely attached) children on several measures of peer competence at the age 3 years 6 months. In other studies (in some cases based on the same children at different ages), these researchers found several indicators of superior social competence in Type Bs through to the nursery school years (Pastor, 1981; LaFreniere and Sroufe, 1985). It was found that Type Bs rated higher than Type Cs on measures of social participation adapted from Parten (1932) (although there were no differences between Bs and As in this respect). Lyons-Ruth et al. (1993) found that infant attachment status at 18 months was the strongest single predictor of problematic peer relations among 5-year-old preschoolers. In particular, children classified at the earlier age as having Type D attachments were disproportionately represented among hostile preschoolers at the later age.

Once again, it is tempting to conclude that the quality of attachment does indeed underlie aspects of later social relations. However, as discussed in chapter 3 the problem with this inference is that it fails to deal with the possibility of continuities in the parent–child relationship (Lamb and Nash, 1989; Lamb et al., 1985; Lewis and

Feiring, 1989) which could themselves be due to some third factor, such as the child's characteristics.

Temperament

Prominent among the child's characteristics is her or his temperament. Intuitively, it seems plausible that if an individual is, say, hostile and aggressive, then she or he may not excel in interpersonal relations and may even be rejected by peers; on the other hand, a calm, warm and outgoing person might stand a better chance of gaining popularity.

As we have already seen in chapter 2, temperament is not independent of other factors in the child's social world. The relations among temperament, attachment, emotional self-regulation and peer relations are complex (Cassidy and Berlin, 1994; Hartup and van Lieshout, 1995; Rubin et al., 1990), but there is evidence, for example, that children who are initially fussy, overactive and difficult to soothe are at greater risk of negative social behavior in the preschool, and in turn risk isolation and disaffection during middle childhood (Rubin et al., 1990). Rubin et al develop an elaborate theoretical model of the relations among ecological setting conditions, parenting behavior and beliefs, temperament and the development of interpersonal competencies.

The Limits and Dangers of Social Competence

Important as social competence may be, it has been stressed here that it is difficult to define. This problem becomes even more substantial when we attempt to place it in cultural context. Most of the work discussed above has been concerned with children growing up in Western nations – indeed, usually in North America. The requirements of social competence in America (or in different communities within America) might be quite different from those expected in say, Sweden (or in different communities within Sweden) and still more so from those expected in other, non-Western, cultures. Oppenheimer (1989) argues that many of the abilities that have been suggested as dimensions of social competence are really measures of children's abilities to deal with the demands of particular social environments: in this sense, they may concern conformism and social desirability rather than social competence. Drawing on Bronfenbrenner's (1979) framework, Oppenheimer (1989) argues that what the developing person is conforming to reflects the values and goals of the social structures in which he or she is situated.

There is strong evidence that different personal and social qualities are regarded quite differently in different societies. In Western cultures, for example, independence is often held to be a desirable individual characteristic (see chapter 2). In contrast, in some traditional cultures social competence is gauged in terms of the individual's acknowledgement of shared responsibility within the family system and ethnic community, obedience, and deference to elders and social superiors (Greenfield, 1994; Smith and Bond, 1994; Triandis, 1994). An illustration is provided by Nsamenang and Lamb's (1993) study of Nso children in Cameroon. While playfulness is seen almost as synonymous with positive social adjustment by many Western parents and researchers, 99 percent of Nso parents interviewed by Nsamenang and Lamb regarded "playfulness" as undesirable in the young.

Cultural differences can be found at the very core of how one is expected to behave toward peers. In a classic series of studies, Bronfenbrenner (1970) compared children in the Soviet Union with agemates from Western nations (England, Switzerland, West Germany and the US) on measures of how they would respond to moral or social transgressions by their peers. The children from the (then strongly collectivist) USSR showed a high degree of acceptance of the adult culture, and a marked willingness to apply social pressure to modify the behavior of wayward peers, even to the extent of bringing transgressors to the attention of the authorities; the children from the other countries tended to regard behavioral choices as a more individual matter, "none of my business", and were loath to intervene. Thus an aspect of social competence in one culture would be to respect the autonomy of one's peers, and in another to exert pressure on them to comply.

This is not to say that social competence does not exist, nor that some of the skills identified as advantageous in Western studies will be invariably irrelevant to children's peer acceptance in other societies. However, if social competence is defined in general terms as an ability to organize one's social behavior adaptively then it is clear that the constituent elements and their application may vary widely with social context. The features usually assumed in studies of Western children's social competence tend to reflect the ideological values of those societies.

A possible liability of the notion of social competence is that it can attract prescriptivism. Social competence sounds like such a self-evidently desirable property that it is tempting to confuse it with moral worth and to assume that it expresses an objective standard that all ought to be encouraged to match. We have already seen that a cross-cultural perspective places a check on this notion.

Consider also the risks of misreading the meaning of a particular set of behaviors. For example, solitary play may be a sign that a child is neglected or isolated. However, there is an important qualification on this interpretation: much depends upon what the child is doing when solitary (Rubin, 1982a, b). A kindergartener who spends a lot of time alone in less mature functional or dramatic activities might well be at risk of developmental problems; a child who is engaged in a lot of constructive play may be quite competent in terms of social skills and social understanding (Fonzi and Tassi, 1988; Rubin, 1982b; Rubin and Pepler, 1980). Intervening to divert a child away from all forms of solitary play and make him or her more "socially competent" may be counterproductive.

Of course, research such as Rubin's can help avoid unduly simplistic diagnoses of a child's social behavior. The point is that we need to proceed cautiously. To take another example, shyness in children is sometimes perceived as problematic. But shyness may or may not warrant intervention (Rubin and Asendorpf, 1993; Rubin et al., 1990). It is not established that shyness is predictive of serious maladjustment or antisocial behavior later on (cf. Asher and Parker, 1989). We are also not too sure what we are intervening in: is shyness a matter of inadequate opportunities to develop social skills, as some intervention programmes assume, or is it a constitutional variable, as Kagan's (1989) research suggests (see chapter 2)?

Summary

There are individual differences in how children form and maintain peer relations. Multiple factors appear to be involved, ranging from seemingly superficial characteristics such as personal name and physical appearance, through the influence of family and school regimes. An important, if conceptually elusive, focus of much current research is social competence. Researchers vary in its definition, and differ in its measurement; most acknowledge its importance to human development, but it is clear that it is not an homogeneous body of skills that can be appraised in the same way in all people, irrespective of social context and developmental status. There is evidence to indicate that variability in the kinds of behaviors required for successful social participation in some peer contexts is associated with differences in social-cognitive processing, family relations, and temperament.

Conclusions

Social life begins in the family unit, a small group within which the child makes his or her first discoveries about dealing with others. The values and interpersonal processes of this unit are influenced by its place in the larger social system and, in turn, are associated with individual differences in the social behaviors of the new member(s) it introduces to the community. In looking back on the literature summarized in the chapter, we find repeated evidence of countervailing forces: one group of theorists stresses the importance of family influences, another reminds us that children are not infinitely malleable but each has his or her own unique characteristics that have an impact upon how other people treat him or her; some reseachers point to continuities from home to the outside world, others reveal parallel developments, still others stress divergent demands in different contexts; some point to conflicts among social engagements, others identify complementarities. These and other perspectives are not generated to make life difficult for the student who would like a clear answer! They reflect the remarkable diversity of forces and multiple interacting processes entailed in the early stages of social life. Progress toward understanding these complex interactions forms part of the challenge and excitement of developmental social psychology.

Further reading

Asher, S. R. and Coie, J. D. (eds) (1990) *Peer Rejection in Childhood*. Cambridge: Cambridge University Press.

Among the most pressing practical issues relating to children's peer relations and social competence is an understanding of why some children are rejected by their peers in order to develop effective means of intervention. Contributors to this book review theory and research concerning the behavior, social cognitive processes, and social contexts of rejected, withdrawn, and lonely children and discuss issues in intervention research.

Baumrind, D. (1989) Rearing competent children. In W. Damon (ed.), *Child Development Today and Tomorrow*. San Francisco: Jossey-Bass.

As well as a thorough review of her own research, Baumrind responds to Lewis's (1981) critique, and makes the interesting proposal, after Bronfenbrenner, that the greater instability of contemporary societies intensifies the need for firm family structures. She discusses, too, the relationship between her account of parental responsiveness and that of Bowlby and Ainsworth.

Boer, F. and Dunn, J. (eds) (1992) *Children's Sibling Relationships: developmental and clinical issues*. Hillsdale, NJ: Erlbaum.

A useful collection of recent European and North American research into the nature and contexts of sibling relationships, including several chapters on disabled siblings.

Bornstein M. H. (ed.) (1991) *Cultural Approaches to Parenting*. Hillsdale, NJ: Erlbaum.

A valuable set of essays on the commonalities and varieties among parental roles and behavior in different societies.

Dunn, J. and Plomin, R. (1990) *Separate Lives: why siblings are so different*. New York: Basic Books.

Siblings growing up in the same family are often quite different. Why? Dunn and Plomin review the contributions of the multiple factors involved, including genetic differences, parent–child relationships, differential experiences within the family, and extra-familial influences.

Erwin, P. (1993) *Friendship and Peer Relations in Children*. Chichester: Wiley.

An excellent review of research into the factors influencing peer relations: a developmental social psychological text.

Greenfield, P. M. and Cocking, R. R. (eds) (1994) *Cross-cultural Roots of Minority Child Development*. Hillsdale, NJ: Erlbaum.

In this chapter, it has been stressed that social development is intimately affected by the prevailing social structures within which children live. This book provides diverse perspectives on the socialization of children growing up as members of minority groups in American, European, African, and Asian societies.

Hartup, W. W. and van Lieshout, C. F. M. (1995) Personality development in social context. *Annual Review of Psychology*, 46, 655–87.

Although stressing that the relationships among temperament, personality, social context, and social development remain major challenges, Hartup and van Lieshout draw on recent evidence to illustrate important directions in what they regard as the dawn of a new era of research into personality development.

Hetherington, E. M. and Clingempeel, W. G. (1992) *Coping with Marital Transitions: a family systems perspective*. Monographs of the Society for Research in Child Development, 57 (2–3), no. 227.

Establishing the importance of family relations raises the converse question of what happens when the family is disrupted, especially as is the case for almost one half of contemporary children, when their parents divorce. This monograph provides a review of the literature with new findings revealing a higher incidence of developmental problems for children in divorced families.

McGurk, H., Caplan, M., Hennessy, E. and Moss, P. (1993) Controversy, theory and social context in contemporary day care research. *Journal of Child Psychology and Psychiatry* 34, 3–23.

Given the importance of early social relationships, especially with the primary caregivers, to social and cognitive development, it is not surprising that there has been a great deal of controversy in scientific and popular literature concerning the effects of placing young children in the care of persons and institutions outside the family. Much research has been directed toward discovering the consequences, and McGurk and colleagues review the state of the art.

Patterson, C. J. (1992) Children of lesbian and gay parents. *Child Development*, 63, 1025–42.

Most of the research reviewed in this chapter is based on homes organized around conventional heterosexual parents. What are the implications for child development of having parents who are gay? Patterson reviews a growing body of evidence.

Schneider, B. H., Attili, G., Nadel, J. and Weissberg, R. P. (eds) (1989) *Social Competence in Developmental Perspective*. Dordrecht: Kluwer.

Discussions of the conceptual and empirical issues in the study of social competence. This is an unusually embracing collection, drawing together researchers from diverse backgrounds.

White, D. and Woollet, A. (1992) *Families: a context for development*. London: Falmer Press.

A valuable overview of the diversity of family contexts. The authors examine traditional and contemporary patterns of family life, including useful discussions of adoption, reproductive technology, single parenting, reconstituted families, cultural variations, stress, health, and abuse within the family.

Chapter 5

The Development of Gender

Some of them achieve a considerable art in their work. A good needleworker is almost as highly valued in a family as a good hunter.
(Shepovalova, 1930/1993, p. 20)

In earlier chapters, we have seen that before the child is born, people have invested effort, resources, and emotion in preparing for its arrival. Parents look forward to their newborn, and the infant enters a social context that manifests certain expectations about it.

We come now to an important qualification of that description. Unfortunately, sometimes, some children turn out to be an instant disappointment to their parents. It is apparent at birth that they cannot fully live up to the desires and expectations held of them, and that they are destined to be second-class citizens. Other children with precisely the same handicap are welcomed happily enough by their parents, but still face the prospect of entering in due course a wider social environment which will be prejudicial to their advancement.

These children are called girls. Being born a girl is a decided liability in many societies. In extreme cases, this failing is met with by death: from at least the first century BC, there are records of "exposure" of female infants, that is, abandoning them in the wilds (Keuls, 1985) and many female infants in parts of the Third World today are killed at birth (Hausfater and Hrdy, 1984; Hrdy, 1988). Elsewhere, the availability of more sophisticated health systems means that in some cases parents are able to detect and abort the female fetus, thus pre-empting the problem. In other contexts, the arrival of female children is a cause of severe marital discord, largely reflecting the mother's perceived culpability in getting the sex of her progeny wrong. An anthropologist working in contemporary Greece found:

> Rural people especially feel resentful when they have more than one daughter. In Stira, a woman told me that when her daughter-in-law gave birth to three girls and no sons, her husband was so angry that when she returned from the hospital he locked the door of his house and would not let her in. (Beyene, 1989, p. 96)

If we accept the premise of ethological and attachment theorists that parents are generally predisposed to care for and protect their infants, then this hostility to a particular subset may tell us something about the power of socially generated belief systems.

These practices may sound rather remote, perhaps even a little reprehensible, to many readers from other cultures. However, the difference may be one of degree rather than kind. Surveys of Western parents-to-be reveal that a majority would prefer to have a boy, especially if they are talking about their first child (Hoffman, 1977). Disappointment with the onset of a girl may be expressed in more subtle ways in Western families. Consider these excerpts from transcripts of the conversations among mother, father, and medical staff in a British hospital in the minutes immediately following birth (taken from Macfarlane, 1977, p. 60ff).

Family 1
> *Doctor:*   Come on, junior. Only a lady could cause so much trouble. Come on, little one [baby is delivered].
> *Mother:*   A girl.
> *Doctor:*   Well, it's got the right plumbing.

Mother:	Oh, I'm sorry darling.
Father:	[laughs]
Doctor:	What are you sorry about?
Mother:	He wanted a boy.
	Well, Dr M., I was right, I had a sneaky feeling it was a girl, just because I wanted a boy.
Father:	Well, it will suit your mum, won't it?
Mother:	[*laughs*]
Doctor:	Often tactically best to have a girl first – she can help with the washing up.

Family 2

Father:	It's a boy!
Midwife:	It's a girl.
Mother:	It's a girl! Oh, it's not is it?
Father:	Very nice, I got my things sorted out wrong.
Mother:	Oh.
Midwife:	Beautiful, absolutely lovely.
Mother:	Oh.
	I wanted a boy.
Father:	Take it easy – that's it.
Mother:	It can't play rugby. Everyone said it was going to be a boy. What are we going to put her in?
Father:	Yeah – no, I wasn't disappointed.
Mother:	No, it wasn't a boy. I know what Ma will do – bitch.
Father:	No, Oh dear, oh dear.

Oh dear, indeed. Of course, they are only joking (aren't they?), just as Mohammed Ali was only joking when he reportedly said: "People ask me how many children I have and I say one boy and seven mistakes" (*The Australian*, November 2, 1992). But, oddly enough, none of the parents Macfarlane studied who *did* have boys spent the early moments of their child's life fretting about his sex and reassuring each other that things would work out.

It is certainly the case that girls born in the West and in many other societies are unlikely to suffer purposeful parental attempts to murder them, and may to the contrary be treated with love and devotion, but their prospects for equal social status to their brothers are none the less curtailed. Females, in all known societies, attain on average less social power, occupational and political status than their male counterparts (Bem, 1993; Eibl-Eibesfeldt, 1989; Gregor, 1990; Triandis, 1994). Why?

Before we begin to consider answers, it should be recorded that the news is not all good for males, either. Male neonates are less often disposed of by their parents, but are still more likely to die in infancy and at every other stage of the lifespan. Males are more likely to suffer a host of genetic disorders. Males are much more likely to be involved in accidents, to suffer stress-related illnesses, to be imprisoned, to be sent off to die for their country. Males die, on average, about seven years earlier than females (Eibl-Eibesfeldt, 1989; Harrison, 1978). It is true that males achieve sociopolitical power, but part of the price is that there are always other males eager to displace them, and the male-dominated world can be a tough and destructive one. Why?

Gender is fundamental to our existence and our interactions as human beings. It is therefore a fundamental topic for developmental social psychologists. Virtually every aspect of social life is affected by the gender of the participants, and we will find that the gender factor reappears time and time again throughout this book.

This chapter outlines some of the attempts that have been made to answer the "why" questions above. The chapter is organized in five main sections. The first section considers sex differences, concentrating mainly on the discrepancies between popular beliefs and actual research-based findings. The next three sections review in turn three of the major theoretical perspectives that guide much of the research into gender role development, namely: biological theories, social learning theory, and cognitive developmental approaches. In the final section, aspects of the social context of gender role development are considered, including the ways in which parents organize children's daily lives, the place of gender in peer interactions, and the influence of schools.

A note on terminology

The terms sex and gender will be treated as interchangeable here; this is not the unanimous practice among specialists in this area. Some social scientists have argued for a distinction between sex and gender, holding that one refers to the biological distinction, and the other to the social construction. Unfortunately, there is not an established practice as to which refers to which. On balance, "gender" tends to be treated as a social construct. But it is not easy to maintain a strict definition even between these notions: the very fact that we label and attach value to the concept of biological (genital) sex is itself a social decision – something we agree collectively is salient and meaningful; conversely, the assumptions or values we share and transmit about gender are based on a biological differentiation.

Sex (or gender) roles are the collection of behaviors and responsibilities that a given society holds as appropriate to members of a specific sex: that is, sex roles are socially shared expectations (Eagly, 1987). In some societies, sex roles are rigidly prescribed with a dichotomy maintained between, say, a male role of head of family and breadwinner and a female role of wife and mother. In many societies, sex roles were traditionally organized in this way but nowadays these constraints are probabilistic rather than absolute, and departures are tolerated to an extent. Even so, there are strong public expectations about some of the things that males and females can and cannot do and these have profound implications for the kinds of activities, relationships, goals, and careers that are collectively endorsed. We will encounter many examples in this and later chapters. It remains the case in most post-industrial Western societies, for example, that males occupy the overwhelming majority of senior positions in industry, social services, education, and government, while females are much more likely to undertake responsibility for child care. Part of the explanatory task is to determine how these differences in roles relate to differences in capacity.

Sex Differences: How Extensive Are They?

Clearly, there are physical differences between the sexes in terms of sexual apparatus, reproductive capacity, size, strength, and so on. These factors are implicated in the development of gender roles, and different theories account for them in different ways, as will become clearer below. For the moment, we will concentrate on psychological differences.

It would not provide a conclusive answer to our "why" question if we were able to locate clear sex differences in psychological abilities, but it would certainly help. Suppose we had evidence that males possessed superior intellects, with advantages in specific skills that are helpful when mastering the environment and scrambling to the top of the corporate ladder, or that females were uniquely equipped with mental attributes that suited them to domestic servitude and occupational subordination. Or suppose there was evidence of substantial personality differences between the sexes, such that males were more aggressive and females more compliant. Indications of consistent divergence in these respects might encourage us to locate in biology the explanation of differences in male and female behavior and status. What does the available evidence tell us?

The overwhelming conclusion to be drawn from the literature on sex differences is that it is highly controversial! A basic problem is that, for every topic that has been addressed extensively (e.g., by several different sets of researchers), there are contradictory findings; some find a male advantage in a given domain, some find a female advantage, and some find none at all. This is problematic, but consider the contexts in which researchers conduct and report their work. On the one hand, there is the nonsignificant results barrier to publication. While the *rhetoric* of science holds that the quality of the investigation is the critical consideration in acceptance for publication, and that findings of no differences between groups may contribute to the accumulation of knowledge, the *practice* of science is sometimes different: researchers do not bother to submit nonsignificant findings, often anticipating that they will not be considered sufficiently interesting to warrant publication (Maccoby and Jacklin, 1974; Rosenthal, 1993). Another grey area in reporting reflects the fact that sex differences may not always be of interest to a researcher investigating, say, the development of some personality characteristic or intellectual attribute, and so she or he may not test for them.

The Science and Politics of Finding Sex Differences

Another worrying possibility is that there may be ideological biases at work in the review process. What would *you* do with a finding of a sex difference on some measure of intellectual capacity in favor of males? Or females? Are your feelings about these matters affected at all by your own gender, or your gender ideology? Your integrity is not in doubt – but how confident are you about other psychologists?

Certainly, other psychologists give us cause for concern. Eagly and Carli (1981) found some evidence that, among studies of social influence, sex differences (with females rated as more influenceable) were more likely to be reported by *male* authors. Explaining these findings is not easy. The obvious charge of male chauvinist piggery is implausible: social scientists, male or female, tend to be more liberal on these kinds of issues than the general population. But even if we assume that wicked males are stacked up in the gender research laboratories, scheming to demonstrate the influenceability of the second sex, it is not clear how their biases could be transmitted to the subjects, especially since the personnel responsible for administering the tasks (i.e., the research assistants) in psychological research is often female-dominated (the men have the top jobs, but that is another story; see chapter 18). Alternatively, we might assume that some disgruntled female investigators are covering up gender differences that they find unpalatable. What do you think is going on?

Putting these disconcerting thoughts aside for the moment, consider the interpretation of findings of sex differences when they *are* obtained. If different investigators report apparently contradictory findings (Dr A discovers males are more prosocial, while Dr B finds females are more prosocial), we cannot assume that they necessarily cancel each other out (everybody, or nobody, is prosocial). It does not always solve the problem to look for a third investigator who found a sex difference, on the tennis match principle that two out of three settles the matter. Obviously, we would wish to assess the quality and measures used in the respective studies. But this gets us into still more difficult terrain, since psychologists do not always agree on what constitutes quality.

Social psychologists have begun to address these matters through the statistical techniques of meta-analysis. In a meta-analysis, an investigator aims to interpret multiple findings across the numerous studies that accumulate with sustained research interest in a particular field. Meta-analysis not only provides overall quantification of the available findings, but also takes into account the quality problem, at least to the extent that it can measure the degree of homogeneity among results. If homogeneity is not obtained, then the meta-analyst attempts to uncover the factors which might explain seeming inconsistencies in the body of literature. For example, perhaps males are more prosocial in some contexts, and females more prosocial in others. This helps to explain variability among findings, and generates hypotheses for more focused investigation in future research. In fact, through pursuing these kinds of questions, sex difference research has provided a major impetus to the development of this methodology (see Eagly, 1987).

Differences in Personality and Social Behavior

Expecting differences

Widespread stereotypes maintain that there are personality differences between males and females. For example, studies of undergraduates' beliefs about the attributes of the "typical" man or woman reveal a high degree of agreement that men are more aggressive, more independent, more competitive and more self-confident, while women are more emotionally expressive, more nurturant, and more gentle (Rosenk-rantz et al., 1968). Broverman et al. (1970) found that mental health workers (including clinical psychologists and psychiatrists) not only held similar stereotypes, but also integrated them with their conceptions of psychological wellbeing. For these professionals, the attributes associated with healthy, mature, and socially competent men were assertiveness and autonomy, while well-adjusted women were expected to be more submissive, less assertive, and less competitive.

Since the 1970s we have had a major wave of feminism, and extensive challenges to traditional beliefs about the characteristics of the sexes have been aired in many quarters: it is reasonable to expect corresponding changes in popular stereotypes. In fact, however, further studies conducted in the US during the 1980s have shown that the sex stereotypes are quite robust (Bergen and Williams, 1991; Leuptow, 1985; T. Ruble, 1983). Bergen and Williams (1991) found a correlation of 0.90 between stereotypical values associated with the sexes in 1972 and those of 1988, a remarkably high degree of similarity. We know that in some respects the US is an unusual society, so perhaps the picture is different elsewhere? It appears not: Williams and Best (1990), in a study of sex stereotypes in 25 countries from the Americas, Asia, Africa, Europe, and Oceania found some variations, but overall the gender stereotypes uncovered in American research tended to be representative of gender stereotypes held around the rest of the planet.

Finding, and not finding, differences

Research into sex differences in personality attributes does not support the stereotypical expectations very consistently. Differences in the expected direction are usually found on measures of physical aggression (Maccoby and Jacklin, 1974), but the findings are mixed with respect to nonphysical aggression, and in some areas of indirect aggression females score higher (this issue is addressed in greater detail in chapter 12).

Similarly, stereotypes of greater feminine nurturance would lead us to expect sex differences on measures of empathy and prosocial behavior, but such differences are not found invariably and where they are they tend to be associated with situational factors (Eisenberg and Mussen, 1989; see chapter 13 for fuller discussion). On the basis of the stereotypes, we might expect sex differences in *conformity*, such that males should show greater independence. As already noted, there are slight sex differences in the literature, to some extent associated with the gender of the authors as well as the subjects, but it should be added that where they are obtained they are usually small (Eagly and Carli, 1981).

Locating differences

In fact, where sex differences in personality are found, they tend to be confounded with variations in actual relative status of males and females. For example, in situations where males are in charge and females are subordinate, it is not surprising that sex differences in conformity or perceived conformity are obtained (Eagly and

Wood, 1982). More generally, if we test adult men and women engaged in traditional roles, some sex differences on personality measures may emerge (though usually not strongly) but the causal direction is difficult to establish. Did she become a home-oriented mother because she is a nurturant sort of person, or vice versa? Did he achieve professional attainment because of inherent aggressiveness, or vice versa? As we will see in chapter 18, there is evidence to suggest that these kinds of personality characteristics vary, in each sex, according to life-stage and other circumstances. A possible explanation emerges here for the gender differences in *authors'* discoveries that Eagly and Carli (1981) detected. It could be that female researchers are more likely to focus upon, or have better access to, situations in which females have a more equal status to males: if so, they may be less likely to find sex differences.

Overall, the evidence does not reveal strong and consistent sex differences in personality, at least on the major variables that we associate stereotypically with each sex. Yet there is little disagreement that males and females tend to have different life-courses. Perhaps the explanation lies in cognitive differences?

Cognitive Differences

Research into cognitive differences between the sexes has concentrated on mathematical, spatial, and linguistic abilities. Much the same picture emerges here as that sketched for personality, above: there are strong stereotyped expectations about differences, and minimal evidence to support them.

Mathematical abilities

We all know that males are better than females at mathematics. But researchers have been unable to come up with much evidence to validate our "knowledge." Hyde et al. (1990) conducted a meta-analysis of a large number of studies of sex differences in mathematical ability, based on millions of subjects. Contrary to what we all think we know, gender differences were quite small. Among the general population (as opposed to groups of students) there was a significant difference: but it was in the opposite direction to the stereotype. Among school children, in middle childhood no sex differences in mathematical ability were found, but during adolescence they were detectable in certain areas – particularly problem-solving tasks, where males outscored females.

This finding is open to interpretation, but its relatively late developmental appearance at least allows for the possibility that there are other factors than genetic inheritance involved (see Hyde et al., 1990, for further discussion). For example, Jacobs and Eccles (1992) in a large American study found evidence of an association between mothers' gender stereotypes about children's abilities in mathematics (and other domains), and their children's performance and self-perceptions. Similarly, Lummis and Stevenson (1990), in large studies in Taiwan, Japan, and the US, found that mothers believed at first grade that there were sex differences in mathematical ability, although the researchers found reliable differences emerging only at around fifth grade. The evidence indicates that the difference in mathematical abilities is not a massive one, but it may be important because of its implications for other educational attainment and for expectations.

Spatial abilities

Another stereotype is that males have superior spatial abilities to females. Men rate their own everyday spatial abilities higher than females rate theirs (Lunneborg, 1982). Both men and women expect men to be better at remembering directions and locations (Crawford et al., 1989). In general, research into sex differences in spatial abilities *does* indicate some superiority to males in respect of some, though not all, spatial tasks (Anderson, 1987; Linn and Petersen, 1985). However, within-sex variability is typically large (Anderson, 1987). On the basis of a meta-analysis, Linn and Petersen (1985) conclude that boys tend to score higher on visual–spatial and mental rotation tasks.

It has been pointed out that many spatial tasks are themselves stereotyped as masculine, and so it is conceivable that people undertake them with gender-biased expectations about their own performance, which may then affect their performance (Anderson, 1987). However, in a study of young adults' responses to one spatial task which does reveal sex differences (Piaget's horizontality of water-level task), Robert (1990) found that both sexes perceived the task itself as neutral – but none the less there was a sex difference in performance, in favor of males. Interpretations of research into sex differences in spatial ability are varied and controversial but what is clear is that, when significant differences are found, they are usually small.

Linguistic differences

Yet another stereotype holds that females have greater verbal abilities than males. Everyone seems to like this one, perhaps because it seems only fair to let females be good at something. Brownmiller (1984, p. 107) concludes that research has shown that "from infancy little girls excel in verbal skills." In fact, once again the evidence does not support this myth about little girls. Plomin and Foch (1981), for example, found that sex differences account for only about 1 percent of the variance in measures of verbal ability among children. Fairweather (1976) shows that there is little support for the widespread belief that females are superior to males in language acquisition. Summaries of studies of sex differences in language find mixed patterns of results, but meta-analyses show that any difference is "so small that it can effectively be considered to be zero" (Hyde and Lynn, 1988, p. 67).

We have to admit to another minor professional embarrassment in this connection. It transpires that there is an additional sex of author effect in respect of sex differences in linguistic ability. Hyde and Lynn (1988) found that research reports in which evidence of female verbal superiority was obtained were written by *females*. They suggest that, as with the findings of Eagly and Carli (1981) above, a plausible explanation is that investigators may elect to test in situations more congenial to their sex. In any case, the size of the effect was small. (For readers who wish to pursue the sex of author effect, Eagly, 1987, p. 144, discusses it more fully, and concludes that it is not a robust one.)

Summary

Sex differences in measures of personality, cognitive abilities, and linguistic proficiency are widely assumed but rarely found. When they are found they tend to be quite small. The overlaps between the sexes means that many females score higher on ability measures than many males, even in cases where overall mean differences are sometimes reported. While it is true, as Eagly (1987) argues, that even a small finding should not necessarily be dismissed as trivial, there is a strong tendency in some areas of the sex difference and sex role literature to interpret modest differences in means as massive dichotomies in practice, and this is not justified by the evidence. Furthermore, where differences are established in the adult literature (such as in the water-level task) it remains difficult to determine to what extent they are due to inherent, biologically given differences, to social expectations and developmental opportunities, or to some interaction among these factors (cf. Robert, 1990).

A preliminary review of sex differences in attributes does not furnish a ready basis for explaining differences in roles. How, then, can we account for indisputable differences in everyday behaviors, professional attainment, and differential values attached to each sex? Let us look now at the three major theoretical perspectives.

Biological Accounts of Sex Role Differences

It seems to be more than a coincidence that people keep arriving in one or the other gender package. Nature has clearly arranged something quite fundamental in this aspect of our lives, and the arrangements are connected directly to our collective future; we need males and females to ensure the continuity of the species. These facts, the facts of life, are so basic that we may take them for granted. As a result, we may underestimate their implications for the organization of our lives. We view the world through sophisticated consciousness, we are aware of options and choices that we make in terms of our personal behavior, and we like to think of our lives as being, to some extent at least, under our volitional control.

But we do not make the biological choice to be male or female, and we have very limited control over the hormonal allocations or reproductive roles that arise from this essential dimorphism. Could the whole pattern of gender role *behavior* be a natural outcome of the biological facts?

Some influential approaches to the study of sex roles maintain that this is indeed the case. It is argued that gender roles have taken shape gradually in the course of human evolution as part of our broader adaptation to the environment, and that each sex is equipped, in instincts and in physical attributes, for particular types of activity and responsibility. Sociobiologists, for example, hold that males and females developed different social roles as a function of their respective contributions to reproduction and domestic labor (Barash, 1982; Wilson, 1975, 1978). Males' relative physical strength and greater lung power made them better fitted to the pursuit of wildlife and the defence of territory and kin; females' childbearing and milk-production capacities rendered them best suited for nurturant roles. Thus, the male became the hunter and fronted up to the harsh external environment, while the female took care of the home and the children, concentrating on needlework and related duties (though presumably not fortifying her spatial skills in the course of them).

These patterns, it is argued, should not be regarded merely as fleeting precursors to our more complex and more advanced contemporary societies. Historically, over 90 percent of human evolution occurred in the context of hunting and gathering societies and the couple of hundred years or so of industrial society accounts for only a fraction of the species' evolution (Eibl-Eibesfeldt, 1989; Rossi, 1977). Surely, argue some biological theorists, whatever we learned and wrote slowly into our genetic codes over generations of adaptation must weigh more heavily on the scales of human nature than a few years' experience with high-tech gadgetry of the late twentieth century?.

Parental Investment Theory and Sex Roles

Sociobiologists draw upon parental investment theory (Kenrick, 1994; MacDonald, 1988d; Trivers, 1972, 1985; Wilson, 1978; see chapters 1 and 3) as part of their explanation of sex differences in behavior. Like male and female animals, men and woman need each other if they are to reproduce, but their respective orientations toward sexual congress conflict. As we have seen, the basic idea is that reproduction is inexpensive for the male, but costly for the female. As a result, according to the sociobiologists, our social structures and patterns of behavior have evolved around an uneasy compromise.

Wilson (1978) argues that the family emerged among humans as males and females struggled to establish a deal whereby the female trades reproductive capacity in return for male protection. Females have one advantage in this context, and that is that they can be confident that any offspring which they produce is their own genetic material; males lack this certainty. In order to ensure that any child in which he invests protection is actually his, the male needs to preclude his female from other males. Sociobiologists maintain that it is not surprising that males in virtually all societies are concerned with the control of female sexuality: males wish to preserve their genetic prerogatives in reproduction (Archer, 1992; Daly and Wilson, 1987; Low, 1989; see also chapter 16). At the same time, before she undertakes the major investment of pregnancy, the female needs to be assured that the father will stay around to provide for his dependents. And so society came to be organized in sexually exclusive domestic partnerships (or polygynous set-ups, where a man has several wives). Among the consequences for behavioral patterns is that males and females play different courtship roles: she dresses up and decorates herself to draw his interest, but she also affects coyness and plays hard to get, because she needs time to assess his commitment. He is the hunter in pursuit of a conquest, keen to demonstrate his potential as a protector, and so he adopts aggressive, commanding postures.

Sociobiologists point to strong similarities between this account and widespread patterns of contemporary sexual relations. In Western and many other societies, women *do* dress up and use make-up more than men, and both males and females place great emphasis upon female physical attractiveness (Buss, 1987; Jackson, 1992). Females find attractive in men characteristics associated with the provision of resources, such as being ambitious, hardworking and demonstrating a good earning capacity (Buss, 1987; Feingold, 1992; see chapter 16). Men, it is argued, still do take the initiative much more frequently, both in commencing relationships and in conducting sex lives. Men, in all known societies, are more sexually promiscuous than women (Oliver and Hyde, 1993). Women, in all known societies, are more likely to be the principal caregiver and to prepare food for consumption by the rest of the family (Rossi, 1977).

Sociobiologists argue that male dominance in contemporary societies arises out of males' innate aggressiveness. Wilson (1975, p.50) draws upon evidence of male aggression, greater male spatial ability, and greater female verbal skills to assert that "even with identical education and equal access to all professions, men are likely to continue to play a disproportionate role in political life, business, and science".

Finally, sociobiologists can offer an explanation of the differential value attached to male and female offspring. Males have the potential to go out and accrue resources, vital to survival and reproduction of one's genes. Males have longer reproductive life spans, and each can in principle stamp his genetic message home countless times. Females have less scope to chase wild beasts and defend their territory, and the frequency of reproduction is much lower. Hence, if you wish to ensure reproduction of your genes, better to have a son. In fact, one of the main reasons parents in traditional and Western societies give for preference for sons include continuity of the family name (Orubuloye, 1987), while the main benefits of having daughters are perceived as help with household chores ("she can help with the washing up," as the doctor on p. 161 explained). The theory does not hold that all females are devalued: those whose attributes indicate high reproductive potential (i.e., young, with smooth skin, good muscle tone, lustrous hair, curvaceous) should be highly sought after: they are almost as valuable as a good hunter/provider.

Biological Differences in Early Behavior

That biological differences exist between the sexes is a truism, contested by no one. How strong their relationship may be to psychological variables is more controversial, and there are many unsettled issues. If there are biologically given sex differences in behavior, we might expect to find some sign of them before any impact of social experiences. (Effects of biological factors are not necessarily restricted to infancy or early childhood, of course. We will defer to later chapters discussion of the implications of sexual development during adolescence.) In chapter 2, we saw that temperament theorists have postulated several dimensions of behavioral responsivity which are held to be the inherited cornerstones of personality. Are there, then, early emerging sex differences in temperament? The evidence indicates that on most measures, there are not. Two large-scale Australian studies of temperament among infants (Sanson et al., 1985) and toddlers (Prior et al., 1987), respectively, found virtually no reliable sex differences in temperament (as rated by mothers; one exception was that boys in the Prior et al. study were rated as slightly more willing to approach novel stimuli than girls). There is some evidence of higher activity levels in male infants by the end of the first year (Kohnstamm, 1989) but this is difficult to disentangle from possible observer bias. Parents and other raters may *expect* boys to be more active (Condry and Condry, 1976; Rubin et al., 1974).

There is no dispute that males and females have different chromosomal compositions (females are XX, males are XY), that their reproductive organs are formed from different tissues, that the external genitalia are more pronounced in one sex, that the balance of fat to muscle weight is different and that differentiating secondary sexual characteristics normally develop during adolescence. Some biologically oriented theorists have argued that these characteristics give rise to differences in abilities and behavior.

For example, it has been suggested that the presence of the Y chromosome elicits more information from the genetic blueprint (Hutt, 1978; Ounsted and Taylor, 1972), leading to slower maturation in the male with the benefit that greater phenotypic variation is expressed in that sex. This, it is proposed, explains the fact that the extremes of human abilities are more often manifest by males – allegedly, greater proportions of retarded and gifted individuals are male. Hutt (1978) argues also that chromosomal differences give rise to differences in spatial and verbal ability.

Greater amounts of the hormone testosterone are produced in the male fetus once the testes form, at about 6 weeks (Money and Ehrhardt, 1972), whereas females produce greater amounts of oestrogen. It has been argued that these hormones underlie differences in behavior between the sexes, including male aggressiveness and female nurturance. Two forms of evidence have been drawn upon: animal research and case studies on individuals born with or accidentally subjected to exceptional physical misfortunes. For example, researchers have administered doses of testosterone to pregnant monkeys and then observed the behavior of the female offspring, finding that they exhibited greater amounts of rough and tumble play, and were more aggressive toward other animals (Young et al., 1964).

Experiments with children's sex

Although ethical constraints prevent this kind of experimentation with humans, trial and error in medical science sometimes yield accidentally useful evidence. Such was the case during the 1940s and 1950s when many obstetricians in the US administered synthetic hormones, closely resembling natural male hormones, to pregnant women in order to minimize the risk of spontaneous miscarriage. Unfortunately, it was discovered belatedly that this treatment led in many cases to the birth of girls with masculinized external genitalia. The problem was tackled surgically early in life, and the girls were usually treated with hormone therapy. Nevertheless, Money and Ehrhardt (1972) report that these children tended to exhibit masculine patterns of play behavior and interests, such as greater involvement in physical activities and preferences for vehicles and blocks rather than dolls.

Money and Ehrhardt (1972) also report the intriguing case of identical twin boys who were born as normal males but one suffered an accident during circumcision in which his penis was destroyed. The traumatized parents were initially unsure of what to do, and for several months continued to treat the child as a boy. However, when the child was 17 months old they decided to follow advice to have him undergo surgical reconstruction as a female. The parents had to confront many difficult issues, not least the reactions of family and friends in their rural American community. Nevertheless, both of the twins appeared to adjust and to develop sex role identities consistent with their surface characteristics. The mother reported that the (now) girl seemed to be "daintier," "neat and tidy," and "feminine." Her brother developed as a robust little boy, protective toward his sister. Money and Ehrhardt (1972) did note that the girl had abundant physical energy and was somewhat tomboyish, but these are not unusual characteristics of females in middle childhood, and the researchers perceived her as indisputably a girl; in their view, she provided convincing evidence that gender identity is open at birth and for some time thereafter.

The story of these twins is often recounted as an illustration of the relative malleability of sex role characteristics. However, follow-up research with the girl when she reached her teens did not support this picture so clearly. Diamond (1982) found that the girl was experiencing an unhappy adolescence, with few friends, uncertainty about her gender, and expressing the view that boys have a better life. She looked rather masculine. Diamond's conclusion was that biology had ultimately proven irrepressible.

Problems with Biological Explanations

On first sight, biologically oriented theories appear plausible. They converge with everyday observations that males and females look, sound, and act differently, and they are consistent with traditional beliefs about the nature of sex differences. Nevertheless, a number of criticisms have been leveled against them.

Sayers (1982) argues that sociobiologists betray circular reasoning. They use value-laden concepts of present human society to characterize animal behavior, and then infer that accounts of animal behavior generalize to humans. Sayers points out that sociobiologists borrow terms from the vocabulary of the *human* sexual double standard ("coyness" and "philandery") to describe the sexual patterns of animals, and then take it as confirmation of their theory when coyness and philandery are discovered in humans (who are taken to be behaving just like animals).

We have already seen that some of the sociobiologists' assumptions about sex differences in cognitive, verbal, and spatial abilities, and possibly even aggression, are not strongly supported. Sternglanz and Nash (1988) dispute another sociobiologists' assumption that promiscuity enhances a male's prospects of ensuring the continuity of his genes. They point out that a male philanderer who moves on after mating, leaves a partner who could then mate with and be impregnated by someone else: in these circumstances, male dominance (i.e., gaining the status which allows first access to the female) is not such an advantage after all since the love-'em-and-leave-'em male may not be around long enough to ensure pregnancy. Furthermore, when the mother is left alone to rear the offspring, there are greater risks to the child – for example, impoverishment, reduced intellectual and social stimulation – thus decreasing the dependent's survival prospects. Again, even in sociobiological terms, this would appear to be maladaptive.

Sayers (1982) also rejects accounts of male dominance as reflecting greater male physical strength and innate male aggressiveness. If physical strength alone were critical to social status, we would all have a lot more respect for the elephant. Rather more importantly, she notes that there is evidence that behavior among animals, including dominance patterns, may be learned, and that dominance among animals is not always associated with greater strength or aggressiveness. She points out that much of human dominance is oriented around "status seeking" – prestige, reputation, acclaim – and that status presupposes values. Values are culturally produced, and culture is unique to humans.

Finally, sociobiological theories of sex role differences tend to overlook one of the most remarkable features of human evolution: that we have developed the capacity to transform our environments and hence, arguably, ourselves (Bem, 1993).

Summary

Some of the facts drawn upon by exponents of biological accounts of sex role acquisition are incontrovertible: we enter the world as members of a sex. Given the evidence of the integral importance of biological endowment and social development seen in earlier chapters, it would be a bold step to assert now that the fundamental biological difference has no implications for behavior or development. Males, on average, inherit greater physical strength and females are designed to carry children. The problem with some versions of biological and sociobiological theories is that they seem to assume that this is just about all that we inherit. Biological theories stress the demands of parenting and the possible implications of possible differences in abilities, but have little to say about the other distinguishing characteristic that has evolved in this species: its ability to articulate, share, reflect upon, and change its social practices. These theories tend to play down, too, the variabilities in human sex role organization. Turning now to social learning theory, we find an example of an approach that gives much more weight to the environment.

Social Learning Theory and Sex Roles

Imagine a hefty young woman, with the stamina of a horse and the strength to carry heavy loads of domestic produce up a mountainside. Whatever this person's virtues, she would face difficulties establishing her sexual attractiveness in a Western culture where the standards of female desirability attach greatest value to those who fall in the range petite to voluptuous. Yet among the Kwoma of Papua New Guinea such a woman would be highly prized and widely desired by males (Whiting, 1941).

We can suppose that Sharon Stone would not be a crowd-puller at Kwoma parties. Different people, at different times, in different locations, have radically different conceptions not only of physical desirability but also of role-appropriate behavior. This suggests the possibility that sex role standards, and sex role development, are the products of local norms and social pressures rather than innate determinism. Social learning theorists (Bandura, 1977; Mischel, 1970; Perry and Bussey, 1984) hold that sex role learning is the outcome of the accumulating learning experiences that the individual has in a particular social environment.

According to early formulations of this theory, socializing agents, such as parents, teachers, peers, and the mass media, convey repetitive messages about the importance of sex role appropriate behavior. The child is rewarded for behaving in certain ways, and punished for behaving in others. The socializing agents also provide many illustrations of what is expected and examples of the consequences of conforming or failing to conform to the norms. As discussed in chapter 1, the principal mechanisms of development stipulated by social learning theorists include reinforcement, observational learning, and self-regulation. Indeed, in one of the earliest formulations of the theory, Bandura and Walters (1963) drew on examples of sex role learning to illustrate the generalizability of their account, noting that parents in many cultures present their offspring with direct example and instruction in appropriate gender role behaviors, and provide them with play materials – such as toy kitchens, dolls, and cooking utensils for girls – thus wittingly or unwittingly fostering imitation of adult role behavior (p. 48). The social learning theory of sex role development has inspired a great deal of research, much of it concerned with the processes of reinforcement and modeling. Bandura and his colleagues subsequently developed a modified version of social learning theory, now called social cognitive theory (Bandura, 1986; Bussey and Bandura, 1992; see chapter 1); a summary of this perspective will be presented shortly.

Reinforcement

The findings concerning reinforcement of sex-typed behavior are not as clear cut as might be expected. Maccoby and Jacklin (1974) examined scores of studies concerned with various aspects of parental socialization practices. Evidence of consistent sex differences was not forthcoming. Many investigations yielded no sex differences, and others were contradictory or difficult to interpret. In general, the evidence did not support the hypothesis that parents reward boys more for aggressive or competitive behavior, or that they punish girls more for these behaviors. Some (but not much) evidence emerged to indicate that boys were more likely to be punished for aggression, and one clear difference was that boys were much more likely than girls to receive physical punishment for misdeeds. No sex differences obtained in studies concerned with parental encouragement of independence and autonomy. The authors were led to conclude that, contrary to their expectations that there would be blatant and powerful shaping forces at work, there actually appears to be "a remarkable degree of uniformity in the socialization of the two sexes" (1974, p. 348).

Subsequent research has qualified, though not refuted, this conclusion. One limitation of the evidence available to Maccoby and Jacklin's extensive review was that most of the studies were conducted with mothers, and Maccoby and Jacklin suggested that fathers may play a more determining role. Some research supports their speculations. Langlois and Downs (1980) had preschool children play with strongly sex-typed toys, instructing them to play with them in the sex appropriate manner. Once the subject was happily into his or her role play, the experimenters brought one of his or her parents, who was unaware of the instructions to the child. Mothers appeared not to differentiate their responses, and were equally warm to sons or daughters in same-sex or opposite-sex play. But fathers were far more sensitive to gender role proprieties. While they were positive toward their children in sex-appropriate play, they were overtly hostile when they found them engaged in cross-sex behavior. Fathers disparaged cross-sex play with verbal and behavioral ridicule. These reactions were strongest when their sons were crossing the gender boundaries.

Even so, the assumption of differential reinforcement across the board proves difficult to sustain. Subsequent analyses indicate that the presence or absence of a father makes little difference to boys' sex role development, and none to girls' (Stevenson and Black, 1988). More generally, Lytton and Romney (1991) conducted a meta-analysis of a large number of studies of parental treatment of boys and girls, and found surprisingly few sex differences. For example, there were no reliable differences according to sex of child with respect to measures of parental warmth, amount of interaction, encouragement of achievement or dependency, restrictiveness and disci-pline, and clarity of communication. There was one area where sex differences did hold up, and that was the encouragement of sex-typed activities. Yet even here the magnitude of the effect was modest. This comes as a surprise because most psychologists would agree on the importance of the parents as principal contributors to socialization. Perhaps the focus on reinforcement is misleading, and the main social learning mechanism is a slightly different one: modeling?

Modeling

As we saw in chapter 1, social learning theorists maintain that observing others, and the consequences of others' behavior, is one of the most economical means of gathering information about social norms and expectations. According to Perry and Bussey (1984, p. 278), for example: "Sex-role stereotypes are acquired mainly through observational learning." Certainly, there is evidence that parents tend to encourage their same-sex children to join them in traditionally sex-typed activities, such as cooking and shopping for mothers and daughters, car washing and fishing for fathers and sons (Bandura and Walters, 1963; Huston, 1983; Lytton and Romney, 1991). Fathers begin to make themselves more prominent in their sons' lives during the second year by talking to them more than to daughters (Lamb, 1977). By middle childhood, fathers tend to interact more with their sons than their daughters (Sears, 1965).

In these ways, the social environment begins to make different models more prominent according to the sex of the child. In addition, according to Bandura (1977, 1986), the child attends selectively to models, taking into account both the sex of the model and the sex typicality of the model's actions. Research supports both claims (Bussey and Bandura, 1984; Bussey and Perry, 1982; Perry and Bussey, 1979). Perry and Bussey (1979) demonstrated that when 8–9-year-old children watched a series of adult models engage in choices between sex-neutral activities (such as selecting an apple or a pear, a pencil or an eraser) their own choices subsequently were in line with the proportion of same-sex models that revealed a particular preference.

Children will imitate the same-sex model – but not always. Barkley et al. (1977) reviewed 81 studies testing the same-sex hypothesis, and found that the hypothesis was supported in only 18. A critical factor seems to be the sex *labeling* of the modeled behavior (Masters et al., 1979). In a toy-choice experiment with 4–5-year-olds, Masters et al. (1979) found that children were less influenced by the model's sex than by the gender label attached to the toy. In this study, children played most with a toy labeled as appropriate to their own sex yet modeled by a member of the opposite sex; it seemed to the authors that children reasoned along the lines that "if this is so good that even *they* play with it, then this is the toy for me."

One problem which remains for an account based on modeling is that the sex role orientations of children turn out not to be very strongly correlated with those of their parents (Huston, 1983). Parental modeling may make a contribution (though the processes are still little understood), but seem not to be the sole explanation. Let us consider another suspect, the media.

The Media

The mass media provide a plentiful source of sex role models. The media, especially television, are prominent in children's daily lives from infancy, and children spend enormous amounts of time in their presence. When media content is examined, it turns out to be highly stereotyped. Television producers appear to have much in common with the parents and medical professionals that we encountered at the beginning of the chapter: they prefer males. In most areas of television, whether entertainment or informational, males outnumber females 7: 3 (Butler and Paisley, 1980; Durkin, 1985). Even developing nations' infanticide practices have not resulted in gender imbalances on the scale of Western television.

Males are shown in more dominant roles with higher occupational status, while females are more often presented as subordinate, in a narrow range of traditional feminine occupations such as housewife, secretary, and nurse (Durkin, 1985, 1986a). In television commercials, women are more likely to be shown using products, especially domestic products, while men are depicted receiving their services or pronouncing on the merits of the products; this pattern of findings has been obtained repeatedly in studies in North America, Britain, Italy, Australia and elsewhere (Davis,

1990; Furnham and Bitar, 1993; Furnham and Voli, 1989; Livingstone and Green, 1986; Lovdal, 1990; Manstead and McCulloch, 1981; Mazzella et al., 1992). Commercials for children manifest sex stereotypes in even their use of formal features: ads for boys are action packed with fast pace and dramatic sound effects, while those for girls are gentler, with more fades and softer music (Welch et al., 1979). Similar patterns can be found in other media to which children and adolescents are exposed, such as radio advertisements (Furnham and Schofield, 1986), toy catalogues (Schwartz and Markham, 1985), the lyrics and format of rock music videos (Hansen and Hansen, 1990), and the content of teen magazines (Evans et al., 1991; Peirce, 1993).

These findings are provocative, but do they demonstrate an effect of media content upon gender role development? Of course, they do not: the critical test is to discover whether there is a relationship between viewing such material and the acquisition of particular beliefs and behaviors. At this point, the story becomes much less clear.

Some studies have reported associations between amount of viewing of television and measures of traditional sex role beliefs (e.g., Beuf, 1974; Frueh and McGhee, 1975; Levy, 1989; Morgan, 1982). That is, the more television a child watches, the more ready she or he is to endorse traditional beliefs. It is tempting to conclude that this confirms that exposure to stereotyped content brings about the corresponding beliefs in impressionable young minds. But, lest you are tempted, have a chat with a first-year psychology student: she or he will remind you that correlation does not equal causation. It could be that highly sex-typed children like to watch lots of television because they find there confirmation of their own limited world views. Furthermore, the correlations or other statistical effects are not very strong. Beuf (1974) provides no quantitative data; Frueh and McGhee (1975) found a weak relationship; Morgan (1982) found weak to modest relationships that varied with age and sex in ways that are not easy to interpret. Levy (1989) found evidence of a moderate relationship such that a preference for entertainment television was associated with greater gender role knowledge among boys, but not girls; girls preferring educational television displayed greater gender role flexibility than other girls.

Other studies have found a minimal or no relationship between amount of television viewing and sex role attitude (Meyer, 1980; Perloff, 1977; Zuckerman et al., 1980) and at least one has reported the unexpected finding that high viewers score *lower* on a test of sex stereotype acceptance (Cheles-Miller, 1975). Durkin (1985) reviews research in this field in greater detail, and concludes that the evidence for a linear relationship between amount of television viewing and degree of sex typing or stereotyped beliefs is not persuasive.

Interestingly, the evidence is a little stronger that television can sometimes contribute to gender role development in the opposite direction: that is, that it can help to promote more open and more egalitarian sex role attitudes and beliefs. Several experimental studies (Davidson et al., 1979; Flerx et al., 1976; Jeffery and Durkin, 1989; McArthur and Eisen, 1976), and at least one large scale field experiment (Johnston and Ettema, 1982), have found that children sometimes alter their attitudes as a result of exposure to counter-stereotyped television content.

The most ambitious of these studies is the *Freestyle* project, conducted in several

American states in the late 1970s (Johnston and Ettema, 1982; Williams et al., 1981). Broadcasters and psychologists worked together to produce a 13-part series for 9–12-year-olds, in which nontraditional opportunities and activities were modeled and discussed. Short- and medium-term (9 months after viewing) changes were measured, and a significant shift in the direction of nontraditional sex role attitudes was obtained. Impressive as this study and its results are, the largest changes were obtained in conditions where teachers were also involved and led discussions about the material, and the least effective condition was ordinary home viewing without adult input (i.e., the condition closest to mere modeling). Furthermore, in this and most other studies, it proved easier to change attitudes than behavior (see also Huston, 1983).

Overall, while it is easy to pick fault with the popular media's representations of the sexes, it is less easy to demonstrate that they have much effect on the young viewer/ reader. Media content *might* be implicated in sex role development, but if so, the processes appear likely to be more complex than modeling. Children *select* their models. Duck (1990) found that school children, when asked who they would most like to be like, frequently picked media figures but the choice of celebrity appeared to reflect the young person's own characteristics. One of Duck's subjects, a 14-year-old girl high in self-esteem, chose Meryl Streep as her ideal: "She is in my opinion an excellent actress. I admire this. She plays her roles to perfection and isn't worried about what people think." A 15-year-old boy with low self-esteem and dislike of his stepfather identified as his ideal Raistagen: "Raistagen is a character from a *Dungeons and Dragons* game and he can cast spells. I just like the way he seems not to have any feelings" (both examples from Duck, 1990, p. 25).

Problems with Social Learning Theory

One of the limitations of social learning theory is that it is essentially adevelopmental. That is, it holds that the processes of learning are much the same at any age, and development is equated with the accumulation of knowledge and behaviors. The theory does not account very well for the fact that children's sex role beliefs appear to undergo substantial changes (Durkin, 1985; Huston, 1983; Stangor and Ruble, 1987) and at times are more rigid than those of their parents. For example, parents with liberal sex role beliefs, and parents with nontraditional roles (such as a mother who is also a professional worker, or a father who is the primary caregiver), often find to their consternation that their 6-year-old insists on a very traditional division of the sexes, maintaining that mommies look after children and pops go out to work.

Another problem with some studies of modeling, pointed out by Katz (1987), is that they are often somewhat removed from natural situations. Katz argues that experiments in which adults are used to model toy play overlook the fact that in real life parents are more likely to illustrate *adult* rather than child behavior – and models of adult behavior may not be especially relevant to children in the early stages of gender role development. Hence, while modeling may be important at some points in development, its influence may depend on the child's level of knowledge and interest.

Summary

One of the clearest strengths of social learning theory is its acknowledgment of the social environment. Social learning theorists have been principally responsible for directing attention to the numerous components of the social context that convey subtle or stark gender role messages. It is clear that examples of sex role norms provided by others make at least some contribution to the discoveries of each new generation. Social learning theorists have little to say about why the social context is constituted this way: that is, the theory scarcely addresses the question of why one sex is valued more than the other, except that it is a sociocultural fact (see Jackson, 1992, p. 35f.) Research into the effects of the principal mechanisms emphasized by the theory (parental reinforcement, modeling) has not led consistently to the conclusion that they have major influence. This is surprising – in fact, so surprising that the unreliable performance of the data is often overlooked, and sex role development is widely "blamed upon" the environment regardless of the evidence. It seems that something is still missing; cognitive developmentalists have an interesting suggestion.

Cognitive Developmental Theories and Sex Roles

One of the common characteristics of the theories we have considered so far is the implicit assumption that the individual acquiring a sex role knows which one to develop: that is, the child knows that he or she is male or female, and proceeds accordingly to learn the appropriate role. But where does this knowledge come from and how important is it to the developmental process? The cognitive developmentalist's answer is that it comes from the same source as all knowledge: the child's active construction of an understanding of the world within which he or she interacts.

The seminal exponent of the cognitive developmental account of sex role acquisition is Kohlberg (1966), although subsequent work has also been influenced by a model based on information-processing theory. We will consider each of these approaches in turn. Bandura's social cognitive theory also re-enters the debate in this area, and some findings from this perspective are considered later.

Kohlberg and the Self-socialization of Gender Roles

Working within a Piagetian framework, Kohlberg proposed that the whole process finds its origins in the child's "concept of physical things – the bodies of himself and of others – concepts which he relates in turn to a social order that makes functional use of sex categories in quite culturally universal ways" (1966, p. 82). This is not an instantaneous process, but a gradual one which progresses through three stages during early childhood. The stages Kohlberg outlined are:

Gender labeling (approximately 2–3½ years).   During this stage, the child slowly becomes aware that he or she is a member of a particular sex. At first, this knowledge constitutes little more than a label for the child, equivalent to a personal name. The child begins to discover which other individuals fall into the same category, and elaborates his or her gender labels to include terms such as *man, woman, boy, girl*. But knowledge is not perfect. Sometimes children of this age assign sex incorrectly to other people (Thompson, 1975), and the implications of the labels are much less evident to the child; for example, many 3-year-olds are unaware that membership of a particular sex is usually a lifelong characteristic (Slaby and Frey, 1975).

Gender stability (approximately 3½–4½ years)   Children gradually become aware of the durability of their own gender, and can predict accurately what their sex will be when they grow up. However, children are still dependent largely upon their physical concept of gender. If a person is superficially transformed – for example, by donning the clothes of the opposite sex – the child in this intermediate stage is prone to assume that the person has changed gender (Emmerich et al., 1977). Recall that, according to Piaget, children of this age are seduced by perceptual transformations: they think that liquid transferred to a taller but thinner beaker is "more" because it looks taller (see chapter 1). On a similar basis, transformation of appearance may lead the 4-year-old to believe that a person who was recently a girl or boy has switched sex. McConaghy (1979) found that if a doll was dressed in transparent clothing, so that its male or female genitals were visible, children of this age regarded it as a boy or a girl according to the sex-typing of its most obvious physical appearance, its clothing. The British author, Jan Morris (1974), in her account of her transsexuality, reports that she (then he) was somewhere between the ages of 3 and 4 years "when I realized that I had been born into the wrong body, and should really be a girl. I remember the moment well, and it is the earliest memory of my life" (p. 3).

Gender consistency (approximately 4½–7 years)   During this stage, children come to understand the permanency of gender and the fact that a person's gender is constant even if he or she temporarily wears opposite-sex clothes or engages in opposite-sex activities. Gender is now seen as consistent over time and across contexts. Cognitive developmental theory predicts that these insights should be established around the same time as other conservation abilities, and some evidence is consistent with this prediction (Kohlberg, 1966).

A central tenet of the cognitive developmental approach is that the child's cognitive efforts are the foundation of gender role development. Conceptual awareness is regarded as the cause rather than the outcome of processing the environment for sex role information. As the child's conceptual understanding increases, so he or she is motivated to seek out more information about the details of his or her gender role. One useful means of acquiring this information is to look for potential models of sex-appropriate behavior.

Like social learning theory, then, the cognitive development account of sex role acquisition regards modeling as an important element. In contrast to social learning theory, though, the proposal here is that modeling the behavior, attitudes, and values associated with a particular gender role develops as a secondary consequence of cognitive construction. These details of gender-appropriate characteristics are sought actively rather than imbued passively, and the crucial factor is how children process information rather than its sheer availability (Martin, 1991).

Self-socialization and selective attention to gender-related information

Some interesting experimental evidence supports this aspect of Kohlberg's account. Slaby and Frey (1975) administered a measure of gender constancy to 2–5-year-olds, and divided the children into low or high stages. They showed the children a silent film of adult models simultaneously carrying out a series of simple activities. The actors were presented on a split screen, with a male on one side and a female on the other. The researchers measured the amount of visual attention the child gave to each side of the screen.

Now, if a child is indifferent to the sex of an observed model, then there should be no evidence of attentional bias. Among the sample as a whole, attention should be distributed roughly evenly between the male and female actors. If a child is drawn to relate to models of the same sex, then boys should watch the male and girls the female. However, if children only begin to watch the same-sex model as a consequence of constructing a conceptual understanding that they are members of a particular gender category and that they will remain members of this category, then we would expect the same-sex bias to be most marked among those who have attained high levels of gender constancy. This was exactly the pattern found for boys, and the results for girls were in the same direction, although they did not reach statistical significance. In a similar experiment, Ruble et al. (1981) investigated the relationship between gender constancy and responsiveness to television toy commercials which represented attractive toys as either for boys or for girls. They found that high gender constancy preschoolers were more likely to be sensitive to the implicit message of the ads, and this affected both their inclination to play with the toys and their judgments of which sex they were appropriate for. This evidence is consistent with the view that children construct their sex role knowledge through purposeful monitoring of the social environment.

A growing body of research adds further support to the claim that children's gender-role knowledge becomes more complete and more accurate with age, and that as they develop they are motivated to seek out information and organize their own behavior to ensure mastery of their traditional gender role: that is, children engage in self-socialization (Ruble, 1987; Slaby and Frey, 1975; Stangor and Ruble, 1987). This theory provides for a more complex perspective on the possible involvement of media in sex role development. An important consideration may be what the children bring with them to their media use (including their existing stereotypes and gender schematic processing biases, rather than the mere accumulation of stereotypes that they find there; cf. Calvert and Huston, 1987; Durkin, 1984, 1985).

Gender Schematic Processing Theory

Another cognitive developmental theory, *gender schematic processing theory* (Martin, 1991; Martin and Halverson, 1981, 1983, 1987), also emphasizes the child's active processing of gender-related information. However, this theory diverges from Kohlberg's in a crucial respect. Martin and Halverson propose, like Kohlberg, that children do strive to discover more about their gender group and the values and behaviors that go with it, but that the process begins when the child discovers his or her own sex rather than upon the attainment of gender constancy.

According to this theory, once children have a gender identity, they look increasingly to the environment for information with which to build and enrich the appropriate gender schema, an organized body of knowledge about the attributes and behaviors associated with a specific gender. This schema provides a basis for interpreting the environment and selecting appropriate forms of behavior. In this way, the child's self-perception becomes sex-typed.

Martin and Halverson propose that children's initial gender schemata are organized around a simple ingroup/outgroup dichotomy. Children are concerned initially to learn which objects and behaviors are appropriate for which sex. Subsequently, they focus on their own sex schema because this is integral to their need to establish a self-concept. Hence, this model holds that children first identify certain activities as sex-typed, and then concentrate on learning more about the activities that are appropriate to their own sex; correspondingly, they pay less attention to the details of activities associated with the opposite sex. Boys, for example, learn that doll play is designated as "for girls," and so they avoid dolls and acquire relatively little further knowledge about them.

One attraction of this theory is that it provides an explanation of the resilience of children's sex role beliefs and attitudes. The proposal is that children process gender-related information schematically: they admit data that are consistent with their schema and disregard or reject data that are inconsistent with them. If children encounter an adult engaged in some activity stereotypically associated with the opposite sex, they may fail to take the information on board. Several experiments have demonstrated that when children view pictures or watch films of individuals in cross-sex activities (such as a male acting as a nurse, or a female as a doctor) they variously miss the point, distort the information, or forget it swiftly (and insist that the man was the doctor, the woman the nurse; cf. Carter and Levy, 1988; Cordua et al., 1979; Liben and Signorella, 1993; Martin and Halverson, 1983; Stangor and Ruble, 1989).

The theory also accounts for the finding noted above that children appear to be more influenced by the sex-appropriateness of an activity performed by a model than by the sex of the model (Barkley et al., 1977; Masters et al., 1979). Children appear to work according to a schema (*"this is for boys/ girls"*) rather than unqualified imitation (*"do everything that grown-ups do"*). Indeed, it is interesting that Masters et al. (1979) found that children were more influenced by verbal labels of sex-appropriateness than by the actual sex of the model, a finding which suggests that children do process the information according to rules and regularities. Bradbard et al. (1986) found also that children explored novel objects more and remembered more about them if they were labeled gender-appropriate. Preschoolers who know the gender labels tend to spend more time playing with same-sex peers and also have greater knowledge of gender stereotypes (Fagot, 1985; Fagot et al., 1992). Studies of older children demonstrate that children perform better at tasks which have been labeled gender-appropriate (Davies, 1986; Hargreaves et al., 1985), findings which suggest that children organize their behavior around their conceptions of what is involved in being a boy or a girl. Labeling effects can be accommodated by other theories of sex role development (including social learning theory), but they fit particularly comfortably with models which emphasize the active construction of a knowledge base to guide future discoveries.

Is Gender Constancy Irrelevant to Sex Role Development?

As mentioned above, the critical difference between Martin and Halverson's theory and that of Kohlberg is that the former maintains that the organization of gender schematic knowledge begins as soon as children have some awareness of their gender group membership, and does not depend on the establishment of gender constancy. Much current research and debate in the field of sex role development centres on the question of whether the cognitive achievement of gender constancy really does guide other developments and social behavior. There is dispute among cognitive developmentalists, and between cognitive developmentalists and social learning theorists over this issue.

Carter and Levy (1988) found that gender schemas predict children's sex-typed cognitions and behavior better than gender constancy. Other studies have failed to find a clear relationship between gender constancy and sex-typing or preferences (Bussey and Bandura, 1984; Fagot, 1985; Marcus and Overton, 1978). These accumulating findings led Bussey (1983), from a social learning theory perspective, and Carter and Levy (1988), from an information-processing perspective, to suggest that the notion of gender constancy does not appear after all to be an especially important aspect of early sex role development.

From a social learning (or strictly speaking, social cognitive) theory perspective, Bandura and colleagues find studies pointing to a lack of a clear relationship between gender constancy and gender-linked behavioral preferences quite unsurprising (e.g., Bussey and Bandura, 1992, p. 1238). Bussey and Bandura argue that gender development begins as a result of "predominantly external sanctions" (such as parental controls) but shifts gradually to a self-regulated process governed by perceptions of anticipated outcomes, perceptions which are mediated by the social environment. According to this perspective, the major mechanism whereby standards regulate conduct is self-evaluation.

To test the relative importance of self-evaluation and gender constancy, Bussey and Bandura (1992) had preschoolers decide whether they would feel "real great" or "real awful" if they played with each of a variety of same-sex or opposite-sex toys. The results showed that between 3 and 4 years both boys and girls developed anticipatory approving self-reactions for same-sex behavior and disapproving reactions for cross-sex behavior. By the age of 4, boys felt great about playing with dump trucks and robots, but were not at all comfortable with kitchen sets and baby dolls; girls showed the opposite preferences. These findings are particularly interesting since the experimenters had arranged things so that the children thought that they were registering responses anonymously (i.e., the results cannot be explained easily in terms of demand characteristics and self-presentation). Across a number of tasks, children's self-evaluative reactions were consistent predictors of gender-linked behavior, whereas gender constancy and gender knowledge scores were not. Bussey and Bandura (1992) conclude that children learn early in life the sanctions against cross-sex behavior, and start to regulate their own behavior accordingly.

However, Stangor and Ruble (1989), from a self-socialization perspective, argue that gender schemata and gender constancy may represent different underlying processes. They suggest that gender schemata are concerned with the organization of information, while gender constancy provides a motivational dimension to sex role development (once you know that your future is inextricably linked to your gender group, you are motivated to do things which are relevant to your self-concept). Hence, the growth of gender schemata should affect cognitive variables, such as memory, while increases in gender constancy should be associated with motivationally relevant variables, such as activity choice and the distortion of gender-related information. In an experiment with 4–10-year-olds, Stangor and Ruble obtained support for these predictions. Memory for gender role consistent pictures increased with age, and preference for same-sex toys was greater in children who had attained gender constancy. These authors stress the importance of *both* cognitive and motivational factors in sex role development.

Problems for Cognitive Developmental Theories of Sex Role Development

Although cognitive developmental approaches are currently the most influential among developmental psychologists studying gender role development, they do have a number of limitations. First, like social learning theorists, the cognitive developmentalist has little to say about the question of *why* the sexes are differentially valued (Bem, 1993). In the lopsided tradition of cognitive developmental work (see chapter 1), this is treated as just another interesting datum the inquisitive constructivist has to acquire. In contrast to social learning theory, it has relatively little to say about the relationships between children's development and the surrounding culture (Bem, 1993; Frieze et al., 1978). The environment is taken as a given, and universal cognitive developments are held to promote acquisition of information. Martin and Halverson (1981, p. 1130), for example, see sex role development as the result of normal cognitive processes "developing with little effort and requiring only minimal socialization input" (although Martin, 1991, modifies this view).

Second, most of the cognitive developmental models tend to assume the framework of *individual* social cognition (see chapter 9), the central idea being that of the individual looking out at society and trying to work out what is going on. One problem with this is that cognitive development itself proceeds in an interactive context, and the construction of social role knowledge is a collective activity. This does not mean that cognition is irrelevant, but simply that there is a pressing need for studies of sex role knowledge as a *social* achievement (Lloyd and Duveen, 1993). Bem (1989, 1993) argues that the bases for gender differentiation are not, as Kohlberg proposes, in the child's mind, but in the child's socially organized experiences. For example, although as we saw above, children are developing the awareness of appropriate gender labels by their third year, Bem (1989) found that only about one-half of a sample of American 3–5-year-olds was able to identify correctly the sex of toddlers photographed nude. Those who did have this knowledge performed better on a gender conservation test. This suggests the possibility that rather than originating in the child's "concept of physical things – the bodies of himself and of others" (Kohlberg, 1966), gender role knowledge depends at least in part upon social experiences, and on the ways the culture organizes gender differentiation.

Third, the relationship between cognition and behavior presents problems, as pointed out by Huston (1985). Huston argues that if cognitions are major determinants of gender role development, then at least after the first few years, we should expect to find a positive correlation between gender concepts and sex-typed preferences, behavior, and identity. But these relationships appear not to be strong. For example, both boys and girls appear to develop their gender role cognitions in the same order and at approximately the same pace, but there are differences between the sexes in terms of the strength of their stereotypes and the developmental curves of their sex-typed preferences. Boys tend to have stronger stereotypes and greater resistance to opposite-sex activities (Bussey, 1983; Durkin, 1985; Huston, 1983, 1985), and boys tend to display monotonically increasing preferences for masculine activities and masculine self-images throughout childhood (Perry et al., 1984), while girls actually move away from feminine preferences and identity during middle childhood (Archer, 1984). As Huston stresses, this pattern among girls has been found in many studies conducted at different points in the twentieth century, and it seems to reflect something more than contemporary sensitivity to sex role inequities.

Huston raises a further problem. If cognitions are major determinants of behavior, then it follows that by changing cognitions – for example, by persuading children that their sex role stereotypes and beliefs are unduly restrictive – then we should bring about changes in behavior. We saw earlier that in general it is not easy to dissuade children of their traditional stereotypes, and greater success has been reported in attempts to change concepts than attempts to change behavior or behavioral intentions. We will see in chapter 18 that similar phenomena obtain among young adults with respect to sharing domestic duties: many couples agree theoretically upon the desirability of egalitarianism in the home, but few succeed in practice in distributing household chores equally. The concepts may have changed, but reality proves more robust.

Huston (1985) argues that, under the influence of cognitive developmental theory, recent research has concentrated too much on concepts and cognitions at the expense of behavior, activities, and interests. She points out that preferences for particular activities, which we have seen emerge very early, are likely to foster sex segregation from the preschool years. The central point for Huston is that conceptual knowledge may develop from play and other activities rather than preceding them.

Summary

Cognitive developmental theories of sex role development emphasize the constructive processes of the child as an active seeker of social information. These theories take as a starting point the discovery that one is a member of a particular gender, and hold that this is followed by a lengthy process of cognitive investigation. Although these models have been the most productive in recent years, they have not resolved all of the puzzles of sex role acquisition and there are areas of neglect and continuing controversy. Cognitive developmental theories say relatively little about biological factors, and downplay the issue of gender role variability among different communities and cultures. External sources of information are not entirely disregarded, but the stress is on internal organization which guides attention and constrains the assimilation of new data. Emotional and motivational features of gender role development have also been relatively neglected in these theories (although greater attention is paid to them in recent discussions, for example, Martin, 1991; Stangor and Ruble, 1989). Bussey and Bandura's (1992) study, conducted from outside the cognitive developmental camp but incorporating cognitive processes in a model which assumes reciprocal determinism, points to the importance of self-evaluation as a mediating factor and the relationship between self-evaluation and gender constancy remains contentious. Huston's (1985) critique illustrates very clearly that there is more to gender than cognition, and progress in this field is likely to depend on the success of investigators addressing the interconnections between social context and developmental social understanding. We turn to some of the relevant issues next.

The Social Contexts of Sex Role Development

We have now considered in outline three of the major theoretical perspectives on sex role development. Each merits more extensive attention (and further readings are suggested below), but it will already be clear that none offers a fully adequate account of why and how we acquire gender roles. Ultimately, it is likely that a successful theory of sex role acquisition will incorporate aspects of each of these theories, and then go beyond them.

With these theoretical perspectives in mind, we look now a little more closely at the social contexts within which gender roles are acquired. We will consider aspects of family organization, peer relations, and schooling. It becomes clear that social contexts are organized around sex-typing, and that direct and indirect encouragement certainly occurs. However, as we proceed, pause now and then to consider the extent to which the evidence to be summarised below is compatible with *each* of the main theoretical perspectives outlined so far.

What do Parents Encourage?

Recall that Lytton and Romney (1991) found that although there was little overall evidence that parents reinforced boys and girls differentially on several measures, they did find a significant (though not large) difference with respect to the encouragement of sex-typed activities. It is helpful to consider just how fundamental some everyday parental encouragement may be.

Parents dress children differently. There has been some relaxing of the exclusivity of certain controls in recent decades, but by and large girls and boys still wear clothes and hairstyles that leave it unambiguous to which sex they belong. Even infants and toddlers whose facial appearance does not make their gender obvious are often dressed in clothes or colours which provide powerful cues. To some extent, what children wear may seen relatively trivial, compared, say, to how people behave toward them. But appearance marking is one of the most common ways humans have of signifying the importance of particular social categories – and it is established for most of us, from very early in life. This affords a pervasive visible reminder that gender is important (Intons-Peterson, 1988; Jackson, 1992; Martin, 1991).

Parents establish sex-typed physical environments for their children. From the earliest physical handling, boys and girls are treated differently, with boys experiencing more varied and more intense stimulation, and girls experiencing greater consistency and stability in interactions with their caregivers (Yarrow et al., 1975). Rheingold and Cook (1975) examined the bedrooms of boys and girls, aged 1–5 years. They found marked differences in decor and content. There were more toys in the boys' rooms, and the toys were allocated in clear, if unsurprising, ways. Boys had more vehicles, machines, weapons, animals, sports equipment, educational, and scientific toys, but girls did well for dolls and miniature domestic appliances. As Rheingold and Cook (1975) point out, children spend a lot of time in their rooms. They wake up in them, they are surrounded by their contents as they go to sleep, and it has to be concluded that they engage in a lot of sex-typed play in them.

Parents encourage children to pursue different activities. This is true from quite early in life. A clever experimental technique to demonstrate this was introduced by Will et al. (1976). They presented a boy aged 6 months to adults who were then observed while playing with the infant. One of the convenient characteristics of babies of this age is that it is virtually impossible to identify their gender unless they are naked or wearing sex-typed clothes. So Will et al. (1976) presented the child in sex-typed clothes: half of the subjects met the child as "Beth", dressed in pink, and half met "Adam", dressed in blue. Three toys were available: a train, a doll, and a fish. Will et al. found that the doll was most often handed to "Beth", and there was a tendency for Beth to receive more smiles. There were no sex differences with respect to the other toys, nor on other measures of behavior toward the child, such as vocalizing or touching. An extension and refinement of the study by Smith and Lloyd

(1978) found that "boys" were more likely handed a hammer, while girls were more likely to be given a doll. The adults encouraged physical action in boys more than girls. Smith and Lloyd used both boys and girls as infants, and so they were able to examine their data for effects due to actual sex of child: there was none. Subsequent research has shown that effects of gender labeling do not always occur, but they are likely in situations of uncertainty (i.e., when the adult knows little else about the child other than his or her gender; see Stern and Karraker, 1989, for a review).

Parents also seem to encourage sex-typed behaviors in everyday settings. Fagot (1978) observed families with toddlers and found that children were differentially reinforced (with smiles, praise, greater attention) for the kinds of activities traditionally associated with their sex. Girls were positively reinforced for doll play, dressing up, dancing, assisting with domestic tasks, and signs of dependency, such as following a parent around the home, whereas boys were reinforced for block play and gross motor activities. The children received negative feedback for cross-sex activities, such as running and jumping (girls) and playing with dolls (boys). Recall the exclamation of the mother on p. 161, who perceived a shortcoming of her newborn daughter that: "It can't play rugby." This mum probably would not be too pleased if later her daughter favored rugby over doll play. Caldera et al. (1989) found that parents gave more positive nonverbal responses to their 18–23-month-old children picking up toys when the selected object was sex-appropriate, and more negative responses if it was traditionally associated with the opposite sex. Parents vary in terms of the extent to which these matters are important to them and how firmly they endorse traditional stereotypes. Fagot et al. (1992) found that mothers who were more traditional tended to have toddlers who had mastered gender labels.

What do Peers do?

Perhaps it is not surprising that children raised in sex-typed rooms, guided toward sex-typed behaviors, and keen to discover more about what it means to be a boy or a girl should tend to favor sex-typed activities. When they begin to mix with peers, they are likely to encounter individuals of very similar backgrounds and interests. Certainly, during the early years, children's play does display sex-typing. By the age of 2, children opt for sex-appropriate toys more often than opposite-sex toys (Fagot, 1974). By the age of 3, sex differences are well established, with boys preferring gross motor and vehicle play while girls favor play with dolls and household utensils (Fagot, 1974; O'Brien et al., 1983; Perry et al., 1984; Smith and Daglish, 1977). Given the impetus to find sympathetic environments and useful materials, where is a young person to turn? In practice, the outcome is that: "If you like playing dolls, you will end up playing mostly with girls. Or, if you choose to play with girls, you will often find them in the doll corner" (Huston, 1985, p. 6; figure 5.1). In other words, the child seeks like-minded peers with similar resources. The peers themselves are likely to entertain strong sex role stereotypes, possibly as a function of the kinds of social cognitive developments discussed above (cf. Stern and Karraker, 1989).

Maccoby (1990) makes a strong case for attention to the peer contexts of sex role

Figure 5.1   If you choose to play with girls, you will find them in the kitchen area.

development, pointing out that sex differences emerge primarily in social situations such as peer settings rather than in individual tests. Children soon begin to demonstrate preferences for same-sex playmates and segregate into predominantly same-sex groups, in which they do not welcome adult interventions to encourage them to be nice to the opposite sex. Peers are alert to any suggestion of cross-sex behavior. For example, in the Langlois and Downs (1980) study described earlier (see p. 175), the experimenters compared peer and maternal reactions to preschoolers' play with opposite-sex toys. They found that when boys played with girls' toys, mothers were tolerant but their (male) peers ridiculed and even hit them. From early childhood, gender is not just another thing to learn about, but a vital social category that determines whom one mixes with and how one behaves. Once a little boy has his blocks, his football, his cars, and his Martian-zapper he may not need much parental reinforcement to keep going – in fact, it soon becomes difficult to stop him. The critical variable may not be vertical reinforcement so much as horizontal social engagement.

What do Schools Encourage?

While family and peers are important features of the child's social microsystem, another major variable comes into play when she or he reaches the first stages of entry into the exosystem – which for most is via the school. Schools also highlight the significance of gender and furnish a lot of information about sex roles (Meece, 1987). Schooling is important because it ushers in not simply more formal structures to daily life but also raises, with increasing emphasis, prospects of the future – of what you are going to be when you grow up. Meece (1987) reviews extensive evidence to demonstrate that schools maintain widely sex-biased practices in terms of the opportunities and advice (including career counselling) they provide. In later chapters, we consider some of the processes in more detail. But for the moment, note that many teachers and educational policy-makers are well aware and deeply concerned about this issue. However, if they try to instigate changes, such as promoting scientific classes among girls or other nontraditional pursuits for boys, then they are typically met with considerable resistance at the peer level.

Even getting home from school tells you something about the meaning of your gender. For example, a large study of families in Nottingham found that girls were more often collected from school or instructed to come straight home than were boys (Newson and Newson, 1976). Once home, girls were more likely to bring friends into the house rather than play in the neighborhood. Of course, if girls are in the house much of the time, they are more likely to be enrolled to assist in domestic chores. Meanwhile, their brothers, returning home at a more leisurely pace, are more likely to be exposed to nonsupervised play activities, which may foster more exploratory and greater assertiveness in the male peer culture.

To return briefly to theoretical matters, all of these contextual considerations may appear to favor explanations of gender role differentiation based on the force of external influences. These kinds of findings are often drawn upon to support theories (or sometimes, intuitions) of the "molding" or "conditioning" of gender. But in fact they simply extend our *description* of the nature of the social contexts in which children acquire gender, rather than account for the developmental and social processes involved. A sociobiological determinist might comment that it is entirely consistent with his or her theory that communities would organize themselves (and hence their children's experiences) in ways consistent with the dictates of nature; sociobiologists who admit an interaction of nature and environment would argue that the adaptiveness of the species allows for accommodations to specific local conditions (for example, a traditional community at an early stage of economic development may need to perpetuate relatively rigid role divisions in order to distribute manual labour and domestic responsibilities efficiently, while a modern community might relax these patterns in order to increase the availability of female labour for technological industry; see MacDonald, 1988b, for related discussion).

From other theoretical perspectives, it can be pointed out that in the face of all of these parental efforts, peer practices, and educational experiences, we should bear in mind that the child is neither passive nor empty. As Scarr (1992) emphasizes (see chapter 3), individuals gravitate toward their own preferred environments. Perhaps little boys like more robust toys and games because of the nature of their motor development. Social development is far more than a matter of being guided into socially approved activities; children have to develop a conceptual understanding of the social world and their place in it. As cognitive developmental theories emphasize, in order to extract generalities from even these highly repetitive play structures, means of assimilating and organizing social knowledge are required at some point. Similarly, although cognitive developmentalists rarely address issues concerning *adult* understanding, it is perfectly compatible with a cognitive approach to assume that the mature person's knowledge and comprehension is drawn upon in order to support the discoveries of the next generation. Overall, while it is important as part of our understanding of social development to take note of the sheer pervasiveness of gender-related experiences, the explanation of their origins, correlates, and consequences remains a major theoretical challenge.

Summary

There is extensive evidence that parents organize children's environments, appearance and activities with gender in mind and that the character of much of everyday life, from its very beginnings, is sex-typed. But the character of everyday life is also highly social. That is, it includes a developing person who is actively involved in choosing among behavioral options (rather than just receiving them from above), and who is striving to understand the socially shared meanings of being a "boy" or a "girl"; furthermore, this developing person enjoys time spent with others of similar status and interests. As a result, peer activities are often organized around gender specific preferences. Once the major arrangements have been put into place, continuing encouragement from parents may not always be required, which may be why Lytton and Romney (1991) found evidence of only modest differences in parental reinforcement. The most justifiable conclusion we can make at this stage concerning the relationship between social context and gender role development is that it is a complex, multifactorial, and dynamic affair that research has only begun to disentangle (Katz, 1987).

Conclusions

This is not really the conclusion of our dealings with sex roles. As indicated at the beginning of the chapter, gender is a critical social variable – sometimes a matter of life and death, and invariably a major factor in determining a person's options and life-course. Several of the issues introduced here will resurface time and time again in relation to other topics. Developmental social psychology cannot be pursued indifferently to the gender of the subjects.

What we have seen so far is that people attach values to other people according to their gender. Stereotypes about gender differences are widely shared through most communities, despite the fact that they are poorly supported by research evidence. Newcomers are expected to learn where they fit in, and what the appropriate role is – and most do so.

Different theories have been proposed to account for these patterns of human social organization and belief. Three of the main theoretical orientations have been introduced. Sociobiological theory makes an important contribution by attempting to locate gender role differences in historical–evolutionary context: these are issues that are often neglected by mainstream psychological theories. On the other hand, sociobiological explanations in this area have tended either toward the cavalierly deterministic or have simply left open the question of the processes that are involved in reconstructing gender in each new generation. Social learning theory maintains the importance of the social environment and emphasizes the potency of observational and modeling processes; however, this theory does not have a lot to say about developmental differences in reasoning about gender. Cognitive developmental theories do address developmental changes, and stress the relevance of children's cognitive schemata which constrain which aspects of the social environment they attend to, and what they make of it. Although this is the most favored theory among many developmentalists, it is relatively indifferent to variations in social context and social outcomes.

In the final section of the chapter, we have seen that the kind of social world in which the child lives does have important implications for his or her development. This point is consistent with each of the major theories, though no one accounts fully for learning about social life through participation. There is much more to be discovered about the development of gender.

Further reading

Bem, S. L. (1993). *The lenses of gender: transforming the debate on sexual inequality*. New Haven, Conn.: Yale University Press.

An important perspective on the polemics and the meanings of gender research. Bem draws together her own and others' work from social and developmental psychological studies of gender and sets it in (American) political and cultural context.

Cahan, E. D. (1991) Science, practice, and gender roles in early American child psychology. In F. S. Kessel, M. H. Bornstein and A. J. Sameroff (eds) *Contemporary Constructions of the Child: essays in honor of William Kessen*. Hillsdale, NJ: Erlbaum.

Readers contemplating a future in developmental social psychology will find it interesting to review the gender issues that, historically, have influenced the careers of women and men in developmental and social topics. In particular, should men handle the theory, women the practicalities?

Eagly, A. H. (1987) *Sex Differences in Social Behavior: a Social-role Interpretation*. Hillsdale, NJ: Erlbaum.

Eagly advances a theory of sex differences which holds that socially shared expectations about men's and women's specific roles in everyday settings are the foundations of sex-typed behavior.

Golombek, S. and Fivush, R. (1994) *Gender Development*. Cambridge: Cambridge University Press.

A succinct overview of research into several different areas pertaining to gender development, including prenatal influences, hormonal factors, stereotypes, social experiences, and psychopathology.

Intons-Peterson, M. (1988) *Children's Concepts of Gender*. Norwood, NJ: Ablex.

This book provides a useful review of theories of gender concepts, and very interesting findings on young children's reliance on appearance cues – especially hair and clothing – to differentiate gender.

Liben, L. S. and Signorella, M. L. (eds) (1987) *Children's Gender Schemata*. San Francisco: Jossey-Bass.

Six useful discussions of cognitive dimensions of gender development.

Serbin, L. A., Powlishta, K. K. and Gulko, J. (1993) *The Development of Sex Typing in Middle Childhood*. Monographs of the Society for Research in Child Development, 58 (2), no. 232.

Sex role development during middle childhood has been relatively neglected as a research topic, but these authors suggest that this may be an important period for closer study because of the integration of cognitive and affective dimensions of development it entails. Serbin et al. show that extensive knowledge of gender stereotypes is acquired during the years 5–12, and that there are individual differences in flexibility of gender role beliefs and attitudes. Confirming the multifaceted nature of development, they conclude that no single causal factor accounts for all changes and variability, though important influences can be identified.

Chapter 6

Language Development I: Origins and Course

The striking fact is that it is the most ordinary everyday uses of language, with parents, brothers and sisters, neighborhood children, in the home, in the street and the park, in the shops and the trains and the buses, that serve to transmit, to the child, the essential qualities of society and the nature of social being.
> (Halliday, Language as a Social Semiotic, 1978).

Try inviting a friend to meet you on Saturday night for a party without using words.
> (Sherif and Sherif, An Outline of Social Psychology, 1956)

On June 16, 1976, around 15,000 students began a march to protest about the language of instruction used in their schools. At some point on their journey, they were stopped by the police. The police threw tear gas cannisters into the crowd to disperse them and then began firing. Nobody knows exactly how many children were killed or injured on that day and during the riots that ensued through the next week, but even official figures admit to about 140 dead, and 1,000 injured (Geber and Newman, 1980).

The children were South Africans, residents of Soweto, and they were protesting about the imposition of the Afrikaans language in their education. To them, Afrikaans was the language of Apartheid. They had other concerns and complaints, but the language issue was central because of its symbolic significance. Their willingness to take a public and very dangerous stance on the issue is a powerful confirmation of a point made several years earlier by the linguist Halliday that: "A speaker who is made ashamed of his own language habits suffers a basic injury as a human being; to make anyone, especially a child, feel so ashamed is as indefensible as to make him feel ashamed of the colour of his skin" (1968, p. 165).

Most of us, most of the time, take language for granted. Yet our worlds are heavily dependent upon language: most of what we know or learn is transmitted linguistically and much of our social involvement is mediated linguistically. Even *Mr Bean* has to speak sometimes. Language is so pervasive in our daily lives that it is almost transparent – until threatened or lost. When it is threatened, as it was for the children of Soweto, its integral presence in our social existence is highlighted. When it is absent, as in the cases of individuals with mental impairment or trauma, a major lifeline to the rest of the community is lacking, with profound consequences.

Language is integral to social being, and being social makes language possible. There would be little value in devoting oneself to acquiring a language that no one else knows. The critical advantages of language include the facts that it enables us to make contact with others, to learn from what they have already found out, to coordinate joint behavior, to evaluate and compare experiences, to record past events and predict future possibilities, to influence and inform, and to organize social environments. For these reasons, language stands out as demanding a central place in the attentions of social and developmental psychologists.

The Neglect of Language

It is rather surprising, then, to look back on the history of these fields of social and developmental psychology and discover that researchers in the former long ignored language and that researchers in the latter had to be led (back) to study it by someone from a different discipline, linguistics. Social psychologists' neglect of language is a particularly curious anomaly, since much of social life and social interaction is conducted through language. Although taken as central by one of the early leaders of social psychology (Wundt, 1900–1920; see Farr, 1983), its popularity as a research topic waned during the middle of the twentieth century, and, as mentioned in chapter

1 it remains possible – in fact, rather easy – to find introductory social psychology textbooks that have no chapter or even index entry on language.

This oversight may be due to a number of reasons (Fraser and Scherer, 1982; Moscovici, 1972). Language, especially language in social interaction, is difficult to measure and to manipulate. It thus poses a risk to experimental social psychologists keen to establish the rigor of the discipline in the face of hostility from colleagues committed to scientific enquiry into the workings of rats and computers. Another reason may be that language clashes have not been an everyday preoccupation within the United States, where one language is spoken by a clear majority of the huge population; this may change with the increasing prominence of some other languages (such as Spanish, or the preservation of some Native Indian languages), but, historically speaking, relations among different language groups have been less salient than elsewhere. Since much of the leading work in social psychology is undertaken in the US, this may have affected the general directions of the field. Fraser and Scherer (1982) point out that it is no coincidence that much of the impetus for recent work on the social psychology of language has come from Europe and Canada, from researchers working in communities where language conflicts are more prevalent. Fortunately, such work has done much to remedy the situation, and recent years have seen a healthy growth of social psychological research into language (see Giles and Robinson, 1990) and the relationship between everyday language and social psychological theories and processes (Semin, 1987).

For their part, developmental psychologists have always maintained some interest in language (Guillaume, 1927; Lewis, 1963; Stern and Stern, 1928; Vygotsky, 1962; Wallon, 1942; Werner, 1948), though during the middle of the twentieth century it became peripheral in this field, too. In Europe, Piaget's guiding emphasis on cognitive development led to a preoccupation with logical operations rather than what Piaget saw as the "merely verbal"; in the US, the leading protagonists of behaviorism were not especially sympathetic to the study of abstract structures called grammar and invisible properties such as meaning. Although one of Piaget's earliest books (1926) was entitled *The Language and Thought of the Child*, language served primarily in this and later studies as a lens through which Piaget aimed to inspect the child's thought, rather than a focus in its own right. Following Piaget, much of developmental psychology has been concerned with what the child *thinks* rather than what the child *says*. However, for reasons that will be elaborated shortly, developmentalists have revived their interest in language since the 1960s, and the study of child language acquisition is now one of the largest and most active research areas in psychology.

In this and the following chapter, we will be considering the acquisition and use of language. In this chapter, we examine language as a phenomenon that children come somehow to acquire – that is, as something that children *know*. As with other topics, the major theoretical perspectives have emphasized environmental, biological, and cognitive factors, respectively. Each will be reviewed below, and a summary of language acquisition research will be provided. The debates arising highlight basic controversies about the nature of the human mind and its development. But these turn out only to be the starting point because, as we will see in the next chapter, some of the major questions that the field has begun only recently to address concern what happens when minds get together, as, for example, when adults and young language learners interact. In the next chapter, then, we will examine language as a feature of social interaction – that is, as something that children (and their co-interactants) *do*. We will also consider language as something that children *have*, in the sense that it is an attribute that signifies they are a member of a particular speech community or group – and as such, prone to be appraised in terms of the social stereotypes held of that group. Knowing, doing, and having language are by no means independent, and throughout it will be seen that language development is closely tied to activity in social contexts.

Language as Knowledge

How children acquire language is one of the key mysteries facing scientific enquiry into humans. One of the reasons the topic excites so much interest is that many regard language as a defining characteristic of our species – a capacity that distinguishes us sharply from other creatures, and gives us enormous evolutionary advantages. Through studying the acquisition of language, we address some of the core puzzles of human nature. Indeed, many would agree with Chomsky (1972, 1986, 1988) that the study of language is the most viable route that scientists have for discovering the properties of the mind. Chomsky points out that other things the mind is alleged to do, such as thinking, are not manifest directly, whereas the products of linguistic capacity are relatively accessible, and can be observed, recorded, and analyzed.

As already indicated, there are several theoretical approaches to the explanation of language acquisition, and we will consider only a few of them here. It is worth mentioning now that the whole field is intensely controversial, characterized by claim and counter-claim, and continuously opening new and challenging topics for further enquiry. In order to understand some of the central debates, it is useful to follow the main arguments in a quasi-historical structure. To preview, the history of child language study in the past couple of decades began with a resounding dismissal of learning theories (behaviorism) and a widespread enthusiasm for a proposed alternative, the nativist theory of Noam Chomsky. The larger part of the chapter will be concerned with this biological theory and the research that it inspired. However, in due course, enthusiasm for nativist theory was tempered somewhat as investigators began to consider the relationships between language development and other developments in the child. This led to a resurgence of cognitive developmental approaches. Support for the "cognition hypothesis" waxed and waned, too, but this perspective did contribute to a broadening of research attention, with the outcome that researchers began to study the contexts of language development more generally. Attention was drawn increasingly to children's interactive involvements with other language users as possible sources of information, motivation, and feedback about language – and language acquisition theory and research became increasingly social.

In the present chapter, then, we will consider some of the strands of this progress, dealing in turn with learning theory, Chomsky's biological theory, and cognitive developmental theory (or the "cognition hypothesis"). Social interactional approaches to language acquisition are discussed in the next chapter. Necessarily, this review will be very selective, with an emphasis on issues relevant to developmental social psychology.

Learning Theory and Language Development

Learning theorists regard language as learned in much the same way that anything else is learned – through processes of reinforcement and modeling. If we take as a starting point the reasonable observation that children invariably learn the language of the community in which they happen to grow up, then there are strong preliminary grounds for suspecting a link between the environment and the product. If we listen to early language users, it is obvious that children try to imitate things that others say; if they get it wrong, then they are encouraged to practice, perhaps by repeating a more careful enunciation modeled by a parent.

Elaborate theories of language learning have been based on the presumed power of these processes. It has been proposed that children learn initially the meanings of vocabulary as a function of repeated exposures to words and their referents, allowing them to build up a set of associations for a specific term (Mowrer, 1954; Staats, 1968). In this vein, Staats (1968) describes an informal experiment in which he taught his cat, Max, the meaning of the word *no* by classical conditioning procedures. Classical conditioning in this instance consisted of hitting the pet with a newspaper whenever it did anything unacceptable and shouting "NO!" Once Max got the point, his behavior could be controlled by the word (the conditioned stimulus) alone.

Staats maintains that children learn the meanings of words in similar ways: they come to associate them with particular experiences until they become so familiar that they can serve as surrogates for the experiences. Then, once a word is known, it can serve as the unconditioned stimulus to promote further word learning. For example, suppose that (as a result of procedures similar to Max's lessons) a child has learned the meaning of the word *bad*. Later, he hears the word *evil*, at first a meaningless term for him:

> He is then told by a parent or teacher that EVIL MEANS BAD and he repeats this to himself several times. These experiences would constitute conditioning trials . . . Through this conditioning the new word EVIL, would come to elicit the same meaning response as the word BAD. It would not be necessary that the word EVIL ever be paired with an unlearned aversive stimulus. (Staats, 1968, p. 25)

Whether this model really explains how the child learns what other people's words mean is contentious; it certainly seems fortuitous that this hypothetical learner knows what *means* means before getting onto other words. But even if we beg that question for a moment, it is clear that classical conditioning does not readily explain how children begin to *produce* words. (Max, as far as we know, never spoke to Staats again after his humiliating treatment.)

To account for production, some behaviorists turn to operant conditioning. Recall that the basic notion of operant conditioning is that behaviors that elicit positive reinforcement will be repeated. Applying this principle to the child's early vocal noises, we might expect that when an infant accidentally hits upon a sound that appears similar to one that her parents would like to hear her say, then she will be reinforced. If the baby emits the syllable *da*, parents may seize enthusiastically upon this welcome token of affiliation, and tease out repetitions until the child is able to say *dada* at will. Skinner (1957) proposed that more elaborate processes based on this principle could explain how parents shape children's vocal repertoire into the language of the local community. According to Skinner, language behavior could be explained exclusively in terms of environmental effects upon the organism, including both reinforcement and imitation. However, although he developed an ambitious theoretical account of this position (Skinner, 1957), he did not conduct any empirical research of his own to test it with children.

Social learning theory

Traditional learning theory accounts of language development fell into disfavor by the 1960s for reasons that will become clearer in the next section. However, social learning theorists have developed more elaborate and more persuasive accounts in recent years. Social learning theorists acknowledge that language acquisition and use entails more complex structures than early learning theorists recognized, but argue that these can be accounted for in terms of modeling, reinforcement, and feedback (Whitehurst and DeBaryshe, 1989).

For example, Moerk (1991, 1992) has developed a skill learning model, based on a theoretical synthesis of behavioristic learning theory, social learning theory, and elements of Piagetian cognitive developmental theory. Essentially, Moerk's position is that language learning depends on continuous feedback cycles within which the "trainer" (normally, the parent) invites a response from the child and then provides feedback to the response. To return to an example from above, the parent may say "Dada" in order to prompt the child to make a similar noise. A very young speaker might respond "Da," whereupon the trainer emphasizes "Dada . . . Dada . . . Dada." This provides the child with opportunities to learn by comparing his or her attempts with a modeled utterance. Moerk (who provides more extensive evidence of parental interventions in early language experiences) regards the child as an active participant in the learning process, but stresses that it is a *learning* process, much like the transmission of any other aspect of culture to a new generation.

Summary

Traditional learning theories and more recent social learning theories have in common that they regard language development as proceeding according to general principles of learning. Early theorists emphasized classical and/or operant conditioning as essential mechanisms, while more recent approaches place more stress on modeling and feedback.

A Biological Theory of Language Acquisition

As with many of the topics we will be addressing in this book, at the opposite end of the theoretical continuum there is a radically different explanation of how learning comes about, an explanation based in biology. In the case of language, nativist arguments have been developed more extensively and had greater impact than have biologically oriented accounts of other areas of human social behavior. This is due largely to the influence of the American linguist, Noam Chomsky.

Chomsky sees the overriding goal of his discipline as providing an explanatory model of the grammar of language. Ultimately, he seeks a universal grammar, that is, a grammar of sufficient abstraction as to be able to characterize the core rules that all languages follow. Chomsky's own eminence as a scientist is due primarily to the revolution he initiated in linguistics with the introduction of a new grammatical model (transformational generative grammar) that seemed to explain important facts about language structure in ways that previous linguistic theories had not. He also achieved early notoriety (Chomsky, 1959) with the publication of a vigorous, polemical critique of Skinner's (1957) text in which he argued that behaviorism could account for none of the interesting properties of language and that it fundamentally underestimated what was involved in acquiring language.

Introductions to the goals and methods of theoretical linguistics are available elsewhere (e.g. Radford, 1988), but for present purposes it will be useful just to sample the kinds of properties of language that linguists get excited about, because they turn out to have implications for how we conceive of the task facing the child as language learner.

Linguistics and Language Structure

An overall purpose of linguistics is to describe and explain the grammatical structure of language. For many linguists, a central component of language is *syntax*, or the set of rules governing permissible word orders. The rules are of interest for at least three reasons. One, they form a complex, interdependent system which is very difficult to describe and explain. Two, complex as the rules may be, all normal language users know them. Three, we can use them creatively to produce and understand an infinite number of new sentences. If we wish to understand the properties of the human mind, these qualities of language make it an excellent place to start.

Let us take some simple examples. Consider sentences 1 and 2.

1   Mitterrand addressed the nation.
2   Mitterrand the addressed nation.

We know at once that there is something wrong with 2, while 1 is well formed. Sentence 1 exemplifies a basic structure of English: the declarative sentence (consisting of subject–verb–object). Sentence 2 is close, but very minor variations of the word order render it ungrammatical. This simple contrast provides a reminder of just how transparent our knowledge of language is; we scarcely notice the rules governing everyday usage, unless we encounter a violation or error. Yet clearly there is some sense in which we follow the rules, both in producing language and comprehending it.

Consider next sentence 3:

3   The nation was addressed by Mitterrand.

Sentence 3 conveys essentially the same meaning as sentence 1, yet they differ by much more than the location of one word. How is 3 (the passive) related to 1 (the declarative)?

Suppose we wished to create a question corresponding to sentence 1. The simplest way to do so in spoken English is to change the intonation:

4   Mitterrand addressed the nation?

Another way of expressing the question, and one which avoids the ambiguities of 4, is as follows:

5   Was the nation addressed by Mitterrand?

Obviously, we have exactly the same words as in sentence 3, but by reordering them in line with the rules of English question formation, we change the meaning. If we try to work out the pattern, we see quickly that to obtain the question all we need to do is invert the subject (*the nation*) and the auxiliary verb (*was*). This seems to be a general rule, because it works elsewhere, too:

6   The Chancellor was satisfied.
6a Was the Chancellor satisfied?
7   The Soviet Union was dismantled.
7a Was the Soviet Union dismantled?

But if we try this rule on sentence 1, we run into problems:

1   Mitterrand addressed the nation
1a Addressed Mitterrand the nation?

Perhaps we could solve this difficulty by using the strategy that seemed to work so well for sentences 5–7, namely stick an auxiliary (*was*) at the beginning?

1b Was Mitterrand addressed the nation?

Obviously, this does not work. In fact, we have to do something quite different to form the question here, an operation described by some linguists as *do*-insertion (the appropriate tense of *do* is inserted):

1c   Did Mitterrand address the nation?

How do we know why 1a and 1b are incorrect, and 1c is perfectly well formed? How do we know that alongside *do*-insertion, we need to make a corresponding adjustment to address*ed*?

Consider a further sentence:

8   I told you that irritating Chirac can be unhealthy.

One reading of 8 is that a person called Chirac, who is irritating, suffers sometimes from ill health. But another is as a warning that to irritate Chirac can have unhealthy consequences for you. The whole structure is ambiguous. Many other illustrations are possible; the above is actually a variant of a more famous example from Chomsky, *Flying planes can be dangerous*. Another you might care to disentangle is *Cleaning ladies can be delightful* (from Aitchison, 1992). These kinds of ambiguities tell us something very important about language structure: that there must be relations among the elements of a sentence that are not apparent on the surface.

Take another example:

9   Mitterrand, after a glass of Chardonnay, addressed the nation.

Notice that we do not interpret this sentence as meaning that a glass of Chardonnay addressed the nation. We recognize a structural link between *Mitterrand* and *addressed* – even though it is not apparent from the surface juxtapositions. Again, there seems to be some underlying structure that is easily accessible to an English speaker.

Finally, consider sentences 10 and 11, from Chomsky (1986):

10   I wonder who the men expected to see them.
11   The men expected to see them.

What is interesting about these examples is that in 10 *them* is referentially dependent upon *the men* (i.e. it refers to the same people), while in 11 *them* refers to some other people or objects. How are we able to understand the different meanings of *them* in structures that are so similar? Or, in Chomsky's terms: "How does every child know, unerringly, to interpret the clause differently in the two cases?" (1986, p. 8).

The goals of linguistics include the development of theories of the linguistic rules that govern structures such as the above (and all of the other sentences we understand or produce). This is a formidable task and there is much debate about how best to characterize the rules. One of Chomsky's principal early arguments was that we need to distinguish between the *surface* structure (the actual arrangement of words that we hear or see) and the *underlying* (or deep) structure in which the grammatical relations are specified. This distinction helps to account for ambiguous sentences such as *Flying planes can be dangerous* by proposing that, while the surface structures are identical, the underlying structures are different. It is also possible to characterize the relationship between active and passive versions of a sentence (such as 1 and 3, above) in this way: perhaps they share a common underlying structure and rules for word combination relate the surface forms to this structure.

The linguist's goal, according to Chomsky, is to formulate a precise account of the rules that govern these and all other permissible word combinations in a language. For present purposes, the details are less important than the conclusion, which surely must be that any language is an extraordinarily intricate structure – so much so that linguists are still a long way from achieving agreement about the properties of grammar. Since his early work, Chomsky has revised his own theory of grammatical structure several times, and many others have developed variants or proposed completely different models. The controversies among linguists reflect not wilfulness but the sheer magnitude of the task of developing an adequate model of the rules of language.

Language and Creativity

Another obvious but intriguing property of language is that it enables us to produce and understand new statements. Take the sentence *Foreign growers eye the tree-lined streets of Paris* (from *Le Monde*, December 6–7, 1992). You may never have encountered this particular word combination before, but its meaning is easily grasped by virtue of your knowledge of the rules of English (and perhaps a little contextual information concerning sluggish business in the French tree-planting industry). This creative property is, in Chomsky's view, one of the most important features of our language capacity. It is not restricted to the sub-editors of *Le Monde*: much of our everyday language consists of new sentences in this sense.

Now, behaviorists maintain that all that we know is brought about by learning, but Chomsky points out that through language we are engaged extensively in the production and comprehension of *novel* utterances. Skinner (1957) was aware of this problem, and tried to account for it in terms of "stimulus generalization" and the combination of "units" of previously learned language. Chomsky (1959) was dismissive of these notions, arguing that the first is too broad a description to be meaningful and the second fails to come to terms with the facts of underlying structure in language (for example, the fact that the same combination of units can have two possible readings, as illustrated in the ambiguous sentences above).

Implications of Grammatical Analysis for the Study of Development

The study of formal grammar is only for the dedicated, but Chomsky pointed out that there is an important sense in which all of us are linguists. We may not be able to describe the structures of our language using the technical apparatus of the professionals, but we do know whether a sentence is correctly formed or not, and we produce and understand language that honors the rules quite effortlessly all the time. It seems that we have a tacit knowledge of the rules, or linguistic *competence*. Sometimes our linguistic *performance* lets us down – we make mistakes, we change our mind or pause mid-sentence, we commit minor speech errors, and so on – but (by reference to our underlying competence) we can correct these if we wish and we can distinguish between errors and well-formed sentences in the language of others.

Still more intriguing is the fact that even quite young people have much if not all of this knowledge. A normal 5-year-old, for example, might not know as many words as you, but she or he can produce an inordinate amount of well-formed strings of language, and rarely seems to find the task problematic. Chomsky points out that "the young child has succeeded in carrying out what from the formal point of view, at least, seems to be a remarkable type of theory construction" (1959, p. 58).

This achievement is undertaken quite rapidly. The child begins to use productive speech at around age 12–18 months, and by 5 years or so has a good grasp of the basic rules of her or his language, and is using it fluently and creatively. Indeed, virtually all normal children manage this, whether they are growing up in a middle-class home in Europe, an Aboriginal community in outback Australia, or a ghetto in Washington, D C.

Who teaches the rules? Presumably not the parents. Unless they are professional linguists, most parents are not familiar with the rules governing passive sentences, the formation of questions, the referential constraints upon pronouns, the analysis of structural ambiguity, and so on. (If they *are* professional linguists, they spend too much time arguing about the details of the rules to be of much use to their children.) Worse, parents like any other language users, are likely to show the performance limitations mentioned above – interruptions, false starts, errors and so on – so that the available data modeled for the child are in some respects impoverished or degenerate, consisting of "fragments and deviant expressions of a variety of sorts" (Chomsky, 1965, p. 201).

The only way in which the child could discover the rules of language so swiftly in the face of these impediments, Chomsky proposed, is by way of innate knowledge:

> A consideration of the grammar that is acquired, the degenerate quality and narrowly limited extent of the available data, the striking uniformity of the resulting grammars, and their independence of intelligence, motivation, and emotional state, over wide ranges of variation, leave little hope that much of the structure of the language can be learned by an organism initially uniformed as to its general character. (1965, p. 58)

The child must know something (indeed, quite a lot) about the structure of language in advance of exposure to it, so that she or he can recognise it and construct and evaluate a grammar to match it. Since Spanish children learn Spanish and Indonesian children learn Indonesian, it follows that the "advance knowledge" must be quite abstract – that is, it must consist of rules that fit every known language at some level. Again, the ultimate purpose of linguistics, according to Chomsky, is to work out what these rules must be – hence the search for a universal theory of grammar. According to Chomsky, the contribution of psychologists is to find out how the rules are implemented as children acquire their first language.

Broadly speaking, the nativists' view is that certain parameters are set by the innate principles of grammar with which every normal child is endowed. Specifying these parameters is a tricky business, and tends to vary with each new model of grammar that linguists propose (interested readers can pursue the details further in Atkinson, 1987; Goodluck, 1991). But the basic idea is that the child knows (implicitly) in advance that language will embody certain structures and constraints; this reduces the amount of learning required by restricting it to those aspects of the grammar that are unique to the particular language the child encounters. Note that linguistic experience *is* required for these processes to operate: first, some exposure to an actual language is necessary to "trigger" (Chomsky, 1980) them and, second, the particular selection of rules and any local variants can only be discovered through involvement in the language.

Summary

One of the most influential theories of language acquisition emerged from the field of linguistics. Chomsky argued that the structures of grammar can only be accounted for in terms of abstract, underlying rule systems. Most linguists accept this claim as a starting point, although there is continuing debate about exactly what the rules are and how we might characterize them. Chomsky went on to propose that, if it is difficult for formal linguists to determine the rules, then the normal child's success in mastering most of them within just a few years in early childhood – in the face of poorly informed teachers and degenerate input – appears all the more impressive an achievement. Chomsky's explanation of this mystery is that the child already knows much of the relevant information in advance, in the form of a biologically given faculty for language which sets limits on the possible rules that the child might infer from exposure to a language.

The Study of Child Language

Chomsky's ideas inspired a huge amount of research into child language development in the 1960s and 1970s, and the field has continued to grow rapidly since that time. There are now several periodicals devoted exclusively to the study of child language and an enormous number of publications appear annually in these and other developmental literature. The field is highly specialized and often focused on very technical arguments, with the result that it tends to stand aside from much other developmental work. While it would require an additional book to address all of the issues and findings that emerge, the general implications of child language research are important for developmental social psychology for at least two main reasons. First, advances in understanding any one area of development contribute to our general picture of the nature and processes of development as a whole. The findings of developmental psycholinguistics have fundamental implications for the broader field because they test the limits of traditional theories (cf. Maccoby,1992), especially learning theories and cognitive developmental theory. As research progresses, the study of language acquisition may provide analogies and insights that are productive in the study of other domains of development.

Second, as understanding of language acquisition has advanced, it has become overwhelmingly clear that the processes are inextricably linked to the development of social interaction; this means that specialists in social development may have a role to play in illuminating the links between language and social development. To be honest, interchanges between language acquisition researchers and other investigators of social development have not been extensive so far, but there are encouraging signs of overlap and mutual interest, and we will consider some of these in the following chapter.

Does Language Grow?

Chomsky argues that the development of language in the child is best thought of as a form of mental growth, analogous to the growth of physical organs such as the liver. Equipped with specialized advanced knowledge of the general rule structures (sometimes called a language acquisition device, or LAD), the child's capacity to acquire language is triggered by exposure to a specific language. From then on it grows, largely according to a biologically preprogrammed schedule. Indeed, Chomsky maintained, along with Lenneberg (1967), that like other forms of biological growth, nature dictates that language acquisition is best achieved within certain periods of development. If the child is not exposed to language during the sensitive period, then he or she may not be able to learn it adequately if it is made available in the environment later. This argument is similar to the reasoning of ethologists and some attachment theorists concerning the evolutionary bases of critical periods in the early lifespan: the assumption is that the species is designed to allow phases for the establishment of specific patterns which both facilitate acquisition and ensure that the developing organism is sufficiently robust to meet later environmental variations (Bornstein, 1989). Nativists (e.g. Pinker, 1994) draw on the theory of natural selection to explain the origins of language in the species, pointing out that language gives us evolutionary advantages, is found in all known human societies, but is not developed among our closest neighbors on the evolutionary scale.

Some of the early studies of language development provided findings that are consistent with the idea of language growing, and with the claims of a sensitive period. We will concentrate for the moment on the growth of language, and return to issues concerning the sensitive period later.

In one sense, researchers could scarcely fail to find evidence of growth: nobody disputes that children produce very little language at first, and that in due course they know a great deal. Even so, if we look closely, we find that there is much more to the process than merely additive development.

Charting linguistic production in early childhood

Children's earliest recognizable language is typically in the form of single words. The development of the first 10 words or so is relatively slow, taking place from the latter part of the first year and proceeding gradually over the next few months. During this period, children begin to use single words to express linguistic relations such as possession, location, negation, interrogation (Barrett, 1989; Chumak-Horbatsch, 1994; Rodgon, 1976).

By around 18–20 months, most infants have a productive vocabulary of around 50 words, and now enter a period of "vocabulary explosion" (Barrett, 1989; Nelson, 1973). Shortly after the beginnings of this phase, they begin also to produce simple word combinations, usually achieved by combining two or three of their earlier words. Beyond this the number of elements in the child's utterances increases, and the complexity of the structures advances. By no means everyone agrees that these developments reflect biological preprogramming, but most accept that impressive changes are taking place that amount to much more than the steady addition of new elements.

Brown (1973) and his associates conducted an intensive study of the productive early language development of three American children, Adam, Eve, and Sarah. One of their principal measures was the mean length of utterance (MLU). The MLU is based on the number of morphemes in the child's utterances. A morpheme is the smallest meaningful unit of language. For example, the word *cookies* includes two morphemes, the stem *cookie*, and the plural inflection, *-s*. The word *cry* consists of one morpheme, while the word *crying* consists of two. The number of morphemes in an utterance provides a crude but useful indicator of its linguistic complexity. The language of a child whose typical utterances are of the form *cookie* or *baby cry* (whose MLU would be less than 2) could reasonably be assumed to have rather less knowledge of the rules than a child producing 10 morpheme utterances like *The cows are running away from the farm*.

Brown (1973) proposed a model of early child language development in which progress involved a series of five stages, marked by increments in MLU. Stage I begins when the child's MLU passes 1.0 (i.e. when some multiword utterances occur), and ends when it reaches 2.0. The subsequent stages are indicated by increases in the MLU of 0.5. Some young speakers can pack quite a lot into their single words. Consider the output of a Greenlandic 2-year-old (studied by Fortescue, 1984/ 85) who, around the time of entry into Stage II, was producing multi-morphemic utterances such as "tattuus-sinaa-nngil-angut" (*We cannot be so crowded together in it*) and "anartarfilerisu-u-pput" (*they are the sewage collectors*) .

Brown found that the pace of development varied markedly among his three English-learning subjects, but that the structural characteristics of the children's speech at any one stage was very similar. Most of his analyses were concerned with Stages I and II. In addition, he reviewed a number of independent studies that were becoming available of children learning Finnish, Swedish, German, Hebrew, Samoan, Japanese, Korean, Russian, and Luo (spoken in a province of Kenya).

Structures of early language

Some intriguing properties of early language were identified by these analyses. First, all of the children's many utterances could be classified into a small set of basic semantic and grammatical roles. These included the expression of nomination (e.g. *that ball*), recurrence (*more book*), possession (*Adam ball*), agent–action (*Adam hit*), and attribution (*big ball*). That is, children seemed to have some simple rules for permissible word combinations, and to use them to create a good many different expressions. Second, later developments within the stage consisted of expansions and conjunctions of the existing structures, such as agent–action–object (*Adam hit ball*), and agent–action–object–location (*Adam hit ball there*) – rather like new shoots growing out of established branches. Third, children produced mainly content words (nouns, verbs, adjectives) and ignored minor parts of speech (such as prepositions, articles) and inflections (like the plural marker *-s*, the past tense *-ed*); the little extras emerge later, like a plant reaching maturity. Fourth, instances of gross errors of word order (*ball the Adam there hit*) were virtually nonexistent, a phenomenon which suggests the whole process is highly constrained – just as the unfolding of our physical structures normally follows a standard programme. Fifth, very much the same characteristics identified in the English learning subjects could be found in Stage I children in each of the other languages studied, supporting the prediction that the developments are universal.

The emergence of grammatical morphemes

Development during Stage II, when some of the missing elements of Stage I begin to appear, proves equally interesting. Brown (1973) charted the emergence of 14 basic grammatical morphemes, minor parts of speech such as inflections (*-ing*, *-ed*, *-s*), elementary prepositions (*on*, *in*). He discovered that although the *pace* of development varied from individual to individual, the *order* of appearance was consistent across children, a finding which was replicated with a larger sample by de Villiers and de Villiers (1973). Why should this be the case? Brown (1973, p. 272) remarks: "Some factor or some set of factors caused these grammatical morphemes to evolve in an approximately consistent order in these children."

An obvious candidate is parental speech: perhaps the parents made the morphemes differentially available and the order of emergence corresponds with frequency of adult use? This would be consistent with learning theories of language acquisition. But Brown's analyses of parental speech demonstrated no relationship with children's output. An alternative possibility is that order of acquisition reflects the relative linguistic complexity of the morphemes. The evidence here was more encouraging: Brown found that both grammatical and semantic complexity were better predictors of order of emergence than parental frequency.

So, detailed study of the language of young children confirmed that quite extraordinary developmental processes were taking place, and suggested that it would be unproductive to attempt to account for these in terms of the direct effects of parental instruction or modeling. Other research seemed to confirm that the traditional behaviorist assumptions of imitation and reinforcement could explain very little.

Language and Imitation

Fraser et al. (1963) had 2- and 3-year-old children imitate a set of simple English sentences, such as *I am very tall, I showed you the book, I can see a cow*. They found that the children's responses typically left something out. Examples include *I very tall, Very tall, I show book, Show you the book, See cow, Cow*. What is left out and what is included, of course, correspond closely to the grammatical properties uncovered in the spontaneous speech of young children, as characterized in the analyses of Adam, Eve, and Sarah, above. This experiment is easily replicated and if you have access to a toddler you might (with parental permission) try it out yourself. It demonstrates convincingly that "imitation" involves active, selective processes on the part of the young child.

Lenneberg (1962) presents a case study of a boy who was unable to speak at all yet could understand language addressed to him. It is difficult to explain this child's achievement as a consequence of imitation followed by differential reinforcement. Bloom et al. (1974), in a longitudinal study of six children in the early stages of language acquisition, found individual differences in tendency to imitate: some children imitated a lot, others very little. More recently, Tager-Flusberg and Calkins (1990) analysed the proportions of utterances by normal, Down's syndrome and autistic children that were imitative or spontaneous, and compared the grammatical complexity of the two types. If imitation is the principal means through which advanced language is acquired, then it could be expected to be associated with greater utterance length and complexity than is found in spontaneous speech. But these investigators found the opposite, with MLUs and grammatical complexity higher in spontaneous speech than in imitated.

Perhaps the strongest evidence against imitation as an explanation of language acquisition is simply that children come up with forms that they are most unlikely to have heard in the speech of caregivers, such as *allgone shoe, mices, runned*, and so on (Marcus et al., 1992; McNeill, 1970). Take this astute description of the 1991 television version of the Gulf War by an American 4-year-old: "If the watcher plane sees a bad guy, it radio-shacks to the bomber plane, and the bomber plane blewns it up" (from Baron, 1992, p. 1). Imitation scarcely appears an adequate means to account for the productive manner in which this child seems to be working out his theory of language and the other interesting things that grown-ups do.

Language and Reinforcement

It might be argued from a learning theory perspective that nobody would expect early imitations, especially of complex stimuli, to be perfect. But once the attempt is made, the parent is likely to intervene to shape and then reinforce improvements, gradually molding the child's language. A number of further problems confronts this account.

First of all, Brown et al. (1969) and Brown and Hanlon (1970) reported that by and large parents do not correct grammatical errors in children's speech. Instead, they focus on the *truth value* of what the child is saying. In one instance, Eve said of her mother "He a girl", and the mother responded affirmatively "That's right"; grammatical correctness seemed to be much less salient to the mother than the conceptual accuracy. Elsewhere, children came up with "grammatically impeccable" statements such as *There's the animal farmhouse*, or *Walt Disney comes on on Tuesday*, only to receive negative feedback because the building was a lighthouse and the programme appears on a different day. Several other studies have since supported the claim that direct corrections or instruction about grammar are quite rare (Hirsh-Pasek et al., 1984; Morgan and Travis, 1989; Shatz and Ebeling, 1991). Brown et al. remark that if parental interventions are concentrated on truth and accuracy, it is something of a paradox that the typical product of this kind of training schedule ends up telling lies grammatically!

When parents do attempt to intervene at the linguistic level, and to correct an ungrammatical or poorly pronounced utterance by the child, the usual outcome is parental frustration rather than child compliance (Braine, 1971; McNeill, 1970). Many amusing anecdotes of thwarted parental language lessons have been reported in the literature, but among the best known is the following:

> *Child:*   Nobody don't like me.
> *Mother:*   No, say "nobody likes me."
> *C:*   Nobody don't like me.
> *[eight repetitions of this exchange]*
> *M:*   No, now listen carefully; say "nobody likes me."
> *C:*   Oh! Nobody don't likes me.
> (McNeill, 1970, pp. 106–7)

It is perhaps unfortunate that this child's parent was a linguist rather than a developmental social psychologist, since some attention to his peer relations and psychosocial distress might have been more pressing than a grammar lesson. Nevertheless, he demonstrates vividly the obstacles facing direct adult attempts at language instruction. McNeill encapsulated the feelings of the first wave of nativist research into child language when he concluded: "Not only is there nothing calling for behaviorist principles in language acquisition, but when situations favorable to response learning are examined, such as imitation or overt practice, one finds no effects that behaviorist principles can explain" (1970, p. 112).

Continuing Progress in the Study of Syntactic Acquisition

Inspired by these early demonstrations, researchers went on to examine more closely, through observational and experimental studies, how children's knowledge of the rules of grammar develop. Careful study of different structures, such as the negative, questions, passives, coordination, relative clauses, and so on, were conducted and, although there is much dispute about the details and the underlying processes, there is general agreement that the acquisition of grammar is a rich, intricate, and relatively swift achievement in which children formulate and revise rules about permissible syntactic structures.

Research into children's early questions, for example, reveal that they seem to progress in ways roughly similar to those we tried out with sentences 1, 4, 5, 6 and 7, above. Very early questions use the simplest of techniques, namely changing the intonation: "See hole? Sit chair?" Soon, children experiment with one or two *wh*-words, usually *what* and *where* ("Whatthat?" "Where Mummy?" "What kitty doing?"). Gradually, they increase their repertoire of *wh*- words (*why, why not, who, when*). For a while, the *wh*- word is the main marker that a question is intended: there are no other modifications of word order and few uses of auxiliary verbs ("What the dollie have?" "Why not me sleeping?"). It is some time before children begin to try out *do*-insertion, and their early attempts differ from adult standards ("*What did you doed?*" "*Why he don't know how to pretend?*") (examples based on Klima and Bellugi, 1966; see also Barrett, 1989; Tyack and Ingram, 1977).

Other research showed that children find it easier to comprehend the active version of a sentence before the passive (Bever, 1970; Maratsos et al., 1985). Even so, some evidence suggests that children begin to use the more complex passive construction as early as the third year, despite its relative infrequency in parental speech (see Marchman et al., 1991, for a review and new data). Children have been found to be able to make the kinds of subtle discriminations between reflexives and pronouns entailed in sentence structures similar to those in sentences 10 and 11, above, by around the age of 4–6 years (Goodluck, 1991; McKee et al., 1993). Children of this age could identify the correct picture to accompany sentences such as "*Is the daddy monkey scratching himself with a stick?*" versus "*Is the daddy monkey scratching him with a stick?*" (McKee et al., 1993). These kinds of achievements do not prove that acquisition is due to innate knowledge, but they do establish that syntactic development reflects extraordinary skills – skills which are possessed by every normal child (see Galligan, 1992; Goodluck, 1991; Stevenson, 1988; for fuller reviews).

Semantic Development

Most of the work we have touched on so far has been concerned with syntax. Another vital component of language is *semantics*, or meaning. Semantic development also provides evidence of quite extraordinary achievements. We noted earlier that a vocabulary explosion begins toward the end of the second year. From then on, new word learning proceeds at a rapid pace. The rate of vocabulary acquisition has been estimated at approximately nine new words per day – or about one every one and a half waking hours (Carey, 1978). It seems unlikely that Staats' cat could have withstood a learning schedule on this scale, and you could wear out a family's newspaper supply whacking this amount of linguistic sense into your feline companion. Similarly, it is difficult to imagine how a child's parents could provide classical conditioning experiences at a sufficient rate.

Still more importantly, it is evident that children do not need this level of intervention to help them acquire new words. Several experimental studies have demonstrated that 2–5-year-olds can learn (or *fast map*) new words on the basis of just one or two exposures to pairings of the word and object or attribute (Carey and Bartlett, 1978; Dickinson, 1984; Dollaghan, 1985; Rice et al., 1990). Even in the fleeting context of television programmes, children of this age can acquire new word meanings swiftly (Rice and Woodsmall, 1988).

This is not to say that the child's initial acquisition of a word's meaning is identical to that understood by adults. Again, studies in both naturalistic contexts and experiments show that children's early meanings tend to be partial and not a simple consequence of adult instruction.

Over-extension and under-extension

A common feature of early vocabularies, for example, is known as *over-extension*: the child uses a word to refer to more things or features than is appropriate in the adult language (Clark, 1993; Shatz, 1994). A French child used the word *bebe* to refer initially to babies, but subsequently applied it to small statues and figures in small pictures; an English child used the word *fly* to refer not only to flies but also to specks of dirt, small insects, his own toes, crumbs of bread, and a toad (Clark, 1973a).

Less common (or less noticeable) is the related phenomenon of *under-extension*, whereby a child uses a general term only to refer to a specific object (e.g. *car* is used exclusively for the family vehicle). Although there is much controversy within child language study about the underlying developmental processes that account for these patterns (cf. Barrett, 1989; Clark, 1983, 1993; Elsen, 1994), it is clear that children's and adults' meanings are not perfectly aligned.

Lexical organization and innovation

Subsequent semantic development provides further evidence that children organize their word knowledge differently from adults. Several experiments have shown that preschoolers sometimes confuse the meanings of related words, such as antonyms *more* and *less* (Donaldson and Balfour, 1968; Palermo, 1973), *before* and *after* (Clark, 1971). Some common words which have multiple meanings tend to be understood by young children only in their dominant sense, and acquisition of the more subtle, derived senses is achieved slowly during middle childhood (Campbell and MacDonald, 1983; Durkin et al., 1986a). Mastering the semantic interrelations among words also develops over several years (Aitchison, 1987; Pease et al., 1993).

Young children also reveal another form of independence as language users in *lexical innovation*, or the creation of new words (Becker, 1994; Chukovsky, 1925; Clark, 1982, 1993). When the child wishes to express a meaning for which she or he does not have a suitable word, then one may be constructed. Among many examples cited by Clark (1982) are a German child, aged 3 years 11 months, who was talking about playing music and created the verb *musiken* (to music); a French 2-year-old who invented *c'est déconstruit, c'est bulldozé* (it's unbuilt, it's bulldozed); and an American 2-year-old who watched his mother feed his baby sister and reported to his father that *Mommy nippled Anna*. Clark argues that children follow a general rule to the effect that any concrete noun can be used as a verb for talking about related activities.

In sum, as researchers turned their attention to other aspects of language development, especially semantics, further impressive attainments of the young learner became apparent. The pace of vocabulary acquisition is remarkable, but underlying the quantitative increases are subtle and not yet fully understood reorganizational changes as children expand and revise their word meanings. Much of children's work in semantic development is covert, not taught directly by adults and often not even noticed except when the child comes up with errors or innovations.

Although there is once again controversy concerning the theoretical explanation of semantic development (see Carey, 1982; Clark, 1983, 1993; Pease et al., 1993), one issue which became much more salient to researchers as they began to pursue this area of language acquisition was that it seemed to lead them, time and time again, to . . . well, the rest of the child. It is difficult to study semantic development without having to address the relationship between lexical knowledge and cognitive and perceptual knowledge. How does the child's development of spatial, quantitative, temporal, and causal vocabulary relate to his or her spatial, quantitative, temporal and causal understanding? It seems unlikely that anyone would go around learning words for things quite independently of learning about the things themselves. But which comes first, language or concept? At this point, the focus on language as a topic in its own right begins to blur. These kinds of concerns led to new developments in the field during the 1970s, and we turn to them shortly. Before moving on, however, we need to return to one of the other central claims of biological accounts of language acquisition, namely that the whole process is preprogrammed to occur during a particular period of development.

Is there a Sensitive Period for Language Acquisition?

In support of a biological account of the origins of language, Lenneberg (1967) pointed to the species-specific anatomical and physiological basis for language, to evidence of cerebral specialization for language functions, to the uniformity of the developmental course of language acquisition, and to the fact that even severely mentally handicapped individuals often achieve a degree of linguistic skill that exceeds their other cognitive competencies. Recall also that research showed subsequently that human infants are capable of discriminating categorically among speech sounds (chapter 2), a facility which would seem to tie in with what nature has in store as the principal means of communication among the species (see Jusczyk and Bertoncini, 1988; Kuhl, 1993).

Lenneberg (1967) proposed that the critical period for acquiring language extended from about one year to puberty. Most contemporary researchers regard the term "critical" as too strong a claim since (as we will see shortly) there is certainly evidence that individuals can make some progress in language acquisition beyond this range. But it remains possible that there is a sensitive period, an optimal time for exposure to the task.

Although many of the details remain unsettled, there is little dispute among researchers that the kinds of developmental phenomena sketched above do tend to occur at roughly the same time in normally developing children all around the world. There are important differences in terms of the rate of acquisition of particular structures according to the complexity of their expression in the target language (Slobin, 1985) but all agree that the toddler years witness substantial linguistic achievements usually resulting in reasonable levels of fluency by the age of 5 or so. This provides circumstantial evidence in support of the Lenneberg–Chomsky assertion of a sensitive period, but does not settle the matter. There is abundant evidence that language development continues past the age of 5, for example (Durkin, 1986b; Karmiloff-Smith, 1986). However, there is abundant evidence that *physical* development continues past the age of 5, too, and this does not lead scientists to reject a role for biology in physical development. Later progress is not in itself a major problem for nativist theories.

A stronger test would involve inhibiting a person's opportunities to learn language during the supposed sensitive period (say, pre-adolescence) and then attempting to teach that person a language belatedly. Another would be to teach a new language to individuals within and beyond the sensitive period, and compare their progress. Both tests have been performed. The first involves studying the language development of feral children and the victims of extreme child abuse. The second involves studies of second language acquisition.

A case study in language acquisition post-puberty

The best-known case is that of Genie, a young woman who was found as a teenager in her Los Angeles home, where she had been kept in a cupboard throughout her childhood with scant human contact other than her deranged father or brother occasionally throwing food in. In stark contrast to children in normal circumstances whose early vocalizations are greeted with parental enthusiasm, Genie was savagely discouraged from making any sounds at all. When she was $13\frac{1}{2}$ years old, her mother managed to escape, taking Genie with her. At this age, Genie neither produced nor understood language and even cried silently. Among extensive remedial assistance and instruction, Genie was taught to use language, and her development was scrutinized closely by a team of psycholinguists, making her a candidate for "the most tested subject in history" (Curtiss et al., 1975).

Here is an example of Genie's language at the age of 18, almost five years after her liberation:

Genie:	Marsha give me square.
Researcher:	When?
G:	In the class. Marsha give me in the class. Marsha in the class.
R:	Which class?

G: One class, two class, three class.
R: What does Marsha do in class?
G: Draw.
R: What does Marsha draw?
G: Sun.
(Curtiss et al., 1975, p. 147)

Genie's language development was slow, and after about five years her sentences were short. Important aspects of English grammar were absent, most notably the use of auxiliary verbs, question formation, and pronouns, and she had difficulties comprehending complex syntax. Her vocabulary expanded and she could maintain a conversation, but her use of intonation was poor, and only people who knew her well could understand much of what she was trying to say. Yet on some other cognitive measures, Genie showed faster development, attaining most aspects of concrete operational intelligence within four years of her freedom. In certain perceptual tasks she performed at normal levels, and in others she had high-level competence (Curtiss, 1989). Curtiss interprets these discrepancies as indicating that the left hemisphere had atrophied due to lack of language stimulation in early childhood. In short, Genie did make some progress with language, but the outcome was incomplete; this is consistent with at least a weak version of the sensitive period hypothesis.

Second language acquisition within and beyond the sensitive period

The second test of the sensitive period hypothesis suggested above was to compare the second language learning progress of adults and children placed in a foreign community. Snow and Hoefnagel-Hohle (1978) conducted such a study with a group of American families temporarily resident in The Netherlands. This enabled them to compare the progress of children aged 8–10 years, adolescents (12–15 years) and adults. The subjects were assessed at three-monthly intervals during their first year in the country. Contrary to what might be expected on the basis of the sensitive period hypothesis, the adolescents and the adults outperformed the younger subjects on a range of pronunciation, grammatical, and translation tasks. Long (in press) reviews several other studies of younger and older subjects learning a variety of second languages, and in most cases the older subjects fared better.

Long points out, however, that most of the available studies have assessed development during the *early* stages of exposure to the new language. He argues that experienced language users may have a temporary advantage. It could be that adults outperform children initially because they have superior cognitive abilities which they could apply to any task to relative advantage; but ultimately language acquisition may involve other, covert processes which unfold over time, if they are still accessible, and it may be here that younger individuals have an advantage. Long also reviews evidence from longer-term studies of second language acquisition, and here the evidence is decidedly in the opposite direction: only individuals who start to learn a second language before the age of 15, and ideally before the age of 6, achieve native-like proficiency. In one example, Johnson and Newport (1989) compared the English language skills of immigrant American adults whose first languages were Chinese or Korean. Success in English was closely related to age of entry to the US: the younger the individual upon arrival, the better her or his grammatical abilities.

Summary

The excitement of Chomskyan claims led to widespread interest in the study of child language. Investigations of spontaneous production, imitations, and comprehension supported the view that normal language acquisition does involve rapid progress, implicit rule formulation, continuous revision and reorganization of specific linguistic knowledge. An analogy with biological growth seemed, to many, to fit rather well the miracle of language acquisition.

But others had their doubts. Note that the theoretical origins of much of this work came from outside the discipline which normally undertakes principal responsibility for studying the human mind. Psychologists reacted vigorously to Chomsky's ideas in the 1960s and 1970s and, although many were sympathetic, others were skeptical of claims about the relationship between linguists' representations of grammar and the structures and processes in people's heads as they produce and understand language. In particular, cognitive developmental psychologists began to challenge the plausibility of the innatist theory as an account of how children acquire language; we consider next some of their objections.

Cognitive Developmental Approaches to Language Acquisition

In summarizing research into semantic development, above, we saw that it proved difficult to study children's lexical knowledge for very long without considering more general theories of cognitive development. This led to a new twist in language acquisition research: the possibility that language learning emerged not from an innate grammatical specification but from a constructed cognitive basis.

Clearly, children do not go around emitting bursts of increasingly intricate syntax just for the fun of exercising their language faculty; among other things, they have meanings to convey and negotiate. The child's meanings must be related to her or his conceptual understanding, and conceptual understanding is the stuff of mainstream cognitive developmental psychology. Indeed, Brown (1973), although concluding that the structures of Stage I speech were probably universals, felt that they were extensions of a universal level of early intelligence, namely the sensorimotor stage of Piagetian theory, rather than an innate knowledge of grammar. He pointed out, for example, that nomination (*that ball*) depends on the ability to recognize objects and actions; specifying location requires spatial knowledge (*ball there*), agent–action expressions depend on grasping the relationship between an actor and an event (*Adam hit ball*).

At around the same time, researchers of early word meaning began to explore other links between semantic development and cognition. Clark (1973a) argued that much of the child's early word meanings were "mapped onto" previously acquired perceptual and conceptual knowledge. Clark (1973b) showed that children's comprehension of simple spatial relational terms (such as *in*, *on*, and *under*) seemed to reflect nonlinguistic strategies for dealing with the environment. Children tended to respond to instructions to put something *in* a container before they could respond correctly to instructions to put something *on* the container; this order of acquisition seemed to correspond to an early nonlinguistic tendency to put objects in containers (reflecting the child's active engagement with the physical environment), rather than the abstract semantic properties of the words themselves. Each of these claims led to a flurry of objections and further research, but they also led to a more general interest among language acquisition researchers in the role of cognition. And this led back to the dominant theory of cognitive development, Jean Piaget's.

Piaget on Language Acquisition

According to Piaget, language is just one manifestation of a more general symbolic capacity developing toward the end of the sensorimotor period. The driving force of development is held to be the construction of intelligent thought, and from Piaget's perspective language comes "from outside" (1971, p. 72) and is therefore not fundamental. In an early work, he remarked that: "with children thought is indeed more original in its character than language" (1929, p. 39), an article of faith which may explain why decades later he found it hard to embrace the enthusiasm for linguistic creativity as emphasized by Chomsky. For Piaget, it is inconsistent with his theory of unified stage structures to give language a special place.

One of the clearest statements of the Piagetian perspective on language development is provided by Sinclair-de-Zwart (1969, pp. 330–331) who comments: "Much of the need for postulating specific, innate linguistic structures seems to vanish if one considers language acquisition within the total cognitive framework and, in particular, within the frame of the symbolic function." Sinclair-de-Zwart's (1967) own research addressed the relationship between what Piagetians regard as one of the major cognitive attainments, namely conservation (see chapter 1), and aspects of linguistic development. She compared French-speaking conservers, non-conservers, and children who were intermediate on conservation tasks, on linguistic comprehension and production tasks concerned with size terms and comparatives (*beaucoup, plus que*).

Conservation status made no difference to performance on comprehension tasks, which most subjects could handle well. But on production tasks, where the subject was prompted to describe a relationship, there were marked differences between conservers and non-conservers. Conservers used comparatives very frequently (*le garçon a plus que la fille* – the boy has more than the girl), whereas the nonconservers typically used absolute terms (*le garçon a beaucoup, la fille a peu* – the boy has a lot, the girl has little). A subsequent attempt to teach nonconservers how to use comparatives proved very difficult, and even when the terms were used very few subjects showed corresponding improvements in conservation performance. Sinclair-de-Zwart concluded that the acquisition of the syntax of comparison (terms like *more than, less than, as much as*) is very closely linked to cognitive progress from preoperational to concrete operational thought.

The Cognition Hypothesis

The suggestion that the idea of innate structures could vanish became very popular for a while in developmental psycholinguistics as part of a general reaction against the nativist camp, and in the 1970s several different positions were propounded concerning the ways in which broader cognitive and perceptual development might affect linguistic development (Bates, 1976; Beilin, 1975; Clark, 1973a, b; Cromer, 1974; Nelson, 1974; Macnamara, 1977; Sinclair-de-Zwart, 1969). Space does not permit a full review of these arguments here, but they have in common the assumption that cognitive developments precede and set limits for language acquisition. Cromer (1974; reprinted in Cromer, 1991) distinguished usefully between strong and weak versions of this "cognition hypothesis." According to the strong version, language development is entirely dependent on cognitive development, closely following it in time and reflecting its structures in detail. According to the weak version, we are able to use particular linguistic structures "only when our cognitive abilities enable us to do so."

The strong version of the cognition hypothesis is another manifestation of lopsided developmentalism (see chapter 1). The stages of cognitive development are presumed to determine the content of all that is learned. In fact, Cromer concluded that there is not much support for the strong version, since studies of language acquisition were revealing processes and reorganizations that were not easily explained in terms of existing models of cognitive development.

Cromer (1974) favored instead the weak version of the hypothesis. This version is moderately lopsided, too, since it assumes all constraints are internal and one dimension of the developing mind sets all the limits. However, Cromer did not develop this claim very far, and it is difficult to see how it could account for detailed relationships between particular cognitive capacities and specific linguistic knowledge or processes. Curtiss (1989) points out that to specify how children recognise and exploit the structural principles that are held to be common to cognition and language is scarcely trivial – and this has not yet been done by any of the cognitive developmental models of language acquisition. In fact, one of the most extensive empirical investigations of links between cognitive development and language development, conducted by a researcher very sympathetic to Piagetian theory, found evidence only of modest correlations and was forced to conclude that a direct relationship could not be found (Beilin, 1975).

Problems for the cognition hypothesis

Strong and weak versions of the cognition hypothesis remain influential, but there are at least three main problems facing this perspective. The first is that even its proponents were swift to qualify it, and most acknowledged that language has unique properties not easily accounted for by other models of cognitive development. For example, Sinclair-de-Zwart later modified her position on the extent to which Piagetian theory could account for language acquisition, retreating to the claim that "the closest link between language and intelligent activity dealing with reality is to be found during the earliest period of language learning" (1973, p. 12). But since some of the most distinctive features of language (such as structure-dependent rules) are not present during the earliest period, this does not amount to a very strong challenge to theories, such as Chomsky's and other nativists', that assume highly specific properties to language.

Even at the earliest stages, it is not clear that a particular cognitive development invariably precedes the relevant language development. Yarrow et al. (1975) report only weak (and sometimes negative) correlations between measures of early language development and measures of cognitive development. Gopnik (1984) tested the relationship between the development of the object concept (a major achievement of the sensorimotor period, according to Piaget) and the use of *gone* (identified by Brown and others as a very common word in early language use). Rather than *gone* appearing after the establishment of the object concept (as Piagetian theory would predict), Gopnik found that children used the word frequently *as they developed* the concept, suggesting that they use it to help encode the concept. Similar results were obtained in a cross-linguistic extension of this work, involving English-speaking and Korean-speaking children (Gopnik and Choi, 1990). The latter study also yielded evidence that object categorization emerged later in Korean children, and the authors relate this to differences in the ways appearance and disappearance are expressed in the two languages. Nouns are emphasized less in Korean, and this may lead children to pay less attention to the kinds of object categorization that nouns encode.

The second problem is that evidence from individuals who suffered exceptional abuse or deprivation as children, or intellectual impairment or trauma, points to a dissociation between the development of combinatorial linguistic abilities (i.e. syntax) and conceptual and semantic knowledge (Curtiss, 1989). That is, some children develop good syntactic and morphological skills alongside very poor vocabulary and propositional ability, while others develop reasonably good – sometimes even exceptional – cognitive abilities yet never master the basic rules of syntax. (We have already considered Genie; Curtiss provides several other fascinating case studies.) In his later work, Cromer (1991) acknowledged evidence of dissociation as a major stumbling block for the cognition hypothesis.

The third reason why the cognition hypothesis became less influential was that just as language acquisition researchers had found that language was in some way related to the rest of the child, so they discovered next that the child is related to other people. The contexts of language acquisition are diverse, but they invariably involve other language users. As Dore (1985) comments, cognitive psychology in general is biased toward the study of the individual and is limited – Dore suggests "incapable" (p. 55) – as a basis for explaining something as inherently social as linguistic development. This brings us to a whole new wave of language acquisition research, leading to a more social framework, to which we turn in the following chapter.

Summary

Cognitive developmentalists tend to regard most changes in the child's capacities as constrained by general cognitive progress. In response to the nativist surge in developmental psycholinguistics during the 1960s and 1970s, cognitive developmentalists, especially Piagetians, proposed that language should be seen as a symbolic capacity regulated by the child's cognitive level. The strong version of this hypothesis was swiftly abandoned, in light of evidence of linguistic structures for which existing models of cognitive development had no obvious counterpart. The weak version of the hypothesis survives, though the ontogenetic sequence of related concepts and vocabulary is disputable, and even leading protagonists (such as Cromer, 1991) acknowledge that the hypothesis faces difficulties in explaining the evidence from exceptional children of a dissociation between cognitive and linguistic abilities.

Conclusions

We have just touched the surface of language acquisition, but it is clear that it is a remarkable achievement, not easily explained in terms of traditional developmental theories. In several respects, Chomsky's nativist arguments that language is an innate, species-specific faculty stand up best and, in fact, most researchers working in this field agree that some biological endowments must be implicated. A lot of controversy remains over exactly what these might be and how richly structured they are.

Another interesting feature of Chomsky's case which is worth noting is that it reveals an unusual side to a biological theory. While biological theories are often associated with deterministic assumptions (for example, that a species' development or behavior is determined by its genes), Chomsky's view is that the biologically given specificity of the human language capacity is what makes possible our creativity and freedom (cf. Chomsky, 1972). Indeed, Chomsky castigates environmental theories (such as Skinner's) for attributing causation to external forces (social determinism), and for failing to acknowledge the richness of the organism.

But there is still another aspect to language development, one which is represented inadequately by learning theories and ignored or discounted by nativist and cognitive developmental theories: other people. We saw that Chomsky's reasoning was, in a nutshell, if this is so difficult for linguists, how does a child do it? In other words, Chomsky sees the child as a kind of mini-linguist, much as Piagetians see the child as a mini-scientist. The Piagetian response, in another nutshell, is that since the child is doing so much anyway it is perfectly conceivable that learning to symbolize and to sign can be incorporated into general constructive procedures. Both see the individual child as the driving force, and neither sees a great deal of interest in the social context. In the next chapter, we consider some different positions on this issue.

Further reading

Barrett, M. (1989) Early language development. In A. Slater and G. Bremner (eds), *Infant Development*. Hillsdale, NJ: Erlbaum.

An excellent account of the emergence of early vocabulary and the beginnings of combinatorial speech.

Clark, E. V. (1993) *The Lexicon in Acquisition*. Cambridge: Cambridge University Press.

An advanced but accessible review of the past two decades' research into children's vocabulary development. Clark presents an influential theory of her own and amasses data from several different languages to identify common paths followed by young word learners.

Cromer, R. F. (1991) *Language and Thought in Normal and Handicapped Children*. Oxford: Blackwell.

A careful exposition and assessment of the cognition hypothesis, the work it inspired and its limitations as a theory of language acquisition.

Gibson, K. R. and Ingold, T. (eds) (1993) *Tools, Language and Cognition in Human Evolution*. Cambridge: Cambridge University Press.

Multidisciplinary perspectives on the origins of language, with useful discussions of the links among language, gesture, and tool use.

Gleason, J. B. (ed.) (1993) *The Development of Language*, 3rd edn. New York: Macmillan.

Well-written, up-to-date chapters on the main areas of language acquisition.

Goodluck, H. (1991) *Language Acquisition: a linguistic introduction*. Oxford: Blackwell.

A lucid integration of linguistic theory and language acquisition research, with a particular emphasis on recent Chomskyan grammar.

Moerk, E. L. (1992) *A First Language Taught and Learned*. Baltimore: Brookes.

Rejecting nativist theories of language acquisition as premature, one-sided, and, "a considerable setback to the field", Moerk reports a detailed microanalytic study of the interactions between Eve (of Brown's sample) and her mother, and argues strongly that language *is* taught. Interestingly, Moerk rests his case finally on a biological metaphor, comparing language instruction to kiss feeding in some bird species, whereby the mother premasticates food to simplify its digestion by the young.

Piatelli-Palmarini, M. (ed.) (1980) *Language and Learning: the debate between Jean Piaget and Noam Chomsky*. London: Routledge and Kegan Paul.

The dispute between the Chomskyan and Piagetian camps culminated in a full-scale debate arranged near Paris in 1975, with each of the protagonists and his eminent supporters present. Although there were representatives from linguistics, developmental psychology, philosophy, artificial intelligence, neurobiology, and anthropology, no social psychologists seem to have been invited. Nevertheless, the outcome is a stimulating volume, in which some of the leading scientists of language and cognition outline and discuss their ideas; intriguingly, none of them considers the relevance of the observation that people use language to communicate with other people.

Chapter 7

Language Development II: Social Dimensions of Acquisition and Use

Language is not limited to organic correlates; it has social and technical ones as well. There is no a priori reason for giving precedence to one at the expense of the other or for claiming that one is more fundamental than the other. There is less justification than ever for this sort of precedence now that we know how important a role the social factor must have played in the evolution of the species.

(*Moscovici*, The Psychosociology of Language, *1972*)

One thing I am sure of, from these twenty-one transcripts and my longitudinal records of Adam, Eve, and Sarah, is that just as children will not be pushed, parents will not be discouraged. Put off for the moment by an undiagnosably irrelevant response, they retreat only to return to that attack at a better time. Again and again in the twenty-one transcripts a particular sentence type elicits a nonsequitur *or a blank stare, and the adult gives it up — for the time being.*

(*Brown*, "The maintenance of conversation," *1980*)

In chapter 6, we focused on the question of the origins of language in the individual child. Does language learning depend on parental training and reinforcement? Does the language faculty grow like other organs? Or is language mapped onto cognitive development? We saw that as researchers sought answers to these questions they were led increasingly to take account of the interconnections between language and other developmental processes in the child. In this chapter, we take account of another level of interconnection: that between the child and other people.

The nativists' hostility to learning theory explanations of language acquisition, together with early demonstrations such as Brown's (1973) that parental examples or instruction could not account for order of acquisition, had brought about a general downplaying of the social environment. However, particularly as researchers studied development naturalistically in children's everyday contexts, it became difficult to sustain this lack of interest in whom the child was talking to, and what they said. Investigations of these questions led to a whole new wave of child language research, focusing very much on the social contexts of acquisition and on the ways in which language is put to use by children and their caregivers in social interaction.

This chapter is organized in three main sections. In the first, we continue the acquisition question, asking: could social interaction provide the foundation for language learning? The answer is "maybe"; some thought at first that a return to parents' input could uncover a tutorial basis within which children are taught language, but some maintain that parental speech is of minimal relevance, and others argue that in some respects parental speech may even complicate the learner's task still further. In many respects, the mechanisms of acquisition still remain a mystery, but one outcome of this social redirection is that greater attention has begun to be paid to children's *use* of language, and this is now an important research topic in its own right. In the second section, we review some of the ways in which children learn to use language, focusing on conversational development, including referential communication (in which a speaker adapts his or her speech to take account of the listener's perspective) and the emergence of politeness conventions. Finally, in the third section, we move from the micro-processes of interaction to consider differences and adaptations at the macro-level of language varieties. We ask: do differences between language styles result in developmental differences, and how do members of different linguistic communities relate to others? By this stage, we begin to make contact again with mainstream social psychology, because many anecdotal and observational findings concerning attitudes toward language style can be accounted for in terms of a particular social psychological model of language use.

Language Acquisition in its Social Contexts

It became clear in the previous chapter that there are many different methodologies for studying language acquisition. Much has been gained by means of experimental studies, concerned with aspects of comprehension or production. As with all good psychological experiments, these techniques enable the researcher to identify a specific research question, to design appropriate stimulus materials and to manipulate the conditions under which the subject responds. But child language researchers rapidly became interested in studying the child's language in more naturalistic environments, too, in order to chart the emergence of particular structures and meanings and to investigate the relationships between what the child was doing and what she or he was saying.

The latter kinds of studies began to uncover individual differences in the early course of language acquisition (e.g. Lieven, 1978; Nelson, 1981b), arguably a problem for nativist theories which hold that language development is a biologically preprogrammed universal. That there are differences in *pace* of acquisition was not the issue: researchers began to find that there appeared to be different *routes* into language. For example, Nelson (1973) found that some infants emphasized object labels in their early vocabularies. She called these "referential" children, and argued that their approach to language was analytic and information oriented. Other children had fewer labels but more action words, pronouns and personal–social expressions. Nelson called these "expressive" children, and proposed that they had a more holistic, message-oriented style of language learning.

Other studies also revealed individual differences in mothers' interactional styles (Ellis and Wells, 1980; Howe, 1981; McDonald and Pien, 1982; Pine, 1990) and variability across contexts (Wells, 1986), indicating that language development might well be affected by aspects of the environment. Still more crucially, such studies showed that linguistic interactions between parents and young children were rich, highly structured and meaningful social contexts (Howe, 1981; Lock, 1980). Interactions involving early language did not occur out of nowhere, but continued a longstanding mutual interest that had been developing from the very beginnings of the parent–child relationship. It began to appear implausible that these interactions were irrelevant to the processes of language acquisition.

And so the environment began to come back into the picture. This new shift of interest led initially to a development analogous to the cognition hypothesis, and it was first thought that there might be a "social basis" to language acquisition.

A Social Basis to Language Acquisition?

One line of argument is based on continuities from the prelinguistic period to early language. As we saw in chapter 2, parents and infants alternate their vocal behaviors well before the child begins to use or comprehend language, seemingly engaging in "protoconversations." It has also been found that the transition period from prelinguistic communication to first words involves increasingly sophisticated uses of gestures as the child strives to make him or herself better understood (Bates et al., 1975; Bullowa, 1979; Marcos and Pezé, 1989; Murphy and Messer, 1977; Zinober and Martlew, 1985). In the course of sharing meanings, parents appear particularly sensitive to early attempts by the infant to coordinate gesture and vocalization (Martinsen and Smith, 1989). Harris et al. (1995) found a positive correlation between the first appearance of pointing and the first understanding of object words.

The development of joint attention and formats: assisting language acquisition?

We also saw in chapter 2 that parents strive to share infants' attention. They monitor what the infant is doing and what he or she is looking at, and join in. It is possible that these activities have implications for early language development. Once joint attention is achieved, parents exploit it with structured, repetitive exchanges that allow for the practice of simple verbal skills and the emphasis of new labels (Bruner, 1983a,b). Several researchers have demonstrated that parents tend to make verbal reference to objects or actions which have been established as the focus of joint attention (Collis, 1977; D'Odorico and Franco, 1985; Messer, 1983, 1994). An interesting study by Baldwin and Markman (1989) showed that infants attended longer to objects which had been labeled, suggesting that the use of labels signifies something worth taking note of. Furthermore, the extent to which mothers vary in the frequency of their joint attention, or the focus they emphasize, has been found in several studies to correlate at least moderately with individual differences in aspects of early language use by the child (Akhtar et al., 1991; Goldfield, 1986, 1990; Smith et al., 1988; Tomasello and Todd, 1983). For example, Goldfield (1985/ 86) found in case studies of a referential and an expressive child that their mothers had distinct styles of interaction, such that the referential child's mother was more likely to label and describe toys, while the expressive child's mother focused more on interpersonal issues and was more socially expressive.

Shared attention is exploited in relation to other language skills, such as conversation. Bruner and his colleagues proposed that parents and children jointly evolve *formats*, or rule-bound activity routines, within which the child has many opportunities to relate language to familiar play. Parents and infants play simple give-and-take or hide-and-seek games, in the course of which the adult uses the same words many times and sets up turns for the child. In this way, shared frameworks or "scaffolds" are constructed which may help the child to discover how to use language and to understand the rules of dialogue (Bruner, 1978, 1983a). One format which is very popular in many homes is picture book reading (figure 7.1), and in a longitudinal case study, Ninio and Bruner (1978) found that mothers used labels extensively and inserted them skillfully into the dialogue in ways which appeared "well suited to the teaching of labelling" (p. 6). Research by Whitehurst and his colleagues has shown that gains in early language development can be brought about by having parents implement specific teaching strategies in the course of picture book reading (Whitehurst et al., 1988, 1994).

Speech Addressed to Children

Yet another line of argument has been based on the nature of speech addressed to children. Recall that Chomsky (1965) held that one of the reasons language acquisition was so impressive was that the actual data available to the child were degenerate, exposing the learner to "fragments and deviant expressions," making a difficult task

Figure 7.1   Picture book reading: this activity involves joint attention, pointing gestures, and verbal labeling.

all the more obscure. These assumptions seemed very persuasive when Chomsky first articulated them. They followed naturally from Chomsky's account of the underlying complexity of natural language, and from his competence–performance distinction. Unfortunately, they overlooked an important piece of evidence. When adults speak to children, they tend to modify their language.

In fact, a number of studies demonstrated that, in comparison with adult–adult speech, adults speaking to infants and toddlers tend to provide much shorter utterances, to simplify the syntax, to raise the pitch for emphasis, and to repeat or paraphrase much of what they say (Messer, 1981; Phillips, 1973; Snow, 1972). In the light of this kind of evidence, which became abundant in the early 1970s, it began to seem that, quite contrary to Chomsky's speculations, parents and other adults provide "language lessons" to young learners (Levelt, 1975; Snow, 1972). Indeed, it first appeared that the lessons were skillfully graded, such that as the child's linguistic abilities advanced, the parents raised the level of their input. It was suggested that parents "fine tune" the structure of their language so that "the input is closely tailored to the child's linguistic requirements" (Cross, 1977, p. 154). The distinctive speech register that adults adopt when speaking to children has been called *motherese* or *parentese*, although it is by no means unique to parents. It was demonstrated subsequently that even children modify their speech to younger children (Dunn and Kendrick, 1982; Sachs and Devin, 1976; Shatz and Gelman, 1973; Trehub et al.,

1994; Zukow, 1989). We noted evidence in chapter 2 that infants prefer to listen to this form of modified speech.

In contrast to Chomsky's LAD, Bruner (1983a, b) proposed that a major factor underlying language acquisition was a LASS, or Language Acquisition Support System. Moerk (1989) has argued still more strongly that "the LAD was a lady," namely the lady who does most of the talking to the child (the mother). The mother, in Moerk's view, not only simplifies input but also breaks it down into helpful illustrative segments for the learner to practice and build upon. In a re-analysis of Brown's transcripts for his subject Eve, Moerk (1991) found many instances of corrective feedback in maternal responses to child utterances, thus challenging one of the fundamental tenets of the nativist camp (see also Bohannon and Stanowicz, 1988; Demetras et al., 1986; Moerk, 1992).

In sum, language acquisition seems to represent an extension – albeit a very sophisticated extension – of the processes of meaningful interaction that caregiver and child have constructed over several months. Many parents (especially those willing to be subjects of research) tend to be very interested in their children, and work hard to achieve joint attention with them. Parents know the names for more things than the child does, and often set up formats of joint play in which they introduce labels and get the child to practice them. Parents (and others) adjust the complexity of language to the children.

Does this provide an explanation for the mystery of language acquisition? Unfortunately, as with everything else in the study of language, things proved not to be so straightforward.

Some Problems for the Social Basis Perspective

While the involvement of (at least some) parents in language acquisition processes is established by these kinds of studies, the actual mechanisms by which development comes about are still obscure (Durkin, 1987b; Hayes, 1984; Shatz, 1981, 1994). It might be helpful to extend Cromer's (1974, 1991) distinction between strong and weak versions of the cognitive hypothesis (chapter 6) to the social basis hypothesis. A strong version of the hypothesis would hold that language acquisition is entirely dependent upon social support; a weak version holds that social experience certainly has something to do with language acquisition, but it acknowledges that "social" behavior is bidirectional rather than a deterministic, externally controlled process (see chapter 1).

Several problems confront the strong version. These concern the renewed enthusiasm for parents as teachers and the assumption of continuity from prelinguistic interaction to language. First, the relationship between gestural development and the emergence of language is not consistent across children. Zinober and Martlew (1985) in two detailed longitudinal studies found that their subjects followed different routes from gesture to words but by around 20 months had achieved equivalent linguistic status. Studies of maternal gestures and language found that the relationship was not always obvious (Schaffer et al., 1983; Schnur and Shatz, 1984).

Second, where relationships are found between parental language and children's vocabulary, they tend to be clearest in respect of very early language. Barrett et al. (1991) and Hart (1991) found with respect to vocabulary development that there was a strong relationship between maternal input and children's first few words, but as the child's vocabulary increased the relationship weakened. Rome-Flanders et al. (in press), in a substantial longitudinal study, found no correlation between parental scaffolding attempts and subsequent vocabulary development.

Third, early findings suggesting that parents fine tune their linguistic input also proved not to be consistent with the evidence (Cross, 1977; Gleitman, et al., 1984; Newport et al., 1977). The complexity of parental syntax did not correlate very well with developments in children's language. Gleitman et al. (1984) did find some evidence of positive relationships between the complexity of maternal speech and aspects of syntactic development among children aged 18–21 months, but the same pattern did not hold for a sample aged 24–25 months. Thus, some degree of correlation may be there when language is minimal, but it reduces or even disappears as language gets going. There is reasonably consistent evidence of a moderate correlation between maternal use of *yes/no* questions and child use of auxiliaries, but the causal direction is not easily determined (see Richards and Robinson, 1993). It is important to note that even where correlations between input and output are found, they are based only on *rate* of development (Shatz, 1981), and therefore do not tell us a great deal about the structures of the child's grammatical knowledge. The fact that one child uses, say, auxiliaries (*be, is, are*) more frequently than another does not necessarily mean that the second child lacks the relevant grammatical knowledge, only that she uses it less frequently.

Fourth, the fact that parents modify their speech does not confirm that this brings about acquisition. It has also been found that adults use a similar speech style when talking to pet dogs (Hirsh-Pasek and Treiman, 1982), and Prince Charles is rumored to lecture his vegetables in this fashion: none of these addressees learn language. Cross-cultural studies have revealed some communities in which parents do not modify their language to their infants to anything like the extent found in studies of middle-class Westerners (Heath, 1983; Pye, 1986; Schieffelin, 1990) and other communities in which parents use culture-specific routines that seem to be motivated more by the need to preserve folklore rather than by intuitive attempts to teach language structure (Reger and Gleason, 1991). Bornstein et al. (1991b) report that, among middle-class samples, French mothers address their infants much less frequently in the modifed speech register than do American parents, and use normal adult–adult conversational tones more frequently in child-addressed speech than do American mothers. In another cross-linguistic study, Bornstein, et al. (1992) report some similarities and some differences among the contents and interactive strategies of maternal speech to infants in Argentina, France, Japan, and the US. Yet in all of these cases the children turn out to learn language anyway.

Another useful test of the impact of parental speech would be to compare the language development of twins or triplets, who are presumably exposed to pretty much the same input. Schaerlaekens (1973) conducted such a test with two sets of Dutch triplets, and found that there were considerable individual differences among the children in terms of both the pace of development and the structures of their early grammars. It is difficult to explain these findings in terms of fine tuning or direct environmental shaping of language acquisition. For these and a variety of other reasons, the idea of fine tuning and parental language lessons has now been largely abandoned (see Snow, 1986).

In short, research into the relationship between language acquisition and early social interaction has not uncovered an easier route for the child into the mysteries of language that was once predicted (see also Camaioni et al., 1984; Collis, 1985; Schaffer, 1989b). Does this mean that the social context of language acquisition is (a) irrelevant to the achievement itself, and (b) not deserving of further research? Not necessarily. For example, there is persuasive evidence that the provision of certain types of input, such as *recasting* (in which the adult elaborates an expression initially provided by the child) may trigger the use of new syntactic forms (Baker and Nelson, 1984; Nelson, 1977; Nelson et al., 1995; Pemberton and Watkins, 1987; Whitehurst et al., 1988). This indicates that adult input can be useful as a catalyst to the learner who is ready to proceed, though it leaves open the question of whether it is *necessary* in the normal course of acquisition (cf. Baker and Nelson, 1984; Nelson et al., 1984). It also leaves unsettled the question of what children themselves contribute to the acquisition process and how children cope with the diversity, complexity and sometimes impoverished nature of input in everyday circumstances. Many mysteries remain, but it appears likely that a social explanation will be required which takes account of both environmental stimuli *and* the child's own activity.

Language as Interaction

Although the vast amount of research into the social basis of language acquisition has not come up with the results anticipated, it has led to a major reorientation in how we conceive of children's language and their involvements with other language users. Specifically, it has focused attention on the fact that language *use* in childhood is predominantly social – that is, it is undertaken most of the time with other people (not all of the time, since children like to practice language on their own, when they go to bed; see Kuczaj, 1983). It has begun to expose to enquiry the nature of the social–linguistic interactions that children and their caregivers engage in. Language is not only something children know, but something they *do*. It will be argued below that, on closer inspection, these interactions turn out not to be a matter of harmonious tuning, but complex, multi-level transactions involving a certain amount of "fumbling and bumbling" (Robinson, 1984) and a good deal of work by the learner. Hence, rather than being irrelevant to language acquisition, a social perspective raises the possibility that the achievement may actually be *more* remarkable than was earlier supposed in the first waves of Chomsky-inspired psycholinguistics.

The non-simplicity of parental language

It has often been concluded that because, on some measures, parental speech to infants is simpl*er* than adult–adult speech that it is simple *per se*. But this does not follow logically. For example, psychobiology may be simpler than social psychology (it involves fewer variables, more straightforward causal theories, a more limited vocabulary), but that does not mean that it is a simple topic. It does not follow phenomenologically, either: that is, parentese may appear "simple" to those of us who already know the language, but things might be different from the perspective of the learner. In fact, early analyses suggested that in some respects parentese is quite complex (Newport et al., 1977). Wexler (1982) points out that there has been a tendency to equate "short" with simple (i.e., most researchers agree that, on average, sentences addressed to young children are shorter than sentences addressed to adults). Many of the short utterances consist of single words or interjections; many of the full sentences are imperatives or questions (Gleitman and Wanner, 1982). Since not all of the grammatical structures children have to learn are short, this limitation of the input actually provides *less* information to the learner than he or she will need. Similarly, since the child needs to learn to produce the simplest, active declarative sentences before advancing to questions and other complicated forms, then it seems unhelpful to swamp him or her with instructions and interrogatives.

There are other ways in which parental modifications, motivated by social–communicative or pedagogical goals, may complicate the nature of the linguistic model the child is encouraged to work with (Durkin, 1987b). To take a concrete example, one familiar speech modification of adults talking to children is the substitution of a proper name for a personal pronoun. A mother might say "Give it to Mummy" or "David do it" (Conti-Ramsden, 1989; Durkin et al., 1982). This speech adjustment has been reported among parents of a number of languages, including English, Japanese, Romanian, and Serbo-Croat (Ferguson, 1977; Jocic, 1976). On first sight, such a modification might appear linguistically helpful, since it gets around the rather difficult problem of determining who is the referent of a personal pronoun. In the space of moments, "I" can be me as I speak, or you as you take the floor – or someone else if she joins our conversation. Learning the meaning of *I* (or *you*) poses a considerable challenge, and the acquisition of personal pronouns is a problematic area of early grammar for many children (Bamberg et al., 1991; Charney, 1980; Chiat, 1986; Oshima-Takane, 1992).

However, parental speech modifications in this area are not consistent. Sometimes they use proper names, sometimes they use pronouns, and sometimes they mix them both together in the same utterance (e.g., "I think Mummy might have to blow hers," where *I*, *Mummy*, and *hers* all refer to the same person; see Durkin, 1987b, for further examples). Durkin and colleagues argue that the parent's motivation is to facilitate immediate communication and behavior management rather than to help with language acquisition. Consistent with this interpretation, Conti-Ramsden (1989) found that when parents were in an experimental condition which explicitly required them to teach a particular task they increased substantially the frequency with which they used proper names. None the less, the modification has a consequence for the child's language, since he or she, too, soon starts to use it, coming up with utterances like "David want one" (by David) or "Mummy give me" (to Mummy; see Durkin et al., 1982). Baron (1992, p. 112) reports a 2-year-old's request to her mother "Please carry you", meaning *Please carry me*, and closely related to her mother's constant refrain "I don't always need to carry you, Sara." Atkinson (1986, p. 106) quotes another young speaker (age not given) who violated a general principle of adult grammar with the retort: "I said mummy night-night."

Durkin (1987b) comments that parents and child language researchers often greet these early utterances by the child as cute idiosyncracies or manifestations of intermediate grammars. The point is that children may well work on the data provided by their caregivers (motivated by purposes of social control) and initially incorporate them into their own language (we might speculate what, for example, mummy had just said to Atkinson's informant). In due course – through processes that are scarcely understood – children have to discard these patterns, in order to approximate to the target language.

Rather than parents being naturally attuned teachers of language, then, it seems to be the case that once they attempt (deliberately or intuitively) to teach they introduce further complications or even ungrammatical expressions into the setting (see Durkin et al., 1986b; see also, Durkin, 1993, for similar arguments with respect to parental teaching of number words and counting). A further example is provided in an interesting case study by Chafetz et al. (1992) who analyzed the speech of a mother and father in the course of interactions with their young children. These investigators found that when the parents, who spoke normal grammatical English to adults, set about teaching language (for example, names for things, syntax) they introduced ungrammatical structures (such as "she a puppet," "is that shoe," "orange go there," "you no break them") which were not part of their dialect. Studies of sibling speech to infants and toddlers have also shown that on closer inspection the modifications introduced here are not invariably simplifications or helpful scaffolds (Dunn and Kendrick, 1982; Mannle et al., 1991).

In short, language input to young language learners is not simple, but departs from adult–adult language in interesting ways. Some of it, as Chomsky observed, is fragmentary and deviant. Since it is not simple and not finely tuned, since different members of the family (e.g., parents *v.* siblings) produce different versions of it, and since children are also exposed to large doses of "regular" language (i.e., via overhearing adults, via television), quite how they make sense of it all becomes a greater mystery than we first thought. Part of the answer may lie in social interaction, but it may be that the *mis*understandings between language learners and their partners are more important than the theories of attunement and harmony supposed.

Parent–child misunderstanding

Perhaps one of the most important findings of recent research into parent–child interactions is that they do *not* consistently understand each other perfectly well after all. As Service et al. (1989, p. 34) remind us "to err is only human," and mothers and babies do err regularly. This has important implications for what they do next. For example, Golinkoff (1983) shows that infants on the verge of the transition to speech are often misunderstood by their parents. These miscommunications frequently lead to episodes of negotiation, wherein each party tries to clarify. Parents reformulate their utterances, or attempt to guess at what the child means. Infants use gestures and other attention-orienting devices to help make clearer what they want, and in so doing discover that other people do not invariably understand their signals. Service et al. (1989) show that parents will work very hard to remedy miscommunications, using every trick they can think of to get their point across. Golinkoff (1983) comments that if children did not experience communication failures then they could reasonably assume that all they ever need to do is to want something, make any kind of signal, and what they want should appear.

With respect to language use and development, Durkin (1987b) has argued that misunderstandings and mismatches are inevitable and central to the dynamics of progress. He suggests that they occur not simply because two or more individuals (parent and child) have competing goals, but also because the intersections among social–cognitive purposes and language structure lead to conflicts which must eventually be resolved. Conflict, mismatches, and misunderstandings occur in parent–child linguistic interactions in a number of ways (Brown, 1980; Dore, 1985; Durkin et al., 1986; Ochs, 1991; van Rijt-Plooj and Plooj, 1993; Robinson, 1984; Shatz, 1981; Sylvester-Bradley, 1981). Tizard and Hughes (1984), on the basis of extensive naturalistic home-based data, suggest that children respond to partial understandings and gaps in their knowledge by actively seeking more information: that is one reason, they suggest, why preschoolers ask so many questions. Ochs (1991) develops a persuasive case that resolving the misunderstandings that arise in everyday interactions are central to the coordination of linguistic, social, and cultural knowledge: "From this point of view, misunderstandings are not loci in which social life breaks down. Rather, to the contrary, misunderstandings structure social life"(1991, p. 60). From a different perspective, Mannle et al. (1991) reach a similar conclusion about the effects of sibling speech, showing that when talking to their infant siblings preschoolers tended to be less solicitous and less prone to repair breakdowns but more directive and more prohibitive. Mannle et al. speculate that these characteristics may be beneficial to the learner because they provide communication pressure to resolve misunderstandings.

How is language development possible in the course of social interactions?

Parent–child interactions no doubt include elements of both harmonious shared attention and sequences of constructive misunderstanding. Overall, it seems plausible that misunderstanding is more productive, since if the child is always perfectly well understood and the meanings of others are readily apparent, then she or he has little need to improve her or his communication skills (cf. Brown, 1973; Golinkoff, 1983; Snow, 1989). It is interesting to note that Gleitman et al. (1984) found a near perfect positive correlation between maternal *unintelligibility* and the frequency of verbs (a measure of early linguistic sophistication) in their younger subjects' utterances, a finding that they prefer to dismiss as "garbage" (p. 64), but one which begins to make perfect sense if we assume that children have to work to make sense of the fumblings and bumblings of social life. (I would not want to stretch the analogy too far, but perhaps it will help to reflect on your own learning experiences in other difficult domains. A colleague of mine insists that students learn better with dreadful lecturers, because the bewilderment, anxiety and frustrations arising from taking their courses motivate the victims to do a lot of work on their own.)

Exactly how language emerges out of these complex interchanges remains difficult to disentangle, but it is likely that both the child and her or his co-interactants each play a role. Powerful factors promoting progress appear to be the child's desire to communicate with others (cf. Schaffer, 1989b) and the child's motivation to organize and make sense of language itself (Durkin, 1987b; Robinson, 1984; Karmiloff-Smith, 1992; Shatz, 1981). We will consider evidence on this point in a moment, but note first that such a position does not necessarily contradict nativist claims of a strong biological component to language acquisition. As we saw in chapter 6, nativists do allow for a role of linguistic experience to set off the innate mechanisms. However, nativists tend to discount the involvement of parentese. Wexler (1982, p. 311), for example, concludes that the speech modifications of parentese cannot be helpful to the language learner and must therefore contribute toward other functions, not to grammar learning. But this does not follow: the fact that something is unhelpful does not mean it is irrelevant, only unhelpful. By analogy, closed doors are unhelpful to infants seeking access to consumables in the kitchen, but they are very relevant.

It may in any case be too strong a claim that parentese is unhelpful. Suppose instead we accept that, like most naturalistic language use, it is complex, with special complications arising because parents adapt it for a variety of management, pedagogical, and social–cognitive reasons (Durkin, 1987b). How then do children deal with it to begin to learn language? It may be that they set about working on it, actively seeking or inviting information and manipulating the data available.

For example, although we have seen that parents often produce the names for things that children are attending to, they are by no means consistent in how they do this or what they focus upon. Baldwin (1993) engineered situations in which adults playing with infants provided new names for novel toys. In one condition, the experimenter waited until the child was focused on one of the new toys and then labelled it ("It's a *toma*"). In another condition, the experimenter waited until the child was focused on one toy, but then looked at a toy *in her own hand* and labelled that ("It's a *peri*"). In the latter (discrepant) condition, the child's attention was oriented toward one toy, and a label was uttered, but the label happened not to be relevant to the focus of attention. If infants are dependent upon adult support to work out the meanings of new words, then we should expect massive errors among subjects in the discrepant condition when it comes to testing comprehension of the novel term: they should assume that the *peri* is the toy that they (not the adult) are playing with.

In fact, Baldwin found little evidence of this error among infants aged 1 year 4 months and above. By 18 months, children in the discrepant condition were more likely to identify the *experimenter's* toy as a *peri*. How did the infants determine what was the referent of the experimenter's utterance? They resorted to a familiar procedure for resolving uncertainty (chapter 2): they looked at her, and monitored the direction of her gaze. It appeared that the children realised that there was some ambiguity in the adult's speech, and actively sought clarification. Rather than relying solely on parental fine tuning, the infants themselves "seem to be tuned to whether or not someone is talking about the object they themselves are focused upon, and when not, they do not link the label they hear to the object of their own regard" (Baldwin, 1993, p. 413).

There is other evidence that young language learners strive actively to obtain and evaluate linguistic information. Goldfield (1990) found that, at 20 months, children with a high proportion of nouns in their vocabularies (referential children) were much more likely than those with a lower proportion (expressive children) to point out objects to their mothers. Goldfield's conclusion is that the referential children use pointing as a means of eliciting names for things during the period of vocabulary explosion. Shatz and Ebeling (1991), in a study of six English 2-year-olds observed over six months, investigated the production of language learning behaviors. These included language lessons (in which the child solicited or received direct instructions), practice, metalanguage (comments about language), and revisions (partial repetitions of previous utterances in order to clarify or correct). They found that such behaviors were very frequent throughout the period studied (on average, about 55 per hour). Most were initiated spontaneously by the child, and the main category of language learning behavior was revision. Importantly, children tended to produce utterances that were more grammatical on their second attempts. Shatz and Ebeling (1991) maintain that 2-year-olds listen to their own speech and compare it to an internal model that they are developing on the basis of the language they hear from others. Interestingly, Kuczaj (1983) reports that the frequencies with which children practice elements of language alone in their cribs and in social contexts are highly correlated, a finding which suggests that when children are working on language they rely on both their own resources and what they can find out from others. Again, in Shatz and Ebeling's study, progress was not instantaneous and there were decrements as well as improvements, suggesting to the investigators that children do not straightforwardly correct their utterances toward the input model (1991, p. 310). This is probably not surprising, if we take note of the inconsistencies and complexities of the input model.

Social Perspectives on Language Acquisition: a Summing Up

In this and the previous chapter, we have charted a lengthy course through the stormy history of child language theory and research, and I am afraid we have not answered fully the interesting question we began with: how can children come to know language? At present, the field cannot provide a complete answer – but the question gets more interesting all the time. We have seen that a full gamut of theoretical positions has been incited by this fascinating topic, and it should be stressed that eloquent and forceful expositions of each are still current in the research field. Early learning theories of language acquisition proved unequal to the task of accounting for the phenomenon (though recent versions appear more robust; cf. Moerk, 1992; Whitehurst and DeBaryshe, 1989). Nativist theories highlighted the complexity and specificity of the achievement, and no satisfactory answer has yet been forthcoming to Chomsky's insistence that there are features of language that cannot be accounted for in terms of current models of cognition or social interaction. Cognitive developmental approaches were important because they reminded the field that language is intimately connected to thought, but the connections have not turned out to be the orderly sequence predicted by the cognition hypothesis.

Social interactional theories started from the assumption that the connections between language and social context were so transparent as to afford an easy way in – but this overlooked the problem that if language were redundant, no one would need it. It is also contradicted by increasing recent evidence that social–linguistic interaction between child and caregivers involves multi-level factors, and leads often to mismatches and misunderstandings. Social life, as we were warned in chapter 1, is something of a battlefield. Even at the micro-level of linguistic interaction we find that parents "return to the attack" (Brown, 1980) and engage in prolonged skirmishes with opponents who have wills of their own. One of the most important outcomes of all this is that social processes have come to be recognised as central to language acquisition, and this may increase the prominence of the topic in the future of developmental social psychology.

Language in Use: Conversational Development

We turn now from arguments about the origins of linguistic ability to studies of the development of language in use. Much of the Chomsky-inspired research into language acquisition was concerned with grammatical rules, focusing attention on children's early progress with the awesome technicalities of syntax and, later, semantics. However, Hymes (1974) pointed out that while possession of this formal structural knowledge may be impressive, it would not guarantee that the child could hold a conversation:

> A child from whom any and all of the grammatical sequences of a language might come with equal likelihood would be, of course, a social monster. Within the social matrix in which it acquires a system of grammar, a child acquires also a system of use regarding persons, places, purposes, other modes of communications, etc. – all the components of communicative events, together with the attitudes and beliefs regarding them. (Hymes, 1974, p. 75)

Research into the characteristics of popular and unpopular children supports Hymes's observation. Children who lack pragmatic skills tend to be isolated and rejected by their peers (Donahue and Prescott, 1988; Gottman et al., 1975; Putallaz and Gottman, 1981). The social rules are at least as important to the use of language as the grammatical, and possibly just as complex. The social rules are fundamental to virtually everything else we do in interpersonal interaction, since conversation is the most widely used mode of social interaction (Ervin-Tripp and Mitchell-Kernan, 1977; Shatz, 1994; Siegal, 1991). Conversation is one of the most readily confirmed universals of language acquisition – no child acquires language without conversing with someone (Dore, 1985; Hayes, 1984). The development of conversational skills involves not only the acquisition of formal syntactic and semantic knowledge, but also the ability to relate one's utterances appropriately to the utterances of others, to understand one's conversational partners' perspectives and intentions, to take account of politeness conventions.

Communicating as Partners: the Development of Conversational Skills

As discussed earlier, although children are involved in conversation-like interactions from well before the advent of language, their contributions to the maintenance of the conversation are necessarily limited. When they do begin to produce speech, their utterances are short and, where conversations are sustained, much of the work is done by the caregiver. Even so, the relatively limited participation of a 1-year-old in a verbal conversation does reveal some impressive early abilities. As mentioned in chapter 6, although children may produce only single-word utterances, they can use them in conversationally appropriate ways (Barrett, 1989). For example, the formulaic "whassat?" enables them to ask questions, and their early vocabulary can be drawn upon to reply to questions from adults (so that infants can begin to respond to enquiries such as "What do you want now?," "What's that?," "Where's mommy?"). They can also use single words to offer *comments*; Barrett (1989) gives the example of a baby picking up an empty cup, looking inside it and then turning to her mother and exclaiming: "*Gone.*" Children less than 2 years of age show in their responses to others that they can differentiate questions from non-questions (Allen and Shatz, 1983; Ervin-Tripp, 1970; Shatz and McCloskey, 1984).

Children of this age seem to be aware that adult communications require responses, and they try to provide them, even if they sometimes mismatch the formal content with the behavior. Shatz and McCloskey (1984) describe various instances of young children responding to questions or instructions (such as "Do you want a cookie?," "Pick up your toys") with the word "no," a useful syllable which they have presumably received often enough in response to their own requests. But the children said "no" even though their actual behaviors indicated acceptance (taking the cookie) or compliance (picking up the toys). The social response appears to be imperfectly aligned with linguistic knowledge. McTear (1984) comments that in such instances children seem to be following the rule "if there is a question, give an answer, even if you do not understand it."

During the third year, increased vocabulary knowledge means that children are better able to provide more accurate responses to adult questions and prompts; they also monitor adult language and behavior for cues as to which kind of verbal response is appropriate (Shatz, 1994; Shatz and McCloskey, 1984). However, they still have to develop skills in the procedural contingencies of conversation. Kaye and Charney (1980), in a study of American mothers' and 2-year-olds' conversations, found that, although children at this age could respond relevantly and smoothly to maternal utterances, they produced *turnabouts* far less frequently than their partner. A turnabout is a contribution to conversation which takes up the previous speaker's topic and then extends it ("Two hippos! What does the other hippo say?"). A turnabout shows more proactive social involvement in the conversation, since it offers one's partner a means to come back in, and take another turn. Learning to produce and respond to turnabouts appears, not surprisingly, to be closely tied to social experience, and in turn to promote further conversational development. Wells (1985), for example, found that the extent to which mothers produce conversational strategies such as turnabouts was correlated with aspects of conversational development during the preschool years, including initiations by the child.

During the preschool years, children's abilities to sustain conversation increase and they learn to initiate, respond and develop a topic (Dore, 1978; Ervin-Tripp, 1970; Foster, 1986; Garvey, 1984; Luszcz and Bacharach, 1983; McTear, 1984, 1985; Mueller, 1972). By at least the age of 3, they demonstrate abilities in monitoring the conversations of others (Dunn and Shatz, 1989; Shatz, 1994), and responding to points where they become the topic (for example, where their name comes up; see Forrester, 1988). The analysis of young children's spontaneous conversations with friends often reveals psychological capabilities and insights that are missed in formal, laboratory-style testing (Dunn, 1988a, 1993; Shatz, 1994; Shugar, 1993).

Verbal interchanges with peers become increasingly cooperative and, providing the topic is sufficiently motivating, preschoolers can maintain conversations involving several turns (French et al., 1985). However, at this stage, children's conversations still include high proportions of nondialogue speech (Piaget, 1926; Schober-Peterson and Johnson, 1991). That is, children playing side by side will engage in self-directed talk in which they appear oblivious to the presence of others, or sometimes they take turns but fail to link their utterances thematically to those of their partner. Consider this interchange between two American male preschoolers:

>   *A:*   Meet that bad guy.
>   Haaa.
>   *B:*   Bkkk.
>   We're missing in the American Air Force.
>   We're missing into the American Air Force.
>   *A:*   Oh no.
>   Into the Roby Howery.
>   *B:*   Fires ready.
>   Bkkkk!
>   Missiles ready.
>   Bkkkk!
>   *A:*   Yaaaaah!
>   *B:*   I'm riding.

A: Yaaboosh!
B: I'm riding in the American Air Force plane.
(Schober-Peterson and Johnson, 1991, p. 164)

Well, maybe you need to be there, but it is clear that the exchange lacks features of topic development and cohesion that would assure older speakers that they were making contact. The following conversation between another pair of 4-year-olds looks on first glance to reflect somewhat better coordination:

A: It's a bird
B: Is this it?
A: No.
(adapted from Glucksberg et al., 1975, p. 321).

Here, we have turn-taking and topic maintenance. The only drawback is that the conversationalists are taking part in an experiment in which they are physically separate and cannot see each other. *B* had no idea what *A* was looking at – but, rather like the younger children above, answered "no" anyway.

Into the school years, conversational skills are still developing, as children acquire more subtle techniques for shifting the focus of a discussion and for elaborating topics (McTear, 1985; Schober-Peterson and Johnson, 1993; Wanska and Bedrosian, 1985). Conversational skills intersect with other social developments, such as increasing interests in friendships; research shows that among school-aged children friends not only talk more but also engage in more connected discourse (Foot et al., 1977; Gottman and Parkhurst, 1980). Schooling itself brings a whole new set of linguistic challenges, including participation in the diverse dialogues of the classroom (Edwards and Mercer, 1986; Edwards, 1990; Wells, 1985; Willes, 1983). One particular conversational challenge facing the child as she or he moves into the larger social environment has attracted a considerable amount of research attention, and that is the development of referential communication skills.

Understanding Others' Perspectives and Intentions

One valuable way in which we exploit language is to share knowledge. In order to do so successfully, we need to be aware of how to formulate messages, to determine what our conversational partner needs and adjust the message accordingly, and to detect when problems, gaps, and miscommunications arise. These are demanding requirements, yet they occur – simultaneously or in close succession – in many of our conversations. To test the development of such abilities, Glucksberg and Krauss (1967) devised a *referential communication task*, in which two children sit on either side of an opaque screen with one child acting as speaker and the other as listener. Each participant has an identical set of blocks, and each block has an unusual (and difficult to describe) shape drawn on its upper surface. The speaker has to select and arrange some of the blocks, and then to communicate to the listener so that she or he can construct an identical arrangement.

Preschool children find aspects of this task very difficult, even though they understand the basic purpose of the game (they perform adequately when easy to describe, familiar objects are used). The children (*A* and *B*) in the interchange above (Glucksberg et al., 1975) were taking part in a referential communication task. Glucksberg et al. found that it is not that young subjects cannot label the odd configurations – they generate novel or idiosyncratic names for them – but the problem appears to be that they do not take account of the listener's perspective. Thus, if a 4-year-old decides upon the label "mother's dress," "drapeholder," or "coffee pot" for a particular shape, then she simply refers to it with that term, seemingly oblivious to the fact that her partner has no idea what she means. Across several trials, older children swiftly improve their performance as a result of feedback, but 4- and 5-year-olds remain quite ineffective. When children of this age range are asked to explain why they had problems communicating with their partner, they tend to blame the listener (Robinson and Robinson, 1981; Sonnenschein and Whitehurst, 1984).

The referential communication task provides an interesting laboratory test of the child's ability to handle an array of linguistic, cognitive, and social demands – demands that are analogous to aspects of many authentic conversational interchanges. Careful manipulation enables experimenters to determine which factors children give weight to, which they disregard, and how these change with development or as a function of other situational variables. There is evidence that the quality of a child's performance in this task is associated with subsequent verbal skills development (Robinson, 1981). It is also a relatively easy procedure to replicate. Not surprisingly, it has attracted a lot of research attention.

Variants and extensions of referential communication tasks have been used widely, and the evidence points fairly consistently to the period from 5 to 7 years as an important developmental period (Robinson and Whittaker, 1986). In addition to their limitations as senders of messages in such tasks, 5-year-olds also reveal problems as listeners. They interpret ambiguous instructions as though they have only one meaning or fail to recognize that incomplete instructions are inadequate (Lloyd, 1991; Markman, 1977; Pynte et al., 1991; Robinson, 1981; Sakata, 1987; Whitehurst and Sonnenschein, 1981). They are confident of their ability to understand instructions that are actually inadequate (Flavell et al., 1981). They are less able to distinguish effective clarification questions from poor ones (Bearison and Levy, 1977). They tend not to be accurate in assessing their own understanding (Brownell et al., 1988; Robinson and Robinson, 1981). By the age of 7 or 8, children begin to provide more helpful descriptions, mentioning differences among the stimuli (Kahan and Richards, 1986), and they now provide fuller information to listeners unfamiliar with the materials (Sonnenschein, 1986).

Referential communication, language skills, and social context

Why should developments in the ability to handle referential communication tasks come about during the years 5–7? No doubt a range of factors is involved, including concurrent developments in language skills in general, and cognitive developments underlying improved perspective-taking abilities. However, Robinson and Whittaker (1986) review evidence showing that young children already have many of the requisite abilities, yet fail to exploit them. Several researchers have shown that it is possible to improve children's performance in verbal referential communication tasks by asking them to focus on differences among referents, by pointing out the ambiguity of their instructions, by guiding them to reformulate inadequate instructions, and by providing information about the listener's noncomprehension (Lefevbre-Pinard et al., 1982; Robinson, 1981; Robinson and Robinson, 1985; Robinson and Whittaker, 1986; Sonnenschein and Whitehurst, 1984). It has also been found that alerting children to the speaker's *intentions* – for example, warning them that the speaker might try deliberately to deceive or trick them – can result in better detection rates for inadequate messages (Ackerman, 1981; Bonitatibus et al., 1988).

Robinson and Whittaker (1986) moved beyond the laboratory to provide interesting findings suggestive of a link between the child's changing social context and his or her referential communication performance during this period. In an analysis of the speech of a group of British children recorded at home and at school, they found several differences between language demands in the two contexts. Conversation at school was more adult-centered, while conversation at home was more child-centered. At school, children received complex and lengthy instructions more frequently; teachers were more likely than parents to ask "display" questions (questions to which the adult already knew the answer); teachers favor an interrogative technique whereby they ask questions in a series of increasing specificity. These distinctive new discourse requirements may encourage children to distinguish between message and meaning, waiting for longer to make sure that they follow what the adult is saying, and becoming accustomed to people pressing for further information. In a follow-up experiment, Whittaker and Robinson (1987) showed that deliberate interventions, in which an adult continued to ask questions until an answer was supplied, promoted children's understanding of ambiguity.

Research into the development of referential communication skills has provided an illuminating source of insights into the priorities of young children communicating with others. Robinson and Whittaker's findings indicate that it may well be associated with variations in linguistic experiences.

The Emergence of Politeness

There are other important social constraints upon language use, including the requirement that one adapt the way one speaks according to the status of the listener. We have already touched upon one aspect of speech adaptation, namely speech addressed to young children, and found that even 2-year-olds show some sensitivity to this requirement. But this is only one of many ways in which language is modified according to social context. Others are called upon in adapting the content of one's speech for different partners. Again, research indicates that at an early age children are sensitive to this requirement, altering the length, structure, and focus of their speech according to whether they are talking to an adult or a peer (Martlew et al., 1978) and reserving some kinds of talk for inside the house, others for outside (Heath, 1983). To participate successfully in different contexts, the language user needs to discover the politeness conventions: it is not polite to talk to a grandparent using the vernacular that might be appropriate in the street.

Politeness is expected of language users in most cultures, especially young language users. Consider requests. It would be syntactically and semantically correct to say "I want another piece of cake" – but this would not necessarily be the pragmatically appropriate way to ensure you get what you want. Young children often do formulate their requests in this or similarly blunt manners ("gimmecookie!"), but then find that they receive feedback. Politeness is one area where parents are very prone to intervene in language behavior, providing direct and indirect instruction from relatively early in the child's life. For example, in many homes preschoolers who do not say *please* and *thank you* are swiftly reminded to do so (Becker, 1988; Garvey, 1984; Greif and Gleason, 1980). Becker found that parents' favored strategy for eliciting the appropriate pragmatic adaptation is to coax the child indirectly: "What do you say?," "What's the magic word?," "Daddy is talking to you." Although direct techniques were employed as well ("Say please"), indirect methods were more frequently successful in prompting the child to "correct" his or her pragmatic error.

Children learn early in life to modify their speech according to the status and activity of the addressee. Older people are approached more politely (Axia and Baroni, 1985) and adults who are busy are approached more deferentially (Ervin-Tripp et al., 1984). Children also learn relatively early the meaning of polite speech, such as indirect requests. Ledbetter and Dent (1988) found that by the age of 5, children responded appropriately to indirect requests. But some of the finer subtleties of politeness are still being acquired during the school years. For example, Baroni and Axia (1989) found that children's awareness of the rules governing polite request forms (including the best way to ask for a piece of cake) developed during the years 5–7. Younger children tend to think that adding "please" is sufficient to make an utterance polite ("give me some cake – please"), while in the early school years children become increasingly aware of the benefits of making requests indirectly ("Dad, I feel hungry").

Recognizing that indirect requests are more polite involves awareness of a *pragmatic convention* (Brown and Levinson, 1987). The convention is rarely stated explicitly, but most adult language users know it and can evaluate others' requests (as, for example, parents do when reminding their child to say "please"). Garton and Pratt (1990) provide evidence that 8–12-year-olds can differentiate among various forms of request ("I want my football", "Can I have my football, please?"), and predict their effectiveness and the likelihood of use (they also recognise that some forms may be polite, but will not always work). By mid-childhood, children appear to have attained a good deal of subtle information about how one should phrase requests, and are aware that there are different expectations concerning how to formulate a request to an adult versus a request to a peer (Baroni and Axia, 1989; Garton and Pratt, 1990; Wilkinson et al., 1984).

Summary

Conversational development begins *before* the child starts using language. Most of the child's linguistic experiences and activities occur in conversational contexts. As researchers have begun to study the development of conversational skills they have found that there is much more to language acquisition than the inordinately complex task of mastering the formal rules of grammar. During the preschool years, children develop increasing competence in the initiation and maintenance of conversation, but there are further challenges ahead as they move into the less child-centered discourse of school. During the early school years, they face the difficulties of relating their output to other people's perspectives and knowledge, and experimental studies of referential communication show that this is a multidimensional task which may be facilitated by particular strategies of adult conversational partners. Finally, conversational development entails participation in a socially regulated domain, where the child must learn about the contextual appropriateness of particular speech styles and the means of satisfying the politeness conventions of the broader community.

Language as an Attribute: Social Status and Language Style

So far, we have seen that language is a challenging thing to *learn*, and a tricky thing to *use*; now we will see that it is a precarious thing to *have*. In this final section, we turn to the significance of the particular language or language variant that the child acquires. One way in which language relates to the social context is as a marker of social status and affiliation (J. R. Edwards, 1986, 1989; Giles and Powesland, 1975; Robinson, 1972). We saw at the beginning of chapter 6 the brutal extremes which language clashes can reach, but overt and subtle conflicts between language groups are by no means restricted to South Africa; contemporary examples can be found in Belgium, Canada, Spain, Wales, and elsewhere. Different dialects or accents are also strongly associated with status and prejudice, and it will be seen shortly that this has implications for the development and opportunities of children and young people. Before addressing these issues, it will be useful to consider briefly the question of whether particular languages or dialects have inherent superiority – for example, are some languages more complex or richer, do some language variants promote greater cognitive skills?.

Are there Qualitative Differences among Languages?

When languages are analyzed in terms of their formal rule structures and expressive potential, linguists find no basis for claiming that any one language is superior to any other (Edwards, 1989; Pinker, 1994). It simply does not make linguistic sense to claim that French is better than English, Japanese better than Italian, Spanish better than Swedish. The same point holds when variants within a language – different dialects – are examined. Certainly, there are differences in the relative prestige accorded to different dialects, but these social and attitudinal values do not reflect the inherent superiority of a particular language variety.

The deficit–difference argument

This point was argued forcibly in an influential study by Labov (1972) of the logic of black English vernacular (BEV), as spoken by black people in some US cities. Previous work (e.g., Bereiter and Engelmann, 1966) had led some researchers to the conclusion that black speakers were linguistically disadvantaged, speaking an impoverished form of English which did not equip them well for the conceptual demands of the educational system. Indeed, black children often appeared to investigators to be distressingly inarticulate. These liabilities seemed to help explain their poor performance in school and on other achievement measures, relative to whites. Teachers were widely advised that black children did not have enough language, and that a priority of the school had to be to compensate for this deficit.

However, Labov demonstrated that quite elementary methodological adjustments – such as the use of a black interviewer instead of a white – resulted in dramatic changes in the fluency of young black subjects. Furthermore, when their language was analyzed, Labov found that the differences between BEV and standard English were superficial rather than substantive. To take one example of many discussed in Labov (1972), where a standard English speaker would say "He doesn't know anything," a BEV speaker would say "He don't know nothing" (p. 226). There is no grammatical basis for concluding that one of these forms is more complex; Labov notes that several (higher status) European languages express negatives in the same way as BEV. BEV, he concludes, is not an accumulation of errors but a systematic and highly structured variant. Unfortunately:

> Teachers are now being told to ignore the language of black children as unworthy of attention and useless for learning. They are being taught to hear every natural utterance of the child as evidence of his mental inferiority. As linguists, we are unanimous in condemning this view as bad observation, bad theory, and bad practice. (Labov, 1972, p. 240)

Labov was justified in claiming a rare consensus among linguists and sociolinguists on the latter point. Subsequent studies of nonstandard dialects in England (Trudgill, 1975), Ireland (Edwards, 1989), and Scotland (Macaulay, 1977; Romaine, 1984) have supported his view that dialectical variations are best regarded as differences rather than deficiencies. J. R. Edwards (1986) points out that this conclusion is not surprising if one accepts that all human beings are born with a roughly similar capacity to acquire language.

Differences and Prejudices

While linguists are virtually unanimous in regarding language varieties as differences rather than hierarchies, out in the real world traditional prejudices are alive and well. Edwards quotes as a representative example a Canadian teacher from one of his studies who maintains "Blacks have a slang language all their own. They will not use proper English when opportunity arises" (1986, pp. 152–3).

In most countries, beliefs about what is "proper" reflect the fact that different dialects have different status. In France it is Parisian French, in Greece it is Athenian, in Britain it is Received Pronunciation (RP or BBC English), in the US it is "network" English, in Norway Oslo predominates, and so on. In each case, the particular dialect or accent that a speaker uses is often sufficient to evoke in other members of the community a social stereotype which goes far beyond language itself (Edwards, 1989).

The potency of these stereotypical associations has been demonstrated in a number of experimental studies exploiting the *matched-guise* technique, first introduced by Lambert and colleagues (Lambert, 1967; Lambert et al., 1960). In a matched-guise experiment, subjects listen to recordings of a speaker reading a passage in two or more different accents, dialects, or languages. The subjects, of course, are unaware that it is the same speaker (normally someone who is perfectly bilingual or bidialectal). After each passage, they rate the speaker on a number of dimensions, such as intelligence, plausibility, persuasibility, sincerity, friendliness, sense of humour, likeability, warmth, and so on. Thus, in a typical experiment, the subjects are rating the same person, who is using the same tone of voice, and reading the same or comparable material – but in different dialects or languages.

The results show consistently that "proper" (i.e., high social status) speech is more favorably evaluated on most measures. For example, Lambert et al. (1960) found that both French- and English-speaking undergraduates in Montreal rated English guises (at that time, the higher-status language in that community) more favorably than French. Where regional dialects and accents are more subtly differentiated, as is the case through the United Kingdom, listeners tend to have a hierarchy of evaluations. Giles (1973) found that British secondary school children evaluated arguments from different guises in declining order of quality (moving down from Received Pronunciation, South Welsh, Somerset to Birmingham). Giles's subjects were drawn from South Wales and Somerset, and so their rankings cannot be explained simply in terms of an ingroup bias: instead, people tend to know their place in the linguistic scheme of things. The main exception to the overall pattern is that speakers of lower-status varieties are sometimes rated higher on measures of personal warmth and sincerity, consistent with the stereotype that members of the lower orders are simple – but decent and affectionate.

The finding of deference to high-status speech varieties has been widely replicated. Members of lower socioeconomic status or minority groups in Canada, the US, Britain, Sweden, Norway, and elsewhere have been found to devalue their own speech style in matched-guise experiments or in interviews and ethnographic studies (Edwards, 1989; Gabrielsen, 1984; Romaine, 1984). People what don't talk proper tend to be keenly aware of the fact. Should they overlook the matter, it is likely to be impressed upon them by others. A particularly important source of feedback is the school where, as Edwards's illustration above indicates, many teachers tend to hold stereotyped and often negative views of particular language varieties (see Edwards, 1979, 1989; Williams, 1976, for extensive additional evidence). Edwards (1989) argues that the stereotypes evoked by language variety influence teachers' expectations of the pupil, thus risking the initiation of a process of self-fulfilling prophecy.

Parental concerns about language style

Not surprisingly, given the perceived associations between language variety and social attainment, many parents tend to be concerned about the language style their children acquire. However, parental concerns can be manifest in various ways: some are anxious to steer their children away from lower-status speech styles; others are keen to ensure that their children do not lose the social identity that is expressed in their dialect or accent.

Avoidance of lower-status speech tends to be more common among parents who have upwardly mobile aspirations for their children. Parents can be quite vigorous in their remedial actions when confronted with signs of the presumed inferior speech style. Romaine (1984, p. 127) cites an example of a Scottish child whose mother was so outraged by her use of the vernacular *ken* that she hit her across the face so hard that the child lost a tooth.

That's nothing compared to the linguistic uproar among the parents in Westfield, a small town in Massachussetts, who in 1992 learned that their primary school had assigned a couple of teachers with foreign accents to teach first- and second-grade classrooms. Some 403 residents of the town wanted them reassigned somewhere else, fast, and got up a petition to the school board to demand their removal. Apparently, the parents feared that the children would pick up the teachers' accents (Raskin, 1992). Of course, anyone who has spent ten minutes with the children of migrants knows that they acquire the majority community accent, but neither everyday observation nor the assembled wisdom of several distinguished professors of language science who were consulted by the local media were enough to assuage the anxieties of the linguistically perturbed parents of Westfield.

Yet, although several studies have shown that speakers of lower-status language varieties recognize social prejudices against their speech and sometimes denigrate it themselves, it is also found that people are sometimes reluctant to change their variety by adopting a higher-status one. This is a fraught issue for many migrant groups, for example, where adopting the language of the host country has economic attractions but could be perceived simultaneously as betraying one's background (Carranza and Ryan, 1975; Edwards, 1989).

It is also a recurrent issue among members of lower socioeconomic status (SES) groups as their children progress through the educational system. Edwards (1989) recounts an example of a Cockney grandmother who remarked that if her grandchild were to talk in a "la-di-da" (RP) accent, his mates would label him "a queer." Romaine (1984, p. 127) interviewed a Scottish child who told her that his local dialect was "corrected" by his neighbors: "'cause see they've got a boy four called Andrew and they don't want him to learn the bad habits and they're always checking me for saying it ... When I say – I don't know if it's right or wrong – I say like, if I done something today, they go: you *did* and they do it like that all the time'." So, there can be pressures to relinquish or avoid a speech style from one quarter, but there can be equally emphatic guidance from another to preserve or adopt it. This can lead to tensions for the recipient of linguistic counsel: Gabrielsen (1984) reports an upper middle-class adolescent in a southern Norwegian city who complains that at home she is told off for speaking "ugly" (i.e. using peer language) while at school her friends castigate her for talking "nicely" (i.e. in Oslo Norwegian). If you grew up with a regional or working-class speech style, you will know that at university you speak differently; but what do you do on those occasions where people who know you in one context (home) meet people who know you in the other (education)?

Shifting speech style

Individuals are sometimes averse, then, to altering their speech style, and are sometimes trapped in the tensions between the competing linguistic preferences of the different groups with which they are involved. Yet in other contexts, people make definite shifts toward the language style of another group. For example, fragments of the language of a minority group, such as Caribbean Creole or Punjabi in Britain, are occasionally adopted by some of the young people of the mainstream society, as an expression of their rejection of the Establishment or as a means of consolidating peer group identification (Hewitt, 1986; Rampton, 1991). Rampton found that white adolescents in the South Midlands of England sometimes referred to outsiders from other schools or communities as "gorras" (derived from the Punjabi *gore*, white person), irrespective of the colour of their skin. "Acting black" (adopting Creole slang and speech style) was considered to be cool and tough, a more radical statement.

Adolescence appears to be an especially important phase in this respect. Although debate continues as to whether the prepubertal years are a sensitive period for language acquisition, adolescence is a sensitive period in a different respect, namely the acquisition of language styles expressing group identification (Cheshire, 1982; Labov, 1972; Milroy, 1980). Romaine (1984, p. 104f.), in a review of work conducted in the US, Britain, and Sweden, concludes that during the adolescent years the use of slang, nonstandard syntax, and socially stigmatized phonological forms is at its maximum. Swearing is particularly important among many adolescents: it serves as a symbol of vernacular identity (Cheshire, 1982), helping to mark the distinctiveness of the peer group from adult respectability and to consolidate friendships. Rampton (1991) found that white British youths used Punjabi swear words as part of the banter of close friendships. Male adolescents often find it difficult to express positive feelings toward peers directly – and so they swear at them, obliquely emphasizing mateship and macho complicity.

Entertainers appear to have a special talent for accommodation to other accents. Nigel Kennedy, the English violinist, is noted for having acquired working-class "Sarf London" speech in early adulthood, overcoming the heritage of an elite education as a gifted child at the Yehudi Menuhin school, in the course of which he was exposed to continuous input of RP. Mel Gibson, the Australian actor, now speaks with an American accent, and it has become stronger as his star roles in extremely successful Hollywood cop movies have accumulated.

These anecdotes and field observations are very interesting and remind us that, to some extent, the social markings of language are adjustable. If circumstances required, a person *could* opt to modify his or her dialect in the direction of another speech community. But we have seen movements in various directions: some people favor a shift "upwards" (toward higher-status speech), while others become entrenched in or intensify their community dialect, and yet others prefer to adopt the speech styles of lower-status or marginalized groups. Perhaps to a lesser degree, most of us find we modify or entrench our speech style according to context: talking to our peer group, to our family, to our work associates, to people above and to people below us in the social strata. How can we account for these patterns and for the particular directions chosen?

Accommodation Theory: Language Study Meets Experimental Social Psychology

Giles (1979, 1980; Giles and Smith, 1979; Giles et al., 1987; Thakerar et al., 1982) has forged one of the major links between language study and experimental social psychology by developing a theoretical model of these speech accommodation processes. According to Giles's *speech accommodation theory*, speakers converge or diverge in response to other speakers as a function of social perceptions and intergroup relations. Following Tajfel (1981), Giles argues that we categorize the social world and perceive ourselves as members of social groups. Our group's characteristics and standing are central to our social identity. Social identity may be positive or negative as a function of how our group stands in social comparison to other groups. We are motivated to seek a positive social identity, and we strive to achieve it by finding dimensions which afford favorable comparisons with other groups. When interlocutors from different groups (with different speech styles) desire each other's approval, then they converge their speech patterns; when they seek to differentiate from each other socially, then they will diverge their speech patterns.

This theory would account well for most of the examples above. It is also consistent with the events in Soweto that we considered in the previous chapter. The issue of the language of instruction was a principle reason for the uprising (Geber and Newman, 1980). Among black South African students, radicals preferred to speak English while more conservative students preferred to speak their own languages – but neither opted to speak in Afrikaans, the language of the group perceived as the major oppressor in the society (Geber and Newman, 1980). When serious threats were made to impose the language of this resented outgroup upon them, the Soweto students took to the streets to preserve their social identity. Ironically, a couple of decades later Afrikaaner speakers found themselves in a linguistic mirror-image when the association between their language and Apartheid led to widespread stigmatization of their tongue. In 1994, for example, as majority rule approached, Coca Cola proposed to drop Afrikaans from its products, and Afrikaaner speakers protested vigorously at the perceived threat to their linguistic identity (Taylor, 1994). Although the political situation has changed, the linguistic response is very similar, with the Afrikaaners now striving to maintain the psycholinguistic distinctiveness of their group.

Giles and his co-workers have provided experimental support for accommodation theory in a number of studies with adults, and some with high school-aged children. Unfortunately, developmental work on accommodation processes has been sparse, but there are experimental and observational data to indicate that they begin early and have important implications for social adjustment through childhood and especially into adolescence.

Street and Cappella (1989) investigated aspects of speech accommodations in 3–6-year-olds who were interacting with an unfamiliar adult. These investigators examined patterns of interpersonal adaptation as manifest in the temporal structure and verbal complexity of the children's speech. Speech rates and response latencies (time to take turns) were found to be associated with measures of verbal responsiveness. Children who are highly verbally responsive take note of what the other person is saying and build upon it (Adult: "This looks like a house"; Child: "Yes, it is a very big house"). During the interaction, these children proved better able to adapt the pace of their speech to the pace set by the adult in the immediately preceding minute.

At the intergroup level, quite young children can be observed to segregate themselves by language, as Doyle (1982) reports for French- and English-speaking preschoolers in Montreal. Children's willingness to converge appears to be affected by relative intergroup status, as Giles would predict. For example, a study of 3- and 4-year-old Punjabi/English speakers in a British preschool found that the children rarely chose the "wrong" language intentionally to address another speaker (Moffatt and Milroy, 1992) . That is, the (minority group) bilingual speakers converged readily to the interlocutor's language. Very occasionally, they would poke fun at a monolingual English addressee by speaking in Punjabi (deliberately diverging). In another mixed-language setting, Aboud (1976) taught individual Chicano and Anglo-American children a new game. The children were attending a bilingual school and all had some knowledge of both Spanish and English. Once the subject knew the game, she or he was placed with two agemates who asked to be taught to play. One child asked in Spanish, one in English. The Chicano children, whose first language was Spanish, showed convergence: 71 percent adopted the language of the English listener. The Anglo-American children tended not to converge: only 17 percent spoke in Spanish or used some Spanish words.

Cheshire (1982) describes the case of an English teenager, a chronic truant, who was not very well integrated into his peer group but none the less actually increased the proportion of his nonstandard vernacular extensively in school. She interprets this as consistent with Giles's accommodation theory: the boy loathed school and was deliberately seeking to diverge from the language of his teachers.

Exceptional children provide interesting evidence concerning the factors that might underlie accommodation processes. Baron-Cohen and Staunton (1994) investigated whether autistic and normally developing children whose mothers were non-English acquired the accent of their parents or their English peers (the children were brought up in England). While most of the normally developing children acquired English accents, most of the autistic children acquired their mothers' non-English accent. Baron-Cohen and Staunton (1994) suggest that autistic children may have an impaired theory of mind (awareness of others' mental states; see chapter 9) and may be oblivious to the attitudes they evoke from others (their peers) and hence fail to shift their accent toward them.

The importance of intergroup relations to speech accommodation is made clear in a study by Abrams and Hogg (1987). These researchers demonstrated that biases toward or against a particular speech variety can be relative. In a matched-guise experiment, Scottish adolescents from Dundee showed outgroup negativity when evaluating speakers with Glaswegian accents; when contrasted with Dundee accents, Glasgow speakers were rated less favorably on measures of solidarity, social status and job prospects. However, when the Glasgow accents were contrasted with RP accents (the sound of the oppressors south of the border), then the Dundee subjects rated their fellow Scots *more* favorably. The authors interpret the findings in the light of social psychological theories of group processes (Tajfel's and Turner's, 1979, social identity theory and Turner et al.'s, 1987, self-categorization theory) which hold that the definition of groups as in- or out- is sensitive to which contrasts are salient in a particular context. When the main difference is urban origin, it matters whether you come from Dundee or Glasgow; when the higher-order social category of nationality becomes pertinent, then it matters more whether you come from Scotland or England.

Summary

Although there is little scientific basis for assumptions that one language is superior to another, there are strong socially shared values about language varieties which influence people's evaluations and expectations of others. From a developmental perspective, these prejudices are particularly important in educational contexts. From early in life, people adjust their language behavior in different social circumstances. They converge or diverge as a function of respective social status, social–cognitive intepretations of the situation, and social goals. Developmental processes underlying these patterns of behavior have not, as yet, been investigated extensively but available evidence establishes that they can begin in childhood and are possible well into adulthood.

Conclusions

In this and the previous chapter, we have considered language as something that children know, do, and have. As stressed at the outset, these are not independent features, and developments in each are inextricably interwoven with developments in the others. There are many ways of examining language, and many ways in which it permeates social life. The arguments here have been, first, that language acquisition is an extraordinary achievement, and one which can only be understood with reference to the social context; second, that analyses of language use also illuminate something of the complexities of the social context and the diversity of skills that children need to coordinate to participate effectively in the fundamental mode of human social interaction, conversation; third, that language is a prominent social marker, one which identifies a person as part of a particular social group and hence has profound implications for how she or he relates to others. It is not surprising, then, that people do not respond indifferently to threats by outsiders to impose a new language upon them, as we saw in chapter 6. Perhaps it is surprising, though, that social psychologists disregarded language for so long; of course, with a developmental social psychological perspective scope for improvement emerges.

Further reading

Garton, A. F. (1992) *Social Interaction and the Development of Language and Cognition*. Hove, UK and Hillsdale, NJ: Erlbaum.

An extensive overview of social processes in language development. Garton discusses the major theories of language development and examines the mutual implications of cognitive development, language development, and social interaction.

Giles, H. and Robinson, W. P. (1990) *Handbook of Language and Social Psychology*. Chichester: Wiley.

An excellent compendium of perspectives on the links between social psychology and language, demonstrating that much progress has been made in recent years to compensate for longstanding neglect. Unfortunately, only one paragraph is devoted to development in children, although there are useful chapters on language in education and language in the elderly. The collection indicates the range of topics to be addressed by a developmental social psychology of language.

Edwards, J. R. (1989) *Language and Disadvantage*, 2nd edn. London: Cole and Whurr.

A lucid and well-illustrated account of the significance of social attitudes to language and their implications for developmental social psychological and sociolinguistic processes in education.

McTear, M. F. (1985). *Children's Conversation*. Oxford: Blackwell.

A valuable synthesis of different disciplinary approaches to the study of conversation, illustrating the intricacies of conversational development at home and school.

Shatz, M. (1994) *A Toddler's Life: becoming a person*. New York: Oxford University Press.

A rich, longitudinal case study of the interweaving of language development, social understanding, and social behavior in an American toddler.

Chapter 8

The Development of Nonverbal Communication

As {facial expressions} guide you through life, it is as well to keep them up to peak performance by exercising them every morning. Begin with glowering and growling. Followed by displeasure and pleasure, nonchalance and discomfiture. And before finishing up with tittering and laughing be sure to give cowardice and inferiority a good workout, just in case your bravery and superiority are not up to scratch that day. Strict privacy should be observed during practice sessions as regretfully these facial expressions in quick combination demonstrate certifiability.

(Donleavy, The Unexpurgated Code, 1975)

Bill Clinton, in the early stages of the 1992 US Presidential campaign, was understandably keen to impress voters with his general likeability. Since he was going to be appearing in the press a lot, and in countless news fragments on TV, he needed to be able to demonstrate his worthiness even when he had no opportunity to say anything. As a result, he hit upon what we have seen to be one of the fundamental nonverbal means of attracting others' attention, a simple facial display that he had probably discovered as a baby to have all sorts of positive effects upon people: he smiled. He must have been under considerable pressure, rushing around the States, fronting up to several public meetings a day, negotiating hard behind the scenes, watching the opinion polls, deflecting intrusive journalists, and more – but he kept on smiling.

Clinton, like most politicians, knew the power of nonverbal communication. Many top figures in politics and the media are so well aware of the importance of this aspect of their public appearance that they take coaching from specialists in nonverbal behavior, often using videotape to study and rehearse their performances very carefully. Not only does this provide lucrative employment for applied social psychologists, but it also demonstrates people's sensitivities to the precarious nature of our nonverbal displays. Used effectively, the nonverbal channel can complement or strengthen the message we wish to get across – but a slight facial slip can undermine a skillfully worded sentence, and the wrong posture can belie a whole presentation.

For these and related reasons, the study of nonverbal communication has traditionally occupied a prominent place in the work of social psychologists (Argyle, 1988a; Ekman and Friesen, 1975; Feyereisen and de Lannoy, 1991; Kendon, 1986; Rutter, 1984; Scherer and Ekman, 1982). Surprisingly, the topic has been less to the fore in developmental psychology where, as we have just seen in chapters 6 and 7, the study of communicative development has been focused primarily upon language. However, as psycholinguistic investigators became increasingly interested in the precursors and social contexts of language, greater attention has been paid to nonverbal means of communication. Simultaneously, several researchers have begun to investigate developmental antecedents of nonverbal behaviors initially studied in adults. Specialists in neighboring disciplines, especially ethology, have long maintained the importance of nonverbal communication among children, and have provided valuable techniques for studying its uses in children's social environments.

Hence, a growing body of research into the development of nonverbal communication is now available, and in this chapter we will consider this work in three main sections: *output, intake,* and *interaction.* Under *output* we will examine work on expressive skills, the display side of nonverbal communications. Under *intake,* we will examine work on receptivity and sensitivity to the nonverbal skills of others. *Interaction,* the final section, encompasses two broad issues concerned with the uses of nonverbal skills in interpersonal contexts. First, returning to a theme already familiar, we consider the interpersonal contexts within which children acquire and develop their nonverbal skills. Second, we consider aspects of the interaction between communicative channels, that is between nonverbal communication and linguistic behavior.

Familiar theoretical perspectives will recur during this chapter. Since Darwin's (1872) account of the expression of emotions in humans and animals, the thesis that nonverbal communication reflects innate propensities has been very influential in this field of study. However, there are some inter-family, gender-related, and cultural variations in the control and use of nonverbal behaviors which have led others to emphasize the contributions of learning and social context. While there has been continuing debate among exponents of these positions (see Buck, 1982; Scherer and Ekman, 1982, for fuller discussions), it will become clear that they are not necessarily mutually exclusive. As in many other aspects of social development, we will see also that cognitive developmental and social–cognitive perspectives are becoming increasingly prominent in the explanation of nonverbal communication among children.

Definition

First, we need to consider the definition of nonverbal communication. For present purposes we will adopt that of Mayo and La France (1978): "Nonverbal communication refers to behaviors other than verbal which enable a child increasingly to understand and to be understood by members of his or her social community." A key element of this definition is the stress on the shared nature of the systems: nonverbal *communication* is meaningful because it serves social functions.

It may help to clarify why communication is stressed here if we note that nonverbal behaviors can have non-communicative functions, too, such as the use of laughter as a tension-releaser (Sroufe and Waters, 1976) or the lowering and raising of eyebrows to aid optical convergence or increase the visual field (Camras, 1982; Ekman, 1979). Although these developments are interesting in their own right, in this discussion we will be concerned primarily with the social, communicative aspects of nonverbal behavior.

Output: Expressive Nonverbal Communication

Nonverbal communicative displays serve a number of purposes, but the two most fundamental are the expression of emotion and the sharing of referential meaning. We consider each of these in turn in this section. Both are pressing social concerns of the infant and caregivers and it is important to recognise that the beginnings of the child's active contributions in these respects can be found in nonverbal communication well before the child is able to interact linguistically.

Nonverbal Expression of Emotion

One of the first things we need to communicate to others is how we feel and what we want. In chapter 2, it was shown that the normal infant is equipped with very effective means of nonverbal communication to handle these tasks: crying and smiling. Darwin (1872) hypothesized that means of communicating emotions in this way evolve because of their adaptive value. He argued that specific facial expressions echo facial actions that once served a direct survival function – such as baring one's teeth in anger (in earlier times, our predecessors would have actually attacked with their teeth). A species stands a greater chance of survival if its members can share information about perils and pleasures and can coordinate responses to environmental contingencies. As already discussed, early emerging nonverbal expressions play major roles in promoting the proximity of the caregiver and enhancing early social interaction, all of which increases survival prospects. Recent research indicates that there may be an array of universal nonverbal emotional expressions which are detectable readily even in quite young infants.

Universals of nonverbal expression

If Darwin's hypothesis that the form of emotional expressions is innate is correct, then we might expect to find that they occur universally and that they emerge early in development. There is considerable evidence of both. Studies of adults obtain high levels of agreement as to the meaning of facial displays of basic emotions (happiness, sadness, disgust, anger, surprise, and fear), and this holds across a wide range of cultures (Ekman, 1992, 1994; Ekman et al., 1987). It seems that just about everyone recognizes the meaning of a smile, much as Bill Clinton anticipated.

Studies of normal infants show that they are capable of producing a set of discrete, recognizable emotions appropriate to situations (Camras et al., 1991; Izard, 1994; Izard and Malatesta, 1987; Izard et al., 1980, 1987). Izard has proposed an influential theory, *differential emotions theory*, which views the emotions and their interrelations as an organized system in which innate, neuromuscular patterns (facial expressions) are associated with specific emotions. Izard argues that, like many innate phenomena, these relationships can be detected early in life. For example, Izard et al. (1980) videotaped 1–9-month-olds responding to events ranging from pleasant interactions with their mothers to much less enjoyable inoculations and blood tests. Adult raters, blind to the stimulus, who viewed slides or videotapes of the babies were able to distinguish emotional expressions such as joy, sadness, interest, surprise, anger, disgust and fear, usually to good levels of reliability. Izard argues (1994) that these basic emotions correspond to analogous expressions in adults, and that they emerge so early because they are biologically preprogrammed, adaptive features of the species with fundamental importance to socioemotional development.

To take just one example of the clarity of early nonverbal expression, Chiva (1983) and Rosenstein and Oster (1988) tested young infants' reactions to different tastes, including sweet, acidic, and salty. Babies' facial expressions leave little doubt as to how they respond to these sensory experiences, and it is obvious from Chiva's illustrations that their responses are quite spontaneous (see figure 8.1). Further, studies of children without opportunities to observe and model others' emotional expressions, such as individuals born blind or deaf-and-blind, reveal that they laugh, smile, cry, frown and stamp their feet in anger in much the same way as non-handicapped children; similarly, children born blind cover their faces when embarrassed (Eibl-Eibesfeldt, 1970). This is not to suggest that there are no changes from infancy to adulthood, or that environmental context is irrelevant. Izard and colleagues

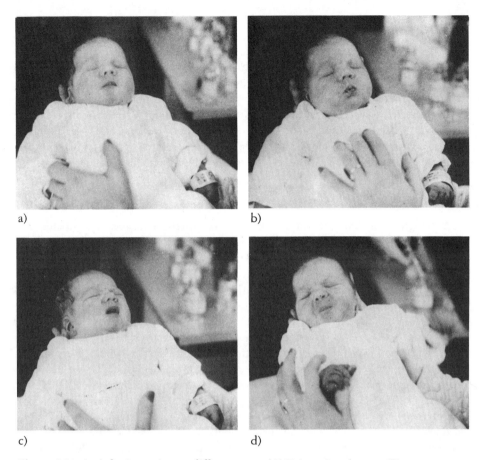

Figure 8.1   An infant's reactions to different tastes: (A) Evian mineral water; (B) a sugary liquid; (C) a salty liquid; (D) an acidic (citrus) liquid.
(*Source: Chiva, 1983*)

accord a role to experience and socialization processes, but maintain that "Basically, the changes are from instinctlike expressions to more restricted and controlled emotion signals" (Camras et al., 1991).

Recent research indicates, however, that although some infants' facial expressions can be easily interpreted, others are perceived as more ambiguous (Camras et al., 1991; Oster et al., 1992). In particular, Oster et al. (1992) found that expressions of pleasure, interest, and surprise seem to be detectable quite early in life, but more negative expressions such as fear, anger, sadness, and disgust are less readily judged by adults. It may be that the earliest expressions reflect some of the most powerful hedonistic responses of the organism (experiencing pleasure) while later developments are concerned with more subtle discoveries about the vagaries of the environment.

Age-related Developments

During the preschool years, nonverbal displays are frequent, and individual differences in the production of particular types of expression are relatively stable (Montagner et al., 1984; Unzner and Schneider, 1990). But nonverbal communication is not mastered completely within the first few years of life. When children are asked to *produce* specific facial expressions – "look happy," "show me a sad face" – performance increases with age (Field and Walden, 1982). When children attempt to *control* their expressive communication, further evidence of developmental changes emerges.

Control of emotional displays

Although it is often useful to be able to express emotions nonverbally, and sometimes irrepressible, there are also many occasions on which we find it appropriate to control the display. The rules of display (when to smile, whom to touch, how to show gratitude, what is polite) vary with culture (Ekman, 1992; Ekman and Friesen, 1975), but they are vitally important to the conduct of everyday social life. How do you deal with a well-intentioned grandparent who, knowing your interest in what she perceives as the undifferentiated mass of "pop" music, gives you a copy of *Kylie Minogue's Greatest Hits* as a birthday present? Or, what face do you present to your peers when you have received an A+ for an assignment on which everyone else struggled to get into the C range? Social context often demands that we handle or mask the emotions that we experience (Lewis, 1993; Saarni and von Salisch, 1993).

Ekman (1978) classified three main types of display behaviors that adults adopt, namely *simulation* (displaying feelings when you have none), *inhibition* (displaying no feelings when in fact you are experiencing them), and *masking* (covering a feeling with the expression of one that you are not actually experiencing). From a developmental perspective, important questions arise concerning the emergence of these social skills.

Recent research has begun to chart developmental progress in these respects. In a large-scale longitudinal study of children from infancy through to the toddler years, Malatesta-Magai and her colleagues (Malatesta et al., 1986, 1989; Malatesta-Magai, 1991; Malatesta-Magai et al., 1994) have revealed that even during the first year children show increases in the display of positive emotions. As the child moves into the second year, two new facial expressions commonly emerge, both seemingly associated with the regulation of negative affect: biting the lower lip (associated with anxiety) and compressing the lips tightly (associated with anger control). By the third year, although the range and frequency of expressive behaviors does not reduce, the behaviors themselves become more muted.

With slightly older children, other researchers manipulate situations in which different types of display are socially desirable. Reissland and Harris (1991) studied pairs of siblings (aged from 20 months to 5 years) engaged in competitive games in the presence of their mother. Almost all of the children showed signs of pride upon winning, but 5-year-olds were more likely than 3-year-olds to attempt to mask their reactions: already, they demonstrate an awareness that it is not good to be seen gloating.

Saarni (1984) presented school-aged children, who had helped an adult in an interview, with gifts that were inappropriate to their ages (such as a boring baby toy). Just the day before, the children's participation in the same task had been rewarded with more interesting things, such as money or candy. On receipt of the unappealing gift, Saarni found that it was easier to detect disappointment in the faces of younger boys than older, and that older subjects tended to engage in more transitional expressions – that is, expressions which fell somewhere between simulated delight and honest disappointment. Shennum and Bugental (1982) had school-aged children pretend to be interviewees for an amateur television talk show, and questioned them about their likes and dislikes. The twist was that the subjects were prompted to give the opposite of their true feelings, feigning positive affect for disliked topics, and so on. Interestingly, the results showed that although most subjects could control their emotional displays, the younger children (6 years) tended to overshoot the mark, giving highly exaggerated exhibitions of the pretend emotion.

Thus, it does appear that children learn the need for some nonverbal techniques for controlling the display of emotions quite early, although mastering them may proceed over the next few years. In a further illustration, Cole (1986) used a similar methodology to Saarni (1984) in two experiments with children aged 3–9 years, and found that even the younger subjects were able to control the display of mild negative emotions. Development during the school years includes gaining greater skill in managing a repertoire of behaviors that are available from early on. This is not an instantaneous achievement, but one which involves gradual progress through middle childhood (DePaulo and Jordan, 1982; Saarni, 1984, 1988; Schneider and Josephs, 1991) (see figure 8.2).

Not all children appear to acquire display rules at the same pace. Casey and Schlosser (1994) found that children diagnosed as "externalizers" (manifesting overt behavioral problems such as hyperactivity or aggression) reacted to praise from peers with displays of surprise and hostility, and were less aware of their facial displays than were nondiagnosed children.

Physiology, social cognition, and social presence

Learning to control nonverbal displays is challenging for a number of reasons. Mastery of the fine facial musculature is demanding: even adults sometimes find it difficult to inhibit or mask a facial expression of a sentiment they would rather not disclose (Ekman and Friesen, 1975). Another integral ability is that of perspective-taking, since one is only motivated to control a display if one is aware of how one appears to others. Feldman et al. (1979) proposed that both of these tasks should be difficult for younger children – the first because of maturational constraints on the development of the facial muscular control, and the second because of social–cognitive limitations in developing understanding of others' perspectives.

Feldman et al. (1979) had people in three age groups (6, 13, and 16 years) act as stimulus persons in an experiment designed to test these developmental predictions. Each individual was filmed unobtrusively while consuming a drink. The drink was prepared so that it was either pleasant or distinctly unpleasant. The consumer's task

Figure 8.2   An 8-year-old struggles to provide the socially desirable smile in response to a seriously underwhelming present.

was to try to convince an interviewer that the drink actually tasted good. Remember that Chiva's subjects, above, show convincingly that children are equipped from very early in life with means of expressing their reactions to tastes. An additional manipulation was that some subjects were face to face with the interviewer (public condition) and some were alone, but addressed their remarks to a tape recorder, ostensibly for an interviewer to listen to later on (private condition). This allowed for a test of the sensitivity of nonverbal displays to another's perspective. Consider Bill Clinton's smile again: it is unlikely that it was quite so pronounced when he was doing radio interviews from his hotel bedroom after a tough day on the campaign trail. The developmental question is when and how successfully do people begin to vary their nonverbal display according to the social context?

The recordings of the stimulus persons' avowals of drinking pleasure were later played to raters, blind to the quality of the drink and to whether the recording was made in public or private conditions. The raters' task was to evaluate on a Likert scale exactly how much they thought the stimulus person really enjoyed the drink. The results confirmed the developmental prediction, with observers finding it easier to discern the degree of truthfulness in the 6-year-olds than in either of the older groups. However, at all three age levels, the stimulus persons were rated as more pleased with the drink when they could be seen (public condition) than when they believed themselves to be alone.

In a similar study, Morency and Krauss (1982) found that children's abilities to control their deceptive expressions on pleasant stimuli lags behind their abilities to feign pleasant displays in reaction to unpleasant stimuli. These researchers suggest that in daily life children are more likely to be encouraged by parents and others to simulate a pleasant affect than an unpleasant one ("No, dear, we don't tell Granny to stuff her present"). Again, these findings suggest that even relatively young children do have some control over their nonverbal behavior, and that development during the school years is concerned with acquisition of the more subtle dimensions of personal management and discoveries about situational appropriateness of specific behaviors.

Why do these kinds of changes come about? Complex interactions among physiological, social–cognitive, and interpersonal processes are suggested by recent research. Through putting on a socially desirable face, we may change the nature of our emotions, regulating them in line with others' standards (Masters, 1991). For example, it is possible that through feigning an emotion we go some way toward experiencing it. Try bringing about a bilateral upwards extension of your outer lip regions (smiling broadly) for a few moments: you may find that you feel at least a little happier. According to the *facial feedback hypothesis* (Ekman, 1992; Ekman et al., 1983; Tomkins, 1962, 1963), expressions may contribute to the experience of an emotional state by affording neurological information derived from the changes in facial musculature. When adults are asked to adapt their face (for example, pull eyebrows down and together, narrow lips and press them together) they report emotional changes in the direction of the facial display. Cecil and Masters (unpublished study reviewed in Masters, 1991) found that children (age range unspecified) who were encouraged to disguise an initially sad affect with a positive or neutral facial expression subsequently performed more successfully on a problem-solving task than did control subjects who were not required to modify their facial displays. Schneider and Josephs (1991) found that, among 3–6-year-olds, children often smile following failure, and at the same time look toward another person (such as the experimenter). It seems that children learn quite early that the interpersonal situation requires the display of positive, if rueful, affect even when it contradicts internal feelings. Lewis (1993) reports that children in the same age range prove quite competent in masking deception in contexts where they risk exposure of their own misdemeanors; self-preservation appears conducive to the practice of display control skills!

Understanding and reacting appropriately to the social context prove important dimensions of the development of nonverbal communication, and we return to them

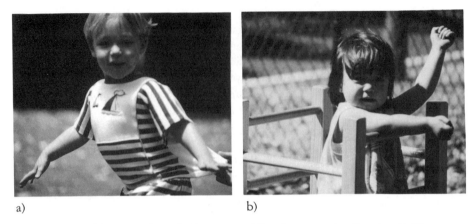

a)   b)

Figure 8.3 Toddlers provide symbolic gestures: (A) a plane preparing for take off; (B) driving a car.

later. But we turn now to another aspect of output which is also closely integrated with cognitive developments: the use of symbolic gestures.

The Development of Symbolic Gestures

As well as expressing emotional reactions to the social world, the child has a cognitive and empirical interest in things that he or she is encountering. One way in which the young child manifests these concerns socially is through nonverbal gestures and symbols. By these means, the child is able to share or direct the attention of the caregiver and, in due course, to represent aspects of the environment. Researchers have demonstrated that by the end of the first year infants have begun to integrate their first signalling system (crying) with other meaningful nonverbal actions, such as reaching for or pulling at the caregiver, or pointing at something that the infant wants (Gustafson and Green, 1991).

Acredolo and Goodwyn (1988) interviewed parents of 16–18-month-old infants about the children's use of nonverbal gestures, and found many examples of clear symbolic uses, such as sniffing to indicate a flower, panting to represent a dog, and smacking the lips to request food. These behaviors illustrate early awareness not only that gestures can stand for things but also that gestures can be shared with other people (see figure 8.3).

Pointing

One of the first manifestations of shared gestures, as well as one of the most useful, is the point: using the outstretched arm and index finger to focus attention on a particular referent. Pointing is the nonverbal equivalent of saying "this," "that," "look there." It is very much a social gesture, since the point of pointing is to guide someone

Figure 8.4 Infant makes point.

else's attention, and, of course, like all gestures it is one that we have to interpret (i.e., when others use a point to orient *our* attention) as well as give. In this section, we are concerned with output and will concentrate on the production of pointing, but we return later to infants' comprehension (intake) of points.

The production of pointing gestures is significant because it is an effective method whereby the infant can register his or her interest in specific features of the surroundings (Murphy and Messer, 1977) (figure 8.4). This ability appears to be attained by around the first birthday. In a cross-sectional observational study of mother–infant dyads, Murphy and Messer found only rare uses of points by babies at 9 months, but considerably more at 14 months. Leung and Rheingold (1981) found that by just over 12 months a majority of infants pointed. Both of these pairs of investigators speculate that the origins of pointing may lie in reaching, one of the infant's earliest reflexive actions upon the environment. The baby learns that it can grasp and manipulate interesting objects. In time, the baby reaches toward objects outside of its immediate presence. These early reaches fail in their direct purpose (the objects are too far away) but may have an impact upon the caregiver, who detects the child's interest and sometimes assists by bringing the required object within range. Through repeated interactions of this sort, the child comes to discover that the indicative, reaching gesture communicates needs and interests to others. Gradually, reaching diminishes in frequency while pointing becomes more common (Leung and Rheingold, 1981).

At a little over one year, then, the child is using pointing skillfully and socially. Rather less is known of the development of pointing during the toddler and preschool years, although there are interesting issues here concerning the use of points in peer interactions. We know, for example, that pointing can be used with an affective force as well as a referential purpose, marking someone out for especial attention or derision, but how and when children begin to use the gesture in this way has been little studied.

Another interesting feature of pointing is that it shows some degree of awareness of another's perspective. I point in order to encourage you to orient your visual field in a particular direction, and this implies my recognition of your perceptual independence. The fact that 12-month-olds have some sense of this suggests an intriguing early ability to take another's perspective. However, this does not mean that infants' understanding of pointing and perceiving are identical to those of adults, and a charming anecdotal report by van der Geest (1981) suggests that there are further developments through early childhood in terms of the integration of this nonverbal communication and social–cognitive competencies. Van der Geest describes an incident in which his 7-year-old son tried to direct his attention to a car, some 100 metres away, by pointing at the vehicle. After pointing appropriately, "Joost corrected his nonverbal behavior by pointing much higher and saying to me: 'No! I will point some higher because you are much bigger than me'" (p. 1521).

Summary

The output of nonverbal communication is a strong feature of infant social capacity from the beginnings of life. It was recalled from an earlier chapter that very young babies are equipped to communicate by means of crying, and we saw further in this section that there is a range of other emotional expressions, such as joy, sadness, interest, surprise, anger, and disgust, that are produced in reliably recognizable forms within the first few months of life. Learning to control emotional displays is an important dimension of the development of social competence, and one that involves the coordination of self-knowledge, physiology, and social–cognitive awareness; research indicates that control begins early but develops throughout childhood.

By around the age of 12 months, infants are beginning to use symbolic gestures, such as pointing, to communicate specific interests and over the next few months they come increasingly to use conventional (shared) gestures for familiar objects and events. The fact that their gestures come to take forms also used by caregivers suggests that they are taking account of, and interpreting accurately, some of the meanings of others' nonverbal communications – and this brings us to the closely connected topic of intake.

Intake: Decoding the Nonverbal Communicative Signals of Others

As nonverbal communicators, we are continuously both sending and receiving signals. So far, we have considered the child's capacities to send messages, and have acknowledged that caregivers are often able and willing to interpret these. But the child has also to learn what is meant by the nonverbal signals of others. Intake includes acquiring particular forms of expression and symbolization as well as learning how to monitor others' nonverbal behaviors for cues as to how they are reacting – and possibly as a basis for how to act oneself. We will consider these processes first in respect of infants, and then of preschool children.

Intake during Infancy

Investigators have found that within the first weeks of life, infants are sensitive to the nonverbal displays of others. Later in infancy, they demonstrate comprehension of nonverbal communications and they begin to use the cues offered by others' nonverbal behavior to help interpret ambiguous or novel situations.

Discrimination among nonverbal behaviors

One of the best-known demonstrations is Meltzoff and Moore's (1977) study of 12–21-day-old babies' imitations of facial expressions presented by adults. Meltzoff and Moore found that not only did the infants imitate tongue protrusion, mouth opening and lips pursing, but also that there was an increase in these expressions in the child's repertoire even after the adult had resumed a passive expression. Field et al. (1982) demonstrated equally clearly that neonates can imitate emotional expressions, such as surprise, happy, and sad, and Meltzoff and Moore (1989) showed that they can imitate non-oral gestures (such as head movements).

Several other experiments using habituation paradigms have shown that during the next two or three months infants become able to discriminate among happy, sad, surprise, smiling and frowning expressions (Barrera and Maurer, 1981; Kuchuk et al., 1986; Nelson and Horowitz, 1983, Young-Browne et al., 1977). By manipulating the relationship between a film presentation and a soundtrack so that an angry or happy face was accompanied by an angry or happy voice, researchers have found that infants of 7 months show attentional preference for those conditions in which the two modalities correspond (Soken and Pick, 1992; Walker-Andrews, 1986). These findings reveal a remarkable sensitivity to facial and vocal cues from the beginnings of life, but of course they do not indicate that the *meanings* of the expressions and tones are the same for the infant as they would be for older individuals.

Nelson (1987) shows that there are reasons for caution before imputing understanding of emotional expressions to young infants. These include the limitations of the infant's visual system (which make it improbable that very young infants are reacting to the same visual information as older individuals), limitations in the infant's knowledge of faces, and methodological problems inherent in testing reactions to faces out of emotional context in laboratory studies. Nelson (1987) argues that although perceptual discrimination is available early, understanding develops more slowly during the first two years of life, involving "a complex interaction of sensory and cognitive maturation, experience, and, perhaps, biological preparedness" (p. 906).

However, as has been stressed in earlier chapters, the adult's expression and the infant's reaction may none the less have meaning within the caregiver–infant *dyad*, partly because the adult will often act *as though* the child understands, sharing her or his feelings of surprise, joy, and sadness, and partly because the child appears to express through imitation a recognition that the other person is "like me" and that some experiences are being shared (Meltzoff and Gopnik, 1993; Meltzoff and Moore, 1992). For these reasons it appears that the role of imitation in the acquisition of nonverbal communicative behavior is more complex than a matter of the infant simply absorbing whatever goes on around him or her. Meltzoff and Moore (1992) argue that the processes of discerning and imitating others' nonverbal behaviors are means of entering the social world, and in particular of determining the identity of specific individuals with whom the newcomer interacts. People's perceptual properties have much in common, and the infant may require techniques for disambiguating them. Nonverbal imitations provide an activity-based technique for checking out, which Meltzoff and Moore (1992) suggest is the preliminary equivalent of asking: "Are you the one who usually sticks your tongue out at me?"

Comprehending others' gestures: pointing revisited

As well as discriminating among emotional expressions, the infant has to learn to understand nonverbal referential communication. We considered above the child's first productions of the pointing gesture, for example, and noted that this is also a gesture that is used in communicating with infants and thus presents a comprehension task. In fact, understanding what someone is doing by pointing is initially quite difficult.

Several investigators have reported that young infants tend to respond to a point by staring at the end of the index finger (cf. van der Geest, 1981; Murphy and Messer, 1977) (figure 8.5A). Murphy and Messer (1977) found that learning to follow a point (that is, to look in the correct direction) develops gradually during the period 9–14 months, and performance varies according to whether the gesture relates to a location directly in front of the child (the easiest condition) or to locations across the child's midline or away from both parent and child (figure 8.5B). By the middle of the second year, children appear to be able to respond quite appropriately to points (Leung

a)

b)

Figure 8.5 Responding to points: (A) young infant stares at point; (B) older infant follows point.

and Rheingold, 1981; Murphy and Messer, 1977), an achievement which involves an impressive coordination of at least two nonverbal mechanisms (gesture and gaze). Again, however, little is known of young children's understanding of social meanings of pointing, such as being pointed at.

Social referencing in infancy

One way in which we can gauge whether infants are able to discern meaning in other people's nonverbal expressions is to investigate whether they adapt their behavior in line with the signals available. Young children's intake of others' nonverbal cues in this sense has been studied by developmentalists in recent years under the general title of *social referencing* (Campos and Sternberg, 1981; Desrochers et al., 1994; Feinman, 1982; Feinman and Lewis, 1983; Walden, 1991; Walden and Ogan, 1988). Social referencing denotes a monitoring process that most of us exploit at least occasionally, and that is the use of other people's reactions to help us to interpret a situation and guide our own responses. For example, in Latane and Darley's well-known study of social influences upon helping behavior, students in a room that was gradually filling up with smoke tended to react to the situation according to the nonverbal responses of the other people in the room (who were actually confederates of the experimenters). If the confederates manifested indifference – by shrugging their shoulders – the subject was less likely to leave or call for help.

In similar ways, infants have been found to take account of parental reactions before determining their own response to ambiguous or uncomfortable circumstances. Sorce et al. (1985) found that 1-year-olds faced with the visual cliff (i.e., an apparatus which contains the illusion of a steep decline in the middle) would cross the "cliff" if their mother at the other side displayed positive facial emotion, but would stop if she presented a negative face. Infants have also been found to vary their willingness to interact with objects (Klinnert, 1984; Rosen et al., 1992; Walden and Ogan, 1988) or unfamiliar people (Feinman and Lewis, 1983; Klinnert et al., 1986) according to the nonverbal reaction of their mothers to the objects or events. Skilled parents and preschool teachers know that the best way to pre-empt a crying episode after an accident is for the adult to act as if the matter was minor or amusing; in contrast, an expression of anguished empathy is sure to elicit a corresponding wail.

Walden and Ogan (1988) found that at around 10 months, there is a change in where the infant looks when making social reference to the parent. Prior to that age, looks tend to be indiscriminate to any part of the adult's body, but at around 10 months they become increasingly concentrated upon one region – not surprisingly, the face. As we might expect on the basis of research reviewed in chapter 2, the infant appears now to be well aware of the special informational value of this part of the body. At around this age, infants are also improving their understanding of causality (Desrochers et al., 1994). Mundy et al. (1992) found that, with 20-month-olds, once joint attention has been established with the caregiver there is a greater likelihood of affect being shared than in other interactions (such as requests).

Even in infants, social referencing is not focused exclusively upon parents. Camras and Sachs (1991) studied infants aged 10–19 months in a day care center, and found that the children were alert to the facial expressiveness of the center staff (who integrated particular displays into their activities at the request of the experimenters). Interestingly, even at this age children showed differential attention to those caretakers who prior observations had revealed to be more expressive in normal day-to-day work in the center. It seems that infants are soon aware of the relative utility of different social reference points.

Feinman and Lewis (1983) and Walden (1991) point out that the phenomena that have captured infancy researchers' attention in this respect are already well known to social psychologists under different labels, such as *social comparison, attribution*, and *attitude formation*. From the first year or so, children appear to refer to others for feedback on how they are performing (social comparison), for possible explanations of unfamiliar events (attribution), and for cues as to how one should feel (attitudes). If, as the above research suggests, social referencing is widely exploited by children, then it is likely to provide not only opportunities to discover how adults react to particular stimuli and events, but also how adults react repetitively to particular aspects of the social environment – in other words, it provides a basis for acquiring elements of the culture (Campos et al., 1989). Nonverbal communication serves as a vehicle through which these social processes can begin at a very early age.

Intake during the Preschool and School Years

During the toddler and preschool years, children become able to make quite fine distinctions in the intake of nonverbal behavior (Philippot and Feldman, 1990; Walden, 1991). Social referencing is used extensively, with infants becoming increasingly wary of dealing with novel phenomena without a glance at their parents to check (Walden and Ogan, 1988). Presumably, this reflects numerous opportunities to discover that parents often have an opinion about what one should and should not touch. By around two years, children begin to negotiate with their parents in response to social referencing, often expressing their own perspective (Walden, 1991).

Preschool and older children can be tested on their recognition of different emotional expressions, and the results of several studies show gradual improvements during middle childhood (Bugental et al., 1992; Bullock and Russell, 1984, 1985; Kestenbaum, 1992; Knowles and Nixon, 1989; Odom and Lemond, 1972; Stifter and Fox, 1987). However, even when children make errors on the tasks employed they tend to be systematic (Bullock and Russell, 1985; Knowles and Nixon, 1989; Manstead, 1993), rarely confusing an emotional expression with its opposite. Manstead (1993) had 4–9-year-old children identify (from a set of photographs) the nonverbal expression of a story character who had just had an experience that could be expected to result in happiness, excitement, surprise, sadness, anger, or fear. He found that most children did well on the happy and sad scenarios, but there were age-related differences for each of the other emotional expressions. Error patterns revealed a tendency to pick "happy" in response to the positive vignettes and "sad" in response to the negative vignettes. These findings suggest that children's conceptual organization of emotions may be broader than adults' (a point to which we return in chapter

9) and that development during mid-childhood includes increasing differentiation among the nuances of emotional expression.

Children's reactions to humor also reveal responsiveness to the nonverbal behavior of others. When in the company of another child of approximately the same age, laughter and smiling at jokes is enhanced relative to the responses of solitary children (Chapman et al., 1980). Social referencing and display norms are again implicated: Chapman et al. report that children suppress laughter if exposed to humorous stimuli in the presence of an adult experimenter who displays no amusement.

Differentiating culture-specific nonverbal communications

There are many nonverbal symbolic gestures that are specific to culture. For example, if you are Italian, you may know the signals for "Go away, I'm clean," or for "Two events/people coming together," "Against the evil eye," and "a thin person." But suppose that you have an Italian family background yet live in another society: could your cultural heritage impede your acquisition of nonverbal fluency in your new country? Pearce and Caltabiano (1982) tested the ability of Italian-Australian (born in Australia but with one or more Italian parents) and Anglo-Australian children to decode a number of specific Italian gestures. The results suggest that by around the age of 6, Italian-Australian children are becoming "bi-gestural," able to decode the gestures of the dominant Anglo-Australian community as competently as other children but superior to them in their understanding of Italian gestures. Exposure to different nonverbal systems does not appear to inhibit these children's development.

Use of nonverbal cues in social perception

Children can exploit nonverbal cues to make inferences about an individual's personality. Keating and Bai (1986) presented American children aged 4–7 years with pairs of facial photographs of adult models where one member posed unsmiling, with a lowered brow (dominant expression) and the second model posed with a raised brow and a smile (appeasing expression). Earlier work with adults had confirmed that these expressions were perceived as dominant or appeasing, respectively, by members of Western and non-Western cultures (Keating et al., 1981). The children were read short stories concerning some issue of social relations between the individuals, and had to indicate who would take the dominant role. For example, the two people are going on a trip together – who will be the leader? Or, the two people work in the same office – who is the boss? The children selected the predicted face significantly more often, indicating that at this relatively early age they were sensitive to the dominance cues in the expression.

Intake of these aspects of nonverbal display is not restricted to peer observations. Soppe (1991) showed older children (aged 8–13 years) brief videotapes of adults who were described as teachers, and who adopted either dominant or submissive nonverbal styles of self-presentation. Children completing personality questionnaires about the teachers ascribed attributes consistent with the nonverbal displays, perceiving the dominant figures as better teachers. Neill (1991) reviews extensive evidence from studies of teacher–pupil interactions which confirms that children in the classroom are sensitive to nonverbal aspects of the adult's behavior, and that this has direct implications for teachers' success. Even quite young school children can pick out the tentative body language of the trainee teacher on her or his first weeks in the role (and then they take the opportunity to get their revenge on grown-ups).

Social familiarity and nonverbal decoding

As we saw under "Output", the developments during middle childhood tend to be concerned with the subtleties and nuances of nonverbal communications. For example, there appear to be gradual developments in children's abilities to exploit "leakage" to determine when someone else is hiding or masking an emotion or meaning (DePaulo and Jordan, 1982; Feldman et al., 1982). Evidence suggests that direct experience of the person whose nonverbal cues are being decoded is an important mediator of nonverbal intake in the early years. Abramovitch (1977) showed 3–5-year-olds video tapes of the face and upper torso of their own mothers or female strangers. The adult was interacting with another person, and the child's task was to tell the experimenter if the adult was talking to a friend or a stranger. The children were able to guess correctly whether their mother knew her co-interactant, but were unable to do so for the unknown female stimulus person.

Abramovitch and Daly (1979) followed up this work by using children as stimulus persons. They point out that children in preschools spend a lot of time interacting with their classmates, and that the ability to interpret nonverbal behavior would be of obvious value in this social context. In this study, they presented 4-year-olds with video tapes of either classmates or unfamiliar agemates interacting with adults or peers who were familiar or unknown. Subjects saw only the silent film of the face and upper torso of the stimulus child, and had to identify the age and relationship (known/unknown) of the co-interactant. As in Abramovitch's earlier study, the subject's familiarity with the stimulus person proved critical: children were significantly better at identifying the age and relationship of the person with whom their classmates were interacting, but were not successful when the stimulus persons were unfamiliar.

Summary

The intake of nonverbal communication can also be detected from very early in life. Infants can imitate facial expressions and actions within the first few weeks, and they can discriminate among different expressions. Early in the second year, infants learn to orient their visual attention appropriately to follow a pointing gesture. Although the ways in which infants learn to attach meaning to different expressions and gestures is not yet fully understood, it is clear that they come soon to exploit other people's nonverbal behaviors as part of the ways in which they attempt to understand complex and ambiguous situations. In particular, the precursors of familiar social psychological processes such as social comparison, attribution, and attitude formation can be found in infants' and toddlers' scrutiny of adult nonverbal cues. During the preschool and

Figure 8.6 Nonverbal communication takes place in a social context.

school years, children's abilities to decode others' nonverbal signals become increasingly sensitive, working initially from persons better known to the child.

Interaction

Although it is useful to distinguish between the output and intake of nonverbal communication, in practice of course the two are closely linked and advances in one respect are likely to have consequences for development in the other. More generally, nonverbal communication is acquired in interactive contexts, where both output and intake proceed in close succession, and involves interaction both between individuals and between systems. In this section, we will consider nonverbal communication in interaction (figure 8.6). We note first the importance of interpersonal context for early progress. Then we consider some aspects of the ways in which nonverbal communication is used in interaction, especially early peer interactions. Next, we turn to interaction between systems, examining the mutual implications of nonverbal communication and language. At least two important issues arise in this connection: one, since nonverbal communication precedes language, it is possible that it affects the nature of the language acquisition process itself, and two, since children (like adults) eventually use both channels of communication simultaneously it is of interest to ask what happens when the channels conflict.

Acquiring Nonverbal Communication in a Social Context

It seems an unlikely coincidence that most people would develop roughly the same set of symbolic gestures or the same set of skills for controlling the display of emotions, and follow similar principles in putting them into effect, without input from others. For example, the fact that infants make a transition from reaching gestures to pointing may well reflect the fact that just as they are learning about the effects of their striving to reach things, their caregivers happen to be using pointing gestures frequently for much the same purpose: eventually, the child seems to incorporate the parental gesture to a meaning that he or she had already formulated (Leung and Rheingold, 1981; Murphy and Messer, 1977). Output and intake interact and the behavior of the more skilled partner has implications for the forms of nonverbal communication the child learns.

Acredolo and Goodwyn's (1988) investigation of infants' use of symbolic gestures which was mentioned earlier, also points to a direct contribution of parental behavior. In a longitudinal study, these researchers followed a set of infants from 11 to 20 months, and had their mothers keep regular diaries of the children's nonverbal behavior. In this way, they were able to trace antecedents of the symbols the children used. They found that in approximately 50 percent of instances the gestures took a form that mirrored an action specific to a familiar interaction routine between parent and child (such as sniffing for "flower"). Furthermore, just as adults are keen to interpret early vocalizations as language-like, so they respond to gestures and expressions as though they have the meanings associated with them in adult interactions (Feyereisen and de Lannoy, 1991). Hence, any preliminary but contextually-appropriate attempt at a sniff for a flower, flapping arms for a bird or butterfly and so on, stands a good chance of being greeted approvingly and acted upon.

There is strong empirical evidence that learning about the control of emotional displays emerges as the product of mutually influential interaction (Malatesta-Magai, 1991). To illustrate, let us reconsider some of the developments outlined by Malatesta and her colleagues that we listed above: specifically, the increase in the display of positive emotions during the first two years of life.

Malatesta et al. (1989) found that this development was related to maternal behavior. As mothers monitored their babies' behavior they reacted to the child's expressiveness with facial responses of their own – often positive displays such as joy and interest. The emergence of displays of joy and interest by the baby during the period 2–7 months was associated with high levels of the same expressions in maternal behavior. Malatesta et al. (1989) found that children of different attachment types displayed different nonverbal behaviors. Insecurely attached children showed more inhibited anger expression (compressed lips), while securely attached children looked toward their mother more frequently. Several other studies have found associations between children's nonverbal behavior and aspects of parental behavior or parental well-being (Cassidy et al., 1992; Cole et al., 1992; Hinde and Tamplin, 1983; Lutkenhaus, 1984; Montagner et al., 1984). For example, Cole et al. (1992) found that the 2-year-olds of depressed mothers showed more evidence of frustration and suppression of tension. Montagner et al. (1984) found an association between parental nonverbal behavior and the child's behavioral profile. Parents who exhibit non-threatening physical warmth to their child tend to have offspring who offer more appeasement gestures to their peers. Montagner found also that stresses upon the mother (due to illness, serious disruption of her ovarian cycle, work or family discord) led to discordant behavior toward the child which in turn affected the child's behavioral pattern at preschool.

The ways in which children learn about the control of emotional expression is related to the social context and to social understanding. Saarni (1989) argues that as children come to realize that what they really feel may not always correspond with what they actually express, they develop subtle new interactive strategies which enable them to control emotional–expressive behavior in socially appropriate ways. In her view, the development of emotional behavior cannot be separated from the social context where information about emotional expression can be acquired *directly* through adult direction, *indirectly* through observation, or through the *social transmission* of behavioral expectancies. Parental involvement and imitation have already been demonstrated in the several studies cited above. An example of the impact of social expectancies of nonverbal communication can be found in children's willingness to display emotional expressions to different people. Saarni reports that children aged around 7 years tended to indicate that they would prefer to display their true feelings to adults rather than to peers, while children aged 10 and 13 years took the opposite stance. Children who preferred to disclose to adults were concerned about possible peer derision or betrayal, while children who preferred to show their feelings to peers saw adults as either less trustworthy or more troublesome. Although this does not test directly how nonverbal behavior is managed in these different social contexts, it does suggest that children differentiate among them and act accordingly.

The Social Contexts of Individual Differences in Expressiveness

If children acquire and practice nonverbal communicative skills in social contexts, it follows that differences among contexts may be associated with differences among children. There is strong evidence that this is the case (Halberstadt, 1991). Halberstadt reviews a growing body of research into individual differences in expressiveness. Expressiveness refers to the pattern of an individual's nonverbal output across situations: in brief, some people use nonverbal behaviors a lot and present them emphatically, some use them far less.

Halberstadt reports evidence that individual differences in expressiveness in children are associated with differences in their parents. She argues that this is explicable in terms of family interaction styles: if parents express themselves vividly, they model, prompt, and reinforce similar displays in their children. Interestingly, her own and others' research with subjects aged from preschool to early adulthood suggests a cross-over effect over time. Young children from highly expressive families tend not only to be expressive in their own output but also to be relatively good decoders of others' signals; it appears that the everyday involvement in expressive behaviors confers an early advantage. However, among older subjects, the advantage in decoding shifts to people from less expressive homes, who now outscore more expressive peers when it comes to judging others' emotions via nonverbal cues. Halberstadt's interpretation is that although intake skills may develop more slowly in children growing up in low-expressive families, the fact that they have to work harder, on the basis of less frequent and less intense displays, leads ultimately to greater sensitivity to the subtle cues that people emit.

Halberstadt's ecological account also helps to explain cultural differences in expressiveness. Why do some people gesticulate energetically over their tagliatelli, while others sit somberly behind the wheels of their Volvos? She argues, on the basis of cross-cultural research (rather than the national stereotypes I have injected purely for illustrative purposes), that cultural and societal norms affect family expressiveness and the wider socialization contexts in which children acquire their nonverbal styles.

Gender differences and social context

Many studies of nonverbal communication in children and adults report sex differences (Halberstadt, 1991; Hall, 1984; Neill, 1991; Noller, 1986), and meta-analyses indicate that these differences are larger than other sex differences (cf. Eagly, 1987). Buck (1981) reports that girls tend to be more accurate senders of emotions. Females from the school years on are often found to be better at disguising emotions, especially negative emotions, than are males (DePaulo and Jordan, 1982; Feldman et al., 1979). Female children smile more frequently, even when they are responding to a negative experience (Cole, 1986; Saarni, 1984). Studies of young adults indicate a sex difference in preference for style of nonverbal behavior in the opposite sex: females tend to prefer males who adopt dominant stances, males are equally attracted to dominant and submissive females (Sadalla et al., 1987). In general, adult females tend to reveal higher skills in terms of nonverbal decoding and expressiveness (Eagly, 1987; Hall, 1984).

These findings could be interpreted as reflecting either innate differences in nonverbal competencies or as the outcome of differential socialization experiences. As usual, this proves difficult to unravel, but quite a lot of evidence points to the latter. Adults, parents or otherwise, smile more at girl infants (Fogel et al., 1988; Malatesta et al., 1989). Rosen et al. (1992) found, in an experimental study, that mothers' facial expressions of negative emotions such as fear were less intense when directed at female infants than at male infants. It may be that parents expect more robust and dramatic expressions from boys and thus cue them with stronger examples, while sociability is prized in girls, who receive more smiles.

Acredolo and Goodwyn (1988) found that girl infants tended to use gestures more than boys, and argue that this may be related to differences in parental style of interaction with males and females. Girls in Cole's (1986) study were more likely to smile when dissimulating in social conditions than in nonsocial, an outcome which suggests that the behavior is moderated by perceived social desirability. Particularly interesting are the findings of Shennum and Bugental's (1982) study, discussed above, in which children were asked to pretend reactions to topics that were opposite to their true feelings. Shennum and Bugental found that girls overshot the mark when inhibiting negative affect, while boys with increasing age became better at "neutralizing" their negative affect. This suggests that girls respond to others' expectations that they display pleasant emotions, while boys learn that in these kinds of circumstances they are expected to mask or inhibit their feelings.

It seems that an important axis around which nonverbal behavior is differentiated by gender concerns social power and assertiveness. Schieffelin (1990) comments that in her observations of the Kaluli people she found that from early in the child's life mothers encourage boys to take physically assertive stances and their daughters to take compliant and nurturing stances. In general, boys learn during mid-childhood to repress displays of vulnerability and sadness, though they may in some contexts be reinforced for demonstrating anger and dominance (Buck, 1981; Fuchs and Thelen, 1988; Halberstadt, 1991). Linfors (1992) raises the interesting suggestion that in contemporary Western societies sex roles may be changing more rapidly on overt measures, such as verbal behavior and publicly expressed attitudes, but much more slowly on the nonverbal level.

Nonverbal Communication and Peer Interactions

Interaction with others is essential to develop an appreciation of the effects and limits of one's nonverbal capacities. It was stressed in chapter 2 that babies learn a lot about their properties (such as crying and smiling) as a result of their effects on other people. Eibl-Eibesfeldt (1988) describes how infants and toddlers experiment with nonverbal behaviors by testing the reactions of others. Toddlers provoke each other, snatching or withholding objects, pushing and shoving and so on, seemingly in order to find out how others will respond and to discover the limits upon interpersonal behavior. These exploratory tests are not just occasional incidents but the very basis of the child's entry into the social world. This becomes particularly clear when we examine how children initiate, maintain, and regulate peer interactions. During their early experiences of peer relations in nurseries and child-care settings, language is not well developed but children have much to communicate and much to discover about each other. Nonverbal behavior is fundamental to the regulation of interpersonal relations at this stage of engagement with the larger social world (Eckerman et al., 1989; Schaffer, 1984b).

Initiating peer interactions

For example, faced with the problem of making contact and coordinating actions with a peer with whom one cannot speak, there are two or three useful nonverbal strategies that one can adopt. The first is to look at him or her (Dubon et al., 1981; Eckerman et al., 1975; Verba and Musatti, 1989). The second is to copy his or her actions (Brenner and Mueller, 1982; Dubon et al. 1981; Eckerman et al., 1989;

Nadel-Brulfert and Baudonnière, 1982; Nadel and Fontaine, 1989; Uzgiris, 1981; Wallon, 1949). The third is to give or take an object (Eckerman et al., 1989; Verba and Musatti, 1989; see figure 8.7). The first strategy may well lead to the second or third, since establishing mutual eye-contact often precedes more direct interaction (Finkelstein et al., 1978).

A longitudinal observational study of pairs of toddlers revealed that from 16 to 32 months a marked increase occurs in the extent to which the children's acts are socially coordinated (Eckerman et al., 1989). The main mechanisms for achieving this developmental change include joint manipulation of objects and imitation of each other's play actions. Often, these are integrated into turn-taking games and gestural control of the playmate's actions (for example, indicating where the partner should climb, requesting or accepting a toy, getting someone to stop). Bakeman et al. (1990) found that !Kung infants, whose caregivers tend to ignore them while they are playing, try to involve others in their activities by offering them objects. Studies of slightly older children (3–6 years) reveal that they too tend to begin peer interactions by first watching the other child's behavior and then approaching and joining in the ongoing activity (Promnitz, 1992).

Maintaining and regulating peer interactions

In detailed observational studies of the early peer interactions of French preschoolers, Montagner and his colleagues (Montagner et al., 1984) show that children develop individual profiles of nonverbal behavior before their second birthday, and that these determine how they fit into the social structure of the nursery. Some children display predominantly *appeasement* behaviors (smiling, offering, stroking, kissing). Figure 8.7 illustrates appeasing actions; note that as the cookie is accepted the initiator inclines his head and upper body in a solicitous, unthreatening posture. Other children are more prone to take *agonistic* stances (threatening by clenching the teeth, frowning, making assertive noises, hitting, or taking away), and still others tend to *fearfulness/ withdrawal* (moving away from other children, crying in response to aggression by others), or *isolation* (standing alone, crying alone, sucking fingers and toys). Although most children at this age are capable of most of these behaviors, distinct personal patterns or profiles are readily detectable (Montagner et al., 1984).

Importantly, the pattern an individual develops has substantial implications for how she or he relates to peers. Individuals with high appeasement profiles often emerge as very popular and become leaders (recall Bill Clinton's smile versus George Bush's dour dismay in the final pre-election weeks). Agonistic children become feared and avoided, and withdrawn children enter a spiral of social isolation, lack opportunities to develop confidence in interpersonal skills, and are more likely to be victimized by the agonistic peers than are the leader-like appeasers. Promnitz (1992), in an extension of Montagner's methodology to the study of older children (Australian preschoolers), found very similar patterns and reports that one of the main changes with age was for the behavioral strategies to become more complex and sequential in comparison to the single actions of very young children.

Thus, nonverbal communication is much more than a set of party tricks or

a)

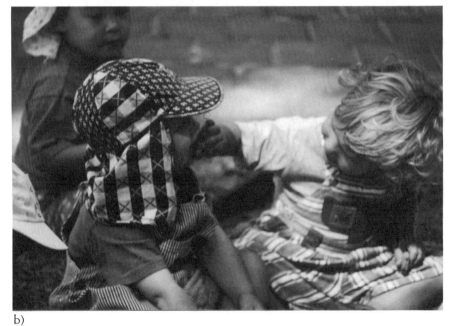

b)

Figure 8.7   Early peer interactions frequently involve objects.

substitute for language: individual performance here has considerable impact upon the beginnings of out-of-home social life. From the toddler years, social competence in the peer community is related to skill in nonverbal encoding and decoding (Montagner et al., 1984; Philippot and Feldman, 1990; Promnitz, 1992). Although few studies have investigated directly the consequences of these early patterns for later development, studies of older children, adolescents and young adults reveal an association between social skills, socioemotional adjustment and nonverbal behavior (Edwards et al., 1984; Feldman et al., 1982; Halberstadt, 1986, 1991; Rutter and O'Brien, 1980), findings which suggest that early patterns may have long-term consequences.

Interpersonal Distance

Another basic form of nonverbal communication occurs in terms of where we locate ourselves in relation to others. This is very much a skill that is inseparable from interaction, since by definition it is concerned with the space between or among people, and each party makes a contribution to establishing, maintaining, or modifying the shared distance. By adulthood, most of us are intuitively aware of the appropriate uses of interpersonal distance. We know, for example, that it is acceptable to be physically close to intimates while rather more distance is normally expected in interactions with casual acquaintances.

Hall (1966) categorized four major levels of interpersonal space, or *distance zones*, that he observed to be characteristic of social interactions among American adults. These are:

1 The *intimate zone*, typical of individuals with a close personal relationship (such as family members, lovers), in which the persons may actually be in contact (e.g., holding hands or embracing) or only a small distance apart (up to about 18 inches).

2 The *personal zone*, typical of people who know each other (such as friends), in which the persons stand between 18 inches and 4 feet apart.

3 The *social distance* zone, typical of people in relatively formal or functional interactions (such as teacher and students, shopper and shopkeeper), in which the individuals stand between 4 and 12 feet apart.

4 The *public distance* zone, typical of strangers at meetings or in public places, in which the individuals stand 12 or more feet apart.

These distances may be modified according to the number of people present, or other physical factors. At a well-attended meeting, a popular entertainment place or in a lift, complete strangers may tolerate much smaller interpersonal distances than they would opt for in an open space. Nevertheless, most of us have a sense of the amount of personal space that is comfortable in a given social situation, and we feel uncomfortable if that expectation is violated (for example, if a stranger comes and sits exactly next to us in a large, empty waiting room. And starts to smile).

How and when do we learn about the conventions of interpersonal distance? Even in infancy, children demonstrate personal space requirements. As we saw in chapter 2, some of the central social relationships, such as those with primary caregivers, are characterized by relatively high levels of very close contact. The intimate zone is established at birth. Yet infants have means of communicating their displeasure at excessive or unwanted intrusions into their personal space, such as gaze aversion, withdrawal, whimpering, and we saw that within the first year they direct these nonverbal behaviors increasingly to strangers.

Relations with peers are also marked by selective use of space. Even among toddlers, children reflect privileged relationships by greater proximity (Eckerman and Stein, 1982; Baudonnière, 1988; Baudonnière et al., 1989), and joint play behaviors involve a great deal of direct body contact, such as touching, pushing and pulling, and facial displays (Promnitz, 1992). Legendre (1987, 1989) points out that during this period, children's use of interpersonal space needs to be analyzed in terms of the microsystem of their current social environment. For example, in the nursery, children with low social competence may often seek proximity to adults, irrespective of the degree of familiarity with those adults. Since the adults are frequently in the company of other children, this means that a simple measure of a given child's proximity to peers might exaggerate the quality of the peer relationship. The children happen to be standing close to each other only because each is close to the adult. When peer proximity is measured away from the adult's presence, then it turns out that those with low interactive competencies are often excluded. Legendre suggests that the low social competence children do not have the same nonverbal skills in sharing attention to interesting objects or tasks that we saw above facilitate more successful peer interactions during the early years.

Personal space and development

There is some difference of opinion in the literature concerning changes in the amount of interpersonal space required by children. Several investigators, using a variety of measures, including behavioral, paper-and-pencil representations and figure placements, have obtained evidence that the amount of personal space required *decreases* steadily during middle childhood and early adolescence (Jones and Aiello, 1973; Meisels and Guardo, 1969; Severy et al., 1979). On the other hand, researchers point out that in some contexts younger children tend to pack together while older children prefer to space themselves as adults do. For example, Hoffer (1981, p. 43) comments that first-graders attending social gatherings, such as a mass, cram into the front pews so tightly that they resemble "a pack of gerbils huddling together on a chilly night." But Hoffer observed that by around the age of 9 or so adult-like spacing arrangements prevail. On this evidence, personal space requirements seem to increase with age.

The resolution of these conflicting findings may depend on taking into account the nature of the social relationship involved. In a task where the child is dealing with distance between self and stranger, younger children may be more wary. Severy et al. (1979) speculate that the increasing acceptance of the physical proximity of others may reflect the gradual reduction of stranger anxiety, and they point out that their own and others' findings reveal that decreasing space occurs later with stranger referents than with familiar referents. Another possible factor may be that older individuals find it prudent to concede greater amounts of space to toddlers, since they are prone to move around more unpredictably and more vigorously: best to keep your distance if they are carrying a paintbrush or a plate of jelly and ice-cream. In laboratory tasks or real-world settings where children are dealing with peers, then group processes may play a role, such that proximity is sought to liked (ingroup) individuals and distance established from outgroups (Hoffer, 1981). Development may consist of gradual increases in the amount of personal space accepted among friends as a function of increasing physical size, increasing social cognitive awareness of others' perspectives and needs, and awareness of adults' standards.

Adults themselves give children feedback about interpersonal spacing conventions. In an imaginative field experiment, Fry and Willis (1971) had children act as confederates, and sent them out to stand next to adults in bus queues. The children, aged 5, 8 and 10 years, were instructed to stand as close as possible to the grown-ups without actually touching them. You can probably anticipate the results. When a 5-year-old sidles up to you, the tendency is to smile affectionately; when a 10-year-old does so, the inference is that the child is being rude or inconsiderate. Fry and Willis found that older children were more likely to elicit negative reactions (frowns, stares, adult moving away).

Learning about interpersonal distance continues into adulthood, and appears to be integrated with greater understanding of social hierarchies. Watch the spontaneous spacing arrangements the next time you attend a departmental function that involves students from different years. Lott and Sommer (1967) found that seating distances reflected academic rank, with students from the higher years sitting closer to each other than to lowly first years. This is difficult to explain in terms of mere familiarity effects (the senior students would have known each other for longer) since there was also a tendency for senior students to sit away from the academics (whom presumably they knew reasonably well). It seems that even psychologists are prone to differentiate among themselves and adjust their interpersonal distances as a function of relative status and group identification.

Nonverbal Communication and Language Development

As we saw in chapter 7, there is controversy concerning the ontogenetic relationship between nonverbal communication and language acquisition, with some researchers maintaining that there is a continuity from early nonverbal behaviors to language, and others arguing that language represents a discontinuous leap. Another important issue concerns the relative status of each channel as both are developing. Clearly, the nonverbal has developmental priority, in that it is exploited from the beginnings of life, well before recognizable and meaningful language is used. On the other hand, the emergence of language affords a whole new set of communicative possibilities, making it possible to talk about things that are not present, to communicate with someone without needing to look at them (e.g., shouting to a parent in another room), and to share labels for interesting things. Does this mean that nonverbal communication loses its significance as language develops?

There is little evidence to suggest that nonverbal skills atrophy with the emergence of language. In some contexts, such as laboratory tasks involving multiple choices among toys, infants show an increase in vocal reference and a decline in gestural reference during the second year (Bretherton et al., 1981a). However, in other interactions nonverbal communications are still used extensively. For example, visual social referencing does not decrease with the advent of language, but at least up to 3 years the two increase concurrently (Walden, 1991). Acredolo and Goodwyn (1988) argue that the development of symbolic gesturing and language during the second year are intimately connected. They stress that both begin to appear at about the same time and that they serve a similar range of communicative functions in similar social contexts. The two modes of communication also tend to complement each other, such that if the child wishes to refer to an object then he or she uses either a word or a symbol, but not both simultaneously: "It is as though the child's desire to communicate is supreme, with the choice of which modality to use depending on whatever works within his or her particular social environment" (Acredolo and Goodwyn, 1988, p. 464).

During the next year or two, children continue to integrate verbal and nonverbal information economically and efficiently. Marcos (1991) shows that 18-month-olds resort to nonverbal gestures (such as pointing and reaching) when verbal communications with their mothers break down or falter. Von Raffler-Engel (1981) illustrates the interweaving of lexical and nonverbal behavior with an interesting example of an Italian 3-year-old who had one word, *kappa*, for both *scarpa* (shoe) and *schiaffo* (slap). To distinguish his meaning in a particular use, he marked the second (slap) sense with a stern facial expression (decidedly similar to the expression used by his father when the matter of dispensing slaps came up). As children become increasingly adept conversationalists, they gain skills in complementing or supplementing verbal utterances with appropriate gestures and expressions (see van der Geest, 1981; von Raffler-Engel, 1981; Tomasello et al., 1985). There is also evidence that competence in discriminating among nonverbal expressions is correlated positively with verbal ability, at least among younger school-aged children (Knowles and Nixon, 1989).

Nevertheless, the relationship between the channels may change with age. Consider your own interpretation of conflicting messages, that is, instances when a person says one thing ("I really like your new hairstyle"), while his face displays some signs of negativity (it would be a he, of course, since males are not so good at dissimulating). Under these circumstances, most of us tend to discount the verbal message as mere politeness, and to interpret the nonverbal signals as conveying the true sentiment. In much of informal and formal interaction, we seek actively cues to the underlying feelings and motives of other people. Obviously, with social experience we discover that people do not always mean what they say. As a result, adults tend to place greater weight on visual (especially facial) information than the verbal (DePaulo et al. 1978; Volkmar and Siegel, 1982).

This task is complicated by the fact that most people are aware of at least some aspects of nonverbal presentation. Hence, they try to control them by using socially appealing behaviors such as smiling. If they overdo it, we become suspicious. Bill Clinton ran into problems in the early stages of his campaign because he smiled *too much* while selling his agenda; as a result, he acquired the nickname Slick Willy.

But while adults are distrustful of what they hear when it is contradicted by what they see, young children demonstrate precisely the opposite bias. When presented with conflicting messages in verbal and nonverbal channels, they appear to be highly "literal minded" (Bugental et al., 1970), and place greater weight on the words. In evaluating a communication from someone who has a friendly face but says something unfriendly, children interpret the communication as negative. This occurs even when the adult is familiar, and may be the source of considerable mismatch in parent–child communication. Bugental et al. (1970) interviewed parents about films of their interactions with kindergarten-aged children, and found that many were surprised to discover that messages they had intended as jocular were actually interpreted as criticisms by the child.

Volkmar and Siegel (1982) tested children's (aged 1 to 3 years 6 months) reactions to an adult who presented messages that involved channel complementarity (i.e., what he said was consistent with his facial display and gestures) or channel discrepancy. For example, in the complementary condition the experimenter put on a warm, friendly face, gestured manually to the child to approach, and said "come here." Alternatively, in the discrepant condition, while maintaining the same nonverbal appearance, he told the child to "stay away." In the discrepant condition children typically complied with what was being said rather than what was being displayed visually.

A possible explanation of these kinds of findings is that younger children find it difficult to decenter from one channel and interpret a message from the other one simultaneously (DePaulo and Rosenthal, 1978; Piaget and Inhelder, 1966). However, this explanation does not account for the predominance of the verbal channel. We would not interpret adults' greater reliance on the nonverbal channel as reflecting a failure to decenter, and it may be that children's suppression of information available from a hitherto extensively used channel tells us something about the demands of early language. Perhaps language dominates for a while because it is an especially complex and challenging developmental task.

Summary

It was stressed earlier that nonverbal communication is meaningful because it is used in relation to others. Developmental research establishes that it is an integral feature of social life from infancy and it forms the principal communicative mechanism during the crucial period of entry into the peer community. The kinds of nonverbal skills that a child acquires, the extent and adequacy of their use, their symbolic and functional significance all depend upon or are influenced by interactions with others.

Interactions with others, however, can be effected in more than one channel of communication. This raises the interesting question of how different channels are related. By the toddler years *both* forms of communication are available and used extensively. Young children are able to exploit either mode to convey a specific meaning. Linguistic communication without nonverbal communication is rare in early childhood (children do not become immobile, stoney-faced automatons every time they begin to speak), and communicative development involves a continuous interaction between the two channels. Although typically complementary, the two channels are sometimes contradictory and as life goes on, we discover more frequently that people do not always mean what they say. Research indicates a developmental shift in terms of the relative weight attached to verbal versus nonverbal cues to the meaning of a person's message: in the case of conflicting information, young language users tend to believe what they hear, older individuals tend to rely on what they see.

Conclusions

While language acquisition has been a boom area of developmental research in the past couple of decades, the study of nonverbal communicative development has been growing quietly beside it. Communication is a defining characteristic of social behavior, and the pervasiveness of nonverbal communication throughout childhood interactions makes it a major topic for the attention of developmental social psychologists. Research reviewed in this chapter is making important advances. Once again, a complex interplay between innate and experiential factors is indicated. Infants certainly bring into the world effective means of nonverbal expression and they show early abilities to differentiate among nonverbal cues in the social environment; but the course of development implicates other competencies (including social–cognitive skills) and is influenced by opportunities, examples, and expectations in the child's social context.

Further reading

Baudonnière, P.-M., Garcia-Werebe, M.-J., Michel, J. and Liégeois, J. (1989) Development of communicative competencies in early childhood: a model and results. In B. H. Schneider, G. Attili, J. Nadel and R. P. Weissberg (eds), *Social Competence in Developmental Perspective*. Dordecht: Kluwer.

These researchers present a model of the development of competence in peer communication during the first five years which allocates a principal role to nonverbal behaviors. They focus on qualitative and quantitative reorganizations of communicative behavior as the child strives increasingly to relate her or his activities to those of playmates.

Camras, L. A. (1992) Expressive development and basic emotions. *Cognition and Emotion*, 6, 269–83.

Camras reviews and then challenges Izard's differential emotions theory of infant emotions. She proposes an alternative framework, based on dynamical systems theory, which attaches greater weight to contextual factors in the development of expressive repertoires.

Feldman, R. S. and Rime, B. (1991) *Fundamentals of Nonverbal Behavior*. Cambridge: Cambridge University Press.

A set of state-of-the-art essays on several aspects of nonverbal communication, with several chapters on developmental perspectives.

Feyereisen, P. and de Lannoy, J.-D. (1991) *Gestures and Speech: psychological investigations.* Cambridge: Cambridge University Press.

An integrative review of research into the relations between gesture and speech, drawing on social psychological, neuropsychological, ethological, and developmental literatures. Contains a useful discussion of the implications of preverbal communication for language acquisition.

Hoffer, B. L. and St Clair, R. N. (eds) (1981) *Developmental Kinesics: the emerging paradigm.* Baltimore: University Park Press.

Although now a little old, the ideas and issues raised in this book provide a thoughtful basis for further studies in the development of nonverbal communication.

Neill, S. (1991) *Classroom Nonverbal Communication.* London: Routledge.

A comprehensive and well-illustrated account of the nature of nonverbal communication in the school, considering its place in teacher–child and peer interactions.

Chapter 9

Social Cognition I: Understanding the Social World

Linda: Who sits by you?
Jean: Pam.
Linda: Do you like Pam?
Jean: No. Do you?
Linda: No, she's too mean.
        (Two 6-year-olds at school, quoted by Rizzo,
Friendship Development among Children in
School, *1989)*

We have seen ample evidence that the child's world is a social one from the very beginnings of life. But how does the child *understand* the properties and actions of other people? How does the child conceive of the relationship between the self and others? Understanding people is one of the most difficult things that human beings have to do, yet it is also an endeavour that seems to motivate us extensively (M. Bennett, 1993; Fiedler, 1996; Fiske and Taylor, 1991; Heider, 1958; Kelley, 1972; Leyens, 1983; Leyens and Dardenne, 1996). Linda and Jean, above, seem already to have entered into the spirit of things, but what do they understand of what they are saying?

Understanding others is difficult for several reasons. For one, people are capable of an infinite variety of behaviors, making what they do hard to categorize and predict. For another, the laws of the social world are less reliable than those of the physical world. If, for instance, you push an object off a table, the law of gravity dictates what it will do; but if you push a friend off a table, her reaction could be to reciprocate, to bite your ankle, to tickle your toes, to run away, to get back up, to burst into tears, to burst into laughter, to call for assistance, or to sit on a high-backed chair next time you are around.

A further problem is that some of the most interesting properties and processes of people – such as their thoughts, intentions, and emotions – are not directly observable and relate to their outward appearance in quite complex ways. Your dislodged friend could burst into laughter to mask embarrassment, to please you, to frustrate you, to allay your anticipation of the revenge she fully intends to exact or because she finds the incident amusing.

Yet another complication is that "people perceive back" (Fiske and Taylor, 1991, p. 18). Unlike liquid transferring from one size beaker to another, the social objects we try to make sense of are very often doing much the same to us, and adjusting their behavior because of what they think we think they think . . . You can bet that Pam has her own views of Linda and Jean.

Finally, understanding other people is difficult because we tend to have emotional reactions toward them, and vice versa. Cognition about the social world is "hot," something which we cannot easily detach from affect. Linda and Jean may begin to act differently toward Pam now that they have agreed upon a shared diagnosis, and if Pam gets to hear of their appraisal, her response is likely to involve more than registering a new fact. (In due course, and in relation to another incident, we find that she calls Jean a "dummy," an epithet which Jean says that she finds unspeakable. Then Jean calls Pam a dummy; read Rizzo, 1989, for further details.)

Difficult as it may be to understand other people, we find the task very motivating. Some individuals are driven to extraordinary lengths by this task: they train to become psychologists. But the concerns of the psychologist are merely the institutionalized extreme of a natural activity. There are strong adaptive reasons why most humans attempt at least some level of understanding of their fellows, since the ability to differentiate between friends and enemies may make a primitive but critical contribution to survival and is essential to mediate more complex navigations of the social environment (Cairns and Cairns, 1988). We need regularly to determine with whom we should interact, from whom we can obtain useful information, with whom it is advantageous to cooperate, how others interpret situations, what their motives are and what they might do next. We need to know who is mean and who is not and what to do if someone calls us a dummy. In dealing with these matters, virtually everybody is a psychologist.

In this and the following two chapters, we will be concerned with some of the activities of lay psychologists, discussing the rapidly expanding field of research into what is known as *social cognition*. Social cognition is a focal topic for developmental social psychologists, and research into social cognition forms the theoretical backdrop to much contemporary investigation of a whole range of developmental topics. We will encounter social cognitive theories or perspectives repeatedly in other chapters of this book. The purpose of chapters 9–11 is to introduce the main themes of social cognitive work.

What is social cognition? Two research orientations

The first point to stress is that the term "social cognition" is used in different ways by different investigators. Probably the most widely used sense is that of social cognition as *cognition about social phenomena*: "The object of study concerns how people make sense of other people and themselves" (Fiske and Taylor, 1991, p. 14). Adopting this definition, much recent research in social and developmental psychology has attempted to test and extend cognitive theories by applying them to social domains. For example, as we saw in chapter 1, traditional cognitive developmental psychology, such as the work of Piaget and his followers, was concerned primarily with the child's understanding of physical and spatiotemporal relations. Valuable advances in the study of developmental social cognition have been achieved as researchers have begun to use Piagetian or similar stage-sequence models to account for children's reasoning about people, interpersonal relations, institutions, and societal structures. We will consider some of this work later in the present chapter. For the moment, this orientation can be referred to as *individual* social cognition: in the standard cognitive metaphor, the individual is conceived of as observing, interpreting, and judging the world which, in this case, happens to be the social world. Fiske and Taylor (1991) comment that the social perceiver in this sense is represented as something of a hermit.

A less widely used sense of the term social cognition is that of *cognition as a product of social interaction*. Although less widely used, this interpretation has by no means been ignored and it has been the focus of a good deal of insightful research, especially in European developmental social psychology. This work, which will be discussed in more detail in chapter 11, is concerned with the ways in which involvement with other people – adults or peers – affects, promotes, and guides the development of cognitive abilities. In some ways, this sense of social cognition brings more radical implications for social psychology and for psychology more generally, since it proposes a shift in attention from the individual processor often assumed by psychologists as the object of enquiry, and fosters instead the notion of cognitive activity as founded in (or at least, influenced by) interpersonal processes. It asserts that "Human knowledge is a social product" (Forgas, 1981c, p. 1). In this orientation, we are moving toward a truly *social* cognition: rather than the individual looking out, people are out there together, participating in a social world and affected by its processes.

Although these two definitions differ in emphasis, and have led to different research directions, they are not mutually exclusive. At present, they provide orientations for a wide range of enquiries, some veering more toward one sense of social cognition, some toward the other. Our task in reviewing them would be easier if we were to settle on just one direction but then, as we have just agreed, understanding people is difficult, and in the long run it will not help us to narrow arbitrarily our focus to just one perspective. Hence, while we will begin with research focused on how the individual conceives of the social world, it will become clear that this process ("individual" social cognition) itself is influenced by input and guidance from others ("social" social cognition). Similarly, while we see later that the outcomes of social interaction may often be cognitive gains, the resolution of these social products depends upon the constructive mental activity of the individual.

In the present chapter, we address some of the social knowledge that children have to attain and aspects of developmental progress involved. We begin with one of the most prominent objects of social cognition: the self. As seen in chapters 2 and 3, differentiating the self from others is a major task of early childhood. In the first section, we consider some of the cognitive and affective aspects of these developments. In the second section, we consider the development of understanding of others, discussing in turn the infant's sensitivity to the differences between people and things, and the child's knowledge of others' personal characteristics, mental processes, and emotions. In the third section, we consider developmental perspectives on a social psychological theory which offers a useful link between cognitions about self and cognitions about others, namely social comparison theory.

Chapter 10 is concerned with the development of social reasoning processes and knowledge of the social structure. Chapter 11 examines theories and research concerned with the processes of learning through interaction.

Developing a Concept of Self

Lewis (1990) suggests that achieving identity, in the sense of acquiring a set of beliefs about the self (a *self-schemata*), is one of the core developmental tasks of a social being. It is not an instantaneous achievement, but one which progresses through several levels of complexity, and indeed continues to develop through the lifespan. At the very beginning of life, it is unlikely that the neonate distinguishes itself from its environment, but within the first few months it becomes able to distinguish self from other and, as we will see shortly, to gain some awareness of its own continuity through time.

These early achievements, which Lewis and his colleagues call the *existential self*, constitute important bases for social development. However, at this stage the infant's self-knowledge is comparable to the self-knowledge of members of other species (e.g. monkeys have comparable understanding). One of the distinguishing characteristics of human self-knowledge is that we become *aware* that we have it: that is, we are conscious of our existence and our uniqueness (Buss, 1992). This awareness is central to the development of identity and hence to the social cognitive processes whereby we determine what our own characteristics are and how we relate to others. Lewis and colleagues describe this level of self-knowledge as the *categorical self*.

Discovering the Self in Infancy and Early Childhood

Knowledge of the self may not on first sight appear a particularly social achievement. It seems to be a matter of the individual "looking in" to appraise her or his own characteristics. However, distinguishing the self from others presupposes some social knowledge, at the very least that "there are more than one of us around and that I am separate from the rest." Wallon (1949) argued that the infant's initial lack of a distinction between her or his own world and that of others reveals a complete immersion in the social environment from the outset; from this basis, the child gradually achieves an awareness of self.

One crucial source of information about our uniqueness is our interactions with others (Baldwin, 1902; Cooley, 1902; Fogel, 1993; Heider, 1958; Lewis and Brooks-Gunn, 1979; Mead, 1934; Wallon, 1949; Youniss, 1994). At the beginnings of life, this may be a matter of relating to the useful entities who come along when we cry, providing food, comfort, and stimulation and discovering discrepancies between what we can do on our own and what we can do with them or get them to do for us (see chapter 2). From these experiences we derive a sense of subjectivity, the feeling that we are a source of action separate from others (Grusec and Lytton, 1988; Hattie, 1992; Lewis and Brooks-Gunn, 1979).

Development of self-recognition

Knowledge of the self as subject (the sense of "I") is only part of the early developmental task. Most philosophers and psychologists who have addressed this topic agree that the other side of self-concept development is awareness of the self as object; that is, as a "me" that I and others perceive (Baldwin, 1902; Cooley, 1902; Damon and Hart, 1988; Harter, 1983; Hattie, 1992; Higgins, 1987; James, 1890; Wallon, 1949). One component of the "me" – and the one which has attracted most research attention with respect to infancy – is the physical self.

How could we investigate the development of knowledge of the physical self among subjects who cannot speak? One simple but effective technique, adapted from research with animals, involves testing infants' reactions to images of themselves in a mirror (Amsterdam, 1972; Gouin-Decarie et al., 1983; Lewis and Brooks-Gunn, 1979). Lewis and Brooks-Gunn (1979), for example, had mothers unobtrusively smudge the nose of their infant with a spot of rouge. The infants were then placed near a mirror and the experimenters measured the amount of "nose-directed behavior" the subject displayed. Infants below the age of 12 months were often amused by what they seemed to regard as another child but showed virtually no interest in the novel

Figure 9.1   Self-recognition? This infant stares fixedly at lipstick smudged on her nose.

features (i.e., they did nothing to their nose). During the second year children were increasingly likely to take some action, such as reaching for their face and touching or rubbing the mark (figure 9.1).

Visual recognition is, of course, only one aspect of the development of self-knowledge, but it appears to correlate highly with others and it is integrated with other important aspects of development, such as emotional experiences and cognitive growth (Lewis and Brooks-Gunn, 1979). For example, the earliest manifestations of self-recognition in the latter part of the first year co-occur with the infant's increasing understanding of the permanence of objects and with the organization of emotional experiences around specific individuals, such as wariness of strangers, happiness in the presence of attachment figures (see chapter 3). During the second year, as infants gain greater knowledge of the self–other distinction, they begin also to develop emotions that reflect relations with others – emotions such as guilt, empathy, embarrassment (Izard, 1978; Zahn-Waxler et al., 1992) – and they develop more sophisticated modes of representing social knowledge, especially through symbolic representation and language.

The development of self-definition

Toward the end of infancy children begin to construct a representation of the self as an objective entity, in Lewis's (1990) terms, the *categorical self*. This builds upon the knowledge of self as an enduring, unique phenomenon and provides a focus for the gradual elaboration of the individual's unique properties. These processes involve cognitive and linguistic developments that themselves entail interaction with other people. Other people are important because they help to define our properties, partly by adjusting their behavior to accommodate their expectations of us (for example, according to our gender or perceived temperament), partly by reacting to things we do, and partly by labeling what they see in us. Cooley (1902) captured the significance of others' perceptions in his notion of the "looking glass self," the idea that how we come to see ourselves is at least partially a reflection of how others see us.

As toddlers, children begin to learn words which reflect self-awareness and help to organize their knowledge of self (such as names, personal pronouns; Durkin et al., 1982; Shatz, 1994; van der Meulen, 1991; Stern, 1985). Another, related, aspect of developing self-definition is found in the individual's perception of property relations. Recognizing or deciding that something is "mine" presupposes some differentiation of "me" from everything else (Lewis, 1990; van der Meulen, 1991). Children's behavior reveals that they begin to understand the rules of possession quite early in life, probably during the second year, and that these rules are implicated in early social relations such as sibling quarrels (Dunn, 1988b, p. 68f). By their third year, children refer to a wide variety of self-characteristics, including internal processes (feelings and perceptions), appearance, opinions, and volition (Dunn and Brown, 1991; van der Meulen, 1991; Shatz, 1994).

Self and others' treatment of self

On the basis of Lewis and Brooks-Gunn's (1979) work it is possible to chart normative patterns of infants' development of reactions to self-reflections in mirrors. However, evidence suggests that the extent to which the child follows the normal course is affected by aspects of his or her relations with the primary caregiver. Pipp et al. (1992) found that among 2- and 3-year-olds, the extent and complexity of infant self-knowledge was related to attachment type: once again, the securely attached infants were more advanced.

In an interesting clinical report, Kernberg (1987) describes several examples of infants and toddlers who demonstrate precocious, delayed, or bizarre reactions to their reflections, and in each case there are exceptional characteristics to their relationship with their mother. For example, a mother of three who was suffering depression displayed cold, strained behavior toward her 4-year-old daughter, cheerful engagement with her 2-year-old daughter, and glum, mechanistic responses to her 9-month-old son. When the mirror reactions of her children were tested, the older daughter seemed indifferent and had little interest in her reflection (unlike most 4-year-olds); the 2-year-old shared her mirror reflection laughingly with her mother (in contrast to most children of this age, who often show an adverse reaction to the image). The 9-month-old:

> looked at the mirror without a smile and did not react to the mirror with the vividness and enthusiasm of "the other child" characteristic of this age. He reflected the mother's

depression as she handled him in a rather mechanical and impersonal way and with a rather serious expression on her face. (Kernberg, 1987, p. 337)

In short, infants' and young children's reactions to their own mirror reflections reveal not only cognitive progress in the acquisition of a self-concept but an affective orientation which may be influenced by the child's principal social relationships.

Development of Self-concept beyond Early Childhood

The preschool years

During the preschool years and beyond, part of social cognitive development is concerned with learning more about the characteristics of one's self. This includes learning about both external and internal properties. When self-descriptions of young children are elicited, they tend to be focused predominantly upon visible, tangible properties or possessions: "I've got black hair and brown eyes," "I've got my own bike" (Damon and Hart, 1988). Slightly older preschoolers emphasize more their activities: "I can ride my bike," "I play with my dog." Even 3-year-olds, though, have concepts of selves and others that generalize across time: they can identify people who are "naughty," and can report on consistencies in their own responses to situations (Eder, 1989). They become increasingly aware of standards of behavior and begin to regulate their own, recognizing and organizing information about what they "should" and "should not" do (Kopp, 1991; Thompson, 1990). Before long, children begin to make these descriptions on a comparative basis: "I can run faster than my sister," "I am bigger than Marie." This process, known to social psychologists as *social comparison*, is an integral aspect of self-knowledge henceforth, and we will consider more fully what is involved later in the chapter.

Recent cognitive developmental research has shown that young children do become aware also of internal psychological processes. During the preschool years, children are beginning to develop a "theory of mind" (cf. Astington et al., 1988; Frye and Moore, 1991; Leekam, 1993; Shatz, 1994; Wellman, 1990). They are aware that they, and other people, have mental processes, such as thought, perception, and memory. By around the age of four, children are able to indicate that the place where this kind of thing goes on is the head (Flavell et al., 1980; Johnson and Wellman, 1982). They can distinguish among their own mental representations, recognizing that it is possible to imagine or dream of objects yet acknowledging that these things cannot be touched, while real things can be (Estes et al., 1989). They understand that sensory experiences, such as seeing or hearing, can produce mental representations, such as knowledge or inferences (Chandler et al., 1989; Pratt, 1993; Pratt and Bryant, 1990; Wimmer et al., 1988). In other words, the preschooler's self-concept already includes some awareness of his or her own psychological properties and processes.

The extent to which children grasp the continuity of the self during this period is uncertain. Recall from chapter 5 that toddlers may not be confident of the durability that older people take for granted, such as gender. Cowan (1978) summarizes unpublished work by Piaget in which children were asked to order pictures of themselves taken at yearly intervals: 3- and 4-year-olds were unable to achieve the correct order, and appeared to see little relationship between the self of even a few days ago and the self at the point of testing. (There is scope for a good research project on the effects of home videos on this aspect of self-concept development!)

The school years

During middle childhood and into adolescence, the self-concept becomes more highly differentiated. Advancing cognitive and linguistic abilities mean that children are able to understand and use a broader array of concepts and terms to describe themselves and other people. Elicited self-descriptions now include many more references to internal, psychological characteristics, such as competencies, knowledge, emotions, values, and personality traits (Damon and Hart, 1988; Eder, 1989; Livesley and Bromley, 1973; Markus and Nurius, 1986; Montemayor and Eisen, 1977; Selman, 1980; Yuill, 1993). Self-disclosure (the verbal communication of private thoughts and feelings) increases during this period (Erwin, 1993).

Alongside the development of these abilities, the child's social world is changing markedly by virtue of the engagement in the formal educational system (Hattie, 1992; Higgins and Parsons, 1983; Valsiner, 1989a). Schooling highlights others' expectations about how the individual should develop. The self now becomes involved with an institution, which both confers a new category ("I go to Hampstead Primary") and provides a social context in which new goals are set and comparisons with others (peers) are prompted. This makes evaluation of the self all the more salient, and we turn to this topic shortly.

The development of the self-concept, then, is a multifaceted social cognitive process which continues through middle childhood, and beyond. Adolescence is a particularly important period for self-understanding and the development of personal identity (see chapter 15), and concerns with the nature of one's self and one's purposes in life resurface continually through adulthood (see chapters 18 and 19).

The Social Context of Self-knowledge

As already stressed, development of a self-concept (or concepts) is an inherently social activity. The achievement of self-knowledge does not pop unaided out of an inquisitive little head, eagerly but independently formulating terms to capture noteworthy phenomena. Children are engaged in interactions with more mature beings who are very interested in them, and who provide both context and guidance. We need other people in order to determine what is distinctive about our own self. This does not mean that the individual is incapable of independent discovery, reasoning, and the synthesis of information about the self, but it does mean that we are affected by other people's emphases on social and psychological properties, and by their expectations about who we should become. To illustrate, let us consider how other people might be involved in several of the dimensions of self-development.

Self, others, and public characteristics

Awareness of the self is prompted in the course of exchanges with others who try to control or influence behavior. There are many conflicts between children and their parents during the second and third years as children strive to exploit their developing abilities and their widening interests in the world around them while parents try to regulate their behavior (Dunn, 1988b; Heckhausen, 1994). Preschoolers show keen awareness of self-concerns in respect of behavioral opportunities among peers: "It's my turn!"

In these kinds of social contexts, children often receive information from others concerning their public characteristics. Parents approve or disapprove of particular actions, they suggest goals and encourage aspirations, they joke about events and activities in which the child participates. Dunn (1988b) argues that in these everyday ways, children receive continuously large amounts of information about their "self" and their relations to others. Self-definition develops in the course of interactions which arise from the child's concerns with meeting his or her own interests, and the sense of self-efficacy that grows with success in gaining influence (Bandura, 1986).

Emotional regulation in social contexts

Emotions are pivotal to the self, conferring meaning on our experiences and providing the motivational force of our continuing discoveries (Cicchetti et al., 1991; Parke, 1994; Saarni, 1989, 1990; Sroufe, 1979). In earlier chapters, we have seen much evidence of the importance of emotions in social development: in the course of forming attachments, in the mastery of nonverbal communication, in the development of social competencies. Understanding and regulating emotion depend crucially on social engagement (Campos et al., 1983; Cassidy et al., 1992; Izard and Kobak, 1991; Parke, 1994; Trevarthen, 1993). Caregivers provide the principal social contexts, and the infant's early experiences of emotional regulation are often negotiated in the course of interactions with the mother (Field, 1994; Thompson, 1994). As discussed in chapter 8, in emotionally ambiguous situations infants often look to their caregiver for nonverbal cues as to how to react (social referencing). Several studies of children's early uses of the language of emotion have also shown associations between children's productions and the language of their caregivers (Bretherton et al., 1986). For example, much of parents' early reference to emotion is focused on the child's feelings, including physical discomforts, arousal, likes and dislikes, often with the apparent intention of guiding or controlling the child's affective state (Dunn and Brown, 1991, 1994; Dunn et al., 1987). Between 18 and 36 months children begin to label their own emotions and those of others (usually, with self-reference emerging first; Bretherton and Beeghly, 1982; Shatz, 1994).

Parke (1994; Parke et al., 1993) proposes that parents' reactions to the child's emotional displays may inform her or him what is socially acceptable, and how to define the self ("Big boys don't cry.") Important emotional constraints upon self-presentation, such as pride, shame, and guilt, are intimately related to the acquisition of social norms, and the awareness that other people evaluate behavior (Harris, 1989a;

Stipek et al., 1992b; Zahn-Waxler et al., 1991). For example, Semin and Papadopou-lou (1990) show that mothers themselves feel a social obligation on behalf of their child to ensure that the correct emotion is displayed. They presented mothers with short vignettes describing accidents that their child might commit in public (such as dropping a bottle in a supermarket, spilling soup in a restaurant). Mothers were asked to indicate how embarrassed the child would feel and how embarrassed they would feel. The degree of embarrassment the child was expected to feel was positively correlated with the child's age. The degree of embarrassment the mother herself anticipated was negatively correlated with the degree of embarrassment she expected her child to feel. In other words: "the less the child displays emotion, the more the mother does" (p. 117). The mother is prompted to advise the child of the problem, leading to corrective actions toward the child which give him or her opportunities to learn about emotional responses to situations. In short, learning how to define and regulate the emotional facets of the self is closely interwoven with the social context.

Developing a self with, despite, and because of other people

Having stressed that other people make important contributions to the contexts and processes of self-development, it should also be emphasized that external influences are not omnipotent and that relationships are not unidirectional. Malatesta-Magai's (1991) longitudinal studies of early emotional development indicate that both parties (parent and infant) learn to cope with and influence the emotional behavior of the other as part of the dialogue of the early social relationship. The self is not constructed as a direct function of parental or teacher's decree (the demands of parenting and teaching would be greatly alleviated if it were). Indeed, there are many respects in which there are mismatches between external appraisal and self-definition. For example, through middle childhood to adolescence, the correlations between individ-uals' self-ratings and ratings of those individuals by others on a number of important dimensions tend to be quite low (Cairns and Cairns, 1988). This may well be quite adaptive for at least some individuals, since they are able to sustain positive impressions of themselves that are not widely shared.

Similarly, the social cognitive conflicts arising from diverging perspectives of the self may generate contexts within which individuals formulate self-definitions that *reflect* others' ascriptions but do not necessarily *accept* them. For example, parents tell their children "you are too cheeky," "you are lazy," "you are very good at maths," and so on. These appraisals may not always be agreed: a child may feel she is not cheeky but unusually mature for her age; another may regard himself as a bit of a thinker, and therefore temperamentally unable to assist with household chores. Accepting or rejecting these descriptors makes self-definition a social endeavour, rather than a unilateral definition by external forces.

There is evidence that the cognitive elaborations incurred by dealing with other people's evaluations may actually increase the salience and accessibility of the labels they apply. Lord et al. (1992) had children (aged 8–10 years) complete a task in which they had to decide whether each of a series of trait adjectives applied to them. Some of the adjectives were positive, some were negative. Subsequently, the words they had been working with were embedded in a much longer set of descriptors, and the children were required to identify any words among this larger set that they had made a decision about in the previous, self-descriptive, task. Children who had negative reputations in the eyes of parents or teachers were more likely than peers with more positive reputations to remember deciding whether they had unlikeable traits – especially unlikeable traits that they claimed they did *not* have.

Thus, the looking glass – others' perceptions of the self – *affects* us but does not simply *shape* us. In fact, what emerges in self-development is a complex social product which for most individuals includes a sense of both actual and ideal (Higgins, 1987). The discrepancy between what is and what ought to be may be one of the fundamental meeting places of social cognition and affect. Higgins argues that the process achieves its potency through emotional pressures from parents who establish expectations about the ideal self, a "guide" toward what they believe the child should be striving to become. As the child becomes aware of the risks of love withdrawal upon disappointing one's parents, so he or she is motivated to monitor an internalized notion of their standards. Any discrepancy between the actual and the guide is potentially painful.

Research with children indicates that generally they perceive less distinctiveness in relation to their parents than in relation to their peers, possibly because they find it more difficult to react against the opinions and values of others to whom they feel very close than others with whom they interact less frequently (Oosterwegel and Oppenheimer, 1993). Based on retrospective data obtained from American undergraduates, Higgins (1987) reports that awareness of discrepancies between one's actual and one's ideal self is associated with emotional problems, especially depression and anxiety.

Self-concept and Culture

The self-concept emerges in different ways in different cultures (Damon and Hart, 1988; Kim and Choi, 1994). For example, we noted above that references to one's own possessions is an early marker of selfhood in Western children. This emphasis is not universal. Whiting and Edwards (1988) report that in several of the societies they studied in a large cross-cultural project, children do not own toys and claims of "mine" are rare. Damon and Hart (1988) in a study of children in a Puerto Rican fishing village found that although these subjects were developmentally on a par with Americans of the same age, they tended to define their actions with reference to their *effects* on others rather than the relative *superiority* of their actions in comparison with others.

Greenfield (1966), in the course of conservation experiments with unschooled Wolof children in Senegal, found that subjects were baffled when asked (in their own language) "Why do you *think* or *say* that thus and such is true?" The children could explain their conservation responses, but Greenfield reports that they seemed to be lacking in Western self-consciousness: they saw no distinction between their own thoughts about something and the thing itself. Children's theories of mind, and the relationship between mind and self, may vary with culture.

Western cultures tend to recognize the self as a legitimate focus for attention (Wicklund and Frey, 1980), but there is variety among cultures in terms of the acceptability of public preoccupation with self. Even among Western societies, for example, self-disclosure tends to be more prevalent in some cases than in others. It is more common among Americans than Germans, and still less common among the British (see Erwin, 1993). In some other cultures, any overt emphasis on the self is viewed with suspicion. Among Chinese people, for example, it is regarded as an unhealthy expression of individualism (Bond and Hwang, 1986; Stevenson, 1991). Chinese people tend to value self-effacement and to endorse group-oriented self-concepts more than individualistic concepts (Triandis, 1991).

A striking illustration of cultural differences in self-understanding is provided by van den Heuvel et al.'s (1992) study of children in The Netherlands. These investigators elicited Dutch, Turkish, and Moroccan 10–11-year-olds' self-descriptions in order to test the prediction that the children's concepts would reflect the individualistic or collectivistic orientation of their respective cultures. As expected, the Western children used many more psychological statements than did their Eastern peers; also consistent with predictions, the Turkish and Moroccan children employed substantially more references to social aspects of the self. The authors conclude that, despite the fact that all of their subjects were drawn from similar, low socioeconomic environments within Amsterdam, inter-cultural differences lead to profoundly different ways of looking at the self. The *content* of social cognition varies with social group.

The Development of Self-esteem

Differentiating oneself from others is not merely a cognitive achievement. It concerns also one's sense of reality and worth (Cairns and Cairns, 1988). Not surprisingly, we tend to attach salience and values to the self. If we did not, our survival prospects would be dim, since we would be less disposed to take care of the self, protect it from discomforts and danger, and get it what it wants. There is evidence that attaching high value to the self may contribute to children's resilience in the face of stress (Ruble and Thompson, 1992). Because we have an affective commitment to the self, it is something of an oversimplification to attempt to distinguish between self-concept and self-esteem (Damon and Hart, 1988). Hattie (1992) argues that while a conceptual distinction is possible, in practice most measures have failed to discriminate the two.

Harter's (1987, 1988) work has been among the most successful in uncovering the interweaving of conceptual and affective knowledge of the self. She shows that in the early years, children tend to regard the self favorably:

> I am a boy, my name is Jason. I live with my mother and father in a big house. I have a kitty that's orange and a sister named Lisa and a television set that's in my own room. I'm four years old and I know all my A.B.C.s. Listen to me say them, A, B, C, D, E, F,

G, H, J, L, K, O, M, P, R, Q, X, Z. I can run faster than anyone. I like pizza and I have a nice teacher. I can count up to 100, want to hear me? I love my dog, Skipper. I can climb to the top of the jungle gym. I have brown hair and I go to preschool. I'm really strong. I can lift this chair, watch me! (quoted in Harter, 1988, p. 49)

Jason seems to be enjoying himself and the things he can do, even if his estimations of his accomplishments (such as knowledge of the alphabet) tend to stray from empirical reality. Harter argues that at this stage, children's self-concepts display little organization and little negativity. Children have not yet formulated a global concept of self-worth, but make judgments about the self in relation to a number of specific domains. As a result, their self-descriptions consist of lists of disjointed features, usually focused on possessions, attributes, and attainments, with a pervasively positive attitude.

As the individual becomes increasingly aware of her or his uniqueness, so she or he becomes increasingly aware of others' appraisals and expectations. During middle childhood, self-definitions typically include evaluative components, or *self-affects* (Harter, 1983, 1988). Harter maintains that these affective orientations are influenced by others' reactions to the self and by assessments of self-competence (assessments which are themselves often based on comparisons with others). The developing individual now expresses pride in some characteristics and achievements, and shame or feelings of inadequacy in respect of others:

I'm in the fifth grade this year at Rockland Elementary School. I'm pretty popular. That's because I'm nice and helpful, the other girls in my class say that I am. I have two girlfriends who are really close friends, and I'm good at keeping their secrets. Most of the boys are pretty yukky. My brother Jason is younger and I don't feel that way about him, tho' sometimes he gets on my nerves too. But I control my temper most of the time and don't get too angry and I'd be ashamed of myself if I got really mad at him. (Lisa, older sister of Jason, quoted in Harter, 1988, p. 49)

Integrating domains of self-knowledge

From about the age of 8, children have the cognitive and emotional maturity to be able to integrate information concerning several domains of their lives into a global concept of self-worth (Marsh et al., 1991). Harter (1987) had children rate themselves in five areas (scholastic competence, athletic competence, social acceptance, physical appearance, and behavioral conduct) as well as provide a more general measure of their self-esteem. She found that where children perceived a discrepancy between their own competence and the importance they attached to a given domain, the more likely it was that their global self-esteem would be low; on the other hand, children who perceived themselves as not very competent in some domains but who regarded those domains as relatively unimportant tended to maintain high self-esteem. For example, someone who fares well in school subjects but poorly in athletics may hold the opinion that athletic accomplishments are relatively unimportant to her, and thus suffer no serious threat to her global self-esteem.

One domain which appears especially important, however, is that of physical appearance. Children of either sex who were unhappy with how they looked tended to have low self-esteem. If we were to consider this finding in purely cognitive terms, it might appear surprising: after all, as we have seen, children's social knowledge progresses from a relatively external orientation in early childhood to a more abstract, psychological orientation in middle childhood. Why should a relatively superficial aspect of self, such as outward appearance, correlate more reliably with global self-esteem than substantive features, such as competencies and conduct? The briefest reflection on the social contexts of development identifies plausible candidates for the sources of appearance-based anxieties; good looks are highly valued in most cultures (Berscheid, 1986; Jackson, 1992; Langlois and Roggman, 1990). Young children themselves display biases in social perception according to the attractiveness of the target (Alley and Hildebrandt, 1988; Erwin, 1993; see chapter 2 on infants' attractiveness biases). Conceptions of physical appearance, which derive from comparisons with real and idealized social standards, are established relatively early in life as valued dimensions of selfhood.

Confirming the suggestion above that experiences associated with school may have an impact on the developing self-concept, there is evidence that self-esteem tends to reduce somewhat during the early years of schooling (Ruble, 1994). Initially optimistic appraisals of one's capacities and prospects tend to be challenged by discoveries of one's limitations, by the experiences of setbacks and difficulties in new educational tasks, and by social comparisons with peers who may be ahead in some domains (Marsh, 1985; Marsh et al., 1984). Marsh (1985) points out that this decline should not be interpreted as necessarily a "bad" thing, since the glowing self-concepts of younger children may be unrealistic.

Summary

Learning about the self is one of the primary tasks of social cognitive development. Distinguishing self from environment begins early in infancy (chapter 2), but this is the beginning of a protracted process in which the developing individual has to build up an enduring and multifaceted body of knowledge about his or her own properties and capacities. The self is more than a matter of a data base, but is an affective foundation for personal and interpersonal development. Constructing an understanding and evaluation of the self is closely dependent upon interactions with, and input from, other people. Other people introduce the conceptual and vocabulary framework within which self-definition is elaborated in the relevant culture, and provide feedback and focus throughout. While this context is influential, it has been argued here that it is not wholly deterministic: the individual develops through interaction with rather than subordination to the social environment.

Knowledge of Others

Learning about the self is closely interwoven with learning about other people (Damon and Hart, 1988; Dunn and Brown, 1994; Erwin, 1993; Harris, 1989a). There are several dimensions to this task, and it is one that people work on from infancy through adolescence, and beyond. It involves distinguishing people from other things, discovering the characteristics of individuals, and learning that others have an independent psychological existence (and hence that they might see and experience things differently from us). We consider each of these in this section.

Distinguishing People from Other Things

One of the infant's earliest social cognitive discoveries is that people are different from other things. It seems obvious to us that there are important distinctions between these two classes of entity (people and things), but then we have a lot of experience of both. Adults have a great deal of conscious knowledge about the nature of people and the properties of objects, knowledge which is accumulated, organized, and shared over a long time. Infants have much less experience, lack the ability to articulate this kind of knowledge, and cannot discuss existential matters with their caregivers. How do they understand the different natures of people and things?

Before considering possible answers to this mystery, it is interesting to note that for many developmental psychologists, the question feels more comfortable framed with a different emphasis. That is, do infants realize that people are a special class of things? The reason is that the central focus of infancy research until fairly recently has been on the infant's cognitive and perceptual functioning. Piaget (1936; see chapter 1) saw infancy as the sensorimotor stage of development, during which the child passes through a series of six substages of constructive discoveries about the environment and her or his relationship to it. For Piaget, the fascinating questions included how the infant discovered constancies and causalities, such as the permanence of objects, the continuity of form, size constancy, means–ends relationships and so on.

Following Piaget's inspiration, this work has generated many ingenious techniques for investigating infants' understanding (Bremner, 1994, Harris, 1989b; Willatts, 1989, provide useful reviews of Piaget's original ideas and of more recent work). The nature of the experimental paradigms developed in the course of this research tradition has been such that, typically, they involve taking infants out of their normal social contexts and testing solitary performance with objects. Although this is a useful research tactic for some purposes, one drawback is that these studies have become so fundamental to the study of infancy that they are sometimes confused with the fundamentals of the infant's world itself, as though the primary tasks of early life were to work out a theory of object permanence, master the phenomena of space and time, learn about causality – and *then* turn one's attention to the still more tricky things, such as other people. Piaget himself acknowledged that studying the infant's involvement with and feelings about other people "is much more difficult than studying his cognitive functions" (Piaget and Inhelder, 1966, p. 21) and, although he touched on this matter in passing, it never achieved prominence on his agenda for infancy research. As far as Piaget was concerned, the infant only became interested in people and their differences from other phenomena during the latter part of the first year, after the achievement of object permanence. However, more recent work has called this assumption into question.

There is abundant evidence, discussed in chapter 2, that infants are very interested in people from the beginnings of life. In itself, this does not establish that they perceive a difference between people and other objects. People are among the most interesting of stimulus configurations because they possess distinctive facial contours, interesting sound-producing devices and food-administering apparatuses, but this does not mean that infants are aware of their internal properties such as subjectivity, intentionality, and feelings (Sylvester-Bradley, 1986).

But supposing we found that infants respond differently to people and to objects? Or that they vary their reactions to a person according to whether she behaves as a person or as a virtually inanimate object? There is evidence of both outcomes. Richards (1974) reported informally that observations of very young infants showed that they react differently to interesting objects and to people. With the former, they concentrate attention, scan the object visually. When interacting with a person, the infant's posture becomes less tense, the eyes widen, the mouth opens, the face is more mobile, and smiling is more common. Sylvester-Bradley (1986) replicated these findings in a study of 10-week-old infants' responses to face-to-face interaction with their mother and to solitary experience with a wooden ball that moved jerkily across their field of vision. Each infant underwent both experimental conditions, with order counterbalanced. Much as Richards described, the babies oriented "socially" toward the mother, adjusting their facial behavior and looks, and were slightly (though non-significantly) more likely to reach out toward the novel object. Richards (1974) comments that it would be very helpful to an infant to "know" when she or he was communicating with a person rather than doing something with a thing.

Studies using Tronick et al.'s (1979) "still face" paradigm (see chapter 2), in which mothers interact with their infant at first normally, using face, voice and touch, and then present a still, neutral face and refrain from touching, usually show that infants are dissatisfied with inanimate people. Visual attention declines, movements toward the mother decrease, and sometimes the child shows distress or annoyance. Broerse et al. (1983) and Gusella et al. (1988) found that with 3-month-olds, the crucial variable appears to be whether the mother touches the infant – at this age, much of their communication depends on tactile involvement and physical movement. With 6-month-olds, however, the lack of facial animation was sufficient to cause upset: infants of this age looked and smiled less at their mothers and grimaced more.

Legerstee (1991) studied a group of infants from the age of 3 to 25 weeks, observing their vocalizations in the presence of their mother, a female stranger or a doll, each of whom was either active or passive. Analysis of the audio tapes revealed that the babies' sounds varied with condition. Melodic sounds (which have speechlike variability in contour and pitch) were much more frequent when interacting with the active, talking mother than in other conditions; emotional sounds (such as crying, fussing, laughing)

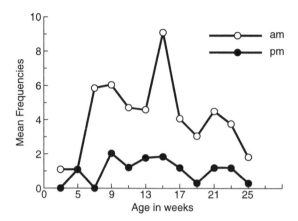

Figure 9.2   Infants' melodic sounds in response to an
active mother (AM) or passive mother (PM) during the
first six months.
(*Source*: Legerstee, 1991)

were much more likely in the presence of a person than a doll. Charting production of
melodic sounds over time provides persuasive evidence of a relationship between the
behavior of infant and communicative partner (see figure 9.2). In short, babies do
respond differently to people and things from very early in life, and increasingly so
during the first year.

These developments need to be understood in social context. They involve more
than the infant studying the world and discovering that people are especially
interesting: as has been firmly established in earlier chapters, people themselves are
very interested in infants and in how infants are reacting to them. In an interesting
variant of the "still face" paradigm, Murray and Trevarthen (1986) had mothers
interact with their 2-month-old infants via a video system, set up so that they could
interact face to face with eye contact. However, on some occasions the mother
interacted with the live baby, and on others with a replay of the baby's responses to
her earlier input (but which she was led to believe was "live"). Thus, the babies'
actions were identical in form in the two conditions, but moment-by-moment
responsiveness to the mother was quite different. There was a marked shift in how the
mothers spoke to the child. For example, they asked fewer questions, repeated their
utterances less frequently, and made fewer child-centered statements. Of course,
mothers do not expect their 2-month-olds to have a literal understanding of what
they are saying, but the important finding is that they like to *feel* that the child is
attending to them. Mothers' comments after the experiment revealed their discomfort
at the sensation that their infant seemed no longer to be reacting to and communicating with them as people: "I felt she wasn't responding to me. There was a barrier, you
know; it was as though I wasn't there and I just felt, well, either, she's not hearing
me or she's not seeing me" (Murray and Trevarthen, 1986, p. 26). The researchers

conclude that this is strong evidence that the infant is communicative and an active contributor to the interactional process.

Debate continues about how much of an active contribution the child makes to the interaction and about exactly what kind of a representation of the categorical distinction between people and objects a very young infant could make (see Frye, 1989; and Sylvester-Bradley, 1986). However, two points are agreed. The first is that babies are responsive to both people and objects from birth (Frye, 1989). The second is that caregivers have expectations about the nature and development of the infant, and are keen to involve it in their world; adults – at least in some cultures – attribute meaning to the infant's actions and vocalizations and respond to them as though the child wished to participate in meaningful discourse.

The Development of Person Perception

Just as children come to discover aspects of their own physical, mental and emotional properties, so they come to relate their new knowledge to their understanding of others. For example, although children's early language about mental states tends to be more frequently concerned with their own experiences, they make many appropriate references to the psychological states of others (Bretherton and Beeghly, 1982; Moore et al., 1994). Similarly, children's early theories of mind are applied to their own mental processes but also to those of others (Pratt, 1993). This aspect of social cognitive development is important because of course children cannot have direct experience of other people's internal states.

Several researchers have elicited or tested children's descriptions of their friends or other people and investigated age-related changes in the kinds of characteristics that are mentioned or understood (Barenboim, 1981; Damon and Hart, 1988; Livesley and Bromley, 1973; Newman, 1991; Oppenheimer and De Groot, 1981; Peevers and Secord, 1973; Scarlett et al., 1971; Spurgeon et al., 1983). Overall, these studies show that younger children refer most often to external phenomena, such as the person's physical appearance, dress, possessions, while from around 7 or 8 years there is increasing reference to internal psychological properties, such as personality traits, needs, motives, and attitudes. Similar patterns are found also when children are asked to define trait terms or to describe people they have not previously met who are engaged in social interactions (Flapan, 1968; Yuill, 1992). Flapan (1968) had children describe people in movie scenes, and she found that 6-year-olds recounted relatively superficial aspects of the scenes while children of 9 years and older used inferences and psychological terms to explain the characters' behavior.

This pattern is so reliable that the "concrete-to-abstract shift" has been widely taken to be a central feature of social cognitive development during middle childhood (Barenboim, 1981; Erwin, 1993; Feldman and Ruble, 1981). A related development is that, when asked to explain a person's behavior, young children often appear to give more weight to external factors than internal. For example, Ruble et al. (1979) had subjects aged from 4 years to adult watch an actor select an item from an array, and then tell the experimenter why the actor liked the item chosen. The younger subjects tended to explain the choice on the basis of the properties of the item ("the chocolate was nice," "it looked good"), while adults explained choices in terms of the person ("he likes chocolate.") It seemed that for the preschoolers, influence resided in the entity, while for the adults the important factor was the internal psychological processes of the actor. Similar results were obtained when children had to explain their own choices. Thus, both person description tasks and tasks which involve comparing the perceived import of person versus situational factors seem to converge in the finding that younger children focus more on the concrete and external than on the internal and unobservable.

One distinction between self- and other-descriptions which should be noted is that children are much more likely to include self-referent descriptions when talking about others than they are to make references to specific others when describing the self (Damon and Hart, 1988; Honess, 1980). Thus, when describing a friend, a child might say "He lends me his computer games," or when describing their mother they say things like "She is easy to handle ... Like if I want to go over to my friend's house, I usually can trick her into saying yes" (Damon and Hart, 1988, p. 188). Descriptions of self might include references to similar characteristics ("I share things," "I know how to get around people") but focus is on personal generalities rather than the individuals with whom one interacts. Damon and Hart suggest that this is a fundamental difference between self- and other-perception: understanding of another person usually includes a strong element of "how she affects me," while understanding of the self tends to focus on "what I think of me."

Perceptions of Others and Conceptions of Friendship

Person perception studies which require children to describe others often use friends as the focus of attention. Given the importance of friends to children's social worlds, it is of interest to discover not only how they conceive of other people who happen to be peers but also how they understand the nature of friendship itself. Several studies have addressed this issue (Berndt, 1981, 1983; Bigelow, 1977; Erwin, 1985, 1993; Rizzo, 1989; Selman, 1980; Serafica, 1982; Youniss and Volpe, 1978) and, despite differences in methodology and coding techniques, there is broad agreement among these researchers that there are qualitative changes in conceptions of friendship from kindergarten to the teenage years. Several theorists relate concepts of friendship to broader cognitive development, often drawing on Piagetian stages as the basis for their model (Bigelow, Erwin, Selman, Youniss).

Erwin (1993, pp. 48–9) summarizes the main developments emerging from this work as follows. Younger children (up to around the age of 7 or 8) tend to describe friends and friendships with reference to relatively concrete factors, such as common activities, mutual assistance, and propinquity ("he's my friend because he lives next door and we play together.") At this stage, the child's concerns are immediate and practical and the focus is on recent events rather than enduring dispositional properties. During the next few years, there is an increasing emphasis upon reciprocity and the obligations of friendships. Children incorporate their growing awareness of others' psychological distinctiveness into their understanding of their own relation-ships. In adolescence, this interest in psychological characteristics is consolidated and elaborated: young people think of friendships in terms of interpersonal dependencies and exchange of confidences, and incorporate awareness of the complexity of personalities into their accounts of how relationships work.

Clearly, there are important developmental changes in how children account for friendship. However, as Duck (1992) points out, the order of considerations they seem to attend to (appearance, followed by behavior, followed by attitudes and personality attributes) corresponds rather well to the steps that *adults* typically undertake in the development of relationships. To some extent, social cognitive competencies in this domain interact with natural constraints: appearance and behavior are salient, readily observable (cf. Barenboim, 1981). It would be very unusual to become acquainted with someone first by a detailed insight into his or her psychological processes, then to learn about his or her behavior and, finally, to find out what he or she looks like.

There is some evidence of sex differences in friendship conceptions. For example, among pre-adolescents, Spurgeon et al. (1983) found that most girls' friendships were explained as based on internal psychological reasons, while boys saw their friendships in roughly equal proportions as involving internal psychological reasons or contractual reasons. In general, girls' friendships from middle childhood on do tend to be more intimate and confiding than those of boys, who are more likely to organize their activities in larger groups (Buhrmester and Furman, 1987; Erwin, 1993).

Developmental and Social Perspectives on Person Perception

Clearly, there are age-related differences in the content of person-descriptions elicited from children. However, whether this tells us the full story about the development of understanding of others' properties is debatable, and on closer inspection the notion of a concrete to abstract, external to internal shift has been called into question (Miller and Aloise, 1989). Even preschoolers demonstrate some awareness of the internal, affective meaning of social relations, warning peers who commit transgressions that "I won't be your friend any more" (Corsaro, 1993). Several researchers have shown that by at least the age of 5 years children can use information about a person's *psychological* attributes to predict how he or she will behave in another situation (Bennett, 1985–86; Berndt and Heller, 1985; Yuill, 1993).

This issue brings us to an interesting example of the benefits of cross-fertilization between social and developmental psychologists which has led to recent progress in this area. Consider first the inherent differences in approach between developmental and social psychologists. Uncovering age-related differences in a task such as person-description is a natural focus for the developmentalist. At the same time, the study of person-perception is also a major traditional focus of the social psychologist. Yet these two approaches often proceed independently, with only token acknowledgment of each other's concerns. Developmentalists tend to study changes presumed to take place within the individual over time, typically applying cognitive developmental frameworks in order to identify underlying shifts in intellectual capacities; developmentalists often pay relatively modest attention to the social contexts in which individuals make their judgments of other people. Social psychologists, on the other hand, tend to concentrate their attention on adults' social perceptions, investigating external influences upon impression formation (such as social stereotypes, or contextual information manipulated experimentally) as well as motivational factors within the observer; social psychologists attend only infrequently to the origins of the phenomena they study.

In an interesting exception to this tradition of mutual disregard, Feldman and Ruble (1981) show how the two approaches can be fused to mutual advantage. For example, in one study Feldman (reported in Feldman and Ruble, 1981, pp. 201–3) solicited children's descriptions of characters presented via video tape. This technique, as we have seen, reveals age-related differences, with children over 8 years or so producing more "psychological" accounts. Feldman replicated this pattern of results but also found a strong effect of a motivational factor. She varied the task by having some subjects simply describe the actor (the method used in earlier studies) while others were led to believe that they would shortly be interacting with the person on the tape. In this condition, both younger (5–6 years) and older (9–10 years) subjects made substantially more abstract, psychological descriptions than did their peers who anticipated no interaction with the target.

Two examples of the different kinds of descriptions provided by the 5–6-year-olds illustrate how person-perception varies according to the perceiver's motivations:

> *No future interaction expected*:
> She was throwing balls into the bucket. She was throwing Frisbees at the target. She has dark hair. She went into another room.

> *Future interaction expected*:
> She is good at games and she's probably nice. She tries very hard. I think she likes to play games.
> (Feldman and Ruble, 1981, p. 202).

Hence, a social motivational variable (potential interaction with the target) affects the depth of interpersonal appraisal, even among quite young subjects. As Feldman and Ruble stress, most developmental approaches have tended to overlook this factor, presenting person-description tasks "cold" as though equivalent, to say, an object-description task. This has implications for the kinds of findings obtained since the perceiver's social purpose with respect to the perceived is demonstrably influential. On the other hand, Feldman did also find substantial age effects, confirming that in many contexts an individual's developmental status will influence how he or she responds to a social perception task.

Other illustrations of the interaction of social context and developmental changes are provided by Benenson and Dweck (1986) and Stromquist and Strauman (1991). Benenson and Dweck had children provide explanations of success or failure in social (e.g., peer popularity) and academic domains (e.g., school grades). As in other studies, they found increasing use of internal, trait descriptions with age (from 5 to 10 years); however, there was a lag between domains, such that trait descriptions emerged first for the social domain. The authors argue that, because children have greater experience of social relations, their understanding in this domain precedes that in the academic domain. Similarly, using a person-description task, Stromquist and Strauman (1991) found that the development of children's social constructs during middle childhood tends to reveal greater accessibility of child-related concepts but not of adult-related concepts. The investigators suggest that this reflects children's increasing independence of adult supervision and more time spent with peers. Both studies indicate that organization of social knowledge is affected by shifts in the social context. Development in the perception of others, then, reflects both cognitive progress and social experience (Higgins and Parsons, 1983; Yuill, 1993).

Person, situation, and development

While the research just summarized establishes that social variables can usefully be taken into account in developmental studies of person-perception, further developmental investigation indicates that the kinds of tasks borrowed from social psychology may incur their own biases. In fact, an analysis of young children's perceptions of the causes of people's behavior leads to the conclusion that social psychologists' dichotomy between personal and situational influences may oversimplify accounts of the nature of the ways in which young subjects perceive the relationship between individuals and external factors (Miller and Aloise, 1989).

Miller and Aloise argue that the methodology favored in person-perception tasks (verbal descriptions) may lead to an underestimate of young children's capacities. Among other limitations, these tasks are ambiguous in terms of what is required of the respondent. For example, these authors point out that in Flapan's (1968) task, mentioned above, the subject is requested specifically to tell the investigator "what you saw" in the film. What you see is a person carrying out a series of activities, and it is perfectly reasonable to describe those highly salient activities, as kindergarten subjects do. (In fact, Miller and Aloise note that, even so, Flapan did obtain some psychological descriptions from her younger subjects.) Another problem for young children may be that inferences about *stable* attributes, such as traits, may be difficult since they involve familiarity with people's behavior over time – an experiential basis which is not extensive in preschoolers nor easily grasped by them. Miller and Aloise propose that young children can take account of temporary psychological states, such as intentions and emotions, if motivated to do so (as in Feldman and Ruble's study, above), and that they can take account of situational influences, though they are most likely to be influenced by aspects of the situation that have been made salient by the research procedure.

Overall, the intersection of developmental and social psychology around the topic of person-perception has been fruitful in leading to a greater awareness of the complexity of young children's perception of people and their relationships to their surroundings. It also establishes, unsurprisingly but often overlooked, that the processes of person-perception in adults do not arise fully formed out of nowhere. Finally, it indicates that social psychologists' dichotomy between the person and the situation may incur oversimplifications of the perceived relationships between internal and external factors by even the youngest of subjects.

Understanding Others' Mental Processes: Perspectives, Intentions, and Emotions

A basic requirement of social knowledge is that we recognize that each person has his or her own perspective on the world, and that these may be quite distinct from our own. To appreciate this, we have to understand that other people are social subjects, that they have perspectives, thoughts, intentions, and feelings that underlie their behavior yet are not directly accessible to us. Much of contemporary social psychology is concerned with precisely these aspects of interpersonal understanding.

From a developmental psychologist's orientation, understanding others' perspectives relates to longstanding issues concerning the quality of child thought and the nature of social discovery. A standard tenet of Piagetian psychology, for example, has been the claim that the preschool child (in the preoperational period) has a profound intellectual limitation in respect of other people's perspectives. This issue has attracted a lot of attention within developmental psychology, because it is quite critical to accounts of how the child understands the objective world and her or his relationship to it.

Visual perspective-taking in childhood

According to Piaget, the preoperational child is *egocentric*, tending to view the world from his or her own point of view and failing to take into account other possible perspectives. Several classic demonstrations of this apparent deficiency have been provided by Piaget and his collaborators (see chapter 1). These include the three mountains task (Piaget and Inhelder, 1966) in which the child is required to identify the photograph of the model that best represents the visual perspective of the experimenter, who views the mountains from a different position to the subject. As is well known, Piaget found that children below the age of 8 years manifest a strong bias toward selecting the photograph that represents their *own* perspective.

Intriguing as these demonstrations are, the considerable controversy that Piaget's claims inspired among developmentalists has led to a good deal of research which demonstrates quite convincingly that the problem does not lie in a blanket inability to take another's perspective (Bremner, 1993). It has been shown that even infants can exploit another's line of visual regard to guide their own looking around a room, and similar findings have been obtained with respect to 1- and 2-year-olds' reactions to pointing (Butterworth and Grover, 1988; Murphy and Messer, 1977). Children as young as 9–12 months also use pointing both to obtain objects and to share attention with another person (Bruner, 1983a). These findings suggest that young children are aware that other people have independent visual perspectives, and that other people can be useful as cues to interesting things or as joint interpreters of those things. Consistent with this interpretation, it has been found that autistic children (whom many believe to lack an awareness of other people's perspectives) fail to use pointing to share information (Baron-Cohen, 1989; Goodhart and Baron-Cohen, 1993). In addition, several investigators using modified versions of the three mountains task, employing scenarios that are simpler and more familiar to young children, have obtained evidence of good perspective-taking ability in 3- and 4-year-olds (Borke, 1975; Hughes and Donaldson, 1979; Light and Nix, 1983).

Although interesting issues remain in terms of explaining developmental changes in tasks such as the three mountains task and other classic Piagetian tasks (see Cox, 1991, for a more extensive review), the important point for present purposes is that the upshot of much developmental critique of Piaget's stronger claims has been to assert the child's social context as a critical variable. Donaldson (1978) argues that provided the test situation makes human sense to the young subject, children can differentiate among perspectives. Cox (1991, p. 50) points out that in normal face-to-face interaction even among adults we may not need to have a mental picture of another's point of view to be able to recognize that he or she does have a different perspective to ours.

Social role-taking perspectives in childhood

Recognizing another person's visual perspective is only one aspect of perspective-taking, and it could be argued that it depends more on cognitive computation than interpersonal understanding (cf. Shantz, 1983). There are many further respects in which social interactions call for an appreciation of how things appear from another's perspective (Selman, 1976, 1980). These include recognizing other people's expectations and desires, predicting how they might react, and understanding what they mean to communicate. In this sense, how people "see" the world encompasses much more than their visual perceptions. Selman points out that the ability to take account of others' perspectives in these respects is integral to a wide range of human social behaviors, including joint problem-solving, communication and persuasion, sympathizing and empathizing, and understanding of fairness and justice.

Using techniques adapted from moral developmental research (discussed in more detail in chapter 14), Selman (1976) solicited children's reasoning about a set of social dilemmas in which conflicting feelings might be invoked. For example, subjects are asked to consider a story about a child, Holly, who is confronted with an urgent choice between climbing up a tree to save a friend's distressed kitten and honoring an earlier promise to her father that she would never again engage in reckless tree-climbing behavior. The subject is asked a series of role-taking questions: does Holly know how her friend feels about his kitten? How will Holly's father feel if he finds out she climbed the tree? What would you do? and so on.

Taking a cognitive developmental approach, Selman characterizes children's responses in a series of five stages. The model is subtle and richly illustrated, but an essential theme is that of a gradual, qualitative progress from egocentric reasoning to

Box 9.1   Selman's stages of social role-taking

Stage 0: Egocentric viewpoint (*age range 3–6*)[a]

Child has a sense of differentiation of self and other but fails to distinguish between the social perspective (thoughts, feelings) of other and self. Child can label other's overt feelings but does not see the cause-and-effect relation of reasons to social actions.

Stage 1: Social informational role-taking (*age range 6–8*)

Child is aware that other has a social perspective based on other's own reasoning, which may or may not be similar to child's. However, child tends to focus on one perspective rather than coordinating viewpoints.

Stage 2: Self-reflective role-taking (*age range 8–10*)

Child is conscious that each individual is aware of the other's perspective and that this awareness influences self and other's view of each other. Putting self in other's place is a way of judging his/her intentions, purposes, and actions. Child can form a coordinated chain of perspectives, but cannot yet abstract from this process to the level of simultaneous mutuality.

Stage 3: Mutual role-taking (*age range 10–12*)

Child realizes that both self and other can view each other mutually and simultaneously as subjects. Child can step outside the two-person dyad and view the interaction from a third-person perspective.

Stage 4: Social and conventional system role-taking (*age range 12–15+*)

Person realizes mutual perspective-taking does not always lead to complete understanding. Social conventions are seen as necessary because they are understood by all members of the group (the generalized other) regardless of their position, role, or experience.

[a] Age ranges for all stages represent only an average approximation.
Source: Selman, 1976

an eventual understanding of the complexities of mutual perspective-taking within a social system organized around conventions and normative expectations. A summary is provided in box 9.1.

As an example of a young child's response to the task, consider this interviewee (age not specified, but classified as Stage 0, around 4–6 years):

> *Q:* What do you think Holly will do, save the kitten or keep her promise?
> *A:* She will save the kitten because she doesn't want the kitten to die.
> *Q:* How will her father feel when he finds out?
> *A:* Happy, he likes kittens.
> *Q:* What if her father punishes her if she gets the kitten down?
> *A:* Then she will leave it up there.
> *Q:* Why?
> *A:* Because she doesn't want to get into trouble.
> (modified from Selman, 1976, p. 303)

Selman comments that this interviewee appears to focus on the act of saving the kitten, and assumes that everyone else sees things this way. When pressed about breaking a promise to the father, the child lurches to a quite different viewpoint, and seems to be quite unaware of the inconsistency.

Subsequent research has supported the broad developmental claims of Selman's model, showing that individuals progress gradually to higher stages over time, with little evidence of regression to lower stages (Gurucharri and Selman, 1982; Oppenheimer, 1989; Selman, 1980). This establishes that the framework deals with a meaningful conceptual development. The next question concerns how perspective-taking might relate to other aspects of social development.

Perspective-taking and social behavior

The relationship between perspective-taking ability and the development of social behavior is not straightforward. Some studies have found evidence that children with more advanced role-taking skills are more likely to volunteer appropriate prosocial assistance to peers when necessary (Hudson et al., 1982) and to be more popular (Kurdek and Krile, 1982; Spence, 1987). But others have failed to obtain a consistent relationship between popularity and perspective-taking (Musun-Miller, 1993; Oppenheimer, 1989). Training in perspective-taking skills with the goal of improving social competence has led to mixed outcomes, sometimes resulting in progress (Chalmers and Townsend, 1990; Chandler, 1973) and sometimes not (see Shure, 1982).

These findings indicate that social perspective-taking is unlikely to be the only attribute or social cognitive ability that is implicated in harmonious peer relations. Selman himself does not predict a straightforward relationship, and argues that the critical factor in social performance may not be simply the stage of reasoning that the individual child has reached but the ways in which he or she *uses* perspective-taking skills in everyday interactions (Selman, et al., 1982). Shure (1982) argues that in addition to the ability to take someone else's perspective, successful social interaction often requires *knowing what to do* to resolve a problem. In such circumstances, perspective-taking skills may be necessary but not sufficient.

Role-taking involves many considerations which vary from situation to situation

(Damon, 1983; Erwin, 1993). Damon (1983, p. 126) suggests that rather than conceiving of perspective-taking as a general *ability* that children acquire, it is more useful to regard it as a frequent *activity* in which children consider perspectives other than their own. These perspectives could involve disparate concerns, such as the other's thoughts, feelings, vision, interpersonal relations, goals, expectations – a whole range of issues that come up in different situations as people interact. The extent to which children engage in taking perspectives, Damon holds, may well be associated with success in resolving social problems and gaining from interactions with others. The importance of viewing it as a multifaceted process is that it leads us to conceive of it not as a "driving force" of social cognition and social behavior but as a set of skills which themselves grow out of what the child knows about social interactions.

Understanding Others' Intentions

In making sense of events in the social world, one of the primary considerations we have to take into account is other people's intentions. This task is complicated because intentions are not always directly observable. If it is true that young children's social cognitions are dominated by concrete and external cues, then we should expect that their understanding of others' intentions would be weak. Some evidence appears consistent with this view. For example, Astington (1986) found that children's comprehension of the language of intention (e.g., terms like *intends to, means to, plans to, would like to, on purpose*) was quite poor at the age of 5 and develops markedly over the next few years. She concludes that the concept of intention emerges in middle childhood.

However, other research has found evidence of the ability to label, recognize or infer other people's intentions somewhat earlier. As already noted, young children do have a theory of mind, and this may provide a basis for attributing mental properties and goals to others (cf. Leekam, 1993). Toddlers' language contains many references to their own and others' intentions (Brown, 1973; Wells, 1985), suggesting that they have some practical awareness of the relevance of intentionality to everyday behavior. Interestingly, there is evidence that the child's social context can influence the pace of development of theory of mind. Perner et al. (1994) found that children from larger families tended to perform more successfully on theory of mind tasks than did peers from smaller families. The researchers argue that sibling interactions stimulate the social cognitive processes by providing a richer data base of relevant experiences.

Toddlers' language contains many references to intentionality (Dunn, 1988a; Piaget, 1932; Shultz, 1980). Whether this linguistic practice amounts to a grasp of intentionality equivalent to that of adults is questionable (Astington, 1986). It could be argued that children are using verbal routines that they have found useful in excusing their actions ("I didn't do it on purpose, Mum"), without necessarily understanding fully the meaning of the concepts they express. However, Shultz et al. (1980) found that 3–5-year-olds could distinguish reliably between the errors of a peer that were intentional and those that were induced by equipment or tricky tasks. For example, children understood the effects of distorting spectacles upon the response of another child who, wearing the glasses, tried in vain to point at a particular object. They recognized that speech errors were not deliberate when attempting to copy tongue twisters (*she sells sea shells by the sea shore*). In this and related studies, Shultz and colleagues found that young children's judgments of the intentionality of action outcomes were equally accurate for their own and others' behavior. Yuill (1984) found that even 3-year-olds were aware that individuals are more pleased when the outcomes of their actions matched their intentions than when there was a mismatch, a finding which indicates quite sophisticated coordination of purpose and satisfaction in understanding other people's actions.

In fact, in some respects, preschoolers' attributions of intentionality *exceed* those of older people. M. C. Smith (1978) had 4-, 5- and 6-year-olds describe the behavior of people in short films, where the behavior was sometimes voluntary (such as sitting down), sometimes involuntary (such as sneezing) and sometimes prompted acciden-tally (such as tripping over an object). Four-year-olds saw nearly all the acts as intentional, while by 6 years children tended to discriminate voluntary and involun-tary acts along the same lines as adults.

This finding points to more than an interesting error in young children's perceptions of causality. Miller and Aloise (1989) argue that the extensive evidence of early use (even overuse) of intentionality contradicts the picture of social cognitive development as consisting essentially of an external to internal shift during mid-childhood. Instead, "the main developmental task seems to be learning when *not* to use the psychological causes that the child has preferred to use since toddlerhood" (p. 267; emphasis added). In a review of the literature, Miller and Aloise show that there are several illustrations of preschoolers' use of intentionality and other internal phenomena to account for others' behavior in preference to external factors.

Hence, children do appear to understand something of intentionality from early in the preschool years. While by no means establishing that their understanding is equivalent to that of older individuals, this interest in the psychological causes of behavior is entailed in their interpretations of the social world.

Understanding Others' Emotions

A related social cognitive development concerns insight into others' emotions. Some understanding of other people's feelings is a facility that we expect to be within the competencies of most normal human beings (Harris, 1989a). In considering the emergence of emotional self-regulation, above, the importance of other people's input was stressed. Correspondingly, children's understanding of other people's emotions is closely tied to their understanding of their own (Bretherton et al., 1986; Dunn and Brown, 1991, 1994; Harris, 1989a; Shatz, 1994).

In part, as seen in chapter 8, decoding others' emotions depends on sensitivity to nonverbal cues. In part, as discussed earlier in this chapter, it depends upon coming to understand and attend to the language of emotion (and Bretherton and Beeghly, 1982, found that the emergence in infancy of reference to other people's emotions tended to follow swiftly upon, or in some cases to appear simultaneously with, reference to those of the self). Integral to these processes are the social cognitive abilities to *represent* abstract phenomena such as emotion and to comprehend the *causes* of emotional responses. Harris (1989a) argues that an important dimension of the process of emotional understanding is an imaginative leap from the experience of one's own feelings to the representation of how others feel, and that this is closely connected to the child's developing theory of mind (Harris and Saarni, 1989).

To understand the causes of other people's emotions involves taking into account situational and personality factors. Several studies by Gnepp and her colleagues indicate that aspects of the ability to handle complex information of these kinds develops gradually during middle childhood (Gnepp, 1983; Gnepp and Gould, 1985). Gnepp gives children conflicting cues about a person's response to a situation, and asks them to describe how he or she is feeling. For example, subjects may be presented with a picture of a child awaiting inoculation in a doctor's chair, smiling as the needle approaches, or another of a child smiling while holding a broken bicycle. Given these ambiguous scenarios, preschool children tended to rely on the facial cues. Preschoolers found it difficult to reconcile the conflicting information, while older children were more inclined to attach greater weight to the situation, and could offer complex accounts of the discrepancy ("she's . . . smiling, trying to hide her fear from the doctor").

Similarly, during middle childhood individuals become more adept at incorporating personality factors into their interpretations. Given a child whom previous information has revealed to be an affable extrovert and who is now placed in a mildly embarrassing situation (his shoes are different colours), older children (8- and 10-year-olds) were more likely to predict his reaction along personality lines ("[he's happy] because he got all this fun and attention . . . he wants people to laugh at him") (Gnepp and Chilamkurti, 1988). Gnepp (1989) proposes a model of the development of emotional inferences, suggesting that the process begins quite early, but is developed and refined over a long period, continuing into adulthood. Even adults are sometimes socially insensitive to others' feelings, and this research suggests that their responses need to be understood in a developmental social psychological perspective.

Summary

We have seen in earlier chapters that the infant is very interested in people; in this section, evidence has been reviewed which suggests that infants are aware of differences between people and other things, and especially interested in people behaving like people. Infants' cognitive representations of the social world remain controversial, but it is clear that understanding other people is closely interwoven with understanding of the self. Once again, we find that children are aware of others' internal processes — thoughts, perspectives, intentions, and feelings — from an early age. This awareness is elaborated with age. During the school years, children provide more complex descriptions of others, paying increasing attention to enduring psychological properties. Throughout, while the child works actively to construct a social understanding, including exploring the similarities between his or her own psychological processes and those of others, this developmental progress itself takes place in an interpersonal context, where others expect the child to participate in social life and draw attention to salient aspects of the social world.

Social Comparison

At several points when considering the development of self-knowledge and the interpretation of ambiguous situations, we noticed that children often compare themselves with others. The interweaving between self and others in understanding the social world brings us finally to an important social cognitive process which permeates both our sense of personal identity and the interpersonal and intergroup relationships into which we enter: social comparison (Festinger, 1954).

Social comparison is the process whereby people compare their own attributes, behavior, achievements, and understanding with those of other people. Suppose, for example, that you receive the information that you have scored 73 out of a possible 100 on a test of digital dexterity. What do you conclude? That your fingers are hot stuff? That you fall a long way short of manual perfection? Without some indication of normative performance on the test, it is difficult to interpret your raw score. A common response to feedback is to ask how others fared: "Well, what did Sam get?"

The process is not restricted to performance evaluations. Celebrating, or recovering from, this social comparison of manual aptitude, you go to the movies. You see *Final Statement*, starring Kevin Costner, and conclude that it is a light but entertaining film. Later, your intellectual friends who attend only subtitled angst, preferably in black and white, scoff at your seduction by Hollywood pap. You revise your opinion and buy a season ticket for the Arts cinema. But then you read Kevin Costner's audience figures. You change your mind: you identify with the masses, not the obscurantist elite, and the millions of people who contribute to box office supremacy cannot all be wrong. You await eagerly, but quietly, *Final Statement II*.

You are experiencing the everyday oscillations of social comparison. Festinger's (1954) social comparison theory holds that in contexts where there is no firm objective criterion of performance or opinion we look to other people to determine a basis for evaluating ourselves and our ideas. Gergen (1977) stressed the volatile sensitivities of this process: "What is 'true' about self depends on those available for comparison. In the presence of the devout, we may discover that we are ideologically shallow; in the midst of dedicated hedonists, we may gain awareness of our ideological depths" (p. 153). Your pitiful indecision about your movie preferences shows how readily you are influenced by the opinions of whoever is available for comparison.

In practice, we may not always find the process so dramatic because we have preferred strategies for finding reliable comparison markers: we identify individuals and groups that we perceive as similar or superior to us, and orient our judgments around theirs (Tajfel, 1981; Wheeler, 1991; Zanna et al., 1975). We do occasionally make "downward" comparisons, too, but these tend to reflect self-enhancing goals (sometimes, it is refreshing to cast an eye over those above whom we shine) or coping mechanisms (if things are really bad, it may help to know that others are worse off; see Gibbons and Gerrard, 1991; Wills, 1991).

Social comparisons are one social cognitive mechanism by which the individual can establish and validate his or her personal and social identity and obtain confidence in the accuracy of his or her beliefs (Hogg and Abrams, 1988; Rijsman, 1983; Turner, 1991). Social comparison is a prerequisite to observational learning (Bandura, 1986; Berger, 1977; Butler, 1989a, b), since modeling our behavior upon others requires at the very least that we notice a discrepancy between how they do things and what we do. How we respond to social comparisons depends on both achievement motivation (Veroff, 1969) and social integration (Erwin, 1993).

Social Comparisons in Childhood

If these processes are so basic to adults' social cognition, what role might we expect them to play in development, which is by definition concerned with making and validating new understandings? Ruble and Frey (Ruble, 1983; Ruble and Frey, 1991) propose that social comparison processes are central to the task of self-socialization. In the course of discovering society's rules and expectations, the child needs to determine how one is supposed to behave (norm acquisition) and how well one is doing (self-evaluation). Typically, self-evaluation involves comparing one's own characteristics and behaviors with those of others.

When do social comparisons begin?

Veroff (1969) doubted whether young children would engage spontaneously in social comparison processes, and maintained that only "considerable reinforcement" from family members could bring about such a development. Among other considerations, he pointed out that social comparison could be risky for a young child, because it is in the nature of things that most of the people available for comparison will be older and more proficient in most domains.

However, subsequent research indicates that some social comparison does occur among preschool children. For example, at this age, children are keenly aware of who is getting what when some critical resource (such as a pile of sweets) is being shared out, and unfavorable comparisons result in swift remedial action. Preschoolers often make statements like "I'm bigger/older/better/smarter than you" (Chafel, 1986; Mosatche and Bragonier, 1981; Ruble, 1983). Occasionally, they appear mildly bemused by the whole process, but their verbal play indicates a growing consciousness of the utility of comparisons:

> *Joshua:*   I'm five and three-quarters.
> *Tom:*   No you're six, six.
> *Joshua:*   So I must be six and three-quarters. That makes you taller than me. But . . .
>   that makes me taller than you. But someday you might be taller than me.
> (Ely and McCabe, 1994)

Figure 9.3 Preschoolers engage in social comparison.

Joshua may not be precise on the details but he certainly appears to be attuned to the spirit of social comparison as well as sensitive to the instability of the social environment. Young children also use social comparisons to organize social activities (Butler, 1989a; Jennings, 1993). They compare what they and others are doing and express both their solidarity ("I'm drawing a picture as well") and mutual differences ("Your shoes are red, but mine are blue") (cf. Gottman and Parkhurst, 1980) (figure 9.3).

Developmental changes

On the other hand, the interpretation and use of social comparison information may be limited among younger children. The kinds of social comparison just described, for example, appear to reflect interests in the mastery of tasks, the comparison of tangible properties, and the general attractions of "joining in," rather than careful mutual evaluations and appraisals of how well one is doing (Ruble and Frey, 1991). In a series of experimental studies, Ruble and her colleagues found that below the age of 7 years information obtained from social comparisons had minimal impact on self-evaluations. For example, in one study, kindergarten, 7-year-olds and 9-year-olds played a ball-throwing game in which the experimenters manipulated the outcome so that all subjects successfully hit the target two out of four times (Ruble et al., 1980). To help interpret this ambiguous outcome, subjects received information about how same-sex peers had performed, with some being told that other kids performed better, some being told that they had exceeded their peers' scores, and a control group receiving no feedback. The children were then asked to predict how they would perform on another round of the game. It was stressed that the number of prizes they could receive was contingent upon both performance and *accuracy* of prediction. Even so, only the oldest subjects made use of social comparisons (e.g., "I must be pretty good because I can beat all of the others.") The kindergarten subjects' responses were unaffected by experimental condition.

Ruble (1983) and Ruble and Frey (1991) argue that children below the age of 7 may have the understanding of basic capacities, sufficient interest in peer performance, and some of the processing strategies that are necessary to make social comparisons. However, they may find it more difficult to focus on abstract properties of another person (such as ability) than on concrete attributes (such as possessions). They may also be less inclined to take into account the *stability* of people's skills (for good reason, since many of the preschooler's own skills do change quite rapidly; cf. Suls, 1986). And young children may give greater priority when evaluating others to detectable *similarities* rather than differences, since having something in common is a useful foundation for friendship formation at this age ("do you like ice cream, too?")

Comparisons and competencies

Ruble and Flett (1988) found that the extent to which children use social comparison also interacts with their competence in the task at hand. In a mathematics activity where they received initially only vague feedback about how they were doing, children aged 7, 9 and 11 years were given opportunities to gain more information about their performance from either social comparisons (how their peers were doing) or self-comparisons (how they had done on previous administrations). Most children spent more time making comparisons with others. This tendency may explain why, when self-reports of abilities (such as in mathematics, spelling) are collected longitudinally, individuals tend sometimes not to rate themselves as getting any better. They may actually be improving, but because they compare themselves with peers who are developing alongside them, they are less sensitive to their own advances (Cairns and Cairns, 1988).

However, among Ruble and Flett's two older groups, children with *high* levels of ability did behave differently from their peers. They focused more attention on comparisons with their own prior performances. This finding indicates that as self-knowledge increases, those who are moving ahead of the crowd become more likely to base self-evaluations – at least in achievement-related domains – on principled information rather than global comparisons. It is also likely that when social comparisons are made by older individuals, the selection of a relevant comparison group becomes much more principled.

Social Comparison and Social Context

Similarity

In order to make a meaningful social comparison, it is useful to select a suitable reference point. To return to your digital dexterity score, it is unlikely that you would evaluate your performance by comparing it with that of, say, very young infants, or very old people, or individuals with specialized manual skills, such as professional typists. However, if you happen to *be* a professional typist, or a very old person, then other members of your social category may well serve as relevant comparison points. In short, the most useful social comparisons are those we make in reference to individuals or groups who are in some respects similar to us (Festinger, 1954; Rijsman, 1983).

Similarity plays a central role in the development of social comparisons. By the early school years, children already demonstrate a preference for similar others when making social comparisons (Erwin, 1993; France-Kaatrude-Smith, 1985). Similarity is a critical variable in social selectivity (e.g., friendship choice; cf. Duck, 1988b; Erwin, 1993). Erwin (1993) points out that the larger contexts of children's social relationships promote relations among similar persons; for example, through age stratification at school, and socioeconomic and cultural stratification by neighborhood. In this context, Erwin proposes, social comparison may be functional because it facilitates the establishment of social identity (by evaluating who one is similar to, and by promoting the likelihood of social approval from similar others), and also because it reduces areas of conflict among people. By developing informal or formal associations with similar others, we establish a sense of trust and shared meanings. We generate a common frame of reference for appraising our own behavior and attributes and those of outsiders.

Society, school, and values

The developments that Erwin outlines make it clear that social comparison is not solely an individual process. Formulating a social comparison reflects the individual's social context, both in terms of who and what is worth taking into account and in terms of the presupposed values that are entailed in the comparison.

There is evidence that any shift toward the competitive use of social comparisons during middle childhood may be associated with the social context within which the child is developing. Butler and Ruzany (1993) compared urban and kibbutzim Israeli children (ages 4–8 years), investigating the subjects' reasons for glancing at their peers' work, or their interpretations of why an unfamiliar child might watch someone else's work. The younger children were more likely to give mastery reasons ("I wasn't sure what we were meant to do, so I wanted to check.") However, among the older children there was an urban *v.* kibbutz difference, such that the urban children were more likely to give competitive, ability-based comparisons ("I wanted to see who did the best flower.") The authors conclude that the more competitive environment of the urban school guides children to use social comparisons as sources of relative ability assessments.

Deciding who we compare ourselves with and what we accept as relevant criteria is likely to be influenced by the need to develop and preserve personal and social identity (Rijsman, 1983; Tajfel, 1981; Turner et al., 1987). In school contexts, social comparisons tend often to be more motivating to successful pupils than to their less able peers (DePaulo, et al. 1989; Monteil, 1988, 1993). Monteil and Huguet (1991) and Huguet and Monteil (1992) show that pupils' responses to social comparisons vary according to both their own scholastic history (good or poor) and the academic status of the task area in which the comparison is being made. Pupils who are generally low achieving but who attain in relatively devalued school subjects (such as drawing, manual and technical education, music and physical education) tend to *revalue* the disciplines that are less highly regarded by the dominant culture. Thus, low-ability pupils attribute greater memory, imagination, and reflective capacities to performance in the devalued subjects than do their more successful peers (Huguet and Monteil, 1992). At the same time, these pupils accept the broader school culture which equates success with intelligence. Hence, they perceive a weaker link between memory, imagination, reflection, and intelligence than do successful pupils.

In other words, in striving for bases for social comparisons which preserve self-esteem, less able pupils appear to develop outlooks which revalue competencies that they feel they do possess, even though they accept the prevailing view of themselves as less intelligent than others. Monteil and Huguet (1991) show that these social cognitive processes can impact upon school performance. The same task (recall and recognition of a set of geometrical forms) was presented to subjects as either a drawing task (low-value school subject) or a geometry task (high-value school subject). Under these conditions, good pupils performed better in the geometry task than they did in the drawing task, while for poor pupils the reverse was true.

Interestingly, the good pupils outperformed the poor pupils *only in the geometry condition*: their results in the drawing version of the task were similar. However, when the subjects were led to believe that their performances in the drawing task would be subject to social comparisons with able peers, there were marked differences in response. The good pupils raised their act, while the poor pupils did significantly worse. DePaulo et al. (1989) report similar findings. It appears that the process and effects of social comparison vary according to where one is (or where one perceives oneself to be) in the relevant social/ achievement hierarchy.

Summary

Social comparisons enable us to find out how we are progressing relative to others and to ascertain the reliability of our opinions and beliefs. Through social comparisons, the social environment affects not only our self-concepts and goals but the very framework within which we organize our understandings of the social world. Social comparisons are employed from an early age, but they appear to develop in sophistication through childhood, and in this respect are integrated with other social cognitive developments, such as person understanding and knowledge of social status.

The kinds of criteria we employ in social comparisons, and our readiness to adjust our behavior as a result, are themselves affected by the social context and what we perceive our position in it to be. We determine our position by reference to interpersonal and intergroup criteria. Group criteria appear to become especially important with development, as the individual's relationship to the social world becomes more differentiated and the relevance of similar others is firmly established.

Conclusions

We began this chapter with two children chatting about a third. On first sight, their remarks seem slight, if a little unsociable. But as we chart just some of the developments of social cognition it becomes clear that a great deal of complex intellectual discovery precedes and succeeds the casual peer evaluations of early school children. By this age, children have already undergone a lengthy period of discovery about self and others; these processes are far from complete, and we saw that they continue through childhood (in later chapters, we will see that concepts of self develop through adolescence and adult life, too). The children we began with have begun to conceptualize people in terms of underlying properties and attributes; they have some sense of other people's abilities to think, to engage in purposeful activity and of individual differences in personality traits. It remains unsettled just how profound the psychological insights of the 6-year-old are; it is agreed that the young child has much to learn, and that interactions with other people will be vital both as sources of labels and as illustrations of social variety. What is established clearly by the available research is that, from childhood on, social cognition is highly motivating: we desire to find out about other people, and we are especially keen to find out how we compare with them.

Understanding the social world includes more than discovering the attributes and abilities of individuals. The child has also to learn about the causes of behavior, of the roles that people enact, the nature of social institutions and power relations within them, and the meaning and correlates of particular social categories. We turn to these issues in the next chapter.

Further reading

Bennett, M. (ed.) (1993) *The Child as Psychologist: an introduction to the development of social cognition*. New York: Harvester Wheatsheaf.

Several thoughtful and provocative essays on current issues in social cognitive development, including children's theories of mind, the interrelationship of cognitive and social elements in the development of emotion, children's theories of personality, the acquisition of social rules, event knowledge, and societal understanding, as well as valuable critiques of the state of the art in introductory and concluding chapters.

Bretherton, I. (1990) Open communication and internal working models: their role in the development of attachment relationships. In R. A. Thompson (ed.), *Socioemotional Development. Nebraska symposium on motivation, 1988*. Lincoln: University of Nebraska Press.

In examining the development of attachment in chapter 3, we noted Bowlby's emphasis on the infant's early representation (working model) of the relationship with a caregiver. Bretherton provides a theoretical synthesis of this construct and more recent work on the development of social cognition, especially understanding of self, others, and social events.

Damon, W. and Hart, D. (1988) *Self-understanding in Childhood and Adolescence*. Cambridge: Cambridge University Press.

An excellent overview of developmental and social psychological theories of the self, together with the presentation of an elaborate model of the development of self-understanding.

Garber, J. and Dodge, K. A. (eds) (1991) *The Development of Emotion Regulation and Dysregulation*. Cambridge: Cambridge University Press.

The editors and contributors review the difficulties of definition and measurement in this resurgent field, and present diverse evidence from recent research into the coordination of biological, cognitive, and interpersonal processes in regulating emotion.

Harris, P. L. (1989) *Children and Emotion: the development of psychological understanding*. Oxford: Blackwell.

An original and insightful account of the relations among the child's developing knowledge of self, the interpersonal contexts of development, and understanding of emotion.

Suls, J. and Wills, T. A. (eds) (1991) *Social Comparison: Contemporary Theory and Research*. Hillsdale, NJ: Erlbaum.

Reviews of recent work on social comparison processes, including a developmental chapter by Ruble and Frey, and several discussions of the conditions under which social comparisons are made and interpreted. This book provides a good example of intriguing social psychological issues that raise many questions for developmental research.

Zebrowitz, L. A. (1990) *Social Perception*. Milton Keynes: Open University Press.

A tale of how the author went to college with nudists, sweater hoarders, hippies, men-haters, and depressives, and emerged, inevitably, as an experimental social psychologist. Also very good on the developmental and cultural aspects of social perception.

Chapter 10

Social Cognition II: Social Reasoning and Societal Knowledge

Interviewer: What are you like?
Child: I'm not as smart as most kids.
Interviewer: Why is that important?
Child: It takes me longer to do my homework.
        (child interviewed by Damon and Hart, Self-understanding in Childhood and Adolescence, *1988, p. 63)*

We call them "Ostschweine" (east pigs) over there. Sometimes we go to the observation platforms along the Wall and shout at them.
        (child interviewed by Davey, A Generation Divided, *1987, p. 52)*

These children seem to be telling us something about their understandings of their respective social worlds. Damon and Hart's (1988) subject has a firm handle on the social cognitive developments we considered in the previous chapter. He or she volunteers self-descriptions with reference to internal, psychological properties (being "smart"), and employs social comparisons (with "most kids") in order to locate his or her own prowess in the domain under consideration. But two other dimensions of social cognition are reflected here as well. First, the interviewee is thinking about causal relations. The gross inconvenience to daily life associated with excessive duration of homework has to be accounted for somehow, and the explanation adopted here is in terms of personal deficiency: lack of smartness causes slow performance. Second, the child's choice of details when asked to describe the self suggests a clear awareness of societal criteria. Presumably, he or she accepts that smartness, speed of homework completion, and scholastic attainment more generally *matter*. Perhaps if probed further he or she would be able to explain that these things matter because they influence where we end up in society. In other words, the subject seems to have an at least implicit knowledge that the social world is a structured one, with different people occupying different slots.

Davey's (1987) subject is in no doubt that they do. This child was growing up in Berlin in the 1980s, before reunification. Helped by the highly visible reminder of social categorization that the local environment provided, the interviewee provides a robust statement of intergroup relations. It appears that this interviewee not only divides people into different slots, but also has strong views about their relative worth.

In this chapter, we consider in more detail the kinds of social cognitive developments that underpin such outlooks. The chapter is organized in two main sections. In the first section, we examine the development of thinking about causal relations, or *attribution theory*. We consider how children deal with the fact that, for many social events and attainments, there are several potential factors involved in explaining what has happened. We consider the relationship between causal explanation and affective reaction: for example, how is the child who concludes that she is not smart enough likely to feel about herself? How is the child who is told that he is not making enough effort likely to react to another opportunity? We will see that in fact there is a good chance that it will be a *she* who reaches the former conclusion (lack of ability) and a *he* who is advised of the latter problem (lack of effort).

In the second section, we turn to research on the development of knowledge about social roles and social structure. An important domain of social cognitive development concerns discovering the roles, relationships, hierarchies, and distinctions around which human lives are organized. These are often quite abstract notions and they pose many challenges to the newcomer to society. What exactly is entailed, for example, in being a police officer, a Queen, a boss? From where do authorities derive their status and what constraints, if any, should there be on the use of their powers? What do social concepts such as nationality and ethnic group mean to developing children, and why do children sometimes regard members of outgroups unfavorably (as *Ostschweine*, or similar)? We will see that understanding social structures, roles, and categories is not an instantaneous development but one that proceeds gradually through childhood, reflecting cognitive and affective developments and the influence of the social context.

Attribution Theory

Human beings seek constantly to explain events taking place in the world around them. This is so common a process that we often engage in it automatically, inferring a cause for an event without really "thinking" about it. If you have noticed any other persons passing by during the past hour or so, you have probably formulated some explanation for their movements: she was looking for a book on another library shelf, they were *en route* to a lecture, he was about to get a coffee or meet a friend. Similarly, if a stranger accosts you in the street and gives you free sachets of McDonald's tomato ketchup, you might well contemplate possible motivations for her generosity; if you receive an exam result that was worse than expected you might ask what went wrong; if an apple fell upon your head, you might invent a theory of gravity, or just wonder who threw it.

In explaining events, we *attribute* outcomes to particular causes. Noticing passers-by, you assume that they are moving because they wish to get somewhere else (i.e., you infer that their behavior is purposeful). You might suspect the ketchup donor is an agent of a fast-food outlet, "giving" you lots of tomato goo to whet your appetite for the burgers that you could purchase to accompany it along the pleasure-detecting sensors of your digestive tract; the exam result probably reflects malice or incompetence on behalf of the examiners, and so on.

Some of the explanations we generate for events are virtually automatic; others may be more deliberated. The point for the moment is that we engage in causal analysis very frequently – indeed, it is hard to resist doing so. Since the early work of Heider (1944, 1958) and Ichheiser (see Rudmin et al., 1987) social psychologists have taken these kinds of explanatory processes to be central to people's cognitive orientation toward the social environment. Heider proposed that they reflect our need to render the environment predictable, controllable and meaningful: without explanations, the world would be a bizarre and tumultuous succession of arbitrary experiences.

Attributions are Lay Theories

In making attributions, or causal explanations, we are applying our own lay theories of how things work. *Attribution theory* is the label for the causal explanations of the lay person. Attribution theory has been the focus of an explosion of research attention in experimental social psychology during the past two decades or so (for introductions see Fiske and Taylor, 1991; Hewstone, 1989; Hewstone and Fincham, 1996). Much of this work has been concerned with the cognitive processes of the adult social perceiver, and several models treat attributional processes as analogous to the operations of a scientist or a computer, whereby a series of logical operations are applied to a set of possible causes to arrive at an explanation of a given event.

In one influential early model, Kelley (1967, 1972) likened attributional reasoning to the application of an analysis of variance. According to this approach, in striving to explain a social event, such as someone shouting aggressively at another person, the lay theorist considers the *distinctiveness* of the action (does she shout at everyone, or just this individual?), the *consistency* of the action (does she shout at him frequently?), and the *consensus* (does everyone shout at him?) Different explanations of why she is shouting at him in a particular instance are arrived at according to the answers to each question (or, in ANOVA terms, the level of each factor). For example, if Marie shouts only at Karl, and does so every day, and everyone else shouts at him, then an observer might infer that Karl has a social skills deficit (or, in lay terms, is a real jerk). If Marie shouts at most people including Karl, and nobody else is shouting, then the observer might infer that Marie has a difficult temperament.

Exactly how and when attributions occur among adults are subjects of continuing controversy among investigators of adult social cognition. For developmentalists, interest turns naturally to the origins of these processes (Fincham, 1981; Harris, 1981; Kassin and Pryor, 1985). Indeed, as we will see below, attention to the development of attributions may help to explain some of the problems and anomalies that have cropped up in the experimental literature concerned with adults. The key questions include: when do children begin to analyse events in terms of underlying causes? Do the patterns of attributions change with development? What implications do attributions have for behavior? Are attributions affected by the social contexts of development?

Early awareness of causality

Some sense of causality appears to emerge quite early in infancy (Frye, 1991; Premack, 1991). Leslie (1982), using visual attention measures, found that 4–8-month-old infants discriminated between simple spatial events that appeared to be causally related (e.g., one object bumps into another, and the latter moves) and similar events which have less clear causes (e.g., the second object moves without any apparent cause). There is a lot of evidence that infants can not only learn to control aspects of their environment, but seem to take pleasure in the discovery of cause–effect relations and find them highly motivating (Jennings, 1991, 1993; Messer et al., 1986; Sullivan and Lewis, 1988; Watson, 1972). Sullivan and Lewis (1988), for example, placed 1-year-olds in an apparatus where they learned to move a tiller which triggered the presentation of a slide and some music from *Sesame Street*. About 70 percent of the subjects worked out how to do this within a few minutes, and were visibly engrossed in and excited by the contingencies they had discovered.

During the next year or so, children become increasingly likely to display pride in their own accomplishments (Bullock and Lutkenhaus, 1988; Lutkenhaus and Bullock, 1991; Stipek et al., 1992b). Bullock and Lutkenhaus (1988) observed children aged between 17 and 32 months engaged in block-building and cleaning tasks with specific goals (such as completing a tower, cleaning a blackboard). The researchers were particularly interested in whether the children showed any concern for the outcome of the task. Even at 17 months, many did (although this varied with the nature of the task), but by 32 months virtually all children did so. Using similar games, Stipek et al. (1992) found clear increases in a social orientation after the age of 21 months: children from this age responded to success with positive affect (smiling) and to failure with aversion (e.g., looking away from the experimenter). Mastery awareness appears to be developing during the first three years, and it is swiftly related to other people's reactions.

By around the age of 3–4 years, children are able to differentiate between outcomes that they have caused and outcomes that are random. Schneider and Unzner (1992) had preschoolers play games in which skilled actions could trigger a sound and light display, or games in which similar displays occurred every now and again but with no causal relationship to the player's actions. The children liked the displays and greeted them with visible signs of pleasure; however, these positive reactions to the random effects began to diminish with experience, while positive reactions to the effects brought about by their own skills were sustained across several trials. This evidence indicates that preschoolers are aware of causality in their own actions, and are motivated to control outcomes. As discussed in chapter 9, there is also a growing body of evidence to confirm that preschoolers are aware of *others'* mental states and activities as causal bases for their actions. Indeed, interactions with others, such as conversations, may serve both to furnish the toddler with examples of causality and to provide contexts in which to discuss it; Dunn (1993), for example, found that references to causality, including psychological causes, were common in 3-year-olds' conversations with parents and siblings.

Some understanding of causality, then, develops quite early. But the social world is a multifarious environment, and it is often the case that a given event could be explained in terms of different causes. Another challenge to social understanding is working out which is the most plausible cause. This involves acquiring the rules of attribution.

Using Attributional Rules

Many developmental studies have been conducted to determine when and how children are able to use some of the attributional principles that Kelley and others have claimed are involved in adult causal reasoning. One of Kelley's central interests was how people deal with events for which there are more than one possible cause. For example, if you walk into a cold room, you might infer that someone has left a window open, *or* that the air-conditioner is running; if you encounter a person who is cold toward you, you might infer that you have offended her, *or* that she has some personal problems which are affecting her mood. To help find suitable explanations, you could engage in the ANOVA type reasoning above. Once you have hit upon a plausible cause (you hear the whirr of the air-conditioner, you remember that you have failed to repay a longstanding debt to this person, perhaps she has had another row with Karl), then you may cross the other possible causes off the list. In Kelley's terms, you are following the *discounting principle*.

The discounting principle holds that the role of a given cause in producing a given effect is discounted if other plausible causes are also present. We tended earlier to discount the pure altruism motive to account for our tomato ketchup benefactor once we learned she worked for McDonalds; a different cause then seemed somehow more plausible. Of course, it is remotely possible that she really *is* an inherently kind person, it could be that the window in the air-conditioned room has been left open, and it could be that your frosty friend resents your dilatory attitude toward loan repayment but has also fallen out with her lover. The point is that you may not keep all causes in mind once you have identified a plausible and salient one: you discount the other(s). Often, it is economical and ecologically adaptive to discount. If you still believe that people giving you "free" gifts in the shopping mall are motivated by their internal predispositions to generosity, then you may not be equipped with the most adequate social cognitive repertoire for setting foot in the wicked world outdoors.

Research testing Kelley's claim among adult subjects has yielded mixed results (see Fiske and Taylor, 1991; Kruglanski et al., 1978; Reeder, 1985), though it is certainly agreed that we sometimes use the discounting principle. To do so, we need to be able to assess the relative significance of the multiple sufficient causes that might be involved. For example, if you view a celebrity endorsing a product in a television commercial you might accept that the product is every bit as remarkable as he or she proclaims; alternatively, you might infer that he or she is being paid a whopping fee to appear in the ad, and will say anything if the price is right. You are using the discounting principle. How do children fare with the rather abstract computation of discounting?

Children and the discounting principle

Some early studies of children's attributional reasoning indicated that younger subjects may not use the discounting principle (Karniol and Ross, 1976; Shultz et al., 1975; Smith, 1975). For example, Smith (1975) presented children with stories in which a central character played with a toy. In one version, toy choice was spontaneous, while in another the child was induced to play with it (e.g., an adult offered a reward for doing so, or commanded the child to play with it). Subjects were asked to decide which character really liked the toy. Now, if you use the discounting principle, you should reason that the child who was ordered or cajoled into playing with it may not have really liked it, whereas the child who opted for the toy voluntarily must presumably find it attractive. This is exactly how older children reasoned. Kindergarten subjects, however, showed no evidence of discounting. Karniol and Ross (1976), using a similar paradigm, even found evidence of what they called an "additive principle" in younger subjects' responses, such that some children interpreted playing with a toy after adult direction indicated greater liking.

On the other hand, interesting studies suggest that the discounting principle can be employed from an early age. Lepper et al. (1973) provided preschool children with some new felt pens, and monitored the amount of time the children used them in their classroom free play periods. Then, some children were led to believe that they would receive an award if they continued to play regularly with the pens. The initial cause for playing with the pens was that they were fun, but now the experimenters had manipulated an alternative cause: working to get an award. Here, use of the toy appeared to be "overjustified." Before long, the initial cause seemed to be discounted by these subjects, and they played less with the toys than did peers in conditions where the award was given unexpectedly or where there was no award.

Although the Lepper et al. (1973) experiment indicates that young children can discount some factors underlying their own behavior, it is less clear that they apply the principle when interpreting the actions of others. Kassin and Pryor (1985) review literature which produces mixed results in this respect, pointing to an interesting paradox that children's behavior might be mediated by the discounting principle even though they lack the cognitive abilities to understand and apply it elsewhere. In order to explain the development of this form of attribution, Kassin and Lepper (1984) propose that children's use of the discounting principle reflects both cognitive developmental status and social experience (such as whether the situation about which they are being questioned is a familiar one).

Kassin and Ellis (1988) tested this proposal in a pair of experiments in which 5–7-year-olds and 8–10-year-olds were first given experiences which were designed to heighten their awareness of possible varieties of motives for taking particular actions. For example, they were offered choices between chocolate chips and tasteless crackers, or between fruit drinks and water. (Decades of meticulous research have confirmed that under these conditions children favor chocolate and fruit juice.) Subjects were next either *commanded* to consume the less appealing substance or offered a *reward* for doing so. Place yourself in the child's position and you can see that this is quite a good way to discover the discrepancies between what a person *wants to do* and what a person *has to do*.

The children then went on to view tapes of other children being induced to take particular options by adults using either commands or rewards. The activities in the tapes were either similar to or different from those the child had just been involved in. The subjects were asked to say what the stimulus child in the tape *really* liked, and to explain the reasons for their answer. Kassin and Ellis found that although discounting was not used extensively, it was used most by those subjects assessing choices which were familiar to them, especially when there was an inverse relation between extrinsic pressure and internal motivation. When the activity was unfamiliar, subjects were least likely to discount; that is, observing an adult *command* a child to engage in an unfamiliar activity did not lead them to suppose that the child might actually be uninterested in the activity.

Several subsequent studies lead to the conclusion that preschoolers can discount when the external cause is made highly salient (Aloise and Miller, 1991; Karniol and Ross, 1979; Lepper et al., 1982; Newman and Ruble, 1992; Shultz and Butkowsky, 1977; see Miller and Aloise, 1989, for a fuller review). For example, Aloise and Miller (1991) found that preschoolers discounted a hypothetical child's interest in Toy A when a "big, mean brother" declared that if the child played with A he could later play with Toy B. Even preschoolers knew that the child did not really care for Toy A, and seemed to appreciate that sometimes you have to go through the motions to satisfy a longer-term aim (in this case, getting to play with Toy B).

Preschoolers, then, *can* discount but may not always do so. Miller and Aloise (1989) point out that the tendency sometimes not to discount is consistent with their view (discussed in chapter 9) that young children *do* have an understanding of – even a preference for – internal causes of behavior. If preschoolers tend to attribute someone's persistence in an activity to that person's interest or enjoyment rather than discount these motivations and conclude that the person has been coerced by an adult, then this is not easily explained by the hypothesis that children of this age are dominated by perceptions of external factors.

Attributional Biases

Important as these inferential processes may be to social cognition, one limitation of the models sketched so far is that they assume that the social cognitive agent is a cool, rational observer whose priority is to gain an accurate understanding of cause–effect relations in the social environment. In practice, human motivations are rarely this simple (Darley and Goethals, 1980) nor so context-free (Costanzo and Dix, 1983; Kassin and Pryor, 1985). For a start, having invested so much in the development of a self, we are inclined to look out for its interests. This heartfelt commitment may affect the way we appraise our own performances.

In fact, a lot of experimental research in the study of attribution theory demonstrates that we have a self-serving bias to regard our own successes favorably (as due to our inherent qualities), while distancing ourselves from responsibility for our failures (someone or something interfered with our performance). That is, we have a tendency to attribute causality for success to internal factors ("I did it!,") and causality for failure to external factors ("They stopped me," "You cheated!") Unless, of course, we are observing someone else's performance: then, we tend to work the other way around, attributing their success to external and their failure to internal factors (see Fiske and Taylor, 1991; Sabini, 1995; Zebrowitz, 1990, for reviews of research into attributional biases among adults). Some evidence suggests that teachers may be particularly prone to attributional bias: they tend to explain their pupils' success as due to their teaching skills, and their students' failures as due to lack of effort (Gosling, 1994). "Obviously," comment Darley and Goethals, "the possibilities for distortion, for deceiving oneself, and for attempting the same with others are many" (1980, p. 29).

The fundamental attribution error

One bias that is of particular interest from a developmental social psychological perspective is the so-called "fundamental attribution error" (Jones, 1979; Ross, 1977). The fundamental attribution error refers to the tendency of adults "to underestimate the impact of situational factors and to overestimate the role of dispositional factors in controlling behavior" (Ross, 1977, p. 183). In other words, when observing others' behavior, people are sometimes prone to attribute causality to individuals' own motives and qualities, rather than to the circumstances in which they act.

In early demonstrations of this phenomenon, Jones and Harris (1967) had American students read an essay about Fidel Castro, the communist President of Cuba, supposedly written by another student. The American government of the time was not favorably disposed toward the "red menace" of communism so close to its shores. In different conditions, the essay was either pro- or anti-Castro, and the author was reported to have written it through choice *or* in order to satisfy the prejudices of a lecturer who would be assessing it. Subjects who were told that the essay was written under constraint none the less tended to rate it as at least partially reflecting the author's *own* opinions. Subjects seemed, in short, to disregard the situation and to overestimate the personal commitment of the author. This does appear to reflect a person-centered bias in adults' explanations of social events, at least among Westerners (see Fiske and Taylor, 1991, for additional examples and discussion).

Attributional biases in children

Although the study of attribution processes has led in recent years to some convergence of social and developmental psychologists around this topic, once again the traditional orientation of each approach has led to a difference in emphases and methods, and in some cases to surprisingly different conclusions. An ironic outcome pointed out by Kassin and Pryor (1985) is that an attributional tendency which social psychologists have come to regard as a bias inherent in normal adult reasoning strategies – namely, the fundamental attribution error – can appear from a developmental perspective as a manifestation of sophisticated information-processing.

As we saw in chapter 9, many cognitive developmental researchers have concluded either that young children are not very good at inferring intention or that they may not always realize that it is appropriate to do so. In contexts where causality could be attributed to a person or a situation, younger children tend often to opt for the latter (as in Ruble et al., 1979; see also Higgins and Bryant, 1982). From this perspective, coming to discover individuals' responsibility for their actions could be seen as an achievement, the product of sustained social cognitive development. But, as indicated above, the outcome of this lengthy process is interpreted by social psychologists, in some circumstances at least, as a fundamental "error". In a nutshell, if the *adult* attributes responsibility to the actor, then she or he is suspected of bias for failing to give adequate weight to the situation; but if the *child* attributes responsibility to the situation, we infer that she or he may not grasp the fact that people have internal cognitive processes and intentions.

This seeming contradiction is, as Kassin and Pryor (1985) suggest, an irony rather than a folly. The developmental perspective has in fact contributed to social psychologists' recent explanations of the fundamental attribution error; they tend now to regard it as acquired rather than automatic and to stress its adaptive value (cf. Fiske and Taylor, 1991), social desirability (Beauvois and Dubois, 1988) and cross-cultural variability (Fletcher and Ward, 1988; Zebrowitz, 1990). For example, Beauvois and Dubois (1988) report that children are more likely to attribute internal responsibility to an actor in conditions where they are made aware of adult expectations than when they are expressing freely their own point of view; this suggests that Western children come to learn that adults think of people as responsible for their actions (i.e., that adults make the fundamental attribution error) and that they are expected to follow suit.

Similarly, the social psychological perspective has broadened developmental approaches to the explanation of causality, by raising important questions about where children are disposed to seek causes, how social reinforcement may encourage them to focus on internal factors, and how relevant patterns of reasoning change (Beauvois and Dubois, 1988; Costanzo and Dix, 1983). As already indicated, recent evidence has challenged the view that young children cannot take account of internal causes of behavior (Miller and Aloise, 1989), though it may well be the case that situational factors and interpersonal expectations influence whether they focus on internal or external considerations. One possible social transaction which might make internal attributions increasingly salient, for example, is *evaluation* (Beauvois, 1984). That is, as children gain more experience of being evaluated (in school, at home, in other social contexts) so they may come to focus more on individuals' capacities and efforts. As a result, the external process which initially happens *to* the child may be taken over as one that she or he applies in turn when accounting for the observed behavior of others. Dix et al. (1986) investigated parents' attributions for children's behavior and found that adults were more likely to explain children's conduct in terms of internal dispositions as the child grew older. Dix et al. suggest that parental attributions may provide cues to their children about how to explain behavior.

Higgins and Parsons (1983) point out that evidence that even 4- and 5-year-old children can make dispositional attributions under certain conditions indicates that the weight they give to person versus situation may itself be influenced by their own experiences and circumstances. For example, preschoolers find that their own, and their peers', behavior is often controlled by external forces (grown-ups). This social context could well guide them to look first toward the situational control of a person's actions. It is not that they are incapable of contemplating personal choice, it is just that it is not that salient a factor in their daily lives. Children in the early school years experience greater liberty to choose activities and playmates. Their newfound increase in personal freedom may enhance their perception of volitional control of behavior.

Attributional biases and intergroup relations

Another important emphasis made by social psychologists is that attributional biases can be associated with intergroup tensions and stereotype confirmation (Rosenfield and Stephan, 1981). For example, in addition to their discomfort with red Cubans, some white Americans do not like black Americans or Mexican-Americans, and the sentiments are occasionally reciprocated. In a study of several hundred American high school students, Stephan (1977) found that adolescents explaining negative or positive behaviors in hypothetical stimulus persons made more favorable attributions to members of their own group than to members of other ethnic groups. Told that a white person had worked hard on a project, white subjects attributed the effort to industriousness (i.e., an internal attribution); told that a black person had worked hard, white subjects attributed the effort to the influence of a strict supervisor (i.e., an external attribution). Mexican-Americans also showed ingroup favoritism (although the results were less clear cut for black Americans). Among non-prejudiced individuals, however, no evidence of attributional biases in these kinds of tasks is found (see Rosenfield and Stephan, 1981). We consider the emergence of ethnic prejudice in more detail later, but for the moment it should be clear that the processes of formulating attributions are influenced, like many other aspects of social cognition, by the social contexts in which they are invoked.

Attributions and Achievement-related Behavior

One of the major applications of accounts of attributional processes in the young concerns achievement-related behavior, especially in educational contexts. When we approach an educational task, we have some expectancy about the outcome, and in due course we may well receive feedback about our performance that will either confirm or challenge our expectation. Consider how a person might react to a disappointingly negative examination result. One possibility is to attribute causality to some other party, such as an examiner, or a poor teacher; another is to feed the bad news into our self-concept, and conclude that we are not as smart as we thought.

In short, in the face of success or failure information, we are likely to invoke attribution theories to help us to explain the outcome. Weiner and his associates (Weiner, 1972, 1979, 1986; Weiner et al., 1971) have developed an influential model of the social cognitive processes thought to be engaged in achievement-related attributions, and this model has stimulated a great deal of empirical research, particularly in educational settings (Bar-Tal, 1978, 1979; Frieze, 1981).

The model is based on the assumption that beliefs about the causes of success and failure mediate the relationship between feedback and subsequent performance. According to Weiner, when we try to explain a success or failure, we are likely to attribute it to one or more of four causes: ability, effort, task difficulty, or luck. These causes can be categorized in relation to three dimensions. The first dimension is that of *internality–externality*. Was the outcome due to my performance (internal) or to unusually difficult circumstances (external)? The second dimension is that of *stability*. Was the outcome what I typically achieve (stable) or was it a fluke (unstable)? The third dimension is *controllability*. Could I have worked any harder (controllable) or was I ill at the time of the exam (uncontrollable)?

Any achievement-related outcome, such as a particular success or failure, could be explained by different options within this attributional framework, and the choice of options has both cognitive and affective consequences. Let us imagine that you attribute an unhappy examination outcome to an internal factor: effort. The *cognitive* consequence is that you have identified a variable that needs attention if you are to improve your performance next time. The *affective* consequence is that you feel some shame or self-disappointment. Fortunately, in this instance you have pinpointed a causal factor which is both unstable and controllable; you could raise your effort and expect to do better next semester. The dent to your self-esteem is not irremediable, because you reason: "I am as smart as the best of them; I just need to get my act together."

Suppose instead that you had attributed the failure to an ability (such as your innately low level of intelligence). In this case, you have a bigger problem, since you have diagnosed yourself as lacking a vital quality, and a rather stable one which it is difficult to control (you cannot opt to become cleverer next semester). Following this ability attribution, you are likely to have lowered cognitive expectations. After all, you feel that you do not have the ability to succeed. In this case, your affective reaction is likely to be one of reduced self-esteem, at least in respect of this area of achievement. This is a more serious dent, because you are really beginning to question whether you can make it. As you drag yourself back to your studies, you have a foreboding of further cognitive catastrophe and a profound sense of personal deficiency. Like Damon and Hart's interviewee at the beginning of the chapter, you have reached the conclusion that "I am not as smart as most students."

Clearly, different attributions for the same outcome have the potential to bring about quite different expectations about future performance. Bar-Tal (1978) illustrates some of the possibilities in figure 10.1. (Note that for expository purposes, this figure deals only with the internal–external and stable–unstable dimensions.)

As mentioned, a large amount of research has been conducted to test this model (or variants of it), and it has proven fruitful and applicable in a number of contexts. First, several studies which have solicited subjects' explanations of performances have found that people do engage in spontaneous causal thinking (Weiner, 1985) and that they tend to employ the factors taken by Wiener to be central, especially ability, effort and task difficulty (although others are drawn upon, too; see Bar-Tal et al., 1984; Frieze, 1981; Little, 1985). Second, research has confirmed that people's affective reactions to success or failure tend to be consistent with predictions following from Weiner's model; for example, individuals feel greater pride about successes attributed to ability or effort (internal factors) than to those attributed to external factors, while greater shame is experienced in reaction to failures attributed to internal causes (Frieze, 1981; Nicholls, 1976; Weiner et al., 1978). Third, and perhaps most importantly, the attributions people make affect their expectations for subsequent performances. For example, Dweck and Repucci (1973) found that children who attributed outcomes to internal causes were more likely to persevere in a task than were children who made external attributions. In these ways, individuals can bring about successes or failures in ways which are consistent with their own understanding of the causes of outcomes (see Skinner, 1991).

Development of achievement-related attributions

Although attributional models of achievement have obvious implications for education and have been widely applied, it should be borne in mind that this approach is not inherently *developmental* – that is, it does not take directly into account the possibility that the processes may operate differently according to the individual's level of development. In fact, there are good reasons to expect developmental differences, not least because the essential concepts of the Weiner framework (ability, effort, luck, task difficulty) are quite abstract and therefore not readily employed by younger children.

As we have seen, from infancy, children are motivated toward mastery. The antecedents of the affective reactions outlined by Bar-Tal (1978 figure 10.1) can be

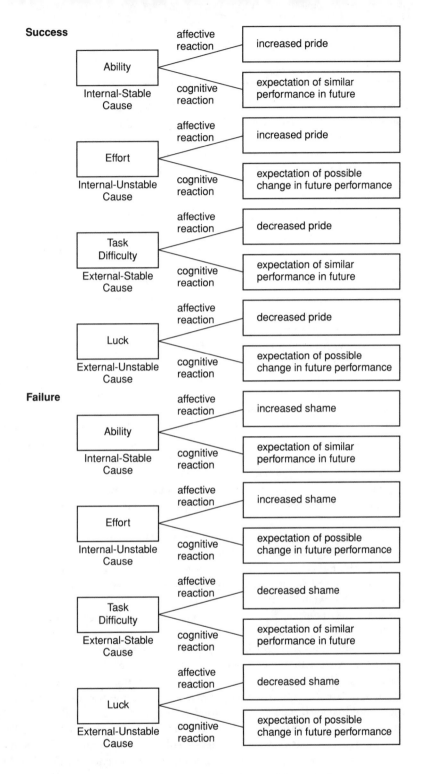

Figure 10.1 Possible causal attributions for success and failure and their affective consequences.
(*Source*: Bar-Tal, 1978)

found very early in life. Heckhausen (1988) reports that infants in their second year displayed pride at their accomplishments (e.g., building a tower), though at this stage there was little evidence of shame at failure. Hence, there may be an early connection between achievement and affect, but the question remains as to whether children reason about the causes of their performances by using concepts such as ability, effort, and so on.

Several researchers have found that young children (around the age 5–7) do not appear to differentiate among these notions as clearly as do older individuals. In particular, they tend to be "learning optimists" (Dweck and Elliot, 1983), overestimating their own capabilities (Eshel and Klein, 1981; Stipek, 1984). Ask a 5-year-old to estimate how many items he will be able to remember from a list, and his prediction will typically be far greater than the number actually recalled (Yussen and Levy, 1975). Recall Jason's enthusiastic list of his skills and achievements in chapter 9. Yee and Brown (1992) provide evidence that this tendency occurs in group contexts, too, with 5-year-olds in arbitrarily adult-created teams insisting that theirs is best, notwithstanding empirical evidence to the contrary (e.g., the other team won).

Nicholls (1978a, 1979; Nicholls and Miller, 1985) found that causal attributional schemes develop over several years from early childhood to around the age of 12. He had subjects aged 5–13 watch films in which actors performed educational tasks with either successful or failed outcomes (Nicholls, 1978a) or provide explanations of their own educational successes or failures (Nicholls, 1979). In these kinds of task, Nicholls found that younger children tend not to distinguish very clearly between effort and ability. They assume that people who try harder must be smarter, even if they achieve poorer outcomes than others. Similarly, Nicholls and Miller (1985) found that many young children believed that effort could influence the outcome of a task that was actually wholly dependent upon luck (picking the correct card from a set facing downwards).

Nesdale and Pope (1985), in a study of 4- and 7-year-olds, found that at both ages the children attributed successes and failures to the ease or difficulty of the task, respectively, rather than to internal processes. Thus, there was no evidence within this age range of self-serving attributional biases. The researchers suggest that young children may not have clearly differentiated concepts of effort, ability and luck. Task difficulty may be a more accessible notion, since all children have lots of experiences of things that are easy or difficult to do.

Stipek and DeCotis (1988), testing 6–13-year-olds' understanding of the emotions associated with achievement outcomes, found again that although most children understood a link between attribution and emotion in such contexts, younger subjects did not differentiate according to whether an outcome was due to ability, effort, or luck. Children aged 6 and 7 years old appeared to assume that all of these factors were to some extent controllable, and felt that a person should be equally ashamed following failure caused by low ability as failure caused by low effort. Similarly, they felt that one could be just as proud of a successful outcome attributed to luck as to a success attributed to effort or ability.

Nicholls (1978a) charts development as follows. At first, children's differentiation among effort, ability and luck is rather weak. Gradually, during mid-childhood, they come to recognize a relationship between effort and outcome but still do not recognize that ability could interact with effort – for example, that a very smart person could achieve a successful outcome in an educational task with less effort than her peers might have to put in. In due course, children begin to take note of ability intermittently, but treat it as one factor among several, rather than one with implications for others. Systematic use of ability, and correct inferences about ability on the basis of effort and outcome, is found among 12-year-olds, though – according to Nicholls's (1978a) data – not ubiquitously. Consistent with the increasing reference to internal properties, during middle childhood children become less likely to explain outcomes in terms of luck (Skinner et al., 1988).

Another reason why younger children may attach less weight to stable factors such as ability is that, in *their* personal experiences and social lives, ability is not actually very stable. Higgins and Parsons (1983) note that preschoolers undergo relatively rapid development in a number of their own capacities. Furthermore, if they look to their older siblings, they find impressive evidence that people seem to be able to do all sorts of things better just by getting a bit older. In addition, their parents are well aware of the pace of development and may provide recurrent prompts to "try again" until the child exhibits progress. On the basis of these observations and experiences, why would one infer that ability is stable?

It appears that not only are the possible computations involved in explaining success or failure quite complex (for example, the Weiner matrix involves several different factors which could interact in different combinations) but the social environments within which children are prompted and guided toward causal explanations are themselves changeable. Nevertheless, as we see next, most children can draw emotional implications from their own successes or failures.

Attributions and Learned Helplessness

If a causal attribution about an achievement-related outcome affects how a person approaches similar tasks in the future, it is easy to see how initial bad news could set the scene for lowered expectations. Having failed your driving test once, you might be still more apprehensive the next time around; if things go wrong again, you begin to feel quite inept behind the wheel; a third or fourth "regret to inform you" and deep despair begins to set in. By the time you take your ninth test, you no longer believe you can pass, whatever you do. By now, you are contemplating repairing your bicycle, although you doubt your roadworthiness even on two wheels.

At this stage, you are beginning to exhibit what Seligman (1975) calls *learned helplessness*, the belief that one's outcomes are independent of one's actions. Since we have seen consistent evidence that from infancy onwards human beings are highly motivated to achieve mastery and control of their environments, it is clear that encountering situations in which this appears impossible could be very distressing. Seligman and colleagues' work with animals and clinical patients shows that persistent failure to achieve any sense of effectiveness in important task areas can lead to an overwhelming sense of futility, often accompanied by profound depression (Peterson and Seligman, 1984).

Learned Helplessness in Children

Research with children has shown that some individuals are susceptible to developing patterns of learned helplessness (Dweck, 1991; Dweck and Elliott, 1983; Dweck and Leggett, 1988; Seligman et al., 1988). Consistent with the adult literature, children who exhibit learned helplessness have also been found to be more prone to suffer negative affect and depression (Fincham et al., 1987).

According to Dweck and her colleagues, some children are *mastery oriented*; these individuals respond to negative outcomes with increased perseverance, attributing failures to unstable internal causes (such as lack of effort) or external factors (such as poor test conditions) rather than to stable internal deficiencies (such as lack of ability). As figure 10.1 indicates, the emotional and cognitive reactions of these children to setbacks are not likely to inhibit future performances since they infer that they can obtain a better result by increasing their effort or avoiding disadvantageous circumstances.

Children suffering from learned helplessness, on the other hand, display a quite different pattern of attributions. They interpret their failures as reflecting internal and stable causes, especially lack of ability. As figure 10.1 shows, once an attribution for failure is focused on the supposed stable limitations of the actor, self-defeating emotions and expectations are likely to follow. Dweck's and others' research demonstrates that this is indeed what happens. For example, children who manifest learned helplessness tend to regard themselves as less able than their peers even in respect of tasks in which they have previously performed as well as or better than those peers (Dweck, 1978; Dweck and Elliott, 1983; Phillips 1984). When undertaking classroom work in groups, helpless children whose team is unsuccessful tend to learn least from the activity (Abrami et al., 1992).

This pattern is not restricted to evaluations of academic performance and predictions of academic success. Heyman et al. (1992) found that, among 5- and 6-year-olds, children who had received criticism of their work (a painting) not only tended to downgrade their products but also were more likely to make global negative self-judgments, even to see themselves as "not a good person". Fincham and Hokoda (1987) found that children who are neglected and rejected in social situations among peers are also prone to develop learned helplessness styles of attribution to account for their interpersonal experiences and social prospects.

In due course, children suffering setbacks in work or social relations, believing that it is not within their competence to achieve success, become less motivated and reduce their efforts and minimize their goals. In this way, they gradually fulfil their own expectations of helplessness (Seligman et al., 1988). Fincham et al. (1989) found that, on both self-report measures and teacher ratings collected over a two-year period, learned helplessness is relatively stable in late childhood.

The onset of learned helplessness

Exactly how early children are at risk of developing patterns of learned helplessness and how the processes develop are not clearly established. On the one hand, since some of the concepts underlying attributions are rather abstract, we might not expect younger children to employ notions such as ability in appraising their own behavior and its outcomes. Rholes et al. (1980) compared children aged 5, 7, 10, and 12 years in a task in which they were given feedback about their success or failure; only the oldest subjects began to show patterns of helplessness (performance decrements after repeated failure).

On the other hand, we know that from infancy setbacks can be frustrating. If a task is in the realm of things that the child expects to be able to handle, it may be disturbing to discover incompetence. Subsequent research has confirmed that preschoolers and early school-aged children can develop symptoms of learned helplessness, especially if they receive negative feedback or experience other difficulties in tasks which are familiar to them. Boggiano et al. (1993) set up a context in which children had to correct an out-of-focus slide projector. This is a simple enough physical task for primary school-aged children (Sullivan and Lewis's 1-year-olds could probably work it out with a bit of practice). But Boggiano et al. had rigged the machine so that it simply could not be focused. In this context, 8-year-olds showed helpless responses. Heyman et al.'s (1992) study, above, revealed helplessness in still younger subjects. Overall, research points toward the possibility of early onset of helplessness in at least some domains, although it is likely that with social cognitive development children may come to represent their perceived weaknesses and strengths in more differentiated ways. For example, they may develop more complex understandings of the relationship between intelligence and performance, and refine their knowledge of what cannot be done because of relative immaturity versus individual differences in competence.

The Social Contexts of Attribution

So far, we have seen several illustrations of the utility of attributional approaches in helping to investigate how individuals think about causal relations. However, in terms of the distinction introduced at the beginning of chapter 9, this work is predominantly located in the tradition of *individual* social cognition: the individual looks out at the world and tries to compute an understanding of what is going on. Research into attribution theory has been criticized for this preoccupation with the individual subject (Deschamps, 1983; Forgas, 1981b; Hewstone, 1989; Hewstone and Jaspars, 1984; Tajfel, 1981). Hewstone and Jaspars (1984) argue for a more social approach to explaining attributions. They stress that attributions are social in *origin* (they arise in social interactions), social in *reference* (they are about people, often people perceived as members of social categories), and they are social in the sense that they are *shared with other members of one's group* (that is, group members tend to use similar explanatory frameworks).

As an example of the social origins of attributions, we might return to Heckhausen's (1988) findings above that infants displayed pride at success. It turns out that there is a social context to this expression. Heckhausen also reported that this reaction typically occurred *in response to exaggerated praise by the mother*. Similarly, Stipek et al. (1992b) found that before the age of 2 years children show anticipation of adult reactions to their successes and failures. It seems that from the beginnings of life, other people provide cues as to how to interpret or respond to causal relations. Stipek et al. propose that early development is oriented around the internalization of adults' reactions.

Another social dimension to attributional processes is revealed in children's biases as a function of their liking for the person about whom the attribution is made. Hymel (1986) investigated 7- and 10-year-olds' explanations for the behavior of their peers. Subjects were asked to imagine circumstances in which a (named) classmate performed a positive or negative behavior, such as helping the subject to pick up some dropped papers, failing to invite the subject to a party, or ignoring the subject in the lunch room. In accounting for the behaviors, children were more likely to attribute positive actions to stable causes when performed by a child they liked. Negative actions were attributed to stable causes when performed by a child they disliked. If a liked child was under consideration for a negative act, children were more likely to excuse it or attribute it to unstable causes ("He didn't really do it to be mean, it was just a joke.") The attributional process is influenced by social context.

The social contexts of learned helplessness

Why do some individuals develop a mastery orientation while others fall victim to the vicious cycle of learned helplessness? One possibility is that these are innate personality differences; maybe some people are just prone to give up too readily. However, this does not appear a very promising explanation since, as noted above, learned helplessness has often been observed in individuals who are initially competent – even above average – in certain domains.

In fact, Dweck et al. (1978) demonstrated experimentally that it is possible to manipulate a "mastery" or a "helpless" outcome from an achievement task by varying the feedback given to the subject. They had 12-year-olds complete anagrams, designed so that half were easy and half were difficult. As the children "failed" on the difficult word tasks, those in the Mastery condition were told that they were not trying hard enough (thus highlighting an unstable cause for the outcome), while those in the Helpless condition were told that their answers were not up to the required standards (conveying the implication that they were not smart enough for the task – a stable cause). Subsequently, the children were asked to explain their performance. The results showed a marked difference between conditions, with the Mastery children attributing failure primarily to lack of effort, and the Helpless children attributing it to lack of ability.

This experimental demonstration raises the possibility that different children receive different feedback about their successes and outcomes in classrooms and other contexts, and that this social input guides them toward particular attributional styles.

The closely related concept of self-efficacy (belief in one's ability to perform a skill or action; see chapter 1) also appears to be influenced by social context (Garber et al., 1991; Skinner, 1991). For example, Garber et al. (1991) found that the children of depressed mothers perceived themselves as having low self-efficacy in helping others deal with emotional problems.

Again, there is persuasive evidence that this does happen extensively, in both the formal (school) and informal (home) contexts in which children receive feedback about their educational progress (Dweck and Elliott, 1983; Holloway and Hess, 1985; Parsons et al., 1982; Seligman et al., 1988). In a well-known field experiment, Rosenthal and Jacobson (1968) showed that by inducing in teachers the belief that some children in their classes were brighter than average, those children's IQ scores were raised substantially in an end-of-year test (the children were actually selected at random). Although this experiment has been subjected to methodological criticism, few dispute that teachers do have different expectations of different pupils, and that they communicate these expectations directly and indirectly, and that children are sensitive to the messages conveyed (see Gibbons, 1981; Minuchin and Shapiro, 1983).

Children may acquire and share their interpretations of their own and their peers' academic behavior. Listening to children's spontaneous accounts of peers' performances provides hints of the influence of the social context. Little (1985) found that adult-sounding attributions about behavior (e.g. "he's naughty," "she mucks around," "he talks during lessons") were used frequently by children to account for achievement levels within classrooms, a finding which suggests that teachers' emphases on these matters are a salient component of school socialization. Seligman et al. (1988) also report intergenerational similarities in explanatory style, particularly between children and their mothers. Once children have an academic expectation about a peer, then they may transmit and reinforce it. For example, Harris et al. (1992) had pairs of previously unacquainted 9–13-year-old boys work on building tasks. Some of the subjects were told that their partner was in a special class for his behavior ("Apparently he gets in trouble a lot for disrupting the class, talking when he shouldn't, not sitting in his chair and acting silly.") The boys who had been forewarned that their partner was a bit of a troublemaker were less friendly toward them, talked less, and put less effort into the joint task. For their part, the alleged problem kids found the task less enjoyable, judged their dyad as not doing so well, and took less credit even for good performances. It seems that when your peers expect poor things of you, you begin to fulfil their expectations.

Gender, attributions, and helplessness

A crucial example of the ways in which the social context may influence the development of attributional styles concerns gender. Several studies have revealed a sex difference in terms of the attributional feedback that children are likely to receive. Negative feedback to girls tends to be concerned predominantly with ability-related matters (analogous to Dweck et al.'s 1978 experiment, when negative messages are given, they are focused on discrepancies with expected standards). Negative feedback to boys is often couched in terms of unstable characteristics (such as not trying hard enough). Thus, girls more often receive feedback which may lead them to reflect on their lack of relevant ability, while boys receive feedback which stresses their misbehavior (Dweck 1978; Meece, 1987; Minuchin and Shapiro, 1983).

Walkerdine (1986) illustrates this with excerpts from teachers' comments on specific pupils:

> *On girls*:
> Quiet. Gets on very well, sits down and gets on with it. Very rarely makes mistakes. Very tidy handwriting.
>
> Very, very hard worker. Not a particularly bright girl but everything she presents is very high. Her hard work gets her to her standards.
>
> She's not a high flier. But she plods along and does quite well – a very nice personality.
>
> *On boys*:
> Damian . . . covered the work as well. He's been in Greece . . . He's interested because he comes up and says he's bored . . . and that's the reason why he makes a lot of mistakes.
>
> I would say he is the brightest child in the class, but again is someone who needs to be encouraged. He can be very rude, and can be obstreperous with other children rather than the teacher. But he has a very good ability, very interested in everything, a very good general knowledge and has an all-round ability with a lot of potential.

Consider again figure 10.1, and note the different consequences of inferring – or accepting someone else's inference – that you do not have the ability (are "not particularly bright") versus you are not putting in the necessary effort to realize your potential.

On first sight, this kind of thing may appear to be a rather sexist practice on the part of teachers, but the explanation is somewhat more complex. If we consider the different routes of sex role development discussed in chapter 5, we are reminded that children do not arrive at school as uniform receptacles, ready to be filled up by the system; instead, they have already undergone extensive socialization experiences and bring certain gender-associated characteristics with them. Among these are the greater physical robustness of boys and the greater social skills of girls. The practical consequence of this for the teacher is that, on average, boys *do* tend to generate more behavioral problems in the classroom, and as a result invite more attention. Girls, on average, are less of a management problem, and so teachers may find when they have to address girls' work their focus is more likely to be on content rather than behavior, running the risk that the girl may begin to infer that she lacks ability. Meanwhile, the self-esteem of her disorderly neighbor is less threatened, since he can reason that he could handle all this stuff if he wanted too, and that getting told off for messing around is all part of the fun.

These processes are not necessarily divided absolutely around gender; it is quite probable that *within*-sex variability in attributional style could be explained by reference to the same patterns. Well-behaved children of either sex are more likely to attract attention as a result of committing an error than a misdemeanor. Even so, research reveals a greater incidence of self-derogation and learned helplessness among girls than boys ((Burger and Hewstone, 1993; Dweck et al., 1978, 1980; Frey and Ruble, 1987; Stipek and Hoffman, 1980).

Attributional retraining

Learned helplessness is a liability but not necessarily an immutable one. Several researchers have demonstrated that training children to attribute failures to effort rather than to ability and successes to ability rather than chance factors can lead to improved performance and persistence in the face of setbacks (Craske, 1985; Dweck, 1975; Gatting-Stiller et al., 1979; Ho and McMurtie, 1991; Schunk, 1983; Schunk et al., 1987) and similar results have been obtained with undergraduate students (Wilson and Linville, 1985). If you know anyone who has developed a learned helplessness orientation toward statistics, you might draw this encouraging application of developmental social psychology to his or her attention. The fact that attributions can be retrained underlines once more the proposition that attributions are closely related to social processes, rather than the computations of a solitary cognitive agent.

Culture and Attributions

Hewstone and Jaspars (1984, see above) maintained that attributions are social in the sense that they are shared with other members of one's group. One test of this proposal would be to compare the explanatory frameworks of members of different cultural groups. Several such analyses have been conducted, and they support the claim that these social cognitive processes reflect the sociocultural context. Bond and Hwang (1986), for example, report that Hong Kong Chinese students explaining behavior mention relationships more frequently than do American students, but mention internal need considerations less frequently. The pattern of their attributions appears to reflect the greater emphasis upon collective responsibilities within Chinese cultures (see also Hofstede, 1983; Triandis, 1991).

Nicholls (1978b), comparing the attributions for success and failure of Maori (Polynesian minority) and Pakeha (white majority) children in New Zealand, found that both ethnic groups displayed a stereotypical bias toward regarding Maori stimulus persons as less able than their white counterparts. Miller (1984) investigated American and Indian (Hindu) children's accounts of people's behaviors, and discovered a divergence in attributions with age: that is, during their teens Americans were more likely to make dispositional attributions, while Hindu subjects were more likely to emphasize the context within which the hypothetical person was acting. Cashmore and Goodnow (1986), comparing Anglo-Australian and first-generation Italian-Australian children's explanations of competency across a range of academic skills, found that the Italian boys placed greater stress on effort. The researchers interpret this emphasis as reflecting a socio-cultural orientation among migrant parents toward the upward mobility of their children. The parents stress hard work as a means of fulfilling this aspiration (especially for boys), and the children (especially the boys) come to see this as strongly associated with success.

These findings indicate that the elements entered into an attributional judgment may vary across cultures in terms of both content and weight. One cultural group may attach great importance to abilities, such as intelligence, mechanical aptitude, while another may regard effort and loyalty as the supreme virtues. One society may emphasize individual responsibility, another may stress collective duty or the omniscience of supernatural forces. All of the evidence suggests that children acquire the explanatory frameworks of their culture, including the biases and stereotypes held within that culture (see also Ben-Ari et al., 1994). The ways in which cultural experience influence the nature and development of attributional reasoning open crucial questions at the intersection of developmental and social psychological research (cf. Hewstone, 1989, chapter 7). Future investigations in this area should enrich our understanding of the extents to which social cognitive processes reflect and transcend the structures of the social context.

Summary

The study of attributional processes has been a major area of research activity in developmental social psychology. As well as addressing important questions about how developing individuals understand causal relations in the social world, it also has wide-ranging practical applications in educational and clinical–developmental contexts. There are several models of attribution theory in the adult literature, and two of these – Kelly's ANOVA model and Weiner's model – have proven especially fruitful sources of developmental research. In both cases, research has pointed increasingly to social influences on the ways in which individuals formulate attributions. The social context influences whether and when children make person or situational attributions, and the social context influences the kind of attributional style (mastery or helpless) that a child develops in particular domains.

Knowledge of Social Roles and Social Structure

We have seen (chapter 9) that social cognitive development includes learning about the psychological and social characteristics of self and others, and (this chapter) comprehending the underlying reasons for people's behavior. These discoveries, demanding as they may be, are only part of the knowledge and understanding that are involved in developmental social cognition. Becoming a member of a society also calls for an understanding of people's social roles, and the ways in which these roles fit into the broader societal organization. We turn now to developmental aspects of social role knowledge. In this section we will consider aspects of the development of knowledge of occupational roles and societal structure and the emergence of knowledge and attitudes concerning macro-social categories, such as nation and ethnic group.

Developmental Changes in Reasoning about Social Structures

Much work in this field has drawn upon Piagetian frameworks to test for qualitative changes in children's reasoning about roles and institutions. Furth's (1980; Furth and Kane, 1992) and Berti and Bombi's (1988) studies provide rich examples of the strengths of this approach. Furth interviewed English school children aged between 5 and 12 years about their understanding of particular roles, such as the policeman, the Queen, and of institutions, ranging from the corner shop to the government. Berti and Bombi interviewed Italian children about aspects of the economic system.

Although there are some differences in detail and principle between their approaches, both Furth (1980) and Berti and Bombi (1988) depict development in a series of sequential stages, maintaining that progress in understanding involves a series of transitions from an initially undifferentiated and perceptually dominated understanding at around the age 5 to a more sophisticated grasp of the complexities of societal relations by the age of 11 or so. For example, most of Furth's younger subjects perceived an inalienable link between wearing a police uniform and being a policeman, and insisted that without this apparel, a man could not be a policeman. Five-year-olds regarded the process of shopping as made possible by adults' seemingly unlimited access to money and by the generosity of the shopkeeper who not only gives you things for money but also provides yet more money (change) to facilitate subsequent shopping. Berti and Bombi (1988) obtained similar findings, with preschool children identifying the source of money as "Daddy's trouser pockets."

In the course of middle childhood, theories of how shops operate are enriched as children come to understand the rituals of payment, but even so the notion of profit margins is rarely grasped and the destination of funds in the till is uncertain. Furth found that 7–8-year-olds often suppose it is given to poor or blind people, or collected (in England at least) by the Queen. Although understanding improves by the age of 10–11 years, there is still little or no awareness of considerations such as the expenses of running the shop. Similarly, Berti (1993) found that many 9- and 10-year-old children saw no connection between bank deposits and bank loans, believing that funds placed on deposit were simply locked in a safe until the owner wanted them back. Many subjects regarded interest as a form of prize that banks awarded customers for their wisdom in choosing to associate with their particular institution. Furth (1980) demonstrated analogous and at least equally protracted development in understanding of the notion of government.

Among several illuminating examples of developments in children's understanding of societal structure is Berti and Bombi's (1988, pp. 158–64) account of children's responses to the question "Who owns the bus?" The researchers charted five broad levels of reasoning.

Level 1: The bus belongs to the passengers   At this level, ownership seems to reflect the child's relationship to the conveyance, mediated by key individuals:

> Francesa (5:5) *The buses belong to Mummy and Grandma.* Are they the owners of the bus? *Yes.* Do they own just one bus or all of the buses that go through Marghera? *All of them . . .* But the man who drives the bus, how does he come to be driving it? *Because the mummies have to go out.*

Level 2: The bus belongs to the driver   At this level, a more differentiated conception is emerging in which the child perceives links between external people's actions and outcomes:

> Michela (6:3) *The bus belongs to the driver.* So he's the owner? *Yes.* And what did he do to become the owner? *He learnt to drive.*

Level 3: The bus belongs to a "boss" or the council   Some children at this level reasoned that the driver studied to earn the money to purchase the bus; others believed that there would be a boss sitting in a factory or council office somewhere who directs operations. Thus, children now display some awareness of institutional structures in society.

Levels 4 and 5: More advanced conceptions about the council or the state   In late childhood or early adolescence, interviewees were able to account for organizations which run the buses, describing entry to them as dependent upon training or election. Eventually, they became able to articulate accounts of the nature of public ownership:

> How did the council become the owner of the bus? (Cristina, 12:2): *In the beginning Marghera was just a few factories which belonged to private owners; then by investing money the council provided what the people needed. In the beginning they ran up debts, but then with the money from taxes the debts were paid off.*

Similar results have been obtained in an extension of this study with New Zealand children (Cram and Ng, 1994). Clearly, children's conceptual grasp of social roles and institutions does undergo dramatic – though not necessarily rapid – changes between the preschool years and early adolescence. Further evidence is provided when children's understanding of authority relations is probed.

Understanding authority

Young children appear to find the *concept* of giving orders difficult (although my colleague, John Hattie, Professor of Education and father of three preschoolers, advises that they are very good at the *practice*). For example, Berti and Bombi (1988, p. 55) report this exchange between an interviewer and Elsa, a 5-year-old Italian:

> Do you know what it means to give orders? *No.* Doesn't the Mother [this term was used to refer to the nuns who taught in the school] *ever tell you to do something? Yes.* What does she ask you to do? *To go and dry the spoons, to look after a child's bag, to bring in the trolley.* Do you think a child can tell a Mother what to do? *Yes.* What could a child tell a Mother to do? *Mother, I have to pee.* Is that an order? *Yes.*

It appears clear that Elsa does not conceive of an order in quite the same way that older individuals do. Berti and Bombi found that children's accounts of the role and authority of the "boss" were very limited at this age.

Gradually they became aware of the idea of someone in authority, but remained confused about the specific nature of the boss's role. For example, they confused the boss of the nursery with the driver of the nursery bus, or they insisted that the caretaker was the boss of the school. Only at around the age of 8 years did children begin to understand that the boss had institutional status to exercise authority over others, though even at this stage children were often unable to distinguish between the boss of a factory and the owner of a factory.

There are, then, changes in children's cognitive mastery of social roles and structures. Cognitive developmentalists such as Furth (1980) and Berti and Bombi (1988) interpret the lengthy developments in reasoning that they have uncovered as consistent with Piagetian stage theory. Berti and Bombi point out (p. 58), for example, that constructing an understanding of the hierarchy of authority relations draws on similar cognitive abilities to those identified by Piaget (1927) in his study of the development of seriation.

The Social Contexts of Role and Societal Understanding

Although there are cognitive developments in children's accounts of roles and institutions, there are also clear indications above that children formulate their views with reference to their own experiences (cf. Emler and Dickinson, 1993; Higgins and Parsons, 1983). To all practical intents and purposes, money *does* come from Daddy's pocket; Mummy, Grandma, and the school caretaker *do* seem to have a lot of influence over the way the world runs, and who has ever seen a policeman without a uniform on? Furthermore, the opportunity to learn more about these matters might well be influenced by what other people say and do. Parents are prone to reveal from time to time that: "I'm not made of money, you know!" And buses can be found to have a will of their own (as can be tested by waiting for one when you are in a hurry). Cram and Ng (1994) found that understanding of societal relations such as public ownership was heightened by peer discussion.

Social experiences, then, may play an important role in the emergence of social cognitive understanding. There is evidence that preschoolers can understand authority relations in domains directly familiar to them. Laupa and Turiel (1993) tested children aged from preschool through to early adolescence on their conceptions of the limits of the school principal's authority. They found that 93 percent of the subjects were aware that their principal did not have authority over other schools. Asked about the principal's authority in non-school contexts (such as the park or the home) even the youngest subjects regarded his or her legitimacy as restricted to the school (although kindergarten children were not too sure about who had the upper hand in the park).

The content and processes of social concept development may be affected by the social context within which one is growing up (Emler et al., 1990; Jahoda, 1984). Further evidence that this is the case is provided by cross-cultural studies. Jahoda

(1983) found that Zimbabwean 9–11-year-olds who had personal involvement in small-scale trading showed more sophisticated understanding than European (Scottish, English, and Dutch) agemates in a test of comprehension of the concept of profit. Ng (1983) found that children in Hong Kong, one of the centres of capitalist enterprise demonstrated more advanced understanding of the ideas of bank loans and interest than had children in earlier European studies. A subsequent investigation of New Zealand children found that they were developing at about the same pace as Europeans (Ng, 1985). It remains to be seen whether a replication of the Hong Kong study post-1997 will show that financial precocity can be tempered by macro-systemic intervention.

Coming to understand authority relations may involve more than dispassionate cognitive appraisal. Emler et al. (1987a) investigated 6–12-year-old Scottish and French children's understanding of the role of the teacher. Consistent with Berti and Bombi's (1988) pattern of results summarized above, they report that by about 11 years children had come to recognize the hierarchy of authority relations within the school. Children of this age understood that the head teacher had authority over teachers and that teachers were required to honor certain rules governing correct conduct. They held that it was inappropriate for teachers to allow their own personal preferences to influence how they administered school procedures with respect to individual pupils.

More importantly, Emler and colleagues also obtained evidence of cross-cultural differences in terms of the children's views of the obligations of those holding authority within the school. The Scottish children believed that teachers had to enforce regulations irrespective of their personal feelings about the fairness of the rules. Viewed alone, this finding might appear to support a standard cognitive developmental interpretation that advancing moral reasoning ability enabled the children to recognize objective constraints upon the actions of authority and led to the acceptance of the need for a societal consensus about codes of behavior (see chapter 9). However, the French children reasoned quite differently, maintaining that the teacher should do what was fair, irrespective of what the rules maintained. In both sets of subjects there were developmental changes, but the precise content of the views held by the older children appeared to reflect differences in the values held in their sociocultural contexts (i.e., their different societies).

Emler et al. (1990) report similar findings with respect to comparisons among American, British, and French children's judgments of the fairness of income inequalities. In general, middle-class children were able to advance more elaborate justifications for income inequality and were more resistant to the idea of greater income equality across occupations, although there was some tendency for British children to stress social class differences while Americans placed more store on educational attainment. Middle-class children also tended to estimate the salary differentials among unskilled and professionally qualified jobs as higher than did the working-class children. Following Tajfel (1984), Emler et al. suggest that when making social comparisons among social categories, people tend to emphasize differences which favor their own category and to de-emphasize differences which do not. Since income differentials usually favor the middle-classes, middle-class subjects are inclined to accentuate them, while working-class subjects are more likely to play them down.

One marked difference between French children and the other nationals was that working-class French children estimated the income of road sweepers as especially low. Emler et al. (1990) point out that this is consistent with Tajfel's account, too, since the road sweepers familiar to their Parisian subjects came from a North African immigrant minority community, and (white) working-class subjects may have perceived these people as belonging to a lower status group and therefore one from which they would wish to emphasize their social distance.

The Development of Conceptions of International and Ethnic Relations

As well as learning about people's characteristics and capacities, understanding social roles and relative status, and discovering the structures of societal organization, children have also to distinguish among people and societies on the basis of yet other criteria, including nationality and ethnic category. In these respects, we find clear evidence of an interaction between affect and cognition.

One of the earliest studies of children's concepts of nation was conducted by Piaget and Weil (1951). They found that among children aged around 7 years the concept was very limited and rather confused, a finding that was supported and extended by Jahoda (1962, 1963). In a sense, it is not surprising that nationality would be a somewhat elusive concept for young children – it is a relatively intangible property, and at this age experience of different nations may be limited.

Nevertheless, from an early age children have some sense of positive and negative *values* attached to different nationalities. Tajfel and Jahoda (1966) studied 6–12-year-olds in Austria, Belgium, England, Italy, The Netherlands, and Scotland, testing them on knowledge of factual information about other countries and also their likes and dislikes among different peoples. Although the children's factual knowledge was patchy, the investigators found that the younger children showed a distinct preference for individuals whom they perceived as members of their own national group. This preference became less marked with age, but was still present in some countries.

In more recent work, Barrett and Short (1992) investigated English school children's images of people from other European countries, namely France, Germany, Spain, and Italy. Working with 5–10-year-olds, the researchers found that the younger children (5–7 years) had limited factual knowledge about the different countries, and even some fundamental uncertainties about their own. For example, a majority of the younger children were of the opinion that, although the country in which they lived (i.e., England) was big, it was not as big as a place called London; most of the younger children did not know what languages were spoken by the citizens of France, Germany, Spain, and Italy. They did have some idea of the favored diets of these peoples, associating the French with "snails," "garlic," and "french bread" and Italians with "spaghetti," "pasta," "seafood" and "pizza." More importantly, the children had evaluative opinions about the four foreign nations. A clear rank-order of preferences emerged, such that the French and Spanish were liked most, followed by Italians, and the Germans were liked least.

Where could these prejudices have originated and how might they be acquired by the young? The idea that somebody is "good" or "bad" because he or she belongs to a particular national group reflects in part a fairly modest level of cognitive development (cf. Milner, 1984). But, of course, it is not hard to find older persons with much the same views, and the relationship between children's values and adults' suggests some process of social transmission. Tajfel (1981, p. 206) comments that these kinds of studies reveal "the very high sensitivity of young children to the more primitive aspects of the value systems of their countries." While this certainly appears to be part of the explanation (and the part which comes most readily to mind for the social psychologist), closer inspection indicates that there are other (developmental) dimensions to the story.

The Development of Ethnic and National Prejudice

Ethnic prejudice is "an organized predisposition to respond in an unfavorable manner toward people from an ethnic group because of their ethnic affiliation" (Aboud, 1988, p. 4). Aboud (1988) outlines a number of theoretical approaches to the explanation of the origins of prejudice, of which two will be considered here: what she calls the *social reflection theory*, and her own social cognitive developmental theory.

The social reflection theory of prejudice

This theory, as sketched by Aboud, holds that people are a product of their social context, and that part of the process of socialization includes learning the attitudes and stereotypes that reflect the power relations of one's society. Since not everyone in a given society has exactly the same values, the process may be qualified by relative intergroup status: the specific focus of one's prejudices is likely to reflect the status of one's own group. Tajfel's account, above, is an example of a social reflection theory. According to Aboud, such a theory would predict that young children are initially without prejudice, but that they come to acquire them through social learning processes.

Certainly, it is easy to find a background to young children's affective reactions toward foreigners. Think about the context within which Barrett and Short's (1992) subjects arrived at their views about the respective merits of the Germans, French, and other Europeans. The English have long regarded the Continent as a place at constant risk of being cut off by fog in the Channel, and the British tabloid press is notorious for its exposition of anti-foreigner sentiment. As Barrett and Short note, the Second World War is still a recurrent theme of entertainment fiction in Britain, which may help account for sustained antipathy toward the Germans. Jingoism is scarcely unique to Britain, of course. Most nations proceed on the assumption that they constitute the finest society on the planet: a guide to Chinese school teachers, for example, recommends that "China should be perceived by children as superior to any other country" (Stevenson, 1991, p. 93). Hence, proponents of the social reflection theory can point easily to prejudice in the adult community, and to a likely correspondence between some adult attitudes and those of some of the younger generation. Consider this 11-year-old West German girl's complaints:

> These foreigners are taking our jobs. Look at all our unemployment here – and it's because of them! Pretty soon this will be a Turkish city if we don't do something. When I walk home from school, I see a Turk, a German, a German, then a Turk, a Turk, and another Turk. They're all over, and then they're even rude to us Germans. (Davey, 1987, p. 55)

Wherever we live, we have all heard some adults express this kind of sentiment. It is tempting to infer that we are listening indirectly to this interviewee's parents.

Plausible as the social reflection theory might seem on first consideration, however, Aboud (1988) points out that it cannot account for all of the available evidence. First, she reviews research which shows that children's views and values are not invariably direct replicas of those of their parents. Second, there are changes with age in the nature and intensity of children's prejudices which are not predicted by the theory (we will examine these in more detail below). Third, not all members of a given social category are equally prejudiced against members of other groups, and the social reflection theory has little to say about the causes of individual differences. Fourth, the theory does not explain why children of minority groups often demonstrate preferences for an outgroup over their own group (often in contrast to their parents' preferences). Finally, the theory rests on a counter-intuitive implication. If (as the theory maintains) knowledge of relative group status is a prerequisite to the emergence of prejudice, then it follows that the young child must *first* grasp the hierarchies of the social order and *then* attach values to particular groups within it. This seems improbable, and in fact is not fully supported by research findings, such as Barrett and Short's (1992) evidence that firm prejudice can be found even in children who know little more about the international order than that some people prefer pasta to rice.

A social cognitive theory of the development of prejudice

Aboud (1988) develops an alternative social cognitive developmental theory of prejudice which predicts, in direct contrast to the social reflection theory, that prejudice should be stronger in *younger* children. Her reasoning is that two overlapping sequences of development influence how the child orients toward others. One is a gradual transition from affective to perceptual to cognitive processes, and the other is a shift in focus from the self to groups to individuals.

Aboud argues that children are dominated initially by their emotions and needs, and that reactions to other people will be influenced by how they fit with these considerations. As discussed in chapter 3, even infants display affective preferences for those who are familiar and wariness of strangers. Aboud proposes that over the next few years this differentiation extends so that children maintain a distrust of people who are different and hence unpredictable. Next, children begin to distinguish among people in terms of how similar or dissimilar they are to oneself; dissimilar people are disliked. Features such as skin color, facial appearance, clothing, language afford straightforward means of comparing self and others. Subsequently, with cognitive development, children become able to understand social categories, learn labels, and understand the meaning of differences among peoples. Hence, there is a shift from a focus on self to an awareness of one's group membership, and then to the differences among groups.

At first, this leads to exaggerated appraisals, such that one group (the ingroup) is regarded very favorably, while outgroups are viewed as decidedly negative. With advances in social understanding, however, prejudice should begin to reduce, since the child is now capable of recognizing the arbitrariness of ethnic affiliation and the reciprocity of perceptions (i.e., if you are a foreigner to me, perhaps I am a foreigner to you). The kinds of social cognitive developments in person-perception discussed in chapter 9 also mean that the child becomes increasingly ready to take account of a person's inner qualities and to recognize individual differences. These developments promote a further shift, from an orientation to simple group distinctions to a broader sensitivity to individual variabilities. The outcome of these new social cognitive achievements is less intense ethnic prejudice by middle childhood (cf. Aboud, 1988, p. 22ff).

Aboud's theory: the empirical evidence

Aboud's theory provides a stimulating example of a developmental perspective on social cognitive processes. It makes specific predictions which can be tested in both experimental and field research, and much of the evidence is consistent with her theory. In a review of a large amount of research conducted in North America and a smaller amount in other parts of the world, she shows that children first demonstrate ethnic *awareness* at around the age of 4–5 years (e.g., they can distinguish accurately between photographs of black and white people), and that over the next few years they become better able to distinguish reliably among particular ethnic groups (Chinese, Native American Indians, Hispanics, and so on).

Children also begin to demonstrate ethnic *prejudice* at around the age of 4 years. Using variants of techniques developed by Horowitz (1939) and Clark and Clark (1947), researchers present children with figures or dolls exemplifying different ethnic groups. The subjects are asked a series of questions intended to tap their awareness of ethnic distinctions (e.g., which doll looks like you?) and also their attitudinal preferences (which is the good doll? who would you like to play with? which is the bad doll?). In general, research has supported the conclusion that children aged between 4 and 7 years tend to show the strongest ethnic favoritism in such experiments (Aboud, 1988). Barrett and Short (1992) (using interview methods rather than the dolls task) report that negativity toward foreigners was stronger among their younger subjects. Doyle et al. (1988) found that English-speaking Canadian children showed greater flexibility and less negativity with age in their attitudes toward French-speaking children.

Ethnic minority children's evaluations

There is an important qualification upon the picture emerging so far, however, and it is that not all children show an ingroup bias. In the dolls task, among subjects aged 4–7 years, white children tend to prefer the white doll but, in white-dominated societies, many *black* children tend to prefer the white doll, too. Clark and Clark (1947), testing black and white American children from the segregated South and from racially mixed schools in Massachusetts, found that not only did white children show an ingroup bias but that 60 percent of black children thought a white doll was a "nice" color, while only 38 percent thought a brown doll was a nice color (with a slight regional difference, such that the northerners were more "pro-white" than the southerners). Although this early study was limited somewhat in methodology – for example, there appears to have been no attempt to balance the race of the experimenters – subsequent research has produced similar findings. To take just one of many possible examples, Vaughan (1963, 1964a, b), in a series of studies in New Zealand found that Pakeha (European) 4- and 6-year-olds showed marked and increasing ingroup preferences, while their Maori agemates showed far weaker and declining ingroup preferences. Aboud (1988) concludes that after the age of 7 years, ingroup bias becomes less marked in white children, while black children become less negative toward their own group. Both shifts would appear to be consistent with Aboud's social cognitive developmental explanation, in that after the age of 7 years children can be assumed to have greater ability to reflect on the issues and to take more factors into account.

One prominent factor which does appear to be influential throughout is the relative status of different ethnic groups within the society. Most of the research which Aboud reviews is based upon North American, British, Australasian, and South African communities. It appears that children are, as Tajfel comments above, sufficiently sensitive to ethnic stratifications within their societies that they guide their early categorizations and preferences. Consider another West German child: "I don't mind the Italians or the Yugoslavs. But I hate the Turks. I can't understand them. They're not like us and don't belong here" (Davey, 1987, p. 54).

With age, the picture becomes more complex with the result that both dominant-ethnicity prejudice and within-group denigration by minorities reduce (as Aboud's theory predicts). Furthermore, there is evidence that these patterns are themselves sensitive to broader sociocultural shifts. For example, Vaughan (1987) reports that Maori children of all age levels have become more positive about their own group since the advent of a greater ethnic consciousness within New Zealand society and the emergence of a "Brown power" movement.

In sum, it appears that children's social cognitions about ethnic identity do undergo developmental shifts. Aboud's is one of the most elaborate accounts of the processes involved. However, as she acknowledges, the child's reasoning capacities develop within, and are applied to, particular societal structures at particular times and places.

The conditions obtaining beyond the child – and beyond his or her family – affect the content and the processes of social cognitions. Furthermore, the child's evaluative orientation toward particular groups may influence how much information he or she builds up about them and how it is interpreted. For example, Barrett and Short (1992) and Lambert and Klineberg (1967) both found that descriptions of foreign peoples became more diverse with age, and that children became more knowledgeable about groups which they regarded positively.

Summary

Several important research programs have begun to show the relevance of cognitive developmental, especially Piagetian or neo-Piagetian, frameworks for investigating children's understanding of social roles, societal and economic structures, and international and inter-ethnic relationships. In each case, these approaches highlight age-related differences in the sophistication of children's thinking about the broader social world, and it is clear that there are profound changes from the preschool years to early adolescence in these areas of social cognition. At the same time, it is also clear that the development of children's reasoning in these domains is affected by their social contexts. We have seen that there are cross-cultural differences in the pace of development of economic understanding and in the ideological presuppositions which children bring to bear on their interpretation of authority relations at school. There is an interaction between developmental changes in thinking about broad social categories such as race or nationality and the child's own social experiences and the status of his or her group.

Conclusions

The *content* of social knowledge that the normal child has to acquire is enormous, ranging from a complex body of information about the internal and external properties of human beings (including self and others) to a vast amount of detail about the roles, relationships, structures, and mechanisms of society. The *processes* whereby children acquire this information, and the sources that influence their progress, are equally complex, involving developments in reasoning ability, language, and interpersonal relations. Although the principal focus of this chapter has been on individual social cognition (what the developing individual learns about the social world), it has also been stressed throughout that this aspect of development is inseparable from the social context. In the next chapter, we consider more fully the relationship between social context and the development of social reasoning processes.

Further reading

Aboud, F. E. (1988) *Children and Prejudice*. Oxford: Blackwell.

A developmental social psychological analysis of the emergence and amelioration of ethnic prejudices, including thorough reviews of the literature and careful accounts of measurement problems in this area.

Boggiano, A. K. and Pittman, T. S. (eds) (1992) *Achievement and Motivation: a social–developmental perspective*. Cambridge: Cambridge University Press.

Advanced reviews of theory and research concerning the links among motivation, social cognition, and achievement, with particular reference to educational contexts.

Davey, T. (1987) *A Generation Divided: German children and the Berlin wall*. Durham, NC: Duke University Press.

Although not specifically concerned with any social cognitive developmental theories, Davey's interviews with East and West German children provides many telling illustrations of the intertwining of development, social context, and intergroup relations.

Pryor, J. B. and Day, J. D. (eds) (1985) *The Development of Social Cognition*. New York: Springer-Verlag.

A set of advanced essays on attribution, social judgment, moral development, and the social contexts of cognitive development.

Chapter 11

Social Cognition III: Social Interaction and Cognitive Development

*Now where do you think this one goes? . . . No, try
again . . . Ye-es! That's correct . . . Very good!
I bet you'll go to second grade next year!*
  *(Child teaching child; from Ellis and Rogoff, "The
    strategies and efficacy of child vs. adult teachers,"
                                                    1982)*

In the previous chapter we saw that cognitive developmental psychology, especially Piagetian stage theory, has proven a useful framework within which to study aspects of the development of social cognition in childhood. However, we also noted some limitations and some factors that Piagetians and other cognitive developmentalists tend to neglect. In particular, the orientation of cognitive developmental work in this area has tended to maintain the metaphor of the child as a "mini-scientist" who sets out to investigate the properties of the objective world and to construct a theory (or successive theories) about how things work. Social cognition, from this theoretical perspective, is merely another, albeit interesting, domain to which the child applies his or her cognitive capacities, constructing theories about the properties of people and institutions in much the same way that he or she would construct theories about the properties of the spatiotemporal environment. Among the drawbacks of this approach are the assumptions that development occurs chiefly as a result of activities *within* the individual.

Another way of examining social cognition is as a social *process*: that is, as something that occurs in the course of interaction, and which is prompted and regulated by relations among persons. Rather than coming to understand the world through independent enquiry, hypothesis formulation, and testing, the child might find it useful (indeed, inevitable) to exploit the knowledge and insights of others. Social cognition in this sense, then, refers to activities and outcomes in which individuals gain through working with others. As we will see, "others" may include people with more advanced understanding, such as parents or teachers, and people of about the same level of understanding (or even misunderstanding), namely one's peers.

This chapter discusses theoretical and empirical work investigating cognitive development as a social process, or at least as a process which derives much of its motivation and direction from social interactions. Three important theorists have inspired recent investigations in this field. The first, perhaps paradoxically in the light of the above comments, is Piaget. Piaget's theory is widely admired, and sometimes viewed with suspicion, for the sheer range of elements it embraces. Among these is a distinct recognition of the relevance of social interaction to cognitive development. As will be elaborated in the first main section of this chapter, neo-Piagetian researchers have retrieved, reinstated, and revitalized this often overlooked strand of the theory.

The second thinker who has had a great deal of influence over recent directions in the study of social processes and cognition is the Russian psychologist, Vygotsky. In the second section, we consider Vygotskyan perspectives on the social nature of thought. As will be seen, Vygotsky regarded the origins of all significant mental functions as occurring between people rather than within individuals. Some differences of emphasis will be highlighted as we examine neo-Piagetian and Vygotskyan accounts of social processes and cognitive development, but there are also overlaps. This leads us to the question of the extent to which the two theorists have engendered approaches which are complementary rather than contradictory. We address this issue in the third section.

Although both neo-Piagetian and Vygotskyan theories have much to say about the social dimensions of cognitive activity, much of their work remains focused on learning about physical and spatiotemporal phenomena. The social side of their frameworks concerns interactions among learners, or between learners and tutors, but what is being learned usually consists of the standard fare of mainstream developmental psychology: conservation, construction, object manipulation, early scientific concepts, and so on. How can we begin to understand the social nature of learning about *social* phenomena? At this point, it proves helpful to turn to social psychology. In the final section of the chapter, we consider the developmental implications of a social psychologist whose ideas have begun to influence research into the acquisition of social knowledge: Moscovici. Moscovici's provocative theory of social representations is concerned with the ways in which societies formulate and transmit shared understandings about the world and our relationships to it; we examine the development of these processes in childhood.

Neo-Piagetian Theory and Social Cognition

Much of Piaget's work was concerned with how the child comes to understand the physical, spatial, and temporal world. For Piaget, at the centre of cognitive development is *activity* – the child's own constructive efforts to understand and represent the causal processes of the environment. In one of his early books, concerned with the development of moral reasoning, Piaget (1932) (discussed in more detail in chapter 14) did accord an important role to social factors. In that text, Piaget emphasized the importance of peer interaction for moral development, proposing that cognitive disagreement among peers instigated awareness within the child that there could be more than one perspective on a given problem. Taking more perspectives into account should, according to Piagetian theory, promote decentering – the ability to apprehend more than one aspect of a task at a time – which should in turn promote the search for a better level of understanding. Despite this early emphasis in Piaget's own writings and occasional returns to the theme later (and see also Piaget, 1929), neither Piaget nor his followers asserted social interaction as a primary focus of subsequent research (see Chapman, 1988; Light, 1983, for discussions).

However, in the 1970s another group of researchers, based like Piaget in Geneva, drew on developments in social psychology to formulate a new theme for cognitive developmental research: the constructive nature of social interaction (Doise and Mugny, 1984; Doise and Palmonari, 1984; Doise et al., 1975). Doise and Mugny (1984) point out that experimental social psychologists were well aware of discrepancies between individual and group performance in a diversity of tasks. Sometimes group performances exceed the total of the same (or the same number of) individuals working separately, indicating that there may be cognitive, practical and motivational gains through group collaboration (cf. Kelley and Thibaut, 1969; Moscovici and Paicheler, 1973; Wilke and van Knippenberg, 1996). Although it is not invariably the case that group performances are superior to the efforts of individuals working separately, it is a sufficiently common finding that Doise and Mugny drew attention to its developmental implications. If it is possible that adults can gain insight into

Figure 11.1　There may be cognitive, practical, and motivational gains through peer collaboration.

problems and share solutions in the course of group activity, what might be the consequences for children?

One possibility is that children could profit from working in social contexts on specific problems if their partners happen to have more relevant knowledge than they do. We will consider this possibility shortly. But Doise et al. (1975) advanced a more radical proposal, namely that through working together on a problem, two or more children could achieve a level of understanding that neither had attained independently. That is, that through social interaction children could construct knowledge that they did not already possess (figure 11.2).

These researchers (sometimes known as the "social Genevans") agree with Piaget that cognitive development involves the restructuring of previous understanding. But while Piaget attributes progress to the individual child striving to organize and advance his or her knowledge, Doise and colleagues hold that "elaboration [of understanding] is as social as it is individual in nature" (Doise and Mugny, 1984, p. 26). A critical claim is that this social activity generates competing interpretations. Development is not the product of imitation or accepting someone else's authority, but the resolution of *sociocognitive conflict* arising from the exposure to contradictory perspectives on the same problem (Doise and Mugny, 1984; Mugny and Doise, 1978, 1979). For cognitive gains to be achieved, more is involved than steering children to joint activities: there must also be a confrontation between different perspectives (Perret-Clermont, 1980). Consistent with Piaget's early arguments noted above, Doise and Mugny (1984) maintain that this confrontation leads to *disequilibrium*, an instability due to contradictory hypotheses, which the child is motivated to resolve for both cognitive and social reasons. Cognitive reasons include the drive for understanding, which Piagetians take to be a fundamental necessity, and social reasons include the desire to relate to others, to participate in shared activities, and to achieve mutual agreement about the nature of the experienced world.

Perret-Clermont and her colleagues encapsulate the way in which this approach draws upon yet goes beyond traditional Piagetian theory:

> The child's activity is essential to his cognitive development; however, this activity is in constant interplay with the activity of others. The individual is, as it were, the "co-author" of the development of his intelligence. His partners are the persons, adults or children, with whom he interacts. (Perret-Clermont et al., 1984, p. 64)

Social Interaction and Cognitive Development: the Evidence

Several experimenters have shown that children can make cognitive gains through participation in tasks which lead individuals to confront initially incorrect hypotheses with the ideas of others (see, for example, Bearison, 1982; Doise and Hanselmann, 1990; Mackie, 1980; Perret-Clermont and Schubauer-Leoni, 1981; Rijsman et al., 1980). In an early illustration, Doise et al. (1975), using the conservation of liquid task, found that 6–7-year-olds working together (in twos or threes) performed at a higher level than they had done individually in pre-tests. Furthermore, initially nonconserving children who worked with children who could conserve subsequently performed at a higher level on post-tests than children who did not participate in the collaborative sessions.

A possible objection is that the children who improved their performance had merely learned to imitate the behavior of more competent peers, and have not actually advanced their cognitive abilities. However, the children were able to provide explanations of their judgments at a higher level than at the outset, making reference now to considerations such as reversibility, compensations for changes in height or width and so on – a finding which suggests that definite insights had been gained.

Experiments with dyads in which both participants are initially unable to handle the task and provide different responses are particularly revealing in this respect. Ames and Murray (1982) selected 6- and 7-year-olds on the basis of pre-tests in which they had failed standard conservation of length or volume tasks. Some children were paired with peers who had also failed to conserve but gave a different answer (e.g., one said that the liquid transferred to a new vessel was more, one said that it was less). Others were placed in conditions where correct answers were modeled, or they were required to "pretend" that the correct answer was the opposite of the one they had given, or they were given corrective feedback. The social interaction subjects showed marked gains at immediate and delayed post-tests, while subjects in the other conditions did not, leading the authors to conclude that a critical component of the equilibration process is the conflict between children's beliefs, irrespective of the content of those beliefs (figure 11.2).

Later work using similar experimental paradigms has shown that gains acquired through social interaction in Piagetian-type tasks can be generalized, leading to higher performance in other Piagetian tasks (Perret-Clermont, 1980) and to tasks using different material and formats from those used at pre-test (Valiant et al., 1982). Improved performance as a result of social interaction on more advanced cognitive tasks has also been demonstrated with older children and adolescents (Aboud, 1989; Blaye et al., 1992; Gilly and Roux, 1984, 1988; Light et al., 1994).

This is not to say that any pair of conflicting opinions will invariably lead to cognitive gains. Doise and Mugny (1984), following Piaget, stress that what a child can discover is constrained by what he or she currently knows: "In order that a new structure can integrate with less advanced structures, the latter must of course exist" (p. 26). Hence, cognitive conflict is most likely to occur and to give rise to insights when the discrepancy between the old (the child's previous understanding) and the new (ideas constructed in the course of social interaction) is not too large (see also Perret-Clermont, 1980).

Social Marking and Sociocognitive Conflict

Another important factor in the dynamics of cognitive development, according to Doise and Mugny, is the phenomenon of *social marking*. Social marking refers to "the correspondences which may exist between, on the one hand, the social relations presiding over the interactions of persons actually or symbolically present in a given situation, and on the other hand, the cognitive relations bearing on certain properties of the objects through which these social relations materialize" (Doise, 1989, p. 395). In some situations, social norms give rise to the same outcome as cognitive rules. For example, suppose one had to divide a quantity, such as the contents of a bottle of blackcurrant juice, among several salivating friends. Each has fingers clenched firmly around a beaker and is watching carefully to ensure that the distribution is equitable. Here, the *social expectation* that everyone should get the same amount and the *logical task* of determining equal-sized portions result in the same division.

This may seem fairly unremarkable, but the notion of social marking becomes more interesting when there is a conflict between the social rule and the understanding available as a result of one's current level of cognitive ability. To illustrate, suppose one knows and accepts the social norm that, among peers, each should get an equal share, but one is not yet fully cognisant of the fact that distributing equal amounts of liquid into differently shaped vessels does not affect the actual amount. That is, the social rule says we should all get the same, but your tall, thin beaker conveys the distinct impression that you are receiving much more juice than I am. Here, for the nonconserving child, there is a discrepancy between the social regulation and her intellectual understanding. Could confronting this discrepancy stimulate cognitive progress?

To test this possibility, Doise et al. (1981) constructed a variant of the conservation

Figure 11.2 Conservation of length: two heads better than one?

of liquid experiment in which they drew children's attention to the social rule by telling them that they had worked equally hard as a peer and that both deserved the same reward (equal amounts of a drink). Two equal amounts were poured into identical beakers and then, once the subject had confirmed their equality, the contents of one were transferred to a differently shaped beaker. The children were encouraged to discuss the transformation. Compared to control subjects for whom no emphasis was placed on social rights, initially nonconserving 4–6-year-olds showed significant gains on a post-test of conservation ability. Similar advantages of social marking were obtained even when the other partner was symbolically, rather than physically, present (i.e., the child was told to provide equal shares for herself and an absent collaborator). It appears that the mental effort required to achieve social harmony (a fair outcome for each) did indeed instigate cognitive progress (better scores on a conservation test).

Other work on social marking has found comparable effects in perspective-taking and spatial transformation tasks (Doise and Mugny, 1984; Doise et al., 1978; Girotto, 1987; de Paolis et al., 1981) and tests of logical reasoning (Gilly and Roux, 1984, 1988). For the social Genevans, these findings establish social marking as an important aspect of the social dynamics of cognitive development (Doise and Mugny, 1984; de Paolis et al., 1987). To repeat: the important point is not that children come to absorb social regulations, but that cognitive progress is promoted as an outcome of the sociocognitive conflict between what they know of these regulations and other concepts they are still constructing. Doise (1989) shows how this developmental social psychological perspective marries well with social psychological theorizing (such as that of Gergen, 1985) which stresses the influence of the social transmission of meanings on the construction of systems of understanding within societies (figure 11.3).

Conflict over Sociocognitive Conflict

It is a fitting irony that not all of Doise et al.'s peers agree with them, and that there is currently some controversy concerning exactly which features of social interaction may promote cognitive development – controversy which is generating further advances in this field of research. There is dispute about the relative importance of interpsychological versus intrapsychological processes (Emler and Valiant, 1982). Some researchers maintain that imitation plays a more important role than Doise, Mugny, Perret-Clermont and their collaborators acknowledge (see Fortin, 1985; Robert and Lacroix, 1984; Winnykamen, 1990). Gilly and Roux (1988) argue that the crucial mechanism may not be sociocognitive conflict but better internal representation of the task to hand.

Russell (1982) objects that children will not benefit from sociocognitive conflict unless the correct answer emerges in the course of their deliberations, and in his own work with paired conservers and nonconservers, he found that typically the conserver's answer was adopted. Also consistent with this view, Bijstra at al. (1991) found that intermediate conservers could profit from attempting jointly to solve a conservation task. However, the source of their success appeared not to be sociocognitive conflict

Figure 11.3   Shared social expectations may heighten understanding of quantities.

but the opportunity to confirm together that which they had learned from the pre-test (i.e., from being questioned with a modified procedure). Bijstra et al. conclude that it is the presence of the correct answer rather than the active resolution of conflict that leads to improved performance in these dyads. (Perret-Clermont et al., 1984, p. 57, respond to this kind of challenge: "But how does the subject come to recognize the partner's answer as correct and to accept it?")

However, other researchers have found that the presence or construction of the correct answer during the deliberations is largely irrelevant to whether children gain from peer interaction. In studies of 8–12-year-olds' understanding of elementary scientific concepts such as floating, sinking, and motion down an incline, Howe and her colleagues (Howe et al., 1990, 1992) report that the most productive conditions were those in which the peers' initial ideas were different. Although different (conflicting) ideas promoted cognitive gains, the relative quality of the ideas did not matter: that is, the participants stood to gain irrespective of whether their peer offered ideas that were more or less advanced or around the same level as their own. Furthermore, these investigators found no correlation between the achievement of jointly constructed advancement during the interactions and level of performance at post-tests administered one month later. Howe interprets this as indicating that most of the growth occurred after the interaction was concluded (1992, p. 245).

Notice that Howe and colleagues' findings present a problem for interpretations of the sociocognitive conflict studies which argue that the real mechanisms of learning are either imitation or the internalization of social products (cf. Howe, 1992, p. 246). If gains are attained in the absence of socially generated correct answers, then *intra*psychological processes of the individual must presumably be implicated. (See Doise and Mugny, 1991, and Howe, 1992, for an interesting sociocognitive debate over this issue.)

Certainly, it is clear that conflict is not the only social means of promoting cognitive gains (Beaudichon et al., 1988; Carugati and Gilly, 1993; Crook, 1994; Grossen, 1994; Maffiolo, 1993; Perret-Clermont and Nicolet, 1988). For example, Light et al. (1994) report that in some of their studies, although advantages were obtained by children working in pairs, there was not much evidence of disagreement or argument in some tasks; indeed, in one experiment these investigators demonstrated gains on a computer-based task as a consequence of the mere presence of a peer who took no other part (consistent with a well-known effect in the adult social psychological literature; Bond and Titus, 1983; Zajonc, 1965).

In short, the study of the processes involved in sociocognitive conflicts among children has become a fertile field of enquiry, but has generated some conflicts in its own right. At present, there are some contradictions in the literature and disputes over the relative importance of different factors.

Summary

The social Genevans have emphasized the relevance of peer interactions to cognitive development, and shown that two (or more) young minds can generate insights that neither had independently. Both social and cognitive factors appear to motivate efforts to resolve sociocognitive conflicts. In some studies, gains have been obtained only when the correct answer is available during the interaction, either because one participant already understands the task or because experimental procedures ensure that the answer becomes apparent; in other studies, gains have been found after the interaction, irrespective of the quality of ideas advanced during the task itself. Note for the moment that, while the researchers in this tradition are certainly interested in social processes between subjects, the focus of what children are working on in most of this work has been physical and spatial tasks (such as traditional Piagetian conservation or coordination tasks) rather than social concepts. We return to this issue later, but first let us consider another account of social interaction and cognitive development which identifies the principal mechanism of change not in conflict, but in collaboration.

Vygotskyan Theory and Social Cognition

Vygotsky was a Russian psychologist whose major works were first published in the 1920s and 1930s, the period following the Soviet revolution and a time during which Marxist theory influenced thinking in most areas of the social sciences in that country. Although he died at an early age in 1934, the force of his ideas is such that Vygotsky has had dominant influence in Soviet and East European developmental psychology since that time (Davydov and Radzikhovskii, 1985; Zinchenko, 1985).

With the translation into English of his major texts since the 1960s, Vygotsky's work has become increasingly disseminated in the West and has attracted considerable interest among researchers of developmental social cognition (Rogoff, 1990; Wertsch, 1985; Wertsch and Tulviste, 1992).

Vygotsky incorporated key tenets of Marxist ideology into psychology, drawing particularly upon the notions of dialectics and historical materialism (see Cole and Scribner, 1978; Newman and Holzman, 1993; van der Veer and Valsiner, 1991, for fuller accounts). He was centrally interested in the dynamics of the developmental tensions between the individual and society, a relationship which he regarded as the intersection of nature and culture. Through participation in social activity, he proposed, the individual becomes immersed in practices which gradually transform his or her own capabilities. Thus, Vygotsky regarded cognitive development as characterized by an active internalization of problem-solving processes that are originally shared. Vygotsky maintains: "Any function in the child's cultural development appears twice, or on two planes. First it appears on the social plane, and then on the psychological plane" (1981, p. 163). In contrast to the Piagetian metaphor of the child as a scientist, for the Vygotskyan the child is better conceived of as an apprentice (Rogoff, 1990), acquiring the knowledge and skills of his or her culture through guided collaboration with those who already have the knowledge and skills.

Vygotsky's (1962) account of the developmental relations between thought and language is pivotal to his view of the relations between the individual and society. He argued that thought and language derive from distinct origins but become interwoven in the course of the child's development. The integration of language with thought is a particularly important development because language – as a social tool – brings society's evolved understandings into the child's realm of thinking:

> *The nature of the development itself changes,* from biological to sociohistorical. Verbal thought is not an innate, natural form of behavior but is determined by a historical-cultural process and has specific properties and laws that cannot be found in the natural forms of thought and speech. ... It is only to be expected that on this level the development of behavior will be governed essentially by the general laws of the historical development of human society. (Vygotsky, 1962, p. 51)

Cognition is social, in Vygotsky's view, because its development is interwoven with social activity, itself mediated by the social instrument of language.

The Zone of Proximal Development

One of Vygotsky's most stimulating ideas is that of *the zone of proximal development.* In a provocative discussion, he pointed out (1978; translation of work published in 1935) that it is a standard assumption of developmental psychologists, and of measurement-oriented psychologists more generally, that only those things that subjects can perform *on their own* are indicative of their underlying mental abilities. Consider just how basic and widespread this assumption is: in most areas of quantitative psychology, the respectable conditions for testing a subject would be to isolate him or her and to ensure that his or her responses are not contaminated by the input of others.

While Vygotsky did not condemn this practice, he did argue that it is somewhat naive to imagine that it tells us the full story of a given subject's capabilities. He argued that the very procedures that a good experimentalist would attempt rigorously to preclude – such as offering leading questions, demonstrating a solution, collaborating with the testee – may in fact provide opportunities to discover important additional information about the subject. Specifically, we might find that the subject can succeed or perform at a higher level in the social context. Furthermore, we may well find differences among subjects in terms of their capacity to profit from interpersonal assistance.

These considerations led Vygotsky to formulate the concept of the zone of proximal development, which refers to: "the distance between the actual developmental level as determined by independent problem solving and the level of potential development as determined through problem solving under adult guidance or in collaboration with more capable peers" (1978, p. 86). Vygotsky describes the zone of proximal development as consisting of embryonic capacities that have not yet fully developed but are in the process of development: "the 'buds' or 'flowers' of development rather than the 'fruits' of development" (p. 86).

The notion of a zone of proximal development is appealing because it represents a domain which reflects both the individual's own capacities and the structures made available to him or her through participation in a particular social environment. Cole (1985), for example, illustrates how the concept of the zone of proximal development can help to account for the ways in which cultural practices are transformed into cultural differences in cognitive processes.

Vygotskyan Accounts of Cognitive Development: the Evidence

There is a growing body of research examining the effects of collaborative learning and the nature of the zone of proximal development. We will consider just one of the major themes of this work, namely the role of instruction in development. Vygotsky saw the contributions of a more advanced tutor as a key to cognitive progress. Such partners could be adults or peers, and researchers have investigated processes in both contexts.

Adults as tutors: experimental tasks

Wertsch et al. (1980) addressed Vygotsky's thesis that the order of emergence of any new function is first social, second psychological (individual). They had 2-, 3- and 4-year-olds and their mothers complete a reconstruction task, in which the goal was to build a replica of a model of a truck, using a set of pieces of different shapes and colors. The task was set up so that at certain stages it was essential to consult the model (to determine the exact layout of a set of colored squares representing the "cargo"), while at others it was possible to work out the correct shape from the interlocking features of the pieces alone (i.e., knowledge of vehicle shapes in general would suffice to guide the subject to place the wheels below the body of the truck).

When it came to consulting the model, the investigators found an interesting social developmental shift. First, a lot of looks by the child to the model were preceded by maternal looks to the model; in about 90 percent of instances, when the mother looked at the model, the child looked too. The children appeared to exploit social reference (see chapter 8) to guide them in dealing with a complex situation. Second, the frequency of mother-guided looks declined significantly with age, supporting the Vygotskyan prediction of an ontogenetic shift from other-regulation to self-regulation (Wertsch et al., 1980, p. 1220). Third, the older children appeared to extract the relevant information from the maternal looks more efficiently, a finding which suggests that these children had a more developed grasp of the strategic utility of information from an adult.

Scaffolding

Wood et al. (1976) introduced the metaphor of "scaffolding" to help describe the ways in which caregivers organize their interventions around the child's progress, guiding attention toward relevant aspects of a task (e.g., what to do next), supporting efforts with minor interventions (e.g., handing over components or tools) and providing a structure within which specific stages can become manageable. Wood et al. (1978) found that different mothers, in a construction task with 4- and 5-year-olds, used instructional strategies of varying levels of specificity, ranging from general verbal encouragement through to direct demonstration of a relevant action. No one single strategy guaranteed learning, but the most effective maternal instructors turned out to be those who combined general and specific interventions according to the child's progress. For example, the mother might begin with a general instruction and stay at that level of advice until the child ran into difficulties; then, she would interject with a more specific instruction or demonstration. This style allows the child considerable autonomy but provides carefully placed guidance at the boundaries of his or her abilities – or at the edges of his or her zone of proximal development.

Moss (1992) summarizes a longitudinal series of investigations of maternal scaffolding during the infancy to preschool period which indicate three recurrent dimensions to mothers' scaffolding strategies. One is the tendency to stay "one step ahead" of the child, introducing new skills that the child will not actually be able to handle unaided for some time. The second is the consolidation of useful tactics that the child has already demonstrated. The third is to attempt to inhibit actions that they consider developmentally immature. For example, working with a child of less than a year on an activity such as playing with blocks, mothers may attempt to encourage the acquisition of new skills, such as establishing a simple sequence or putting one on top of another. At the same time, they try to consolidate existing skills, such as paying attention to one's partner and to joint activity (which we saw in chapter 2 develops during the first year). Finally, they try to divert the infant from relatively low-level sensorimotor responses, such as sticking the blocks in his or her mouth. With older children, the same scaffolding dimensions are relevant, though the content is more advanced: a 3-year-old might be encouraged to concentrate on perceptual knowledge (such as the shape and colour of the blocks), but discouraged from low-level nonverbal responses or from simply labelling the blocks with words that she or he has been using for some time. The mother is working continuously to edge the child forward, to maintain useful tactics, and to discard previously functional but now immature behavior.

In other investigations of scaffolding, Rogoff et al. (1984) had mothers and their 6- or 8-year-olds carry out two classification tasks: a "home" task (sorting grocery items) and a "school" task (sorting photographs of common objects, such as machines, tools, domestic articles). They found that mothers provided more intense instruction to the younger children, but this was particularly marked in the school condition. It appears that mothers have an expectation that school activities will be difficult and tune their instruction to the learner's needs in his or her zone of proximal development. Pratt et al. (1992) also had parents engage in a school task (helping their child with long division mathematics problems), and found that the adults generally gave more support around difficult task components and to children with lower initial skills. Pratt et al. found also that variation among parents in terms of their scaffolding skills was associated with variation in outcomes in the children's performances, and that authoritative parents (in Baumrind's sense; see chapter 4) tended to have superior scaffolding skills.

Adults as tutors: naturalistic contexts

The above studies concern relatively contrived activities, similar to everyday domestic routines or school work, but set up especially for the purposes of the experiment. Other research has investigated adult–child tutorial processes in more naturalistic contexts. Similar findings emerge.

Saxe et al. (1987) studied the relationships between American mothers' everyday involvements in their preschoolers' early number activities and the children's number development. They found that mothers generally saw learning about numbers as desirable, and attempted to direct the children's efforts in this domain quite often. But, broadly consistent with a Vygotskyan account, the involvement was generally tailored to the child's current level of ability and to guiding the child toward higher levels of understanding. For example, one everyday number activity in many homes consists of counting the stairs. Saxe et al. found that as children became more proficient at this task, mothers would intervene to extend their understanding. After a count, they might ask: "How many stairs have you counted?", thus encouraging the child to go beyond rote number recitation to state the numerosity of the set. When children were able to respond appropriately to this kind of request, mothers would lift the demands still higher, asking the child to predict how many stairs would have been climbed if he or she went one more.

Greenfield and Lave (1982) studied the learning processes of Zinacanteco Mexican girls acquiring traditional weaving skills from more practiced women in their community. The girls initially spend over half of their time watching the skilled teachers, and they begin to weave by cooperating with the teachers. As they become more involved and more competent, cooperative activity increases for a while until the girl is able to take personal responsibility for the work. Again, the investigators found that the adults scaffolded the task, providing just the right amount of help to enable the girl to complete it successfully. The adults also guided task selection, ensuring that easier activities were attempted earlier in the developmental sequence. Interestingly, the adults did not see themselves as playing a major role in the learning process, believing the Zinacanteco girls learn to weave "by themselves." In short, as Vygotskyan theory would lead us to expect, scaffolding processes can be found in naturalistic, everyday contexts and seem closely linked to the transmission between generations of culturally valued competencies.

Peers as tutors

Findings from studies of peer tutoring, that is, training experiments in which children are paired with agemates or slightly older children who already have greater skill in the task at hand also show gains due to collaboration. In general, the tutee's cognitive performance improves following the tutorial session (Kerwin and Day, 1985). For example, Barnier (1989) obtained improvements in the performance of 6–7-year-olds on spatial and perspective-taking tasks by exposing them to brief training sessions led by 7–8-year-old tutors. Phelps and Damon (1989) obtained similar effects in mathematical and spatial tasks with 10–11-year-olds, and found that gains were stronger when the collaboration required formal operational reasoning rather than rote learning or imitation. Cazden et al. (1979), in a series of case studies of peer teaching among 8–9-year-olds, report that the most successful teachers were those who (like the mothers in Wood et al.'s study above) were able to vary their verbal strategies from the general to the specific according to the tutee's needs. One outcome of these findings has been a strong increase among educators in the potential for peer tutoring and collaborative learning in schools (Foot et al., 1990; Goodlad and Hirst, 1989; Kerwin and Day, 1985; Slavin, 1990). There is also evidence that tutoring others promotes gains in the *tutor* (Barron and Foot, 1991; Goodlad and Hirst, 1989; Kerwin and Day, 1985; Smith, 1993).

Peer tutoring and social context

Teaching a peer is itself a demanding responsibility, involving interpersonal awareness, conceptual competency in the task at hand, and communicative skill (Barron and Foot, 1991; Crook, 1994; Ellis and Gauvain, 1992; Rogoff, 1990). Ellis and Gauvain (1992) reasoned that it is difficult to disentangle the relative import of each of these components when working within just one culture, where prevailing norms may influence the relative values attached to individual versus group achievement. For example, in some Western societies, such as America, individual attainment is highly prized and, within a group, competition over ideas and opinions is considered legitimate practice. In some other cultures, there is a greater emphasis upon collective success, mutual respect and responsibility for others' progress (Nsamenang and Lamb, 1994; Rabain-Jamin, 1994; Tietjen, 1994). One such culture is that of the Navaho people of northern Arizona. Ellis and Gauvain (1992) compared the performance of Navaho children, who lived on a Navaho reservation, with that of Euro-American children from rural Virginia on a peer tutoring task involving a complicated maze game.

An interesting manipulation in this study was that some of the tutors themselves worked collaboratively. Nine-year-olds were first trained in the task and then, either in pairs or alone, had to teach a 7-year-old (from the same culture) parts of the game. Ellis and Gauvain expected that the paired teachers should be more successful, because their joint role should elicit greater verbalization than in the case of a solitary teacher. This proved to be the case, with tutees in the paired conditions receiving twice as much information as children in the solitary teacher conditions, and the paired conditions led to superior learning. Navaho and Euro-American children did equally well. However, there were between-culture differences in how the teachers operated. The Euro-American children employed far more verbal instructions while a great deal of the Navahos' instruction was nonverbal. Navaho teachers were more patient, spending more time pausing than the Euro-Americans, and one apparent consequence of this was that the Navaho children made significantly fewer errors. Navaho teachers were also more content to sit by and observe while their partner taught part of the task; when Euro-American children found their services temporarily unnecessary they were inclined to become distracted or simply to wander off. Overall, although collaboration was beneficial in both cases, the mechanisms of interaction showed considerable differences between cultures.

Summary

Vygotsky's theory emphasizes the benefits of collaboration with a more skilled tutor, an individual who can facilitate the transition from the individual's zone of proximal development to new levels of skill and comprehension. The tutor can be a parent, teacher or even a peer, provided that she or he has the requisite competence in the tasks being worked on, and sufficient sensitivity to the learner's needs to adjust instruction appropriately. Both experimental and naturalistic studies have provided evidence that such interactions can lead to improvements in children's abilities. Note that, again, the kinds of things that children are learning about in the Vygotskyan studies tend to be spatiophysical tasks rather than social concepts.

Conflict, Complementarity, and Oversights among Neo-Piagetian and Vygotskyan Perspectives

So far, we have evidence from the social Genevans that conflicting viewpoints can promote cognitive gains, and evidence from Vygotsky-inspired studies that collaboration with a skillfully attuned tutor can guide and extend development. Are these propositions in conflict, or do they simply describe different possibilities which might be experienced by any learner according to circumstances? In some contexts, you might achieve new insights into a cognitive problem through discussing it with someone with a very different point of view. Elsewhere you might advance your skills in a new task if an expert monitors your progress and lends a helping hand whenever you run into difficulties. Much depends on the nature of the domain, and the goals of the participants. Viewed this way, it soon becomes clear that, although there are differences in emphasis, there are overlaps in the concerns of each of the two perspectives we have been considering. We will see shortly that there are also gaps in research which neither approach has closed yet. In this section, we consider the extent to which these accounts are competing or complementary, and we review some of the gaps in current enquiry. First, a note of caution should be introduced: it cannot be concluded that social interaction is guaranteed always to bring about cognitive gains.

Some Limits on the Benefits of Partners, Tutors, and Teams

We saw earlier that not all experimenters have obtained cognitive gains as a result of juxtaposing learners. Let us consider now some of the variables that appear to influence the nature of the outcome. Recent research points to at least two broad factors: the kind of relationship the participants have (friendly or unfamiliar) and their relative status (expert or novice).

Variabilities in interpersonal relations

It has been objected that one limitation of both the social Genevan and Vygotskyan theories is that both presuppose a rather benign interpersonal environment (Goodnow, 1990; Moss, 1992). In the first case, individuals are taken to express different points of view in good faith and then set about finding the best way to resolve them; in the second, helpful tutors team up with eager tutees to yield maximum learning outcomes. We all know that in real life this is not always what happens: in some circumstances, people confronted with an opposing point of view invest ego in their opinions, dig their heels in, get hot under the collar, refuse to budge, exploit their knowledge as a source of power and control, and so on.

As yet, these processes have not been extensively studied among children in sociocognitive conflict experiments or peer collaborative exercises. However, there is some evidence from sociocognitive conflict studies that disagreements between best friends are more likely to promote cognitive gains than are disagreements between lukewarm friends or nonfriends (Aboud, 1989), a finding which suggests that a benign environment characterized by mutual respect and goodwill may well be an optimal context for progress when a conflict has to be resolved (see also Azmitia and Perlmutter, 1989). Similarly, Azmitia and Hesser (1993) found that joint task performance between *siblings* led to greater mastery by the younger child than did joint task performance with an unrelated older child. It seems that the familiarity and the willingness to exchange information that siblings may generate can be effective foundations to learning. Goodnow's (1990) point is that benign environments cannot be assumed everywhere that children get together with others.

In fact, in some cases, a benign environment may not be a productive one. Foot and Barron (1990) showed that peer tutoring between friends can involve the allocation of greater amounts of time and management resources to the social aspects of the task. In their study (in which children taught peers the rules for ecologically correct behavior in the countryside) there was no advantage to pairing friends rather than nonfriends as tutors. These findings suggest that amiability can sometimes impede progress, as can be confirmed by any student who has ever joined friends for a coffee break in the Library at mid-morning and finally returned to her or his books mid-afternoon.

With respect to tutorial processes, Goodnow herself (1988a, 1990) has shown that transmission of skills from expert to learner in one naturalistic context – household chores – is not always plain sailing, and that "resistance is open and prolonged" (Goodnow, 1990, p. 279). There seems to be something about washing the dishes and tidying one's room that is decidedly inimical to the harmonious dynamics of the zone of proximal development. Goodnow points out that in these contexts children are remarkably swift to discover one of the benefits of incompetence – if you wait long enough, a grown-up will do it for you. This was not what Vygotsky had in mind!

Status and partnership

Another complication of joint endeavors is that relative status can have an impact on progress. For instance, one of the negative consequences of *parental* instruction is that the adult, by virtue of her or his authority and superior competencies, can sometimes dominate to the point that the child becomes demotivated. Deci et al. (1993) found that, among 6- and 7-year-olds, excessive maternal control of a joint task was negatively correlated with the child's intrinsic motivation; mothers who demonstrated autonomy supportiveness (that is, let the child get on with it when they could see that she or he was capable of doing so) drew more successful responses from their children.

In a peer tutoring task, Verba and Winnykamen (1992) obtained other evidence that the interpersonal dynamics and expectations of the participants affected the social processes. Classmates were paired as novices and experts, where "experts" were created by pre-training them on the task. But the experimenters also varied whether expert–novice status was consistent with the subjects' everyday classroom status: half of the experts were children who were high achieving and half were low achieving. When the two characteristics were consistent – a high-achiever was trained as the expert – then the interaction took on a directive character, guided by the better-informed peer who provided relevant information, explanations, and instruction. In contrast, when the subject who was trained as an expert was one of the normally low achieving children, the interaction tended to be more cooperative.

Verba and Winnykamen's (1992) explanation is that the low achiever finds the management responsibilities of tutorial status unfamiliar and uncomfortable. As a result, he or she is more hesitant, leading the high achiever, despite being allocated the novice role, to intervene to help organize the task. At times, when the low achiever–expert runs into trouble, the high-achiever adopts what Verba and Winnykamen call a "reverse tutor" function – taking over the interaction and seeking to put things right, teaching the tutor how to tutor.

In other studies with peers as experts, investigators have provided further evidence that social status considerations play a role. Fraysse (1991) found that novices' willingness to accept the guidance of a peer tutor depended upon whether they had been made aware that the peer knew more than they did. Children who were ignorant of their partner's expertise were less likely to submit to his or her advice. Duran and Gauvain (1993) found that, among 5-year-olds, greater gains were attained when children were paired with an expert agemate rather than an expert older child. These authors suggest that for social comparison purposes 5- and 6-year-olds are oriented toward peers (we saw other evidence of this possibility in chapter 9), and find ability comparisons with older children irrelevant because they know that older people are usually better at most tasks.

Some studies of collaborative learning in educational contexts have found that joint activities can occasionally lead to *poorer* outcomes than individual work (Salomon and Globerson, 1989; Wiersema and van Oudenhoven, 1992). Salomon and Globerson also relate these findings to interpersonal factors, pointing out that, in contrast to short experiments, teams in classrooms have a history of relationships: they know each other, have likes and dislikes, sustain mutual expectations, make social comparisons, and so on. In such contexts, a variety of social processes can occur. Salomon and Globerson (1989, pp. 94–6) identify some of these:

1 The "free rider" effect (one or more team members leave it to the others to get things done).
2 The "sucker" effect (one or more especially productive members are depended on increasingly by the rest – until they wise up, and adjust their behavior, too).
3 "Status differential" effects (the more able individuals gain prestige and influence within the team, resulting in the less able reducing their involvement, and thus losing potential gains from interaction).
4 "Ganging up on the task" effects (few members really want to do the task anyway, so they agree to minimize their efforts and "go through the motions").

These processes are well known to social psychologists who investigate small group processes (van Avermaet, 1996; Wilke and van Knippenberg, 1996) but have not been investigated systematically in either neo-Piagetian or Vygotskyan studies of the social contexts of cognitive activity. It is important to bear in mind that they are not inevitable (some dyads and some teams operate very successfully), but nevertheless they are possible outcomes of social interaction, depending on features of the situation and the participants. There is scope for a fuller integration of developmental and social psychological theories around these issues.

In sum, it appears that responses to peer interactions will vary with the relative knowledge and the relative status of the participants. Responses to parental "help" will vary with the extent to which the task is appealing and the extent to which the child's autonomy and skills are respected. The success or otherwise of social interactions around cognitive tasks and problem-solving appears to be affected by interpersonal relations and motivation (a point acknowledged by Doise and Mugny, 1984).

Multiple Processes of Social Interaction

It may be misleading to seek *the* process in social interaction which promotes cognitive development. The social Genevans have been criticized for an overemphasis on conflict, as though this were the exclusive mechanism of development (Forrester, 1992). Vygotskyans have been criticized for stressing the external regulation of learning, largely ignoring or skirting the fact that the success of the tutor depends upon responding to the internal activities of the pupil (Davidson, 1992). As research accumulates, it becomes clear that a variety of factors affects the outcome of social problem-solving and that what works in one context may be less efficacious in another (Amigues and Agostinelli, 1992; Azmitia, 1988; Beaudichon et al., 1988; Kerwin and Day, 1985; Tudge and Rogoff, 1989; Verba and Winnykamen, 1992). Several developmentalists have concluded that the two theories are complementary rather than competing (Butterworth, 1982; Kerwin and Day, 1985; Tudge and Rogoff, 1989).

To consider how conflict and collaboration may interweave, let us examine three different studies, with subjects of different developmental levels and quite different concerns. In the first, Azmitia (1988) found that when children were paired in a construction task using Lego materials gains were most marked for novices working with peers who were already "expert" with the materials. In this study, gains were associated with opportunities to observe or be guided by the expert, rather than with conflict about how to proceed. But construction tasks involve the acquisition of procedural skills (such as the best ways to use Lego bricks) rather than conceptual understanding (such as conservation of length). In the second, Howe et al. (1991, 1992) ran experiments which involved older peers collaborating on relatively challenging physics concepts. Here, observational learning and direct tutoring were largely irrelevant. In this context, the prompt to reflect on the underlying ideas appeared more important than emulating someone else's behavior or insights.

In a third study, Forman and Cazden (1985) focus on the issue of different task demands to offer a reconciliation of Piagetian and Vygotskyan accounts of the nature and outcomes of social interaction. They tested 9-year-olds' performances in an experiment designed to test understanding of chemical reactions. They propose that some phases of joint work call for cooperation, while others direct attention to conflicting opinions. For example, early in the procedures the subjects had to set up the apparatus (a construction-type task). This promoted the laying out and sharing of materials and joint planning of experiments to be conducted. Here, the participants had to construct and implement a joint experimentation plan that would be tested later on in the task. This is closer to the collaborative enterprise that a Vygotskyan would see as one of the benefits of social interaction.

Later, when the subjects reached the stage where they could conduct the experiments, conflicting points of view became more apparent. They disagreed about matters such as which element or combination of elements would lead to particular reactions. Now, because the children reached different conclusions, they were forced to acknowledge information that challenged their own inferences as well as data that supported them. This obliged them to try to integrate the data into a convincing argument in support of their own point of view. Given that their partners could point to evidence in support of their position, good counter-arguments also had to be constructed. This manifests the kinds of intellectual disequilibrium and active pursuit of a resolution that a Piagetian would predict.

Having reached a sociocognitive conflict, however, progress among Forman and Cazden's subjects seemed to depend upon the gradual internalization of jointly achieved solutions. Following one pair of subjects longitudinally over a period of months, the researchers found that for a while the boys could achieve the necessary level of deductive reasoning to explain the chemical reactions only when working together, by guiding, prompting, and correcting each other. Subsequently, one subject demonstrated that he could generate the solutions alone, and in due course his partner also internalized the process – much as Vygotskyans would foretell.

At the risk of deriving from Forman and Cazden an interpretation rather more simplistic than they would care to articulate, the eventual outcome looks like 2 to 1 to Vygotsky. Except, of course, that science is never static, and it remains possible that either or both of the nascent chemists might become dissatisfied with his existing level of understanding and so go on to generate further problems to explore and explain – thus balancing things out for the neo-Piagetians.

The Zone of Developmental Social Psychological Development

Perhaps the major contribution of both the social Genevan and Vygotskyan schools has been to reassert the importance of the social context and social processes of cognitive development. If we consider the predominance of traditional Piagetian and information-processing models in developmental psychology which investigate cognitive development as though it were in principle detachable from the child's involvement with others, then the return of the social to centre stage (Light, 1986) is a healthy corrective.

Nevertheless, as we have seen, each theory has its limitations. The social Genevans, while stressing the importance of sociocognitive conflict, have not investigated closely the actual processes that are involved as children negotiate new understandings. For example, little work has been conducted on the verbal and nonverbal aspects of sociocognitive interchanges. The Vygotskyans, on the other hand, have examined interpersonal interactions in some detail but – notwithstanding Vygotsky's concern with the interrelations of thought and language – offer only superficial accounts of how language is actually used in the course of social interactions (see Forrester, 1992, for a critique).

Reflecting awareness of these drawbacks, theoretical developments in this field are focusing on two related aspects of developmental social cognition. First, both Genevans and Vygotskyans have converged on the importance of the achievement of *intersubjectivity* (Blaye et al., 1992; Davidson, 1992; Forman, 1992; Perret-Clermont et al., 1991; Rommetveit, 1985; Wertsch, 1985). Intersubjectivity refers to the achievement of a shared understanding, in which each participant has at least some awareness of how the other represents and thinks about the task to hand. This is a truly *inter*psychological (between minds) process, though how it comes about, and how it changes with development, is still little understood (cf. Crook, 1994; Forman, 1992; Grossen, 1994). Closer connections to the growing literature on parents' social cognitions – especially, parental beliefs, ideas and expectations – may yield productive frameworks, since this literature is also concerned with "mutual cognitions" (Goodnow and Collins, 1990; Maccoby and Martin, 1983), but with a focus on the mature partner.

A large part of the answer to how these processes occur may be obtained through the second main emphasis, which is on the ways in which language is used in social cognitive interactions (Davidson, 1992, 1986; Durkin, 1986b, 1987b; Garton, 1992; Hickmann, 1985; Forrester, 1992; Siegal, 1991). Language provides a means for making understandings public, for transmitting, challenging, analysing, rejecting, accepting, improving, and speculating. Several researchers have argued that conversation is the essential context in which cognitive abilities are engaged and transformed through inter-individual processes (Forrester, 1992; Galimberti, 1992; Siegal, 1991). Light et al. (1994), in analyses of the verbal strategies of children in joint computer-based tasks, provide evidence that explicit formulations of plans and use of negotiation are associated with successful outcomes. It remains to be seen if this is true of other tasks, and to develop micro-level analyses of the operation of social cognitive and developmental psycholinguistic processes in such engagements.

Summary

Social interaction between children is not invariably productive. Tudge and Rogoff (1989, p. 35) express a fundamental point succinctly: "It is unlikely that merely sitting next to another person will enhance a child's skills." The success of joint efforts depends on a variety of factors, but prominent among them are the nature of the task, the perceived relative status of the participants, the motivations and interpersonal relations of the participants and the small group dynamics they engender. The social aspects of cognitive interaction do not constitute just *one* process (such as conflict or tutorship), and the dimensions highlighted by social Genevan and Vygotskyan perspectives respectively are likely both to be involved. These theories may be complementary rather than contradictory. But it is also clear that there are important aspects of social cognitive interaction that neither school has investigated very thoroughly, namely the achievement of intersubjectivity and the role of language.

As has been stressed above, it remains ironic that while both of the approaches we have been considering here are concerned with social aspects of cognition, neither pays a great deal of attention to the social *content* of cognition, that is, to the subjects' understanding of social phenomena. We turn in the next section to another development, originating primarily in European social psychology, which has begun to meet this challenge.

The Development of Social Representations

The various investigations of social cognitive development that we have been examining since chapter 9 have adopted one of two orientations. One emphasis has been upon the individual's attempts to make sense of the social world. For example, we considered in chapter 9 attempts to apply traditional cognitive developmental frameworks to children's developing concepts of persons, roles, and societal structure. Similarly, in chapter 10, we examined research concerned with the individual's inferences about causality in the social domain. The second emphasis, which has been to the fore in the present chapter, has been upon the interactions among individuals sharing or transmitting knowledge about the world – usually, the physical world (such as conservation tasks, coordination of perspectives, construction of objects). As Butterworth (1982, p. 11) comments, these two approaches offer us, respectively, a "theory of social knowledge" and a "social theory of knowledge."

But there is a logical and empirical need for a theory which offers both components – that is, a *social* theory of *social* knowledge. Clearly, developing such a theory is especially challenging, since it requires attention simultaneously to the processes of development, to the complex nature of the phenomena that are being acquired, and to the interactions between these. One promising line of investigation arises from attempts to extend Moscovici's (1976, 1981, 1984) theory of social representations into the developmental domain.

Social Representations

The term *social representations* refers to shared understandings of the social world: "a set of concepts, statements and explanations originating in daily life in the course of inter-individual communications. They are the equivalent, in our society, of the myths and belief systems in traditional societies; they might even be said to be the contemporary version of common sense" (Moscovici, 1981, p. 181). Social representations are, for Moscovici, the "essence of *social* cognition" (p. 103): they are not only the sum of our knowledge about the world and our relationships to it but they also provide the framework within which we share, transmit, and reflect upon our understandings.

In these ways, social representations help render the unfamiliar familiar. That is, they provide us with means of objectifying and categorizing the complex phenomena of the universe we encounter (by labeling and defining them), and they provide us with anchors (established concepts) to which we can relate new experiences. Knowledge, according to Moscovici, is meaningful *because* it is social, and it is constructed through social activity: "We derive only a small fraction of our knowledge and information from the simple interaction between ourselves and the facts we encounter in the world. Most knowledge is supplied to us by communication which affects our way of thinking and creates new concepts" (1988, p. 215).

The concept of social representations is rather abstract and there is some debate among social psychologists as to exactly what is entailed and how amenable it is to empirical test (cf. Hogg and Abrams, 1988; Leyens, 1983; Potter and Litton, 1985; see also an interesting exchange between Jahoda, 1988, and Moscovici, 1988). By and large, the idea has not gone down well in the individualistic tradition of North American social psychology and, by and large, Moscovici is correspondingly unimpressed by the reluctance of American psychologists to address the possibility of cognitive representations that extend beyond the individual. From the perspective of a developmental social psychology, however, Moscovici's central tenet is quite compatible with a major theme, namely that: "Our everyday life is interwoven with that of other people who act on us. The reason we know our life is that we create it day by day" (Moscovici, 1988, p. 229). Indeed, for the developmentalist, it seems obvious that the prime testing ground for the theory of social representations should be the developmental contexts within which social life is (re)constructed (Corsaro, 1993; Duveen and Lloyd, 1990). Verges (1987), for example, demonstrates that in at least some contexts, adults' social representations are relatively stable while children's are subject to change and reorganization – this makes children's formulations all the more useful as sources of evidence on the origins and course of social representation.

Social Representations in Childhood

We considered in chapter 10 studies by Emler et al. (1987a, 1990) which indicated that how children conceive of social roles and societal processes is not a straightforward function of level of cognitive development, but varies according to the society in which the child is developing and the child's own status within that society (e.g., social class). Emler et al. (1990, p. 65) propose that:

> When we ask children about such matters as why certain income levels or differences exist, it is unlikely that we are simply accessing their own moral judgment capacities, constructed according to universal laws of cognitive organization and discovered by us in this kind of research at various stages of completion. It is more likely that we are also accessing their understanding of their culture's framework of legitimations for the status quo: children are repeating society's justifications . . . Hence, we would argue that these children are providing us with social representations.

In ethnographic studies of "the underlife of the nursery school" Corsaro (1990, 1993) develops an account of the role of social representations in developmental social cognition in which he argues that participation in peer activities reflects children's attempts to transform the puzzling and ambiguous features of the adult world into the familiar routines of peer culture – motivated, as Moscovici would predict, to make the unfamiliar familiar. By looking closely into the social activities of Italian and American preschoolers, Corsaro found evidence that the children deal with the rules imposed by adults by incorporating them into their own collective practices.

For example, in the Italian nursery, the teachers prohibited children from bringing personal objects to school. From the perspective of a 4-year-old this presumptuous constraint makes little sense (the whole point of having personal objects is that they are fun to play with), but the children know that grown-ups set the rules. So, the sensible thing to do is to smuggle small playthings in, concealed in one's pockets. Of course, having got around the system it is essential to share the achievement with one's peers, who can appreciate the risks undertaken and the delights of the illicit goods. This calls for discretion, and all disclosures have to be made out of sight of the agents of repression. But through these defiant arrangements, the rules themselves are given meaning and are transformed into a basis for social organization. Corsaro holds that children are trying to make sense of the adult rule by anchoring it in the collective security of their own culture. As they begin to incorporate the rule, and find ways of working around it, so they themselves lend it a form of objectivity: it influences how they organize their shared activities. By avoiding someone's authority and persuading your peers to avoid her authority, you confirm her authority. In this way, through working jointly within the rules that adults impose, children begin to reconstruct jointly a social representation of how the world (or their fragment of it) is regulated.

Social representations of mental illness

A fascinating study in the development of social representations is presented by de Rosa (1987), who investigated children's ideas about mental illness. De Rosa suggests that one of the attractions of social representations for the developmentalist is that it serves to link accounts of historical/cultural processes with individual ontogenesis. Her own findings provide a clear example.

Using clinical interview and projective techniques, de Rosa elicited Italian children's representations of what it meant to be a mad person. Madness presents a classic instance of something which is unfamiliar and difficult to explain, and the interest lies in how people attempt to render the idea familiar and interpretable. Consistent with the theory of social representations, she found that children attempt to locate this concept in regions which already make sense to them. At around the age of 5 or 6, children anchor the concept of madness to their early understandings of deviance and violent criminality: essentially, the mad person is regarded as a dangerous bad guy. By around 8 or 9 years, children can entertain etiological hypotheses about underlying causes, although these tend to be relatively concrete ("she's on drugs," "he was hit on the head by lightning and went crazy"); at this stage, the mad person is represented as affected by forces beyond his or her control. By early adolescence, de Rosa's subjects were more likely to draw on psychological concepts, suggesting that mad people have suffered inner disturbances, "externally the madman behaves normally and, physically, he is like everyone else, only he thinks about things that don't exist" (adolescent subject quoted by de Rosa, 1987, p. 110). Now, the representation of madness incorporates ideas of social difficulties, the madman as isolated or as victim. De Rosa points out that the developmental shifts in representations of madness parallel the historical shifts in medical representations: mental illness was first thought of as a dangerous deviance, then as an organic disease and, more recently, as a psychological and social illness.

Particularly interesting aspects of children's representations are captured in their drawings. Figure 11.4 presents examples from a much larger set in de Rosa (1987). Notice that although there are clear signs of increasing conceptual sophistication with age, one feature which remains relatively constant is the idea of the mentally ill person as deviant and threatening. De Rosa suggests that this ambiguity (more profound understanding, yet continuing discomfort) itself reflects an ambiguity in the wider community's perception and treatment of mentally ill people.

Cross-cultural comparisons would be of interest. For example, do children from societies with different medical beliefs have different representations of madness? Are Italian mad people more chic than Belgian or British mad people? (Notice the designer clothes of the buffoon, the transvestite's Gucci bag, and the sensuous eyes and fashionably coiffured brain of the neurotic.) Even so, from this one culture alone de Rosa's evidence supports the thesis that social representations of the unfamiliar are anchored in the familiar, shared by members of a community, and subject to developmental change.

Social Representations *of* Development

Social representations are more than a body of shared knowledge which new members of a society have to acquire. As stressed above, they also provide the framework within which knowledge is organized and transmitted. Hence, an important aspect of social representations as they bear on development is that *development itself is something about which any society has social representations*. In other words, a society has a belief system, a set of expectations and explanations, concerning what children are like and what should be done with them. These social representations influence the contexts in which the young are raised.

For example, contemporary industrialized societies tend to value highly a human property which cannot be observed directly but which is thought to be present – to varying degrees – in most people. The property is called *intelligence*. We (psychologists as much as lay people) do not know exactly what intelligence is, but we tend to share the belief that it is a good thing and that the more one has of it, the better. In other words, this rather mysterious attribute is rendered familiar by *objectifying* it: calling it "intelligence" (and developing tests which aim to measure it). The idea of intelligence now becomes rather "ordinary and immediately present" (Moscovici, 1981, p. 190).

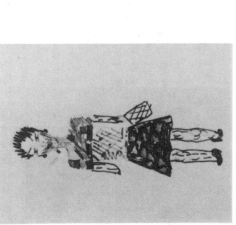

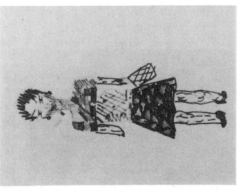

a)

b)

c)

d)

e)

Figure 11.4 Children's representations of mental illness. (A) Madman drawn by 5-year-old upper-class boy from Rome (stereotype deviant: murderer); (B) madman drawn by 7-year-old lower-class girl from Rome (stereotype deviant: drunkard); (C) madman drawn by 9-year-old upper-class girl from Rome (stereotype: buffoon); (D) madman drawn by 13-year-old lower-class girl from Rome (stereotype deviant: transvestite); (E) mad woman drawn by 16-year-old lower-class girl from Rome (stereotype: medical case, neurotic individual obsessed by problems).

(*Source:* de Rosa, 1987)

You could conduct an armchair test of just how fully you share the social representation of intelligence by imagining that you had to explain the concept to a member of a nontechnological culture who has never heard of such an idea. It seems perfectly obvious to you, but may be quite obscure – or plain daft – to someone with a different system of representations.

According to Moscovici, familiar representations serve as anchors, firm bases in our networks of understanding to which we can link new and troubling ideas. Suppose, for instance, we observe that different individuals appear to have different amounts of intelligence. How could we make sense of this variability? Mugny and Carugati (1985) and Carugati (1990) found that lay people (their subjects were from a Western culture, Italy) have a complex, multidimensional representation of intelligence, but that one powerful and widely shared assumption was that the attribute is attained as a *gift* of nature. Again, the notion of a gift is a familiar enough anchor from other areas of social understanding. Pause for a moment to consider your dialogue with the person who has never heard of *intelligence*. Suppose that his or her culture has no practice of *gifts*, either; it becomes clear just how much we build upon representations that can be assumed within our own culture but may not be universal.

By linking our representations of gifts to our representations of intelligence we can achieve a more elaborate account of individual differences. Carugati proposes that giftedness serves as a reference around which parents and teachers construct explanations for differences in intelligence. The elaborate construct of intelligence is anchored first to this more readily graspable notion; but once it is anchored (represented as a gift), it can become objectified in its turn. Now, individuals are categorized according to the amount of intelligence they have been given, and they are labeled as *bright* or *dull*. Since the property of brightness or dullness is taken to predict subsequent attainments, the gift of nature becomes a property which determines the child's capabilities: "In the process of objectification the differences which were originally effects have been transformed into causes" (Carugati, 1990, p. 139).

Having built up these representations, the ways in which we employ them may affect the ways in which we admit new members to our culture. For example, we saw in the work on attributions and achievement in chapter 10 that once a person has been distinguished as *bright* or *dull*, expectations about his or her future performance are generated and transmitted, and may well influence how he or she approaches tests of intellectual capability.

Other research in the social representations tradition confirms that adults have wide-ranging representations of childhood and development, and that these guide them in the establishment of particular domestic and educational practices (e.g., D'Alessio, 1990; Emiliani et al., 1981; Molinari and Emiliani, 1990; Selleri et al., 1995). (In fact, as you will know only too well if you have ever confessed at a party that you are a psychologist, people have social representations of our profession, too; see de Paolis, 1990. But don't even begin to explain to the person who hasn't heard of *intelligence* and *gifts* what we do for a living.)

Social Representations and Social Attributions

The theory of social representations has also been drawn upon to place attribution theory in a more social framework. Hewstone and Jaspars (1984), who we saw in chapter 10 stress that explanatory structures tend to be shared among members of a group, propose that these causal reasons are embedded in social representations. To test this possibility, Hewstone et al. (1982) first compared the social representations of 16-year-old boys attending either a British elite, fee-paying public school or a state (comprehensive) school. Among other differences, the public school boys saw themselves as hardworking and oriented toward high academic standards; the comprehensive school students saw themselves as less privileged than the public school boys. Not surprisingly, then, the two samples had distinct social representations of the social world.

The subjects were required next to provide attributions for success or failure within the educational system. The public schoolboys attributed the failure of one of their own group to achieve satisfactory university entry results to lack of effort, while they saw similar outcomes for comprehensive school pupils as due to lack of ability. There appeared to be a group-serving bias, to the effect that "They fail because they're stupid, we fail because we don't try" (Hewstone et al., 1982, p. 256). The comprehensive pupils attributed the successes of public school individuals to luck – again, an attribution which helps to explain unfavorable differentials in group achievements while maintaining ingroup esteem. Thus, attributions were not the product of "cold" computations based on the objective application of causal models. Instead, they reflected the collective assumptions (social representations) that each group had constructed to account for its place in the social hierarchy. The repositories of explanations which are drawn upon are couched in terms which maximize a positive social identity (see also Devos et al., 1994; Emiliani and Molinari, 1994).

Overall, these several, diverse, attempts to relate the theory of social representations to social cognition in the young appear promising in that they help uncover the social nature of thought about social relations: a *social* social cognition. On the other hand, it has to be said that, although independent studies have worked with different age groups, there have been only limited attempts so far to forge a *developmental* dimension to the theory. Moscovici (1990) himself acknowledges overlaps between his theory and those of both Piaget and Vygotsky, but places more emphasis on the imposition of culture upon the young mind than on any qualitative transformations in how the young are able to formulate and elaborate their social representations. A developmental component is certainly not incompatible with the theory in principle, but it has not yet been taken very far in practice.

Summary

Social representations are collective understandings of the nature of the social world. Proponents of this theory hold that representations are not simply bodies of knowledge that new members of a society have to acquire, but they form the very frameworks within which social beings organize their thinking. They influence the kinds of contexts in which children experience the world, reflecting adults' social representations of what is involved in childhood and development. Several different studies support the thesis that the ways in which children understand aspects of their social environment can be accounted for in terms of social representations. At the same time, few would dispute that the concept of social representations is a difficult one and it has been suggested here that further work is needed to elaborate the developmental implications of the theory. The benefits of future theory and research on this topic may be a fuller account of the nature of social cognitive development as a social process.

Conclusions

In chapters 9–11, we have considered a broad range of issues concerned with the development of social cognition. As was suggested at the beginning of chapter 9, there are different interpretations of the term social cognition, and these lead to different research traditions. Some focus on the conceptual difficulties confronting the individual trying to understand the social world, and others concentrate on the interdependence of people in achieving understanding of anything. Each approach makes a valuable contribution, and continuing progress in this challenging field is likely to draw upon more than one perspective – just as children do. It is already clear from the past couple of decades of research into social cognitive development that the intersection of social and developmental psychology in this area can be a very fruitful one, with benefits for both subdisciplines. Developmentalists have attained a broader and more social topic area through responding to the growth of social cognitive research in social psychology; social psychologists are beginning to take note of developmental investigations of interpsychological processes in cognitive activity. The continuing expansion of social cognitive research may prove to be one of the most productive meeting grounds of the two disciplines, and a fertile location for the growth of developmental social psychology.

Further reading

Baron, R. M. and Misovich, S. J. (1993) An integration of Gibsonian and Vygotskyan perspectives on changing attitudes in group contexts. *British Journal of Social Psychology*, 32, 53–70.

A stimulating example of the application of developmental theories to standard social psychological topics, including group socialization and attitude change.

Doise, W. and Mugny, G. (1984) *The Social Development of the Intellect*. Oxford: Pergamon.

One of the principal statements of the social Genevan position, elaborating the links to mainstream Piagetian theory and reviewing a large number of the early studies of sociocognitive conflict and cognitive development.

Dunn, J. (1988) *The Beginnings of Social Understanding*. Oxford: Blackwell.

A rich, if deceptively readable, account of the interpersonal context of early social knowledge, emotional development, and moral discourse.

Duveen, G. and Lloyd, B. (1990) *Social Representations and the Development of Knowledge*. Cambridge: Cambridge University Press.

Several applications of the theory of social representations to developmental issues, including gender role acquisition, knowledge of social relations, emotional understanding, and concepts of childhood.

Fiske, S. T. and Taylor, S. E. (1991) *Social Cognition*, 2nd edn. New York: McGraw-Hill.

A thorough discussion of individualistic approaches to social cognition. Aimed at an advanced level readership, but well structured and clearly written, with a comprehensive bibliography.

Rogoff, B. (1990) *Apprenticeship in Thinking: cognitive development in a social context*. New York: Oxford University Press.

An important account of the implications of social interaction for cognitive development. Developing the concept of the child as apprentice, Rogoff draws upon and extends Vygotskyan theory with findings from parent–infant communication, cross–cultural studies, and laboratory experiments of adult–child and child–child collaboration.

Winegar, L. T. (ed.) (1989) *Social Interaction and the Development of Children's Understanding*. Norwood, NJ: Ablex.

This collection provides a variety of perspectives on the role of other people in supporting, challenging, and stimulating children's developing social understanding; several authors draw on Vygotskyan theory.

Wertsch, J. V. and Tulviste, P. (1992) L. S. Vygotsky and contemporary developmental psychology. *Developmental Psychology*, 28, 548–57.

A useful overview of Vygotsky's ideas and their impact on recent developmental research.

Chapter 12

The Development
of Aggression

*Those who argue dogmatically against all forms of
corporal punishment find themselves urging a variety
of psychological reprisals against the child –
withdrawal of approval or privileges, the
humiliation of an early bedtime and so on. There is
no evidence to suggest that these more protracted
forms of punishment, which can waste a good deal of
a busy parent's time, cause less long-term damage
than a swift clip across the ear or a few smart slaps
to the backside. Commonsense suggests the contrary.
Raise your hand once and show you mean business!
It is likely you will never have to raise it again.*
    From The Authorised Childcare Handbook, *in*
    McEwan, The Child in Time, *1987)*

In July, 1992, a 9-year-old boy shot and blinded his uncle's cow. In response, his uncle swore to kill him. The family lived in northern Lebanon, where an oath of honour is regarded as irrevocable. To show he meant business, the uncle carried out his vow, slitting the throat of the boy in front of his parents. The boy's brother and father retaliated using a Kalashnikov assault rifle, killing the uncle, his wife and their son. Nine neighbors who attempted to intervene in the dispute were wounded.

Around the same time, a schoolboy in Sydney took a chunk of thigh out of a classmate with his machete, the Mafia blew up another senior judge in Sicily, the IRA left three dead, naked, and mutilated traitors at a roadside in Northern Ireland, neo-Nazis in Rostock set fire to the hostels of immigrant workers, there were several hundred rapes a day in the United States, and the Serbs continued the ethnic cleansing of Bosnia, displacing millions of people from their homes and committing countless atrocities on a scale not witnessed in Europe since the Second World War.

Why do people do things like this to others? These are among the uglier manifestations of a capacity for aggression that most human beings seem to possess to some degree. An interview study of British primary school children found that 51 percent of the sample reported having had at least one serious fight within the previous year (Boulton, 1993); research in Norway reveals that approximately one child in seven is involved in bully/victim problems during the school year (Olweus, 1993); in many schools in urban America, children have to be frisked or run through metal detectors at the gates to ensure that they are not carrying guns, knives, or other deadly weaponry into class.

We encounter aggression regularly, not only in news reports of atrocities and in our daily television entertainment, but also in everyday social transactions, in the competitive world of work, in politics, in sport, on the roads, and at home. Not every instance of real-world aggression involves physical violence, but most are intended to cause harm of some kind and many affect the quality of people's lives in minor to major ways. Given the salience of aggression in our lives, we hear often common-sense theories of its origins and of how to deal with it. One of the most favored, of course, is that it is all/ partly due to what we watch on television; we will consider this issue in some detail. Others include naive biological theories, such as that all males are inherently aggressive; we will consider sex differences in aggression, too. Everyday responses to aggression are often rooted in these theories, as in the assertion that a swift clip around the ear of a truculent child works wonders (usually followed up with "it never did me any harm.")

Not always content to rely upon common sense, social psychologists have been involved extensively in the pursuit of explanations of aggression and in attempts to find ways to reduce its frequency and severity. Developmental psychologists have charted the emergence of aggression in childhood, the roles it plays in the development of social relations, and its correlates in socialization practices.

In this chapter, we consider first the problem of defining aggression. This turns out to be more than an academic nicety, since deciding exactly what we mean by the term has substantial implications for how we interpret – and deal with – some forms of behavior that are widespread in younger children that might not be quite as undesirable as they first appear. Following definition, an outline of the development of aggression through childhood is sketched. Then, we consider some of the most influential theoretical explanations that have been advanced to account for the emergence and functions of aggression. In particular, we turn to ethology and sociobiology for perspectives on the adaptive purposes of aggression, to the frustration–aggression hypothesis, whose proponents hold that aggression occurs when goal-directed behavior is blocked, to social learning theory for ideas and evidence relating to some of the environmental factors associated with aggression (including the mass media), and then to social cognitive approaches which emphasize the role of interpretations in guiding behavior. In the final section of the chapter, we consider four aspects of social context which are associated with individual differences in aggression, namely the family, the peer group, gender, and culture.

Defining and finding aggression

What exactly is aggression? Looking at the examples we began with, aggression might be defined as behavior that causes harm to another party. In this vein, Buss (1961, p. 1) proposes that aggression is "a response that delivers noxious stimuli to another organism." Unfortunately, this concise statement provides only an approximate definition. First, there are instances of human behavior which we would recognize as aggressive where harm is caused to objects or property rather than organisms. For example, many forms of vandalism do not involve direct physical harm to persons. Second, there may be instances where harm to other organisms or objects is accidental or even well motivated: a surgeon amputating a limb to prevent the further spread of cancer would be delivering noxious stimuli to the patient, but few would see her intervention as aggressive. Third, humans sometimes enact behaviors which do not actually result in harm, but were certainly intended to: a bomb placed in a public place failing to detonate, a dart thrown into a crowd of soccer supporters only to fall to the ground, a kick that just misses the target, would all constitute aggressive behavior yet the noxious stimuli never make contact with the organisms intended.

A crucial aspect of these behaviors is the *intent* of the actor. Distinguishing intent allows us to differentiate among the acts listed above in a more useful way, and most scientists working in this area tend to incorporate intentionality in their definition (Ferguson and Rule, 1983; Geen, 1990; Mummendey, 1996). Geen (1990, p. 3) suggests adding the element of *expectancy*, that is, the belief that there is a better than zero chance that the act one is taking (setting the bomb, propelling the dart, swinging one's leg) will actually result in some harm to someone or something. Hence, an enriched working definition of aggression can be formulated as follows: "Aggression involves the delivery of noxious stimuli by one party to other organisms or objects, under conditions in which the actor intends to harm the target and the actor expects the noxious stimuli to have their intended effect" (modified from Geen, 1990, pp. 2–3).

Note that we can *see* (observe, record, count, measure the force of) aggression, but we can usually only *infer* intention or expectation. This is important in terms of determining when it is accurate to label a particular act or set of acts as aggressive.

The issue poses a challenge to the scientist observing or manipulating human behavior, since it raises questions about how we can test for processes that are not directly observable. An analogous problem faces any of us confronted by a seemingly aggressive provocation, since one of the critical factors determining how we react to the behavior of others is the inferences we make about the intentions and motives underlying that behavior.

Modes of aggressive and nonaggressive behavior

There are different ways in which people behave aggressively. A common distinction is that between hostile and instrumental aggression (Buss, 1961; Rule, 1974). Hostile aggression refers to actions where the central intent is to cause harm to someone or something; for example, two children might beat up another in the playground. Instrumental aggression refers to behavior in contexts where the actor has some broader goal which entails hurting another in order to reach it; for example, a girl wrenches a plaything from a friend's hand, hurting his fingers.

There are also forms of behavior which appear aggressive, yet may not be. Particularly important among these for developmental social psychologists is *rough and tumble play*. Rough and tumble play (henceforth R & T) is found in many cultures, and is especially popular among boys (Fagot, 1985; Goldstein, 1992; Whiting and Edwards, 1988). It emerges among preschoolers but still occurs among adolescents; you can even observe it first hand in student common rooms and other places where young adults gather to entertain themselves. On first consideration, the inclination of many young children to engage in R & T may appear to confirm fears that aggression is "built in" to human beings. The sight of preschoolers hitting, chasing, and wrestling with each other often distresses parents and many well-intentioned educators.

However, on closer examination, the significance of R & T is somewhat more complex. A number of careful studies has found that this form of behavior is quite distinct from aggression (Blurton Jones, 1972; DiPietro, 1981; Hinde, 1988; Humphreys and Smith, 1987; Pellegrini, 1988; Smith and Connolly, 1980; Sutton-Smith, 1988). First, R & T is a form of *play* and, as is typical of play activity, it is entered into voluntarily and pleasurably. The participants keep coming back for more, and wear broad smiles over their faces (see figures 12.1 and 12.2). The victims of true aggression rarely have anything to laugh about, and usually strive to distance themselves from their assailant. Second, R & T serves a number of positive functions for young children, including social affiliation, developing cooperative and turn-taking skills, and joint problem-solving (see Pellegrini, 1988; Rubin, 1982b). Third, R & T leads to actual aggression and injury only very rarely, and typically as a consequence of the actions of children low in social competence (DiPietro, 1981; Pellegrini, 1988). Fourth, children who are seriously aggressive and prone to hurt others are *less* likely to become involved in R & T play, largely because their peers avoid them (Goldstein, 1992).

Note that, above all, the *intentions* of children engaged in R & T are quite remote from those of individuals enacting aggression. In the former, the idea is to have fun;

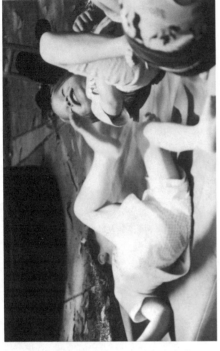

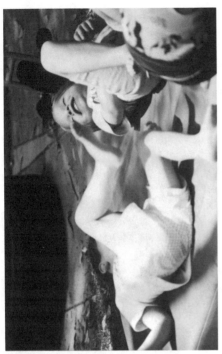

Figure 12.1 Three 4-year-old boys engage in rough-and-rumble play: moments later, they contemplate what to do next.

Figure 12.2   Adolescent males engage in rough-and-tumble play. Each boy in turn is thrown into the river by his friends. He protests vigorously, swims around a bit, and then resumes his place in the line to be thrown in again. The girls watch, squeal, and giggle.

in the latter, the idea is to hurt someone, to appropriate someone else's property, or to dominate. If someone is hurt in the course of R & T, the participants often apologize and assure him or her that there was no intent to harm (Whiting and Edwards, 1988). When school-aged children are asked about their relations with other children with whom they engage in R & T, it turns out that they *like* the individuals: R & T is something you do with your friends (Humphreys and Smith, 1987). These considerations, we will see later, are important, because R & T has often been measured as though it were a form of aggression.

Outline of the Development of Aggression

Infancy

Some aggressive behavior can be observed in quite young children. Observational studies of children during the second year of life reveal that many of the conflicts between children around this age revolve around objects, especially when one child attempts to remove an interesting toy from another (Campbell and Ewing, 1990; Caplan et al., 1991; Howes et al., 1993; Kolominskii and Zhiznevskii, 1992; Zahn-Waxler et al., 1990). Hence, early aggression appears to be instrumental: the aim is to acquire a desired object rather than to inflict harm upon another. Broch (1990, p. 47) describes an incident in an Indonesian village where a girl who wanted to suckle her mother's breast became angry upon discovering that there was no milk for her. To the amusement of bystanders, the dissatisfied consumer squeezed the breast vigorously with her hands.

The Preschool Years

Early aggressive acts have a social character. Hay and Ross (1982), for example, observed that conflicts between children often began with a verbal exchange, indicating that the parties were aware of each other as animate beings. Toddlers would sometimes become aggressive in order to retrieve a toy once they found that one of their peers had become interested in it, even though they had previously discarded it – and then throw it away again once they had put paid to the opposition. Caplan et al. (1991) found similarly that many conflicts over toys occurred even when a duplicate was available nearby.

Goodenough (1931) had 45 mothers keep records of outbursts of anger in their 2–5-year-old children. The findings indicated that early expressions of anger tended to be relatively unfocused tantrums, often prompted by discomfort in the course of routine care (such as being bathed). But by around the age of 4 years these kinds of outbursts were increasingly likely to be directed at specific people, especially playmates. From the age of 4, direct physical aggression tends to become less frequent, but verbal aggression (taunting, teasing, name calling) becomes more common and retaliatory aggression also increases during the early school years (Hartup, 1974).

Middle Childhood Onwards

By the primary school years, individual differences in proneness to aggression are well established and these tend to remain stable into adolescence (Farrington, 1994; Lerner at al., 1988; Parke and Slaby, 1983; Olweus, 1979, 1980) and beyond (Caspi et al., 1987; Huesmann et al., 1984; Magnusson, 1988). Individuals prone to aggressiveness are also more likely to demonstrate negative emotional behaviors. Lerner et al. (1988) found that aggression during middle childhood emerged as the best predictor of adolescent adjustment problems, and Caspi et al. (1987) found that individuals who were aggressive in middle childhood tended as adults to have unhappy and conflict-ridden relations with their partners and their own children.

The *scope* for aggression increases with age. Older individuals have more mechanisms available for acting aggressively. Not only do they have bigger, stronger, and better coordinated bodies, and in some cases access to more dangerous weapons, but they have also increasing competence in nonphysical means of aggression, such as verbal and nonverbal communications, and more sophisticated social understanding (so that, for example, they have a better sense of what will hurt someone else's feelings).

Overall, while its forms may vary and its complexity increase with age, aggression emerges early in life and individuals who score high on this variable are likely to continue to do so and to display other social developmental problems. With this overview of the developmental course in mind, we need now to consider why aggression emerges, and why some individuals are more aggressive than others. Many theories have been advanced to account for aggressive behavior in humans and other species. Among these, four broad perspectives have particular relevance to developmental social psychology, namely biological theories, the frustration–aggression hypothesis, social learning theory and, more recently, social cognitive approaches.

Biological Theories and Aggression

There are several different perspectives on aggression that locate the principal source of this kind of behavior in biology. These include instinct theories such as that of McDougall (1908), Freudian psychoanalytic theory, ethological approaches such as those of Lorenz (1963), Ardrey (1966, 1970), and sociobiological theories such as those of Wilson (1975, 1978). We will consider ethological and sociobiological accounts here (see Mummendey, 1996, and Parke and Slaby, 1983, for fuller discussions of the earlier perspectives).

Ethologists such as Lorenz (1963) and Ardrey (1966) view aggression as the outcome of innate forces, themselves the product of evolutionary adaptation. Lorenz, for example, was confident that the human predilection for violent aggressiveness emerged out of the adaptive defence strategies of our pre-human ancestors. Ardrey (1970) regarded aggression as contributing to the full development of the individual, promoting the competition that he saw as essential to natural selection. Ethologists see aggression as a primary drive manifest in specific patterns of behavior (cf. Eibl-Eibesfeldt, 1989). Eibl-Eibesfeldt points to nonverbal displays such as the threat stare, agonistic postures, fist clenching and teeth baring, which are found in virtually all human societies (as well as in many animals), as illustrations of a biologically given capacity which may be triggered by external stimuli, such as territorial incursions, resource disputes, and relationship conflicts. Ethologists do not all see aggression as leading inevitably to mutual destructiveness – since they accept that it can be moderated by cultural traditions, education, and social regulation – but they do regard it as a powerful internally motivated drive.

In a closely related perspective, sociobiologists see aggression as a mechanism of social competition, elicited under conditions where there are mutually disadvantageous needs for access to some resource: that is, where two or more parties want the same thing and there is not enough to satisfy everybody. The use of aggression is a principal strategy to ensure one's own, and one's offsprings', survival. Barash (1982) points out that few animals compete for air, which is available in adequate supply, but severe competition is prone to erupt over food, water, nesting sites, and mates. He characterizes these competitions as taking one of two basic forms, namely *scramble* and *contest*.

In a scramble, participants strive to grab as much of the critical resource as they can, paying little heed to the needs and behaviors of their competitors. The winner (the individual, group or species which maximizes its inclusive fitness) is the party which accumulates most. Young children playing supposedly team sports, such as soccer, often display scrambling, in that they mass around the ball, chasing and kicking it in a fairly random fashion without regard to the broader strategies of the game, still less the desires of their playmates. Adults can be observed to engage in scramble competitions in the early stages of department store sales, upon seeking entrance to the conveyances of public transport systems during the rush hour, or during the opening of a float on the stock market. In China in 1992 there were riots as would-be investors scrambled to grab the first shares to become available in the newly authorized stock exchange.

One liability of scrambling is that the resource itself can be used up, damaged or obscured by the very processes of acquisition. If you and I scramble to grasp the same garment during the sale, we may tear it to shreds before getting it to the till, or if we veer simultaneously into the same space on the freeway, we might incur a mutually disadvantageous collision. In Egypt in 1993 it was admitted that Tutankhamun's tomb and other treasures were in danger of destruction as egyptologists plundered them for materials and tourists trundled remorselessly through. Scrambling is wasteful. So, by and large, humans tend to engage in more sophisticated ways of determining access to valued resources: we fight over them.

In contest competition, the participants interact directly with each other to establish some means of deciding who gets how much access to the resources at stake. Often, the mechanism involves some form of aggression whereby the parties conduct a dispute and then the victor gains the goods. Consider the ways in which human beings settle minor and major conflicts over resources. We struggle to outdo each other within the systems that regulate access to rewards, such as education and career advancement, we fight over property, possessions, and privileges and, if the worst comes to the worst, we go to war. Ethologists and sociobiologists are fond of pointing out that the history of our species is a seemingly relentless story of escalating intergroup violence focused upon issues of wealth, commodities, trade routes and territory. In fact, confirming our evolutionary acceleration beyond lesser species, we have reached the stage where we *do* behave aggressively with the air itself: witness the spread of acid rain as one European country allows its industries to create pollutants that fall over a neighbor, or the major powers' engagement in nuclear experiments that release radiation into the planet's wind currents.

According to the sociobiologist, then, aggression is a fundamental, adaptive characteristic of nearly all living things (Barash, 1982). In this view, human beings can be expected to be aggressive when crucial resources are limited, when experiencing pain or discomfort, where social systems are disrupted, and when strangers appear. All of these circumstances are potentially threatening to one's survival, and maintaining inclusive fitness demands that one acts aggressively to protect or advance one's interests. The issue is not whether we like to think of ourselves in these harsh functional terms, but whether the explanation fits. And there are data which are consistent with the overall account. From infancy onwards, we react warily to strangers, we fight over resources, and we get mad when things go wrong. All of the nasty events described at the beginning of the chapter could easily be interpreted as battles among internally aroused organisms over the possession of resources, such as the Lebanese uncle's cow or the question of who should run Sicily, Northern Ireland, and the remnants of Yugoslavia. The fact that there were almost 30 full-scale wars raging around the planet in 1995 alone speaks to the popularity of aggression as a means of problem-solving among humans.

Biological Factors and Aggression

There is other evidence of links between biology and aggression. The presence of certain hormones, especially the male hormone testosterone, is associated with aggression. Administering testosterone to young animals leads to an increase in their aggressive behavior, while castrating the animals (which reduces the natural production of testosterone) leads to a reduction in aggressiveness (Tieger, 1980). Similarly, adolescent boys prone to aggression and antisocial behavior have been found to have significantly higher levels of testosterone in their blood (Olweus, 1985; Susman et al., 1987). Olweus's interpretation is that the presence of the hormone stimulates the young male to the point of irritation, thus making him susceptible to impulsive and aggressive responses to provocations.

Temperament is also associated with aggressive behavior. Children who are identified as "difficult" babies tend to be rated high on aggression during the preschool and early school years (Bates et al., 1985; Prior, 1992). Hyperactivity is a reliable predictor of aggressiveness in children aged 8 to 11 (Farrington, 1994), and evidence from twin studies has been interpreted as demonstrating that hyperactivity is genetically transmitted (Goodman and Stevenson, 1989a, b).

Some Problems for Biological Accounts

Although ethological, sociobiological, and other biological theories have intuitive appeal and are consistent with some of the available evidence concerning aggression, there are none the less some problems for these approaches. Biological factors seem to contribute antecedent conditions rather than direct causes of aggression, and the relationship with actual behavior is by no means unidirectional.

First, the relationship between hormones and aggressive behavior is not as straightforward as might be expected. The association between hormones and behavior seems to act in both directions, so that behaving aggressively can heighten naturally produced hormones (Geen, 1990; Jacklin, 1989). The correlation is not always obtained: although Susman et al. (1987) found a relationship between hormonal levels and aggressiveness in boys, the same relationship did not obtain for girls — yet in this study the measured levels of aggressiveness did not differ significantly between the sexes. Second, although a child with a naturally difficult temperament may be at risk of developing aggressive tendencies, much depends upon how the immediate social context accommodates to his or her needs (McCord, 1994); difficult children with responsive parents are likely to fare more favorably than those with cold and rejecting parents (Thomas et al., 1968). Olweus (1993) reports that although temperamental factors were associated with the development of the aggressive reaction patterns characteristic of school bullies, they were less influential than aspects of parenting. Third, it is implausible that biological factors can account straightforwardly for one of the defining characteristics of aggression, namely intent to injure (Perry and Bussey, 1984), since intention depends upon appraisal of specific contexts and actions.

Perry and Bussey (1984, pp. 208–10) suggest that biological factors, such as hormonal levels, temperamental characteristics, and physical capacities, may increase the chances that certain children will adopt aggressive responses to frustrating or provoking circumstances, but that social contingencies influence what happens next. At least occasionally, children are likely to find aggressive responses productive, and they will be rewarded by getting what they want. This may lead them to re-use the successful behaviors, indeed even to seek out opportunities to do so.

Summary

Ethologists and sociobiologists see the primary causes of aggression as located in biology. They point to analogies between animal aggression and human aggression, pointing out that it typically occurs in situations where there is competition for resources. Although the uses of aggression may often be tied to adaptive purposes, it is difficult to disentangle biological influences from the social learning experiences and the situations in which aggression arises (Perry and Bussey, 1984). Some biological theorists do not dispute this point, and argue that learning mechanisms, cultural variations, and social strategies to control aggression are perfectly compatible with the proposition that there is a biologically given drive (cf. Eibl-Eibesfeldt, 1989).

The Frustration–Aggression Hypothesis

Dissatisfied with earlier biological theories, Dollard et al. (1939) proposed that aggression is caused not by instinct but by frustration: "the occurrence of aggressive behavior always presupposes the existence of frustration and . . . the existence of frustration always leads to some form of aggression" (p. 1). Frustration, Dollard et al. maintained, occurs when some ongoing, goal-directed activity is blocked. This hypothesis too has intuitive appeal, and it appears on first sight to offer an explanation that accounts for a wide range of manifestations of aggression, from infants' outrage at the indignities of being bathed, through toddlers' eruptions over toys taken away, to riots in the streets of Los Angeles, Bradford, or Johannesburg by people seething at the perceived injustices of their societies.

Dollard et al.'s work had considerable impact on early social and developmental psychologists studying aggression. As is often the case with all-embracing theories of complex social behaviors, it soon ran into problems. For example, everyday observation and research reveals that frustration does not always lead to aggression (Berkowitz, 1994). Individuals react to frustration in various ways, including crying, laughing, becoming depressed, avoiding the problem, trying harder – and, indeed, simply coping. Thus, childhood frustrations turn out not to be strong predictors of aggression (Sears et al., 1966), some preschool children suffering frustrations have been found to regress to less constructive behaviors, including giving up (Barker et al., 1941), and in several experimental studies children experiencing or observing frustrated efforts have been found to respond more energetically to the task in hand (Endsley, 1967). These kinds of objections led to an early modification of the hypothesis (Miller, 1941) to the effect that it was proposed that frustration *sometimes* causes aggression, although aggression was claimed to be the dominant response.

This weaker formulation does enjoy some support. Experimental studies with both children (e.g., Davitz, 1952; Mallick and McCandless, 1966; Otis and McCandless, 1955) and adults (e.g., Geen, 1968) confirm that aggressive responses can sometimes be increased or intensified following frustration. Even infants, if frustrated by having their limbs held to prevent movement, begin to display facial anger (Campos et al., 1983). Haskins (1985) found that children who had attended a cognitively oriented preschool program were more aggressive during their first year at school than their peers who had attended regular day-care centres; Haskins interpreted the findings as reflecting the frustration suffered by the cognitive-program group on finding themselves confronted with more able peers and less individual attention from their teachers.

Problems with the Frustration–Aggression Hypothesis

Some people behave aggressively in the absence of frustration, such as soldiers under orders or voracious property developers espying another part of the old city not already under their control. Further, people respond aggressively to attack, whether physical or verbal (Geen, 1990). While it is arguable that being attacked is likely to incur a form of frustration (i.e., a physical attack disrupts whatever one was doing prior to the assault, a verbal attack is a threat to the positive aspects of the self-image one might wish to maintain), Geen argues that a more plausible explanation of aggressive responses in such contexts is that they are prompted by negative affective arousal; the aversive nature of arousal may motivate aggression by energizing dominant responses.

Summary

The frustration–aggression hypothesis states that aggression (sometimes) occurs as an outcome of the frustration incurred when an individual's goals are blocked. There is little doubt that this is true of some instances of aggression, but there are many instances where the theory does not explain responses to frustration.

Social Learning Theory and Aggression

In contrast to theories which attempt to explain human aggression in biological or drive terms, social learning theorists offer what they regard as a more optimistic account (Bandura, 1973; Eron, 1994), with principal emphasis on the environmental causes – factors which could be modified. In Bandura's view, aggressive behaviors are learned, not innately given (1973, p. 61). To understand the origins of aggression, he argues, our focus should be on the predisposing conditions rather than predisposed individuals (p. 67). Moreover, aggression is "learned through essentially the same processes as those regulating the acquisition of any other form of behavior. People learn by observation and by direct experience." (p. 68).

A central proposition of all learning theories is that the consequences of an action are powerful determinants of whether that act is subsequently repeated or avoided. We saw above that early forms of aggression tend to be instrumental. In instances where a toddler achieves a successful outcome from an instrumental aggression – that is, where the child gets the toy she wanted – then the child is receiving positive reinforcement. Similarly, if a victim in the playground discovers that by counter-attacking he can repel the bully, he is obtaining a positive outcome. There is considerable evidence to confirm that young children learn from exactly these kinds of encounters, and are prone to increase their aggressiveness accordingly (Patterson and Cobb, 1973; Turner and Dodd, 1980). Perry et al. (1990) found that school-aged children were well aware of the tangible benefits of aggression.

However, while acknowledging the effects of reinforcement, Bandura (1973) proposes that a still more fundamental means of learning about aggression is through social transmission, particularly via modeling. Modeling has a number of consequences, including the acquisition of new patterns of behavior, the inhibition or disinhibition of previously learned behavior, and the social facilitation of behavior. We saw in chapter 1 that Bandura and Walters (1963) had argued persuasively that modeling is a more efficient means of social transmission than reinforcement or extinction of spontaneous behaviors. By observation, we can profit from the expertise that others have acquired rather than re-invent the wheel individually.

Importantly, mere exposure to modeled behaviors and their consequences is not held in itself to be sufficient to explain the instigation of aggressive acts by the observer. As also stressed in chapter 1, a key element of Bandura's theory is the proposal that the individual exercises control over his or her own behavior through self-regulatory mechanisms. In respect of aggression, he maintains that people enact or curb aggressive responses at least partly as a function of the associated feelings of self-satisfaction and self-worth. In addition, individuals assess their self-efficacy. For example, we may all know how Jean-Claude van Damme handles interpersonal discord, but some of us might pause before testing our observational learning of martial arts techniques and hurtling through the air to disable an aggressor twice our size.

According to Bandura, there are three major sources of aggressive behavior. These are the aggression modeled within the family, the subculture within which a person lives, and the mass media (1973, p. 93). There is evidence to support Bandura's claim that each of these is associated with aggressive behavior in some individuals. For the moment, we will consider research relating to the third factor, namely the symbolic modeling of violence in the media, since it is in this connection that most of the experimental evidence concerning the effects of aggressive models has been obtained. This topic provides an important example of the relevance of developmental social psychology to vital practical and policy issues in society.

Learning about Violence via the Mass Media

There is little doubt that the mass media, most notably television, do contain much violent imagery. Some disturbing associations are almost self-evident. For example, American TV presents high levels of violence (Comstock and Paik, 1991), and America has the highest homicide rate among Western nations (Huesmann and Miller, 1994). Could there be a causal connnection? Common sense dictates that there must be, and much research seems to support this conclusion.

In a series of studies reported in the early 1960s, Bandura and his colleagues tested the effects upon children's behavior of observing live and filmed models commit aggressive acts. For example, Bandura et al. (1963) placed nursery school children in a situation where they watched a model behave aggressively toward an inflatable toy doll (a Bobo doll). Some children watched a real live adult undertake the aggression, others watched a filmed adult, and others saw the model dressed up as a cartoon cat. The reasoning was that the more remote the model from reality, the less likely it was that children would imitate. Two other conditions were included, one in which there was no model at all, and one in which the model behaved nonaggressively.

Children in all experimental conditions were mildly frustrated and then placed in a room with the Bobo doll and a few implements of aggression, identical to objects used by the models. Children in the no model and nonaggressive model conditions performed a certain amount of aggression, but children in the other conditions performed more. Importantly from Bandura's perspective, not only did the children aggress but they aggressed *in the same way* that they had observed the model to aggress. They picked the Bobo doll up and threw it in the air, they hit it with a hammer, kicked it, sat on it and so on – just as the model had done. Consistent with predictions, there was more direct imitation of the live model, followed by the filmed model, and then the cat. On the other hand, if all aggressive acts were taken into account (i.e., including actions that were not modeled) then the cartoon cat condition actually elicited the greatest number of aggressive responses, a finding which has led many to infer that cartoons are particularly bad for children (although, as mentioned, the stimulus was actually a person dressed up as a cartoon character).

The processes of observational learning are powerful, and these studies provided an influential stimulus to other researchers interested in the effects of aggressive models, especially in the media. Numerous replications and extensions of the early paradigms have been reported, usually confirming that children will imitate modeled behavior (see Bandura, 1973, and Comstock and Paik, 1991, for reviews). Bandura's essential claim that children can learn about aggressive behaviors by observing the actions of others is well supported.

Subsequently, other researchers employed different methodologies to test further the possible link between media exposure and aggressive behavior in the young. In an ambitious and pioneering correlational field study, Eron et al. (1972) followed the entire third-grade (age 9) population of a small semi-rural community in Hudson River Valley, New York, measuring each individual's television viewing habits and aggression. The same individuals were re-tested a decade later. This allowed the investigators to look at the relations among variables simultaneously (e.g., does amount of viewing at the age of 9 correlate with aggression at 9 years?) and longitudinally (e.g., does amount of viewing at the age of 9 correlate with aggression at the age of 19?). The findings indicated that preference for violent TV at the age of 9 was positively correlated with rated aggressiveness at age 19. Furthermore: "coupled with the lack of a relation between third grade aggression and a preference for violent television (at age 19), this significant correlation supports the hypothesis that *preferring to watch violent television is a cause of aggressive behavior*" (Eron et al., 1972, p. 257, emphasis added).

Another approach is that of the field experiment, in which captive audiences are exposed to different levels of television violence over a fixed period of time and then their social behavior is observed. One of the most careful field experiments is that of Leyens et al. (1975). These investigators exposed a literally captive audience of delinquent Belgian adolescents (living in a corrective institution) to a diet of either aggressive movies (including *Bonnie and Clyde*, *The Dirty Dozen*) or neutral movies (*Lily*, *La Belle Américaine*) every night for a week. Compared to pre-viewing baselines, the boys in the aggressive movie condition increased their physical aggression in the week following exposure, while the boys in the neutral condition showed very little aggression. Leyens et al. (1975) comment that "It seems as if the films evoked among the spectators the kind of aggression they had been exposed to" (p. 352).

There are many more studies available that have reached similar conclusions. A lot of psychologists believe that violence in the media does cause or evoke violence in the young audience. If you have the time, check out other textbooks in social or developmental psychology for their accounts of the relationship between the media and aggression. Most likely, you will find a statement to the effect that television violence causes aggression, or that, although the matter has not been established conclusively, most psychologists interpret the available evidence as pointing strongly to a causal link. You might consult another source of clear opinion on this matter: your daily newspaper. If it has anything in common with the British press analyzed by Cumberbatch (1991) it will probably offer you regular articles on the topic of TV violence, and around 83 percent of these will confirm that it is a major social problem. *USA Today* (October 22, 1993) typified these recurrent concerns in an article headed "Taking aim at TV violence", highlighting the warnings of the US Attorney General, Janet Reno, who avowed: "I want to challenge television to substantially reduce its violent programming now or else the government will have to intervene." The article cited statistics allegedly provided by the American Psychological Association that the average child watches up to 8,000 TV murders and 100,000 other acts of violence by the end of grade school. Not surprisingly, the judge in the Bulger case in Britain (in which two 10-year-old boys were found guilty of the brutal murder of a 2-year-old) commented: "I suspect that exposure to violent video films may, in part, be an explanation" (Mr Justice Morland, quoted in the *Sunday Times*, November 28, 1993).

Psychological consensus, common sense, and legal authorities point, then, to the harmful effects of viewing media violence. Important policy issues seem to follow; government intervention in the media is not a step taken lightly in a democratic society, as Reno's ominous "make my day" warning to the television industry illustrates. But how persuasive is the evidence?

Does Violence in the Media Cause Aggression in the Viewer?

It would require at least chapter length discussion to evaluate all of the arguments about the effects of TV violence and a hefty book to describe the thousands of studies that have addressed the topic. Hence, the following is necessarily an abbreviated overview of some of the central issues.

While most psychologists accept that observational learning of many phenomena, including aggression, can be induced in children in certain circumstances, there is disagreement over the implications of this finding for actual behavior outside the laboratory. Clearly, the Bobo doll experiments have strong demand characteristics (Orne, 1962; Manstead and Semin, 1996). Where else in life does a 5-year-old find a powerful adult actually showing you how to knock hell out of a dummy and then giving you the opportunity to try it out yourself? In the experimental procedure, the *model* frequently articulated aggressive ideas ("sock him in the nose," "kick him," "pow!"), and in some versions of these studies the target doll has the invitation "Hit me" in large letters across his tummy. (Of course, viewers of *Sesame Street* have higher literacy skills and so, trapped by their own competencies, they hit him.) Furthermore, the Bobo doll has a great virtue over other targets of aggression: he does not hit back. Nor does the Bobo doll suffer pain. He just keeps bouncing up for more fun. In short, while the internal validity of experimental studies of observational learning of "aggression" is often good, the external validity is highly suspect.

Another problem with much of the social learning research into the effects of media violence is apparent from the faces of the children in Bandura et al.'s study. Blurton Jones (1972, p. 123) comments that although Bandura and colleagues do not distinguish between playfighting and genuine aggression, illustrations in Bandura et al. (1963) make it clear that the children were enjoying themselves (often, they were smiling), and other measures such as "gun play" make it clear that R & T accounted for at least part of the dependent measures in this classic experiment. If, as we considered above, R & T is not really aggression at all, but a virtually universal form of robust interaction that may have some positive payoffs for social skills development, then the fact that TV "violence" (such as a woman dressed up as a cat hitting an inanimate doll) elicits slightly more of it may not be as disturbing as we first thought.

Similarly, there are problems with correlational findings. Studies that report associations between amount of viewing and amount of aggression are open to the challenge that the relationship could be explained in the reverse direction (maybe aggressive people elect to watch aggressive media) or as a function of some third factor (perhaps neglectful parents allow both excessive TV viewing and high levels of aggression). Eron et al.'s (1972) study aimed to go beyond these criticisms by testing associations longitudinally, and as we saw above did present evidence that seemed to support the "TV causes aggression" claim. However, there are serious problems with the measures employed in the study. First, information on the children's viewing preferences was obtained by asking their parents to nominate the child's three favorite programs. Unfortunately, this is a very indirect measure of exposure to aggressive content and it runs the risk that parents' reports of their child's preferences could be mediated by their own influence over viewing choice. Second, the classification of the programs is open to criticism. For example, *Bugs Bunny*, *Wells Fargo*, and *M-Squad* were all grouped in the same "violent" category (while *Donald Duck*, *Bonanza*, and *Dennis the Menace* fell into "nonviolent"). Third, the measure of peer-rated aggressiveness is weak (Noble, 1975). Children were asked to nominate peers who met the following criteria: does not obey the teacher, starts a fight over nothing, gets very mad at a bully, will always fight back if someone hits him first, is rude to the teacher, takes other boys' things without asking, gives dirty looks and sticks his tongue out at other boys, swears when another boy annoys him. It is arguable whether some of these are really aggression; we thought tongue protrusion was quite cute when we found babies doing it in chapter 8. Another problem with the study was the high attrition rate – over 55 percent of the sample disappeared between the first two phases – meaning that we cannot tell whether the minority that remained accessible was representative. More generally, it has to be noted that where correlations have been found between amount of viewing and amount of aggression, they have typically been quite weak (usually around 0.1, though up to 0.31 in the Eron study), indicating that at most only a small proportion of the variance in human aggressiveness is associated with (but again, not necessarily caused by) viewing violent TV content (Freedman, 1984; Parke and Slaby, 1983).

Leyens et al. (1975) concluded on the basis of their findings that the violent movies' content evoked similar behavior in their incarcerated subjects. However, this is a generous analogy, since in *Bonnie and Clyde* and *The Dirty Dozen* the aggression is heavily dependent upon the use of machine guns, grenades and other weaponry, and a lot of people die. These instruments and outcomes were not found in the boys' dormitories. What was reported was an increase in a range of measures such as physical threat (defined as attack without physical contact), physical attack (physical contact of sufficient intensity to potentially inflict pain upon the victim), verbal aggression, yelling, self-aggression verbal (making statements such as "Boy, am I crazy"), and several others. Out of context, it is difficult to interpret the meanings of the specified behaviors, and some seem decidedly close to R & T play (as acknowledged by Leyens et al., 1975, p. 359), just as one would expect to find among a group of male early adolescents. Threats are often issued among groups of peers of all ages; the researchers did not differentiate serious from jocular threats. Yelling and declaring that one is crazy could reflect serious pathology or simply adolescent boisterousness. A further problem is that the observers in the study appear not to have been blind to the condition they were scoring; obviously this may have made them especially sensitive to manifestations of aggression in one condition, and somewhat less so in the other.

Let us put the issue in perspective by recalling that children actually grow up in the real world, involved with real people in complex, meaningful, and emotionally driven relationships – as much other evidence in the field of developmental social psychology demonstrates. It could be that the real world plays a far greater role in the development and modification of aggression than do the mass media. Studies in South Africa and North America, for example, indicate that aggression is more likely among children growing up in aggressive communities (Lidell et al., 1994; Sinclair et al., 1994). Is it really plausible that Saddam Hussein's predilection for genocide is the long-term consequence of watching too much TV violence (probably imported American war films) during his impressionable years? Is it really plausible that the violence on the streets of America – a society which in recent decades has suffered the rapid breakdown of the family system, huge inequalities of wealth, endemic racism, unfettered access to guns, serious drug problems – is due to the adverse effects of too much exposure to *Bugs Bunny*, or even *Miami Vice*? (But which problem would you prefer to tackle if you were a senior American politician?) The behavior of the 10-year-old murderers in the Bulger case defies simplistic explanation, but the main evidence presented in court concerning the boys' media use was that one of them turned his head away whenever anything violent came up on television; rather more substantial evidence was provided that both boys had long-term histories of maladaptive social behavior and that they came from discordant family backgrounds. Unfortunately, a discordant family background "is not so easily turned off as a television set" (Cummings et al., 1985, p. 506).

Of course, nobody has proposed that TV violence is responsible for *all* aggression; the issue is how much? On the basis of the findings available so far, it is difficult to conclude that it can be very much. Huesmann and Miller (1994) acknowledge that we can dismiss the naive idea that "the current level of interpersonal violence in the United States and other Western nations is solely due to or even primarily due to the long-term exposure of our youth to scenes of violence in the dramatic media" (p. 155). In fact, when adolescents' television involvement is entered as a factor in multivariate studies of the correlates of antisocial and problematic behavior, there is evidence of an unexpected relationship: the *greater* the involvement with the medium, the *lower* the engagement in and approval of deviant or unconventional behavior (Jessor and Jessor, 1977).

The above critique is based on only a fraction of the available studies, and many relevant issues have not been discussed here (Bandura, 1973, provides well-argued replies to some of the objections raised above). The fact that some research has flaws or is open to alternative interpretations does not in itself disconfirm the hypothesis it was testing. Many psychologists – indeed a majority – have reached a quite different conclusion about this topic. Some get quite aggressive about it. Many believe, in their heart-of-hearts, that no matter what quibbles one might have about individual studies, there *must* be an adverse effect due to watching violent TV content. The main point for the moment is that the topic is contentious, and that widely cited "proof" of the effects of media violence is at least open to criticism – a point which is overlooked in many orthodox psychology treatments of the topic, most press coverage and many politicians' throwaway cures for society's ills. I urge the interested reader not to accept, compliantly, the skeptical account summarized here, but to rush to the library, dig out the relevant journals and read critically the best studies you can find until you come across one that does not suffer from demand characteristics, implausible analogies to real-life violence, confounding variables, weak to negligible effects or the possibility of alternative explanations. (At this point, it will be very late at night, you will be tired and frustrated so, please, as you venture into the darkness, thinking "I'll show that crazy textbook writer a thing or two about TV aggression," do beware of all the non-TV-viewing delinquents who are prowling the streets.)

Back to social learning theory

Where does all of this leave social learning theory as an account of human aggression? In my opinion, the arguments above do not do a great deal of harm to the theory itself; they merely suggest that it is possible that one of the most publicized applications has proven to be something of a red herring. Social learning theorists *have* demonstrated that observational learning is one way in which children can learn about aggression. This does not demonstrate that observational learning from the media is a principal route into real aggression in real circumstances, but whatever the resolution of this controversy, it remains plausible that observation plays a role elsewhere – for example, in learning from real people such as one's parents or other members of one's cultural group. (Saddam's sons – the "cubs" – have a pretty mean reputation, too: one of us should contact their father and enquire what kind of home life they had as children, and what they viewed.) We will see later that there is certainly evidence of an association between aggression and social context, and it is possible that social learning theory may continue to make a contribution to understanding the learning processes involved.

Summary

Social learning theory has proven one of the most productive psychological perspectives on aggression. As with other behaviors, the social learning theorist sees aggression as the outcome of observational and reinforcement processes, mediated by information-processing and self-regulation. Many studies have demonstrated that children will, under certain circumstances, imitate the aggressive behavior of models, especially powerful and attractive models. One of the best known applications of social learning theory is to the investigation of the effects of exposure to TV violence. Arguments have been reviewed for and against the hypothesis that viewing TV violence causes aggression in the viewer. The reader has been encouraged to arrive at an independent conclusion.

Social Cognitive Developmental Perspectives on the Development of Aggression

We noted earlier that retaliatory aggression becomes more common among children past the toddler years. Hartup (1974) argues that these shifts in the character of aggressive behavior reflect cognitive developments. Children develop role-taking skills which enable them to infer others' intentions. Hence, if attacked, the child is now able to attribute deliberate purpose to the assailant, and responds in kind. For understandable reasons, aggression is a form of behavior that children appear to distinguish among the myriad activities of their social world quite early in life (Coie and Pennington, 1976; Younger et al., 1985). As the sociobiologist would remind us, there is considerable adaptive value in recognizing aggression and those who are most prone to it. However, even in the toddler period, children appear to be aware of subtle social rules governing when and against whom aggression is acceptable. Dunn (1988b) reports that among 18–20-month-olds, appeals to parents for help or comfort in the aftermath of aggressive exchanges with siblings were rarely made by the child who had initiated the aggression. Children appeared to be following the principle: "If my sibling hurts me, I can appeal for help and . . . I am likely to get it. But if I hurt my sibling, I am unlikely to get help" (p. 69).

Among preschoolers, still more complex assessments of aggression can be found. Contrary to Piagetian-based predictions that children below around the age of 7 years would fail to take intentionality into account when judging aggressive behavior, several studies have found that kindergarten-aged subjects – in common with older children and adults – do vary their judgments according to whether the assailant is motivated by considerations of personal gain or prosocial goals, or by justifiable or unjustifiable goals (Ferguson and Rule, 1988; Rule et al., 1974). Changes in this respect appear to be related to cognitive development. Children below around the age of 7 tend to be less sensitive to cues differentiating intentional from accidental provocations; they are likely to react equally aggressively to both, while older children are more aggressive in response to what they perceive as deliberate provocations (Shantz and Voydanoff, 1973).

In situations where aggression is a common mode of social action, then it may be rational and adaptive to respond aggressively. There is evidence that in such contexts individuals select and appraise particular courses of action according to moral cognitions. In an analysis of urban American adolescents' accounts of violence in their own lives, Ward (1988) shows that many young people evaluate and justify behaviors with reference to what is fair and equitable. For example, one subject told how she was bullied and verbally abused by a peer in front of her friends, leading eventually to her fighting back:

She pushes me and that was it, like if I had done something to her personally, I could see it. I could see her not liking me or something. But I hadn't done anything to her . . . I wasn't going to stand there. I felt I was in the right, because she was the one to initiate the fight, but when she did, I just happened to finish it. I think she was in the wrong and she knew it. She had to know that. (Ward, 1988, p. 186)

Ward reports that a substantial proportion of justifications were couched in terms of rectification: putting right a wrong incurred by others' actions. Her interviewees often accounted for a violent incident with reference to notions of "should/shouldn't," "ought to/not supposed to," "fair/unfair," and "hurt." This suggests a social cognitive dimension to aggression, placing these inferences and choices about responses in the context of the individual's system of moral values.

Social Information-processing

Other research indicates that social cognitive inferences are implicated extensively in children's responses to the acts of others. In one of the most productive applications of the information-processing perspective to social development, Dodge and his colleagues (Dodge, 1980, 1991; Dodge and Frame, 1983; Dodge et al., 1986) developed an experimental procedure wherein subjects viewed the video-taped activities of pairs of actor boys involved in play activities. In each case, one boy committed some behavior which resulted in a negative outcome for the other boy (such as knocking over his play materials or spilling paint on his artwork). In some instances, the behavior was hostile (the provocateur was portrayed as acting maliciously); in others, it was accidental; in still others, it had a prosocial motive (for example, the boy tries to help his peer win a painting competition by adding a few strokes to his work – only to discover later that this made the work ineligible); in a fourth condition, the reasons for the behavior were left ambiguous, and contradictory cues were available.

The vignettes were pre-tested to ensure high agreement among adult judges on the intentions being portrayed. However, the intentions were not so accessible to children. Dodge et al. (1984) found that 5-year-olds judged the actions correctly less than half of the time, and accuracy increased gradually through the elementary school years. They found also that aggressive boys were less accurate in interpreting the intentions of the actor, and were biased toward attributing hostility toward him. Using similar materials, Dodge and Somberg (1987) compared the interpretations of 8–10-year-old boys who were selected (on the basis of peer and teacher ratings) as either rejected–aggressive or adjusted–nonaggressive. These subjects were tested under conditions in which they were relaxed or under threat (the threat was manipulated by allowing them to "overhear" a boy confederate of the experimenter say that if he had to join the subject then he would get into a fight with him). In the relaxed trial, aggressive boys' attributions of hostility to the actors did not differ significantly from those of the nonaggressive boys. However, in the post-threat trials, the aggressive boys were much more likely to attribute hostile motives to the actors on screen, while the nonaggressive boys did not change their attributional tendencies.

Dodge and Somberg (1987) suggest that cognitive, affective, and physiological processes may each be implicated in boys' reactions to threat. In the cognitive realm, sensitivity to threatening stimuli might prime subsequent expectations: once an individual is perceived as dangerous, one tends to be wary of his future behavior and to "read" his every move as potentially hostile. In the affective realm, a basic consequence of threat is that it makes one feel uncomfortable; when uncomfortable, people may tend to make defensive attributions, because they are motivated to protect themselves. At the physiological level, one effect of arousal may be that it increases the availability of cognitions that are consistent with the arousal; when subject to some kind of interpersonal provocation, one is more likely to entertain hostile thoughts than to generate kind thoughts about the provocateur. In actual contexts of aggression and hostility, the authors argue, these various factors may act in concert to pre-empt more advanced logic and lead the child to resort to more basic and more impulsive response patterns.

Several studies have shown that aggressive boys are more prone to respond to provocations aggressively (Asarnow and Callan, 1985; French and Waas, 1987; Graham and Hudley, 1994; Waas, 1988). They tend also to be more likely than other children to perceive aggression as a useful strategy, an effective means of getting what one wants (Boldizar et al., 1989; Perry et al., 1986).

Summary

Social cognitive approaches to the study of aggression have come to the fore in recent years, pointing to the possibility that attributional biases may make some individuals more vulnerable to provocation and more inclined to conjecture aggressive responses as a means of dealing with conflicts. This work is theoretically exciting because it is striving to account for the links among cognition, affect, and action. Unlike the theories discussed above, the social cognitive approach in general has the attraction that it addresses developmental issues, investigating changes in the reasoning held to underlie some types of aggressive behavior. On the other hand, information-processing approaches tend to have less to say than other theories about the social contexts within which aggression occurs.

We turn now to some aspects of the contexts that seem to be reliably associated with individual differences, considering in turn, the family, peers, gender, and culture. It should be clear that the fact that aggression occurs in contexts is scarcely evidence for or against any particular theory, and it will be shown that the different theories we have discussed can each account for at least some aspects of the relationships discovered.

The Social Contexts of Aggression

The Family

One of the principal locations in which individuals learn about aggression is the family. Numerous studies have found associations between characteristics of the family, especially child-rearing style, and aggressive behavior in the young (Bandura, 1973; Loeber and Dishion, 1984; MacKinnon-Lewis et al., 1994; Montagner et al., 1984; Olweus, 1980; Patterson, 1980, 1982; Straus et al., 1980). The consensus emerging from this work is that parents who are cold, punishment-oriented, and rejecting tend to have children who exhibit higher than average levels of aggression. Of course, this relationship can be read the other way around: highly aggressive children tend to end up with disenchanted parents who have to turn on the pressure to keep them in line. In other words, the causal direction is difficult to determine and in fact we will see that the evidence points to bidirectional influences.

There are several ways in which parental behavior might affect children's propensity to aggress. One is via high levels of punishment. Notwithstanding the common-sense view endorsed in *The Authorised Childcare Handbook*, above, raising your hand to show you mean business increases the chances you will have to raise your hand again, still higher. Physical punishment of children is indeed widespread. In the US, for example, over 90 percent of parents acknowledge that they have spanked their children, and an overwhelming majority feels that it is sometimes justified (Flynn, 1994). For many children, punishment is frustrating, and violent punishment is likely to arouse strong emotional reactions; the child subjected to this kind of discipline may generate still greater aggressiveness (Weiss et al., 1992). Children who bully others at school tend to have more punitive parents (Olweus, 1993). The act of punishing violently provides a model of a particular means of resolving problems and conflicts (Bandura, 1973; Leach, 1993; Parke, 1977; Skinner, 1973; Walters and Grusec, 1977). Consider the experiences of these mothers, talking about their 1-year-olds:

> I smack her bum. She just turns around and gives you one back.

> I smack his legs ... But even when you smack him sometimes, he doesn't take any notice of you, he just does it again. And if you smack him he turns around and smacks you back. (Newson and Newson, 1963, p. 109)

Interestingly, patterns of punishment within a family (i.e., as meted out by mothers and older siblings) are positively correlated (Bryant, 1992), and when preschoolers are asked to comment on parent–child conflicts and advise on suitable forms of parental response they usually elect for disciplinary techniques similar to those they experience at home (Wolfe et al., 1982).

Cognitive dissonance and aggression in the home

Among slightly older children, there is also the possibility that being on the receiving end of punishment can arouse cognitive dissonance (Aronson, 1992), the state of tension occurring when a person holds two mutually contradictory cognitions. Aronson (1992) argues that when children are punished for aggressive behaviors they experience dissonance, wanting to commit the aggressive act but simultaneously struggling to suppress it. In order to reduce the dissonance, Aronson proposes, the child reasons, in effect, that "I would really like to hit my sister, but my mother will beat the pants off me if I do." In these circumstances, the aggressive behavior is held back temporarily until more favorable circumstances present themselves (e.g., when mum isn't looking). But the child's fundamental reasoning that aggression is a good way to deal with interpersonal discord is unaltered, it has simply been curtailed because of the external constraint. Consistent with this account, Aronson and Carlsmith (1963) found that with young children threats of mild punishments are more effective than threats of severe punishments. Aronson (1992) suggests that under mild punishment the child is less likely to generate an external justification for changes in behavior; instead, he or she might reason "Well, I don't really like to hit my sister" – internalizing a counter-aggressive value and discounting external factors.

Cognitive dissonance may lurk also in parents' judgments of the effects of environmental examples of aggression. Consider this: most studies find that about 70 percent of parents believe TV violence has a negative effect on their children by encouraging aggression (Wober and Gunter, 1988). It's a matter of common sense. Yet, as noted above, Flynn (1994) found that over 90 percent of parents believe that real life violence administered by themselves is justifiable and even constructive. That's a matter of common sense, too. But common sense has led us to an apparent paradox, that fictional violence is bad, while real-life violence is good. Perhaps attributional bias (chapter 10) is helpful here. If we assume that external influences (such as TV) are responsible for negative outcomes and self-directed actions (such as firm parenting) are responsible for positive outcomes, balance may be restored. Ask a few parents!

Aggression and domestic climate

The recurrence of violence in the home, whether or not the child is the target, is stressful to the child (Crockenberg, 1985; Cummings and Cummings, 1988; El-Sheikh and Cummings, 1992; Leach, 1993), and the resultant arousal can provoke aggressive responses (Cummings et al., 1981; Geen, 1990). Growing up in a conflict-ridden, aggressive domestic climate can establish an impression that this kind of behavior is normative (Straus et al., 1980). Some parents are more tolerant of aggressive behavior in their children, some directly encourage it ("go on, hit him back"), and there is evidence that this permissiveness is associated with greater amounts of aggression by the child (Sears et al., 1966).

Aggression in the home is not restricted to parent–child interactions. In Canadian (Abramovitch et al., 1982) and British (Dunn and Munn, 1986) studies, over

25 percent of interactions between preschool siblings were conflictual and antagonistic. Dunn (1991) observes that even quite young children are highly competent in discerning exactly what will annoy or upset their siblings, and this knowledge is exploited in the emotional forum of the family home. Most of the points raised above about the possible correlates and consequences of parental aggression (frustration, modeling, norm setting) hold for sibling influences, too. Dunn and Munn (1986) report that the frequency of aggressive behaviors in second born children whom they followed from 18 months to 36 months was correlated with the frequency of aggression observed in the children's older brother or sister 6 months earlier.

Bidirectionality in parent–child aggression

As we have seen in earlier chapters, the family is an interactive social unit, and participants' behaviors are interrelated. If your big sister keeps picking on you, you retaliate; but in so doing you confirm her perception that you are a troublesome little wretch, and that she will have to step up the discipline to keep you in line. Similarly, if a parent treats her or his child as a nuisance or a problem, the child may respond by antisocial behavior, and the negative aspects of the relationship may escalate (Patterson, 1980). As also seen in relation to several earlier topics, parenting behavior itself may develop in response to characteristics of the child. Disruptive children may provoke coercive responses (Lytton, 1990).

Patterson (1980) found that aggressive boys present their mothers with more than twice the rate of aversive behaviors of nonproblem boys. This means that the hour-by-hour stresses of parenting are considerably more demanding for the mother of an aggressive child, and that she may feel compelled to punish her son more frequently, a behavior to which such children are prone to react aversively. Patterson (1986) found also that American mothers' perceptions of their school-aged sons' behavior as aggressive and academically unsatisfactory correlated fairly strongly with measures of their rejection of the child. Eisenberg and Fabes (1994) found that mothers' punishment reactions were correlated with their ratings of the children's negative affect and lack of attentional control (with the latter factor especially relevant in boys).

Hence, the possibility arises that parent–child relationships which – for whatever reason – become problematical are likely to be associated with increased aggressiveness in the child, which in turn is likely to make the parent reject the child. Possibly, the mother feels that the unsatisfactory behavior of her child means that she has failed as a parent, an outcome which is unlikely to enhance the relationship. Patterson comments: "It is our impression that the point at which the parent labels the child as deviant is accompanied by an increase in aversive reactions and a commensurate decrease in supportive positions" (1986, p. 90). This shift in interpersonal perception leads to a further reduction in positive interactions but an increase in negative feelings. The genesis of antisocial and aggressive behavior may be located not simply in antecedent conditions but in interpersonal processes.

In sum, the family context is strongly associated with individual differences in aggressiveness. This relationship could be interpreted in terms of all of the theories we considered above. The sociobiologist could point to adaptive pressures, the frustration–aggression theorist could emphasize the stresses and impediments to action within the domestic setting, the social learning theorist would emphasize the role-modeling and reinforcement processes, and the social cognitivist would emphasize the joint construction of norms, attributions for behavior, and the scope for evaluating the efficacy of particular responses.

Peer Groups

Another important social context for the development of aggression is the peer group. It is clear that children make important discoveries about the effects of their own and others' aggressiveness through peer interactions. Ethological and other observational studies of preschool groups typically reveal that agonistic behavior is intimately connected to the establishment of social hierarchies and social rules among young children (Kolominskii and Zhiznevskii, 1992; Lauer, 1992; Montagner et al., 1984; Pettit et al., 1990; Promnitz, 1992; Strayer, 1992). Aggression is one means of resolving conflicts and asserting status, and it is a common feature of preschoolers' interactions. With development, children tend to constrain within-group aggressiveness, and it is less common among cohesive groups of peers (Pettit et al., 1990).

But what happens between groups? Recall the boys at Robber's Cave, whom we left in chapter 4, constructively setting up camp, proudly sharing their newfound social identities, and working eagerly toward joint goals (Sherif and Sherif, 1956). Well, I did mention that there were *two* groups.

At first, the groups (the Rattlers and the Eagles) were separated, and we saw in chapter 4 that they concentrated on organizing their collective duties, and in the course of these social structures began to emerge. After studying the formation of ingroup structures, the experimenters let each learn that there was another group in the park, and arranged a few competitive activities. A tournament was set up, and the experimenters tell us that "to a man" each of the boys expressed fervent commitment to the idea of establishing his group's superiority. The Sherifs had it in mind to introduce an element of frustration, already known from Dollard et al.'s (1939) work to be useful for inciting problems. However, such intervention proved unnecessary, because as soon as the groups got together the sparks started to fly.

A tug-of-war contest was held, and the Eagles were not at all pleased to find themselves defeated. To restore the balance, they thought it would be a good idea to burn the Rattlers' flag. When the Rattlers found the ashes of their emblem the next morning, they were hopping mad, and vowed to get their own back. Reciprocal conflagration ensued.

Then things really started to warm up. Raids were staged on each other's cabins, physical skirmishes broke out, "unfavorable invectives" were hurled between the groups, and finally the Rattlers looted a pair of their enemy's jeans and displayed them on a pole as "The Last of the Eagles." The experimenters meanwhile were busy measuring friendship preferences and intergroup stereotypes. The details are worth reading, but for present purposes it will suffice to say that the Eagles and the Rattlers did not like each other at all.

Just a few days earlier, most of these All-American boys had not even met each other, although they did have much in common in terms of social backgrounds, age, and interests. As far as we know, they were not psychopaths, just ordinary WASPs. It seems that intergroup rivalry can engender quite ferocious antipathies. (Incidentally, I am afraid that there was no TV in the park, and TV was still in its very early years in the US, falling far short of the levels of violence we take for granted in American popular entertainment these days.)

The Sherifs' subjects were just on holiday, but this imaginative field experiment illuminates processes that we can see regularly in other contexts. Some parts of Los Angeles and other large US cities are marked off, by graffiti and other boundary symbols, to indicate that only members of certain groups can enter; if outgroup representatives do stray in, they are dealt with very violently. Tajfel (1979) argues that the formation of intense intergroup rivalries and subsequent aggression reflects the operation of several social psychological processes, including the reduced salience of personal relations and individual characteristics in the group context, a within-group shift toward uniformity in behavior, the construction of shared perceptions of the outgroup, and social comparisons. Social norms about aggression may be generated by members of a group in the context of specific events. Mummendey (1996) illustrates this with reference to an incident in West Germany where young squatters faced police attempting to evict them. The police smashed into the house the youths were occupying and tried to drag them out of the building. The squatters responded by throwing stones at the police. Meanwhile, sympathizers outside set cars alight, tore up cobblestones and erected barricades. It is probable that none of the individuals would have engaged in these behaviors alone, but in the group context norms emerged to which participants tended to conform. Tajfel objects that ethologists rarely analyze social processes at this level, and thus ignore a crucial social psychological dimension of human aggression.

In short, another important aspect of the social context of aggression may be the peer group. Aggression may serve a function in organizing relative status within the group, although this appears also to be subject to developmental changes, and high levels of within-group aggression are not conducive to cohesion among older children and adolescents. Even among older individuals, however, high levels of aggression are instigated, sometimes rather easily, as a result of intergroup rivalries.

Gender Differences in Aggression

Most of the aggressive events noted at the beginning of this chapter appear to have been committed by males. It was the male members of the Lebanese family who resorted to Kalashnikovs to settle family discord, most of the serious street violence of the world's cities is committed by males, men lead their countries into war. There is little dispute that males take the lead in the commission of serious physical aggression (Bjorkqvist and Niemala, 1992; Maccoby and Jacklin, 1974; Parke and Slaby, 1983). A high proportion of inter-sex fighting among primary school children is initiated by boys teasing girls, and disrupting their play (Boulton, 1993). Boys are more likely than girls to be involved as bullies and victims (Olweus, 1993). For this reason, most of the theory and research into sex differences in aggression has been based on the assumption that aggression is, if not a male preserve, a predominantly masculine phenomenon. In fact, we will see shortly that there are grounds for rejecting the assumption of greater male aggressiveness as an oversimplification. First, let us consider possible explanations of gender differences in physical aggression.

Nature versus nurture

As you might by now expect, sex differences in aggression raise nature–nurture controversies. Some biologically oriented theorists and some feminists have argued that sex differences in aggression reflect innate characteristics; others argue that socialization and role constraints influence how aggression is manifest.

Ethologists maintain that sex differences in aggression are a clear example of the influence of *non*-environmental factors. They stress hormonal differences between the sexes, and emphasize evidence of different physiological responses to aggressive contexts between men and women. For example, Eibl-Eibesfeldt (1989) summarizes evidence that while both sexes respond to provocation with raised blood pressure, men's blood pressure decreases if they have the opportunity to retaliate, while women's remains heightened; the reverse happens if the only response option is conciliatory behavior. This suggests that men are predisposed to obtain release from their internal symptoms by aggressive means, while females prefer to talk things over.

Sociobiologists account for sex differences in aggression in terms similar to those encountered in chapter 5, namely parental investment theory. Barash (1982) maintains that the disparity between males and females in respect of parental investment means that males are selected for a high degree of direct male–male competition for access to females. If most males are preprogrammed to engage in as much reproductive activity as possible, the scope for conflict over the finite supply of female partners is considerable. Along these lines, Thornhill and Thornhill (1992) argue that rape may be a maladaptive side-effect of the generally adaptive male mating strategy which drives him toward persistent attempts at copulation. They point out that rapists are predominantly men who have less success in societally legitimized means of gaining access to females such as having status and money (most rapists are young and poor). Parental investment theory also predicts that there will be some conditions under which the female can be expected to behave aggressively, and these include threats to her inclusive fitness as represented in her young: "in fact, this explains the well-known nasty disposition of a sow with her cubs" (Barash, 1982, p. 349).

From the nurture side, Tieger (1980), in a detailed rebuttal of biologically based accounts of sex differences in aggressiveness, shows that most of the reliable differences in the literature concern adults, and that when the studies focused on children are examined carefully (in meta-analyses) the evidence of consistent sex differences among children below the age of 5 years is negligible. Tieger argues that sex differences are better explained as the outcome of socialization processes in which males are expected and encouraged to become more aggressive. In general, male children are allowed or encouraged to wander further from the home (Whiting and Edwards, 1988), to play with weapons (Goldstein, 1992), to engage in physical activities and sports, and to maintain a tough persona (Kimmel, 1987; Parke and Slaby, 1983).

Sex differences in peer activities

Everyday observation might lead us to be skeptical of Tieger's (1980) conclusion that there is little evidence of sex differences in early childhood aggression. One needs only to watch a group of preschoolers to see the propensity for physical aggression among little boys: they are usually tearing around the playground, pushing and shoving each other and engaging in robust activity of all sorts. Surely this demonstrates something fundamental about sex differences in orientation toward violent aggression?

Not necessarily. As we saw above, what is typically witnessed in the school yard is rough-and-tumble play, and there are good grounds for challenging the casual assumption that R & T is aggressive. The same point can be extended to boys' preferences for war toys (Goldstein, 1992). Goldstein points out that play with weapons is motivated by a variety of concerns, including sociability (after all, other boys are playing with them, too), mastery of the environment, physical coordination, fantasy, arousal, and imitating the behavior of adults. Importantly, when boys are interviewed about gun play, they are apt to distinguish between play and real fighting (Goldstein, 1992).

Seemingly aggressive play and ostensibly violent toys are likely to elicit reactions from adults who are concerned with what the children are learning. Since the principal caregivers of the young are females (see chapter 18), they are likely to interpret the play from a female perspective, which is generally hostile to physical aggression (Gilligan and Wiggins, 1988; Goldstein, 1992; Huesmann et al., 1992). What, then, do mothers and preschool staff do when they encounter boyish "aggression"? They try to stamp it out, wresting little play-scrappers apart, shaking them, scolding them, and propelling them to distant areas of the playground, thereby reminding children of the brute fact of life that adults are more powerful. A likely consequence is that the repressed activity goes "underground," becoming part of male peer culture that is protected from adult – especially adult female – interference. Oettingen (1985), for example, found in a study of German kindergarten children that when the teacher was around the boys engaged in no R & T, but when she was absent, things returned to normal.

In these ways, robust physical interaction may become integrated with sex role development, and this may have implications for the types of peer interaction and the modes of aggression that boys and girls experience. During the primary school years, children of both sexes tend to differentiate the appropriate target of their aggression, each focusing primarily upon same-sex peers (Cairns et al., 1989a; Fry, 1992). Moller et al. (1992) found among Canadian school boys that, by late childhood, peer popularity was associated with masculine play behavior; in such a context, when aggressive behavior occurs, it is likely to be associated with macho displays. The peer culture evolves collective standards against which aggressive behavior is evaluated. Similarly, Rauste von Wright (1989), in a study of Finnish 15–16-year-olds, found that among boys, there was a tendency to regard fighting as a mark of courage and strength, while among girls fighting was typically regarded as a very inappropriate form of behavior. For girls, social expectations may require that when hostile emotions arise they should be controlled or at least displayed more decorously. For example, Zahn-Waxler et al. (1994) found that 4-year-old girls' reactions to hypothetical social conflicts showed higher levels of anger than did boys'; however, the girls' anger responses were accompanied by lower levels of aggressiveness than boys', and by higher levels of prosocial reaction.

Where are *the sex differences in aggression?*

A closer look at research into sex differences reveals that, although the differences usually – but not always – indicate greater male aggression, the magnitude is not great (Hyde, 1984). There is considerable overlap, such that some females are more aggressive than some males, and there are many situations in which females are just as likely as males to react aggressively (Frodi et al., 1977). In a large study of American and Israeli children aged 18 months to 4 years, observed in 12 different day-care or kibbutzim settings, Lauer (1992) found that "variability is the rule." Ranking children on agonistic behavior revealed that boys on average held higher ranks than girls, but members of both sexes held high, medium, and low ranks and in four of the 12 groups, the average ranks of males and females were virtually identical.

Among older subjects, a critical variable may be the type of aggression that is examined. Bjorkkvist and Niemala (1992) argue that there is a sense in which focusing only on physical aggression may itself reflect the imposition of a masculine perspective on this field of enquiry. Bjorkkvist and Niemala (1992) raise a number of problems for this traditional assumption, including the questions: how do we compare male–male aggressive acts with female–female aggressive acts? Which causes greater distress, direct or indirect aggression? Is the motivation to hurt as important an indicator as the act itself? Which is worse: physical or psychological pain? These investigators recommend distinguishing among physical aggression (hitting, kicking, shoving, etc.), verbal aggression (yelling, calling names, threatening) and indirect aggression. Among prominent means of indirect aggression are gossiping or telling bad or false stories about someone, becoming friends with another peer as a means of revenge on a former friend, planning secretly to bother someone, saying to others "let's not be with him/her," telling someone's secrets to a third party, and so on (Bjorkvist et al., 1992). Who do you think does more of this kind of aggression?

Bjorkvist et al. (1992) report a series of studies with Finnish children and adolescents, aged 8, 11, 15, and 18 years. Based on peer estimates, males and females were compared on measures of the three types of aggression just outlined. Males were rated higher on physical aggression, and there were no reliable differences on verbal aggression. At all ages except 8 years, females scored significantly higher on the measures of indirect aggression (the 8-year-olds did not seem to have yet developed very many means of indirect aggression).

There are at least three plausible and complementary reasons why adolescent females should engage in more indirect aggression than males. First, males tend to be stronger and there are limits to how much of the social environment females can dominate by direct, physical aggression. Second, adolescent females' peer interactions are often organized around smaller and more intimate groupings, and indirect aggression may be particularly effective in these contexts (Bjorkqvist et al., 1992; Lagerspetz and Bjorkqvist, 1994). Interestingly, there is evidence from experimental studies that females may sometimes be more ready to behave aggressively when in groups and especially if they perceive threats to the norms of the group (Rabbie et al., 1992). Third, sex role stereotypes represent physical aggression and toughness as masculine attributes (chapter 5), and the display of such tendencies is likely to be decreasingly appealing to girls approaching womanhood because they are not "lady-like" (Tieger, 1980). In fact, Rauste von Wright (1989) found that verbal aggression among female adolescents was often focused on matters relating to femininity and appearance. One study of elderly adults found little evidence of sex differences in aggression, except that men tended to be rated as less aggressive than women when measured on a scale of female aggressive techniques (Turner, 1992).

Aggression in adult male–female relations

One of the most disturbing and perplexing expressions of aggressive behavior arises in the context of male–female relations, such as dating and domestic life. Take the following confession:

> And I flung a teakettle across the room. We had an apartment with one of those folding doors that was plastic. And I ripped it down. I mean this was physical, physical anger. The strength that I didn't know that I had just ripped it down because I was calling attention to the fact that I was so angry. And I left. I just left and that was it. I walked out of the marriage. There was never any thought of reconciliation. (interviewee in Campbell, 1993, p. 48)

In professional life, this violent individual was vice president of a major American bank – a very respectable high achiever with a strong sense of commitment, yet capable of volatile eruptions behind closed doors ("physical, physical anger") and of abrupt marital desertion. Fortunately, she did not physically harm her husband on this occasion.

Is she atypical? Perhaps the most surprising finding of several studies of domestic and date violence in the US and the UK is that men are more often the *recipients* of this kind of violence than the perpetrators (Archer and Ray, 1989; Arias et al., 1987; Cate et al., 1982; Deal and Wampler, 1986; Farrington, 1994). Of course, frequency should not be confused with severity. Certainly, women are more likely to be seriously hurt or intimidated by courtship or domestic violence than men (Unger and Crawford, 1992).

One explanation is that male violence is likely to have more serious consequences, and that men will therefore exert greater restraint (Archer and Ray, 1989; Arias et al., 1987). There are cultural constraints inhibiting male aggression against females (cf. Geen, 1990, pp. 136–7), at least in the courtship process. For example, Ohbuchi and

Izutsu (1984) demonstrated that men were more likely to retaliate aggressively against an unattractive woman than an attractive one; it could be that during courtship males' attraction to their partner is one factor which constrains aggressiveness.

How does aggression emerge in male–female relations? Part of the answer may rest in the characteristics and backgrounds of the offenders; for example, there is evidence that males who beat their partners have histories of experiencing parental disharmony, have been physically aggressive in their teens, and have histories of relationship difficulties (Farrington, 1994). Cultural factors, such as prevailing sexist attitudes and acceptance of violence against women, may also contribute (see Campbell, 1993; and Unger and Crawford, 1992). But while these factors may help explain predispositions toward aggression in some men, actual incidents of violence need to be understood in the context of the dynamics of the interpersonal relationships in which they occur.

In this respect, Campbell (1993) develops the interesting thesis that the meanings of aggression differ for males and females and that this itself can contribute to continuing tensions. She argues that males have learned to see aggression primarily as an instrumental force (serving to meet goals, including the dominance of others) while females see it as expressive (reflecting some emotional tension). These patterns would be consistent with the different gender-related patterns of aggression found during childhood and adolescence, discussed above. Campbell (1993) argues that when men encounter aggression in women, they tend to interpret it as a threat to their dominance which they meet in an instrumental way – by counter-attack; for some men at least, this escalates into physical attack. Campbell holds that when women encounter male aggression, they try fruitlessly to identify the expressive cause, and then turn to self-criticism and self-modification as a means of appeasement. Actual outbursts of physical violence by females may be related more to this internal frustration than deliberate intent to injure: notice that the teakettle missed, fists do not.

There is another factor that may be relevant to many instances of female violence in dating: namely, what the male was doing before she struck out. Much female violence in these contexts is enacted in self-defence against sexual abuse (Unger and Crawford, 1992). There are few instances of male victims of date rape. (We return to this topic in chapter 17).

In sum, although there are sex differences in physical aggressiveness, they may not be as strong or as pervasive as popular stereotypes (and a good deal of scientific theory) would have us believe. Explaining them proves more challenging than attributing behavior straightforwardly to biological differences or to sociocultural expectations that females must always be nonaggressive and deferent. Unfortunately, research into gender differences in aggression has been hampered until recently by simplistic assumptions that the phenomenon is peculiar to one sex. Aggression can be found in both males and females, though its manifestation and its severity depends on the actor's perception of effectiveness in particular contexts, on peer group norms, and on interpersonal power relations.

Cross-cultural Differences in Aggression

Most societies and communities experience conflicts, but there is a very wide range of variation in the ways these are manifest and resolved (Bandura, 1973; Bolton, 1973; Cook, 1992; Fry, 1988, 1992; Montagu, 1974; Robarchek and Robarchek, 1992; Rosenfield and Stephan, 1981; Ross, 1992; Whiting and Edwards, 1988; Whiting and Whiting, 1975). The Robarcheks (1992) describe the lifestyle of the Waorani, a people of the Ecuadorian Amazon who, with a homicide rate of 60 percent, appear to be the most warlike society ever studied. (Studying them involves some risks.) These people are so ferocious that they will attack adjoining groups even when heavily outnumbered. They are so hostile that if one of them takes ill they attribute the inconvenience to witchcraft on the part of the neighbors, and deal with that by rushing the putative sorcerer's house at night, killing as many of the occupants as possible. The only positive aspect of the Waorani's traditional way of life seems to be that they enjoy a low population density in the large territory of the Amazon basin.

Although Western nations seem to have contributed more than their fair share to humanity's history of violent discord, even among these there are considerable variations. Ross (1992) compares Northern Ireland and Norway, two European societies with radically different ways of dealing with internal conflicts. In Northern Ireland, some 3,000 people have died in the past 20 years as a direct result of the Troubles, and extensive damage has been done to property. Norway records relatively low homicide, suicide and violence rates. In Ross's view, the contrast between these societies is only partly explained by historical factors, and he attributes greater weight to patterns of male socialization, to differences in class structures and ideologies, and to cultural differences in attitudes toward violence. Tajfel (1979; see above) would no doubt point out that Norway lacks the intergroup structures found in Northern Ireland. Clearly, there are culturally linked differences in the use of aggression even among societies that have many other characteristics in common.

Culture and sex differences

Inter-cultural variations in aggression also provide another perspective on the issue of sex differences. There are some, though not many, communities with high levels of female physical aggression. Cook (1992) provides a colorful account of the women of Margarita, an island off the coast of Venezuela, who engage in ferocious physical fighting with other women and occasionally with men:

> If a man bothers me, I slap him in the face or I hit him over the head with a bottle. Once my women friends and I threw a guy on the ground because he was being disrespectful. (p. 153)

> My husband is a fisherman. He is very strong . . . If he ever disrespected me, I would wait until he slept and throw boiling oil on him. (p. 154)

If you really want to hurt another woman, you punch her in the breast. If you want to hurt a man, you strike him in the testicles. But with a woman, you hit her in the breast because it really hurts. (p. 156).

Yet for all their exceptional prowess in this domain, the women of Margarita occupy traditional status in other respects, with relatively little formal power and continuously subject to male transience. The men practice polygyny if they wish and often leave their partners or the community altogether, so that females end up with responsibility for child care. Female Margaretino society is tough because women are left to deal with family survival in a harsh environment, and the women adjust by behaving aggressively. In other words, an adequate explanation of the females' exceptional physical aggression needs to take into account the ecological system in which it occurs.

Similar conclusions emerge from studies of the children of the Kaulong of Papua New Guinea, who are encouraged to adopt certain gender-differentiated practices in their early play, whereby boys may play roughly with other boys, but not with girls. However, girls are allowed to play rough with boys and are encouraged to act aggressively toward them. Toddler girls may strike blows with sticks. Boys are prohibited from returning a girl's attack, and so their only option is to run for it. The girls are encouraged to keep up the attack by chasing the fleeing victim (Goodale, 1980).

To Western eyes, this may appear to be the precursor to chivalry and chauvinism, whereby males' implicit power over females is qualified by social restraints upon how the superior status may be used. But this is not the preparatory function of such behavior among the Kaulongese. Instead, children in this culture appear to be rehearsing elements of a quite different approach to female–male relations. Goodale explains that male-initiation of courtship is considered an act of rape, for which the aggressor is punished by death (or marriage). Women have almost complete choice in the selection of their spouse and once they have made their choice they enlist their brothers and male cousins to assist in the persuasion of the often reluctant husband-to-be: "The groom may be forcibly restrained in the same house with the bride who has chosen him for as long as it may take him to accept his fate and pay off the guards with shells so they can leave" (Goodale, 1980, p. 135). Thus, sex differences are encouraged in the aggressive behavior of Kaulong children, and the sex differences (with reciprocal aggression fostered among male peers) are similar to those found in many other cultures. On first sight, they look like universals, but their meaning corresponds to somewhat distinctive patterns of adult power relations in their society.

Cultural differences and theories of aggression

How can we explain these variations among societies in terms of the major theories we have been considering? Before concluding that cross-cultural variations in patterns of aggressiveness put paid to any nature theories of this human characteristic, it should be noted that the kinds of findings just noted are quite compatible with some expositions of sociobiological theory. For example, Eibl-Eibesfeldt (1989) and

MacDonald (1988b) argue that fitness in human societies requires a complex interaction of biologically influenced mechanisms and adaptation to specific economic and social controls. In some circumstances (such as social groups characterized by relatively low levels of genetic relatedness and high sexual competitiveness) it would be adaptive to socialize children for aggressiveness; in others (such as the advantaged members of industrialized societies during periods of economic progress) it would be optimal to develop close, affectional, and child-centered family ties within which to promote the instrumental competence of the young and underpin their upward mobility. So, ethological/sociobiological and social learning theory explanations are not necessarily incompatible. In fact, as we look more closely at different societies we also find evidence that is compatible with frustration–aggression theory and with social cognitive approaches.

Certainly, there is strong evidence that the adults of different communities prepare their children for the local conditions (Cook, 1992; Fry, 1992; Kornadt, 1990; Triandis, 1994). For example, Kornadt (1990) examined the relationship between adolescent aggressiveness and maternal style. He administered an Aggression Thematic Apperception Test to adolescents from five cultures: Germany, Switzerland, Japan, Bali, and Batak. Subjects were required to give their immediate responses to a series of potential provocations and stresses. Kornadt reports substantial differences between Western and Eastern subjects, with German and Swiss children scoring over twice the levels of aggression of their Japanese, Balinese, and Batak agemates.

When mothers from these cultures were probed about their reactions to child misbehavior, there was an equally clear pattern of results. Mothers in the less aggressive societies were prone to respond by exonerating the child, or gradually conceding to the child; mothers in the Western cultures were more easily frustrated and became angry, setting the scene for escalating conflict (Kornadt, 1990, p. 163). This would suggest that cultural practices encourage particular modes of reasoning about conflicts, and that some of these interpersonal styles are prone to incur frustration. The Western children also scored higher than the Eastern children on measures of the inhibition of aggression, indicating that not only were aggressive responses more common in the former but also that they attempted, at least sometimes, to repress them.

Internecine strife tends to be self-perpetuating. Once a community is into serious aggression its members are likely to develop correspondingly aggressive outlooks and behavior to ensure their own survival. In other words, social cognition comes back into the picture. Kornadt (1984) suggests the possibility that different attributional biases are engendered in different cultural contexts. This returns us to the definition of aggression, and reminds us that inferring intention is based on culturally relevant knowledge and social psychological processes.

Summary

Variations in aggressiveness can be found associated with family context, peer group processes, gender roles, and different cultures. Some communities engage in aggression even to the extent that their population size is threatened; some communities reveal higher levels of physical aggression among females than is typically found in Western research. Interesting as this variability is, it does not provide a straightforward basis for deciding among the explanatory strengths of the different theories we have been considering. To be sure, it is compatible with relativistic perspectives, such as social learning theory, but some current ethological and sociobiological theories acknowledge ecological adaptations, and cognitive and social cognitive theorists can point to underlying interpretive processes that may be implicated in quite diverse manifestations of aggressive behavior. As we examine aggression in its social contexts, it becomes clearer that it is a multidetermined behavior, enacted in different ways in different places for different reasons.

Conclusions

We have considered just some of the major theoretical approaches to aggression and some of the social contexts in which it is elicited. Each theory has something to offer, but none has yet provided a completely satisfactory account of the development and functions of this almost universal human social characteristic. This may well be because there are many forms of aggression, many circumstances in which it occurs, and many stimuli which can instigate it. But at least this survey of perspectives and evidence enables us to return to the perspective with which we began the chapter, and to reflect on the extent to which common sense withstands scientific enquiry.

It is, as Ian McEwan's sources reveal, common sense that a swift clip around the ear will teach a child a lesson. But the lesson seems to be to hit back. Common sense has a good many other pronouncements to offer about aggression, including the fact that males are invariably more aggressive than females, and that television causes violence. Scientific analysis does not always yield evidence to support these widely shared beliefs. Often, the evidence which is available can be interpreted comfortably by more than one theory. The theoretical debate is important because it is directed toward uncovering the reasons underlying one of human beings' most dangerous capacities. The complexity of the debate may at least make us wary of settling for common-sense explanations.

Further reading

Bandura, A. (1973) *Aggression: a social learning analysis.* Englewood Cliffs, NJ: Prentice Hall.

The classic statement of the social learning approach to aggression, written in a vigorous, polemical style.

Bjorkqvist, K. and Niemala, P. (eds) (1992) *Of Mice and Women: aspects of female aggression.* San Diego: Academic Press.

An excellent collection of discussions of sex differences in aggression in humans and other species, drawing on psychological, biological, anthropological, and other evidence .

Comstock, G. and Paik, H. J. (1991) *Television and the American Child*. San Diego: Academic Press.

A careful and detailed review of research into the effects of TV violence, reaching the conclusion that it can cause aggression in the (American) child.

Cumberbatch, G. and Howitt, D. (1989) *A Measure of Uncertainty: the effects of the mass media*. London: Libbey.

A careful and detailed review of research into the effects of TV violence, challenging the conclusion that it is a cause of aggression.

van der Dennen, J. and Falger, V. (eds) (1990) *Sociobiology and Conflict: evolutionary perspectives on competition, cooperation, violence and warfare*. London: Chapman and Hall.

Useful discussions of recent developments in sociobiological theory and its applications to the study of aggression in animals and humans. Readers interested in the politics of academic debate will find the final chapter on reactions to sociobiology stimulating.

Geen, R. G. (1990) *Human Aggression*. Milton Keynes: Open University Press.

A thorough review of theories and research in aggression, emphasizing the intrapersonal contexts within which aggression occurs, and including a useful discussion of the relationship between health and aggression.

Pepler, D. J. and Rubin, K. H. (eds) (1991) *The Development and Treatment of Childhood Aggression*. Hillsdale, NJ: Erlbaum.

While much theory and research has been focused on the origins and development of aggression, a crucial related question concerns the issue of whether it is viable to intervene and modify such behavior. Contributors to this volume review recent progress in treatment and its theoretical implications.

Chapter 13

The Development of Prosocial Behavior

Those who find it naturally hard to wield authority over their children should seriously consider the systematic use of treats and rewards. The promise of chocolate in return for, say, good bedtime behaviour is, on balance, worth the minor damage to teeth which will in any case soon replace themselves. In the past, too much has been demanded of parents who have been exhorted to inculcate altruism in their children at all costs. Incentives, after all, form the basis of our economic structure and necessarily shape our morality; there is no reason on earth why a well-behaved child should not have an ulterior motive.

(*from* The Authorised Childcare Handbook, *in* McEwan, The Child in Time, *1987*)

In mid-1992, as the people of Bosnia were being slaughtered and purged from their homeland, a British TV reporter covering the war enacted a brave deed of interpersonal kindness. ITN's Michael Nicholson smuggled an 8-year-old orphan out of the country, forging her name in his passport in order to pass her off as his daughter. Clearly, there was some risk to Nicholson, in that he could have been arrested by authorities who were hardly likely to be generous toward a foreign journalist in these circumstances, and in that he faced problems back in the UK, where the immigration office considered prosecuting him for importing an alien. Why take so much trouble for a stranger?

Back in the 1970s, a talented young Polish surgeon earning in his home country the equivalent of $40 a month was offered a position in an American hospital on a six-figure salary. In addition to the money and an affluent lifestyle, such a job offered professional prestige, superior resources, opportunities to work with talented and highly skilled colleagues. Yet the doctor, Zbigniew Religa, chose to stay at home, and spent the next couple of decades establishing and sustaining a very busy clinic. He wanted to help his fellow Poles. Why not help a few Americans and accumulate a lot of hard currency into the bargain?

All over the world, people can be found helping others in small to large ways. People donate to charities, assist a neighbor, promote the interests of a friend or protégé, visit a sick relative, give coins to a beggar on the street, hold the door open for an elderly person and so on. We tend to regard helping others as manifestations of civilized social behavior, as components of the moral fabric of our societies (Rest, 1983). Yet in a fundamental respect, helping others appears to differ from many of our other social behaviors in that it does not seem to serve our *own* interests. In this chapter, we consider possible explanations for prosocial behavior, and examine its development.

Intuitively, it appears easier to account for aggression than it is to account for prosocial behavior (Batson, 1991, p. vii). Aggression serves the interests of the person we hold dearest: the self. Looking after the self seems to be a primary feature of human motivation, reflected pervasively in the many things we do to acquire resources, status, opportunities, and return for effort. Batson points out that the assumption of "universal egoism" (i.e., the idea that, for each of us, the incentive underlying our actions is self-benefit) is embedded in all of the dominant theoretical traditions of at least Western philosophy, economics, and psychology, from Aristotle, through Adam Smith and Karl Marx to Sigmund Freud. *The Authorised Childcare Handbook* (McEwan, 1987 above) elucidates the sentiments of a whole culture based on the idea. It is paramount across psychology, where the belief that organisms are prone to repeat behaviors which they have found elicit positive rewards is well entrenched (Krebs, 1987; Skinner, 1973). But why do things for *others*? The fact that prosocial behavior seems to fly in the face of self-interest has traditionally posed a serious problem for philosophers and psychologists interested in the factors that motivate human behavior. It certainly perplexed Darwin (1859), who feared that the theory of natural selection could be undermined by this curious inclination of some creatures to help others.

We will consider theoretical responses to this challenge below. First, it should be mentioned that prosocial behavior is a phenomenon of interest to both social psychologists and developmental psychologists, and has attracted a great deal of attention in each field. In large part, these research efforts have proceeded independently. Social psychologists have tended to focus on the situational factors and normative expectations which appear to influence helping behavior, while developmentalists have concentrated on changes, investigating age-related variations in the frequencies of particular helping responses and in the understanding of others' needs and of appropriate interventions. Brown and Herrnstein (1975) pointed out some time ago that the persistent mutual lack of interest of the two subdisciplines working on the same broad topic has led not only to failures to exploit others' insights, but even to an ironic paradox in the conclusions emerging. The paradox is that while developmentalists see their subjects as becoming increasingly sophisticated prosocial beings over time, social psychologists tend to regard their subjects as capable of great variation in prosocial responses as a function of situational influences – influences which may in some circumstances lead to decidedly unhelpful responses from supposedly mature people. The irony is that the same subjects – college students – serve often as the pinnacle of the developmentalist's scale and as the focus of the social psychologist's experimental manipulations.

So far, two paradoxes, but there are more to come. Prosocial behavior is a curious phenomenon with many uncharted aspects. Nevertheless, in recent years, it has become the focus of increasingly active and fruitful research endeavors, which will be introduced here. We consider first the matter of definition. Next, a brief overview of the developmental course of prosocial behavior is presented, showing essentially that it tends to increase in frequency during childhood and may vary during later parts of the lifespan. We turn then to theoretical perspectives on altruism and prosocial behavior, including sociobiological, social learning and social cognitive approaches. As elsewhere, there are differences in emphasis among these theories and some disagreements, but it will become clear that at least some of the discrepancies reflect differences in levels of analysis rather than diametrically opposed accounts of the same phenomena. With the different theories in mind, we consider aspects of the social contexts of prosocial behavior, addressing issues relating to family socialization practices, gender, situational influences, and cross-cultural variability.

Defining and finding prosocial behavior

Defining prosocial behavior and the related concept of altruism poses similar difficulties to those we found with the definition of aggression. Merely to identify overt behavior does not appear to be completely adequate: we want also to know about the underlying intentions of the actor. Discovering the underlying intentions is difficult, partly because we are not always accurate in inferring the causes of even our own behavior (Fiske and Taylor, 1991; Gelfand and Hartmann, 1980; Nisbett and Wilson, 1977), and partly because people tend to present themselves in socially desirable ways.

In many instances, various possible intentions could be attributed to individuals behaving prosocially. One way of explaining interpersonal generosity without abandoning the otherwise widely applicable motive of self-interest is to propose that the consequences of the behavior actually are rewarding to the person performing the prosocial act. In Nicholson's case, for example, one could impute cynical and self-interested motives: people in the media tend to relish publicity, and some journalists will do anything for a good story. This does not seem a very plausible explanation in this instance (for reasons to which we will return), but there are certainly occasions when we do behave helpfully toward others for motives connected to self-interest.

Suppose, for example, you help another student to collect materials for an essay. On the face of it, generous behavior, but beneath your benevolent exterior you might find it gratifying that the recipient now regards you favorably. Dr Religa states firmly that his motives for staying in Poland were that "In America I would have been one of many, many doctors and my presence wasn't necessary. Here I felt needed" (quoted in Nagorski and Wiecko, 1993). Or suppose you are a socially concerned rock megastar, and you volunteer to perform for no fee at a concert intended to collect funds to save a rainforest on the other side of the planet. Are you really indifferent to the happy side-effect that the event (and your impeccable Greenness) will be televised worldwide to an anticipated audience of two billion, days before your latest CD is released (which, as it happens, is printed on mechanically flattened globs of oil, and prettily packaged in half a South American country's worth of paper and cellophane wrapping)? Even private generosity (you send an anonymous donation to a charity) can be attributed to self-interest, since the reward could be the smug glow of self-congratulation upon recognizing that you are kinder than everyone else, or the prospects for a briefer stay in Purgatory, or the alleviation of some of the guilt you feel because you eat three meals a day while others are starving. There is evidence from experimental studies of adults that people are more likely to act prosocially when they believe that doing so will lead to a relief of their *own* discomfort at the victim's plight (Cialdini et al., 1987).

On the other hand, this miserable self-interest interpretation does not always feel credible. Indeed, experimental studies of adults show that empathetic individuals will help victims even when they have been assured that they will receive a pleasant, mood-enhancing experience *regardless of whether they help or not* (Batson, 1991). Place yourself in Nicholson's position, face to face with the distraught, parentless children trapped in the midst of a truly horrendous situation where their lives could easily be lost at any moment. Wouldn't you want to *do something*? Wouldn't there be some powerful internal feeling telling you that you had to help? Note that Nicholson would in any case have experienced the mood-enhancing experiences of (a) flying out of Bosnia and (b) having important stories to broadcast when he got home, regardless of what he did about the orphan.

Nicholson's actions appear distinct from those of European political leaders who, a year later, made a great show of transporting a couple of dozen photogenically injured children from the same war zones to hospitals in other countries. The recipients of this aid were obviously in need but represented only a minute proportion of the casualties. Many critics interpreted the children's salvation as political tokenism, using the discounting principle (see chapter 9) to contrast the highly publicized helpfulness of the politicians with their modest actions on diplomatic and strategic levels.

It seems plausible that kindness toward others may sometimes be motivated by selfless concern for others and sometimes by self-interest. For this reason, it has been proposed (e.g., Staub, 1978) that we distinguish between behavior which helps others but may well have some payoff for the helper, and behavior which helps others without intentional benefit to the helper and even at some cost to the helper. The former is usually referred to as prosocial behavior and the latter is sometimes described as altruism. As stressed, it is often difficult to distinguish precisely between the two, but it is useful to bear in mind that prosocial behavior can be motivated by a variety of reasons, only one of which may be altruistic intent.

Examples of prosocial behavior include giving, sharing, cooperating, and protecting. Of course, these kinds of behavior are not necessarily rendered uninteresting or unimportant by the consideration that they may sometimes be motivated by some return to the actor. As social beings, we may value less an ostensibly helpful act which is prompted by the self-interest of our benefactor, but from a scientific perspective it remains of interest to account for the relations among behaviors and motives. Indeed, even from the perspective of the layperson, there are advantages to living in a community where people behave prosocially, for whatever reason, rather than run around committing acts of violent aggression as a result of sincerely intended malevolence. One major consideration promoting research into prosocial behavior is the possibility that our societies might be enhanced if there was more of it.

Outline of the Development of Prosocial Behavior

Infancy

Some sensitivity to others' discomfort may be present very early in life. It was mentioned in chapter 2 that infants exposed to cries of peers will often begin to cry themselves. These kinds of findings have led Sagi and Hoffman (1976) to claim that there is an inborn empathetic distress reaction. Particularly interesting are the findings of Martin and Clark (1982) that exposure to recordings of his or her own cries did not prompt a calm infant to cry and, if he or she was crying, resulted in the child stopping. These investigators found also that the cries of older infants (11 months) and of an infant of another species (a chimpanzee) did not lead to crying in neonates. In the very young, the reaction appears to be peer-specific.

The infant's differentiation of self and others is limited (chapter 2), and many of the baby's concerns are oriented around the gratification of immediate needs. None the less, infants as young as 8–12 months can be observed to offer to share objects with peers and parents (Escalona, 1973; Hay and Murray, 1982; Hay et al., 1991; see also chapter 8). This seems to constitute a form of prosocial behavior, even altruism, in that it involves at least temporary self-sacrifice to the benefit of another. In fact, the sacrifice does appear to be very temporary: the infant often demands the swift return of the object (Rheingold et al., 1976). Similarly, although children below the age of a year are sometimes responsive to the distress of others, their reactions indicate that they may fail to differentiate exactly who is suffering. Hoffman (1987) describes an 11-month-old who observed a peer fall over, looked on sadly, "and then put her thumb in her mouth and buried her head in her mother's lap, as she does when she herself is hurt" (p. 51).

Toddlers and Preschoolers

During the second and third years, children will sometimes offer nurturance to siblings or peers in distress (Dunn and Brown, 1991; Radke-Yarrow and Zahn-Waxler, 1984; Zahn-Waxler and Kochanska, 1990; Zahn-Waxler et al., 1992). They pat or hug someone who is crying, or offer food or toys to appease upset peers (figure 13.1). In an experimental study, Levitt et al. (1985) found that children aged 29–36 months were sensitive to the principle of reciprocity (discussed in more detail later). These investigators placed ten pairs of toddlers in a play context where they were separated by a gate and one member of the dyad had a set of toys. After a while, the situation was reversed, so that the previously toy-deprived child now had the goods. Levitt et al. (1985) found that the likelihood of the second child sharing the toys was contingent upon the behavior of the first: if the first child did not share, the second child did not either.

Dunn et al. (1981) obtained maternal reports of the frequency with which 2–4-year-olds offered comfort to their recently arrived younger siblings, and found that about two-thirds of them did so at least occasionally, some very frequently. In a study conducted in a preschool, Eisenberg-Berg and Neal (1979) questioned 4- and 5-year-olds about their spontaneous helping, sharing or comforting behaviors. During a 12-week period, most of the children initiated some prosocial behaviors, and a familiar experimenter asked them to explain the reasons behind their action ("How come you gave that to John?", "Why did you help Marissa?"). A variety of different types of reasons was elicited, ranging from hedonistic (where some selfish gain was expected), through stereotyped socially desirable responses ("It's nice to help") to a focus on the needs of others ("He's hungry"). The most common types of reasons were needs of others (24.5 percent of responses) and pragmatic orientation (justifying the behavior on some practical grounds, which also accounted for 24.5 percent of responses). Selfish reasons were given only 3.9 percent of the time, and stereotyped socially desirable responses were negligible (about 1 percent). Similarly, no child advanced reasons oriented around possible punishment from adults if she or he failed to help. The virtual absence of selfish, socially desirable, and authority-linked explanations is quite striking given the official rhetoric of most preschool settings ("remember caring and sharing"), and the persistently prosocial messages of *Sesame Street*.

Figure 13.1   Very young children can demonstrate concern for others.

The School Years

Most measures of prosocial behavior and empathy tend to reveal increases during the primary school years (Bryan, 1975; Green and Schneider, 1974; Lennon and Eisenberg, 1987; Rushton, 1975). During this age range children include more prosocial descriptors (*helpful, considerate*) in person-perception tasks (Livesley and Bromley, 1973), a development which could reflect both changes in the depth of understanding of the perceiver, and changes in the behavior of the peers they are describing. Individual differences in children's prosocial behavior show some stability during middle childhood (Rushton, 1980), and prosocial tendency is a reasonably good predictor of social adjustment. In particular, children who are rated low on prosocial measures are more likely to be rejected by peers and to adopt antisocial roles, such as the bully (Pulkinnen and Tremblay, 1992; Vitaro et al., 1990), while children rated high seem better equipped to overcome behavior problems (Tremblay et al., 1992).

The presence of siblings in the family may promote the development of at least some aspects of prosocial behavior. As noted above, Dunn et al. (1981) found that many preschool children offered emotional support to younger siblings. Jiao et al. (1986) studied children aged 4–10 years in rural and urban locations in China, a country where the state discourages parents from having more than one child. Comparing "only children" with peers who have siblings, Jiao et al. (1986) found that the former scored consistently lower on cooperation and higher on self-centered behavior.

Adolescence

In later childhood and into adolescence, the pattern of development is somewhat less clear. Some studies report continuing increases of prosocial behavior into adolescence (e.g., Green and Schneider, 1974), while others find that by this age children tend to be less helpful (Radke-Yarrow et al., 1983). In accounting for age differences, a lot depends upon how the behavior is measured. For example, those prosocial behaviors that require insight into another's perspective may not be so common in the very young because of their relative social cognitive limitations, while simple acts of sharing may be influenced more by the immediate context than by the developmental level of the participants (Miller et al., 1991). Life itself has become more complex by adolescence and, although older individuals may have a fuller understanding of the reasons for helping, they may also be sensitive to a host of interpersonal and situational variables that influence whether one actually does help. There is some evidence (reviewed by Zahn-Waxler et al., 1991) that girls may be more subject to these expectations and that those who are most responsive (i.e., who develop higher levels of empathy and prosocial behavior) are more likely to suffer guilt and depression in adolescence.

Adulthood

There have been few studies directly concerned with developmental changes in prosocial behaviors during adulthood. However, changes in adult role demands (discussed in more detail in chapters 18 and 19) may be associated with variations in helping and these may interact with gender. For example, the traditional male breadwinner may in young adulthood find himself behaving in competitive, assertive, and self-seeking ways in the workplace in order to fulfill his responsibilities to care and provide for his dependent family; in contrast, a woman accepting the traditional wife and mother role may find that her nurturance toward others peaks during early to middle adulthood, the period when she has the greatest obligations toward the wellbeing of her dependents. In later life, there may be changes in people's involvements with others, possibly associated with greater nurturance during the grandparental years. Midlarsky and Hannah (1989), in a donation study with subjects ranging in age from 5 to 75 years, found that elderly people were the most generous.

Summary

Prosocial behavior tends to increase with age during childhood. Moore and Underwood (1981) comment that this is one of the most replicable findings in developmental social psychology. The developments are varied, but recurrently important factors appear to be both experience and understanding of other people and their needs. Developments during later childhood and adolescence are difficult to characterize, partly because of individual differences and partly because of the increasing diversity of social tasks and circumstances that young people have to deal with. Similar observations could be made of adult development, though there is some evidence of an increase in older adults in certain forms of generosity toward others.

With this outline in mind, we need now to consider possible theoretical bases for explanations of prosocial behavior. Three major approaches to explanation will be summarized: the *sociobiological*, which holds that altruism, where it exists, is prepro-gramed by nature, *social learning theory*, which maintains that, like other behaviors, prosocial responses are learned, and *social cognitive* perspectives, which emphasize the mediating influence of social reasoning abilities, interpersonal understanding, and problem-solving competencies. Although each approach has its own distinctive emphasis and leads to a focus on specific issues that may be of less interest to the others, it should be stressed that they are not necessarily mutually exclusive (Sharabany and Bar-Tal, 1982), and we will consider possible interrelations later.

Sociobiological Theory and Prosocial Behavior

"It is always nice to be nice to someone else. But it is unlikely to be adaptive" (Barash, 1982, p. 67). According to the sociobiologist, prosocial behavior is explicable ultimately in terms of advantage to the prosocial agent. If it was not, it would simply die out, because nature does not include arrangements for the perpetuation of the self-sacrificing.

Yet many patterns of behavior can be found in the natural environment which do involve the seeming paradox of self-sacrifice. Some species of insects respond to threats to their territory by discharging venom into the intruders, losing most of their viscera in the process and dying shortly afterwards; the females of some bird species feign injury, staggering around as though suffering a broken wing, in order to distract predators from the nest containing their offspring; mongooses have "sentinels" who stand out in the sun to divert threat from other members of their group foraging in the shade; in a celebrated human example, the elder members of traditional Inuit families reportedly will volunteer to remain behind when depletion of food sources requires the rest of their extended family to move on: the grandparents feel that they will be a burden on the younger family members and opt to stay put, and die (see Barash, 1982; Harcourt, 1991; Trivers, 1985; Wilson, 1975, for fuller discussions of these and related examples).

However, each of these ostensibly self-sacrificial acts does have a payoff. It promotes the survival of one's kin. According to sociobiologists, individuals are motivated to maximize not simply their individual fitness but their *inclusive* fitness, which includes both their own survival *and* their representation in the next generation. Consider it this way: if members of a genetic group were all absolutely selfish, with each individual looking out only for its own immediate interests, then that group's long-term survival prospects would be jeopardized relative to those of a competing group which did practice some level of mutual aid. The other group would be taking care of its young, for example, maximizing the likelihood of genetic continuity, while the "selfish" group would be whooping it up, gobbling all the available resources, but at the expense of neglecting the next generation.

This is an oversimplification, but the essential point for present purposes is that, according to the sociobiologist, an individual may be prepared to make some personal sacrifice if it increases the survival prospects of others carrying his or her genes. In the *long* term, survival of the fittest is about continuity of the species rather than the indulgences of a single cohort. To this end, it follows that prominent among the recipients of prosocial behavior would be one's immediate family (who share the greatest amount of genetic material), then the extended family. Much evidence from other species (and we will consider some from humans later) confirms the adage that, when it comes to helpfulness, blood is thicker than water (Barash, 1982).

Even so, creatures (including humans) sometimes help non-relatives. How can a biological theory explain this phenomenon? One variant of the sociobiological approach maintains that assistance to conspecifics outside of one's own immediate family can be better explained as a function of the evolution of genes which promote *reciprocal altruism* (Trivers, 1971, 1985). In Trivers' view, species whose members help each other are likely to increase their collective and individual survival prospects. If I help you today, there may be no immediate return to me, but in due course I might find that you or some other helpful member of the species comes to my aid. In this way, we find it advantageous to help one another. An illustration is provided by male baboons without a sexual partner, who sometimes team up with other males suffering a similar disadvantage. One of them will then attack a male who is enjoying the company of a female; while these two are fighting, the first male sneaks in and mates with the female. Hence, one of the hitherto unpartnered males achieves a hasty dash at the fun side of reproductive endeavor while his collaborator must see how he fares in a scrap. As deals go, this arrangement seems imbalanced, but there is a payoff for the patient pugilist: research shows that, over time, individual males who give aid in this way are more likely to receive aid in return (Hinde, 1982).

These helpful actions are not a matter of cognitive deliberation or environmentally induced learning, but reflect the forces of evolution, within which a form of behavior, altruistic or otherwise, will evolve only if it is mediated by genes whose consequence is to increase the inclusive fitness of the bearer (Barash, 1982; Trivers, 1985). It is plausible that prosocial behavior would have been advantageous to early humans, who lived in social structures involving division of labor and cooperation in the capture and distribution of large game (Krebs, 1987). Research confirms that it remains true of human communities today that children and adults are more likely to offer prosocial assistance to friends than to unfamiliar individuals (Bierhoff, 1994; Farver and Branstetter, 1994; Hartup and van Lieshout, 1995; Youniss, 1994).

One of the theoretical strengths of the sociobiological approach is that it takes note of the interrelationship among events in a larger system. Sacrifices which appear anomalous if examined in purely local terms may be explicable if we take them as manifestations of a broader adaptive pattern: "they pay off in the long run" (Krebs, 1987, p. 87). Trivers (1985) argues that the emotions of gratitude and sympathy as well as the human sense of fairness and mutual obligation probably emerged in the species as means of regulating long-term relationships in which we could expect to exchange the roles of helper and recipient frequently. Emler (1990) extends the argument to propose that one of the reasons why personal reputations have such significance among human social networks is that our dependence on reciprocal altruism prompts an interest in gathering knowledge about who is, and who is not, helpful, reliable, and likely to reciprocate any favors we perform.

Problems with Sociobiological Accounts of Prosocial Behavior

One problem with biologically based explanations of altruism and prosocial behavior is that they do not account very well for individual differences (Eisenberg and Mussen, 1989; Sharabany and Bar-Tal, 1982). Why are some members of a community, group, or family more altruistic than others? Eisenberg and Mussen (1989) argue that individual differences are better explained with reference to different socialization experiences, variations in cognitive processes and emotional responsiveness, and situational determinants. We will consider evidence in relation to each of these later. However, it should be recognized that the fact that sociobiologists do not address these matters extensively does not necessarily invalidate their explanations of the issues that they do address. Trivers (1985), for example, argues that a complex psychological framework for the regulation of prosocial expectations should be favored by natural selection since it enables humans to deal with the problems of potential instability in social relations due to the fact that cheating (failing to reciprocate prosocial behavior) sometimes has short-term advantages.

Another limitation of the sociobiological approach is that it does not offer a very extensive basis for explaining *changes* in prosocial behavior and reasoning with age. The framework might allow the prediction that prosocial behavior should increase with age, since capacities mature, but it does not lend itself to a more comprehensive account of development, nor explain the possible reduction in prosocial behavior during adolescence. Again, this is a level of analysis outside of the remit of most sociobiologists, rather than a phenomenon which undermines the whole basis of their approach, although several sociobiological authors have stressed the scope for synthesis with psychological treatments of these topics (Krebs, 1987; MacDonald, 1988d; Trivers, 1985). Both social learning theory and social cognitive approaches address relevant questions, and we consider these in the following sections.

Summary

Sociobiological accounts of prosocial behavior and altruism offer an explanation for the apparent paradox of behavioral propensities which do not serve the immediate self-interests of the actor. Theorists focus on the commitment to those with shared genetic material and on the collective advantages of mutual aid. This approach has the strength that it addresses issues concerned with the longer-term functional significance of helpful behavior. It has the limitation that it says relatively little about the developmental and social psychological factors entailed in becoming prosocial.

Social Learning Theory and Prosocial Behavior

Social learning theorists explain most human behaviors in terms of environmentally induced learning (see chapter 1). In respect of prosocial behavior, social learning theorists again emphasize the two main processes held to underlie all learning: reinforcement/punishment and observational learning.

Reinforcement and Punishment

As we have already seen, prosocial behavior appears to present a paradox to reinforcement theorists as much as it does to biologically oriented scientists, since the basic premise of the learning theorist is that humans are pleasure-seeking organisms, motivated by the prospect of reward. The solution to this paradox has generally been couched either in terms we have already noted, namely by proposing that some internal reward *is* obtained, such as a change of affect (Aronfreed, 1968; Rosenhan, 1972), or by emphasizing the power of extrinsic rewards to increase prosocial behavior. For example, several studies have shown that the frequency of donations or other helping behaviors made by children can be increased by adult praise or the administration of candy (Gelfand et al., 1975; Midlarsky et al., 1973; Mills and Grusec, 1989; Warren et al., 1976). Other studies in this tradition have shown that punishment (i.e., where the subject receives some aversive stimulus, such as witnessing someone else's pain) can sometimes increase prosocial responses (Aronfreed, 1968; Gelfand and Hartmann, 1980). Punishment can also reduce prosocial acts (e.g., if the child is criticized for acting prosocially; Rushton, 1980).

However, the fact that these contingencies can increase or reduce the frequency of prosocial behavior in laboratory experiments is not in itself a demonstration that this is how such behavior is acquired in the natural environment. One problem is that children could be responding to the demand characteristics of the experiment rather than developing selfless insights into the needs of others. They might anticipate that the experimenter will return shortly and want to know how much they gave (Siegal, 1982). Another problem is that if the reinforcement is removed, then we should expect the behavior to revert to base-line levels of frequency (Grusec, 1983). In practical terms, this would mean that, throughout life, we would need at least intermittent reinforcement to ensure the continuation of prosocial behavior, unless some other processes are involved. For the social learning theorist, candidate processes include internalization and generalization, processes which depend at least in part on opportunities to learn from watching others.

Observational Learning

Many experimental studies have demonstrated that children will imitate prosocial models (Bryan, 1975; Grusec et al., 1978; Rice and Grusec, 1975; Rushton, 1975). The typical method employed is to place the child subject in a game where she or he is able to win tokens; prior to or during the game the child witnesses a model (usually an adult or older child) also play the game and then donate some of the winnings to a charity. Children in the model condition usually donate more than children in control conditions. Consistent with social learning theory predictions, certain characteristics of the model such as personal warmth, power, and positive affect (upon behaving prosocially) are sometimes associated with greater modeling effects (Bryan, 1975; Grusec, 1983).

Rushton (1975) examined the effects of the congruence or otherwise of the model's words and actions. Children saw a model who, after winning some tokens in a bowling game, preached in favor of selfishness ("keep the lot yourself") or generosity ("give half to charity"). The model then *acted* either selfishly or generously. In both of the conflict conditions (i.e., where the model preached generosity but acted selfishly, or preached selfishness but actually donated) children were more likely to follow what the model *did* rather than what she *said*.

Some researchers of children's responses to television began in the 1970s to broaden the search from the possible effects of aggression to examine the consequences of watching prosocial content, such as *Sesame Street*, *Mister Rogers' Neighborhood* and miscellaneous similar programs designed to inculcate caring and sharing in the young viewer. In general, the evidence from both laboratory and field studies supports the conclusion that watching such programmes may be associated with increases in helpfulness, cooperation, and sharing among children (van Evra, 1990; Huston-Stein and Friedrich, 1975). In fact, some reviewers of the research have concluded that television is more effective (brings about more reliable changes) in this domain than in that of aggression, possibly because prosocial programs are usually designed with the express goal of teaching, while aggressive content is usually included simply to entertain (van Evra, 1990; Hearold, 1986). Some caution is due before leaping to the conclusion that regular doses of *The Muppets* and friends will eventually solve all of the world's problems. It is generally found that any effects associated with TV content are amplified if significant adults embellish the program message (Huston-Stein and

Friedrich, 1975) — a finding which is not contradictory to social learning theory predictions — and it remains difficult to ensure that children will opt to watch prosocial content when there is action-packed melodrama available on the other channel (see van Evra, 1990, for further discussion).

It is interesting to consider *why* modeling should promote prosocial behavior. Remember, we are talking here about self-sacrificial actions: why should observing others give up something make the same or similar concessions more appealing to the onlooker? Perry and Bussey (1984, p. 247) outline a number of possible reasons. First, models can teach children what is appropriate; correspondingly, children may fear censure for failing to act in a socially desirable manner. Second, observing the consequences of others' prosocial acts may alleviate concerns about the possible adverse effects of such behavior; if no harm came to the helper, perhaps it is safe for me to help, too. Third, models can provide illustrations of the positive consequences of being prosocial (such as people displaying gratitude and admiration). Perhaps the European political leaders who observed public responses to Michael Nicholson's prosocial actions inferred that they in their turn could attract some favorable evaluations by displaying a measure of helpfulness.

Problems with the Social Learning Theory of Prosocial Behavior

The social learning framework generated a great deal of interesting research into children's prosocial behavior during the 1970s, and clearly makes an important contribution by demonstrating the potential influence of extrinsic factors, such as reinforcement and others' examples. In contrast to sociobiological approaches, it offers a plausible basis for explaining individual differences in prosocial behavior, since it could be argued that different child-rearing environments are responsible for variations (and we will see evidence that supports this view below). However, one limitation of at least the initial work in this paradigm was that it paid relatively little attention to children's understanding of the *reasons* for prosocial behavior (cf. Bryan, 1975; Siegal, 1982). Another problem, reflecting the theory's general bias to treat knowledge as accumulated rather than as subject to qualitative changes, is that it does not offer a *developmental* perspective (cf. Sharabany and Bar-Tal, 1982). Learning about prosocial behavior is often assumed to be pretty much the same process for a 2-year-old and an adolescent. Note also that each of the reasons Perry and Bussey, above, advance to explain why models might be effective is based on the notion of some anticipated reward to the learner; i.e., this is primarily a "self-interest" theory, and we saw earlier that it is controversial whether *all* prosocial behavior is self-interested.

Summary

Social learning theories offer explanations for prosocial behavior with an emphasis on environmental factors, such as reinforcement or punishment and the observation of social approval for the actions of prosocial individuals. Cognitive processes are entailed in this account, since it is stressed that learners must attend to the model's behavior and store representations of it, as well as retrieve this information to organize their own behavior around it in relevant instances (see chapter 1). This approach goes further toward accounting for individual differences in prosocial behavior, since it deals with differences in observational experiences and rewards. On the other hand, the theory says relatively little about why prosocial behavior comes about in the first place and little about developmental changes.

Social Cognitive Developmental Perspectives on Prosocial Behavior

Social cognitive approaches focus on the reasoning presumed to underlie prosocial behavior. At present, although much work has been oriented around social cognitive dimensions, and it is probably fair to say that this is now the dominant theoretical orientation within the field, there is no one unifying theory that offers a systematic interrelationship of propositions and predictions intended to account for all of the phenomena of prosocial behavior. Instead, work in this tradition is influenced variously by traditional cognitive developmental psychology (especially Piagetian) and by developmental investigations of processes initially identified in the experimental social psychological literature, such as social perceptions and attributions.

Since Latane and Darley's (1970) influential early study of the cognitive aspects of prosocial behavior, social psychologists have acknowledged that in responding to a situation in which help might be required a lot of information has to be processed rapidly. Prosocial action involves several fundamental cognitive processes, including perception, reasoning, problem-solving, and decision-making (Eisenberg and Mussen, 1989), as well as awareness of the expectations and norms governing interpersonal behavior (Bierhoff, 1996). From a developmental perspective, this raises the questions of how these competencies emerge and how they change. We will consider just some aspects of development, focusing on changes in reasoning ability, understanding of social norms, the growth of empathy and, finally, the social cognitive consequences of being helped.

Cognitive Development and Prosocial Behavior

Cognitive developmentalists assume that the acquisition of the relevant reasoning competencies is not instantaneous or cumulative, but subject to the broader principles of qualitative change that are taken to be central to intellectual progress through childhood. A strong version of the cognitive developmental approach holds that "the developmental trend of the individual is the movement from a phase of being illogical, egocentric, and selfish-hedonistic to a phase of being logical, empathetic, and moral"

(Sharbany and Bar-Tal, 1982, p. 64). This would predict increases in prosocial behavior with age during childhood, and, as we have seen, there is evidence of such a relationship, although its strength is a matter of debate.

It is clear that very young children's perception of distressing events is sometimes quite limited (Eisenberg and Mussen, 1989). For example, as noted above, at around 12 months some children react to others' misfortunes by consoling *themselves*. Zahn-Waxler et al. (1992) found that with the development of self-recognition (one of the major landmarks in early social cognition; see chapter 9) children in their second year became more likely to display concern for others. Preschool children are less sensitive than older individuals in interpreting subtle cues of another's distress (Barnett and Thompson, 1985; Pearl, 1985), but are certainly capable of detecting and responding to overt signs, such as crying.

There is also evidence of developmental shifts in children's understanding of *how* to help. Faced with a distressed peer, younger children tend to prefer adult-mediated help (presumably because they have generally found adults to be the most effective helpers). With age (and social cognitive development), children become increasingly likely to use cognitive strategies (Bernzweig et al., 1993). For example, they might guide the unhappy agemate toward restructuring (encouraging her to tell herself that "it isn't really something to get upset about").

In general, research into prosocial development indicates that perspective-taking ability is moderately associated with prosocial behavior (Eisenberg and Mussen, 1989; Moore and Underwood, 1981; Underwood and Moore, 1982), though causal direction is difficult to determine. Moore and Underwood (1981), in an analysis of studies available to that date, show that the relationship between perceptual perspective-taking (e.g., using measures such as Piaget's three mountains task) and prosocial behavior is usually reduced when age is controlled for statistically. It should be recalled, though, that other research has cast doubt on the meaning of responses to some of the traditional Piagetian perspective-taking tasks (see chapter 9), and it remains to be seen how prosocial behavior relates to performance on perspective-taking tasks which are more sensitive to the abilities of younger children. When measures of *social* perspective-taking ability (such as the ability to predict what someone else is thinking, or to communicate with another person non-egocentrically) are employed, the relationship with prosocial behavior is reasonably strong among older children (Buckley et al., 1979; Dreman, 1976; Iannotti, 1978; Krebs and Sturrup, 1974; Moore and Underwood, 1981).

Attributions about the individual in need of help influence even preschoolers' willingness to provide assistance. For example, Barnett and McMinimy (1988) found that 4-year-olds generally reported more empathy with a story character who was happy as a consequence of observing an acceptable act (such as seeing another child retrieve a ball that was stuck in the mud) than with a child who was happy for an unacceptable reason (such as playing with a kite that he had stolen from a smaller child). There is some basis for inferring causal direction here in that intervention studies have shown that training young children in interpersonal problem-solving skills leads to increases in prosocial behavior (Eisenberg and Mussen, 1989; Spivack and Shure, 1974).

Cognitive development and self-interest

Much of the research into cognitive development and prosocial behavior is focused on how the child comes to understand and react to others' needs. But there is also evidence that cognitive developments may increase the likelihood that children detect more of the benefits to the self in acting prosocially. Lourenco (1993) found that across the age range 5–11 years, children were increasingly likely with age to perceive prosocial behavior in terms of gains to the actor (such as feeling happier). Interestingly, Rigby and Slee (1993) found that children who were more prosocial tended to have higher scores on measures of psychological wellbeing. Although causal direction is difficult to determine, it is possible that, as these authors conclude, virtue is not its own reward – the real attraction could be that it makes you feel better (but see Zahn-Waxler et al., 1991). Social cognitive development could promote awareness of this payoff as well as the more selfless concerns discussed above.

Social Cognitive Development and the Norms of Prosocial Behavior

Social psychologists have identified a number of normative expectations that appear to guide much of prosocial behavior. Prominent among these are the *norm of social responsibility* (that we should help people who need help; Berkowitz and Daniels, 1963), the *norm of reciprocity* (that we should help those who have helped us; Gouldner, 1960); and the *norm of deservedness* (that you get what you deserve out of life; Long and Lerner, 1974). As indicated earlier, social psychological research into these shared understandings has been conducted primarily with adults. But for social norms to impinge upon behavior, they have to be acquired and represented: they form elements of our broader social knowledge (Eisenberg, 1987). A certain amount of developmental work has been undertaken to chart the origins of the phenomena found in laboratory and field studies of adults. We will note some of the findings in respect of each of the norms mentioned.

The norm of responsibility: help those who need help

The norm of social responsibility is widely endorsed in human societies, and often articulated by parents, teachers, and other key contributors to socialization. Among adults, individuals often account for their prosocial behavior with reference to the general expectation of other people that they should help (Berkowitz, 1972). Children seem to acquire this norm at least by middle childhood. Bryan and Walbek (1970) found that by about the age of 8 years, children could understand the norm and acknowledge its import for behavior.

The norm of reciprocity: help those who help you

We have already seen that 2-year-olds honor the principal of reciprocity to some extent (Levitt et al., 1985). Staub and Sherk (1970) found that fourth-grade children were more likely to share crayons with a peer if that peer had earlier been generous to them when he or she had the opportunity to share sweets. In general, while preschoolers are sometimes disinclined to honor this norm, children seem to be aware of its significance by the early school years (Berndt, 1979b). Among 6-, 8- and 11-year-olds, Fishbein and Kaminski (1985) found no age differences in honoring the norm of reciprocity.

Perhaps because most research into prosocial behavior rests on the implicit premise that being prosocial is a nice thing to do, rather less attention has been paid to the development of manipulative uses of the norm of reciprocity: that is, we know little of how and when children may come to discern the advantages of helping others in order to place them under an obligation to reciprocate, and we know little of individual differences in this respect. Reciprocity, however, is known to be moderated by the recipient's perceptions of the motives of the benefactor. For example, Fishbein and Kaminski (1985) found that children were more likely to reciprocate help from peers who they believed to have helped them voluntarily rather than at the prompting of the experimenter.

The norm of deservedness: help those who deserve help

Both children and adults tend to prefer to help those who are in need through misfortune rather than as a consequence of self-neglect or laziness (Barnett, 1975; Berkowitz, 1972). Masters (1971) found that even at 4–5 years children were sensitive to the norm of deservedness, at least as far as it affected their share of things. Subjects in his study were placed in a position where they could donate funds to an absent partner. If the children were given their fair share of the rewards, they donated more to the absentee; but if children saw their classmates get more than them, they gave far less to the absentee. Long and Lerner (1974) showed that subjects (aged around 10 years) who were "overpaid" for their participation in a task, and told that the money they were receiving should really have gone to other kids, were particularly generous when they had an opportunity to donate – it seemed that they wished to restore equity, consistent with their belief in a just world. In a social cognitive developmental study, Damon (1980) provided evidence that children's conceptions of fairness develop through middle childhood, from an initial orientation toward self-interest to an eventual acceptance of considerations of social equality and interpersonal reciprocity. By this stage (in late childhood and early teens), children can take several factors into account in determining how to reciprocate to another's prior helpfulness.

Norms, meanings, and motives in prosocial behavior

The acquisition of norms is an important dimension of coming to represent the shared social understandings and expectations of one's community, but it is not a process which fully explains the development of prosocial behavior (Perry and Bussey, 1984). Perry and Bussey point out that it is often difficult to identify a single norm as the basis for any one prosocial action (for example, as we saw earlier, one might say one helped a fellow student because of one's sense of social responsibility toward the needy, but lurking beneath the surface may be another norm, such as one's anticipation of reciprocity). Conformity may reflect compliance to social influences rather than genuine commitment to the norm (Thibaut and Kelley, 1959; Turner, 1991). In some social contexts, too many norms may exist and they may offer competing prescriptions (Thibaut and Kelley, 1959, p. 140). Imagine a situation in which a child has to deal simultaneously with the following: you should always do what the teacher tells you, you should never rat on a friend, if someone has done wrong she deserves what she gets, look after a friend in trouble. The only way forward, Thibaut and Kelley suggest, is to develop a meta-norm (a norm about norms) that specifies which norms are dominant in which situations. As yet, little is known about how children (or adults) develop meta-norms.

Members of a community sometimes endorse a norm, such as the belief that people get what they deserve, for reasons which seem closer to the maintenance of relative privileges than to prosocial concerns for their fellow humans. Furnham and Proctor (1989) point to the commitment to just world beliefs among conservative South African whites as an illustration of a socially shared belief system which helps them to make sense of the discrepancies between their standard of living and that of their black compatriots. Finally, endorsement or comprehension of particular social norms does not always predict reliably how a person will actually act in a situation where prosocial behavior is possible (Perry and Bussey, 1984; Peterson, 1980).

None of these qualifications means that norms are irrelevant to the development and maintenance of prosocial behavior. On the contrary, they suggest that the phenomenon is more multifaceted than coming to understand another's perspective and determining what is the most appropriate form of help to deliver. The salience of norms indicates that prosocial behavior is interrelated more subtly with a variety of other aspects of social knowledge and communal orientation. It may be that through renewed attention to the norms of prosocial behavior, social and developmental psychologists may be able to strengthen their relationship rather than sustain the divergence that has characterized their involvements in this topic and generated the paradox, discussed at the beginning of the chapter, of the supposedly highly cognitively developed yet allegedly situationally dependent adult (see Bar-Tal et al., 1980; Raviv et al., 1980 for a stage model of the motives for helping behavior in which they place norm-following and generalized reciprocity as reflecting higher levels of cognitive development).

Social Cognitive Development and Empathy

An important focus of much recent social cognitive work has been the role of empathy in prosocial behavior and development. Empathy is the vicarious sensation of someone else's emotional state or condition (Eisenberg and Mussen, 1989). In considering Nicholson's actions in saving the orphan in Bosnia, we imagined how he *felt* in the traumatic circumstances he was reporting. Introspectively, we sense that a powerful motivator for prosocial behavior is how we feel about the plight of the potential recipients of our aid. Some have argued that this affective reaction is a key factor in altruism: "In the same way that genes connect people physically, empathy connects them emotionally" (Krebs, 1987, p. 104; see also Batson, 1991; Blum, 1980; Eisenberg and Miller, 1987).

There is persuasive evidence that empathy motivates some of the prosocial behavior of adults. Batson (1991), arguing that egoistic and empathetic–altruistic motives are distinct, shows in a series of experimental studies that self-interest motives are not sufficient to explain a variety of altruistic behaviors, while an explanation based on the concept of empathetic altruism is consistent with the findings. For example, when subjects are prompted to empathize with a stimulus person their helping scores are substantially higher than other subjects who are prompted to focus on other aspects of the task.

From a developmental perspective, the topic of empathy raises familiar issues of perspective-taking and distinguishing self from others. To share someone else's feelings, one needs to recognize that he or she is separate from the self, and to understand how things appear from his or her perspective. Hoffman (1982, 1983, 1987) has developed an influential account of the interaction of empathetic affect and social cognition in the development of these abilities. He proposes that children progress through four stages, as follows.

Global empathy   Even quite young infants can experience empathic distress as a consequence of the arousal occasioned by someone else's distress. We have already seen examples, such as babies' tendency to cry when other babies around them do so, and Hoffman's own example of the 11-month-old who appeared to console herself when a playmate was upset.

"Egocentric" empathy   As children become able to distinguish self and others, they may still find it difficult to infer another's internal feelings, and may be confused about the appropriate responses to another's distress. For example, one 18-month boy brought his own mother to comfort a distressed friend, even though the friend's mother was present (Hoffman, 1987, p. 51).

Empathy for another's feelings   As role-taking skills develop during the preschool years, children become sensitive to the fact that others' feelings and needs may be different from their own, and they become more responsive to cues about others' feelings. Hoffman suggests (1987, p. 52) that the development of language may play a part here, in that children become capable of labeling an increasing range of emotions. Children can now be empathetically aroused by *information* about another's distress, even when that person is not present.

Empathy for another's life condition   By late childhood, the individual can represent others' distress in still more sophisticated ways, recognizing, for example, that some forms of distress or deprivation can have long-term consequences for the sufferer. The development of social concepts (e.g., of the poor, the disadvantaged) during these years may underpin more elaborate appraisals of others' conditions, and in some cases may provide the stimulus to the emergence of moral and political ideologies as the young person moves into adolescence.

Hoffman's model is rare among developmental approaches in that it combines affect and social cognition in a dynamic framework that allows for their mutual effects. It enjoys considerable support, although it remains the case that the relationship between empathy and prosocial behavior is a complex one (see Eisenberg and Miller, 1987). Certainly, as Batson's work shows, empathetic responses do appear to motivate helping among adults, but in some experimental studies children appear to act according to their impressions of social desirability rather than as a function of their empathetic reactions to a distressing scenario (Eisenberg and Mussen, 1989).

"Better to Give than Receive": Social Cognitive Dimensions of Being Helped

As a child, a friend of mine was selected on the basis of academic competition to attend an elite private secondary school. Her parents could not possibly have afforded the fees, and this was a rare opportunity. Only two girls were admitted per annum on this basis. At the first assembly of the year, the school staff, eager to transmit a sense of prosocial responsibility to their pupils, made a great fuss of announcing the school's generosity and pointing out the recipients, who were known evermore as the "Scholarship Girls." Depending on your social cognitive skills and your level of empathy, you might be able to estimate how the Scholarship Girls felt during the remainder of those long years on the receiving end of prosocial education.

This highlights another of the paradoxes of prosocial behavior: it seems a wonderful thing for people to be kind to others, but it may not always be enjoyable to find oneself in the category of "being helped." In some contexts, people take pains to minimize the discomfort of the recipient by downplaying the significance of their generosity. Eibl-Eibesfeldt (1988) describes how among Yanomami Indians a man might give another a dog as a gift, saying "Take this miserable dog" (even though a quality canine is being dispensed). In Western cultures it is often polite to accompany giving or helping with remarks like "Oh, it's only something small," "It's nothing" (even if it tipped your credit card into the danger zone).

This raises an aspect of helping – the feelings of the recipient – that has been generally disregarded by researchers of prosocial behavior. This is a rather unfortunate neglect in that a supposedly *social* psychological phenomenon has been treated as though it were a one-sided matter (i.e., all attention has been on the giver and his or her motives). It ignores also a crucial developmental aspect of prosocial behavior among humans, which is that at certain phases of the lifespan individuals are perceived to be especially in need of help. One such phase, of course, is childhood (Shell and Eisenberg, 1992); another is old age (see chapter 19). Reactions to being helped have attracted attention only recently, largely as a function of social cognitive approaches to prosocial behavior. Social learning and sociobiological approaches tend to have little to say about this aspect of helping, beyond postulating modeling processes and setting conditions for reciprocity. By focusing on people's understanding of prosocial behavior, the interpretations and reactions of those involved become more salient.

Nadler and Fisher (1986) argue that most instances of being helped contain potentially ambivalent information. On the one hand, there is the positive aspect that someone cares enough to assist, but on the other there is the implicit message of inferiority. The latter aspect poses a threat to self-esteem (Bierhoff, 1994). The extent to which being helped elicits positive or negative feelings in the recipient varies according to his or her social cognitions and the characteristics of the situation. Shell and Eisenberg (1992) extend Nadler and Fisher's model with a developmental perspective. They point out that on a day-to-day basis children typically receive many types of aid, reflecting other people's perceptions of their abilities, needs, and vulnerabilities. This assistance has the potential to provide powerful messages to the child about his or her competencies. These messages may well affect the child's developing sense of self.

Shell and Eisenberg (1992) propose that the effects of being helped upon the child's self-concept and self-esteem are mediated by developmental level. Very young children might not perceive much of the unsolicited help they receive as threatening, since they are less likely to make extended inferences about the helper's picture of them. Even so, we saw in chapters 2 and 9 that the motivation to master the environment is potent from an early age, and almost as soon as they are capable of performing simple tasks toddlers are prone to insist "I can do it on my own!" (Geppert and Kuster, 1983). Nevertheless, toddlers (have to) accept that a great deal of help will be forthcoming, while older children tend to have stronger feelings about which domains they require help in: contrast the reactions of a 4-year-old and a 9-year-old to your offer to hold their hand to assist them crossing the street.

With social cognitive development, children enrich their self-concept and gain increasing insight into the motives and intentions of others. As they do so, they come to understand the implications of help (such as the presumption of inferiority, dependence or laziness in the recipient). Graham and Barker (1990) found that by 5–6 years, children had begun to understand that someone who received more help on his or her schoolwork might be less competent than his or her peers; 4-year-olds did not make this inference. Geppert and Kuster (1983) found that children aged 4–6 years were more likely to show task persistence rather than ask for help, but were inclined to offer help to the experimenter (a move which does no harm to one's self-esteem at all). During middle childhood, the development of the ability to make social comparisons (see chapter 9) is likely to make the implicit meanings of being helped all the more salient. DePaulo et al. (1989) paired children on an educational task, such that subjects of high or low ability were tutored by agemates or children two years older. The most threatening conditions turned out to be those in which tutors and tutees were similar in age and achievement levels. High and low achieving children responded differently to the threat: the high achievers raised their act to compete, while the low achievers performed particularly poorly. Several studies have shown that in this period and into the teens, children are generally reluctant to be seen asking for help in achievement-related areas (Newman, 1990; Newman and Goldin, 1990; van der Meij, 1988; see Shell and Eisenberg, 1992, for a more thorough review). A range of situational and interpersonal factors (such as the norms for the activity, the age and gender of the helper in relation to the age and gender of the helpee) is also likely to affect reactions to assistance (Shell and Eisenberg, 1992).

Problems with Social Cognitive Explanations of Prosocial Behavior

Social cognitive approaches score highly on attention to underlying reasoning but they tend to say very little about the "whys" of prosocial behavior. It is important to investigate how people come to understand and respond to their social world as they find it, but it remains essential, too, to consider why the world is organized as it is, and why human groups sometimes find prosocial behavior adaptive (and sometimes do not). Remember also that other species display prosocial and altruistic behaviors. The social cognitive sophistication of the mongoose sentinel is not thought to be impressive, but its commitment to the reproduction of its genes may be. Sociobiological approaches have much to offer in terms of explaining the longer-term, functional motivations for prosocial actions.

The "lopsidedness" problem (chapter 1) recurs here. Social cognitive explanations are relatively indifferent to variations in the stimulus environment. The emphasis is on stages or transformations *within* the developing child, and the fact that children grow up in very different environments is often treated as mere "noise." The social learning approach demonstrates that variations in this noise can make quite a difference to behavior, and it is possible, though little explored at present, that it makes a difference to the very processes of social cognitive development itself.

Summary

Social cognitive accounts of aspects of the development of prosocial behavior have come to dominate the field in recent years. This broad perspective has the advantage over sociobiological approaches that it addresses the underlying reasoning processes which make complex social behavior possible, situationally relevant, and interpersonally effective. It offers an emphasis on the qualitative cognitive changes which tend to be less central to much of the social learning theory research but which recent evidence indicates may mediate some of the developments in prosocial behavior. Although cognitive approaches often disregard affect, recent work in prosocial development has been enriched by attention to the intersection of thinking and feeling, particularly as exemplified in Hoffman's influential model and by research into the reactions of the recipients of help.

While social cognitive approaches are likely to remain prominent in future work in this field, recognition of their current promise does not preclude or contradict insights from sociobiological or social learning theory perspectives. As Sharabany and Bar-Tal (1982) and MacDonald (1988d) argue, these three theoretical perspectives focus on different levels of analysis, and do not directly challenge each others' premises.

The Social Contexts of Prosocial Behavior

We turn now to aspects of contextual factors in the development of prosocial behavior, considering socialization practices in the family, situational influences, gender differences, and cross-cultural differences. Each of these variables has been found to be associated with individual differences in prosocial behavior. As we consider them, it is useful to consider how each of the above theories would attempt to account for the differences reported.

Socialization Practices and the Family

The family is one of the major *locations* of prosocial behavior: a principal social context within which people feel motivated to help one another (Hartup and van Lieshout, 1995; MacDonald, 1988d). Within the family, there are consistent patterns of the obligatory force and direction of helping. Rossi and Rossi (1990), in a large study of families in the Boston area, found that people's perceptions of their obligations were affected by the degree of relatedness to the self, such that the closer the familial link, the greater the obligation to help. The strongest obligations were evoked between parents and children (directly related), and then the next level was among grandparents, grandchildren, and siblings (all connected to the self through just one link), followed by aunts, uncles, nieces and nephews (two links), and the lowest obligation was to cousins (three links). All of this is perfectly consistent with sociobiological theory, which predicts that concern for those sharing one's genes should be paramount. However, relatively high obligation ratings were also obtained for stepparents and stepchildren, which Rossi and Rossi (1990) point out indicates that the critical factor may be family *position* rather than shared genetic material. This suggests that an adequate explanation would have to take account of social roles, which of course could be addressed from both social learning accounts (e.g., individuals are reinforced for caring for their family) and social cognitive (e.g., people acquire an understanding of the meaning of family ties and are particularly sensitive to the needs of those whom they know well). A sociobiologist might reply that the reasons why these roles and dependencies arise in the first place are to be found in evolutionary adaptation.

Rossi and Rossi (1990) report that the *direction* of helping was also patterned, reflecting economic differentials and lifespan status. Typically, parents provided financial assistance to their adult children rather than the reverse, at least until the younger generation was established in the workforce. As parents enter old age, there is an increase in help provided to them by the younger generation. This may contribute toward an explanation of the evidence of greater generosity in older people that was noted earlier: on the basis of the norm of reciprocity, older people may find it advantageous to be seen to be kind (thereby reminding their kin of how much is now due to them), or becoming the recipient of increased amounts of assistance may intensify their feelings of obligation to others.

Across families, there are variations in the amount of helping, and several studies have found associations between parental values and caregiving style and the prosocial behavior and attitudes of their children (Eisenberg et al., 1992; Feshbach, 1987; Hoffman, 1975; Rubin et al., 1989; Zahn-Waxler et al., 1991). Barnett et al. (1980) found that among undergraduates, individuals with high empathy scores described their parents as having been more affectionate to them as children than did less empathetic subjects. Of course, as with all correlational data, these patterns could be explained in various ways. Perhaps prosocial traits are inherited; perhaps parents provide influential role models; perhaps parents regulate and reinforce desired behaviors; or perhaps parents engage their children in patterns of interaction which promote particular social cognitive understanding and behavioral strategies. At present, it is not resolved exactly how the family context contributes to the development of prosocial behavior, but the evidence is strong that it plays a major role.

Eisenberg and Mussen (1989) point to attachment research, Baumrind's study of the consequences of parental style, the constellation of family relations, and verbal influences as prominent among evidence that the domestic environment may help account for early emerging differences in social competence and reactions to others. As we saw in chapter 3, Type B (securely attached) infants do seem to have an advantage in terms of developing positive relations, and it may be that these children are more likely to develop prosocial dispositions. It is also plausible that from infancy on, children become affectively tuned to their caregivers and this may generate conditions for acquiring patterns of social responsiveness similar to those of the caregiver (Thompson, 1987). For example, while we noted earlier that infants and toddlers will often respond to distress in others by trying to help, Main and George (1985) found that abused toddlers (for whom anger is part of the background of everyday life) showed no signs of empathic concern in response to peer distress. Instead, some showed signs of fear and others threatened or even attacked the already distraught child. The abused children manifest self-isolating and aggressive tendencies similar to those often reported in abusive parents (Frodi and Lamb, 1980; Parke and Collmer, 1975).

Finally, family members tend to talk to one another, and some parents may articulate prosocial values more frequently than others. Verbal messages may promote prosocial reasoning and behavior among children. In the Levitt et al. (1985) study of toddler sharing described above, none of the children shared spontaneously, although their peers stood at the gate, watching forlornly as they played with the toys, and even in some cases straightforwardly asking for a piece of the action. It was only when mothers intervened and encouraged their child to share that prosocial responses were forthcoming. Zahn-Waxler et al. (1979) found that mothers often articulated explanations of principle of why prosocial behavior was desirable as they intervened in specific incidents, and they report that children whose mothers do this more often tend to behave in a more prosocial fashion. Dix et al. (1986), in an experimental study, found that parents were more likely to attribute prosocial behaviors to the child's internal qualities (possibly because this reflects favorably on their own success as caregivers); it may be that parents who verbalize these interpretations guide their children toward increasingly prosocial behavior. Studies of older children in family contexts reveal consistently that dialog with parents plays an important role in facilitating children's interpersonal and social cognitive problem-solving skills (Elias et al., 1985; Shure and Spivack, 1978; Sigel et al., 1980). Siblings, too, often play a prominent role in articulating reasons for sharing and prompting younger children to do so (Dunn and Munn, 1986; Schieffelin, 1990).

Situational Influences upon Prosocial Behavior

Latane and Darley (1970) conducted a series of well-known experiments on bystander effects in emergencies. In one study, these investigators' naive subjects were placed in a room where they were required to complete questionnaires. As they worked, smoke was gradually filtered into the room. In one condition, the subject was alone. In another, the subject was in the presence of confederates of the experimenters who feigned complete indifference to the smoke, and in another the subject was placed with two other naive subjects. Subjects in the presence of the indifferent companions were less likely to take action and waited for longer before leaving the room. Even when all three subjects were naive and had abundant evidence from their senses that something was amiss, they took longer to react than did subjects in the solitary condition.

One reason why people take longer to react when in the presence of others may be that they monitor others for cues to help them interpret ambiguous circumstances. As discussed in chapter 8, from infancy onwards people exploit social referencing to work out how others are reacting and hence how they should react to ambiguous or unfamiliar events. Another reason may be that people may not feel that it is their unique responsibility to intervene — after all, one or more of the others could do something. This phenomenon, known as diffusion of responsibility, is illustrated in other experiments of Latane and Darley's, in which the incidence of helping behavior is compared between subjects who are alone and subjects who are alone but believe themselves to be in contact (e.g., via a speaker system) with others. The solitary subjects, who thought they alone were aware of the emergency, were much more likely to react.

These constraints upon prosocial behavior appear to be acquired by middle childhood. In a variant of the bystander intervention paradigm, Staub (1970) compared the responses of children aged 5–13 years to the screams of a child in an adjacent room, in conditions where they were alone or in pairs. For the younger children, helping was more likely when in pairs, in contrast to findings with adults pointing to diffusion of responsibility effects; for the older children, differences between solitary and paired conditions were much less marked, although overall helping rates were lower. However, Peterson (1983), comparing children aged 6, 9 and 11 years in a similar experiment obtained evidence of greater helping when children thought they were alone. An important variable manipulated by Peterson was competence: if children knew how to help, they were more likely to do so.

The situation back at Robbers' Cave

Let us return for a final time to the Rattlers and the Eagles, who were at the peak of intergroup hostilities in chapter 12. You might have concluded at that point that the boys' use as experimental subjects was spent and that it would be advisable to get them home before they evolved to the next stage of conflict resolution, and tried to nuke each other. But Sherif and Sherif (1956) had still one more experimental manipulation up their sleeves. In the third stage of their study, they introduced some superordinate goals.

The water supply system ran into trouble. (In fact, the experimenters had turned a valve off and stuffed pieces of cloth into the outlet.) A movie was promised but there were inadequate funds to hire it (or so it was claimed). A truck, essential for the supply of picnic ingredients, failed to start (as they tend to, when experimenters remove the spark plugs). In short, a number of problems occurred which obstructed access to resources that everyone – irrespective of group membership – wanted. Furthermore, the most viable solutions were those to which everyone could contribute. It was announced that at least 20 people would be needed to work out what was wrong with the complex water tank system (which was some distance from the camp), and 22 increasingly thirsty boys set off to see what could be done. It was apparent that if everyone contributed a small sum, the money for the movies could be found. If all the boys worked together to tug the truck into action, it might get going again.

And so, for good reasons, the boys, whose intergroup relations had degenerated so rapidly from their opening tug-of-war contest, now found themselves on the same side of the rope, straining toward a common goal. They got the truck started and by the time it came back with the food, the boys were less bothered than they had been earlier about the desirability of separate group facilities. They even prepared and shared out the meal together. The cooperative spirit continued, and the Rattlers and the Eagles tackled other problems around the camp jointly. Each boy chipped in toward the hire of the films (Cowboys and Indians, to be sure, but not followed by intergroup bloodshed). The experimenters got out the stereotype scales and friendship measures, and found that several boys mentioned they were glad of another chance to complete these, as they had "changed their minds" since the last time. The results showed that, while ingroup favoritism remained strong, the outgroup was no longer seen so negatively, and the boys began to concede that the other lot was not so bad after all. In short, even after quite intense intergroup hostilities, it proved possible to bring about a more cooperative climate – to change the nature of the situation – by introducing superordinate goals.

Gender Differences in Prosocial Behavior

Social stereotypes hold that females are more nurturant, more emotional, and more sensitive to the needs of others than are males, who are expected to be tough and assertive (Bem, 1974, 1993; Eagly, 1987; Piliavin and Unger, 1985; Spence and Helmreich, 1978; see chapter 5). Perhaps the Sherifs chose boys for their experiment because they anticipated less prosocial behavior among members of this sex. Both a social learning theory and a sociobiological framework would predict sex differences in prosocial behavior, with females scoring higher. According to sociobiologists, males can be expected to take a protective role toward their family (and other possessions), while females should reveal a nurturant commitment toward persons, especially their children. According to social learning theorists, others' expectations, interventions, and modeling should promote the transmission of cultural norms about female and male behavior. It is pertinent to ask whether there actually is any evidence of sex differences in prosocial behavior and empathy.

The answer is yes and no. Reviews of gender differences in empathy among children and adults find some inconsistencies from study to study, but show that in the main, sex differences tend to turn up when demand characteristics are high (Eagly, 1987; Lennon and Eisenberg, 1987). That is, when subjects have conscious control of their responses (e.g., in paper-and-pencil tasks) and are *aware* that they are being assessed in some way (e.g., in a laboratory), then sex differences are obtained which seem to show greater empathy or helpfulness in females. However, when demand characteristics are low — for instance, if unobtrusive measures are taken of physiological or facial reactions to another's distress — then sex differences disappear. Eagly and Crowley (1986) found that sex differences were associated with the sex-typing of the context in which help was prompted. For example, if the dependent measure is helping a motorist with a flat tire or picking someone up who has collapsed in the subway (contexts which expose the helper to some risk), then males score higher; but if the measure is calling the garage for assistance or volunteering to spend time with handicapped children, then females score higher. Eagly (1987; Eagly and Crowley, 1986) argues that this pattern of results is consistent with a social role explanation of gender differences in prosocial behavior according to which males are expected to present heroic and chivalrous personae (agentic), while females are encouraged to be sympathetic to others' needs and emotions (communal).

Gender role stereotypes appear to influence patterns of caregiving provided to even quite young children. Dunn et al. (1987) found that mothers talking to 12–24-month-old daughters referred more frequently to emotional states than did mothers talking to their sons. Parents reward girls more frequently than boys for helping others (Fagot, 1978). Girls tend in most cultures to be given responsibilities for taking care of others, such as siblings, or assisting in domestic tasks, while boys are often involved in ventures away from the home (Whiting and Edwards, 1988; Whiting and Whiting, 1975). By around the age of 5 years, girls tend to have acquired other-oriented patterns of behavior expected of their sex, such as showing more interest in babies (Berman, 1987; Reid et al., 1989). Consistent with Eagly's

(1987) social role theory, Berman (1987) reports that not only do girls begin to demonstrate increasing responsiveness to infants during the pre- and early school years but also they are still more likely to attend to the baby if an adult observer happens to be around.

Overall, there is little doubt that social stereotypes of sex differences in prosocial behavior endure (see Eagly and Crowley, 1986), but the empirical evidence indicates that in actuality they are not always obtained, are rarely strong, and are better explained in terms of role demands in different contexts of testing rather than inherent divergences between the sexes. Social learning theorists would point to the importance of role models as sources of information about how and when males or females should behave prosocially; social cognitive researchers add that processing this information and determining its applicability in a particular situation are mediated by developing cognitive competencies and social knowledge. The sociobiologist, of course, will insist that the important question remains: *why* did these role expectations evolve in the first place?

Cross-cultural Variations in Prosocial Behavior

There are differences among cultures in the extent to which prosocial behavior and altruism are manifest, and social learning theorists tend to point to these as good evidence of the influence of extrinsic variables upon social learning. Sociobiologists argue that cultural differences are explicable as adaptations to local conditions; however, some loosening of the genetic message has to be acknowledged if we are to account for the possibility that a child born in one community but raised in another is more likely to acquire the prosocial standards of his or her actual rather than inherited environment.

One of the most remarkable inter-cultural contrasts is that between the Waorani people of the Amazon, whom we considered in chapter 12, and the Semai Senoi, an aboriginal people of the Malaysian rainforest. The Waorani, you will recall, have achieved the status of one of the most warlike people on earth. Fighting regularly with neighboring groups as well as among themselves, they are involved almost continuously in animosities and blood feuds resulting in long-term grudges which sustain a cycle of vengeful attacks. The Waorani believe that, when it comes to the crunch, each individual should look after him or herself. If grandparents become a burden, they are often speared to death by their own grandchildren (the Inuit option of staying behind on an ice floe is neither ecologically nor temperamentally congenial to the Waorani). In the event of a raid, each person makes a run for it, with family members disregarding each other and parents abandoning their children in the haste for safety (Robarchek and Robarchek, 1992). The Waorani are not dominated by prosocial motivations; *Sesame Street* might help, but you can see the logistical obstacles to installing the cable service.

The Semai enjoy a much more harmonious existence (Robarchek and Robarchek, 1992). For these people, survival is intimately connected to community cooperation. They perceive the forest environment that surrounds their habitat as a world of unremitting danger, populated by a host of evil forces. As a result, mutual support among members of the community is seen as essential. There is a great stress on sharing, non-aggressiveness, and nurturance.

The children of these distinct societies are immersed in very different value systems and exposed to very different forms of behavior. Not surprisingly, the young of the Semai Hopi community grow up with a much greater propensity to prosocial behavior than do their counterparts in the Waorani.

Other children enter diverse social environments, not all as extreme as the Waorani and Semai worlds, but differing in terms of the expectations, examples and endorsements with respect to prosocial behavior. Hofstede (1983) and Triandis (1991; Triandis et al., 1988) have argued that all cultures involve two organizational tendencies: collectivism (structuring information around ingroups) and individualism (structuring information around individuals). Although both patterns may occur within a society, different societies attach more importance to one or the other. Many Western nations tend to value individualism, with an emphasis on personal responsibility and achievement. Other, collectivist societies, such as the People's Republic of China, stress the obligations of the citizen to her or his community, valuing loyalty, trust and cooperation. These cultural orientations have consequences for socialization, leading to an emphasis on self-reliance for the individualist cultures, and social conformity for the collectivist (Stevenson, 1991; Triandis, 1991). This may in turn lead to variations in the degree of prosocial behavior in the young of the society. The children of one of the leading individualist cultures, the USA, are regarded by some as "singularly deficient in prosocial development" (Perry and Bussey, 1984, p. 234; see also Smith and Bond, 1994). The children of one of the major collectivist cultures, China, have been found in some studies to be better behaved, more deferential to adults, less volatile and less physically aggressive than Western counterparts (Ho, 1986; but see Chen and Rubin, 1992, for contrary evidence). In a comparison of preschoolers in Japan, Taiwan, and Minnesota, Stevenson (1991) reports that prosocial responses such as smiling and friendly gestures toward peers were observed in over 70 percent of interactions among both groups of Asian children, but occurred in only 42 percent of the American interactions.

Eisenberg and Mussen (1989) review a large number of cross-cultural studies testing children's performances in tasks which require cooperation. They conclude that children of all cultures cooperate when cooperation is rewarded – that is, when the group receives rewards that are to be shared. But if the reward system is structured differently, such that only individual rewards are available, then cooperation is less likely. In studies conducted in Mexico, Canada, Israel, Colombia, Korea, Australia, New Zealand, Papua New Guinea, Japan, Greece, the US, and elsewhere, a recurrent finding is that children growing up in small villages or rural communities tend to be more cooperative than their agemates growing up in urban environments.

It appears that there is something about the lifestyle of industrialized cities that promotes more competitive and rivalrous behavior in the young (Rushton, 1980). Further evidence in support of this conclusion is provided by studies of people who move from their traditional environments into urban settings; for example, Aboriginal Australians, Canadian Indians, Mexican-Americans (Eisenberg and Mussen, 1989, pp. 46 –7). In each case, members of these ethnic groups who were raised in the cities tended to score lower on measures of cooperation than their peers who grew up in the respective traditional cultures. Similarly, cultures which make the shift from collectivism to individualism (such as South Korea, Taiwan, Japan) tend to report increases in "selfishness" and other undesirable problems (Triandis, 1991).

Culture and some more paradoxes of prosocial behavior

In many respects, these cross-cultural findings make sense. They support the optimistic intuition that there are simpler ways of life out there, where people are nice to each other and children are raised in social contexts which stress mutual respect and cooperation. Indisputably, there are cultures which come closer to this idyll than do many nations of the post-industrialized West. But many mysteries remain concerning the processes and structures that underlie the evolution of aggressive versus prosocial patterns of existence in different societies. If we return to the definitional issues we considered earlier in the chapter, then we are still faced with the issues of motivation and intention. Do people in the "nicer" communities deploy prosocial behavior for selfless reasons, are they adapting to the system of rewards and punishments that happens to be in place in their environment, or are they maneuvering through the socially prescribed regulations to find the best route to what they want?

Strayer (1980) found variations in the incidence of prosocial behavior among four different preschool groups in Canada, but noted that in general prosocial activities were directed toward friends and toward individuals who had higher ranks in the social hierarchy: "altruism" seemed to function to regulate and control social relations. In a West African study, D'Hondt and Vandewiele (1984) found that many adolescents gave to beggars, which seems a nice thing to do. But, although a variety of explanations was provided, a recurrent theme was the return to the donor. Many Muslim respondents believed that giving alms increased the prospects of paradise after one's death: "He [God] will return it in thousands later, besides forgiving our sins." Others felt that they had a duty of charity, because social inequalities underwrote their relative privilege: "in Senegal, begging is a necessity: who should we give alms to if we did not have beggars?"

To take a more dramatic example, we saw above that the People's Republic of China affords a socialization context within which community obligations and concern for the group are stressed, but what happens when there is a threat to the system? Empirical evidence from June 1989 reveals that cadres of highly socialized troops fulfill their collective obligations to the state by gunning down their dissenting fellow citizens in Tienanmen Square. We know very little about how prosocial regulations are used to control the behavior of members of a community, how the social cognitive processes of participants relate to the social contexts in which they develop, and whether prosocial ideologies can ever be coercive, or exploited for individual gain. Future cross-cultural studies may elucidate the regulatory functions of prosocial activity.

Another interesting puzzle arises from the work of the Robarcheks among the

Waorani and the Semai. As we saw earlier, the thrust of most of the work relating to socialization and cross-cultural variability in aggressive versus prosocial behavior points to the importance of family processes in fostering particular styles of behavior. However, the Robarcheks reveal that this is one area where these two disparate communities have much in common: their socialization practices are virtually identical, with both providing relatively egalitarian social structures, maintaining similar patterns of gender roles, and in both cases revealing an "indulgent and nonpunishing" orientation toward children, with warm and affectionate family relations. Adults of both communities love their kids. Why, then, does this goodwill among kinfolk lead in the case of the Semai to reverence and respect for their elderly while Waorani grandparents face the risk of ending their days by courtesy of a descendant's spear?

Summary

Prosocial behavior varies across social contexts. In this section, we have seen evidence that family regimes and parenting values are associated with individual differences in helpfulness in children, that individuals can be helpful in one situation yet reluctant to intercede in another, and that changing cognitions about the situation (for example, by introducing a superordinate goal) can sometimes bring about the mutual cooperation of hitherto hostile groups. Evidence has been noted of gender differences, though the differences appear best explained as role related rather than biological inevitabilities. Finally, we have seen evidence of cultural variability, sometimes quite enormous, sometimes more subtle, as well as signs of cultural paradoxes – such as a commitment to helpful collectivism along with a bullet for those who get in the way, or a predilection for perpetual strife and treachery accompanied by kind-hearted parenting.

Conclusions

The emergence of prosocial behavior remains a puzzling and controversial feature of human social development. People do things to help others, sometimes at risk of personal loss or danger, sometimes with the prospect of personal rewards and gratification. It is often difficult to disentangle these complex motives, and we are reminded once again that social behavior is typically multidetermined. In this chapter, we have seen that it is possible to find reasons for ostensibly selfless behavior in terms of longer-term adaptive purposes; we have seen that individuals' inclination to behave prosocially can be affected by a variety of situational factors, including modeled examples, sociocultural standards and expectations, as well as anticipated rewards or punishments; we have reviewed advances in social cognitive research which point to the importance of developing abilities to represent and operate upon others' needs and means of meeting them. Future developments in this field are likely to consist in theoretical elaborations of the relationships between the different levels of analysis addressed by these currently influential theories.

Further reading

Eisenberg, N. and Mussen, P. H. (1989) *The Roots of Prosocial Behavior in Children.* Cambridge: Cambridge University Press.

A succinct, balanced, and comprehensive review of the developmental issues in the study of prosocial behavior.

Krebs, D. (1987) The challenge of altruism in biology and psychology. In C. Crawford, M. Smith, and D. Krebs (eds), *Sociobiology and Psychology: ideas, issues, and applications.* Hillsdale, NJ: Erlbaum.

A thoughtful and well-documented discussion of the relationship between sociobiological and psychological accounts of altruism.

Robarchek, C. A. and Robarchek, C. J. (1992) Cultures of war and peace: a comparative study of Waorani and Semai. In J. Silverberg and J. P. Gray (eds), *Aggression and Peacefulness in Humans and Other Primates.* New York: Oxford University Press.

Apart from fascinating accounts of two radically different ways of life, you will want to find out what happened when the missionaries ventured into Waorani territory.

Turiel, E. and Wainryb, C. (1994) Social reasoning and the varieties of social experiences in cultural contexts. *Advances in Child Development and Behavior*, 25, 289–326.

Turiel and Wainryb argue against assumptions of within-cultural homogeneity in respect of prosocial and moral reasoning, and stress that prosocial behavior is not always consistent even within individuals. They present a strong case for viewing culture as but one component of social experience in interpersonal relations.

Chapter 14

Moral
Development

Stowaway traveller, I had fallen asleep on the seat and the ticket inspector was shaking me. "Your ticket!" I was forced to admit that I had not got one. Or the money to defray the cost of the journey there and then. I began by pleading guilty: I had left my identity papers at home and I could no longer remember how I had managed to get past the ticket-puncher, but I admitted that I had entered the carriage on false pretences. So far from challenging the ticket-inspector's authority, I protested aloud my respect for his position and submitted in advance to his decision. At this pole of humility, I could save myself only by reversing the situation; so I revealed that I was summoned to Dijon by important secret reasons which concerned France and possibly humanity. Looked at in this new light, there was no one to be found in the whole train with as much right to occupy a seat in it as myself.

(Sartre, Les mots, 1964)

If you break the law and are caught, you can expect to be punished. Take for example, the matter of contempt of court. Breaching a judge's order is a serious offence, challenging the very fabric of the legal system. A British woman who in 1992 disobeyed an order forbidding her to sell any of her family assets pending divorce proceedings was clearly in contempt of court, and the understandably displeased judge imposed a five-week prison sentence. The sentimental might feel the adjudication was a little harsh given that the woman, having been evicted from her home with four young children, including a baby of only 5 weeks, was desperate for cash and had sold the family's caravan for £340. Nevertheless, she was deemed to have broken the law, and if everyone went around breaking the law, the structures that hold society together would be gravely imperiled.

Another British woman with four children suffered a different mishap at the same time: her home was burned down. Unfortunately, she had not taken out any insurance and was faced with a quite horrendous bill for repairs. Happily, the case was addressed immediately at the highest levels of government, and it was soon announced in the House of Commons that the tens of millions of pounds of costs to be incurred in restoring the residence, Windsor Castle, would be met from the public purse. Although with the benefits of hindsight the unsentimental might say that prior attention to insurance and an efficient sprinkler system would have been prudent, the overriding consideration for the British government was that if the nation's heritage cannot be preserved, the structures that hold society together would be gravely imperiled.

What is involved in your reaction to these social events? I imagine that part of your appraisal includes a swift judgment of what you think is *right* or *wrong*. Pressed to explain, you might focus on matters of justice, fairness, principle, the balancing of individual rights and communal responsibilities, the relationship between the person and the social order, and so on. If you do, then you may be engaging in moral reasoning, one of the hallmarks of a mature social being and one of the major sociocultural processes that enables people to co-exist in regulated communities with mutually agreed frameworks of reference for the evaluation of behavior. One of the most crucial outcomes of socialization is the ability to regulate one's own behavior in ways which are compatible with one's society's standards (Bandura, 1986; Kochanska, 1993; Piaget, 1932). At least part of this achievement depends on being able to understand and apply moral reasoning to one's own and others' behavior. In this chapter, we will be examining the origins and developmental course of this capacity.

Some of the controversies ahead will already be signaled to you in reflecting on the cases just noted. Before proceeding any further, you may care to consider a few more moral issues, as presented in box 14.1. In each case, consider what you regard as the morally justified response. Jot down now the reasoning behind your answer; you may learn about your moral status as we proceed.

How do you *know* what is right or wrong? It turns out once again that attempts to answer this question revolve around the axes of nature, nurture, and social cognitive construction. In the first three sections of this chapter we will consider theoretical approaches that emerge from each of these perspectives. These include biological theories that hold that morality is given by the genes, environmental theories that

Box 14.1 Moral decisions

Answer each question and note the *reasons* for your answers.

1 Are there circumstances in which it is morally defensible not to pay for a train ticket?

2 Should the second- and third-generation children of Turkish migrants to Germany be entitled to claim citizenship of that country?

3 Should American general practitioners be allowed to invest in a specialist pathology clinic (to which they then refer their patients, at a suspiciously frequent pace?)

4 Should universities undertake responsibility for the moral character formation of their students?

5 Should there be more female judges?

6 Should Polish MPs be exempted from the drink-driving laws and speed restrictions that apply to the rest of their compatriots?

7 Does a woman of 18 years have the right to choose her own sexual partner(s)?

maintain that morality is acquired principally as a function of external influences, and cognitive developmental approaches which represent morality as the outcome of internal sequences of intellectual progress akin to other aspects of understanding. The cognitive developmental perspective has been dominant in this field since the 1930s, and so most of our attention will be focused on this orientation. In the later sections of the chapter, we will consider also some of its more recent challenges and modifications, especially issues that have arisen as the social contexts of moral reasoning have come to the fore.

In this respect, too, our preliminary cases signal some of the central issues: how do we account for the fact that different people will have different views of what is right and wrong (Sartre versus the ticket-collector, the judge versus the homeless mother, the Conservative Heritage Secretary versus the Labour MPs who felt that the Queen was rich enough to pay for the restoration herself)? You might even wonder if there are gender issues lurking here, too: perhaps the male judge focused on abstract issues of principle and justice, while the homeless mother focused on the pragmatics of care and responsibility? As we will see, the relationship between gender and moral reasoning has become a controversial issue in this field in recent years. You might ask whether ideology – one's political value system – plays a role; after all, it is not uncommon for persons of different political persuasions to disagree about what is right and wrong (as Conservative and Labour parliamentarians demonstrated in the debate over the castle). Finally, there are cross-cultural concerns. Just as a person who grew up in a state without a monarchy might find aspects of the obeisance of the British to the Royal Family surprising, so there are many other features of different societies' values and moral codes that appear peculiar to outsiders. This variability raises fundamental questions for how we conceive of morality and the processes of acquiring it, and some of these issues will be addressed in the final part of the chapter.

Biological Theories of Morality

Philosophers have long debated whether human beings are endowed with an innate sense of morality. Rousseau (1762) maintained, like your breakfast cereal packet, that "whatever is natural is good" (Cleverley and Phillips, 1987, p. 36), and insisted that children were innately pure, free of original sin; it was only when society got to work on the individual that problems set in. On this basis, he advanced the radical proposal that the goals of education ought to be to encourage liberty, self-expression and self-directed mastery (although he felt that benevolent adults could play a crucial role in setting up the conditions within which children's natural virtue could flourish). In eighteenth-century Europe, Rousseau's views inspired intense controversies, and attracted many followers. His ideas have been echoed through the ideals and practices of progressive educators, such as the Summerhill School in Britain and the deschooling movement in the US during the early 1970s (see Cleverley and Phillips, 1987).

In a related intellectual tradition, many libertarian thinkers also hold that the fundamental human capacity is that of creative self-expression, with unimpeded autonomy over all aspects of one's life and thought, and that if we could organize society to accommodate to these then people should be able to live in systems of mutual respect and tolerance (Chomsky, 1969). Again, the problem – the reason why people are not always good – is seen to lie in the pressures of inequitable societies, the uneven distribution of wealth, and governmental oppression. From this perspective it follows that if we reject the idea of humans as possessing innate qualities, including moral consciousness, then the human "is a fit subject for the 'shaping of behavior' by the state authority, the corporate manager, the technocrat, or the central committee" (Chomsky, 1973, p. 184).

While these libertarian views stress the essential creative autonomy and inherent nobility of the person, another biological approach which has gained ground in recent years is premised on virtually the opposite idea, namely that morality is an involuntary function of species' adaptation and genetic survival. Sociobiologists, as we have seen, argue that behaviors appear and recur because they maximize inclusive fitness. From this point of view, moral reasoning could be regarded as "an epiphenomenon masking self-interest" (MacDonald, 1988c, p. 140). For example, protecting one's children, which we might like to think of as a moral responsibility of all good parents, is actually a fundamental biological imperative, and to default is to jeopardize the prospects of one's own genetic material. You can see readily how prohibitions on incest and within-group homicide can be accounted for in much the same way. Sociobiological theory could offer an explanation for the privileges of vodka-drenched

Polish MPs, tearing merrily up and down the country's highways: those who attain superior places in the dominance hierarchy can write their own rules. Can you see how it could also account for the exclusion of impoverished Turkish migrants from citizenship of affluent Germany? We may dress up these instinctive patterns of social behavior in belief systems and moral codes and attribute to ourselves the dignity of honoring higher principles but, according to the sociobiologist, the reality is that "The genes hold culture on a leash" (Wilson, 1975, p. 53).

Summary

The relationship between morality and human nature is a topic of traditional philosophical dispute. Some have argued that humans are by nature "good", although external factors often constrain or distort their inherent virtues. Others have argued that morality is no more or less than the expression of the underlying forces of adaptation, especially the competition for resources and the need to maximize one's own (or one's group's) inclusive fitness. Biological and sociobiological concerns have rarely been integrated with psychological research in this area. This is in some respects unfortunate, since the basic case that the sheer existence of moral orders reflects something of the longer-term presence and social organization of the species is persuasive, while psychological research has tended only to investigate the transmission or reinvention of morality in new generations – almost as if the broader picture were irrelevant. Psychologists focus on the how questions: how is morality acquired? How does it change? Sociobiologists focus on the why questions: why have human communities found it advantageous to develop moral standards? Their answers are not necessarily mutually incompatible (see MacDonald, 1988c, d), but at present dialog is minimal.

Social Learning Theory and Morality

For the sociobiologist, it is obvious that morality is closely tied to the evolution of the species. For the learning theorist, it "is obvious that the external contingencies of the child's immediate social environment exercise a profound control over its behavior throughout the course of socialization" (Aronfreed, 1968, p. 16), and that this is the source of the child's discovery of morality. Thus, from this perspective, morality is learned, in much the same way as other aspects of social behavior are learned.

Learning theorists point to the considerable range of human standards exhibited in different societies to illustrate what they see as the essential malleability of the process. In one community it is immoral to eat beef, in another it is abhorrent to speak directly to your husband's brother, in another it is unacceptable for a woman to expose her face in male company. Even within a given society, supposed moral standards are readily subordinated to situational demands. Milgram (1974) demonstrated that "ordinary people" would discharge several hundred volts into other ordinary people if required to do so in a laboratory experiment, and pointed to well-documented atrocities of war to emphasize the generality of the process. In Milgram's view "when he merges his person into an organizational structure, a new creature replaces autonomous man, unhindered by the limitations of individual morality, freed of humane inhibition, mindful only of the sanctions of authority" (1974, p. 188). Haney et al.'s (1973) well-known prison experiment showed the readiness with which a normal group of American university students was willing to embrace and enforce the brutal regulations of a punitive organization. The variability and instability of moral codes point, for the learning theorist, to the power of the social environment and the immediate situation.

The proposed mechanisms of learning will by now be familiar: positive reinforcement, punishment, and observational learning (including both modeling and vicarious learning from the feedback that others receive).

Positive Reinforcement and Morality

As we saw in chapter 13, there is evidence that prosocial behavior can be initiated or encouraged by praise or other forms of reward. There is little doubt that behaviors which comply with the basic moral standards of a community often will elicit positive reinforcement, and this is likely to promote their repetition. Perhaps some doctors find the reinforcement of half a million dollars a year enables them to see the desirability of strategic investment in local clinics with greater clarity than is accessible to their increasingly penurious patients. Perhaps some newcomers to the profession observe the benefits accrued by senior colleagues, and as they run the facts through their information processing mechanisms they are led rapidly to the conclusion that this is a behavior to emulate. Learning theorists hold that parents' positive reinforcement (whether purposeful or incidental) of socially sanctioned acts is one of the principal mechanisms through which individuals develop an awareness of right and wrong (Aronfreed, 1968).

Punishment and Morality

A closely related mechanism is punishment, through which agents of socialization are thought to inhibit anti-social behaviors. Punishment, according to Aronfreed, results in conditional anxiety becoming associated with the behavioral and cognitive precursors of a particular act (1968, pp. 54–5). This promotes alternative courses of action, including preference for nonpunished behavior and suppression of any inclination toward the punished act. Aronfreed (1968, chapter 4) provides an excellent review of the effects of punishment upon rats, children, and other behaviorally challenging creatures, and there is little doubt that punishment can have consequences for subsequent behavior. Most parents implement some punishment (whether physical or verbal) at least occasionally in managing child behavior. Experimental studies using the *forbidden toy paradigm* (in which the child receives mild punishment for playing with an attractive toy) demonstrate that even hedonistic motives can be inhibited by negative reinforcement (Parke, 1977). Just how fundamental and how effective punishment is as a means of guiding children to adopt the moral standards of their community, however, is contentious.

As discussed in chapter 12, the drawbacks of punishment include the fact that the intervention itself models a hostile means of dealing with problems. For example, spanking a child illustrates that one way of tackling a conflict is to hit someone. Another limitation is that children swiftly become adept in suppressing the punished act in the presence of the punitive agent, but tend to be all the more prone to engage in it when out of supervision (Walters and Grusec, 1977). Whiting (1959) comments that it might be effective to have a policeman waiting around to ensure that every deviation is punished, but this would require rather a lot of officers, working shifts, to ensure that we are all monitored sufficiently closely – and then the problem remains of who would control the policeman (p. 175). Certainly, some policemen do not like being videotaped at work. Further, the short-term efficacy of punishment may actually be rewarding to the *punisher*, thus rendering the treatment all the more appealing when other problems arise, running the risk of establishing a cycle of coercive and abusive parenting which teaches the child fear and avoidance rather than moral concern (Parke and Collmer, 1975; Patterson, 1982).

Even so, it should be stressed that pointing to limitations of punishment as a source of moral learning does not in itself undermine the social learning theory account *per se*. Both positive reinforcement and punishment can affect the extent to which children exhibit behaviors which are judged morally acceptable or unacceptable. Learning what is right and wrong does appear to involve feedback from others. However, just how far this explanation of moral development takes us is debatable. Does response to reinforcement or punishment indicate that the subject has acquired moral standards, or simply that she has learned about payoffs? For the strict learning theorist, this distinction is not really meaningful, since behavior is regarded as governed by external contingencies rather than abstract and invisible principles or concepts. However, even within learning theory paradigms, it has been demonstrated that verbal *explanations* of why a reinforcement or punishment is being administered increase its effectiveness (see Gelfand and Hartmann, 1980). This suggests that invoking (those invisible) reasoning capacities may be more central to moral development than at least early versions of learning theories cared to admit.

Perhaps more problematic for the learning theorist is the question of just how likely it is that children will spontaneously enact the behaviors that socializing agents can then reinforce. If the child is initially self-centered and hedonistic (seeking pleasurable experiences), his or her actions are not always going to be consistent with the greater good. A 2-year-old might be more interested in stuffing cookies into his mouth than observing family standards for good behavior at the dinner table; a 5-year-old might prefer to play in next-door's cement mixer than comply with her father's stipulation that she keep her clothes nice and clean. How frequently will children "do the right thing," thus allowing caregivers to reward approved acts? Not sufficiently often, according to Bandura and other students of observational learning, who propose instead that a more efficient means of social transmission is for children to watch what others do.

Observational Learning and Morality

We have already seen that much work on the development of prosocial behavior demonstrates that "good behavior" can be increased as a result of exposure to modeled illustrations (chapter 13). Similarly, studies extending the forbidden toy paradigm, in which the child observes a *model* receive punishment for approaching the attractive plaything, show that watching what happens to others can be an effective means of inhibiting behavior (Slaby and Parke, 1971).

Bandura (1973, p. 86) points out that in one of his experiments (Bandura et al., 1963) children were very critical of the aggressive tactics that a model employed. However, when he was seen to be effective and gaining rewards, most of the children selected him as a desirable model for imitation. They did not like what he did (calling it "mean" and "wicked") but they were prepared to do it, too: "Evidently, the utility of aggression rather than its moral value served as the primary basis for emulation" (p. 86).

In subsequent theoretical development, Bandura (1977, 1986) has argued that, as children accumulate social experiences bearing on moral issues, they come to represent to themselves increasingly complex information about standards of behavior, motives, and consequences. Part of the basis for development is processing the explanations offered by adults. In this way, some explanations that may initially have been opaque to the child (such as taking into account a person's intentions when evaluating the moral status of her or his behavior) become more accessible.

Summary

The social learning account of moral development accords a critical role to the input of others, but also regards the child as actively involved in processing the socially derived information and, ultimately, internalizing it so that it comes to govern behavior even in the absence of models or reinforcing agents. The familiar processes highlighted by learning theories (reinforcement, punishment, observational learning) are emphasized. This theoretical perspective does more than other mainstream theories to take into account the variabilities of moral beliefs and practices across families, communities, and cultures. The details and development of the cognitive component, however, remain less of a priority for the social learning theorist than the cognitive developmentalist.

Cognitive Developmental Theories of Moral Development

One of the most influential texts in the history of research into moral development is Piaget's (1932) *The Moral Judgment of the Child*. Although now over 60 years old, this book remains a source of inspiration for many contemporary investigators. Its continuing impact reflects both the theoretical scope of the text and the characteristically imaginative empirical strategies it introduced. As with all of Piaget's work, it is based on the assumptions that the child is an active, exploratory agent who constructs his or her knowledge of any domain and that the course of development entails a logically ordered sequence of stages, involving qualitative transformations of the child's thinking. Piaget rejects both the nativist thesis that morality is inherited and the nurture (or learning) theory that it is received from others. The central focus of Piaget's account, and its later extension by Kohlberg, is the development of reasoning about moral issues.

Piaget and Moral Development

Piaget (1932) depicted morality as developing through three stages: amoral, heteronomous, and autonomous. In the amoral stage of early childhood, the child is virtually oblivious to moral meanings, and his or her behavior is regulated primarily from outside – by adults and older siblings. Most of Piaget's attention was concentrated on the two later stages. He elicited children's reasoning about moral issues by means of clinical interviews, including questions about the rules of games that they played (such as marbles) and by posing simple moral conflicts for children's evaluation. On the basis of their responses, he outlined the characteristics of two developmental stages: the stage of heteronomous morality, and the stage of autonomous morality.

The stage of heteronomous morality

During middle childhood (from approximately 5 to 10 years), the child becomes aware of rules governing behavior, and this insight is the basis of moral understanding, the ability to discriminate "right" from "wrong." From the child's point of view, however, the source of the rules is external: they are given by adults. Thus, moral regulations are understood as one-sided, or *heteronomous*. In interviews with 5- and 6-year-olds, Piaget found that many reported that the rules of marbles and other important matters originate with their fathers or with God.

For a 6-year-old, this perspective is realistic. By and large, adults do tell you what to do, what is acceptable, and what is naughty, and adults command the power to enforce their way of looking at things (cf. Higgins and Parsons, 1983). But because young children are, according to Piaget, egocentric and unable to deal with different perspectives, they tend to comprehend moral rules in ways consistent with their own experiences and outlook. These experiences include being on the receiving end of punishment and control. An efficient way to work out what is wrong is to discover what you get punished for or what you are stopped from enjoying. The pervasiveness of adult regulation is such that children learn to reify adults as the source of authority, with the outcome that commands from above (such as tell the truth, do not steal) are seen as the starting points of obligatory rules: "Right is to obey the will of the adult. Wrong is to have a will of one's own" (Piaget, 1932, p. 188).

One consequence is that rules are regarded by children of this age as rigid and unalterable. When prompted to consider bending rules to fit unusual situations, Piaget's younger interviewees asserted that God would not be pleased, and that it would be cheating. Another consequence is that children in this stage maintain a belief in *immanent justice*, that is, the idea that all transgressions are punished. In this sense, young children believe in a just world, anticipating that misdeeds will be detected by authority (parents or God) and dealt with accordingly.

Acts, intentions, and consequences

Piaget also argued that because children were initially governed by egocentrism, they were dominated by the objective aspects of an event rather than the subjective: that is, they focused on what they could see rather than what might underlie a person's behavior. To demonstrate, Piaget introduced a simple experimental technique which has since stimulated a great deal of controversy. He presented children with brief descriptions of two boys whose actions lead to serious or minor accidents:

> A little boy who is called John is in his room. He is called to dinner. He goes into the dining room. But behind the door there was a chair, and on the chair there was a tray with fifteen cups on it. John couldn't have known that there was all this behind the door. He goes in, the door knocks against the tray, bang go the fifteen cups, and they all get broken!

> Once there was a little boy whose name was Henry. One day when his mother was out he tried to get some jam out of the cupboard. He climbed up on to a chair and stretched out his arm. But the jam was too high up and he couldn't reach it and have any. But while he was trying to get it he knocked over a cup. The cup fell down and broke. (Piaget, 1932, p. 117)

Children were asked to say who was naughtier, John or Henry, and why. Intriguingly, Piaget found that younger children regarded John as the naughtier, and explained that this was because he broke more cups. Only older children began to attribute more importance to Henry's illicit purposes.

Piaget took this to support his broader argument that younger children find it difficult to take others' intentions into account in evaluating the seriousness of a transgression. It is not that children cannot understand the intentions of the actor; Piaget's young subjects refer frequently to the underlying motive ("It wasn't his fault. He didn't do it on purpose," 7-year-old, 1932, p. 123). But this spontaneous insight seems to be overwhelmed by the child's respect for adult authority (p. 125). This is a rather subtle point, not entirely clear in Piaget's own writings and often misinterpreted in later critiques. The central claim is that the child at this stage sees "right" as a matter of obedience, and it is only later, when she or he comes to grasp the necessity for cooperation in the regulation of human affairs, that the relevance of a person's intentions is taken fully into account.

The stage of autonomous morality (or the morality of cooperation)

The child's initial, absolutist concepts are eventually displaced as an awareness of the reciprocal force of moral rules is achieved in late childhood. After assimilating many rules and learning of their implications for their own behavior, children begin to ask whether the rules should also apply to others. Parents of children in this stage gain direct evidence of shifts in moral reasoning as their offspring demand to know why, if they have to go to bed at nine o'clock, grown ups are allowed to stay up as late as they please; or why adults can drink alcohol and they cannot, and so on.

Importantly, Piaget sees discoveries attained through social interaction as fundamental to progress to the advanced stage. Peer interaction in particular provides many experiences of different points of view and encourages a keener sense of the necessity for negotiating rules of conduct. This leads to changes in children's perception of the rigidity of rules and to an implicit understanding of their own (autonomous) input into the maintenance of systems of justice at the peer level. In this way, they come to recognize the motivations for cooperation and fairness in social relations. Notice that Piaget casts moral development in terms of the vertical–horizontal shift in social relations, from adult-commanded to peer-negotiated.

Kohlberg's Theory of Moral Development

After the 1932 book, Piaget's interests shifted increasingly toward the investigation of children's understanding of logical, physical, and spatial matters. Surprisingly, the study of moral development was left largely dormant for almost three decades, until taken up again by the American developmentalist, Lawrence Kohlberg.

Kohlberg found Piaget's basic constructivist theory attractive, but regarded his methodology as lacking rigor and saw his analysis of later development as limited. One of Kohlberg's major contributions was to adapt Piaget's clinical interview technique in order to develop a standardized procedure for eliciting subjects' moral reasoning. Essentially, his technique involves presenting subjects with moral dilemma scenarios; the interviewee is asked to make a decision about what a person should do, and then to explain the basis for the decision. The justification is then submitted to a careful qualitative coding procedure which enables the researcher to classify the moral level of the respondent.

To illustrate, consider one of the best-known of Kohlberg's dilemmas, the case of Heinz:

> In Europe, a woman was near death from a special kind of cancer. There was one drug that doctors thought might save her. It was a form of radium that a druggist in the same town had recently discovered. The drug was expensive to make, but the druggist was charging ten times what the drug cost him to make. He paid $200 for the radium

and charged $2,000 for a small dose of the drug. The sick woman's husband, Heinz, went to everyone he knew to borrow the money, but he could only get together about $1,000, which is half of what it cost. He told the druggist that his wife was dying, and asked him to sell it cheaper or let him pay later. But the druggist said, "No, I discovered the drug and I'm going to make money from it." Heinz got desperate and broke into the man's store to steal the drug for his wife. Should the husband have done that? Why? (Kohlberg, 1963, pp. 18–19)

Kohlberg (1963) interviewed large numbers of American 10–16- year-olds, using this and other moral dilemmas, and on the basis of their responses discerned three broad levels of moral reasoning. The first was a *morality of constraint*, in which the child sees morality as imposed by those with sufficient power; the second, a *morality of convention*, in which the child sees rules and authority as contributing to the maintenance of the social order; and the third, a *postconventional* level, in which the young person sees morality in terms of principles of justice and abstract values. Each level is held to consist of two stages, and Kohlberg claimed that moral development involves sequential, stage-by-stage, progress. Not everyone reaches the higher stages, (indeed, so few reach Stage 6 that Kohlberg later dropped it from the model), but all individuals progress in the same, logical order, with the reasoning of each stage building upon and transcending the reasoning of the preceding stage. A summary of the stages, and illustrations of the kinds of reasoning that they embody, are presented in table 14.1, and see box 14.2.

Kohlberg's theory overlaps with Piaget's, but analyzes more closely developments during adolescence and early adulthood. While Piaget represented development as involving progress from heteronomous thought to reasoning which took account of other individuals' perspectives (similar to Kohlberg's Stage 3), Kohlberg saw progress beyond this as involving appreciation of the systemic needs of society (Stage 4), and later (for some), an appreciation that certain abstract moral principles should hold quite generally, irrespective of the local rules.

Kohlberg's is a classic cognitive developmental theory, offering an ambitious, integrated account of the character and changes of intellectual understanding, based on painstaking analysis of responses to imaginatively devised stimuli. While there are interesting issues raised by the other perspectives we have touched upon, Kohlberg's approach seems to have a distinct edge in terms of attempting to characterize the nature of moral reasoning and account for developmental transformations.

Among the key notions of the theory are the assumptions of *stage unity* (that is, that an individual's reasoning is likely to reflect the same underlying cognitive capacity across a range of moral problems) and *stage-sequence invariance* (that is, that progress to higher stages must always proceed in the same logical order). These assumptions are basic to cognitive developmental theory, reflecting its universalistic orientation: the tenet that human psychological development reflects the logical necessities inherent in the successive organizations of knowledge, irrespective of the content of that knowledge. Note that clear and important predictions arise here. Specifically, we would expect a person tested with a series of different moral dilemma problems to achieve roughly the same stage "score" in each. Further, we would expect developmental

Table 14.1   Kohlberg's moral stages

Level and stage	What is right	Reasons for doing right	Social perspective of stage
Level I: Preconventional Stage 1: Heteronomous mortality	To avoid breaking rules backed by punishment, obedience for its own sake, and avoiding physical damage to persons and property.	Avoidance of punishment, and the superior power of authorities.	*Egocentric point of view.* Doesn't consider the interests of others or recognize that they differ from the actor's; doesn't relate two points of view. Actions are considered physically rather than in terms of psychological interests of others. Confusion of authority's perspective with one's own.
Stage 2: Individualism, instrumental purpose, and exchange	Following rules only when it is to someone's immediate interest; acting to meet one's own interests and needs and letting others do the same. Right is also what's fair, what's an equal exhange, a deal, an agreement.	To serve one's own needs or interests in a world where you have to recognize that other people have their interests, too.	*Concrete individualistic perspective.* Aware that everybody has his own interest to pursue and these conflict, so that right is relative (in the concrete individualistic sense).
Level II: Conventional Stage 3: Mutual interpersonal expectations, relationships, and interpersonal conformity	Living up to what is expected by people close to you or what people generally expect of people in your role as son, brother, friend, etc. "Being good" is important and means having good motives, showing concern about others. It also means keeping mutual relationships, such as trust, loyalty, respect, and gratitude.	The need to be a good person in your own eyes and those of others. Your caring for others. Belief in the Golden Rule. Desire to maintain rules and authority that support stereotypical good behavior.	*Perspective of the individual in relationships with other individuals.* Aware of shared feelings, agreements, and expectations which take primacy over individual interests. Related points of view through the concrete Golden Rule, putting yourself in the other guy's shoes. Does not yet consider generalized system perspective.

table 14.1 continued over

Table 14.1   *continued*

Level and stage	What is right	Reasons for doing right	Social perspective of stage
Stage 4: Social system and conscience	Fulfilling the actual duties to which you have agreed. Laws are to be upheld except in extreme cases where they conflict with other fixed social duties. Right is also contributing to society, the group, or institution.	To keep the institutions going as a whole, to avoid the breakdown in the system "if everyone did it," or the imperative of conscience to meet one's defined obligations (easily confused with Stage 3 belief in rules and authority).	*Differentiates societal point of view from interpersonal agreement or motives.* Takes the point of view of the system that defines roles and rules. Considers individual relations in terms of place in the system.
Level III: Post-conventional or principled			
Stage 5: Social contract or utility and individual rights	Being aware that people hold a variety of values and opinions, that most values and rules are relative to your group. These relative rules should usually be upheld, however, in the interest of impartiality and because they are the social contract. Some nonrelative values and rights like *life* and *liberty*, however, must be upheld in any society and regardless of majority opinion.	A sense of obligation to law because of one's social contract to make and abide by laws for the welfare of all and for the protection of all people's rights. A feeling of contractual commitment, freely entered upon, to family, friendship, trust, and work obligations. Concern that laws and duties be based on rational calculation of overall utility, "the greatest good for the greatest number."	*Prior-to-society perspective.* Perspective of a rational individual aware of values and rights prior to social attachments and contracts. Integrates perspective by formal mechanisms of agreement, contract, objective impartiality, and due process. Considers moral and legal points of view; recognizes that they sometimes conflict and finds it difficult to integrate them.
Stage 6: Universal ethical principles	Following self-chosen ethical principles. Particular laws or social agreements are usually valid because they rest on such principles. When laws violate these principles, one acts in accordance with the principle. Principles are universal principles of justice: the equality of human rights and respect for the dignity of human beings as individual persons.	The belief as a rational person in the validity of universal moral principles, and a sense of personal commitment to them.	*Perspective of a moral point of view* from which social arrangements derive. Perspective is that of any rational individual recognizing the nature of morality or the fact that persons are ends in themselves and must be treated as such.

Source: Kohlberg, 1976

Box 14.2   Should universities undertake responsibility for the moral character formation of their students?

According to Kohlberg's theory, moral development is still proceeding into young adulthood, and participation in stimulating moral discourse may promote higher levels of reasoning. For many people, university education may provide one such context. What role, if any, should the institution and its staff play in furthering the moral development of its intake?

In a provocative article in the *Times Higher Education Supplement*, Joseph Evans, Director of Greygarth Hall, a residential facility for students at the University of Manchester and UMIST, observes that "discipline" and "saying 'no'" have become ugly words these days, and that "sex and drugs are rife among today's students," partly because "the accommodation situation in British universities almost encourages this, as young men and women are thrown together in halls with few if any restrictions" (1994, p. 14). He proposes that the staff of residential halls should intervene to help mold the moral character of the students living there, inculcating a sense of purpose and authority that in his view is sadly lacking in too many of today's young people.

Evans's bold speculations prompt some interesting questions for developmental social psychologists. Can the staff of these institutions impose moral standards heteronomously? If so, would it be best to admit only students at around Stages 1 and 2 of Kohlberg's scheme, as individuals of this level of development are thought to be most responsive to authoritative sources of what is right and wrong?

Could participation in the institution help further students' moral development? Evans argues that it could, since sharing living space and facilities promotes greater sensitivity to the rights of others: "You need only once to take too many potatoes, leaving others short to be told by your table mates that you have excessively asserted your rights to the detriment of others" (p. 15). In other words, living in a hall of residence might help promote Stages 3 and 4 reasoning in which the perspectives of others and the need for shared rules are recognized.

What implications might residentially improved moral development have for students' wellbeing and progress? Evans observes that "Statistics show that results of students in catered halls tend to be a good deal better than those of self-catered ones" (p. 15). Assuming this is true of academic performance, do the benefits generalize to moral development? We know that university students have quite diverse living arrangements. What, then, can we expect for the moral development of students who live in their parental home, alone in bedsits, in shared apartments or houses, or who set up home with partners? What conditions are optimal for the achievement of Stages 5 or 6 moral reasoning?

The reader might care to speculate on the design of rigorous field studies that could further the analysis of residential effects on the moral development of students and test the efficacy of deliberate programs of moral refurbishment, as proposed by Evans. However, points from earlier chapters need to be borne in mind. For example, we have considered arguments that individuals select or even create their own environments: could the licentious and depraved be drawn disproportionately to halls of residence? What role, if any, should we accord to the residents themselves in formulating a moral curriculum? Finally, what are we to make of an anomalous characteristic of the Mancunian students observed by Evans, namely that they have not yet acquired food-sharing skills that we saw in chapter 11 (see figure 11.3) to be within the social-cognitive scope of primary school children?

mental changes always to occur in the same order (i.e., no skipping of stages or regressions), and that this should hold across developmental contexts (e.g., even in different cultures, the underlying cognitive shifts should be much the same). How well supported are these predictions?

Evidence Supporting Kohlberg's Theory

In the 1960s and 1970s, large amounts of research were conducted in the US and in other cultures to test predictions arising from Kohlberg's theory. Much of the work yielded support. Kohlberg (1963) himself tested initially a cross-sectional sample of 7-, 10-, 13-, and 16-year-old American males. Each subject undertook a two-hour interview in the course of which he was questioned extensively about each of a set of ten moral dilemmas. The percentage of answers at each Kohlbergian stage was calculated, and plotted by age. The results showed a reasonable degree of within-subject stage consistency and a pattern of age-related changes, much along the lines the theory would predict. The younger subjects tended to reason predominantly at the lower levels (Stages 1 and 2), and there were higher proportions of Stage 3 and 4 reasoning among the older children. Some of these subjects were followed longitudinally, and re-tested at triennial periods over the next 20 years (Colby et al., 1983). The results of this investigation broadly confirmed the cross-sectional pattern: with increasing age, subjects tended to reach higher stages, and there was little evidence of individuals skipping stages. Many independent studies, using either Kohlberg's scoring techniques or a shorter and more objective procedure developed by Rest (the Defining Issues Test; henceforth, the DIT) have produced corroborative findings, showing reasonably consistently that higher moral reasoning scores are obtained with increasing age (see Rest, 1983).

The next test is to discover whether the same developmental sequence is found in other cultures. There is some evidence to support Kohlberg in this respect, too. For example, Kohlberg (1969) reported that children in Britain, Mexico, Taiwan, Turkey, the US, and Yucatan showed similar sequences of development, although there was some tendency for individuals in the nonindustrialized contexts to proceed through the stages at a slower pace than their Western counterparts. Snarey (1985), in a review of 44 studies completed in 26 different cultures around the globe, concludes that the cross-cultural universality of the model is well supported, with instances of stage skipping and stage regressions sufficiently rare that they could reasonably be regarded as mere measurement error. Edwards (1986), in a critique of a large body of cross-cultural research, stresses that there are a number of remaining questions but essentially concurs that the framework has proven sufficiently adaptable to be useful across quite diverse communities. The remaining questions tend to concern discrepancies in higher stage attainment, and we return to this issue below.

Problems for Cognitive Developmental Theories of Moral Development

Although it is widely acknowledged that Piaget's and Kohlberg's work expanded the scale of moral developmental research, both approaches have been subject to a barrage of theoretical and empirical criticism. We will consider methodological problems, the question of whether the young child really is amoral, the distinction between moral rules and social conventions, and the relationship between moral development and moral behavior.

Methodological problems

One problem which may already have occurred to you is that Kohlberg's methodology, while impressive in scope, must be enormously difficult to implement. Huge amounts of spontaneous and elicited verbal data, possibly varying in many respects from subject to subject, have to be coded and classified – precisely the kind of nightmare that many quantitative psychologists prefer to avoid. Perhaps we should bear in mind that producing huge amounts of complex data is precisely the kind of behavior that human beings are inclined to engage in, and the question of whether we should tackle or avoid such output may tell us much about the relationship between our discipline and people. Kohlberg was prepared to face this challenge, and enriched the study of moral development correspondingly.

Nevertheless, it has been the case that his work has been dogged by criticisms that his scoring procedures are esoteric and subjective (practiced with greatest facility by members of Kohlberg's own research group at Harvard), and unstable (using different criteria at different points in the theory's evolution) (see Kurtines and Greif, 1974; Siegal, 1982, for critiques, and Broughton, 1978; Colby and Kohlberg, 1987; Turiel, 1983, for responses). Among other controversies, there are many who reject Kohlberg's claim of within-subject consistency, and several studies have shown that the same individual can score quite differently across a series of dilemmas (Fishkin et al., 1973; Rubin and Trotter, 1977; Santrock, 1975; see Siegal, 1982, pp. 145–8 for a review). Kohlberg and his collaborators believe that the publication of a very detailed scoring manual addresses many of these concerns (Colby et al., 1987), but the issue remains controversial.

Is the young child really amoral?

Another problem area for the cognitive developmental perspective in general and Kohlberg's model in particular concerns the moral reasoning abilities of the very young child. Piaget saw the child below the age of 5 years as amoral, and directed by older persons. According to Kohlberg, the development of moral reasoning is a very lengthy affair, beginning in middle childhood and progressing into adolescence and beyond. Neither theorist goes into great detail about the preschool child, although there is a certain negativity inherent in both accounts, in that younger children are presumed not to have access to moral concepts and reasons. There is a lot of evidence now available to challenge these assumptions.

Consider Piaget's test of children's reference to intentionality in arriving at moral judgments, the John and Henry vignettes (p. 472, above). Unfortunately, these stories confound different independent variables (Costanzo et al., 1973; Harris, 1981). John's intentions were innocuous and the consequence of his actions serious (a lot of crockery was broken); Henry's intentions were negative but the consequence of his actions relatively minor (only one cup was broken). Other pairings of intention and nature of outcome are not tested. Furthermore, in both cases, the relationship between intention and outcome was accidental (the boys had other goals than the damaging of crockery). Upon close inspection, Piaget's original study turns out not to exemplify the tightest of experimental designs.

Costanzo and colleagues (1973) manipulated the main variables systematically in a 2 × 2 experiment (so that the characters had good or bad intentions and the outcomes were positive or negative). Their results revealed that, just as Piaget had found, younger (kindergarten) children failed to adjust their evaluations according to the intentions of the characters producing negative consequences, while older children did take intention into account. However, when the consequences were positive, kindergarten children were just as likely as older subjects to differentiate according to the character's intentions. Several other studies have shown that preschoolers can take account of the actor's intentions in evaluating the behavior of story characters (Ruffy 1981; Rule et al., 1974) or actual people (such as peers; see the experiment by Shultz et al., 1980, described in chapter 10).

These findings suggest that younger children may after all be able not only to understand information about abstract subjective motives, such as a person's intentions, but also to bring it to bear in moral decision-making. This is important, since the Piagetian and Kohlbergian models maintain that incorporation of the underlying purposes of others into one's moral reasoning is a feature of higher-level cognitive development, and not to be expected of the heteronomous preschooler or preconventional Stage 1 thinker. But perhaps even more important is the discrepancy between conditions in the Costanzo et al. (1973) study. Why should younger children's ability to take intentions into account be revealed in the positive consequences condition but not in the negative consequences condition?

Costanzo and Fraenkel (1987) suggest that the reason may lie in socialization practices. How is a parent likely to react if a child achieves accidentally a positive outcome for malevolent reasons? In such circumstances, parents are likely to focus on the intentions and to criticize the child's motives. In the opposing circumstances, where a good intention leads accidentally to negative consequences, parental feedback may well be ambiguous or downright disapproving. Costanzo and Fraenkel suggest the example of a child intending to help her younger brother out the door, but accidentally knocking him down the stairs. Although the intention was positive, parents may nevertheless be displeased – all the more so in high-damage instances, such as the unfortunate brother breaking his leg. Perhaps this is another tragic example of the ambivalence of sibling relationships, but the daughter's helpful intentions are not likely to appease her parents during the rush to the Emergency Center: she will get a highly memorable telling-off for this behavior.

Children develop early awareness of parents' typical responses to damage, and this highly practical discovery may be more salient to them in judging vignettes involving negative consequences than their ability to infer intentions. It is not that the ability is absent, but that it is *pre-empted* by knowledge of real-world social constraints. In experimental studies with children and adults, Costanzo and his colleagues demonstrate several other examples of the pre-emptive force of social norms (see Costanzo and Fraenkel, 1987).

Morality and social convention

Another departure from the Piaget–Kohlberg tradition is based on a challenge to the notion of stages as autonomous, self-contained structures that are brought to bear in the same way on all types of problems. Turiel (1983) argues instead that knowledge is organized in domains, and that "Development within a domain entails reorganizations of thought, so that separate developmental sequences can be identified for each domain" (p. 20). In particular, Turiel draws a distinction between the moral domain and the social conventional domain. The domain of moral knowledge is concerned with matters of individual rights, harm to persons, and the comparative treatment of individuals. The domain of social convention is concerned with matters of behavioral uniformities that enable individuals within a community to coordinate their behavior.

To illustrate, the rule that you should not kill other people falls within the moral domain; this proscription is obligatory, applicable to everyone, and impersonal, in the sense that it is not based on individual preferences or inclinations (see Turiel, 1983, pp. 35–6). In contrast, the rule that you should not eat dinner with your fingers falls within the domain of social conventions; this rule reflects what people expect of us and serves to coordinate social behavior, but it is essentially arbitrary, and applicable only within certain cultures under certain eating conditions.

Turiel maintains that in both cases, domain knowledge is derived from social experiences. However, moral knowledge is based on an understanding of the consequences of an action for other persons; for example, hitting someone causes pain to the recipient, and this renders the act intrinsically unacceptable. Social conventional knowledge is based on understanding the characteristics of the social system, which involves a recognition that not only are conventions maintained by consensus but also that they could be changed by consensus (we might agree to dispense with cutlery to deal with barbecued chicken wings) or vary with local circumstances (only a Westerner would tackle chapattis with a knife and fork).

If distinguishing the domains of morality and social convention seems to depend on rather fine philosophical distinctions, the striking discovery of Turiel and his collaborators' work is that they are perfectly accessible to preschoolers. For example, young children designate certain behaviors (such as lying, stealing, hitting) as wrong even in the absence of an explicit rule, while accepting that other transgressions (such as chewing gum in class, eating lunch with fingers, addressing a teacher by her or his first name) would be OK if there was no rule against them (see Turiel, 1983, chapter 4). In one study, Weston and Turiel (1980) found that a clear majority of 5–11-year-olds responded that it would be wrong for a school to permit children to hit others in the playground, indicating that children of this age range can weigh a moral value over institutional authority (thus contradicting both the Piagetian view of early morality as heteronomous and the Kohlbergian view that principles outweigh conventions only in the later stages of adolescent moral reasoning).

The following preschoolers' responses to incidents in the nursery illustrate the distinctions Turiel has in mind:

> *Moral obligation*:
> (*Interviewer*: Did you see what just happened?) *Child*: Yes. They were playing and John hit him too hard. (Is that something you are supposed to do or not supposed to do?) Not so hard to hurt. (Is there a rule about that?) Yes. (What is the rule?) You're not to hit hard. (What if there were no rule about hitting hard. Would it be right to do it then?) No. (Why not?) Because he could get hurt and start to cry.

> *Social convention*:
> (Did you see what just happened?) Yes. They were noisy. (Is that something you are supposed to or not supposed to do?) No. (Is there a rule about that?) Yes. We have to be quiet. (What if there were no rule. Would it be right to do it then?) Yes. (Why?) Because there is no rule.
> (based on Turiel, 1983, p. 49)

Several other studies confirm that children distinguish between moral and social conventional transgressions, and view the former as more serious (Arsenio and Ford, 1985; Barbieri and Griguolo, 1993; Much and Shweder, 1978; Nucci and Nucci, 1982; Smetana, 1981; Smetana and Braeges, 1990; Song et al., 1987; Tisak and Turiel, 1988). (There is additional evidence that young children can also distinguish between moral rules and *prudential* rules, such as "Tie your shoelaces," "Put on your sunscreen before you play at the beach;" see Smetana, 1993; Tisak, 1993).

Turiel's theory extends and qualifies cognitive developmental accounts of morality, rather than rejecting them entirely. This picture of children's moral understanding has problematic implications for earlier research into moral development, since Turiel points out that most previous investigators have failed to distinguish between morality and social conventions. Hence, models which represent morality as achieved only quite late in childhood or adolescence may actually be recording progress in the understanding of social conventions; the basis of moral knowledge, according to Turiel, is available much earlier.

Turiel's theory, incidentally, also provides a response to the social learning theorist's argument that morality is essentially subordinate to situational demands, as exemplified by the willingness of subjects to persist in applying electric shocks in the Milgram (1974) experiment. Turiel (1983, pp. 203 ff) argues that the experiment involves both moral and social conventional concerns. He points out that inspection of the transcripts of Milgram's studies reveals that most subjects did experience considerable conflict, and that moral concerns about the wellbeing of the victim were prominent. Turiel analyzes subjects' responses as a function of the coordination of two different domains (moral and social organizational), and shows that when the organizational demands were lowered (e.g., when the experimenter was no longer present) administration of shocks was less likely, and if the organizational demands were disrupted (e.g., two experimenters gave contradictory instructions) administration ceased.

The relationship between moral reasoning and moral behavior

Perhaps the most enduring debate over Kohlberg's theory in particular relates to the question of the relationship between moral reasoning and moral behavior (Emler, 1983; Higgins and Parsons, 1983; Kutnick, 1986; Siegal, 1982; Straughan, 1986). Put simply, we might expect — or hope — that people who attain higher levels of reasoning are inclined toward higher standards of behavior. Kohlberg himself suggested that this was the case: "To act in a morally high way requires a high stage of moral reasoning. One cannot follow moral principles (Stages 5 and 6) if one does not understand or believe in them" (1976, p. 32). Kohlberg stressed that moral stage was not the only determinant of moral behavior — other factors such as social conventions, perception of risk, and self-interest enter into the equation — but nevertheless he was convinced that moral stage was a "good predictor" of action.

Over the years, psychologists have puzzled over this issue. Long before Kohlberg's work, a large-scale study of American school children's moral behavior pointed to marked inconsistencies in individuals' conduct from situation to situation (Hartshorne and May, 1928). Subjects aged 8–16 years were asked about their behavior in contexts in which they could steal, cheat, or lie. How a child responded to one item was found to bear only modest relationship to how he or she would respond to another. A child who might cheat in the regular classroom might be more honest at Sunday school; another who stole from home would be trustworthy at the boys' club, and so on. Even in similar domains, there was little consistency, with subjects behaving honestly on one speed test and dishonestly on another. Overall, intercorrelations were quite weak. These findings are often cited by social learning theorists as indicative of the importance of situationally specific reinforcement rather than generalized moral stages (e.g., Aronfreed, 1968; Mischel, 1976).

There has been debate about Hartshorne and May's methodology and analyses (Burton, 1963; Emler, 1983). However, if we move a few decades on from their work, and turn to research designed to test Kohlberg's position and using more sophisticated methodologies and statistical techniques, the evidence for a strong link between moral level and moral action is still not well established. Many studies find an association (Blasi, 1980), but it is rarely a powerful one (see Kutnick, 1986; Siegal, 1982, for more detailed reviews). Richards et al. (1992), for example, found a curvilinear relationship, such that children classified as either Stage 1 or Stage 3 were less likely than Stage 2 children to be rated by their teachers as displaying conduct disorders. On a Kohlbergian thesis, we should expect a trend toward better behavior with advancing moral maturity.

Of course, it is possible for a low-level moral reasoner to behave impeccably simply by conforming to authority. Only in cases of conflict between convention and moral principle should we expect a more advanced thinker to distinguish him or herself from the compliant masses. In this respect, there is some evidence that postconventional thinkers are disproportionately represented among radical groups. For example, Haan et al. (1968) found that a high percentage of students arrested in a sit-in protest over issues of free speech at UC Berkeley were Stage 5 reasoners. Presumably, the postconventional individuals knew that it was against the law to take over campus administration buildings, but felt that there was a higher principle, the protection of liberty, which must be upheld regardless of majority opinions.

But the distribution of the sit-in group was bi-modal, with many Stage 2 thinkers involved, too. And there were many other Stage 5 students at the university who did not take part in the protests. Brown and Herrnstein (1975) speculate that an important additional determinant of action may be how people perceive the situation. They add: "actions, without context, cannot be rank-ordered for morality" (p. 329).

The fact of the matter is that when people start perceiving situations and interpreting contexts, a large array of other social psychological processes come into play, including selective attention, self-serving attributional processes, awareness of social conventions and ideology. With a bit of imagination, it is never too difficult to find a higher principle to justify one's actions. Jean-Paul Sartre, at the introduction to this chapter, was only reporting the fantasies of his childhood, but note how easily the ticketless 7-year-old's initial law-and-order mentality was upgraded to first-class, highly principled travel once he was able to perceive the situation in terms of his responsibilities to France and possibly humanity.

Human beings are very good at providing justifications for behavior they find attractive. Bandura (1979, p. 351) notes that people do not usually embark on contentious actions until they have convinced themselves of the morality of their behavior. Some politicians (pick your own favorites and listen carefully) sit at the pinnacle of moral flexibility and can justify anything, in colloquial or grand terms as the occasion requires. Even the lowest forms of political action, such as firebombing of immigrant hostels, can be justified in terms of abstract general principles, such as the alleged superiority of the white race. In March, 1993, David Gunn, a Florida doctor, was shot and killed outside a clinic in which he performed abortions. The director of an anti-abortion group, "Rescue America," commented "While Dr Gunn's death is unfortunate, it's also true that quite a number of babies' lives will be saved" (Krum, 1993). From this perspective, saving babies' lives certainly seems an admirable thing, and if serving this higher principle brings about conflict with a law then surely one has to consider "the greatest good for the greatest number"?

Abstract moral dilemmas such as those posed by Kohlberg may be far less prevalent in real life. People are quite adept at not suffering from them. Consider, for example, the affair between Soon-Yi Previn and Woody Allen which exercised the collective moral anxieties of the mass media in 1992. Soon-Yi was the adopted daughter of Woody's estranged partner, Mia Farrow, and sister to Mia's several other adopted children. Should Soon-Yi and Woody have had such a relationship? Should the media have publicized it? Should you and I be discussing it? Much depends on your perspective.

Woody, whose cultural contributions over the years make it indisputable that he is a postconventional reasoner, said himself that he saw no "great moral dilemma" (*Time* magazine, August, 1992) pertaining to this relationship. Soon-Yi was over the age of consent (and, remember, when answering question 7 in box 14.1 you said *of course* an 18-year-old woman has the right to choose: only some kind of Hartshorne and May moral chameleon changes position with every new problem). The relationship was entered into without coercion, and Woody – who did not share an apartment with Mia during their relationship – felt that he was never a father figure to Mia's several adopted children.

Are there any absolutes here? Where is the boundary between being a mother's lover and her children's stepfather? How do we weight the older male's obligations against the free choice of an autonomous young woman? Who has the greater responsibility to the younger children: the non-stepfather or the half-sister? Perhaps you have the answers, but where do they come from: a universal moral code? Your faith (or lack of it)? Prevailing societal values? Gender role ideology? We will explore some of these issues further below, but it is already clear that the relationship between moral behavior and moral reasoning ability is somewhat complicated. This, incidentally, is not Kohlberg's fault – he was trying to understand people, not design them – but it does raise issues that his theory does not address very adequately.

Summary

Cognitive developmental theories focus on the reasoning presumed to underlie morality. Following Piaget, they attempt to uncover stages in the development of moral understanding. Kohlberg in particular has provided an elaborate stage-sequence account of these developments which has proven a fruitful, if controversial, basis for many subsequent studies. Many of these studies provide support, indicating that moral reasoning does increase broadly in sophistication with age, and there is some evidence that this holds true across a wide range of cultures. On the other hand, fundamental premises have been challenged: there are disputes about methodology, there is evidence that preschool children can take more factors into account in moral judgment than either Piaget or Kohlberg assumed; there is a persuasive argument that these thinkers failed to distinguish between morality and convention (a distinction which is available to young children); and, above all, there are the problems of the imperfect relationship between moral reasoning and moral behavior together with evidence that people can be very flexible when it comes to finding moral justifications for their own actions.

The Social Contexts of Moral Development and Behavior

We turn now to look more closely at the social contexts within which morality is acquired and applied. Cognitive developmental perspectives remain prominent throughout this discussion because many investigations of social factors impinging on moral reasoning have been conducted to test or challenge Kohlbergian ideas. We will consider issues relating to the family, gender, ideology, and culture.

The Family and Moral Development

Children's first – and most extensive – exposure to moral regulations is in the context of the family (Dunn, 1988b; Janssens and Gerris, 1992; Kelley and Power, 1992; Siegal, 1982; Smetana, 1989; Speicher, 1994; Zahn-Waxler and Kochanska, 1990). Emler and Hogan (1981) speculate that the beginnings of morality, or at least attunement to the rules of one's community, are to be found in the processes of attachment formation, and they note that securely attached infants have been found to be more willing to comply positively to parental directives. Damon (1988) points out that family rule enforcement often presents a "double message" (p. 51) to the effect that behavior which is wrong here is wrong in general. According to Piaget, the regulations enforced upon the young child in the family establish little more than motor regularities. But closer inspection reveals considerable sensitivity of even quite young children to moral injunctions.

The rights and wrongs of everyday life

Dunn (1988b; Dunn and Brown, 1991, 1994), for example, shows in observational studies of young children at home that there are many domestic interchanges about matters of right and wrong, in the course of which parents express regulations and constraints upon children's behavior and children attempt to reconcile their interests and desires with adult control. This includes learning to take responsibility for one's actions:

> Child, 21 months, spills milk on floor, looks at Mother.
> M: Oh dear, oh dear!
> C: Look!
> M: Look! Yes!
> C: [*rubbing at spill with hand*]: Rub it in. Rub it in. [*To observer*] I done it. I done it.
> (Dunn, 1988b, p. 29)

Before long, children begin to take a more sophisticated perspective on responsibility, learning the early lessons that it is advantageous where possible to attribute it to someone else ("Oh no I didn't. She done it," child age 30 months, quoted in Dunn, 1988b, p. 29), to make excuses ("Sorry. Sorry. Sorry. I don't mean to," 26-month old, p. 32; "we only making it up," 30-month old, p. 33) as well as to attempt to justify behavior, and occasionally to question rules. Indeed, children as young as 3 years in Dunn's study were arguing with their parents about the reciprocal application of rules ("Why don't you go wash *your* hands?," child, 36 months, to mother, p. 35). Recall that understanding the mutual significance of rules is thought by both Piaget and Kohlberg to be a much later achievement. Dunn shows also that children this young proffer moral judgments about the behavior of others (such as siblings) and condemn in moralistic language ("Naughty!") disapproved actions.

From a somewhat different perspective, Kagan (1989) arrives at overlapping conclusions about the incipient moral sensitivities of toddlers. Kagan claims that the "central psychological victories" of the latter half of the second year of life are "(1) an appreciation of the standards of proper behavior and (2) an awareness of one's actions, intentions, states, and competences" (p. 236). In experimental and observational studies, he shows a marked tendency of children of this age to detect and comment on anomalies and flaws in the physical environment (such as small holes in clothing, minor cracks in household implements, broken toys, often reacted to with exclamations such as "Oh-oh"). In a related longitudinal study, Lamb (1991) found that internal state words (such as *happy*, *sad*, *hungry*, *sleepy*, *scared*, etc.) and morally evaluative words (*good*, *bad*, *dirty*, *yucky*, and *nice*) emerged in children's early vocabularies within 2–4 months of the peak of their awareness of standards. Lamb found no evidence that maternal use of these terms preceded their appearance in the children's vocabulary, but rather that mothers used the words more in response to their child's growing interest.

While Dunn sees early moral sensibilities as closely tied to the interpersonal negotiations of the family, Kagan sees these developments as the outcome of maturational processes and the emergence of self-awareness, which he regards as possibly triggered by social interaction but preprogramed to emerge virtually independently of context. Although the developing relations among conceptual understanding, vocabulary use, and social interactions call for further research, the evidence from both Dunn and Kagan indicates strongly that moral awareness is available and is implemented in daily life before the end of the child's second year.

Family context and beyond in the development of morality and social conventions

Discoveries in the family context (figure 14.1) appear important to the discovery of the distinctions among moral, social conventional, and prudential rules (Smetana, 1993). Kelley and Power (1992), in observational studies of American families, provide extensive evidence that children's distinctions among different types of transgressions tend to be very similar to those of their parents, and in particular to those articulated by their mothers. Other research with older children indicates a

Figure 14.1   Siblings can be a source of moral guidance.

continuing relationship between parental moral values and those of their children
(Janson et al., 1992; Siegal, 1982; de Veer and Janssens, 1991; Walker and Taylor,
1991). A key component appears to be the parents' interactive styles. For example,
Janssen et al. (1992) and Walker and Taylor (1991) found that children whose parents
used inductive or Socratic styles (encouraging the child to formulate his or her own
moral accounts) tended to score higher on tests of moral reasoning.

At the same time, parental action and emphases alone cannot explain fully the
nature of children's moral reasoning. Even as parents present and illustrate rules and
conventions, children are active in working out what is at stake. An interesting study
by Ross et al. (1990) suggests that parental interventions may not always illuminate
the elementary principles of justice. Ross et al. (1990) observed mothers' interventions
in conflicts among peers, and found that when mothers intervened, they usually did
so *in favor of the other child*. Presumably, this reflects social norms that one does not
always act in blatant support of one's own progeny. But the mothers were inconsistent
in terms of whether they endorsed rights of ownership versus current possession,
sometimes insisting that a toy be returned to its owner and at other times insisting
that a peer be allowed to continue to play with a toy irrespective of whose property it
was. In the midst of life's little battlefields, mothers seemed to be more concerned
with restoring harmony than with consistent moral pedagogy. This raises the
possibility that in order to make sense of moral rules, children may have to play a
major constructive role.

There is also evidence that early experience outside of the family, especially of
institutional organization, can promote differentiation between different types of rule

violations. Siegal and Storey (1985) compared preschoolers who had been enrolled in day care for 18 months or more ("veterans") with new entrants of the same age range. The children were asked to rate the naughtiness of sets of moral (such as hitting, taking another child's apple) and social conventional transgressions (not putting toys in their right place, eating ice cream with a fork). Both groups of children perceived moral transgressions as naughtier than social transgressions, but the veterans were less likely than the newly enrolled to regard social transgressions as naughty, and were less likely to advocate punishment for these kinds of misbehaviors. Siegal and Storey suggest that the experience of day care may nurture greater independence and thus promote a preference for adult discrimination in rule enforcement (moral rules are accepted, but some of the social conventions like where to put your toys are a bit of a drag).

Overall, then, experimental studies of preschoolers' use of intention cues and observational studies of toddlers' involvement in moral activities reveal that much more takes place before the periods of development covered by Piaget and Kohlberg's stages. Dunn comments that while the 2- or 3-year-old has "no place" in Kohlberg's model, studying the very young in their everyday worlds reveals evidence of nascent moral understanding, including knowledge of others' feelings, anticipation of the consequences of behavior and of likely reactions to one's behavior, and of moral negotiations in which acts are evaluated, excused, mitigated, and denied. A serious limitation of both Piaget's and Kohlberg's theories of moral development is that they underestimate the knowledge and abilities of the preschooler, and fail to incorporate the early social developmental contexts of morality into their models.

Gender and Morality

Yet another area of controversy that has developed around Kohlberg's model concerns the possibility of gender differences in moral reasoning. We saw in chapter 5 that boys and girls live, to some extent, in different social worlds. They experience different social expectations, different opportunities, and different constraints. If, as cognitive developmental theories suppose, moral development draws upon experience, could these differences lead to different moralities?

Piaget (1932, pp. 72f) found that the play of the Swiss girls he interviewed was oriented around games such as *ilet cachant* ("you're it") or *marelle* (a form of hopscotch), which had much more elementary rule structures than the games of their male peers. Piaget felt that the girls' games were so simple as to be hardly worth wasting research time on (p. 73) and, although he concluded that girls eventually achieved similar moral outcomes to boys, he did observe that there was reason for "suspecting them of being less concerned with legal elaborations" (p. 78).

Some subsequent research found differences between males and females on Kohlbergian measures of moral development (Haan et al., 1976; Holstein, 1976; Kohlberg and Kramer, 1969). For example, in a longitudinal study of adolescents, Holstein reported that the most frequent score for girls was around Stage 3, while the most frequent score for boys was around Stage 4.

Look at it this way: one possible conclusion is that females' moral reasoning is inferior to that of males. Such an inference has far-reaching implications for the selection of personnel for responsible positions in society. Surely we would not engage the morally deficient in any area of employment where the principles of justice have to be applied (for example, in promotions, hiring and firing, contract negotiations, and indeed in the legal system itself, where "elaborations" are invoked all the time)? Of course, this is certainly taking the implications of Piaget's and Kohlberg's evidence far further than either of these scientists would intend or approve. However, put theory aside for the moment and face facts. If you look at the gender distribution of the senior judiciary in your country, I predict you will find that about 5 percent is female. To take just one example from a legal system highly regarded by the rest of the world, 22 top judges were appointed in Britain in 1992; two of these were female (*Guardian*, January 11, 1993).

Is this coincidence or was Piaget right about difficulties with legal elaborations? I hear you spluttering apoplectically about sexist biases in the system, the old boys' network and so on. But all that is beside the point if females really do attain, on average, lower moral reasoning scores. The old boys could simply be doing their job, selecting the capable, purging the limited.

Not surprisingly, the topic has aroused heated controversy. Gilligan (1977, 1982) argued that the very basis of Kohlberg's framework – the focus on the development of concepts of justice – is based on a male way of looking at things, and thus introduces a bias against females in the instrumentation and scoring procedures. In fact, much of Kohlberg's early work was conducted with male subjects only, and most of his dilemmas involved male characters as the principal actors, possibly making it easier for male subjects to relate to them. If we locate our analyses in the preserve of one sex, we run the risk of overlooking different phenomena and processes that may be more prevalent in the other.

Return to Piaget (1932) for a moment, and consider what he might have concluded about sex differences in morality if, instead of concentrating on the use and interpretation of rules in marbles and (to a much lesser extent) hopscotch, he had analyzed the interpersonal relations that the children engaged in *around* their games. Subsequent research in the US by Lever (1978) and Borman and Kurdek (1987) confirmed Piaget's finding that boys tend to be much more involved in rule-based competitive games than do girls, but showed also that girls' activities reflected relationship issues – matters such as cooperation and interpersonal intimacy – much more than did boys'. Perhaps if Piaget had regarded *relating to others* as more central to morality than *relating to rules* the field of moral development would have progressed in a quite different direction.

Promoting a change of direction, Gilligan argues that different upbringings do engender different moral orientations. She argues that males are socialized to be independent and achievement oriented, and thus preoccupied with issues such as a fair return, equality of treatment, and the application of abstract principles to resolve conflicts of interest. Females are socialized to be nurturant and to maintain a sense of responsibility toward others. In terms of Kohlberg's model, this means that male socialization is directed toward Stage 4 reasoning (maintaining the social order, fulfilling the duties to which you have agreed), while female socialization is directed toward Stage 3 (the morality of interpersonal concordance, living up to what those close to you expect of you). Kohlberg treats the ability to *detach* oneself from the situation one is judging as a measure of advanced morality, while the female's role is organized around *attachment*, and concern for others' welfare. It may be "unfair" that "the very traits that have traditionally defined the 'goodness' of women, are those that mark them as deficient in moral development" (Gilligan, 1982, p. 18).

Consider the judge and the mother at the beginning of the chapter. Which do you find the superior moral action: dispassionately enforcing the letter of the law according to one's analysis of the principle at stake, or committing a minor transgression to feed your children? According to Gilligan, your response is likely to reflect a justice or a care orientation.

Moral reasoning in a female preserve

Gilligan argued that females' moral reasoning emerges not as deficient but as a "different voice," and one that has not been listened to very carefully in hitherto male-dominated moral developmental research. Toward a remedy, she elicited the reasoning of a group of female subjects facing a substantial real-life moral dilemma: whether or not to continue a pregnancy. This issue, she reasoned, poses a central conflict for women, between on the one hand the right to personal choice and on the other hand the convention linking femininity with self-sacrifice and care for others. She interviewed 29 American women aged between 15 and 33 and identified three levels of reasoning.

Level 1 is governed by *self-interest*. Women at this level justify their decisions in terms of their own needs and survival, responding for example that having the baby might restrict one's personal freedom, or having a baby could provide a good excuse to get married and leave home. This is akin to Kohlberg's preconventional level, where moral reasons are dominated by rewards or punishment. At Level 2, *self-sacrifice*, the woman reasons primarily with respect to others' needs, suggesting that she ought to have or abort the baby because of her partner's wishes, or that she ought to place the child's rights above her own. This reasoning is akin to Kohlberg's conventional level, with the individual deferring to social norms and expectations. Finally, at Level 3, *care as a universal obligation*, women achieve a balance between care for others and the well-being of the self.

One woman classified at this level explained: "The decision has got to be, first of all, something that the woman can live with . . . one way or another, or at least try to live with, and it must be based on where she is at and other significant people in her life are at" (p. 96). Following Kohlberg's criteria, this level of reasoning would probably be classified as Stage 3, but Gilligan argues that it reflects reasoning which is abstract and principled, and therefore postconventional. The critical point is that Kohlberg's schema fails to hear this care-oriented voice, because its justice orientation neglects the female way of looking at things.

Of course, Gilligan's data are derived from females only, and it is possible that males involved in abortion decisions would demonstrate very similar responses.

Similarly, it is an open empirical question whether a female judge would imprison a father who defied a court order and sold off property to meet his child-care responsibilities. However, in some of her own research with both female and male subjects, Gilligan and Attanucci (1988) asked subjects to think about real-life moral conflicts they had experienced and then to rate the extent to which they focused on justice or care concerns. Both sexes used both orientations, but men tended more toward a justice focus, while women tended more toward a care focus.

Reactions to Gilligan's position

Gilligan's critique and her new model have in turn generated a lot of debate. One major problem is that sex differences in moral reasoning turn out to be much less clear cut than Gilligan first supposed. While some studies have found differences in favor of males, most have not. Walker (1984) found sex differences in only eight out of 54 studies conducted in the United States (and a couple of these were in favor of females). Snarey (1985), in a review of 17 cross-cultural investigations conducted in 15 different countries, found sex differences in only three studies, and comments that only one of these was clearly interpretable. Thoma (1986), reviewing a large number of studies which had employed the DIT (see above, p. 478), found evidence of a slight female superiority.

Other evidence brings into question the assertion that moral reasoning based on a care orientation is a mode of social cognition that is peculiar to females, or as Unger and Crawford (1992, p. 50) put it, questions "whether the different voice is a *woman's* voice." Gilligan and Attanucci's (1988) report has been criticized for sampling and design limitations, and a larger investigation conducted by Ford and Lowery (1986) failed to obtain reliable sex differences in justice versus care orientations.

An impressive study by Walker et al. (1987) interviewed 80 Canadian children and their parents about both real-life and hypothetical dilemmas and found that only a minority of subjects reasoned consistently with one orientation, that most showed no clear preference, and that the evidence for sex differences was slight. Interestingly, evidence did emerge from this study that individuals who scored high on a Kohlberg-related measure of moral level tended to use *both* a justice and a care orientation.

Finally, it is important to note that the gap between moral reasoning and moral behavior is not narrowed by Gilligan's model. If women have a care orientation, this does not appear to inhibit their use of decidedly uncaring interpersonal strategies, such as indirect aggression (see chapter 12). The fact that females score higher than males on measures of indirect aggression does not necessarily vitiate Gilligan's account, but to accommodate the evidence of female superiority in this respect we would presumably have to represent "caring" as a dimension that females are more likely to find salient; but which end of the dimension (caring versus uncaring) is actually invoked in a particular social setting may be variable. Furthermore, if females are more oriented toward caring than justice issues, we might expect that females should be less outraged than males by evidence of injustice in society (such as gender imbalance in the appointments of senior judiciary). But there is no such evidence (Adams, 1992; Averill, 1983; Kelly and Breinlinger, 1995).

Gilligan's account reappears shortly, but for the moment the most appropriate conclusion appears to be that her critical perspective opened up the study of moral development in important ways by broadening conceptions of what morality is and how it should be measured. But, like most research seeking sex differences in cognitive performance, it has not exposed a major discrepancy in male and female moral reasoning.

Morality and Ideology

Another problem for Kohlberg's theory is the relationship between moral reasoning and political ideology. Let us return to the incinerated remains of Windsor Castle, and consider the moral dilemma facing the British government. The year 1992 was not a good one for the British economy, which was in the midst of a severe recession; large sectors of the population were suffering as a result of high unemployment and record bankruptcies. In this context, should the government have agreed to use public funds to pay for the repairs, or should it have required Her Majesty to use some of her own enormous wealth for this purpose?

A monarchist might respond in favor of governmental expenditure, offering the justification that the royal heritage is a symbol of the British nation, and that at times of crisis it is imperative for the people to rally to support the Crown; the castle belongs to the nation, and it should fall to the community in general to meet the costs of preserving its heritage. A republican might object that the allocation of public funds for the benefit of an extremely privileged household reflects an extravagantly inequitable distribution of a society's resources, and that taking public funds to pay for repairs to a castle while millions live below the poverty line is an affront to the rights of all human beings to live in dignity and to partake from society's resources according to need. The monarchist and the republican could probably spend an evening elaborating these arguments, but we have a sense of their differences.

If we classify the above parties according to Kohlberg's model, then our hypothetical monarchist comes out somewhere in Level II (conventional). The monarchist used justifications based on conformity to society's hierarchy, maintaining the social order, and interpersonal concordance. Peter Brooke, the Heritage Secretary at the time, appealed to the latter when he remarked that "The heart of the nation went out to the Queen. It is a traumatic experience for anyone to see their home in flames." This shows a commitment to being a good person, loyal and helpful, exactly what one would expect of a Stage 3 thinker. Our hypothetical republican, however, shows a higher level of justification. She appeals to principles beyond mere legal obligations to the ruler, emphasizing the equal rights of all people and rejecting unfair distribution of wealth in favor of the greatest good to the greatest number. This is postconventional reasoning, and would score somewhere around Stages 5–6.

The respective scores of our monarchist and our republican seem perfectly congenial to persons of a liberal political outlook. They are inclined to view the opposition as "morally stunted" (cf. Emler and Hogan, 1981), and application of this purportedly objective scientific theory appears to confirm their assessment. Once again, the Tories are exposed for the low level of intellect that decent thinking people always suspected. But here lies the problem: is Kohlberg's theory really a context-free, universalistic account of qualitative differences in human reasoning or is it at heart an endorsement of the value system of the liberal–humanist Western thinker (which Kohlberg happened to be)? Several critics have made exactly this objection (Emler and Hogan, 1981; Simpson, 1974; Sullivan, 1977).

Emler et al. (1983) have argued that moral reasoning and political attitudes represent overlapping domains (p. 1075). They provided a provocative illustration of the overlap by having Scottish students of different political perspectives (right, left, and moderate) complete the DIT once from their own perspective and once from an opposing perspective. They found that right-wing and moderate respondents achieved significantly higher principled reasoning scores when completing from the perspective of a radical. Markoulis (1989) obtained comparable findings in a similar study with Greek political activists.

These results pose a challenge to Kohlbergian theory, since cognitive developmentalists maintain that individuals should not be able to understand the reasoning of persons at higher stages. If a "morally stunted" right-winger can articulate refined left-wing reasoning, then the argument that selection of principled reasoning is more a matter of political orientation than cognitive level receives support. Cognitive developmentalists have responded to Emler et al.'s case by objecting to their methodology on the grounds that the right-wing respondents may not truly have understood the principled arguments in the fake condition, but simply have picked out ideas that seemed to them to embody the woolly anti-establishment rhetoric of the left ("fancy sounding, rather vague, considerations questioning the existing social order," Thornton and Thornton, 1983, p. 78). Think of our republican's arguments: she fretted about the rights of all human beings to live "in dignity" and advocated sharing in society's resources "according to need." Our conservative might regard these phrases as typical of the vacuous nonsense talked by wet do-gooders – but easy enough to recognize.

To resolve this argument, it would be helpful to test right- and left-wing thinkers' selection of moral reasons in relation to authentic political issues. Sparks and Durkin (1987) conducted such a test with British university students during the miners' strike of 1984–5. This lengthy period of industrial discord was seen by many as the critical battle between Thatcherism and union power, and aroused a great deal of political debate throughout the country. Sparks and Durkin (1987) focused on two issues around which right- and left-wing thinkers had divergent positions. The first was the police use of roadblocks to prevent striking miners from moving around the country to support picket lines. The second was the question of whether the union executive ought to call a ballot of all members before proceeding to strike action. Left- and right-wing students were asked to rate the importance of conventional (social order, law) and postconventional (democratic principles, individual rights) concerns with respect to each issue. Their responses are illustrated in figure 14.2.

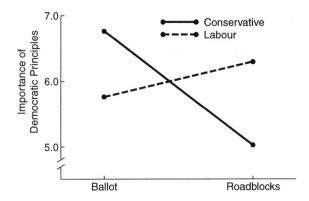

Figure 14.2   Perceived importance of democratic principles
to Conservative and Labour voters of the issues relating to a
national ballot and police roadblocks.
(*Source*: Sparks and Durkin, 1987)

On the first issue, roadblocks, right and left differed in the traditional direction: the right saw individual rights as less important (favoring instead the preservation of the social order). However, on the second issue, the ballot, a quite different pattern was obtained: here, the conservatives saw individual rights as very important (indicating acceptance of a postconventional argument), while the left rated individual rights as somewhat less pressing.

The crucial matter seemed to be the orientation of the respondent to the status quo. When the status quo is in one's favor, one tends to endorse law-and-order reasons for maintaining it; when the status quo is contrary to one's position, one evokes postconventional reasons for rejecting it. Usually, conservatives find the status quo preferable to change, and so their political orientation leads them often to use conventional arguments. Markoulis (1989) found that when a leftish government is in power (as with the Greek socialists), then left-wing respondents are more likely to endorse status quo arguments. As Emler argues, these kinds of findings do not settle the question of whether political orientation and morality are the same thing, but they do make it hard to tell the difference.

Feminism, morality, and ideology

In a fundamental respect, much of the dispute about gender and morality that we have already considered is also a debate about ideological issues. In fact, Gilligan's work itself, and the reactions to it, provide an intriguing case study of the intersection of psychological and ideological concerns. These revolve around a classic dilemma for feminists that, on the one hand, to argue for equality between the sexes entails challenging traditional beliefs about inherent differences between the sexes, while, on the other hand, taking a "no difference" position could devalue women's experiences and perspectives, perhaps even accepting that the benchmark is measures of male competencies (cf. Vasudev, 1988, p. 240; similar issues are discussed by Bem, 1993; Eagly, 1987; Sayers, 1986). Sayers argues that there is an inherent contradiction in Gilligan's stance, which is essentially that she charges Kohlberg with failing to accord equal rights to women and men as individuals (she called him "unfair" above), while she herself maintains simultaneously that women are not as concerned with individual rights as are men. Sayers (1986, p. 19) objects that Gilligan may unwittingly be fostering sex stereotypes that are prejudicial to women (such that women are more empathic and better attuned to relationship issues). After all, what is the best role for a caring, empathic sort of person who is heavily into attachment? Not a High Court judge.

From a quite different perspective, a stimulating if slightly irreverent discussion by MacDonald (1988c) provides evidence of just how readily Gilligan's argument can be incorporated into theoretical accounts with which she is unlikely to be sympathetic. MacDonald interprets Gilligan's work as a promising example of *sociobiological* investigation. Gilligan, he points out, was concerned with a real-life dilemma with real costs for the participants – a good test of whether self-interest or abstract principles prevail. In fact, MacDonald argues, it is quite clear that self-interest wins out (as sociobiological theory predicts), with all of the interviewees choosing the decision that suited their interests, and then justifying the option with reference to moral criteria (several of which both MacDonald and Gilligan regard as self-deceptive justifications). MacDonald comments that "Since Gilligan wants to see her subjects in a sympathetic light, she casts their reasoning into an ethic of care and responsibility," but in his view what she has really demonstrated is once again the triumph of self-interest "chosen according to reasons which make the actor feel good about himself/ herself" (1988c, p. 156).

Who said moral development was boring? What these debates do confirm is that issues of right and wrong are difficult to extract from the social context, and that the search for pure psychological structures that are independent of the respective positions of people and groups in the social order remains elusive.

Culture and Morality

The final demonstration of the complex interrelationship between morality and social context comes with respect to culture. It is indisputable that different cultures have different moralities, and a perpetual debate within this field – indeed, within the study of human nature more generally – concerns the extent of these differences and their implications for our conceptions of human capacities and plasticity.

We saw above that there was a certain amount of cross-cultural evidence to support the basic framework of Kohlberg's model. On many analyses, the model does appear to hold up reasonably well across cultures, with people reasoning at Stages 1–4 being found in most environments, and with most individuals who are studied longitudinally progressing through the stages in the predicted sequence (cf. Snarey, 1985).

Unfortunately, the story does not end there. One problem concerns the higher stages (5 and 6), which turn out to be rare in most cultures, and seemingly absent in many (Huebner and Garrod, 1993; Snarey, 1985). Again, evidence does emerge of differential progress, such that individuals in middle-class, industrialized environments tend to proceed faster and in some cases to higher terminal levels than people growing up in non-industrialized societies (Edwards, 1982, 1986; Snarey, 1985). This poses problems for a supposedly universalistic theory.

There are a number of possible explanations for this finding, and we will consider just two. One is that some cultures simply do not provide the need to engage in complex reasoning about justice, since the regulatory mechanisms and social practices of the community are at a simpler, pre-industrial level: on this view, Western morality is supreme. The second is that Kohlberg's theory is itself culture-bound, presuming quite inappropriately that the values and preoccupations of liberal-educated middle-class Westerners form the summit of human moral capacity.

Western morality as supreme

One interesting version of the "Western morality as supreme" perspective, as discussed by Snarey (1985, p. 227), is the hypothesis of social evolutionism, a mild version of which is embraced by Kohlberg in some of his earlier writings. This is the notion that human morality has evolved from its primitive predecessors in earlier communities to the level of "principled" sophistication we enjoy today in Western societies. It may be that the complex formal systems for the pursuit of justice and adjudication of disputes that are institutionalized in Western societies provide more opportunities and stimulus to take account of the variety of perspectives on a given moral issue; ultimately, this may foster higher-level reasoning.

Snarey (1985) outlines a number of arguments against this interpretation, including (a) cross-cultural psychological evidence that the cognitive structures of preliterate folk societies are often very intricate, sometimes posing a challenge to Western psychologists' apparatus; (b) the fact that members of all cultures have to resolve conflicts in ways which accommodate the rights and needs of competing groups or individuals (very much the kind of problem that Kohlberg maintains facilitates postconventional reasoning); and (c) the fact that US samples do not always occupy the top positions in cross-cultural comparisons of moral development scored according to Kohlberg's criteria.

Western civilization, as Ghandi once said, would be an excellent idea. Of course, Kohlberg is not arguing that the cumulative conditions of existence that fostered the growth of Chicago, the city in which he conducted his original research, were directly responsible for the emergence of postconventional reasoning. (If you visit Chicago, it is best not to go out looking for postconventional reasoners after dark.) But nevertheless there is an element of cultural bias in the assumption that hierarchies of moral thought identified in the West exemplify the higher capacities of human cognition and the most elevated attainments of the moral capacity of the species. Kohlberg eventually distanced himself from this interpretation, maintaining that it is not meaningful to interpret differences in group means on a moral development test with differences in the relative moral worth of cultures (Kohlberg et al., 1983). For the present, there is no clear evidence that life in the West promotes higher moral reasoning – only that there is a tendency for the citizens of industrialized societies to progress more rapidly and, in some cases, to score more highly on Kohlbergian measures.

Kohlberg's model as culture biased

Another possibility, then, is that the Kohlbergian model is insensitive to modes of moral reasoning that exist in other cultures but are infrequent in the West. For example, Snarey (1985) summarizes data from studies conducted in collectivist cultures (Israeli kibbutzim, India, Taiwan, New Guinea, and Kenya) in which subjects demonstrate principled reasoning that assumes different shared values from those of many Westerners, such as obligatory parent–child dependencies, community responsibilities, and a belief in the unity of all life, including animals.

Shweder (1991, p. 221) argues more strongly that Kohlberg's research strategies leave him "methodologically doomed" to impose stage classifications upon informants from other cultures that both distort the meaning of what they have to say and fail to take account of implicit structures in their views of their own social order. Shweder describes an interesting case study based on an interview he conducted with a Babaji, an orthodox Hindu informant in India. The interview included a version of the Heinz dilemma (with "Heinz" translated to Ashok). This vignette raises particular issues for the Babaji since Hindu dharma prohibits stealing for oneself or one's family under any circumstances. The Babaji responds that Ashok should not steal the drug and, using clinical interview techniques, Shweder proceeds to elicit his reasoning:

> I: But his wife is going to die!
> B: There is no way within Hindu dharma to steal even if a man is going to die.
> I: But doesn't Hindu dharma prescribe that you try to save a person's life?
> B: Yes. And for that you can sacrifice your blood or sell yourself, but you cannot steal.
> I: Why doesn't Hindu dharma permit stealing?
> B: If he steals it is a sin, so what virtue is there in saving a life? Hindu dharma keeps a man from sinning.
> (Shweder, 1991, p. 206)

The case is interesting, among other reasons, because Shweder invited Kohlberg to classify the Babaji's moral stage. Kohlberg (acknowledging some difficulties) placed the man at around Stage 3/4, essentially on the grounds that his reasoning reflected a commitment to honoring the conventions (the religious dharma) of his community.

Shweder argues in contrast that Kohlberg's coding criteria prevent him from taking into account the underlying reasoning that reflects the mind of a man with a conceptually sophisticated understanding of his own culture. While the passage above might appear superficially to reflect quite low-level reasoning in Kohlberg's terms (a punishment orientation), if we take into account the Hindu belief system then it is apparent that rather more complex thought is implicated. Specifically, Hindus believe that sinful actions have invariably deleterious consequences, and so to commit a major sin like stealing will lead ultimately into further errors, confusion, and suffering

(Shweder, 1991, p. 207). Shweder argues that in this (and other respects elsewhere in the interview) the Babaji demonstrates a commitment to nonrelative objective values, based on human and spiritual dignity, that transcend immediate circumstances. This, in Shweder's view, is postconventional thought, since the Babaji subscribes to principles that must be upheld irrespective of laws and local opinions.

Shweder (1991) develops a social communication approach to moral socialization which holds that "local guardians of the moral order persistently and powerfully trace for children the boundaries of normative reality and assist the children in stepping into the frame" (p. 191). The implications of such assistance for the structure of moral cognition are illustrated further in an experimental study, also comparing Hindu and Western thought, by Miller and Bersoff (1992).

Cultures, justice, and interpersonal responsibilities, and more missing train tickets

Miller and Bersoff (1992) point out that, traditionally, moral developmentalists have tended to accept a philosophical distinction between justice and interpersonal responsibilities. Justice is concerned with matters of rights that are held to obtain cross-situationally, even universally, while interpersonal responsiveness is a matter of personal choice.

For example, consider Ben, who steals a ticket from the pocket of another person. Most of us would regard this as contravening principles of ownership and privacy. But consider Ben on another occasion where he fails to turn up to deliver the ring to his best friend's wedding. Virtually everybody would regard this as reprehensible but, if you are a Westerner, you might well place this default in the area of interpersonal responsibility: Ben has let down a friend, but he has not clearly breached a principle of justice. Indeed, we have laws against the first kind of behavior (stealing), but only social ostracism for the second (letting down a friend).

This may be a peculiarly Western way of looking at these matters. Miller and Bersoff (1992) compared American and Indian subjects' (aged 8, 12, and 21 years) responses to offences such as the above, and found that while people from both societies were in agreement that the theft was a moral contravention, there were inter-cultural differences over the defaulting best man. Specifically, Americans tended to classify this kind of behavior as a problem within the interpersonal domain, while Indians almost invariably rated it as a moral matter.

This is interesting, but you might be wondering whether this is only a rather academic matter of how we label values, since people from both communities were in agreement that both behaviors were undesirable, and in fact ratings of seriousness of the behaviors did not differ between groups. However, consider the implications for social life if one feels that obligations to others are governed by moral imperatives. Better still, consider the implications in cases where a moral stricture and an interpersonal one are in conflict.

For example, suppose Ben is in Los Angeles (or Mysore) and needs to get to San Francisco (or Bombay) to serve as best man. His ticket has been stolen, and his only means of replacing it is to steal someone else's. What should Ben do? He is faced with two options: the *justice* choice, which is not to steal even though it means letting his friend down, or the *interpersonal* choice, which is to honor his commitment to his friend, even though it means stealing the ticket.

In the face of this kind of conflict, the inter-cultural differences were particularly marked. Indians resolved in favor of the interpersonal choice about 84 percent of the time, while Americans selected this option only 39 percent of the time. Recall that the groups agreed in their ratings of the seriousness of each offence, so we cannot attribute the difference to Americans' inherent unreliability as wedding guests or to Indians' disregard for property rights. The authors argue that there is cross-cultural variability in the priority given to interpersonal expectations: "Indians possess an alternative postconventional moral code in which interpersonal obligations are seen in as fully principled terms as justice obligations and may be accorded moral precedence over justice obligations" (Miller and Bersoff, 1992, p. 551). The Hindu religion emphasizes social duties as the foundation of society. Interestingly, Miller and Bersoff did not find age differences in the patterns of responses, which would seem to indicate that access to the "postconventional" code is attained very early among Hindus. Like 7-year-old Jean-Paul Sartre, they can see higher-level reasons than the uniform of the ticket collector.

If this is correct, then cultural differences in morality may amount to much more than a matter of pace or terminal point of development. Individuals are immersed in the social practices and value systems of their community from very early in life, and the justifications they advance in moral reasoning tasks may reflect accommodations to cultural knowledge (or social representations; cf. Emler, 1987) rather than the independently formulated logic of justice.

Does this bring us back full cycle to the learning theorist's position that what is moral depends primarily upon where one happens to be in the world, and that moral development is essentially an accumulation of externally driven reinforcements? Turiel (1983, 1989a, b; Turiel and Wainryb, 1994) warns that theories which envisage culture shaping behavior (cultural determinism) often overlook the fact that individuals *think* about their culture and that, in any society, social life includes many tensions between the personal and the communal as well as many conflicts among different individuals' conceptions of reality. In Turiel's view, it is an oversimplification to speak of *the* morality of a society. Emler (1987) responds to these kinds of arguments with the claim that the actual content of social cognition is affected by culture, and that all human knowledge of any significance is socially based.

Summary

Aspects of morality vary with family, gender, ideology, and culture. There are differences in perspective and differences in content of moral reasoning according to social context. Much of the debate among psychologists working in this area concerns the issue of whether there are differences in *quality*. Several different positions have been reviewed here, and these highlight controversies that are likely to continue in the post-Kohlbergian era.

Conclusions

Distinguishing right from wrong seems quite clear cut until you start to think about other people. If morality is seen as instinctively endowed, then the perspectives of others are not a major problem since we need only discriminate those who contribute to our inclusive fitness (i.e., those we can cooperate with to gain more resources) and those who threaten it (i.e., by competing for resources we want); the former are good, the latter bad. Although this sounds simplistic, there is extensive evidence in human history that this is how we have organized morality.

Similarly, if morality is externally imposed, for example by superior forces who reinforce and model acceptable behaviors, then the perspectives of others are relevant in so far as we come to share (internalize) them. Although this sounds straightforward, there is extensive evidence from diverse human communities that many of the beliefs and values cherished by one group appear absurd or appalling to outsiders, supporting the view that local influences help determine the moralities we acquire.

Strong versions of each of the above approaches preclude the involvement of the very capacity that distinguishes humans from lower species: thought (cf. Turiel, 1983, p. 165). Dissatisfaction with this oversight led Piaget and later cognitive developmentalists to cast the emergence of morality in a very different basis: not nature, not society, but reason. The development of moral reasoning was seen as closely tied to other people's perspectives, since insight into these was thought by Piaget to promote conflicts which were eventually resolved by transition to new and superior stages of understanding. Both Piaget and Kohlberg see morality as a social achievement, although one that is constrained by the developmental level of the individual.

Recent developments in the study of morality are primarily concerned with the complexities of bringing other people into the picture. Other people turn out to be relevant to early engagement with the moral order; we saw that recent studies by Dunn and others suggest that children are actively involved in moral practices and discourse from infancy onwards. Other people are relevant in a different sense, too, in that some challenges to Kohlberg (such as Shweder's) have highlighted the need for closer attention to the social cognitive structures underlying different cultural groups' moral orders. Within the cognitive developmental camp, it has been argued (by Turiel) that Kohlberg's theory sets morality too broad, failing to take account of the distinction between morality and social convention, and thus overlooking the significance of the child's participation in social actions. From a different perspective, it has been argued (by Gilligan and followers) that Kohlberg's conception of morality is not broad enough, failing to take account of the care orientation, arguably more common among females but accessible to both sexes, yet largely neglected in traditional cognitive developmental models. Explaining how people decide what is right and wrong remains one of the core areas of developmental social psychology, and one that is likely to profit from the continuing controversy engendered by the diversity of perspectives it attracts. What did you decide about the judges in the end?

Further reading

Darley, J. M. and Shultz, T. R. (1990) Moral rules: their content and acquisition. *Annual Review of Psychology*, 41, 525–56.

Arguing that "social and cognitive psychology have let developmental psychology down" in failing to provide useful models of adult moral reasoning, Darley and Shultz analyze the rules used in evaluating moral issues and discuss the possible advantages of computational modeling in this area.

Emler, N. (1987) Socio-moral development from the perspective of social representations. *Journal for the Theory of Social Behavior*, 17, 371–88.

A forceful attack on cognitive developmental approaches to morality, arguing that the constructivist model is "entirely inappropriate" for the explanation of social development, and sketching an alternative based on Moscovici's theory of social representations.

Gilligan, C., Ward, J. V., Taylor, J. M., with Bardige, B. (eds) (1988) *Mapping the Moral Domain: a contribution of women's thinking to psychological theory and education.* Cambridge, Mass.: Harvard University Press.

A collection of essays and research findings elaborating Gilligan's account of two moral "voices," and presenting illustrations of its application to a variety of developmental contexts, from adolescent reasoning to the social outlooks of women in elite occupations.

Huebner, A. and Garrod, A. (1991) Moral reasoning in a karmic world. *Human Development*, 34, 341–52.

An account of the moral reasoning of young Buddhist monks in Tibet, revealing quite striking differences between the basic assumptions of the karmic world and those of Western, especially Kohlbergian, theories of morality.

Kochanska, G. (1993) Toward a synthesis of parental socialization and child temperament in early development of conscience. *Child Development*, 64, 325–47.

A review of theory and research concerning the emergence of conscience, attempting to account for individual differences with reference both to parenting behavior and temperamental variations.

Kohlberg, L. and Diessner, R. (1991) A cognitive developmental approach to moral attachment. In J. L. Gewirtz and W. M. Kurtines (eds), *Intersections with Attachment.* Hillsdale, NJ: Erlbaum.

An integration of Kohlberg's theory with aspects of attachment theory, discussing the role of early affective experiences in the emergence of the moral self.

Minuchin, P. and Shapiro, E. K. (1983) The school as a context for social development. In E. M. Hetherington (ed.), *Handbook of Child Psychology:* Vol. 4: *Socialization, personality, and social development.* New York: Wiley.

An additional aspect of the social context of moral development not discussed above is the school. Minuchin and Shapiro point out that the school is a moral system, providing an institutional framework and behavioral models for moral learning. They review several studies indicating links between school regime and moral development, as well as intervention attempts based on Kohlbergian theory to promote higher-level moral reasoning.

Shweder, R. A. (1991) *Thinking through Cultures: expeditions in cultural psychology*. Cambridge, Mass.: Harvard University Press.

Written expressly for readers with souls, this book demonstrates the strengths of cultural psychology and presents fascinating analyses of the implicit meanings of people's responses to moral dilemmas.

Turiel, E. (1983) *The Development of Social Knowledge: morality and convention*. Cambridge: Cambridge University Press.

A landmark in the field of socio-moral development, elaborating the distinction between morality and convention and providing a new stage-sequence model of the acquisition of social knowledge. Among other features, this book provides a lucid discussion of the divergences between social learning and constructivist theories.

Chapter 15

Adolescence I: Transitions

If you plod along and do the same boring old thing your whole damn life you'll die a boring old fart.
        (American adolescent, interviewed by Lightfoot,
    "Constructing self and peer culture," 1992, p. 243)

We are saying these things now, but we shall end up jumping through the hoop.
        (Spanish adolescent, interviewed by Maquieira,
    "Boys, girls and the discourse of morality," 1989,
                                            p. 54)

If someone describes you as "behaving like an adolescent," he or she is unlikely to be paying you a compliment. Adolescence is not a period of the life-cycle which attracts favorable reviews in the popular media, and there are people who go out of their way to minimize social contact with those perceived to be suffering from the condition. It has been suggested that adolescents are among the most stigmatized of social groups (Elliott and Feldman, 1990; Offer et al., 1988; Rice, 1990). You would be justified in assuming that what your accuser has in mind is something like the cluster of personality attributes popularly associated with *Beavis and Butthead.*

Adolescence is also something of a problem area for developmental psychologists: the main theories (especially cognitive developmental) tend to focus on earlier periods of the lifespan, representing the teenage years as the culmination of intellectual transformations that are more interesting to study in younger members of the species. Although there are many valuable contributions to the study of aspects of adolescent development, it is fair to conclude, with Hill (1993), that at present we lack a unified theory of this phase of life. Social psychologists find adolescents of occasional interest *because* they are a problem (e.g., if they smoke, drink, get pregnant, take drugs, commit crimes) since this generates opportunities for field tests of mainstream theories of attitude formation, social influence, persuasion, and causal attribution and so on with subjects who are old enough to fill out questionnaires and who are usefully packaged in classroom-sized experimental cells. On the other hand, the developmental aspects of adolescence are not always prominent in social psychological approaches.

If psychologists feel a little awkward and unsure of themselves in the face of adolescents, this may mean that there is much to learn from them (adolescents). In this and the next two chapters, we will address some of the key issues in adolescent development. The present chapter begins by considering when and what adolescence is. Although these questions prove difficult to answer precisely, it is clear that adolescence is a dynamic period, a period of change. There are changes not simply within the young person, but within his or her whole social structure. We consider some of the changes in biological status, cognitive capacities and interests, the self-concept, identity formation, relationships with parents, and relationships with peers. Chapter 16 discusses adolescent sexuality, and entry into the adult world (via work or unemployment). Chapter 17 deals with social and developmental *problems* associated with adolescence.

When and What is Adolescence?

Despite the familiarity of the term *adolescent* in everyday language, it proves remarkably difficult to define precisely what such a creature is. When does adolescence begin, for example? As a first stab, we might suggest that it starts at the age of 13 (i.e., entrance into the "teens"). But this chronological criterion fails to take account of the maturational differences among young people. One person of 12 years may be more advanced in physical development than another of 14; one girl may start her periods at the age of 11, while another may be in her mid-teens or older before this major physical change comes about: which of these are adolescents and which are not? There is no known psychological criterion that correlates perfectly with age, and no psychological state that is universally recognized as the marker of adolescence (although there are certainly some social stereotypes that others hold of adolescents, and we return to these later).

It is equally difficult to determine when adolescence ends. Does reaching the age of 20 years signify anything concrete and universal about a person's developmental status? Perhaps we might opt instead for an economic criterion, such as achieving independent income – but how then do we categorize individuals who continue (or return to) tertiary education into their 20s or beyond, or the huge proportions of contemporary young people who are cast onto the unemployment heap, perhaps never to reach financial autonomy? Societal criteria can be arbitrary, too (such as acquiring the vote, which can occur at different age points in different societies, and may not always be exploited by the recipient), or applicable only to subsets of the population and at widely varying age points (such as marriage).

Era, Culture, and Adolescence

To appreciate the scale of the variation it is helpful to consider adolescence from historical and cross-cultural perspectives. Historically, adolescence as it is thought of in the West is a relatively recent phenomenon and one that is subject to continuing change (Ben-Amos, 1994; Hurrelmann, 1989; Furstenberg, 1990; Modell and Goodman, 1990; Youniss and Smollar, 1989). In pre-industrial society, age differentiation was rarely so salient, and people of all ages were involved in many of the same daily activities. This is not to say that relative age was ignored or irrelevant (most societies have regarded young people as developing and learning; cf. Aries, 1962; Pollock, 1983), but it is the case that with the industrial revolution and the development of more elaborate societal infrastructures, age segregation became increasingly common. Adults went out of the home to work in factories, and children were stratified, usually by age and ability, within the educational system. As industrial requirements advanced, increasingly specialized skills were required of the workforce, leading to longer and more finely graded periods of training and to the extension of education beyond puberty. In this way, the transition to adulthood became longer and longer, creating or highlighting the phase of life we now see as adolescence.

Cultures that have not undergone industrialization, or have evolved through somewhat different histories, afford quite different experiences to their young. Among the Sambia of Papua New Guinea the beginning of adolescence is marked quite dramatically, for males, by initiation into nosebleeding rites – painful rituals that are believed to help purge the male of female pollutants (Savin-Williams and Berndt, 1990). Among some African hunter-gatherer peoples, adulthood is considered to be attained for males once they can participate successfully in the hunt and for females once they menstruate or become pregnant (Turnbull, 1989). In some Aboriginal communities in the Northern Territory of Australia, the relatively brief period of adolescence is regarded as ended when a person marries and has children – often in the late teens (Burbank, 1988). It is not that relative age is irrelevant in Aboriginal society, but the transition period is less protracted.

Adolescence and Change

These difficulties in identifying the boundaries of adolescence are multiplied when we try to determine exactly what goes on *within* adolescence. For many contemporary children, adolescence brings a set of major life changes, related to biology, social status, and organizational context (Simmons et al., 1987). We will see later in the chapter that the biological changes have implications for how the young person relates to others. Changes in social status are also far reaching, and somewhat ambiguous; on the one hand, the adolescent is moving beyond the dependent and relatively controlled period of childhood; on the other hand, he or she is not yet regarded or treated as an independent adult.

Changes in organizational context typically involve the transition from junior to high school, which in most educational systems means moving from small, familiar settings to large, more impersonal ones. Simmons et al. (1987) note that in a sample of Milwaukee adolescents they studied, the mean school size increased as a result of this transition from 466 to 1,307. And, of course, the young person's status in school shifts from being one of the senior pupils in a manageable environment to becoming one of the naive newcomers in an anonymous bureaucracy.

In this respect, the young person is undergoing one of the more general consequences of adolescence, namely a change in *group membership* (Lewin, 1952). The individual who was a "child" is now *en route* to becoming an "adult," one of the principal shifts in social categories in most societies. Lewin stressed that this "social locomotion" necessitates a change in the life position of the person involved, and that it is a move into a more or less unknown position. After all, one has concrete evidence of what it is like to be a child, but adulthood lies ahead, vicariously familiar in parts but still containing many uncertainties. Hence: "The unfamiliar can be represented psychologically as a cognitively unstructured region. This means that region is not differentiated into clearly distinguishable parts. It is not clear therefore where a certain action will lead and in what direction one has to move to approach a certain goal" (Lewin, 1952, p. 137). Not surprisingly, this scenario presents many challenges to the young person. "Life ahead" must always contain some uncertainties for persons of any age, but the salience of the future is amplified for adolescents because of the transition in social categories that he or she is undergoing.

In short, we like to believe that we know one when we see one, but *adolescent* is an inherently fuzzy concept. It labels a diversity of young people, and covers a lengthy developmental span. For this reason, most psychologists tend to describe adolescence in general terms as a period of transition between childhood and adulthood, acknowledging that the boundaries (and indeed the experiences) of this part of the life-cycle can be subject to considerable individual variation. Nevertheless, as a starting point, we can accept that this is a period of change, with consequences for how the young person thinks of him or herself and how he or she relates to others and to the broader society. We consider next some of the biological changes and their correlates, and then we review some of the cognitive developments of adolescence.

Biological Development in a Social World

The physical changes of puberty are among nature's most emphatic reminders of its contributions to human development. Individuals experience critical physical developments and these are associated with changes in self-perception and behavior as well as changes in others' expectations. We will review these for each sex in turn.

Female development

Some have suggested that the physical changes of adolescence are more stressful for girls, and the larger part of recent research into the intersection of biological changes and social development has been focused on females for this reason. Most researchers observe that the onset of menstruation is an ambivalent event (Brooks-Gunn, 1991; Katz, 1979; Moore, 1995; Ruble and Brooks-Gunn, 1982). On the one hand, it is an irrefutable sign of maturation, and maturation is generally regarded as a positive; on the other hand, it is negatively associated with blood and physical discomfort. A Finnish study found that girls who began their periods early (by the age of 12) were more likely than peers maturing at an average or late pace to suffer psychosomatic stress symptoms during their adolescence (Aro and Taipale, 1987).

On first sight, such findings appear to indicate a unidirectional effect of biology on social development. However, it proves very difficult to separate physical changes from aspects of the sociocultural context. Even the beginning of menstruation, seemingly an endogenous physical development, is affected by aspects of the macro- and micro-systems in which the young woman lives. There is evidence that the timing of menarche (onset of first period) varies as a function of general social conditions, such that girls in more affluent societies (with better nutrition) tend to start earlier (Bullough, 1981). Other social commitments and choices can also affect this transformation: girls who train excessively in some physical activity, such as ballet or sport, tend to start later (Frisch, 1983; Warren, 1983).

So, physical context and behavioral choices can moderate the pace of physical development. But surely the impact of the change when it comes about confirms a direct effect of biology on psychology? Not necessarily. Belsky et al. (1991) propose that rather than treat pubertal timing as the independent variable, researchers should consider the extent to which it may be conceived of as the *dependent* variable – that is, as an outcome affected by other factors in the developing person's social context. They suggest that girls who grow up in conditions of protracted family stress (including parental conflict, marital instability and divorce) may experience behavioral and psychological problems. As we know from earlier chapters, attachment insecurity is more likely under these conditions, and we have seen many examples of associations between family problems and developmental difficulties. Belsky et al. (1991) take the argument a step further, proposing that these stressors could well have somatic consequences, predisposing girls to internalizing disorders and hence lowered metabolism. Lowered metabolism leads to weight gain, and weight gain leads to early menarche.

By this chain of reasoning, the seemingly biological given is located in a developmental social framework. In a test of the model, Moffitt et al. (1992) analyzed data from a large longitudinal study of New Zealand girls, whose physical, psychological, and family histories had been recorded at regular intervals from birth to the age of 16 years. The results provided some support. In particular, family conflict and father absence were associated with earlier onset of menarche.

At the very least, it becomes clear that physical and social changes intertwine. Aro and Taipale (1987) found also that early maturing girls are more likely to begin dating earlier. As a result, they are drawn into more mature, out-of-home activities at an earlier age than many peers. They tend to begin drinking and smoking earlier, which may incur additional stresses.

Menarche and social expectations

Another variable mediating adjustment to menstruation is shared social beliefs about the process. Most societies have organized myths, rituals, and taboos around menstruation (Beyene, 1989; Douglas, 1966; Gillison, 1980; Goodalle, 1980). Among the Gimi people of Papua New Guinea, for example, menstruation is associated with danger and death, and a girl's first menses are believed to symbolize her father's dead child, the appropriate treatment for which is held to be seclusion and ritual incantations (Gillison, 1980). In Western societies, menstruation is often regarded negatively by women ("the curse," Attwood, 1994), and our mythologies acquire ominous scientific titles, such as Pre-Menstrual Syndrome.

Shared beliefs appear to be incorporated into the developmental process (Brooks-Gunn and Reiter, 1990; Moore, 1995). Ruble (1977) provided late adolescent women with false information, supposedly based on EEG readings, about the proximity of their next period. Although all the women were actually about six or seven days away from menstruation, some were told that their period would start within a day or two, some were told that they were mid-cycle, and others (i.e., the control group) were given no information. All of the subjects completed measures of mood and physical discomfort. There were no differences in mood reported, but women in the first group (period imminent) registered higher levels of physical discomfort, including pain, greater water retention, and eating disturbances.

This does not, of course, signify that all premenstrual distress is spurious or induced by cultural mythologies. It is plausible that the subjects did regularly experience discomfort around the time of their periods and news that another was due invoked a cluster of negative symptoms associated with the event – just as the phrase "End of Year Examinations" can stir visceral reactions in the student at any point on the academic calendar. However, this experiment does point again to the interweaving of biology, cognition, and social context. Other evidence confirms that many girls approach the menarche fuelled with negative, socially shared anticipation, and indicates that those with the most negative pre-menarcheal expectations also report the most negative experiences after the menarche (Brooks-Gunn and Reiter, 1990; Brooks-Gunn and Ruble, 1982).

Male Development

The available evidence on the developmental social psychological correlates of male physical development points similarly to interactions between biological change and social expectations. Many years ago, Jones and Bayley (1950) found in an American study that early-maturing boys tended to be regarded more favorably by their peers and by adults, and tended to develop more positive self-images than late-maturing boys. While genetic endowment and environmental experiences are both relevant, it may be overinterpreting the data to assume that the social advantages to early-maturing males are due exclusively to their accelerated progress through puberty. In a longitudinal study, Weisfeld et al. (1987) found that boys who enjoyed dominance status among their peers in adolescence had actually been dominant since at least 6 years of age. Weisfeld and his colleagues propose a sociobiological explanation, arguing that the critical factor may be bodily form, and that males with a strong athletic physique (who tend also to mature earlier) are likely to attain dominance because, as with other species, humans instinctively acknowledge the superiority of those better equipped to cope with the environment, to survive, and to reproduce.

The psychological correlates of one of the major biological outcomes of male adolescence – spermarche, or the first ejaculation of seminal fluid – are difficult to investigate for ethical and practical reasons (Downs and Fuller, 1991; Gaddis and Brooks-Gunn, 1985). However, it is possible to collect retrospective data (adult males' recall of their adolescent experiences) and Downs and Fuller (1991) conducted one such study with a large sample of American men. The fact that most of the subjects could recall spermarche and many reported "flashbulb memory" effects (clear memories of where, how, and when it occurred) indicates something of the developmental significance of the event. Once again, social context appears important in terms of preparing the young person for this development: about one-third of the respondents had no information that spermarche would occur, and almost 80 percent of the sample told nobody about it when it did occur. Fathers in particular seem reluctant to discuss pubertal development with their children (Brooks-Gunn and Reiter, 1990). This contrasts with girl's responses to menarche, in that a majority do discuss it with either their mother or another female confidante (Brooks-Gunn and Ruble, 1982).

Cognitive and Social Cognitive Developments in Adolescence

Adolescence is a time of transitions and, in approaching most of life's transitions, people seek information about what is about to happen and strive to organize their understandings as events unfold (Ruble, 1994). For adolescents, the search for information about the self and the future is associated with major new developments in reasoning capacity. Piaget (1972; Piaget and Inhelder, 1966) viewed adolescence primarily in cognitive developmental terms, representing it as the final, *formal operational* stage of his model of intellectual development. According to Piaget and his colleagues, a person in the formal operational stage becomes able to reason in a more abstract fashion than hitherto. She or he can now formulate ideas and hypotheses without a dependence upon immediately available concrete representations; like a true scientist, the adolescent can imagine alternative outcomes to a problem, and can test the possibilities systematically. Although there are many difficulties with the details of Piaget's model of adolescent thought (see Keating, 1990; McKinney and Vogel, 1987), it is generally agreed that the developments in reasoning capacity in adolescence enable – indeed, compel – the young person to think about the phenomena of the material and social world and her or his place in it in greater depth, and often with greater intensity. However, this does not necessarily entail that the adolescent's theory of self is invariably a "better" one (Harter, 1983, p. 315). One of the consequences of the cognitive advances of adolescence is that the young person has a greater capacity to focus on the self, but this preoccupation can introduce its own distortions: indeed, adolescents often enter a new phase of egocentrism.

Adolescent egocentrism

One notion arising from Piaget's account that has particularly interesting implications for how we understand adolescent social relations is that of adolescent egocentrism. The supposed egocentrism of the preoperational child was discussed in chapter 1, where it was stressed that the label is intended to describe a cognitive orientation (a focus on one's own point of view) rather than anti-social selfishness. Although the inability to take another's perspective is, according to Piaget, transcended during the concrete operational period of mid-childhood, there is still a sense in which older children and adolescents fail to place their own cognitions in perspective. As the adolescent gains increasingly sophisticated understanding of the way the world works, so she becomes immersed in her own new insights. One consequence is that she attaches excessive weight to these, and fails to appreciate that other people may have their own, different, theories and concerns. Although the adolescent recognizes the thoughts of others "he fails to differentiate between the objects toward which the thoughts of others are directed and those which are the focus of his own concerns" (Elkind, 1967, p. 184).

A correlate of this form of egocentrism, proposed by Elkind (1967, 1985), is that young adolescents are prone to entertain feelings, of an *imaginary audience* – a sense of being on show, with the rest of the world focused on their thoughts, feelings and behavior. Elkind points to the heightened self-consciousness of young adolescents as an indicator of the validity of this concept. Adolescent preoccupation with style of dress, physical stature, acne quota, encouragement or eradication of bodily hair, dancing around in one's bedroom pretending to be a rock star surrounded by delirious fans, and so on, could all be interpreted as tokens of the same perception that other people are watching and evaluating. Although the content may be banal, the process is important, because it suggests one of the ways in which anticipation of others' scrutiny may influence our social behavior.

A closely related feature of adolescent thought proposed by Elkind is the *personal fable*. The young person is so preoccupied with his or her own thoughts and significance to an imaginary audience that he or she develops a sense of personal uniqueness and permanence. This gives rise to the egocentric belief that one is above many of the world's mundane demands and risks: "I am different," "it won't happen to me," "I won't jump through society's hoops."

Empirical tests have supported Elkind's claim that these manifestations of egocentrism tends to peak in early adolescence (Adams and Jones, 1981; Elkind and Bowen, 1979; Goosens, 1984; Lechner and Rosenthal, 1984; Ryan and Kuczowski, 1994). Incorporating our cognitions of other people's views may be especially salient during this phase because of heightened intellectual powers, but the tendency may never be entirely lost — even as adults we tend to anticipate others' reactions to our appearance, ideas, possessions and behavior, attributing to "them" greater interest in us than they may actually sustain. The difference may be that adults see themselves as opera stars in the shower rather than rock idols in the bedroom (see Singer, 1992).

The Development of Self-understanding in Adolescence

By early adolescence, the young person is able not only to reflect in more sophisticated ways upon the physical and social world but also to consider more profoundly her or his own self, and the relationship between self and environment. For one thing, the young person is increasingly aware that she or he is changing; this entails awareness that one has a past as well as a present. We saw in chapter 9 that in early adolescence children begin to formulate descriptions of the self in more general and more abstract terms, a development which indicates reflective abilities which transcend observations of one's immediate state and activities. Nevertheless, these self-descriptions do not necessarily form a unified whole: contradictions and inconsistencies are detectable, and these continue into mid-adolescence. Harter (1986) found that children below the age of about 14 or 15 not only provided mutually contradictory self-descriptions, but appeared oblivious to the conflicts.

Although social cognitive progress is occurring, it is not independent of social context. Some of the institutional transitions of early adolescence — especially the shift to high school — appear to have unsettling consequences for at least some young people's self-understanding during this period. For example, Materska et al. (1987) compared children around the shift from primary to secondary school on measures of the coherence of their self-representations. Subjects aged 10–11 years, 11–12 years, 12–13 years, and 13–14 years were asked to assess themselves from their own point of view and from the points of view of their teachers, parents, and friends. The 11–12-year-olds, just entering a junior high school, displayed least coherence across these representations: that is, they tended to reveal inconsistencies between how they saw themselves and how they felt others saw them. Materska et al.' interpret this as due to the impact of the school transition, temporarily disrupting the child's organization of self-concept.

Some broad patterns can be discerned in adolescent self-understanding. After a period of some diffuseness and self-contradiction in self-description, the adolescent generates a more unified self-image (Damon, 1983; Harter, 1986; Selman, 1980). Self-understanding becomes increasingly psychological (Damon, 1983; Harter, 1986), drawing on abstract and internally focused concepts. Adolescents become more aware of their volitional and self-evaluative powers, recognizing that they can take control over their own behavior and thinking (Broughton, 1978; Damon, 1983). Through these social cognitive processes, Damon (1983) holds, the adolescent comes to attribute stable psychological, social, and personality characteristics to the self.

As discussed in chapter 9, developing self-understanding is not a purely intellectual task. It is one with intense affective significance for the individual – deciding who one is and who one might become are hot topics rather than cold cognitions. Furthermore, it is not a task that the individual embarks on alone, coolly detaching him or herself from other people and societal structures in order to make a few objective decisions about life. Deciding who one is to become tends to attract a lot of advice, possibly from conflicting sources, and substantial input from reality, in the form of school grades, peer feedback, and career prospects. In the face of these, adolescents experience emotional tasks and social negotiations, and the sense of self and self-worth can vary as a result.

Self-esteem in adolescence

There is little doubt that the period of adolescence does present substantial challenges to the developing person, many of which are stressful (Fend and Schroer, 1985; Lau, 1990). The multiple stresses of early adolescence have consequences for how the young person feels about her or himself, and particularly for self-esteem. Self-esteem denotes the individual's sense of worth as measured on dimensions which she or he values (Hattie, 1992). It was mentioned above that the transition to high school is associated with changes in self-*concept*, and Simmons and Blyth (1987) found that self-*esteem* drops substantially around this time, especially in girls. Many girls are experiencing not only the institutional shift, but the onset of menstruation and accompanying physical changes together with changing parental and peer attitudes (see p. 509).

The picture emerging from research concerning reactions to these stresses is that there are considerable individual differences in coping and that these interact with contextual factors, such as parental expectations and support, and school regime (Eskilson et al., 1986; Fend and Schroer, 1985; Petersen et al., 1991). For example, in large-scale studies of German adolescents, Fend and Schroer (1985) found that young people were sensitive to both parental and school pressure to achieve; but parental pressure had impact (on self-concept and text anxiety) irrespective of school climate, while school pressure contributed primarily for those children not already under high pressure from parents. Overall, however, while many individuals report lower self-esteem in early adolescence, it is rarely a permanent drop and not the beginnings of a terminal decline. During the teenage years and into early adulthood, self-esteem increases with age (Marsh, 1989; McCarthy and Hoge, 1982; O'Malley and Bachman, 1983).

Is Adolescence a Period of Storm and Stress?

Occasional scrutiny of adolescents may lead to the conclusion that they are suffering not from diminution of self-esteem but from a woeful spate of self-indulgent volatility, out of all proportion to their actual place in the scheme of things. Part of the popular stereotype of adolescents is that they are unable or unwilling to curb the rampant energies and emotional instabilities that correlate with youth. With the surge of hormones, the growth of secondary sexual characteristics, the stimulus of genital arousal, the pressures of educational and career choices, the temptations of drugs, the sway of the peer group, the conflicting messages of the mass media, the lure of Satan, suicide and debauchery in rock music, the impending trials of adulthood, the state the world is in today, the sheer social gaucheness of being 15, and the eruption of pimples – is it any wonder that adolescents sometimes freak out?

Probably not, but in fact, only a minority does. Although stereotypes associate adolescence with rebellion and intense personal turmoil, research indicates that these extreme symptoms are by no means universally experienced (Adams and Gullotta, 1989; Hauser and Bowlds, 1990; R. M. Lerner and Galambos, 1984; Rice, 1990). Following the hour-by-hour emotional states of American 9–15-year-olds, Larson and Lampman-Petraitis (1989) found no evidence of increased emotionality with the onset of adolescence. The myth that adolescence is a period of storm and stress has been endorsed by a variety of influential theoreticians since the early work of the psychologist and educator G. Stanley Hall in 1904. Hall (who was himself strongly influenced by Darwin) depicted human development as analogous to evolutionary development, and saw adolescence as akin to eras of turbulence, "*sturm und drang*," preceding the emergence of a new political order. He regarded the instability, anguish, and intensity of adolescence as a necessary precursor to the establishment of adult equilibrium.

Hall's ideas are now part of popular culture: many parents expect that adolescents will undergo a period of storm and stress (Goodnow and Collins, 1990). However, the research findings suggest that, typically, only about 5–15 percent of the adolescent population report severe psychological disturbances (Kazdin, 1990; Offer et al., 1988; Rutter et al., 1976; Seiffge-Krenke, 1985) – a large number of young people, but by no means a majority. In the light of the undeniable pressures upon adolescents, the remarkable thing about these results is the infrequency of serious malaise.

Adolescence as Identity Crisis

Lay images of teenage turmoil, then, do not hold for the majority of the adolescent population. Another popular notion about adolescence is that it involves an identity crisis as the young person struggles to decide who she or he is and wants to become. This idea, which originates in the writings of Erikson (1959, 1968), has been subjected to extensive empirical investigation. While there is much dispute about the details, the view that one of the central developmental tasks of adolescence is to achieve a sense of personal identity has been widely accepted in the wake of Erikson's theory (Baumrind, 1987; Kroger, 1989).

Erikson views adolescence as a critical period for the formation of a sense of personal identity. He represents this stage as involving a conflict between the need to attain a sense of self-integration (ego identity) and the need to meet the diffuse external demands of society and determine one's place within it (identity diffusion). For Erikson, adolescence is a period of psychosocial moratorium during which the individual asks (and keeps asking) "Who am I?" and "Where am I going?" It is only through the resolution of these uncertainties that an individual becomes equipped for the next stage of human development, attaining the psychological intimacy of adult relationships.

Identity status

Research by Marcia (1966) has elaborated on Erikson's account and identified four different types of identity status found among adolescents:

1   *Identity diffusion*: an identity status characterized by the avoidance of commitment, indecision about major life issues such as vocation, ideology, religion.
2   *Identity foreclosure*: a status of preliminary commitment and value orientation, but characterized by the tentative acceptance of others' (such as parents or teachers) values rather than self-determined goals (e.g., selecting school options because an adult says that they are worth while).
3   *Moratorium*: a status of intense identity crisis characterized by active attention to major decisions, exploration of possibilities for the future (occupational, political, social, sexual) but not yet resolved in firm commitments.
4   *Identity achievement*: individuals with this status have resolved their crises and made firm commitments to ideals and plans.

In a study of American males aged between 12 and 24 years, Meilman (1979) obtained evidence that these statuses were broadly age related, such that younger people tended to be classified as experiencing identity diffusion or foreclosure while from the age of 18 increasing proportions of young men were classified as identity achievers. However, at all ages, only small proportions of subjects were found to be experiencing moratorium, the supposed peak of the crisis. Two obvious questions arise here. First, are researchers making the common "malestream" assumption (cf. Griffin, 1986) that male development is the standard, which we can expect females to share or against which we can measure their deviance? Second, just how common is the moratorium experience?

Gender, identity, and intimacy

With respect to the first question, although many studies have included female subjects, there does seem to have been something of a bias in focus on male identity issues. Erikson (1968) had warned that females are different on the grounds that they postpone their identity development until they have secured a man whose name they will accept, whose occupation determines their social status, and whose lineage they will help perpetuate. Gilligan (1982) argues that because of these differences in orientation we should expect that the achievement of *intimacy* to be a late-emerging concern for males (as Erikson's model predicts) but somewhat earlier for females, since the social constraints upon their development lead them to fuse identity and intimacy: "the female comes to know herself as she is known, through her relationships with others" (1982, p. 12). Consistent with this view, Douvan and Adelson (1966) found that identity development during adolescence was more problematic for girls, many of whom failed to define their identity very fully because they expected the matter to be settled later, by marriage.

The answer to the question of whether the pace of male and female identity development differs is not straightforward, partly because identity development itself proceeds in relation to several different content areas (e.g., vocational, sexual, sex role, religious, ideological) and, at any one time, an individual may be at different statuses in respect of different areas (Archer, 1982; Hill, 1993; Waterman, 1982). None the less, there is some support for the claim that interpersonal relations and intimacy are more salient among adolescent and young adult females (Adams and Gulotta, 1989; Beckett, 1986; Bilsker et al., 1988; Blyth and Foster-Clark, 1987; Gilligan, 1982). Marcia (1980) acknowledges that, when applied to females, Erikson's model and the identity status approach work "only more or less" (p. 178).

Even so, the issue is still more complex because of social presentational factors that may influence how young people of either sex respond to questions about psychological intimacy. Stereotypically, exploration and sharing of emotions are acceptable in females but suspect in males (see chapter 5). Since young people are well aware of these kinds of gender-related expectations, they may feel that it is socially desirable to present themselves correspondingly in interviews and questionnaires. Finally, the dangers of misunderstanding female development via a new stereotype should be borne in mind. For example, Beckett (1986) shows that, although concerns with relationships are prominent among the identity issues of female adolescents, they are expressed and experienced in different ways by different individuals. It is an oversimplification to speak of *the* female route to identity formation.

Does everyone experience identity crisis?

Returning to the second question above, namely the universality or otherwise of crisis, we have already seen that in fact only about a minority of adolescents suffers symptoms of serious psychological adjustment difficulty. However, Erikson stressed that the moratorium may be intense without being anguished, and he regarded it as a psychologically healthy process rather than a potentially catastrophic pathology. The experiences of conscious attempts at self-definition, dealing with contradictory values and self-images, and striving to create a sense of personal order are reported by substantial proportions of adolescents, increasingly so with age (Montemayor and Eisen, 1977; van der Werff, 1985). To this extent, Erikson's highlighting of identity concerns appears well justified. Whether everyone experiences a fully fledged moratorium remains unsettled (Hill, 1993). What does emerge from research in this tradition is that identity development is by no means a short-term process but one that proceeds through adolescence and continues at least into young adulthood (Damon, 1983; Hill, 1993; Waterman, 1982). In chapter 18 theories and evidence will be discussed which indicate that identity development is a life-long affair (as Erikson would predict).

Family, class, and ethnic correlates of identity status

It was stressed above that achieving a sense of identity is not the process of a cognitive isolate but depends on interactions between a developing individual and her or his social context. Not surprisingly, there is evidence that both micro- (e.g., family) and macro- (e.g., class and culture) factors are associated with identity development. Adams et al. (1994) review findings pointing to an influence of family styles, such that diffused youths tend to come from rejecting and detached families, foreclosure youths tend to come from strongly child-centered and conformist families, while moratorium and identity achieving youths tend to come from warm, supportive families that encourage independence and initiative. Since there tends to be an association of identity status with age (i.e., most people do not remain in identity diffusion indefinitely) presumably family styles and any effects they may have are not absolute, though many questions remain about the longitudinal dynamics of identity status changes in different family environments.

Some evidence points to possible class differences in identity development. Munro and Adams (1977) found that, with respect to religious and political identity, college students lagged behind agemates who had already joined the workforce; they concluded that tertiary education (typically the preserve of the middle classes) may extend the moratorium period. It is possible that the college environment promotes the exploratory and questioning aspects of the moratorium more than do the unskilled and low-skilled environments of people who enter the workforce earlier. However, Adams et al. (1994) comment that this study does not rule out the possibility that the moratorium of young employees comes still later, as they begin to reconsider the benefits of employment and their prospects. This remains to be tested but, on either interpretation, differences in identity status seem likely to be associated with differences in economic status.

Similarly, ethnic and cultural context have implications for identity development (Hitch, 1983; Rosenthal, 1987; Spencer and Dornbusch, 1990; Weinreich, 1983). For example, some investigators have found that ethnic minority adolescents are less likely to have achieved advanced identity status than are their peers from the dominant culture (see Chapman and Nicholls, 1976, for a comparison of European and Maori New Zealanders, and Tzuriel and Klein, 1977, for a study of European versus Oriental

Israelis). In a sense, ethnic minority adolescents have to face *threats* to their identities because part of who they are becoming may be devalued by the dominant social group(s) (cf. Weinreich, 1983).

However, these factors do not always result in developmental differences in identity formation. Rosenthal et al. (1983), comparing Anglo-Australian, Greek Australian, and Italian Australian adolescents, found no differences among these groups. Weinreich (1983), comparing immigrant (West Indian and Asian) British youth with native English, found no difference between boys from the immigrant and native backgrounds, and only slight differences between girls from both backgrounds. Kitwood (1983) develops an interesting argument that the traditional Muslim background provides a different basis for the personal and social processes of adolescence, one that is so profound that it pre-empts ethnic and identity confusion among Muslims growing up in Western cultures. In some traditional Muslim communities, for example, the notion of an individual and independent self is circumscribed by a strong sense of place within an extended family, which itself is perceived as part of a community, which in turn is part of Islam. Each person has a sense of individuality but it is highly specified within the structures of the social group. Weinreich (1983) reports that Asian adolescents had very low identification conflicts with their parents, while West Indian girls had high levels.

These findings – that identity statuses sometimes do and sometimes do not differ between ethnic groups – do not, of course, "cancel each other out," but underscore the possibility that identity development interacts with ethnic context. Rosenthal and Hrynevich (1985) did find that 14–16-year-old Greek and Italian Australians reported that in some social contexts (such as in the company of their family or immigrant friends) they felt their ethnic identity strongly, while in other contexts (such as the school environment or with Australian friends) they were more aware of their Australian identity. For these young people, the sense of cultural cohesion and the importance of maintaining links with other members of their ethnic group increased across this agespan, indicating that ethnic identity may become more salient during the period in which the adolescent is working on interpersonal relationships and her or his relation to the broader social context.

Rosenthal (1987) points out that in respect of each of the important dimensions of adolescent identity development (such as physical and sexual self-image, egocentrism and the imaginary audience, vocational choice) members of ethnic minority groups have to deal with both differences and similarities between their group and others in their society. The outcomes are variable, sometimes leading to developmental turbulence as the individual strives to determine an identity (or set of identities) among conflicting pressures and expectations but also promoting greater flexibility among individuals who learn to deal effectively with varied contexts. Rosenthal stresses that there is not *one* route to identity among minority adolescents, but "the adolescent who can wholly ignore his or her ethnic background is a rare creature" (1987, p. 179).

Summary

It is difficult to determine the boundaries of adolescence, and the experiences vary with cohort, gender, and broader social status. Adolescence is a period of many transitions, including physical, cognitive, personal, and social status. These factors interact: we saw that even the pace and "effects" of puberty are moderated by interpersonal and sociocultural phenomena, and the emergence of new intellectual capacities have consequences for self-perception and self-understanding. Although popular myths of adolescence as a time of turmoil are not widely supported, forming a sense of identity is certainly an important developmental task of this phase of life. It is an emotionally laden challenge and one which cannot be separated from the individual's social context. Major components of identity (sex role, race, occupational, ideological) are only meaningful in comparison to others and in relation to socially shared categories. There is some support for the Eriksonian distinction among different identity statuses, although progress through these appears to be highly variable as a function of gender, race, and family context.

Relations with Parents

As already stressed, becoming an adolescent is not an experience contained within the individual, but is a development which has implications for all of the other significant people in her or his life. The family in particular is the location of major changes, and some have argued that the period of adolescence involves changes for the family unit as radical as those of the initial transition into parenthood (Kreppner, 1992). These changes present many challenges to the family as a system, and some of these are reflected in parent–child relations. In this section, we consider the generation gap, the pursuit of autonomy, and the nature of adolescent–parent conflicts.

The Generation Gap

We are all familiar with the notion of the "generation gap". The twentieth century has seen social and technological changes at such a pace that the assumptions and routines of any one generation appear outmoded within just a few years. It seems inevitable that people who grew up in primitive times – for example, when TV sets were in black and white, the video recorder had not been discovered, and schools still taught spelling – would find it virtually impossible to communicate with their contemporary teenage progeny, alien beings who can be contacted only while changing discs in their Walkman, whose literary abilities are stretched to their limits in the task of decoding the latest rap lyrics, who take the miracles of information technology for granted, who sneer at parental theories of how to get-on-in-the-world and who know everything about sex and drugs.

It is common sense that parents and their adolescent children experience a huge gulf in their outlooks, values, and lifestyles, and that their interactions are founded in mutual incomprehension and distrust. But we have found common sense to be deficient as an account of human social development in earlier chapters, and a similar conclusion is promoted by the study of parent–adolescent relations. In fact, it turns out that the generation gap (like storm and stress) is largely mythical (Brown, 1990): parents and their adolescents *do* communicate and get on quite well much of the time. In a very large study of adolescents in ten countries, including Australia, Bangladesh, Hungary, Israel, Italy, Taiwan, Turkey, United States, and West Germany, Offer et al. (1988) found that in each location over 91 percent of teenagers denied holding a grudge against their parents, and similar proportions rejected the ideas that their parents were ashamed of them and that their parents would be disappointed in them in the future. Du Bois-Reymond (1989), in a Dutch study, reported that 96 percent of adolescents say that they are satisfied with the situation at home. Youniss (1989), summarizing a number of American investigations, reports that when adolescents are asked to describe how "close" they feel to their parents, responses are very close for both mothers and fathers.

There *are* differences between generations, but they tend to be restricted to specific spheres of activity. For example, young people often favor different hairstyles and clothes to those of their parents, and may have different tastes in entertainment. Even these differences are not absolute – a pair of Levi's jeans would be equally unexceptional in the wardrobes of a 40-year-old or her 17-year-old son, and in the 1990s young people periodically return to the rock music of the 1960s. In a German study, researchers found that parents frequently adopted the leisure interests of their adolescents, and were out at the same discotheques (cf. Neubauer and Melzer, 1989). Where differences do exist they tend to be visible – concerned with style and fashion – and easily available to stereotype formation processes. Members of the younger generation sometimes *look* different, but in the less immediately obvious but more substantial domains of moral and political values, social beliefs and attitudes, then the congruence between parents and their teenagers tends to be much greater (Adams et al., 1994; Neubauer and Melzer, 1989; Rice, 1990; Speicher, 1994).

The Pursuit of Autonomy

As we saw above, Erikson depicts adolescence as a time of identity formation during which the individual strives toward personal autonomy. Many other theorists recognize adolescence as a time of autonomy seeking (Berndt, 1979a; Blos, 1962; Douvan and Adelson, 1966; A. Freud, 1958), but as Steinberg and Silverberg (1986) point out, each theorist seems to define autonomy according to different criteria. Erikson and Blos conceived of it as a process of individuation, Freud as a developing sense of detachment from parents, Berndt as resistance to parental or peer pressure, and yet others focus on other concerns (see Ryan and Lynch, 1989; Steinberg and Silverberg, 1986). This variety led Steinberg and Silverberg to propose that the development of autonomy is not a unidimensional achievement, but actually involves progress in different domains, and that the pace of development may not be consistent across domains.

They focused on three aspects of autonomy:

1 *Emotional autonomy*, in which the individual relinquishes childish dependence upon her or his parents.
2 *Resistance to peer pressure*, in which the individual becomes able to act upon his or her own ideas, rather than conform to those of peers.
3 *Subjective sense of self-reliance*, in which the individual feels free of excessive dependency upon others, takes initiative, and has a feeling of control over his or her life.

Intuitively, one might expect these variables to be positively correlated. As individuals gain in emotional autonomy, so they might be expected to increase their ability to withstand peer pressure and to strengthen their sense of self-reliance. But this was not what Steinberg and Silverberg found. Working with a large cross-sample of American 12–16-year-olds, they discovered that as emotional autonomy increased, resistance to peers *declined*: "Simply put, adolescents who are most emotionally autonomous in the face of pressure from their parents are least able to remain autonomous in the face of pressure from their friends to engage in antisocial behavior." (Steinberg and Silverberg, 1986, p. 847).

In fact, the patterns of development of the three different types of autonomy appear to be different. Particularly interesting are the indications that for most people in early adolescence, one dependency (upon parents) is "traded" for another (upon peers). As a result, during mid-adolescence there is a tendency to be more dependent upon peers than is the case for younger children.

Ryan and Lynch (1989) obtained similar findings in a separate study also employing Steinberg and Silverberg's measure of emotional autonomy (EA). However, Ryan and Lynch argued that the measure really reflects *emotional detachment* rather than developments in self-regulation. Their findings showed that the higher individuals score on EA, the less connected or secure they feel with their family. In their view, rather than a "trade" of parental dependency for peer dependency, those individuals who become particularly dependent upon peers are actually compensating for the lack of emotional support at home. It is not that they are seeking detachment, but that they lack (or believe they lack) the emotional support and acceptance from their parents that would enable them to deal more comfortably with the processes of individuation. Ryan and Lynch, drawing on attachment theory, argue that "individuation is not something that happens from parents but rather with them"(1989, p. 341). Their view is that just as the securely attached infant is able to venture from the parental base, so the securely attached adolescent is able to address the challenges of self-determination; those without this sense of support turn to peers.

Gender and autonomy

Another important finding in Steinberg and Silverberg's (1986) study concerned sex differences. Again, intuition and folklore might lead us to expect a difference in favor of males: there is a stereotypical expectation that males will become more independent and assertive during adolescence. In contrast, Steinberg and Silverstein found that, on all measures, girls scored higher than boys. The authors suggest that there are two plausible reasons for this finding. First, autonomy may be stereotypically associated with males because the issue is certainly very salient for them during this period, but that one of the reasons it is salient is that they actually experience considerable difficulty in establishing it. Second, stereotypes of adolescents' characteristics and preoccupations may be out of date: perhaps contemporary young people, sensitive to gender role changes, are less likely to conform to traditional values in the search for self-definition.

Adolescent–Parent Conflicts

As individuals strive for greater autonomy, their relations with those who hitherto held authority over them come increasingly into focus – and often under strain. Popular stereotypes paint adolescents as resentful of adult authority, and several studies do reveal increases in parent–child conflicts from early adolescence (Furman and Buhrmester, 1992; Laursen, in press; Montemayor, 1983; Paikoff and Brooks-Gunn, 1991; Rigby and Rump, 1981; Steinberg and Hill, 1978; Youniss and Smollar, 1985). Wish et al. (1976) asked US college students to recollect the typical parent–adolescent relationship and the subjects likened it to the relationship between a guard and a prisoner. Clearly, the young person's felt need to express his or her autonomy and the parents' sense of responsibility for their offspring's development can, and often do, lead to clashes.

Why should adolescent conflict occur? Laursen and Collins (1994) point out that each of the major theoretical traditions in developmental psychology can offer an explanation. Cognitive developmentalists might point to the newly achieved powers of hypothetical reasoning which enable the young person to contemplate and articulate alternatives to the status quo. For example, Peterson et al. (1986) found an association between cognitive developmental status and intensity of arguments with parents, such that formal operational adolescents were more likely to have heated arguments. Ethologists and sociobiologists would see some conflict around the pubertal stage as adaptive, since it prompts the young person to spend more time with his or her peers and forms part of the status realignments of entry into adulthood (see Steinberg, 1993). Social learning theorists might argue that adolescents have experienced vicarious exposure to conflict as a means of problem-solving, together with intermittent reinforcement obtained when parents yield to their own conflictual demands.

Collins and Laursen (1992; Laursen and Collins, 1994) develop an alternative account, drawing on equity theory (Berscheid, 1986; Kelley et al., 1983), which holds that relationships are established and maintained by parties engaging in consistently rewarding exchanges. The amount of emotional investment that both adolescent and parent have in their relationship means that they are both inclined to preserve it. They do have to accommodate some changes as the adolescent strives for autonomy, and this can lead to conflicts at times, but generally not so intense as to destroy the relationship. As we have seen, despite the conflicts, most adolescent–parent relationships do survive, and are positively regarded by both parties.

Smetana (1993; Smetana et al., 1991) suggests that parent–adolescent conflicts reflect the parties' different roles in the family and their attempts to coordinate conflicting social cognitive perspectives. In a study of adolescents' and parents' attitudes to authority, Smetana (1988) found that *both* sides felt that they were the victims in many confrontations. Adolescents felt that their rights were being curtailed or abrogated by parents; parents felt that their adolescents often defaulted in their moral obligations to the family. Importantly, Smetana (1988) found that shifts in attitudes to authority were not global: that is, during adolescence, young people were more likely to identify certain aspects of life as properly under their control than their parents', but continued to accept that other domains were the legitimate preserve of parents. For example, issues in what Smetana called the personal domain (such as sleeping in late at the weekend or watching MTV) and the multifaceted domain (such as dressing unconventionally or associating with friends whom the parents do not like) were seen by adolescents as their prerogatives. On the other hand, issues in the moral and social conventional domains (such as stealing pocket money, lying, hitting siblings, not cleaning up after a party; see chapter 14) were accepted as areas where parental authority should prevail. Barber (1994), Meuss (1989), and Neubauer and Melzer (1989) report similar findings in studies of American, Dutch, and German adolescents, respectively. Adolescent–parent discord is more likely to arise over a piece of toast left on the TV set than anything they watch in the News.

In two-parent families, the adults themselves undertake different responsibilities concerning adolescent supervision. Smetana (1988) and Youniss and Smollar (1985) in the US, Hortacsu (1989) in Turkey, Meuss (1989) in The Netherlands, and an Australian study by Noller and Callan (1990) all found differences in the areas handled by mothers and fathers. Mothers tend to be concerned more with the interpersonal domain, and fathers with preparation for the outside world. These orientations tend to be reflected in the types of conflicts that arise between mothers and fathers and their adolescent children.

Summary

Not surprisingly, the adolescent's transition toward adulthood has consequences for his or her relationship with parents, hitherto the overriding social relationships of most young people's lives. Some lay expectations – particularly the notion of a generation gap – turn out not to be very well supported. On the other hand, conflicts certainly arise in most homes with adolescents. To place these in perspective, we should bear in mind that conflicts arise also in most homes with 2-year-olds, live-in relatives, or indeed any collection of more than one person. Conflict, as we have seen elsewhere, is a part of social life. The conflicts of adolescence can take on an added intensity because of the crucial social developmental change that affects both parties, namely the beginnings of separation and the establishment of autonomy. Some degree of conflict is inevitable and psychologically healthy (cf. Montemayor, 1983, 1986; Smetana and Asquith, 1994), and likely to be balanced by underlying concordance on many of the substantive issues of life.

If it has struck you that it appears contradictory to report earlier that most adolescents get on reasonably well with their parents and yet to reveal now that there is an increase in discord during this period, then the resolution may lie in the perceived depth and significance of the disputes: not all disagreements result in the parties rejecting the relationship itself. Where conflict becomes severe, however, then developmental problems for the young person are a likely outcome, and we return to this issue in chapter 17.

Peers in Adolescence

While the nature of the adolescent's relationship with her or his parents is changing, the place of peers is increasing (Brown, 1990; Fine et al., 1990; Steinberg and Silverberg (1986). Lewin (1952) saw as fundamental to the social locomotion of adolescence changes in both physical context (i.e., the young person ventures into more activities in more diverse settings away from the parentally controlled environment) and in social surroundings (as the peer group and other affiliations become more valued). These shifts are not due solely to the attractive pull of external forces. As Bronfenbrenner (1970, p. 101) observes, parents also give their adolescent offspring implicit or explicit guidance to the effect "Don't bug us! Latch on to your peers!" In this section, we consider the increasing salience of peers in adolescence, the phenomenon of peer conformity, and the interdependencies among changing relationships with peers, parents, and other people.

The Increasing Salience of Peers in Adolescence

Many researchers have found that peers and peer-oriented activities do become more important to the individual during adolescence (Adams et al., 1994; Berndt, 1979a; Brown et al. 1993; Bush et al., 1994; Gaiser and Muller, 1989; Palmonari et al., 1989; Rice, 1990; Steinberg, 1993). Particularly prominent among the social processes entailed is that of identification with a peer *group*. Brown (1989, 1990) points out that adolescents have many peers, but not all are part of any one individual's peer group. He proposes that peer groups be conceptualized at three levels: dyads (pairs of close friends or lovers), cliques (groups of several individuals who interact frequently), and crowds (larger collectives of people with similar images and affinities – in American teen culture, for example, these include *jocks*, *brains*, *druggies*, and others).

In a survey of 600 16–18-year-olds in Bologna, Palmonari et al. (1989) found that

90 percent of their subjects saw themselves as belonging to a peer group. The majority participated in what Palmonari et al. called informal groups, that is groups constituted on the basis of the mutual interests of the members, rather than adult direction. Palmonari et al.'s informal groups are the equivalent of Brown's cliques. These groups tended to meet in the streets or coffee shops. Rather less people in this age range participated in formal groups, that is, groups constituted to fulfill clear goals (such as religious, political, or sports commitments) with adult leadership. Virtually all those who were members of peer groups regarded that affiliation as an important aspect of their lives. Peer group involvement affects the physical settings of the adolescent's life – from home to coffee shop, street, shopping mall, video arcade – and the interpersonal contexts (Brown, 1989; Fine et al., 1990; Griffiths, 1991; Palmonari et al., 1989).

While popular stereotypes represent adolescent peer relations as potentially danger-ous, it is the *lack* of peer involvement which is unusual in this age range, and may perhaps place the individual at greater risk. As Kirchler et al. (1991) point out, if adolescents are not able to develop peer relations and stick exclusively to their family, then they may face problems in developing their adult autonomy and in handling relations with other adults. Buhrmester (1992) found that adolescents who enjoyed close relationships with peers tended also to be less prone to anxiety and depression.

If peers in general, and peer groups in particular, are so salient, do these alignments bring about heightened social conformity? Yet another component of lay stereotypes of adolescents is that they tend to submit slavishly to peer group influences. Conformity is a phenomenon of longstanding interest to social psychologists, and we turn now to consider the possibility that it is especially powerful during the transition to adulthood.

Peer Conformity

Everyday observation supports the impression that if being a gothic is in, everyone gets sun-shy, wears black garments and dyes their hair; trouser legs contract or expand dramatically with each generation, and you can bet that, if someone invented laser beam zippers, no self-respecting jeans could be worn in public without one – whatever the risk. While the occurrence of group convergence in these matters is easy to detect, it is not clear that this is a peculiarly adolescent phenomenon: adults have equally pronounced dress codes (try wearing business clothes on campus). More interesting is the issue of psychological conformity, that is, adherence to the beliefs, values, and behaviors of others.

Again, we know that adults are sometimes vulnerable to group influence in these respects (Asch, 1951; van Avermaet, 1996; Sherif, 1935). In Asch's classic study, adults' judgments of the lengths of lines were influenced by preceding judgments made by confederates of the experimenter. Even when the choice of the group contradicted evidence from the senses, about one-third of subjects conformed to the group. In a developmental version of this experiment with subjects aged between 7 and 21 years, Costanzo and Shaw (1966) found that conformity peaked at around the ages 11–13 years.

Other studies using different methodologies have produced similar findings. Coleman (1974) found that young adolescents conceived of peers who did not belong to the group in predominantly negative terms, while older (over 15) subjects showed significantly more constructive evaluations (admiring people for not acting "like sheep"). Berndt (1979a) tested children and adolescents' reactions to hypothetical scenarios in which they had to imagine that adults or peers were encouraging them to commit an antisocial transgression such as stealing candy or a prosocial act such as helping someone with schoolwork. He found that conformity to adults' suggestions diminished with age, but responses to peer pressure followed a more complex course. Conformity to *prosocial* pressures from peers was most likely at around the age 11–12, consistent with Costanzo and Shaw's finding and with their explanation that children of this age have developed a strong sense of the necessity for rules. However, conformity to *antisocial* suggestions peaked at the age 14–15, seemingly reflecting aspects of the struggle for autonomy from parents.

It appears, then, that adolescent conformity is not an absolute condition but a form of social accommodation that varies according to situation and developmental status (Brown, 1989; Hartup, 1983). Moreover, peer pressure itself is not a blanket covering all aspects of social behavior. Brown (1989, 1990) suggests that peer influence may operate in different ways at the different levels of peer involvement identified above (dyads, cliques, and crowds). For example, imagine a situation in which your dyadic partner may not want to go to the football match, while your clique does; but your crowd thinks it's nerdish to be interested in sport. In the face of these countervailing pressures, it is an oversimplification of the notion of peer group influence in adolescence to imagine that it operates unilaterally and accounts for every activity or choice that young people make.

Adolescents' perceptions of peer pressure

It is revealing to consider how adolescents themselves conceive of peer pressure. Often, they report that they do not feel under peer pressure (du Bois-Reymond and Ravesloot, 1994). Brown et al. (1986) found that adolescents differentiated among the domains in which they felt it. As might be expected, appearance (clothes and hair) came top of the list, followed closely by social involvement (dating, frequenting the same places). Pressure to engage in misconduct (smoking, drinking, having sex) increased in early adolescence, but none the less it was rated significantly lower than appearance and social involvement concerns at all ages.

Lightfoot (1992) found that some adolescents were dismissive of popular notions of peer pressure: "There's all this crap about being accepted into a group and struggling and making an effort to make friends and not being comfortable about your own self-worth as a human being . . . the idea of peer pressure is a lot of bunk" (p. 240). Instead, Lightfoot's subjects reported that they were interested to see how their peers did things, including how they got their kicks, but this appeared to be more part of a process of the joint creation of shared knowledge and subcultural meanings than a response to peer inducement.

Peers, conformity, and social comparisons in adolescence

Lightfoot's findings are consistent with Ruble and Frey's (1991) account of the development of social comparison processes (discussed in chapter 9), which holds that one factor influencing how one reacts to comparisons is the stage of expertise one has in the relevant domain. Adolescents have much to master, and in novel activities it may be more important initially to find out from others what is possible rather than to compete for attainment.

Another, closely related, aspect of social comparison among peers is the salience of group identity. Tajfel (1981) points out that early work on social comparisons accepted Festinger's primary concern with *inter-individual* comparisons. Tajfel objects that this emphasis leads to neglect of an important dimension of an individual's self-definition, namely that fact that he or she is a member of numerous social groups. He argued that the characteristics of one's group achieve most of their significance in relation to perceived differences from other groups.

The group formations and social identities of adolescents provide strong illustrations of these processes. Part of identity-seeking in adolescence consists, for many, in strong identification with a particular group or subculture, distinguished by its differences from the adult society and other adolescent groups. Obvious examples in Western societies in recent decades include mods, rockers, hippies, skinheads, punks, and gothics. Members of these groups have rigorous internal evaluative criteria, are scornful of outsiders, and most profess antipathy toward the mainstream (encapsulated in the spirited T-shirt slogan "Die yuppie scum").

Unfortunately, these real world groups are somewhat less studied by developmental and social psychologists than transient groups (e.g., created in university laboratories), partly because researching them incurs access difficulties. It is not the done thing to crate a bunch of bikies into the Psychology Department. They also present methodological problems (running an experiment may not be the best way to tap the reasoning processes of disaffected youth). However, a notable exception is a study by Widdicombe and Wooffitt (1990), in which the investigators studied social comparison processes among British punks, gothics, and hippies.

The subjects of the study were interviewed in their own preferred environments, such as the Kings Road, London, an "Acid Daze" festival, and a rock festival. Widdicombe and Wooffitt (1990) found that in each group social identities were highly differentiated and based on finely drawn social comparisons. These included comparisons with outgroups, as well as among the ingroup (based on criteria such as length of membership and age). For example, a punk commenting on the outgroups gothics and skinheads felt that these latter associations lacked depth and subcultural identity: "I dunno, pathetic anyway, 'cos it doesn't, l-like, I think being a gothic and being a skinhead is not a way of life really, is it?" Lack of commitment and durability was despised by members of all groups, and older members tended to draw unfavorable comparisons between the present and a more meaningful past, when being a gothic, hippie, or punk stood for something. Newer members ("Eighties punks," "mini-goths") were suspect. A gothic comments: "It's going downhill really. And a lot of really naff people are latching on to it because they like the style."

The study of social comparisons in everyday adolescent settings confirms the prevalence of such processes in the real world but also highlights dimensions that are easily overlooked in laboratory contexts. In particular, Widdicombe and Wooffitt's (1990) study impresses the significance of the *duration of involvement* in a particular group and of the importance that group members attach to the *authenticity of commitment* – whether one is just "doing" punk (etc.) or really "being" it. This is consistent with laboratory-based findings that individuals or subgroups emerge within social groups who best represent or embody the norms of the group (Hogg and Turner, 1987).

Conformity generally signifies a desire to be accepted by some social group (Hogg and Turner, 1987; Turner, 1991). The fact that this pattern of behavior is somewhat heightened in early to mid-adolescence does point to the importance of the peer community for the young person. Nevertheless, despite the stereotype, conformity is not ubiquitous and part of the developmental achievement of later adolescence is to establish one's autonomy from peer pressures (Berndt, 1979a; Coleman, 1974; Steinberg and Silverberg, 1986). While conformity to peers tends to be regarded (by adults) with some suspicion, the process appears to be significant as an element of coming to terms with the extra-familial social environment and it is an oversimplification to represent all, or even the majority, of peer influence as negative.

Peers, Parents, and Other Social Relationships

When we first considered family and peer relationships in early childhood (chapter 4), it became clear that there were many overlaps and mutual implications. In the same way, research shows that during adolescence identification with peers and family is not an "either/or" phenomenon (Bo, 1994; Brown et al., 1993; Hirsch et al., 1994; Kirchler et al., 1991). Kirchler et al. (1991), working with 770 Italian adolescents, found that those individuals who felt strongly identified with their peers also felt strongly committed to their family. Brown et al. (1993), in a study of almost 4, 000 US adolescents, obtained evidence that the kind of parenting style which the young person experienced was associated with the adolescent's social behaviors and choices, which influenced the kinds of peer crowds to which he or she was drawn.

Several studies of adolescents' social networks have been undertaken in the US (Cauce et al., 1994; Furman and Buhrmester, 1992; Garbarino et al., 1978; Hunter and Youniss, 1982) and Europe (Bo, 1989; Gaiser and Muller, 1989; Neubauer et al., 1994). These studies produce consistently the finding that the people rated as most significant by adolescents are core family members (especially, but not only, parents). Peers are rated as increasingly significant with age – though they do not overtake parents – and throughout, contact with other adults is perceived as valuable. Wintre et al. (1988) report that by the age of 17 years peers are more likely to be nominated as sources of advice in relation to peer group problems. Even so, parents are by no means out of the picture. They are still included as important intimate relationships, and remain the principal reference point for advice on major decisions (such as careers).

It would be an oversimplification to assume that the adolescent's interpersonal existence is located entirely between the two occasionally countervailing poles of parents and peers. Youniss and Smollar (1985) suggest that parents may themselves undergo something of a role change as their adolescents develop, becoming more similar to friends than authority figures. Young people interact with many others, including siblings, members of the extended family, neighbors, teachers, coaches, supervisors in youth clubs, shopkeepers, other caretakers (Bo, 1989, 1994; Hamilton and Darling, 1989; Gottlieb and Sylvestre, 1994; Matsuda, 1989; Neubauer et al., 1994) and they relate vicariously to a wide range of people through the mass media, at least some of whom they may regard as very significant. Adolescents' social networks are rarely independent of parents' social networks (i.e., teenagers and their parents tend to know a lot of people in common), and media use is often a family activity.

Summary

Peers do become increasingly important to adolescents, and they spend more time with them. In some contexts, early to mid-adolescents tend to conform to peer expectations and values, though these are not invariably in conflict with parental values and, when they are, the differences tend to be over relatively superficial issues such as grooming and entertainment preferences. Overall, adolescents' increasing involvement in peer relationships does not displace the relationship with parents, though it does serve different functions and does present its own challenges. Hill (1993) remarks that there is no "closed budget" on the number of relationships that a young person can have, and that the changes that are coming about reflect an increased differentiation as the young person finds different types of social stimulation, personal satisfaction, and interpersonal support from different individuals.

Conclusions

The next time someone likens you to an adolescent, you can respond that he or she is ill informed. Even if you are gawky, self-preoccupied and spotty, with *The Cure* in big letters across your chest, it would be unfair to suggest that you are analogous to persons in the adolescent phase of life (unfair to adolescents, that is). The fact of the matter is that adolescents are a diverse group of people, and that popular stereotypes underestimate their variety and exaggerate their liabilities – as stereotypes tend to do. Certainly, adolescents do have to cope with wide-ranging pressures, emanating from within and without, and they are in a period of many transitions. But research indicates that, in general, they cope quite successfully, with far less anguish and turmoil than is widely supposed. There are important developments in the social world of adolescents as relations with parents and peers adjust, but there is little evidence that for the majority this entails a radical division and a rejection of the family.

Further reading

Brown, B. B. (1989) The role of peer groups in adolescents' adjustment to secondary school. In T. J. Berndt and G. W. Ladd (eds), *Peer Relationships in Child Development*. New York: Wiley.

Brown provides a lucid discussion of the conceptual issues involved in studying adolescent peer groups, and shows that these are dynamic, multi-level contexts which reflect individual members' choices and aspects of the surrounding social environment.

Feldman, S. S. and Elliot, G. R. (eds) (1990) *At the Threshold: the developing adolescent*. Cambridge, Mass.: Harvard University Press.

A substantial collection of 19 well-informed and well-written essays on diverse aspects of contemporary adolescent experiences in the United States, with occasional useful references to other societies. In addition to extensive literature reviews, a particular attraction of this book is that each author outlines issues and directions for future research and policy.

Hill, P. (1993) Recent advances in selected areas of adolescent development. *Journal of Child Psychology and Psychiatry*, 34, 69–99.

A valuable overview of work on family life, peer relations, the impact of divorce, identity, and the correlates of hormonal changes in adolescence.

Kroger, J. (1989) *Identity in Adolescence: the balance between self and other*. London: Routledge.

A fuller account of Erikson's theory and work following from it, as well as useful discussions of other psychoanalytic and cognitive developmental perspectives on identity formation.

Nestemann, F. and Hurrelmann, K. (eds) (1994) *Social Networks and Social Support in Childhood and adolescence*. Berlin: de Gruyter.

Twenty-five chapters from an international authorship, discussing research into the functions of adolescent family and peer relations.

Rosenthal, D. A. (1987) Ethnic identity development in adolescents. In J. S. Phinney and M. J. Rotheram (eds), *Children's Ethnic Socialization: pluralism and development*. Newbury Park: Sage.

An insightful discussion of the dynamics of ethnic identity development among adolescents, highlighting the intersection of developmental changes and the boundaries within and between cultures.

Chapter 16

Adolescence II: Entering the Adult World

Some mothers might have encouraged the intimacy from motives of interest, for Edward Ferrars was the eldest son of a man who had died very rich; and some might have repressed it from motives of prudence, for, except a trifling sum, the whole of his fortune depended on the will of his mother. But Mrs Dashwood was alike uninfluenced by either consideration. It was enough for her that he appeared to be amiable, that he loved her daughter, and that Elinor returned the partiality.
(*Austen,* Sense and Sensibility, *1813)*

The measure of a man is the thickness of his wallet.
(*Campbell,* Men, Women, and Aggression,
1993)

Some friends of mine, middle-aged, liberal people who enjoyed relaxed and good-humoured relations with their two adolescent children, showed characteristic tolerance when Jerry, their oldest, reached the stage where he wanted to bring his girlfriend to stay overnight. Frank advice about contraception was forthcoming, and the granny flat was made available. The young woman, already well known to the parents, was made to feel very welcome, and she was treated as a member of the family whenever she chose to stay. I think my friend Steve was rather pleased with his son: the girlfriend was decidedly good looking, and all the indications were that the physical side of the association was very energetic. In Steve's view, Jerry was a lad to be proud of.

You can probably guess what happened some two years later, when Jerry's younger sister, Danica, now 17, decided that she too had a deep and meaningful relationship that called for the occasional accommodation of her loved one, Mark. Parent–child conflict shot across the Likert scale like never before, and unprecedented turbulence rattled the household. Jerry himself felt obliged to advise his sister that guys are all too often out for only-one-thing, and that she really ought to think carefully about this involvement. Mark was amiable enough, he loved Danica, and she returned the partiality, but my friends were uninfluenced by these considerations. They did not want some horny juvenile getting his paws on *their* daughter.

The moral is that life isn't fair. Not many textbooks will advise you of this harsh fact, but I thought you would wish to know. It is a useful consideration to bear in mind as we study the transition into adult life because many of the principal concerns of this phase are to do with getting what you want or, in technical parlance, with the developmental tasks of adolescence and early adulthood. The snags are that there are rules about what you can do, there are obstacles to what you can have, and there are a lot of other people who want the same things. This makes life tough, but interesting.

In this chapter, we consider the young person's first steps into the larger social world. There are two main sections. In the first, we look at aspects of adolescent sexuality and the search for a partner. In the second, we focus on the approach and entry to the world of work, considering variations in attainment and aspirations, future orientation, career development and early work and unemployment experiences. Sexual and vocational development are often conceived of as functions of individual progress, but it will become very clear that these seemingly personal matters are inseparable from social context.

Sexuality and Social Context

The development of sexuality provides a key demonstration of the intersection of biology, identity, interpersonal, and societal factors in adolescence. Sex reflects biological changes to the physical apparatus but is a social activity. Even if you do it by yourself, as about 95 percent of male adolescents and upwards of 60 percent of female adolescents do (Hyde, 1990), it is an area of behavior riddled with social values. That is why many people are reluctant to discuss their masturbatory experiences and all but Madonna opt not to do it in public. For the early adolescent, sexual arousal occasions unfamiliar and disruptive feelings which may appear detached from the self "and is almost 'watched' by the adolescent as it 'happens,' but later on it is taken for granted, owned, as part of one's own being" (Pine, 1985, p. 120). During early to mid-adolescence many Western children add a more directly social dimension to their sexual experiences, and start doing things with others (Katchadourian, 1990). Sex with another person is very special among our social activities, because it is one of the most exposed, literally and figuratively (Chilman, 1980). In this respect, it is a precarious experience for the adolescent, who is dealing with profound developments in his or her sense of self and, in the course of sexual involvement, rendering that self vulnerable.

The ways in which the compelling forces of sexual maturation are expressed, or repressed, vary enormously according to the social context in which the young person is developing. Variabilities are associated with other dimensions of social life and belief: for example, adolescents who are strongly involved in a religion tend to be less precocious in their sexual activities (Billy et al., 1994; Jessor and Jessor, 1977; Sheeran et al., 1993). More generally, cross-cultural studies of sexual behavior and attitudes among young people confirm considerable variation in patterns of sexual involvement. Even among people growing up in Western societies, there are differences in the extent and nature of sexual experiences by a given age point. Luckey and Nass (1969) compared the sexual attitudes and activities of college students in the US, Canada, Britain, Germany, and Norway, and found that the North American students tended to be slightly more conservative than their European counterparts.

Among the Europeans, the British tended to be the most enthusiastic and most experienced. This was manifest not only in the frequency of young people reporting that they had had sexual intercourse (63 percent of females, 75 percent of males in the UK; 35–60 percent of females, 54–67 percent of males in the other countries), but also in the prevalence of more specialized sexual activities. For example, the researchers found that in most countries approximately 5 percent of young people had engaged in acts of spanking, but the British took a world lead in this practice, scoring over 17 percent (for both sexes). That is a lot of spanking. The reader may care to speculate what features of British public and educational life nurture this particular form of affiliative behavior, but the point is that despite common apparatuses, different peoples express their sexuality in somewhat different ways.

The Double Standard

The different responses to Jerry and Danica's respective forays into the world of adult relationships are by no means unusual. A survey of West German youths, for example, found that while only 15 percent of males believed that their parents would absolutely forbid them from bringing a girl home overnight, 32 percent of females knew that their parents would play merry hell (or the German equivalent). While almost half of the males thought that their parents would allow the arrangement with some hesitation, only about one-third of the females anticipated such an outcome (Neubauer and Meltzer, 1989). The double standard is alive and well.

Culture and biology: a reminder

Why is male sexuality endorsed and female sexuality constrained? Clearly, there are sociocultural values attached to female chastity (though this too is subject to marked inter-cultural variations). Even in the Western cultures with more liberal sexual attitudes, our traditions and our media still transmit the message repeatedly that the female body is to be prized and possessed – but that, like all possessions, it becomes less valuable second-hand. In contrast, the male is encouraged to regard himself as a predator and sexual conqueror. Hence, we could begin to explain the double standard in terms of social expectations and differential socialization. What Steve saw as admirable in his son, he perceived as quite alarming in his daughter.

On the other hand, says the sociobiologist, *why* do cultures organize things in this way? The sheer ubiquity of this bias, and the facts that virtually all societies accord greater respect to male promiscuity than female, and that where polygyny (multiple marriage) is practiced it is most often organized in favor of male prerogatives (cf. Hinde, 1988), are often pointed to by sociobiologists as evidence of the organizing force of evolution (Thornhill and Thornhill, 1992). Perhaps Steve's seemingly inequitable parenting is just one more demonstration of the sociobiological thesis that males will strive to control the reproductive activities of females (Archer, 1992; Low, 1989). When the opportunity for casual sex arises, substantially more males than females leap at it. In an imaginative field experiment, Clark (1990) had attractive research assistants approach opposite-sex undergraduates and ask for a date, and enquired of some whether they would be interested in having sexual intercourse later in the evening. High numbers of both sexes agreed to the date, and almost half of the males thought hopping into bed would be perfectly acceptable, too. But no females accepted the latter proposition. In a second study, other subjects were called up by their own friends and asked if they would be interested in a date with a gorgeous friend who happened to be visiting town. If they wanted, they could sleep with the visitor. Almost everyone accepted the date, but again the males were much more amenable to the idea of sleeping with the newcomer. (In case you were wondering what happened next, Clark assures us that "Each subject was immediately debriefed.")

This is clearly the kind of study for which students make good subjects, and at least the males at Florida State University proved compliant, though scarcely wimps. Clark's findings remind us of three facts of life. One is that you should never believe a good offer from a social psychologist during semester. The second is that males and females have very different attitudes toward sexual congress. The third fact of life is so disturbing that we need to prepare for it; for the moment, we will concentrate on the second.

The imbalance in sexual attitudes and behavior is so widely established that it does seem a good candidate for the status of a social universal, and it is certainly consistent with a sociobiological explanation. However, a closer inspection of the processes of heterosexual relations in adolescence also illustrates the potency of socially shared expectations (whatever their ultimate origins).

Social scripts for sexuality

It is not really surprising to anyone familiar with heterosexual courtship patterns that sexual involvement can be an emotionally fraught experience. The very fact of our familiarity with these aspects of interpersonal relations itself reveals something of the influence of socially shared understandings about how males and females should behave toward one another sexually. Gordon and Gilgun (1987) characterize the regulations governing heterosexual relations as social scripts, shared expectations about the standard course of events. Part of the problem is that there are at least two scripts, one for males and one for females.

A male script

One male script highlights pursuit and conquest. Hence, boys seek to initiate relationships, and tend to do so with girls who are younger, perhaps because it is easier to control or influence individuals younger than oneself. As already noted, a critical aspect of the male script is to have the female, but once this is achieved retention of her services is not always a priority. Some young males sum up the whole process as the "Three Fs." If you do not know what this means, ask an adolescent male.

Within this script, the act of sex itself is relatively unambiguous. For males, first sexual intercourse is typically a highly regarded event, by both the individual and those with whom he confides (Gordon and Gilgun, 1987; Miller and Simon, 1980; Zani, 1991). (In fact, he may well confide the information as widely as possible.) Young males' comments on their first intercourse are usually positive (Sorenson, 1983). Of course, there could be a variety of reasons why this is the case: the experience could well be a very enjoyable one, but it could also be one that is *expected* to be enjoyable. The adolescent male may feel obliged to report in favorable terms in order to confirm his new status and masculinity (Mosher and Tomkins, 1988).

A female script

A widely shared female script is in some respects complementary, but in other respects it may be radically discrepant. Traditionally, she is expected to find a male of status who can protect and provide for her, and win her more prestige among her same-sex peers: to this extent, an older boy is a better catch than an agemate. She is expected to be cautious in sexual matters, and to resist initial advances. Sexuality is ambiguous for females: while *he* has made it, *she* has been made, laid, scored. *Other people's* preconceptions are negative and this matters: "Girls have got to keep quiet about sex and think it's something to be ashamed of" (teenage girl, interviewed by Lees, 1989, p. 27). Furthermore, girls may hear pessimistic reports of what to expect: "My mum does talk about it. When mum explains it she talks like she's carrying a heavy load" (teenage girl, interviewed by Lees, 1989, p. 35). Not surprisingly, then, adolescent females' reports of first intercourse tend to be more anxious (Carns, 1973; Cvetkovitch and Grote, 1980; Gordon and Gilgun, 1987; Sorensen, 1983).

At the same time, for many females the concept of sexuality is associated with love and intimacy (Moore and Rosenthal, 1991). Hence, if she does choose to have sexual intercourse, then it may well be a manifestation of her belief in the importance and durability of the relationship. Girls are more likely to lose their virginity with longstanding partners with whom they anticipate a continuing relationship, while boys are more likely to lose their virginity to partners whom they cease to see shortly afterwards (Kallen and Stephenson, 1982; Traeen et al., 1992; Zani, 1991). Girls engaging in their first experiences of sexual intercourse with males who opt not to see them again are often seriously distressed by what they perceive as a violation of the intimacy (Gordon and Gilgun, 1987).

The scripts above are clearly somewhat oversimplified. They disregard individual differences, and research shows that adolescent orientations toward dating vary with gender role orientation, such that it is only the highly traditionally sex types who subscribe to the traditional scripts (McCabe, 1982; Mosher and Tomkins, 1988). Not all young males would subscribe to the hyper-macho slogan: "You're not a 'real man' until you catch the clap" (Mosher and Tomkins, 1988, p. 72). Many young males do experience a great deal of emotion and commitment in their love relationships (McCabe, 1982). Similarly, the female script over-romanticizes what are likely to be more complex motives among dating teenage girls, which include variously competition for social status ("look who I've caught"), fun, companionship, entry to adulthood, and sexual exploration (McCabe, 1984). The scripts, like television programs, might be changed, and there are some signs that contemporary Western societies are undergoing changes. Consistent with the double standard, many surveys of adolescent sexual behavior still show that more males than females report sexual activities, but in recent decades, there has been a definite narrowing of the gap (Gordon and Gilgun, 1987; Shea, 1984). Nevertheless, many of the tensions and trials of male–female relations may have their starting points in the scripts that young people acquire.

Coercion and Rape

A still more serious problem is that the male script may sometimes lead to sexual coercion of the female. If males feel that they have to take the initiative to obtain sex, then some may come to see putting pressure on the female as part of the sequence. In a large survey of US adolescents, Ageton (1983) found that around 5–7 percent of females reported being the victim of one or more sexual assaults within the previous year. By late adolescence, quite high proportions of American college women (around 20–5 percent) report that men with whom they have been on dates have attempted to force them to have intercourse (Kanin and Parcell, 1977) and about one-third of these attempts succeeded. Kanin (1969) reports corresponding figures from male students, of whom 25 percent admitted that they had attempted to force a woman to have intercourse to the point where she cried and pleaded with the perpetrator to stop. Although these are problems that women have to face at any age, it appears that adolescence is a particularly vulnerable period. It is also the period in which males are most at risk of committing sexual assault: Ageton (1983) found that more than 50 percent of offenders were in the 16–19 years age range.

In part, this problem seems to occur because of different social cognitions about sexual relations, social behavior, and even about the meaning of clothing. For example, if a young woman chooses to wear tight jeans or a short skirt, this may simply reflect her response to current fashions; yet some males may regard her dress as deliberately provocative or even an invitation to sex (Goodchilds et al., 1988). Similarly, traditional role playing leads to cruel outcomes if a young male feels that because he has taken a girl out and spent money on her, then he is entitled to his reward (Goodchilds et al., 1988). Some males may not be responsive to negative feedback from females (Lipton et al., 1987), or may even interpret reluctance as a preliminary gambit, all part of the script but not meant seriously. Hyde (1990) notes that some rapists have even been reported to ask the victim whether she had an orgasm: an enquiry which indicates a pretty fundamental difference in reasoning about the event.

A closely related factor is the male's attitudes toward women. Kanin (1985) found that among a sample of college-aged men who admitted to date rape there was a strong tendency toward manipulative and assertive tactics (such as trying to get the woman drunk, or threatening to end the relationship), and a general disregard for female rights. Feminist theorists tend to interpret rape as an expression of male power and dominance (Brownmiller, 1975; Hyde, 1990). The fact that most rapists are young (under 25) is consistent with the view that males in the transition to the adult male role are among the most confused about sexuality and the most prone to commit rape as a proof of their "manhood" (Hyde, 1990). I know that Steve abhors rape, and I doubt that Jerry's relations with women have ever involved physical coercion. But it could be argued that the culture of conquest implicit in Steve's attitudes reflects and contributes to a wider social climate which is hostile to women's rights.

Finally, although rape is often considered in terms of the pathology of the individual attacker, there is also a clear social component in the sense that rape is shared among males, both symbolically and actively. For example, part of sexual socialization in some male peer contexts includes exchange of advice along the lines of "When she says 'no,' she really means 'yes'" (Hyde, 1990). The strongest predictor of adolescent male involvement in rape is belonging to a peer group which endorses and encourages sexual aggression (Ageton, 1983). Estimates of the proportions of rapes that are committed by two or more men attacking together vary, but most sources concur that they are frequent (cf. Gregor, 1990; Hyde, 1990; Unger and Crawford, 1992) and clinical findings indicate that the social context of a gang can increase the likelihood of participation in rape (Blanchard, 1959). Gregor (1990) shows that in some societies gang rape is a traditional mechanism of male dominance:

> It at once expresses the subordinate status of women and the solidarity of men. It is the sanction by which men as a group keep women as a group from participating in the

religious and political system as equals ... It is an overwhelming and supremely effective symbol of gender inequality. (pp. 492–3)

Gang rape is used also as a means of brutality between communities. Perhaps the most horrendous contemporary illustration of the ability of rapists to persuade other rapists that what they are doing is commendable is provided in warfare, such as the case of Serbian atrocities against the women and children of Bosnia. Presumably, not every Serbian male grows up to regard rape as his privilege and duty, yet in extreme this behavior is elicited and condoned on a virtually nationwide scale.

At the age of 22, Borislav Herak was the first Serb to stand trial for these offences, charged with 16 rapes and 32 murders. All of the rapes were committed in groups, a procedure that seems "natural": "Herak is puzzled when you ask him why they preferred to gang-rape their victims. He says that was just the way it was done. Their commander told them it was good for morale to rape Bosnian women" (O'Kane, 1993a). Situational factors and intergroup relations can be very potent influences upon male behavior toward females.

Not Fitting the Regular Script: Gay Adolescents' Development

Heterosexual scripts are so pervasive in most cultures as to be almost overlearned, but what happens to young people who find that they cannot organize their sexual interests to fit in with majority expectations? The study of homosexual development is relatively sparse, partly because it is disputed whether homosexuality can be identified in adolescence, especially since many people experiment with both same-sex and opposite-sex encounters during this period, and many people who may experience homosexual attraction none the less remain homosexual virgins during their teens (see Savin-Williams, 1990; Sullivan and Schneider, 1987). In addition, practical and ethical issues and homophobic prejudices in the broader community often make it difficult to conduct research directly with young gay subjects. Conservative education authorities are unlikely to approve research projects that focus on homosexual relationships or interests, many parents may refuse consent for their children to participate in such projects, and many potential subjects may be reluctant to disclose their sexuality in the context of a survey or interview – all the more so in the context of a longitudinal study, where identification would be necessary to facilitate follow-up. Kitzinger (1987) and Savin-Williams (1990) remark that there are also risks for the researchers who might elect to work in this area, because they may be regarded as "guilty by association" (with a stigmatized group) or even suspected of pedophiliac motivations.

The research which is available indicates that homosexual development can pose enormous stresses which can be devastating to some, but that many young gay people meet these challenges and develop surprisingly robust self-concepts. Most young homosexual people are well aware that they do not match the socially approved script for sexual relationships, and for many the consequences include "learning to hide" (Martin, 1982): avoiding disclosure, limiting social contact, and finding sex through anonymous encounters. Male homosexuals have "failed" the script because they are not motivated toward sexual appropriation of females, and their masculinity is subject to question (stereotyped as "poofters" or "fags"). Female homosexuals are at odds with the script because they do not wish to marry and may not have children (Gordon and Gilgun, 1987).

A critical factor for most young homosexuals is the perceived or anticipated reactions of others (Martin, 1982; Martin and Hetrick, 1988; Rotheram-Borus et al., 1991; Savin-Williams, 1990). These reactions include parental hostility and rejection, the loss of friendships, public ridicule, and physical assaults. AIDS education materials often convey the message that homosexuality is unhealthy, and Savin-Williams (1990) recounts instances of gay teenagers being condemned by their peers as "AIDS factories." Gordon and Gilgun (1987) point out that the discovery of homosexuality in their offspring is threatening for many parents, some of whom may panic about their own sexuality, while some fear for the stigmatization that the child will have to endure: "Your mother and I have no further reason to live. I don't know what the hell we have done to deserve the treatment we are getting. Terry, you were our only hope" (from a subject interviewed by Heron, quoted in Savin-Williams, 1990, p. 139). All in all, while sexual preference might appear to be a personal matter involving the individual and his or her consensual partners, the reality is that it is a highly social matter. Social rejection can have severe consequences (significantly associated with the high incidence of suicide or suicidal attempts among gay youths), while social acceptance (by peers or parents) can promote much more positive reactions and self-acceptance (Rotheram-Borus et al., 1991; Savin-Williams, 1990).

Savin-Williams (1990), in a study of gay and lesbian American youths, found that his sample enjoyed predominantly positive self-images, and appeared to be coping well in their society. In this study, the extent to which young gay males had "come out" (disclosed their homosexuality to their friends and/or family) was associated with higher levels of self-esteem. Such individuals appeared able to evaluate themselves in positive terms despite hostility in some sectors of the community, either refusing to accept the negative attitudes of others or finding coping resources to deal with it (Savin-Williams, 1990, p. 131). The pattern for lesbians was somewhat different, but parental (especially maternal) acceptance was associated with feeling comfortable with gay sexual orientation. It appears that departures from the script can be accommodated, but this requires both personal resilience and a supportive social context.

Choice of Mate

One of the other principal outcomes of adolescent sexuality and dating is mate selection and marriage. At this point in life, a training in developmental social psychology is indispensable. In many societies, marriage is an overt, negotiated transaction among families based on exchange of property, status considerations and political affiliations (Nsamenang, 1987; Rao and Rao, 1986; Tapper, 1991; Vaidyan-athan and Naidoo, 1990). Some traditional peoples are wary of love marriages because they are perceived as involving too much emotional attachment, and this is suspected to be a transient disturbance (Broch, 1990, p. 150). In Western societies, we like to think of marriage as the consolidation of freely chosen romantic partnership, and we cite love as the principal factor we are looking for in choosing a partner (Buss et al., 1990). However, social psychological research reveals that in practice there are several constraints which actually do much the same job for Westerners as the elders of societies which favor arranged marriages.

First, even within large-scale societies, people are organized by family background, income level, and educational opportunities into social strata, and it is within these contexts that prospective partners are encountered, as Jane Austen knew very well: mate selection tends to be *homogamous* (within the same group: Eshelman, 1985; Morgan, 1981; Stroebe and Stroebe, 1984). A woman attending a university during her early young adulthood is quite likely to find there, or in the social and occupational circles she joins thereafter, a future spouse who is also tertiary educated and with similar values and aspirations.

Second, once sorted into social strata, people do not choose mates at random, but appear to honor a set of social psychological principles which help to determine compatibility. This brings us back to the third fact of life underscored by Clark's (1990) study of date-accepting American undergraduates, above. The third fact of life would seem to be that no one can be trusted: a large number of male and female subjects were telephoned, and some of these must have had a boyfriend or girlfriend, yet over 90 percent were interested in the date with a stranger.

The reason is that people on the dating scene are busily engaged in calculations and comparisons. Before making a final commitment (or the first of a series of final commitments) they evaluate their options. Social cognitive processes and biases which have been developed through the early part of the lifespan are drawn upon extensively in the course of mate selection. For example, we have seen at several points that from early childhood individuals are influenced by physical attractiveness biases, and not surprisingly these predilections come prominently into play in the mating arena (Jackson, 1992; Sprecher et al., 1994; Walster et al., 1966). Walster et al. (1966) set up a mass blind date, pairing up hundreds of American students at a dance. Halfway through the evening, newly paired couples were asked to fill out a questionnaire, rating the physical attractiveness of their partner and how much they liked him or her. (This is a big night out, everyone is in her or his best clothes, new partners are being met, the drinks are subsidized – and at 10.45 everyone sits down to fill out a questionnaire. Is there clearer support for Sears's, 1986, compliant wimp hypothesis?) The results showed high correlations between subjects' ratings of liking and ratings of physical attractiveness. Subjects' ratings of liking also correlated, though not so highly, with independent ratings of their partner's attractiveness.

Once the physical attractiveness principle has been obeyed, interpersonal relations are mediated by market forces. That is, while you might find someone in the range of Tom Cruise or Greta Scacchi a promising starting point, so does everyone else. Given this advantage, the initial target of your affections is likely to have stringent requirements of his or her own, and a critical question could be whether what you have to offer is as marketable as his or her selling points.

If this seems an unduly calculating account of the course of romance, perhaps you have not started dating yet. Certainly, most social psychological theories of mate selection assume that social exchange processes (Berscheid, 1986; Thibaut and Kelley, 1959) are pivotal to courtship. As Stroebe and Stroebe (1984) elaborate, in the exchange hazards of the dating game, if an attractive woman chooses to go out with a less attractive man, then the relationship is imbalanced and there is always the risk that she may opt later for a more attractive replacement; on the other hand, if she starts up with an exceptionally attractive man, *he* could be drawn away by a still more attractive woman. The solution is to find someone of about your own level of attractiveness – and research confirms that this is what most people do (Jackson, 1992). The Stroebes observe that this does not actually prevent individuals from "giving themselves away below market value" (1984, p. 260), but it is very likely that if such a risk occurs then other parties, such as parents and peers, will bring pressure to bear to avert it. Jane Austen was an astute reporter of these processes, but the same influences seem to hold in our more liberal age: Sprecher and Felmke (1992) found that the durability of adolescents' and young people's romantic relationships is influenced by whether or not parents and peers approve of the choice of partner. (Incidentally, Danica's Mark found the heat too much; the relationship broke up quite swiftly and I gather he moved on to a young woman who was living away from home. I wish I could give you a happier ending, but at least this lends further support to the "life isn't fair" hypothesis.)

Cultural differences in mate preferences

There are inter-cultural differences in mate preferences. Buss et al. (1990) conducted a massive study to investigate the features sought in mates by young people in 37 cultures around the globe, including samples from Africa, Asia, Europe, North America, South America, and Oceania. The findings indicate considerable variations among cultures, with no two samples showing precisely the same preference ordering. However, cultures did cluster around the traditional–modern continuum, with people in Asian and African countries tending to attach value to homekeeping potential and desire for home and children, while people in the Western nations attached greater value to love, character, and emotional maturity. Variation among cultures was found also with respect to chastity, with people in some countries rating this toward the top of their criteria (China, India) while their agemates in many other nations (Australia, New Zealand, Scandinavia, the Americas) rated it at or near the bottom.

Cross-cultural constancies in mate preferences

Two preferences which transcended cultures, however, concerned appearance and earning power. Buss et al. (1990) found consistently that men expressed a preference for mates who are physically attractive, while women favored mates who show ambition–industriousness and other signs of resource–acquiring potential. Trivers

(1985) adds the interesting statistic that, in the United States, those males who marry in a given year earn on average nearly 50 percent more money than males of the same age who do not marry. (Life isn't fair if you're an impoverished male, either.)

Again, these findings are consistent with both sociobiological and sociocultural theories of mate selection (Feingold, 1992; Jackson, 1992). Sociobiologists hold that what we perceive as attractive (such as youthful appearance, interesting curves, financial status) is correlated with fertility and reproductive value. This theory predicts greater survival chances for the offspring of the beautiful and the powerful, who should in their turn inherit the genes that afford good looks and success in the competition for resources. Feingold (1992) observes that variables *not* associated with reproductive success (such as sense of humor, "personality") are not associated with sex differences in mate preference either. Steve found it especially heartening that his son Jerry had won the affections of a very good looking young woman; he did not care that Danica's Mark was handsome, but he did complain that, among other failings, Mark had no job. Read the personal ads (Deaux and Hanna, 1984), and you will see that everyone wants a partner with a GSOH (good sense of humor) – but, in addition, he usually wants a younger woman with looks, and she wants a slightly older man with "sophisticated tastes" (read *thick wallet*).

Preferences are not in dispute, but explanation is. An alternative account (called generally the "sociocultural theory" by Jackson, 1992) draws on elements of social learning theory and models of social cognition to emphasize the repetitive environmental stress on particular images of female beauty and male power/wealth. On this theory, it could be argued that the enhanced social fortunes of the offspring of attractive and rich couples are a product of the environmental advantage that comes with prestigious parenthood. Social cognitive factors could be implicated in that anyone smart enough to work out how the world works would realize that the attributes of one's partner have implications for individual and joint social status, and hence should attend selectively to the requisite features in surveying the field. Bar-Tal and Saxe (1976), for example, found that subjects rated photographed individuals more favorably on measures of intelligence and professional standing if the person's opposite sex *partner*, also in the photograph, was physically attractive. Readers in a marketing phase of life should rest assured that, if the state of affairs described by any of this research seems to you to be in any sense repugnant or unromantic, you retain the prerogative of marrying someone poor and ugly. But don't introduce him or her to your folks.

Summary

Adolescence is a phase of life during which biology remits powerful messages. The sexual messages are often experienced as intensely personal and private, but a brief consideration of sexual development demonstrates that it is fundamentally social. Societal context has implications for the manner in which a young person expresses his or her sexuality, and becoming sexual has fundamental implications for how one relates to others – not only sexual partners, but also the family and society more generally. Sexual development is potentially fraught because of the vulnerability of the young person entering into qualitatively new relationships and also because of the ambiguities and contradictions inherent in social expectations about sexual relations. Traditional scripts familiar to adolescents provide a basis for entry (for some) into the world of adult sexual relationships, but whether it is an optimal basis is open to review. We have seen that the heterosexual scripts effectively exclude a substantial minority of the adolescent population. Gay youths often have to come to terms with widespread hostility toward their sexuality, but recent research indicates that many do so successfully and that an important influence upon their adjustment is the degree of social support from significant persons in their lives, especially their families. Returning to heterosexual partnerships, we saw that the initiation of a long-term partnership, including marriage, is an outcome of complex social negotiations rather than the straightforward effects of some biologically preordained sexual attraction. In chapter 18, we examine some of the developmental social psychological processes *within* marriage.

Attainment and Aspirations

One reason why adolescence is such an important phase in the lifespan is that critical choices are made during this period which have major implications for the individual's future life direction. How well a person performs in the educational system, what he or she aspires to do as an adult have long-term consequences (Henderson and Dweck, 1990). In this section, we will consider some of the contextual factors influencing opportunities and development, the relationship between adolescents' cognitions of the future and their social contexts, the development of vocational interests, and early experiences of work and unemployment.

Family, School, and Ethnic Backgrounds

Many studies have shown that the educational attainment and aspirations of adolescents are associated with aspects of the family and school environments that they experience (Bo, 1994; Coleman, 1987; Dornbusch et al., 1987; Lau and Leung, 1992; Marjoribanks, 1987, 1991; Shavit and Williams, 1985). It helps to come from a stable, affluent, affectionate, cognitively stimulating home with educationally aware parents. Adolescents from lower socioeconomic families aspire to relatively low-status occupations while those from middle-class backgrounds set their sights higher (Entwhistle, 1990; Keating, 1990; Marjoribanks, 1979; Roberts and Parsell, 1989). Ethnic background is important, too (Chao, 1994; Luster and McAdoo, 1994; Ogbu, 1994; Schneider et al., 1994; Stevenson and Lee, 1990). In a study of educational achievement in the British Midlands, Scarr et al. (1983) found that West Indian school children lagged behind their peers of English and Asian backgrounds, and the gap grew larger from mid-childhood to adolescence. In the US, many studies show that African-American and Hispanic American adolescents perform on average less well than white students, and all these groups perform less well than Asian-American students (Luster and McAdoo, 1994; Schneider et al., 1994).

These findings identify *correlates* of achievement, but what are the psychological mechanisms whereby the adolescent raises or lowers his or her goals and performance? We have already encountered principal candidates in earlier chapters: they include style of parenting, and the formulation of expectations. There is evidence that authoritative parenting fosters higher levels of educational performance (Baumrind, 1987; Dornbusch et al., 1987; Steinberg, 1993). As discussed in chapter 4, the authoritative parent establishes guidelines and goals, but does so in consultation with the child and is prepared to discuss the reasons for them; this sets conditions in which the young person has recurrent opportunities to negotiate directly and responsibly about his or her performance. Similarly, parental aspirations guide the young person's expectations about his or her future (Marjoribanks, 1987). We saw in chapter 10 that expectations can have a powerful effect upon performance, and that the family is one of the chief sources of influence in the development of positive or negative attributional styles (see also Henderson and Dweck, 1990). Steinberg (1993) points out that in many Asian-American homes, attainment and effort are highly valued and individual responsibility for success is emphasized. Finally, families whose values are congruent with those of the school provide the young person with consistent messages about the mainstream goals of their community and the most effective means of attaining them (Kurdek and Sinclair, 1988; Steinberg, 1993).

Engel et al. (1987) observe that, while the rhetoric of modern, competitive societies stresses individual opportunities and achievement and endorses the prospect of each person earning his or her rewards in life, the reality is not quite so clear cut. Instead, individuals have different starting points and different conditions, according to the family context into which they happen to be born. This includes how far up the ladder their parents are, and how far the parents believe it is realistic for their children to progress.

Orientation toward the Future

An important cognitive change of adolescence is intricately enmeshed in developments in identity and social relations. This is the perception of future time. Theorists such as Lewin and Erikson both saw awareness of time perspective as one of the fundamental developmental changes of this part of the life-cycle. Lewin (1952) stressed the adolescent's orientation toward time because of its implications for the young person's representation of the scope of the life space ahead. Erikson (1968) emphasized the anxieties associated with thinking about the future, which might bring desired changes or unforeseen challenges. Time becomes important not simply because of cognitive advances but because of affective uncertainties which are likely to be stimulated by other people laying great store on "the future," and encouraging the adolescent to conceive of longer-term goals and decisions

The future does become much more salient for adolescents (Gesell et al., 1956;

Poole and Cooney, 1987; Silbereisen and Noack, 1988). This is not always a comfortable sensation:

> What adults would like us to do is to think a great deal about the future. We are expected to be the generation of the future, but what about our present? They don't understand our present and in addition they don't allow us to have it. (Spanish adolescent, interviewed by Maquieira, 1989, p. 40)

There are individual differences in the extent to which adolescents conceive of the future, and these differences are associated with differences in personal progress (Poole and Cooney, 1987). How adequately an adolescent prepares for his or her adulthood will reflect in part his or her *future time perspective* (Verstraaten, 1980; de Volder and Lens, 1982). Future time perspective (FTP) refers to the individual's awareness of the structure of the future and the relationship between present activities and choices and later outcomes. Attainment at school has been found to be positively associated with FTP: individuals who sustain an awareness of the connection between schoolwork and exam results are likely to fare better than peers who disregard this link (Cartron-Guerin and Levy, 1980; de Volder and Lens, 1982).

FTP in turn is associated with aspects of the individual's family context (Pulkkinen, 1990; Trommsdorff, 1983, 1986), institutional experience (Greene, 1990), and sociocultural environment (Seginer, 1988, 1991). Pulkkinen found that higher future time orientation among 20-year-olds was related to positive retrospective appraisals of family life, and especially to the amount of interest that parents had shown in their development and plans during adolescence. Not surprisingly, but importantly, young people who experience interest and input from significant adults tend to develop clearer and more positive plans for their own adulthood. Conversely, young people who experience lack of interest and lack of guidance tend to develop weaker FTP (Agarwal et al., 1983), and those who encounter serious negative feedback – such as failure in university entrance examinations – suffer some undermining of their FTP (Bouffard et al., 1983).

This is another manifestation of the consequences of vertical relationships in social development, as discussed in earlier chapters. There are also important horizontal factors at work. Greene (1990) argues that many of the experiences of adolescence are shared, and that as a result members of a particular cohort come to engender common expectations of what will happen in their lives, and when. Greene found that with increasing age, adolescents develop a shared life-course perspective with greater agreement about the kinds of events that they will experience. This contrasts with the notions of early adolescents, who often have idiosyncratic anticipations about their futures, but it comes increasingly to resemble adult expectations and the viable options within the adolescents' society. Greene (1990) argues that adolescents of the same cohort acquire shared norms about what the future holds for them.

This conclusion is supported also by comparisons of the FTP of Arab Israelis, Jewish urban and Jewish kibbutzim adolescents (Seginer, 1988, 1991). Seginer found that the Arab youth had the strongest future orientation, the urban youth were intermediate, and the kibbutzim youth had the lowest scores on most dimensions.

Seginer comments that these differences closely parallel the subjects' social milieus. The Arab Israelis are part of a generation seeking social and personal change which is not readily available in their present circumstances: hence, they look to a future in which new opportunities might be sought. The urban Jewish youth are growing up in a more stable middle-class environment, but recognize that maintaining their social status is their own responsibility. The kibbutzim youth are developing in collectivist environments which are expected to meet their future needs without a great deal of preparation.

In sum, understanding time and the future seems on first sight a cognitive achievement (and indeed in yet another seminal work, Piaget, 1927, treated the child's conception of time as an individual intellectual quest). Yet dealing with time in adolescence is not the outcome of purely intrapsychological progress, but is affected by both the extent of domestic and institutional experience the individual has and the perceptions and expectations shared with peers. The social context in which one grows up affects the construction of future time perspective, the cognitive and affective basis for one's personal goals.

Work and Adolescence

If seeking autonomy is one of the driving themes of adolescent development, societies often arrange things so that one of the principal routes to autonomy is economic independence: getting a job. Winefield and Winefield (1992) point out that in order to progress to the kinds of social relations and attachments that are associated with adulthood, the individual needs to establish the appropriate financial resources. In order to attain these, the young person needs to determine how she or he will join the workforce.

Vocational development

Choosing a job or career is a developmental task which depends in part upon the young person's conceptualization of her or his abilities and preferences, and the pursuit of a match between these and job requirements. Early research into occupational choice (Ginzberg et al., 1951) indicated that this was a developmental process that took several years, from childhood into adolescence. Ginzberg *et al.* depicted development as proceeding through three stages. In the initial *fantasy stage* of early to mid-childhood, the child translates his or her impulses into career choices: for example, a child might desire to drive a train, and so he declares that he will become a train driver. In the second, *tentative stage* of late childhood through the teens, individuals begin to think about their interests, capacities, and values; for example, one of Ginzberg's subjects decided that because she had always loved sports she would become a physical education teacher. In the third, *realistic stage*, of late adolescence and into early adulthood, the individual shifts from a focus on subjective needs and interests to an appraisal of what the world has to offer. The males in Ginzberg's sample tended to view the college period as a time to assess the job market, their qualifications and prospects, and to narrow their occupational search.

And the females? Well, as Erikson and Gilligan would predict (see chapter 15), they were looking to get married, preferably to very successful young men, and so jobs didn't matter so much – though college was certainly expected to help them broaden their social experience. Scandalous to enlightened postmodernists, and we might take heart from more recent findings such as a large Canadian study by King (1989) in which it was found that virtually every adolescent girl now has a definite career plan, often more clearly formulated than boys'. On the other hand, if we look at the specific careers favored, we find that they tend in many cases to remain within strictly traditional lines. Adolescents have gender stereotypes for particular academic subjects: you can probably work out how they classify woodwork, engineering, physics, chemistry and maths versus English, biology, psychology, French, and sociology (but in case of difficulty see Archer and Freedman, 1989; Weinreich-Haste, 1981).

Studies in different parts of the world reveal consistency in adolescents' preferences for occupations: traditional gender associations prevail. Feather and Said (1983) found this pattern among Australian high school students (especially so among males). Hammond and Dingley (1989), in a study of Belfast sixth formers, found that girls aspired to lower-status occupations than boys, and only 1.2 percent elected for a nontraditional career such as engineering (which attracted over 15 percent of boys). Sastre and Mullet (1992), in an investigation of 14-year-old Spanish adolescents' occupational preferences, found that, although many factors were implicated, a significant concern for many girls was the traditional femininity of the work.

More detailed stage theories of career choice and development have been developed since Ginzberg et al.'s early work, the most prominent of which is Super's (1980, 1985), which also posits a stage theory of vocational self-concept but places development in a larger, lifespan framework and holds that important developments continue well into adulthood. Like Ginzberg, Super views adolescence as a crucial period in the development of vocational goals. He sees the mid- to late teens as a period of *crystallization*, during which the young person is formulating a vocational self-concept and narrowing down his or her options. This is followed by a stage of *specification* (in the late teens to early 20s) during which a specific choice is made. (Career development does not cease at this point; we return to this topic, and to the Ginzberg interviewees' outmoded ideas, in chapter 18).

An alternative approach is that of Holland (1985), which emphasizes the matching of personality characteristics and job qualities. Holland identified six basic personality orientations – *realistic, investigative, artistic, social, conventional*, and *enterprising* – and proposed that successful career choice depends on finding the occupational environment which best matches the individual's particular composition. A person scoring high on artistic characteristics might find a career as a photographer or illustrator would suit him; a person with a high investigative orientation might find her optimal employment as a researcher or journalist, and so on.

As you might expect, these theories are often criticized for not taking the real world into account. For example, someone with a psychology degree might feel that she or he (scoring high on at least five of Holland's sub-scales and most other criteria of employability) would be well matched to a position as say, a psychologist. But finding the job is another matter, dictated in large measure by the prevailing conditions of the economy, demographic fluctuations in demand, and the quality of the competition. McDonald's, meanwhile, has filled up with younger assistants. Life, as we have agreed, isn't fair.

In the face of the real world of boom–bust economies and rapid fluctuations in workforce demand, Ginzberg's, Super's, and Holland's vocational theories may seem irrelevant. However, if you place yourself in the position of our hypothetical psychology graduate, then it is possible to conclude quite the opposite: that is, that developmental and individual differences *are* important elements of preparation for work. The psychology graduate, like many other prospective entrants to the workforce, has undergone a gradual process of formulating her or his interests, capabilities, and skills, has evaluated the extent to which these match occupational requirements, and may well judge these personal adjustments to be very meaningful. Problems occur when societal constraints inhibit the realization of the aspirant worker's needs and potential. The nature of human development would not be a problem if people could be accommodated comfortably in whichever boxes the macro-system presents them with, or if they could be discarded without complaint. Because this proves not to be the case, we are reminded once again that socialization is much more than a matter of molding people to fit into preordained slots. Hence, a developmental perspective should not be lost sight of as we turn now to more recent research on the transition to work and unemployment. (Before we do so, a word of reassurance. The psychology example was purely for illustrative purposes. Psychology graduates tend to do relatively well in the job market, and there are still careers in this field. Which seems fair, after all.)

Transitions to work and unemployment

Broadly speaking, the quality of adolescence varies according to the economic circumstances in which people are growing up. For example, Offer et al. (1988) in their ten-nation study, found moderately strong positive relationships between countries' Gross National Product (GNP) and their adolescents' emotional tone: straightforwardly, "the wealthier the country, the better the adolescent mood" (p. 104). Similarly, GNP was strongly correlated with quality of social relationships. Higher proportions of young people in the affluent countries, such as West Germany, Italy, USA, Australia, seemed to be enjoying life than are their agemates in poorer nations such as Bangladesh.

However, as we have just seen, it is also the case that even in the advanced nations the experiences of adolescence and early adulthood are changing as a function of ructions in the world economy. Many Western countries have suffered serious and protracted recessions in recent years, and one outcome has been that job markets have reduced dramatically. This has direct consequences for young people: it means that it is difficult, perhaps impossible, to find employment. As a result, it is probably misleading to generalize about *the* transition into the world of work, since the entry paths are so varied and sometimes so elusive. In the following sections, we will consider aspects of development first in adolescents who do find employment, and then in those who become unemployed or underemployed.

Work and adolescent development

In a short-term longitudinal study, Steinberg et al. (1982) investigated the consequences of part-time employment among a sample of Californian high school students who were undertaking the kinds of "McJobs" that students find in their summer vacations and out-of-school hours. The study found that there were, as expected, some gains in aspects of personal development, including self-management skills and reliability. However, there were also some less wholesome outcomes. After a period on the edges of the workforce, the subjects had picked up some cynical attitudes about the value of work (they were more likely to agree with items such as "Anyone who works harder than he or she has to is a little bit crazy"), and were accepting of unethical business practices (including offsetting the indignity of a low salary by taking little things from the workplace). There were also costs in terms of lowered school and family involvement and reductions in the quality of friendships. Subsequent studies of American adolescents have shown that there is an element of self-selectivity involved in the process – that is, young people who are already experiencing some adjustment difficulties are more likely to seek high amounts of part-time work, but that "working appears to make a bad situation worse" (Steinberg et al., 1993) especially with respect to school participation and attitudes toward education. Other dubious consequences of early work include precocious affluence (too much money for consumer goods at an early age), work-related stress, proneness to smoke and abuse alcohol, reduced sleep, lower exercise rates, and less satisfying leisure activities (Bachman and Schulenberg, 1993; Steinberg et al., 1993). Similar conclusions emerge from a study of young adolescents in a very different cultural context, namely street traders in Lagos, Nigeria (Oloko, 1994). In this case, lack of adult supervision placed children at risk of enticement into delinquent activities.

Rather than assume that part-time work is invariably a negative phenomenon, it should be borne in mind that other aspects of the young person's social ecology may influence outcomes (Fine et al., 1990). Much may depend on the reasons for working (e.g., to fund consumerism or to make a contribution to family income) and the approval or disapproval of the adolescent's parents.

Joining the workforce in a full-time capacity

Moving from school to full-time employment is a major life transition with implications for the young person's self-concept, goals, and understanding of society (Devos et al., 1994; Sarchielli, 1984; West and Newton, 1984). Devos et al. (1994) found that the social representations of 16–18-year-old Swiss people varied according to their work status. Subjects in this study were asked to elaborate on their representations of "the young." Those who had already joined the workforce as apprentices tended to represent young people in terms of things that they *do* (social activities, relations with the opposite sex, driving), while youths of the same age who were still at school focused more on cognitive and affective attributes (compassion, solidarity, idealism, future orientation). Sarchielli (1984) found, among young Italian work entrants, that the early stages of employment were associated with a shift from rather idealistic and global expectations about the self-fulfillment of work to a more pragmatic orientation toward job security and the constraints of hierarchical control. We noted in chapter 15 that the transition from junior to high school involves a reverse of status – from being one of the senior members of the old institution to a novice in the new one – and a similar readjustment is incurred upon entering the workplace.

The transition has its benefits. Sarchielli's subjects, and those of West and Newton's (1984) British study, all regarded access to money as a decidedly welcome development. Most responded also that they felt more grown-up, more self-confident, and had a broader outlook on the world. However, West and Newton report that these findings were qualified by sex differences. In general, the transition to work was perceived as more positive by males. The reasons appeared to involve both the interaction of individual and job, and the implications for family life. Young male employees were more likely to be in jobs which offered formal training (such as apprenticeships), they enjoyed the interactions with other people and greater independence from parental regulation. Females more often received informal training only, more often felt alienated from the workplace and were less likely to report changes in their home life. This latter finding is consistent with evidence discussed above that girls' freedom is more often curtailed during adolescence. Another pervading reason, to which we will return, was differences in expectations for adult roles: the males saw their future work role as central, the females saw marriage and children as the important things ahead.

Underemployment and unemployment

In some European countries, about 20 years ago, all school leavers could reasonably have expected to find work. Today, less than one-third will make it: "Nowadays, in many parts of Britain, most 16-year-olds' only scope for choice is between educational programs and training schemes. Access to adult employment has been delayed, maybe for ever in some cases" (Roberts and Parsell, 1989, p. 369). Similar problems afflict young people, especially from lower socioeconomic groups, in the US (Fine et al., 1990; Rice, 1990), Australia (Winefield and Winefield, 1992), and elsewhere.

One consequence of this societal downturn has been that many young people have to defer entrance into occupational life, typically by prolonging their education. Some have argued that this in turn protracts the dependency of the young, curtailing their willingness to take responsibility for their own decisions and to demonstrate initiative. For example, Andersson (1990) found that among a large sample of Swedish 21-year-olds, only 25 percent gave an unconditional "yes" in response to the question "Do you regard yourself as an adult?" In further studies with Swedish adolescents, Andersson found that only a minority responded to hypothetical dilemmas with strategies that indicated self-reliance as opposed to compliance to adult instruction.

Another consequence of hard economic times is distributed unequally. Some families are hit by unemployment or serious income loss (due to fewer hours worked, reduced wages, etc.), while others are not. While the direct impact is upon the parent or parents who have been retrenched or downgraded, inevitably parental loss of income has implications for the family as a whole, incurring austerity and emotional instability (Jahoda et al., 1933; McGhee and Fryer, 1989). With respect to adolescence, the question arises as to whether these negative alterations in family context are likely to lead to negative developmental outcomes.

On first consideration, this might appear a plausible prediction: perhaps family stresses impact upon the adolescent and make him or her more prone to transgress. Evidence from a study of adolescents in Berlin, however, suggests that the consequences of family income change interact with family style. Galambos and Silbereisen (1987) classified families as high or low on a measure of parental acceptance (i.e., the extent to which adolescents feel comfortable in expressing themselves to their parents, and perceive their parents as supportive). The adolescents also completed a scale measuring their proneness to transgression (such as inclination to steal things, to lie, to disregard rules, etc.). They found that those adolescents enjoying high parental acceptance were least prone to transgression, while the low acceptance group was most at risk. Income gain appears to be particularly propitious for the low acceptance subjects. The authors suggest that this may be because this kind of change enhances the adolescent's perception of the status of his or her parents.

When the adolescent him or herself is unemployed, this can have negative consequences on family interactions. In an Australian study, Patton and Noller (1991) found that both parents and adolescents perceived their families as less cohesive when the adolescent was out of work.

Mental health and employment status

Several studies have found that unemployment has negative consequences for the mental health of young people (Donovan and Oddy, 1982; Feather and Barber, 1983; Feather and O'Brien, 1986; Patton and Noller, 1984; Warr et al., 1985). For example, Warr et al. (1985), in a British study, found that the average distress scores as measured by the General Health Questionnaire (GHQ) of unemployed males and females were 0.9 and 1.1, respectively, while a comparable study of employed young people had obtained scores of 0.65 and 0.75 for males and females respectively (Banks and Jackson, 1982). How the individual interprets his or her situation appears to be critical. Ullah (1990), in a study of unemployed Western Australian youth, found that psychological distress was associated with subjective financial strain rather than with the actual amount of income received.

Unemployment has effects on young people before they enter the job market. Hendry (1989) summarizes findings from studies conducted with Scottish youth, demonstrating that people about to join the job market were well aware of the problems of finding a job and approached the prospect of work feeling insecure and prepared to entertain staying in jobs that they found unpleasant. As a male apprentice in Germany observed "It doesn't mean shit, what kind of work I do! The main thing is I am not unemployed and can earn money" (quoted by Heitmeyer and Moller, 1989, p. 305). Ullah and Brotherton (1989) found that psychological distress (measured by the GHQ) was as high among young people in their final years of school as it was among youngsters already unemployed, and that level of distress was associated with the expected difficulty of finding a job.

Some adolescents react to the prospects of unemployment with symptoms of learned helplessness (Feather, 1983, 1986). They express low levels of confidence that they will find a job, and estimate the time spent searching to be lengthy. Feather (1986) found that a number of factors predicted helplessness. Consistent with other findings on the social contexts of helplessness that we considered in chapter 10, these included the individual's own prior attainment history (i.e., his or her school performance), the kinds of guidance received, and family factors, including social class and paternal employment. Attributions for unemployment were important, too: adolescents who believed in personal responsibility for employment progress tended to be less likely to show helplessness and pessimism than did peers who believed that unemployment was not the fault of the individual concerned.

While unemployment is associated with mental health and life satisfaction problems, having to settle for a job below the new worker's expectations or capabilities is also problematic. O'Brien (1990) reviews extensive research which demonstrates that repetitive performance of boring low-level jobs tends to induce depression, a low sense of self-efficacy and other maladjustment. Winefield and Winefield (1992), in Australian studies, found that on measures of psychological wellbeing young people who were dissatisfied with low-status and low-skilled jobs were no better off psychologically than the unemployed.

Wallace's (1989) study of young people in the Isle of Sheppey, UK, is particularly interesting in this regard because she interviewed her subjects at three stages: shortly before, one year after, and four years after leaving school. The Isle of Sheppey had unemployment at twice the UK average. Wallace reports that many young people's entry into the world of work was often discontinuous with their earlier expectations, sometimes because jobs turned out to be less enjoyable than expected, sometimes because individuals had to settle for lower-level jobs than they had sought, and sometimes because they were unemployed or able only to obtain occasional casual work. Contrary to popular images of the young unemployed as passive and aimless, Wallace found a variety of responses, including some overt rejection of the lower strata of the world of work: "There's Tesco's, the shirt factory, and shit like that. Boring, repetitive jobs, sewing jeans and stacking shelves. I wouldn't do a lot of factory work unless I was really desperate because I would think it was a waste of my life" (adolescent female, quoted by Wallace, 1989, p. 359). However, when she saw a subset of her initial sample some four years on, Wallace found that at least half of them had experienced becoming "really desperate." Many were not doing the jobs they had initially desired, and most seemed to have forgotten their earlier aspirations. By this stage they had come to accept whatever work they could find:

> It's a real crusher, especially if you're out of work 2 years like I was. In the end. You're
> so hopeful at first. When I first got unemployed, I remember, it was when Thatcher first

got in and you could see jobs disappearing then ... Oh, it's a real killer being unemployed for 2 years. See, it's not just me now, it's them [indicating his girlfriend and child] I got to think of." (adolescent male, quoted by Wallace, 1989, p. 363)

Unemployment and disaffection with society

One consequence of adolescent unemployment is that the afflicted individuals feel excluded from the adult world (Hendry, 1989; O'Brien, 1990; Wallace, 1989). This has consequences for self-image and orientation toward the social structure. Perhaps if you think about the matter, you might predict that the victims would react angrily. (It really isn't fair.) In some contexts, this does occur, with disaffected youths developing hostile attitudes toward society and the "system" (Breakwell, 1986). Palmonari (1980) describes the reactions of some groups of Italian students who perceive that the adult world will have no place for them, and who categorize themselves as the "unguaranteed." Their response is to reject the values of the status quo and attack the system directly, through subversive activity.

On the other hand, there are literally millions of jobless youngsters out there in most of the larger contemporary economies; not all are challenging the "system." Based on British research, Hendry (1989) concludes that apathy and a sense of isolation are more likely than collective rebellion. Social psychologists could help account for this pattern of reactions in terms of *relative deprivation theory* (Sabini, 1995). Briefly, relative deprivation theory holds that people tend to compare themselves with others around them – people of neighboring social status. From this perspective, for the unemployed youth casting an eye over his or her peers, life may seem bad, but then everybody else's life is pretty tough, too. Aronson (1992, p. 270) summarizes the implications of relative deprivation theory: "Revolutions are not usually started by people whose faces are in the mud." Instead, he suggests, revolutions are initiated by those who have raised their faces above the mud and compared their situation with those of people doing better. O'Brien (1990) points out that hostile and protesting kinds of reaction to youth joblessness are more typical of those who have recently entered the world of unemployment, or who are not yet unemployed but are simply aware that this is what society promises them. Thus, individuals who have a basis for comparison based on recent experiences or the vantage point of preparation for work, may become disgruntled. However, as the debilitating effects of long-term unemployment set in, and the mud settles, then young people may lose any sense that they could affect their own circumstances (Hendry, 1989; O'Brien, 1990).

Summary

Of all the transitions of adolescence, preparation for adult work roles is particularly crucial to the direction and quality of the individual's future life. In this section, we have seen that aspirations and possibilities are circumscribed by social context. In part, the story begins before adolescence, reflecting the status of the family and the expectations and demands of the home. Developmental changes in self-understanding and self-definition are reflected in the emergence of a vocational self-concept, but the implementation of this is negotiated with others and ultimately constrained by the economic realities of the society in which the young person is developing. Early experiences of work may have consequences for the adolescent's development, though whether these are positive or otherwise depends greatly on the quality of the workplace. Early experiences of unemployment also have consequences. There is little evidence yet that they are ever experienced as positive, and the form of response (apathy, anger, rebellion) varies across different societies in ways that are still poorly understood.

The trouble with adolescents: a final comment on cohort changes

It was stressed in chapter 15 that adolescence is difficult to define, that in many respects the experiences of adolescence are historical products that are subject to continuous shifts. Adolescence is a fascinating but challenging period to study. One correlate of this is that it is also a very difficult period about which to make generalizations and predictions. Baethge (1989) makes the interesting point that if we evaluate the collective field of youth studies over the past few decades in terms of its foresight and reliability, then it does not fare well.

Social scientists studying young people in the 1960s, Baethge notes, gave no notice of the far-reaching upsurge of revolutionary political involvement and disaffection with bourgeois society that was to spread across Western societies by the end of that decade. In the 1970s, the fervor and force of youth radicalism was widely acknowledged, especially among sociological researchers, only to be replaced by the apparent apathy and withdrawal of the next upcoming adolescents. Just as observers were becoming aware of this trend, the Peace Movement and the Greens captured the enthusiasms of large numbers of young people. And these in turn were succeeded by embracement during the 1980s of Yuppiedom and the fruits of free enterprise capitalism. In the 1990s, recession-daunted adolescents are often said to have become cynical and hopeless.

Of course, each generation actually contains a plurality of political and social perspectives, and we should be wary of accepting caricatures as adequate representations of whole populations of young people. Baethge's argument is that no one "snapshot" of youth should be taken as the essence of this phase of the lifespan; instead, the experience and resolution of adolescence will continue to change as societies themselves change. Life proceeds in social contexts.

Conclusions

Adolescence is a period of change: physical, cognitive, interpersonal, and institutional. In chapter 15, we saw that there are shifts in the balance of power at home and transitions from the domestic context toward external, peer-oriented settings. In this chapter, we have considered entry into new, uncertain, and often highly sensitive relationships in the sexual arena, and the first steps into the world of work or nonwork. Throughout, the broader society impinges, partly through the transmission of socially shared beliefs about how a young person should behave, and partly through establishing the material conditions within which the adolescent experiences the transitions. With the diversity of factors at play, it is perhaps not surprising that there is no unifying theory of adolescent development, but it also becomes clear why this phase of life is attracting a greatly increased amount of research attention and why it provides ample scope for research perspectives drawing on the diverse strands of developmental social psychology.

Further reading

Hurrelmann, K. and Engel, U. (eds) (1989) *The Social World of Adolescents: international perspectives.* Berlin: de Gruyter.

Twenty-three chapters based on research from around the world, providing theoretical discussions of issues relating to adolescents' social networks, lifestyles, values, peer groups, relations with parents and other adults, education, and careers.

Lent, R. W., Brown, S. D., and Hackett, G. (1994) Toward a unifying social cognitive theory of career and academic interest, choice and performance. *Journal of Vocational Behavior*, 45, 72–122.

A framework for understanding the formulation and development of career plans, based on Bandura's social cognitive theory. This monograph provides a good example of theory building in relation to complex real world choices that involve person, situation, and performance.

Peterson, A. C. and Mortimer, J. T. (eds) (1994) *Youth Unemployment and Society.* Cambridge: Cambridge University Press.

Drawing on evidence from the United States and Europe, the contributors assess the impact of high rates of youth unemployment on individuals' development and societal organization.

Chapter 17

Adolescence III: Problems

"What's it going to be then, eh?"
        (Burgess, A Clockwork Orange, *1972)*

"Yo soy el vato que control todo" ("I am the crazy guy who controls everything")
        (Luis, aged 10 years; member of a Los Angeles street gang, quoted by Colvin, Los Angeles Times, *1993)*

In chapter 15 it was emphasized that adolescence is often stereotyped as a period of stress and turbulence, and yet the evidence is not consistent with this stereotype. It may seem paradoxical to reveal now that much research work on adolescent development is focused on problems (Coleman, 1989; Compas et al., 1995; Hill, 1993; McCord, 1990). On the one hand, we have seen that many adolescents prove resilient in the face of the numerous challenges and stresses they have to deal with; on the other hand, it will be shown in this chapter that many adolescents engage in behaviors which involve risks, and that for a minority the risk-taking can have serious consequences.

It is important to bear in mind that the negative outcomes to be discussed here are not universals of adolescent development, although many – even a majority – of adolescents may have to resolve issues that relate to them. For example, we will see that almost all adolescents commit minor crimes, but rather smaller numbers become "delinquents;" almost all adolescents consume alcohol at some point, yet fewer pursue the route to serious substance abuse and narcotic dependency; almost all female adolescents worry about their body image and their weight, but only a small proportion suffers from anorexia or bulimia; quite a lot of young people have sexual relations, but not all become premature parents.

Dealing with problematic issues and behaviors is part of adolescence, and to that extent normative. One reason why the study of problem behavior among youth is important is that it is intimately connected to the processes of change, both within the individual and his or her society (cf. Jessor and Jessor, 1977, pp. 4–5). It was argued in chapter 1 that change should be to the fore in a developmental social psychology, and there are good grounds for taking problems as indicators of change. Problems tell us something about the shifting goals and priorities of the individual, and they reveal the values and regularities of her or his societal context. Reactions to pregnancy, or to sexual activity, or to alcohol consumption reflect the age stratification of societal values. Each of these activities is permissible – indeed, often expected – among adults, but they are considered inappropriate behaviors for adolescents. Yet, as visible correlates of adulthood such activities have a potential attraction for adolescents: "engaging in such behaviors can serve to mark a transition in status, their occurrence representing a developmental change toward, or a claim upon, a more mature status" (Jessor and Jessor, 1977, p. 41).

Another reason why problems of adolescents are compelling topics for research is that this phase of the life-cycle is perceived as the last opportunity to ensure that the young grow up as the adult society would prefer. Reicher and Emler (1986) suggest that the recurrent fears about the contemporaneous generation of youth and the correlated nostalgia for the golden age of our own teens reflect the developmental importance of adolescence, marking a critical stage in an individual's acceptance or rejection of the society in which he or she lives. They point out that the survival of the existing social order requires the reproduction of the society's values and patterns of behavior among new generations. Perhaps perversely, adult society does not want adolescents to accept all of them too quickly.

In this chapter, we will consider first a general theoretical model of problem behavior in adolescence that has influenced much recent research. Then, we review specific problem areas: delinquency and health problems (including drug use, pregnancy, and eating disorders). An important general point is that adolescents experiencing problems and engaging in problem behaviors rarely experience them singly – that is, an individual may suffer several problems simultaneously – and at various points we will consider the interplay and intercorrelations among problems.

Jessor and Jessor's Model of Adolescent Problem Behavior

The Jessors (1977) proposed a developmental social psychological model of the interplay of factors which they hypothesized to account for the genesis of problem behavior in adolescence as experienced in the West. These factors include the antecedent variables which form the young person's developmental context (including family status and structure, socialization influences), "social psychological" variables (including the individual's personality, and his or her perception of the social environment), and sets of behavioral options that are available to the adolescent, some of which are sanctioned by adult authority (such as academic performance), and some are not (such as smoking dope). Their model is illustrated in figure 17.1. Note that some of the arrows in the model are bi-directional, representing the authors' commitment to an interactional perspective which holds that behavior, personality, and perceptions of the environment have mutual implications. Thus, a young person might become involved in, say, sexual activity because of predisposing personality characteristics, but involvement in the activity (or activities – she probably will not want to stop) may then affect aspects of her personality development (she may become a more overtly sexual being) which may correlate with changes in her perceptions of the social environment (she might become more oriented toward finding sexual partners, or may reassess her views of parental control over her social life).

In a major longitudinal project with adolescents in a small US city, the Jessors found clear patterns in psychosocial development during adolescence which supported their model and pointed to important interrelationships. They found that in what they termed the personality variables, there was a general decline in the value attached to achievement, in intolerance of deviance and in religiosity, accompanied by an increase in the value of independence and in social criticism (rejection of the values of the mainstream society). In relation to the perceived environment, there was a decline in parental controls and an increase in peer support and peer approval of deviant behavior. These personal and interpersonal changes were accompanied by predictable developments in actual behavior: there was an increase in problem behaviors such as heavy drinking, sexual experience, general deviance, and drug use, and a decline in conventional behaviors, such as church attendance.

Importantly, then, adolescent problem behaviors need to be seen in the broader context of young people's social development and social goals. According to the Jessors, although the behaviors may well be problematic, they are also functional: they are motivated to resolve some of the central challenges of the transitions of youth, and

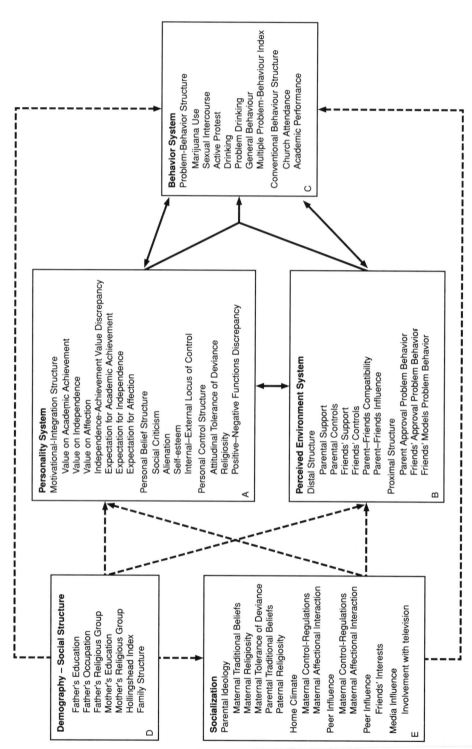

Figure 17.1 The conceptual structure of Jessor and Jessor's (1977) problem-behavior theory.

to increase autonomy over one's own life. Luis, above, says that he would like to control "everything."

Transition proneness

The Jessors introduced the important concept of "transition proneness" (cf. 1977, pp. 41–2) to describe the tendency of some young people to transgress precociously the age-related regularities of behavior. They argued that "the greater the transition proneness, the earlier the likelihood of engaging in transition behavior" (p. 42). In a similar vein, Stattin and Magnusson (1989) propose that an important mediating variable is the adolescent's self-perception as more adult than her or his agemates. This affects selection of friends and social activities, which are chosen in order to express or bolster this belief in relative maturity. In turn, selection of a particular social milieu affects the values, practices, and opportunities to which one is exposed. Luis provides an extreme example. According to Colvin (1993), Luis was enlisted by a gang of drug dealers and acquired eagerly the gang's tattoo, which he had placed on his neck. He aspired to realize the values of his peers, declaring that he aimed to become the "biggest, meanest, toughest *cholo*" in the neighborhood. In return for his commitment, his new peers dressed him in man-sized trousers and extra-large T-shirts that hung down to his knees: public symbols of the mature status they believed he deserved.

The family and adolescent problems

There are interrelations among adolescent problem behaviors, and a common underlying factor appears to be the family context (Compas et al., 1995; DuBois et al., 1994; Jessor and Jessor, 1977; Johnson, 1986; Meuss, 1994). (Luis's mother, incidentally, had left the home, and he grew up with his father and brother – until his brother was killed in gang warfare.) Different types of family processes appear to be associated with different problem outcomes. Steinberg (1990) and Barber (1992) distinguish between psychological control and behavioral control. Barber argues that the developing individual needs both psychological autonomy and behavioral regulation, and that different families afford different systems in these respects. Families which deprive the adolescent of opportunities to develop autonomy (i.e., families where the parents maintain excessive psychological control) may place the young person at risk of withdrawal and internalized problems. On the other hand, families which allow plenty of autonomy but fail to offer behavioral guidelines, Barber argues, place the adolescent at risk of externalized problems. The salience of the family context will be demonstrated frequently as we turn now to some of the major problems that adolescents face.

Delinquency

The universal fascination with delinquency is a good example of how social problems tell us about the social values and tensions of a society. Almost everyone has something to say about juvenile delinquents: the causes, the impact, the solutions. Every Prime Minister or President promises once during his or her tenure of office to "crack down" on delinquents. (The promise is usually uttered only once, because the problem proves to be more intractable than it appears during the stage of pre-election omniscience.) Juveniles seem to be of broader interest than other age groups of criminals, perhaps because the emergent criminal is perceived as the symbolic retribution for society's ills: the payoff for economic deprivation, or the outcome of slack disciplinary techniques in schools and homes.

Adolescence is a period of peak involvement in certain types of crimes (particularly property-related crimes, including theft, break-ins, car damage, and violence). There is also a strong association between criminal status in adolescence and later criminality. For example, in a large longitudinal study of males born in Philadelphia in 1945, Wolfgang et al. (1987) found that of the nondelinquent adolescents, 81 percent remained non-offenders at the age of 30, while of the juvenile chronic offenders, 45 percent were chronic offenders as adults.

Defining Delinquency

Defining juvenile delinquency proves elusive. There are relatively straightforward legal criteria, typically that a juvenile delinquent is a person under the age of 18 who has been convicted of a criminal act. But note that this definition effectively classifies delinquents *post hoc* – that is, after they have been apprehended. How should we regard those who do not get caught? Self-report data indicate that the latter group may well be much larger. Gold (1970) solicited American adolescents' confidential reports of their involvement in illegal acts, and found that over 80 percent admitted to some transgression. Kirchler et al. (1991) found that a substantial proportion of Italian youth acknowledged problems with "microcriminality," that is, involvement in illegal acts such as vandalism, shop-lifting, etc. Over 90 percent of males in a New Zealand study admitted some delinquent activity prior to the age of 18 (Moffitt, 1993). Reviewing a variety of self-report findings, Hollin (1990, p. 3) concludes: "It can be stated that most young people will, at some time in their early life, commit a criminal act."

A further definitional complication arises from the fact that getting caught does not always result in being placed in court. Some young offenders may be sent home with a warning from the police. We will see shortly that characteristics of the offender appear to predict whether he or she will receive this treatment or a more severe one.

What, then, are the characteristics of delinquents and how can we explain their involvement in crime? The overriding conclusion emerging from the available research is that there is no simple answer to this question, and no single variable that can be identified as the "cause" of this widespread societal problem: juvenile delinquency is multidetermined. Nevertheless, there are several factors that stand out as closely associated with delinquency, and we consider several of them below, including individual differences (personality, cognitive and moral development, school performance), demographic status (class, race, gender), and family environment. Finally, we turn to a developmental social psychological theory of the motivations and contexts of delinquent behavior, Emler's "reputation management theory."

Individual Differences

Personality

A natural starting point is to ask what is wrong with the delinquents, and to attempt to identify their deficiencies. One limitation of approaches that focus on individual pathology is that it is difficult to identify constellations of attributes or behavioral styles that are unique to delinquents. Comfort (1950), for example, outlines several categories of personality that we might expect to recur among the delinquent population. These include:

1 The "inadequate psychopath," an unpredictable and malleable individual who drifts into activities along with the crowd,
2 The "aggressive egocentric," a domineering, intolerant sort of person, driven by selfish ambition.
3 The "ethical aberrant," characterized by a severe impairment of moral responsibility and a determination to get his or her own way.
4 The "fantasy delinquent" or the "fantasy aggressor," who seeks to live out destructive impulses arising from inner psychical conflict.
5 The "addictive psychopath," who turns to alcohol or drugs to cope with personal inadequacies and lurches into a destructive spiral of crises.
6 The "paranoid psychotic," a person with an overwhelming grudge against society or some sector of it.

Not a bunch whom one would rush to engage in casual discourse upon a chance encounter downtown late on a Saturday night. However, Comfort was describing categories of *politicians*, a class of beings whom he regards as tolerated delinquents. He comments: "Unfortunately, all the old-style criminologists' categories are as recognizable in the Establishment itself as they are in the approved school or in Brixton. The difference lies chiefly in the choice of a condemned or an accepted mode of expressing them" (p. 47).

Are delinquents any different from other members of the community? There is certainly evidence that particular constellations of antisocial personality features found from as early as the preschool years are predictive of delinquency in youth and criminality beyond (Farrington, 1992, 1994; Farrington and West, 1990; Magnusson, 1988; Spivack et al., 1986). Farrington and West's (1990) study, a longitudinal examination of 400 London males from the age of 8 to 32 years, provides strong evidence that boys who were scoring high on measures of general trouble-causing, conduct problems, dishonesty, anger, impulsiveness, and truancy were likely to sustain similar patterns of behavior into adulthood and to end up in trouble with the law. Magnusson's (1988) study of Swedish youths shows similarly a strong relationship between early aggressiveness and later criminality.

Somewhat paradoxically in the light of these findings, comparisons of the social skills of delinquents and non-delinquent peers have not revealed consistently strong differences (see Hollin, 1990), and at least two studies have found that self-reports of delinquency and measures of social difficulty do not correlate (Furnham, 1984, with a sample of secondary school children, Renwick and Emler, 1991, with a sample of incarcerated delinquent males). In fact, Renwick and Emler (1991) compared delinquents' self-reports of social difficulties (e.g. "making friends," "dating," "keeping a conversation going") with data collected earlier from university students. They found that both the overall mean difficulty and the difficulty with specific social activities were remarkably similar. Perhaps this indicates that undergraduates can be more useful in the study of real world problems than we surmised in chapter 1, but it does not increase confidence that we are identifying characteristics *unique to* the officially delinquent population.

Cognitive and moral development

There are at least two ways in which cognitive development might be implicated in the genesis of delinquency. First, delinquents are by definition doing something wrong, they are violating the standards and laws of their community. It could be that those who break the law have a deficient grasp of the regulations governing accepted behavior: in short, they could be morally retarded. Second, individuals who are less intellectually able may find the criteria of success within the school system less attainable, less rewarding, and less motivating. Hence, they have greater prospects than their peers of finding themselves alienated from the system.

As we saw in chapter 14, the relationship between moral reasoning and social behavior is a complex one, and this turns out to be no less true for delinquents. Certainly, several studies have found differences between delinquents and age-matched controls on measures of moral reasoning, such as Rest's Defining Issues Test (DIT; see chapter 14), with delinquents scoring lower (Emler, 1984). However, as Emler (1984) comments, these studies have often been conducted with incarcerated delinquents, and it is difficult to disentangle any effects due to institutionalization. Living in a prison might depress anyone's moral reasoning ability (as the Zimbardo prison experiment suggests). It is also possible that the less intellectually able are more prone to getting caught (leaving the morally sophisticated delinquents still on the loose). An alternative basis for a comparison would be based on self-reported delinquency, which would allow for more differentiated tests of the relationship between frequency of offences and moral reasoning independent of institutional status.

Such a study was conducted by Emler et al. (1978). They compared a group of male inmates of a Scottish borstal with a group of non-incarcerated boys matched on age, socioeconomic status, and urban background, with each sample completing a self-report measure of delinquency, a test of verbal intelligence, a Piagetian measure of operational thought, and the DIT. The borstal youths scored higher on the self-report measure of delinquency, and lower on the DIT. However, the measure of intelligence did not discriminate between the groups, and the differences on the Piagetian measures were rather modest (although in favor of the controls). Importantly, the measure of moral reasoning (DIT) did not correlate with self-reported delinquency scores for either group or across the sample as a whole. In a quite different study conducted with 10-year-old Finnish children judged by their peers to be either aggressive or nonaggressive, Keltikangas-Jarvinen (1989) also found no correlation between moral judgment and aggressive behavior. Together, these findings do not provide much support for explanations of delinquency based on cognitive or moral developmental level, although as Emler et al. (1978) acknowledge, there are many remaining questions for research in this context. Emler (1984) points to a related problem confronting moral developmental explanations of delinquency, which is that while there is little evidence of differences in moral reasoning between the sexes (see chapter 14), there is strong evidence of sex differences in delinquent involvement. Still more generally, Binder (1988) raises the familiar question of the relationship between moral cognition and behavior, and asks whether it is reasonable to expect a straightforward relationship between responses to a test of moral reasoning and actual behavior on the streets.

School performance

Many studies have shown that delinquents tend to have poor school records (Engel and Hurrelmann, 1989; Hargreaves, 1967; Hindelang et al., 1981; Reicher and Emler, 1986; West and Farrington, 1973, 1977). A ready explanation of this pattern of results might be that delinquents are less intelligent than their peers. Some have advanced such an interpretation, drawing on evidence that delinquents are sometimes found to score lower on IQ tests than do their peers – about 8 points less on average (Quay, 1987), though not always (see Emler et al., 1978, above). Unfortunately, this finding is clouded by the considerations that if delinquents do not enjoy school, they may not find school tests very motivating, and thus may not be interested in giving their best performance on an IQ assessment administered by an unfamiliar middle-class professional. It is generally accepted that IQ tests are not culture-free, and so they may be less sensitive to the abilities of youngsters from lower socioeconomic status and nonwhite backgrounds than to those of the groups upon whom they have been standardized. Further, as noted above, the delinquents who get tested have also been caught and institutionalized. This could mean that their intellectual performance is inhibited by the relentless boredom of the circumstances in which they now find themselves, but there could also be other aspects of selectivity: for example, at the various steps of the judicial process, from preferring charges to sentencing, the system itself could be less sympathetic to seemingly duller individuals so that disproportionate numbers end up inside. Or, still more simply, it could be that only the dumb get caught: there could be some very bright delinquents still at large (as Comfort, above, maintains).

Nevertheless, there are good reasons for including school failure as part of the explanation of delinquency. Reicher and Emler (1986) found that there was a wide ideological and attitudinal gap between high school children who were succeeding and those who were failing. While the former tended to see the system as fair and purposeful, the latter viewed school as a waste of time, a con within which one is duped into working hard to no avail in the face of entrenched prejudices that obstruct the advancement of people of working-class background. Not surprisingly, the former were broadly committed to success within the system, while the latter consciously rejected scholastic achievement. In the words of an ex-skinhead from the East End of London: "Exams are fucking stupid and they build up a class barrier" (Daniel and Maguire, 1972, p. 47). We return to the implications of disenchantment with school below.

Socioeconomic Status

Class

One of the most controversial topics in the investigation of juvenile delinquency is the relationship between class and criminal involvement. When official records (e.g., arrest rates, seriousness of offences) are taken as the dependent measures, delinquency is usually found to be more common in lower socioeconomic groups (Wolfgang et al., 1987). When self-reports are taken into account, the picture becomes more confused. For example, several studies comparing self-reported criminal activities of American youths from different socioeconomic backgrounds found no significant differences (see Wolfgang et al., 1987). Thus, debate revolves around the possibilities of differential involvement (i.e., lower-class individuals commit more crime) versus differential selection (i.e., the police and the legal system are more disposed to prosecute lower-class individuals).

Obviously, the discrepancy between official records and self-report data raises the possibility that one measure may be more reliable and more valid than the other. Intuitively, one might suspect self-reports as an indicator of criminal activity – who would voluntarily admit to a string of antisocial and criminal acts? But in fact, there is good evidence that, providing confidentiality is assured, young people are surprisingly frank in their admissions, and very respectable levels of reliability have been attained in self-report measures (Emler, 1984; Hindelang et al., 1981). The validity of measures of criminal activity, whether official records or self-report, is more difficult to determine. It is certainly accepted by all parties that much more crime occurs than is recorded officially. Hence, it is likely that self-report measures may be closer to the truth. If this is the case, then the fact that self-report data reduce social class differences in participation suggests the possibility that differences in conviction may have something to do with biases in either policing or judicial systems or both.

Another source of information on this issue comes from studies of delinquency and race.

Race

In white-dominated societies, delinquency is more common among nonwhites. For example, in the US, blacks and chicanos have substantially higher delinquency rates than whites (Hindelang et al., 1981). In South Australia, Aboriginal people constitute about 1.2 percent of the general population but 28.1 percent of youths in detention are Aboriginal (Gale et al., 1990). Similar patterns emerge in Britain (Carr-Hill and Drew, 1988).

The explanation of racial difference in delinquency rates is complex. The first point to be stressed is that the imbalances described above are derived from official records, based on arrests and prosecutions. When self-report data are taken into account, then the overall differences between the races in criminal involvement are dramatically reduced (Hindelang et al., 1981). As in the interpretation of class differences above, criminologists have inferred that prejudices among the police and judicial systems may contribute to the differential statistics concerning punishment. It is difficult, for example, to avoid the conclusion that Los Angeles police have been especially zealous in recent years in the apprehension of black suspects.

Gale et al.'s (1990) Australian study reveals that at each stage of contact with the legal system, Aboriginal youths – compared to adolescents of other ethnic backgrounds – are disproportionately likely to be sent on to the next stage. Thus, of those youths stopped by the police, Aboriginals are more likely to be arrested (rather than cautioned); of those arrested, Aboriginals are more likely to be referred to court; of those appearing in court, Aboriginals are more likely to be sent to detention centers; of those in detention centers, Aboriginals are more likely to be re-incarcerated subsequently. Gale et al.'s analyses indicate that the crucial point in the sequence is the decision to arrest, and they report anecdotal evidence and police statements which indicate that, for the same offence, a white youth will be cautioned while an Aboriginal youth will be arrested.

Self-report data in the US do reveal some racial differences, particularly in the commission of serious crimes and especially violence. Blacks are more likely to be involved in serious offences against the person (Hindelang et al., 1981; Tracy, 1987). Of course, evidence of differential involvement merely describes the problem rather than explains it. We still need to know what factors associated with some minority group youths' socialization and what aspects of the day-to-day circumstances of their lives place them at greater risk of criminal participation. In America, Australia, Britain and other white-dominated societies, black people tend to be disproportionately represented among the very poor, and hence vulnerable to a multitude of stresses associated with economic deprivation, lack of employment opportunities, family pressures, and inadequate education.

Gender

Traditionally, males are more likely to become delinquent than are females (Canter, 1982; Emler, 1984; Hindelang et al., 1981; Hudson, 1989; Rutter and Giller, 1983). Why should this be the case? Once again, explanations range from the biologically determinist to the environmental molding. On the biological side, it has been argued that males are prone to violent aggression (see chapter 12), and thus more prone to become involved in antisocial activities of this kind. It has also been asserted that females are innately deficient in criminal capacities. Lombroso and Ferrero (1900) proposed that females were not as evolutionarily advanced as males, and lacked the intellect and initiative to participate in criminal activity.

It is more plausible that there may be an interaction between biological characteristics and social context. For example, boys are more vulnerable to a range of stress factors throughout development, and this may place young males at special risk when they encounter difficulties in their social contexts, such as family discord. Since one outcome of family discord is often that the father departs, this may have a particularly negative impact upon the development of boys (Rutter and Giller, 1983). Among girls, there is evidence that reaching pubertal status early may be associated with greater risk of involvement in delinquent activities, though chiefly among girls in mixed-sex schools (Caspi et al., 1993), indicating that the consequences of physical development may vary according to social context.

Still more important appear to be social expectations concerning how males and females should behave, and how misdemeanors should be treated. In respect of behavior, Reicher and Emler (1986) in a study of Scottish adolescents, found that delinquents were characterized as tough, strong, unemotional, cruel, and "hard." Clearly, these are stereotypically masculine properties, and the authors speculate that one of the reasons why delinquency may be less popular among girls is that such attributes are in direct opposition to those of the traditional feminine stereotype. Studies of girls' positions in teenage gangs show that they are usually a numerical minority, and that they have peripheral status (often as sex objects) from which they are not expected to participate in the heavy action, such as inter-gang fights (Daniel and Maguire, 1972; Lagree and Fai, 1989).

The surrounding culture is also likely to maintain social values relating to male and female behavior: delinquency is often considered a "normal" problem for males, but "abnormal" in females (Hudson, 1989). Willemsen and van Schie (1989) point out that sex-role stereotypes could be expected to influence social attitudes toward delinquent behavior in either of two seemingly mutually contradictory ways. On the one hand, since much criminal activity is stereotypically masculine (e.g., aggressive), criminal behavior by males will be seen as conforming to the male gender stereotype and hence reflecting stable internal causes; this should lead to more negative evaluations of males committing crimes. On the other hand, when a female commits a stereotypically male crime, she is deviating from her sex role, and this may be interpreted as a token of maladjustment; this inference should lead to more negative evaluations of female criminals.

In a study of Dutch adolescents' and adults' reactions to different types of crimes,

Willemsen and van Schie (1989) found that violent crimes by boys were deemed to merit more severe punishment than the same crimes by girls (consistent with the first hypothesis). However, for less gender stereotyped offences such as shoplifting or fare dodging there were no differences in the treatments recommended for either sex, while for minor misdemeanors such as staying away from home all night after a party or hanging around discos, respondents were more likely to recommend some kind of intervention (e.g., seeing a social worker) for girls than for boys (consistent with the second hypothesis). It seems, conclude the authors, that these kinds of things are "something a 'decent' girl ought not do" (p. 631). When delinquent behavior is consistent with the masculine stereotype, this stereotype becomes salient in attributing responsibility and determining punishment – to the disadvantage of the male offender; when the behavior is gender neutral then sex bias in punishment is less likely but girls are perceived as in greater need of remedial assistance.

Feminism and equal opportunities in crime

Finally on gender, the interesting possibility arises that as societies move away from the narrower constraints of traditional gender roles then we should expect to see corresponding shifts in crime participation rates (thus debunking the sexist assertions of Lombroso and colleagues). In fact, some relatively recent statistics do show that increasing numbers of young females are becoming involved in delinquency, a finding which has led to some media speculation that this may be one of the more negative outcomes of feminism. In a provocative text, Adler (1975) advanced the thesis that the growth of female criminality was but one token of a new female assertiveness, and she pointed to instances of female bank robbers and other "sisters in crime" to support her case.

Reviews of the growing literature on female juvenile delinquency do not support this interpretation. Both Berger (1989) and Hollin (1986) conclude that there are no data to confirm the culpability of feminism. Studies have found little evidence of an association between female delinquency and commitment to nontraditional attitudes toward female roles. In both sexes, there is some evidence that involvement in criminality is moderately associated with masculinity, but it remains the case that males are more involved than females irrespective of their degree of masculinity (Berger, 1989).

It may be, however, that female delinquents who fail to conform to feminine stereotypes are particularly likely to receive punitive treatment. Hudson (1989) reviews evidence indicating that girls whose physical appearance and dress style are not stereotypically feminine are treated more severely by the courts. Analyses of the treatment in European courts of boys and girls facing charges relating to status offences (i.e., having sexual relations below the legal age limit) show that girls are dealt with more severely (see Appendix to Cain, 1989). Accounts of corrective institutions for girls reveal that the staff perceive part of their duties as focused on curing the inmates of insufficient femininity, and preparing them for normal housewife roles (Ferrari-Bravo and Arcidiacono, 1989; Kersten, 1989).

Family Environment

Given the importance of family processes that we have seen so frequently in this book, it is not surprising to find that they emerge as one of the key variables associated with delinquency. In one of his earliest works, Bowlby (1944) was struck by a recurrent pattern in the family histories of a sample of juvenile delinquents that he had been working with. In many cases, during the preschool years, some disruption had occurred to the security of the boy's relationship with his mother. Subsequent research has demonstrated repeatedly that delinquency is more common among children growing up in homes suffering from protracted marital discord and/or paternal absence (Baker and Mednick, 1984; Dornbusch et al., 1985; Farrington, 1992; Loeber and Stouthamer-Loeber, 1986; Patterson et al., 1989; Rutter and Giller, 1983). It is also more common where parent–child relationships lack affection, and where parenting styles are harsh, erratic, neglectful or abusive (Dishion et al., 1994; Rutter and Giller, 1983; Shaw and Scott, 1991; Widom, 1989; Wilson, 1980). Studies in Britain (Wilson, 1980) and America (Patterson et al., 1989) report that parents of delinquents tend to be poor monitors of their adolescent sons' activities. Often, they did not know where the boys were, who they were hanging around with, or what they did. The mother below is commenting on her teenage son, but her remarks may also reveal something of her own management style:

> "He's not bothered, he always mixes with the wrong children, there's a lot of boys around here – the one he calls his best friend I don't like. He's a daredevil if another boy says anything ... You don't always know where they are – you can't always see what they're up to." (mother interviewed by Wilson, 1980, p. 215)

If one or both of the parents have a criminal record, there is a greater probability that their son will become delinquent (Farrington, 1992; Robins, 1979). Baker and Mednick (1984), in an analysis of data recorded in the Danish National Police Register, found that the influence of parental criminality appeared to be additive: if both mother and father had a criminal record, then the incidence of criminality in their sons was dramatically increased.

Overall, evidence on the families of delinquent youths tends to confirm Barber's (1992) thesis that there is a relationship between lack of behavioral regulation and participation in problem behaviors. Other evidence reviewed above indicates that factors such as socioeconomic status, gender, race, poor school performance, and personality characteristics may also be risk factors. However, while this helps us to understand the setting conditions, it has also been stressed above that not all persons who are at risk actually become delinquent. What are the motivations and interpersonal contexts which underlie initiation and continued involvement in delinquency? To address this issue, we need to consider a developmental social psychological theory.

Delinquency as a Positive Choice: the Reputation Management Theory

It was noted earlier that delinquents tend to have poor relations at and with school. Emler (1984) reports evidence that measures of delinquency and attitudes to school/authority correlate quite highly. It is tempting to pursue the causal question: which comes first, negative attitudes toward school or involvement in delinquency? But Emler develops an intriguing alternative account, suggesting that negative attitudes toward school and delinquent behavior are expressions of the same underlying motivation, namely the need to establish a social identity. He argues that "individuals may choose between alternative identities *with the delinquent alternative as a positive choice* rather than simply a failure to choose the other alternative" (1984, p. 222, emphasis added).

The idea that delinquent behavior could be a deliberate, purposeful, and valued choice contrasts with theories which attempt to account for delinquency in terms of individual pathology or the influence of adverse socialization experiences. Emler (1984) argues that one of the major tasks all individuals face in social life is to present the self in ways which make sense both to self and others. For this reason, he proposes, all people are motivated to develop and maintain a reputation, a public record of one's behavior and worth. For those who stand to gain within the mainstream, then the criteria of a good reputation are determined in accord with the values of the system, such as educational success and career advancement. Others, finding this route closed or distrusting the system's claims that compliance will lead to later rewards, reject the socially sanctioned values and opt to fend for themselves.

The social contexts of delinquent activity

Reicher and Emler's (1986) account predicts that the locus of delinquent activity should be the peer group – and there is abundant evidence that it is (Agnew, 1991; Henngeler, 1989). Interview studies with delinquents themselves reveal consistently that they find social support, ideas for action and bravado from group involvement:

"I don't act so hard when I am on my own." (Scottish male, aged 15, quoted by Reicher and Emler, 1986, p. 35)

"Just because other people were doing it, and if I was on my own I wouldn't know what to do." (Scottish male, aged 15, quoted by Reicher and Emler, 1986, p. 35)

"You're just one of the mob going to look for fights every other night . . . you couldn't just walk around by yourself and beat up Pakis, you wouldn't half get a beating if you went round on your own doing things you would have done with the mob. Don't say you would 'ave run around Brick Lane punching Pakis on your jack." (ex-skinhead, interviewed by Daniel and Maguire, 1972, pp. 31–2).

Table 17.1   British delinquents' accounts of degree of group involvement and admission rates for delinquent activities (*n* = 40)

Scale	Group involvement[a]	Admission rate (%)
Drugs	3.12	7.5
Theft	3.29	52.5
Aggression	3.24	58.6
Vandalism	3.16	43.6
Status	3.00	39.5
Minor/nuisance	2.73	36.7

[a] On a scale from 1 to 4.
Source: Emler et al., 1987b

In self-report questionnaire studies with Scottish adolescents, Emler et al. (1987) found that across a wide range of offences there was a high degree of social involvement at the time they were committed (see table 17.1), and no offence that was predominantly solitary. Girls were even more likely than boys to commit offences in company. In a study of the street gangs of Paris, Lagrée and Fai (1989) reach very similar conclusions.

Reputation, both individual and collective, recurs frequently in adolescent gang members' accounts of their motivations (Campbell, 1993; Goldstein, 1994). Campbell (1993) reports that violent gangs with which she worked in New York maintained scrapbooks of newspaper clippings about their exploits. In a city near you there will be reputation-earning statements of identity sprayed on walls, bus shelters, telephone booths, and train sides.

Drawing on the data from Wolfgang et al.'s Philadelphia study, Rand (1987) found that young males who joined a gang were more delinquent than those who did not: 81 percent of the sample became delinquent after joining a gang, although there was no difference between the seriousness of offences committed before and after joining a gang. Leaving a gang coincided for many with the end of their delinquency.

Reicher and Emler (1986) argue that the peer context is important to all adolescents for similar reasons: it is essential to the social process of constructing a social identity. Within nondelinquent groups, involvement in criminal activity might lead to exclusion; for the delinquent group, it is a criterion of inclusion. In both cases, actions do not take on meaning until they have an audience of like-minded others, people who regard themselves as belonging to the same group and sharing a similar fate. The authors point out that the large bureaucratic environments of contemporary high schools provide ideal conditions for creating and nurturing such social configurations.

Summary

As forewarned, there is not a simple answer to the question of what causes delinquency. Delinquency is multidetermined and the explanation of delinquency in one young person may differ from that for another. Evidence of individual deficiencies in delinquents is somewhat mixed. Farrington and West's (1990) prospective data relating to the continuity of antisocial tendencies from childhood to adulthood are impressive. However, this does not locate the problem in the child, like a disease (see Farrington, 1991), since there is also likely to be continuity in the young person's family and social environment. We also encountered evidence that these factors are strongly linked to the emergence of delinquency. Findings in respect of other attributes, such as social skills, cognitive and moral development, sometimes indicate lower scores in delinquents, but some of the studies may be confounded by situational differences (testing inmates versus people in normal environments) and motivational factors (incarcerated youths may not feel favorably disposed toward investigators whom they may perceive as part of the system). Where most of these lines of investigation converge is in terms of the young person's relationships to and within school: prospective delinquents tend, often from early childhood, not to get on very well with their peers and the institution.

Demographic characteristics, such as social class, race, and gender, are associated with official delinquency, and may be associated, though somewhat less strongly, with unofficial or hidden delinquency. It should be stressed that class, race, and gender are risk factors rather than guarantees. Furthermore, it is likely that any risk arises from aspects of the social contexts of individuals within these social categories, particularly with respect to family processes and peer relations.

The reputation management theory places delinquency in social and developmental context. It holds that individuals strive to establish a reputation in circumstances affected by their standing and performance in the community. Reputation is tied closely to the attainment of social identity, which we saw in the previous chapter is a major developmental task of early to mid-adolescence. For some, the mainstream does not allow for the possibility of a successful conventional reputation, and alternative reputations become attractive. Initiation and maintenance of a delinquent reputation is a social affair, involving reference to peer standards and peer evaluation.

Health Problems

Adolescence is an important but neglected period with respect to the development of health-related behavior (Millstein and Litt, 1990). It is neglected because, compared to other phases of the lifespan, it tends to be a relatively healthy one, with lower levels of mortality and morbidity (Chassin et al., 1987). It is none the less important because it is a time of new discoveries and exploratory behavior, some of which may establish patterns that endure well into adulthood with potentially serious long-term implications. For example, use of nicotine, alcohol, and other drugs are often initiated in adolescence (Chassin et al., 1987) while previous patterns of positive health behaviors, such as exercise, may be altered. In addition, some health risks, such as eating disorders, are especially frequent among adolescents. In this section, we consider drug use, pregnancy, and eating disorders.

Drug Use in Adolescence

Most Westerners take drugs. Among the most highly regarded are alcohol, tobacco, and tranquillizers; among the most reviled are marijuana, cocaine and its derivatives, and heroin. Societal attitudes to drugs are a complex affair: some are highly valued as leisure products for adults, others are endorsed and dispensed by the medical profession even though they are known to create dependencies or deleterious side effects, and others are universally condemned (see Howitt, 1991, for a historical account of the vagaries of theories and policies relating to drug abuse). With respect to adolescence, concerns arise because people of this age range are presumed not to have the maturity to handle the effects of the substances that adults enjoy. We will focus here primarily on the two most dangerous drugs: alcohol and tobacco. These drugs are important partly because of their inherent risks, and partly because they serve often as "gateways" to other drug use (Blaze-Temple and Lo, 1992). It will become clear that some of the factors associated with risky uses of these substances are also associated with the use of illegal drugs, which we will consider more briefly.

Alcohol

Alcohol is one of the most dangerous drugs used in contemporary societies, and it is one of the most widely accepted. US data reveal that around 90 percent of high school students have tried alcohol, and over 60 percent are drinking regularly (Adams et al., 1994). This makes it the most common drug used by this age group, contrasting with cocaine at 17 percent (with about 5 percent using regularly) and heroin at around 1 percent.

In most countries, the age at which one can consume alcohol in licensed premises is determined by law – often 18 years, sometimes older. One consequence of this legal boundary is that drinking is regarded by the young as a definitively adult activity. Hence, for individuals dealing with the transition to adulthood, one way to accelerate progress is to start drinking (Jessor and Jessor, 1977) and findings confirm that those who develop earlier physically and psychosocially start to use alcohol earlier (Stattin and Magnusson, 1989). Alcohol and transition proneness seem intimately related.

Other functions of alcohol consumption (and of other drug use) may include coping. One liability of the use of alcohol as a coping aid is that the adolescent may not learn other coping skills (Newcomb and Bentler, 1989). Still another prominent reason for drinking alcohol is to get drunk. Substantial proportions of adolescents acknowledge this as a legitimate goal of the activity. Pulkkinen and Narusk (1987) found that 25 percent of Finnish teenage boys, 16 percent of Finnish teenage girls, 14 percent of Estonian boys and 4 percent of Estonian girls expressed strong acceptance of becoming drunk as a purpose of drinking. Among 15-year-old New Zealanders, Connolly et al. (1992) found that 68 percent anticipated that it was very likely that they would get drunk in the future.

Alcohol and the peer context

Pulkkinen and Narusk's (1987) subjects also stressed the importance of drinking as a social custom – and the youth of most countries outside of Islam are highly likely to make the same observation. Drinking is expected in peer contexts, and through adolescence social life is organized increasingly around drinking sites (Bush, 1990). Becoming a drinker facilitates making friends, especially with members of the opposite sex (Fondacaro and Heller, 1983; Halebsky, 1987; Pulkkinen and Narusk, 1987; Silbereisen and Noack, 1986). It also establishes one's credentials as part of a social group. In many Western societies, alcohol is so pervasive in social activity that those who decline to partake sometimes find they attract negative reactions or direct pressure to join in (Bush, 1990).

Drinking is a highly social activity in adolescence. Bush (1990) reports that young people consume more alcohol outside the home (i.e., at gatherings with peers), and that the amount of alcohol consumption tends to increase with the size of the group (a phenomenon that can easily be tested by observational research in suitable premises). Indeed, Newcomb and Bentler (1988) found that heavy drinking youths tended to have relatively high levels of social integration compared to their peers. While drinking may be a normal part of social development, the social context can also provide the setting conditions for the emergence of problem drinking and related dangerous behaviors. For example, Klepp et al. (1987), in an American study, found that while most adolescents had experience of peers who drink and drive, those who admitted to the highest levels of drinking and driving in their sample were also the subjects most likely to have several friends who drink and drive.

Alcohol and the parental context

Although drinking is popularly blamed on the peer group, findings of numerous studies reveal strong links between parental use of alcohol and adolescent involvement (Foxcroft and Hull, 1991; Hill et al., 1992; Jessor et al., 1994; Mori et al., 1987; Newcomb and Bentler, 1989; Vicary and Lerner, 1986; Woodside, 1988). Many youngsters have their first drinks with parents (Vicary and Lerner, 1986). Parents may act as role models, and in cases of serious alcohol dependency may well be less competent and less involved caregivers, thus increasing the motivations to seek alcohol as a source of support or relief from problems.

In their study of Finnish and Estonian youth, for example, Pulkkinen and Narusk (1987) found that in both countries more than two-thirds of their samples had seen their father drunk (and 15 percent of Estonians, 37 percent of Finns had seen their mothers drunk). Striking differences in experience of alcohol among teenagers were related to whether or not parents drank. In homes where alcohol was never used by parents, 42 percent of girls and 35 percent of boys had never tried it, and the majority had only slight experience of it. These researchers conclude that cognitions relating to alcohol use are formed on the basis of observations of parental behavior.

Other evidence indicates that parents who drink excessively often acquiesce in the face of their teenagers' drinking (Barnes and Farrell, 1992; Foxcroft and Hull, 1991).

It may be that parents accommodate to the process as part of the general shift in their relations with their children in the transition to adulthood, as discussed in chapter 15. Stattin and Magnusson (1989) found that the parents of early maturing girls were less severe in their reactions to the girls' drinking, and were more likely to expect that their daughters would become involved in drinking. The authors suggest that because early maturing girls *look* as though they are more mature than their peers they are assumed to be more likely to be drawn to adult behaviors.

Finally, another important aspect of parental involvement may be the degree of supportiveness that they show to the child during adolescence (Compas et al., 1995; Kliewer et al., 1994; Meuss, 1994). Low levels of perceived family support are associated with disrupted family functioning, parental role stress – and adolescent drinking (Barnes and Farrell, 1992; Fischer and Wampler, 1994; Meuss, 1994).

Smoking

Just about everybody has heard that smoking is a serious health risk. The robustness of smokers' practices in the face of self-injury and widespread social disapprobation makes this group of people an important source of evidence on the potency of social psychological processes in adolescence.

Awareness of the dangers of smoking is well established in contemporary children by the end of the primary school years (Goddard, 1990; Peterson and Peterson, 1986; de Vries and Kok, 1986). Children of this age understand the health consequences and are particularly sensitive to its implications for the wellbeing of their parents. Yet when adolescents are tested, their understanding of the long-term effects is sometimes found to be poor (Eiser et al., 1989). About half of young people who smoke begin experimenting with the practice below the age of 12 (Rice, 1990) and almost 70 percent of high school students have tried it, with around 30 percent inhaling regularly (Adams et al., 1994). Smoking is second only to alcohol as a popular drug among this age group. Why do adolescents take up a habit that only a few years earlier they understood to be dangerous and unpleasant? Once again, the evidence points to transition proneness, the influence of social context (especially parents and peers), and to social cognitive adjustments.

Smoking and the family context

As with most problem behaviors, the family stands out as a principal context for acquiring smoking. Studies have consistently found a strong link between parental smoking or other drug use and child initiation (Stanton et al., 1994). Many children receive their first cigarette from their parents (Royal College of Physicians, 1983). The critical consideration may not be parental approval (even smoking parents often disapprove of the habit), but parental behavior. Grube et al. (1986) found, in Irish samples, that parental *approval* of smoking had little effect (though in some cases, parental *dis*approval was associated with adolescent smoking, possibly because of reactance on the part of the child; cf. Brehm, 1981); on the other hand, Grube et al. (1986) found that if parents themselves smoked, then adolescents were more likely to smoke. Correspondingly, Peterson and Peterson (1986) found, in an Australian sample, that if parents quit smoking, then their adolescent children were much less likely to approve of smoking or to have friends who smoked. Siblings' smoking habits have also been found to be associated with involvement (Goddard, 1990). Engel et al. (1987) found that social conflict within the family was strongly associated with the use of legal drugs including tobacco.

Smoking and the peer context

There is considerable evidence that initiation into smoking is also affected by the peer context. Young people who smoke tend to have friends who smoke (Conrad et al., 1992; Eiser et al., 1991; Goddard, 1990; Waldron et al., 1991). It is very likely that peer selection may reflect rather than cause similar interests (Brown, 1990; Savin-Williams and Berndt, 1990). Even so, young smokers sometimes attribute their habit to peer expectations (Morgan and Grube, 1989; Rice, 1990; Semmer et al., 1987) and to their own perceived lack of self-efficacy in refusing cigarettes offered by peers (Conrad et al., 1992). Rowe et al. (1992) demonstrate that the transitions from nonsmoker to trier to regular smoker among the young display the characteristics of a social contagion process: the stages of an epidemic in which a certain number of contacts are exposed to the bug, and then a predictable proportion go on to develop the more serious consequences.

There are at least three ways in which peer involvement contributes to the onset of smoking. First, as indicated earlier, taking up behaviors associated with adulthood may serve as a marker of the transition to maturity, and it may be important within the peer context to prove one's standing in this respect (Jessor and Jessor, 1977; Semmer et al., 1987; Silbereisen and Noack, 1988). Silbereisen and Noack provide a telling anecdotal example of how cigarettes can become a medium for adolescent social interaction. A 16-year-old German boy comments: "The best way to make contact is to ask somebody for a cigarette, and then tear the filter off, and then crumble the cigarette – she just must realize that I mean something else" (1989, p. 162). More generally, these investigators show that early use of tobacco and other substances is aimed predominantly at integrating the adolescent into the peer community (which in turn is striving to adopt some of the practices of the adult community).

Second, peer groups may foster the sharing of particular sets of social attitudes. An important contemporary example is the increase in smoking among teenage girls. Traditionally, more males than females smoked, but recent studies among Western adolescents find consistently a swing in the opposite direction (Goddard, 1990; Waldron et al., 1991). Waldron et al. surveyed over 11,000 American adolescents and found that girls who smoked were more likely to share a host of less conventional attitudes (toward society and education) and were also less likely to participate in sports. Girls may also share the (incorrect) view that smoking helps reduce weight (Abraham and Llewellyn-Jones, 1992). Again, peer influence is not monolithic, and there is evidence that adolescents with high self-efficacy are less likely to be susceptible to peer influences to take up drugs such as tobacco (deVries et al., 1988; Lawrance, 1988; Stacy et al., 1992).

Third, peers may help generate a social cognitive basis for self-attributions and expectations about the smoking habit. Eiser and his colleagues (Eiser, 1985; Eiser et al., 1987) have argued that information provided by other cigarette smokers may influence the reasoning of novice smokers. The taste of tobacco and the inhalation of smoke are not instantly pleasurable sensations for first timers; indeed, the early experience of smoking is likely at best to be an ambiguous experience. Eiser et al. (1987) point out that interpretation of ambiguous feelings can be influenced by environmental cues, including how other people label the experience (Schacter and Singer, 1962). Veteran smokers may tell the learner that the practice is enjoyable and rewarding: "it calms your nerves," "it clears the brain," "picks you up," and so on. Similarly, veterans may relate how difficult it is to give up, and Eiser suggests this may persuade teenagers who have not yet reached the stage of pharmacological dependence to believe that cessation would be uncomfortable. Eiser et al. (1987), in a study of over 10,000 British adolescents, found that teenagers who were smoking relatively low numbers of cigarettes (four or five a day) anticipated serious difficulties in stopping, felt that they craved a smoke, and had brand preferences. Compared to non-smokers, smokers were more external in their health beliefs (they believed that health was more a matter of luck and external events than self-determination), and the more addicted a young person believed him or herself to be, the more likely he or she was to agree that smoking had a calming effect. In short, Eiser and colleagues propose that a constellation of beliefs about smoking is socially shared, transmitted from experienced smokers to novices, and that these social cognitions provide a base for attributions and expectancies about the effects of the addiction and the chances of escaping from it.

It is worth reiterating here a point from chapter 15. Peer influence is not invariably oriented toward risk and antisocial behavior (Brown, 1990). If positive peer attitudes toward smoking tend to be correlated with the adoption of smoking, then the converse is implied, too: negative peer attitudes toward smoking may dissuade some from taking it up. Waldron et al.'s (1991) finding that boys who were keen on sports were less likely to smoke provides a clear illustration. By and large, people who are interested in fitness are likely to discourage their peers from the habit.

Other drugs

In Western nations, the next most popular substance is marijuana. A majority of US high school students report that they have tried this though many, like President Clinton, did not persist. Around 20–30 percent say that they use it regularly (Adams et al., 1994; Shedler and Block, 1990; Steinberg, 1993). A recent British study found that over one-fifth of 15- to 16-year-olds acknowledge having used illegal drugs such as marijuana, solvents, glue, and psilocybin, and one-tenth had used one or more of these substances within the month immediately prior to testing (Smith and Nutbeam, 1992). High rates of psilocybin use have been found to cause deleterious effects on advanced study, leading to higher levels of compliance, dependence on rote learning and intellectual timidity (Ushrum et al., 1993).

It was mentioned earlier that drugs which cause the greatest public concerns, such as heroin and cocaine, are used by only a minority of adolescents. In America, large-scale surveys reveal that only about 2–4 percent of young people have ever used crack and around 1 percent have dabbled in heroin (Steinberg, 1993). Of course, 4 percent of American youth amounts to a large number of people, but by no means a majority of these continue to use illicit drugs – although, as elsewhere, the use of solvents and stimulants appears to be increasing (Adams et al., 1994).

Invariably, the family and peers emerge as key factors in explaining adolescent use of illegal drugs. As with legal drugs, there is often found to be serious interpersonal conflict within the family of illegal drug users (Baumrind, 1991; West, 1987). In a Swiss study, Uchtenhagen and Zimmer-Hofler (1985, 1987) compared the family backgrounds of 215 heroin addicts and 513 controls, finding that the addicts were much more likely to come from broken homes, to have spent time with foster parents and/or in institutions as children, to have left home at an early age, and to have family members who have problems with alcohol or drugs. Uchtenhagen and Zimmer-Hofler report that 95.8 percent of the peers of their heroin addicts used drugs, while only 16.6 percent of the peers of their control subjects used them. Smith and Nutbeam (1992) found that children of single parents were more likely to be involved in illegal drug use.

The extent to which the family serves as an effective buffer against other stresses again emerges as a factor in drug use. In a study of African-American and Puerto Rican adolescents' drug use, Brook et al. (1993) found that drug-resistant youths tended to have positive relations with their parents (secure attachment), which in turn was associated with the internalization of parental attitudes and behavior. Drug-resistant youth were also more achievement-oriented.

Although the reputation management theory has not been applied extensively to drug use in adolescents, it seems plausible that using illegal substances is one way to establish credentials among a peer group. There is evidence that some subcultural groups use drugs as a component of a more general expression of their social identity. For example, in a Bermudian study, West (1987) investigated a subgroup of young black students who were disaffected with the school system and who tended also to have unstable family structures. These adolescents favored reggae music, Rastafarian hairstyles, and marijuana, which West suggests may represent important features of their social cohesion and their rejection of the dominant culture of the island.

Adolescent drug use in perspective

It has been stressed above that some amount of drug use during adolescence is very common. Indeed, it is so common that some researchers have concluded that a degree of experimentation is normative (Baumrind, 1987; Furby and Beyth-Marom, 1992; Shedler and Block, 1990). Shedler and Block (1990) produce findings from a longitudinal study of young Californians which lead them to posit a U-shaped relationship between psychosocial adjustment and drug use. Across a number of measures of wellbeing and adjustment, Shedler and Block found that individuals who had tried drugs such as marijuana once or twice were better adjusted than individuals who never tried drugs at all, and those who used drugs frequently revealed a more negative cluster of personality and emotional characteristics. These investigators argue that trying new experiences, even with some degree of risk attached, may not be pathological but part of normal, psychologically healthy development. On the other hand, frequent to excessive use may be motivated by maladjustment, and the desire to "numb out" feelings of inadequacy (Shedler and Block, 1990, p. 626). A controversial feature of Shedler and Block's analysis is the proposal that abstainers may also be maladjusted, in that they remain detached from the contemporary practices of their peers.

Overall, explaining drug use, whether legal or illegal, remains a challenge to applied developmental social psychologists but certain factors have been identified clearly in recent research. Experimentation is closely aligned with developmental concerns: at least part of adolescents' motives appears to be the desire to attain adult status and share adult pleasures. Choice of drugs is influenced by parental and peer practices, and there is evidence that the norms shift with time and culture (as revealed, for example, in Shedler and Block's data on the widespread social acceptability among contemporary Western youth of marijuana). Personality differences and psychological wellbeing are predictive of excessive use, and social developmental contexts (such as parenting received) are in turn predictive of psychological wellbeing. Social cognitions are implicated, in terms of young people's formulations of the attractions of drugs, their justifications of involvement and their representations of the obstacles to cessation.

Adolescent Pregnancy

The development of sexuality in adolescence was discussed in chapter 16. We turn now to one of the more problematic consequences of this activity: pregnancy. It is interesting to find again that there are cultural variations in the likelihood of this outcome. The US, for example, sustains one of the highest incidences of this variable among its young: approximately one in 10 American teenage females becomes pregnant each year (Jaffe and Dryfoos, 1980; Langer and Warheit, 1992; Sommer et al., 1993), a figure which is exceeded elsewhere only by Hungarians (Gilchrist and Schinke, 1987). In most Western countries, teenage pregnancy is seen as a major social problem, and in the US it is a virtual epidemic.

The fact that adolescent pregnancy tends to be regarded as a problem reminds us of the arbitrariness of the definition of adolescence. The message from biology is relatively clear: the girl has developed physically to the stage where she is capable of conception. The message from society is more ambivalent. In fact, as Davis (1980) points out, the gulf between what biology makes possible and what society renders acceptable has tended to increase in industrialized societies as the age of the menarche has dropped while the age of approved parenthood has risen. We do not find comparable media concern or government inquiries into the incidence of pregnancy among women in their 20s, for example. Yet in some eras, and today in some societies, it has been considered perfectly appropriate for girls in their teens to conceive shortly after reaching the menarche (see Weisfeld and Billings, 1988).

In contemporary Western societies, teenage pregnancy is regarded as problematic for a variety of reasons. Consistent with the Jessors' (1977) notion of transition proneness, some have suggested that the maternal role has been regarded as almost sacred, and that as a result acquiring the status "too soon" is perceived as a near sacrilege (cf. Lieberman, 1980). More pragmatically, there are concerns about possible effects upon the mother's mental health, given that she may be subjected to stigmatization, financial stresses, and the demands of a dependent infant. There are concerns about the impact upon the child, whose developmental context may be limited by the relative immaturity of the mother and, in many cases, by the fact that the mother will be a single parent and poor (Parke and Tinsely, 1987). Adolescent mothers have been found to be less knowledgeable about child care and development, to experience the role as more stressful and to be less adaptive and less patient as parents than older women (Culp et al., 1991; Garcia Coll et al., 1987; McLoyd et al., 1994; Sommer et al., 1993). There are also concerns about the consequences for the broader society, especially in terms of welfare payments. In fact, research generally confirms that early motherhood leads to a curtailment of the adolescent's education, career prospects and to a reduction in her aspirations (Dillard and Pol, 1982; Furstenberg et al., 1989; Gilchrist and Schinke, 1987; Presser, 1980) as well as to greater likelihood of educational disadvantage and future delinquency in the offspring (Brooks-Gunn and Furstenberg, 1986). Termination is a widely favored alternative: in the US, about 500,000 adolescents obtain abortions each year.

Why become pregnant?

The "how" question is dealt with in other books, but given the availability of contraception and the option of sexual restraint, the "why" question stands out as an important one for developmental social psychologists, and has attracted a lot of applied research. Traditional lay views of young girls who become pregnant are that it reflects their personal failings – perhaps due to a lack of moral fibre or sexual restraint. (Some might apportion blame to the father, too: but researchers, with some exceptions, have tended to follow lay opinion that the male simply cannot be held responsible for his urges.)

As with many social behaviors, there are several factors involved in becoming pregnant (Shea, 1984). Some teenagers may lack the cognitive abilities to predict the causal relationship between sexual intercourse and later pregnancy and many lack adequate factual knowledge (Brooks-Gunn, 1993; Cvetkovich and Grote, 1981). For example, Brooks-Gunn (1993) reports that two-thirds of adolescents were ignorant of which time in the monthly cycle pregnancy is most likely. Many subscribe to the adolescent fable that "it won't happen to me" (Zelnik and Kantner, 1979), and most are quite surprised when it does (Brooks-Gunn and Furstenberg, 1989).

Some instances of adolescent pregnancy provide an illustration of the complexity of the attitude–behavior relationship, well known to social psychologists. Furstenberg

(1980), in a study of over 400 pregnant teenagers in Baltimore, found that almost half of his sample stated that it was very important for a woman to wait until marriage to have sex (remember: these are *pregnant* teenagers). Probing this discrepancy between professed values and current condition revealed the justifications that "everyone else is doing it," and that doing it "once in a while" should not result in conception. The worst you might expect is to get a little bit pregnant. Similarly, while both male and female adolescents believe that they should take responsibility for using birth control rather than assuming that their partner will do so, US data reveal that less than two in ten young males actually do take an active role in contraception, even to the minimal extent of asking their partner if she is protected (Shea, 1984).

Another possibility is that adolescents lack the social and communicative skills that enable them to use contraception effectively (Lawrance et al., 1990; Shea, 1984). Access to contraception may involve communications, major or minor, with others ranging from parents, through family doctor, clinic, chemist to partner – any one of which may be problematic for the young person. Lawrance et al. (1990) report that pregnant teenagers acknowledge difficulties in this respect.

Research tends not to support the popular assumption that girls who become pregnant are any less well adjusted than agemates who do not (Shaffer et al., 1978). It has been suggested that girls who become pregnant might be better looking, because (as seen several times in earlier chapters) physical attractiveness attracts, and better looking people tend to start dating earlier, have sex earlier, and marry earlier (Cvetkovich and Grote, 1980).

The social contexts of adolescent pregnancy

Rather than locate the "problem" in the young woman, it is instructive to examine the social context in which she is developing. It should not come as a surprise to discover that several studies have found that the family environments of teenagers who become pregnant are often very stressful (prior to the pregnancy), with high incidences of alcohol-related problems and single parenthood (Adams et al., 1994). Oz and Fine (1988), in an Israeli study, found that teenage mothers were more likely to have experienced foster care, family violence, alcohol abuse in the family, and poorer education.

Of course, not all girls in stressful families become pregnant, but it may be that these circumstances increase the likelihood of risk-taking, and afford less information and counsel concerning the means of avoiding pregnancy (i.e., in Barber's terms, above, they offer less behavioral regulation). In an adverse social environment, the meaning of pregnancy for the individual may not be congruous with the meaning attached to it by others. For example, Baumrind (1987) points out that while many black American adults endorse Jesse Jackson's slogan "Babies should not have babies," to some black American teenagers pregnancy may actually appear an attractive option because it provides a route – a means of transition – into the adult world that is not otherwise easily accessed by the disadvantaged.

The example of the US serves to illustrate the influence of the broader social context. According to Brooks-Gunn (1993), adolescent participation in sexual relations is generally considered not socially acceptable in America. Nevertheless, it is engaged in with much the same enthusiasm recorded elsewhere. We noted in chapter 16 some evidence from a cross-national survey to indicate that American adolescents may lag slightly behind their counterparts in other Western countries in age of initiation and frequency of sexual intercourse, but the difference is not massive (and may be confounded with social class). The US is no more generous in the provision of welfare to teenage mothers than other countries, and less so than many European countries (Gilchrist and Schinke, 1987). However, social mores in the US may make it more difficult for some parents to address sexual matters with their adolescents, and the organization of contraceptive services and counseling appears, at least until recently, to have been less geared to the needs of the young than they are in other countries (Gilchrist and Schinke, 1987; Jaffe and Dryfoos, 1980). In contrast, in some European countries (such as Finland; see Utriainen, 1989) social attitudes toward sex are more liberal and information and advice to teenagers correspondingly more freely available.

The impact of adolescent pregnancy upon family relations

Not surprisingly, the occurrence of a teenage pregnancy itself has effects upon the existing family. It can evoke parental reactions ranging from fury and horror, through rejection, disappointment, and distress, to empathy and support. Interestingly, some of the effects appear to be in terms of enhanced relationships. Teenager–mother conflict often subsides by mid-pregnancy, possibly because the mother is reliving her own pregnancy or perhaps because the "trouble shared" strengthens the relationship (Adams et al., 1994). In some communities, extended family structures provide supportive contexts for the adolescent mother as well as new, instructional roles for her mother. For example, Wilson (1989) reports that in poor black families in some parts of the US, the extended family facilitates the teenage mother's participation in self-improvement activities, while ensuring that the total amount and quality of day care available to the baby is high. This not only benefits the new mother, but also underlines the value of the extended family itself.

In short, becoming pregnant clearly indicates changes in the behavior of the young woman; but the values attached to the changes are also inextricably related to her relations with others, to her general social status, and to her future opportunities and responsibilities. Pregnancy shifts the predominantly interpersonal nature of adolescent sexuality into the public domain (Lieberman, 1980): everyone knows, or could soon know, what she has been doing. As a result, other parties now become involved as judges and decision-makers about the young person's sexuality and fertility. Support from key individuals – not least the child's father – may make a considerable difference to the quality of parenting the young mother is able to provide (Crockenberg, 1987).

Eating Disorders

Eating disorders such as *anorexia nervosa* (severely limiting the intake of food) and *bulimia nervosa* (binge eating followed by self-induced purging) pose serious physical and psychological health risks to the young person (Abraham and Llewellyn-Jones, 1992; Halmi, 1987). Inadequate or disrupted dietary behavior during the growth period of adolescence is particularly precarious, with short- and long-term consequences for the development of secondary sexual characteristics and menstrual cycles (Abraham and Llewellyn-Jones, 1992). Some 5–10 percent of anorexics die from malnutrition, and both anorexics and bulimics suffer recurrent illnesses, intestinal disorders, and general debilitation (Abraham and Llewellyn-Jones, 1992; Halmi, 1987). The exact prevalence of the disorders is difficult to ascertain, since not all cases are likely to be drawn to the attention of professionals, and bulimics in particular tend to be secretive about their dieting/purging patterns (Fairburn et al., 1986). However, specialists in the field agree on three points: (a) the incidence of both disorders appears to have increased in recent decades; (b) both are substantially more frequent among females; and (c) both are predominantly phenomena of adolescence and early adulthood (Abraham and Llewellyn-Jones, 1992; Hsu, 1989; Johnson and Connors, 1987). As with other adolescent problem behaviors, the causes of eating disorders are not fully understood, but certain correlates can be identified. These include the family, peers, and the broader culture.

Eating disorders and the family

Numerous clinical reports have shown an association between family processes and anorexia. The families of anorexic girls have been found to tend toward overprotectiveness and perfectionism, enmeshing the girl in an interpersonal environment tense with suppressed conflicts and high aspirations (Grigg et al., 1989; Halmi, 1987; Minuchin et al., 1978). There is evidence that anorexia is more common among girls from middle- and upper-middle-class backgrounds – for example, the disorder is more frequent among college students than the general young female population (Abraham and Llewellyn-Jones, 1992) – and this pattern would be consistent with an explanation in terms of more regulated and more demanding family contexts. Of course, parents rarely want to see their daughter starving herself to the point of serious ill health, and one interpretation is that the girl's behavior is part of a power struggle within the family whereby she is striving to find some means of attaining personal control (Calam et al., 1989; Grigg et al., 1989; Minuchin et al., 1978). However, most families have tensions, and many adolescents of either sex have to struggle to assert their autonomy. Only a small proportion becomes anorexic, and most of these are girls. Thus, family discord may be a factor, but not necessarily the whole explanation.

An alternative possibility, proposed by Crisp (1982), is that anorexia reflects an attempt to avoid adulthood by inhibiting the body's maturation. As mentioned, anorexia can interrupt a young woman's menstrual cycles, and it reduces the amount of body fat available. Notice that this hypothesis posits very much the reverse of a factor we have seen associated with other adolescent problem behaviors, namely transition proneness. On Crisp's account, the anorexic teenager is striving to *delay* adulthood rather than accelerate entrance. Consistent with this view, Damon and Hart (1988) report analyses of anorexic adolescents' self-concepts which indicate that the sense of agentic self is less developmentally advanced in these girls than in nonanorexic peers.

Eating disorders and peers

One of the most interesting studies of peers and eating disorders is that of Crandall (1988), conducted with female undergraduates resident in an American university. Crandall followed these young women's eating patterns over an academic year, and found that binge eating was roughly synchronized. That is, if your friends are bingeing, then there is a greater likelihood that you will, too. Over the year, eating patterns of the residents became increasingly similar. Binge eating was correlated positively with peer popularity. Crandall suggests that processes of social contagion are at work.

Eating disorders and broader societal influences

Another possibility is that the family and peers are but means of conveying broader sociocultural expectations. Parents may share views about what constitutes an ideal physique, and may communicate these to their children (Attie and Brooks-Gunn, 1989; Paxton et al., 1991). There is evidence that appearance anxieties among college-age women have their antecedents in dissatisfaction with appearance during childhood and adolescence (Keelan et al., 1992; Nolen-Hoeksema and Girgus, 1994); it seems plausible that young females are aware of and compare themselves to socially shared representations of attractive forms. There is also evidence that people in general share views of what it is socially desirable for females to *eat*. Basow and Kobrynowicz (1993) found that American male and female college students who watched video tapes of a young woman eating different sizes of meals rated the target as more socially appealing when she ate lightly. A woman seen eating a meatball hoagie of approximately one foot in length, accompanied by several cheese sticks, a heap of french fries, followed by a piece of cake and all washed down by a large Coke was not seen as a frontrunner for Miss Pennsylvania. Sensitivity to shared beliefs about desirable female eating patterns is reflected in social contexts. For example, Mori et al. (1987) found that female students socializing with an attractive male (actually a confederate of the experimenters) ate less than when they were interacting with an unattractive male or a female.

Where do parents and peers get their ideas from? This emphasis could in turn be related to a more general preoccupation with these qualities that is pervasive in most societies and in our mass media. Silverstein and her colleagues (Silverstein et al., 1986a) report interesting evidence of an association between the ways in which popular media represent women's ideal body shapes and the incidence of suboptimal weight in young college women. These investigators analyzed photographs in popular US women's magazines from the 1900s to 1980 and found, with some fluctuations, a general decline in the curvaceousness of the models depicted over this period. They then examined the records of American university health centres, where most women undergo a medical upon entrance to tertiary education. During eras when the thin ideal predominated in the media, doctors recorded increased incidences of under-weight female undergraduates.

Obviously, we should beware the trap of overinterpreting correlational evidence. The relationship here could be in the opposite direction to that which first tempts: the magazines could be *reflecting* changing fashions rather than causing them. In today's media, it would be difficult to pick up a copy of *Cleo, Cosmopolitan* or *New Woman* that did not contain at least one article connected to slimming and countless photographs of slender females, but whether these contents determine or manifest contemporary preoccupations is not easily disentangled. See, for example, the readers' letters pages, and consider the magazines' circulation figures. Correspondingly, it would be unwarranted to assume that we could liberate young females of tubular aspirations simply by manipulating the extent to which they are exposed to Cindy Crawford and Helena Christiansen. Even so, Silverstein et al.'s evidence is important because it points to broad cultural shifts in ideal body images. Unger and Crawford (1992) remark that Western societies also manifest prejudice and discrimination against overweight women – for example, media comments about *Roseanne* often relate to her size rather than her personality. This suggests the possibility that processes beyond the individual, and beyond her immediate social context, may play a role in the genesis of eating disorders. Certainly, high proportions of contemporary young women report levels of dissatisfaction with their body shape or parts of the body, and high proportions restrict their food intake or try out diets intermittently (Abraham and Llewellyn-Jones, 1992; Jackson, 1992).

In this connection, it should be noted that high proportions of young men also express dissatisfaction with their bodies (95 percent in a study described by Mishkind et al., 1987). Male responses sometimes include dieting but also exercising in pursuit of the mesomorphic ideal, occasionally assisted by steroids. Mishkind et al. speculate that increases in this kind of behavior are also related to broader cultural shifts which may be reflected in the media (for example, increasing international assertiveness and, in the US, the *Rambo* mentality that a tough guy could have done better in Vietnam). At present, male eating patterns and other body concerns tend to be less studied.

Most adolescents watch television and read popular magazines, but not all become anorexic or bulimic. At present, we do not have a comprehensive account of why adolescent females (and a small number of adolescent males) suffer from severe eating disorders. Jackson (1992) points out that evidence of greater female vulnerability to psychopathologies concerned with body image is consistent with a sociocultural theory that societies place greater store on female physical attractiveness *and* with sociobiological theory that female appearance is more important to the species because the features of youthful female attractiveness are highly correlated with reproductive value. Although much remains to be explained, the evidence does indicate that an adequate account will be both developmental (to account for the vulnerability of adolescents) and social (to account for the interactions between the young person, her interpersonal context, and the broader society).

Suicide

Suicidal behavior becomes much more common in adolescence than in earlier stages of the lifespan, increasing monotonically with age during the teens (Masten and Braswell, 1991; Shaffer, 1974, 1986). Further, the incidence of suicide among adolescents has been increasing, especially among the youth of the developed nations (Cairns et al., 1988; Fabian, 1986; Masten and Braswell, 1991).

Cognitive and social cognitive developments may contribute part of the explanation (Masten and Braswell, 1991). Younger children may suffer from depression, but may be less able to sustain a continuously hopeless outlook, and less capable of formulating and carrying out a suicide plan. Chandler (1994; Ball and Chandler, 1989) has compared adolescents who had attempted suicide with nonsuicidal peers (including peers suffering from emotional distress), and found that the suicidal subjects had a much weaker sense of personal continuity – a measure similar to future time perspective, discussed in chapter 16. Harter (1990) summarizes unpublished research which indicates a link between low self-esteem – especially as a result a sense of failing to meet one's own or others' expectations – and suicidal ideation in adolescents.

Cognitive factors alone cannot account for adolescent suicide. In two large studies of suicidal behavior in American youths, Cairns et al. (1988) found that highly aggressive individuals were much more at risk of attempting suicide. The authors suggest that violent acts and suicidal behavior are not mutually exclusive but may be part of a cluster of long-term characteristics. It may be that suicidal youths have greater difficulties with impulse control and when suffering from depression are prepared to act out negative feelings toward the self.

It also seems unlikely that cognitive factors could account for sex differences in the patterns of suicide. Several studies have shown that females are more prone to attempt suicide – but males are more likely to succeed (Hawton, 1986; Morgan et al., 1975; Pfeffer, 1986). Among girls who attempt or commit suicide, pregnancy is sometimes indicated as a major factor (Lieberman, 1980). Cairns et al. (1988) found that aggressiveness was associated with suicidal behavior in adolescents of both sexes, and the severity of suicidal behavior was not significantly different between males and females. However, there was a difference in manner of suicide: males were more likely to hang themselves, females were more likely to overdose on drugs.

Once again, family factors turn out to be closely associated with the likelihood of suicide among young people. In an American study of adolescents who had attempted suicide, Tishler et al. (1981) found that the most commonly reported precipitating factors were problems with parents (52 percent), siblings (16 percent), school (30 percent), and peers (15 percent). Summerville et al. (1994), working with a sample of African-American youths who had attempted suicide, found that 67 percent classified their families as maladaptive. A substantial proportion of adolescents committing suicide had a relative who had either committed or attempted suicide (Holden, 1986; Shaffer, 1974). It would appear that the social proximity of a suicidal person serves to make the option salient, and perhaps reduces inhibitions against the taboo (Fabian, 1986).

One factor which may prompt or compound family difficulties for some adolescents is acculturation problems. For example, Zayas (1987) reports that Hispanic teenage females in the US are particularly at risk of suicide attempts, and are prone to engage in them at an earlier age than other teenagers. Once again, these young people place family discord at the top of their list of reasons, and Zayas argues that critical problems arise because of the tensions due to reconciling a traditional, religious ideal of *marianismo* (stressing the chaste, sacrificing, and nurturant qualities of the Virgin Mary) with the pressures to accommodate to the majority culture, itself undergoing change with respect to female roles. These countervailing forces result in parent–child conflict, identity problems, depression, and suicide attempts.

Interrelations among Adolescent Problem Behaviors

It is by now clear that the same factors – especially family and peer relations – are associated with each of the problem behaviors we have considered here. On this basis, we might expect that if an adolescent is prone to problem behavior in one domain (say, smoking) then he or she is likely to be prone to problems in others (such as drinking, delinquency, substance abuse, unprotected sex). Furthermore, since each of these problems is associated with stress, difficulties in one area is likely to set the conditions for experimentation in another. For example, if a young person has reached a level of problem drinking, then she might be more likely to participate in illegal activities such as driving under the influence, or to find that her school performance is deteriorating; as problems accumulate, the temptation to find relief via another stimulant or a narcotic may increase. Similarly, indulging in substance abuse may affect cognitive abilities. Luis, discussed above, was into tobacco and marijuana at the age of 10, and confessed: "I can't think as good as I used to" (Colvin, 1993). In short, there are good grounds for predicting intercorrelations among measures of problem behavior in adolescents.

This prediction is supported (Compas et al., 1995; Jessor, 1993). For example, with respect to substance abuse, a recurring finding of studies conducted in the US (Newcomb and Bentler, 1988), Canada (Smart et al., 1992), Australia (Commonwealth Department of Health, 1987), Germany (Silbereisen and Kastner, 1985), and Bermuda (West, 1987) is that a small proportion of young people uses several different drugs. This subset is the most at risk of serious drug abuse problems (West, 1987). Adolescents who engage in high levels of drug use tend to be precocious in several other respects, including early school leaving and marriage (Newcomb and Bentler, 1988). They are also most likely to be involved in a wider range of unconventional behavior (Jessor and Jessor, 1977; Osgood et al., 1988), sexual risk taking (Cooper et al., 1994) and delinquency (Compas et al., 1995; Neighbors et al., 1992; Smart et al., 1992). Intensive involvement in part-time work shows a linear association with a number of problem behaviors, including substance abuse and delinquency (Bachman and Schulenberg, 1993; Steinberg et al., 1993), and Bachman and Schulenberg suggest that excessive work involvement may itself be another manifestation of transition proneness.

When problem behaviors and symptoms, such as mental distress, hostility, suicidal thoughts, delinquency, school drop out, sexual risk-taking, are examined in the same individuals, there is clear evidence that these are strongly interrelated (Colten et al., 1991; Neighbors et al., 1992).

Summary

In respect of health-related behavioral choices, the transition period of adolescence brings challenges and risks. Most young people meet these through observation, and experimentation; some young people experience more profound difficulties. Not all of the health-related problems of adolescents that we have considered here can be explained in the same ways, and each entails taking several variables into account. However, the same variables recur: the developmental difficulties of shifting from childhood to adulthood, family experiences, and peer involvements. Finally, we have seen that many of the stressors associated with adolescent problem behaviors are intercorrelated.

Conclusions

As emphasized at the beginning of the chapter, not all young people become delinquent, become premature parents, use legal or illegal drugs to dangerous levels, suffer eating disorders, or attempt suicide. However, most young people have to face issues relating to several of these problem areas, and negative outcomes are statistically higher among adolescents. It is important to discover which factors are associated with serious difficulties and to begin to explain the processes involved.

In the case of each problem area we have considered it is clear that behaviors are multidetermined, and it is rare that we can point to one factor alone as the "cause" of an adolescent problem or transgression. Several social and demographic factors are associated with delinquency, for example, but no one of them guarantees that a young person will become a delinquent.

However, some of the key variables can be identified very clearly, and we have persuasive evidence of their interconnectedness. Time and time again, family and peer relations come to the fore. The major external institution of adolescence, the school, is also prominent. Although much remains to be uncovered about the processes, two developmental social psychological models prove insightful. First, the relevance of the Jessors' emphasis on problem behavior as a normative aspect of the transition to adulthood in age-stratified societal contexts has been shown repeatedly in relation to several of the activities that adolescents are sometimes keen to embrace – like, with, and to the chagrin of, their parents. Second, Emler's reputation management theory of delinquency helps to explain the motivations and criteria of problem behavior, relating two of the key factors of adolescent social development, the search for identity and the significance of peers.

Further reading

Abraham, S. and Llewellyn-Jones, D. (1992) *Eating Disorders: the facts*. Oxford: Oxford University Press.

A well-written review of medical and psychological research into the causes and consequences of eating disorders.

Cain, M. (ed.) (1989) *Growing up Good: policing the behaviour of girls in Europe*. London: Sage.

A stimulating set of essays on the lifestyles and legal treatments of young women who depart from social norms, including delinquents, prostitutes, and substance abusers.

Compas, B. E., Hinden, B. R., and Gerhardt, C. A. (1995) Adolescent development: pathways and processes of risk and resilience. *Annual Review of Psychology*, 46, 265–93.

A concise but thorough review of recent themes in research into adolescent problem behavior, its development and social contexts. Topics covered include aggression, delinquency, and depression.

Elliott, D. S., Huizinga, D., and Menard, S. (1989) *Multiple Problem Youth: delinquency, substance use, and mental health problems*. New York: Springer-Verlag.

A detailed longitudinal study of delinquent behavior and substance use among a representative sample of adolescent Americans, analyzing the initiation and course of multiple problem behaviors.

Farrington, D. P. (1992) Explaining the beginning, progress, and ending of antisocial behavior from birth to adulthood. In J. McCord (ed.), *Facts, Frameworks and Forecasts: advances in criminological theory*, vol. 3. New Brunswick: Transaction.

The author reviews theoretical and empirical issues in the study of delinquency, including a summary of the Cambridge Study, and sketches his own theory of offending.

Furby, L. and Beyth-Marom, R. (1992) Risk taking in adolescence: a decision-making perspective. *Developmental Review*, 12, 1–44.

This paper considers adolescent risk-taking from a decision-making perspective, according to which individuals arrive at a behavioral choice after processing the options, the possible consequences of the options, and the desirability and likelihood of those consequences. Furby and Beyth-Marom's analyses lead to the conclusion that what is perceived by adults as risk-taking may sometimes appear advantageous to young people in this developmental stage.

Griffin, C. (1993) *Representations of Youth: the study of youth and adolescence in Britain and America*. Cambridge: Polity Press.

A critical analysis of the ways in which adolescence is represented in contemporary Western societies, this book discusses the construction of images of young people's problems, the status and treatment of minority groups, and ideological influences on youth research.

Howitt, D. (1991) *Concerning Psychology: psychology applied to social issues*. Milton Keynes: Open University Press. Chapter 4: The creation of a social issue: the case of drug abuse.

A lively account of the craven submission of psychologists to medical model theories of drug abuse. Howitt argues that the notion of drug abuse is socially constructed. Well worth reading before your next seminar on drugs and adolescents.

McCord, J., Tremblay, R. E., Vitaro, F., and Desmarais-Gervais, L. (1994) Boys' disruptive behavior, school adjustment, and delinquency: the Montreal prevention experiment. *International Journal of Behavioral Development*, 17, 739–52.

The antecedents and setting conditions of delinquency and antisocial behavior in adolescents are well established. A crucial practical issue becomes: what can be done to help youngsters identified as at risk, and their families? This paper reports the promising findings of a longitudinal intervention project.

Shedler, J. and Block, J. (1990) Adolescent drug use and psychological health: a longitudinal inquiry. *American Psychologist*, 45, 612–30.

In the context of a report of the findings of a longitudinal study, Shedler and Block identify psychological differences between frequent drug users, occasional experimenters, and abstainers. The antecedents of the differences are examined in relation to early childhood characteristics and the style of parenting experienced. Developmental social psychological issues are discussed, including the interrelationships of shifting social norms and individual adjustment, and the implications for social policy are outlined.

Chapter 18

Adulthood I: Development, Relationships, and Roles

Was this what it came to — that you could never escape? That certain things were doomed to continue, generation after generation?
(*Tyler*, Dinner at the Homesick Restaurant,
1982)

As we progress through the early part of our lives toward adulthood, we experience many of our tasks as preparatory. In both formal (e.g., educational) and informal (e.g., socializing) spheres, we and others assume that we are gathering skills and knowledge to equip us for autonomous existence as adults. However, while our autonomy may well increase upon reaching adulthood and our responsibilities and opportunities change, development does not cease. Throughout life, one thing that can be reliably predicted is change:

> Over time, we are what we were, but we are also different. From at least the moment of birth to at least the moment of death, every living organism is part of that interwoven process of development at every level from the societal to the cellular and in whatever mode of reality we choose to consider – biological, social, personality, cognitive. Furthermore, each of those levels and each of those realities is, in turn, coexisting and coterminous with some state of all of the others. Life is intimately grounded in relationships. (Blank, 1982, p. 3)

In this and the following chapter, we will be concerned with some aspects of the changes of adulthood. The extent and complexity of developmental social psychological progress through the mature life-cycle are such that it would require another – and very large – book to consider all of the relevant issues and research. Instead, the scope here will be more modest, but there are two complementary reasons why a text concerned with developmental social psychology should address issues in adulthood. First, many of the themes that have recurred through chapters on the earlier parts of the lifespan remain central topics in the study of adult social development and behavior: these include interpersonal relationships, social reasoning, social roles, and adaptation to societal constraints and institutions. A developmental approach would be incomplete without attention to the changes and continuities of the greater part of the lifespan.

Second, many of the topics and the whole of the subjects (i.e., human beings) that form the preserve of social psychology have developmental histories and futures. Responses to change (such as joining or leaving the workforce, marriage, transition to parenthood) may have substantial consequences for an individual's relations with others, and for the beliefs, attitudes, and social reasoning that he or she develops. People do not function as social beings in adevelopmental contexts, but bring to any new relationship or role their accumulated understanding, skills, and expectations, which in turn may be modified by the novel experiences. A social approach would be incomplete without attention to the changes and continuities that both precede and result from human interdependencies (Costanzo, 1992; Nesselroade, 1992; Pratt and Norris, 1994; Ruble, 1994).

This chapter is organized into two main sections. As a starting point, it is useful to consider how developmentalists have approached adult development. Although there is a variety of models and emphases, developmental accounts tend to stress the sequential, stage-like nature of progress from young adulthood to old age. The first section presents an overview of this kind of approach, paying particular attention to one influential model that combines both developmental and social psychological perspectives. One theme which stands out clearly from a developmental social account of adult development is the importance of relationships to other people and to institutions; in the second section, we consider relationships and roles in respect of both the micro-systems of the family and the macro-system of the society. Throughout, it will be clear that one fundamental social category – namely gender – has major implications for how people organize their adult life-course. In the following chapter, we turn to aspects of social psychological processes and developments during two particular phases of the life-cycle, middle age and older adulthood respectively.

Adulthood and Development

It is often remarked in developmental psychology texts that until relatively recently, the field was predominantly child-oriented: even adolescence tended to be a neglected period, and development was implicitly assumed to have stopped at adulthood. Some developmentalists insist that this is as it should be. Bower (1979) concludes an impressive account of child development (which he calls human development) with the suggestion that the idea of changes after the age of 20 does "some violence to the idea of development," and he adds that he knows of "no evidence indicating genuine developmental change in the adult's basic world view, whether of the self, the social world, or of the physical world. Indeed, what little evidence there is indicates that such changes do not take place" (p. 432). Presumably, Bower would be happy enough with the dismemberment of people, discussed in chapter 1, that leads developmentalists to hand over to other specialisms – such as social psychology and cognitive psychology – at this age point.

Part of the reason why Bower expresses such reluctance to embrace the idea of changes in adulthood may be that he is comfortable with the metaphor of the child as a mini-scientist, an inquisitive agent who has spent some 20 years developing his or her "basic world view," and now has it pretty firmly established. It is odd that the mini-scientist, all alone, is able to reach this plateau so rapidly, in contrast to professional scientists who have spent collectively thousands of years formulating, testing, rejecting, and revising their basic world views – and are still not happy with them. Another reason may be that Bower, although maintaining that humans are basically social animals, feels that the terminus of social development is *"relative autonomy within the social order"* (p. 359; emphasis added) and that this ("the last stage of social development;" p. 361) is the outcome of intrapsychological attainment in late adolescence rather than social processes. Even if we restrict consideration primarily to Western societies, we find extensive evidence to rebut Bower's (and many other traditional developmentalists') assumptions about the absence of development beyond the teens.

People do not live in laboratories, but in domestic environments, workplaces, and societies. Each of these not only provides opportunities for change and development, but absolutely demands it. Social developmentalists studying the stages of the family life-cycle tend to agree with Cunningham and Antill (1984) that their impact on the individual's social and personality development is at least equal to the impact of the stages of cognitive growth upon intellectual development, and that these social experiences and adjustments do continue throughout the lifespan. In the workplace, standing still means falling behind. In many other societal contexts, there are subtle to stark variations in what is expected and endorsed of adults of different ages and stages. Many examples will be provided in this and the following chapter, but first it will be useful to consider another perspective on development after the age of 20, a developmental social psychological model of the broad sweep of changes that need to be taken into account in studying the lifespan.

Levinson's Seasons of a Man's Life

Levinson (1978, 1986) has developed an influential account of adult development based around a series of phases that he believes occur in each individual's life-cycle. Levinson distinguishes among the terms life*span* (which simply labels the period from birth to death), life-*course* (which refers to the flow of the individual's life over time, the particular directions, events, and achievements that she or he experiences), and life-*cycle*. The latter incorporates the notions of a *journey* following some basic sequence, and of *seasons*, predictable periods of completion and rebirth as we move through life. For Levinson, this is an important notion because he stresses that the psychological characteristics of an individual at a given stage can only be understood in terms of their connection to the whole framework of the life-cycle.

Levinson developed his model initially on the basis of a series of detailed interviews of 40 American men in mid-life (ages 35–45). The men were selected to represent four different social categories, namely blue-collar factory workers, executives, academic scientists, and novelists. Let us acknowledge the obvious straightaway: 40 middle-aged American men, even from different social strata, probably do not reflect the totality of the human experience, and the retrospective interview method is not without limitations. Given the intensive nature of the data-collection procedures, the sampling restriction is understandable, and subsequent research, some of which is discussed later, has included different social groups (such as American women). Self-reports on personal changes over time are problematic because what a person recalls may not reflect accurately his or her subjective experiences of some decades earlier (Hart, 1992; Vaillant, 1977); again, this points to the need for complementary research using different methodologies, and we consider examples below.

Each of Levinson's subjects was asked to review his life so far, focusing on critical choices and their consequences. From their responses, Levinson extrapolated four broad periods (or seasons) each with a set of subperiods that he maintains are experienced by most people. The first period is childhood and adolescence, which we have already seen to bring an ample array of developmental tasks and challenges. We will concentrate here on Levinson's account of the developmental sequence of adulthood.

The three main (and partially overlapping) seasons of adulthood, according to Levinson, are (a) early adulthood (extending from approximately 17 to 45 years); (b) middle adulthood (approximately 40 to 65 years); and (c) older adulthood (60 years onwards). Of course, it is indisputable that everybody follows this chronological order; what makes the model interesting is the account of the self-perceptions and social orientations that Levinson claims characterize the changing seasons of life, and the insistence that these are broadly age-related and predictable: "although each human life is unique, everyone goes through the same basic sequence" (Levinson, 1986, p. 4). In considering the sequence, we will follow Levinson's initial emphasis on male lives, but bear in mind that he sees the same pattern holding for females, and we will turn shortly to research concerned specifically with female adult development.

Early adulthood

Early adulthood begins with the substage of *early adult transition* (17–22 years), during which the individual seeks autonomy from parents and forms what Levinson calls the Dream – a vision of his life goals that provides motivation and excitement in respect of the future. A man at this stage might envisage attainment in his profession, the acquisition of material wealth, sporting achievement, etc. How the individual relates to his Dream is critical: "If the Dream remains unconnnected to his life it may simply die, and with it his sense of aliveness and purpose" (1978, p. 92).

The next substage is the period of *entering the adult world* (22–28) where the individual is struggling to forge a pathway into the world of work and to establish a special personal relationship (for example, by getting married). This is followed by the *age 30 transition* (28–33), where the individual undergoes a moderate degree of self-questioning prior to moving into the final substage of this season, *settling down* (33–40). In this substage, the individual finds his niche in society, makes a commitment to advancement in a particular career, accepting the terms of his life.

An important feature of the early adulthood season is the selection of a mentor, an older and more experienced co-worker or boss who provides advice on career advancement. Levinson sees this relationship as crucial and complex. It is crucial because the mentor offers guidance, goals, and support to the young person; it is complex because it involves the positive affect of friendship and assistance together with the negative features of self-doubt, competition and displacement. In many respects, Levinson's mentor is the adult equivalent of Vygotsky's skilled tutor (see chapter 11) and a new attachment figure. Mentoring relationships are often intense, but transient. They usually last between two and 10 years, and sometimes end with ill feelings on both sides. The younger person may begin to resent interventions that are increasingly seen as smothering or unnecessary; the mentor perceives rebellion and ingratitude.

Middle adulthood

The second major season is that of midlife, from around age 40 to 60. Again, Levinson depicts this period as consisting of a series of substages. First is the *midlife transition* (40–45). This is a period of crisis, according to Levinson, during which the individual reviews his life structure, history, and prospects, asking did I achieve my dream, was it the right dream, was it worth it? Some 32 of the 40 men in Levinson's sample described this time as one of at least moderate turbulence. There are several triggers for the crisis, including awareness of physical decline, a sense of aging, death of parents or friends, children growing up and leaving home, and coming to terms with aspects of the self that may have been repressed or disregarded in earlier years while the individual was struggling to achieve career advancement. Levinson sees part of the task here as reconciling the masculine and feminine elements of one's personality, often reflected in the greater acknowledgment of key relationships during this period.

Levinson's subjects were aged 35–45, and so his basis for developments sub-sequently is speculative. He proposes that the midlife transition is followed by a substage of seeking a new balance, during which the individual resolves some or all of the preceding conflicts, possibly choosing new directions (which can be manifest in a new job, a reorientation toward work, a new spouse). None of these changes, of course, affects only the individual man progressing through his lifespan. His family, peers, workmates, and employers all have a perspective and a claim upon him – and the diversity of these means that the experience of entering middle adulthood can vary greatly in degree of comfort and harmony.

One other feature of the model which should be emphasized is that each major seasonal boundary is accompanied by a period of transition (the early adult transition, the midlife transition, the age 50 transition, and so on). During a transition, the individual is concluding an existing life-structure and creating the possibility of a new one (e.g., "I am no longer a dependent youth, but I am becoming an independent young adult"). If you have undergone any such transitions, you might agree that they are not instantaneous; Levinson claims that each lasts about five years, and points out (1986, p. 7) that this means almost half of our adult lives is spent in developmental transitions. As stressed above, the one thing we can be sure of is change.

Seasons of Women's Lives

Subsequent researchers (and, reportedly, Levinson's own team in work in progress) have turned to women's lives to determine whether the same framework fits. Roberts and Newton (1987) provide a review of four separate studies (unpublished US doctoral dissertations) conducted by female investigators with a total of 39 female interviewees. Of course, there is a risk in such a research strategy that attempting to view women through a framework originally constructed to account for men's lives could be loaded, so that female subjects' progress might seem deficient against some arbitrary male benchmark, or that important dimensions of women's lives might be overlooked altogether. However, on the first issue the results point to greater complexity rather than deficiency. On the second, scientists can never be sure what they have overlooked, but the investigators (chiefly female researchers interested in the generalizability of Levinson's model) could be presumed to be attuned to this possibility and particularly concerned to identify areas where the women's lives revealed patterns different from those among men.

Roberts and Newton (1987) conclude that, in broad terms, the age-related structures of women's lives reveal very similar developmental progress to those of men. In all cases, the period from the age of 17 to 22 involved a transition much the same as those experienced by Levinson's subjects. In almost all cases, the women experienced an age 30 transition. The "Dream" – so fundamental to Levinson's male subjects' entry into the adult life-cycle – was also critical for virtually all of the women.

However, there were subtle but meaningful differences. For a start – and it is quite an important start – women's Dreams asserted different priorities from those of Levinson's subjects. Very few women placed occupations as the primary component. Even a study concerned with attorneys who did attribute importance to their careers found that marriage was considered primary (unpublished thesis by Adams, 1983, cited in Roberts and Newton, 1987). In general, the women's Dreams were more complex and more diffuse than men's, often reflecting a split between individual goals and relational obligations. While Levinson's male subjects saw their lives as likely to be organized in terms of individual career goals plus supportive families, women constructed Dreams around relationships with husbands and family and the subordination of personal needs. Part of *her* Dream was *his* success.

There were also differences concerning the place of the mentor in women's and men's lives. Levinson (1978, p. 98) stressed that while the role of the mentor is crucial, for many women such a person may be difficult to find. The research summarized by Roberts and Newton (1987) confirms this expectation. Even women who aspired to professional success, who did have professional careers, and who did sometimes identify role models, tended not to find mentors. Some found that their male partners served this function in early adulthood, but apparently this rarely endured and was abandoned by the women by the age 30 transition. However, while the mentor was either not sought or not available, almost all of the subjects described their early to middle adult lives as concerned substantially with the search for the "special man" – again, suggesting the importance of relationships in women's life-structures. (And the poignancy of their aspirations – Roberts and Newton report that special men were not abundant.)

As indicated, the age 30 transition was found to be as important in the women's lives as it was for Levinson's subjects. Interestingly, individual adjustments through this transition seemed to reflect a dialectical tension with options pursued earlier. Women who had placed marriage and motherhood as their major concerns in their twenties tended to develop more individualistic goals for the next decade, while women who had been career oriented in early adulthood now focused on marriage and family (Roberts and Newton, 1987, p. 159). The thirties proved to be a less clearly defined period for many women and, unlike Levinson's interviewees, few women reported this as a time of settling down – if anything, the transitory instability of the transition continued. One reason may be that for women the establishment of career seniority during this period may be less clear cut, affording a less objective basis for "settling down."

Overall, aspects of Levinson's age-related model hold up reasonably well, at least for the small samples of American women studied in these intensive investigations.

Women do appear, like men, to experience adult life as structured in "seasons" and, like men, experience periods of transition during which they review and sometimes redirect their progress. Yet at the same time, the priorities of women's lives are often different from those of men, according greater significance to relationships than to occupational roles and – perhaps because of their willingness to orient the dreams around others – incurring greater risk of disappointment and developmental tension as their investments in others' goals conflict with their personal needs.

Summary

Levinson holds that there is an underlying order to the human life-cycle, characterized by qualitatively different phases or "seasons" that are closely associated with the biological and social changes of age. Each season has its own character and each individual constructs a life-structure according to his or her unique circumstances, but the life-course gains much of its meaning from the overall seasonal framework. Although Levinson's study involved data collection from a small group of individual men, who were part of a particular birth cohort, in a particular country, and who experienced development within a particular social, economic, and political order, subsequent research with women has tended to support his claims of the universality of at least the main structures and sequence of the seasons of adult life. To state the obvious, cross-cultural replications are needed, but the approach serves usefully to illustrate the scale and complexity of adult development. Furthermore, the model provides for a link between *intra*personal development and social context, that is, between the individual's changing sense of self and his or her changing relations to others. We turn next to relationships and roles.

Relationships and Roles in Adulthood

According to Levinson (1978), each developmental stage involves interrelated biological, psychological, and social adjustments, but central to a person's life-structure at any one point will be his or her family and work roles, and development is fundamentally interwoven with changes in these. In this section, we look more closely at the nature of some of the key relationships and roles in adulthood.

We have seen in previous chapters that human development is inseparable from relationships. Other people matter to us affectively and cognitively from the very beginnings of life, with the consequence that who we are, how we change, and what we become depends crucially upon the multifaceted adjustments we make as participants in the ever-changing social world. Relationships themselves are essentially developmental, and human social development proceeds in the context of personal relationships (Hay, 1988). It would be surprising if all this were to stop at our 21st birthday.

Clearly, it does not. Throughout adulthood, as Levinson's work emphasizes, the fundamentals of our lives are reflected in and affected by our relationships to others.

The central social relationships of childhood (to parents and siblings) may change with maturity but they do not disappear. New relationships may well be formed (romantic, professional, friendship, parenthood) and are likely to have profound implications for how we understand our selves and the meanings of our lives.

Life-cycle and Personal Organization

One of the crucial themes arising from Levinson and colleagues' research is that where a person is in terms of the life-cycle has extensive repercussions for his or her social priorities and personal organization. How a person thinks about other people, society, and his or her relationship to it are among the very basics of social psychology, yet the fact that these are continuously evolving and changing is often overlooked. To take a couple of concrete examples, consider a person's life-goals and concerns, and a person's gender role orientation. Research indicates that in both respects there are changes with age and life-stage. Nurmi (1992), in a large study of Finnish adults aged 19–64 years, found that while younger people were focused on goals related to education and family, middle-aged adults were more concerned about their children's lives, and older adults were concerned with matters of health, retirement, and the state of the world. Social goals and concerns are closely related to the main developmental tasks that the individual is facing.

Similarly, while social psychologists tend to treat individual differences in gender role orientation as constants (i.e., some people are highly masculine, others are androgynous, etc.), lifespan research reveals that the true picture is far more complicated and that within-individual differences occur over time. In an American study, for example, Feldman and Aschenbrenner (1983) found that both males and females showed increased femininity scores shortly after the birth of their first child, presumably reflecting the heightened salience of nurturance in their lives after this event. An Australian investigation found that women's femininity scores were highest during the unmarried dating stage, and lowest during the married and employed stage (Cunningham and Antill, 1984). McCreary (1990) found in prospective and retrospective studies with young and elderly British adults that individuals tended to rate masculine and feminine attributes lowest in the chronologically earliest of the developmental tasks, while both sexes rated their masculinity and femininity higher in the later phases. In short, even seemingly definitive personal characteristics may vary through the lifespan as a function of interactions among the individual, other people, and role requirements.

Development and the Social Clock

Expectations about how a person *should* develop are conveyed to the individual through a diversity of social sources. Neugarten et al. (1965) introduced the notion of the *social clock* to describe the sociocultural constraints upon many aspects of development during adulthood. The social clock refers to the age-related norms and expectations that guide and constrain personal behavior and choices through the lifespan, sometimes prodding us forward ("It's time you settled down and got a proper job," "Isn't your Julie thinking of getting married yet?"), sometimes holding us back ("You're just not ready for marriage") and sometimes phasing us out ("Do you really think it's dignified to wear jeans at your age?")

Aspects of these norms vary with culture and era. The "right time" for marriage in some countries and social classes is generally held to be the late teens or early twenties, while for young middle-class people in many Western nations it is thought to be the mid-twenties or later. Within cultures there may be shifts over time in terms of how strongly people endorse particular expectations (Neugarten and Neugarten, 1987). American adults sampled in the 1970s showed much less agreement over the best age points to complete education, to marry, to become grandparents, to retire, and so on than did their counterparts a generation earlier (Rosenfeld and Stark, 1987).

People who look younger than they are seem to get a particularly raw deal from the social clock. On the one hand, they know their age and in so far as life is organized around institutions (school, college, entry to work, etc.) they are likely to progress "on time." But other people may often perceive them differently. Zebrowitz et al. (1993) found that babyfaced people were perceived by others as more childlike.

Relationships

Recall Hartup's (1989b) distinction between vertical and horizontal relationships that we first considered in chapter 4. In early childhood, the major relationships (i.e., with one's caregivers) are vertical (with asymmetries of power, knowledge, and dependency). From middle childhood, horizontal relationships (i.e., with peers) become increasingly important, although vertical relationships certainly do not cease. In adulthood, relationships intensify along *both* axes: the horizontal relationship with one's partner has major significance for the emotional and practical organization of life while, as a parent, the adult inverts her or his position on the vertical dimension, now taking the senior status and with it the responsibilities of care and provision. Yet at the same time, as an employee, early adulthood often involves a return to the junior position in a social structure and, for many, middle adulthood may be oriented around upward progress on this dimension. Adult development involves multiple shifts in respect of relationships and status, and its course depends not only upon the intrapersonal adjustments of the individual assessing his or her progress, but also upon the social and societal contexts within which the person is developing.

Attachment through the Lifespan

In understanding adult relationships, we return to a concept that we have already found to be prominent in the study of social development in childhood: attachment. It was noted in the introduction to attachment in chapter 3 that this relationship should not be considered unique to parents and young children. Parent–child

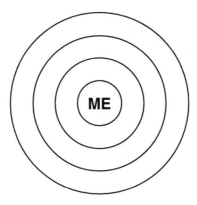

Figure 18.1 A social convoy diagram. With yourself in the center, place in the immediately adjacent circle the names of those people without whom life would be difficult to imagine. Then, in the next circle, place those who are not absolutely crucial to your existence but who still rate as very important to you. In the outer circle, place those members of your social network who are not included in the inner circles but are still close enough and important enough to you that they should be represented in your network.
(*Source*: modified from Levitt, 1991)

attachments tend to be enduring, commonly regarded as important through the lifespan of each party (Antonucci, 1990; Antonucci and Akiyama, 1994; Kobak and Sceery, 1988; Levitt, 1991; Main et al., 1985; Rossi and Rossi, 1990). Of course, the nature of the relationship changes, taking on a continuing ambivalence because from adolescence onwards we strive also for autonomy and independence. Levinson comments that the process of separation from parents continues through life, and is never completed (1978, p. 74). Bowlby (1988) himself held that the attachment system exerts powerful effects upon adjustment and wellbeing from the cradle to the grave. As we move through the lifespan, we form new attachments, such as strong friendships and romantic partnerships.

The benefits of attachments

As with the infant–parent relationship, one of the benefits of attachment at any stage of the lifespan is that it affords a secure base from which to tackle life's stresses (Bowlby, 1988; Levitt, 1991). A simple but effective way to illustrate the importance of attachments in adulthood is to consider for yourself figure 18.1. Imagine yourself in the center and then place in the inner circle those individuals to whom you feel "so close that it's hard to imagine life without them." In the middle circle place those persons who are "not quite as close but who are still very important", and in the outer circle place those who do not quite belong in the closer circles but nevertheless are "close enough and important enough" to warrant a place in your social network.

Once you have completed the figure, consider next who are the people in life in whom you are most able to confide, who provide reassurance, who would care for you in illness, who respect you and to whom you would turn for advice or financial assistance. Not surprisingly, these are likely to be the people you have nominated for the inner circle. Levitt (1991) reports a series of studies, with subjects at different stages of the lifespan from recent parenthood to old age and from different cultural groups (including Anglo- and Spanish-Americans), which reveal considerable consistency among responses to this kind of task. Most people enter only a small number of individuals into the inner circle, and these are typically family members – spouses if they exist, and then parents or children. In-laws rarely make it to the inner circle, but they, other family members and friends appear regularly in the middle or outer circles. Other means of measuring attachments in adults include structured interviews about the individual's early relationships with her or his parents (Kobak and Sceery, 1988; Main et al., 1985; Pratt and Norris, 1994). The presence of at least one close relationship seems to be related fundamentally to personal wellbeing (Antonucci, 1990; Levitt, 1991).

From attachments to attachments

Most people do not remain at home with their initial attachment figures for the rest of their lives. Although these attachments continue, new ones are formed – for example, with spouses or partners. To what extent is it valid to draw analogies between the parent–child attachment considered in chapter 3 and the relationship between an adult couple? Bowlby (1973, 1988) proposed that the child's "working model" of the initial relationship should influence his or her formulations about subsequent relationships – does this hold even in adulthood?

Shaver and his colleagues (Hazan and Shaver, 1987; Reis and Shaver, 1988; Shaver et al., 1988) have pointed to marked similarities between romantic love as experienced by adults and the characteristics of attachment identified by Bowlby and others. Both relationships involve intense orientation toward a specific other, proximity seeking, extensive eye contact, the provision of caregiving, discomfort or distress at separation, and grief at loss. Hazan and Shaver (1987) show that adult romantic relationships exemplify three major patterns that are very similar to the Ainsworth typology of mother–infant relationships, namely secure, anxious/ambivalent, and avoidant (see chapter 3). Securely attached lovers tend to find close personal relationships comfortable and rewarding, and are not continuously nagged by the fear that their partner will abandon them or demand too much. Anxious/ambivalent adults experience uncertainty in their relationships, afraid that their partner does not love them enough and might leave, and sometimes putting too much pressure on the partner. Avoidant lovers find getting close to people threatening, and are reluctant to commit themselves fully to another. Shaver and colleagues' research shows that the proportions of individuals falling into each of these categories is also remarkably similar to the distribution of attachment types typically reported in infancy studies (see chapter 3), with about 56 percent secure, 19 percent anxious/ambivalent, and 25 percent avoidant.

Feeney and Noller (1992) and Feeney et al. (1993) obtained similar distributions in studies of Australian undergraduates. Feeney et al. (1993) found also that avoidant subjects reported fewer and less intense love experiences. Anxious/ambivalent subjects had more but less enduring affairs, and the secure types came out best again, with more satisfying and loving relationships. Attachment type also predicted attitudes toward casual sex: the avoidant subjects were more accepting of such practices, presumably because they prefer uncommitted relationships. Feeney and Noller (1992) found that when romantic relationships broke up, persons of different attachment styles differed in their reactions. The avoidant were relieved while the anxious/ambivalent soon found themselves in love with a new partner (see also Simpson, 1990).

Do early attachments determine the character of later attachments?

As seen in chapter 4, there is extensive evidence of a relationship between the quality of early attachment and other aspects of social and cognitive development, although inferences of direct causality are suspect. Mainstream attachment theorists hold that the first relationship is the foundation upon which subsequent relationships are built. Alternatively, it is possible that the interpersonal environment which promoted the initial attachment (e.g., the presence of a sensitive caregiver) is relatively continuous.

Levitt (1991) argues that attachment relationships through the lifespan are not simply a matter of a sequence of links where the quality of later relations is mediated directly by the quality of the initial parent–child attachment. Instead, individuals enter relationships with a host of expectations (cf. Argyle et al., 1985; Duck, 1988b; Ginsburg, 1988; Hazan and Shaver, 1987; Sabatelli and Pearce, 1986). Levitt suggests that these expectations are derived partly from individuals' previous experiences of relationships (including earlier attachments) but also from their general social cognitive development (especially their understanding of people), from their perceptions of the broader social norms governing relationships (for example, culturally shared beliefs about how lovers should behave) and from their ideology (such as traditional, egalitarian, feminist, and so on).

Hence, the interaction of the quality of early relationships and the quality of later relationships is manifold, and of course each new relationship that an individual forms brings together not only that person's own developmental history but also her or his partner's. It is also important to remember from research into attachments in infancy (chapter 3) that not all of an individual's attachments to different people fall into the same type. We saw that a child could be securely attached to one parent, yet anxious/avoidant with another. Sternberg and Beall (1991) point out that many adults find that their relationships vary: with one partner, you may experience an insecure attachment, but with the next a secure one (we like to think of you settling down eventually). Sternberg and Beall (1991) comment also that a serious limitation of much work on adult attachment styles is that the demand characteristics are strong, requiring the subject to generalize about her or his relationships and, in several studies, to recall aspects of the very early relationship with her or his parents. This runs the risk of inflating measures of association, as the same person fills out two questionnaires about how she or he relates to people, and at least one of the instruments depends on the subject's fuzzy memories of early childhood.

Nevertheless, Rossi and Rossi (1990), in a three-generational study of American families, did find several indications of associations between early family experiences and relationship development in adult life. For example, the marital happiness of the first-generation parents was related to the marital happiness of their children, and this in turn was related to the marital happiness of the next generation. People who grew up in happy, cohesive families tended to establish positive relationships with their own partners and to internalize high levels of commitment to both domestic and civic involvement. Similarly, Norris and her colleagues (unpublished data summarized in Pratt and Norris, 1994, pp. 103f) have found that, among older people, the more positive their earlier attachment relationships, the more positive their reports on their current social relationships. Child language researcher Marilyn Shatz (1994, p. vii) comments incidentally on her own orientation to her first grandchild: "Determined to relive the wonderfully satisfying relations I had shared with my own grandmother, I quickly warmed to my new role when Ricky was born, and I happily gave much time and energy to developing an affectionate relationship with him." These findings are consistent with the attachment theorists' predictions. Although there are remaining questions about the applicability of the attachment construct to adult relationships (cf. Sternberg and Beall, 1991), the evidence does point to at least some degree of intergenerational continuities (Benoit and Parker, 1994) and some tendency among individuals toward similarities in their relationships. With this in mind, we turn next to one of the major institutions of domestic and civil involvement: marriage.

Marriage

"Marriage," says Billy Connolly, "is a wonderful invention – but then again, so is a bicycle repair kit." Although marriage costs more than a bicycle repair kit and is less reliable, it remains one of the most popular social inventions. Most societies organize domestic practices and property laws around marriage, and the institution is endorsed by social custom, the state, the mass media, and popular expectations. Most people grow up expecting to marry, and most do. We considered in chapter 16 some of the considerations involved in selecting a mate, and now we turn to the consequences.

In contemporary Western societies, over 90 percent of adults marry at least once (Perlmutter and Hall, 1992; Peterson, 1989). Although the formalities are increasingly disregarded by younger generations in some Western countries, the majority of even those who do not legally marry still enter into long-term heterosexual pair-bonding arrangements that are decidedly similar in structure and functions to those of a husband and wife (Reibstein and Richards, 1992). Marriage, or some very similar arrangement, is crucial to societal and personal life for most adults in most societies.

One of the reasons marriage is a wonderful invention is that so much is expected of it (Reibstein and Richards, 1992). Reibstein and Richards suggest that the contemporary Western marriage ideal is of an exclusive relationship which meets all of the primary emotional and sexual needs of the partners. It is expected to be the central relationship of their adult lives lasting, like the diamonds recommended at the onset of the commitment, forever. Reibstein and Richards (1992, p. 43) argue that the relative liberalization of sexual attitudes and behaviors in the late twentieth century and individuals' freedom to enter into or depart from marriages of choice mean that the idealized expectations of the relationship are now stronger than ever. In order to assert the special nature of the relationship in social contexts where sexual involvements among the unmarried are commonplace, marriage is expected to provide *everything*: love and sharing are crucial themes, and fidelity and sexual exclusiveness are regarded as vital.

Marriage as a developmental social change

Marriage is related to social development in complex ways. For a start, as Levinson (1978) points out, most people who enter into the institution are not ready for it. Individuals who marry in their twenties may have some experience of sexual activity, but much less of developing and sustaining long-term relationships: "Given the fundamental importance of these tasks, it is astonishing that nature's timing is so bad: we must choose a partner and start a family before we quite know what we are doing or how to do it well" (p. 107). Nevertheless, marriage can bring about change. Folklore has it that it can "settle a man down" (Goodnow and Collins, 1990) – and some evidence is consistent with this belief. Teachman et al. (1994) found in the US that married men spent less time unemployed than do single men, and that during any given month married men are between 50 percent and 100 percent more likely to take a job than unmarried men.

Second, marriage has consequences for existing relationships, especially those with parents. Komarovsky (1987) describes how the "silver cord" of long-term attachments (e.g., to parents) can affect the nature of the relationship a person establishes with another (e.g., a spouse). Many recently married people in Komarovsky's study of American blue-collar workers described tensions due to the pull of parents on their wives or husbands, and many young adults found it difficult to restructure their lives fully around a spouse. Some, for example, would continue to eat meals regularly at their mother's home, or insist on taking their parents or other family members out on social events with their new spouse. In a charming illustration, Palmer (1991) describes how Yehudi Menuhin, who grew up in a strongly matriarchal American Jewish family devoted to his wellbeing, headed for his first marriage vaguely assuming that his parents would not thrust him out of their house. It took a forceful intervention at the wedding by his father-in-law to alert him to the fact that getting out of the parental house would be strongly recommended in these circumstances. Not all transitions to independence are so abrupt, but marriage (or cohabitation) is usually associated with radical changes in the fundamentals of the individual's familial structure (Levinson, 1978).

Third, a married person's subsequent development is intimately tied to the development of his or her partner. Levinson summarizes: "A couple can form a lasting relationship that furthers his development only if it furthers hers . . . If in supporting his Dream she loses her own, then her development will suffer and both will later pay the price" (1978, p. 109). John McEnroe is reported to have advised Tatum O'Neal that "No wife of mine is going to make movies while our children are left with a stranger." She filed divorce papers shortly afterwards.

Marriage: correlates and course

We saw in chapter 16 that getting to the altar is the outcome of delicate social psychological negotiations wherein the respective parties assess each other's qualities and arrive at a conclusion about relative worth. Feingold (1992) observes that, while appearance and status may be important factors in mate *selection*, the couple then has to live together. At this point, other developmental social psychological factors are implicated. Like all relationships, marriage is not static (Duck, 1988b; Komarovsky, 1987; Reibstein and Richards, 1992). Both parties are developing and changing, and the nature of the relationship changes as a result. In many marriages, the trend is downwards: dissatisfaction with the relationship increases over time (Perlmutter and Hall, 1992; Reibstein and Richards, 1992). Yet for many others, marital satisfaction is maintained or even increased over the life-cycle (Bengston et al., 1990). Some findings indicate that patterns of marital satisfaction may in general follow a U-shaped curve: high in the early and later stages, but dipping in the middle (Bengston et al., 1990; Rollins and Feldman, 1981). The fact that in many cases the perceived quality of this fundamental relationship varies over time reminds us once more of an important point about the social psychological study of adult development: lives and relationships undergo continuous change. One of the major correlates of downturns in marital satisfaction, for example, is the arrival of children: as will be elaborated below, the readjustments of family relationships and roles entailed in this development can be far reaching.

While there are many factors associated with the success and/or durability of marriages, prominent among them seem to be commitment to marriage as an institution (Bengston et al., 1990), the ability to accommodate to changes in one's spouse (Kurdek, 1993), to be supportive and to maintain good communication patterns (Antill and Cotton, 1987; Argyle, 1992a; Argyle and Henderson, 1985; Burns and Dunlop, 1992), to find ways to resolve conflicts (Gottman, 1994) and, perhaps less profound but seemingly integral to maintenance, to keep up the routines of partnership (Duck, 1988b). Gender is an important factor: more women report dissatisfaction with their marriages than do men (Unger and Crawford, 1992). We will consider some possible reasons shortly.

Social cognition and marital satisfaction

One important social psychological variable associated with marital satisfaction is the nature of the attributions made about one's partner's behavior. It was pointed out in chapter 10 that, from childhood on, people are motivated to seek causal explanations for their own and other people's actions. We saw also that the same behavior can be "explained" in different ways according to whether one attributes it to person or situation, to stable or unstable characteristics, to internal or external causes, and so on. These are interesting enough social cognitive processes in the laboratory, but what happens when you apply them to your loved one?

Fincham and Bradbury (1993) investigated longitudinally the relationship between married people's attributions about their partner and their marital satisfaction. Subjects were asked to consider aspects of negative behavior in their spouse, such as "criticizing something you say," "acting cold and distant." As with most interpretations of social behavior, there is ambiguity here. Did you say something stupid, or is your partner unduly critical? Is he cold and distant, or have you upset him? Fincham and Bradbury found that husbands and wives who blamed their partner's negative behavior on *internal* characteristics ("my husband's behavior was due to something about him," "that's the type of person she is") reported higher levels of dissatisfaction with the marriage one year later. The social cognitive constructions that are generated within the micro-system of the husband–wife pair have important consequences for the dynamics and development of the relationship.

Marital status and wellbeing

Marriage is associated with psychological and physical health benefits. On average, married people tend to be healthier than those who are not (Anson, 1989; Bengston et al., 1990; Cramer, 1993; Mastekaasa, 1995; Wood et al., 1989). Unfortunately, the causal direction underlying this relationship is not so straightforward that scientists are able to recommend marriage as invariably more beneficial than bicycle repair kits. Part of the difference between married and unmarried people's health may be accounted for by the possibility that unhealthy individuals are less likely to seek or find partners in the first place (Mastekaasa, 1992). After all, the lovely and the loaded tend to live well, and are less exposed to malnutrition, hazardous environments, depression, and other health threats associated with lower social status. It is also difficult to determine the relative contribution of direct benefits of partnership (e.g., one spouse cares for the other if he or she is ill) versus the indirect benefits of a companionate relationship.

Parenthood

The marital relationship is also likely to undergo changes as a result of enlarging the family, through parenthood. For many, this involves a major role transition. The shift in status has radical consequences for how the individual conceives of herself (Baker, 1989; Deutsch et al., 1988; Nicolson, 1986; J. Smith, 1991) or himself (Levinson, 1978), and for how she or he relates henceforth to the new family and the broader society (Cowan and Cowan, 1988; Feldman and Nash, 1984; Goodnow and Collins, 1990; Palkovitz and Sussman, 1988; Ruble et al., 1988). Becoming a parent is a public undertaking, in that the individual is likely to be evaluated (by self and others) in terms of the socially shared criteria for being a "good mother" or "good father" (Goodnow and Collins, 1990). Consistent with the self-socialization theory of gender role development (see chapter 5) mothers-to-be actively seek information on what the role change will entail, and how to perform (Deutsch et al., 1988). One mother, interviewed by Nicolson (1986), described the experience as being "jolted into change." Presumably this informant was not familiar with Bower's (1979) view that the idea of adult transformations does violence to the concept of development.

Attachment again

One of the most obvious changes is that the parent takes a new position in the attachment system. Many of the characteristics definitive of the *infant's* attachment, such as desiring proximity, distress at absence, security, and relaxation in the presence of the attachment figure (see chapter 3) are also found in the new parent (Newman and Newman, 1988). However, the Newmans point out that the experience of attachment as parent also has new features, not least the sense of responsibility toward the dependent infant, leading both to satisfaction upon fulfilling the child's needs and to anxiety and strain when it proves difficult to work out what the needs are. The asymmetries of the relationship also mean that the adult has a new social capacity: the opportunity and responsibility to exert authority. How she or he integrates this potentiality into family life has long-term implications for the parent–child relationship and for the child's development. Hence, the developmental social psychological processes we have considered in earlier chapters are now experienced from a different perspective. But there appears to be a degree of continuity, too, in that new parents' reports of their personal attachment histories correlate with the attachment types found in their own infants (Feeney et al., 1994; Main, in press).

Parental stresses and social expectations

Obviously, becoming a parent involves many stresses and new role demands (Belsky and Pensky, 1988; Brazelton, 1988; Grossman, 1988; Terry, 1992; Tessier et al., 1992). But how an individual responds to these demands appears in part to be mediated by his or her experiences and expectations. For example, longitudinal studies of American (Field et al., 1985b; Heinicke and Guthrie, 1992) and Swedish women (Mothander, 1992) have found that how positively the mother-to-be adjusted to pregnancy is associated with psychosomatic adjustment and role satisfaction up to one year after birth. It appears that the pressures of the maternal role interact with the social cognitions of the woman; Mothander (1992) argues that as the mother deals with the practical demands of caregiving, her internal representations become intertwined with the actual needs of the infant and other environmental demands. The outcomes of this process of adaptation may in turn contribute to the quality of the mother's early relationship with her infant. American findings indicate that mothers who are dissatisfied with their role are more prone to reject the child, and their children are more likely to become difficult (Lerner and Galambos, 1985), thus setting the conditions for a continuous cycle of stressful interactions.

Although becoming a parent has implications for the adult's self-concept and adjustment, these processes do not occur in a social vacuum. Where the parents cohabit, for example, we saw in chapter 4 that the addition of a new member to the family has consequences for the whole system of relationships, not least the fact that the parents can now spend less time in joint leisure activities. In general, Western studies show a decline in the level of satisfaction with the marriage after the arrival of the first child (Belsky and Pensky, 1988; Reibstein and Richards, 1992; Ruble et al., 1988). In studies of American and Canadian couples, Ruble et al. (1988) found that many women pre-birth expected higher levels of egalitarianism in the home than actually turned out to be the case post-birth.

There is strong evidence that the character of the couple's relationship that precedes parenthood has implications for how the couple meets this challenge, and in turn for the quality of their interactions with the child (Cox et al., 1989; Goldberg, 1990; Goldberg and Easterbrooks, 1984; Heinicke and Guthrie, 1992; van de Rijt-Plooj and Plooj, 1993; Tessier et al., 1992). Heinicke and Guthrie found that couples showing the most positive pre-birth interactions, and who were able to deal with their conflicts in the context of mutual respect, were more likely to adjust positively to the advent of the child. Cox et al. (1989), in a review of the literature, conclude that the degree to which the partners establish a confiding relationship predicts maternal warmth and the husband's feelings about his paternal role.

It is also sometimes the case, though, that the partners in an otherwise unhappy marriage will opt to stay together not simply "for the kids' sake" but because the parental role itself has such meaning and value for the individual that it outweighs the perceived shortcomings of the marital relationship (Levinson, 1978). This kind of adjustment underscores the relevance of Levinson's concept of life-structure, and the fact that any one dimension of a person's relationships and roles needs to be understood within the larger structured framework of the life-cycle. A person might be disappointed with the unfolding of one relationship (such as her marriage) yet be prepared to sustain or suffer it because of the value she attaches to another relationship (with her child) and to a role (motherhood) that she strongly expected to be part of her life-cycle.

Division of labor in the home

A critical aspect of the development of a marital or partnership arrangement is the division of domestic labour. In many societies and cultural groups, the rules here are very clearly established by tradition (Di Domenico et al., 1987). The respective parenting roles are related integrally to gender role beliefs and stereotypes that we have seen in earlier chapters begin to take shape early in life and continue to develop and to affect social behavior through childhood and adolescence. Part of the feminine stereotype is the attribution of nurturance and fondness of children; part of the masculine stereotype is the notion of the protector and provider (Feldman and Aschenbrenner, 1983). The assumption that this entails a division of responsibilities such that the man will continue in his occupation while the woman will give up or reduce out-of-home work to look after the children remains firmly entrenched for many, resulting in a "father-dominated and mother-centered" household (New and Benigni, 1987). In many macro-systems, life is organized in congruence with these beliefs and expectations. In particular, few societies provide sufficient paternity leave arrangements to allow men to take principal responsibility for caregiving if they wish to do so (Sweden is a rare exception), and few provide sufficient child care support services to enable women to return to full-time work after the birth.

Hence, while it was seen in chapter 5 that parents constrain the environments within which children acquire their sex roles, the structure of parental roles is itself influenced by sociocultural context. In many traditional societies, the authority of the father's role is underwritten and supported by the culture (Ho, 1987; New and Benigni, 1987; Nsamenang, 1987). In others, it is modified by changing social expectations – for example, the belief in several Western societies that the "new father" should be more involved than his predecessors in child care and domestic work (Pleck, 1987). In still others, his role is almost undermined by societal developments. Schwalb et al. (1987) show how the stringent occupational demands upon workers in modern Japan mean that many fathers (about 19 percent of male white-collar employees) are physically separated from their families due to work transfers, and others are psychologically separated by work-related stress and excessive hours, the cumulative outcome of which is a reduction in the clarity of the paternal role and a corresponding devaluation.

Is the domestic division of labor changing?

A succinct exposition of the traditional perspective is voiced by an American father interviewed (in the late 1950s) by Komarovsky (1987, p. 52) who asserted unequivocally: "No son of mine will wash dishes." In some contemporary industrialized societies, *attitudes* appear to be shifting somewhat on this issue toward greater equality (in Australia, Russell, 1983; in Germany, Nickel and Kocher, 1987; in the UK, Lewis and O'Brien, 1987; in the US, Wright et al., 1992).

At the level of *behavior* – actually implementing the role adjustments that egalitarian ideologies call for – things get a little fuzzier. Several studies have found that the sex role ideology of the couple is associated at least modestly with the extent of participation of the male in domestic labour (Coltrane and Ishi-Kuntz, 1992; Hardesty and Bokemeier, 1989; New and Benigni, 1987; Pleck, 1983; Wright et al., 1992). If the couple believes in egalitarian role arrangements, then the male is more likely to contribute, though probably not to an equal extent.

When both partners are working, there is, on average, a slight increase in the amount of time men spend on housework, and a more substantial decrease in the amount of time women devote to it (Presland and Antill, 1987). But women still generally end up retaining principal responsibility for these chores: the norm for husbands' contributions to the housework has been found in several studies of families in North America, Europe and Australia to be between 20 and 30 percent (Berardo et al., 1987; Callan and Noller, 1987; Horne and Lupir, 1987; Hwang, 1987b; Wright et al., 1992). Interestingly, there seem to be some gender differences in perceptions of this distribution. While both sexes attribute less housework to husbands and both sexes agree on the rank order of husbands' contributions to different tasks, when a couple is tested, the male tends to estimate his contributions some 25 percent higher than his partner does (Wright et al., 1992).

Perhaps the subtlety of male housework behaviors renders them most salient to the practitioner but less apparent to his cohabitee. Lewis et al. (1982) noted that fathers are said to be "highly participant" in caregiving when they do things that are simply taken for granted in the mother's work. In general, men's participation in what are traditionally regarded as "feminine" household tasks is low (Starrels, 1994). However, as Jackson (1987) and Cowan and Cowan (1988) point out, it would be an oversimplification to attribute these imbalances in gender allocations to sheer male villainy. Evidence from Britain (Jackson, 1987; McGhee and Fryer, 1989), Australia (G. Russell, 1983, 1989), Italy (New and Benigni, 1987), and the US (Cowan and Cowan, 1988; Jump and Haas, 1987; Lamb et al., 1987) reveals that there are equally potent female constraints upon what men do around the house: "Many husbands have a delicate sense of the point at which "help" becomes trespassing, and women are unlikely to give up their command of the home territory any more willingly than men have allowed women full admission to the world of work" (Jackson, 1987, p. 54). Many women tend at least as firmly as men to adhere to *la via vecchia* (the traditional way of life) when it comes to domestic organization (New and Benigni, 1987), and in some cases are more likely to report dissatisfaction with the marriage if the husband becomes substantially involved in household chores (see Lamb et al., 1987). Cowan and Cowan's (1988) data from US families indicate that the increased involvement of men in the workplace following parenthood is often a *result* rather than a cause of their reduced opportunities to become involved in the parental role during the first two years of the child's life.

The pattern of male–female differences in domestic labor does not appear to vary greatly with social class (Lamb et al., 1987; Saraceno, 1980; Wright et al., 1992). As Wright et al. (1992) put it, there is little support in their data for the image of "the egalitarian and enlightened yuppie who cooks elegant meals and pushes a stroller in the park" (1992, p. 276). Middle-class men in their study did no more or less housework than working-class men. However, there are marked differences among countries. In Wright's study, Swedish men were involved in housework considerably more than American men. This finding is interesting because it suggests the impact of deliberate social policy changes upon domestic gender behavior. The Swedish government has since the 1970s pursued a commitment to gender equity, reflected in tax systems, child care provision, family support (Haas, 1981; Wright et al., 1992), while in the US family policies have been somewhat different, including a Presidential veto of federal support for child care centres (Cowan and Cowan, 1988).

Overall, then, Connolly is correct: marriage is a remarkable invention and it is one that affects profoundly the social development of an overwhelming majority of people. Finding a partner, evolving a new and central attachment, acquiring new role demands, adjusting to an intimately shared lifestyle, achieving a new position on the parent–child axis, and the many other changes of domesticity are quite basic to the structure and processes of adult life.

Other Relationships

Although marriage and parenthood may typically be central to the organization of the life-structure, other relationships are often important through adulthood. These include sibling relationships, friendships, and affairs.

Siblings

For many people, relations with siblings remain a vital feature of their social network throughout the lifespan (Bank, 1992; Cicirelli, 1989). For obvious reasons, sibling relationships tend to last longer than parent–child relationships, and may well be the most enduring attachments of a person's life. Sibling relationships are exceptional among horizontal relationships in terms of the sheer extent of shared experiences (as well as shared genetic material). The nature of the relationship and its perceived importance to the participants varies, and is affected by many factors including life decisions (e.g., moving to different locations for work reasons) and new relationships (not everyone gets on with their in-laws). Although involvement with siblings varies from the apathetic to the intense (Bank, 1992), most adults studied in Western investigations report feeling close to siblings in at least some respects (Cicirelli, 1989).

Friendship

As seen in earlier chapters, relations with peers (horizontal relations, in Hartup's terms) are significant to individuals from very early in life, and undergo qualitative and structural changes as a function of development and social opportunities during childhood and adolescence. But, of course, their significance does not end with adulthood, and friendships remain important aspects of social involvement throughout life. Exactly what friendship means among adults proves difficult to determine (Hays, 1988), since people use the term to describe relations as varied as occasional co-conversationalists in the pub, associates met from time to time for specific purposes such as playing sport, and intimate, confidence-sharing dependencies between individuals who maintain the relationship over many years. It is clear, though, that friendships are dynamic relationships, continuously evolving and dependent upon repeated interactions between the partners and appropriate adjustments in each to changes in the other (Duck and Miell, 1986; Hays, 1988).

Gender differences in adult friendships are common. Both sexes tend to continue the style of interpersonal relations emerging during later childhood and adolescence, with adult male friendships being characterized more by "side by side" interactions, and female relationships exhibiting a more "face to face" character (Wright, 1982). Levinson (1978) came to the tentative conclusion that close friendship with a man or woman is rarely experienced among American men; he suggested that men may have broad social networks but few intimate relationships. Unger and Crawford (1992) review several studies which confirm that women's friendships tend to be more intimate, more intense, and generally more important to the people involved.

Close cross-sex friendships are reported by less than one-third of adults (Hays, 1988). People's explanations of the obstacles to cross-sex friendships are perhaps not surprising – they include sexual tensions, social discouragement, and the lack of things in common (Hays, 1988) – but they are none the less forceful reminders of the pervasiveness of gender role differences that are well entrenched and widely reinforced in adult social life.

Some evidence indicates that involvement in friendships is associated with physical and mental wellbeing (House et al., 1988; Lewittes, 1988). Although an association such as this could be interpreted in different ways, it does appear that friendships confer the benefits of emotional support as well as structure and meaning beyond work. Men's relative distance from friendship may therefore be disadvantageous, and arguably a contributing factor to the greater vulnerability to ill health and the lower longevity of males.

Affairs

Affairs seem more the stuff of gossip, newspapers, and novels than developmental social psychological research, but perhaps psychologists should be less aloof from the real world. In Britain, for example, Royality is tarnished and cabinet ministers resign, with some regularity, upon production of hotel receipts, photographs, telephone transcripts or "love" children, and in America Presidents are greatly embarrassed by allegations of clandestine encounters with persons naked under their trench coats. Shocking as these revelations and claims may be, they do not seem to reflect patterns of social behavior unique to the ruling classes. Reibstein and Richards (1992) estimate that between 50 and 75 percent of men and slightly less women engage in extramarital affairs at some points in their marriage. This indicates a pervasive social phenomenon, presumably meaningful and with impact on the conduct of everyday lives, and it may reflect social values rather than scientific purpose to pretend that this sort of thing does not go on, or at least does not warrant attention.

Certainly, affairs are more mysterious inventions than marriage, and rather more difficult to research. There are practical and ethical obstacles to subject recruitment. However, investigations such as Reibstein and Richards (1992), based on case studies, uncover a variety of reasons and precipitating circumstances. These authors show that each partner's developmental history of relationships, his or her model or script of marriage, and the stage of the marital cycle can all influence the likelihood of having an affair (or a series of affairs).

Gender stands out again as an important factor. One of the reasons men are slightly more likely to have affairs, for example, is that the organization of marital roles means that they spend more time outside the household and have greater opportunities to meet other potential partners (e.g., through work). Another is that men, on average, appear to handle the emotional demands of extramarital relationships more comfortably: Reibstein and Richards argue that men find it easier to "segment" their lives, demarcating compartments such as work, marriage, and affairs which can be kept relatively distinct. Drawing on Gilligan's (1982) account of women's greater commitment to interpersonal relationships, Reibstein and Richards suggest that women find having affairs stressful because they are more prone to contemplate the impact of their actions upon others (such as their husband or children). The double standard prevails in this domain, too, with greater social hostility to women who have affairs and generally more outraged reactions from husbands who feel that they have been betrayed. Of course, as we have seen in earlier chapters, explanations of the origins of the double standard are controversial.

Affairs, by definition, coexist with marriage – at least for a time. Their consequences for the marriage can be varied. Reibstein and Richards (1992) review cases in which the marital correlates of an affair were positive, negative, or neutral. In some cases, marriages were strengthened by the joint or individual resolution of the aftermath of an affair; in others, the establishment of new boundaries seemed to enhance each partner's view of him or herself and the relationship; in others, involvement in or discovery of an affair was associated with the rapid or gradual dissolution of the marriage. Again, these outcomes vary with the developmental status and responsibilities of the individuals concerned and the nature of their relationships – Reibstein and Richards suggest that there are no easy formulas for predicting outcomes.

Relating to the Broader Community

The developmental social psychological processes discussed in earlier chapters remain important features of the young adult's broadening involvement in society. To illustrate, we consider here two familiar themes. First, attachment reappears yet again, this time with an emphasis on how attachment style may be implicated in dealing with social organizations and societal trauma. Second, we examine how social comparisons are drawn upon and influenced by the new priorities of adult life.

Attachment and societal involvement

Attachments can be found outside of the family and sexual pairings. People become attached to other people, to places, to symbols and concepts. Attachment to places again shows evidence of a need for secure bases from which to deal with the world. An obvious example is the home (see also chapter 19), but it is easy to find space attachments in other contexts. That is why, if you attend a lecture or seminar in the same room with the same people every week, you will notice that many people strive to sit in the same location that they occupied previously; try violating their attachments, and you will have an opportunity to observe agonistic nonverbal displays. Somner (1969) found that people in public spaces such as campuses mark out the territories to which they have become attached, and in general other people respect their markers (e.g., you do not take a library space if someone has left a notepad at it). Indeed, Feshbach (1991) has proposed that in due course individuals' attachment relationships have ramifications for their attachment to their nation, and in a retrospective study of Americans he found evidence of an association between the quality of early attachments to fathers and the adults' degree of patriotism (commitment to the fatherland).

Kirkpatrick (1992) points out that there is a striking resemblance between the infant's attachment to a parent and many adults' commitment to a religious figure, such as God, Buddha, or other supernatural beings: "The religious person proceeds with faith that God . . . will be available to protect him or her when danger threatens; at other times, the mere knowledge of God's presence and accessibility allows him or her to approach the problems and difficulties of daily life with confidence" (p. 6) – much the same service that a Mum or Dad provides to an infant. Kirkpatrick and Shaver (1992) found that adults classified as secure, avoidant, or anxious/ambivalent (on the basis of their own reports of their experiences in love relationships) reported different types of religious commitment. The secure had greater religious commitment and more positive images of God, the avoidant were more likely to describe themselves as agnostic, and the anxious/ambivalent were more likely to report having had a glossolalia experience (speaking in tongues).

Attachment styles have been found to be predictive of how individuals react to traumatic societal events. We saw in chapter 3 that the standard means of measuring infants' attachment type is to place them in a moderately stressful situation. In a timely piece of applied developmental social psychology, Mikulincer et al. (1993) studied the reactions of young Israeli adults to a situation at the very high end of the stress scale, the Iraqi attacks during the Gulf War. Many of their subjects lived in areas directly targeted for Scud missile bombardment. Once again, attachment style predicted reactions. Compared to secure individuals, ambivalent subjects were more distressed, and avoidant people suffered greater somatization, hostility, and trauma-related avoidance. Coping strategies varied, too. Those with secure attachment styles sought support from others, while ambivalent people became more emotional and avoidant people attempted to create a psychological distance between themselves and the events.

Social comparisons in early adulthood

As the young adult develops new roles and new relationships, he or she is likely to use social comparison processes to collect evidence on how he or she is faring relative to others. As we saw in chapter 9, social comparison theory was initially developed within an adevelopmental context, as part of experimental social psychology. Subsequent theory and research have led to broader, developmental perspectives on social comparison examining both its emergence in childhood (Ruble, 1983) and changes through adulthood (Ruble and Frey, 1991; Suls, 1986). Ruble and Frey (1991) propose that, as people move through the lifespan, their social comparison reference points will vary as a function of several factors, including the particular phase of skill acquisition they have reached in the relevant domain, the importance they attach to the activity, the availability of comparative information, and the implications of each type of comparison for self-esteem.

One context in which we could expect social comparisons to be particularly salient is in early to middle adulthood, while the individual is striving to establish his or her place in the world. Ruble and Frey suggest that the uncertainties of this period should render people especially alert to the achievements and attributes of those whom they regard as their peers or near-peers. One of the classic early experimental demonstrations of the effects of social context on social comparisons (Morse and Gergen, 1970) involved students at the University of Michigan who were suckered into applying for a position as a research assistant at the Institute of Social Research. Each applicant completed a form in the company of another "applicant." The latter was of course a confederate of the experimenters, and he turned up either as "Mr Clean" (smartly dressed in a dark suit) or "Mr Dirty" (wearing a smelly sweatshirt, ripped trousers, no socks and carrying a well-thumbed copy of a smutty paperback). When self-esteem ratings were collected, subjects exposed to Mr Clean did not feel too good about themselves, especially among those whose own characteristics were more toward the Mr Dirty end of the sartorial spectrum. It seems that the social environment can induce social comparisons that have an impact on the individual's self-perceptions.

Real life provides many examples of the affective salience of social comparisons in the course of ladder-climbing. Consider the British composer, Sir Andrew Lloyd Webber (of *Cats*, *Evita*, and *Phantom of the Opera* fame). Some readers may say it's the kind of stuff their parents like, but Webber's success is plain for all to see: his shows run in London and New York for years, everything he writes sets him up for royalties *ad infinitum* and he pulls in about a million pounds a day, and that's before he leaves the house. He is very happy with the way things have turned out, but how do his peers (or would-be peers) cope with social comparisons? The novelist Jonathan Coe is frank:

> "It's so annoying to see someone overrated and making so much money, isn't it? Without you being able to see what's so good about it. I think it's also a kind of rage that people, people like me feel, because we genuinely do think we're better than him, but the financial evidence is so glaringly to the contrary." (quoted in C. Bennett, 1993)

Social comparisons, especially upward social comparisons, can be painful but motivating to adults seeking to establish their place in society.

In general, research supports Ruble and Frey's (1991) point about the importance of context. In an interesting illustration of the influence of social circumstances upon the salience of different components of one's self-concept, Kite (1992) found that non-traditional age university students who were asked to provide self-descriptions were significantly more likely to mention *age* than were students in the normal undergraduate age range. The selectivity of social comparisons was again demonstrated in this study. Kite found that the self-descriptions of academic staff in the same institution did not contain the same high level of age references as the mature students, despite similarities in age range. Presumably, self-descriptions entail comparisons with people in the same *social* category (i.e., other students), rather than people who happen to be in the immediate *physical* environment.

Summary

Blank's (1982) observation that life is intimately grounded in relationships is amply supported wherever we look in adulthood. We have seen here that the nature and development of relationships are affected by many variables, including the structural and value organization of the societal macro-system, interpersonal expectations and social cognitions, and the practicalities of social roles. Relationships and roles change through the life-cycle. Attachment remains a key concept in accounting for relationships during adulthood, partly because existing attachments continue to hold significance, partly because important new ones are formed to partners, and partly because many adults now shift to a new position as they become parents. Long-term partnerships, such as marriage or its near-equivalents, have major consequences for most people's social development. Other relationships (such as siblings and friendships) are also important for many. Virtually everybody has to accommodate to some of the demands of the broader society, and these processes themselves are affected by or entail new developments in attachment relationships and social cognitions. We turn in the final section to consider more closely the principal form of societal involvement, work.

Work in Adulthood

For many people, work is one of the defining attributes of their adult lives. The social psychology of work is too large a field to attempt to summarize here (see Argyle, 1989), but it is important to recognize the interrelations between work role and adult development. Work is associated with wellbeing, social identity, social contact, physical and mental activity, economic status, sense of purpose, personal fulfillment, and is sought actively by the majority of adults (Argyle, 1989, 1992a; Furnham, 1990; Jahoda, 1981; Levinson, 1978; Llewelyn and Osborne, 1990; Lodge, 1988). A work role is one of the key connections a person maintains between his or her micro-system (the family) and the macro-system (society).

We have already seen that work is developmental. Critical steps *en route* to one's work role are actually taken before adulthood, and we have considered some of these in chapter 16. We have also seen earlier in this chapter, in Levinson's model, that the organization of the life-cycle is intimately connected to the individual's work role, both in terms of the structure of life at a particular time and in terms of the continuing progress of his or her role (from junior to senior, trainee to supervisor, mentored to mentor). There are many routes through the world of work (as well as many people excluded from it; see chapter 16). The outcomes are varied: "At best, his occupation permits the fulfillment of basic values and life goals. At worst, a man's work life over the years is oppressive and corrupting, and contributes to a growing alienation from self, work and society" (Levinson, 1978, p. 45).

That may hold for a man's work, but what about a woman's? There are numerous factors associated with development through work, but one of the most fundamental is, of course, gender.

Work and Gender

To state the obvious, both sexes *work* as adults. A key difference is that men are more likely to do it outside the home and to get paid, or get paid more, for it. In most societies, males are expected to aspire to a full-time occupation, to achieve within it, and to adopt a "provider" role toward their family. The extent to which these traditional expectations are endorsed by contemporary men in different societies and cultures is uncertain. Among recent American samples, for example, they appear to be only weakly supported by white, middle-class men (Thompson and Pleck, 1987) though held somewhat more strongly among black men and among women (Cazenave and Leon, 1987). Nevertheless, the practical reality is that most men who can do so find an entry to the workforce, take up full-time employment and remain (or strive to remain) employed until they reach retirement age.

Studies of career development (e.g., Levinson, 1978; Super, 1980, 1985) show that for most men it is an oversimplification to represent entering the world of work as a swift and firm transition of early adulthood. Instead, it is a gradual social psychological process that extends across many years, in which the individual first struggles to sort out interests and to find the occupation and opportunities to meet them, and then strives to establish himself with the necessary skills and occupational identity. Even by the age 30 transition, this process is often incomplete. By the mid-life transition, the individual is likely to have peaked in terms of occupational attainment, and has new adjustments to make as he makes his place in the middle adult generation, as well as reviewing whether he has attained his Dream, and whether it still matters.

For women, the picture is somewhat different, and currently in a state of flux. In the traditional family and in many contemporary traditional societies, the primary adult female role has been held to be that of mother. External work, although not precluded, was seen as subordinate to this principal commitment, so that a woman was expected to withdraw from the workforce for several years to fulfill her maternal purpose. Women were expected to take part-time employment as a supplement to family income rather than the main source. It is difficult to decide which tense to use in describing these assumptions because, of course, they are still widely held, and they affect the contexts within which contemporary women may elect to work. For example, Hartnett and Bradley (1986) report European Community statistics according to which 37 percent of women were in part-time employment, compared to 5 percent of men. Even so, in most parts of the Western world, women are now entering the workforce in substantially higher proportions and tend to report at least equal satisfaction with work as do men (Hartnett and Bradley, 1986; Unger and Crawford, 1992). This generally positive attitude to external work contrasts with abundant evidence that women's attainment within the workplace is markedly lower than that of men (cf. Unger and Crawford, 1992). Thus, both men and women find benefits in work, and there is overlap between the sexes in the need for the economic, social, and psychological benefits of work — but there seems to be a crucial difference in terms of achievement.

Achievement and Gender

The French writer Christen (1991, p. 50) cites US statistics, rather gleefully, to demonstrate that there is one woman in 600 in a leadership position. French data, he adds, point to the same conclusion, that there are virtually no women at the top of any significant occupational hierarchy. In Christen's view, these findings confirm the triumph of human nature over culture: *la différence* is destiny.

The imbalance in favor of males is not quite so extreme as the figures in which Christen rejoices. More typically, females account for about one in 20 of senior occupational hierarchies, and this is subject to variation among fields and appears to be changing in contemporary societies with shifts in the direction of greater equity (Unger and Crawford, 1992). Overall, though, he has a point, and one which is undisputed by most commentators: namely, that males tend to dominate the workplace. Given the fundamental importance of work to social status, economic autonomy and personal fulfillment, this discrepancy raises vital questions for developmental social psychology: how is the gender differentiation of the workplace brought about, and how is it sustained? Christen's view is that testosterone rules, but let us consider some social psychological variables which have attracted researchers' attention over the past couple of decades.

Fear of success

One possibility that seemed plausible initially was the proposal that women have been socialized to fear success. Horner (1972) presented students with the initial line of a story which they were requested to complete: *After first term finals, Ann finds herself at the top of her medical school class.* (In the version given to male subjects, the name was changed to John.) About two-thirds of female subjects continued the description of Ann in quite unfavorable terms: she was seen as unfriendly, unattractive, snotty, probably wearing glasses, heading for a nervous breakdown, and (in the late 1960s) wearing her skirt too long. Among the male subjects, less than 10 percent of attributions to John were negative. Horner concluded that young women had been socialized to fear success on the grounds that it would make them appear unfeminine and unloveable.

However, as Unger and Crawford (1992, p. 471) point out, the initial appeal of the message the study seemed to send was such that its limitations were widely overlooked. It is quite possible that the demand characteristics of the procedure elicited subjects' knowledge of cultural stereotypes rather than their own anxieties. Subsequent research has found overall there are no reliable sex differences in fear of success (Feather and Raphelson, 1974; Paludi, 1979; Weinreich-Haste, 1984), and that whether it is elicited or not depends considerably upon the stimulus materials and context, rather than the sex of the subject (Unger and Crawford, 1992).

Gender bias in evaluation

Another possibility was that sex role stereotypes lead people to evaluate male and female performances differently. An often-cited example is the work of Goldberg (1968), who had female students evaluate scholarly articles, telling some subjects that they were written by men, others that the authors were women. Goldberg reported a bias such that supposedly female authors' work was rated less favorably. However, the differences were not strong, and attempts to replicate and extend the work led to conflicting results (see Durkin, 1987b, for a review).

In a much more rigorous experiment, based on Weiner's model of attribution theory, Deaux and Emswiller (1974) found some tendency of male and female subjects to rate male success as due to ability and female success as due to luck. It was shown in chapter 10 that attributing success to internal or external factors has consequences for future performance expectations; if women's success is due to luck, then we might expect different results on other occasions. But again, attractive as this explanation may seem, the differences in Deaux and Emswiller's study were not great, and further research into gender biases and attributions yielded a mass of inconsistent findings (discussed in more detail in Durkin, 1987b).

Furthermore, field studies of performance evaluation in real-world occupational settings have found either no effect due to sex of rater or ratee (Wexley and Pulakos, 1982) or *more favorable* ratings of females (Gupta et al., 1983; Mobley, 1982; Peters et al., 1984). Die et al. (1990) found no obvious bias (no sex difference) in male managers' ratings of other male and female managers, though female managers rated other females more favorably than other males. (Of course, if the female managers' ratings were valid, then the males who failed to detect a difference may have been biased against acknowledging female superiority.) There is rather stronger evidence of bias against females at the selection stage (Terborg, 1977; Unger and Crawford, 1992), but this is not sufficient to explain differential attainment between the sexes once into an occupation.

Of course, being rated as competent or even superior does not guarantee that an individual will receive recognition and advancement. She might find that a promotions committee takes "other factors" into account – and these are rarely made explicit or open to candidates and researchers! Die et al. (1990) found that women managers *felt* discriminated against. Chi-Ching (1992), in a study of women managers in Singapore, reported that young female career entrants, although admitted to the same initial grade as their male peers, were often assigned support roles. Perhaps young women are more likely to be guided into assistant positions rather than leadership. Although it should be added that Singapore is in a transition phase from a traditional society to a modern capitalist trading center, and the generalizability of this finding needs to be tested in other cultures, this finding is consistent with the arguments of Eagly (1987). Eagly maintains that, despite the increasing presence of women in the North American workforce, the socially shared tendency to perceive women as communal (selfless, concerned with ·others) and men as agentic (assertive, controlling) still survives, and influences the kinds of specific skills that women and men seek and are expected to have in the workplace.

Developmental social expectations

The question remains of where these expectations come from. Eagly (1987, p. 132) acknowledges a contribution from earlier experiences, but stresses that learning role expectations continues throughout life, and concludes that "better predictors of adult sex differences can be achieved by focusing on the contemporaneous causes active in adult life rather than on childhood socialization." But this may be to underestimate the importance of developmental goals and histories as well as to overlook the developmental backgrounds to the contemporaneous causes themselves. In fact, it proves very difficult to separate social and developmental factors.

Women entering the workplace may have lower expectations about their futures than do their male counterparts – expectations which have a realistic basis if they take note of the obstacles to their advancement and the track records of their predecessors (Redgrove, 1987; Unger and Crawford, 1992). These obstacles may reflect others' assumptions about sex differences in occupational development.

An interesting account developed by Wetherell et al. (1987) suggests that part of the explanation may lie in the ideology that young people formulate as they approach the critical life transition of occupational entry. Wetherell et al. (1987) interviewed final year Scottish university students about their expectations and beliefs concerning gender role issues in the workplace and in domestic organization. As one might expect, these relatively highly educated people tended, irrespective of gender, to profess strong egalitarianism, consistent with the kinds of views that are espoused in liberal educational settings. No doubt the commitment to female–male equality was sincere, but under the surface were a number of qualifications and concerns that appeared to reflect social representations of practical limitations upon individuals' choices. For example, although everyone was in favor of equal opportunity at work and avowed that there were no sex differences in ability, most felt that there was a problem in respect of childrearing:

> *Male*: "I mean there are other considerations like by and large women are probably better for bringing up children in the home so uh you know if they're all working then they are not going to be able to do that which . . . you know wouldn't be good."

> *Female*: "I said that to some friends the other night who have got children and they said yeah well that's what we thought as well and one of them was high up in management but once her children came along that was it, she just, all these maternal urges came surging out of her and she just couldn't go back to work again." (passages from Wetherell et al., 1987, p. 62)

Although several interviewees anticipated maternal surges overwhelming them in due course, paternal impulses were expected to be better controlled:

> *Male*: "in other words if my wife was adamant that she wanted to go out to work, uh, and if I were 90 per cent convinced that I wanted to go out to work, then it is possible that I would look after the children. But I would say that it's unlikely that I would

marry a person who would be so closeted in her views anyway. So you know, it's not really likely to happen. I will be going out to work." (Wetherell et al., 1987, p. 63).

Overall, the respondents sustained an ideology of "unequal egalitarianism." They appeared to manage self-presentational goals (i.e., the desire to be seen as egalitarian) alongside representations of practical limitations (perhaps due to biologically given urges and surges or to perceived employers' stereotypes) which led them, however reluctantly, to anticipate inequality in the real world outside the campus. As the respondent above indicates, women who thought differently were taken to be "closeted in their views."

It is interesting to compare the comments of Wetherell et al.'s subjects with those of Ginzberg et al.'s (1951) pre-feminist interviewees at Columbia University whom we encountered in chapter 16. The majority of these young women, the educated American elite of the 1940s, felt that marriage and serious work were incompatible, and reported "I'd like to have children right away; really on the whole I would rather not think of working ... only if it's necessary" (p. 165). Wetherell *et al.*'s Scottish subjects had a late twentieth-century awareness that working *is* necessary and an ideology that held that women are perfectly capable of performing successfully in it; but these views remain qualified by an expectation, shared with their sisters of the 1940s (and with their prospective partners), that it was their responsibility to look after the children.

Similar findings have been reported in recent American and Australian studies of university and high school students (Feather and Said, 1983; Jackson et al., 1992; Komarovsky, 1985; Schroeder et al., 1992). Feather and Said (1983), for example, found sex differences among Australian adolescents' expectations about the likelihood of quitting work to get married, to care for children (females most likely) or to find a better position (males most likely). Schroeder et al. (1992) observe that while young women's beliefs about career and family roles may be becoming more egalitarian than those of earlier generations, "their behavioral intentions are not" (p. 287), and a majority sustains an expectation that working life will be discontinued to accommodate children. Since this expectation is actually inconsistent with demographic trends in contemporary workforces (i.e., most women continue to work through early parenthood, and this pattern is predicted to increase), Schroeder et al. highlight an important practical and research issue for the next few decades: investigating the developmental social psychological processes involved in young women's adjustments to structural changes in work and family arrangements.

In a study of senior American university students aiming to enter a variety of occupational fields, Jackson et al. (1992) also asked subjects to indicate their expected first salary and their salary by the time they reached career peak. In general, women anticipated less than men at both points, and the discrepancy was especially marked in male-dominated occupations, such as engineering. The one exception was among social scientists – psychologists and the like – where women envisaged salaries higher than their male peers expected. It could be that women who have had more extended intellectual involvement in issues of gender roles and equity (which might be the case among social scientists) develop atypical self-concepts and future expectations.

By and large, women's expectations of lower pay and lesser advancement are perfectly rational, since across many fields women *are*, on average, paid less than men and the senior ranks are dominated by men. Bem (1993) points out that the lack of child care provision in most workplaces sustains practices from times when women were virtually excluded from the world of employment; in Bem's view these practices situate men and women in different and unequal places in the social structure and this inequality provides the sexes with different daily social experiences which in turn lead to very different ways of construing social reality. Jackson et al. (1992) suggest that women and men may adopt different referents for social comparison – each focusing on their own sex. If this is the case, then their early career expectations would be different, and these authors point out that there is good evidence that career attainment correlates with career expectations.

Role conflict and role uncertainty

Another important factor influencing female achievement at work underlines the connections that have been stressed at several points in this chapter between personal relationships and societal involvement: role conflict. Most individuals experience conflicts among different role demands. For example, being a "good," involved father may clash with the time requirements of achievement in competitive employment. But women tend to suffer this kind of role conflict (between family and work) more severely. First, many experience the "double shift" phenomenon (Llewelyn and Osborne, 1990; Martin and Roberts, 1984), whereby they have one job outside the home and another in it (as indicated by the statistics on the distribution of household labour, discussed earlier). Second, if they aspire to high involvement in their careers they are exposed to societal expectations that the maternal role should be a priority (McCartney and Phillips, 1988; Schwartz, 1989; Unger and Crawford, 1992; Willard, 1988). You may remember the difficulties faced by successive female US Attorney General nominees early in 1993; these women's career advancement was curtailed (they had to withdraw from consideration for this prestigious post) because of admissions that they had hired illegal immigrants to assist in child care duties – problems that had never arisen when men had been screened for high office. Role conflicts are experienced by the individual but fostered by the society (see Condor, 1986; Marshall, 1986, for interesting discussions of the research implications of role uncertainty among contemporary women).

Women who experience role conflict around these issues often report that they feel they are not living up to their own standards for a good wife or mother (Greenberger and O'Neil, 1993; Willard; 1988) and they find plenty of advice from well-meaning others to exacerbate the conflict. A developmental psychologist who experienced these reports:

> People let you know in subtle and not so subtle ways that you will never be mother of the year. A friend is surprised that your baby is attached to you. A relative asks how you can leave to go to an important conference. A colleague tells you that his wife is staying

home, because they think it's important for their child. It does not feel good to know that others do not think you are a good mother. (McCartney and Phillips, 1988)

One solution to role conflict is to reduce one of the roles. We have already seen from Wetherell et al.'s (1987) data the kinds of advice women can expect to receive from their partners under these circumstances. Many studies show that where a potential conflict arises between family responsibilities and career advancement, women are more likely than men to subordinate the job to the family (Rosin and Korabik, 1990; Russell et al., in press; Unger and Crawford, 1992). This decision can have negative consequences for the woman's occupational status. Women taking part-time employment are deemed to be on the "mommy track" and find themselves treated as less central to their workplace (Barker, 1993; Schwartz, 1989).

What we can conclude here is that all this is for real. Differential achievement between the sexes remains a fact of the late twentieth-century workplace, but one that is only partially explained by current psychological theory and research. Deterministic biological theories of male supremacy do not appear to be consistent with readily available evidence that some women do achieve and excel over men even in the face of strong sociocultural obstacles, and have been doing so increasingly in recent years (see Unger and Crawford, 1992). On the other hand, some of the most straightforward "molding" theories of ubiquitous prejudice against women are not as well supported as first anticipated, and recent directions point to a developmental social explanation, involving a variety of factors including prejudice, barriers, and role conflicts, but also socially shared ideologies and scripts about appropriate role behavior that have been in the process of construction since early childhood and continue to develop through the lifespan. The young woman's Dream makes its contribution to the unfolding of her reality. It would be surprising if it were otherwise, since it would mean that the intensive socialization experiences of the first two decades of a woman's life had had no consequences. In short, by taking only a snapshot of the processes operating upon women as members of the workforce we may run the risk of overlooking the developmental contexts within which these obstacles and prejudices occur.

Summary

A person's work role is central to his or her social definition. Work is central to the life-cycle, in that much of the earlier stages is oriented around preparation for it, and much of adulthood is oriented around doing it and developing within it. Work intersects with gender, and there are stark overall differences in terms of achievement and opportunities at work. Explanations for these differences are sometimes rather glib: they are attributed to biological destiny or social molding. It has been argued here that, while biases in selection and reward may be implicated, the dynamics of gender differentiation in the workplace depend substantially on developmental social psychological processes. These include the expectations and life-cycle plans that individuals acquire in the course of childhood and adolescence and the intersection of these with other developmental processes of adulthood, especially domestic organization and parenthood. The choices, expectations, and goals that men and women formulate with respect to their occupations are themselves influenced by other social factors, including overt and covert messages from others about what is desirable in this domain, and broader constraints deriving from the societal macro-system. People formulate their life plans with reference to socially shared beliefs, and thereby sustain and perpetuate those beliefs.

Conclusions

Adult development involves life-cycle transitions as sketched in theories such as Levinson's, and these intersect with the myriad social processes of involvement with other people and institutions. The life-cycler keeps an eye on the social clock, a sociocultural consensus about what is normative for individuals in particular age groups. The critical social relationships of attachments are not discarded with adulthood but undergo new developments (in the continuing process of separation from parents) and admit new members (as people meet spouses and become parents themselves). Involvement with the world of work is another fundamental step toward adult self-definition and a crucial direction post in the life-course; we have seen that the direction is likely to reflect the individual's gender. These relationships, roles, and the institutions that endorse them have major impact upon how the individual conceives of him or herself and how he or she relates to society. In the face of all these developments, it is difficult to accept the view of some developmentalists that there are no significant changes after the age of 20, and difficult to endorse the working practices of some social psychologists which assume that all interesting social processes are conveniently encapsulated in the undergraduate population.

Further reading

Blank, T. O. (1982) *A Social Psychology of Developing Adults.* New York: Wiley.

A provocative and wide-ranging assessment of the implications of adult development for mainstream social psychology.

Duck S. (1992) *Human Relationships*, 2nd edn. London: Sage.

A wide-ranging account of human relationships, with discussion of communicative processes, emotions, families, friendships, and how these matters can get you into court.

Fletcher, G. J. O. and Fincham, F. D. (eds) (1991) *Cognition in Close Relationships.* Hillsdale, NJ: Erlbaum.

A collection of advanced discussions of research into the social cognitive processes involved in intimate relationships.

George, L. K. (1990) Social structure, social processes, and social-psychological states. In R. H. Binstock and L. K. George (eds), *Handbook of Aging and the Social Sciences*, 3rd edn. San Diego: Academic Press.

An analysis of the interactions between social structure and personal change during later life, with particular emphasis on determinants of wellbeing and the self-concept.

Larson, R. W., Richards, M. H., and Perry-Jenkins, M. (1994) Divergent worlds: the daily emotional experience of mothers and fathers in the domestic and public spheres. *Journal of Personality and Social Psychology*, 67, 1034–46.

If, as discussed in this chapter, family and work roles are so important to a person's social adjustment and development, what influences would we expect these different domains to have on their emotional experiences? How positively do mothers experience domestic versus external work activities? Is the relationship the same for fathers? Larson et al. provide intriguing findings based on a sample of 55 American families.

Levinson, D. (1978) *The Seasons of a Man's Life*. New York: Ballantine.

Whatever your season and whatever your gender, this book repays reading as an overview of theoretical issues in lifespan development, as an impressive example of the successful application of clinical interview techniques, and as an intriguing source of material on the progress of individual lives.

Merriam, S. B. and Clark, M. C. (1993) Work and love: their relationship in adulthood. *International Journal of Behavioral Development*, 16, 609–27.

In this chapter we have seen that love and work are two of the major foci of most adults' lives, but relatively little research has attempted to uncover the relationship between the two over time. Using qualitative and interview data collection techniques, Merriam and Clark identify three different relational patterns of work and love and discuss their significance for personal growth.

Chapter 19

Adulthood II: Middle Age and the Later Years

Mae West was told, on her eightieth birthday, that she looked like a woman half her age:

"Can you imagine that?" she said. "Jesus Christ, she thinks I look forty years old? She said I look half my age, that's forty. Why would someone say that?"

"She meant it as a compliment to you."

"What a vicious bitch. What a thing to say."

(Leonard, Mae West: empress of sex, *1991)*

We turn in this final chapter to two specific periods of the life-cycle: middle age and later adulthood, respectively. Although these phases occupy chronologically as much of the lifespan as does childhood, they have been traditionally much less focal to developmental research. Similarly, because middle-aged and elderly people tend to be less common among undergraduate populations, they have also been less frequently involved in social psychological studies. As we consider recent research into these phases of life, it may become clear that this neglect is unwarranted and disadvantageous to both subdisciplines.

In Western and many other societies, aging is significant. Kite et al. (1991) found that when Americans are asked to describe others, age stereotypes are even more likely to be invoked than are gender stereotypes. Middle age and old age both have stereotypical associations, and neither period is represented popularly as a good time. Notice that childhood has its drawbacks, adolescence is disapproved of, and no one wants to get old: this leaves only a few years for socially approved existence, and you are expected to work yourself toward the grave just to get established during this period. But, as with many other topics we have addressed so far in the lifespan, it turns out that the stereotypes and common-sense assumptions are not wholly valid. In this chapter, we will consider first some of the expectations and tribulations of middle age, discovering that, although there certainly are new developmental demands through these years, they are not invariably the time of despair and loss that is sometimes anticipated. Finally, we turn to the social worlds of older people where again stereotypes abound, new social expectations and influences come to bear, but people's capacities and behavior do not always conform with them.

Middle Age

The Midlife Transition

The midlife transition is one of the most fraught in Western societies. While you can buy birthday cards specifying just about any age, the big sellers are 21 and 40. The 21sts are swamped with messages of promise and optimism, the 40ths are steeped in consolation, ambivalent reassurances that life is just beginning or teasing reminders that it has just ended. It is not surprising that in the midst of this popular and commercial sentiment, many people approach midlife with a sense of dread.

Is there a midlife crisis?

As noted in chapter 18, Levinson (1978) reported that 80 percent of his sample experienced moderate or severe personal turbulence during midlife. Levinson interpreted these feelings as the outcome of psychodynamic tensions among the individual's needs for attachment and separation, the resurfacing of a need for creativity that is often repressed in order to achieve in the workplace, the retrospective comparisons between a man's Dream and the reality that his life has become. In

Levinson's view, these developments – although often painful – are perfectly normal, part of a developmental process through which the person achieves a new stability. He argues that those who do *not* experience the midlife crisis are likely to pay the price later on.

Levinson provides some detailed illustrations of men's midlife crises, and there is little doubt that some individuals do experience this as a period of severe personal difficulty. However, recall that his sample was a small one, and restricted to particular sets of men in just one society. Subsequent research has raised questions about the generality of the feelings that Levinson's subjects experienced.

The notion of a midlife crisis has something in common with that of mother–infant bonding (discussed in chapter 3), or the generation gap (discussed in chapter 15). It is a readily graspable idea, encapsulated in a succinct (and, in this case, rather desperate-sounding) label, and therefore easily transferable from academic psychology to the popular media. One of the virtues of Levinson's (1978) book is that it is very readable, and it strikes many a chord among general readers (perhaps especially among middle-aged men from Western societies). It became a best-seller. As a result, the "midlife crisis" took on a talk show status, which may or may not be a good test of scientific validity.

As the "midlife crisis" found its way from Levinson's pages to *The New York Times*, *Paris Match*, and the *Daily Mirror*, everyone began to feel entitled or obligated to have one. It is easy enough to contract: any and all symptoms of personal dissatisfaction or discomfort experienced by a middle-aged person can be categorized as due to "midlife crisis." The problem of course is that people of all ages suffer occasional depression, self-doubt, sexual uncertainty, misgivings about the future. Are these phenomena more prevalent or more intense among the middle-aged?

They certainly were in several of Levinson's subjects, but other research indicates that most periods of life are experienced as difficult by some people (Vaillant, 1977). Uncertainty about the direction of one's life and the meaning of achievements is often experienced in *early* career (Baruch et al., 1983; Costa and McCrae, 1980). Several studies have found that substantial proportions of middle-aged people actually feel *more* positive about this phase of their life than earlier ones (Clausen, 1981; Long and Porter, 1984). Self-report questionnaire studies with somewhat larger samples than Levinson's indicate that, while many people acknowledge some reassessment in middle-age, only about 12 percent feel that they have experienced a crisis (Farrell and Rosenberg, 1981). In short, the midlife crisis does not appear to be as universal as Levinson's data first indicated, and it may be that the time and the extent to which people experience uncomfortable self-assessments is subject to variability as a function of personality, social context, and cohort.

Nevertheless, even if midlife is not invariably experienced as traumatic, it does involve shifts in the individual's perceptions of self and relations to others. At the personal level, a fundamental social cognitive development of middle age is the realization that the final authority for life rests with the individual, and many people at this stage find that the array of life choices made and remaining becomes more salient (Gould, 1978; Levinson, 1978; McAdams, 1992; Rodeheaver and Datan, 1981). Middle age also involves changes in relationship structures within the family.

Midlife and the family

Within the family, middle-aged adults often discover that their own development depends in part upon the development of their children (Pratt and Norris, 1994; Rodeheaver and Datan, 1981; Troll, 1989). Parents have to adjust to the fact that as their own physical strengths and attractions may be going into decline, those of their adolescent children will be increasing. Parents also have to come to terms with the impending absence or relentless presence of their maturing offspring. Rodeheaver and Datan (1987) argue that both of these states – the empty and crowded nest, respectively – lead to developmental issues for the middle-aged parents.

The empty nest   The empty nest refers to the period following the departure of grown-up children. Clearly, this incurs basic changes in family structure and relations, and it is popularly associated with distress and a sense of psychological emptiness for the parents, especially the mother. Research demonstrates to the contrary that the empty nest phenomenon is not experienced as negative by a majority. Many find the conclusion of childrearing responsibilities liberating, and welcome the opportunities for closer relationship with the partner, and the scope for personal fulfillment through new work roles or a return to education (Cooper and Gutmann, 1987; Lowenthal and Chiriboga, 1972). Recent research indicates that the extent to which women report empty nest distress is cohort-related, and more typical of women who reach maturity during historical periods when traditional roles are emphasized (Adelmann et al., 1989). The upshot of most investigations of this topic is clear: if you are a young college-aged student who has recently left your nest, and are worried about how the wrinklies are coping without you, you are probably suffering from a severe dose of adolescent egocentrism (see chapter 15). Back home, they are doing fine, and will be happier still when you stop hassling them for money.

The crowded nest   For many contemporary parents, a greater problem may be the "crowded nest" (Datan, 1980): the children grow up, but opt *not* to leave home. Providing a telling example of the impact of the macro-system on lifespan development, in economies where house prices are beyond the reach of younger generations, crowded nests proliferate and young people reside with their parents into their mid-twenties and beyond (Glick and Lin, 1986). One reason that the crowded nest may be problematic is that it defies the dictates of the social clock established by the preceding generations, which holds that by late middle age adults can expect to be freed of their dependents. Another may be that, although the parent–child relationship has been becoming less vertical (in Hartup's terms; see chapter 4) since the child's adolescence, it is difficult for the older party to adjust to virtual horizontal equality, especially since in material respects the parents are still doing much of the providing. Research confirms that there are many conflicts between middle-aged parents and their adult children who live at home, and these often relate to matters of personal responsibility (such as domestic chores, the younger person's hours or sex life) that might reflect parental difficulty in adjusting to their offsprings' autonomy (Clemens and Axelson, 1985).

Midlife and Gender

As might be expected in light of the substantial differences in male and female life-courses, midlife is experienced somewhat differently according to sex. This reflects both sociocultural factors, especially stereotypes about middle-aged women and men, and biological factors, such as the menopause (which itself is subject to socioculturally determined expectations).

Social stereotypes and midlife

Social stereotypes of different age groups are prevalent, though subject to cultural and gender differences. The social clock is imposed more stringently upon women than men. Images and stars in the mass media illustrate the assumption that males can be perceived as retaining attractiveness and prestige until an older age than women (Durkin, 1986a). When middle-aged people remarry, it tends to be considered socially acceptable, even admirable, for men to choose wives considerably younger than themselves, but not for women to select substantially younger partners (Unger and Crawford, 1992). Articles about Elizabeth Taylor, Joan Collins, and Cher in the popular press, for instance, point continuously to the 20 or so years' discrepancy between their ages and those of their current male partners, often with the implication that some crucial social boundary has been transgressed. The American actor Glenn Close had the gossip columnists burbling in 1995 when she announced a double whammy: planning to marry a man who was both a few years younger than her *and* considerably less wealthy. (As was explained in chapter 15, life isn't fair.)

In English-speaking cultures, the phrase "mutton dressed as lamb" is used commonly to derogate middle-aged or older women who dress fashionably. Tina Turner is invariably described in the press as an "aging rock granny" as though to highlight an assumed incongruence between middle age and the vigor of her music and stage performances. Elsewhere, these kinds of constraints are still more direct. For example, among traditional Greek islanders, there is a widespread expectation that older women should wear subdued and dark clothes, and widows should wear black continuously. Beyene (1989, p. 124) recounts an instance of the ways in which these pressures are experienced and accommodated:

> one of the women in the village who was in her early fifties, bought a burgundy blouse from a vendor who came to Stira once a week. Even though the color looked nice on her, a week later she exchanged the blouse for a dark blue one because she was afraid that people would ridicule her for wearing a color inappropriate for her age.

Why are there stronger prohibitions upon middle-aged women's sexual and personal expression than on middle-aged men's? We can point to powerful social pressures at work, but why do they arise in the first place? A sociobiological explanation would be that because middle-aged women are less able to contribute to the reproductive process, social groups act to distance them from the mating arena – better for young men to find fertile young partners. Men, by contrast, have the advantage that they can continue to father children until much later in life and so their dalliances with younger females are approved. Barbra Streisand's close friendship with André Agassi seemed to incite grave concern in the gossip columns, perhaps because it threatened to violate these traditions: athletic young males are expected to hunt younger females and mature women should content themselves with their family responsibilities.

On the other hand, since women have been traditionally disadvantaged in terms of gaining economic autonomy it follows that a majority of middle-aged women will have lower economic status than male counterparts and therefore be rated as a weaker bet in the competition for resources. This theory would predict that the older women who do attract younger men will be those who have compensating economic merits, though it probably still helps to look like Cher, who makes sure she does. Another possibility is that since the traditional male role is associated with dominance and provider responsibilities, a young man who enters a partnership with an older woman may be perceived as foregoing central criteria of his gender role identity, whereas a young woman attaching herself to an older man is assumed to be complying with the traditional role of subordination.

These explanations give different weight to inherited social characteristics versus socially constructed role expectations, but they may not be mutually exclusive. As has been stressed in previous discussions of gender relations, sociobiological, sociocultural, and social cognitive accounts are often compatible with the same data, and it is possible to conceive of theoretical syntheses. Many issues which arise here remain open to future research.

Additional caregiving responsibilities for midlife women

Role conflict for women was considered in chapter 18 with respect to family and occupational activities. An extra dimension to many women's responsibilities in midlife occurs if their parents' or other elderly relatives' health declines in old age. At this point, the "double shift" can become a triple shift. Traditional expectations about caregiving responsibilities lead many women into patterns of *serial caregiving* (Logue, 1993), whereby they are providing domestic support not only to their husband, children and elderly relative, but then to other elderly relatives. For example, Logue reviews findings that many women help to take care of their ill father, and then after his death take care of their widowed mother. These responsibilities incur considerable stress, and this takes its toll on women's health and sometimes their work performance – or their employer's perceptions of their work performance (Logue, 1993). Doress-Waters (1994) describes the syndrome as a "caregiving pile-up." Although some men may undertake similar responsibilities, organization of work and family roles, females' greater involvement in family relationships, and socially shared expectations about the female life-cycle, all converge to promote the likelihood that women will become the primary serial caregivers. Logue comments that the "mommy track" keeps running long after a mother has completed her own childrearing tasks.

The menopause

For many Western women, menopause is perceived negatively and associated with psychosomatic distress. Neugarten et al. (1963) surveyed the beliefs of young American women (in their 20s and 30s) about menopause, and found that about half of their sample anticipated that it would lead to depression and marital difficulties. Carroll (1983) asked women to identify the first thing that came to mind when they heard the word "menopause" and found that a high proportion of responses included references to loss of youth, depression, hot flashes, empty nest, over-the-hill, and – not to be excluded from something Levinson's interpreters had just popularized for men – midlife crisis. However, the event itself proves to be somewhat more variable. While some women certainly do experience negative physiological symptoms during this transition, a majority of those who have actually passed through it regard it retrospectively as a relatively minor transition, in many cases a positive one (Neugarten et al., 1963).

Cross-cultural evidence reveals once again that a transition assumed within some Western cultures to be inevitably uncomfortable is actually regarded – and experienced – very differently in different locations (Beyene, 1989; Griffen, 1982). Beyene (1989) reports that among the Mayan Indian people of Yacatan, Mexico, it is very rare for women to experience any negative symptoms during menopause. Indeed, Beyene found that medical workers whom she interviewed were surprised that anyone would expect otherwise:

> Dona Conchita [a midwife] seemed puzzled by my questions. She did not understand why I was probing to find out if women had any discomfort or problems at this stage. She thought that I was trying to tell her that menopause was abnormal, so she threw the question back at me and wanted to know about women where I lived. (p. 118)

Beyene found that Mayanese village women simply did not know what hot flashes were (p. 122), creating something of a problem for biologically based, medical models which assume universal effects of hormonal changes. Menopause in the Yacatan community is not considered a development to lament but the women regard menstruation as a nuisance, and its cessation liberating. Beyene's conclusions are very similar to those suggested when we considered the menarche (chapter 15), indicating that a range of biocultural factors (environment, diet, fertility patterns) interact with socially shared interpretations and expectations.

Summary

Midlife is a period of physical and social changes, and it is a period subject to strong sociocultural expectations. Like adolescence, it is a somewhat stigmatized phase, with lay stereotypes and mass media images depicting it as a time of profound crisis and severe loss. Research findings are rather mixed on the question of whether the supposed midlife crisis is experienced universally, but there is little support for the notion that such midlife reassessments as may occur are typically pathological:

some proportion of middle-aged people may experience some turbulence but most appear to emerge from the transition feeling relatively positive about themselves. There are pressures upon middle-aged people to conform to the criteria of the local social clock, to organize their social lives, even to select their clothes according to what is deemed appropriate. There are often major changes in the family lives of middle-aged people, reflecting altered relationships with their now adult or near-adult children. There are biological changes, too, though interesting evidence suggests that much of the impact of these will depend upon how they are interpreted within a particular sociocultural context. Overall, midlife is a period of change and readjustment but, as we have seen many times in earlier chapters, the nature and consequence of the changes are integrally interwoven with the individual's social relationships and roles.

Development in Later Life

Aging is a biological fact, but its impact upon the individual and her or his life is mediated by a number of social and societal factors. These include the cultural norms and expectations about the consequences and correlates of age (the social clock again) as well as state-, market-, and family-related institutions (Hagestad, 1990; Mayer and Muller, 1986; O'Rand, 1990; Pratt and Norris, 1994). For example, *when* a person withdraws from the workforce is influenced by state regulations (such as statutory retirement ages and pension entitlements), by market forces (which dictate that some positions or skills are surplus to requirements, and which affect the viability of the retiree's finances), and by her or his partner's retirement (which may prompt joint retirement, or necessitate that the employee remain in the workforce for as long as possible to compensate for the lost income of the retired spouse). As with every other stage of the life-cycle, the experiences of becoming elderly are interwoven with changes in interpersonal relations and in the socially shared expectations and institutional constraints of the broader society. In this final section, we will consider just a few of these factors, focusing on the implications of aging for social relations.

Two overriding points may be made about developmental social psychology and older people. First, it is useful to recall here some of the concerns about a social psychology based predominantly upon the investigation of undergraduates (chapter 1). Blank (1982) argues that research with the elderly is almost bound to improve the ecological validity of social psychology, partly because it draws the researcher out of the laboratory – it is easier to study older people in their usual habitats than on campus – and partly because it tends to generate questions of practical import (such as retirement, widowhood). Second, if we think back to aspects of development from childhood and adulthood, we see enormous variation in important respects. People have different characteristics, grow up in different circumstances, are subject to different influences, make different choices and decisions, and pursue different goals with varying degrees of success. It is hardly to be expected that the latter phases of these processes should result in homogeneity: there is a great deal of diversity among older people (Pratt and Norris, 1994). It remains the case that social psychological research into older people and the phenomena of aging is a minority pursuit, but there is plenty of evidence to support Blank's view that a developmental social psychology will be enriched by further study of people beyond midlife.

Aging and Culture

The meaning of age varies dramatically across cultures, from being virtually irrelevant in some to being highly elaborated in others (Fry, 1985; Keith, 1990; Rosenmays, 1985; Tout, 1989). In many traditional societies, specific chronological age has little meaning, partly because the years are not counted. In some cases, social seniority is determined not by age but by generation; in instances where the two conflict (for example, a biological aunt is younger than her niece) then generation counts for more than years (Keith, 1990, p. 96). On the other hand, Keith points out that in societies which have organized citizenship relations that transcend kinship ties (such as the advanced industrial nations), chronological age is a significant basis for social differentiation.

The values attached to age also vary with culture and with role. When President Ronald Reagan was in his 70s, public criticism often centered on his age and alleged senility as much as his policies (this was unfair: President Reagan's intellect remained unchanged with age). If a person in his 70s finds his way into the Chinese government, he is viewed suspiciously by his seniors because youngsters are felt to be prone to hot-heatedness. Fry (1985) and Tout (1989) review historical and anthropological evidence to show that in many societies elderly people have retained status, authority, and active social involvement, but that these characteristics are modified by economic stresses. For example, nomadic peoples tend to be less empathetic toward their elderly, because with increasing frailty they pose an encumbrance on the mobility of the community; some traditional cultures have become less caring toward the elderly since Western religions (with self-help ethics) were imposed; many societies in Africa, South America, and Asia have undergone rapid social changes in recent years, leading to the breakdown of the extended family and the reduction of care for older members. To take an extreme example, the Ik people of Uganda, who suffered major economic and social upheavals, became so hostile to their elderly that they resented the interventions of outsiders who offered assistance and medication which belonged, in their view, to the living not the "dead" (Turnbull, 1989).

Even within Western societies of broadly comparable economic conditions, there is variation in attitudes and policies toward the elderly. In Europe, for instance, they range from the view in Greece that people tend to be full of vigor into their late 70s and should properly be involved in and cared for by the family (Amira, 1990) to the Danish system which maintains a level of state-funded institutional support that would seem generous by most comparisons yet which leads to structural separation from relatives and greater problems of loneliness among the elderly (Jamieson, 1990). In the US and other advanced nations, there is a growing focus on older people because of the demographic fact that they will continue to increase as a proportion of the population over the next few decades. This raises a bottom-line question not dissimilar to the Ik's concerns: "Can we continue to spend up to 26 per cent of the federal budget on benefits and services to an older population?" (Torres-Gil, 1992, p. 2). Seeking answers to this question is leading to a reassessment of the status, needs, and capacities of the elderly. In the West, this has to begin from the premise that older people are often the targets of negative stereotypes and beliefs.

Stereotypes of the Elderly

It was noted earlier that middle age is a moderately stigmatized period of the life cycle. As you might expect, stereotypes of the elderly are still more negative. Becoming old is considered such a liability that, from around the age 30 transition, people are complimented on *not* looking their age. This is not necessarily always welcome, as Mae West illustrates above, but try telling a Western adult that he or she looks several years *older* than his or her chronological age. While this advice would be received positively by many adolescents, studies of Americans have found that when adults are asked to identify their subjective age (i.e., the age that they feel they are, feel they look, and would most prefer to be) then those in the middle to elderly years tend to specify an age some years below their actual chronological age (Barnes-Farrell and Piotrowski, 1989; Montepare and Lachman, 1989). Becoming elderly is particularly resisted, and stronger reluctance to acknowledge chronological age is found among females.

The stereotypes that people hold of the elderly are not wholly negative. Schmidt and Boland (1986) found that there are multiple stereotypes, ranging from "perfect grandparent," "sage" at the positive end to "bag lady," "vagrant," "shrew" at the negative. Obtaining similar findings, Hummert (1990) found that younger adults do not see the negative stereotypes of the elderly as necessarily typical of all elderly. Even so, there are many negative attributes associated with aging, and stereotypes and attitudes toward older people are manifest in many quarters. For example, the entertainment media demonstrate a common response to stigmatized groups: they ignore them. Not very many older people appear in the entertainment media, and their frequency in television is proportionately less than their frequency in society (Davis and Davis, 1985; Huston et al., 1992). Where they are included, the images that are conveyed are often unfavorable (Gibson, 1993). If the *Golden Girls* come to mind as something of an exception, it is because they *are* an exception – the representation of older women as intelligent, witty and sociable is not widespread in the media. More commonly, images of older women are used in advertising as fear-inducers to stimulate younger women to purchase a skin product, commence a diet, or submit to liposuction.

Stereotypes of the elderly tend to include negative components irrespective of the age group of the perceiver, though children's and adolescents' stereotypes of older people are particularly unfavorable (Ahammer and Baltes, 1972; Goldman and Goldman, 1981). The Goldmans interviewed over 800 children, aged 5–15 years from Australia, England, Sweden, and the US about their views of old age. There were variations among samples, but two general patterns were very clear: children of all ages were much more likely to say negative things about the elderly than positive, and this tendency became even stronger with age of interviewee. Between 90 and 100 percent of 15-year-olds described the old in negative terms.

The authors comment that the figures "do not convey the revulsion and often disgust expressed about old age by many children of all ages. Descriptions of wrinkled skin, sickness, feebleness and increasing fragility were often accompanied by grimaces and emotional negativisms" (p. 408). Negativity was not restricted to physical descriptions, but also included psychological attributes (moody, bad tempered, impatient, falling behind the times, slow to understand or react), and social/emotional characteristics (isolation, going to bed early, dependence, withdrawal, financially restricted). The causes of aging were predominantly seen as biologically based ("They've spent their time, spent their use. Their body is now very old and worn out like a biro, when it comes to an end just throw it away", 15-year-old English boy).

Explanations of negativity toward the aged

Why is old age perceived as a liability in our societies? One reason may be that older people are generally regarded as less physically attractive (Jackson, 1992), and, as we have seen, attractiveness is associated with social rewards in many societies. Mae West, at 80, may have resented being taken for a 40-year-old but none the less in her later years she spent up to several hours a day putting on make-up and squeezing into corsets. Jackson points out that prejudice against the elderly and the physical associations of old age is consistent with sociobiological arguments that as people lose their reproductive capacities (which of course correlates with looking older) then their perceived social worth diminishes.

Other reasons may include the older person's changing status with respect to both the outside world of work, and the family. When a person retires, he or she has diminished authority, a less clear economic role, and possibly reduced income; these are important criteria of personal status in Western societies. Similarly, within the family, mature status is typically associated with heading (or heading jointly) a nuclear unit (Keith, 1990). Younger adults orient their social activities with a view to entering such arrangements (i.e., to choosing a partner) and then devote the central chunk of adulthood to establishing and maintaining the unit. But in due course, the unit fragments as the offspring set off to repeat the cycle, and this leaves the older people bereft of the social structures that have been so important to their lives.

Social consequences of stereotypes and expectations of the elderly

Stereotypes of old people, their characteristics and limitations, appear to influence how other people evaluate and interact with them, but the relationship is not always as straightforward as might initially be predicted. There is some evidence that the stereotypes evoked lead to negative outcomes in certain contexts. In an experimental study Avolio and Barrett (1987) found that subjects evaluating a tape-recorded interviewee for a supervisory position were less favorable when told the candidate was aged 59 than when told he was 32. However, the fact that we know the negative stereotypes does not necessarily mean that we perceive all actual instances of members of a social category as conforming to them. For example, the demonstration that the mass medium of television represents a sector of the population negatively does not predict that attitudes of viewers correspond. Wober and Gunter (1982) investigated a sample of British adults' impressions of old people in real life and in TV and found little evidence of a relationship between the two, a finding which suggests that viewers are able to form their own opinions, presumably based on sources of information other than television (such as real people).

One might suspect that not all of Goldman and Goldman's (1981) young subjects, who were so repulsed by their images of old age, would actually hold all the old people they *knew* (such as their grandparents) in such low regard. Few children maintain the strict stereotype–behavior correspondence of the young Ik boy, described by Turnbull (1989), who entertained his friends by practicing with drumsticks on his elderly grandfather's bald head and repaid the old man's irritating frailties by hitting him so hard that he collapsed. Most studies in European and North American societies find that grandparents are described by children and adolescents in predominantly positive terms and that interactions with them are valued (Battistelli and Farneti, 1991; Ruoppila, 1991; Tyszkowa, 1991; Werner, 1991). Similarly, research indicates that while old people are themselves prone to hold negative views of old people, they reserve the negatives for *other* old people rather than accepting them as accurate self-descriptors (Blythe, 1979; Luszcz and Fitzgerald, 1986).

Furthermore, although social appraisals vary according to the age of the target, this does not invariably lead to overt negativity toward the elderly. Blank (1982) points out that hostile attributions are made of some people receiving state welfare (who are seen as bums, scroungers, freeloaders, etc.), but if the recipients are elderly, then these negative evaluations are much less likely. However, Blank suggests that older people are subject instead to "love prejudice," such that their entitlements may be acknowledged but at the price that they are regarded as less competent and less autonomous because of their perceived dependency. Recall from chapter 13 that a potential downside of prosocial behavior is that it can undermine the self-esteem of those being helped. An illustration of love prejudice is provided in a newspaper advertisement for a British charity, described by P. K. Smith (1991), in which a frail, white-haired elderly woman is depicted, alongside the slogan: "Adopt a granny: Help the Aged." Another example can be found in lifespan developmental texts, which sometimes provide the supposedly reassuring news that older people can still have sexual relations "with dignity." Since when has dignity been a criterion?

Love prejudice appears to be particularly marked in contexts involving the provision of services for the elderly. Coupland and Coupland (1990) report that in interactions they studied between older women (aged 70–87) and women in their thirties, the older participants spoke about painful topics (ill health, loneliness, bereavement, etc.) 16 percent of the time, seemingly supporting the stereotype that the elderly are miserable, and preoccupied with negative experiences. However, the researchers report that closer inspection reveals that the *younger* women play an active role in eliciting this information from them, either by raising painful issues directly or by protracting the topic when it comes into the conversation. Similarly, Revenson (1989) found that doctors with high contact with elderly patients rated older people as less well adjusted and in greater need of support than did low contact doctors. It may be that the social stereotype guides both participants toward areas of pain and adjustment difficulties, and renders them especially salient when they crop up.

Social Comparisons and Self-esteem among the Elderly

Bandura (1986) suggests that, because of cohort shifts in social experiences and skill practice, older people who make social comparisons with younger generations are at greater risk of being forced to negative inferences about their own self-efficacy than are their peers who compare their performance with their own earlier abilities. However, this may depend upon the domain under consideration. As discussed earlier, Ruble and Frey (1991) propose that people's social comparison reference points vary as a function of several factors, including how much skill they have in the relevant activity, how important it is to them, the availability of comparative information, and the implications of each type of comparison for self-esteem.

For example, they point out that people in late middle age who have attained a plateau in one area of their lives (such as their work role) sometimes take up new activities (such as leisure pursuits) as sources of new challenges. In some cases, these individuals seek quite deliberately to compare themselves with younger people, and may find the comparison rewarding. Ruble and Frey quote a 65-year-old interviewee, from a study of people who took up running in their later years, who said that after watching participants in a 10km race she "wanted to see if ladies my age could do it" (1991, p. 81).

There is little doubt of the availability and dissemination of negative stereotypes of the elderly in Western societies, but it would be an oversimplification to infer that this means that all social interactions with the elderly are correspondingly negative, or that the elderly invariably succumb to socially shared beliefs about their stage of life and regard themselves as discarded or peripheral. Many older people adjust very positively to changes in themselves and their circumstances (Baltes and Baltes, 1990; Gibson, 1993; Lerner and Gignac, 1992; Pratt and Norris, 1994). In fact, studies of self-esteem among the elderly reveal that it does not diminish with age, and may even increase moderately compared to earlier years (Baltes and Baltes, 1990; Bengston et al., 1985; Brandtstadter et al., 1993). Baltes and Baltes (1990) suggest several reasons for this finding, including the possibilities that levels of aspiration change through the life-cycle, and that social comparison processes may lead older people to orient their comparison standards to their peers rather than the younger population. As with most social processes, there are tensions between others' expectations and individuals' development, self-perceptions, capacities, and goals.

Physical, Cognitive, and Linguistic Developments in Old Age

When we considered stereotypes of adolescents in chapter 15, we found that in many respects the empirical evidence failed to support the mythology. Very similar findings emerge with respect to beliefs about the elderly. Researchers have investigated physical changes, cognitive abilities, and linguistic capacities in the elderly.

Physical changes

Tout (1989) remarks that aging is sometimes regarded as a kind of prolonged terminal illness with no cure, and as we saw above lay stereotypes often associate old age with sickness, continuous decline, and diminished physical and mental capacities. Although there are certainly gradual reductions in physical capacities with age, in contemporary Western societies a majority of old people actually enjoy good health and are not the disproportionate drain on medical services that is widely assumed (Rowland, 1991; Torres-Gil, 1992; Tout, 1989). Davis and Davis (1985) observe that poor health increases with age among fictional TV characters on a markedly greater scale than it does among elderly people in the real world. Not surprisingly, health does tend to vary with socioeconomic status, to the disadvantage of the poor, and some illnesses become more common among the elderly, not as a direct result of chronological advancement but as a consequence of health risks undertaken earlier in life (e.g., smoking, excessive sun exposure).

Cognitive changes

Similarly, it is something of a myth that all old people suffer from fundamental intellectual decline (Baltes and Schaie, 1976). Older people do tend to perform less well than younger adults on tasks dependent upon processing speed (Luszcz, 1992; Salthouse, 1990), and cross-sectional studies of mental abilities usually report moderately lower scores in the elderly. However, there are several reasons for pausing before assuming that serious reductions in intellectual performance are inevitable with age.

First, intelligent behavior in the real world typically involves several capacities, and people may be able often to compensate for diminutions in one (say, processing speed) by adjustments in another (say, judgments based on experience). Second, cross-sectional comparisons of different age groups may confound age differences with cohort effects (Baltes, 1987). That is, a sample of contemporary old people may have experienced a very different developmental context, and very different educational services, from those of a sample of contemporary young adults; supposed "IQ" differences between such samples may actually reflect differences in familiarity and practice. In a longitudinal study, Schaie and Hertzog (1983) compared groups of Americans born in different decades, testing their performance on a series of mental ability tests when they reached particular age ranges. These investigators found that cohort effects were as strong as age effects.

Third, changes in performance with age appear to be mitigated by practice. Older people who maintain active use of a skill or ability tend to continue to perform well in it, in some cases better than younger people who have not practiced (Baltes et al., 1986; Shaie, 1983, 1990).

Fourth, there are some aspects of intellectual performance – particularly what is sometimes called "crystallized intelligence" (the ability to store and manipulate learned information) – which gradually *increase* with age through adulthood and often remain high well into old age (Baltes and Baltes, 1990; Horn and Donaldson, 1980).

Social cognitive abilities provide a good example of intellectual capacities that may be maintained or actually increase with age. As seen in earlier chapters, the social cognitive competencies that underlie interpersonal understanding have a long developmental history. In some respects, the achievements of youth provide a basis for continuity in social understanding in adult life. For example, studies of person perception in adulthood reveal that the emphasis on psychological characteristics shows little change from young adulthood to old age (Dolen and Bearison, 1982; Fitzgerald and Martin-Louer, 1983–84; Pratt and Norris, 1994). On the other hand, adult life affords many opportunities to experience the complexity of the social environment, and the diversity of viewpoints and interests within it. Blanchard-Fields (1986) found that in generating solutions to hypothetical interpersonal problems adolescents were prone to focus on one reading of the conflict, while middle-aged adults showed sensitivity to both perspectives and strove to provide answers that met both parties' needs. Pratt et al. (1987), comparing young, middle-aged and older adults' responses to moral dilemma tasks found no evidence of decline with age, but did obtain some evidence of increasingly complex reasoning about personal moral dilemmas among the oldest group (60–75 years).

Overall, older people's intellectual capacities are rarely the wasteland that lay stereotypes represent. Although there may well be changes in the relative strengths of different abilities and variations in the opportunities and motivations to use them (Baltes et al., 1986), researchers of the aged have arrived at similar conclusions to those of recent investigators of infants: it is quite surprising what subjects at these extremes of the lifespan can do!

Language and the elderly

It was stressed in chapter 6 that language is central to social being. It is sometimes claimed that language abilities decline in later years, and there is evidence that elderly individuals (mid-70s onwards) perform less well than younger people on some psycholinguistic tasks, particularly those which involve speed and substantial memory or inferential demands (Coupland and Coupland, 1990; Pratt and Norris, 1994; Schaie, 1983). However, as the Couplands comment, age effects have not been obtained consistently, and they are rarely large. Although some elderly individuals suffering from specific impairments may have linguistic problems, most older people maintain good language ability.

But language is social and this means that *others'* beliefs and attitudes may be reflected in the linguistic experiences of older people. There is evidence from experimental social psychological studies that older speakers are perceived less favorably than younger speakers, even when other features (such as content) are held constant (Ryan and Laurie, 1990). Furthermore, when people talk to the elderly, the "old dear syndrome" (Blank, 1982) often comes clearly into play. Speech to older people exhibits features similar to those found in parentese (speech to young children; see chapter 7). People tend to use more questions and repetitions than when talking to younger adults, to raise their pitch and volume, and to reduce the complexity of their syntax (Ashburn and Gordon, 1981; Caporael, 1981, Caporael and Culbertson, 1986; Montepare et al., 1992). Coupland and Coupland (1990) suggest that this varies according to context and role. For example, nurses may be especially prone to adopt such a speech style as a function of their practical concerns rather than interpersonal sensitivities.

Using the framework of Giles's accommodation theory (see Thakerar et al., 1982, and chapter 7), the Couplands propose that the extent to which a speaker addressing the elderly over-accommodates or under-accommodates may contribute directly to intergenerational conflicts and problems. Over-accommodation can lead to the elderly addressee feeling demeaned (spoken to like a child); under-accommodation can lead to excessively regulative talk, with the speaker failing to give sufficient attention to the older person's needs. Consistent with this interpretation, Ryan et al. (1991) found that when adults caring for the elderly use patronizing speech modifications (such as "Poor dear," "Good girl") then the carers are perceived as less respectful and less nurturant.

However, there is at least one more area of language use in which older people may have decided strengths, and that is oral narrative production (Kemper et al., 1990; Pratt and Norris, 1994). Narratives involve the schematic organization of large amounts of verbal information. Kemper et al. (1990) found that older adults' personal narratives tended to be rated as of better quality than those of young adults. Pratt and Norris (1994) point out that although there is growing evidence of special competence among older people in this respect, it may be a form of competence which is becoming devalued in contemporary societies by the ever-increasing presence of mass media such as television and radio.

In sum, there are changes and adjustments in respect of physical, mental, and linguistic capacities in older adulthood, but an overriding conclusion has to be that, while subject to considerable individual differences, these developments are not normally as dramatic as stereotypes of the elderly convey. Individual differences reflect a variety of factors, including cohort, experiences, health, and personal choices. All of these developments take place in social contexts which influence what opportunities are available and what is perceived as normative.

Relating to Society and Social Life in the Later Years

As noted earlier, the point at which a person withdraws from the workforce is influenced by a combination of societal, interpersonal, and personal considerations. For most, retirement does involve major changes. Not surprisingly, given the centrality of work role to social identity and to the organization of daily life, many people experience retirement as a time of loss (Anson et al., 1989; Atchley, 1991). On the other hand, there are potential benefits to leaving work, including liberation from disliked aspects of the job, increased leisure time, and the possibility of spending more time with the family; some of the work-related achievement goals of earlier phases of adulthood may be far less salient toward the end of working life (Levinson, 1978), and new goals may replace them (Heckhausen, 1986). People approaching retirement are likely to be aware of both the losses and gains. Pratt and Norris (1994) suggest that many retired people enter a kind of psychosocial moratorium analogous to that experienced by adolescents formulating an identity (chapter 15). Just like young people preparing for a new phase of life, retirees explore their options, try out new activities, reconsider who they are and what they want out of life.

Anson et al. (1989) reasoned that men and women weighing up these factors could be expected to arrive at different conclusions. Specifically, they predicted that both sexes would see retirement as incurring losses, but that women would perceive greater benefits, partly because retirement spells an end to the role conflict and "double shift" experienced by many female employees (see chapter 18), and partly because women's traditionally greater involvement in family life would mean that they could expect to find it easier and more rewarding to spend more time in family activities. Consistent with these predictions, in a large sample of Israeli people tested two months prior to retirement, Anson et al. (1989) found no evidence of sex differences in attitudes toward *losses* in retirement: both sexes anticipated major losses. There were differences between the sexes in terms of expectations of *gains* due to retirement. Here, as predicted, women had more positive attitudes than men.

One consequence of the changes of old age is that some elderly people in Western societies begin to *disengage* from social and physical involvement (Cumming and Henry, 1961). Cumming and Henry, who studied disengagement processes among a sample of elderly Americans, represented this process as a developmental inevitability, something that people elect for as they become aware of their declining capacities and the nearness of death. Indeed, they maintained that this was the optimal mode of adjustment to old age. In contrast, as indicated earlier, research in other cultures shows that some elderly people retain status and involvement (for example, as chiefs and other leaders) for a very long time (Tout, 1989). Even among Western societies, such as Australia, Britain, New Zealand, and North America, disengagement does not appear to be the norm among elderly people, who often maintain high social involvement through community organizations and churches (Braithwaite, 1992; Koenig, 1992; Peterson, 1989; Pratt and Norris, 1994). In Canadian research, Norris (1993) obtained no evidence of a pervasive negative impact of retirement on wellbeing and life satisfaction. In an American study, Langer and Rodin (1976) found that the extent to which the elderly residents of nursing homes were encouraged to take responsibility for their own care was significantly related to wellbeing and longevity (active people fared better than disengaged). Similarly, a study of several thousand elderly Japanese people found that individuals who maintained a high level of physical activity tended to score highest on measures of morale and life satisfaction (Yaguchi et al., 1987).

Two variables which stand out as critical to wellbeing and satisfaction in the later stages of the lifespan are two which we have seen are important from infancy onwards, namely personal control and social involvement (Braithwaite, 1992; Gurin and Brim, 1984; Nurmi et al., 1992). Higher self-efficacy is associated with wellbeing among the elderly (Holahan and Holahan, 1987; Pratt and Norris, 1994). When asked to identify the most important considerations of quality of life, older people consistently place relationships, social networks, and health at the top of their lists (Ferris and Branston, 1994). Maintenance of the key relationships, such as spouse, siblings, children, grandchildren, and friends has been found in numerous studies to be closely associated with life satisfaction and health (Arber and Evandrou, 1993; Cicirelli, 1989; George, 1990; Tomlin and Passman, 1989; Wright, 1994).

In short, remaining an actively involved social being is as important in later life as at any earlier stage, although the areas of life (work, family, community, other leisure) in which an individual prefers to be active are subject to individual differences. These findings are important in the light of the increasing proportions of Western populations which will live to an old age in coming decades (Hagestad, 1990; Torres-Gil, 1992). Hagestad (1990) points out that, with improved health services and better nutrition, large numbers of people now have retirements which last around as long as one-half of their active working lives. This makes retirement and old age important phases of the lifespan on a historically unprecedented scale: a very clear example of the effects of large-scale societal changes on individuals' lives. As we have seen, the contexts within which an older person's social life is conducted are circumscribed by social expectations and prejudices.

Mass Media Use by the Elderly

One other area of societal involvement which should be mentioned concerns media use, especially television, which plays an important part in the daily lives of most contemporary older people (Fouts, 1989; Huston et al., 1992; Rubin and Rubin, 1982; Wober and Gunter, 1988). Fouts (1989) points out that amount of television viewing is related curvilinearly to age, with the largest amounts of viewing in the first and last few years of life. Based on surveys of television use among the elderly, Fouts shows that viewing during this phase of the lifespan is, like earlier viewing, a purposeful activity reflecting the individual's interests, needs, and social context. For example, elderly people with high social involvement tend to watch television both as a social activity in itself (i.e., with friends or family) and as a source of information and ideas which then feed into her or his social life; people with lower levels of life satisfaction, mobility, and social involvement tend to use television more as a means of passing time and as a source of vicarious companionship through which they experience "parasocial interaction," or the illusion that they are making contact with other people (Davis and Kubey, 1982). In general, older viewers like television though, like other viewers, they select particular types of content that appeal to them (Huston et al., 1992; Wober and Gunter, 1988). For example, older people often report liking older stars, such as Bob Hope, Lawrence Welk, and George Burns (Davis and Kubey, 1982), although whether this is because the stars are elderly or because they have been familiar to the viewer for a long time is less easily determined.

Mares and Cantor (1992) found that elderly (over 70 years) television viewers differed in their reactions to television depictions of old people. Elderly subjects who were lonely and subjects who were not lonely watched materials including lonely or nonlonely elderly people. Lonely subjects preferred lonely characters and felt better after they had watched them; nonlonely subjects preferred nonlonely characters. The increased happiness among the lonely subjects after viewing lonely stereotypes on TV is consistent with social comparison theory, according to which downward social comparisons (i.e., with people who are even worse off than you are) can be ego-enhancing.

No evidence has emerged that excessive exposure to television content turns elderly people into violent thugs. It *has* been argued, though, that excessive exposure to relentless crime portrayals and other alarming representations of the social world leads to undue fears among the elderly that there is a mean and hostile world out there (Gerbner et al., 1980). Gerbner et al. found that older characters on TV are more likely than younger characters to be depicted as victims of crime, and that the more television viewing elderly subjects reported, the more likely they were to express fear of victimization. Since elderly people are statistically at *lower* risk of becoming victims of street crime and assault than other age groups (the highest risk group is young males), this suggests an effect of television exposure. But it turns out not to be that straightforward. First of all, the statistical relationship was not a very powerful one. Second, other studies have found that fear of crime is better predicted by actual crime levels in one's neighborhood. For example, in a study in Toronto, Doob and MacDonald (1979) found that people who lived in higher crime areas tended to have greater fear of victimization *and* higher TV viewing habits. What do you do if your locality is too dangerous to venture into during the evenings?

Overall, television is a prominent and subjectively valued part of life for many elderly people. It has been suggested that it may become still more important. Developments in mass media, especially the advent of interactive television, may well increase the contribution it makes, so that it could become "real" company, providing a means of re-entry for older people into the community (Comfort, 1977, p. 138).

The Family and the Elderly

From the beginnings of life to the end, the family is pivotal to social existence. In older life, the household unit typically contracts — even the crowded nest empties sometime. Nevertheless, relationships and homes remain central. We noted in chapter

18 that attachments are important throughout life, and this is clearly the case for the elderly. Even attachment to places remains important and – again contrary to elements of stereotypes about the elderly – most older people prefer to remain in their own homes, with only about 5 percent moving into residential institutions (Arber and Evandron, 1993, Bury and Holme, 1991; Comfort, 1977; Rowland, 1990; Wright, 1994). The secure base of familiar territory has cognitive and affective significance during this period as much as earlier ones. To take an extreme example, in Chernobyl, an area devastated by the world's worst nuclear accident and now an exclusion zone, the very elderly are moving back in defiance of local regulations. By late 1993, over 760 old people were recorded as living there and interviewees declared that they did not want to live anywhere else (Radford, 1993).

Personal adjustment in old age is interwoven with social involvement with the rest of the family, including one's spouse, children and grandchildren. Although there is variation among couples, there is some tendency for older married couples to report greater satisfaction with their relationship Cole, 1984). This could reflect increased dependency upon the other for companionship and the fact that participants in a long-term marriage have much in common in terms of shared experiences and achievements; it is also likely that people who stay married for a long time do so *because* they are satisfied with the relationship.

Nevertheless, within elderly couples, there is evidence of a sex difference such that women tend to be less satisfied with marriage than men (Cole, 1984). It may be that older men, after a lifetime of side-by-side peer relations and a traditional breadwinner role, find it difficult to meet their wives' needs for a full-time, close and emotionally intimate relationship. Consistent with this inference, Imamoglu et al. (1993), in a study of Swedish and Turkish couples around retirement age, found that women in both countries anticipated greater loneliness in retirement.

Gender differences are evident in family relations involving the elderly in a number of ways. Komarovsky (1987) and Rossi and Rossi (1990) found that, across a wide range of topics, ties among women were stronger, more frequent and more reciprocal than those among men, and that these links held together the social and emotional fabric of the extended family: "There is, all told, a steadier beat to the quality of the relationships between women in the family than between men or cross-sex pairs" (Rossi and Rossi, 1990, p. 499). Adult daughters are more likely to visit their parents than are sons, and contact is more frequent with mothers than fathers (Hoffman et al., 1897; Komarovsky, 1987). Men tend to report less satisfaction with the grandparental role than do women (Thomas, 1986).

Loss of partner

For couples, one partner will eventually be left alone as the other dies. Because of sex differences in longevity, the remaining partner is most often the widow, but about 1 in 6 widowed people is the husband.

Loss of a spouse is generally rated as the most traumatic life-event an individual can experience. First, the loss is a major emotional trauma, involving the termination of a central attachment. Parkes (1986; Parkes and Weiss, 1983) draws on Bowlby's attachment theory to explain the processes of reaction to bereavement. Like the child separated from a parent, the widowed person undergoes a sense of shock and numbness, followed by an intense, agonized yearning for the lost partner. This is followed by a long period of despair and depression, until eventually the individual can begin to reorganize and rebuild her or his life.

Second, one of the underlying difficulties for the widowed person is that she or he has lost much of the unifying basis of the life structure: the fundamental relationship and role around which much of life has been organized so far. Nearly every aspect of daily life is affected by loss of a partner. Alongside the emotional trauma, widowed people may suffer a profound blow to their social identity, since the family upon which it was based is radically altered (Stroebe and Stroebe, 1986). They also acquire a new identity with negative connotations: the very label *widow(er)* is a continuous reminder of death (Llewelyn and Osborne, 1990). In turn, these shifts in identity have consequences for the individual's connections to the social world outside the household: widowed people find often that much of social life is organized around couples (Lopata, 1979).

Once again, evidence indicates that how people cope with this major life transition and loss is influenced by social involvement and by gender. Several studies have found that women who adjust more successfully to widowhood tend to have strong relations with others, usually her adult children, sometimes other family members or friends (Field and Minkler, 1988). This is consistent with the more general finding that social support – or the perception that social support is available – contributes to the wellbeing of elderly people (Antonucci, 1990). Social support is not a panacea for the many problems of widowhood, but it does provide a more favorable context for dealing with them (Lund, 1989).

Men are more prone to suffer serious ill health and death following bereavement (Bury and Holme, 1991; Stroebe and Stroebe, 1987). On the other hand, men are more likely to remarry (Aizenberg and Treas, 1985; Stroebe and Stroebe, 1987), a fact which may reflect, variously, their relative advantage as scarcer parties in the older marriage market, their greater need for a domestic partner (since it is difficult for men to achieve psychological intimacy outside the home), or their experience that on the whole marriage is beneficial. Lopata (1979) found that widows are less interested in remarriage, for a variety of reasons including reluctance to resume the subordinate role in a traditional relationship, fear of experiencing the stresses of widowhood another time around, and a belief that their deceased husbands were irreplaceable.

Summary

The older person is the subject of some of the strongest and most negative social stereotypes, and there are powerful sociocultural influences which undoubtedly do affect the conditions of older people's lives and their involvement in society. However, the stereotypes are often misplaced and their consequences are mitigated by the behavior of actual people whose abilities and goals may often contradict popular assumptions. While there are enormous variations among personal lives and circum-stances, a key factor in wellbeing and later development appears to be relationships with others: active social involvement generally predicts wellbeing and positive adjustment, even to some of the most painful events of later life.

Conclusions

In concluding this examination of social development through the adult lifespan, the importance of relationships to others emerges prominently – as it does at every other period of life (Blank, 1982; Fogel, 1993). Who one is, how one changes, where one is going are all dependent upon relations with others and upon how one responds to the expectations of the social world. Part of the task of a developmental social psychology is to draw together and extend our still only fragmentary understanding of how these processes operate.

As research continues into social development during adulthood, it is difficult to maintain the traditional developmentalist's assumption that development ceases at 20, and to support the traditional social psychologist's implicit faith that social processes are pretty much a constant from student days to retirement. It contradicts abundant evidence to conceive of the object of our enquiry as a discrete cognitive isolate who develops theories of the world like a dispassionate scientist (a doubly misleading metaphor, since scientists are never isolates and are only dispassionate about things that do not interest them). It defies the nature of life itself to regard change as peripheral and to treat developmental status as irrelevant to interaction. Developmental psychology and social psychology have done respectable jobs of taking the bits apart; the future of developmental social psychology rests in reassembling them.

Further reading

Baltes, P. B. and Baltes, M. M. (eds) (1990). *Successful Aging: perspectives from the behavioral sciences*. Cambridge: Cambridge University Press.

A valuable collection of essays on psychological and physiological aspects of aging, from the early adult transition through to old age. The emphasis is on the optimal conditions for aging, including discovering the antecedents of the "happy octogenarian."

Bengston, V. L., Reedy, M. N., and Gordon, C. (1985) Aging and self-conceptions: personality processes and social contexts. In J. E. Birren and K. W. Schaie (eds), *Handbook of the Psychology of Aging*. 2nd edn. New York: Van Nostrand.

A penetrating review of the conceptual and methodological issues in studying the development of self among older people.

Braithwaite, V. (1992) The ageing experience: loss, threat or challenge? In P. C. L. Heaven (ed.), *Life Span Development*. Sydney and London: Harcourt Brace Jovanovich.

A readable and thorough review of literature on the challenges of late adulthood and the individual and social psychological variables associated with adjustment.

George, L. K. (1990) Social structure, social processes, and social-psychological states. In R. H. Binstock and L. K. George (eds), *Handbook of Aging and the Social Sciences*, 3rd edn. San Diego: Academic Press.

An analysis of the interactions between social structure and personal change during later life, with particular emphasis on determinants of wellbeing and the self-concept.

Pratt, M. W. and Norris, J. E. (1994) *The Social Psychology of Aging*. Oxford: Blackwell.

An excellent example of the benefits of fusing social psychological and developmental approaches to the study of aging, providing extensive coverage of developments in social cognition, moral reasoning, and communication.

Taylor, A. (1986) Sex roles and aging. In D. J. Hargreaves and A. M. Colley (eds), *The Psychology of Sex Roles*. London: Harper & Row.

A useful review of research into the relationship between sex role orientation and the life-cycle, pointing to the conclusion that sex-typing diminishes in old age.

References

Aboud, F. E. (1976) Some social developmental aspects of language. *Papers in Linguistics*, 9, 15–37.

Aboud, F. E. (1988) *Children and Prejudice*. Oxford: Blackwell.

Aboud, F. E. (1989) Disagreements between friends. *International Journal of Behavioral Development*, 12, 495–508.

Abraham, S. and Llewellyn-Jones, D. (1992) *Eating Disorders: the facts*. Oxford: Oxford University Press.

Abrami, P. C., Chambers, B., D'Apollonia, S., Farrell, M., and De Simone, C. (1992) Group outcome: the relationship between group learning outcome, attributional style, academic achievement, and self concept. *Contemporary Educational Psychology*, 17, 201–10.

Abramovitch, R. (1977) Children's recognition of situational aspects of facial expression. *Child Development*, 48, 459–63.

Abramovitch, R. and Daly, E. M. (1979) Inferring attributes of a situation from the facial expressions of peers. *Child Development*, 50, 586–9.

Abramovitch, R., Pepler, D., and Corter, C. (1982) Patterns of sibling interaction among preschool-age children. In M. Lamb and B. Sutton-Smith (eds), *Sibling Relationships: their nature and significance across the lifespan*. Hillsdale, NJ: Erlbaum.

Abrams, D. (1989) Differential association: social developments in gender identity and intergroup relations during adolescence. In S. Skevington and D. Baker (eds), *The Social Identity of Women*. London: Sage.

Abrams, D. and Hogg, M. A. (1987) Language attitudes, frames of reference, and social identity: a Scottish dimension. *Journal of Language and Social Psychology*, 6, 201–13.

Ackerman, B. P. (1981) Performative bias in children's interpretations of ambiguous referential communications. *Child Development*, 52, 1224–30.

Acredolo, L. and Goodwyn, S. (1988) Symbolic gesturing in normal infants. *Child Development*, 59, 450–66.

Adams, D. (1992) Biology does not make men more aggressive than women. In K. Bjorkqvist and P. Niemala (eds), *Of Mice and Women: aspects of female aggression*. San Diego: Academic Press.

Adams, G. R. and Gullotta, T. (1989) *Adolescent Life Experiences*. Pacific Grove, Calif.: Brooks/Cole.

Adams, G. R. and Jones, R. M. (1981) Imaginary audience behavior: a validation study. *Journal of Early Adolescence*, 1, 1266–75.

Adams, G. R., Gullotta, T. P., and Markstrom-Adams, C. (1994) *Adolescent Life Experiences*, 3rd edn. Pacific Grove, Calif.: Brooks/Cole.

Adamson, L. B. and Bakeman, R. (1985) Affect and attention: infants observed with mothers and peers. *Child Development*, 56, 582–93.

Adelmann, P. K., Antonucci, T. C., Crohan, S. E., and Coleman, L. M. (1989) Empty nest, cohort, and employment in the well-being of midlife women. *Sex Roles*, 20, 173–89.

Adler, F. (1975) *Sisters in Crime: the rise of the new female offender.* New York: McGraw-Hill.

Adorno, T. W., Frenkel-Brunswik, E., Levinson, D. J., and Sanford, R. N. (1950) *The Authoritarian Personality.* New York: Harper.

Agarwal, A., Tripathi, K. K., and Srivastava, M. (1983) Social roots and psychological implications of time perspective. *International Journal of Psychology*, 18, 367–80.

Ageton, S. S. (1983) *Sexual Assault among Adolescents.* Lexington: Lexington Books.

Agnew, R. (1991) The interactive effects of peer variables on delinquency. *Criminology*, 29, 47–72.

Ahammer, I. and Baltes, P. (1972) Objective versus perceived differences in personality: how do adolescents, adults and older people view themselves and each other? *Journal of Gerontology*, 27, 46–51.

Ahrens, R. (1954) Beitrag zur Entwiklung der Physiognomie und Mimikerkennens. *Zietschrift für Experimentelle und Angewandte Psychologie*, 2, 414–514, 599–633.

Ainsworth, M. D. S. (1967) *Infancy in Uganda: infant care and the growth of love.* Baltimore: Johns Hopkins University Press.

Ainsworth, M. D. S. (1969) Object relations, dependency and attachment: a theoretical review of the infant–mother relationship. *Child Development*, 40, 969–1025.

Ainsworth, M. D. S. and Bell, S. M. (1970) Attachment, exploration and separation: illustrated by the behaviour of one-year-olds in a strange situation. *Child Development*, 41, 49–67.

Ainsworth, M. D. S. and Bowlby, J. (1991) An ethological approach to personality development. *American Psychologist*, 46, 331–41.

Ainsworth, M. D. S. and Wittig, B. A. (1969) Attachment and exploratory behavior of one-year-olds in a strange situation. In B. M. Foss (ed.), *Determinants of Infant Behaviour*, vol. 4. London: Methuen.

Ainsworth, M. D. S., Bell, S. M., and Stayton, D. J. (1971) Individual differences in strange situation behavior of one-year-olds. In H. R. Schaffer (ed.), *The Origins of Human Social Relations.* London: Academic Press.

Ainsworth, M. D. S., Bell, S. M., and Stayton, D. J. (1974) Infant–mother attachment and social development: "socialisation" as a product of reciprocal responsiveness to signals. In M. P. M. Richards (ed.), *The integration of a child into a social world.* Cambridge: Cambridge University Press.

Ainsworth, M. D. S., Blehar, M., Waters, E., and Wall, E. (1978) *Patterns of Attachment.* Hillsdale, NJ: Erlbaum.

Aitchison, J. (1987) *Words in the Mind: an introduction to the mental lexicon.* Oxford: Blackwell.

Aitchison, J. (1992) *The Articulate Mammal: an introduction to psycholinguistics*, 3rd edn. London: Routledge.

Aizenberg, R. and Treas, J. (1985) The family in later life: psychosocial and demographic considerations. In J. E. Birren and K. W. Schaie (eds), *Handbook of the Psychology of Aging*, 2nd edn. New York: Van Nostrand.

van Aken, M. A. G. (1994) The transactional relations between social support and children's competence. In F. Nestemann and K. Hurrelmann (eds), *Social Networks and Social Support in Childhood and Adolescence.* Berlin: de Gruyter.

Akhtar, N., Dunham, F., and Dunham, P. J. (1991) Directive interactions and early vocabulary development: the role of joint attentional focus. *Journal of Child Language*, 18, 41–9.

Allen, R. and Shatz, M. (1983) "What says meow?" The role of context and linguistic experience in very young children's responses to "what" questions. *Journal of Child Language*, 10, 321–35.

Alles-Jardel, M. and Genest, E. (1989) Communication and cooperation among young children. In B. H. Schneider, G. Attili, J. Nadel, and R. P. Weissberg (eds), *Social Competence in Developmental Perspective.* Dordecht: Kluwer.

Alley, T. R. and Hildebrandt, K. A. (eds) (1988) *Social and Applied Aspects of Perceiving Faces.* Hillsdale, NJ: Erlbaum

Allport, G. W. (1937/1961) *Pattern and growth in personality.* New York: Holt, Rinehart and Winston.

Allport, G. W. (1968) The historical background of modern psychology. In G. Lindzey and E. Aronson (eds), *The Handbook of Social Psychology*, vol. 1. Reading, Mass.: Addison-Wesley.

Aloise, P. A. and Miller, P. H. (1991) Discounting in preschoolers: effect of type of reward agent. *Journal of Experimental Child Psychology*, 52, 70–86.

Ambrose, J. A. (1961) The development of the smiling response in early infancy. In B. M. Foss (ed.), *Determinants of Infant Behaviour.* London: Methuen.

Ames, G. J. and Murray, F. B. (1982) When two wrongs make a right: promoting cognitive change by social conflict. *Developmental Psychology*, 18, 894–7.

Amigues, R. and Agostinelli, S. (1992) Collaborative problem-solving with a computer: how can an interactive learning environment be designed? *European Journal of Psychology of Education*, 7, 325–37.

Amira, A. (1990) Family care in Greece. In A. Jamieson and R. Illsely (eds), *Contrasting European Policies for the Care of Older People*. Aldershot: Avebury.

Amsterdam, B. (1972) Mirror self-image reactions before age two. *Developmental Psychology*, 5, 297–305.

Anderson, C. A. (1989) Temperature and aggression: ubiquitous effects of heat on occurrence of human violence. *Psychological Bulletin*, 106, 74–96.

Anderson, N. S. (1987) Cognition, learning, and memory. In M. A. Baker (ed.), *Sex Differences in Human Performance*. Chichester: Wiley.

Anderson, S. A. (1985) Parental and marital role stress during the school entry transition. *Journal of Social and Personal Relationships*, 2, 59–80.

Andersson, B.-E. (1989) Effects of public day-care: a longitudinal study. *Child Development*, 60, 857–66.

Andersson, B.-E. (1990) Are adolescents given a relevant preparation for the adult role? A Swedish perspective. *European Journal of Psychology of Education*, 5, 45–57.

Andersson, B.-E. (1992) Effects of day-care on cognitive and socioemotional competence of thirteen-year-old Swedish schoolchildren. *Child Development*, 63, 20–36.

Anson, O. (1989) Marital status and women's health revisited: the importance of a proximate adult. *Journal of Marriage and the Family*, 51, 185–94.

Anson, O., Antonovsky, A., Sagy, S., and Adler, I. (1989) Family, gender, and attitudes toward retirement. *Sex Roles*, 20, 355–69.

Antaki, C. and Naji, S. (1987) Events explained in conversational "because" statements. *British Journal of Social Psychology*, 26, 119–26.

Antill, J. K. and Cotton, S. (1987) Self disclosure between husbands and wives: its relationship to sex roles and marital happiness. *Australian Journal of Psychology*, 39, 11–24.

Antonucci, T. C. (1990) Social supports and social relationships. In R. H. Binstock and L. K. George (eds), *Aging and the Social Sciences*, 3rd edn. San Diego: Academic Press.

Antonucci, T. C. and Akiyama, H. (1994) Convoys of attachment and social relations in children, adolescents, and adults. In F. Nestemann and K. Hurrelmann (eds), *Social Networks and Social Support in Childhood and Adolescence*. Berlin: de Gruyter.

Antonucci, T. C. and Levitt, M. J. (1984) Early prediction of attachment security: a multivariate account. *Infant Behavior and Development*, 7, 1–18.

Arber, S. and Evandrou, M. (1993) Mapping the territory: ageing, independence and the life course. In S. Arber and M. Evandrou (eds), *Ageing, Independence and the Life Course*. London: Jessica Kingsley.

Archer, J. (1984) Gender roles as developmental pathways. *British Journal of Social Psychology*, 23, 245–56.

Archer, J. (1992) Childhood gender roles: social context and organisation. In H. McGurk (ed.), *Childhood Social Development: contemporary perspectives*. Hove: Erlbaum.

Archer, J. (1996) Evolutionary social psychology. In M. Hewstone, W. Stroebe, and G. M. Stephenson (eds), *Introduction to Social Psychology*, 2nd edn. Oxford: Blackwell.

Archer, J. and Freedman, S. (1989) Gender-stereotypic perceptions of academic disciplines. *British Journal of Educational Psychology*, 59, 306–13.

Archer, J. and Ray, N. (1989) Dating violence in the United Kingdom: a preliminary study. *Aggressive Behavior*, 15, 337–43.

Archer, S. (1982) The lower age boundaries of identity development. *Child Development*, 53, 1551–6.

Ardrey, R. (1966) *The Territorial Imperative*. New York: Atheneum.

Ardrey, R. (1970) *The Social Contract*. London: Collins.

Argyle, M. (1988a) *Bodily Communication*, 2nd edn. London: Methuen.

Argyle, M. (1988b) Social relationships. In M. Hewstone, W. Stroebe, J.-P. Codol, and G. M. Stephenson (eds), *Introduction to Social Psychology: a European perspective*. Oxford: Blackwell.

Argyle, M. (1989) *The Social Psychology of Work*, 2nd edn. Harmondsworth: Penguin.

Argyle, M. (1992a) *The Social Psychology of Everyday Life*. London: Routledge.

Argyle, M. (1992b) Does nonverbal communication cause happiness? In F. Poyatos (ed.), *Advances in Nonverbal Communication: sociocultural, clinical, esthetic and literary perspectives*. Amsterdam: John Benjamins.

Argyle, M. and Dean, J. (1965) Eye-contact, distance and affiliation. *Sociometry*, 28, 289–304.

Argyle, M. and Henderson, M. (1985) *The Anatomy of Relationships*. London: Heinemann.

Argyle, M., Henderson, M., and Furnham, A. (1985) The rules of social relationships. *British Journal of Social Psychology*, 24, 125–39.

Arias, I., Samios, M., and O'Leary, K. D. (1987) Prevalence and correlates of physical aggression during courtship. *Journal of Interpersonal Violence*, 2, 82–90.

Aries, P. (1962) *Centuries of Childhood*. London: Jonathan Cape.

Aro, H. and Taipale, V. (1987) The impact of timing of puberty on psychosomatic symptoms among fourteen- to sixteen-year-old Finnish girls. *Child Development*, 58, 261–8.

Aronfreed, J. (1968) *Conduct and Conscience: the*

socialization of internalized control over behavior. New York: Academic Press.

Aronoff, C. (1974) Old age is prime-time. *Journal of Communication*, 24, 86–7.

Aronson, E. (1992) *The Social Animal*, 6th edn. New York: W. H. Freeman.

Aronson, E. and Carlsmith, J. M. (1963) The effect of severity of threat on the devaluation of forbidden behavior. *Journal of Abnormal and Social Psychology*, 66, 584–8.

Arsenio, W. F. and Ford, M. E. (1985) The role of affective information in social-cognitive development: children's differentiation of moral and conventional events. *Merrill-Palmer Quarterly*, 31, 1–17.

Asarnow, J. R. and Callan, J. W. (1985) Boys with peer adjustment problems: social cognitive processes. *Journal of Consulting and Clinical Psychology*, 53, 80–7.

Asch, S. E. (1951) Effects of group pressure on the modification and distortion of judgments. In H. Guetzkow (ed.), *Groups, Leadership and Men*. Pittsburgh: Carnegie.

Asendorpf, J. B. (1992) A Brunswikean approach to trait continuity: application to shyness. *Journal of Personality*, 60, 53–77.

Ashburn, G. and Gordon, A. (1981) Features of a simplified register in speech to elderly conversationalists. *International Journal of Psycholinguistics*, 8, 7–31.

Asher, S. R. and Coie, J. D. (eds) (1990) *Peer Rejection in Childhood*. Cambridge: Cambridge University Press.

Asher, S. R. and Parker, J. G. (1989) Significance of peer relationship problems in childhood. In B. H. Schneider, G. Attili, J. Nadel, and R. P. Weissberg (eds), *Social Competence in Developmental Perspective*. Dordrecht: Kluwer.

Asher, S. R., Parkhurst, J. T., Hymel, S., and Williams, G. A. (1990) Peer rejection and loneliness in childhood. In S. R. Asher and J. D. Coie (eds), *Peer Rejection in Childhood*. Cambridge: Cambridge University Press.

Aslin, R. N. (1987) Visual and auditory development in infancy. In J. D. Osofsky (ed.), *Handbook of Infant Development*. New York: Wiley.

Astington, J. W. (1986) Children's comprehension of expressions of intention. *British Journal of Developmental Psychology*, 4, 43–9.

Astington, J. W., Harris, P. L., and Olson, D. R. (eds), (1988) *Developing Theories of Mind*. Cambridge: Cambridge University Press.

Atchley, R. (1976) *The Sociology of Retirement*. Cambridge, Mass.: Schenkman.

Atchley, R. (1991) *Social Forces and Aging: an introduction to social gerontology*. Belmont, Calif.: Wadsworth.

Atkinson, M. (1986) Learnability. In P. Fletcher and M. Garman (eds), *Language Acquisition*, 2nd edn. Cambridge: Cambridge University Press.

Atkinson, M. (1987) Mechanisms for language acquisition: learning, parameter-setting and triggering. *First Language*, 7, 3–30.

Attie, I. and Brooks-Gunn, J. (1989) The development of eating problems in adolescent girls: a longitudinal study. *Developmental Psychology*, 25, 70–9.

Attili, G. (1989) Social competence versus emotional security: the link between home relationships and behavior problems in preschool. In B. H. Schneider, G. Attili, J. Nadel, and R. P. Weissberg (eds), *Social Competence in Developmental Perspective*. Dordrecht: Kluwer.

Attwood, M. (1994) *The Robber Bride*. London: Virago.

Austen, J. (1813). *Sense and Sensibility*. London: T. Egerton.

Averill, J. R. (1983) Studies of anger and aggression: implications for theories of emotion. *American Psychologist*, 38, 1145–60.

van Avermaet, E. (1996) Social influence in small groups. In M. Hewstone, W. Stroebe, and G. M. Stephenson (eds), *Introduction to Social Psychology*, 2nd edn. Oxford: Blackwell.

Avolio, B. J. and Barrett, G. V. (1987) Effects of age stereotyping in a simulated interview. *Psychology and Aging*, 2, 56–63.

Axia, G. and Baroni, M. R. (1985) Linguistic politeness at different age levels. *Child Development*, 56, 918–27.

Azmitia, M. (1988) Peer interaction and problem solving: when are two heads better than one? *Child Development*, 59, 87–96.

Azmitia, M. and Hesser, J. (1993) Why siblings are important agents of cognitive development: a comparison of siblings and peers. *Child Development*, 64, 430–44.

Azmitia, M. and Perlmutter, M. (1989) Social influences on children's cognition: state of the art and future directions. In H. W. Reese (ed.), *Advances in Child Development and Behavior*, vol. 22. New York: Academic Press.

Bachman, J. G. and Schulenberg, J. (1993) How part-time work intensity relates to drug use, problem behavior, time use, and satisfaction among high school seniors: are these consequences or merely correlates? *Developmental Psychology*, 29, 220–35.

Baethge, M. (1989) Individualization as hope and as disaster: a socioeconomic perspective. In K. Hurrelmann and U. Engel (eds), *The Social World of*

Adolescents: international perspectives. Berlin and New York: de Gruyter.

Bailey, S. L., Flewelling, R. L., and Rachal, J. V. (1992) Predicting continued use of marihuana among adolescents: the relative influence of drug-specific and social-context factors. *Journal of Health and Social Behavior*, 33, 51–66.

Bakeman, R. and Adamson, L. B. (1984) Coordinating attention to people and objects in mother–infant and peer–infant interaction. *Child Development*, 55, 1278–89.

Bakeman, R. and Adamson, L. B. (1986) Infants' conventionalized acts: gestures and words with mothers and peers. *Infant Behavior and Development*, 9, 215–30.

Bakeman, R. and Brownlee, J. (1980) The strategic use of parallel play: a sequential analysis. *Child Development*, 51, 873–8.

Bakeman, R. and Brownlee, J. R. (1982) Social rules governing object conflicts in toddlers and preschoolers. In K. H. Rubin and H. R. Ross (eds), *Peer Relationships and Social Skills in Childhood.* New York: Springer-Verlag.

Bakeman, R., Adamson, L. B., Konner, M., and Barr, R. (1990) !Kung infancy: the social context of object exploration. *Child Development*, 61, 794–809.

Baker, D. (1989) Social identity in the transition to motherhood. In S. Skevington and D. Baker (eds), *The Social Identity of Women.* London: Sage.

Baker, N. D. and Nelson, K. E. (1984) Recasting and related conversational techniques for triggering syntactic advances by young children. *First Language*, 5, 3–32.

Baker, R. L. and Mednick, B. R. (1984) *Influences on Human Development: a longitudinal perspective.* Boston: Kluwer.

Baldwin, D. (1993) Infants' ability to consult the speaker for clues to word reference. *Journal of Child Language*, 20, 395–418.

Baldwin, D. and Markman, E. M. (1989) Establishing word–object relations: a first step. *Child Development*, 60, 381–98.

Baldwin, J. M. (1902) *Social and Ethical Interpretations in Mental Development.* London: Macmillan.

Ball, L. and Chandler, M. (1989) Identity formation in suicidal and nonsuicidal youth: the role of self-continuity. *Development and Psychopathology*, 1, 257–75.

Baltes, P. B. (1983) Life-span developmental psychology: observations on history and theory revisited. In R. M. Lerner (ed.), *Developmental Psychology: historical and philosophical perspectives.* Hillsdale, NJ: Erlbaum.

Baltes, P. B. (1987) Theoretical propositions of life-span developmental psychology: on the dynamics between growth and decline. *Developmental Psychology*, 23, 611–26.

Baltes, P. B. and Baltes, M. M. (eds) (1990) *Successful Aging: perspectives from the behavioral sciences.* Cambridge: Cambridge University Press.

Baltes, P. B. and Schaie, K. W. (1976) On the plasticity of intelligence in adulthood and old age – where Horn and Donaldson fail. *American Psychologist*, 31, 720–5.

Baltes, P. B., Dittman-Kohli, F., and Dixon, R. A. (1986) Multidisciplinary propositions on the development of intelligence during adulthood and old age. In A. B. Sorenson, F. E. Weinert, and L. B. Sherrod (eds), *Human Development across the Life Course: multidisciplinary perspectives.* Hillsdale, NJ: Erlbaum.

Bamberg, M., Budwig, N., and Kaplan, B. (1991) A developmental approach to language acquisition: two case studies. *First Language*, 11, 121–41.

Bandura, A. (1971) *Social Learning Theory.* Morristown, NJ: General Learning Press.

Bandura, A. (1973) *Aggression: a social learning analysis.* Englewood Cliffs, NJ: Prentice Hall.

Bandura, A. (1977) *Social Learning Theory*, 2nd edn. Englewood Cliffs, NJ: Prentice Hall.

Bandura, A. (1979) Psychological mechanisms of aggression. In M. von Cranach, K. Foppa, W. Lepenies, and D. Ploog (eds), *Human Ethology: claims and limits of a new discipline.* Cambridge: Cambridge University Press.

Bandura, A. (1986) *Social Foundations of Thought and Action: a social cognitive theory.* Englewood Cliffs, NJ: Prentice Hall.

Bandura, A. and Rosenthal, T. L. (1966) Vicarious classical conditioning as a function of arousal level. *Journal of Personality and Social Psychology*, 3, 54–62.

Bandura, A. and Walters, R. H. (1959) *Adolescent Aggression.* New York: Ronald Press.

Bandura, A. and Walters, R. H. (1963) *Social Learning and Personality Development.* New York: Holt.

Bandura, A., Ross, D., and Ross, S. A. (1963) Imitation of film-mediated aggressive models. *Journal of Abnormal and Social Psychology*, 66, 3–11.

Bank, S. (1992) Remembering and reinterpreting sibling bonds. In F. Boer and J. Dunn (eds), *Children's Sibling Relationships: developmental and clinical issues.* Hillsdale, NJ: Erlbaum.

Banks, M. H. and Jackson, P. R. (1982) Unemployment and risk of minor psychiatric disorder in young people: cross-sectional and longitudinal evidence. *Psychological Medicine*, 12, 789–98.

Barash, D. P. (1977) *Sociobiology and Behavior.* London: Heinemann.

Barash, D. P. (1982) *Sociobiology and Behavior,* 2nd edn. London: Heinemann.

Barber, B. K. (1992) Family, personality, and adolescent problem behaviors. *Journal of Marriage and the Family,* 54, 69–79.

Barber, B. K. (1994) Cultural, family, and personal contexts of parent–adolescent conflict. *Journal of Marriage and the Family,* 56, 375–86.

Barbieri, M. S. and Griguolo, M. (1993) Context and quantitative dimension of social conventional transgressions: is it more serious at home or at school? *European Journal of Psychology of Education,* 8, 105–17.

Barden, R. C., Ford, M. E., and Jensen, A. G. (1989) Effects of craniofacial deformity in infancy on the quality of mother–infant interactions. *Child Development,* 60, 819–24.

Barenboim, C. (1981) The development of person perception in childhood and adolescence: from behavioral comparisons to psychological constructs to psychological comparisons. *Child Development,* 52, 129–44.

Barglow, P., Vaughn B. E., and Molitor, N. (1987) Effects of maternal absence due to employment on the quality of infant–mother attachment in a low-risk sample. *Child Development,* 58, 945–54.

Barker, K. (1993) Changing assumptions and contingent solutions: the costs and benefits of women working full- and part-time. *Sex Roles,* 28, 47–71.

Barker, R., Dembo, T., and Lewin, K. (1941) Frustration and regression: an experiment with young children. *University of Iowa Studies in Child Welfare,* 18, no. 1.

Barkley, R. A., Ullman, D. G., Otto, L., and Brecht, J. M. (1977) The effects of sex typing and sex appropriateness of modeled behavior on children's imitation. *Child Development,* 48, 721–5.

Barnes, G. M. and Farrell, M. P. (1992) Parental support and control as predictors of adolescent drinking, delinquency and related problem behaviors. *Journal of Marriage and the Family,* 54, 763–76.

Barnes-Farrell, J. L. and Piotrowski, M. J. (1989) Workers' perceptions of discrepancies between chronological age and personal age: you're only as old as you feel. *Psychology and Aging,* 4, 376–7.

Barnett, M. A. (1975) Effects of competition and relative deservedness of the other's fate on children's generosity. *Developmental Psychology,* 11, 665–6.

Barnett, M. A. (1987) Empathy and related responses in children. In N. Eisenberg and J. Strayer (eds), *Empathy and its Development.* Cambridge: Cambridge University Press.

Barnett, M. A. and McMinimy, V. (1988) Influence of the reason for the other's affect on preschoolers' empathic response. *Journal of Genetic Psychology,* 149, 153–62.

Barnett, M. A. and Thompson, S. (1985) The role of perspective taking and empathy in children's Machiavellianism, prosocial behavior and motive for helping. *Journal of Genetic Psychology,* 146, 295–305.

Barnett, M. A., Howard, J. A., King, L. M., and Dino, G. A. (1980) Antecedents of empathy: retrospective accounts of early socialization. *Personality and Social Psychology Bulletin,* 6, 361–5.

Barnier, G. (1989) L'effet-tuteur dans des situations mettang en jeu des rapports spatiaux chez des enfants de 7-8 ans en interactions dyadiques avec des pairs de 6-7 ans. *European Journal of Psychology of Education,* 4, 385–99.

Baron, N. S. (1992) *Growing up with Language: how children learn to talk.* Reading, Mass.: Addison-Wesley.

Baron-Cohen, S. (1989) Perceptual role-taking and protodeclarative pointing in autism. *British Journal of Developmental Psychology,* 7, 113–27.

Baron-Cohen, S. and Staunton, R. (1994) Do children with autism acquire the phonology of their peers? An examination of group identification through the window of bilingualism? *First Language,* 14, 241–8.

Baroni, M. R. and Axia, G. (1989) Children's meta-pragmatic abilities and the identification of polite and impolite requests. *First Language,* 9, 285–97.

Barrera, M. E. and Maurer, D. (1981a) Recognition of mother's photographed face by the three-month-old infant. *Child Development,* 52, 714–16.

Barrera, M. E. and Maurer, D. (1981b) Discrimination of strangers by the three-month-old. *Child Development,* 52, 558–563.

Barrera, M. E. and Maurer, D. (1981c) The perception of facial expressions by the three-month-old. *Child Development,* 52, 203–6.

Barrett, M. (1989) Early language development. In A. Slater and G. Bremner (eds), *Infant Development.* Hillsdale, NJ: Erlbaum.

Barrett, M. and Short, J. (1992) Images of European people in a group of 5–10 year old English school children. *British Journal of Developmental Psychology,* 10, 339–63.

Barrett, M., Harris, M. and Chasin, J. (1991) Early lexical development and maternal speech: a comparison of children's initial and subsequent uses of words. *Journal of Child Language,* 18, 21–40.

Barron, A.-M. and Foot, H. C. (1991) Peer tutoring and tutor training. *Educational Research,* 33, 174–85.

Bar-Tal, D. (1978) Attributional analysis of achievement-related behavior. *Review of Educational Research,* 48, 259–71.

Bar-Tal, D. (1979) Interactions of teachers and pupils.

In I. H. Frieze, D. Bar-Tal, and J. S. Carroll (eds), *New Approaches to Social Problems: applications of attribution theory*. San Francisco: Jossey-Bass.

Bar-Tal, D. and Saxe, L. (1976) Perceptions of similarly and dissimilarly attractive couples and individuals. *Journal of Personality and Social Psychology*, 33, 772–81.

Bar-Tal, D., Goldberg, M., and Knaani, A. (1984) Causes of success and failure and their dimensions as a function of SES and gender: a phenomenological analysis. *British Journal of Educational Psychology*, 54, 51–61.

Bar-Tal, D., Raviv, D., and Leiser, T. (1980) The development of altruistic behavior: empirical evidence. *Developmental Psychology*, 16, 516–24.

Barth, J. M. and Parke, R. D. (1993) Parent–child relationship influences on children's transition to school. *Merrill-Palmer Quarterly*, 39, 173–95.

Bartsch, K. and Wellman, H. (1989) Young children's attribution of action to beliefs and desires. *Child Development*, 60, 946–64.

Baruch, G., Barnett, R., and Rivers, C. (1983) *Lifeprints*. New York: McGraw-Hill.

Basow, S. A. and Kobrynowicz, D. (1993) What is she eating? The effects of meal size on a female eater. *Sex Roles*, 28, 335–49.

Bates, E. (1976) *Language and Context*. New York: Academic Press.

Bates, E., Camaioni, L., and Volterra, V. (1975) The acquisition of performatives prior to speech. *Merrill-Palmer Quarterly*, 21, 205–26.

Bates, J. E. (1989) Concepts and measures of temperament. In G. A. Kohnstamm, J. E. Bates, and M. K. Rothbart (eds), *Temperament and Personality*. Chichester: Wiley.

Bates, J. E., Marvinney, D., Kelly, T., Dodge, K. A., Bennett, D. S., and Pettit, G. S. (1994) Child-care history and kindergarten adjustment. *Development Psychology*, 30, 690–700.

Bates, J. E., Maslin, C. A., and Frankel, K. A. (1985) Attachment security, mother–child interaction, and temperament as predictors of behavior-problem ratings at age three years. In I. Bretherton and E. Waters (eds), *Growing Points of Attachment Theory and Research*. Monographs of the Society for Research in Child Development, 50 (1–2), no. 209.

Bateson, P. (1987) Biological approaches to the study of behavioral development. *International Journal of Behavioral Development*, 10, 1–22.

Batson, C. D. (1991) *The Altruism Question: toward a social-psychological answer*. Hillsdale, NJ: Erlbaum.

Battistelli, P. and Farneti, A. (1991) Grandchildren's images of their grandparents: a psychodynamic perspective. In P. K. Smith (ed.), *The Psychology of Grandparenthood: an international perspective*. London: Routledge.

Baudonnière, P.-M. (1987) Interactions dyadiques entre enfants de 4 ans: inconnus, familiers at amis. Le role du degré de familiarité. *International Journal of Psychology*, 22, 347–62.

Baudonnière, P.-M. (1988) *L'évolution des compétences à communiquer chez l'enfant de 2 à 4 ans*. Paris: Presses Universitaires de France.

Baudonnière, P.-M., Garcia-Werebe, M.-J., Michel, J., and Liégeois, J. (1989) Development of communicative competencies in early childhood: a model and results. In B. H. Schneider, G. Attili, J. Nadel, and R. P. Weissberg (eds), *Social Competence in Developmental Perspective*. Dordecht: Kluwer.

Baumrind, D. (1967) Child care practices anteceding three patterns of preschool behavior. *Genetic Psychology Monographs*, 75, 43–88.

Baumrind, D. (1971) Current patterns of parental authority. *Developmental Psychology Monographs*, 4 (1) pt 2.

Baumrind, D. (1972) An exploratory study of socialization effects on black children: some black–white comparisons. *Child Development*, 43, 261–7.

Baumrind, D. (1987) A developmental perspective on adolescent risk taking in contemporary America. In C. E. Irwin (ed.), *Adolescent Social Behavior and Health*. New Directions for Child Development, no. 37. San Francisco: Jossey-Bass.

Baumrind, D. (1989) Rearing competent children. In W. Damon (ed.), *Child Development Today and Tomorrow*. San Francisco: Jossey-Bass.

Baumrind, D. (1991) The influence of parenting style on adolescent competence and substance use. *Journal of Early Adolescence*, 11, 56–95.

Bearison, D. (1982) New directions in studies of social interaction and cognitive growth. In F. Serafica (ed.), *Social Cognitive Development in Context*. London: Methuen.

Bearison, D. J. and Levy, L. M. (1977) Children's comprehension of referential communication: decoding ambiguous messages. *Child Development*, 48, 716–20.

Beattie, G. W. (1983) *Talk: an analysis of speech and nonverbal behaviour in conversation*. Milton Keynes: Open University Press.

Beaudichon, J., Verba, M., and Winnykamen, F. (1988) Interactions sociales et acquisition de connaissances chez l'enfant: une approche pluridimensionelle. *Revue Internationale de Psychologie Sociale*, 1, 129–141.

Beauvois, J.-L. (1984) *La psychologie quotidienne*. Paris: Presses Universitaires de France.

Beauvois, J.-L. and Dubois, N. (1988) The norm of

internality in the explanation of psychological events. *European Journal of Social Psychology*, 18, 299–316.

Becker, J. (1988) The success of parents' indirect techniques for teaching their preschoolers pragmatic skills. *First Language*, 8, 173–82.

Becker, J. A. (1994) "Sneak-shoes", "sworders" and "nose-beards": a case study of lexical innovation. *First Language*, 14, 153–71.

Becker, J. M. T. (1977) A learning analysis of the development of peer-oriented behavior in nine-month-old infants. *Developmental Psychology*, 13, 481–91.

Beckett, H. (1986) Cognitive developmental theory in the study of adolescent development. In S. Wilkinson (ed.), *Feminist Social Psychology: developing theory and practice*. Milton Keynes: Open University Press.

Beebe, B., Jaffe, J., Feldstein, S., Mays, K., and Alson, D. (1985) Interpersonal timing: the application of an adult dialogue model to mother–infant vocal and kinesic interactions. In T. M. Field and N. A. Fox (eds), *Social Perception in Infants*. Norwood, NJ: Ablex.

Befu, H. (1986) Social and cultural background for child development in Japan and the United States. In H. Stevenson, H. Azuma, and K. Hakuta (eds), *Child Development and Education in Japan*. New York: W. H. Freeman.

Beilin, H. (1975) *Studies in the Cognitive Basis of Language Development*. New York: Academic Press.

Bell, R. Q. (1968) A reinterpretation of the direction of effects in studies of socialization. *Psychological Review*, 75, 81–95.

Bell, R. Q. and Harper, L. V. (1977) *Child Effects on Adults*. Lincoln: University of Nebraska Press.

Belle, D. (ed.) (1989) *Children's Social Networks and Social Supports*. New York: Wiley.

Belsky, J. and Pensky, E. (1988) Marital change across the transition to parenthood. In R. Palkovitz and M. B. Sussman (eds), *Transitions to Parenthood*. New York: Haworth.

Belsky, J. and Rovine, M. (1987) Temperament and attachment security in the Strange Situation: a rapprochement. *Child Development*, 58, 787–95.

Belsky, J. and Rovine, M. (1988) Nonmaternal care in the first year of life and the security of infant–parent attachment. *Child Development*, 55, 718–28.

Belsky, J., Lang, M., and Rovine, M. (1985) Stability and change in marriage across the transition to parenthood: a second study. *Journal of Marriage and the Family*, 47, 855–66.

Belsky, J., Rovine, M., and Taylor, D. G. (1984) The Pennsylvania infant and family development project, III: the origins of individual differences in infant–mother attachment: maternal and infant contributions. *Child Development*, 55, 718–28.

Belsky, J., Steinberg, L., and Draper, P. (1991) Childhood experience, interpersonal development, and reproductive strategy: an evolutionary theory of socialization. *Child Development*, 62, 647–70.

Bem, D. J. and Allen, A. (1974) On predicting some of the people some of the time: the search for cross-situational consistencies in behavior. *Psychological Review*, 81, 506–20.

Bem. S. (1974) The measurement of psychological androgyny. *Journal of Consulting and Clinical Psychology*, 42, 155–62.

Bem, S.L. (1983) Gender schema theory and its implications for child development: raising gender-aschematic children in a gender-schematic society. *Signs: Journal of Women in Culture and Society*, 8, 598-616.

Bem, S. L. (1989) Genital knowledge and gender constancy in preschool children. *Child Development*, 60, 649–62.

Bem, S. L. (1993) *The Lenses of Gender: transforming the debate on sexual inequality*. New Haven, Conn.: Yale University Press.

Ben-Amos, I. K. (1994) *Adolescence and Youth in Early Modern England*. New Haven: Yale University Press.

Ben-Ari, R., Schwarzwald, J. and Horiner-Levi, E. (1994) The effects of prevalent social stereotypes on intergroup attribution. *Journal of Cross-cultural Psychology*, 25, 489–500

Benenson, J. F. and Dweck, C. S. (1986) The development of trait explanations and self-evaluations in the academic and social domains. *Child Development*, 57, 1179–87.

Bengston, V. L., Reedy, M. N., and Gordon, C. (1985) Aging and self-conceptions: personality processes and social contexts. In J. E. Birren and K. W. Schaie (eds), *Handbook of the Psychology of Aging*, 2nd edn. New York: Van Nostrand.

Bengston, V. L., Rosenthal, C. and Burton, L. (1990) Families and aging: diversity and heterogeneity. In R. H. Binstock and L. K. George (eds), *Aging and the Social Sciences*, 3rd edn. San Diego: Academic Press.

Bennett, C. (1993) Don't cry for Sir Andrew. *Guardian*, 18 July.

Bennett, M. (1985/86). Developmental changes in the attribution of dispositional features. *Current Psychological Research and Reviews*, 4, 323–9.

Bennett, M. (1993) Introduction. In M. Bennett (ed.), *The Child as Psychologist: an introduction to the development of social cognition*. New York: Harvester Wheatsheaf.

Benoit, D. and Parker, K. C. H. (1994) Stability and

transmission of attachment across three generations. *Child Development*, 65, 1444–56.

Berardo, D. H., Sheehan, C. L., and Leslie, G. R. (1987) A residue of tradition: jobs, careers, and spouses' time in housework. *Journal of Marriage and the Family*, 49, 381–90.

Bereiter, C. and Engelmann, S. (1966) *Teaching Disadvantaged Children in the Pre-school*. Englewood Cliffs, NJ: Prentice Hall.

Bergen, D. J. and Williams, J. E. (1991) Sex stereotypes in the United States revisited. *Sex Roles*, 24, 413–23.

Berger, R. J. (1989) Female delinquency in the emancipation era: a review of the literature. *Sex Roles*, 21, 375–99.

Berger, S. M. (1977) Social comparison, modeling, and perseverance. In J. M. Suls and R. L. Miller (eds), *Social Comparison Processes: theoretical and empirical perspectives*. Washington, DC: Hemisphere.

Berkowitz, L. (1972) Social norms, feelings, and other factors affecting helping and altruism. In L. Berkowitz (ed.), *Advances in Experimental Social Psychology*, vol. 6. New York: Academic Press.

Berkowitz, L. (1994) Is something missing? Some observations prompted by the cognitive-neoassociationist view of anger and emotional aggression. In L. R. Huesmann (ed.), *Aggressive Behavior: current perspectives*. New York: Plenum Press.

Berkowitz, L. and Daniels, L. R. (1963) Responsibility and dependency. *Journal of Abnormal and Social Psychology*, 66, 429–36.

Berman, P. W. (1987) Children caring for babies: age and sex differences in response to infant signals and to the social context. In N. Eisenberg (ed.), *Contemporary Topics in Developmental Psychology*. New York: Wiley.

Berndt, T. J. (1979a) Developmental changes in conformity to peers and parents. *Developmental Psychology*, 15, 608–16.

Berndt, T. J. (1979b) Lack of acceptance of reciprocity norms in preschool children. *Developmental Psychology*, 15, 662–3.

Berndt, T. J. (1981) Relations between social cognition, nonsocial cognition, and social behavior: the case of friendship. In J. H. Flavell and L. Ross (eds), *Social Cognitive Development: frontiers and possible futures*. Cambridge: Cambridge University Press.

Berndt, T. J. (1983) Social cognition, social behavior, and children's friendships. In E. T. Higgins, D. Ruble and W. Hartup (eds), *Social Cognition and Social Development: a socio-cultural perspective*. Cambridge: Cambridge University Press.

Berndt, T. J. and Heller, K. A. (1985) Measuring children's personality attributions. In S. R. Yussen

(ed.), *The Growth of Reflection in Children*. New York: Academic Press.

Berndt, T. J. and Perry, T. B. (1986) Children's perceptions of friendships as supportive relationships. *Developmental Psychology*, 22, 640–8.

Bernzweig, J., Eisenberg, N., and Fabes, R. A. (1993) Children's coping in self- and other- relevant contexts. *Journal of Experimental Child Psychology*, 55, 208–26.

Berry, J. M. and West, R. L. (1993) Cognitive self-efficacy in relation to personal mastery and goal setting across the life span. *International Journal of Behavioral Development*, 16, 351–79.

Berscheid, E. (1986) The question of the importance of physical attractiveness. In C. Herman, M. Zanna and E. Higgins (eds), *Physical Appearance, Stigma, and Social Behavior: the Ontario symposium*, vol. 3. Hillsdale, NJ: Erlbaum.

Berti, A. E. (1993) Fifth-graders' ideas on bank functions and interest before and after a lesson on banking. *European Journal of Psychology of Education*, 8, 183–93.

Berti, A. E. and Bombi, A. S. (1988) *The Child's Construction of Economics*. Cambridge: Cambridge University Press.

Beuf, A. (1974) Doctor, lawyer, household drudge. *Journal of Communication*, 24, 142–5.

Bever, T. (1970) The cognitive basis for linguistic structure. In J. Hayes (ed.), *Cognition and the Development of Language*. New York: Wiley.

Beyene, Y. (1989). *From Menarche to Menopause: reproductive lives of peasant women in two cultures*. New York: State University of New York Press.

Bierhoff, H. W. (1994) On the interface between social support and prosocial behavior: methodological and theoretical implications. In F. Nestemann and K. Hurrelmann (eds), *Social Networks and Social Support in Childhood and Adolescence*. Berlin: de Gruyter.

Bierhoff, H. W. (1996) Prosocial behaviour. In M. Hewstone, W. Stroebe, and G. M. Stephenson (eds), *Introduction to Social Psychology*, 2nd edn. Oxford: Blackwell.

Bigelow, A., MacLean, J., Wood, C., and Smith, J. (1990) Infants' responses to child and adult strangers: an investigation of height and facial configuration variables. *Infant Behavior and Development*, 13, 21–32.

Bigelow, B. J. (1977) Children's friendship expectations: a cognitive-developmental study. *Child Development*, 48, 246–53.

Bijstra, J. O., van Geert, P., and Jackson, A. E. (1989) Conservation and the appearance–reality distinction: what do children really know and what do they answer? *British Journal of Developmental Psychology*, 7, 43–53.

Bijstra, J. O., Jackson, S., and van Geert, P. (1991) Progress to conservation: conflict or correct answer? *European Journal of Psychology of Education*, 6, 291–301.

Billy, J. O. G., Brewster, K. L., and Grady, W. R. (1994) Contextual effects on the sexual behavior of adolescent women. *Journal of Marriage and the Family*, 56, 387–404.

Bilsker, D., Schiedel, D., and Marcia, J. (1988) Sex differences in identity status. *Sex Roles*, 18, 231–6.

Binder, A. (1988) Juvenile delinquency. *Annual Review of Psychology*, 39, 253–82.

Birdwhistell, R. L. (1971) *Kinesics and Context: essays on body-motion communication.* London: Allen Lane.

Bjorkqvist, K. and Niemala, P. (1992) New trends in the study of female aggression. In K. Bjorkqvist and P. Niemala (eds), *Of Mice and Women: aspects of female aggression.* San Diego: Academic Press.

Bjorkqvist, K., Osterman, K., and Kaukiainen, A. (1992) The development of direct and indirect aggressive strategies in males and females. In K. Bjorkqvist and P. Niemala (eds), *Of Mice and Women: aspects of female aggression.* San Diego: Academic Press.

Blakemore, J. E. O. (1990) Children's nurturant interactions with their infant siblings: an exploration of gender differences and maternal socialization. *Sex Roles*, 22, 43–57.

Blanchard, W. H. (1959) The group process in gang rape. *Journal of Social Psychology*, 49, 259–66.

Blanchard-Fields, F. (1986) Reasoning on social dilemmas varying in emotional saliency: an adult developmental perspective. *Psychology and Aging*, 1, 325–33.

Blanck, P. D. and Rosenthal, R. (1982) Developing strategies for decoding "leaky" messages: on learning how and when to decode discrepant and consistent social communications. In R. S. Feldman (ed.), *Development of Nonverbal Behavior in Children.* New York: Springer-Verlag.

Blank, T. O. (1982) *A Social Psychology of Developing Adults.* New York: Wiley.

Blasi, A. (1980) Bridging moral cognition and moral action: a critical review of the literature. *Psychological Bulletin*, 88, 1–45.

Blaye, A., Light, P., and Rubtsov, V. (1992) Collaborative learning at the computer: how social processes "interface" with human–computer interaction. *European Journal of Psychology of Education*, 7, 257–67.

Blaze-Temple, D. and Lo, S. K. (1992) Stages of drug use: a community survey of Perth teenagers. *British Journal of Addiction*, 87, 215–25.

Blehar, M. C., Lieberman, A. F., and Ainsworth, M.

D. S. (1977) Early face-to-face interaction and its relationship to later mother–infant attachment. *Child Development*, 48, 195–203.

Bloom, K. and Lo, E. (1990) Adult perceptions of vocalizing infants. *Infant Behavior and Development*, 13, 209–19.

Bloom, K., D'Odorico, L., and Beaumont, S. (1993) Adult preferences for syllabic vocalizations: generalizations to parity and native language. *Infant Behavior and Development*, 16, 109–20.

Bloom, L., Hood, L., and Lightbown, P. (1974) Imitation in language development: if, when, and why. *Cognitive Psychology*, 6, 380–420.

Blos, P. (1962) *On Adolescence.* New York: Free Press.

Blos, P. (1979) *The Adolescent Passage.* New York: International Universities Press.

Blum, L. A. (1980) *Friendship, Altruism and Morality.* London: Routledge and Kegan Paul.

Blurton Jones, N. (1972) Categories of child–child interaction. In N. Blurton Jones (ed.), *Ethological Studies of Child Behaviour.* Cambridge: Cambridge University Press.

Blyth, D. A. (1982) Mapping the social world of adolescents: issues, techniques, and problems. In F. C. Serafica (ed.), *Social-cognitive Development in Context.* New York: Guilford.

Blyth, D. A. and Foster-Clark, F. (1987) Gender differences in perceived intimacy with different members of adolescents' social networks. *Sex Roles*, 17, 689–718.

Blythe, R. (1979) *The View in Winter.* New York: Harcourt Brace Jovanovich.

Bo, I. (1989) The significant people in the social networks of adolescents. In K. Hurrelmann and U. Engel (eds), *The Social World of Adolescents: international perspectives.* Berlin and New York: de Gruyter.

Bo, I. (1994) The sociocultural environment as a source of support. In F. Nestemann and K. Hurrelmann (eds), *Social Networks and Social Support in Childhood and Adolescence.* Berlin: de Gruyter.

Boer, F. (1990) *Sibling Relationships in Middle Childhood: an empirical study.* Leiden: DSWO Press, University of Leiden.

Boer, F. and Dunn, J. (eds) (1992) *Children's Sibling Relationships: developmental and clinical issues.* Hillsdale, NJ: Erlbaum.

Boer, F., Goedhart, A. W., and Treffers, P. D. A. (1992) Siblings and their parents. In F. Boer and J. Dunn (eds), *Children's Sibling Relationships: developmental and clinical issues.* Hillsdale, NJ: Erlbaum.

Boggiano, A. K., Barrett, M., and Kellam, T. (1993) Competing theoretical analyses of helplessness: a social developmental analysis. *Journal of Experimental Child Psychology*, 55, 194–207.

Bohannon, J. N. and Stanowicz, L. B. (1988) The issue of negative evidence: adult responses to children's language errors. *Developmental Psychology*, 24, 684–9.

Bohlin, G. and Hagekull, B. (1993) Stranger wariness and sociability in the early years. *Infant Behavior and Development*, 16, 53–67.

du Bois-Reymond, M. and Ravesloot, J. (1994) The role of parents and peers in the sexual and relational socialization of adolescents. In F. Nestemann and K. Hurrelmann (eds), *Social Networks and Social Support in Childhood and Adolescence*. Berlin: de Gruyter.

Boldizar, J. P., Perry, D. G., and Perry, L. C. (1989) Outcome values and aggression. *Child Development*, 60, 571–9.

Bolton, R. (1973) Aggression and hypoglycemia among the Qolla: a study in psychobiological anthropology. *Ethnology*, 12, 227–57.

Bond, C. F. Jr and Titus, L. J. (1983) Social facilitation: a meta-analysis of 241 studies. *Psychological Bulletin*, 94, 265–92.

Bond, M. H. and Hwang, K.-K. (1986) The social psychology of Chinese people. In M. H. Bond (ed.), *The Psychology of the Chinese People*. Hong Kong and Oxford: Oxford University Press.

Bonitatibus, G., Godshall, S., Kelley, M., Levering, T., and Lynch, E. (1988) The role of social cognition in comprehension monitoring skills. *First Language*, 8, 287–98.

Booth, C. L., Rose-Krasnor, C., and Rubin, K. H. (1991) Relating preschoolers' social competence and their mothers' parenting behaviors to early attachment security and high-risk status. *Journal of Social and Personal Relationships*, 8, 363–82.

Borke, H. (1975) Piaget's mountains revisited: changes in the egocentric landscape. *Developmental Psychology*, 11, 240–3.

Borman, K. M. and Kurdek, L. A. (1987) Grade and gender differences in and the stability and correlates of the structural complexity of children's playground games. *International Journal of Behavioral Development*, 10, 241–51.

Bornstein, H. (1989) Cross-cultural developmental comparisons: the case of Japanese–American infant and mother activities and interactions. What we know, what we need to know, and why we need to know. *Developmental Review*, 9, 171–204.

Bornstein, M. H. (1989a) Between caretakers and their young: two modes of interaction and their consequences for cognitive growth. In M. H. Bornstein and J. S. Bruner (eds), *Interaction in Human Development*. Hillsdale, NJ: Erlbaum.

Bornstein, M. H. (1989b) Sensitive periods in development: structural characteristics and causal interpretations. *Psychological Bulletin*, 105, 179–97.

Bornstein, M. H., Gaughran, J. M., and Segui, I. (1991a) Multimethod assessment of infant temperament: mother questionnaire and mother and observer reports evaluated and compared at five months using the Infant Temperament Measure. *International Journal of Behavioral Development*, 14, 131–51.

Bornstein, M. and Tamis-Lemonda, C. S. (1990) Activities and interactions of mothers and their firstborn infants in the first six months of life: covariation, stability, continuity, correspondence, and prediction. *Child Development*, 61, 1206–17.

Bornstein, M. H., Tal, J., Rahn, C., Galperin, C. Z., Pecheux, M.-G., Lamour, M., Toda, S., Azuma, H., Ogino, M., and Tamis-Lemonda, C. S. (1992) Functional analysis of the contents of maternal speech to infants of 5 and 13 months in four cultures: Argentina, France, Japan, and the United States. *Developmental Psychology*, 28, 593–603.

Bornstein, M. H., Tamis-Lemonda, C. S., Pecheux, M.-G. and Rahn, C. W. (1991b) Mother and infant activity and interaction in France and in the United States: a comparative study. *International Journal of Behavioral Development*, 14, 21–43.

Bornstein, M. H., Toda, S., Azuma, H., Tamis-Lemonda, C., and Ogino, M. (1990) Mother and infant activity and interaction in Japan and in the United States: II. A comparative microanalysis of naturalistic exchanges focused on the organisation of infant attention. *International Journal of Behavioral Development*, 13, 289–308.

Bouffard, L., Lens, W., and Nuttin, J. R. (1983) Extension de la perspective temporelle future en relation avec la frustration. *International Journal of Psychology*, 18, 429–42.

Boukydis, C. F. Z. (1985) Perception of infant crying as an interpersonal event. In B. M. Lester and C. F. Z. Boukydis (eds), *Infant Crying: theoretical and research perspectives*. New York: Plenum.

Boukydis, C. F. Z. and Burgess, R. (1982) Adult physiological response to infant cries: effects of temperament of infant, parental status, and gender. *Child Development*, 53, 1291–8.

Boulton, M. J. (1993) Proximate causes of aggressive fighting in middle school children. *British Journal of Educational Psychology*, 63, 231–44.

Bower, T. G. R. (1979) *Human Development*. San Francisco: Freeman.

Bowlby, J. (1944) Forty-four juvenile thieves: their characters and home life. *International Journal of Psycho-Analysis*, 21, 154–78.

Bowlby, J. (1953) *Child Care and the Growth of Love*. Harmondsworth: Penguin.

Bowlby, J. (1969) *Attachment and Loss, vol. 1: Attachment*. London: Hogarth.

Bowlby, J. (1973) *Attachment and Loss, vol. 2: Separation*. London: Hogarth.

Bowlby, J. (1980) *Attachment and Loss, vol. 3: Loss, sadness and depression*. Harmondsworth: Penguin.

Bowlby, J. (1988) *A Secure Base: parent–child attachment and healthy human development*. New York: Basic Books.

Bradbard, M. R., Martin, C. L., Endsley, R. C., and Halverson, C. F. (1986) Influence of sex stereotypes on children's exploration and memory: a competence versus performance distinction. *Developmental Psychology*, 22, 481–6.

Bradley, B. S. (1989) *Visions of Infancy: a critical introduction to child psychology*. Cambridge: Polity Press.

Braine, M. D. S. (1971) On two types of models of the internalization of grammars. In D. I. Slobin (ed.), *The Ontogenesis of Grammar*. New York: Academic Press.

Braithwaite, V. (1992) The ageing experience: loss, threat or challenge? In P. C. L. Heaven (ed.), *Life Span Development*. Sydney and London: Harcourt Brace Jovanovich.

Brandtstadter, J., Wentura, D., and Greve, W. (1993) Adaptive resources of the aging self: outlines of an emergent perspective. *International Journal of Behavioral Development*, 16, 323–49.

Braten, S. (1992) The virtual other in infants' minds and social feelings. In A. Heen Wold (ed.), *The Dialogue Alternative*. Oslo: Scandinavian University Press.

Brazelton, T. B. (1988) Stress for families today. *Infant Mental Health Journal*, 9, 65–72.

Breakwell, G. M. (1986) *Coping with Threatened Identities*. London: Methuen.

Brehm, S. S. (1981) Oppositional behavior in children: a reactance theory approach. In S. S. Brehm, S. M. Kassin, and F. X. Gibbons (eds), *Developmental Social Psychology: theory and research*. New York: Oxford University Press.

Brehm, S. S., Kassin, S. M., and Gibbons, F. X. (eds) (1981) *Developmental Social Psychology: theory and research*. New York: Oxford University Press.

Bremner, G. (1984) *Infancy*. Oxford: Blackwell.

Bremner, G. (1993) Spatial representation in infancy and early childhood. In C. Pratt and A. F. Garton (eds), *Systems of Representation in Children: development and use*. Chichester: Wiley.

Brenner, J. and Mueller, E. (1982) Shared meaning in boy toddlers' peer relations. *Child Development*, 53, 380–91.

Bretherton, I. (1978) Making friends with one-year-olds: an experimental study of infant–stranger interaction. *Merrill-Palmer Quarterly*, 24, 29–51.

Bretherton, I. (1987) New perspectives on attachment relations: security, communication, and internal working models. In J. D. Osofsky (ed.), *Handbook of Infant Development*. New York: Wiley.

Bretherton, I. (1990) Open communication and internal working models: their role in the development of attachment relationships. In R. A. Thompson (ed.), *Socioemotional Development: Nebraska symposium on motivation, 1988*. Lincoln: University of Nebraska Press.

Bretherton, I. (1992) The origins of attachment theory: John Bowlby and Mary Ainsworth. *Developmental Psychology*, 28, 759–75.

Bretherton, I. and Ainsworth, M. D. S. (1974) Responses of one-year-olds to a stranger in a strange situation. In M. Lewis and L. A. Rosenblum (eds), *The Origins of Fear*. New York: Wiley.

Bretherton, I. and Beeghly, M. (1982) Talking about internal states: the acquisition of an explicit theory of mind. *Developmental Psychology*, 18, 906–21.

Bretherton, I., Bates, E., McNew, S., Shore, C., Williamson, C. and Beeghly-Smith, M. (1981a) Comprehension and production of symbols in infancy: an experimental study. *Developmental Psychology*, 17, 728–36.

Bretherton, I., Fritz, J., Zahn-Waxler, C., and Ridgeway, D. (1986) Learning to talk about emotions: a functionalist perspective. *Child Development*, 57, 529–48.

Bretherton, I., Prentiss, C., and Ridgeway, D. (1990) Family relationships as represented in a story-completion task at thirty-seven and fifty-four months of age. *New Directions for Child Development*, 48, 85–105.

Bretherton, I., Stolberg, U., and Kreye, M. (1981b) Engaging strangers in proximal interaction: infants' social initiative. *Developmental Psychology*, 17, 746–55.

Bril, B., Zack, M., and Nkounkhou-Hombessa, E. (1989) Ethnotheories of development and education: a view from different cultures. *European Journal of Psychology of Education*, 4, 307–18.

Brim, O. G., Jr (1968) Adult socialization. In J. Clausen (ed.), *Socialization and Society*. Boston: Little, Brown.

Brim, O. G., Jr and Kagan, J. (1980) Constancy and change: a view of the issues. In O. G. Brim, Jr and J. Kagan (eds), *Constancy and Change in Human*

Development. Cambridge, Mass.: Harvard University Press.

Broch, H. B. (1990) *Growing up Agreeably: Bonerate childhood observed*. Honolulu: University of Hawaii Press.

Brody, G., Stoneman, Z., and Burke, M. (1987) Child temperaments, maternal differential behavior, and sibling relationships. *Developmental Psychology*, 23, 354–62.

Broerse, J., Peltola, C., and Crassini, B. (1983) Infants' reactions to perceptual paradox during mother–infant interactions. *Developmental Psychology*, 19, 310–16.

Bronfenbrenner, U. (1970) *Two Worlds of Childhood*. Harmondsworth: Penguin.

Bronfenbrenner, U. (1979) *The Ecology of Human Development: experiments by nature and design*. Cambridge, Mass.: Harvard University Press.

Bronfenbrenner, U. (1988) Interacting systems in human development. Research paradigms: present and future. In N. Bolger, A. Caspi, G. Downey, and M. Moorehouse (eds), *Persons in Context: developmental processes*. Cambridge: Cambridge University Press.

Bronfenbrenner, U. and Crouter, A. C. (1983) The evolution of environmental models in developmental research. In W. Kessen (ed.), *Handbook of Child Psychology: history, theories, and methods*, vol. I. New York: Wiley.

Bronfenbrenner, U., Alvarez, W. F., and Henderson, C. R., Jr (1984) Working and watching: maternal employment status and parents' perceptions of their three-year-old children. *Child Development*, 55, 1362–79.

Bronson, W. C. (1974) Mother–toddler interaction: a perspective on studying the development of competence. *Merrill-Palmer Quarterly*, 20, 275–301.

Bronson, W. C. (1981) Toddlers' behavior with age-mates: issues of interaction, cognition, and affect. In L. Lipsett (ed.), *Monographs on Infancy*, vol. 1. Norwood, NJ: Ablex.

Brook, J. S., Whiteman, M., Balka, E. B., and Hamburg, B. A. (1993) African–American and Puerto Rican drug use: personality, familiar, and other environmental risk factors, *Genetic, Social, and General Psychology Monographs*, 118, 417–38.

Brookhart, J. and Hock E. (1976) The effects of experimental context and experimental background on infants' behavior toward their mothers and a stranger. *Child Development*, 47, 333–40.

Brooks-Gunn, J. (1985) Maternal beliefs about children's sex-typed characteristics as they relate to maternal behavior. In I. E. Sigel (ed.), *Parental Belief Systems: the psychological consequences for children*. Hillsdale, NJ: Erlbaum.

Brooks-Gunn, J. (1991) How stressful is the transition to adolescence for girls? In M. E. Colten and S. Gore (eds), *Adolescent Stress: causes and consequences*. New York: Aldine de Gruyter.

Brooks-Gunn, J. (1993) Why do adolescents have difficulty adhering to health regimes? In N. Krasnegor, L. Epstein, S. B. Johnson, and S. J. Yaffe (eds), *Developmental Aspects of Health Compliance Behavior*. Hillsdale, NJ: Erlbaum.

Brooks-Gunn, J. and Furstenberg, F. F. (1986) The children of adolescent mothers: physical, academic and psychological outcomes. *Developmental Review*, 6, 224–51.

Brooks-Gunn, J. and Furstenberg, F. F. (1989) Adolescent sexual behavior. *American Psychologist*, 44, 249–57.

Brooks-Gunn, J. and Paikoff, R. L. (1992) Changes in self feelings during the transition towards adolescence. In H. McGurk (ed.), *Childhood Social Development: contemporary perspectives*. Hove: Erlbaum.

Brooks-Gunn, J. and Reiter, E. O. (1990) The role of pubertal processes. In S. S. Feldman and G. R. Elliott (eds), *At the Threshold: the developing adolescent*. Cambridge, Mass.: Harvard University Press.

Brooks-Gunn, J. and Ruble, D. (1982) The development of menstrual-related beliefs and behaviors during early adolescence. *Child Development*, 53, 1567–77.

Broughton, J. M. (1978) The cognitive-developmental approach to morality: a reply to Kurtines and Greif. *Journal of Moral Education*, 8, 81–96.

Broverman, I. K., Broverman, D. M., Clarkson, F. E., Rosenkrantz, P. S., and Vogel, S. R. (1970) Sex-role stereotypes and clinical judgments of mental health. *Journal of Consulting and Clinical Psychology*, 34, 1–7.

Brown, B. B. (1989) The role of peer groups in adolescents' adjustment to secondary school. In T. J. Berndt and G. W. Ladd (eds), *Peer Relationships in Child Development*. New York: Wiley.

Brown, B. B. (1990) Peer groups and peer cultures. In S. S. Feldman and G. R. Elliott (eds), *At the Threshold: the developing adolescent*. Cambridge, Mass.: Harvard University Press.

Brown, B. B., Clasen, D. R., and Eicher, S. A. (1986) Perceptions of peer pressure, peer conformity dispositions, and self-reported behavior among adolescents. *Developmental Psychology*, 22, 521–30.

Brown, B. B., Mounts, N., Lamborn, S. D., and Steinberg, L. (1993) Parenting practices and peer group affiliation in adolescence. *Child Development*, 64, 467–82.

Brown, P. and Levinson, S. C. (1987). *Politeness: some universals in language use*. Cambridge: Cambridge University Press.

Brown, R. (1965) *Social Psychology*. New York: Free Press.

Brown, R. (1973) *A First Language*. Cambridge, Mass.: Harvard University Press.

Brown, R. (1980) The maintenance of conversation. In D. R. Olson (ed.), *The Social Foundations of Language and Thought*. New York: Norton.

Brown, R. and Fraser, C. (1963) The acquisition of syntax. In C. N. Cofer and B. S. Musgrave (eds), *Verbal Behavior and Learning*. New York: McGraw-Hill.

Brown, R. and Hanlon, C. (1970) Derivational complexity and order of acquisition in child speech. In J. R. Hayes (ed.), *Cognition and the Development of Language*. New York: Wiley.

Brown, R. and Herrnstein, R. J. (1975) *Psychology*. London: Methuen.

Brown, R., Cazden. C., and Bellugi, U. (1969) The child's grammar from I to III. In J. P. Hill (ed.), *Minnesota Symposium on Child Psychology*, vol. 2. Minneapolis: University of Minnesota Press.

Brown, R. J. (1996) Intergroup relations. In M. Hewstone, W. Stroebe and G. M. Stephenson (eds), *Introduction to Social Psychology*, 2nd edn. Oxford: Blackwell.

Brownell, M. D., Trehub, S. E., and Gartner, G. M. (1988) Children's understanding of referential messages produced by deaf and hearing speakers. *First Language*, 8, 271–86.

Brownmiller, S. (1975) *Against our Will: men, women, and rape*. New York: Simon and Schuster.

Brownmiller, S. (1984). *Femininity*. New York: Linden Press.

Bruner, J. S. (1978) Learning how to do things with words. In J. S. Bruner and A. Garton (eds), *Human Growth and Development*. Oxford: Clarendon.

Bruner, J. S. (1983a) *Child's Talk: learning to use language*. Oxford: Oxford University Press.

Bruner, J. S. (1983b) The acquisition of pragmatic commitments. In R. M. Golinkoff (ed.), *The Transition from Prelinguistic to Linguistic Communication*. Hillsdale, NJ: Erlbaum.

Bruner, J. S. and Bornstein, M. H. (1989) On interaction. In M. H. Bornstein and J. S. Bruner (eds), *Interaction in Human Development*. Hillsdale, NJ: Erlbaum.

Bruner, J. S., Goodnow, J. J., and Austin, G. A. (1956) *A Study of Thinking*. New York: Wiley.

Bryan, J. H. (1975) Children's cooperation and helping behaviors. In M. Hetherington (ed.), *Review of Child Development Research*, vol. 5. Chicago: University of Chicago Press.

Bryan, J. H. and Walbek, N. H. (1970) The impact of words and deeds concerning altruism upon children. *Child Development*, 41, 747–57.

Bryant, B. K. (1985) *The Neighborhood Walk: sources of support in middle childhood*. Monographs of the Society for Research in Child Development, 50 (3), no. 210.

Bryant, B. K. (1992) Sibling caretaking: providing emotional support during middle childhood. In F. Boer and J. Dunn (eds), *Children's Sibling Relationships: developmental and clinical issues*. Hillsdale, NJ: Erlbaum.

Bryant, B. K. (1994) How does social support function in childhood? In F. Nestemann and K. Hurrelmann (eds), *Social Networks and Social Support in Childhood and Adolescence*. Berlin: de Gruyter.

Bryant, P. (1974) *Perception and Understanding in Young Children*. London: Methuen.

Buck, R. (1975) Nonverbal communication of affect in children. *Journal of Personality and Social Psychology*, 31, 644–53.

Buck, R. (1981) The evolution and development of emotion expression and communication. In S. S. Brehm, S. M. Kassin, and F. X. Gibbons (eds), *Developmental Social Psychology: theory and research*. New York: Oxford University Press.

Buck, R. (1982) Spontaneous and symbolic nonverbal behavior and the ontogeny of communication. In R. S. Feldman (ed.), *Development of Nonverbal Behavior in Children*. New York: Springer-Verlag.

Buckley, N., Siegal, L. S., and Ness, S. (1979) Egocentrism, empathy, and altruistic behavior. *Developmental Psychology*, 15, 329–30.

Bugental, D. B., Blue, J., Cortez, V., Fleck, K., and Rodriguez, A. (1992) Influences of witnessed affect on information processing in children. *Child Development*, 63, 774–86.

Bugental, D. E., Kaswan, J. W., Love, L. R., and Fox, M. N. (1970) Child versus adult perception of evaluative messages in verbal, vocal and visual channels. *Developmental Psychology*, 2, 367–75.

Buhler, C. (1930) *The First Year of Life*. New York: John Day.

Buhler, C. (1937) *From Birth to Maturity: an outline of the psychological development of the child*. London: Kegan Paul, Trench, Trubner & Co.

Buhrmester, D. (1990) Intimacy of friendship, interpersonal competence, and adjustment during preadolescence and adolescence. *Child Development*, 61, 1101–11.

Buhrmester, D. (1992) The developmental courses of sibling and peer relationships. In F. Boer and J. Dunn (eds), *Children's Sibling Relationships: developmental and clinical issues*. Hillsdale, NJ: Erlbaum.

Buhrmester, D. and Furman, W. (1987) The

development of companionship and intimacy. *Child Development*, 58, 1101–13.

Bukowski, W. M. and Hoza, B. (1989) Popularity and friendship: issues in theory, measurement and outcome. In T. J. Berndt and G. W. Ladd (eds), *Peer Relationships in Child Development*. Chichester: Wiley.

Bullock, A. (1993) *Hitler and Stalin: parallel lives*. London: Fontana.

Bullock, M. and Lutkenhaus, P. (1988) The development of volitional behavior in the toddler years. *Child Development*, 59, 664–74.

Bullock, M. and Russell, J. A. (1984) Preschool children's interpretation of facial expressions of emotion. *International Journal of Behavioral Development*, 7, 193–214.

Bullock, M. and Russell, J. A. (1985) Further evidence on preschoolers' interpretations of facial expressions of emotion. *International Journal of Behavioral Development*, 8, 15–38.

Bullough, V. L. (1981) Age at menarche: a misunderstanding. *Science*, 213, 365–6.

Bullowa, M. (1979) Introduction: prelinguistic communication: a field for scientific research. In M. Bullowa (ed.), *Before Speech: the beginnings of interpersonal communication*. Cambridge: Cambridge University Press.

Burbank, V. K. (1988) *Aboriginal Adolescence: maidenhood in an Australian community*. New Brunswick: Rutgers University Press.

Burger, D. and Hewstone, M. (1993) Young children's causal attributions for success and failure: "self-enhancing" boys and "self-derogating" girls. *British Journal of Developmental Psychology*, 11, 125–9.

Burgess, A. (1972) *A Clockwork Orange*. Harmondsworth: Penguin.

Burman, E. (1994) *Deconstructing Developmental Psychology*. London: Routledge.

Burnham, D. K., Earnshaw, L., and Clark, J. E. (1991) Development of categorical identification of native and non-native bilabial stops: infants, children and adults. *Journal of Child Language*, 18, 231–60.

Burnham, D. K., Earnshaw, L., and Quinn, M. C. (1987) The development of categorical identification in speech. In B. E. McKenzie and R. H. Day (eds), *Perceptual Development in Early Infancy: problems and issues*. Hillsdale, NJ: Erlbaum.

Burns, A. and Dunlop, R. (1992) Divorce. In P. C. L. Heaven (ed.), *Life Span Development*. Sydney and London: Harcourt Brace Jovanovich.

Burns, A., Homel, R., and Goodnow, J. (1984) Conditions of life and parental values. *Australian Journal of Psychology*, 36, 219–37.

Burton, R. V. (1963) The generality of honesty reconsidered. *Psychological Review*, 70, 481–99.

Bury, M. and Holme, A. (1991) *Life after Ninety*. London: Routledge.

Bush, P. J., Weinfurt, K. P., and Iannotti, R. J. (1994) Families versus peers: developmental influences on drug use from Grade 4–5 to Grade 7–8. *Journal of Applied Developmental Psychology*, 15, 437–56.

Bush, R. (1990) The social context of young men's and women's drinking: a psychosocial developmental perspective. In P. C. L. Heaven and V. J. Callan (eds), *Adolescence: an Australian perspective*. Sydney: Harcourt Brace Jovanovich.

Bushnell, I. W. R. (1982) Discrimination of faces by young infants. *Journal of Experimental Child Psychology*, 33, 298–308.

Bushnell, I. W. R., Sai, F., and Mullin, J. T. (1989) Neonatal recognition of the mother's face. *British Journal of Developmental Psychology*, 7, 3–13.

Buss, A. H. (1961) *The Psychology of Aggression*. New York: Wiley.

Buss, A. H. (1992) Personality: primate heritage and human distinctiveness. In R. A. Zucker, A. I. Rabin, J. Aronoff, and S. J. Frank (eds), *Personality Structure in the Life Course: essays on personology in the Murray tradition*. New York: Springer.

Buss, A. H. and Plomin, R. (1984) *Temperament: early developing personality traits*. Hillsdale, NJ: Erlbaum.

Buss, D. M. (1987) Sex differences in human mate selection criteria: an evolutionary perspective. In C. Crawford, M. Smith, and D. Krebs (eds), *Sociobiology and Psychology: ideas, issues and applications*. Hillsdale, NJ: Erlbaum.

Buss, D. M. and associates (1990) International preferences in selecting mates: a study of 37 cultures. *Journal of Cross-Cultural Psychology*, 21, 5–47.

Bussey, K. and Bandura, A. (1984) Influence of gender constancy and social power on sex-linked modeling. *Journal of Personality and Social Psychology*, 47, 1292–1302.

Bussey. K. (1983) A social-cognitive appraisal of sex-role development. *Australian Journal of Psychology*, 35, 135–43.

Bussey, K. and Bandura, A. (1992) Self-regulatory mechanisms governing gender-development. *Child Development*, 63, 1236–50.

Bussey, K. and Perry, D. G. (1982) Same-sex imitation: the avoidance of cross-sex models or the acceptance of same-sex models? *Sex Roles*, 8, 773–84.

Butler, M. and Paisley, W. (1980) *Women and the Mass Media: Sourcebook for research and action*. New York: Human Sciences Press.

Butler, R. (1989a) Interest in the task and interest in peers' work in competitive and noncompetitive conditions: a developmental study. *Child Development*, 60, 562–70.

Butler, R. (1989b) Mastery versus ability appraisal: a developmental study of children's observations of peers' work. *Child Development*, 60, 1350–61.

Butler, R. and Ruzany, N. (1993) Age and socialization effects on the development of social comparison motives and normative ability assessment in kibbutz and urban children. *Child Development*, 64, 532–43.

Butterworth, G. (1982) A brief account of the conflict between the individual and the social in models of cognitive growth. In G. Butterworth and P. Light (eds), *Social Cognition: Studies of the development of understanding*. Chicago: The University of Chicago Press.

Butterworth, G. E. and Grover, L. (1988) The origins of referential communication in human infancy. In L. Weiskrantz (ed.), *Thought without Language*. Oxford: Clarendon.

Buunk, B. (1996) Affiliation, attraction and close relationships. In M. Hewstone, W. Stroebe, and G. M. Stephenson (eds), *Introduction to Social Psychology*, 2nd edn. Oxford: Blackwell.

Byrne, D. (1965) Parental antecedents of authoritarianism. *Journal of Personality and Social Psychology*, 1, 369–73.

Cahan, E. D. (1991) Science, practice, and gender roles in early American child psychology. In F. S. Kessel, M. H. Bornstein, and A. J. Sameroff (eds), *Contemporary Constructions of the Child: essays in honor of William Kessen*. Hillsdale, NJ: Erlbaum.

Cain, M. (ed.) (1989) *Growing Up Good: policing the behaviour of girls in Europe*. London: Sage.

Cairns, R. B. and Cairns, B. D. (1988) The sociogenesis of self concepts. In N. Bolger, A. Caspi, G. Downey and M. Moorehouse (eds), *Persons in Context. Developmental processes*. Cambridge: Cambridge University Press.

Cairns, R. B., Cairns, B. D., Neckerman, H. J., Ferguson, L. L. and Gariepy, J. (1989a) Growth and aggression: 1. Childhood to early adolescence. *Developmental Psychology*, 25, 320–30.

Cairns, R. B., Neckerman, H. J., and Cairns, B. D. (1989b) Social networks and the shadows of synchrony. In G. R. Adams, R. Montemayor, and T. Gullotta (eds), *Biology of Adolescent Behavior and Development*. Newbury Park, Calif.: Sage.

Cairns, R. B., Peterson, G., and Neckerman, H. J. (1988) Suicidal behavior in aggressive adolescents. *Journal of Clinical Child Psychology*, 17, 298–309.

Calam, R., Waller, G., Slade, P., and Newton, T. (1989) Eating disorders and adolescence: relationships with parents. *International Journal of Eating Disorders*, 9, 479–85.

Caldera, Y. M., Huston, A. C., and O'Brien, M. (1989) Social interactions and play patterns of parents and toddlers with feminine, masculine and neutral toys. *Child Development*, 60, 70–6.

Callan, V. (1992) Issues in career development. In P. C. L. Heaven (ed.), *Life Span Development*. Sydney and London: Harcourt Brace Jovanovich.

Callan, V. J. and Noller, P. (1987) *Marriage and the Family*. Sydney: Methuen.

Calvert, S. L. and Huston, A. C. (1987) Television and gender schemata. In L. S. Liben and M. L. Signorella (eds), *Children's Gender Schemata*. San Francisco: Jossey-Bass.

Camaioni, L. (1989) The role of social interaction in the transition from communication to language. In A. de Ribaupierre (ed.), *Transition Mechanisms in Child Development: the longitudinal perspective*. Cambridge: Cambridge University Press.

Camaioni, L. (1993) The social construction of meaning in early infant–parent and infant–peer relations. In J. Nadel and L. Camaioni, L. (eds), *New Perspectives in Early Communicative Development*. London: Routledge.

Camaioni, L., De Castro Campos, M. F. P., and de Lemos, C. (1984) On the failure of the interactionist paradigm in language acquisition: a re-evaluation. In W. Doise and A. Palmonari (eds), *Social Interaction in Individual Development*. Cambridge: Cambridge University Press.

Campbell, A. (1993) *Men, Women, and Aggression*. New York: Basic Books.

Campbell, R. N. and MacDonald, T. B. (1983) Text and context in early language comprehension. In M. C. Donaldson, R. Grieve, and C. Pratt (eds), *Early Childhood Development and Education*. Edinburgh: Grant McIntyre.

Campbell, S. B. and Ewing, L. J. (1990) Follow-up of hard-to-manage pre-schoolers: adjustment at age 9 and predictors of continuing symptoms. *Journal of Child Psychology and Psychiatry*, 31, 871–89.

Campos, J. J. and Sternberg, C. (1981) Perception, appraisal, and emotion: the onset of social referencing. In M. E. Lamb and L. R. Sherrod (eds), *Infant Social Cognition: empirical and theoretical considerations*. Hillsdale, NJ: Erlbaum.

Campos, J. J., Barrett, K. C., Lambe, M. E., Goldsmith, H. H., and Sternberg, C. (1983) Socioemotional development. In M. M. Haith and J. J. Campos (eds), *Handbook of Child Psychology*. Vol 2: *Infancy and developmental psychobiology*. New York: Wiley.

Campos, J. J., Campos, R. G., and Barrett, K. C. (1989) Emergent themes in the study of emotional development and emotion regulation. *Developmental Psychology*, 25, 394–402.

Camras, L. A. (1982) Ethological approaches to non-verbal communication. In R. S. Feldman (ed.), *Development of Nonverbal Behavior in Children*. New York: Springer-Verlag.

Camras, L. A. (1992) Expressive development and basic emotions. *Cognition and Emotion*, 6, 269–83.

Camras, L. A. and Sachs, V. B. (1991) Social referencing and caretaker expressive behavior in a day care setting. *Infant Behavior and Development*, 14, 27–36.

Camras, L. A., Malatesta, C., and Izard, C. E. (1991) The development of facial expressions in infancy. In R. S. Feldman and B. Rime (eds), *Fundamentals of Nonverbal Behavior*. Cambridge: Cambridge University Press.

Canter, R. J. (1982) Sex differences in self-report delinquency. *Criminology*, 20, 373–93.

Caplan, M., Vespo, J., Pederson, J., and Hay, D. F. (1991) Conflict and its resolution in small groups of one- and two- year-olds. *Child Development*, 62, 1513–24.

Caporael, L. (1981) The paralanguage of caregiving: baby talk to the institutionalised aged. *Journal of Personality and Social Psychology*, 40, 876–84.

Caporael, L. and Culbertson, G. H. (1986) Verbal response modes of baby talk and other speech at institutions for the aged. *Language and Communication*, 6, 99–112.

Carey, S. (1978) The child as word learner. In M. Halle, G. A. Miller, and J. Bresnan (eds), *Linguistic Theory and Psychological Reality*. Cambridge, Mass.: MIT Press.

Carey, S. (1982) Semantic development: the state of the art. In E. Wanner and L. R. Gleitman (eds), *Language Acquisition: the state of the art*. Cambridge: Cambridge University Press.

Carey, S. and Bartlett, E. (1978) Acquiring a new word. *Stanford Papers and Reports on Child Language Development*, 15, 17–29.

Carlson, V., Cicchetti, D., Barnett, D., and Braunwald, K. (1989) Disorganized/disoriented attachment relationships in maltreated infants. *Developmental Psychology*, 25, 525–31.

Carlsson, S. G., Fagerberg, H., Horneman, G., Hwang, C. P., Larson, K., Rodholm, M., and Schaller, J. (1979) Effects of various amounts of contact between mother and child on the mother's nursing behavior: a follow-up study. *Infant Behavior and Development*, 2, 209–14.

Carns, D. (1973) Talking about sex: notes on first coitus and the double sexual standard. *Journal of Marriage and the Family*, 35, 677–88.

Carpenter, G. (1975) Mother's face and the newborn.

In R. Lewin (ed.), *Child Alive*. London: Temple Smith.

Carranza, M. and Ryan, E. B. (1975) Evaluative reactions of bilingual Anglo and Mexican American adolescents toward speakers of English and Spanish. *International Journal of the Sociology of Language*, 6, 83–104.

Carr-Hill, R. and Chadha-Boreham, H. (1988) Education. In A. Bhat, R. Carr-Hill, and S. Ohri (eds), *Britain's Black Population: a new perspective*, 2nd edn. Aldershot: Gower.

Carr-Hill, R. and Drew, D. (1988) Blacks, police and crime. In A. Bhat, R. Carr-Hill, and S. Ohri (eds), *Britain's Black Population: a new perspective*, 2nd edn. Aldershot: Gower.

Carroll, J. (1983). Middle age does not mean menopause. *Topics in Clinical Nursing*, 7, 38–44.

Carter, D. B. and Levy, G. D. (1988) Cognitive aspects of early sex-role development: the influence of gender schemas on preschoolers' memories and preferences for sex-typed toys and activities. *Child Development*, 59, 782–92.

Cartron-Guerin, A. and Levy, P. (1980) Achievement and future time perspective among preadolescents: range, nature, and optimism of future plans. *Bulletin de Psychologie*, 33, 747–53.

Carugati, F. (1990) From social cognition to social representations in the study of intelligence. In G. Duveen and B. Lloyd (eds), *Social Representations and the Development of Knowledge*. Cambridge: Cambridge University Press.

Carugati, F. and Gilly, M. (1993) The multiple sides of the same tool: cognitive development as a matter of social constructions and meanings. *European Journal of Psychology of Education*, 8, 345–54.

Casey, R. J. and Schlosser, S. (1994) Emotional response to peer praise in children with and without a diagnosed externalizing disorder. *Merrill-Palmer Quarterly*, 40, 60–81.

Cashmore, J. A. and Goodnow, J. J. (1986) Parent–child agreement on attributional beliefs. *International Journal of Behavioral Development*, 9, 191–204.

Caspi, A., Elder, G. H., Jr, and Bem, D. J. (1987) Moving against the world: life-course patterns of explosive children. *Developmental Psychology*, 23, 308–13.

Caspi, A., Lynam, D., Moffitt, T. E., and Silva, P. A. (1993) Unraveling girls' delinquency: biological, dispositional, and contextual contributions to adolescent misbehavior. *Developmental Psychology*, 29, 19–30.

Cassidy, J. (1986) The ability to negotiate the environment: an aspect of infant competence as related to quality of attachment. *Child Development*, 57, 331–7.

Cassidy, J. (1988) Child–mother attachment and the self in six-year-olds. *Child Development*, 59, 121–34.

Cassidy, J. (1994) Emotion regulation: influences of attachment relationships. In N. A. Fox (ed.), *The Development of Emotion Regulation: biological and behavioral considerations*. Monographs of the Society for Research in Child Development, 59 (2–3), no. 240.

Cassidy, J. and Berlin, L. J. (1994) The insecure ambivalent pattern of attachment: theory and research. *Child Development*, 65, 971–91.

Cassidy, J., Parke, R. D., Butkovsky, L., and Braungart, J. M. (1992) Family–peer connections: the roles of emotional expressiveness within the family and children's understanding of emotions. *Child Development*, 63, 603–18.

Cate, R. M. and Lloyd, S. A. (1988) Courtship. In S. Duck (ed.), *Handbook of Personal Relationships: theory, research and interventions*. Chichester: Wiley.

Cate, R. M., Henton, J. M., Koval, J., Christopher, F. S., and Lloyd, S. (1982) Premarital abuse: a social psychological perspective. *Journal of Family Issues*, 3, 79–90.

Cauce, A. M., Mason, C., Gonzales, N., Hiraga, Y., and Liu, G. (1994) Social support during adolescence: methodological and theoretical considerations. In F. Nestemann and K. Hurrelmann (eds), *Social Networks and Social Support in Childhood and Adolescence*. Berlin: de Gruyter.

Cazden, C., Cox, M., Dickinson, D., Steinberg, Z., and Stone, C. (1979) "You all gonna hafta listen": peer teaching in a primary classroom. In W. A. Collins (ed.), *Children's Language and Communication*, Minnesota Symposia on Child Psychology, vol. 12. Hillsdale, NJ: Erlbaum.

Cazenave, N. A. and Leon, G. H. (1987) Men's work and family roles and characteristics: race, gender, and class perceptions of college students. In M. S. Kimmel (ed.), *Changing Men: new directions in research on men and masculinity*. Newbury Park Calif.: Sage.

Chafel, J. A. (1986) A naturalistic investigation of the use of social comparison by young children. *Journal of Research and Development in Education*, 19, 51–61.

Chafetz, J., Feldman, H. M., and Wareham, N. L. (1992) "There car": ungrammatical parentese. *Journal of Child Language*, 19, 473–80.

Chalmers, J. B. and Townsend, M. A. R. (1990) The effects of training in social perspective taking on socially maladjusted girls. *Child Development*, 61, 178–90.

Chandler, M. (1973) Egocentrism and antisocial behavior: the assessment and training of social-perspective skills. *Developmental Psychology*, 9, 326–32.

Chandler, M. (1977) Social cognition: a selected review of current research. In W. Overton and J. Gallaher (eds), *Knowledge and Development: yearbook of developmental epistemology*. New York: Academic Press.

Chandler, M. (1982) Social cognition and social structure. In F. C. Serafica (ed.), *Social-cognitive Development in Context*. New York: Guilford.

Chandler, M. (1994) Self-continuity in suicidal and nonsuicidal adolescents. *New Directions for Child Development*, 64, 55–70.

Chandler, M., Fritz, A. S., and Hala, S. (1989) Small scale deceit: deception as a marker of two-, three-, and four-year olds' early theories of mind. *Child Development*, 60, 1263–77.

Chao, R. K. (1994) Beyond parental control and authoritarian parenting style: understanding Chinese parenting through the cultural notion of training. *Child Development*, 65, 1111–19.

Chapman, A. J., Smith, J. R., and Foot, H. C. (1980) Humour, laughter, and social interaction. In P. McGhee and A. J. Chapman (eds), *Children's Humour*. Chichester: Wiley.

Chapman, J. W. and Nicholls, J. G. (1976) Occupational identity status, occupational preference and field dependence in Maori and Pakeha boys. *Journal of Cross-Cultural Psychology*, 7, 61–72.

Chapman, M. (1988) *Constructive Evolution: origins and development of Piaget's thought*. Cambridge: Cambridge University Press.

Charlesworth, W. R. (1988) Resources and resource acquisition during ontogeny. In K. B. MacDonald (ed.), *Sociobiological Perspectives on Human Development*. New York: Springer-Verlag.

Charney, R. (1980) Speech roles and the development of personal pronouns. *Journal of Child Language*, 7, 509–28.

Chase-Lansdale, P. L. and Owen, M. T. (1987) Maternal employment in a family context: effects on infant–mother and infant–father attachments. *Child Development*, 58, 1505–12.

Chassin, L., Presson, C. C., and Sherman, S. J. (1987) Applications of social developmental psychology to adolescent health behaviors. In N. Eisenberg (ed.), *Contemporary Topics in Developmental Psychology*. New York: Wiley.

de Chateau, P. (1987) Parent–infant socialization in several Western European countries. In J. D. Osofsky (ed.), *Handbook of Infant Development*. New York: Wiley.

Cheles-Miller, P. (1975) Reactions to marital roles in commercials. *Journal of Advertising Research*, 15, 45–9.

Chen, X. and Rubin, K. H. (1992) Correlates of peer acceptance in a Chinese sample of six-year-olds.

International Journal of Behavioral Development, 15, 259–73.

Cheshire, J. (1982) *Variation in an English Dialect.* Cambridge: Cambridge University Press.

Chiat, S. (1986) Personal pronouns. In P. Fletcher and M. Garman (eds), *Language Acquisition*, 2nd edn. Cambridge: Cambridge University Press.

Chi-Ching, E. Y. (1992) Perceptions of external barriers and the career success of female managers in Singapore. *The Journal of Social Psychology*, 132, 661–74.

Chilman, C. S. (1980) Toward a reconceptualization of adolescent sexuality. In C. S. Chilman (ed.), *Adolescent Pregnancy and Childbearing: findings from research.* Washington, DC: US Department of Health and Human Services.

Chiva, M. (1983) Gout et communication non verbale chez le jeune enfant. *Enfance*, 1–2, 53–64.

Chomsky, N. (1959) Review of Skinner, *Verbal Behavior. Language*, 35, 26–58.

Chomsky, N. (1965) *Aspects of the Theory of Syntax.* Cambridge, Mass.: MIT Press.

Chomsky, N. (1969) Linguistics and politics. *New Left Review*, 57, 21–34.

Chomsky, N. (1972) *Language and Mind.* New York: Harcourt Brace Jovanovich.

Chomsky, N. (1973) *For Reasons of State.* London: Fontana.

Chomsky, N. (1980) *Rules and Representations.* Oxford: Blackwell.

Chomsky, N. (1986) *Knowledge of Language: its nature, origin, and use.* New York: Praeger.

Chomsky, N. (1988) *Language and Problems of Knowledge: the Mangua lectures.* Cambridge, Mass.: MIT Press.

Christen, Y. (1991) *Sex Differences: modern biology and the unisex fallacy.* New Brunswick: Transaction.

Chukovsky, K. (1925) *From Two to Five*, trans. 1963. Berkeley: University of California Press.

Chumak-Horbatsch, R. (1994) Ukrainian single-word use: a case study. *First Language*, 14, 173–94.

Churcher, J. and Scaife, M. (1982) How infants see the point. In G. Butterworth and P. Light (eds), *Social Cognition: studies of the development of understanding.* Chicago: University of Chicago Press.

Cialdini, R. B., Schaller, M., Houlihan, D., Arps, K., Fultz, J., and Beaman, A. L. (1987) Empathy-based helping: is it selflessly or selfishly motivated? *Journal of Personality and Social Psychology*, 52, 749–58.

Cicchetti, D. (1990) The organization and coherence of socioemotional, cognitive, and representational development: illustrations through a developmental psychopathology perspective on Down Syndrome and child maltreatment. In R. A. Thompson (ed.), *Socioemotional Development: Nebraska symposium on Motivation, 1988.* Lincoln: University of Nebraska Press.

Cicchetti, D. and Pogge-Hesse, P. (1981) The relation between emotion and cognition in infant development. In M. E. Lamb and L. R. Sherrod (eds), *Infant Social Cognition: empirical and theoretical considerations.* Hillsdale, NJ: Erlbaum.

Cicchetti, D., Ganiham, J., and Barnett, D. (1991) Contributions from the study of high-risk populations to understanding the development of emotion regulation. In J. Garber and K. A. Dodge (eds), *The Development of Emotion Regulation and Dysregulation.* Cambridge: Cambridge University Press.

Cicirelli, V. G. (1989) Feelings of attachment to siblings and well-being in later life. *Psychology and Aging*, 4, 211–16.

Cillessen, T. and Ferguson, T. J. (1989) Self-perpetuating processes in children's peer relationships. In B. H. Schneider, G. Attili, J. Nadel, and R. P. Weissberg (eds), *Social Competence in Developmental Perspective.* Dordrecht: Kluwer.

Clark, E. V. (1971) On the acquisition of the meaning of *before* and *after. Journal of Verbal Learning and Verbal Behavior*, 10, 266–75.

Clark, E. V. (1973a) What's in a word? On the child's acquisition of semantics in his first language. In T. E. Moore (ed.), *Cognitive Development and the Acquisition of Language.* New York: Academic Press.

Clark, E. V. (1973b) Non-linguistic strategies and the acquisition of word meaning. *Cognition*, 2, 161–82.

Clark, E. V. (1982) The young word maker: a case study of innovation in the child's lexicon. In E. Wanner and L. R. Gleitman (eds), *Language Acquisition: the State of the Art.* Cambridge: Cambridge University Press.

Clark, E. V. (1983) Meanings and concepts. In J. H. Flavell and E. M. Markman (eds), *Handbook of Child Psychology*, vol. 3: *Cognitive development.* New York: Wiley.

Clark, E. V. (1993). *The Lexicon in Acquisition.* Cambridge: Cambridge University Press.

Clark, K. B. and Clark, M. P. (1947) Racial identification and preference in Negro children. In T. M. Newcomb and E. L. Hartley (eds), *Readings in Social Psychology.* New York: Holt.

Clark, R. D. III (1990) The impact of AIDS on gender differences in willingness to engage in casual sex. *Journal of Applied Social Psychology*, 20, 771–82.

Clarke-Stewart, A. (1987) The social ecology of early childhood. In N. Eisenberg (ed.), *Contemporary Topics in Developmental Psychology.* New York: Wiley.

Clarke-Stewart, A. (1989) Infant day care. Maligned or malignant? *American Psychologist*, 44, 266–73.

Clarke-Stewart, A. and Fein, G. G. (1983). Early childhood programs. In P. H. Mussen (ed.), *Handbook of Child Psychology*, vol. 2. New York: Wiley.

Clausen, J. A. (1981) Men's occupational careers in the middle years. In D. H. Eichorn, J. A. Clausen, N. Haan, M. P. Honzik, and P. H. Mussen (eds), *Present and Past in Middle Life*. New York: Academic Press.

Clemens, A. W. and Axelson, L. J. (1985) The not-so-empty nest: return of the fledgling adult. *Family Relations*, 34, 259–64.

Cleverley, J. and Phillips, D. (1987) *Visions of Childhood: influential models from Locke to Spock*. Sydney: Allen and Unwin.

Cobliner, W. G. (1988) The exclusion of intimacy in the sexuality of the contemporary college-age population. *Adolescence*, 23, 99–113.

Codol, J.-P. (1984) Social differentiation and non-differentiation. In H. Tajfel (ed.), *The Social Dimension, vol. 2*. Cambridge: Cambridge University Press.

Cohen, L. J. and Campos, J. J. (1974) Father, mother, and stranger as elicitors of attachment behaviors in infancy. *Developmental Psychology*, 10, 146–54.

Coie, J. D. and Dodge, K. A. (1983) Continuities and changes in children's social status: a five-year longitudinal study. *Merrill-Palmer Quarterly*, 29, 261–82.

Coie, J. D. and Dodge, K. A. (1988) Multiple sources of data on social behavior and social status in the school: a cross-age comparison. *Child Development*, 59, 815–29.

Coie, J. D. and Koeppl, G. K. (1990) Adapting intervention to the problems of aggressive and disruptive rejected children. In S. R. Asher and J. D. Coie (eds), *Peer Rejection in Childhood*. Cambridge: Cambridge University Press.

Coie, J. D. and Pennington, B. F. (1976) Children's perceptions of deviance and disorder. *Child Development*, 46, 400–13.

Coie, J. D., Dodge, K. A., and Coppotelli, H. (1982) Dimensions and types of social status: a cross-age perspective. *Developmental Psychology*, 18, 557–70.

Colby, A. and Kohlberg, L. (1987) *The Measurement of Moral Judgment*. Cambridge: Cambridge University Press.

Colby, A., Kohlberg, L., Gibbs, J., and Liebermann, M. (1983). A longitudinal study of moral development. *Monographs of the Society for Research in Child Development*, 48 (1–2), no. 200.

Colby, A., Kohlberg, L., Speicher, B., Hewer, A., Candee, D., Gibbs, J., and Power, C. (1987) *The Measurement of Moral Judgment*. vol. 2: *Standard issue scoring manual*. Cambridge: Cambridge University Press.

Cole, C. L. (1984) Marital quality in later life. In W. H. Quinn and G. A. Hughston (eds), *Independent Aging: family and social systems perspectives*. Rockville, Md: Aspen.

Cole, M. (1985) The zone of proximal development: where culture and cognition create each other. In J. V. Wertsch (ed.), *Culture, Communication, and Cognition: Vygotskian perspectives*. Cambridge: Cambridge University Press.

Cole, M. (1992) Context, modularity, and the cultural constitution of development. In L. T. Winegar and J. Valsiner (eds), *Children's Development within Social Context*, vol. 2: *Research and methodology*. Hillsdale, NJ: Erlbaum.

Cole, M. and Scribner, S. (1978) Introduction. In L. S. Vygotsky, *Mind in Society: the development of higher psychological processes*. Cambridge, Mass.: Harvard University Press.

Cole, M., Gay, J., Glick, J. A., and Sharp, D. W. (1971) *The Cultural Context of Learning and Thinking*. New York: Basic Books.

Cole, P. M. (1986) Children's spontaneous control of facial expression. *Child Development*, 57, 1309–21.

Cole, P. M., Barrett, K. C., and Zahn-Waxler, C. (1992) Emotion displays in two-year-olds during mishaps. *Child Development*, 63, 314–24.

Coleman, J. C. (1974) *Relationships in Adolescence*. London: Routledge and Kegan Paul.

Coleman, J. C. (1989) The focal theory of adolescence: a psychological perspective. In K. Hurrelmann and U. Engel (eds), *The Social World of Adolescents: international perspectives*. Berlin and New York: de Gruyter.

Coleman, J. S. (1987) Families and schools. *Educational Researcher*, 16, 2–38.

Collins, W. A. (1983) Social antecedents, cognitive processing, and comprehension of social portrayals on television. In E. T. Higgins, D. N. Ruble, D. N. Hartup, and W. W. Hartup (eds), *Social Cognition and Social Development: a sociocultural perspective*. Cambridge: Cambridge University Press.

Collins, W. A. and Gunnar, M. R. (1990) Social and personality development. *Annual Review of Psychology*, 41, 387–416.

Collins, W. A. and Laursen, B. (1992) Conflict and the transition to adolescence. In C. U. Shantz and W. W. Hartup (eds), *Conflict in Child and Adolescent Development*. Cambridge: Cambridge University Press.

Collis, G. M. (1977) Visual co-orientation and maternal speech. In H. R. Schaffer (ed.), *Studies in Mother–infant Interaction*. London: Academic Press.

Collis, G. M. (1985) On the origins of turn-taking: alternation and meaning. In M. D. Barrett (ed.), *Children's Single-word Speech*. Chichester: Wiley.

Collis, G. M. and Schaffer, H. R. (1975) Synchronization of visual attention in mother–infant pairs. *Journal of Child Psychology and Psychiatry*, 16, 315–20.

Colombo, J. and Bundy, R. S. (1981) A method for the measurement of infant auditory selectivity. *Infant Behavior and Development*, 4, 229–31.

Colten, M. E., Gore, S., and Aseltine, R. (1991) The patterning of distress and disorder in a community sample of high school aged youth. In M. E. Colten and S. Gore (eds), *Adolescent Stress: causes and consequences*. New York: Aldine de Gruyter.

Coltrane, S. and Ishi-Kuntz, M. (1992) Men's housework: a life course perspective. *Journal of Marriage and the Family*, 54, 43–57.

Colvin, R. L. (1993) Youngest homeboy wants out. *Los Angeles Times*, 24 July.

Comfort, A. (1950) *Authority and Delinquency: a study in the psychology of power*. London: Routledge and Kegan Paul.

Comfort, A. (1977) *A Good Age*. London: Macmillan.

Commonwealth Department of Health (1987) *Statistics on Drug Use in Australia*. Canberra: Government Publishing Service.

Compas, B. E., Hinden, B. R., and Gerhardt, C. A. (1995). Adolescent development: pathways and processes of risk and resilience. *Annual Review of Psychology*, 46, 265–93.

Comstock, G. and Paik, H. J. (1991) *Television and the American Child*. San Diego: Academic Press.

Condor, S. (1986) Sex role beliefs and "traditional" women: feminist and intergroup perspectives. In S. Wilkinson (ed.), *Feminist Social Psychology: developing theory and practice*. Milton Keynes: Open University Press.

Condry, J. and Condry, S. (1976) Sex differences: a study of the eye of the beholder. *Child Development*, 47, 812–19.

Connolly, G. M., Casswell, S., Stewart, J., and Silva, P. S. (1992) Drinking context and other influences on the drinking of 15-year-old New Zealanders. *British Journal of Addiction*, 87, 1029–36.

Conrad, K. M., Flay, B. R., and Hill, D. (1992) Why children start smoking cigarettes: predictors of onset. *British Journal of Addiction*, 87, 1711–24.

Conti-Ramsden, G. (1989) Proper name usage: mother–child interactions with language-impaired and non-language-impaired children. *First Language*, 9, 271–84.

Cook, H. B. K. (1992) Matrifocality and female aggression in Margariteno society. In K. Bjorkqvist and P. Niemala (eds), *Of Mice and Women: aspects of female aggression*. San Diego: Academic Press.

Cooley, C. H. (1902) *Human Nature and the Social Order*. New York: Scribner.

Cooper, C. R. and Cooper, R. G. (1984) Skill in peer learning discourse: what develops? In S. A Kuczaj (ed.), *Discourse Development: progress in cognitive development research*. New York: Springer-Verlag.

Cooper, K. L. and Gutmann, D. L. (1987) Gender identity and ego mastery style in middle-aged, pre- and post-empty nest women. *Gerontologist*, 27, 347–52.

Cooper, M. L., Pierce, R. S., and Huselid, R. F. (1994) Substance use and sexual risk taking among black adolescents and white adolescents. *Health Psychology*, 13, 251–62.

Coopersmith, S. (1967) *The Antecedents of Self-esteem*. San Francisco: W. H. Freeman.

Cordua, G. D., McGraw, K. O., and Drabman, R. S. (1979) Doctor or nurse: children's perception of sex-typed occupations. *Child Development*, 50, 590–3.

Corsaro, W. A. (1981) Friendship in the nursery school: social organization in a peer environment. In S. R. Asher and J. M. Gottman (eds), *The Development of Children's Friendships*. Cambridge: Cambridge University Press.

Corsaro, W. A. (1990) The underlife of the nursery school: young children's social representations of adult rules. In G. Duveen and B. Lloyd (eds), *Social Representations and the Development of Knowledge*. Cambridge: Cambridge University Press.

Corsaro, W. A. (1993) Interpretive reproduction in the "sculoa materna". *European Journal of Psychology of Education*, 8, 357–74.

Cosgrove, J. M. and Patterson, S. J. (1977) Plans and the development of listener skills. *Developmental Psychology*, 13, 557–64.

Costa, P. T. and McCrae, R. R. (1980) Still stable after all these years: personality as a key to some issues in adulthood and old age. In P. B. Baltes and O. G. Brim, Jr (eds), *Life Span Development and Behavior*, vol. 3. New York: Academic Press.

Costanzo, P. R. (1992) External socialization and the development of adaptive individuation and social connection. In D. N. Ruble, P. R. Costanzo, and M. E. Oliveri (eds), *The Social Psychology of Mental Health: basic mechanisms and applications*. New York: Guilford.

Costanzo, P. R. and Dix, T. H. (1983) Beyond the information processed: socialization in the development of attributional processes. In E. T. Higgins, D. Ruble, and W. Hartup (eds), *Social Cognition and Social Development: a socio-cultural perspective*. Cambridge: Cambridge University Press.

Costanzo, P. R. and Fraenkel, P. (1987) Social influence, socialization, and the development of social cognition: the heart of the matter. In N. Eisenberg (ed.), *Contemporary Topics in Developmental Psychology*. New York: Wiley.

Costanzo, P. R. and Shaw, M. E. (1966) Conformity as a function of age level. *Child Development*, 37, 967–75.

Costanzo, P. R., Coie, J. D., Grumet, J., and Farnill, D. (1973) A reexamination of the effects of intent and consequence on children's moral judgments. *Child Development*, 45, 799–802.

Cotterell, J. L. (1986) Work and community influences on the quality of child rearing. *Child Development*, 57, 362–74.

Cotterell, J. L. (1994) Analyzing the strength of supportive ties in adolescent social supports. In F. Nestemann and K. Hurrelmann (eds), *Social Networks and Social Support in Childhood and Adolescence*. Berlin: de Gruyter.

Coupland, N. and Coupland, J. (1990) Language in later life. In H. Giles and W. P. Robinson (eds), *Handbook of Language and Social Psychology*. Chichester: Wiley.

Cowan, C. P. and Cowan, P. A. (1988) Who does what when partners become parents: implications for men, women, and marriage. In R. Palkovitz and M. B. Sussman (eds), *Transitions to Parenthood*. New York: Haworth.

Cowan, P. A. (1978) *Piaget with Feeling: cognitive, social and emotional dimensions*. New York: Holt, Rinehart and Winston.

Cowles, M. and Davis, C. (1987) The subject matter of psychology: volunteers. *British Journal of Social Psychology*, 26, 97–102.

Cox, M. J., Owen, M. T., Lewis, J. M., and Henderson, K. V. (1989) Marriage, adult adjustment, and early parenting. *Child Development*, 60, 1015–24.

Cox, M. V. (1991) *The Child's Point of View*, 2nd edn. New York: Harvester Wheatsheaf.

Cram, F. and Ng, S. K. (1994) Children's understanding of public ownership. *European Journal of Social Psychology*, 24, 469–80.

Cramer, D. (1993) Living alone, marital status, gender and health. *Journal of Community and Applied Social Psychology*, 3, 1–15.

Crandall, C. S. (1988) Social contagion of binge eating. *Journal of Personality and Social Psychology*, 55, 588–98.

Craske, M. L. (1985) Improving persistence through observational learning and attribution retraining. *British Journal of Educational Psychology*, 55, 138–47.

Crawford, C. (1987) Sociobiology: of what value to psychology? In C. Crawford, M. Smith, and D. Krebs (1987) *Sociobiology and Psychology: ideas, issues and applications*. Hillsdale, NJ: Erlbaum.

Crawford, C., Smith, M., and Krebs, D. (eds) (1987) *Sociobiology and Psychology: ideas, issues and applications*. Hillsdale, NJ: Erlbaum.

Crawford, M., Herrman, D. J., Holdsworth, M., Randall, E., and Robbins, D. (1989) Gender and beliefs about memory. *British Journal of Psychology*, 80, 391–401.

Crisp, A. H. (1982) *Anorexia Nervosa: let me be*. London: Academic Press.

Crockenberg, S. (1985) Toddlers' reactions to maternal anger. *Merrill-Palmer Quarterly*, 31, 361–73.

Crockenberg, S. (1987) Predictors and correlates of anger toward and punitive control of toddlers by adolescent mothers. *Child Development*, 58, 964–75.

Crockenberg, S. B. and McCluskey, K. (1986) Change in maternal behavior during the baby's first year of life. *Child Development*, 52, 857–65.

Cromer, R. F. (1974) The development of language and cognition: the cognition hypothesis. In B. Foss (ed.), *New Perspectives in Child Development*. Harmondsworth: Penguin.

Cromer, R. F. (1991) *Language and Thought in Normal and Handicapped Children*. Oxford: Blackwell.

Crook, C. (1992) Cultural artefacts in social development: the case of computers. In H. McGurk (ed.), *Childhood Social Development: contemporary perspectives*. Hove: Erlbaum.

Crook, C. (1994) *Computers and the Collaborative Experience of Learning*. London: Routledge.

Cross, T. (1977) Mothers' speech adjustments: the contribution of selected child listener variables. In C. E. Snow and C. Ferguson (eds), *Talking to Children: language input and acquisition*. Cambridge: Cambridge University Press.

Culp, R. E., Culp, A. M., Osofsky, J. D., and Osofsky, H. J. (1991) Adolescent and older mothers' interaction patterns with their six-month-old infants. *Journal of Adolescence*, 14, 195–200.

Cumberbatch, G. (1991) Is television violence harmful? In R. Cochrane and D. Carroll (eds), *Psychology and Social Issues: a tutorial text*. London: The Falmer Press.

Cumming, E. and Henry, W. H. (1961) *Growing Old*. New York: Basic Books.

Cummings, E. M. (1987) Coping with background anger in early childhood. *Child Development*, 58, 976–84.

Cummings, E. M. and Cummings, J. S. (1988) A process oriented approach to children's coping with adults' angry behavior. *Developmental Review*, 8, 296–321.

Cummings, E. M., Iannotti, R. J., and Zahn-Waxler, C. (1985) Influence of conflict between adults on the emotions and aggression of young children. *Developmental Psychology*, 21, 495–507.

Cummings, E. M., Iannotti, R. J., and Zahn-Waxler, C. (1989) Aggression between peers in early childhood: individual continuity and developmental change. *Child Development*, 60, 887–95.

Cummings, E. M., Zahn-Waxler, C., and Radke-Yarrow, M. (1981) Young children's responses to expressions of anger and affection by others in the family. *Child Development*, 52, 1274–82.

Cummings, E. M., Zahn-Waxler, C., and Radke-Yarrow, M. (1984) Developmental changes in children's reactions to anger in the home. *Journal of Child Psychology and Psychiatry*, 25, 63–74.

Cunningham, J. D. and Antill, J. K. (1984) Changes in masculinity and femininity across the family life cycle: a reexamination. *Developmental Psychology*, 20, 1135–41.

Curtiss, S. (1989) The independence and task-specificity of language. In M. H. Bornstein and J. S. Bruner (eds), *Interaction in Human Development*. Hillsdale, NJ: Erlbaum.

Curtiss, S., Fromkin, V., Rigler, D., Rigler, M., and Krashen, S. (1975) An update on the linguistic development of Genie. In D. P. Dato (ed.), *Developmental Psycholinguistics: theory and applications*. Washington, DC: Georgetown University Press.

Cvetkovich, G. and Grote, B. (1980) Psychosocial development and the social problems of teenage illegitimacy. In C. S. Chilman (ed.), *Adolescent Pregnancy and Childbearing: findings from research*. Washington, DC: US Department of Health and Human Services.

Cvetkovich, G. and Grote, B. (1981) Psychosocial maturity and teenage contraceptive use: an investigation of decision-making and communication skills. *Population and Environment*, 4, 211–26.

D'Alessio, M. (1990) Social representations of childhood: an implicit theory of development. In G. Duveen and B. Lloyd (eds), *Social Representations and the Development of Knowledge*. Cambridge: Cambridge University Press.

Daly, M. and Wilson, M. (1987) Evolutionary psychology and family violence. In C. Crawford, M. Smith, and D. Krebs (1987) *Sociobiology and Psychology: ideas, issues and applications*. Hillsdale, NJ : Erlbaum.

Damon, W. (1980) Patterns of change in children's social reasoning: a two-year longitudinal study. *Child Development*, 53, 1010–17.

Damon, W. (1983) *Social and Personality Development: infancy through adolescence*. New York: Norton.

Damon, W. (1988) *The Moral Child: nurturing children's natural moral growth*. New York: The Free Press.

Damon, W. and Hart, D. (1982) The development of self-understanding from infancy through adolescence. *Child Development*, 53, 831–57.

Damon, W. and Hart, D. (1988) *Self-understanding in Childhood and Adolescence*. Cambridge: Cambridge University Press.

Daniel, S. and Maguire, P. (eds) (1972) *The Painthouse: words from an East End gang*. Harmondsworth: Penguin.

Daniels-Beirness, T. (1989) Measuring peer status in boys and girls: a problem of apples and oranges. In B. H. Schneider, G. Attili, J. Nadel, and R. P. Weissberg (eds), *Social Competence in Developmental Perspective*. Dordrecht: Kluwer.

Darley, J. M. and Goethals, G. R. (1980) People's analyses of the causes of ability-linked performances. *Advances in Experimental Social Psychology*, 13, 1–37.

Darley, J. M. and Latane, B. (1968) Bystander intervention in emergencies: diffusion of responsibility. *Journal of Personality and Social Psychology*, 8, 377–83.

Darwin, C. (1859) *On the Origin of the Species by Means of Natural Selection, or, the preservation of favored races in the struggle for life*. London: John Murray.

Darwin, C. (1872) *The Expression of Emotions in Man and Animals*. London: John Murray.

Datan, N. (1980) Midas and other midlife crises. In W. H. Norman and T. J. Scaramella (eds), *Midlife: development and clinical issues*. New York: Brunner/Mazel.

Davey, T. (1987) *A Generation Divided: German children and the Berlin wall*. Durham, NC: Duke University Press.

Davidson, E.S., Yasuna, M., and Tower, A. (1979) The effects of television cartoons on sex-role stereotyping in young girls. *Child Development*, 50, 597–600.

Davidson, P. M. (1992) The role of social interaction in cognitive development: a propaedeutic. In L. T. Winegar and J. Valsiner (eds), *Children's Development within Social Context*. Hillsdale, NJ: Erlbaum.

Davies, D. R. (1986) Children's performance as a function of sex-typed labels. *British Journal of Social Psychology*, 25, 173–5.

Davis, A. (1991) The language of testing. In K. Durkin (ed.), *Language in Mathematical Education: research and practice*. Milton Keynes and Philadelphia: Open University Press.

Davis, D. M. (1990) Portrayals of women in prime-time network television: some demographic characteristics. *Sex Roles*, 23, 325–32.

Davis, K. (1980) A theory of teenage pregnancy in the United States. In C. S. Chilman (ed.), *Adolescent Pregnancy and Childbearing: findings from research*. Washington, DC: US Department of Health and Human Services.

Davis, R. H. and Davis, J. A. (1985) *TV's image of the elderly: a practical guide for change*. Lexington: Lexington Books.

Davis, R. H. and Kubey, R. W. (1982) Growing old on television and with television. In D. Pearl, L. Bouthilet, and J. Lazar (eds), *Television and Behavior: ten years of scientific progress and implications for the Eighties*, vol. 2. Washington, DC: US Department of Health and Human Services.

Davitz, J. R. (1952) The effects of previous training on postfrustration behavior. *Journal of Abnormal and Social Psychology*, 47, 309–15.

Davydov, V. V. and Radzikhovskii, L. A. (1985) Vygotsky's theory and the activity-oriented approach in psychology. In J. V. Wertsch (ed.), *Culture, Communication, and Cognition: Vygotskyan perspectives*. Cambridge: Cambridge University Press.

Deal, J. E. and Wampler, K. S. (1986) Dating violence: the primacy of previous experience. *Journal of Personal and Social Relationships*, 3, 457–71.

Deaux, K. and Emswiller, T. (1974) Explanation for successful performance on sex-linked tasks: what is skill for the male is luck for the female. *Journal of Personality and Social Psychology*, 29, 80–5.

Deaux, K. and Hanna, R. (1984) Courtship in the personal column: the influence of gender and sexual orientation. *Sex Roles*, 11, 363–75.

Decarie, T. G. (1974) *The Infant's Reaction to Strangers*. New York: International Universities Press.

DeCasper, A. J. and Fifer, W. P. (1980) Of human bonding: newborns prefer their mothers' voices. *Science*, 208, 1174–6.

DeCasper, A. J. and Spence, M. (1986) Newborns prefer a familiar story over an unfamiliar one. *Infant Behavior and Development*, 9, 133–50.

Deci, E. L., Driver, R. E., Hotchkiss, L., Robbins, R. J., and Wilson, I. M. (1993) The relation of mothers' controlling vocalizations to children's intrinsic motivation. *Journal of Experimental Child Psychology*, 55, 151–62.

Deleau, M. (1990) *Les origines sociales du developpement mental: communication et symboles dans la première enfance*. Paris: A. Colin.

Delgado-Gaitan, C. (1994) Socializing young children in Mexican–American families: an intergenerational perspective. In P. M. Greenfield and R. R. Cocking (eds), *Cross-cultural roots of Minority Child Development*. Hillsdale, NJ: Erlbaum.

Demetras, M. J., Post, K. N., and Snow, C. E. (1986) Feedback to first language learners: the role of repetitions and clarification questions. *Journal of Child Language*, 13, 275–92.

Denham, S. A. (1993) Maternal emotional responsiveness and toddlers' social-emotional competence. *Journal of Child Psychology and Psychiatry*, 34, 715–28.

Denham, S. A., Renwick, S. M., and Holt, R. W.

(1991) Working and playing together: prediction of preschool social-emotional competence from mother–child interaction. *Child Development*, 62, 242–9.

DePaulo, B. M. (1991) Nonverbal behavior and self-presentation: a developmental perspective. In R. S. Feldman and B. Rime (eds), *Fundamentals of Nonverbal Behavior*. Cambridge: Cambridge University Press.

DePaulo, B. M. and Jordan, A. (1982) Age changes in deceiving and detecting deceit. In R. S. Feldman (ed.), *Development of Nonverbal Behavior in Children*. New York: Springer-Verlag.

DePaulo, B. M. and Rosenthal, R. (1978) Age changes in nonverbal decoding as a function of increasing amount of information. *Journal of Experimental Child Psychology*, 26, 280–7.

DePaulo, B. M., Rosenthal, R., Eisentstat, R. A., Rogers, P. L., and Finkelstein, S. (1978) Decoding discrepant nonverbal cues. *Journal of Personality and Social Psychology*, 36, 313–23.

DePaulo, B. M., Tang, J., Webb, W., Hoover, C., Marsh, K., and Litowitz, C. (1989) Age differences in reactions to help in a peer tutoring context. *Child Development*, 60, 423–39.

Deschamps, J.-C. (1983) Social attribution. In J. Jaspars, F. Fincham, and M. Hewstone (eds), *Attribution Theory and Research: conceptual, developmental and social dimensions*. London: Academic Press.

Desrochers, S., Ricard, M., Gouin-Decarie, T., and Allard, L. (1994) Developmental synchrony between social referencing and Piagetian sensorimotor causality. *Infant Behavior and Development*, 17, 303–9.

Deutsch, F. M., Ruble, D. N., Fleming, A., Brooks-Gunn, J., and Stangor, C. (1988) Information-seeking and maternal self-definition during the transition to motherhood. *Journal of Personality and Social Psychology*, 55, 420–31.

Devos, T., Deschamps, J.-C., and Comby, L. (1994) Social insertions and representations of oneself and young people: apprentices and high school students. *European Journal of Psychology of Education*, 9, 55–67.

D'Hondt, W. and Vandewiele, M. (1984), Beggary in West Africa. *Journal of Adolescence*, 7, 59–72.

Diamond, M. (1982) Sexual identity, monozygotic twins reared in discordant sex roles and a BBC follow-up. *Archives of Sexual Behavior*, 11, 181–6.

Dickinson, D. K. (1984) First impressions: children's knowledge of words gained from a single experience. *Applied Psycholinguistics*, 5, 359–74.

Di Domenico, C., de Cola, L., and Leishman, J. (1987) Urban Yoruba mothers: at home and at work. In C. Oppong (ed.), *Sex Roles, Population and Development in West Africa*. Portsmouth: Heinemann.

Die, A. H., Debbs, T., Jr and Walker, J. L., Jr. (1990) Managerial evaluations by men and women managers. *The Journal of Social Psychology*, 130, 763–9.

Diener, E. (1980) Deindividuation: the absence of self-awareness and self-regulation in group members. In P. Paulus (ed.), *The Psychology of Group Influence*. Hillsdale, NJ: Erlbaum.

Diener, E., Fraser, S. C., Beaman, A. L., and Kelem, R. T. (1976) Effects of deindividuation variables on stealing among Halloween trick-or-treaters. *Journal of Personality and Social Psychology*, 33, 178–83.

Dillard, D. D. and Pol, L. G. (1982) The individual economic cost of teenage childbearing. *Family Relations*, 31, 249–59.

Dion, K. K. (1973) Young children's stereotyping of facial attractiveness. *Developmental Psychology*, 9, 183–8.

Dion, K. K. and Berscheid, E. (1974) Physical attractiveness and peer perception among children. *Sociometry*, 37, 1–12.

DiPietro, J. A. (1981) Rough and tumble play: a function of gender. *Developmental Psychology*, 17, 50–8.

Dishion, T. J., Patterson, G. R., and Griesler, P. C. (1994) Peer adaptations in the development of antisocial behavior: a confluence model. In L. R. Huesmann (ed.), *Aggressive Behavior: current perspectives*. New York: Plenum Press.

Dix, T. and Grusec, J. E. (1985) Parent attribution processes in the socialization of children. In I. E. Sigel (ed.), *Parental Belief Systems: the psychological consequences for children*. Hillsdale, NJ: Erlbaum.

Dix, T., Ruble, D. N., Grusec, J. E., and Nixon, S. (1986) Social cognition in parents: inferential and affective reactions to children of three age levels. *Child Development*, 57, 879–94.

Dodge, K. A. (1980) Social cognition and children's aggressive behavior. *Child Development*, 51, 162–70.

Dodge, K. A. (1983) Behavioral antecedents of peer social status. *Child Development*, 54, 1386–99.

Dodge, K. A. (1991) Emotion and social information processing. In J. Garber and K. A. Dodge (eds), *The Development of Emotion Regulation and Dysregulation*. Cambridge: Cambridge University Press.

Dodge, K. A. and Frame, C. L. (1983) Social cognitive biases and deficits in aggressive boys. *Child Development*, 53, 620–35.

Dodge, K. A. and Garber, J. (1991) Domains of emotion regulation. In J. Garber and K. A. Dodge (eds), *The Development of Emotion Regulation and Dysregulation*. Cambridge: Cambridge University Press.

Dodge, K. A. and Price, J. M. (1994) On the relation between social information processing and socially competent behavior in early school-aged children. *Child Development*, 65, 1385–97.

Dodge, K. A. and Somberg, D. R. (1987) Hostile attributional biases among aggressive boys are exacerbated under conditions of threat to the self. *Child Development*, 58, 213–24.

Dodge, K. A., Murphy, R. R., and Buchsbaum, K. (1984) The assessment of intention-cue detection skills in children: implications for developmental psychopathology. *Child Development*, 55, 163–73.

Dodge, K. A., Pettit, G. S., McClaskey, C. L., and Brown, M. M. (1986) *Social Competence in Children*. Monographs of the Society for Research in Child Development, 51 (2), no. 213.

D'Odorico, L. and Franco, F. (1985) The determinants of baby talk: relationship to context. *Journal of Child Language*, 12, 567–86.

Doescher, S. M. and Sugawara, A. I. (1990) Sex role flexibility and prosocial behavior among preschool children. *Sex Roles*, 22, 111–23.

Doise, W. (1989) Constructivism in social psychology. *European Journal of Social Psychology*, 19, 389–400.

Doise, W. and Hanselmann, C. (1990) Interaction social et acquisition de la conservation du volume. *European Journal of Psychology of Education*, 5, 21–31.

Doise, W. and Mugny, G. (1984) *The Social Development of the Intellect*. Oxford: Pergamon.

Doise, W. and Mugny, G. (1991) Doise and Mugny versus Piaget? A rejoinder to Howe, Rodgers & Tolmie. *European Journal of Psychology of Education*, 6, 449–50.

Doise, W. and Palmonari, A. (1984) Introduction: the sociopsychological study of individual development. In W. Doise and A. Palmonari (eds), *Social Interaction in Individual Development*. Cambridge: Cambridge University Press.

Doise, W., Dionnet, S., and Mugny, G. (1978) Conflit sociocognitif, marquage social et developpement cognitif. *Cahiers de Psychologie*, 21, 231–45.

Doise, W., Mugny, G., and Perret-Clermont, A.-N. (1975) Social interaction and the development of cognitive operations. *European Journal of Social Psychology*, 5, 367–83.

Doise, W., Rijsman, J. B., van Meel, J., Bressers, I., and Pinxten, L. (1981) Sociale markering en cognitieve ontwikkeling. *Pedagogische Studien*, 58, 241–8.

Dolen, L. S. and Bearison, D. J. (1982) Social interaction and social cognition in aging. *Human Development*, 25, 430–42.

Dollaghan, C. A. (1985) Child meets word: "fast mapping" in preschoool children. *Journal of Speech and Hearing Research*, 28, 449–54.

Dollard, J. and Miller, N. E. (1950) *Personality and Psychotherapy*. New York: McGraw-Hill.

Dollard, J., Doob, L. W., Miller, N. E., Mowrer, O. H. and Sears, R. R. (1939) *Frustration and Aggression*. New Haven, Conn.: Yale University Press.

Donahue, M. and Prescott, B. (1988) Reading-disabled children's conversational participation in dispute episodes with peers. *First Language*, 8, 247–58.

Donaldson, M. (1978) *Children's Minds*. London: Fontana.

Donaldson, M. and Balfour, G. (1968). Less is more: a study of language comprehension in children. *British Journal of Psychology*, 59, 461–72.

Donleavy, J. P. (1975) *The Unexpurgated Code: a complete manual of survival and manners*. Harmondsworth: Penguin.

Donley, M. G. (1993) Attachment and the emotional unit. *Family Process*, 32, 3–20.

Donovan, A. and Oddy, M. (1982) Psychological aspects of unemployment: an investigation into the emotional and social adjustment of school leavers. *Journal of Adolescence*, 5, 15–30.

Donovan, W. L. and Leavitt, L. A. (1985) Physiology and behavior: parents' response to the infant cry. In B. M. Lester and C. F. Z. Boukydis (eds), *Infant Crying: theoretical and research perspectives*. New York: Plenum.

Dontas, C., Maratos, O., Fafoutis, M., and Karangelis, A. (1985) *Early Social Development in Institutionally Reared Greek Infants*. Monographs of the Society for Research in Child Development, 50, no. 209.

Doob, A. N. and MacDonald, C. E. (1979) Television viewing and fear of victimization: is the relationship causal? *Journal of Personality and Social Psychology*, 37, 170–9.

Dore, J. (1978) Variation in preschool children's conversational performances. In K. Nelson (ed.), *Children's Language*, vol. I. New York: Gardner.

Dore, J. (1985) Holophrases revisited: their "logical" development from dialog. In M. D. Barrett (ed.), *Children's Single-word Speech*. Chichester: Wiley.

Doress-Worters, P. B. (1994) Adding elder care to women's multiple roles: a critical review of the caregiver stress and multiple roles literature. *Sex Roles*, 31, 597–616.

Dornbusch, S., Carlsmith, J., Bushwall, S., Ritter, P., Leiderman, P., Hastorf, A., and Gross, R. (1985) Single parents, extended households, and the control of adolescents. *Child Development*, 56, 326–41.

Dornbusch, S. M., Ritter, P. L., Leiderman, P. H., Roberts, D. F., and Fraleigh, M. J. (1987) The relation of parenting style to adolescent school performance. *Child Development*, 58, 1244–57.

Douglas, M. (1966) *Purity and Danger: an analysis of concepts of pollution and taboo*. London: Routledge and Kegan Paul.

Douvan, E. and Adelson, J. (1966) *The Adolescent Experience*. New York: Wiley.

Dowdney, L., Skuse, D., Rutter, M., Quinton, D., and Mrazek, D. (1985) The nature and quality of parenting provided by women raised in institutions. *Journal of Child Psychology and Psychiatry*, 26, 599–626.

Downs, A. C. and Fuller, M. J. (1991) Recollections of spermarche: an exploratory investigation. *Current Psychology: Research and Reviews*, 10, 93–102.

Doyle, A.-B. (1982) Friends, acquaintances, and strangers: the influence of familiarity and ethnolinguistic background on social interaction. In K. H. Rubin and H. S. Ross (eds), *Peer Relationships and Social Skills in Childhood*. New York: Springer-Verlag.

Doyle, A.-B., Beaudet, J., and Aboud, F. (1988) Developmental patterns in the flexibility of children's ethnic attitudes. *Journal of Cross-cultural Psychology*, 19, 3–18.

Dragonas, T. G. (1987) Greek women's attitudes toward pregnancy, labor, and infant: their significance for intervention. *Infant Mental Health Journal*, 8, 266–76.

Dreman, S. B. (1976) Sharing behavior in Israeli school children: cognitive and social learning factors. *Child Development*, 47, 186–94.

DuBois, D. L., Eitel, S. K., and Felner, R. D. (1994) Effects of family environment and parent–child relationhips on school adjustment during the transition to early adolescence. *Journal of Marriage and the Family*, 56, 405–14.

Du Bois-Reymond, M. (1989) School and family in the lifeworld of youngsters. In K. Hurrelmann and U. Engel (eds), *The Social World of Adolescents: international perspectives*. Berlin and New York: de Gruyter.

Dubon, D. C., Josse, D., and Lezine, I. (1981) Evolution des changes entre enfants au cours des deux premières années de la vie. *Neuropsychiatrie de l'enfance*, 29, 273–90.

Duck, J. M. (1990) Children's ideals: the role of real-life versus media figures. *Australian Journal of Psychology*, 42, 19–29.

Duck, S. (ed) (1988a) *Handbook of Personal Relationships: theory, research and interventions*. Chichester: Wiley.

Duck, S. (1988b) *Relating to Others*. Chicago: Dorsey.

Duck, S. (1989) Social competent communication and relationship development. In B. H. Schneider, G. Attili, J. Nadel, and R. P. Weissberg (eds), *Social Competence in Developmental Perspective*. Dordrecht: Kluwer.

Duck, S. (1992) *Human Relationships*, 2nd edn. London: Sage.

Duck, S. and Miell, D. E. (1986) Charting the development of personal relationships. In R. Gilmour and S. W. Duck (eds), *The Emerging Field of Personal Relationships*. Hillsdale, NJ: Erlbaum.

Dunn, J. (1977) *Distress and Comfort*. London: Fontana.

Dunn, J. (1988a) Relations among relationships. In S. Duck (ed.), *Handbook of Personal Relationships: theory, research and interventions*. Chichester: Wiley.

Dunn, J. (1988b) *The Beginnings of Social Understanding*. Oxford: Blackwell.

Dunn, J. (1991) Sibling influences. In M. Lewis and S. Feinman (eds), *Social Influences and Socialization in Infancy*. New York: Plenum Press.

Dunn, J. (1992) Sisters and brothers: current issues in developmental research. In F. Boer and J. Dunn (eds), *Children's Sibling Relationships: developmental and clinical issues*. Hillsdale, NJ: Erlbaum.

Dunn, J. (1993) Social interaction, relationships, and the development of causal discourse and conflict management. *European Journal of Psychology of Education*, 8, 391–401.

Dunn, J. and Brown, J. (1991) Relationships, talk about feelings, and the development of affect regulation in early childhood. In J. Garber and K. A. Dodge (eds), *The Development of Emotion Regulation and Dysregulation*. Cambridge: Cambridge University Press.

Dunn, J. and Brown, J. (1994) Affect expression in the family, children's understanding of emotions, and their interactions with others. *Merrill-Palmer Quarterly*, 40, 120–37.

Dunn, J. and Kendrick, C. (1982) The speech of 2- and 3-year-olds to infant siblings: baby talk and the context of communication. *Journal of Child Language*, 9, 579–95.

Dunn, J. and Munn, P. (1986) Sibling quarrels and maternal intervention: individual differences in understanding and aggression. *Journal of Child Psychology and Psychiatry*, 27, 583–97.

Dunn, J. and Shatz, M. (1989) Becoming a conversationalist despite (or because of) having an older sibling. *Child Development*, 60, 399–410.

Dunn, J., Bretherton, I., and Munn, P. (1987) Conversations about feeling states between mothers and their children. *Developmental Psychology*, 23, 132–9.

Dunn, J., Kendrick, C., and MacNamee, R. (1981) The reaction of first-born children to the birth of a sibling: mothers' reports. *Journal of Child Psychology and Psychiatry*, 22, 1–18.

Duran, R. T. and Gauvain, M. (1993) The role of age versus expertise in peer collaboration during joint planning. *Journal of Experimental Child Psychology*, 55, 227–42.

Durkin, K. (1984) Children's accounts of sex-role stereotypes in television. *Communication Research*, 11, 341–62.

Durkin, K. (1985) *Television, Sex Roles and Children: a developmental social psychological account*. Milton Keynes and Philadelphia: Open University Press.

Durkin, K. (1986a) Sex roles and the mass media. In D. J. Hargreaves and A. M. Colley (eds), *The Psychology of Sex Roles*. London: Harper and Row.

Durkin, K. (1986b) Language and social cognition during the school years. In K. Durkin (ed.), *Language Development in the School Years*. London: Croom Helm.

Durkin, K. (1987a) Minds and language: social cognition, social interaction and the development of language. *Mind and Language*, 2, 105–40.

Durkin, K. (1987b) Social cognition and social context in the construction of sex differences. In M. A. Baker (ed.), *Sex Differences in Human Performance*. Chichester: Wiley.

Durkin, K. (1993) The representation of number in infancy and early childhood. In C. Pratt and A. F. Garton (eds), *Systems of Representation in Children: development and use*. Chichester: Wiley.

Durkin, K., Crowther, R. D., and Shire, B. (1986a) Children's processing of polysemous vocabulary in school. In K. Durkin (ed.), *Language Development in the School Years*. Beckenham: Croom Helm.

Durkin, K., Rutter, D. R. and Tucker, H. (1982) Social interaction and language acquisition: motherese help you? *First Language*, 3, 107–20.

Durkin, K., Shire, B., Riem, R., Crowther, R. D., and Rutter, D. R. (1986b) The social and linguistic context of early number word use. *British Journal of Developmental Psychology*, 4, 269–88.

Duveen, G. and Lloyd, B. (1990) *Social Representations and the Development of Knowledge*. Cambridge: Cambridge University Press.

Dweck, C. S. (1975) The role of expectations and attributions in the alleviation of learned helplessness. *Journal of Personality and Social Psychology*, 31, 674–85.

Dweck, C. S. (1978) Achievement. In M. E. Lamb (ed.), *Social and Personality Development*. Holt, Rinehart and Winston.

Dweck, C. S. (1991) Self-theories and goals: their role in motivation, personality and development. In R. Dienstbier (ed.), *Nebraska Symposium on Motivation, 1990*. Lincoln: University of Nebraska Press.

Dweck, C. S. and Elliot, E. S. (1983) Achievement motivation. In E. M. Hetherington (ed.), *Handbook of Child Psychology*, vol. 4: *Socialization, personality, and development*. New York: Wiley.

Dweck, C. S. and Leggett, E. L. (1988) A social-cognitive approach to motivation and personality. *Psychological Review*, 95, 256–72.

Dweck, C. S. and Repucci, N. D. (1973) Learned helplessness and reinforcement responsibility in children. *Journal of Personality and Social Psychology*, 25, 109–16.

Dweck, C. S., Davidson, W., Nelson, S., and Enna, B. (1978). Sex differences in learned helplessness. II: The contingencies of evaluative feedback in the classroom. *Developmental Psychology*, 14, 268–76.

Dweck, C. S., Goetz, T. E., and Strauss, N. L. (1980) Sex differences in learned helplessness. IV: An experimental and naturalistic study of failure generalization and its mediators. *Journal of Personality and Social Psychology*, 38, 441–52.

Eagly, A. H. (1987) *Sex Differences in Social Behavior: a Social-role Interpretation*. Hillsdale, NJ: Erlbaum.

Eagly, A. H. and Carli, L. L. (1981) Sex of researchers and sex-typed communication as determinants of sex differences in influenceability: a meta-analysis of social influence. *Psychological Bulletin*, 90, 1–20.

Eagly, A. H. and Crowley, M. (1986) Gender and helping behavior: a meta-analytic review of the social psychological literature. *Psychological Bulletin*, 110, 283–308.

Eagly, A. H. and Wood, W. (1982). Inferred sex differences in status as a determinant of gender differences about social influence. *Journal of Personality and Social Psychology*, 43, 915–28.

Eckensberger, L. H. and Silbereisen, R. K. (1980) *Entwicklung sozialer Kognitionen*. Stuttgart: Klett-Cotta.

Eckerman, C. O. (1993) Imitation and toddlers' achievement of co-ordinated action with others. In J. Nadel and L. Camaioni, L. (eds), *New Perspectives in Early Communicative Development*. London: Routledge.

Eckerman, C. O. and Stein, M. R. (1982) The toddler's emerging skills. In K. H. Rubin and H. S. Ross (eds), *Peer Relationships and Social Skills in Childhood*. New York: Springer-Verlag.

Eckerman, C. O. and Stein, M. R. (1990) How imitation begets imitation and toddlers' generation of games. *Developmental Psychology*, 26, 370–8.

Eckerman, C. O. and Whatley, J. L. (1977) Toys and social interaction between infant peers. *Child Development*, 48, 1645–56.

Eckerman, C. O., Davis, C. C., and Didow, S. M. (1989) Toddlers' emerging ways of achieving social coordinations with a peer. *Child Development*, 60, 440–53.

Eckerman, C. O., Whatley, J. L., and Kutz, S. L. (1975) Growth of social play with peers during the second year of life. *Developmental Psychology*, 11, 42–9.

Eder, R. A. (1989) The emergent personologist: the

structure and content of $3\frac{1}{2}$, $5\frac{1}{2}$, and $7\frac{1}{2}$-year olds' concepts of themselves and other persons. *Child Development*, 60, 1218–28.

Edwards, C. P. (1982) Moral development in comparative cultural perspective. In D. Wagner and H. Stevenson (eds), *Cultural Perspectives in Child Development*. San Francisco: W. H. Freeman.

Edwards, C. P. (1986) Cross-cultural research on Kohlberg's stages: the basis for consensus. In S. Modgil and C. Modgil (eds), *Lawrence Kohlberg: consensus and controversy*. Philadelphia: Falmer Press.

Edwards, D. and Mercer, N. (1986) Context and continuity: classroom discourse and the development of shared knowledge. In K. Durkin (ed.), *Language Development in the School Years*. London: Croom Helm.

Edwards, J. R. (1979) Judgements and confidence reactions to disadvantaged speech. In H. Giles and R. St Clair (eds), *Language and Social Psychology*. Oxford: Blackwell.

Edwards, J. R. (1990) Language in education. In H. Giles and W. P. Robinson (eds), *Handbook of Language and Social Psychology*. Chichester: Wiley.

Edwards, J. R. (1986) Language and educational disadvantage: the persistence of linguistic "deficit" theory. In K. Durkin (ed.), *Language Development in the School Years*. London: Croom Helm.

Edwards, J. R. (1989) *Language and Disadvantage*, 2nd edn. London: Cole and Whurr.

Edwards, R., Manstead, A. S. R., and MacDonald, C. J. (1984) The relationship between children's sociometric status and ability to recognise facial expression of emotion. *European Journal of Social Psychology*, 14, 235–8.

Egeland, B. and Farber, E. A. (1984) Mother–infant attachment: factors related to its development and changes over time. *Child Development*, 55, 753–71.

Eibl-Eibesfeldt, I. (1970) *Ethology: the biology of behavior*. New York: Holt, Rinehart and Winston.

Eibl-Eibesfeldt, I. (1988) Social interactions in an ethological, cross-cultural perspective. In F. Poyatos (ed.), *Cross-cultural Perspectives in Nonverbal Communication*. Toronto: Hogrefe.

Eibl-Eibesfeldt, I. (1989) *Human Ethology*. New York: Aldine de Gruyter.

Eiduson, B. T., Kornfein, M., Zimmerman, I. L., and Weisner, T. S. (1982) Comparative socialization practices in traditional and alternative families. In M. E. Lamb (ed.), *Nontraditional Families: parenting and child development*. Hillsdale, NJ: Erlbaum.

Eimas, P. D., Siqueland, E. R., Jusczyck, P., and Vigorito, J. (1971) Speech perception in infants. *Science*, 171, 303–6.

Eisenberg, N. (1987) The relation of altruism and other moral behaviors to moral cognition: methodological and conceptual issues. In N. Eisenberg (ed.), *Contemporary Topics in Developmental Psychology*. New York: Wiley.

Eisenberg, N. and Fabes, R. A. (1994) Mothers' reactions to children's negative emotions: relations to children's temperament and anger behavior. *Merrill-Palmer Quarterly*, 40, 138–56.

Eisenberg, N. and Miller, P. A. (1987) The relation of empathy to prosocial and related behaviors. *Psychological Bulletin*, 101, 91–119.

Eisenberg, N. and Mussen, P. H. (1989) *The Roots of Prosocial Behavior in Children*. Cambridge: Cambridge University Press.

Eisenberg, N., Boehnke, K., Schuhler, P., and Silbereisen, R. K. (1985) The development of prosocial behavior and cognitions in German children. *Journal of Cross-cultural Psychology*, 16, 69–82.

Eisenberg, N., Fabes, R. A., Bernzweig, J., Karbon, M., Poulin, R., and Hanish, L. (1993) The relations of emotionality and regulation to preschoolers' social skills and sociometric status. *Child Development*, 64, 1418–38.

Eisenberg, N., Fabes, R. A., Carlo, G., Troyer, D., Speer, A. L., Karbon, M., and Switzer, G. (1992) The relations of maternal practices and characteristics to children's vicarious emotional responsiveness. *Child Development*, 63, 583–602.

Eisenberg, R. B. (1976) *Auditory Competence in Early Life*. Baltimore: University Park Press.

Eisenberg-Berg, N. and Neal, C. (1979) Children's moral reasoning about their own spontaneous prosocial behavior. *Developmental Psychology*, 15, 228–9.

Eiser, J. R. (1985) Smoking: the social learning of an addiction. *Journal of Social and Clinical Psychology*, 3, 446–57.

Eiser, J. R., Eiser, C., Gammage, P., and Morgan, M. (1989) Health locus of control and health beliefs in relation to adolescent smoking. *British Journal of Addiction*, 84, 1059–66.

Eiser, J. R., Morgan, M., and Gammage, P. (1987) Belief correlates of perceived addiction in young smokers. *European Journal of Psychology of Education*, 2, 375–85.

Eiser, J. R., Morgan, M., Gammage, P., Brooks, N., and Kirby, R. (1991) Adolescent health behaviour and similarity-attraction: friends share smoking habits (really), but much else besides. *British Journal of Social Psychology*, 30, 339–48.

Ekman, P. (1978) Facial signs. In T. Sebeok (ed.), *Sight, Sound and Sense*. Bloomington, Ind.: Indiana University Press.

Ekman, P. (1979) About brows: emotional and conversational signals. In M. von Cranach, K. Foppa, W.

Lepinies, and D. Ploog (eds), *Human Ethology*. Cambridge: Cambridge University Press.

Ekman, P. (1992) Facial expressions of emotion: new findings, new questions. *Psychological Science*, 3, 34–8.

Ekman, P. (1994) Strong evidence for universals in facial expressions: a reply to Russell's mistaken critique. *Psychological Bulletin*, 115, 268–87.

Ekman, P. and Friesen, W. V. (1975) *Unmasking the face*. Englewood Cliffs, NJ: Prentice Hall.

Ekman, P., Friesen, W. W., and Ancoli, S. (1980) Facial signs of emotional experience. *Journal of Personality and Social Psychology*, 39, 1125–34.

Ekman, P., Friesen, W. W., O'Sullivan, M., Chan, A., Diacoyanni-Tarlatzis, I., Heider, K., Krause, R., LeCompte, W. A., Pitcairn, T., Ricci-Bitti, P. E., Scherer, K., Tomita, M., and Tzavaras, A. (1987) Universals and cultural differences in the judgments of facial expressions of emotions. *Journal of Personality and Social Psychology*, 50, 754–60.

Ekman, P., Levenson, R., and Friesen, W. (1983) Autonomic nervous system activity distinguishes among emotions. *Science*, 221, 1208–10.

Elias, M. J., Ubriaco, M., and Gray, J. (1985) A cognitive-behavioral analysis of parental facilitation of children's social-cognitive problem solving. *Journal of Applied Developmental Psychology*, 6, 57–72.

Elkind, D. (1967) Egocentrism in adolescence. *Child Development*, 38, 1025–34.

Elkind, D. (1985) Egocentrism redux. *Developmental Review*, 5, 218–26.

Elkind, D. and Bowen, R. (1979) Imaginary audience behavior in children and adolescents. *Developmental Psychology*, 15, 38–44.

Elliott, D. S., Huizinga, D., and Menard, S. (1989) *Multiple Problem Youth: delinquency, substance use, and mental health problems*. New York: Springer-Verlag.

Elliott, G. R. and Feldman, S. S. (1990) Capturing the adolescent experience. In S. S. Feldman and G. R. Elliott (eds), *At the Threshold: the developing adolescent*. Cambridge, Mass.: Harvard University Press.

Ellis, R. and Wells, G. (1980) Enabling factors in adult–child discourse. *First Language*, 1, 46–62.

Ellis, S. and Gauvain, M. (1992) Social and cultural influences on children's collaborative interactions. In L. T. Winegar and J. Valsiner (eds), *Children's Development within Social Context*, vol. 2. *Research and methodology*. Hillsdale, NJ: Erlbaum.

Ellis, S. and Rogoff, B. (1982) The strategies and efficacy of child vs. adult teachers. *Child Development*, 53, 730–5.

Ellis, S., Rogoff, B., and Cromer, C. C. (1981) Age segregation in children's social interactions. *Developmental Psychology*, 17, 399–407.

Elsen, H. (1994) Phonological constraints and overextensions. *First Language*, 14, 305–15.

El-Sheikh and Cummings, E. M. (1992) Availability of control and preschoolers' responses to interadult anger. *International Journal of Behavioral Development*, 15, 207–26.

Ely, R. and McCabe, A. (1994) The language play of kindergarten children. *First Language*, 14, 19–35.

Emde, R. N., Gaensbauer, T. J., and Harmon, R. J. (1976) *Emotional Expression in Infancy: a Biobehavioral Study: psychological issues*, vol. 10, no. 37. New York: International Universities Press.

Emiliani, F. and Carugati, F. (1985) *Il mondo sociale dei bambini*. Bologna: Il Mulino.

Emiliani, F. and Molinari, L. (1994) From the child to one's own child: social dynamics and identities at work. *European Journal of Social Psychology*, 24, 303–16.

Emiliani, F., Zani, B., and Carugati, F. (1981) From interaction strategies to social representation of adults in a day nursery. In W. P. Robinson (ed.), *Communication in Development*. London: Academic Press.

Emler, N. (1983) Morality and politics. In H. Weinreich-Haste and D. Locke (eds), *Morality in the Making: thought, action and the social context*. New York: Wiley.

Emler, N. (1984) Differential involvement in delinquency: toward an interpretation in terms of reputation management. In B. A. Maher and W. B. Maher (eds), *Progress in Experimental Personality Research*, vol. 13. New York: Academic Press.

Emler, N. (1987) Socio-moral development from the perspective of social representations. *Journal for the Theory of Social Behaviour*, 17, 371–88.

Emler, N. (1990) A social psychology of reputation. In W. Stroebe and M. Hewstone (eds), *European Review of Social Psychology*, vol. 1. Chichester: Wiley.

Emler, N. and Dickinson, J. (1993) The child as sociologist: the development of implicit theories of role categories and social organization. In M. Bennett (ed.), *The Child as Psychologist: an introduction to the development of social cognition*. New York: Harvester Wheatsheaf.

Emler, N. and Hogan, R. (1981) Developing attitudes to law and justice: an integrative review. In S. S. Brehm, S. M. Kassin, and F. X. Gibbons (eds), *Developmental Social Psychology: theory and research*. New York: Oxford University Press.

Emler, N. and Valiant, G. L. (1982) Social interaction and cognitive conflict in the development of spatial coordination skills. *British Journal of Psychology*, 73, 295–303.

Emler, N., Heather, N., and Winton, M. (1978) Delinquency and the development of moral reasoning. *British Journal of Social and Clinical Psychology*, 17, 325–31.

Emler, N., Ohana, J., and Dickinson, J. (1990) Children's representations of social relations. In G. Duveen and B. Lloyd (eds), *Social Representations and the Development of Knowledge*. Cambridge: Cambridge University Press.

Emler, N., Ohana, J., and Moscovici, S. (1987a) Children's beliefs about institutional roles: a cross national study of representations of the teacher's role. *British Journal of Educational Psychology*, 57, 26–37.

Emler, N., Reicher, S., and Ross, A. (1987b) The social context of delinquent conduct. *Journal of Child Psychology and Psychiatry*, 28, 99–109.

Emler, N., Renwick, S., and Malone, B. (1983) The relationship between moral reasoning and political orientation. *Journal of Personality and Social Psychology*, 45, 1073–80.

Emmerich, W., Goldman, K. S., Kirsh, B., and Sharabany, R. (1977) Evidence for a transitional phase in the development of gender constancy. *Child Development*, 48, 930–6.

Endsley, R. C. (1967) Determinants of frustration and its motivational consequences in young children. In W. W. Hartup and N. L. Smothergill (eds), *The Young Child: reviews of research*. Washington, DC: National Association for the Education of Young Children.

Engel, U. and Hurrelmann, K. (1989) *Psychosoziale Belastung im Jugendalter*. Berlin: de Gruyter.

Engel, U., Nordlohne, E., Hurrelmann, K., and Holler, B. (1987) Educational career and substance use in adolescence. *European Journal of Psychology of Education*, 2, 365–74.

Ennew, J. (1994) Parentless friends: a cross-cultural examination of networks among street children and street youth. In F. Nestemann and K. Hurrelmann (eds), *Social Networks and Social Support in Childhood and Adolescence*. Berlin: de Gruyter.

Entwistle, D. R. (1990) Schools and the adolescent. In S. S. Feldman and G. R. Elliott (eds), *At the Threshold: the developing adolescent*. Cambridge, Mass.: Harvard University Press.

Erickson, M. F., Sroufe, L. A., and Egeland, B. (1985) The relationship between quality of attachment and behavior problems in preschool in a high-risk sample. In I. Bretherton and E. Waters (eds), *Growing Points of Attachment Theory and Research*. Monographs of the Society for Research in Child Development, 50 (1–2), no. 209.

Erikson, E. H. (1950) *Childhood and Society*. New York: Norton.

Erikson, E. H. (1959) *Identity and Life Styles: selected papers*. New York: International Universities Press.

Erikson, E. H. (1968) *Identity: youth and crisis*. New York: Norton.

Eron, L. D. (1994) Theories of aggression: from drives to cognitions. In L. R. Huesmann (ed.), *Aggressive Behavior: current perspectives*. New York: Plenum Press.

Eron, L. D., Huesmann, L. R., Lefkowitz, M. M., and Walder, L. O. (1972) Does television violence cause aggression? *American Psychologist*, 27, 253–63.

Ervin-Tripp, S. (1970) Discourse agreement: how children answer questions. In J. Hayes (ed.), *Cognition and the Development of Language*. New York: Wiley.

Ervin-Tripp, S. (1989) Sisters and brothers. In P. G. Zukow (ed.), *Sibling Interaction across Cultures: theoretical and methodological issues*. New York: Springer-Verlag.

Ervin-Tripp, S. and Mitchell-Kernan, C. (eds) (1977) *Child Discourse*. New York: Academic Press.

Ervin-Tripp, S. M., O'Connor, M. C., and Rosenberg, J. (1984) Language and power in the family. In M. Schulz, C. Kramerae, and W. M. O'Barr (eds), *Language and Power*. Belmont, Calif.: Sage.

Erwin, P. (1985) Similarity of attitudes and constructs in children's friendships. *Journal of Experimental Child Psychology*, 40, 470–85.

Erwin, P. (1993) *Friendship and Peer Relations in Children*. Chichester: Wiley.

Escalona, S. K. (1973) Basic modes of social interaction: their emergence and patterning during the first two years of life. *Merrill-Palmer Quarterly*, 19, 205–32.

Eshel, Y. and Klein, Z. (1981) Development of academic self-concept of lower-class and middle-class primary school children. *Journal of Educational Psychology*, 73, 287–93.

Eshelman, J. R. (1985) One should marry a person of the same religion, race, ethnicity, and social class. In H. Feldman and M. Feldman (eds), *Current Controversies in Marriage and the Family*. Newbury Park, Calif.: Sage.

Eskilson, A., Wiley, G., Muehlbauer, G., and Doder, L. (1986) Parental pressure, self-esteem and adolescent reported deviance: bending the twig too far. *Adolescence*, 21, 501–15.

Estes, D., Wellman, H. M., and Woolley, J. D. (1989) Children's understanding of mental phenomena. In H. W. Reese (ed.), *Advances in Child Development and Behavior*, vol. 22. New York: Academic Press.

Evans, E. D., Rutberg, J., Sather, C., and Turner, C. (1991) Content analysis of contemporary teen magazines for adolescent females. *Youth and Society*, 23, 99–120.

Evans, J. (1994) Sex, drugs and student hall. *The Times Higher Education Supplement*, November 11, pp. 14–15.

van Evra, J. (1990) *Television and Child Development*. Hillsdale, NJ: Erlbaum.

Fabian, S. (1986) *The Last Taboo*. Ringwood: Penguin.

Fagot, B. I. (1974) Sex differences in toddlers' behavior and parental reaction. *Developmental Psychology*, 10, 554–8.

Fagot, B. I. (1978) The influence of sex of child on parental reactions to toddler children. *Child Development*, 49, 459–65.

Fagot, B. I. (1985) Changes in thinking about early sex role development. *Developmental Review*, 5, 83–98.

Fagot, B. I., Leinbach, M. D., and O'Boyle, C. (1992) Gender labeling, gender stereotyping, and parenting behaviors. *Developmental Psychology*, 28, 225–30.

Fairburn, C. G., Cooper, Z., and Cooper, P. J. (1986) The clinical features and maintenance of bulimia nervosa. In K. D. Brownell and J. P. Foreyt (eds), *Handbook of Eating Disorders: physiology, psychology and treatment of obesity, anorexia and bulimia*. New York: Basic Books.

Fairweather, H. (1976) Sex differences in cognition. *Cognition*, 4, 231–80.

Falcone, G. (1992) *Men of Honour: the truth about the Mafia*. London: Fourth Estate.

Fantz, R. L. (1961) The origin of form perception. *Scientific American*, 204, 66–72.

Fantz, R. L. (1963) Pattern vision in newborn infants. *Science*, 140, 296–7.

Farr, R. M. (1983) Wilhelm Wundt (1832–1920) and the origins of psychology as an experimental and social science. *British Journal of Social Psychology*, 22, 289–301.

Farrell, M. P. and Rosenberg, S. D. (1981) *Men at Midlife*. Boston: Auburn House.

Farrington, D. P. (1991) Antisocial personality from childhood to adulthood. *The Psychologist: Bulletin of the British Psychological Society*, 4, 389–94.

Farrington, D. P. (1992) Explaining the beginning, progress, and ending of antisocial behavior from birth to adulthood. In J. McCord (ed.) *Facts, Frameworks, and Forecasts: advances in criminological theory*, vol. 3. New Brunswick: Transaction.

Farrington, D. P. (1994) Childhood, adolescent, and adult features of violent males. In L. R. Huesmann (ed.), *Aggressive Behavior: current perspectives*. New York: Plenum Press.

Farrington, D. P. and West, D. J. (1990) The Cambridge study in delinquent development: a long-term follow-up of 411 London males. In H.-J. Kerner and G. Kaiser (eds), *Kriminalitat: Personli-*

chkeit, Lebensgeschichte und Verhalten. Berlin: Springer-Verlag.

Farver, J. M. and Branstetter, W. H. (1994) Preschoolers' prosocial responses to their peers' distress. *Developmental Psychology*, 30, 334–41.

Feather, N. T. (1983) Causal attributions and beliefs about work and unemployment among adolescents in state and independent secondary schools. *Australian Journal of Psychology*, 35, 211–32.

Feather, N. T. (1986) Employment importance and helplessness about potential unemployment among students in secondary schools. *Australian Journal of Psychology*, 38, 33–44.

Feather, N. T. and Barber, J. G. (1983) Depressive reactions and unemployment. *Journal of Abnormal Psychology*, 92, 185–95.

Feather, N. T. and O'Brien, G. E. (1986) A longitudinal study of the effects of employment and unemployment on school-leavers. *Journal of Occupational Psychology*, 59, 121–44.

Feather, N. T. and Raphelson, A. C. (1974) Fear of success in Australian and American student groups: motive or sex-role stereotype? *Journal of Personality*, 42, 190–201.

Feather, N. T. and Said, J. A. (1983) Preference for occupations in relation to masculinity, femininity, and gender. *British Journal of Social Psychology*, 22, 113–27.

Feeney, J. A. and Noller, P. (1992) Attachment style and romantic love: relationship dissolution. *Australian Journal of Psychology*, 44, 69–74.

Feeney, J. A., Noller, P., and Hanrahan, M. (1994) Assessing adult attachment. In M. B. Sperling and W. H. Brown (eds), *Attachment in Adults: clinical and developmental perspectives*. New York: Guildford Press.

Feeney, J. A., Noller, P., and Patty, J. (1993) Adolescents' interactions with the opposite sex: influence of attachment style and gender. *Journal of Adolescence*, 16, 169–89.

Feingold, A. (1988) Cognitive gender differences are disappearing. *American Psychologist*, 43, 95–103.

Feingold, A. (1992) Gender differences in mate selection preferences: a test of the parental investment model. *Psychological Bulletin*, 112, 125–39.

Feinman, S. (1982) Social referencing in infancy. *Merrill-Palmer Quarterly*, 28, 445–70.

Feinman, S. and Lewis, M. (1983) Social referencing at ten months: a second-order effect on infants' responses to strangers. *Child Development*, 54, 878–87.

Feiring, C. and Lewis, M. (1989) The social networks of girls and boys from early through middle childhood. In D. Belle (ed.), *Children's Social Networks and Social Supports*. New York: Wiley.

Feldman, N. S. and Ruble, D. N. (1981) The development of person perception: cognitive and social factors. In S. S. Brehm, S. M. Kassin, and F. X. Gibbons (eds), *Developmental Social Psychology: theory and research.* New York: Oxford University Press.

Feldman, R. S., Jenkins, L., and Popoola, O. (1979) Detection of deception in adults and children via facial expressions. *Child Development*, 50, 350–5.

Feldman, R. S., White, J. B., and Lobato, D. (1982) Social skills and nonverbal behavior. In R. S. Feldman (ed.), *Development of Nonverbal Behavior in Children*. New York: Springer-Verlag.

Feldman, S. S. and Aschenbrenner, B. (1983) Impact of parenthood on various aspects of masculinity and femininity: a short-term longitudinal study. *Developmental Psychology*, 19, 278–89.

Feldman, S. S. and Nash, S. C. (1984) The transition from expectancy to parenthood: impact of the first-born on men and women. *Sex Roles*, 11, 61–9.

Fend, H. and Schroer, S. (1985) The formation of self-concepts in the context of educational systems. *International Journal of Behavioral Development*, 8, 423–44.

Ferguson, C. (1977) Baby talk as a simplified register. In C. E. Snow and C. Ferguson (eds), *Talking to Children: language input and acquisition*. Cambridge: Cambridge University Press.

Ferguson, T. J. and Rule, B. G. (1983) An attributional perspective on anger and aggression. In R. G. Geen and E. Donnerstein (eds), *Aggression: theoretical and empirical reviews*, vol. 1. New York: Academic Press.

Ferguson, T. J. and Rule, B. G. (1988) Children's evaluations of retaliatory aggression. *Child Development*, 59, 961–8.

Fernald, A. (1985) Four-month-old infants prefer to listen to motherese. *Infant Behavior and Development*, 8, 181–95.

Fernald, A. (1989) Intonation and communicative intent in mothers' speech to infants: is the melody the message? *Child Development*, 60, 1497–510.

Fernald, A. and Kuhl, P. (1985) Acoustic determinants of infant preference for motherese speech. *Infant Behavior and Development*, 10, 279–93.

Fernald, A. and Simon, T. (1984) Expanded intonation contours in mothers' speech to newborns. *Developmental Psychology*, 20, 104–13.

Ferrari-Bravo, G. and Arcidiacono, C. (1989) Compounding misunderstanding: relations between staff and girls in an Italian juvenile prison. In M. Cain (ed.), *Growing up Good*: policing the behaviour of girls in Europe. London: Sage.

Ferris, C. and Branston, P. (1994) Quality of life in the

elderly: a contribution to its understanding. *Australian Journal of Ageing*, 13, 120–3.

Feshback, N. D. (1987) Parental empathy and child adjustment/maladjustment. In N. Eisenberg and J. Strayer (eds), *Empathy and its Development*. Cambridge: Cambridge University Press.

Feshbach, S. (1991) Attachment processes in adult political ideology: patriotism and nationalism. In J. L. Gewirtz and W. M. Kurtines (eds), *Intersections with Attachment*. Hillside, NJ: Erlbaum.

Festinger, L. (1954) A theory of social comparison processes. *Human Relations*, 7, 117–40.

Feyereisen, P. and de Lannoy, J.-D. (1991) *Gestures and Speech: psychological investigations*. Cambridge: Cambridge University Press.

Fiedler, K. (1996) Processing social information for judgements and decisions. In M. Hewstone, W. Stroebe, and G. M. Stephenson (eds), *Introduction to Social Psychology*, 2nd edn. Oxford: Blackwell.

Field, D. and Minkler, M. (1988) Continuity and change in social support between young-old and old-old or very-old age. *Journal of Gerontology*, 43, 100–7.

Field, T. (1979) Differential cardiac responses of 3-month old infants to mirror and peer. *Infant Behaviour and Development*, 2, 179–84.

Field, T. (1985) Neonatal perception of people: maturational and individual differences. In T. M. Field and N. A. Fox (eds), *Social Perception in Infants*. Norwood, NJ: Ablex.

Field, T. (1991) Attachment and early separation from parents and peers. In J. L. Gewirtz and W. M. Kurtines (eds), *Intersections with Attachment*. Hillsdale, NJ: Erlbaum.

Field, T. (1994) The effects of mothers' physical and emotional unavailability on emotional regulation. In N. A. Fox (ed.), *The Development of Emotion Regulation: biological and behavioral considerations*. Monographs of the Society for Research in Child Development, 59 (2–3), no. 240.

Field, T. and Walden, T. A. (1982) Production and discrimination of facial expressions by preschool children. *Child Development*, 53, 1299–311.

Field, T., Guy, L., and Umbel, V. (1985a) Infants' responses to mothers' imitative behaviors. *Infant Mental Health Journal*, 6, 40–4.

Field, T., Muir, D., Philton, R., Sinclair, M., and Dowell, P. (1980). Infants' orientation to lateral sounds from birth to three months. *Child Development*, 50, 295–8.

Field, T., Sandberg, D., Garcia, R., Vega-Lahr, N., Goldstein, S., and Guy, L. (1985b) Pregnancy problems, postpartum depression, and early mother-infant interactions. *Developmental Psychology*, 21, 1152–6.

Field, T., Woodson, R., Greenberg, R., and Cohen, D. (1982) Discrimination and imitation of facial expressions by neonates. *Science*, 218, 179–81.

Filipp, S.-H. and Olbrich, E. (1986) Human development across the life span: overview and highlights of the psychological perspective. In A. B. Sorenson, F. E. Weinert, and L. B. Sherrod (1986) *Human Development across the Life Course: multidisciplinary perspectives*. Hillsdale, NJ: Erlbaum.

Fincham, F. D. (1981) Development dimensions of attribution theory. In J. Jaspars, F. Fincham, and M. Hewstone (eds), *Attribution Theory and Research*, vol. 1. London: Academic Press.

Fincham, F. D. and Bradbury, T. N. (1993) Marital satisfaction, depression, and attributions: a longitudinal analysis. *Journal of Personality and Social Psychology*, 64, 442–52.

Fincham, F. D. and Hokoda, A. J. (1987) Learned helplessness in social situations and sociometric status. *European Journal of Social Psychology*, 17, 95–111.

Fincham, F. D., Diener, C. I., and Hokoda, A. (1987) Attributional style and learned helplessness: relationship to the use of causal schemata and depressive symptoms in children. *British Journal of Social Psychology*, 26, i–7.

Fincham, F. D., Hokoda, A., and Sanders, R., Jr (1989) Learned helplessness, test anxiety, and academic achievement: a longitudinal analysis. *Child Development*, 60, 138–45.

Fine, G. A., Mortimer, J. T., and Roberts, D. T. (1990) Leisure, work, and the mass media. In S. S. Feldman and G. R. Elliott (eds), *At the Threshold: the developing adolescent*. Cambridge, Mass.: Harvard University Press.

Finkelstein, N. W., Dent, C., Gallacher, K., and Ramey, C. T. (1978) Social behavior of infants and toddlers in a daycare environment. *Developmental Psychology*, 14, 257–62.

Fischer, J. L. and Wampler, R. S. (1994) Abusive drinking in young adults: personality type and family role as moderators of family-of-origin influences. *Journal of Marriage and the Family*, 56, 469–79.

Fischer, K. W. and Lamborn, S. (1989) Mechanisms of variation in developmental levels: cognitive and emotional transitions during adolescence. In A. de Ribaupierre (ed.), *Transition Mechanisms in Child Development: the longitudinal perspective*. Cambridge: Cambridge University Press.

Fishbein, H. D. and Kaminski, N. K. (1985) Children's reciprocal altruism in a competitive game. *British Journal of Developmental Psychology*, 3, 393–8.

Fishkin, J., Keniston, K., and MacKinnon, C. (1973)

Moral reasoning and political ideology. *Journal of Personality and Social Psychology*, 27, 109–19.

Fiske, S. T. and Taylor, S. E. (1991) *Social Cognition*, 2nd edn. New York: McGraw-Hill.

Fitzgerald, J. M. and Martin-Louer, P. (1983–84) Person perception in adulthood: a categories analysis. *International Journal of Aging and Human Development*, 18, 197–205.

Flapan, D. (1968) *Children's Understanding of Social Interaction*. New York: Teachers College Press.

Flavell, J. H. (1963) *The Developmental Psychology of Jean Piaget*. New York: Van Nostrand.

Flavell, J. H. and Ross, L. (1981) *Social cognitive development*. Cambridge: Cambridge University Press.

Flavell, J. H., Shipstead, S. G., and Croft, K. (1980) What young children think you see when their eyes are closed. *Cognition*, 8, 369–87.

Flavell, J. H., Speer, J. R., Green, F. L., and August, D. L. (1981) *The Development of Comprehension Monitoring and Knowledge about Communication*. Monographs of the Society for Research in Child Development, 46 (5), no. 192.

Flerx, V. C., Fidler, D. S., and Rogers, R. W. (1976) Sex role stereotypes: developmental aspects and early intervention. *Child Development*, 47, 998–1007.

Fletcher, G. J. O. and Fincham, F. D. (eds) (1991) *Cognition in Close Relationships*. Hillsdale, NJ: Erlbaum.

Fletcher, G. J. O. and Ward, C. (1988) Attribution theory and processes: a cross-cultural perspective. In M. H. Bond (ed.), *The Cross-cultural Challenge to Social Psychology*. Newbury Park, Calif.: Sage.

Flynn, C. P. (1994) Regional differences in attitudes toward corporal punishment. *Journal of Marriage and the Family*, 56, 314–24.

Fogel, A. (1977) Temporal organization in mother–infant face-to-face interaction. In H. R. Schaffer (ed.), *Studies in Mother-infant Interaction*. London: Academic Press.

Fogel, A. (1982) Early adult–infant face-to-face interaction: expectable sequences of behavior. *Journal of Pediatric Psychology*, 7, 1–22.

Fogel, A. (1993) *Developing through Relationships: origins of communication, self, and culture*. New York: Harvester Wheatsheaf.

Fogel, A., Melson, G. F., Toda, S., and Mistry, J. (1987) Young children's responses to unfamiliar infants: the effects of adult involvement. *International Journal of Behavioral Development*, 10, 37–50.

Fogel, A., Toda, S., and Kawai, M. (1988) Mother–infant face-to-face interaction in Japan and the United States: a laboratory comparison using 3-month-old infants. *Developmental Psychology*, 24, 398–406.

Fondacaro, M. R. and Heller, K. (1983) Social support factors and drinking among college student males. *Journal of Youth and Adolescence*, 12, 385–99.

Fonzi, A. and Tassi, F. (1988) Gioco simbolico e strategie di interazione. *Eta Evolutiva*, 29, 79–85.

Foot, H. C. and Barron, A.-M. (1990) Friendship and task management in children's peer tutoring. *Educational Studies*, 16, 237–50.

Foot, H. C., Chapman, A. J., and Smith, J. R. (1977) Friendship and social responsiveness in boys and girls. *Journal of Personality and Social Psychology*, 35, 401–11.

Foot, H. C., Morgan, M. J. and Shute, R. H. (eds) (1990) *Children Helping Children*. Chichester: Wiley.

Ford, M. R. and Lowery, C. R. (1986) Gender differences in moral reasoning: a comparison of the use of justice and care orientations. *Journal of Personality and Social Psychology*, 50, 777–83.

Forgas, J. P. (1981a) Epilogue: everyday understanding and social cognition. In J. P. Forgas (ed.) *Social cognition: perspectives on everyday understanding*. London: Academic Press.

Forgas, J. P. (1981b) Responsibility attribution by groups and individuals: the effects of interaction episode. *European Journal of Social Psychology*, 11, 87–99.

Forgas, J. P. (1981c) What is social about social cognition? In J. P. Forgas (ed.) *Social cognition: perspectives on everyday understanding*. London: Academic Press.

Forman, E. A. (1992) Discourse, intersubjectivity, and the development of peer collaboration: a Vygotskyan approach. In L. T. Winegar and J. Valsiner (eds), *Children's Development within Social Context*. Hillsdale, NJ: Erlbaum.

Forman, E. A. and Cazden, C. B. (1985) Exploring Vygotskian perspectives in education: the cognitive value of peer interaction. In J. V. Wertsch (ed.), *Culture, Communication, and Cognition: Vygotskian perspectives*. Cambridge: Cambridge University Press.

Forrester, M. A. (1988) Young children's polyadic conversation monitoring skills. *First Language*, 8, 201–26.

Forrester, M. A. (1992) *The Development of Young Children's Social-cognitive Skills*. Hove: Erlbaum.

Fortescue, M. (1984/ 85). Learning to speak Greenlandic: a case study of a two-year-old's morphology in a polysynthetic language. *First Language*, 5, 101–14.

Fortin, A. (1985) Apprentissage social et conflit cognitif. *Cahiers de Psychologie Cognitive*, 5, 89–106.

Foster, S. H. (1986) Learning discourse topic management in the preschool years. *Journal of Child Language*, 13, 231–50.

Fouts, G. T. (1989) Television use by the elderly. *Canadian Psychology*, 30, 568–77.

Fox, N. A., Kimmerly, N. L. and Schafer, W. D. (1991) Attachment to mother/ attachment to father: a meta-analysis. *Child Development*, 62, 210–25.

Foxcroft, D. R. and Hull, G. (1991) Adolescent drinking in behaviour and family socialization factors: a meta-analysis. *Journal of Adolescence*, 14, 255–73.

France-Kaatrude, A.-C. and Smith, W. P. (1985) Social comparison, task motivation, and the development of self-evaluative standards in children. *Developmental Psychology*, 6, 1080–9.

Frankel, D. G. and Roer-Bornstein, D. (1982) *Traditional and Modern Contributions to Changing Infant-rearing Ideologies of Two Ethnic Communities*. Monographs of the Society for Research in Child Development, 47 (4), no. 196.

Fraser, C. and Scherer, K. R. (1982) Introduction: social psychological contributions to the study of language. In C. Fraser and K. R. Scherer (eds), *Advances in the Social Psychology of Language*. Cambridge: Cambridge University Press.

Fraser, C., Bellugi, U., and Brown, R. (1963) Control of grammar in imitation, comprehension, and production. *Journal of Verbal Learning and Verbal Behavior*, 2, 121–35.

Fraysse, J.-C. (1991) Effects of social insertion mode on performance and interaction in asymmetric dyads. *European Journal of Psychology of Education*, 6, 45–53.

Freedman, D. (1965) Hereditary control of early social behavior. In B. M. Foss (ed.), *Determinants of Infant Behaviour*, vol. 3. London: Methuen.

Freedman, D. G. and Freedman, N. A. (1969) Differences in behavior between Chinese–American and European–American newborns. *Nature*, 224, 1227.

Freedman, D. G. and Keller, B. (1963) Inheritance of behavior in infants. *Science*, 140, 196–8.

Freedman, J. L. (1984) Effect of television violence on aggressiveness. *Psychological Bulletin*, 96, 227–46.

French, D. C. and Waas, G. A. (1987) Social-cognitive and behavioral characteristics of peer-rejected boys. *Professional School Psychology*, 2, 103–13.

French, L., Lucariello, J., Seidman, S., and Nelson, K. (1985) The influence of discourse content and context on preschoolers' use of language. In L. Galda and A. Pelligrini (eds), *Play, Language and Stories*. Norwood, NJ: Ablex.

Freud, A. (1958) Adolescence. *Psychoanalytic Study of the Child*, 13, 255–78.

Freud, A. and Dann, S. (1951) An experiment in group upbringing. *Psychoanalytic Study of the Child*, 6, 127–68.

Freud, S. (1964) *An Outline of Psychoanalysis. The Standard Edition of the Complete Psychological Works of Sigmund Freud*, vol. 23. London: Hogarth Press.

Freudenberg, R., Driscoll, J., and Stern, G. (1978) Reactions of adult humans to cries of normal and abnormal infants. *Infant Behavior and Development*, 1, 224–7.

Frey, K. S. and Ruble, D. N. (1987) What children say about classroom performance: sex and grade differences in perceived competence. *Child Development*, 58, 1066–78.

Frieze, I. H. (1981) Children's attributions for success and failure. In S. S. Brehm, S. M. Kassin, and F. X. Gibbons (eds), *Developmental Social Psychology: theory and research*. New York: Oxford University Press.

Frieze, I. H., Parsons, J. E., Johnson, P. B., Ruble, D. N., and Zellman, G. L. (1978) *Women and Sex Roles: a social psychological perspective*. New York: Norton.

Frisch, R. E. (1983) Fatness, puberty, and fertility: the effects of nutrition and physical training on menarche and ovulation. In J. Brooks-Gunn and A. C. Petersen (eds), *Girls at Puberty*. New York: Plenum.

Frodi, A. (1985) When empathy fails. Aversive infant crying and child abuse. In B. M. Lester and C. F. Z. Boukydis (eds), *Infant Crying: theoretical and research perspectives*. New York: Plenum.

Frodi, A. M. and Lamb, M. E. (1980) Child abusers' responses to infant smiles and cries. *Child Development*, 51, 238–41.

Frodi, A. M., Lamb, M., Leavitt, L., Donovan, W., Neff, C., and Sherry, D. (1978) Fathers' and mothers' responses to the appearance and cries of premature and normal infants. *Developmental Psychology*, 14, 490–8.

Frodi, A., Macaulay, J., and Thorne, P. R. (1977) Are women always less aggressive than men? A review of the experimental literature. *Psychological Bulletin*, 84, 634–60.

Frueh, T. and McGhee, P. E. (1975) Traditional sex role development and amount of time spent watching television. *Developmental Psychology*, 11, 109.

Fry, A. M. and Willis, F. N. (1971) Invasion of personal space as a function of the age of the invader. *Psychological Record*, 21, 385–9.

Fry, C. L. (1985) Culture, behaviour, and aging in a comparative perspective. In J. E. Birren and K. W. Schaie (eds), *Handbook of the Psychology of Aging*, 2nd edn. New York: Van Nostrand.

Fry, D. P. (1988) Intercommunity differences in aggression among Zapotec children. *Child Development*, 59, 1008–9.

Fry, D. P. (1992) Female aggression among the Zapotec of Oaxaca, Mexico. In K. Bjorkqvist and P. Niemala (eds), *Of Mice and Women: aspects of female aggression*. San Diego: Academic Press.

Frye, D. (1989) Social and cognitive development in infancy. *European Journal of Psychology of Education*, 4, 129–39.

Frye, D. (1991) The origins of intention in infancy. In D. Frye and C. Moore (eds), *Children's Theories of Mind: mental states and social understanding*. Hillsdale, NJ: Erlbaum.

Frye, D. and Moore, C. (eds) (1991) *Children's Theories of Mind: mental states and social understanding*. Hillsdale, NJ: Erlbaum.

Frye, D., Rawling, P., Moore, C., and Myers, I. (1983) Object-person discrimination and communication at 3 and 10 months. *Developmental Psychology*, 19, 303–9.

Fuchs, D. and Thelen, M. H. (1988) Children's expected interpersonal consequences of communicating their affective state and reported likelihood of expression. *Child Development*, 59, 1314–22.

Furby, L. and Beyth-Marom, R. (1992) Risk taking in adolescence: a decision-making perspective. *Developmental Review*, 12, 1–44.

Furman, W. and Buhrmester, D. (1992) Age and sex differences in perceptions of networks and personal relationships. *Child Development*, 63, 103–15.

Furnham, A. (1984) Personality, social skills, anomie and delinquency: a self-report study of a group of normal non-delinquent adolescents. *Journal of Child Psychology and Psychiatry*, 25, 409–20.

Furnham, A. (1990) *The Protestant Work Ethic*. London: Routledge.

Furnham, A. and Argyle, M. (1981) Introduction. In A. Furnham and M. Argyle (eds), *The Psychology of Social Situations*. Oxford: Pergamon.

Furnham, A. and Bitar, N. (1993) The stereotyped portrayal of men and women in British television advertisements. *Sex Roles*, 29, 297–310.

Furnham, A. and Procter, E. (1989) Belief in a just world: review and critique of the individual difference literature. *British Journal of Social Psychology*, 28, 365–84.

Furnham, A. and Schofield, S. (1986) Sex-role stereotyping in British radio advertisements. *British Journal of Social Psychology*, 25, 165–71.

Furnham, A. and Voli, V. (1989) Gender stereotyping in Italian television advertisements. *Journal of Broadcasting and Electronic Media*, 33, 175–85.

Furstenberg, F. F. (1980) The social consequences of teenage parenthood. In C. S. Chilman (ed.) *Adolescent Pregnancy and Childbearing: findings from research*. Washington, DC: US Department of Health and Human Services.

Furstenberg, F. F. (1990) Coming of age in a changing family system. In S. S. Feldman and G. R. Elliott (eds), *At the Threshold: the developing adolescent*. Cambridge, Mass.: Harvard University Press.

Furstenberg, F. F., Brooks-Gunn, J., and Chase-Lansdale, L. (1989) Teenaged pregnancy and childbearing. *American Psychologist*, 44, 313–20.

Furth, H. G. (1980) *The World of Grown-ups: children's conceptions of society*. New York: Elsevier.

Furth, H. G. and Kane, S. R. (1992) Children constructing society: a new perspective on children at play. In H. McGurk (ed.), *Childhood Social Development: contemporary perspectives*. Hove: Erlbaum.

Gabrielsen, F. (1984) *Eg eller je? Ei sosiolingvistisk gransking av yngre mal i Stavanger*. Oslo: Novus.

Gaddis, A. and Brooks-Gunn, J. (1985) The male experience of pubertal change. *Journal of Youth and Adolescence*, 14, 61–70.

Gaiser, W. and Muller, H. U. (1989) The importance of peer groups in different regional contexts and biographical stages. In K. Hurrelmann and U. Engel (eds), *The Social World of Adolescents: international perspectives*. Berlin and New York: de Gruyter.

Galambos, N. L. and Almeida, D. M. (1992) Does parent–adolescent conflict increase in early adolescence? *Journal of Marriage and the Family*, 54, 737–47.

Galambos, N. L. and Silbereisen, R. K. (1987) Influences of income change and parental acceptance on adolescent transgression proneness and peer relations. *European Journal of Psychology of Education*, 1, 17–28.

Galambos, N. L., Almeida, D. M., and Petersen, A. C. (1990) Masculinity, femininity, and sex role attitudes in early adolescence: exploring gender intensification. *Child Development*, 61, 1905–14.

Gale, F., Bailey-Harris, R., and Wundersitz, J. (1990) *Aboriginal Youth and the Criminal Justice System: the injustice of justice?* Cambridge: Cambridge University Press.

Galimberti, C. (1992) Analisi delle conversazioni e studio dell'interazione psicosociale. In C. Gallimberti (ed.), *La conversazione*. Milan: Guerini Studio.

Galligan, R. (1992) Development of language. In P. C. L. Heaven (ed.), *Life Span Development*. Sydney and London: Harcourt Brace Jovanovich.

Garbarino, J. and Kostelny, K. (1992) Child maltreatment as a community problem. *Child Abuse and Neglect*, 16, 455–64.

Garbarino, J., Boston, N., Raber, S., Russell, R., and Crouter, A. (1978) The social maps of children approaching adolescence: studying the ecology of youth development. *Journal of Youth and Adolescence*, 7, 417–28.

Garber, J., Braafledt, N., and Zeman, J. (1991) The regulation of sad affect: an information-processing perspective. In J. Garber and K. A. Dodge (eds), *The Development of Emotion Regulation and Dysregulation*. Cambridge: Cambridge University Press.

Garcia Coll, C. T. (1990) Developmental outcome of minority infants: a process-oriented look into our beginnings. *Child Development*, 61, 270–89.

Garcia Coll, C. T., Hoffman, J., and Oh, W. (1987) The social ecology and early parenting of Caucasian adolescent mothers. *Child Development*, 58, 955–63.

Garmezy, N. (1989) The role of competence in the study of children and adolescents under stress. In B. H. Schneider, G. Attili, J. Nadel, and R. P. Weissberg (eds), *Social Competence in Developmental Perspective*. Dordrecht: Kluwer.

Garner, P. W., Jones, D. C., and Miner, J. L. (1994) Social competence among low-income preschoolers: emotion socialization practices and social cognitive correlates. *Child Development*, 65, 622–37.

Garrison, W. T. and Earls, F. J. (1987) *Temperament and Child Psychopathology*. Newbury Park, Calif.: Sage.

Garton, A. F. (1992) *Social Interaction and the Development of Language and Cognition*. Hove, UK and Hillsdale, NJ: Erlbaum.

Garton, A. F. and Pratt, C. (1990) Children's pragmatic judgements of direct and indirect requests. *First Language*, 10, 51–9.

Garvey, C. (1984) *Children's Talk*. London: Fontana.

Gatting-Stiller, I., Gerling, M., Stiller, K., Voss, B., and Wender, I. (1979) Anderungun der Kausalattribuierung und des Ausdauerverhaltens bei misserfolgsmotiverten Kindern durch Modellernen. *Zeitschrift für Entwicklungspsychologie und Pädagogische Psychologie*, 4, 312–21.

Geber, B. A. and Newman, S. P. (1980) *Soweto's Children: the development of attitudes*. London: Academic Press.

Geen, R. G. (1968) Effects of frustration, attack, and prior training in aggressiveness upon aggressive behavior. *Journal of Personality and Social Psychology*, 9, 316–21.

Geen, R. G. (1990) *Human Aggression*. Milton Keynes: Open University Press.

van der Geest, T. (1981) The development of communication: some nonverbal aspects. In B. L. Hoffer and R. N. St Clair (eds), *Developmental Kinesics: the emerging paradigm*. Baltimore, Md: University Park Press.

Gelfand, D. M. and Hartmann, P. (1980) The development of prosocial behavior and moral judgment. In R. L. Ault (ed.), *Developmental Perspectives*. Santa Monica, Calif.: Goodyear.

Gelfand, D. M., Hartmann, D. P., Cromer, C. C., Smith, C. L., and Page, B. C. (1975) The effects of instructional prompts and praise upon children's donation rates. *Child Development*, 46, 980–3.

Gelman, R. and Gallistel, C. R. (1978) *The Child's Understanding of Number*. Cambridge, Mass.: Harvard University Press.

Georgas, J. (1985) Cooperative, competitive and individual problem-solving in sixth grade Greek children. *European Journal of Social Psychology*, 15, 67–77.

George, L. K. (1990) Social structure, social processes, and social-psychological states. In R. H. Binstock and L. K. George (eds), *Handbook of Aging and Social Sciences*, 3rd edn. San Diego: Academic Press.

Geppert, U. and Kuster, U. (1983) The emergence of "wanting to do it oneself": a precursor of achievement motivation. *International Journal of Behavioral Development*, 6, 355–69.

Gerbner, G., Gross, L., Signorielli, N., and Morgan, M. (1980) Ageing with television: images on television drama and conceptions of social reality. *Journal of Communication*, 30, 37–47.

Gergen, K. J. (1977) The social construction of self-knowledge. In T. Mischel (ed.), *The Self: psychological and biological issues*. Totowa, NJ: Rowman and Littlefield.

Gergen, K. J. (1985) Social constructionist inquiry: context and implications. In K. J. Gergen and K. E. Davis (ed.), *The Social Construction of the Person*. New York: Springer.

Gerth, H. and Wright Mills, C. (1954) *Character and Social Structure: the psychology of social institutions*. London: Routledge and Kegan Paul.

Gerwirtz, J. L. (1961) A learning analysis of the effects of normal stimulation, privation and deprivation on the acquisition of social motivation and attachment. In B. M. Foss (ed.), *Determinants of Infant Behaviour*. London: Methuen.

Gerwirtz, J. L. (1965) The course of infant smiling in four child-rearing environments in Israel. In B. M. Foss (ed.), *Determinants of Infant Behaviour*, vol. 3. London: Methuen.

Gesell, A., Ilg, F., and Ames, L. B. (1956) *Youth: the years from ten to sixteen*. London: Hamish Hamilton.

Gibbons, F. X. (1981) The social psychology of mental retardation: what's in a label? In S. S. Brehm, S. M. Kassin, and F. X. Gibbons (eds), *Developmental Social Psychology: theory and research*. New York: Oxford University Press.

Gibbons, F. X. and Gerrard, M. (1991) Downward comparison and coping with threat. In J. Suls and T. A. Wills (eds), *Social Comparison: contemporary theory and research*. Hillsdale, NJ: Erlbaum.

Gibson, H. R. (1993) Emotional and sexual adjustment

in later life. In S. Arber and M. Evandrou (eds), *Ageing, Independence and the Life Course*. London: Jessica Kingsley.

Gilchrist, L. D. and Schinke, S. P. (1987) Adolescent pregnancy and marriage. In V. B. van Hasselt and M. Hersen (eds), *Handbook of Adolescent Psychology*. New York: Pergamon.

Giles, H. (1973) Communicative effectiveness as a function of accented speech. *Speech Monographs*, 40, 330–1.

Giles, H. (1979) Sociolinguistics and social psychology: an introductory essay. In H. Giles and R. St Clair (eds), *Language and Social Psychology*. Oxford: Blackwell.

Giles H. (1980) Accommodation theory: some new directions. In S. de Silva (ed.), *Aspects of Linguistic Behaviour*. York: University of York.

Giles, H. and Powesland, P. (1975) *Speech Style and Social Evaluation*. London: Academic Press.

Giles, H. and Robinson, W. P. (eds) (1990) *Handbook of Language and Social Psychology*. Chichester: Wiley.

Giles, H. and Smith, P. M. (1979) Accommodation theory: optimal levels of convergence. In H. Giles and R. St Clair (eds), *Language and Social Psychology*. Oxford: Blackwell.

Giles, H., Mulac, A., Bradac, J. J., and Johnson, P. (1987) Speech accommodation theory: the last decade and beyond. In M. McLaughlin (ed.), *Communication Yearbook*, 10. Beverly Hills, Calif.: Sage.

Gilligan, C. (1977) In a different voice: women's conception of the self and of morality. *Harvard Educational Review*, 47, 481–517.

Gilligan, C. (1982) *In a Different Voice: psychological theory and women's development*. Cambridge, Mass.: Harvard University Press.

Gilligan, C. and Attanucci, J. (1988) Two moral orientations: gender differences and similarities. *Merrill-Palmer Quarterly*, 34, 223–37.

Gilligan, C. and Wiggins, G. (1988) The origins of morality in early childhood relationships. In C. Gilligan, J. V. Ward, J. M. Taylor, with B. Bardige (eds), *Mapping the Moral Domain: a contribution of women's thinking to psychological theory and education*. Cambridge, Mass.: Harvard University Press.

Gillison, G. (1980) Images of nature in Gimi thought. In C. P. MacCormack and M. Strathern (eds), *Nature, Culture and Gender*. Cambridge: Cambridge University Press.

Gilly, M. (1989) The psycho-social mechanisms of cognitive constructions: experimental research and teaching perspectives. *International Journal of Educational Research*, 13, 607–21.

Gilly, M. and Roux, J.-P. (1984) Efficacité comparée du travail individuel et du travail en interaction socio-cognitive dans l'appropriation et la mise en oeuvre de règles de resolution chez des enfants de 11–12 ans. *Cahiers de Psychologie Cognitive*, 4, 171–88.

Gilly, M. and Roux, J.-P. (1988) Social marking in ordering tasks: effects and action mechanisms. *European Journal of Social Psychology*, 18, 251–66.

Gilly, M., Blaye, A., and Roux, J.-P. (1988) Elaboracion de construcciones cognitivas individuales en situaciones sociocognitivas de resolucion de problemas. In G. Mugny and J. Perez (eds), *Psicologia social del desarollo cognitivo*. Barcelona: Anthropos.

Ginsburg, G. P. (1988) Rules, scripts and prototypes in personal relationships. In S. Duck (ed.), *Handbook of Personal Relationships: theory, research and interventions*. Chichester: Wiley.

Ginzberg, E., Ginsburg, S. W., Axelrad, S., and Herma, J. R. (1951) *Occupational Choice: an approach to a general theory*. New York: Columbia University Press.

Girotto, V. (1987) Social marking, socio-cognitive conflict and cognitive development. *European Journal of Social Psychology*, 17, 171–86.

Glachan, M. and Light, P. (1982) Peer interaction and learning: can two wrongs make a right? In G. Butterworth and P. Light (eds), *Social Cognition: studies of the development of understanding*. Chicago: University of Chicago Press.

Gleitman, L. R. and Wanner, E. (1982) Language acquisition: the state of the art. In E. Wanner and L. R. Gleitman (eds), *Language Acquisition: the state of the art*. Cambridge: Cambridge University Press.

Gleitman, L. R., Newport, E. L., and Gleitman, H. (1984) The current status of the motherese hypothesis. *Journal of Child Language*, 11, 43–79.

Glenn, N. D. and Weaver, C. N. (1981) The contribution of marital happiness to global happiness. *Journal of Marriage and the Family*, 43, 161–8.

Glick, P. C. and Lin, S.-L. (1986) More young adults are living with their parents: who are they? *Journal of Marriage and the Family*, 48, 107–12.

Glucksberg, S. and Krauss, R. M. (1967) What do people say after they have learned how to talk? Studies of the development of referential communicaiton. *Merrill–Palmer Quarterly*, 13, 309–16.

Glucksberg, S., Krauss, R. M., and Higgins, E. T. (1975) The development of referential communication skills. In F. D. Horowitz (ed.), *Review of Child Development Research*, vol. 4. Chicago: University of Chicago Press.

Gnepp, J. (1983) Children's social sensitivity: inferring emotions from conflicting cues. *Developmental Psychology*, 19, 805–14.

Gnepp, J. (1989) Children's use of personal information to understand other people's feelings. In C. Saarni and P. L. Harris (eds), *Children's Understanding of Emotion*. Cambridge: Cambridge University Press.

Gnepp, J. and Chilamkurti, C. (1988) Children's use of personality attributions to predict other people's emotional and behavioral reactions. *Child Development*, 59, 743–54.

Gnepp, J. and Gould, M. E. (1985) The development of personalized inferences: understanding other people's emotional reactions in light of their prior experiences. *Child Development*, 56, 1455–64.

Goddard, E. (1990) *Why Children Start Smoking*. London: HMSO.

Godde, M. and Engfer, A. (1994) Children's social networks and the development of social competence: a longitudinal analysis In F. Nestemann and K. Hurrelmann (eds), *Social Networks and Social Support in Childhood and Adolescence*. Berlin: de Gruyter.

Gold, M. (1970) *Delinquent Behavior in an American City*. Belmont, Calif.: Brooks/Cole.

Gold, R. (1987) *The Description of Cognitive Development: three Piagetian themes*. Oxford: Clarendon.

Goldberg, P. A. (1968) Are women prejudiced against women? *Transaction*, April, 28–30.

Goldberg, S., Perrotta, M., Minde, K., and Corter, C. (1986) Maternal behavior and attachment in low birth-weight twins and singletons. *Child Development*, 57, 34–46.

Goldberg, W. A. (1990) Marital quality, parental personality, and spousal agreement about perceptions and expectations for children. *Merrill-Palmer Quarterly*, 36, 531–56.

Goldberg, W. A. and Easterbrooks, M. A. (1984) The role of marital quality in toddler development. *Developmental Psychology*, 20, 504–14.

Goldfarb, W. (1945) Effects of psychological deprivation in infancy and subsequent stimulation. *American Journal of Psychiatry*, 102, 18–33.

Goldfarb, W. (1947) Variations in adolescent adjustment of institutionally reared children. *American Journal of Orthopsychiatry*, 17, 499–57.

Goldfield, B. A. (1986) Referential and expressive language: a study of two mother-child dyads. *First Language*, 6, 119–31.

Goldfield, B. A. (1990) Pointing, naming, and talk about objects: referential behaviour in children and mothers. *First Language*, 10, 231–42.

Goldman, B. D. and Ross, H. S. (1978) Social skills in action: an analysis of early peer games. In J. Glick and K. A. Clarke-Stewart (eds), *The Development of Social Understanding*. New York: Gardner.

Goldman, R. J. and Goldman, J. D. G. (1981) How children view old people and ageing: a develop-mental study of children in four countries. *Australian Journal of Psychology*, 3, 405–18.

Goldsmith, H. H. (1989) Behavior-genetic approaches to temperament. In G. A. Kohnstamm, J. E. Bates, and M. K. Rothbart (eds), *Temperament and Personality*. Chichester: Wiley.

Goldsmith, H. H., Buss, A. H., Plomin, R., Rothbart, M. K., Thomas, A., Chess, S., Hinde, R. A., and McCall, R. B. (1987) Roundtable: what is temperament? Four approaches. *Child Development*, 58, 505–29.

Goldsmith, H. H., Rieser-Danner, L. A., and Briggs, S. (1991) Evaluating convergent and discriminant validity of temperament questionnaires for preschoolers, toddlers, and infants. *Developmental Psychology*, 27, 566–80.

Goldstein, A. P. (1994) Delinquent gangs. In L. R. Huesmann (ed.), *Aggressive Behavior: current perspectives*. New York: Plenum Press.

Goldstein, J. (1992) Sex differences in aggressive play and toy preference. In K. Bjorkqvist and P. Niemala (eds), *Of Mice and Women: aspects of female aggression*. San Diego: Academic Press.

Golinkoff, R. M. (1983) The preverbal negotiation of failed messages: insights into the transition period. In R. M. Golinkoff (ed.), *The Transition from Prelinguistic to Linguistic Communication*. Hillsdale, NJ: Erlbaum.

Goodale, J. C. (1980) Gender, sexuality and marriage: a Kaulong model of nature and culture. In C. P. MacCormack and M. Strathern (eds), *Nature, Culture and Gender*. Cambridge: Cambridge University Press.

Goodchilds, J. D., Zellman, G. L., Johnson, P. B., and Giarrusso, R. (1988) Adolescents and their perceptions of sexual interactions. In A. W. Burgess (ed.), *Rape and Sexual Assault*, vol. 2. New York: Garland.

Goodenough, F. L. (1931) *Anger in Young Children*. Minneapolis: University of Minnesota Press.

Goodhart, F. and Baron-Cohen, S. (1993) How many ways can the point be made? Evidence from children with and without autism. *First Language*, 13, 225–33.

Goodlad, S. and Hirst, B. (1989) *Peer tutoring: a guide to learning by teaching*. London: Kogan Page.

Goodluck, H. (1991) *Language Acquisition: a linguistic introduction*. Oxford: Blackwell.

Goodman, R. and Stevenson, J. (1989a) A twin study of hyperactivity. I: An examination of hyperactivity scores and categories derived from Rutter teacher and parent questionnaires. *Journal of Child Psychology and Psychiatry*, 30, 671–89.

Goodman, R. and Stevenson, J. (1989b) A twin study of hyperactivity. II: The aetiological role of genes, family relationships and perinatal adversity. *Journal of Child Psychology and Psychiatry*, 30, 691–709.

Goodnow, J. J. (1988a). Children's household work: its nature and functions. *Psychological Bulletin*, 103, 5–26.

Goodnow, J. J. (1988b). Parents' ideas, actions, and feelings: models and methods from developmental and social psychology. *Child Development*, 59, 286–320.

Goodnow, J. J. (1990) The socialization of cognition: what's involved? In J. W. Stigler, R. A. Schweder, and G. Herdt (eds), *Cultural Psychology: essays on comparative human development*. Cambridge: Cambridge University Press.

Goodnow, J. J. and Collins. W. A. (1990) *Development According to Parents: the nature, sources, and consequences of parents' ideas*. Hillsdale, NJ: Erlbaum.

Goody, E. (1991) The learning of prosocial behaviour in small-scale egalitarian societies: an anthropological view. In R. A. Hinde and J. Groebel (eds), *Cooperation and Prosocial Behaviour*. Cambridge: Cambridge University Press.

Goosens, F. A. (1987) Maternal employment and daycare: effects on attachment. In L. W. C. Tavecchio and M. H. van Ijzendoorn (eds), *Attachment in Social Networks*. Amsterdam: North-Holland.

Goosens, L. (1984) Imaginary audience behavior as a function of age, sex and formal operational thinking. *International Journal of Behavioural Development*, 7, 77–93.

Gopnik, A. (1984) The acquisition of "gone" and the development of the object concept. *Journal of Child Language*, 11, 273–92.

Gopnik, A. and Astington, J. W. (1988) Children's understanding of representational change and its relation to the understanding of false belief and the appearance–reality distinction. *Child Development*, 59, 26–37.

Gopnik, A. and Choi, S. (1990) Do linguistic differences lead to cognitive differences? A cross-linguistic study of semantic and cognitive development. *First Language*, 10, 199–215.

Gordon, S. and Gilgun, J. F. (1987) Adolescent sexuality. In V. B. van Hasselt and M. Hersen (eds), *Handbook of Adolescent Psychology*. New York: Pergamon.

Gordon, S. L. (1989) The socialization of children's emotions: emotional culture, competence, and exposure. In C. Saarni and P. L. Harris (eds), *Children's Understanding of Emotion*. Cambridge: Cambridge University Press.

Goren, C. C., Sarty, M., and Wu, P. Y. K. (1975) Visual following and pattern discrimination of face-like stimuli by newborn infants. *Pediatrics*, 56, 544–9.

Gosling, P. (1994) The attribution of success and failure: the subject/object contrast. *European Journal of Psychology of Education*, 9, 69–83.

Gottlieb, B. H. (1991) Social support in adolescence. In M. E. Colten and S. Gore (eds), *Adolescent Stress: causes and consequences*. New York: Aldine de Gruyter.

Gottlieb, B. H. and Sylvestre, J. C. (1994) Social support in the relationships between older adolescents and adults. In F. Nestemann and K. Hurrelmann (eds), *Social Networks and Social Support in Childhood and Adolescence*. Berlin: de Gruyter.

Gottlieb, L. A. and Mendelson, M. J. (1990) Parental support and firstborn girls' adaptation to the birth of a sibling. *Journal of Applied Developmental Psychology*, 11, 29–48.

Gottman, J. M. (1994) *Why Marriages Succeed or Fail*. New York: Simon and Schuster.

Gottman, J. M. and Parkhurst, J. T. (1980) A developmental theory of friendship and acquaintanceship processes. In A. Collins (ed.), *Minnesota Symposium on Child Psychology*, vol. 13: *Development of cognition, affect, and social relations*. Hillsdale, NJ: Erlbaum.

Gottman, J. M., Gonso, J., and Rasmussen, B. (1975) Social interaction, social competence, and friendship in children. *Child Development*, 46, 709–18.

Gouin-Decarie, T., Pouliot, T., and Poulin-Dubois, D. (1983) Image speculaire et genèse de la reconnaissance de soi: une analyse hierarchique. *Enfance*, 1–2, 99–115.

Gould, R. L. (1978) *Transformations: growth and change in adult life*. New York: Simon and Schuster.

Gouldner, A. W. (1960) The norm of reciprocity: a preliminary statement. *American Sociological Review*, 25, 161–78.

Graham, S. and Barker, G. P. (1990) The down side of help: an attributional-developmental analysis of helping behavior as a low-ability cue. *Journal of Educational Psychology*, 82, 7–14.

Graham, S. and Hudley, C. (1994) Attributions of aggressive and nonaggressive African–American male early adolescents: a study of construct accessibility. *Developmental Psychology*, 30, 365–73.

Gray, W. and Hudson, L. (1984) Formal operations and the imaginary audience. *Developmental Psychology*, 20, 619–27.

Green, F. P. and Schneider, F. W. (1974) Age differences in the behavior of boys on three measures of altruism. *Child Development*, 45, 248–51.

Greenberger, E. and O'Neil R. (1993) Spouse, parent, worker: role commitments and role-related experiences in the construction of adults' well-being. *Developmental Psychology*, 29, 181–97.

Greene, A. L. (1990) Great expectations: constructions of the life course during adolescence. *Journal of Youth and Adolescence*, 19, 289–306.

Greene, A. L. and Larson, R. W. (1991) Variation in stress reactivity during adolescence. In A. Greene, E. M. Cummings, and K. Karraker (eds), *Lifespan Developmental Psychology*. New York: Academic Press.

Greenfield, P. M. (1966) On culture and conversation. In J. S. Bruner, R. R. Olver, and P. M. Greenfield (eds), *Studies in Cognitive Growth*. Chichester: Wiley.

Greenfield, P. M. (1976) Cross-cultural Piagetian research: paradox and progress. In K. F. Riegel and J. A. Meacham (eds), *The Developing Individual in a Changing World: historical and cultural issues*, vol. 1. Chicago: Aldine.

Greenfield, P. M. (1994) Independence and interdependence as developmental scripts: implications for theory, research, and practice. In P. M. Greenfield and R. R. Cocking (eds), *Cross-cultural Roots of Minority Child Development*. Hillsdale, NJ: Erlbaum.

Greenfield, P. M. and Lave, J. (1982) Cognitive aspects of informal education. In D. A. Wagner and H. W. Stevenson (eds), *Cultural Perspectives on Child Development*. San Francisco: W. H. Freeman.

Gregor, T. (1990) Male dominance and sexual coercion. In J. W. Stigler, R. A. Schweder, and G. Herdt (eds), *Cultural Psychology: essays on comparative human development*. Cambridge: Cambridge University Press.

Greif, E. and Gleason, J. (1980) Hi, thanks and goodbye: more routine information. *Language in Society*, 9, 159–66.

Griffen, J. (1982) Cultural models for coping with menopause. In A. Voda, M. Dinnerstein, and S. O'Donnell (eds), *Changing Perspectives on Menopause*. Austin: University of Texas Press.

Griffin, C. (1986) Qualitative methods and female experience: young women frm school to the job market. In S. Wilkinson (ed.), *Feminist Social Psychology: developing theory and practice*. Milton Keynes: Open University Press.

Griffiths, M. (1991) The observational study of adolescent gambling in UK amusement arcades. *Journal of Community and Applied Social Psychology*, 1, 309–20.

Griff, D. N., Friesen, J. D., and Sheppy, M. I. (1989) Family patterns associated with anorexia nervosa. *Journal of Marital and Family Therapy*, 15, 29–42.

Grossen, M. (1988) *L'intersubjectivité en situation de test*. Cousset: DelVal.

Grossen, M. (1994) Theoretical and methodological consequences of a change in the unit of analysis for the study of peer interactions in a problem solving situation. *European Journal of Psychology of Education*, 9, 159–73.

Grossman, F. K. (1988) Strain in the transition to parenthood. In R. Palkovitz and M. B. Sussman (eds), *Transitions to Parenthood*. New York: Haworth.

Grossman, K., Thane, K., and Grossmann, K. E. (1981) Maternal tactile contact of the newborn after various post-partum conditions of mother–infant contact. *Developmental Psychology*, 17, 158–69.

Grossmann, K. E., Grossman, K., Huber, F., and Wartner, W. (1981) German children's behavior towards their mother at 12 months and their father at 18 months in Ainsworth's Strange Situation. *International Journal of Behavioral Development*, 4, 157–81.

Grube, J. W., Morgan, M. and McGree, S. T. (1986) Attitudes and normative beliefs as predictors of smoking intentions and behaviours: a test of three models. *British Journal of Social Psychology*, 25, 81–93.

Grusec, J. E. (1983) The internalization of altruistic dispositions: a cognitive analysis. In E. T. Higgins, D. Ruble, and W. Hartup (eds), *Social Cognition and Social Development: a socio-cultural perspective*. Cambridge: Cambridge University Press.

Grusec, J. E. (1992) Social learning theory and developmental psychology: the legacies of Robert Sears and Albert Bandura. *Developmental Psychology*, 28, 776–86.

Grusec, J. E. and Lytton, H. (1988) *Social Development: history, theory, and research*. New York: Springer-Verlag.

Grusec, J. E., Saas-Kortsaak, P., and Simutis, Z. M. (1978) The role of example and moral exhortation in the training of altruism. *Child Development*, 49, 920–3.

Grych, J. H. and Fincham, F. D. (1990) Marital conflict and children's adjustment: a cognitive contextual framework. *Psychological Bulletin*, 108, 267–90.

Grzelak, J. (1988) Conflict and cooperation. In M. Hewstone, W. Stroebe, J.-P. Codol, and G. M. Stephenson (eds), *Introduction to Social Psychology: a European perspective*. Oxford: Blackwell.

Guardo, C. J. (1969) Personal space in children. *Child Development*, 40, 143–51.

Guerney, L. and Arthur, J. (1984) Adolescent social relationships. In R. M. Lerner and B. L. Galambos (eds), *Experiencing Adolescents: a sourcebook for parents, teachers, and teens*. New York: Garland.

Guerra, N. G., Nucci, L., and Huesmann, L. R. (1994) Moral cognition and childhood aggression. In L. R. Huesmann (ed.), *Aggressive Behavior: current perspectives*. New York: Plenum Press.

Guillaume, P. (1927) Le développement des éléments formels dans le langage de l'enfant. *Journal de Psychologie*, 24, 203–9.

Gupta, N., Jenkins, G. D., Jr, and Beehr, T. A. (1983) Employee gender, gender similarity, and supervisor-subordinate cross-evaluations. *Psychology of Women Quarterly*, 8, 174–84.

Gurin, P. and Brim, O. G., Jr (1984) Change in self in adulthood: the example of sense of control. In P. B. Baltes and O. G. Brim, Jr (eds), *Lifespan Development and Behavior*, vol. 6. New York: Academic Press.

Gurucharri, C. and Selman, R. I. (1982) The development of interpersonal understanding during childhood, preadolescence, and adolescence: a longitudinal follow-up study. *Child Development*, 53, 924–7.

Gusella, J. L., Muir, D., and Tronick, E. Z. (1988) The effect of manipulating maternal behavior during an interaction on three- and six-month-olds' affect and attention. *Child Development*, 59, 1111–24.

Gustafson, G. E. and Green, J. A. (1991) Developmental coordination of cry sounds with visual regard and gestures. *Infant Behaviour and Development*, 14, 51–7.

Gustafson, G. E. and Harris, K. L. (1990) Women's responses to young infants' cries. *Developmental Psychology*, 26, 144–52.

Guttman, D. (1975) Parenthood: a key to the comparative study of the life cycle. In N. Datan and L. Ginsberg (eds), *Lifespan Developmental Psychology*. New York: Academic Press.

Haan, N., Langer, J., and Kohlberg, L. (1976) Family patterns of moral reasoning. *Child Development*, 47, 1204–6.

Haan, N., Smith, M. B., and Block, J. (1968) Moral reasoning of young adults: political-social behavior, family background, and personality correlates. *Journal of Personality and Social Psychology*, 10, 183–201.

Haas, L. (1981) Domestic role sharing in Sweden. *Journal of Marriage and the Family*, 43, 955–67.

Hagestad, G. O. (1990) Social perspectives on the life course. In R. H. Binstock and L. K. George (eds), *Aging and the Social Sciences*, 3rd edn. San Diego: Academic Press.

Halberstadt, A. G. (1986) Family socialization of emotional expression and nonverbal communication styles and skills. *Journal of Personality and Social Psychology*, 51, 827–36.

Halberstadt, A. G. (1991) Toward an ecology of expressiveness: family socialization in particular and a model in general. In R. S. Feldman and B. Rime (eds), *Fundamentals of Nonverbal Behavior*. Cambridge: Cambridge University Press.

Halebsky, M. A. (1987) Adolescent alcohol and sub-stance abuse: parent and peer effects. *Adolescence*, 22, 961–7.

Hall, E. T. (1966) *The Hidden Dimension*. New York: Doubleday.

Hall, G. S. (1904) *Adolescence: its psychology and its relation to physiology, anthropology, sociology, sex, crime, religion and education*, 2 vols. New York: Appleton.

Hall, J. A. (1984) *Nonverbal Sex Differences: communication accuracy and expressive style*. Baltimore, Md: Johns Hopkins University Press.

Halliday, M. A. K. (1968) The users and uses of language. In J. A. Fishman (ed.), *Readings in the Sociology of Language*. The Hague: Mouton.

Halliday, M. A. K. (1978) *Language as a Social Semiotic: the social interpretation of language and meaning*. Baltimore: University Park Press.

Halmi, K. A. (1987) Anorexia nervosa and bulimia. In V. B. van Hasselt and M. Hersen (eds), *Handbook of Adolescent Psychology*. New York: Pergamon.

Hamilton, S. and Darling, N. (1989) Mentors in adolescents' lives. In K. Hurrelmann and U. Engel (eds), *The Social World of Adolescents: international perspectives*. Berlin and New York: de Gruyter.

Hammond, D. and Dingley, J. (1989) Sex differences in career preference of lower sixth formers in Belfast grammar schools. *Journal of Occupational Psychology*, 62, 263–4.

Haney, C., Banks, C., and Zimbardo, P. (1973) Interpersonal dynamics in a simulated prison. *International Journal of Criminology and Penology*, 1, 69–97.

Hansen, C. H. and Hansen, R. D. (1990) The influence of sex and violence on the appeal of rock music videos. *Communication Research*, 17, 212–34.

Hanson, S. L. and Sloane, D. M. (1992) Young children and job satisfaction. *Journal of Marriage and the Family*, 54, 888–900.

Harcourt, A. H. (1991) Help, cooperation and trust in animals. In R. A. Hinde and J. Groebel (eds), *Cooperation and Prosocial Behaviour*. Cambridge: Cambridge University Press.

Hardesty, C. and Bokemeier, J. (1989) Finding time and making do: distribution of household labor in nonmetropolitan marriages. *Journal of Marriage and the Family*, 51, 253–67.

Hareven, T. K. (1989) Historical changes in children's networks in the family and community. In D. Belle (ed.), *Children's Social Networks and Social Supports*. New York: Wiley.

Hargreaves, D. H. (1967) *Social Relations in a Secondary School*. London: Routledge and Kegan Paul.

Hargreaves, D. J., Bates, H. M., and Foot, J. M. C. (1985) Sex-typed labelling affects task performance. *British Journal of Social Psychology*, 24, 153–5.

Harris, B. (1977) Developmental differences in the attribution of responsibility. *Developmental Psychology*, 13, 257–65.

Harris, B. (1981) Developmental aspects of the attributional process. In J. H. Harvey and G. Weary (eds), *Perspectives on Attributional Processes*. Dubuque, Iowa: Wm C. Brown.

Harris, M., Barlow-Brown, F., and Chasin, J. (1995) The emergence of referential understanding: pointing and the comprehension of object names. *First Language*, 15, 19–34.

Harris, M. J., Milich, R., Corbitt, E. M., Hoover, D. W., and Brady, M. (1992) Self-fulfilling effects of stigmatizing information on children's social interactions. *Journal of Personality and Social Psychology*, 63, 41–50.

Harris, P. L. (1989a) *Children and Emotion: the development of psychological understanding*. Oxford: Blackwell.

Harris, P. L. (1989b) Object permanence in infancy. In A. Slater and G. Bremner (eds), *Infant Development*. Hillsdale, NJ: Erlbaum.

Harris, P. L. and Lipian, M. S. (1989) Understanding emotion and experiencing emotion. In C. Saarni and P. L. Harris (eds), *Children's Understanding of Emotion*. Cambridge: Cambridge University Press.

Harrison, J. (1978) Warning: the male sex role may be hazardous to your health. *Journal of Social Issues*, 34, 65–86.

Hart, B. (1991) Input frequency and children's first words. *First Language*, 11, 289–300.

Hart, D. (1992) *Becoming Men: the development of aspirations, values, and adaptational styles*. New York: Plenum Press.

Harter, S. (1983) Developmental perspectives on the self-system. In E. M. Hetherington (ed.), *Handbook of Child Psychology*, vol. 4: *Socialization, personality, and social development*. New York: Wiley.

Harter, S. (1986) Cognitive-developmental processes in the integration of concepts about emotions and the self. *Social Cognition*, 4, 119–51.

Harter, S. (1987) The determinants and mediational role of global self-worth in children. In N. Eisenberg (ed.), *Contemporary Topics in Developmental Psychology*. New York: Wiley.

Harter, S. (1988) Developmental processes in the construction of the self. In T. D. Yawkey and J. E. Johnson (eds), *Integrative Processes and Socialization: early to middle childhood*. Hillsdale, NJ: Erlbaum.

Harter, S. (1990) Self and identity development. In S. S. Feldman and G. R. Elliott (eds), *At the Threshold: the developing adolescent*. Cambridge, Mass.: Harvard University Press.

Hartnett, O. and Bradley, J. (1986) Sex roles and work. In D. J. Hargreaves and A. M. Colley (eds), *The Psychology of Sex Roles*. London: Harper and Row.

Hartshorne, H. and May, M. A. (1928) *Studies in the Nature of Character*, vol 1: *Studies in deceit*. New York: Macmillan.

Hartup, W. W. (1974) Aggression in childhood: developmental perspectives. *American Psychologist*, 29, 336–41.

Hartup, W. W. (1983) Peer relations. In E. M. Hetherington (ed.), *Handbook of Child Psychology*, vol. 4: *Socialization, personality, and development*. New York: Wiley.

Hartup, W. W. (1989a) Behavioral manifestations of children's friendships. In T. J. Berndt and G. W. Ladd (eds), *Peer Relationships in Child Development*. New York: Wiley.

Hartup, W. W. (1989b) Social relationships and their developmental significance. *American Psychologist*, 44, 120–6.

Hartup, W. W. (1991) Social development and social psychology: perspectives on interpersonal relationships. In J. H. Cantor, C. C. Spiker, and L. Lipsitt (eds), *Child Behavior and Development: training for diversity*. Norwood, NJ: Ablex.

Hartup, W. W. (1992) Friendships and their developmental significance. In H. McGurk (ed.), *Childhood Social Development: contemporary perspectives*. Hove: Erlbaum.

Hartup, W. W. and van Lieshout, C. F. M. (1995) Personality development in social context. *Annual Review of Psychology*, 46, 655–87.

Hartup, W. W., French, D. C., Laursen, B., Johnston, K. M., and Ogawa, J. R. (1993) Conflict and friendship relations in middle childhood: behavior in a closed-field situation. *Child Development*, 64, 445–54.

Harwood, R. L. and Miller, J. G. (1991) Perceptions of attachment behavior: a comparison of Anglo and Puerto Rican mothers. *Merrill-Palmer Quarterly*, 37, 583–99.

Hashima, P. Y. and Amato, P. R. (1994) Poverty, social support, and parental behavior. *Child Development*, 65, 394–403.

Haskins, R. (1985) Public school aggression among children with varying day-care experience. *Child Development*, 56, 689–703.

Hattie, J. (1992) *Self-concept*. Hillsdale, NJ: Erlbaum.

Hauser, S. T. and Bowlds, M. K. (1990) Stress, coping, and adaption. In S. S. Feldman and G. R. Elliott (eds), *At the Threshold: the developing adolescent*. Cambridge, Mass.: Harvard University Press.

Hausfater, G. and Hrdy, S. B. (eds) (1984) *Infanticide: comparative and evolutionary perspectives*. New York: Aldine.

Hawton, K. (1986) *Suicide and Attempted Suicide among Children and Adolescents*. Beverly Hills, Calif.: Sage.

Hay, D. F. (1985) Learning to form relationships in infancy: parallel attainments with parents and peers. *Developmental Review*, 5, 122–61.

Hay, D. F. (1988) Overview. In S. Duck (ed.), *Handbook of Personal Relationships: theory, research and interventions*. Chichester: Wiley.

Hay, D. F. and Murray, P. (1982) Giving and requesting: social facilitation of infants' offer to adults. *Infant Behavior and Development*, 5, 301–10.

Hay, D. F. and Ross, H. S. (1982) The social nature of early conflict. *Child Development*, 53, 105–13.

Hay, D. F. and Vespo, J. E. (1988) Social learning perspectives on the development of the mother-child relationship. In B. Birns and D. F. Hay (eds), *The Different Faces of Motherhood*. New York: Plenum Press.

Hay, D. F., Caplan, M., Castle, J., and Stimson, C. A. (1991) Does sharing become increasingly "rational" in the second year of life? *Developmental Psychology*, 27, 987–93.

Hay, D. F., Nash, A., and Pedersen, J. (1983) Interaction between 6-month old peers. *Child Development*, 53, 105–13.

Hayes, A. (1984) Interaction, engagement, and the origins of growth and communication: some constructive concerns. In L. Feagans, C. Garvey, and R. Golinkoff (eds), *The Origins and Growth of Communication*. Norwood, NJ: Ablex.

Hayes, D. P. and Ahrens, M. G. (1988) Vocabulary simplification for children: a special case of motherese? *Journal of Child Language*, 15, 395–410.

Hays, R. B. (1988) Friendship. In S. Duck (ed.), *Handbook of Personal Relationships: theory, research and interventions*. Chichester: Wiley.

Hazan, C. and Shaver, P. (1987) Romantic love conceptualized as an attachment process. *Journal of Personality and Social Psychology*, 52, 511–24.

Hearold, S. (1986) A synthesis of 1043 effects of television on social behavior. In G. Comstock (ed.), *Public Communication and Behavior*, vol. 1. New York: Academic Press.

Heath, S. B. (1983) *Ways with Words: language, life, and work in communities and classrooms*. Cambridge: Cambridge University Press.

Heaven, P. C. L. (1992) Social and economic beliefs in adulthood. In P. C. L. Heaven (ed.), *Life Span Development*. Sydney and London: Harcourt Brace Jovanovich.

Heckhausen, H. (1986) Achievement and motivation through the life span. In A. B. Sorensen, F. E. Weinert, and L. R. Sherrod (eds), *Human Development through the Life Course*. Hillsdale, NJ: Erlbaum.

Heckhausen, J. (1988) Becoming aware of one's competence in the second year: developmental progression within the mother–child dyad. *International Journal of Behavioral Development*, 11, 305–26.

Heckhausen, J. (1994) The development of mastery and its perception within caretaker-child dyads. In D. Messer (ed.), *Mastery Motivation in Early Childhood: development, measurement and social processes*. London: Routledge.

Heider, F. (1944) Social perception and phenomenal causality. *Psychological Review*, 51, 358–74.

Heider, F. (1958) *The Psychology of Interpersonal Relations*. New York: Wiley.

Heinicke, C. H. and Guthrie, D. (1992) Stability and change in husband–wife adaptation and the development of the positive parent–child relationship. *Infant Behavior and Development*, 15, 109–27.

Heitmeyer, W. and Moller, K. (1989) Milieu attachment and erosion as problems of individual socialization. In K. Hurrelmann and U. Engel (eds), *The Social World of Adolescents: international perspectives*. Berlin and New York: de Gruyter.

Henderson, V. L. and Dweck, C. S. (1990) Motivation and achievement. In S. S. Feldman and G. R. Elliott (eds), *At the Threshold: the developing adolescent*. Cambridge, Mass.: Harvard University Press.

Hendry, L. B. (1989) The influence of adults and peers on adolescents' lifestyles and leisure-styles. In K. Hurrelmann and U. Engel (eds), *The Social World of Adolescents: international perspectives*. Berlin and New York: de Gruyter.

Henngeler, S. W. (1989) *Delinquency in Adolescence*. Newbury Park, Calif.: Sage.

Herdt, G. (1990) Sambia nosebleeding rites and male proximity to women. In J. W. Stigler, R. A. Shweder, and G. Herdt (eds), *Cultural Psychology: essays on comparative human development*. Cambridge: Cambridge University Press.

Hess, E. H. (1970) Ethology and developmental psychology. In P. H. Mussen (ed.), *Carmichael's Manual of Child Psychology*, 3rd edn. New York: Wiley.

Hetherington, E. M. and Clingempeel, W. G. (1992) *Coping with Marital Transitions: a Family Systems Perspective*. Monographs of the Society for Research in Child Development, 57 (2–3), no. 227.

van den Heuvel, H., Tellegen, G., and Koomen, W. (1992) Cultural differences in the use of psychological and social characteristics in children's self-understanding. *European Journal of Social Psychology*, 22, 353–62.

Hewitt, R. (1986) *White Talk, Black Talk*. Cambridge: Cambridge University Press.

Hewlett, B. S. (1987) Intimate fathers: patterns of paternal holding among Aka pygmies. In M. E.

Lamb (ed.), *The Father's Role: cross-cultural perspectives*. Hillsdale, NJ: Erlbaum

Hewstone, M. (1989) *Causal Attributions: from cognitive processes to collective beliefs*. Oxford: Blackwell.

Hewstone, M. and Jaspars, J. (1984) Social dimensions of attribution. In H. Tajfel (ed.), *The Social Dimension*, vol. 2. Cambridge: Cambridge University Press.

Hewstone, M. and Fincham, F. (1996) Attribution theory and research: basic issues and applications. In M. Hewstone, W. Stroebe, and G. M. Stephenson (eds), *Introduction to Social Psychology*, 2nd edn. Oxford: Blackwell.

Hewstone, M., Jaspars, J., and Lalljee, M. (1982) Social representations, social attribution and social identity: the intergroup images of "public" and "comprehensive" schoolboys. *European Journal of Social Psychology*, 12, 241–69.

Heyman, G. D. Dweck, C. S., and Cain, K. M. (1992) Young children's vulnerability to self-blame and helplessness: relationship to beliefs about goodness. *Child Development*, 63, 401–15.

Hickmann, M. E. (1985) The implications of discourse skills in Vygotsky's developmental theory. In J. V. Wertsch (ed.), *Culture, Communication, and Cognition: Vygotskyan perspectives*. Cambridge: Cambridge University Press.

Higgins, E. T. (1987) Self-discrepancy: a theory relating self and affect. *Psychological Review*, 94, 319–40.

Higgins, E. T. and Bryant, S. L. (1982) Consensus information and the fundamental attribution error: the role of development and in-group versus out-group knowledge. *Journal of Personality and Social Psychology*, 43, 35–47.

Higgins, E. T. and Parsons, J. E. (1983) Social cognition and the social life of the child: stages as subcultures. In E. T. Higgins, D. N. Ruble, and W. W. Hartup (eds), *Social Cognition and Social Development*. Cambridge: Cambridge University Press.

Higgins, E. T. Ruble, D. N., and Hartup, W. W. (eds) (1983) *Social Cognition and Social Development*. Cambridge: Cambridge University Press.

Hildebrandt, K. A. and Fitzgerald, H. E. (1979) Facial feature determinants of perceived infant attractiveness. *Infant Behavior and Development*, 2, 329–40.

Hill, E. M., Nord, J. L., and Blow, F. C. (1992) Young-adult children of alcoholic parents: protective effects of positive family functioning. *British Journal of Addiction*, 87, 1677–90.

Hill, P. (1993) Recent advances in selected areas of adolescent development. *Journal of Child Psychology and Psychiatry*, 34, 69–99.

Hinde, R. A. (1982) *Ethology: its nature and relations with other sciences*. London: Fontana.

Hinde, R. A. (1988) Ethology and social psychology. In M. Hewstone, W. Stroebe, J.-P. Codol, and G.

M. Stephenson (eds), *Introduction to Social Psychology: a European perspective*. Oxford: Blackwell.

Hinde, R. A. (1992) Human social development: an ethological/relationship perspective. In H. McGurk (ed.), *Childhood Social Development: contemporary perspectives*. Hove: Erlbaum.

Hinde, R. A. and Stevenson-Hinde, J. (1986) Relating childhood relationships to individual characteristics. In W. W. Hartup and Z. Rubin (eds), *Relationships and Development*. Hillsdale, NJ: Erlbaum.

Hinde, R. A. and Tamplin, A. (1983) Relations between mother–child interaction and behaviour in preschool. *British Journal of Developmental Psychology*, 1, 231–57.

Hindelang, M. J., Hirschi, T., and Weis, J. G. (1981) *Measuring Delinquency*. Beverly Hills, Calif.: Sage.

Hirsch, B. J., Boerger, R., Levy, A. E., and Mickus, M. (1994) The social networks of adolescents and their mothers: influences on blacks and whites in single- and two-parent families. In F. Nestemann and K. Hurrelmann (eds), *Social Networks and Social Support in Childhood and Adolescence*. Berlin: de Gruyter.

Hirsh-Pasek, K. and Treiman, R. (1982) Doggerel: motherese in a new context. *Journal of Child Language*, 9, 229–37.

Hirsh-Pasek, K., Treiman, R., and Schneiderman, M. (1984) Brown and Hanlon revisited: mothers' sensitivity to ungrammatical forms. *Journal of Child Language*, 11, 81–8.

Hitch, P. (1983) Social identity and the half-Asian child. In G. Breakwell (ed.), *Threatened Identities*. Chichester: Wiley.

Ho, D. Y. F. (1986) Chinese patterns of socialization: a critical review. In M. H. Bond (ed.), *The Psychology of the Chinese People*. Hong Kong and Oxford: Oxford University Press.

Ho, D. Y. F. (1987) Fatherhood in Chinese culture. In M. E. Lamb (ed.), *The Father's Role: cross-cultural perspectives*. Hillsdale, NJ: Erlbaum.

Ho, R. and McMurtie, J. (1991) Attributional feedback and underachieving children: differential effects on causal attributions, success expectancies, and learning processes. *Australian Journal of Psychology*, 43, 93–100.

Hock, E., Morgan, K. C., and Hock, M. D. (1985) Employment decisions made by mothers of infants. *Psychology of Women Quarterly*, 9, 383–402.

Hoffer, B. L. (1981) Patterns of kinesic development. In B. L. Hoffer and R. N. St Clair (eds), *Developmental Kinesics: the emerging paradigm*. Baltimore, Md: University Park Press.

Hoffman, L. W. (1977) Changes in family roles,

socialization, and sex differences. *American Psychologist*, 42, 644–57.

Hoffman, L. W. (1987) The value of children to parents and childrearing patterns. *Social Behaviour*, 2, 123–41.

Hoffman, L. W., McManus, K. A., and Brackbill (1987) The value of children to young and elderly parents. *International Journal of Aging and Human Development*, 25, 309–22.

Hoffman, M. L. (1975) Altruistic behavior and the parent–child relationship. *Journal of Personality and Social Psychology*, 31, 937–43.

Hoffman, M. L. (1982) Development of prosocial motivation: empathy and guilt. In N. Eisenberg (ed.), *Development of Prosocial Behavior*. New York: Academic Press.

Hoffman, M. L. (1983) Affective and cognitive processes in moral internalization: an information processing approach. In E. T. Higgins, D. N. Ruble, and W. W. Hartup (eds), *Social Cognition and Social Development: a socio-cultural perspective*. Cambridge: Cambridge University Press.

Hoffman, M. L. (1987) The contribution of empathy to justice and moral judgment. In N. Eisenberg and J. Strayer (eds), *Empathy and its Development*. Cambridge: Cambridge University Press.

Hofstede, G. (1983) Dimensions of national cultures in fifty countries and three regions. In J. B. Deregowski, S. Dziurawiec, and R. C. Annis (eds), *Expiscations in Cross-cultural Psychology*. Lisse: Swets and Zeitlinger.

von Hofsten, C. and Siddiqui, A. (1993) Using the mother's actions as a reference for object exploration in 6- and 12-month-old infants. *British Journal of Developmental Psychology*, 11, 61–74.

Hogan, R. and Emler, N. P. (1978) Moral development. In M. E. Lamb (ed.), *Social and Personality Development*. Holt, Rinehart and Winston.

Hogg, M. A. (1992) *The Social Psychology of Group Cohesiveness*. New York: Harvester.

Hogg, M. A. and Abrams, D. (1988) *Social Identifications: a social psychology of intergroup relations and group processes*. London: Routledge.

Hogg, M. A. and Turner, J. C. (1987) Social identity and conformity: a theory of referent informational influence. In W. Doise and S. Moscovici (eds), *Current Issues in European Social Psychology*, vol. 2. Cambridge: Cambridge University Press.

Holahan, C. K. and Holahan, C. J. (1987) Self-efficacy, social support, and depression in aging: a longitudinal analysis. *Journal of Gerontology*, 42, 65–8.

Holden, C. (1986) Youth suicide. *Science*, 233, 839–41.

Holland, J. (1985) *Making Vocational Choice: a theory of careers*. 2nd. edn. Englewood Cliffs, NJ: Prentice Hall.

Hollin, C. (1986) Sex roles in adolescence. In D. H. Hargreaves and A. M. Colley (eds), *The Psychology of Sex Roles*. London: Harper and Row.

Hollin, C. R. (1990) *Cognitive-behavioral Interventions with Young Offenders*. New York: Pergamon.

Holloway, S. D. and Hess, R. D. (1985) Mothers' and teachers' attributions about children's mathematics performance. In I. E. Sigel (ed.), *Parental Belief Systems: the psychological consequences for children*. Hillsdale, NJ: Erlbaum.

Holmberg, M. C. (1980) The development of social interchange patterns from 12 to 42 months. *Child Development*, 51, 448–56.

Holstein, C. B. (1976) Irreversible, stepwise sequence in the development of moral judgment: a longitudinal study of males and females. *Child Development* 47, 51–61.

Honess, T. (1980) Self-reference in children's descriptions of peers. *Child Development*, 51, 476–80.

Hopkins, B. (1989), Culture, infancy and education. *European Journal of the Psychology of Education*, 2, 289–93.

Horan, J. J. and Strauss, L. K. (1987) Substance abuse in adolescence. In V. B. van Hasselt and M. Hersen (eds), *Handbook of Adolescent Psychology*. New York: Pergamon.

Horn, J. L. and Donaldson, C. (1980) Cognitive development in adulthood. In O. G. Brim, Jr and J. Kagan (eds), *Constancy and Change in Human Development*. Cambridge, Mass.: Harvard University Press.

Horne, J. and Lupir, E. (1987) Fathers' participation in work, family life and leisure: a Canadian experience. In C. Lewis and M. O'Brien (eds), *Reassessing Fatherhood: new observations on fathers and the modern family*. London: Sage.

Horner, M. S. (1972) Toward an understanding of achievement-related conflicts in women. *Journal of Social Issues*, 28, 157–76.

Horowitz, R. E. (1939) Racial aspects of self-identification in nursery school children. *Journal of Psychology*, 7, 91–9.

Hortacsu, N. (1989) Targets of communication during adolescence. *Journal of Adolescence*, 12, 253–63.

House, J. S., Landis, K. R., and Umberson, D. (1988) Social relationships and health. *Science*, 241, 540–5.

Howe, C. J. (1981) *Acquiring Language in a Conversational Context*. London: Academic Press.

Howe, C. J. (1992) Social construction and individual development: a reply to Doise and Mugny's rejoinder. *European Journal of Psychology of Education*, 7, 245–7.

Howe, C. J., Rodgers, C., and Tolmie, A. (1990)

Physics in the primary school: peer interaction and the understanding of floating and sinking. *European Journal of Psychology of Education*, 5, 459–75.

Howe, C. J., Tolmie, A., and Rodgers, C. (1992) The acquisition of conceptual knowledge in science by primary school children: group interaction and the understanding of motion down an incline. *British Journal of Developmental Psychology*, 10, 113–30.

Howe, N. and Ross, H. S. (1990) Socialization, perspective-taking, and the sibling relationship. *Development Psychology*, 26, 160–5.

Howes, E. (1989) Friendships in very young children: definition and functions. In B. H. Schneider, G. Attili, J. Nadel, and R. P. Weissberg (eds), *Social Competence in Developmental Perspective*. Dordrecht: Kluwer.

Howes, C. (1990) Can the age of entry into child care and the quality of child care predict adjustment in kindergarten? *Developmental Psychology*, 26, 292–303.

Howes, C. and Hamilton, C. E. (1992) Children's relationships with child care teachers: stability and concordance with parental attachments. *Child Development*, 63, 867–78.

Howes, C. and Olenick, M. (1986) Family and child care influences on toddlers' compliance. *Child Development*, 57, 202–6.

Howes, C., Phillipsen, L., and Hamilton, C. (1993) Constructing social communication with peers: domains and sequences. In J. Nadel and L. Camaioni (eds), *New Perspectives in Early Communicative Development*. London: Routledge.

Howes, C. and Segal, J. (1993) Children's relationships with alternative caregivers: the special case of maltreated children removed from their homes. *Journal of Applied Development Psychology*, 14, 71–81.

Howitt, D. (1982) *Mass Media and Social Problems*. Oxford: Pergamon.

Howitt, D. (1991) *Concerning Psychology: psychology applied to social issues*. Milton Keynes: Open University Press.

Hrdy, S. B. (1988) Daughters or sons? *Natural History*, 88, 64–82.

Hsu, J. K. G. (1989) The gender gap in eating disorders: why are the eating disorders more common in women? *Clinical Psychology Review*, 9, 393–407.

Hubbard, F. O. A. and van IJzendoorn, M. H. (1991) Maternal responsiveness and infant crying across the first 9 months: a naturalistic longitudinal study. *Infant Behavior and Development*, 14, 299–312.

Hubbard, J. A. and Coie, J. D. (1994) Emotional correlates of social competence in children's peer relationships. *Merrill-Palmer Quarterly*, 40, 1–20.

Hudson, B. (1989) Justice or welfare? A comparison of recent developments in the English and French juvenile justice systems. In M. Cain (ed.), *Growing up Good: policing the behaviour of girls in Europe*. London: Sage.

Hudson, L. M., Forman, E. R., and Briuon-Meisels, S. (1982) Role-taking as a predictor of prosocial behavior in cross-age tutors. *Child Development*, 53, 1320–9.

Huebner, A. and Garrod, A. (1991) Moral reasoning in a karmic world. *Human Development*, 34, 341–52.

Huebner, A. and Garrod, A. (1993) Moral reasoning among Tibetan monks: a study of Buddhist adolescents and young adults in Nepal. *Journal of Cross-cultural Psychology*, 24, 167–89.

Huesmann, L. R. and Miller, L. S. (1994) Long-term effects of repeated exposure to media violence in childhood. In L. R. Huesmann (ed.), *Aggressive Behavior: current perspectives*. New York: Plenum Press.

Huesmann, L. R., Eron, L. D., Lefkowitz, M. M., and Walder, L. O. (1984) Stability of aggression over time and generations. *Developmental Psychology*, 20, 1120–34.

Huesmann, L. R., Guerra, N. G., Zelli, A., and Miller, L. (1992) Differing normative beliefs about aggression for boys and girls. In K. Bjorkqvist and P. Niemala (eds), *Of Mice and Women: aspects of female aggression*. San Diego: Academic Press.

Hughes, M. and Donaldson, M. (1979) The use of hiding games for studying the coordination of viewpoints. *Education Review*, 31, 133–40.

Huguet, P. and Monteil, J.-M (1992) Social comparison and cognitive performance: a descriptive approach in an academic context. *European Journal of Psychology of Education*, 7, 131–50.

Hummert, M. L. (1990) Multiple stereotypes of elderly and young adults: a comparison of structure and evaluations. *Psychology and Aging*, 5, 182–93.

Humphreys, A. P. and Smith, P. K. (1987) Rough and tumble, friendship, and dominance in schoolchildren: evidence for continuity and change with age. *Child Development*, 58, 201–12.

Hundeide, K. (1993) Intersubjectivity and interpretive background in children's development and interaction. *European Journal of Psychology of Education*, 8, 439–50.

Hunter, F. T. and Youniss, J. (1982) Changes in functions of three relations during adolescence. *Development Psychology*, 18, 806–11.

Hurrelmann, K. (1988) *Social Structure and Personality Development: the individual as a productive processor of reality*. Cambridge: Cambridge University Press.

Hurrelmann, K. (1989) The social world of ado-

lescents: a sociological perspective. In K. Hurrel-
mann and U. Engel (eds), *The Social World of
Adolecents: international perspectives*. Berlin and New
York: de Gruyter.

Huston, A. C. (1983) Sex typing. In E. M. Hethering-
ton (ed.), *Handbook of Child Psychology*, vol. 4:
Socialization, personality, and development. New York:
Wiley.

Huston, A. C. (1985) The development of sex typing:
themes from recent research. *Developmental Review*, 5,
1–17.

Huston, A. C., Donnerstein, E., Fairchild, H., Feshbach, N. D., Katz, P. A., Murray, J. P., Rubinstein,
E. A., Wilcox, B. L., and Zuckerman, D. (1992) *Big
World, Small Screen: the role of television in American
society*. Lincoln: University of Nebraska Press.

Huston, A. C., Greer, D., Wright, J. C., Welch, R.,
and Ross, R. (1984) Children's comprehension of
televised formal features with masculine and feminine connotations. *Developmental Psychology*, 20,
707–16.

Huston-Stein, A. and Friedrich, L. K. (1975) The
effects of television content on young children. In
A. D. Pick (ed.), *Minnesota Symposia on Child Psychology*, vol. 9. Minneapolis: University of Minnesota
Press.

Hutt, C. (1972) *Males and Females*. Harmondsworth:
Penguin.

Hutt, C. (1978) Sex-role differentiation in social development. In H. McGurk (ed.), *Issues in Childhood
Social Development*. London: Methuen.

Hwang, C. P. (1987a). Cesarean childbirth in Sweden:
effects on the mother and father–infant relationship.
Infant Mental Health Journal, 8, 91–9.

Hwang, C. P. (1987b) The changing role of Swedish
fathers. In M. E. Lamb (ed.), *The Father's Role: cross-
cultural perspectives*. Hillsdale, NJ: Erlbaum.

Hyde, J. S. (1984) How large are gender differences in
aggression? A developmental metal-analysis. *Development Psychology*, 20, 722–36.

Hyde, J. S. (1990) *Understanding Human Sexuality*, 4th
edn. New York: McGraw-Hill.

Hyde, J. S. and Linn, M. C. (1988) Gender differences
in verbal ability: a meta-analysis. *Psychological Bulletin*, 104, 53–69.

Hyde, J. S., Fenneman, E., and Lamon, S. J. (1990)
Gender differences in mathematics performance: a
meta-analysis. *Psychological Bulletin*, 107, 139–55.

Hymel, S. (1986) Interpretations of peer behavior:
affective bias in childhood and adolescence. *Child
Development*, 57, 431–45.

Hymes, D. (1974) *Foundations of Sociolinguistics: an
ethnographic approach*. Philadelphia: University of
Pennsylvania Press.

Iannotti, R. J. (1978) Effect of role-taking experiences
on role-taking, empathy, altruism, and aggression.
Development Psychology, 14, 119–24.

van IJzendoorn, M. H. (1990) Developments in cross-
cultural research on attachment: some methodological notes. *Human Development*, 33, 3–9.

van IJzendoorn, M. H. and Kroonenberg, P. M. (1988)
Cross-cultural patterns of attachment: a meta-analysis of the Strange Situation. *Child Development*, 59,
147–56.

van IJzendoorn, M. H. and Tavecchio, L. W. C. (1987)
The development of attachment theory as a Lakato-
sian research program: philosophical and methodological aspects. In L. W. C. Tavecchio and M. H.
van IJzendoorn (eds), *Attachment in Social Networks:
contributions to the Bowlby–Ainsworth attachment theory*.
Amsterdam: North-Holland.

van IJzendoorn, M. H., Goldberg, S., Kroonenberg, P.
M., and Frenkel, O. J. (1992) The relative effects of
maternal and child problems on the quality of
attachment: a meta-analysis of attachment in clinical
samples. *Child Development*, 63, 840–58.

van IJzendoorn, M. H., van der Veer, R., and van
Vliet-Visser, S. (1987) Attachment three years later.
Relationships between quality of mother–infant
attachment and emotional/cognitive development in
kindergarten. In L. W. C. Tavecchio and M. H. van
IJzendoorn (eds), *Attachment in Social Networks: con-
tributions to the Bowlby–Ainsworth attachment theory*.
Amsterdam: North-Holland.

Imamoglu, E. O., Kuller, R., Imamoglu, V., and
Kuller, M. (1993) The social psychological worlds
of Swedes and Turks in and around retirement.
Journal of Cross-cultural Psychology, 24, 26–41.

Intons-Peterson, M. (1988) *Children's Concepts of Gender*.
Norwood, NJ: Ablex.

Isabella, R. A. (1993) Origins of attachment: maternal
interactive behavior across the first year. *Child Development*, 64, 605–21.

Isabella, R. A., Belsky, J., and von Eye, A. (1989)
Origins of infant–mother attachment: an examination of interactional synchrony during the infant's
first year. *Developmental Psychology*, 25, 12–21.

Izard, C. E. (1978) On the ontogenesis of emotions and
emotion-cognition relationships in infancy. In M.
Lewis and L. Rosenblum (eds), *The Development of
Affect*. New York: Plenum Press.

Izard, C. E. (1994) Innate and universal facial
expressions: evidence from developmental and cross-
cultural research. *Psychological Bulletin*, 115, 288–99.

Izard C. E. and Kibak, R. R. (1991) Emotions system
functioning and emotion regulation. In J. Garber
and K. A. Dodge (eds), *The Development of Emotion*

Regulation and Dysregulation. Cambridge: Cambridge University Press.

Izard, C. E. and Malatesta, C. Z. (1987) Perspectives on emotional development I: differential emotions theory of early emotional development. In J. D. Osofsky (ed.), *Handbook of Infant Development.* New York: Wiley.

Izard, C. E., Hembree, E., and Huebner, R. (1987) Infants' emotional expressions to acute pain: developmental changes and stability of individual differences. *Developmental Psychology,* 23, 105–13.

Izard, C. E., Huebner, R. R., Risser, D., McGinnes, G. C., and Dougherty, L. M. (1980) The young infant's ability to produce discrete emotion expressions. *Developmental Psychology,* 16, 132–40.

Jacklin, C. N. (1989) Female and male: issues of gender. *American Psychologist,* 44, 127–33.

Jackson, L. A. (1992) *Physical Appearance and Gender: sociobiological and sociocultural perspectives.* Albany, NY: State University of New York Press.

Jackson, L., Gardner, P., and Sullivan, L. (1992) Explaining gender differences in self-pay expectations: social comparison standards and perceptions of fair pay. *Journal of Applied Psychology,* 77, 651–63.

Jackson, S. (1987) Great Britain. In M. E. Lamb (ed.), *The Father's Role: cross-cultural perspectives.* Hillsdale, NJ: Erlbaum.

Jackson, S. (1994) Socialization, social support, and social competence in adolescence: the individual in perspective. In F. Nestemann and K. Hurrelmann (eds), *Social Networks and Social Support in Childhood and Adolescence.* Berlin: de Gruyter.

Jacobs, J. E. and Eccles, J. E. (1992) The impact of mothers' stereotypic beliefs on mothers' and children's ability perceptions. *Journal of Personality and Social Psychology,* 63, 932–44.

Jaffe, F. S. and Dryfoos, J. (1980) Fertility control services for adolescents: access and utilization. In C. S. Chilman (ed.), *Adolescent Pregnancy and Childbearing: findings from research.* Washington, DC: US Department of Health and Human Services.

Jahoda, G. (1962) Development of Scottish children's ideas and attitudes about their countries. *Journal of Social Psychology,* 58, 91–108.

Jahoda, G. (1963) The development of children's ideas about country and nationality: the conceptual framework. *British Journal of Educational Psychology,* 33, 47–60.

Jahoda, G. (1983) European "lag" in the development of an economic concept: a study in Zimbabwe. *British Journal of Development Psychology,* 1, 113–20.

Jahoda, G. (1984) The development of thinking about socio-economic systems. In H. Tajfel (ed.), *The Social Dimension,* vol. 2. Cambridge: Cambridge University Press.

Jahoda, G. (1986) A cross-cultural perspective on developmental psychology. *International Journal of Behavioral Development,* 9, 417–37.

Jahoda, G. (1988) Critical notes and reflections on "social representations". *European Journal of Social Psychology,* 18, 195–209.

Jahoda, M. (1981) Work, employment and unemployment: values, theories and approaches in social research. *American Psychologist,* 36, 184–91.

Jahoda, M., Lazarsfeld, P. F., and Zeisel, H. (1933) *Marienthal: the sociography of an unemployed community.* New York: Aldine-Atherton.

James, W. (1890) *The Principles of Psychology.* New York: Henry Holt.

Jamieson, A. (1990) Informal care in Europe. In A. Jamieson and R. Illsley (eds), *Contrasting European Policies for the Care of Older People.* Aldershot: Avebury.

Janssen, A. W. H., Janssens, J. M. A. M., and Gerris, J. R. M. (1992) Parents' and children's levels of moral reasoning: antecedents and consequences of parental discipline strategies. In J. M. A. M. Janssens and J. R. M. Gerris (eds), *Childrearing: influence on prosocial and moral development.* Amsterdam: Swets and Zeitlinger.

Janssens, J. M. A. M. and Gerris, J. R. M. (eds) (1992) *Childrearing: influence on prosocial and moral development.* Amsterdam: Swets and Zeitlinger.

Jarvis, P. A. and Creasey, G. L. (1991) Parental stress, coping, and attachment in families with an 18-month-old infant. *Infant Behavior and Development,* 14, 383–95.

Jeffery, L. and Durkin, K. (1989) Children's reactions to televised counterstereotyped male sex role behaviour as a function of age, sex and perceived power. *Social Behavior,* 4, 285–310.

Jennings, K. D. (1991) Early development of mastery motivation and its relation to the self-concept. In M. Bullock (ed.), *The Development of Intentional Action: cognitive, motivational and interactive processes.* Basel: Karger.

Jennings, K. D. (1993) Mastery motivation and the formation of self-concept from infancy through early childhood. In D. J. Messer (ed.), *Mastery Motivation in Early Childhood: development, measurement and social processes.* London: Routledge.

Jessor, R. (1993) Successful adolescent development among youth in high-risk settings. *American Psychologist,* 48, 117–26.

Jessor, R. and Jessor, S. (1977) *Problem Behavior and Psychosocial Development: a longitudinal study of youth.* New York: Academic Press.

Jessor, R., Costa, F. M., and Donovan, J. E. (1994) *Beyond Adolescence: problem behavior and young adult development*. Cambridge: Cambridge University Press.

Jiao, S., Ji, G., and Jing, Q. (1986) Comparative study of behavioral qualities of only children and sibling children. *Child Development*, 57, 357–61.

Jocic, M. (1976) Types of adaptations in adult speech when communicating with a child. In N. Waterson and C. Snow (eds), *The Development of Communication: social and pragmatic factors in language acquisition*. Chichester: Wiley.

Johnson, C. and Connors, M. E. (1987) *The Etiology and Treatment of Bulimia Nervosa*. New York: Basic Books.

Johnson, C. N. and Wellman, H. M. (1982) Children's developing conceptions of mind and brain. *Child Development*, 53, 222–34.

Johnson, J. and Newport, E. (1989) Critical period effects in second language learning: the influence of maturational state on the acquisition of English as a second language. *Cognitive Psychology*, 21, 60–99.

Johnson, J. E. and Martin, C. (1985) Parents' beliefs and home learning environments: effects on cognitive development. In I. E. Sigel (ed.), *Parental Belief Systems: the psychological consequences for children*. Hillsdale, NJ: Erlbaum.

Johnson, M. H. and Morton, J. (1991) *Biology and Cognitive Development: the case of face recognition*. Oxford: Blackwell.

Johnson, M. H., Dziurawiec, S., Ellis, H., and Morton, J. (1991) Newborns' preferential tracking of face-like stimuli and its subsequent decline. *Cognition*, 40, 1–19.

Johnson, R. E. (1986) Family structure and delinquency: general problems and gender differences. *Criminology*, 24, 65–80.

Johnston, J. and Ettema, J. S. (1982) *Positive Images: breaking stereotypes with children's television*. Beverly Hills and London: Sage.

Jones, E. E. (1979) The rocky road from acts to dispositions. *American Psychologist*, 34, 107–17.

Jones, E. E. and Harris, V. A. (1967) The attribution of attitudes. *Journal of Experimental Social Psychology*, 3, 1–24.

Jones, M. C. and Bayley, N. (1950) Physical maturing among boys as related to behavior. *Journal of Educational Psychology*, 41, 129–48.

Jones, S. E. and Aiello, J. R. (1973) Proxemic behavior of black and white, first, third, and fifth grade children. *Journal of Personality and Social Psychology*, 25, 21–7.

Jones, S. S. and Raag, T. (1989) Smile production in older infants: the importance of a social recipient for the facial signal. *Child Development*, 60, 811–18.

Jump, T. L. and Haas, L. (1987) Fathers in transitions: dual-career fathers participating in child care. In M. S. Kimmel (ed.), *Changing Men: new directions in research on men and masculinity*. Newbury Park: Sage.

Jusczyk, P. and Bertoncini, J. (1988) Viewing the development of speech perception as an innately guided learning process. *Language and Speech*, 31, 217–38.

Kagan, J. (1974) Discrepancy, temperament and infant distress. In M. Lewis and L. A. Rosenblum (eds), *The Origins of Fear*. New York: Wiley.

Kagan, J. (1987) Perspectives on infancy. In J. D. Osofsky (ed.), *Handbook of Infant Development*. New York: Wiley.

Kagan, J. (1989) *Unstable Ideas: temperament, cognition and self*. Cambridge, Mass.: Harvard University Press.

Kagan, J., Arcus, D., Snidman, N., Feng, W. Y., Hendler, J., and Greene, S. (1994) Reactivity in infants: a cross-national comparison. *Developmental Psychology*, 30, 342–5.

Kagan, J., Kearsley, R. B., and Zelazo, P. R. (1978) *Infancy: its place in human development*. Cambridge, Mass.: Harvard University Press.

Kagan, J., Reznick, J. S., and Snidman, N. (1988) Biological bases of childhood shyness. *Science*, 240, 167–71.

Kahan, L. D. and Richards, D. D. (1986) The effects of context on referential communication strategies. *Child Development*, 57, 1130–41.

Kahn, P. H. (1991) Bounding the controversies: foundational issues in the study of moral development. *Human Development*, 34, 325–40.

Kallen, D. and Stephenson, J. (1982) Talking about sex revisited. *Journal of Youth and Adolescence*, 11, 11–24.

Kaltenbach, K., Weinraub, M., and Fullard, W. (1980) Infant wariness toward strangers reconsidered: infants' and mothers' reactions to unfamiliar persons. *Child Development*, 51, 1197–202.

Kandel, D., Mossel, P., and Kaestner, R. (1987) Drug use, the transition from school to work and occupational achievement in the United States. *European Journal of Psychology of Education*, 2, 337–63.

Kanin, E. J. (1969) Selected dyadic aspects of male sex aggression. *Journal of Sex Research*, 5, 42–53.

Kanin, E. J. (1985) Date rapists: differential sexual socialization and relative deprivation. *Archives of Sexual Behavior*, 14, 218–32.

Kanin, E. J. and Parcell, S. R. (1977) Sexual aggression: a second look at the offended female. *Archives of Sexual Behavior*, 6, 67–76.

de Kanter, R. (1988) The children's home: an alternative in childrearing practices in the Netherlands. In B. Birns and D. F. Hay (eds), *The Different Faces of Motherhood*. New York: Plenum.

Karmiloff-Smith, A. (1986) Some fundamental aspects of language development after age 5. In P. Fletcher and M. Garman (eds), *Language Acquisition*, 2nd edn. Cambridge: Cambridge University Press.

Karmiloff-Smith, A. (1992) *Beyond Modularity*. Cambridge, Mass.: MIT Press.

Karniol, R. and Miller, D. T. (1981) The development of self-control in children. In S. S. Brehm, S. M. Kassin and F. X. Gibbons (eds), *Development Social Psychology: theory and research*. New York: Oxford University Press.

Karniol, R. and Ross, M. (1976) The developments of causal attributions in social perception. *Journal of Personality and Social Psychology*, 34, 455–64.

Karniol, R. and Ross, M. (1979) Children's use of a causal attribution schema and the influence of manipulative intentions. *Child Development*, 50, 463–8.

Kassin, S. M. (1981) From laychild to "layman": developmental causal attribution. In S. S. Brehm, S. M. Kassin, and F. X. Gibbons (eds), *Developmental Social Psychology: theory and research*. New York: Oxford University Press.

Kassin, S. M. and Ellis, S. A. (1988) On the acquisition of the discounting principle: an experimental test of a social-developmental model. *Child Development*, 59, 950–60.

Kassin, S. M. and Lepper. M. R. (1984) Oversufficient and insufficient justication effects: cognitive and behavioral development. In J. Nicholls (ed.), *The development of achievement motivation*. Greenwich, Conn.: JAI.

Kassin, S. M. and Lowe, C. A. (1979) On the development of the augmentation principle: a perceptual approach. *Child Development*, 50, 728–34.

Kassin, S. M. and Pryor, J. B. (1985) The development of attribution processes. In J. B. Pryor and J. D. Day (eds), *The Development of Social Cognition*. New York: Springer-Verlag.

Katchadourian, H. (1990) Sexuality. In S. S. Feldman and G. R. Elliot (eds), *At the Threshold: the developing adolescent*. Cambridge, Mass.: Harvard University Press.

Katz, L. F. and Gottman, J. M. (1991) Marital discord and child outcomes: a social psychophysiological approach. In J. Garber and K. A. Dodge (eds), *The Development of Emotion Regulation and Dysregulation*. Cambridge: Cambridge University Press.

Katz, P. A. (1979) The development of female identity. In C. B. Kopp (ed.), *Becoming Female: perspectives on development*. New York: Plenum.

Katz, P. A. (1987) Variations in family constellation: effects on gender schemata. In L. S. Liben and M. L. Signorella (eds), *Children's Gender Schemata*. San Francisco: Jossey-Bass.

Kaye, K. (1977) Toward the origin of dialogue. In H. R. Schaffer (ed.), *Studies in Mother–infant Interaction*. London: Academic Press.

Kaye, K. (1982) *The Mental and Social Life of Babies*. Chicago: Chicago University Press.

Kaye, K. and Charney, R. (1980) How mothers maintain "dialogue" with two-year-olds. In D. R. Olson (ed.), *The Social Foundations of Language and Thought*. New York: Norton.

Kaye, K. and Fogel, A. (1980) The temporal structure of face-to-face communication between mothers and infants. *Developmental Psychology*, 16, 454–64.

Kaye, K. and Wells, A. J. (1980) Mothers' jiggling and the burst-pause pattern of neonatal feeding. *Infant Behavior and Development*, 1, 141–55.

Kazdin, A. E. (1990) Psychotherapy for children and adolescents. *Annual Review of Psychology*, 41, 21–54.

Keating, C. F. and Bai, D. L. (1986) Children's attributions of social dominance from facial cues. *Child Development*, 57, 1269–76.

Keating, C. F., Mazur, A., Segall, M. H. Cysnerios, P. G., Divale, W. T., Kilbride, J. E., Komin, S., Leahy, P., Thurman, B., and Wirsing, R. (1981) Culture and the perception of social dominance from facial expression. *Journal of Personality and Social Psychology*, 40, 615–26.

Keating, D. P. (1990) Adolescent thinking. In S. S. Feldman and G. R. Elliott (eds), *At the Threshold: the developing adolescent*. Cambridge, Mass.: Harvard University Press.

Keelan, J. P., Dion, K. D., and Dion, K. L. (1992) Correlates of appearance anxiety in late adolescence and early adulthood among young women. *Journal of Adolescence*, 15, 193–205.

Keil, L. J., McClintock, C. G., Kramer, R., and Platow, M. J. (1990) Children's use of social comparison standards in judging performance and their effects on self-evaluation. *Contemporary Educational Psychology*, 15, 75–91.

Keith, J. (1990) Age in social and cultural context: anthropological perspectives. In R. H. Binstock and L. K. George (eds), *Aging and the Social Sciences*, 3rd edn. San Diego: Academic Press.

Keller, H., Scholmerich, A., and Eibl-Eisbesfeldt, I. (1988) Communication patterns in adult–infant interactions in Western and non-Western cultures. *Journal of Cross-cultural Psychology*, 19, 427–45.

Kelley, H. H. (1967) Attribution theory in social

psychology. In D. Levine (ed.), *Nebraska Symposium on Motivation*, vol. 15. Lincoln: University of Nebraska Press.

Kelley, H. H. (1971) *Causal Schemata and the Attribution process*. Morristown, NJ: General Learning Press.

Kelley, H. H. (1972) Causal schemata and the attribution process. In E. E. Jones, D. E. Kanouse, H. H. Kelley, R. E. Nisbett, S. Valins, and B. Weiner (eds), *Attribution: perceiving the causes of behavior*. Morristown, NJ: General Learning Press.

Kelley, H. H. (1973) The process of causal attribution. *American Psychologist*, 28, 107–28.

Kelley, H. H. (1983) Perceived causal structures. In J. M. F. Jaspars, F. D. Fincham, and M. Hewstone (eds), *Attribution Theory and Research: conceptual, developmental and social dimensions*. London: Academic Press.

Kelley, H. H. and Thibaut, J. W. (1969) Group problem solving. In G. Lindzey and E. Aronson (eds), *Handbook of Social Psychology*, vol. 4. Cambridge, Mass.: Addison-Wesley.

Kelley, H. H., Berscheid, E., Christensen, A., Harvey, J. T., Huston, T. L., Levinger, G., McClintrock, E., Peplau, L. A., and Peterson, D. R. (eds) (1983) *Close Relationships*. New York: W. H. Freeman.

Kelley, M. L. and Power, T. G. (1992) Children's moral understanding: development and social contextual determinants. In L. T. Winegar and J. Valsiner (eds), *Children's Development within Social Context*, vol. 2: *Research and methodology*. Hillsdale, NJ: Erlbaum.

Kelly, C. and Breinlinger, S. (1995) Identity and injustice: exploring women's participation in collective action. *Journal of Community and Applied Social Psychology*, 5, 41–77.

Keltikangas-Jarvinen, L. (1989) The stability of self-concept during adolescence and early adulthood: a six-year follow-up study. *The Journal of General Psychology*, 117, 361–8.

Keltikangas-Jarvinen, L. (1990. Moral judgments of aggressive and nonaggressive children. *Journal of Social Psychology*, 129, 733–9.

Kelvin, P. (1984) The historical dimension of social psychology: the case of unemployment. In H. Tajfel (ed.), *The Social Dimension*, vol. 2. Cambridge: Cambridge University Press.

Kempe, R. S. and Kempe, C. H. (1978) *Child Abuse*. London: Fontana.

Kemper, S., Rash, S., Kynette, D., and Norman, S. (1990) Telling stories: the structure of adults' narratives. *European Journal of Cognitive Psychology*, 2, 205–28.

Kendon, A. (1986) Some reasons for studying gesture. *Semiotica*, 62, 3–28.

Kenrick, D. T. (1994) Evolutionary social psychology: from sexual selection to social cognition. *Advances in Experimental Social Psychology*, 26, 75–121.

Kermoian, R. and Leiderman, P. H. (1986) Infant attachment to mother and child caretaker in an East African community. *International Journal of Behavioral Development*, 9, 455–69.

Kernberg, P. F. (1987) Mother–child interaction and mirror behavior. *Infant Mental Health Journal*, 8, 329–39.

Kersten, J. (1989) The institutional control of girls and boys: an attempt at a gender-specific approach. In M. Cain (ed.), *Growing up Good: policing the behaviour of girls in Europe*. London: Sage.

Kerwin, M. L. E. and Day, J. D. (1985) Peer influences on cognitive development. In J. B. Pryor and J. D. Day (eds), *The Development of Social Cognition*. New York: Springer-Verlag.

Kestenbaum, R. (1992) Feeling happy versus feeling good: the processing of discrete and global categories of emotional expressions by children and adults. *Developmental Psychology*, 28, 1132–42.

Keuls, E. C. (1985) *The Reign of the Phallus: sexual politics in ancient Athens*. New York: Harper and Row.

Kim, U. and Choi, S. H. (1994) Individualism, collectivism, and child development: a Korean perspective. In P. M. Greenfield and R. R. Cocking (eds), *Cross-cultural Roots of Minority Child Development*. Hillsdale, NJ: Erlbaum.

Kimmel, M. S. (1987) Rethinking "masculinity": new directions in research. In M. S. Kimmel (ed.), *Changing Men: new directions in research on men and masculinity*. Newbury Park, Calif.: Sage.

King, A. J. C. (1989) Changing sex roles, lifestyles and attitudes in an urban society. In K. Hurrelmann and U. Engel (eds), *The Social World of Adolescents: international perspectives*. Berlin and New York: de Gruyter.

Kirchler, E., Pombeni, M. L., and Palmonari, A. (1991) Sweet sixteen . . . Adolescents' problems and the peer group as source of support. *European Journal of Psychology of Education*, 6, 393–410.

Kirkpatrick, L. A. (1992) An attachment-theory approach to the psychology of religion. *International Journal for the Psychology of Religion*, 2, 3–28.

Kirkpatrick, L. A. and Shaver, P. R. (1992) An attachment-theoretical approach to romantic love and religious belief. *Personality and Social Psychology Bulletin*, 18, 266–75.

Kiser, L. J., Bates, J. E., Maslin, C. A., and Bayles, K. (1986) Mother–infant play at six months as a predictor of attachment security at thirteen months.

Journal of the American Academy of Child Psychiatry, 25, 68–75.

Kite, M. E. (1992) Age and the spontaneous self-concept. *Journal of Applied Social Psychology*, 22, 1828–37.

Kite, M. E., Deaux, K., and Miele, M. (1991) Stereotypes of young and old: does age outweigh gender? *Psychology and Aging*, 6, 19–27.

Kitwood, T. (1983) Self-conception among young British-Asian Muslims: confutation of a stereotype. In G. Breakwell (ed.), *Threatened Identities*. Chichester: Wiley.

Kitzinger, C. (1987) *The Social Construction of Lesbianism*. London: Sage.

Klaus, M. H. and Kennell, J. H. (1976) *Parent–infant Bonding*. St Louis: Mosby.

Klaus, M. H. and Kennell, J. H. (1983) *Bonding: the beginnings of parent–infant attachment*. New York: Plume.

Klepp, K.-I., Perry, C. L., and Jacobs, D. R. (1987) Onset, development, and prevention of drinking and driving among adolescents. *European Journal of Psychology of Education*, 2, 421–41.

Kliewer, W., Sandler, I., and Wolchik, S. (1994) Family socialization of threat appraisal and coping: coaching, modeling, and family context. In F. Nestemann and K. Hurrelmann (eds), *Social Networks and Social Support in Childhood and Adolescence*. Berlin: de Gruyter.

Klima, E. S. and Bellugi, U. (1966) Syntactic regulation in the speech of children. In J. Lyons and R. J. Wales (eds), *Psycholinguistics Papers*. Edinburgh: Edinburgh University Press.

Klinnert, M. D. (1984) The regulation of infant behavior by maternal facial expression. *Infant Behavior and Development*, 7, 447–65.

Klinnert, M. D., Emde, R. N., Butterfield, P., and Campos, J. J. (1986) Social referencing: the infant's use of emotional signals from a friendly adult with mother present. *Developmental Psychology*, 22, 427–32.

Knowles, A. D. and Nixon, M. C. (1989) Children's comprehension of expressive states depicted in a television cartoon. *Australian Journal of Psychology*, 41, 17–24.

Kobak, R. R. and Sceery, A. (1988) Attachment in late adolescence: working models, affect regulation, and representations of self and others. *Child Development*, 59, 135–46.

Kochanska, G. (1993) Toward a synthesis of parental socialization and child temperament in early development of conscience. *Child Development*, 64, 325–47.

Koenig, H. G. (1992) Religion and mental health in later life. In J. Schumaker (ed.), *Religion and Mental Health*. Oxford: Oxford University Press.

Kohlberg, L. (1963) The development of children's orientations toward a moral order: I. Sequence in the development of moral thought. *Human Development*, 6, 11–33.

Kohlberg, L. (1966) A cognitive-developmental analysis of children's sex-role concepts and attitudes. In E. E. Maccoby (ed.), *The Development of Sex Differences*. Stanford: Stanford University Press.

Kohlberg, L. (1969) Stage and sequence: the cognitive-developmental approach to socialization. In D. A. Goslin (ed.), *Handbook of Socialization Theory and Research*. Chicago: Rand McNally.

Kohlberg, L. (1976) Moral stages and moralization: the cognitive-developmental approach. In T. Lickona (ed.), *Moral Development and Behavior: theory, research, and social issues*. New York: Holt.

Kohlberg, L. and Kramer, R. B. (1969) Continuities and discontinuities in childhood and adult moral development. *Human Development*, 12, 93–120.

Kohlberg, L., Levine, C., and Hewer, A. (1983) *Moral Stages: a current formulation and response to critics*. Basel: Karger.

Kohnstamm, G. A. (1989) Temperament in childhood: cross-cultural and sex differences. In G. A. Kohnstamm, J. E. Bates, and M. K. Rothbart (eds), *Temperament in Childhood*. Chichester: Wiley.

Kohnstamm, G. A., Bates, J. E. and Rothbart, M. K. (eds) (1989) *Temperament in Childhood*. Chichester: Wiley.

Kolominskii, Ia. L. and Zhiznevskii, B. P. (1992) A sociopsychological analysis of conflicts among children during play. *Journal of Russian and East European Psychology*, 30, 72–86.

Komarovsky, M. (1985) *Women in College: shaping new feminine identities*. New York: Basic Books.

Komarovsky, M. (1987) *Blue-collar Marriage*. New Haven, Conn.: Yale University Press.

Konner, M. J. (1972) Aspects of the developing ethology of a foraging people. In N. Blurton Jones (ed.), *Ethological Studies of Child Behaviour*. Cambridge: Cambridge University Press.

Kontos, S., Hsu, H.-C., and Dunn, L. (1994) Children's cognitive and social competence in child-care centers and family day-care homes. *Journal of Applied Developmental Psychology*, 15, 387–411.

Kopp, C. B. (1991) Young children's progression to self-regulation. In M. Bullock (ed.), *The Development of Intentional Action: cognitive, motivational and interactive processes*. Basel: Karger.

Kornadt, H.-J. (1984) Development of aggressiveness: a motivation theory perspective. In R. M. Kaplan,

V. J. Konecni, and R. W. Novaco (eds), *Aggression in Children and Youth*. The Hague: Martinus Nijhoff.

Kornadt, H.-J. (1990) Aggression motive and its developmental conditions in Eastern and Western cultures. In N. Bleichrodt and P. J. D. Drenth (eds), *Contemporary Issues in Cross-cultural Psychology*. Amsterdam/Lisse: Swets and Zeitlinger.

Korner, A. and Grobstein, R. (1966) Visual alertness as related to soothing in neonates: implications for maternal stimulation and early deprivation. *Child Development*, 37, 867–77.

Korner, A. and Thoman, E. (1970) Visual alertness in neonates as evoked by maternal care. *Journal of Experimental Child Psychology*, 10, 67–78.

Kosky, R. (1987) Is suicidal behaviour increasing among Australian youth? *Medical Journal of Australia*, 147, 194–6.

Kotelchuk, M. (1976) The infant's relationship to the father: experimental evidence. In M. E. Lamb (ed.), *The Role of the Father in Child Development*. New York: Wiley.

Krauthammer, C. (1992) A touch of evil. *The Washington Post* (international edition), week ending August 23, p. 19.

Krebs, D. (1987) The challenge of altruism in biology and psychology. In C. Crawford, M. Smith, and D. Krebs (eds), *Sociobiology and Psychology: ideas, issues and applications*. Hillsdale, NJ: Erlbaum.

Krebs, D. L. and Sturrup, B. (1974) Role-taking ability and altruistic behavior in elementary school children. *Personality and Social Psychology Bulletin*, 1, 407–9.

Kreppner, K. (1987) Attachment inside the family. In L. W. C. Tavecchio and M. H. van IJzendoorn (eds), *Attachment in Social Networks: contributions to the Bowlby–Ainsworth attachment theory*. Amsterdam: North-Holland.

Kreppner, K. (1992) Developing in a developing context: rethinking the family's role for children's development. In L. T. Winegar and J. Valsiner (eds), *Children's Development within Social Context*. Hillsdale, NJ: Erlbaum.

Kreppner, K., Paulsen, S., and Schutze, Y. (1982) Infant and family development: from triad to tetrads. *Human Development*, 25, 373–91.

Kroger, J. (1989) *Identity in Adolescence: the balance between self and other*. London: Routledge.

Kropotkin, P. (1939) *Mutual Aid: a factor of evolution*. Harmondsworth: Penguin.

Kruglanski, A. W., Schwartz, J. M., Maides, S., and Hamel, I. Z. (1978) Covariation, discounting, and augmentation: towards a clarification of attribution principles. *Journal of Personality*, 46, 176–89.

Krum, S. (1993) Doctors take up arms in life-or-death struggle. *The Australian*, March 18.

Kuchuk, A., Vibbert, M., and Bornstein, M. H. (1986) The perception of smiling and its experiential correlates in three-month-old infants. *Child Development*, 57, 1054–61.

Kuczaj, S. A. (1983) *Crib Speech and Language Play*. New York: Springer-Verlag.

Kugiumutzakis, G. (1993) Intersubjective vocal imitation in early mother–infant interaction. In J. Nadel and L. Camaioni, L. (eds), *New Perspectives in Early Communicative Development*. London: Routledge.

Kuhl, P. K. (1993) Innate predispositions and the effects of experience in speech perception: the Native Language Magnet Theory. In B. de Boysson-Bardies, S. de Schonen, P. Jusczyk, P. McNeilage, and J. Morton (eds), *Developmental Neurocognition: speech and face processing the first year of life*. Dordrecht: Kluwer.

Kurdek, L. A. (1993) Predicting marital dissolution: a 5-year prospective longitudinal study of newlywed couples. *Journal of Personality and Social Psychology*, 64, 221–42.

Kurdek, L. A. and Krile, D. (1982) A developmental analysis of the relation between peer acceptance and both interpersonal understanding and perceived social competence. *Child Development*, 53, 1485–91.

Kurdek, L. A. and Sinclair, R. (1988) Relation of eighth graders' family structure, gender, and family environment with academic performance and school behavior. *Journal of Educational Psychology*, 80, 90–4.

Kurtines, W. and Greif, E. B. (1974) The development of moral thought: review and evaluation of Kohlberg's approach. *Psychological Bulletin*, 81, 453–70.

Kutnick, P. (1986) The relationship of moral judgment and moral action: Kohlberg's theory, criticism and revision. In S. Modgil and C. Modgil (eds), *Lawrence Kohlberg: consensus and controversy*. Philadelphia: Falmer Press.

Labov. W. (1972) *Language in the Inner City: studies in Black English Vernacular*. Philadelphia: University of Pennsylvania Press.

Ladd, G. W. (1983) Social networks of popular, average, and rejected children in school settings. *Merrill-Palmer Quarterly*, 29, 283–307.

Ladd, G. W. (1989) Children's social competence and social supports: precursors of early school adjustment? In B. H. Schneider, G. Attili, J. Nadel, and R. P. Weissberg (eds), *Social Competence in Development Perspective*. Dordrecht: Kluwer.

Ladd, G. W. (1990) Having friends, keeping friends, making friends, and being liked by peers in the classroom: predictors of children's early school adjustment? *Child Development*, 61, 1081–100.

Ladd, G. W. and Golter, B. S. (1988) Parents' management of preschoolers' peer relations: is it related to children's social competencies? *Developmental Psychology*, 24, 109–17.

Ladd, G. W. and Price, J. M. (1987) Predicting children's social and school adjustment following the transition from preschool to kindergarten. *Child Development*, 58, 1168–89.

Ladd, G. W., Price, J. M., and Hart, C. H. (1988) Predicting preschoolers' peer status from their playground behaviors. *Child Development*, 59, 986–2.

LaFreniere, P. and Sroufe, L. A. (1985) Profiles of peer competence in the preschool: interrelations between measures, influence of social ecology, and relation to attachment history. *Developmental Psychology*, 21, 56–68.

Lagerspetz, K. M. J. and Bjorkqvist, K. (1994) Indirect aggression in boys and girls. In L. R. Huesmann (ed.), *Aggressive Behavior: current perspectives*. New York: Plenum Press.

Lagrée, J.-C. and Fai, P. L. (1989) Girls in street gangs in the suburbs of Paris. In M. Cain (ed.), *Growing up Good: policing the behaviour of girls in Europe*. London: Sage.

Lamb, M. E. (1975) Fathers: forgotten contributors to child development. *Human Development*, 18, 245–66.

Lamb, M. E. (1976) Interactions between eight-month-old children and their fathers and mother. In M. E. Lamb (ed.), *The Role of the Father in Child Development*. New York: Wiley.

Lamb, M. E. (1977) The development of mother–infant and father–infant attachments in the second year of life. *Developmental Psychology*, 13, 639–49.

Lamb, M. E. and Nash, A. (1989) Infant–mother attachment, sociability, and peer competence. In T. J. Berndt and G. W. Ladd (eds), *Peer Relationships in Child Development*. New York: Wiley.

Lamb, M. E., Hwang, C. P., Frodi, A., and Frodi, M. (1982) Security of mother– and father–infant attachment and its relations to sociability with strangers in traditional and non-traditional Swedish families. *Infant Behavior and Development*, 5, 355–67.

Lamb, M. E., Pleck, J. H., and Levine, J. A. (1987) Effects of increased paternal involvement on mothers and fathers. In C. Lewis and M. O'Brien (eds), *Reassessing Fatherhood: new observations on fathers and the modern family*. London: Sage.

Lamb, M. E., Thompson, R. A., Garnder, W., and Charnov, E. L. (1985) *Infant–mother Attachment: the origins and significance of individual differences in Strange Situation Behavior*. Hillsdale, NJ: Erlbaum.

Lamb, S. (1991) Internal state words: their relation to moral development and to maternal communications about moral development in the second year of life. *First Language*, 11, 391–406.

Lambert, W. (1967) A social psychology of bilingualism. *Journal of Social Issues*, 23, 91–109.

Lambert, W. and Klineberg, O. (1967) *Children's Views of Foreign People*. New York: Appleton–Century–Crofts Meredith.

Lambert, W., Hodgson, R., Gardner, R. C., and Fillenbaum, S. (1960) Evaluational reactions to spoken languages. *Journal of Abnormal and Social Psychology*, 60, 44–51.

Lamborn, S. D. and Steinberg, L. (1993) Emotional autonomy redux: revisiting Ryan and Lynch. *Child Development*, 64, 483–99.

Lamborn, S. D., Mounts, N., Steinberg, L., and Dornbusch, S. (1991) Patterns of competence and adjustment among adolescents form authoritative, authoritarian, indulgent, and neglectful families. *Child Development*, 62, 1049–65.

Landau, R. (1977) Spontaneous and elicited smiles and vocalizations of infants in four Israeli environments. *Developmental Psychology*, 13, 389–400.

Langer, E. J. and Rodin, J. (1976) The effects of choice and enhanced personal responsibility for the aged. *Journal of Personality and Social Psychology*, 34, 191–8.

Langer, L. M. and Warheit, G. J. (1992) The pre-adult decision-making model: linking decision-making directedness/orientation to adolescent attitudes and behaviors. *Adolescence*, 27, 919–43.

Langlois, J. H. and Downs, A. C. (1979) Peer relations as a function of physical attractiveness: the eye of the beholder or behavioral reality? *Child Development*, 50, 409–18.

Langlois, J. H. and Downs, A. C. (1980) Mothers, fathers, and peers as socialization agents of sex-typed play behaviors in young children. *Child Development*, 51, 1237–47.

Langlois, J. H. and Roggman, L. A. (1990) Attractive faces are only average. *Psychological Science*, 1, 115–21.

Langlois, J. H. and Stephan, C. W. (1981) Beauty and the beast: the role of physical attractiveness in the development of peer relations and social behaviour. In S. S. Brehm, S. M. Kassin, and F. X. Gibbons (eds), *Developmental Social Psychology: theory and research*. New York: Oxford University Press.

Langlois, J. H., Roggman, L. A., and Rieser-Danner, L. A. (1990) Infants' differential social responses to attractive and unattractive faces. *Developmental Psychology*, 26, 153–9.

Lapsley, D. K. and Quintana, S. M. (1985) Integrative themes in social and developmental theories of self. In J. B. Pryor and J. D. Day (eds), *The Development of Social Cognition*. New York: Springer-Verlag.

Larson, R. and Asmussen, L. (1991) Anger, worry, and hurt in early adolescence: an enlarging world of negative emotions. In M. E. Colten and S. Gore (eds), *Adolescent Stress: causes and consequences*. New York: Aldine de Gruyter.

Larson, R. and Lampman-Petraitis, C. (1989) Daily emotional states as reported by children and adolescents. *Child Development*, 60, 1250–60.

Latane, B. and Darley, J. M. (1970) *The Unresponsive Bystander: why doesn't he help?* New York: Appleton–Century–Crofts.

Lau, S. (1990) Crisis and vulnerability in adolescent development. *Journal of Youth and Adolescence*, 19, 111–31.

Lau, S. and Leung, K. (1992) Relations with parents and school and Chinese adolescents' self-concept, delinquency, and academic performance. *British Journal of Educational Psychology*, 62, 193–202.

Lauer, C. (1992) Variability in the patterns of agonistic behavior of preschool children. In J. Silverberg and J. P. Gray (eds), *Aggression and Peacefulness in Humans and Other Primates*. New York: Oxford University Press.

Laupa, M. and Turiel, E. (1993) Children's concepts of authority and social context. *Journal of Educational Psychology*, 85, 191–7.

Laursen, B. (in press). Conflict and social interaction in adolescent relationships. *Journal of Research on Adolescence*.

Laursen, B. and Collins, W. A. (1994) Interpersonal conflict during adolescence. *Psychological Bulletin*, 115, 197–209.

Lavery, B., Siegel, A. W., Cousins, J. H., and Rubovits, D. S. (1993) Adolescent risk-taking: an analysis of problem behaviors in problem children. *Journal of Experimental Child Psychology*, 55, 277–96.

Lawrance, L. (1988) Validation of a self-efficacy scale to predict adolescent smoking. *Health Education Research*, 4, 351–60.

Lawrance, L., Levy, S. R., and Rubinson, L. (1990) Self-efficacy and AIDS prevention for pregnant teens. *Journal of School Health*, 60, 19–24.

Leach, P. (1993) Should parents hit their children? *The Psychologist: Bulletin of the British Psychological Society*, 6, 216–20.

Leboyer, F. (1975) *Birth without Violence*. London: Fontana.

Lechner, C. R. and Rosenthal, D. A. (1984) Adolescent self-consciousness and the imaginary audience. *Genetic Psychology Monographs*, 110, 289–305.

Ledbetter, P. J. and Dent, C. H. (1988) Young children's sensitivity to direct and indirect request structure. *First Language*, 8, 227–46.

Ledingham, J. E. (1989) What to do while the kids are growing up: changing instrumentation in longitudinal research. In B. H. Schneider, G. Attili, J.

Nadel, and R. P. Weissberg (eds), *Social Competence in Developmental Perspective*. Dordrecht: Kluwer.

Leekam, S. (1993) Children's understanding of mind. In M. Bennett (ed.), *The Child as Psychologist: an introduction to the development of social cognition*. New York: Harvester Wheatsheaf.

Lees, S. (1989) Learning to love: sexual reputation, morality and the social control of girls. In M. Cain (ed.), *Growing up Good: policing the behaviour of girls in Europe*. London: Sage.

Lefevbre-Pinard, M., Charbonneau, C., and Feider, H. (1982) Differential effectiveness of explicit verbal feedback on children's communication skills. *Journal of Experimental Child Psychology*, 34, 174–83.

Legendre, A. (1987) Transformation de l'espace d'activités et échanges sociaux de jeunes enfants en crèche. *Psychologie française*, 32, 31–43.

Legendre, A. (1989) Young children's social competence and their use of space in day-care centers. In B. H. Schneider, G. Attili, J. Nadel, and R. P. Weissberg (eds), *Social Competence in Developmental Perspective*. Dordrecht: Kluwer.

Legerstee, M. (1991) Changes in the quality of infant sounds as a function of social and nonsocial stimulation. *First Language*, 11, 327–43.

Lehman, D. R., Lempert, R. O., and Nisbett, R. E. (1988) The effects of graduate training on reasoning: formal discipline and thinking about everyday-life events. *American Psychologist*, 43, 431–42.

Lenneberg, E. H. (1962) Understanding language without ability to speak: a case report: *Journal of Abnormal and Social Psychology*, 65, 419–25.

Lenneberg, E. H. (1967) *Biological Foundations of Language*. New York: Wiley.

Lennon, R. and Eisenberg, N. (1987) Gender and age differences in empathy and sympathy. In N. Eisenberg and J. Strayer (eds), *Empathy and its Development*. Cambridge: Cambridge University Press.

Lens, W. and Gailly, A. (1980) Extension of future time perspective in motivational goals of different age groups. *Human Development*, 3, 1–17.

Leonard, M. (1991) *Mae West: empress of sex*. London: Harper Collins.

Lepper, M. R. (1983) Social-control processes and the internalization of social values: an attributional perspective. In E. T. Higgins, D. N. Ruble, and W. W. Hartup (eds), *Social Cognition and Social Development: a socio-cultural perspective*. Cambridge: Cambridge University Press.

Lepper, M. R. and Gilovich, T. J. (1981) The multiple functions of reward: a social-developmental perspective. In S. S. Brehm, S. M. Kassin, and F. X. Gibbons (eds), *Developmental Social Psychology: theory and research*. New York: Oxford University Press.

Lepper, M. R., Greene, D., and Nisbett, R. E. (1973) Undermining children's intrinsic interest with extrinsic rewards: a test of the "overjustification" hypothesis. *Journal of Personality and Social Psychology*, 28, 129–37.

Lepper, M. R., Sagotsky, G., Dagoe, J., and Greene, D. (1982) Consequences of superfluous social constraints: effects of nominal contingencies on children's subsequent intrinsic interest. *Journal of Personality and Social Psychology*, 28, 129–37.

Lerner, J. V. and Galambos, N. L. (1985) Maternal role satisfaction, mother–child interaction, and child temperament: a process model. *Developmental Psychology*, 21, 1157–64.

Lerner, J. V., Hertzog, C., Hooker, K. A., Hassibi, M., and Thomas, A. (1988) A longitudinal study of negative emotional states and adjustment from early childhood through adolescence. *Child Development*, 58, 356–68.

Lerner, J. V., Nitz, K., Talwar, R., and Lerner, R. M. (1989) On the functional significance of temperamental individuality: a developmental contextual view of the concept of goodness of fit. In G. A. Kohnstamm, J. E. Bates, and M. K. Rothbart (eds), *Temperament and Personality*. Chichester: Wiley.

Lerner, M. J. and Gignac, M. A. M. (1992) *Is it Coping or is it Growth? A cognitive-affective model of contentment in the elderly*. In L. Montada, S. H. Fillip, and M. J. Lerner (eds), *Life and Crises and Experiences of Loss in Adulthood*. Hillsdale, NJ: Erlbaum.

Lerner, R. M. and Busch-Rossnagel, N. A. (1981) Individuals as producers of their development: conceptual and empirical bases. In R. M. Lerner and N. A. Busch-Rossnagel (eds), *Individuals as Producers of their Development*. New York: Academic Press.

Lerner, R. M. and Galambos, N. L. (1984) The adolescent experience: a view of the issues. In R. M. Lerner and N. L. Galambos (eds), *Experiencing Adolescents: a Sourcebook for Parents, Teachers, and Teens*. New York: Garland.

Leslie, A. M. (1982) The perception of causality in infants. *Perception*, 11, 173–86.

Lester, B. M. (1985) Introduction: there's more to crying than meets the eye. In B. M. Lester and C. F. Z. Boukydis (eds), *Infant Crying: theoretical and research perspectives*. New York: Plenum Press.

Leung, E. H. L. and Rheingold, H. L. (1981) Development of pointing as a social gesture. *Developmental Psychology*, 17, 215–20.

Leuptow, L. B. (1985) Conceptions of masculinity and femininity: 1974–1983. *Psychological Reports*, 57, 859–62.

Levelt, W. J. M. (1975) *What Became of LAD?* Lisse: Peter de Ridder Press.

Lever, J. (1978) Sex differences in the complexity of children's play and games. *American Sociological Review*, 43, 471–83.

Levevbre-Pinard, M., Charbonneau, C., and Feider, H. (1982) Differential effectiveness of explicit verbal feedback on children's communication skills. *Journal of Experimental Child Psychology*, 34, 174–83.

Levine, M. B. and Willis, F. N. (1994) Public reactions to unusual names. *Journal of Social Psychology*, 134, 561–8.

LeVine, R. (1989) Cultural environments in child development. In W. Damon (ed.), *Child Development Today and Tomorrow*. San Francisco: Jossey-Bass.

Levinson, D. J. (1978) *The Seasons of a Man's Life*. New York: Ballantine.

Levinson, D. J. (1986) A conception of adult development. *American Psychologist*, 41, 3–13.

Levitt, M. J. (1991) Attachment and close relationships: a life-span perspective. In J. L. Gewirtz and W. M. Kurtines (eds), *Intersections with Attachment*. Hillsdale, NJ: Erlbaum.

Levitt, M. J. (1994) Attachment relationships and life transitions: an expectancy model. In M. B. Sperling and W. H. Berman (eds), *Attachment in Adults: clinical and developmental perspectives*. New York: Guilford Press.

Levitt, M. J., Guacci, N., and Coffman, S. (1993) Social networks in infancy: an observational study. *Merrill-Palmer Quarterly*, 39, 233–51.

Levitt, M. J., Weber, R. A., Clark, M. C., and McDonnell, P. (1985) Reciprocity of exchange in toddler sharing behavior. *Developmental Psychology*, 21, 122–3.

Levy, D. G. (1989) Relations among aspects of children's social environments, gender schematization, gender role knowledge, and flexibility. *Sex Roles*, 21, 803–24.

Lewin, K. (1952) *Field Theory in Social Science*. London: Tavistock.

Lewin, K., Lippitt, R., and White, R. K. (1939) Patterns of aggressive behavior in experimentally created "social climates". *Journal of Social Psychology*, 10, 271–99.

Lewis, C. (1981) The effects of parental firm control: a reinterpretation of findings. *Psychological Bulletin*, 90, 547–63.

Lewis, C. and O'Brien, M. (1987) Constraints on fathers: research, theory and clinical practice. In C. Lewis and M. O'Brien (eds), *Reassessing Fatherhood: new observations on fathers and the modern family*. London: Sage.

Lewis, C., Newson, E., and Newson, J. (1982) Father participation through childhood and its relations to career aspirations and delinquency. In N. Beail and

J. McGuire (eds), *Fathers: psychological perspectives*. London: Junction Books.

Lewis, M. (1987) Social development in infancy and early childhood. In J. D. Osofsky (ed.), *Handbook of Infant Development*. New York: Wiley.

Lewis, M. (1989) Cultural differences in children's knowledge of emotional scripts. In C. Saarni and P. L. Harris (eds), *Children's Understanding of Emotion*. Cambridge: Cambridge University Press.

Lewis, M. (1990. Social knowledge and social development. *Merrill-Palmer Quarterly*, 36, 93–116.

Lewis, M. (1993) The development of deception. In M. Lewis and C. Saarni (eds), *Lying and Deception in Everyday Life*. New York: Guilford.

Lewis, M. and Brooks-Gunn, J. (1979) *Social Cognition and the Acquisition of Self*. New York: Plenum Press.

Lewis, M. and Feiring, C. (1989) Infant, mother, and mother–infant interaction behavior and subsequent attachment. *Child Development*, 60, 831–7.

Lewis, M. and Feiring, C. (1991), Attachment as personal characteristic or a measure of the environment. In J. L. Gewirtz and W. M. Kurtines (eds), *Intersections with Attachment*. Hillsdale, NJ: Erlbaum.

Lewis, M., Feiring, C., McCuffog, C., and Jaskir, J. (1984) Predicting psychopathology of six-year-olds from early social relations. *Child Development*, 55, 123–36.

Lewis, M., Young, G., Brooks, J., and Michalson, L. (1975) The beginning of friendship. In M. Lewis and L. A. Rosenblum (eds), *Friendship and Peer Relations*. New York: Wiley.

Lewis, M. M. (1963) *Language, Thought and Personality in Infancy and Childhood*. London: Harrap.

Lewittes, H. J. (1988) Just being friendly means a lot: women, friendship, and aging. *Women and Health*, 14, 139–59.

Leyens, J.-P. (1983) *Sommes-nous tous des psychologues? Approche psychosocialie des théories implicites de la personnalité*. Brussels: Mardaga.

Leyens, J.-P. and Dardenne, B. (1996) Basic concepts and approaches in social cognition I. In M. Hewstone, W. Stroebe, and G. M. Stephenson (eds), *Introduction to Social Psychology*, 2nd edn. Oxford: Blackwell.

Leyens, J.-P. Camino, L., Parke, R. D., and Berkowitz, L. (1975) Effects of movie violence on aggression in a field setting as a function of group dominance and cohesion. *Journal of Personality and Social Psychology*, 32, 346–60.

Liben, L. S. and Signorella, M. L. (1993) Gender-schematic processing in children: the role of initial interpretations of stimuli. *Developmental Psychology*, 29, 141–9.

Lidell, C., Kvalsvig, J., Qotyana, P., and Shabalala, A.

(1994) Community violence among young South African children's involvement in aggression. *International Journal of Behavioral Development*, 19, 613–28.

Lieberman, E. J. (1980) The psychological consequences of adolescent pregnancy and abortion. In C. S. Chilman (ed.), *Adolescent Pregnancy and Childbearing: findings from research*. Washington, DC: US Department of Health and Human Services.

Lieven, E. (1978) Conversations between mothers and young children: individual differences and their possible implications for the study of language learning. In N. Waterson and C. Snow (eds), *The Development of Communication*. Chichester: Wiley.

Light, P. (1983) Social interaction and cognitive development: a review of post-Piagetian research. In S. Meadows (ed.), *Developing Thinking: approaches to children's cognitive development*. London: Metheun.

Light, P. (1986) Context, conservation and conversation. In M. P. M. Richards and P. Light (eds), *Children of Social Worlds*. Cambridge: Polity Press.

Light, P. (1993) Developing psychologies. In M. Bennett (ed.), *The Child as Psychologist: an introduction to the development of social cognition*. New York: Harvester Wheatsheaf.

Light, P. and Glachan, M. (1985) Facilitation of individual problem solving through peer interaction. *Educational Psychology*, 5, 217–25.

Light, P. and Nix, C. (1983) "Own view" versus "good view" in a perspective-taking task. *Child Development*, 54, 480–3.

Light, P., Littleton, K., Messer, D., and Joiner, R. (1994) Social and communicative processes in computer-based problem solving. *European Journal of Psychology of Education*, 9, 93–109.

Lightfoot, C. (1992) Constructing self peer and culture: a narrative perspective on adolescent risk taking. In L. T. Winegar and J. Valsiner (eds), *Children's Development within Social Context*, vol. 2: *Research and methodology*. Hillsdale, NJ: Erlbaum.

Linfors, B. (1992) The other sex: How are women different? Gender, dominance, and intimate relations in social interaction. In K. Bjorkqvist and P. Niemala (eds), *Of Mice and Women: aspects of female aggression*. San Diego: Academic Press.

Lingle, J. H., Geva, N., Ostrom, T. M., Leippe, M. R., and Baumgardner, M. H. (1979) Thematic effects of person judgments on impression formation. *Journal of Personality and Social Psychology*, 37, 674–87.

Linn, M. C. and Petersen, A. C. (1985) Emergence and characterization of sex differences in spatial ability: a meta-analysis. *Child Development*, 56, 1479–98.

Lipton, D. N., McDonel, E. C., and McFall, R. M. (1987) Heterosocial perception in rapists. *Journal of Consulting and Clinical Psychology*, 55, 17–21.

Little, A. (1985) The child's understanding of the causes of academic success and failure: a case study of British schoolchildren. *British Journal of Education Psychology*, 55, 11–23.

Livesley, W. J. and Bromley, D. B. (1973) *Person Perception in Childhood and Adolescence*. London: Wiley.

Livingstone, S. and Green, G. (1986) Television advertisements and the portrayal of gender. *British Journal of Social Psychology*, 25, 149–54.

Llewelyn, S. and Osborne, K. (1990) *Women's Lives*. London: Routledge.

Lloyd, B. and Duveen, G. (1993) The development of social representations. In C. Pratt and A. F. Garton (eds), *Systems of Representation in Children: development and use*. Chichester: Wiley.

Lloyd, P. (1991) Strategies used to communicate route directions by telephone: a comparison of the performance of 7-year-olds, 10-year-olds and adults. *Journal of Child Language*, 18, 171–89.

Lock, A. (1980) *The Guided Reinvention of Language*. New York: Academic Press.

Lodge, D. (1988) *Nice Work*. Harmondsworth: Penguin.

Loeb, R. C., Horst, L., and Horton, P. J. (1980) Family interaction patterns associated with self-esteem in preadolescent girls and boys. *Merrill-Palmer Quarterly*, 26, 205–17.

Loeber, R. and Dishion, T. J. (1984) Boys who fight at home and school: family conditions influencing cross-setting consistency. *Journal of Consulting and Clinical Psychology*, 52, 759–68.

Loeber, R. and Stouthamer-Loeber, M. (1986) Family factors as correlates and predictors of juvenile conduct problems and delinquency. In M. Tonry and N. Morris (eds), *Crime and Justice*, vol. 7. Chicago: University of Chicago Press.

Logue, B. J. (1993) To Grandmother's house we go? Around the bend on the "mommy track". *Applied Behavioral Science Review*, 1, 47–67.

Lombroso, C. and Ferrero, W. (1990) *The Female Offender*. New York: Appleton.

Long, G. T. and Lerner, M. J. (1974) Deserving, the "personal contract," and altruistic behavior by children. *Journal of Personality and Social Psychology*, 29, 551–6.

Long, J. and Porter, K. L. (1984) Multiple roles of midlife women: a case for new direction in theory, research, and policy. In G. Baruch and J. Brooks-Gunn (eds), *Women in Midlife*. New York: Plenum Press.

Long, M. (1990) Maturational constraints on language development. *Studies in Second Language Acquisition*, 12, 251–85.

Long, M. (in press) The role of the linguistic environment in second language acquisition. In W. C. Ritchie and T. K. Bhatia (eds), *Handbook of Language Acquisition*, vol. 2: *Second language acquisition*. New York: Academic Press.

Lopata, H. Z. (1979) Widowhood and husband sanctification. In L. A. Bugen (ed.), *Death and Dying: theory, research, practice*. Dubuque, Ia: W. C. Brown.

Lord, C. G., Desforges, D. M., Chacon, S., Pere, G., and Clubb, R. (1992) Reflections on reputation in the process of self-evaluation. *Social Cognition*, 10, 2–29.

Lorenz, K. Z. (1935) Der Kumpan in der Umwelt des Vogels. *Journal fur Ornithologie*, 83, 137–213, 289–413.

Lorenz, K. Z. (1943) Die Angeborenen former möglicher Ehfahrung. *Zeitschrift für Tierpsychologie*, 5, 239–409.

Lorenz, K. Z. (1963) *On Aggression*. London: Methuen.

Lott, B. and Sommer, R. (1967) Seating arrangements and status. *Journal of Personality and Social Psychology*, 7, 90–4.

Lourenco, O. M. (1993) Toward a Piagetian explanation of the development of prosocial behaviour in children: the force of negational thinking. *British Journal of Development Psychology*, 11, 91–106.

Lovdal, L. T. (1990) Sex role messages in television commercials: an update. *Sex Roles*, 21, 715–24.

Low, B. S. (1989) Cross-cultural patterns in the training of children: an evolutionary perspective. *Journal of Comparative Psychology*, 103, 311–19.

Lowenthal, M. F. and Chiriboga, D. (1972) Transition to the empty nest: crisis, challenge, or relief? *Archives of General Psychiatry*, 26, 8–14.

Luckey, E. B. and Nass, C. D. (1969) A comparison of sexual attitudes and behaviour of an international sample. *Journal of Marriage and the Family*, 31, 364–70.

Lummis, M. and Stevenson, H. W. (1990) Gender differences in beliefs and achievement: a cross-cultural study. *Developmental Psychology*, 26, 254–63.

Lund, D. A. (ed.) (1989) *Older Bereaved Spouses: research with practical applications*. New York: Hemisphere.

Lunneborg, P. W. (1982) Sex differences in self-assessed everyday spatial abilities. *Perceptual and Motor Skills*, 55, 200–2.

Luster, T. and McAdoo, H. P. (1994) Factors related to the achievement and adjustment of young African American children. *Child Development*, 65, 1080–94.

Luszcz, M. (1992) Memory and ageing: cognitive and functional approaches. In P. C. L. Heaven (ed.), *Life*

Span Development. Sydney and London: Harcourt Brace Jovanovich.

Luszcz, M. A. and Bacharach, V. R. (1983) The emergence of communicative competence: detection of conversational topics. *Journal of Child Language*, 10, 623–37.

Luszcz, M. A. and Fitzgerald, K. M. (1986) Understanding cohort differences in cross-generational, self, and peer perceptions. *Journal of Gerontology*, 41, 234–40.

Lutkenhaus, P. (1984) Pleasure derived from mastery in three-year-olds: its function for persistence and the influence of maternal behavior. *International Journal of Behavioral Development*, 7, 343–58.

Lutkenhaus, P. and Bullock, M. (1991) The development of volitional skills. In M. Bullock (ed.), *The Development of Intentional Action: cognitive, motivational and interactive processes*. Basel: Karger.

Lutkenhaus, P., Grossmann, K. E., and Grossman, K. (1985) Infant–mother attachment and style of interaction with a stranger at the age of three years. *Child Development*, 56, 1538–42.

Lutz, C. A. (1988) *Unnatural Emotions: everyday sentiments on a Micronesian atoll and their challenges to Western theory*. Chicago: University of Chicago Press.

Lyons-Ruth, K., Alpern , L., and Repacholi, B. (1993) Disorganized infant attachment classification and maternal psychosocial problems as predictors of hostile-aggressive behavior in the preschool classroom. *Child Development*, 64, 572–85.

Lytton, H. (1980) *Parent–child Interaction: the socialization process observed in twin and singleton families*. New York: Plenum Press.

Lytton, H. (1990) Child and parent effects in boys' conduct disorder: a reinterpretation. *Developmental Psychology*, 26, 683–97.

Lytton, H. and Romney, D. M. (1991) Parents' differential socialization of boys and girls: a meta-analysis. *Psychological Bulletin*, 109, 267–96.

Ma, H. K. (1988) The Chinese perspectives on moral judgment development. *International Journal of Psychology*, 23, 201–27.

McAdams, D. P. (1992) Unity and purpose in human lives: the emergence of identity as a life story. In R. A. Zucker, A. I. Rabin, J. Aronoff, and S. J. Frank (eds), *Personality Structure in the Life Course: essays on personology in the Murray tradition*. New York: Springer.

McArthur, L. Z. (1982) Judging a book by its cover: a cognitive analysis of the relationship between physical appearance and stereotyping. In A. H. Hastorf and A. M. Isen (eds), *Cognitive Social Psychology*. New York: Elsevier.

McArthur, L. Z. and Eisen, S. V. (1976) Television and sex-role stereotyping. *Journal of Applied Social Psychology*, 6, 329–51.

Macaulay, R. S. (1977) *Language, Social Class and Education*. Edinburgh: Edinburgh University Press.

McCabe, M. P. (1982) The influence of sex and sex role on the dating attitudes and behavior of Australian youth. *Journey of Adolescent Health Care*, 3, 29–36.

McCabe, M. P. (1984) Toward a theory of adolescent dating. *Adolescence*, 19, 159–70.

McCarthy, J. D. and Hoge, D. R. (1982) Analysis of age effects in longitudinal studies of adolescent self-esteem. *Developmental Psychology*, 18, 372–9.

McCartney, K. and Phillips, D. (1988) Motherhood and child care. In B. Birns and D. F. Hay (eds), *The Different Faces of Motherhood*. New York: Plenum Press.

McCartney, K., Scarr, S., Phillips, D., Grajek, S., and Schwartz, J. C. (1982) Environmental differences among day care centers and their effects on children's development. In E. F. Zigler and E. W. Gordon (eds), *Day Care: scientific and social policy issues*. Boston: Auburn House.

McClelland, D. C. (1992) Is personality consistent? In R. A. Zucker, A. I. Rabin, J. Aronoff, and S. J. Frank (eds), *Personality Structure in the Life Course: essays on personology in the Murray tradition*. New York: Springer.

Maccoby, E. E. (1992) The role of parents in the socialization of children: an historical overview. *Developmental Psychology*, 28, 1006–17.

Maccoby, E. E., and Jacklin, C. N. (1974) *The Psychology of Sex Differences*. Stanford: Stanford University Press.

Maccoby, E. E. and Jacklin, C. N. (1987) Gender segregation in childhood. In H. W. Reese (ed.), *Advances in Child Development and Behavior*, vol. 20. New York: Academic Press.

Maccoby, E. E. and Martin, J. A. (1983) Socialization in the context of the family: parent–child interaction. In E. M. Hetherington (ed.), *Handbook of Child Psychology*, vol. 4: *Socialization, personality, and development*. New York: Wiley.

McConaghy, M. J. (1979) Gender permanence and the genital basis of gender: stages in the development of constancy of gender identity. *Child Development*, 50, 1223–6.

McCord, J. (1990) Problem behaviors. In S. S. Feldman and G. R. Elliott (eds), *At the Threshold: the developing adolescent*. Cambridge, Mass.: Harvard University Press.

McCord, J. (1994) Aggression in two generations. In L. R. Huesmann (ed.), *Aggressive Behaviour: current perspectives*. New York: Plenum Press.

McCreary, D. R. (1990) Self-perceptions of life-span

gender-role development. *International Journal of Aging and Human Development*, 31, 135–46.

McDavid, J. W. and Harari, H. (1966) Stereotyping of names and popularity in grade-school children. *Child Development*, 37, 453–9.

MacDonald, K. B. (1988a) Socialization in the context of the family: a sociobiological perspective. In K. B. MacDonald (ed.), *Sociobiological Perspectives on Human Development*. New York: Springer-Verlag.

MacDonald, K. B. (1988b) The interfaces between sociobiology and developmental psychology. In K. B. MacDonald (ed.), *Sociobiological Perspectives on Human Development*. New York: Springer-Verlag.

MacDonald, K. B. (1988c) Sociobiology and the cognitive-developmental tradition in moral development research. In K. B. MacDonald (ed.), *Sociobiological Perspectives on Human Development*. New York: Springer-Verlag.

MacDonald, K. B. (1988d) *Social and Personality Development: an evolutionary synthesis*. New York: Plenum.

McDonald, L. and Pien, D. (1982) Mother conversational behaviour as a function of interactional intent. *Journal of Child Language*, 9, 337–58.

McDougall, W. (1908) *Introduction to Social Psychology*. London: Methuen.

McEwan, I. (1987) *The Child in Time*. London: Picador.

Macfarlane, A. (1977) *The Psychology of Childbirth*. London: Fontana.

McGhee, J. and Fryer, D. (1989) Unemployment, income and the family: an action research approach. *Social Behaviour*, 4, 237–52.

McGillicuddy-De Lisi, A. V. and Subramanian, S. (1994) Tanzanian and United States mothers' beliefs about parents' and teachers' roles in children's knowledge acquisition. *International Journal of Behavioral Development*, 17, 209–37.

McGillicudy-De Lisi, A. V. (1985) The relationship between parental beliefs and children's cognitive level. In I. E. Sigel (ed.), *Parental Belief Systems: the psychological consequences for children*. Hillsdale, NJ: Erlbaum.

McKee, C., Nicol, J., and McDaniel, D. (1993) Children's application of binding during sentence processing. *Language and Cognitive Processes*, 8, 265–90.

Mackie, D. (1980) A cross-cultural study of intra-individual and inter-individual conflicts of centrations. *European Journal of Social Psychology*, 10, 313–18.

McKinney, J. P. and Vogel, J. (1987) Developmental theories. In V. B. van Hasselt and M. Hersen (eds), *Handbook of Adolescent Psychology*. New York: Pergamon.

MacKinnon-Lewis, C., Volling, B. L., Lamb, M. E., Dechman, K., Rabiner, D., and Curtner, M. E.

(1994) A cross-contextual analysis of boys' social competence: from family to school. *Developmental Psychology*, 30, 325–33.

McLoyd, V. C., Jayartne, T. E., Ceballo, R., and Borquez, J. (1994) Unemployment and work interruption among African American single mothers: effects in parenting and adolescent socioemotional functioning. *Child Development*, 65, 562–89.

Macnamara, J. (1977) On the relation between language learning and thought. In J. Macnamara (ed.), *Language Learning and Thought*. New York: Academic Press.

McNeill, D. (1966) Developmental psycholinguistics. In F. Smith and G. A. Miller (eds), *The Genesis of Language*. Cambridge, Mass.: MIT Press.

McNeill, D. (1970) *The Acquisition of Language: the study of developmental psycholinguistics*. New York: Harper and Row.

McTear, M. F. (1984) Structure and process in children's conversational development. In S. A. Kuczaj (ed.), *Discourse Development: progress in cognitive development research*. New York: Springer-Verlag.

McTear, M. F. (1985) *Children's Conversation*. Oxford: Blackwell.

Maffiolo, D. (1993) From a social to a cultural approach in the study of cognitive activities: the fundamental role of semiotic systems. *European Journal of Psychology of Education*, 8, 487–500.

Magnusson, D. (1988) *Individual Development from an Interactional Perspective: a longitudinal study*. Hillsdale, NJ: Erlbaum.

Main, M. (1983) Exploration, play, and cognitive functioning related to infant–mother attachment. *Infant Behavior and Development*, 6, 167–74.

Main, M. (ed.) (in press) *A Typology of Human Attachment Organization Assessed in Discourse, Drawings and Interviews*. Cambridge: Cambridge University Press.

Main, M. and Cassidy, J. (1988) Categories of response to reunion with the parent at age 6: predictable from attachment classifications and stable over a 1-month period. *Developmental Psychology*, 24, 415–26.

Main, M. and George, C. (1985) Responses of abused and disadvantaged toddlers to distress in agemates: a study in the day care setting. *Developmental Psychology*, 21, 407–12.

Main, M. and Solomon, J. (1986) Discovery of a disorganized disoriented attachment pattern. In T. B. Brazelton and M. W. Yogman (eds), *Affective Development in Infancy*. Norwood, NJ: Ablex.

Main, M. and Weston, D. (1981) The quality of the toddler's relationship to mother and father: related to conflict behavior and readiness to establish new social relationships. *Child Development*, 52, 932–40.

Main, M., Kaplan, K., and Cassidy, J. (1985) Security

in infancy, childhood, and adulthood: a move to the level of representation. In I. Bretherton and E. Waters (eds), *Growing Points of Attachment Theory and Research*. Monographs of the Society for Research in Child Development, 50 (1–2), no. 209.

Malatesta, C. Z. (1990) The role of emotions in the development and organization of personality. In R. A. Thompson (ed.), *Socioemotional Development: Nebraska symposium on motivation, 1988*. Lincoln: University of Nebraska Press.

Malatesta, C. Z., Culver, C., Tesman, J. R., and Shepard, B. (1989) *The development of emotion expression during the first two years of life*. Monographs of the Society for Research in Child Development, 54 (1–2), no. 219.

Malatesta, C. Z., Grigoryev, P., Lamb, C., Albin, M., and Culver, C. (1986) Emotion socialization and expressive development in preterm and full-term infants. *Child Development*, 57, 316–30.

Malatesta-Magai, C. (1991) Development of emotion expression during infancy: general course and patterns of individual difference. In J. Garber and K. A. Dodge (eds), *The Development of Emotion Regulation and Dysregulation*. Cambridge: Cambridge University Press.

Malatesta-Magai, C., Leak, S., Tesman, J., Shephard, B., Culver, C., and Smaggia, B. (1994) Profiles of emotional development: individual differences in facial and vocal expression during the second and third years of life. *International Journal of Behavioral Development*, 17, 239–69.

Mallick, S. K. and McCandless, B. R. (1966) A study of catharsis of aggression. *Journal of Personality and Social Psychology*, 4, 591–6.

Mangelsdorf, S. C. (1992) Developmental changes in infant–stranger interaction. *Infant Behavior and Development*, 15, 191–208.

Mannle, S., Barton, M., and Tomasello, M. (1992) Two-year-olds' conversations with their mothers and preschool-aged siblings. *First Language*, 12, 57–71.

Manstead, A. S. R. (1993) Children's representation of emotions. In C. Pratt and A. F. Garton (eds), *Systems of Representation in Children: development and use*. Chichester: Wiley.

Manstead, A. S. R. and McCulloch, C. (1981) Sex-role stereotyping in British television advertisements. *British Journal of Social Psychology*, 20, 171–80.

Manstead, A. S. R. and Semin, G. R. (1996) Methodology in social psychology: turning ideas into actions. In M. Hewstone, W. Stroebe, and G. M. Stephenson (eds), *Introduction to Social Psychology*, 2nd edn. Oxford: Blackwell.

Maquieira, V. (1989) Boys, girls and the discourse of morality. In M. Cain (ed.), *Growing up Good: policing the behaviour of girls in Europe*. London: Sage.

Maratsos, M., Fox, D., Becker, J., and Chalkley, M. (1985) Semantic restrictions on children's passives. *Cognition*, 19, 167–91.

Marchman, V. A., Bates, E., Burkhardt, A., and Good, A. B. (1991) Functional constraints on the acquisition of the passive: toward a model of the competence to perform. *First Language*, 11, 65–92.

Marcia, J. (1966) Development and validation of ego-identity status. *Journal of Personality and Social Psychology*, 3, 551–8.

Marcia. J. (1980) Identity in adolescence. In J. Adelson (ed.), *Handbook of Adolescent Psychology*. New York: Wiley.

Marcos, H. (1991) Reformulating requests at 18 months: gestures, vocalizations and words. *First Language*, 11, 361–75.

Marcos, H. and Pezé, A. (1989) L'adaptation de la demande à la situation sociale chez le bébé. *Revue Internationale de Psychologie Sociale*, 2, 37–49.

Marcus, D. E. and Overton, W. F. (1978) The development of cognitive gender constancy and sex-role preferences. *Child Development*, 49, 434–44.

Marcus, G. F., Pinker, S., Ullman, M., Hollander, M., Rosen, T. J., and Xu, F. (1992) *Overregularization in language acquisition*. Monographs of the Society for Research in Child Development, 57, no. 228.

Marcus, R. F. (1991) The attachments of children in foster care. *Genetic, Social, and General Psychology Monographs*, 117, 365–94.

Mares, M.-L. and Cantor, J. (1992) Elderly viewers' responses to televised portrayals of old age. Empathy and mood management versus social comparison. *Communication Research*, 19, 459–78.

Marjoribanks, K. (1979) *Families and their Learning Environments: an empirical analysis*. London: Routledge.

Marjoribanks, K. (1987) Ability and attitude correlates of academic achievement: family-group differences. *Journal of Educational Psychology*, 79, 171–8.

Marjoribanks, K. (1991) Family and school correlates of adolescents' aspirations: ability–attitude group differences. *European Journal of Psychology of Education*, 6, 283–90.

Markman, E. M. (1977) Realizing that you don't understand: a preliminary investigation. *Child Development*, 48, 986–92.

Markoulis, D. (1989) Political involvement and socio-moral reasoning: testing Emler's interpretation. *British Journal of Social Psychology*, 28, 203–12.

Markova, I. (1990) Causes and reasons in social development. In G. Butterworth and P. Bryant (eds),

Causes of Development: interdisciplinary perspectives. New York: Harvester.

Markus, H. and Nurius, P. (1986) Possible selves. *American Psychologist*, 41, 954–69.

Marsh, H. W. (1985) Age and sex effects in multiple dimensions of preadolescent self-concept: a replication and extension. *Australian Journal of Psychology*, 37, 197–204.

Marsh, H. W. (1989) Age and sex effects in multiple dimensions of self-concept: preadolescence to early adulthood. *Journal of Educational Psychology*, 81, 417–30.

Marsh, H. W., Barnes, J., Cairns, L., and Tidman, M. (1984) The Self Description Questionnaire (SDQ): age and sex effects in the structure and level of self-concept for pre-adolescent children. *Journal of Educational Psychology*, 76, 940–56.

Marsh, H. W., Craven, R. G., and Debus, R. (1991) Self-concepts of young children 5 to 8 years of age: measurement and multidimensional structure. *Journal of Educational Psychology*, 83, 377–92.

Marshall, J. (1986) Exploring the experiences of women managers: towards rigour in qualitative methods. In S. Wilkinson (ed.), *Feminist Social Psychology: developing theory and practice*. Milton Keynes: Open University Press.

Martin, A. D. (1982) Learning to hide: the socialization of the gay adolescent. In S. C. Feinstein, J. G. Looney, A. Z. Schwartzberg, and A. D. Sorosky (eds), *Adolescent Psychiatry: developmental and clinical studies*, vol. 10. Chicago: University of Chicago Press.

Martin, A. D. and Hetrick, E. S. (1988) The stigmatization of the gay and lesbian adolescent. *Journal of Homosexuality*, 15, 163–83.

Martin, C. L. (1991) The role of cognition in understanding gender effects. *Advances in Child Development and Behavior*, 23, 113–49.

Martin, C. L. and Halverson, C. F., Jr (1981) A schematic processing model of sex typing and stereotyping in children. *Child Development*, 52, 1119–34.

Martin, C. L. and Halverson, C. F., Jr (1983) The effects of sex-typing schemas on young children's memory. *Child Development*, 54, 563–74.

Martin, C. L. and Halverson, C. F. (1987) The roles of cognition in sex role acquisition. In D. B. Carter (ed.), *Current Conceptions of Sex Roles and Sex Typing: theory and research*. New York, Praeger.

Martin, G. B. and Clark, R. D. (1982) Distress crying in neonates: species and peer specificity. *Developmental Psychology* 18, 3–9.

Martin, J. and Roberts, C. (1984) *Women and Employment*. London: HMSO.

Martinsen, H. and Smith, L. (1989) Studies of vocalization and gesture in the transition to speech. In S. von Tetzchner, L. S. Siegel, and L. Smith (eds), *The Social and Cognitive Aspects of Normal and Atypical Language Development*. New York: Springer-Verlag.

Mastlew, M., Connolly, K. J., and McCleod, C. (1978) Language use, role and context in a five year old. *Journal of Child Language*, 5, 81–99.

Maslin-Cole, C., Bretherton, I., and Morgan, G. A. (1993) Toddler mastery motivation and competence: links with attachment security, maternal scaffolding and family climate. In D. J. Messer (ed.), *Mastery Motivation in Early Childhood: development, measurements and social processes*. London: Routledge.

Mastekaasa, A. (1992) Marriage and psychological well-being: some evidence on selection into marriage. *Journal of Marriage and the Family*, 54, 901–11.

Mastekaasa, A. (1995) Age variations in the suicide rates and self-reported subjective well-being of married and never married persons. *Journal of Community and Applied Social Psychology*, 5, 21–39.

Masten, A. S. and Brawell, L. (1991) Developmental psychopathology: an integrative framework for understanding behaviour problems in children and adolescents. In P. R. Martin (ed.), *Handbook of Behaviour Therapy and Psychological Science: an integrative approach*. Oxford: Pergamon.

Masters, J. C. (1971) Effects of social comparison upon children's self-reinforcement and altruism toward competitors and friends. *Developmental Psychology*, 5, 64–72.

Masters, J. C. (1991) Strategies and mechanisms for the personal and social control of emotion. In J. Garber and K. A. Dodge (eds), *The Development of Emotion Regulation and Dysregulation*. Cambridge: Cambridge University Press.

Masters, J. C., Ford, M. E., Arend, R., Grotevant, H. D., and Clarke, L. V. (1979) Modeling and labeling as integrated determinants of children's sex-typed imitative behavior. *Child Development*, 50, 364–71.

Matas, L., Arend, R. A., and Sroufe, L. A. (1978) Continuity of attachment in the second year: the relationship between quality of attachment and later competence. *Child Development*, 49, 547–56.

Materska, M., Garot, M.-H., and Ehrlich, S. (1987) Les désorganisations de la representation de soi à l'entrée au college. *European Journal of Psychology of Education*, 1, 61–77.

Matheny, A. P., Jr, Riese, M. L., and Wilson, R. S. (1985) Rudiments of infant temperament: newborn to 9 months. *Developmental Psychology*, 21, 486–94.

Matsuda, S. (1989) Significant partners in childhood and adolescence. In K. Hurrelmann and U. Engel (eds), *The Social World of Adolescents: international perspectives*. Berlin and New York: de Gruyter.

Matthews, K. A. (1981) "At a relatively early age . . . the habit of working the machine to its maximum capacity": antecedents of the Type A coronary-prone behavior pattern. In S. S. Brehm, S. M. Kassin, and F. X. Gibbons (eds), *Developmental Social Psychology: theory and research*. New York: Oxford University Press.

Maurer, D. (1985) Infants' perception of facedness. In T. M. Field and N. A. Fox (eds), *Social Perception in Infants*. Norwood, NJ: Ablex.

Maurer, D. and Salapatek, P. (1976) Developmental changes in the scanning of faces by young infants. *Child Development*, 47, 523–7.

Mayer, K. U. and Muller, W. (1986) The state and structure of the life course. In A. B. Sorensen, F. E. Weinert, and L. R. Sherrod (eds), *Human Development and the Life Course: multidisciplinary perspectives*. Hillsdale, NJ: Erlbaum.

Mayo, C. and La France, M. (1978) On the acquisition of nonverbal communication: a review. *Merrill-Palmer Quarterly*, 24, 213–28.

Mazzella, C., Durkin, K., Cerini, E., and Buralli, P. (1992) Sex role stereotypes in Australian television advertisements. *Sex Roles*, 26, 243–59.

Mead, G. H. (1934) *Mind, Self, and Society: from the standpoint of a social behaviorist*. Chicago: University of Chicago Press.

Meece, J. L. (1987) The influence of school experiences on the development of gender schemata. In L. S. Liben and M. L. Signorella (eds), *Children's Gender Schemata*. San Francisco: Jossey-Bass.

Meerum Terwogt, M. and Olthof, T. (1989) Awareness and self-regulation of emotion in young children. In C. Saarni and P. L. Harris (eds), *Children's Understanding of Emotion*. Cambridge: Cambridge University Press.

Mehler, J. and Dupoux, E. (1994) *What Infants Know: the new cognitive science of early development*. Oxford: Blackwell.

Mehler, J., Bertoncini, J., Barriere, M., and Jassik-Gerschenfel, D. (1978) Infant recognition of mother's voice. *Perception*, 7, 491–7.

van der Meij, H. (1988) Constraints on question asking in classrooms. *Journal of Educational Psychology*, 80, 401–5.

Meilman, P. W. (1979) Cross-sectional age changes in ego identity status during adolescence. *Developmental Psychology*, 15, 230–1.

Meisels, M. and Guardo, C. J. (1969) Development of personal space schemata. *Child Development*, 49, 1167–78.

Meltzoff, A. N. (1985) The roots of social and cognitive development: models of man's original nature. In T. M. Field and N. A. Fox (eds), *Social Perception in Infants*. Norwood, NJ: Ablex.

Meltzoff, A. N. and Gopnik, A. (1993) The role of imitation in understanding persons and developing a theory of mind. In S. Baron-Cohen, T. Tager-Flusberg, and D. J. Cohen (eds), *Understanding Other Minds: perspectives from autism*. Oxford: Oxford University Press.

Meltzoff, A. N. and Moore, M. K. (1977) Imitation of facial and manual gestures by human neonates. *Science*, 198, 75–8.

Meltzoff, A. N. and Moore, M. K. (1989) Imitation in newborn infants: exploring the range of gestures imitated and the underlying mechanisms. *Developmental Psychology*, 25, 954–62.

Meltzoff, A. N. and Moore, M. K. (1992) Early imitation within a functional framework: the importance of person identity, movement, and development. *Infant Behavior and Development*, 15, 479–505.

Meltzoff, A. N. and Moore, M. K. (1993) Why faces are special to infants – on connecting the attraction of faces and infants' ability for imitation and cross-modal processing. In B. de Boysson-Bardies, S. de Schonen, P. Jusczyk, P. McNeilage, and J. Morton (eds), *Development Neurocognition: speech and face processing the first year of life*. Dordrecht: Kluwer.

Mendelson, M. J., Aboud, F. E., and Lanthier, R. P. (1994) Personality predictors of friendship and popularity in kindergarten. *Journal of Applied Developmental Psychology*, 15, 413–35.

Merton, R. K. (1957) *Social Theory and Social Structure*. Glencoe, Ill.: Free Press.

Messer, D. J. (1981) Non-linguistic information which could assist the young child's interpretation of adults' speech. In W. P. Robinson (ed.), *Communication in Development*. London: Academic Press.

Messer, D. J. (1983) The redundancy between adult speech and nonverbal interaction: a contribution to acquisition? In R. M. Golinkoff (ed.), *The Transition from Prelinguistic to Linguistic Communication*. Hillsdale, NJ: Erlbaum.

Messer, D. J. (1994) *The Development of Communication*. Chichester: Wiley.

Messer, D. J. and Collis, G. M. (in press) Early interaction and cognitive skills: implications for the acquisition of culture. In A. Lock and C. Peters (eds), *The Evolution of Symbolic Behaviour*. Oxford: Oxford University Press.

Messer, D. J. and Vietze, P. M. (1984) Timing and transitions in mother–infant gaze. *Infant Behavior and Development*, 7, 167–81.

Messer, D. J., McCarthy, M. E., McQuiston, S.,

MacTurk, R. H., Yarrow, L. J., and Vietze, P. M. (1986) Relation between mastery behavior in infancy and competence in early childhood. *Developmental Psychology*, 22, 366–72.

van der Meulen, M. (1991) Toddlers' self-concept in the light of early action theory. In M. Bullock (ed.), *The Development of Intentional Action: cognitive, motivational and interactive processes*. Basel: Karger.

Meuss, W. (1989) Parental and peer support in adolescence. In K. Hurrelmann and U. Engel (eds), *The Social World of Adolescents: international perspectives*. Berlin and New York: de Gruyter.

Meuss, W. (1994) Pyschosocial problems and social support in adolescence. In F. Nestemann and K. Hurrelmann (eds), *Social Networks and Social Support in Childhood and Adolescence*. Berlin: de Gruyter.

Meyer, B. (1980) The development of girls' sex-role attitudes. *Child Development*, 51, 508–14.

Midlarsky, E. and Hannah, M. E. (1989) The generous elderly: naturalistic studies of donations across the lifespan. *Psychology and Aging*, 4, 346–51.

Midlarsky, E., Bryan, J. H., and Brickman, P. (1973) Aversive approval: interactive effects of modeling and reinforcement on altruistic behavior. *Child Development*, 44, 321–8.

Mikulincer, M., Florian, V., and Weller, A. (1993) Attachment styles, coping strategies, and posttraumatic psychological distress: the impact of the Gulf War in Israel. *Journal of Personality and Social Psychology*, 64, 817–26.

Milgram, S. (1974) *Obedience to Authority: an experimental view*. London: Tavistock.

Miller, C. L. (1988) Parents' perceptions and attributions of infant vocal behaviour and development. *First Language*, 8, 125–42.

Miller, J. G. (1984) Culture and development of everyday social explanation. *Journal of Personality and Social Psychology*, 46, 961–78.

Miller, J. G. and Bersoff, D. M. (1992) Culture and moral judgment: how are conflicts between justice and interpersonal responsibilities resolved? *Journal of Personality and Social Psychology*, 62, 541–54.

Miller, N. and Gentry, K. W. (1980) Sociometric indices of children's peer interaction in the school setting. In H. C. Foot, A. J. Chapman, and J. R. Smith (eds), *Friendship and Social Relations in Children*. Chichester: Wiley.

Miller, N. E. (1941) The frustration–aggression hypothesis. *Psychological Review*, 48, 337–42.

Miller, P. and Simon, W. (1980) The development of sexuality in adolescence. In J. Adelson (ed.), *Handbook of Adolescent Psychology*. New York: Wiley.

Miller, P. A., Bernzweig, J., Eisenberg, N., and Fabes, R. A. (1991) The development and socialization of prosocial behavior. In R. A. Hinde and J. Groebel (eds), *Cooperation and Prosocial Behaviour*. Cambridge: Cambridge University Press.

Miller, P. H. (1993) *Theories of Developmental Psychology*, 3rd edn. Oxford: W. H. Freeman.

Miller, P. H. and Aloise, P. A. (1989) Young children's understanding of the psychological causes of behavior: a review. *Child Development*, 60, 257–85.

Mills, R. S. L. and Grusec, J. E. (1988) Socialization from the perspective of the parent–child relationship. In S. Duck (ed.), *Handbook of Personal Relationships: theory, research and interventions*. Chichester: Wiley.

Mills, R. S. L. and Grusec, J. E. (1989) Cognitive, affective, and behavioral consequences of praising altruism. *Merrill-Palmer Quarterly*, 35, 299–326.

Millstein, S. G. and Litt, I. F. (1990) Adolescent health. In S. S. Feldman and G. R. Elliott (eds), *At the Threshold: the developing adolescent*. Cambridge, Mass.: Harvard University Press.

Milner, D. (1984) The development of ethnic attitudes. In H. Tajfel (ed.), *The Social Dimension*, vol. 1. Cambridge: Cambridge University Press.

Milroy, L. (1980) *Language and Social Networks*. Baltimore: University Park Press.

Minuchin, P. P. and Shapiro, E. K. (1983) The school as a context for social development. In E. M. Hetherington (ed.), *Handbook of Child Psychology*, vol. 4: *Socialization, personality and social development*. New York: Wiley.

Minuchin, S., Rosman, B., and Baker L. (1978) *Psychosomatic Families: anorexia nervosa in context*. Cambridge, Mass.: Harvard University Press.

Mischel, W. (1968) *Personality and Assessment*. New York: Wiley.

Mischel, W. (1970) Sex-typing and socialization. In P. H. Mussen (ed.), *Carmichael's Manual of Child Psychology*, vol. 2. New York: Wiley.

Mischel, W. (1973) Toward a cognitive social learning reconceptualization of personality. *Psychological Review*, 80, 252–83.

Mischel, W. (1976) *Introduction to Personality*, 2nd edn. New York: Holt, Rinehart and Winston.

Mischel, W. (1977) On the future of personality measurement. *American Psychologist*, 32, 246–54.

Mischel, W. (1979) On the interface of cognition and personality: beyond the person-situation debate. *American Psychologist*, 34, 740–54.

Mishkind, M. E., Rodin, J., Silberstein, L. R., and Striegel-Moore, R. H. (1987) The embodiment of masculinity: cultural, psychological, and behavioral dimensions. In M. S. Kimmel (ed.), *Changing Men: new directions in research on men and masculinity*. Newbury Park, Calif.: Sage.

Mizukami, K., Kobayashi, N., Ishi, T., and Iwata, H. (1990) First selective attachment begins in early infancy: a study using telethermography. *Infant Behavior and Development*, 13, 257–71.

Mobley, W. H. (1982) Supervisor and employee race and sex effects on performance appraisals: a field study of adverse impact and generalizability. *Academy of Management Journal*, 25, 598–606.

Modell, J. and Goodman, M. (1990) Historical perspectives. In S. S. Feldman and G. R. Elliott (eds), *At the Threshold: the developing adolescent*. Cambridge, Mass.: Harvard University Press.

Moerk, E. L. (1989) The LAD was a lady and the tasks were ill-defined. *Developmental Review*, 9, 21–57.

Moerk, E. L. (1991) Positive evidence for negative evidence. *First Language*, 11, 219–51.

Moerk, E. L. (1992) *A First Language Taught and Learned*. Baltimore: Brookes.

Moffatt, S. and Milroy, L. (1992) Punjabi/English language alternation in the early school years. *Multilingua*, 11, 355–85.

Moffitt, T. E. (1993) Adolescence limited and life-course-persistent antisocial behavior: a developmental taxonomy. *Psychological Review*, 100, 674–701.

Moffitt, T. E., Caspi, A., Belsky, J., and Silva, P. A. (1992) Childhood experience and the onset of menarche: a test of a sociobiological model. *Child Development*, 63, 47–58.

Molinari, L. and Emiliani, F. (1990) What is an image? The structure of mothers' images of the child and their influence on conversational styles. In G. Duveen and B. Lloyd (eds), *Social Representations and the Development of Knowledge*. Cambridge: Cambridge University Press.

Moller, L. C., Hymel, S., and Rubin, K. H. (1992) Sex typing in play and popularity in middle childhood. *Sex Roles*, 26, 331–9.

Money, J. and Ehrhardt, A. A. (1972) *Man and Woman, Boy and Girl*. Baltimore: Johns Hopkins University Press.

Montagner, H., Restoin, A., Ullman, V., Rodriguez, D., Godard, D., and Viala, M. (1984) Development of early peer interaction. In W. Doise and A. Palmonari (eds), *Social Interaction in Individual Development*. Cambridge: Cambridge University Press.

Montagu, M. F. A. (1974) Aggression and the evolution of man. In R. E. Whalen (ed.), *The Neuropsychology of Aggression*. New York: Plenum Press.

Monteil, J.-M. (1988) Comparaison sociale. Stratégies individuelles et médiations socio-cognitives. Un effet de différenciations comportementales dans le champ scolaire. *European Journal of Psychology of Education*, 3, 3–18.

Monteil, J.-M. (1993) *Soi et le contexte: constructions autobiographiques, insertions sociales et performances cognitives*. Paris: A. Colin.

Monteil, J.-P. and Huguet, P. (1991) Insertion sociale, categorisation sociale et activités cognitives. *Psychologie Française*, 36, 35–46.

Montemayor, R. (1983) Parents and adolescents in conflict: all families some of the time and some families most of the time. *Journal of Early Adolescence*, 3, 83–103.

Montemayor, R. (1986) Family variation in parent–adolescent storm and stress. *Journal of Adolescent Research*, 1, 15–31.

Montemayor, R. and Eisen, M. (1977) The development of self-conceptions from childhood to adolescence. *Developmental Psychology*, 13, 314–19.

Montepare, J. M. and Lachman, M. E. (1989) "You're only as old as you feel": self-perceptions of age, fears of aging, and life satisfaction from adolescence to old age. *Psychology and Aging*, 4, 73–8.

Montepare, J. M., Steinberg, J., and Rosenberg, B. (1992) Characteristics of vocal communications between young adults and their parents and grand parents. *Communication Research*, 19, 479–92.

Moore, B. and Underwood, B. (1981) The development of prosocial behavior. In S. S. Brehm, S. M. Kassin, and F. X. Gibbons (eds), *Developmental Social Psychology: theory and research*. New York: Oxford University Press.

Moore, C., Furrow, D., Chiasson, L., and Patriquin, M. (1994) Developmental relationships between production and comprehension of mental terms. *First Language*, 14, 1–17.

Moore, S. (1995) Girls' understanding and social constructions of menarche. *Journals of Adolescence*, 18, 87–104.

Moore, S. and Rosenthal, D. (1991) Adolescents' perceptions of friends and parents' attitudes to sex and sexual risk taking. *Journal of Community and Social Psychology*, 1, 189–200.

Moran, G., Pederson, D. R., Pettit, P., and Krupka, A. (1992) Maternal sensitivity and infant–mother attachment in a developmentally delayed sample. *Infant Behavior and Development*, 15, 427–42.

Morelli, G. A. and Tronick, E. Z. (1991) Efe multiple caretaking and attachment. In J. L. Gewirtz and W. M. Kurtines (eds), *Intersections with Attachment*. Hillsdale, NJ: Erlbaum.

Morency, N. L. and Krauss, R. M. (1982) Children's nonverbal encoding and decoding of affect. In R. S. Feldman (ed.), *Development of Nonverbal Behavior in Children*. New York: Springer-Verlag.

Moreno, J. L. (1934) *Who Shall Survive?* Washington,

DC: Nervous and Mental Disease Publishing Company.

Morgan, B. S. (1981) A contribution to the debate on homogamy, propinquity, and segregation. *Journal of Marriage and the Family*, 43, 909–21.

Morgan, H. G., Pocock, G., and Pottle, S. (1975) The urban distribution of non-fatal deliberate self-harm. *British Journal of Psychiatry*, 126, 319–28.

Morgan, J. L. and Travis, L. L. (1989) Limits on negative information in language input. *Journal of Child Language*, 16, 531–52.

Morgan, M. (1982) Television and adolescents' sex-role stereotypes: a longitudinal study. *Journal of Personality and Social Psychology*, 43, 947–55.

Morgan, M. and Grube, J. W. (1989) Adolescent cigarette smoking: a developmental analysis of influences. *British Journal of Developmental Psychology*, 7, 179–89.

Mori, T., Togawa, K., Aoyama, K., and Shimizu, T. (1987) Parental background related to drinking behavior of university student drinkers. *Journal of Human Development*, 23, 1–14.

Morris, J. (1974) *Conundrum*. New York: Henry Holt.

Morse, S. and Gergen, K. J. (1970) Social comparison, self-consistency, and the concept of self. *Journal of Personality and Social Psychology*, 16, 148–56.

Mosatche, H. S. and Bragonier, P. (1981) An observational study of social comparison in preschoolers. *Child Development*, 52, 376–8.

Moscovici, S. (1972) Preface. In S. Moscovici (ed.), *The Psychosociology of Language*. Chicago: Markham.

Moscovici, S. (1976) *La psychoanalyse, son image et son public*, 2nd edn. Paris: Presses Universitaires de France.

Moscovici, S. (1981) On social representations. In J. P. Forgas (ed.), *Social Cognition: perspectives on everyday understanding*. London: Academic Press.

Moscovici, S. (1984) The phenomenon of social representations. In R. M. Farr and S. Moscovici (eds), *Social Representations*. Cambridge: Cambridge University Press.

Moscovici, S. (1985) Social influence and conformity. In G. Lindzey and E. Aronson (eds), *Handbook of Social Psychology*, vol. 2, New York: Random House.

Moscovici, S. (1988) Notes towards a description of social representations. *European Journal of Social Psychology*, 18, 211–50.

Moscovici, S. (1990) Social psychology and developmental psychology: extending the conversation. In G. Duveen and B. Lloyd (eds), *Social Representations and the Development of Knowledge*. Cambridge: Cambridge University Press.

Moscovici, S. and Paicheler, G. (1973) Travail, indi-

vidu et groupe. In S. Moscovici (ed.), *Introduction à la psychologie sociale*, vol. 2. Paris: Larousse.

Mosher, D. L. and Tomkins, S. S. (1988) Scripting the macho man: hypermasculine socialization and enculturation. *Journal of Sex Research*, 25, 60–84.

Moss, E. (1992) The socioaffective context of joint cognitive activity. In L. T. Winegar and J. Valsiner (eds), *Children's Development within Social Context*, vol. 2: *Research and methodology*. Hillsdale, NJ: Erlbaum.

Mothander, P. R. (1992) Maternal adjustment during pregnancy and the infant's first year. *Scandinavian Journal of Psychology*, 33, 20–8.

Mowrer, O. H. (1954) The psychologist looks at language. *American Psychologist*, 9, 660–94.

Much, N. C. and Shweder, R. A. (1978) Speaking of rules: the analysis of culture in breach. In W. Damon (ed.), *New Directions for Child Development: moral development*. San Francisco: Jossey-Bass.

Mueller, E. (1972) The maintenance of verbal exchanges between young children. *Child Development*, 43, 930–8.

Mueller, E. (1989) Toddlers' peer relations: shared meaning and semantics. In W. Damon (ed.), *Child Development Today and Tomorrow*. San Francisco: Jossey-Bass.

Mugny, G. and Carugati, F. (1985) *L'intelligence au pluriel: les représentations sociales de l'intelligence et de son développement*. Cousset: Editions Delval.

Mugny, G. and Doise, W. (1978) Socio-cognitive conflict and structuration of individual and collective performances. *European Journal of Social Psychology*, 8, 181–92.

Mugny, G. and Doise, W. (1979) Factores sociologicos y psicosociologicos del desarrollo cognitivo: une nueva ilustracion experimental. *Anuario de Psicologia*, 21, 4–25.

Mugny, G., de Paolis, P., and Carugati, F. (1984) Social regulations in cognitive development. In W. Doise and A. Palmonari (eds), *Social Interaction in Individual Development*. Cambridge: Cambridge University Press.

Muir, D. and Field, J. (1979) Newborn infants orient to sounds. *Child Development*, 50, 431–6.

Mummendey, A. (1996) Aggressive behaviour. In M. Hewstone, W. Stroebe, and G. M. Stephenson (eds), *Introduction to Social Psychology*, 2nd edn. Oxford: Blackwell.

Mundy, P., Kasari, C., and Sigman, M. (1992) Nonverbal communication, affective sharing, and intersubjectivity. *Infant Behavior and Development*, 15, 377–81.

Munn, P. and Dunn, J. (1989) Temperament and the developing relationship between siblings. *International *Journal of Behavioral Development*, 12, 433–51.

Munro, G. and Adams, G. R. (1977) Ego-identity formation in college students and working youth. *Developmental Psychology*, 13, 523–4.

Murphy, C. M. and Messer, D. J. (1977) Mothers, infants and pointing: a study of gesture. In H. R. Schaffer (ed.), *Studies in Mother–Infant Interaction*. London: Academic Press.

Murphy, L. B. (1936) Sympathetic behavior in young children. *Journal of Experimental Education*, 5, 79–90.

Murray, A. D. (1985) Aversiveness is in the mind of the beholder: perception of infant crying by adults. In B. M. Lester and C. F. Z. Boukydis (eds), *Infant Crying: theoretical and research perspectives*. New York: Plenum Press.

Murray, L. and Trevarthen, C. (1986) The infant's role in mother–infant communications. *Journal of Child Language*, 13, 15–29.

Mussen, P. (1987) Longitudinal study of the life span. In N. Eisenberg (ed.), *Contemporary Topics in Developmental Psychology*. New York: Wiley.

Mussen, P. H. and Haan, N. (1982) A longitudinal study of patterns of personality and political ideologies. In D. H. Eichorn, J. A. Clausen, N. Haan, M. P. Honzik, and P. Mussen (eds), *Present and Past in Middle Life*. New York: Academic Press.

Musun-Miller, L. (1993) Social acceptance and social problem solving in preschool children. *Journal of Applied Developmental Psychology*, 14, 59–70.

Nadel, J. and Fontaine, A.-M. (1989) Communicating by imitation: a developmental and comparative approach to transitory social competence. In B. H. Schneider, G. Attili, J. Nadel, and R. P. Weissberg (eds), *Social Competence in Developmental Perspective*. Dordrecht: Kluwer.

Nadel, J. and Peze, A. (1993) What makes imitation communicative in toddlers and autistic children? In J. Nadel and L. Camaioni, L. (eds), *New Perspectives in Early Communicative Development*. London: Routledge.

Nadel-Brulfert, J. and Baudonnière, P. M. (1982) The social function of reciprocal imitation in 2-year-old peers. *International Journal of Behavioral Development*, 5, 95–109.

Nadel-Brulfert, J., Baudonnière, P. M., and Fontaine, A.-M. (1983) Les comportements sociaux imitatifs. *Recherches de Psychologie Sociale*, 5, 15–29.

Nadler, A. (1991) Help-seeking behavior: psychological costs and instrumental benefits. In M. Clark (ed.), *Review of Personality and Social Psychology*, vol. 12. Newbury Park, Calif.: Sage.

Nadler, A. and Fisher, J. D. (1986) The role of threat to self-esteem and perceived control in recipient reaction to help: theory development and empirical validation. In L. Berkowitz (ed.), *Advances in Experimental and Social Psychology*, vol. 19. San Diego: Academic Press.

Nagorski, A. and Wiecko, A. (1993) Passing the hat in style. *Newsweek*, September 27, 33.

Nance, J. (1975) *The Gentle Tasady: a Stone Age people in the Philippine rain forest*. New York: Harcourt Brace Jovanovich.

Nash, A. (1988) Ontogeny, phylogeny, and relationships. In S. Duck (ed.), *Handbook of Personal Relationships: theory, research and interventions*. Chichester; Wiley.

Neighbors, B., Kempton, T., and Forehand, R. (1992) Co-occurence of substance abuse with conduct, anxiety, and depression disorders in juvenile delinquents. *Addictive Behaviors*, 17, 379–86.

Neill, S. (1991) *Classroom Nonverbal Communication*. London: Routledge.

Neisser, U. (1980) On "social knowing". *Personality and Social Psychology Bulletin*, 6, 601–5.

Nelson, C. A. (1987) The recognition of facial expressions in the first two years of life: mechanisms of development. *Child Development*, 58, 889–909.

Nelson, C. A. and Horowitz, F. D. (1983) The perception of facial expressions and stimulus motion by 2- and 5-month-old infants using holographic stimuli. *Child Development*, 54, 868–77.

Nelson, J. and Aboud, F. (1985) The resolution of social conflict among friends. *Child Development*, 56, 1009–17.

Nelson, K. (1973) *Structure and Strategy in Learning to Talk*. Monographs of the Society for Research in Child Development 38, (1–2), no. 149.

Nelson, K. (1974) Concept, word and sentence: interrelations in acquisition and development. *Psychological Review*, 81, 267–85.

Nelson, K. (1981a). Social cognition in a script framework. In J. H. Flavell and L. Ross (eds), *Social Cognitive Development: frontiers and possible futures*. Cambridge: Cambridge University Press.

Nelson, K. (1981b) Individual differences in language development: implications for development and language. *Developmental Psychology*, 17, 170–87.

Nelson, K. E. (1977) Facilitating children's syntax acquisition. *Developmental Psychology*, 13, 101–7.

Nelson, K. E., Bonvillian, J. D., Denninger, M. S., Kaplan, B. J., and Baker, N. D. (1984) Maternal input adjustments and non-adjustments as related to children's linguistic advances and to language acquisition theories. In A. D. Pellegrini and T. D. Yawkey (eds), *The Development of Oral and Written Language in Social Contexts*. Norwood, NJ: Ablex.

Nelson, K. E., Welsh, J., Camarata, S. M., Butkovsky,

L., and Camarata, M. (1995) Available input for language-impaired children and younger children of matched language levels. *First Language*, 15, 1–17.

Nesdale, A. R. and Pope, S. (1985) Young children's causal attributions and performance expectations on skilled tasks. *British Journal of Developmental Psychology*, 3, 183–90.

Nesselroade, J. R. (1992) Adult personality development: issues in assessing constancy and change. In R. A. Zucker, A. I. Rabin, J. Aronoff, and S. J. Frank (eds), *Personality Structure in the Life Course: essays on personology in the Murray tradition*. New York: Springer.

Nestemann, F. and Hurrelmann, K. (eds), *Social Networks and Social Support in Childhood and Adolescence*. Berlin: de Gruyter.

Nestemann, F. and Niepel G. (1994) Social support in single-parent families: children as sources of support. In F. Nestemann and K. Hurrelmann (eds), *Social Networks and Social Support in Childhood and Adolescence*. Berlin: de Gruyter.

Neubauer, G. and Melzer, W. (1989) The role of school, family, and peer group in the sexual development of the adolescent. In K. Hurrelmann and U. Engel (eds), *The Social World of Adolescents: international perspectives*. Berlin and New York: de Gruyter.

Neubauer, G., Mansel, J., Avrahami, A., and Nathan, M. (1994) Family and peer support of Israeli and German adolescents. In F. Nestemann and K. Hurrelmann (eds), *Social Networks and Social Support in Childhood and Adolescence*. Berlin: de Gruyter.

Neugarten, B. and Neugarten, D. A. (1987) The changing meanings of age. *Psychology Today*, 21, 29–33.

Neugarten, B. L., Moore, J. W., and Lowe, J. C. (1965) Age norms, age constraints, and adult socialization. *American Journal of Sociology*, 70, 710–17.

Neugarten, B. L., Wood, V., Kraines, R. J., and Loomis, B. (1963) Women's attitudes toward the menopause. *Vita Humana*, 6, 140–51.

New, R. S. and Benigni, L. (1987) Italian fathers and infants. In M. E. Lamb (ed.), *The Father's Role: cross-cultural perspectives*. Hillsdale, NJ: Erlbaum.

Newcomb, A. F. and Bukowski, W. M. (1984) A longitudinal study of the utility of social preference and social impact sociometric classification schemes. *Child Development*, 55, 1434–47.

Newcomb, M. D. and Bentler, P. M. (1988) *Consequences of Adolescent Drug Use: impact on the lives of young adults*. Newbury Park, Calif.: Sage.

Newcomb, M. D. and Bentler, P. M. (1989) Substance use and abuse among children and teenagers. *American Psychologist*, 44, 242–8.

Newcomb, T. M. and Hartley, E. L. (eds) (1947) *Readings in Social Psychology*. New York: Henry Holt.

Newman, F. and Holzman, L. (1993) *Lev Vygotsky: revolutionary scientist*. London: Routledge.

Newman, L. S. (1991) Why are traits inferred spontaneously? A developmental approach. *Social Cognition*, 9, 221–53.

Newman, L. S. and Ruble, D. N. (1992) Do young children use the discounting principle? *Journal of Experimental Social Psychology*, 28, 572–93.

Newman, P. R. and Newman, B. M. (1988) Parenthood and adult development. In R. Palkovitz and M. B. Sussman (eds), *Transitions to Parenthood*. New York: Haworth.

Newman, R. S. (1990) Children's help-seeking in the classroom: the role of motivational factors and attitudes. *Journal of Educational Psychology*, 82, 71–80.

Newman, R. S. and Goldin, L. (1990) Children's reluctance to seek help with schoolwork. *Journal of Educational Psychology*, 82, 92–100.

Newport, E. L., Gleitman, L. R., and Gleitman, H. (1977) Mother, I'd rather do it myself: some effects and noneffects of maternal speech style. In C. E. Snow and C. Ferguson (eds), *Talking to Children: language input and acquisition*. Cambridge: Cambridge University Press.

Newson, J. and Newson, E. (1963) *Patterns of Infant Care in an Urban Community*. Harmondsworth: Penguin.

Newson, J. and Newson, E. (1976) *Seven Years Old in the Home Environment*. Harmondsworth: Penguin.

Ng, S. H. (1983) Children's ideas about the bank and shop profit: developmental stages and the influence of cognitive contrasts and conflict. *Journal of Economic Psychology*, 4, 209–21.

Ng, S. H. (1985) Children's ideas about the bank: a New Zealand replication. *European Journal of Social Psychology*, 15, 121–3.

Nicholls, J. G. (1976) Effort is virtuous, but it's better to have ability: evaluative responses to perceptions of effort and ability. *Journal of Personality and Social Psychology*, 10, 306–15.

Nicholls, J. G. (1978a) The development of the concepts of effort and ability, perception of academic attainment, and the understanding that difficult tasks require more ability. *Child Development*, 49, 800–14.

Nicholls, J. G. (1978b) Development of causal attributions and evaluative responses to success and failure in Maori and Pakeha children. *Developmental Psychology*, 14, 687–8.

Nicholls, J. G. (1979) Development of perception of own attainment and causal attributions for success and failure in reading. *Journal of Educational Psychology*, 71, 94–9.

Nicholls, J. G. and Miller, A. T. (1985) Differentiation of the concepts of luck and skill. *Developmental Psychology*, 21, 76–82.

Nickel, H. and Kocher, E. M. T. (1987) West Germany and the German-speaking countries. In M. E. Lamb (ed.), *The Father's Role: cross-cultural perspectives*. Hillsdale, NJ: Erlbaum.

Nicolson, P. (1986) Developing a feminist approach to depression following childbirth. In S. Wilkinson (ed.), *Feminist Social Psychology: developing theory and practice*. Milton Keynes: Open University Press.

Ninio, A. and Bruner, J. S. (1978) The achievement and antecedents of labelling. *Journal of Child Language*, 5, 1–15.

Nisbett, R. E. and Wilson, T. D. (1977) Telling more than we can know: verbal reports on mental processes. *Psychological Review*, 84, 231–59.

Noble, G. (1975) *Children in Front of the Small Screen*. London: Constable.

Nolen-Hoeksema, S. and Girgus, J. S. (1994) The emergence of gender differences in depression during adolescence. *Psychological Bulletin*, 115, 424–43.

Noller, P. (1984) *Nonverbal Communication and Marital Interaction*. Oxford: Pergamon.

Noller, P. (1986) Sex differences in nonverbal communication: advantage lost or supremacy regained? *Australian Journal of Psychology*, 38, 23–32.

Noller, P. and Callan, V. J. (1990) Adolescents' perceptions of the nature of their communication with parents. *Journal of Youth and Adolescence*, 19, 349–62.

Noller, P. and Patton, W. (1990) Maintaining family relationships at adolescence. In P. C. L. Heaven and V. J. Callan (eds), *Adolescence: an Australian perspective*. Sydney: Harcourt Brace Jovanovich.

Norland, S. and Shover, N. (1977) Gender roles and female criminality: some critical comments. *Criminology*, 15, 547–58.

Norris, J. E. (1993) "Why not think Carnegie Hall?" Working and retiring among older professionals. *Canadian Journal on Aging*, 12, 182–99.

Nsamenang, A. B. (1987) A West African perspective. In M. E. Lamb (ed.), *The Father's Role: cross-cultural perspectives*. Hillsdale, NJ: Erlbaum.

Nsamenang, A. B. and Lamb, M. E. (1993) The acquisition of socio-cognitive competence by Nso children in the Bamenda grassfields of northwestern Cameroon. *International Journal of Behavioral Development*, 16, 429–41.

Nsamenang, A. B. and Lamb, M. E. (1994) Socialization of Nso children in the Bemenda Grassfields of Northwest Cameroon. In P. M. Greenfield and R.

R. Cocking (eds), *Cross-cultural Roots of Minority Child Development*. Hillsdale, NJ: Erlbaum.

Nucci, L. and Nucci, M. (1982) Children's social interactions in the context of moral and conventional transgressions. *Child Development*, 53, 403–12.

Nurmi, J.-E. (1992) Age-differences in adult life goals, concerns, and their temporal extension: a life course approach to future-oriented motivation. *International Journal of Behavioral Research*, 15, 487–508.

Nurmi, J.-E. (1993) Adolescent development in an age-graded context: the role of personal beliefs, goals, and strategies in the tackling of developmental tasks and standards. *International Journal of Behavioral Development*, 16, 169–89.

Nurmi, J.-E., Pullianen, H., and Salmela-Aro, K. (1992) Age differences in adults' control beliefs related to life goals and concerns. *Psychology and Aging*, 7, 194–6.

O'Brien, G. E. (1990) Youth unemployment and employment. In P. C. L. Heaven and V. J. Callan (eds), *Adolescence: an Australian perspective*. Sydney: Harcourt Brace Jovanovich.

O'Brien, M., Huston, A. C., and Risley, T. R. (1983) Sex-typed play of toddlers in a day care center. *Journal of Applied Developmental Psychology*, 4, 1–9.

Ochs, E. (1991) Misunderstanding children. In N. Coupland, H. Giles, and J. M. Wiemann (eds), *"Miscommunication" and Problematic Talk*. Newbury Park, Calif.: Sage.

Odom, R. D. and Lemond, C. M. (1972) Developmental differences in the perception and production of facial expressions. *Child Development*, 43, 359–69.

Oettingen, G. (1985) The influence of the kindergarten teacher on sex differences in behavior. *International Journal of Behavioral Development*, 8, 3–13.

Offer, D., Ostrov, E., Howard, K. I., and Atkinson, R. (1988) *The Teenage World: adolescents' self-image in ten countries*. New York: Plenum Press.

Oghu, J. U. (1994) From cultural differences to differences in cultural frame of reference. In P. M. Greenfield and R. R. Cocking (eds), *Cross-cultural Roots of Minority Child Development*. Hillsdale, NJ: Erlbaum.

Ohbuchi, K. and Izutsu, T. (1984) Retaliation by male victims: effects of physical attractiveness and intensity of attack of female attacker. *Personality and Social Psychology Bulletin*, 10, 216–24.

O'Kane, M. (1993a) A public trial in Bosnia's sniper season. *Guardian*, March 21.

O'Kane, M. (1993b). Giving thanks for little Irma. *Guardian*, August 15.

Oliver, M. B. and Hyde, J. S. (1993) Gender differences in sexuality: a meta-analysis. *Psychological Bulletin*, 114, 29–51.

Oller, D. K. (in press) Development of vocalizations in infancy. In H. Winitz (ed.), *Human Communication and its Disorders*. Norwood, NJ: Ablex.

Oloko, B. A. (1994) Children's street work in urban Nigeria: dilemma of modernizing tradition. In P. M. Greenfield and R. R. Cocking (eds), *Cross-cultural Roots of Minority Child Development*. Hillsdale, NJ: Erlbaum.

Olweus, D. (1979) The stability of aggressive reaction patterns in males: a review. *Psychological Bulletin*, 86, 852–75.

Olweus, D. (1980) Familial and temperamental determinants of aggressive behavior in adolescent boys: a causal analysis. *Developmental Psychology*, 16, 644–60.

Olweus, D. (1984) Stability in aggression and withdrawn, inhibited behavior patterns. In R. M. Kaplan, V. J. Konecni, and R. W. Novaco (eds), *Aggression in Children and Youth*. The Hague: Martinus Nijhoff.

Olweus, D. (1985) Aggression and hormones. Behavioral relationships with testosterone and adrenalin. In D. Olweus, J. Block, and M. Radke-Yarrow (eds), *The Development of Antisocial and Prosocial Behavior: research, theories and issues*. New York: Academic Press.

Olweus, D. (1993) *Bullying at School: what we know and what we can do*. Oxford: Blackwell.

Olweus, D. (1994) Bullying at school: long-term outcomes for the victims and an effective school-based intervention program. In L. R. Huesmann (ed.), *Aggressive Behavior: current perspectives*. New York: Plenum Press.

O'Malley, P. M. and Bachman, J. G. (1983) Self-esteem: change and stability between ages 13 and 23. *Developmental Psychology*, 19, 257–68.

Oosterwegel, A. and Oppenheimer, L. (1993) *The Self-system: developmental changes between and within self-concepts*. Hillsdale, NJ: Erlbaum.

Oppenheimer, L. (1989) The nature of social action: social competence versus social conformism. In B. H. Schneider, G. Attili, J. Nadel, and R. P. Weissberg (eds), *Social Competence in Developmental Perspective*. Dordecht: Kluwer.

Oppenheimer, L. and de Groot, W. (1981) Development of concepts about people in interpersonal situations. *European Journal of Social Psychology*, 11, 209–25.

O'Rand, A. M. (1990) Stratification and the life course. In R. H. Binstock and L. K. George (eds), *Aging and the Social Sciences*, 3rd edn. San Diego: Academic Press.

Orne, M. T. (1962) On the social psychology of the psychological experiment: with particular reference to demand characteristics and their implications. *American Psychologist*, 17, 776–83.

Orubuloye, O. (1987) Values and costs of daughters and sons to Yoruba mothers and fathers. In C. Oppong (ed.), *Sex Roles, Population and Development in West Africa*. Portsmouth: Heinemann.

Osgood, D. W., Johnston, L., O'Malley, P., and Bachman, J. (1988) The generality of deviance in late adolescence and early adulthood. *American Sociological Review*, 53, 81–93.

Oshima-Takane, Y. (1992) Analysis of pronominal errors: a case study. *Journal of Child Language*, 19, 111–31.

Oster, H., Hegley, D., and Nagel, L. (1992) Adult judgments and fine-grained analysis of infant facial expressions: testing the validity of *a priori* coding formulas. *Developmental Psychology*, 28, 1115–31.

Ostrow, R. (1993) Being sick's no fun without mum. *The Weekend Australian*, June 19–20.

Oswald, H., Krappman, L., Uhlerndorff, H., and Weiss, K. (1994) Social relationships and support among peers during middle childhood. In F. Nestemann and K. Hurrelmann (eds), *Social Networks and Social Support in Childhood and Adolescence*. Berlin: de Gruyter.

Otis, N. B. and McCandless, B. R. (1955) Responses to repeated frustrations of young children differentiated according to need area. *Journal of Abnormal and Social Psychology*, 50, 349–53.

Ounsted, C. and Taylor, D. C. (1972) The Y-chromosome message: a point of view. In C. Ounsted and D. C. Taylor (eds), *Gender Differences: their ontogeny and significance*. London: Churchill.

Ouweneel, P. and Veenhoven, R. (1990) Cross-national differences in happiness: cultural bias or societal quality? In N. Bleichrodt and P. J. D. Drenth (eds), *Contemporary Issues in Cross-cultural Psychology*. Amsterdam/Lisse: Swets and Zeitlinger.

Oyama, S. (1986) *The Ontogeny of Information*. Cambridge: Cambridge University Press.

Oz, S. and Fine, M. (1988) A comparison of childhood backgrounds of teenage mothers and their non-mother peers: a new formulation. *Journal of Adolescence*, 11, 251–61.

Paikoff, R. L. and Brooks-Gunn, J. (1991) Do parent–child relationships change during puberty? *Psychological Bulletin*, 110, 47–66.

Palermo, D. S. (1973) More about less: a study of language comprehension. *Journal of Verbal Learning and Verbal Behavior*, 12, 211–22.

Palkovitz, R. and Sussman, M. B. (eds) (1988) *Transitions to Parenthood*. New York: Haworth.

Palmer, T. (1991) *Menuhin: a family portrait*. London: Faber and Faber.

Palmonari, A. (1980) Social differentiation processes and collective representations in adolescents. *Italian Journal of Psychology*, 8, 55–63.

Palmonari, A., Pombeni, M. L., and Kirchler, E. (1989) Peer groups and evolution of the self-system in adolescence. *European Journal of Psychology of Education*, 4, 3–15.

Paludi, M. A. (1979) Horner revisited: how successful must Ann and John be before fear of success sets in? *Psychological Reports*, 44, 1312–19.

de Paolis, P. (1990) Prototypes of the psychologist and professionalism: diverging social representations of a development process. In G. Duveen and B. Lloyd (eds), *Social Representations and the Development of Knowledge*. Cambridge: Cambridge University Press.

de Paolis, P., Carugati, F., Erba, M., and Mugny, G. (1981) Connotazione sociale e sviluppo cognitivo. *Giornale Italiano di Psicologia*, 8, 149–65.

de Paolis, P., Doise, W., and Mugny, G. (1987) Social markings in cognitive operations. In W. Doise and S. Moscovici (eds), *Current Issues in European Social Psychology*, vol. 2. Cambridge: Cambridge University Press.

Papousek, H. (1967) Experimental studies of appetitional behavior in human newborns and infants. In H. W. Stevenson, E. H. Hess, and H. L. Rheingold (eds), *Early Behavior*. New York: Wiley.

Papousek, H. and Papousek, M. (1987) Intuitive parenting: a dialectic counterpart to the infant's integrative competence. In J. D. Osofsky (ed.), *Handbook of Infant Development*. New York: Wiley.

Papousek, M. and Papousek, H. (1989) Forms and function of vocal matching in interactions between mothers and their precanonical infants. *First Language*, 9, 137–58.

Papousek, M., Papousek, H., and Bornstein, M. (1985) Naturalistic vocal environment of young infants: on the significance of homogeneity and variability in parental speech. In T. M. Field and N. A. Fox (eds), *Social Perception in Infants*. Norwood, NJ: Ablex.

Parke, R. D. (1977) Punishment in children: effects, side effects, and alternative strategies. In H. L. Horn and P. A. Robinson (eds), *Psychological Processes in Early Education*. New York: Academic Press.

Parke, R. D. (1994) Process, paradigms, and unresolved problems: a commentary on recent advances in our understanding of children's emotions. *Merrill-Palmer Quarterly*, 40, 157–69.

Parke, R. D. and Bhavnagri, N. P. (1989) Parents as managers of children's peer relationships. In D. Belle (ed.), *Children's Social Networks and Social Supports*. New York: Wiley.

Parke, R. D. and Collmer, C. W. (1975) Child abuse: an interdisciplinary analysis. In E. M. Hetherington (ed.), *Review of Child Development Research*, vol. 5. Chicago: University of Chicago Press.

Parke, R. D. and Slaby, R. G. (1983) The development of aggression. In E. M. Hetherington (ed.), *Handbook of Child Psychology*, vol 4: *Socialization, personality, and social development*. New York: Wiley.

Parke, R. D. and Tinsely, B. J. (1987) Family interaction in infancy. In J. D. Osofsky (ed.), *Handbook of Infant Development*. New York: Wiley.

Parke, R. D., Burks, V. M., Carlson, J. L., Neville, B., and Boyum, L. A. (1993) Family-peer relationships: a tripartite model. In R. D. Parke and S. Kellam (eds), *Family Relationships with Other Contexts*. Hillsdale, NJ: Erlbaum.

Parker, J. G. and Asher, S. R. (1987) Peer relations and later personal adjustment: are low-accepted children at risk? *Psychological Bulletin*, 102, 357–89.

Parker, J. G. and Gottman, J. M. (1989) Social and emotional development in a relational context. In T. J. Berndt and G. W. Ladd (eds), *Peer Relationships in Child Development*. New York: Wiley.

Parkes, C. M. (1986) *Bereavement: studies in grief in adult life*. London: Tavistock.

Parkes, C. M. and Weiss, R. S. (1983) *Recovery from Bereavement*. New York: Basic Books.

Parsons, J. E., Kazcala, C., and Meece, J. (1982) Socialization of achievement attitudes and beliefs: classroom influences. *Child Development*, 53, 322–39.

Parten, M. (1932) Social participation among preschool children. *Journal of Abnormal and Social Psychology*, 27, 243–69.

Pastor, D. L. (1981) The quality of mother–infant attachment and its relationship to toddlers' sociability with peers. *Developmental Psychology*, 17, 326–35.

Patterson, G. R. (1980) *Mothers: the unacknowledged victims*. Monographs of the Society for Research in Child Development, 45 (5), no. 186.

Patterson, G. R. (1982) *Coercive Family Processes*. Eugene, Or.: Castiia Press.

Patterson, G. R. (1986) Maternal rejection: determinant or product for deviant child behavior? In W. W. Hartup and Z. Rubin (eds), *Relationships and Development*. Hillsdale, NJ: Erlbaum.

Patterson, G. R. and Cobb, J. A. (1973) Stimulus control for classes of noxious behaviors. In J. F. Knutson (eds), *The Control of Aggression*. Chicago: Aldine.

Patterson, G. R., DeBaryshe, B., and Ramsey, E. (1989) A developmental perspective on antisocial behavior. *American Psychologist*, 44, 329–35.

Patterson, G. R., Littman, R. A., and Bricker, W. (1967) *Assertive Behavior in Children: a step toward a theory of aggression*. Monographs of the Society for Research in Child Development, 32 (5), no. 113.

Patterson, M. L. (1988) Functions of nonverbal behavior in close relationships. In S. Duck (ed.), *Handbook of Personal Relationships: theory, research and interventions*. Chichester: Wiley.

Patton, W. and Noller, P. (1984) Unemployment and youth: a longitudinal study. *Australian Journal of Psychology*, 36, 399–413.

Patton, W. and Noller, P. (1991) The family and the unemployed adolescent. *Journal of Adolescence*, 14, 343–61.

Paxton, S. J., Wertheim E. H., Gibbons, K., Szmukler, G. I., Hillier, L., and Petrovich, J. L. (1991) Body image satisfaction, dieting beliefs, and weight loss behaviors in adolescent girls and boys. *Journal of Youth and Adolescence*, 20, 361–79.

Pearce, P. L. and Caltabiano, N. L. (1982) Gesture decoding and encoding in children: the effects of ethnicity, age and sex. *Australian Journal of Psychology*, 34, 17–24.

Pearl, R. (1985) Children's understanding of others' need for help: effects of problem explicitness and type. *Child Development*, 56, 735–45.

Pease, D. M., Gleason, J. B., and Pan, B. (1993) Learning the meaning of words: semantic development and beyond. In J. B. Gleason (ed.), *The Development of Language*, 3rd edn. New York: Macmillan.

Peevers, B. H. and Secord, P. F. (1973) Developmental changes in attribution of descriptive concepts to persons. *Journal of Personality and Social Psychology*, 56, 354–63.

Pegg, J. E., Werker, J. F., and McLeod, P. J. (1992) Preference for infant-directed over adult-directed speech: evidence from 7-week-old infants. *Infant Behavior and Development*, 15, 325–45.

Peirce, K. (1993) Socialization of teenage girls through teen-magazine fiction: the making of a new woman or an old lady? *Sex Roles*, 29, 59–68.

Pellegrini, A. D. (1988) Elementary school children's rough-and-tumble play and social competence. *Developmental Psychology*, 24, 802–6.

Pellegrini, A. D. (1989) Children's rough-and-tumble play: issues in categorization and function. *Educational Policy*, 3, 389–400.

Pels, T. (1990) Developmental expectations of Moroccan and Dutch parents. In N. Bleichrodt and P. J. D. Drenth (eds), *Contemporary Issues in Cross-cultural Psychology*. Amsterdam/Lisse: Swets and Zeitlinger.

Pemberton, E. F. and Watkins, R. V. (1987) Language facilitation through stories: recasting and modelling. *First Language*, 7, 79–89.

Pepler, D., Corter, C., and Abramovitch, R. (1982) Social relations among children: comparison of sibling and peer interaction. In K. H. Rubin and H. S. Ross (eds), *Peer Relationships and Social Skills in Childhood*. New York: Springer-Verlag.

Perez, B. (1878). *La psychologie de l'enfant: les trois premières années*, 5th edn. Paris: Alcan.

Pérez-Pereira, M. and Castro, J. (1988) Fenómenos transicionalies en al acceso al lenguaje. *Infancia y Aprendizaje*, 43, 13–36.

Perlmutter, M. and Hall, E. (1992) *Adult Development and Aging*, 2nd edn. New York: Wiley.

Perloff, R. M. (1977) Some antecedents of children's sex-role stereotypes. *Psychological Reports*, 40, 463–6.

Perner, J., Ruffman, T., and Leekam, S. R. (1994) Theory of mind is contagious: you catch it from your sibs. *Child Development*, 65, 1228–38.

Perret-Clermont, A.-N. (1980) *Social Interaction and Cognitive Development in Children*. London: Academic Press.

Perret-Clermont, A.-N. (1981) Conflict and cooperation as opportunities for learning. In W. P. Robinson (ed.), *Communication in Development*. London: Academic Press.

Perret-Clermont, A.-N. and Nicolet, M. (eds) (1988) *Interagir et connaître. Enjeux et regulations sociales dans le développement cognitif*. Cousset: DelVal.

Perret-Clermont, A.-N. and Schubauer-Leoni, M.-L. (1981) Conflict and cooperation as opportunities for learning. In W. P. Robinson (ed.), *Communication in Development*. London: Academic Press.

Perret-Clermont, A.-N., Brun, J., Saada, E. H., and Schubauer-Leoni, M.-L. (1984) Learning: a social actualization and reconstruction of knowledge. In H. Tajfel (ed.), *The Social Dimension*, vol. 1. Cambridge: Cambridge University Press.

Perret-Clermont, A.-N., Perret, J. F., and Bell, N. (1991) The social construction of meaning and cognitive activity in elementary school children. In L. B. Resnick, J. M. Levine, and S. D. Teasley (eds), *Perspectives on Socially Shared Cognition*. Washington, DC: American Psychological Association.

Perry, D. G. and Bussey, K. (1979) The social learning theory of sex differences: imitation is alive and well. *Journal of Personality and Social Psychology*, 37, 1699–712.

Perry, D. G. and Bussey, K. (1984) *Social Development*. Englewood Cliffs, NJ: Prentice Hall.

Perry, D. G., Perry, L. C., and Rasmussen, P. (1986) Cognitive social learning mediators of aggression. *Child Development*, 57, 700–11.

Perry, D. G., White, A. J., and Perry, L. C. (1984) Does early sex typing result from children's attempts to match their behavior to sex role stereotypes? *Child Development*, 55, 2114–21.

Perry, D. G., Williard, J. C., and Perry, L. C. (1990) Peers' perceptions of the consequences that victimized children provide aggressors. *Child Development*, 61, 1310–25.

Peters, L. H., O'Connor, E. J., Weekley, J., Pooyan, A., Frank, B., and Erenkrantz, B. (1984) Sex bias and managerial evaluations: a replication and extension. *Journal of Applied Psychology*, 69, 349–52.

Petersen, A. C., Kennedy, R. E., and Sullivan, P. (1991) Coping with adolescence. In M. E. Colten and S. Gore (eds), *Adolescent Stress: causes and consequences*. New York: Aldine de Gruyter.

Peters-Martin, P. and Wachs, T. (1984) A longitudinal study of temperament and its correlates in the first 12 months. *Infant Behavior and Development*, 7, 285–98.

Peterson, C. and Seligman, M. E. P. (1984) Causal explanations as a risk factor for depression: theory and evidence. *Psychological Review*, 91, 347–74.

Peterson, C. C. (1989) *Looking Forward Through the Lifespan: developmental psychology*, 2nd edn. Sydney and New York: Prentice Hall.

Peterson, C. C. and Peterson J. L. (1986) Children and cigarettes: the effect of a model who quits. *Journal of Applied Developmental Psychology*, 7, 293–306.

Peterson, C. C., Peterson, J. L., and Skevington, S. (1986) Heated argument and adolescent development. *Journal of Social and Personal Relationships*, 3, 229–40.

Peterson, L. (1980) Developmental changes in verbal and behavioral sensitivity to cues of social norms of altruism. *Child Development*, 51, 830–8.

Peterson, L. (1983) Role of donor competence, donor age, and peer presence on helping in an emergency. *Developmental Psychology*, 19, 873–80.

Pettit, G. S., Bakshi, A., Dodge, K. A., and Coie, J. D. (1990) The emergence of social dominance in young boys' play groups: developmental differences and behavioral correlates. *Developmental Psychology*, 26, 1017–25.

Pfeffer, C. R. (1986) *The Suicidal Child*. New York: Guilford Press.

Phelps, E. and Damon, W. (1989) Problem solving with equals: peer collaboration as a context for learning mathematics and spatial concepts. *Journal of Educational Psychology*, 81, 639–46.

Philippot, P. and Feldman, R. S. (1990) Age and social competence in preschoolers' decoding of facial expression. *British Journal of Social Psychology*, 29, 43–5.

Phillips, D. (1984) The illusion of incompetence among academically competent children. *Child Development*, 55, 2000–2016.

Phillips, D., McCartney, K., and Scarr, S. (1987) Child-care quality and children's social development. *Developmental Psychology*, 23, 537–43.

Phillips, J. (1973) Syntax and vocabulary of mothers' speech to young children: age and sex comparisons. *Child Development*, 44, 182–5.

Piaget, J. (1926) *The Language and Thought of the Child*. London: Routledge and Kegan Paul.

Piaget, J. (1927) *The Child's Conception of Time*. London: Routledge and Kegan Paul.

Piaget, J. (1929) *The Child's Conception of the World*. London: Routledge and Kegan Paul.

Piaget, J. (1932) *The Moral Judgment of the Child*. Harmondsworth: Penguin.

Piaget, J. (1936) *The Origin of Intelligence in the Child*. Harmondsworth: Penguin.

Piaget, J. (1970) *Biology and Knowledge*, 2nd edn. Edinburgh: Edinburgh University Press.

Piaget, J. (1971) *Structuralism*. London: Routledge and Kegan Paul.

Piaget, J. (1972) *The Principles of Genetic Epistemology*. London: Routledge and Kegan Paul.

Piaget, J. (1973a) *Main Trends in Psychology*. London: George Allen and Unwin.

Piaget, J. (1973b) The affective unconscious and the cognitive unconscious. *Journal of the American Psychoanalytic Association*, 21, 249–61.

Piaget, J. and Inhelder, B. (1966) *The Psychology of the Child*. London: Routledge and Kegan Paul.

Piaget, J. and Weil, A. (1951) The development in children of the idea of the homeland and of relations with other countries. *International Social Science Bulletin*, 3, 561–76.

Piliavin, J. A. and Unger, R. K. (1985) The helpful but helpless female: myth or reality? In V. E. O'Leary, R. K. Unger, and B. S. Wallston (eds), *Women, Gender, and Social Psychology*. Hillsdale, NJ: Erlbaum.

Piliavin, J. A., Dovidio, J. F., Gaertner, S. L., and Clark, R. D. (1981) *Emergency Intervention*. New York: Academic Press.

Pine, F. (1985) *Developmental Theory and Clinical Process*. New Haven: Yale University Press.

Pine, J. (1990) Maternal style at the early one-word stage: re-evaluating the stereotype of the directive mother. *First Language*, 12, 169–86.

Pinker, S. (1984) *Language Learnability and Language Development*. Cambridge, Mass.: Harvard University Press.

Pinker, S. (1994) *The Language Instinct*. London: Allen Lane.

Pipp, S., Easterbrooks, M. A., and Harmon, R. J. (1992) The relation between attachment and knowledge of self and mother in one- to three-year-old infants. *Child Development*, 63, 738–50.

Pleck, J. H. (1983) Husbands' paid work and family roles: current research issues. In H. Lopata and J.

Pleck (eds), *Research in the Interweave of Social Roles*. Greenwich: Jai Press.

Pleck, J. H. (1987) American fathering in historical perspective. In M. S. Kimmel (ed.), *Changing Men: new directions in research on men and masculinity*. Newbury Park, Calif.: Sage.

Plomin, R. (1987) Developmental behavioral genetics and infancy. In J. D. Osofsky (ed.), *Handbook of Infant Development*. New York: Wiley.

Plomin, R. and Foch, T. T. (1981) Sex differences and individual differences. *Child Development*, 52, 383–5.

Plomin, R. and Rowe, D. C. (1977) A twin study of temperament in young children. *Journal of Psychology*, 97, 107–13.

Plomin, R., DeFries, J. C., and Fulker, D. W. (1988) *Nature and Nurture in Infancy and Early Childhood*. Cambridge: Cambridge University Press.

Pollock, L. A. (1983) *Forgotten Children: parent–child relations from 1500 to 1900*. Cambridge: Cambridge University Press.

Poole, M. E. (1989) Adolescent transitions: a life-course perspective. In K. Hurrelmann and U. Engel (eds), *The Social World of Adolescents: international perspectives*. Berlin and New York: de Gruyter.

Poole, M. E. and Cooney, G. H. (1987) Orientations to the future: comparison of adolescents in Australia and Singapore. *Journal of Youth and Adolescence*, 16, 129–51.

Porter, R. H. and Laney, M. D. (1980) Attachment theory and the concept of inclusive fitness. *Merrill-Palmer Quarterly*, 26, 35–51.

Potter, J. and Litton, I. (1985) Some problems underlying the theory of social representations. *British Journal of Social Psychology*, 24, 81–90.

Pratt, C. (1993) The representation of knowledge and beliefs. In C. Pratt and A. F. Garton (eds), *Systems of Representation in Children: development and use*. Chichester: Wiley.

Pratt, C. and Bryant, P. E. (1990) Young children understand that looking leads to knowing (so long as they are looking into a single barrel). *Child Development*, 61, 973–82.

Pratt, M. W. and Norris, J. E. (1994) *The Social Psychology of Aging*. Oxford: Blackwell.

Pratt, M. W., Golding, G., and Kerig, P. (1987) Lifespan differences in adult thinking about hypothetical and personal moral issues: reflection or regression? *International Journal of Behavioral Development*, 10, 359–75.

Pratt, M. W., Green, D., MacVicar, J., and Bountrogianni, M. (1992) The mathematical parent: parental scaffolding, parenting style, and learning outcomes in long-division mathematics homework. *Journal of Applied Developmental Psychology*, 13, 17–34.

Prechtl, H. R. F. (1984) Continuity and change in early neural development. In H. R. F. Prechtl (ed.), *Continuity of Neural Function from Prenatal to Postnatal Life*. Oxford: Blackwell Scientific.

Premack, D. (1991) The infant's theory of self-propelled objects. In D. Frye and C. Moore (eds), *Children's Theories of Mind: mental states and social understanding*. Hillsdale, NJ: Erlbaum.

Presland, P. and Antill, J. K. (1987) Household division of labour: the impact of hours worked in paid employment. *Australian Journal of Psychology*, 39, 273–91.

Presser, H. B. (1980) Social consequences of teenage childbearing. In C. S. Chilman (ed.), *Adolescent Pregnancy and Childbearing: findings from research*. Washington, DC: US Department of Health and Human Services.

Prior, M. (1992) Development of temperament. In P. C. L. Heaven (ed.), *Life Span Development*. Sydney and London: Harcourt Brace Jovanovich.

Prior, M., Kyrios, M., and Oberklaid, F. (1986) Temperament in Australian, American, Chinese, and Greek infants. *Journal of Cross-cultural Psychology*, 17, 455–74.

Prior, M., Sanson, A. V., Garino, E., and Oberklaid, F. (1987) Ethnic influences on "difficult" temperament and behavioral problems in infants. *Australian Journal of Psychology*, 39, 163–71.

Prior, M., Sanson, A. V., and Oberklaid, F. (1989) The Australian Temperament Project. In G. A. Kohnstamm, J. E. Bates, and M. K. Rothbart (eds), *Temperament and Personality*, Chichester: Wiley.

Prior, M., Sanson, A., Oberklaid, F., and Northam, E. (1987) Measurement of temperament in one to three year old children. *International Journal of Behavioral Development*, 10, 121–32.

Promnitz, J. (1992) Peer interactions in young children. In P. C. L. Heaven (ed.), *Life Span Development*. Sydney and London: Harcourt Brace Jovanovich.

Pulkkinen, L. (1982) Self-control and continuity from childhood to adolescence. In P. B. Baltes and O. G. Brim (eds), *Life-span Development and Behavior*, vol. 4. Orlando, Fla.: Academic Press.

Pulkkinen, L. (1990) Home atmosphere and adolescent future orientation. *European Journal of Psychology of Education*, 5, 33–43.

Pulkkinen, L. and Narusk, A. (1987) Functions of adolescent drinking in Finland and the Soviet Union. *European Journal of Psychology of Education*, 2, 311–26.

Pulkkinen, L. and Tremblay, R. (1992) Patterns of boys' social adjustment in two cultures and at different ages: a longitudinal perspective. *International Journal of Behavioral Development*, 15, 527–53.

Putallaz, M. and Gottman, J. (1981) Social skills and group acceptance. In S. Asher and J. Gottman (eds), *The Development of Children's Friendships*. Cambridge: Cambridge University Press.

Putallaz, M. and Wasserman, A. (1990) Children's entry behavior. In S. R. Asher and J. Coie (eds), *Peer Rejection in Childhood*. Cambridge: Cambridge University Press.

Pye, C. (1986) Quiche Mayan speech to children. *Journal of Child Language*, 13, 85–100.

Pynte, J., Girotto, V., and Baccino, T. (1991) Children's communicative abilities revisited: verbal versus perceptual disambiguating strategies in referential communication. *Journal of Child Language*, 18, 191–213.

Quay, H. C. (1987) Intelligence. In H. C. Quay (ed.), *Handbook of Juvenile Delinquency*. New York: Wiley.

Rabain-Jamin, J. (1989) Culture and early social interactions. The example of mother–infant object play in African and native French families. *European Journal of Psychology of Education*, 4, 295–305.

Rabain-Jamin, J. (1994) Language and socialization of the child in African families living in France. In P. M. Greenfield and R. R. Cocking (eds), *Cross-cultural Roots of Minority Child Development*. Hillsdale, NJ: Erlbaum.

Rabbie, J. M., Goldenbeld, C., and Lodewijkx, H. F. M. (1992) Sex differences in conflict and aggression in individual and group settings. In K. Bjorkqvist and P. Niemala (eds), *Of Mice and Women: aspects of female aggression*. San Diego: Academic Press.

Radford, A. (1988) *Transformational Grammar: a first course*. Cambridge: Cambridge University Press.

Radford, T. (1993) In the forbidden forest. *Guardian*, December 19.

Radke-Yarrow, M. and Zahn-Waxler, C. (1984) Roots, motives, and patterns of children's prosocial behavior. In E. Staub, D. Bar-Tal, J. Karylowski, and J. Reykowski (eds), *Development and Maintenance of Prosocial Behavior*. New York: Plenum Press.

Radke-Yarrow, M., Cummings, E. M., Kuczynski, L., and Chapman, M. (1985) Patterns of attachment in two- and three-year-olds in normal families and families with parental depression. *Child Development*, 56, 884–93.

Radke-Yarrow, M., Zahn-Waxler, C., and Chapman, M. (1983) Children's prosocial dispositions and behavior. In E. M. Hetherington (ed.), *Handbook of Child Psychology*, vol. 4: *Socialization, personality, and development*. New York: Wiley.

von Raffler-Engel, W. (1981) Developmental kinesics:

the acquisition and maturation of conversational nonverbal behavior. In B. L. Hoffer and R. N. St Clair (eds), *Developmental Kinesics: the emerging paradigm*. Baltimore, Md: University Park Press.

Ragozin, A. (1980) Attachment behavior of day-care children: naturalistic and laboratory observations. *Child Development*, 51, 409–15.

Rampton, M. B. H. (1991) Interracial Panjabi in a British adolescent peer group. *Language in Society*, 20, 391–422.

Rand, A. (1987) Transitional life events and desistance from delinquency and crime. In M. E. Wolfgang, T. P. Thornberry, and R. M. Figlio (1987) *From Boy to Man, from Delinquency to Crime*. Chicago: University of Chicago Press.

Rao, P. and Rao, N. (1986) Arranged marriages: an assessment of the attitudes of the college students in India. *Journal of Comparative Family Studies*, 2, 311–25.

Raskin, V. (1992) Accents in classroom. Unpublished report on Linguist e-mail network.

Rauste von Wright, M. (1989) Physical and verbal aggression in peer groups among Finnish boys and girls. *International Journal of Behavioral Development*, 12, 473–84.

Raviv, A., Bar-Tal, D., and Lewis-Levin, T. (1980) Motivations for donation behavior by boys of three different ages. *Child Development*, 51, 610–13.

Redgrove, J. (1987) Applied settings. In M. A. Baker (ed.), *Sex Differences in Human Performance*. Chichester: Wiley.

Reeder, G. D. (1985) Implicit relations between dispositions and behaviors: effects on dispositional attribution. In J. H. Harvey and G. Weary (eds), *Attribution: Basic Issues and Applications*. New York: Academic Press.

Reger, Z. and Gleason, J. B. (1991) Romani child-directed speech and children's language among Gypsies in Hungary. *Language in Society*, 20, 601–17.

Reibstein, J. and Richards, M. (1992) *Sexual Arrangements: marriage and affairs*. London: Heinemann.

Reicher, S. and Emler, N. (1986) The management of delinquent reputations. In H. Beloff (ed.), *Getting into Life*. London: Methuen.

Reid, P. T., Tate, C. C., and Berman, P. W. (1989) Preschool children's self-presentations in situations with infants: effects of sex and race. *Child Development*, 60, 710–14.

Reis, H. T. and Shaver, P. (1988) Intimacy as an interpersonal process. In S. Duck (ed.), *Handbook of Personal Relationships: theory, research and interventions*. Chichester: Wiley.

Reissland, N. and Harris, P. (1991) Children's use of

display rules in pride-eliciting situations. *British Journal of Developmental Psychology*, 9, 431–5.

Renshaw, P. D. and Asher, S. R. (1982) Social competence and peer status: the distinction between goals and strategies. In K. H. Rubin and H. S. Ross (eds), *Peer Relationships and Social Skills in Childhood*. New York: Springer-Verlag.

Renwick, S. and Emler, N. (1991) The relationship between social skills deficits and juvenile delinquency. *British Journal of Clinical Psychology*, 30, 61–71.

Rest, J. R. (1983) Morality. In J. H. Flavell and E. M. Markman (eds), *Handbook of Child Psychology*, vol. 3: *Cognitive development*. New York: Wiley.

Revenson, T. A. (1989) Compassionate stereotyping of elderly patients by physicians: revising the social contact hypothesis. *Psychology and Aging*, 4, 230–4.

Rheingold, H. L. and Cook, K. V. (1975) The content of boys' and girls' rooms as an index of parents' behavior. *Child Development*, 46, 459–63.

Rheingold, H. L., Hay, D. F., and West, M. J. (1976) Sharing in the second year of life. *Child Development*, 47, 1148–58.

Rholes, W., Blackwell, J., Jordan, C., and Walters, C. (1980) A developmental study of learned helplessness. *Developmental Psychology*, 16, 616–24.

Rice, F. P. (1990) *The Adolescent: development, relationships, and culture*, 6th edn. Boston: Allyn and Bacon.

Rice, M. E. and Grusec, J. E. (1975) Saying and doing: effects on observer performance. *Journal of Personality and Social Psychology*, 32, 584–93.

Rice, M. L. and Woodsmall, L. (1988) Lessons from television: children's word learning when viewing. *Child Development*, 59, 420–9.

Rice, M. L., Buhr, J. C., and Nemeth, M. (1990) Fast mapping word-learning abilities of language-delayed preschoolers. *Journal of Speech and Hearing Disorders*, 55, 33–42.

Richards, B. and Robinson, P. (1993) Environmental correlates of child copula verb growth. *Journal of Child Language*, 20, 343–62.

Richards, H. C., Bear, G. G., Stewart, A. L., and Norman, A. D. (1992) Moral reasoning and classroom conduct: evidence of a curvilinear relationship. *Merrill-Palmer Quarterly*, 38, 176–90.

Richards, M. P. M. (1974) First steps in becoming social. In M. P. M. Richards (ed.), *The Integration of a Child into a Social World*. Cambridge: Cambridge University Press.

Richter, L. M. (1990) South African "street children": comparisons with Anglo-American runaways. In N. Bleichrodt and P. J. D. Drenth (eds), *Contemporary Issues in Cross-cultural Psychology*. Amsterdam/Lisse: Swets and Zeitlinger.

Rieser-Danner, L. A., Roggman, L., and Langlois, J. H. (1987) Infant attractiveness and perceived temperament in the prediction of attachment classifications. *Infant Mental Health Journal*, 8, 144–55.

Rigby, K. and Rump, E. E. (1981) Attitudes toward parents and institutional authorities during adolescence. *Journal of Psychology*, 109, 109–18.

Rigby, K. and Slee, P. T. (1993) Dimensions of interpersonal relations among Australian children and implications for psychological well-being. *The Journal of Social Psychology*, 133, 33–42.

Rijsman, J. B. (1983) The dynamics of social competition in personal and categorical comparison-situations. In W. Doise and S. Moscovici (eds), *Current Issues in European Social Psychology*, vol. 1. Cambridge: Cambridge University Press.

Rijsman, J. B., Zoetebier, J. H. T., Ginther, A. J. F., and Doise, W. (1980) Sociocognitief conflict en cognitieve ontwikkeling. *Pedagogische Studien*, 57, 125–33.

van de Rijt-Plooj, H. H. C. and Plooj, F. X. (1993) Distinct periods of mother–infant conflict in normal development: sources of progress and germs of pathology. *Journal of Child Psychology and Psychiatry*, 34, 229–45.

Riksen-Walraven, J. M., Meij, H. T., van Roozendall, J., and Koks, J. (1993) Mastery motivation in toddlers as related to quality of attachment. In D. J. Messer (ed.), *Mastery Motivation in Early Childhood: development, measurement and social processes*. London: Routledge.

Rizzo, T. A. (1989) *Friendship Development among Children in School*. Norwood, NJ: Ablex.

Robarchek, C. A. and Robarcheck, C. J. (1992) Cultures of war and peace: a comparative study of Waorani and Semai. In J. Silverberg and J. P. Gray (eds), *Aggression and Peacefulness in Humans and Other Primates*. New York: Oxford University Press.

Robert, M. (1990) Sex-typing of the water-level task: there is more than meets the eye. *International Journal of Psychology*, 25, 475–90.

Robert, M. and Lacroix, P.-E. (1984) Apprentissage de la conservation par observation: competences reperée et provoquée chez l'enfant. *Psychologie Française*, 29, 198–203.

Roberts, K. and Parsell, G. (1989) Recent changes in the pathways from school to work. In K. Hurrelmann and U. Engel (eds), *The Social World of Adolescents: international perspectives*. Berlin and New York: de Gruyter.

Roberts, P. and Newton, P. M. (1987) Levinsonian studies of women's adult development. *Psychology and Aging*, 2, 154–63.

Robertson, J. and Robertson, J. (1971) Young children

in brief separation: a fresh look. *Psychoanalytic Study of the Child*, 26, 264–315.

Robertson, J. and Robertson, J. (1989) *Separation and the Very Young*. London: Free Association.

Robins, L. N. (1979) Sturdy childhood predictors of adult outcomes: replications from longitudinal studies. In J. E. Barrett, R. M. Rose, and G. L. Klerman (eds), *Stress and Mental Disorder*. New York: Raven Press.

Robinson, E. J. (1981) Conversational tactics and the advancement of the child's understanding about referential communication. In W. P. Robinson (ed.), *Communication in Development*. London: Academic Press.

Robinson, E. J. and Robinson, W. P. (1981) Ways of reacting to communication failure in relation to the development of the child's understanding about verbal communication. *European Journal of Social Psychology*, 11, 189–208.

Robinson, E. J. and Robinson, W. P. (1985) Teaching children about verbal referential communication. *International Journal of Behavioral Development*, 8, 285–99.

Robinson, E. J. and Whittaker, S. J. (1986) Learning about verbal referential communication in the early school years. In K. Durkin (ed.), *Language Development in the School Years*. London: Croom Helm.

Robinson, W. P. (1972) *Language and Social Behaviour*. Harmondsworth: Penguin.

Robinson, W. P. (1984) The development of communicative competence with language in young children: a social psychological perspective. In H. Tajfel (ed.), *The Social Dimension*, vol. 1. Cambridge: Cambridge University Press.

Robson, K. (1967) The role of eye-to-eye contact in maternal–infant attachment. *Journal of Child Psychology and Psychiatry*, 8, 13–25.

Rodeheaver, D. and Datan, N. (1981) Making it: the dialectics of middle age. In R. M. Lerner and N. A. Busch-Rossnagel (eds), *Individuals as Producers of their Development*. New York: Academic Press.

Rodgon, M. (1976) *Single Word Usage: cognitive development and the beginnings of combinatorial speech*. Cambridge: Cambridge University Press.

Roff, J. D. and Wirt, R. D. (1984) Childhood aggression and social adjustment as antecedents of delinquency. *Journal of Abnormal Child Psychology*, 12, 111–26.

Roggman, L. A., Langlois, J. H., and Hubbs-Tait, L. (1987) Mothers, infants, and toys: social play correlates of attachment. *Infant Behavior and Development*, 10, 233–7.

Roggman, L. A., Langlois, J. H., Hubbs-Tait L., and Rieser-Danner, L. A. (1994) Infant day-care, attach-

ment, and the "file drawer problem." *Child Development*, 65, 1429–43.

Rogoff, B. (1990) *Apprenticeship in Thinking: cognitive development in a social context*. New York: Oxford University Press.

Rogoff, B. and Morelli, G. (1989) Perspectives on children's development from cultural psychology. *American Psychologist*, 44, 343–8.

Rogoff, B., Ellis, S. and Gardner, W. (1984) Adjustment of adult–child instruction according to child's age and task. *Developmental Psychology*, 20, 193–9.

Rohrle, B. and Sommer, G. (1994) Social support and social competences: some theoretical and empirical contributions to their relationship. In F. Nestemann and K. Hurrelmann (eds), *Social Networks and Social Support in Childhood and Adolescence*. Berlin: de Gruyter.

Rollins, B. C. and Feldman, H. (1981) Marital satisfaction over the family life cycle. In L. D. Steinberg (ed.), *The Life Cycle: readings in human development*. New York: Columbia University Press.

Romaine, S. (1984) *The Language of Children and Adolescents: the acquisition of communicative competence*. Oxford: Blackwell.

Rome-Flanders, T., Cronk, C., and Gourde, C. (in press) Maternal scaffolding in mother–infant games and its relationship to language development: a longitudinal study. *First Language*.

Rommetveit, R. (1985) Language acquisition as increasing linguistic structuring of experience and symbolic behavior control. In J. V. Wertsch (ed.), *Culture, Communication, and Cognition: Vygotskian perspectives*. Cambridge: Cambridge University Press.

de Rosa, A. S. (1987) The social representation of mental illness in children and adults. In W. Doise and S. Moscovici (eds), *Current Issues in European Social Psychology*, vol. 2. Cambridge: Cambridge University Press.

Rose, S. A. and Ruff, H. A. (1987) Cross-modal abilities in human infants. In J. D. Osofsky (ed.), *Handbook of Infant Development*. New York: Wiley.

Rose-Krasnor, L. (1988) Social cognition. In T. D. Yawkey and J. E. Johnson (eds), *Integrative Processes and Socialization: early to middle childhood*. Hillsdale, NJ: Erlbaum.

Rosen, K. S. and Rothbaum, F. (1993) Quality of parental caregiving and security of attachment. *Developmental Psychology*, 27, 358–67.

Rosen, W. D., Adamson, L. B., and Bakeman, R. (1992) An experimental investigation of infant social referencing: mothers' messages and gender differences. *Developmental Psychology*, 28, 1172–8.

Rosenfeld, A. and Stark, E. (1987) The prime of our lives. *Psychology Today*, 21, 62–72.

Rosenfield, D. and Stephan, W. G. (1981) Intergroup relations among children. In S. S. Brehm, S. M. Kassin, and F. X. Gibbons (eds), *Developmental Social Psychology: theory and research*. New York: Oxford University Press.

Rosengren, K. S., Behrend, D. A., and Perlmutter, M. (1993) Parental influences on children's cognition. In R. Pasnak and M. L. Howe (eds), *Emerging Theories in Cognitive Development*, vol. 2: *Comprehension*. New York: Springer-Verlag.

Rosenhan, D. L. (1972) Learning theory and prosocial behavior. *Journal of Social Issues*, 28, 151–63.

Rosenkrantz, P., Vogel, S., Bee, H., Broverman, I., and Broverman, D. M. (1968) Sex-role stereotypes and self-concepts in college students. *Journal of Consulting and Clinical Psychology*, 32, 287–95.

Rosenmays, L. (1985) Changing values and positions of aging in Western culture. In J. E. Birren and K. W. Schaie (eds), *Handbook of the Psychology of Aging*, 2nd edn. New York: Van Nostrand.

Rosenstein, D. and Oster, H. (1988) Differential facial responses to four basic tastes in newborns. *Child Development*, 59, 1555–68.

Rosenthal, D. A. (1987) Ethnic identity development in adolescents. In J. S. Phinney and M. J. Rotheram (eds), *Children's Ethnic Socialization: pluralism and development*. Newbury Park, Calif.: Sage.

Rosenthal, D. A. and Hrynevich, C. (1985) Ethnicity and ethnic identity: a comparative study of Greek-, Italian-, and Anglo-Australian adolescents. *International Journal of Psychology*, 20, 723–42.

Rosenthal, D. A., Moore, S. M., and Taylor, M. J. (1983) Ethnicity and adjustment: a study of the self-image of Anglo-, Greek-, and Italian-Australian working-class adolescents. *Journal of Youth and Adolescence*, 12, 117–35.

Rosenthal, R. (1993) Cumulating evidence. In G. Kieren and C. Lewis (eds), *A Handbook for Data Analysis in the Behavioral Sciences: methodological issues*. Hillsdale, NJ: Erlbaum.

Rosenthal, R. and Jacobson, L. (1968) *Pygmalion in the Classroom*. New York: Holt Rinehart and Winston.

Rosin, H. M. and Korabik, K. (1990) Marital and family correlates of women managers' attrition from organisations. *Journal of Vocational Behavior*, 37, 104–20.

Ross, G., Kagan, J., Zelazo, P., and Kotelchuk, M. (1975) Separation protest in infants in home and laboratory. *Developmental Psychology*, 11, 256–7.

Ross, H. S., Cheyne, J. A., and Lollis, S. P. (1988) Defining and studying reciprocity in young children. In S. Duck (ed.), *Handbook of Personal Relationships: theory, research and interventions*. Chichester: Wiley.

Ross, H. S., Tesla, C., Kenyon, B., and Lollis, S. P.

(1990) Maternal intervention in toddler peer justice: the socialization of principles of justice. *Developmental Psychology*, 26, 994–1003.

Ross, L. (1977) The intuitive psychologist and his shortcomings: distortions in the attribution process. In L. Berkowitz (ed.), *Advances in Experimental Social Psychology*, vol. 10. New York: Academic Press.

Ross, M. H. (1992) Social structure, psychocultural dispositions, and violent conflict: extensions from a cross-cultural study. In J. Silverberg and J. P. Gray (eds), *Aggression and Peacefulness in Humans and Other Primates*. New York: Oxford University Press.

Rossi, A. S. (1977) A biosocial perspective on parenting. *Daedalus*, 106, 1–32.

Rossi, A. S. and Rossi, P. H. (1990) *Of Human Bonding: parent–child relations across the life course*. New York: de Gruyter.

Rotenberg, K. J., Simourd, L., and Moore, D. (1989) Children's use of a verbal-nonverbal consistency principle to infer truth and lying. *Child Development*, 60, 309–22.

Rothbart, M. K. (1986) Longitudinal observation of infant temperament. *Developmental Psychology*, 22, 356–65.

Rothbart, M. K. (1989) Temperament and development. In G. A. Kohnstamm, J. E. Bates and M. K. Rothbart (eds), *Temperament in Childhood*. Chichester: Wiley.

Rothbart, M. K., Ahadi, S. A., and Hershey, K. L. (1994) Temperament and social behavior in childhood. *Merrill-Palmer Quarterly*, 40, 21–39.

Rothbaum, F., Weisz, J. R., and Snyder, S. S. (1982) Changing the world and changing the self: a two-process model of perceived control. *Journal of Personality and Social Psychology*, 42, 5–37.

Rotheram-Borus, M. J., Rosario, M., and Koopman, C. (1991) Minority youths at high risk: gay males and runaways. In M. E. Colten and S. Gore (eds), *Adolescent Stress: causes and consequences*. New York: Aldine de Gruyter.

Rousseau, J. J. (1762). *Emile*. Republished 1955.

Rowe, D. C., Chassin, L., Presson, C. C., Edwards, D., and Sherman, S. J. (1992) An "epidemic" model of adolescent cigarette smoking. *Journal of Applied Social Psychology*, 22, 261–85.

Rowland, D. (1991) *Ageing in Australia*. Melbourne: Longman Cheshire.

Royal College of Physicians (1983) *Health or Smoking?* London: Pitman.

Rubenstein, J. L. and Howes, C. (1976) The effects of peers on toddler interaction with mother and toys. *Child Development*, 47, 597–605.

Rubenstein, J. L. and Howes, C. (1979) Caregiving

and infant behavior in day care and in homes. *Developmental Psychology*, 15, 1–24.

Rubin, A. and Rubin, R. (1982) Older persons' TV viewing patterns and motivations. *Communication Research*, 9, 287–313.

Rubin, J. Z., Provenzano, F. J., and Luria, Z. (1974) The eye of the beholder: parents' views on sex of newborns. *American Journal of Orthopsychiatry*, 44, 512–19.

Rubin, K. (1974) The relationship between spatial and communicative egocentrism in children and young and old adults. *Journal of Genetic Psychology*, 125, 295–301.

Rubin, K. H. (1982a) Social and social-cognitive developmental characteristics of young isolate, normal, and sociable children. In K. H. Rubin and H. S. Ross (eds), *Peer Relationships and Social Skills in Childhood*. New York: Springer-Verlag.

Rubin, K. H. (1982b) Non-social play in early childhood: necessarily evil? *Child Development*, 53, 651–8.

Rubin, K. H. and Asendorpf, J. B. (eds) (1993) *Social Withdrawal, Inhibition, and Shyness in Childhood*. Hillsdale, NJ: Erlbaum.

Rubin, K. H. and Daniels-Bierness, T. (1983) Concurrent and predictive correlates of sociometric status in kindergarten and grade one children. *Merrill-Palmer Quarterly*, 29, 337–52.

Rubin, K. H. and Mills, R. S. L. (1988) The many faces of social isolation in childhood. *Journal of Consulting and Clinical Psychology*, 56, 916–24.

Rubin, K. H. and Pepler, D. J. (1980) The relationship of child's play to social-cognitive growth and development. In H. C. Foot, A. J. Chapman, and J. R. Smith (eds), *Friendship and Social Relations in Children*. Chichester: Wiley.

Rubin, K. H. and Trotter, K. T. (1977) Kohlberg's moral judgment scale: some methodological considerations. *Developmental Psychology*, 13, 535–6.

Rubin, K. H., Fein, G. G., and Vandenberg, B. (1983) Play. In E. M. Hetherington (ed.), *Handbook of Child Psychology*, vol. 4: *Socialization, personality, and social development*. New York: Wiley.

Rubin, K. H., LeMare, L. J., and Lollis, S. (1990) Social withdrawal in childhood: developmental pathways to peer rejection. In S. R. Asher and J. Coie (eds), *Peer Rejection in Childhood*. Cambridge: Cambridge University Press.

Rubin, K. H., Mills, R. S. L., and Rose-Krasnor, L. (1989) Maternal beliefs and children's competence. In B. H. Schneider, G. Attili, J. Nadel, and R. P. Weissberg (eds), *Social Competence in Developmental Perspective*. Dordrecht: Kluwer.

Rubin, Z. (1980) *Children's Friendships*. Cambridge, Mass.: Harvard University Press.

Ruble, D. N. (1977) Premenstrual symptoms: a reinterpretation. *Science*, 197, 291–2.

Ruble, D. N. (1983) The development of social-comparison processes and their role in achievement-related self-socialization. In E. T. Higgins, D. N. Ruble and W. W. Hartup (eds), *Social Cognition and Social Development: a socio-cultural perspective*. Cambridge: Cambridge University Press.

Ruble, D. N. (1987) The acquisition of self-knowledge: a self-socialization perspective. In N. Eisenberg (ed.), *Contemporary Topics in Developmental Psychology*. New York: Wiley.

Ruble, D. N. (1994) A phase model of transitions: cognitive and motivational consequences. *Advances in Experimental Social Psychology*, 26, 163–214.

Ruble, D. N. and Brooks-Gunn, J. (1982) The experience of menarche. *Child Development*, 53, 1557–66.

Ruble, D. N. and Flett, G. L. (1988) Conflicting goals in self-evaluative information seeking: developmental and ability level analyses. *Child Development*, 59, 97–106.

Ruble, D. N. and Frey, K. S. (1991) Changing patterns of comparative behavior as skills are acquired: a functional model of self-evaluation. In J. Suls and T. A. Wills (eds), *Social Comparison: contemporary theory and research*. Hillsdale, NJ: Erlbaum.

Ruble, D. N. and Thompson, E. P. (1992) The implications of research on social development for mental health: an internal socialization perspective. In D. N. Ruble, P. R. Costanzo, and M. E. Oliveri (eds), *The Social Psychology of Mental Health: basic mechanisms and applications*. New York: Guilford.

Ruble, D. N., Balaban, T., and Cooper, J. (1981) Gender constancy and the effects of sex-typed television toy commercials. *Child Development*, 52, 667–73.

Ruble, D. N., Boggiano, A. K., Feldman, N. S., and Loebl, J. H. (1980) A developmental analysis of the role of social comparison in self-evaluation. *Developmental Psychology*, 16, 105–15.

Ruble, D. N., Feldman, N. S., Higgins, E. T., and Karlovac, M. (1979) Locus of causality and use of information in the development of causal attributions. *Journal of Personality*, 47, 595–614.

Ruble, D. N., Fleming, A. S., Hackel, L. S., and Stangor, C. (1988) Changes in the marital relationship during the transition to first time motherhood: the effects of violated expectations concerning division of household labor. *Journal of Personality and Social Psychology*, 55, 78–87.

Ruble, T. L. (1983) Sex stereotypes: issues of change in the 1970s. *Sex Roles*, 9, 397–402.

Rudmin, F., Trimpop, R. M., Kryl, I.-P., and Boski, P. (1987) Gustav Ichheiser in the history of social psychology: an early phenomenology of social attribution. *British Journal of Social Psychology*, 26, 165–80.

Ruffy, M. (1981) Influence of social factors in the development of the young child's moral judgment. *European Journal of Social Psychology*, 11, 61–75.

Rule, B. G. (1974) The hostile and instrumental functions of human aggression. In W. W. Hartup and J. de Wit (eds), *Determinants and Origins of Aggressive Behaviors*. The Hague: Mouton.

Rule, B. G., Dyck, R., McAra, M., and Nesdale, A. R. (1974) Judgments of aggression serving personal versus prosocial purposes. *Social Behavior and Personality: an International Journal*, 3, 55–63.

Ruoppila, I. (1991) The significance of grandparents for the formation of family relations. In P. K. Smith (ed.), *The Psychology of Grandparenthood: an international perspective*. London: Routledge.

Rushton, J. P. (1975) Generosity in children: immediate and long-term effects of modeling, preaching, and moral judgment. *Journal of Personality and Social Psychology*, 31, 459–66.

Rushton, J. P. (1980) *Altruism, Socialization, and Society*. Englewood Cliffs, NJ: Prentice Hall.

Russell, A. and Finnie V. (1990) Preschool children's social status and maternal instructions to assist group entry. *Developmental Psychology*, 26, 603–11.

Russell, A. and Russell, G. (1994) Coparenting early school-age children: an examination of mother–father interdependence within families. *Developmental Psychology*, 30, 757–70.

Russell, G. (1983) *The Changing Role of Fathers?* St Lucia: University of Queensland Press.

Russell, G. (1987) Fatherhood in Australia. In M. E. Lamb (ed.), *The Father's Role: cross-cultural perspectives*. Hillsdale, NJ: Erlbaum.

Russell, G. (1989) Work/family patterns and couple relationships in shared caregiving families. *Social Behaviour*, 4, 265–83.

Russell, G., Savage, G., and Durkin, K. (in press) Balancing work and family: an emerging issue for private and public sector organisations. *Australian Journal of Social Issues*.

Russell, J. (1982) Propositional attitudes. In M. Beveridge (ed.), *Children Thinking through Language*. London: Edward Arnold.

Russell, J. A. (1989) Culture, scripts, and children's understanding of emotion. In C. Saarni and P. L. Harris (eds), *Children's Understanding of Emotion*. Cambridge: Cambridge University Press.

Russell, J. A. (1994) Is there universal recognition of emotion from facial expression? A review of cross-cultural studies. *Psychological Bulletin*, 115, 102–41.

Rutter, D. R. (1984) *Looking and Seeing: the role of visual communication in social interaction*. Chichester: Wiley.

Rutter, D. R. and Durkin, K. (1987) Turn-taking in mother–infant interaction: an examination of vocalizations and gaze. *Developmental Psychology*, 23, 54–61.

Rutter, D. R. and O'Brien, P. (1980) Social interaction in withdrawn and aggressive maladjusted girls: a study of gaze. *Journal of Child Psychology and Psychiatry*, 21, 59–66.

Rutter, M. (1981) *Maternal Deprivation Reassessed*, 2nd edn. Harmondsworth: Penguin.

Rutter, M. and Giller, H. (1983) *Juvenile Delinquency: trends and perspectives*. Harmonsdworth: Penguin.

Rutter, M. and Quinton, D. (1984) Long-term follow-up of women institutionalized in childhood: factors promoting good functioning in adult life. *British Journal of Developmental Psychology*, 2, 191–204.

Rutter, M., Graham, P., Chadwick, O. F., and Yule, W. (1976) Adolescent turmoil: fact or fiction? *Journal of Child Psychology and Psychiatry*, 17, 35–56.

Ryan, E. B. and Laurie, S. (1990) Evaluations of older and younger adult speakers: influence of communication effectiveness and noise. *Psychology and Aging*, 5, 514–19.

Ryan, E. B., Bourhis, R. Y., and Knops, U. (1991) Evaluative perceptions of patronizing speech addressed to elders. *Psychology and Aging*, 6, 442–50.

Ryan, E. B., Giles, H., Bartolucci, G., and Henwood, K. (1986) Psycholinguistic and social psychological components of communication by and with the elderly. *Language and Communication*, 6, 1–24.

Ryan, R. M. and Kuczowski, R. (1994) The imaginary audience, self-consciousness, and public individuation in adolescence. *Journal of Personality*, 62, 219–38.

Ryan, R. M. and Lynch, J. H. (1989) Emotional autonomy versus detachment: revisiting the vicissitudes of adolescence and young adulthood. *Child Development*, 60, 340–56.

Saarni, C. (1984) Observing children's use of display rules: age and sex differences. *Child Development*, 55, 1504–13.

Saarni, C. (1988) Children's understanding of the interpersonal consequences of dissemblance of nonverbal emotional-expressive behavior. *Journal of Nonverbal Behavior*, 12, 275–94.

Saarni, C. (1989) Children's understanding of strategic control of emotional expression in social transactions. In C. Saarni and P. L. Harris (eds), *Children's Understanding of Emotion*. Cambridge: Cambridge University Press.

Saarni, C. (1990) Emotional competence: how emotions and relationships become integrated. In R.

A. Thompson (ed.), *Socioemotional Development: Nebraska symposium on motivation, 1988*. Lincoln: University of Nebraska Press.

Saarni, C. and von Salisch, M. (1993) The socialization of emotional dissemblance. In M. Lewis and C. Saarni (eds), *Lying and Deception in Everyday Life*. New York: Guilford.

Sabatelli, R. and Pearce, J. (1986) Exploring marital expectations. *Journal of Social and Personal Relationships*, 1, 363–86.

Sabini, J. (1995) *Social Psychology*, 2nd edn. New York: Norton.

Sachs, J. and Devin, J. (1976) Young children's use of age-appropriate speech styles in social interaction and role-playing. *Journal of Child Language*, 3, 81–98.

Sadalla, E. K., Kenrick, D. T., and Vershure, B. (1987) Dominance and heterosexual attraction. *Journal of Personality and Social Psychology*, 52, 730–8.

Sagi, A. and Hoffman, M. L. (1976) Empathic distress in the newborn. *Developmental Psychology*, 12, 175–6.

Sagi, A. and Lewkowicz, K. S. (1987) A cross-cultural evaluation of attachment research. In L. W. C. Tavecchio and M. H. van IJzendoorn (eds), *Attachment in Social Networks: contributions to the Bowlby–Ainsworth attachment theory*. Amsterdam: North-Holland.

Sagi, A., van IJzendoorn, M. H. Azevier, O. Donnell, F., and Mayseless, O. (1994) Sleeping out of home in a Kibbutz communal arrangement: it makes a difference for infant–mother attachment. *Child Development*, 65, 992–1004.

Sagi, A., Lamb, M. E., Lewkowicz, K. S., Shoham, R., Dvir, R., and Estes, D. (1985) Security of mother–infant, father and metaplet attachments among kibbutz-reared Israeli children. In I. Bretherton and E. Waters (eds), *Growing Points of Attachment Theory and Research*. Monographs of the Society for Research in Child Development, 50 (1–2), no. 209.

Sakata, S. (1987) The development of referential communication. *Journal of Human Development*, 23, 31–41.

Salomon, G. and Globerson, T. (1989) When groups do not function the way they ought to. *International Journal of Educational Research*, 13, 89–99.

Salthouse, T. A. (1990) Working memory as a processing resource in cognitive aging. *Developmental Review*, 10, 101–24.

Sameroff, A. J. and Feil, L. A. (1985) Parental concepts of development. In I. E. Sigel (ed.), *Parental Belief Systems: the psychological consequences for children*. Hillsdale, NJ: Erlbaum.

Samuels, C. A. and Ewy, R. (1985) Aesthetic perception of faces during infancy. *British Journal of Developmental Psychology*, 3, 221–8.

Sanson, A. V., Prior, M., and Oberklaid, F. (1985) Normative data on temperament in Australian infants. *Australian Journal of Psychology*, 37, 185–95.

Sanson, A. V., Smart, D. F., Prior, M., Oberklaid, F., and Pedlow, R. (1994) The structure of temperament from age 3 to 7 years: age, sex, and sociodemographic factors. *Merrill-Palmer Quarterly*, 40, 233–52.

Santrock, J. W. (1975) Moral structure: the interrelations of moral behavior, moral judgment, and moral affect. *Journal of Genetic Psychology*, 127, 201–13.

Saraceno, C. (1980) *Il lavore mal diviso?* Bari: De Donato.

Sarchielli, G. (1984) Work entry: a critical moment in the occupational socialization process. In W. Doise and A. Palmonari (eds), *Social Interaction in Individual Development*. Cambridge: Cambridge University Press.

Sartre, J.-P. (1964) *Les mots*. Paris: Editions Gallimard. (Translated, 1964, as *Words*. London: Hamish Hamilton.)

Sastre, M. T. M. and Mullet, E. (1992) Occupational preferences of Spanish adolescents in relation to Gottfredson's theory. *Journal of Vocational Behavior*, 40, 306–17.

Savin-Williams, R. C. (1980) Social interactions of adolescent females in natural groups. In H. C. Foot, A. J. Chapman, and J. R. Smith (eds), *Friendship and Social Relations in Children*. Chichester: Wiley.

Savin-Williams, R. C. (1990) *Gay and Lesbian Youth: expressions of identity*. New York: Hemisphere.

Savin-Williams, R. C. and Berndt, T. J. (1990) Friendship and peer relations. In S. S. Feldman and G. R. Elliott (eds), *At the Threshold: the developing adolescent*. Cambridge, Mass.: Harvard University Press.

Saxe, G. B., Guberman, S. R., and Gearhart, M. (1987) *Social and Developmental Processes in Children's Understanding of Number*. Monographs of the Society for Research in Child Development, 52, no. 2.

Sayers, J. (1982) *Biological Politics: feminist and anti-feminist perspectives*. London: Tavistock.

Sayers, J. (1986) *Sexual Contradictions: psychology, psychoanalysis and feminism*. London: Tavistock.

Scarlett, H. H., Press, A. N., and Crockett, W. H. (1971) Children's descriptions of peers: a Wernerian developmental analysis. *Child Development*, 42, 439–53.

Scarr, S. (1988) How genotypes and environments combine: development and individual differences. In N. Bolger, A. Caspi, G. Downey, and M. Moorehouse (eds), *Persons in Context: developmental processes*. Cambridge: Cambridge University Press.

Scarr, S. (1992) Developmental theories for the 1990s: development and individual differences. *Child Development*, 63, 1–19.

Scarr, S. and McCartney, K. (1983) How people make their own environments: a theory of genotype–environment effects. *Child Development*, 54, 424–35.

Scarr, S., Caparulo, B. K., Ferdman, B. M., Tower, R. B., and Caplan, J. (1983) Developmental status and school achievements of minority and non-minority children from birth to 18 years in a British Midlands town. *British Journal of Developmental Psychology*, 1, 31–48.

Schacter, F. F. and Stone, R. K. (1985) Difficult sibling, easy sibling: temperament and the within-family environment. *Child Development*, 56, 1335–44.

Schacter, S. and Singer, J. (1962) Cognitive, social, and physiological determinants of emotional state. *Psychological Review*, 65, 379–99.

Schaefer, E. S. and Edgerton, M. (1985) Parent and child correlates of parental modernity. In I. E. Sigel (ed.), *Parental Belief Systems: the psychological consequences for children*. Hillsdale, NJ: Erlbaum.

Schaerlaekens, A. (1973) *The Two-word Sentence in Child Language Development*. The Hague: Mouton.

Schaffer, H. R. (1971) *The Growth of Sociability*. Harmondsworth: Penguin.

Schaffer, H. R. (1977) *Mothering*. London: Fontana.

Schaffer, H. R. (1984a) Parental control techniques in the context of socialization theory. In W. Doise and A. Palmonari (eds), *Social Interaction in Individual Development*. Cambridge: Cambridge University Press.

Schaffer, H. R. (1984b) *The Child's Entry into a Social World*. New York: Academic Press.

Schaffer, H. R. (1989a) Early social development. In A. Slater and G. Bremner (eds), *Infant Development*. Hillsdale, NJ: Erlbaum.

Schaffer, H. R. (1989b) Language development in context. In S. von Tetzchner, L. S. Siegel, and L. Smith (eds), *The Social and Cognitive Aspects of Normal and Atypical Language Development*. New York: Springer-Verlag.

Schaffer, H. R. (1990) *Making Decisions about Children: psychological questions and answers*. Oxford: Blackwell.

Schaffer, H. R. (1992) Joint involvement episodes as context for development. In H. McGurk (ed.), *Childhood Social Development: contemporary perspectives*. Hove: Erlbaum.

Schaffer, H. R. and Emerson, P. E. (1964) *The Development of Social Attachments in Infancy*. Monographs of the Society for Research on Child Development, no. 29.

Schaffer, H. R., Collis, G. M., and Parsons, G. (1977) Vocal interchange and visual regard in verbal and pre-verbal children. In H. R. Schaffer (ed.), *Studies in Mother–infant Interaction*. London: Academic Press.

Schaffer, H. R., Hepburn, A., and Collis, G. M. (1983) Verbal and nonverbal aspects of mothers' directives. *Journal of Child Language*, 10, 337–55.

Schaie, K. W. (1983) The Seattle Longitudinal Study: a twenty-one year exploration of psychometric intelligence in adulthood. In K. W. Schaie (ed.), *Longitudinal Studies of Adult Psychological Development*. New York: Guilford.

Schaie, K. W. and Hertzog, C. (1983) Fourteen-year cohort-sequential analyses of adult intellectual development. *Developmental Psychology*, 19, 531–43.

Scheper-Hughes, N. (1990) Mother love and child death in Northeast Brazil. In J. W. Stigler, R. A. Shweder, and G. Herdt (eds), *Cultural Psychology: essays on comparative human development*. Cambridge: Cambridge University Press.

Scherer, K. R. and Ekman, P. (1982) *Handbook of Methods in Nonverbal Behavior Research*. Cambridge: Cambridge University Press.

Schieffelin, B. B. (1990) *The Give and Take of Everyday Life: language socialization of Kaluli children*. Cambridge: Cambridge University Press.

Schiffmann, R. and Wicklund, R. A. (1992) The Minimal Group Paradigm and its minimal psychology. *Theory and Psychology*, 2, 29–50.

Schmidt, D. F. and Boland, S. M. (1986) Structure of perceptions of older adults: evidence for multiple stereotypes. *Psychology and Aging*, 1, 255–60.

Schneider, B., Hieshima, J. A., Lee, S., and Plank, S. (1994) East-Asian academic success in the United States: family, school, and community explanations. In P. M. Greenfield and R. R. Cocking (eds), *Cross-cultural Roots of Minority Child Development*. Hillsdale, NJ: Erlbaum.

Schneider, B. H., Attili, G., Nadel, J., and Weissberg, R. P. (1989) Preface. In B. H. Schneider, G. Attili, J. Nadel, and R. P. Weissberg (eds), *Social Competence in Developmental Perspective*. Dordrecht: Kluwer.

Schneider, K. and Josephs, I. (1991) The expressive and communicative functions of preschool children's smiles in an achievement-situation. *Journal of Nonverbal Behavior*, 15, 185–98.

Schneider, K. and Unzner, L. (1992) Preschoolers' attention and emotion in an achievement and an effect game: a longitudinal study. *Cognition and Emotion*, 6, 37–63.

Schnur, E. and Shatz, M. (1984) The role of maternal gesturing in conversations with one-year-olds. *Journal of Child Language*, 11, 29–42.

Schober-Peterson, D. and Johnson, C. J. (1991) Nondialogue speech during preschool interactions. *Journal of Child Language*, 18, 153–70.

Schober-Peterson, D. and Johnson, C. J. (1993) The performance of eight- to ten-year-olds on measures of conversational skilfulness. *First Language*, 13, 249–69.

Schroeder, K. A., Blood, L. L., and Maluso, D. (1992) An intergenerational analysis of expectations for women's career and family roles. *Sex Roles*, 26, 273–91.

Schunk, D. H. (1983) Ability versus effort attributional feedback: differential effects on self-efficacy and achievement. *Journal of Educational Psychology*, 75, 848–56.

Schunk, D. H., Hanson, A. R., and Cox, P. D. (1987) Peer model attributes and children's achievement behaviors. *Journal of Educational Psychology*, 79, 54–61.

Schwalb, D. W., Imaizumi, N., and Nakazawa, J. (1987) The modern Japanese father: roles and problems in a changing society. In M. E. Lamb (ed.), *The Father's Role: cross-cultural perspectives*. Hillsdale, NJ: Erlbaum.

Schwartz, F. N. (1989) Management women and the new facts of life. *Harvard Business Review*, 89, 65–76.

Schwartz, L. A. and Markham, W. T. (1985) Sex stereotyping in children's toy advertisements. *Sex Roles*, 12, 157–70.

Sears, D. O. (1986) College sophomores in the laboratory: influences of a narrow data base on social psychology's view of human nature. *Journal of Personality and Social Psychology*, 51, 515–30.

Sears, R. B. (1965) Development of gender role. In F. A. Beach (ed.), *Sex and Behavior*. New York: Wiley.

Sears, R. R., Rau, L., and Alpert, R. (1966) *Identification and Child Rearing*. London: Tavistock.

Seginer, R. (1988) Social milieu and future orientation: the case of kibbutz vs. urban adolescents. *International Journal of Behavioral Development*, 11, 247–73.

Seginer, R. (1991) Cross-cultural variations of adolescents' future orientation: the case of Israeli Druze versus Israeli Arab and Jewish males. *Journal of Cross-cultural Psychology*, 22, 224–37.

Seginer, R., Trommsdorff, G., and Essau, C. (1993) Adolescent control beliefs: cross-cultural variations of primary and secondary orientations. *International Journal of Behavioral Development*, 16, 243–60.

Seiffge-Krenke, I. (1985) Die funktion des Tagebuches bei der bewaltigung alterstpischer probleme in der adoleszenz. In R. Oerter (ed.), *Lebensbewaltigung im jugendalter*. Weinheim: Verlagsgesellschaft VCH.

Seitz, V. and Apfel, N. H. (1994) Parent-focused intervention: diffusion effects on siblings. *Child Development*, 65, 677–83.

Seitz, V., Rosenbaum, L. K., and Apfel, N. H. (1985) Effects of family support intervention: a ten-year follow-up. *Child Development*, 56, 376–91.

Seligman, M. E. P. (1975) *Helplessness: on depression, development, and death*. San Francisco: W. H. Freeman.

Seligman, M. E. P., Kamen, L. P., and Nolen-Hoeksema, S. (1988) Explanatory style across the life span: achievement and health. In E. M. Hetherington, R. M. Lerner, and M. Perlmutter (eds), *Child Development in Life-span Perspective*. Hillsdale, NJ: Erlbaum.

Selleri, P., Carugati, F., and Scappini, E. (1995) What marks should I give? A model of the organizaton of teachers' judgements of their pupils. *European Journal of Psychology of Education*, 10, 25–40.

Selman, R. L. (1976) Social-cognitive understanding: a guide to educational and clinical practice. In T. Lickona (ed.), *Moral Development and Behavior: theory, research, and social issues*. New York: Holt.

Selman, R. L. (1980) *The Growth of Interpersonal Understanding*. New York: Academic Press.

Selman, R. L., Lavin, D. R., and Brion-Meisels, S. (1982) Troubled children's use of self-reflection. In F. C. Serafica (ed.), *Social-cognitive Development in Context*. London: Methuen.

Semin, G. (1987) On the relationship between representation of theories in psychology and ordinary language. In W. Doise and S. Moscovici (eds), *Current Issues in European Social Psychology*, vol. 2. Cambridge: Cambridge University Press.

Semin, G. R. and Papadopoulou, K. (1990) The acquisition of reflexive social emotions: the transmission and reproduction of social control through joint action. In G. Duveen and B. Lloyd (eds), *Social Representations and the Development of Knowledge*. Cambridge: Cambridge University Press.

Semmer, N. K., Dwyer, J. H., Lippert, P., Fuchs, R., Clearly, P. D., and Schindler, A. (1987) Adolescent smoking from a functional perspective: the Berlin–Bremen study. *European Journal of Psychology of Education*, 1, 387–402.

Serafica, F. C. (1982) Conceptions of friendship and interaction between friends: an organismic-developmental perspective. In F. C. Serafica (ed.), *Social-cognitive Development in Context*. London: Methuen.

Service, V., Lock, A., and Chandler, P. (1989) Individual differences in early communicative development: a social constructivist perspective. In S. von Tetzchner, L. S. Siegel, and L. Smith (eds), *The Social and Cognitive Aspects of Normal and Atypical Language Development*. New York: Springer-Verlag.

Severy, L., Forsyth, D. R., and Wagner, P. J. (1979) A multimethod assessment of personal space development in female and male, black and white children. *Journal of Nonverbal Behavior*, 4, 68–86.

Shaffer, D. (1974) Suicide in childhood and early adolescence. *Journal of Child Psychology and Psychiatry*, 15, 275–92.

Shaffer, D. (1986) Developmental factors in child and adolescent suicide. In M. Rutter, C. E. Izard, and P. B. Read (eds), *Depression in Young People: developmental and clinical perspectives*. New York: Guilford Press.

Shaffer, D. (1993) *Developmental Psychology: childhood and adolescence*, 3rd edn. Pacific Grove, Calif.: Brooks/Cole.

Shaffer, D., Pettigrew, A., Wolkind, S., and Zaijeck, E. (1978) Psychiatric aspects of pregnancy in school girls: a review. *Psychological Medicine*, 8, 119–30.

Shaie, K. W. (1990) The optimization of cognitive functioning in old age: predictions based on cohort-sequential and longitudinal data. In P. B. Baltes and M. M. Baltes (eds), *Successful Aging: perspectives from the behavioral sciences*. Cambridge: Cambridge University Press.

Shantz, C. U. (1983) Communication. In J. H. Flavell and E. M. Markman (eds), *Handbook of Child Psychology*, vol. 3: *Cognitive development*. New York: Wiley.

Shantz, C. U. and Hobart, C. J. (1989) Social conflict and development: peers and siblings. In T. J. Berndt and G. W. Ladd (eds), *Peer Relationships in Child Development*. New York: Wiley.

Shantz, D. W. (1986) Conflict, aggression and peer status: an observational study. *Child Development*, 57, 1322–32.

Shantz, D. W. and Voydanoff, D. A. (1973) Situational effects on retaliatory aggression at three age levels. *Child Development*, 44, 149–53.

Sharabany, R. and Bar-Tal, D. (1982) Theories of the development of altruism: review, comparison and integration. *International Journal of Behavioral Development*, 5, 49–80.

Shatz, M. (1981) Learning the rules of the game: four views of the relation between social interaction and syntax acquisition. In W. Deutsch (ed.), *The Child's Construction of Language*. London: Academic Press.

Shatz, M. (1994). *A Toddler's Life: becoming a person*. New York: Oxford University Press.

Shatz, M. and Ebeling, K. (1991) Patterns of language learning-related behaviours: evidence for self-help in acquiring grammars. *Journal of Child Language*, 18, 295–313.

Shatz, M. and Gelman, R. (1973) *The Development of Communication Skills: Modifications in the Speech of Young Children as a Function of the Listener*. Monographs of the Society for Research in Child Development, no. 38.

Shatz, M. and McCloskey, L. (1984) Answering appropriately: a developmental perspective on conversational knowledge. In S. A Kuczaj (ed.), *Discourse Development: progress in cognitive development research*. New York: Springer-Verlag.

Shatz, M., Wellman, H. M., and Silber, S. (1983) The acquisition of mental verbs: a systematic investigation of the first reference to mental state. *Cognition*, 14, 301–21.

Shaver, P., Hazan, C., and Bradshaw, D. (1988) Love as attachment: the integration of three behavioral systems. In R. J. Sternberg and M. Barnes (eds), *The Anatomy of Love*. New Haven, Conn.: Yale University Press.

Shavit, Y. and Williams, R. A. (1985) Ability grouping and contextual determinants of educational expectations in Israel. *American Sociological Review*, 50, 62–73.

Shaw, J. M. and Scott, W. A. (1991) Influence of parent discipline style on delinquent behaviour: the mediating role of control orientation. *Australian Journal of Psychology*, 43, 61–7.

Shea, J. A. (1984) Adolescent sexuality. In R. M. Lerner and B. L. Galambos (eds), *Experiencing Adolescents: a sourcebook for parents, teachers, and teens*. New York: Garland.

Shedler, J. and Block, J. (1990) Adolescent drug use and psychological health: a longitudinal inquiry. *American Psychologist*, 45, 612–30.

Sheeran, P., Abrams, D., Abraham, C., and Spears, R. (1993) Religiosity and adolescents' premarital sexual attitudes and behaviour: an empirical study of conceptual issues. *European Journal of Social Psychology*, 23, 39–52.

Shell, R. M. and Eisenberg, N. (1992) A developmental model of recipients' reactions to aid. *Psychological Bulletin*, 111, 413–33.

Shennum, W. A. and Bugental, D. B. (1982) The development of control over affective expression in nonverbal behavior. In R. S. Feldman (ed.), *Development of Nonverbal Behavior in Children*. New York: Springer-Verlag.

Shepovalova, A. (1930/1993) The everyday social environment of Tungus children in the Northern Baikal region. *Journal of Russian and East European Psychology*, 31, 19–36.

Sherif, C. W. (1984) Coordinating the sociological and psychological in adolescent interactions. In W. Doise and A. Palmonari (eds), *Social Interaction in Individual Development*. Cambridge: Cambridge University Press.

Sherif, M. (1935) A study of some factors in perception. *Archives of Psychology*, 27, no. 187.

Sherif, M. (1948) *An Outline of Social Psychology*. New York: Harper.

Sherif, M. and Sherif, C. (1956) *An Outline of Social Psychology*, rev. edn. New York: Harper.

Sherrod, L. R. (1991) Studying infants' lives: competency, context and variability. In F. S. Kessel, M. H. Bornstein, and A. J. Sameroff (eds), *Contemporary Constructions of the Child: essays in honor of William Kessen*. Hillsdale, NJ: Erlbaum.

Shortt, J. W., Bush, L. K., McCabe, J. L. R., Gottman, J. M., and Katz, L. F. (1994) Children's physiological responses while producing facial expressions of emotions. *Merrill-Palmer Quarterly*, 40, 40–59.

Shugar, G. W. (1993) The structures of peer participation in shared activity: frameworks for acquiring communicative knowledge. In J. Nadel and L. Camaioni (eds), *New Perspectives in Early Communicative Development*. London: Routledge.

Shultz, T. R. (1980) Development of the concept of intention. In W. A. Collins (ed.), *Minnesota Symposia on Child Development*, vol. 13. Hillsdale, NJ: Erlbaum.

Shultz, T. R. and Butkowsky, I. (1977) Young children's use of the scheme for multiple sufficient causes in the attribution of real and hypothetical behavior. *Child Development*, 48, 464–9.

Shultz, T. R., Butkowsky, I., Pearce, J. W., and Shanfield, H. (1975) Development of schemes for the attributions of multiple psychological causes. *Developmental Psychology*, 11, 502–10.

Shultz, T. R., Wells, D., and Sarda, M. (1980) Development of the ability to distinguish intended actions for mistakes, reflexes, and passive movements. *British Journal of Social and Clinical Psychology*, 19, 301–10.

Shure, M. B. (1982) Interpersonal problem solving: a cog in the wheel of social cognition. In F. C. Serafica (ed.), *Social-cognitive Development in Context*. London: Methuen.

Shure, M. B. and Spivack, G. (1978) *Problem Solving Techniques in Childrearing*. San Francisco: Jossey-Bass.

Shute, B. and Wheldall, K. (1995) The incidence of raised average pitch and increased pitch variability in British "motherese" speech and the influence of maternal occupation and discourse form. *First Language*, 15, 35–55.

Shweder, R. A. (1991) *Thinking through Cultures: expeditions in cultural psychology*. Cambridge, Mass.: Harvard University Press.

Siegal, M. (1982) *Fairness in Children: a social-cognitive approach to the study of moral development*. London: Academic Press.

Siegal, M. (1991) *Knowing Children: experiments in conversation and cognition*. Hove: Erlbaum.

Siegal, M. and Storey, R. (1985) Day care and children's conceptions of moral and social rules. *Child Development*, 56, 1001–8.

Sigel, I. E. (1985) A conceptual analysis of beliefs. In I. E. Sigel (ed.), *Parental Belief Systems: the psychological consequences for children*. Hillsdale, NJ: Erlbaum.

Sigel, I. E., McGillicudy-DeLisi, A. V., and Goodnow, J. J. (eds) (1992) *Parental Belief Systems: the psychological consequences for children*, vol. 2. Hillsdale, NJ: Erlbaum.

Sigel, I. E., McGillicuddy-DeLisi, A. V., and Johnson, J. E. (1980) *Parental Distancing, Beliefs and Children's Representational Competence within the Family Context*. Princeton, NJ: Educational Testing Service.

Signorella, M. L. (1987) Gender schemata: individual differences and context effects. In L. S. Liben and M. L. Signorella (eds), *Children's Gender Schemata*. San Francisco: Jossey-Bass.

Silbereisen, R. K. and Galambos, N. (1987) Introduction. *European Journal of Psychology of Education*, 2, 307–10.

Silbereisen, R. K. and Kastner, P. (1985) Jugend und Drogen. Entwicklung von Drogengebrauch – Drogenbrauch als Entwicklung? In R. Oerter (ed.), *Lebensbewaltigung im Jugenalter*. Weinheim: VCH.

Silbereisen, R. K. and Noack, P. (1988) On the constructive role of problem behavior in adolescence. In N. Bolger, A. Caspi, G. Downey and M. Moorehouse (eds), *Persons in Context: developmental processes*. Cambridge: Cambridge University Press.

Silverstein, B., Perdue, L., Peterson, B., and Kelly, E. (1986a) The role of the mass media in promoting a thin standard of bodily attractiveness for women. *Sex Roles*, 14, 519–30.

Silverstein, B., Peterson, B., and Perdue, L. (1986b) Some correlates of the thin standard of bodily attractiveness for women. *International Journal of Eating Disorders*, 5, 895–905.

Simmons, R. G. and Blyth, D. A. (1987) *Moving into Adolescence: the impact of pubertal change and school context*. New York: Aldine de Gruyter.

Simmons, R. G., Burgeson, R., Carlton-Ford, S., and Blyth, D. A. (1987) The impact of cumulative changes in early adolescence. *Child Development*, 58, 1220–34.

Simner, M. L. (1971) Newborns' response to the cry of another infant. *Developmental Psychology*, 5, 136–50.

Simpson, E. L. (1974) Moral development research: a case of scientific cultural bias. *Human Development*, 17, 81–106.

Simpson, J. A. (1990) Influence of attachment styles

on romantic relationships. *Journal of Personality and Social Psychology*, 59, 971–80.

Sinclair, J. J., Pettit, G. S., Harrist, A. W., Dodge, K. A., and Bates, J. E. (1994) Encounters with aggressive peers in early childhood: frequency, age differences, and correlates of risk for behavior problems. *International Journal of Behavioral Development*, 17, 675–96.

Sinclair-de-Zwart, H. (1967) *Acquisition du langage et développement de la pensée*. Paris: Dunod.

Sinclair-de-Zwart, H. (1969) Developmental psycholinguistics. In D. Elkind and J. Flavell (eds), *Studies in Cognitive Development*. Oxford: Oxford University Press.

Sinclair-de-Zwart, H. (1973) Language acquisition and cognitive development. In T. E. Moore (ed.), *Cognitive Development and the Acquisition of Language*. New York: Academic Press.

Singer, J. L. (1992) Private experience and public action: the study of ongoing conscious thought. In R. A. Zucker, A. I. Rabin, J. Aronoff, and S. J. Frank (eds), *Personality Structure in the Life Course: essays on personology in the Murray tradition*. New York: Springer.

Sirignano, S. W. and Lachman, M. E. (1985) Personality change during the transition to parenthood: the role of perceived infant temperament. *Developmental Psychology*, 21, 558–67.

Skinner, B. F. (1953) *Science and Human Behavior*. New York: Macmillan.

Skinner, B. F. (1957) *Verbal Behavior*. New York: Appleton–Century–Crofts.

Skinner, B. F. (1973) *Beyond Freedom and Dignity*. Harmondsworth: Penguin.

Skinner, E. A. (1985) Determinants of mother sensitive and contingent-responsive behavior: the role of childrearing beliefs and socioeconomic status. In I. E. Sigel (ed.), *Parental Belief Systems: the psychological consequences for children*. Hillsdale, NJ: Erlbaum.

Skinner, E. A. (1991) Development and perceived control: a dynamic model of action in context. In M. R. Gunnar and L. A. Sroufe (eds), *Self Processes and Development: Minnesota Symposia on Child Psychology*, vol. 23. Minneapolis: University of Minnesota Press.

Skinner, E. A., Chapman, M., and Baltes, P. B. (1988) Children's beliefs about control, means-ends, and agency: developmental differences during middle childhood. *International Journal of Behavioral Development*, 11, 369–88.

Slaby, R. G., and Frey, K. S. (1975) Development of gender constancy and selective attention to same-sex models. *Child Development*, 46, 849–56.

Slaby, R. G. and Parke, R. D. (1971) Effects on resistance to deviation of observing a model's affec-

tive reaction to response consequences. *Developmental Psychology*, 5, 40–7.

Slater, A. (1989) Visual memory and perception in early infancy. In A. Slater and G. Bremner (eds), *Infant Development*. Hillsdale, NJ: Erlbaum.

Slavin, R. E. (1990) *Cooperative Learning: theory, research, and practice*. Englewood Cliffs, NJ: Prentice Hall.

Slobin, D. I. (1985) *The Crosslinguistic Study of Language Acquisition*. Hillsdale, NJ: Erlbaum.

Smart, R. G., Adlaf, E. M., and Walsh, G. W. (1992) Adolescent drug sellers: trends, characteristics and profiles. *British Journal of Addiction*, 87, 1561–70.

Smetana, J. G. (1981) Preschool children's conceptions of moral and social rules. *Child Development*, 52, 1333–6.

Smetana, J. G. (1988) Adolescents' and parents' conceptions of parental authority. *Child Development*, 59, 321–35.

Smetana, J. G. (1989) Toddlers' social interactions in the context of moral and conventional transgressions in the home context. *Developmental Psychology*, 25, 499–508.

Smetana, J. G. (1993) Understanding of social rules. In M. Bennett (ed.), *The Child as Psychologist: an introduction to the development of social cognition*. New York: Harvester Wheatsheaf.

Smetana, J. G. and Asquith, P. (1994) Adolescents' and parents' conceptions of parental authority and personal autonomy. *Child Development*, 65, 1147–62.

Smetana, J. G. and Braeges, J. L. (1990) The development of toddlers' moral and conventional judgments. *Merrill-Palmer Quarterly*, 36, 329–46.

Smetana, J. G., Yau, J., Restrepo, A., and Braeges, J. L. (1991) Conflict and adaptation in adolescence: adolescent–parent conflict. In M. E. Colten and S. Gore (eds), *Adolescent Stress: causes and consequences*. New York: Aldine de Gruyter.

Smiley, P. and Huttenlocher, J. (1989) Young children's acquisition of emotion concepts. In C. Saarni and P. L. Harris (eds), *Children's Understanding of Emotion*. Cambridge: Cambridge University Press.

Smith, B. L., Brown-Sweeney, S., and Stoel-Gammon, C. (1989) A quantitative analysis of reduplicated and variegated babbling. *First Language*, 9, 175–90.

Smith, C. and Lloyd, B. B. (1978) Maternal behavior and perceived sex of infant. *Child Development*, 49, 1263–5.

Smith, C. and Nutbeam, D. (1992) Adolescent drug use in Wales. *British Journal of Addiction*, 87, 227–33.

Smith, C. B., Adamson, L. B., and Bakeman, R. (1988) Interactional predictors of early language. *First Language*, 8, 143–56.

Smith, J. (1991) Conceiving selves: a case study of

changing identities during the transition to motherhood. *Journal of Language and Social Psychology*, 10, 225–43.

Smith, M. C. (1975) Children's use of the multiple sufficient cause schema in social perception. *Journal of Personality and Social Psychology*, 32, 737–47.

Smith, M. C. (1978) Cognizing the behavior stream: the recognition of intentional action. *Child Development*, 49, 736–43.

Smith, M. S. (1987) Evolution and developmental psychology: toward a sociobiology of human development. In C. Crawford, M. Smith, and D. Krebs (eds), *Sociobiology and Psychology: ideas, issues and applications*. Hillsdale, NJ: Erlbaum.

Smith, P. B. and Bond, M. H. (1994) *Social Psychology across Cultures: analysis and perspectives*. Boston: Allyn and Bacon.

Smith, P. K. (1978) A longitudinal study of social participation in preschool children: solidarity and parallel play re-examined. *Developmental Psychology*, 14, 517–23.

Smith, P. K. (1990) Ethology, sociobiology and developmental psychology: in memory of Niko Tinbergen and Konrad Lorenz. *British Journal of Developmental Psychology*, 8, 187–200.

Smith, P. K. (1991) Introduction: the study of grandparenthood. In P. K. Smith (ed.), *The Psychology of Grandparenthood: an international perspective*. London: Routledge.

Smith, P. K. and Connolly, K. J. (1980) *The Ecology of Preschool Behavior*. Cambridge: Cambridge University Press.

Smith, P. K. and Cowie, H. (1992) *Understanding Children's Development*, 2nd edn. Oxford: Blackwell.

Smith, P. K. and Daglish, L. (1977) Sex differences in parent and infant behavior in the home. *Child Development*, 48, 1250–4.

Smith, P. K. and Noble, R. (1987) Factors affecting the development of caregiver–infant relationships. In L. W. C. Tavecchio and M. H. van IJzendoorn (eds), *Attachment in Social Networks: contributions to the Bowlby–Ainsworth attachment theory*. Amsterdam: North-Holland.

Smith, P. K. and Turner, J. (1981) The measurement of shared care and its effects in a sample of nonworking mothers with young children. *Current Psychological Research*, 1, 263–70.

Smith, P. K., Eaton, L., and Hindmarch, A. (1981) How one-year-olds respond to strangers: a two-person situation. *Journal of Genetic Psychology*, 140, 147–8.

Smith, T. E. (1993) Growth in academic achievement and teaching younger siblings. *Social Psychology Quarterly*, 56, 77–85.

Snarey, J. R. (1985) Cross-cultural universality of social-moral development: a critical review of Kohlbergian research. *Psychological Bulletin*, 97, 202–32.

Snow, C. E. (1972) Mother's speech to children learning language. *Child Development*, 43, 549–65.

Snow, C. E. (1986) Conversations with children. In P. Fletcher and M. Garman (eds), *Language Acquisition*, 2nd edn. Cambridge: Cambridge University Press.

Snow, C. E. (1989) Understanding social interaction and language acquisition: sentences are not enough. In M. Bornstein and J. S. Bruner (eds), *Interaction in Human Development*. Hillsdale, NJ: Erlbaum.

Snow, C. E. and Hoefnagel-Hohle, M. (1978) The critical period for language acquisition: evidence from second language learning. *Child Development*, 49, 1114–28.

Soken, N. H. and Pick, A. D. (1992) Intermodal perception of happy and angry expressive behaviors by seven-month-old infants. *Child Development*, 63, 787–95.

Solano, C. H. (1986) People without friends: loneliness and its alternatives. In V. J. Derlega and B. A. Winstead (eds), *Friendship and Social Interaction*. New York: Springer-Verlag.

Solkoff, N., Todd, G. A., and Screven, C. G. (1964) Effects of frustration on perceptual-motor performance. *Child Development*, 35, 569–75.

Sommer, K., Whitman, T. L., Borkowski, J. G., Schellenbach, C., Maxwell, S., and Keogh, D. (1993) Cognitive readiness and adolescent parenting. *Developmental Psychology*, 29, 389–98.

Somner, R. (1969) *Personal Space: the behavioural basis of design*. Englewood Cliffs, NJ: Prentice Hall.

Song, M. Y., Smetana, J. G., and Kim, S. Y. (1987) Korean children's conceptions of moral and conventional transgressions. *Developmental Psychology*, 23, 577–82.

Sonnenschein, S. (1986) Development of referential communication: deciding that a message is uninformative. *Developmental Psychology*, 22, 164–8.

Sonnenschein, S. and Whitehurst, G. J. (1984) Developing referential communication skills: the interaction of role-switching and difference rule training. *Journal of Experimental Child Psychology*, 38, 191–207.

Soppe, H. J. G. (1991) Children's personality judgements of dominant and submissive teachers. *European Journal of Psychology of Education*, 6, 65–71.

Sorce, J., Emde, R., Campos, J., and Klinnert, M. (1985) Maternal emotional signalling: its effect on the visual cliff behavior of 1-year-olds. *Developmental Psychology*, 21, 195–200.

Sorensen, R. (1983) *Adolescent Sexuality in Contemporary Society*. New York: World Books.

Spangler, G. (1990) Mother, child, and situational correlates of toddlers' social competence. *Infant Behavior and Development*, 13, 405–19.

Sparks, P. and Durkin, K. (1987) Moral reasoning and political orientation: the context sensitivity of individual rights and democratic principles. *Journal of Personality and Social Psychology*, 52, 931–6.

Speicher, B. (1994) Family patterns of moral judgment during adolescence and early adulthood. *Developmental Psychology*, 30, 624–32.

Spence, J. T. and Helmreich, R. L. (1978) *Masculinity and Femininity: their psychological dimensions, correlates, and antecedents*. Austin, Tex.: University of Texas Press.

Spence, S. H. (1987) The relationship between social-cognitive skills and peer sociometric status. *British Journal of Developmental Psychology*, 5, 347–56.

Spencer, M. B. and Dornbusch, S. M. (1990) Challenges in studying minority youth. In S. S. Feldman and G. R. Elliott (eds), *At the Threshold: the developing adolescent*. Cambridge, Mass.: Harvard University Press.

Spitz, R. A. (1949) The role of ecological factors in emotional development. *Child Development*, 20, 145–55.

Spitz, R. A. and Wolf, K. M. (1946) The smiling response: a contribution to the ontogenesis of social relations. *Genetic Psychology Monographs*, 34, 57–125.

Spivack, G. and Shure, M. B. (1974) *Social Adjustment of Young Children*. San Francisco: Jossey-Bass.

Spivak, G., Marcus, J., and Swift, M. (1986) Early classroom behaviors and later misconduct. *Developmental Psychology*, 22, 124–31.

Sprecher, S. and Felmke, D. (1992) The influence of parents and friends on the quality and stability of romantic relationships: a three-wave longitudinal investigation. *Journal of Marriage and the Family*, 54, 888–900.

Sprecher, S., Sullivan, Q., and Hatfield, E. (1994) Mate selection preferences: gender differences examined in a national sample. *Journal of Personality and Social Psychology*, 66, 1074–80.

Spurgeon, P., Hicks, C., and Terry, R. (1983) A preliminary investigation into sex differences in reported friendship determinants amongst a group of early adolescents. *British Journal of Social Psychology*, 22, 63–4.

Sroufe, L. A. (1977) Wariness of strangers and the study of infant development. *Child Development*, 48, 731–46.

Sroufe, L. A. (1979) Socioemotional development. In J. Osofsky (ed.), *Handbook of Infant Development*. New York: Wiley.

Sroufe, L. A. (1985) Attachment classification from the perspective of infant–caregiver relationships and temperament. *Child Development*, 56, 1–14.

Sroufe, L. A. and Fleeson, J. (1986) Attachment and the construction of relationships. In W. W. Hartup and Z. Rubin (eds), *Relationships and Development*. Hillsdale, NJ: Erlbaum.

Sroufe, L. A. and Waters, E. (1976) The ontogenesis of smiling and laughter: a perspective on the organization of development in infancy. *Psychological Review*, 83, 173–89.

Sroufe, L. A., Bennett, C., Englund, M., and Urban, J. (1993) The significance of gender boundaries in preadolescence: contemporary correlates and antecedents of boundary violation and maintenance. *Child Development*, 64, 455–66.

Sroufe, L. A., Fox, N. E., and Pancake, V. R. (1983) Attachment and dependency in developmental perspective. *Child Development*, 54, 1615–27.

Staats, A. W. (1968) *Learning, Language and Cognition*. London: Holt, Rinehart and Winston.

Stacy, A. W., Sussman, S., Dent, C. W., Burton, D., and Flay, B. R. (1992) Moderators of peer social influence in adolescent smoking. *Personality and Social Psychology Bulletin*, 18, 163–72.

Stangor, C. and Ruble, D. N. (1987) Development of gender role knowledge and gender constancy. In L. S. Liben and M. L. Signorella (eds), *Children's Gender Schemata*. San Francisco: Jossey-Bass.

Stangor, C. and Ruble, D. N. (1989) Differential influences of gender schemata and gender constancy on children's information processing and behavior. *Social Cognition*, 7, 354–72.

Stanton, W. R., Oei, T. P. S. and Silva, P. A. (1994) Sociodemographic characteristics of adolescent smokers. *International Journal of the Addictions*, 29, 931–25.

Stark, R. E. (1989) Temporal patterning of cry and non-cry sounds in the first eight months of life. *First Language*, 9, 107–36.

Starrels, M. E. (1994) Husbands' involvement in female gender-typed household chores. *Sex Roles*, 31, 473–91.

Stattin, H. and Magnusson, D. (1989) Social transition in adolescence: a biosocial perspective. In A. de Ribaupierre (ed.), *Transition Mechanisms in Child Development: the longitudinal perspective*. Cambridge: Cambridge University Press.

Staub, E. (1970) A child in distress: the influence of age and number of witnesses on children's attempts to help. *Developmental Psychology*, 14, 130–40.

Staub, E. (1978) *Positive Social Behavior and Morality*, vol. 1. New York: Academic Press.

Staub, E. and Sherk, L. (1970) Need for approval,

children's sharing behaviors and reciprocity in sharing. *Child Development*, 41, 243–52.

Stein, N. and Trabasso, T. (1989) Children's understanding of changing emotional states. In C. Saarni and P. L. Harris (eds), *Children's Understanding of Emotion*. Cambridge: Cambridge University Press.

Steinberg, L. (1990) Autonomy, conflict, and harmony in the family relationship. In S. S. Feldman and G. R. Elliot (eds), *At the Threshold: the developing adolescent*. Cambridge, Mass.: Harvard University Press.

Steinberg, L. (1993) *Adolescence*, 3rd edn. New York: McGraw-Hill.

Steinberg, L. and Hill, J. (1978) Patterns of family interaction as a function of age, the onset of puberty, and formal thinking. *Developmental Psychology*, 14, 683–4.

Steinberg, L. and Silverberg, S. B. (1986) The vicissitudes of autonomy in early adolescence. *Child Development*, 57, 841–51.

Steinberg, L., Elmen, J., and Mounts, N. (1989) Authoritative parenting, psychosocial maturity, and academic success among adolescents. *Child Development*, 60, 1424–36.

Steinberg, L., Fegley, S., and Dornbusch, S. M. (1993) Negative impact of part-time work on adolescent adjustment: evidence from a longitudinal study. *Developmental Psychology*, 29, 171–80.

Steinberg, L., Greenberger, E., Garduque, L., Ruggiero, M., and Vaux, A. (1982) Effects of working on adolescent development. *Developmental Psychology*, 18, 385–95.

Stephan, C. W. and Langlois, J. H. (1984) Baby beautiful: adult attributions of infant competence as a function of infant attractiveness. *Child Development*, 55, 576–85.

Stephan, W. G. (1977) Stereotyping: the role of ingroup–outgroup differences in causal attribution. *Journal of Social Psychology*, 101, 255–66.

Stern, C. and Stern, W. (1928) *Die Kindersprache: eine psychologische und sprachtheoretische Untersuchung*, 4th edn. Leipzig: Barth.

Stern, D. N. (1971). A micro-analysis of mother–infant interaction: behavior regulating social contact between a mother and her 3½ month-old twins. *Journal of the American Academy of Child Psychiatry*, 10, 501–17.

Stern, D. N. (1985) *The Interpersonal World of the Infant*. New York: Basic Books.

Stern, D. N., Beebe, B., Jaffe, J., and Bennett, S. (1977) The infant's stimulus world during social interaction. In H. R. Schaffer (ed.), *Studies in Mother–infant Interaction*. London: Academic Press.

Stern, M. and Karraker, K. H. (1989) Sex stereotyping of infants: a review of gender labeling studies. *Sex Roles*, 20, 501–22.

Sternberg, R. J. and Beall, A. E. (1991) How can we know what love is? An epistemological analysis. In G. J. O. Fletcher and F. D. Fincham (eds), *Cognition in Close Relationships*. Hillsdale, NJ: Erlbaum.

Sternglanz, S. H. and Nash, A. (1988) Ethological contributions to the study of human motherhood. In B. Birns and D. F. Hay (eds), *The Different Faces of Motherhood*. New York: Plenum Press.

Stevenson, H. W. (1991) The development of prosocial behavior in large-scale collective societies: China and Japan. In R. A. Hinde and J. Groebel (eds), *Cooperation and Prosocial Behaviour*. Cambridge: Cambridge University Press.

Stevenson, H. W. and Lee, S.-Y. (1990) *Contexts of Achievement*. Monographs of the Society for Research in Child Development, 55 (1–2), no. 221

Stevenson, M. R. and Black, K. N. (1988) Paternal absence and sex role development: a meta-analysis. *Child Development*, 59, 793–814.

Stevenson, R. (1988) *Models of Language Development*. Milton Keynes: Open University Press.

Stewart, L. and Pascual-Leone, J. (1992) Mental capacity constraints and the development of moral reasoning. *Journal of Experimental Child Psychology*, 54, 251–87.

Stewart, R. B. (1983) Sibling interaction: the role of the older child as teacher for the younger. *Merrill-Palmer Quarterly*, 29, 47–68.

Stewart, R. B., Mobley, L. A., van Tuyl, S. S., and Salvador, M. A. (1987) The firstborn's adjustment to the birth of a sibling: a longitudinal assessment. *Child Development*, 58, 341–55.

Stifter, C. A. and Fox, N. A. (1987) Preschool children's ability to identify and label emotions. *Journal of Nonverbal Behavior*, 11, 43–54.

Stipek, D. J. (1984) Young children's performance expectations: logical analysis or wishful thinking? In J. Nicholls (ed.), *The Development of Achievement Motivation*. Greenwich, Conn.: JAI Press.

Stipek, D. J. and DeCotis, K. M. (1988) Children's understanding of the implications of causal attributions for emotional experiences. *Child Development*, 59, 1601–10.

Stipek, D. J. and Hoffman, J. M. (1980) Children's achievement related expectancies as a function of academic performance histories and sex. *Journal of Educational Psychology*, 72, 861–5.

Stipek, D. J., Milburn, S., Clements, D., and Daniels, D. H. (1992a) Parents' beliefs about appropriate education for young children. *Journal of Applied Developmental Psychology*, 13, 293–310.

Stipek, D. J., Recchia, S., and McClintic, S. (1992b)

Self-evaluation in Young Children. Monographs of the Society for Research in Child Development, 57 (1), no. 226.

St James-Roberts, I. and Halil, T. (1991) Infant crying patterns in the first year: normal community and clinical findings. *Journal of Child Psychology and Psychiatry*, 32, 951–68.

Stocker, C. and Dunn, J. (1990) Sibling relationships in childhood: links with friendships and peer relationships. *British Journal of Developmental Psychology*, 8, 227–44.

Straughan, R. (1986) Why act on Kohlberg's moral judgments? (Or how to reach Stage 6 and remain a bastard). In S. Modgil and C. Modgil (eds), *Lawrence Kohlberg: consensus and controversy*. Philadelphia: Falmer Press.

Straus, M. A., Geller, R. J. and Steinmetz, S. K. (1980) *Behind Closed Doors: violence in the American family*. New York: Anchor Press.

Strayer, F. F. (1980) Child ethology and the study of preschool social relations. In H. C. Foot, A. J. Chapman, and J. R. Smith (eds), *Friendship and Social Relations in Children*. Chichester: Wiley.

Strayer, F. F. (1992) The development of agonistic and affiliative structures in preschool play groups. In J. Silverberg and J. P. Gray (eds), *Aggression and Peacefulness in Humans and Other Primates*. New York: Oxford University Press.

Strayer, F. F., Moss, E., and Blicharski, T. (1989) Biosocial bases of representational activity during early childhood. In L. T. Winegar (ed.), *Social Interaction and the Development of Children's Understanding*. Norwood, NJ: Ablex.

Strayer, J. S. (1989) What children know and feel in response to witnessing affective events. In C. Saarni and P. L. Harris (eds), *Children's Understanding of Emotion*. Cambridge: Cambridge University Press.

Street, R. L. and Cappella, J. N. (1989) Social and linguistic factors influencing adaptation in children's speech. *Journal of Psycholinguistic Research*, 18, 497–519.

Stroebe, W. and Stroebe, M. S. (1984) When love dies: an integration of attraction and bereavement research. In H. Tajfel (ed.), *The Social Dimension*, vol. 1. Cambridge: Cambridge University Press.

Stroebe, W. and Stroebe, M. S. (1986) Beyond marriage: the impact of partner loss on health. In R. Gilmour and S. Duck (eds), *The Emerging Field of Personal Relationships*. Hillsdale, NJ: Erlbaum.

Stroebe, W. and Stroebe, M. S. (1987) *Bereavement and Health: the psychological and physical consequences of partner loss*. Cambridge: Cambridge University Press.

Strommen, E. F. (1989) "You're a what?": family member reactions to the disclosure of homosexuality. *Journal of Homosexuality*, 18, 37–58.

Stromquist, V. J. and Strauman, T. J. (1991) Children's social constructs: nature, assessment, and association with adaptive versus maladaptive behavior. *Social Cognition*, 4, 330–58.

Suess, G. J., Grossmann, K. E., and Sroufe, L. A. (1992) Effects of attachment to mother and father on quality of adaptation in preschool: from dyadic to individual organisation of self. *International Journal of Behavioral Development*, 15, 43–65.

Sullivan, E. V. (1977) A study of Kohlberg's structural theory of moral development: a critique of liberal science ideology. *Human Development*, 20, 352–76.

Sullivan, M. W. and Lewis, M. (1988) Facial expressions during learning in 1-year-old infants. *Infant Behavior and Development*, 11, 369–73.

Sullivan, T. and Schneider, M. (1987) Development and identity issues in adolescent homosexuality. *Child and Adolescent Social Work*, 4, 13–24.

Suls, J. (1986) Social comparison processes in relative deprivation: a life-span analysis. In J. M. Olson, C. P. Herman and M. P. Zanna (eds), *Relative Deprivation and Social Comparison: the Ontario symposium*, vol. 4. Hillsdale, NJ: Erlbaum.

Summerville, M. B., Kaslow, N. J., Abbate, M. F., and Cronan, S. (1994) Psychopathology, family functioning, and cognitive style in urban adolescents with suicide attempts. *Journal of Abnormal Child Psychology*, 22, 221–35.

Super, C. M. and Harkness, S. (1982) The development of affect in infancy and early childhood. In D. A. Wagner and H. W. Stevenson (eds), *Cultural Perspectives on Child Development*. Oxford: W. H. Freeman.

Super, D. E. (1980) A lifespan, life space, approach to career development. *Journal of Vocational Behavior*, 13, 282–98.

Super, D. E. (1985) Coming of age in Middletown: careers in the making. *American Psychologist*, 40, 405–14.

Susman, E. J., Inoff-Germain, G., Nottelmann, E. D., Loriaux, D. L., Cutler, G. B., Jr, and Chrousos, G. P. (1987) Hormones, emotional dispositions, and aggressive attributes in young adolescents. *Child Development*, 58, 1114–34.

Sutton-Smith, B. (1988) War toys and aggression. *Play and Culture*, 12, 57–69.

Svejda, M. J., Pannabecker, B. J., and Emde, R. N. (1982) Parent-to-infant attachment: a critique of the early "bonding" model. In R. N. Emde and R. J. Harmon (eds), *The Development of Attachment and Affiliative Systems*. New York: Plenum Press.

Swain, I. U., Zelazo, P. R., and Clifton, R. K. (1993) Newborn infants' memory for speech sounds retained over 24 hours. *Developmental Psychology*, 29, 312–23.

Sylvester-Bradley, B. (1981) Negativity in early infant–adult exchanges and its developmental significance. In W. P. Robinson (ed.), *Communication in Development*. London: Academic Press.

Sylvester-Bradley, B. (1986) Failure to distinguish between people and things in early infancy. *British Journal of Developmental Psychology*, 3, 281–92.

Tager-Flusberg, H. and Calkins, S. (1990) Does imitation facilitate the acquisition of grammar? Evidence from a study of autistic, Down's syndrome and normal children. *Journal of Child Language*, 17, 591–606.

Tajfel, H. (1979) Human intergroup conflict: useful and less useful forms of analysis. In M. von Cranach, K. Foppa, W. Lepenies, and D. Ploog (eds), *Human Ethology: claims and limits of a new discipline*. Cambridge: Cambridge University Press.

Tajfel, H. (1981) *Human Groups and Social Categories: studies in social psychology*. Cambridge: Cambridge University Press.

Tajfel, H. (1984) Intergroup relations, social myths and social justice in social psychology. In H. Tajfel (ed.), *The Social Dimension*, vol. 2. Cambridge: Cambridge University Press.

Tajfel, H. and Jahoda, G. (1966) Development in children of concepts and attitudes about their own and other nations: a cross-national study. *Proceedings of the XVIIIth International Congress of Psychology*, 36, 17–33.

Tajfel, H. and Turner, J. C. (1979) An integrative theory of intergroup conflict. In W. G. Austin and S. Worchel (eds), *The Social Psychology of Intergroup Relations*. Monterey, Calif.: Brooks-Cole.

Takahashi, K. (1986) Examining the Strange Situation procedure with Japanese mothers and 12-month old infants. *Developmental Psychology*, 22, 265–70.

Tal, J. and Bornstein, M. H. (1991) Infant vocal distress: conceptual structure, responsiveness, and sampling in mother and independent observer. In B. M. Lester, J. D. Newman and F. Pederen (eds), *Social and Biological Aspects of Infant Crying*. New York: Plenum Press.

Tapper, N. (1991) *Bartered Brides: politics, gender and marriage in an Afghan tribal society*. Cambridge: Cambridge University Press.

Taylor, P. (1994) Will Afrikaans go the way of apartheid? *The Washington Post*, January 9.

Teachman, J. D., Call, V. A., and Carver, K. P. (1994) Marital status and the duration of joblessness among white men. *Journal of Marriage and the Family*, 56, 415–28.

Terborg, J. R. (1977) Women in management: a research review. *Journal of Applied Psychology*, 62, 647–64.

Terry, D. (1992) Transition to parenthood. In P. C. L. Heaven (ed.), *Life Span Development*. Sydney and London: Harcourt Brace Jovanovich.

Terwogt, M. M., Schene, J., and Koops, W. (1990) Concepts of emotions in institutionalized children. *Journal of Child Psychology and Psychiatry*, 31, 1131–43.

Tessier, R., Piché, C., Tarabulsy, G. M., and Muckle, G. (1992) Mothers' experience of stress following the birth of a first child: identification of stressors and coping resources. *Journal of Applied Social Psychology*, 22, 1319–39.

Teti, D. M. and Ablard, K. E. (1989) Security of attachment and infant–sibling relationships: a laboratory study. *Child Development*, 60, 1519–28.

Thakerar, J. T., Giles, H., and Cheshire, J. (1982) Psychological and linguistic parameters of speech accommodation theory. In C. Fraser and K. R. Scherer (eds), *Advances in the Social Psychology of Language*. Cambridge: Cambridge University Press.

Thibaut, J. W. and Kelley, H. H. (1959) *The Social Psychology of Groups*. New York: Wiley.

Thoma, S. J. (1986) Estimating gender differences in the comprehension and preference of moral issues. *Developmental Review*, 6, 165–80.

Thoma, S. J. (1993) The relationship between political preference and moral judgment development in late adolescence. *Merrill-Palmer Quarterly*, 39, 359–74.

Thomas, A. and Chess, S. (1977) *Temperament and Development*. New York: Brunner/Mazel.

Thomas, A. and Chess, S. (1989) Temperament and personality. In G. A. Kohnstamm, J. E. Bates, and M. K. Rothbart (eds), *Temperament and Personality*. Chichester: Wiley.

Thomas, A., Chess, S., and Birch, H. G. (1968) *Temperament and Behavior Disorders in Children*. New York: New York University Press.

Thomas, J. C. (1986) Gender differences in satisfaction with grandparenting. *Psychology and Aging*, 1, 215–19.

Thomas, R. M. (1992) *Comparing Theories of Child Development*, 3rd edn. Belmont, Calif.: Wadsworth.

Thompson, E. H. and Pleck, J. H. (1987) The structure of male role norms. In M. S. Kimmel (ed.), *Changing Men: new directions in research on men and masculinity*. Newbury Park, Calif.: Sage.

Thompson, L. and Walker, A. J. (1989) Gender in families. *Journal of Marriage and the Family*, 51, 845–71.

Thompson, R. A. (1987) Empathy and emotional understanding: the early development of empathy. In N. Eisenberg and J. Strayer (eds), *Empathy and its*

Development. Cambridge: Cambridge University Press.

Thompson, R. A. (1990) Emotion and self-regulation. In R. A. Thompson (ed.), *Socioemotional Development: Nebraska symposium on motivation, 1988*. Lincoln: University of Nebraska Press.

Thompson, R. A. (1994) Emotion regulation: a theme in search of definition. In N. A. Fox (ed.), *The Development of Emotion Regulation: biological and behavioral considerations*. Monographs of the Society for Research in Child Development, 59 (2–3), no. 240.

Thompson, S. K. (1975) Gender labels and early sex role development. *Child Development*, 46, 339–47.

Thornhill, R. and Thornhill, N. W. (1992) The evolutionary psychology of men's coercive sexuality. *Behavioral and Brain Sciences*, 15, 363–421.

Thornton, D. and Thornton, S. (1983) Structure, content, and the direction of development in Kohlberg's theory. In H. Weinreich-Haste and D. Locke (eds), *Morality in the Making: thought, action and the social context*. New York: Wiley.

Tieger, T. (1980) On the biological basis of sex differences in aggression. *Child Development*, 51, 943–63.

Tietjen, A. M. (1985) Relationships between the social networks of Swedish mothers and their children. *International Journal of Behavioral Development*, 8, 195–216.

Tietjen, A. M. (1989) The ecology of children's social support networks. In D. Belle (ed.), *Children's Social Networks and Social Supports*. New York: Wiley.

Tietjen, A. M. (1994) Supportive interactions in cultural context. In F. Nestemann and K. Hurrelmann (eds), *Social Networks and Social Support in Childhood and Adolescence*. Berlin: de Gruyter.

Tinbergen, N. (1953) *Social Behaviour of Animals*. London: Methuen.

Tinbergen, N. (1973) *The Animal in its World: explorations of an ethologist 1932–1972*. Cambridge, Mass.: Harvard University Press.

Tisak, M. S. (1993) Preschool children's judgments of moral and personal events involving physical harm and property damage. *Merrill-Palmer Quarterly*, 39, 375–90.

Tisak, M. S. and Turiel, E. (1988) Variation in seriousness of transgressions and children's moral and conventional concepts. *Developmental Psychology*, 24, 352–7.

Tishler, C. T., McHenry, P. C., and Morgan, K. C. (1981) Adolescent suicide attempts: some significant factors. *Suicide and Life-threatening Behavior*, 15, 77–90.

Tizard, B. and Hughes, M. (1984) *Young Children Learning: talking and thinking at home and at school*. London: Fontana.

Tizard, B. and Rees, J. (1974) A comparison of the effects of adoption, restoration to the natural mother, and continued institutionalization on the cognitive development of four-year-old children. *Child Development*, 45, 92–9.

Tizard, B. and Rees, J. (1975) The effect of early institutional rearing on the behaviour problems and affectional relationships of four-year-old children. *Journal of Child Psychology and Psychiatry*, 16, 61–73.

Tobin, J. J., Wu, D. Y. H., and Davidson, D. H. (1989) *Preschool in Three Cultures: Japan, China, and the United States*. New Haven: Yale University Press.

Tobin-Richards, M. H., Boxer, A. M., Kavrell, S. A. M., and Petersen, A. C. (1984) Puberty and its psychological and social significance. In R. M. Lerner and B. L. Galambos (eds), *Experiencing Adolescents: a sourcebook for parents, teachers, and teens*. New York: Garland.

Tomasello, M. and Farrar, J. (1986) Joint attention and early language. *Child Development*, 57, 1454–63.

Tomasello, M. and Todd, J. (1983) Joint attention and lexical acquisition style. *First Language*, 4, 197–212.

Tomasello, M., Anselmi, D., and Farrar, M. J. (1985) Young children's coordination of gestural and linguistic reference. *First Language*, 5, 199–210.

Tomkins, S. (1962) *Affect, Imagery, Consciousness*, vol. 1: *The positive affects*. New York: Springer.

Tomkins, S. (1963) *Affect, Imagery, Consciousness*, vol. 2: *The negative affects*. New York: Springer.

Tomlin, A. M. and Passman, R. H. (1989) Grandmothers' responsibility in raising two-year-olds facilitates their grandchildren's adaptive behavior: a preliminary intrafamilial investigation of mothers' and maternal grandmothers' effects. *Psychology and Aging*, 4, 119–21.

Torney-Purta, J. (1990) Youth in relation to social institutions. In S. S. Feldman and G. R. Elliott (eds), *At the Threshold: the developing adolescent*. Cambridge, Mass.: Harvard University Press.

Torres-Gil, M. (1992) *The New Ageing: politics and change in America*. New York: Auburn House.

Tout, K. (1989) *Ageing in Developing Countries*. Oxford: Oxford University Press.

Tracy, P. E. (1987) Race and class differences in official and reported delinquency. In M. E. Wolfgang, T. P. Thornberry, and R. M. Figlio (1987) *From Boy to Man, from Delinquency to Crime*. Chicago: University of Chicago Press.

Traeen, B., Lewin, B., and Sundet, J. M. (1992) The real and the ideal; gender differences in heterosexual behaviour among Norwegian adolescents. *Journal of Community and Social Psychology*, 2, 227–37.

Trause, M. A. (1977) Stranger responses: effects of familiarity, stranger's approach, and sex of infant. *Child Development*, 48, 1657–61.

Trehub, S., Unyk, A. M., and Henderson, J. L. (1994) Children's songs to infant siblings: parallels with speech. *Journal of Child Language*, 21, 735–44.

Tremblay, R. E., Vitaro, F., Gagnon, C., Piché, C., and Royer, N. (1992) A prosocial scale for the Preschool Behaviour Questionnaire: concurrent and predictive correlates. *International Journal of Behavioral Development*, 15, 227–45.

Trevarthen, C. (1977) Descriptive analyses of infant communicative behaviour. In H. R. Schaffer (ed.), *Studies in Mother–infant Interaction*. London: Academic Press.

Trevarthen, C. (1979) Communication and cooperation in early infancy: a description of primary intersubjectivity. In M. Bullowa (ed.), *Before Speech: the beginnings of interpersonal communication*. Cambridge: Cambridge University Press.

Trevarthen, C. (1982) The primary motives for cooperative understanding. In G. Butterworth and P. Light (eds), *Social Cognition: studies of the development of understanding*. Chicago: University of Chicago Press.

Trevarthen, C. (1993) The function of emotions in early infant communication and development. In J. Nadel and L. Camaioni (eds), *New Perspectives in Early Communicative Development*. London: Routledge.

Trevarthen, C. and Hubley, P. (1978) Secondary intersubjectivity: confidence, confiding, and acts of meaning in the first year. In A. Lock (ed.), *Action, Gesture and Symbol: the emergence of language*. London: Academic Press.

Triandis, H. C. (1991) Cross-cultural differences in assertiveness/competition vs. group loyalty/cooperation. In R. A. Hinde and J. Groebel (eds), *Cooperation and Prosocial Behaviour*. Cambridge: Cambridge University Press.

Triandis, H. C. (1994) *Culture and Social Behavior*. New York: McGraw-Hill.

Triandis, H. C., Bontempos, R., Villareal, M., Asai, M., and Lucca, N. (1988) Individualism–collectivism: cross-cultural perspectives on self–ingroup relationships. *Journal of Personality and Social Psychology*, 54, 323–38.

Trivers, R. (1971) The evolution of reciprocal altruism. *Quarterly Review of Biology*, 46, 35–57.

Trivers, R. L. (1972) Parental investment and sexual selection. In B. Campbell (ed.), *Sexual Selection and the Descent of Man*. Chicago: Aldine.

Trivers, R. (1985) *Social Evolution*. Menlo Park, Calif.: Benjamin/Cummings.

Troll, L. E. (1989) Myths of midlife intergenerational relationships. In S. Hunter and M. Sudnel (eds), *Midlife Myths: issues, findings and practice implications*. Newbury Park, Calif.: Sage.

Trommsdorff, G. (1983) Future orientation and socialization. *International Journal of Psychology*, 18, 381–406.

Trommsdorff, G. (1986) Future time orientation and its relevance for development as action. In R. K. Silbereisen, K. Eyforth, and G. Rudinger (eds), *Development as Action in Context: problem behavior in normal youth development*. Berlin: Springer-Verlag.

Tronick, E. Z., Als, H., and Adamson, L. (1979) Structure of early face-to-face communicative intent. In M. Bullowa (ed.), *Before Speech: the beginnings of human communication*. Cambridge: Cambridge University Press.

Trudgill, P. (1975) *Accent, Dialect and the School*. London: Edward Arnold.

Tudge, J. and Rogoff, B. (1989) Peer influences on cognitive development: Piagetian and Vygotskian perspectives. In M. H. Bornstein and J. S. Bruner (eds), *Interaction in Human Development*. Hillsdale, NJ: Erlbaum.

Turiel, E. (1983) *The Development of Social Knowledge: morality and convention*. Cambridge: Cambridge University Press.

Turiel, E. (1989a) Domain-specific social judgments and domain ambiguities. *Merrill-Palmer Quarterly*, 35, 89–114.

Turiel, E. (1989b) The social construction of social construction. In W. Damon (ed.), *Child Development Today and Tomorrow*. San Francisco: Jossey-Bass.

Turiel, E. and Wainryb, C. (1994) Social reasoning and the varieties of social experiences in cultural contexts. *Advances in Child Development and Behavior*, 25, 289–326.

Turnbull, C. (1989) *The Mountain People*. London: Paladin.

Turner, B. F. (1992) Gender differences in old age in ratings of aggression/assertiveness. *Current Psychology: Research and Reviews*, 11, 122–7.

Turner, C. W. and Dodd, D. K. (1980) The development of antisocial behavior. In R. L. Ault (ed.), *Developmental Perspectives*. Santa Monica, Calif.: Goodyear.

Turner, J. C. (1984) Social identification and psychological group formation. In H. Tajfel (ed.), *The Social Dimension*, vol. 2. Cambridge: Cambridge University Press.

Turner, J. C. (1991) *Social Influence*. Milton Keynes: Open University Press.

Turner, J. C., Hogg, M. A., Oakes, P. J., Reicher, S. D., and Wetherell, M. (1987) *Rediscovering the Social Group: a self-categorization theory*. Oxford: Blackwell.

Turner, P. J. (1993) Attachment to mother and behaviour with adults in preschool. *British Journal of Developmental Psychology*, 11, 75–89.

Tyack, D. and Ingram, D. (1977) Children's production and comprehension of questions. *Journal of Child Language*, 4, 211–24.

Tyler, A. (1982) *Dinner at the Homesick Restaurant*. New York: Knopf.

Tyszkowa, M. (1991) The role of grandparents in the development of grandchildren as perceived by adolescents and young adults in Poland. In P. K. Smith (ed.), *The Psychology of Grandparenthood: an international perspective*. London: Routledge.

Tzuriel, D. and Klein, M. M. (1977) Ego identity: effects of ethnocentrism, ethnic identification and cognitive complexity in Israeli, Oriental, and Western ethnic groups. *Psychological Reports*, 40, 1099–101.

Uchtenhagen, A. and Zimmler-Hofler, D. (1985) *Heroinabhangige und ihre «normalen» Altersgenossen*. Bern: Haupt.

Uchtenhagen, A. and Zimmer-Hofler, D. (1987) Psychosocial development following therapeutic and legal interventions in opiate dependence: a Swiss national study. *European Journal of Psychology of Education*, 2, 443–58.

Ullah, P. (1990) The association between income, financial strain and psychological well-being among unemployed youths. *Journal of Occupational Psychology*, 63, 317–30.

Ullah, P. and Brotherton, C. (1989) Sex, social class and ethnic differences in the expectations of unemployment and psychological well-being of secondary school pupils in England. *British Journal of Educational Psychology*, 59, 49–58.

Underwood, B. and Moore, B. (1982) Perspective-taking and altruism. *Psychological Bulletin*, 12, 111–16.

Unger, R. and Crawford, M. (1992) *Women and Gender: a feminist psychology*. New York: McGraw-Hill.

Unzner, L. and Schneider, K. (1990) Facial reactions in preschoolers: a descriptive study. *Journal of Nonverbal Behavior*, 14, 19–31.

Ushrum, M. M., Paistout, S., and Argon, V. F. (1993) "If you'll believe this . . . ": effects of psilocybin use on student compliance. *International Journal of Addiction Studies*, 77, 234–52.

Utriainen, S. (1989) Adolescent pregnancy: standards and service in Finland. *Child Welfare*, 67, 167–84.

Uzgiris, I. C. (1981) Two functions of imitation during infancy. *International Journal of Behavioral Development*, 4, 1–12.

Uzgiris, I. C. (1989) Infants in relation: performers, pupils, and partners. In W. Damon (ed.), *Child Development Today and Tomorrow*. San Francisco: Jossey-Bass.

Uzgiris, I. C. and Hunt, J. McV. (1970) Attentional preference and experience: an exploratory longitudinal study of the effect of familiarity and responsiveness. *Journal of Genetic Psychology*, 117, 109–21.

Vaidyanathan, P. and Naidoo, J. (1990) Asian Indians in Western countries: cultural identity and the arranged marriage. In N. Bleichrodt and P. J. D. Drenth (eds), *Contemporary Issues in Cross-cultural Psychology*. Amsterdam/Lisse: Swets and Zeitlinger.

Vaillant, G. E. (1977) *Adaptation to Life: how the best and brightest came of age*. Boston: Little, Brown.

Valiant, G., Glachan, M., and Emler, N. (1982) The stimulation of cognitive development through cooperative task performance. *British Journal of Educational Psychology*, 52, 281–8.

Valsiner, J. (1989a) *Human Development and Culture: the social nature of personality and its study*. Lexington, Mass.: Lexington Books.

Valsiner, J. (1989b) On the glory and misery of sociobiological perspectives on human development: a selfish book review. *Developmental Psychobiology*, 22, 413–17.

Vandell, D. L. (1980) Sociability with peer and mother during the first year. *Developmental Psychology*, 16, 355–61.

Vandell, D. L. and Mueller, E. C. (1980) Peer play and friendships during the first two years. In H. C. Foot, A. J. Chapman, and J. R. Smith (eds), *Friendship and Social Relations in Children*. Chichester: Wiley.

Vandell, D. L. and Wilson, K. S. (1987) Infants' interactions with mother, sibling, and peer: contrasts and relations between interaction systems. *Child Development*, 58, 176–86.

Vandell, D. L., Henderson, V. K., and Wilson, K. S. (1988) A longitudinal study of children with daycare experiences of varying quality. *Child Development*, 59, 1286–92.

Vandell, D. L., Wilson, K. S., and Buchanan, N. R. (1980) Peer interaction in the first year of life: an examination of its structure, content, and sensitivity to toys. *Child Development*, 51, 481–8.

Vasudev, J. (1988) Sex differences in morality and moral orientation: a discussion of the Gilligan and Attanucci study. *Merrill-Palmer Quarterly*, 34, 239–44.

Vaughan, G. M. (1963) Concept formation and the development of ethnic awareness. *Journal of Genetic Psychology*, 103, 93–103.

Vaughan, G. M. (1964a) Ethnic awareness in relation to minority group membership. *Journal of Genetic Psychology*, 105, 119–30.

Vaughan, G. M. (1964b) The development of ethnic

attitudes in New Zealand school children. *Genetic Psychology Monographs*, 70, 135–75.

Vaughan, G. M. (1987) A social psychological model of ethnic identity development. In J. S. Phinney and M. J. Rotheram (eds), *Children's Ethnic Socialization: pluralism and development*. Newbury Park, Calif.: Sage.

Vaughn, B. E., Egeland, B. R., Sroufe, L. A., and Waters, E. (1979) Individual differences in infant–mother attachment at twelve and eighteen months: stability and change in families under stress. *Child Development*, 50, 971–5.

Vaughn, B. E., Gove, F. L., and Egeland, B. R. (1980) The relationship between out-of-home care and the quality of infant–mother attachment in an economically disadvantaged population. *Child Development*, 51, 1203–14.

de Veer, A. J. E. and Janssens, J. M. A. M. (1992) Victim-oriented discipline and the child's orientation of norms. In J. M. A. M. Janssens and J. R. M. Gerris (eds), *Childrearing: influence on prosocial and moral development*. Amsterdam: Swets and Zeitlinger.

van der Veer, R. and Valsiner, J. (1991) *Understanding Vygotsky: a quest for synthesis*. Oxford: Blackwell.

Verba, M. and Musatti, T. (1989) Minor phenomena and major processes of interaction with objects and peers in day care centres. *European Journal of Psychology of Education*, 4, 215–27.

Verba, M. and Winnykamen, F. (1992) Expert–novice interactions: influence of partner status. *European Journal of Psychology of Education*, 7, 61–71.

Vergeer, M. M. (1987) Interactions in the family, attachment and the birth of a sibling: a quantitative approach. In L. W. C. Tavecchio and M. H. van IJzendoorn (eds), *Attachment in Social Networks: contributions to the Bowlby–Ainsworth attachment theory*. Amsterdam: North-Holland.

Verges, P. (1987) A social and cognitive approach to economic representations. In W. Doise and S. Moscovici (eds), *Current Issues in European Social Psychology*, vol. 2. Cambridge: Cambridge University Press.

Veroff, J. (1969) Social comparison and the development of achievement motivation. In C. P. Smith (ed.), *Achievement-related Motives in Children*. New York: Russell Sage.

Verstraaten, D. (1980) Levels of realism in adolescent future time perspective. *Human Development*, 23, 177–91.

Vicary, J. R. (1984) Adolescent drug and alcohol use and abuse. In R. M. Lerner and B. L. Galambos (eds), *Experiencing Adolescents: a sourcebook for parents, teachers, and teens*. New York: Garland.

Vicary, J. R. and Lerner, J. V. (1986) Parental attributes and adolescent drug use. *Journal of Adolescence*, 9, 115–22.

de Villiers, J. G. and de Villiers, P. A. (1973) A cross-sectional study of the acquisition of grammatic morphemes in child speech. *Journal of Psycholinguistic Research*, 2, 267–78.

Vine, I. (1983) Sociobiology and social psychology – rivalry or symbiosis? The explanation of altruism. *British Journal of Social Psychology*, 22, 1–11.

Vitaro, F., Gagnon, C., and Tremblay, R. E. (1990) Predicting stable peer rejection from kindergarten to Grade One. *Journal of Clinical Child Psychology*, 19, 257–64.

de Volder, M. L. and Lens, W. (1982) Academic achievement and future time perspective as a cognitive-motivational concept. *Journal of Personality and Social Psychology*, 42, 566–71.

Volkmar, F. R. and Siegel, A. E. (1982) Responses to consistent and discrepant social communications. In R. S. Feldman (ed.), *Development of Nonverbal Behavior in Children*. New York: Springer-Verlag.

de Vries, H. and Kok, G. (1986) From determinants of smoking behavior to the implications for a prevention programme. *Health Education Research*, 1, 85–94.

de Vries, H., Dijkstra, M., and Kulhman, P. (1988) Self-efficacy: the third factor besides attitude and subjective norm as a predictor of behavioural intentions. *Health Education Research*, 3, 273–82.

Vuorenkoski, V., Wasz-Hockert, O., Koivisto, E., and Lind, J. (1969) The effect of cry stimulus on the temperature of the lactating breast of primipara: a thermographic study. *Experientia*, 25, 1286–7.

Vygotsky, L. S. (1962) *Thought and Language*. Cambridge, Mass.: MIT Press.

Vygotsky, L. S. (1978) *Mind in Society: the development of higher psychological processes*. Cambridge, Mass.: Harvard University Press.

Vygotsky, L. S. (1981) The genesis of higher mental functions. In J. V. Wertsch (ed.), *The Concept of Activity in Soviet Psychology*. Armonk, NY: Sharpe.

Waas, G. A. (1988) Social attributional biases of peer-rejected and aggressive children. *Child Development*, 59, 969–75.

Walden, T. (1991) Infant social referencing. In J. Garber and K. A. Dodge (eds), *The Development of Emotion Regulation and Dysregulation*. Cambridge: Cambridge University Press.

Walden, T. and Ogan, T. (1988) The development of social referencing. *Child Development*, 59, 1230–40.

Waldron, I., Lye, D., and Brandon, A. (1991) Gender differences in teenage smoking. *Women and Health*, 17, 65–90.

Walker, L. J. (1984) Sex differences in the development

of moral reasoning: a critical review. *Child Development*, 55, 677–91.

Walker, L. J. and Taylor, J. H. (1991) Family interactions and the development of moral reasoning. *Child Development*, 62, 264–83.

Walker, L. J., de Vries, B., and Trevethan, S. D. (1987) Moral stages and moral orientations in real-life and hypothetical dilemmas. *Child Development*, 58, 842–58.

Walker-Andrews, A. S. (1986) Intermodal perception of expressive behaviors: relation of eye and voices? *Developmental Psychology*, 22, 373–7.

Walkerdine, V. (1986) Post-structuralist theory and everyday social practices: the family and the school. In S. Wilkinson (ed.), *Feminist Social Psychology: developing theory and practice*. Milton Keynes: Open University Press.

Wallace, C. (1989) Social reproduction and school leavers: a longitudinal perspective. In K. Hurrelmann and U. Engel (eds), *The Social World of Adolescents: international perspectives*. Berlin and New York: de Gruyter.

Wallace, W. A. (1993) *Theories of Personality*. Boston: Allyn and Bacon.

Wallon, H. (1942) *De l'acte à la pensée*. Paris: Flammarion.

Wallon, H. (1949) *Les origines du caractère chez l'enfant*, 2nd edn. Paris: Presses Universitaires de France.

Walster, E., Aronson, V., Abrahams, D., and Rottman, L. (1966) Importance of physical attractiveness in dating behavior. *Journal of Personality and Social Psychology*, 4, 508–16.

Walters, G. C. and Grusec, J. E. (1977) *Punishment*. San Francisco: W. H. Freeman.

Wanska, S. K. and Bedrosian, J. L. (1985) Conversational structure and topic performance in mother–child interaction. *Journal of Speech and Hearing Research*, 28, 579–84.

Ward, C. (1981) Prejudice against women: who, when, and why? *Sex Roles*, 7, 163–71.

Ward, J. V. (1988) Urban adolescents' conceptions of violence. In C. Gilligan, J. V. Ward, J. M. Taylor with B. Bardige (eds), *Mapping the Moral Domain: a contribution to women's thinking to psychological theory and education*. Cambridge, Mass.: Harvard University Press.

Warr, P. B., Banks, M. H., and Ullah, P. (1985) The experience of unemployment among black and white urban teenagers. *British Journal of Psychology*, 76, 75–87.

Warren, M. P. (1983) Physical and biological aspects of puberty. In J. Brooks-Gunn and A. C. Petersen (eds), *Girls at Puberty*. New York: Plenum Press.

Warren, S. F., Rogers-Warren, A., and Baer, D. M.

(1976) The role of offer rate in controlling sharing by young children. *Journal of Applied Behavior Analysis*, 9, 491–7.

Wartner, U. G., Grossman, K., Fremmer-Bombik, E., and Suess, G. (1994) Attachment patterns at age six in South Germany: predictability from infancy and implications for preschool behavior. *Child Development*, 65, 1014–27.

Wasz-Hockert, O., Michelsson, K., and Lind, J. (1985) Twenty-five years of Scandinavian cry research. In B. M. Lester and C. F. Z. Boukydis (eds), *Infant Crying: theoretical and research perspectives*. New York: Plenum Press.

Waterman, A. S. (1982) Identity development from adolescence to adulthood: an extension of theory and review of research. *Developmental Psychology*, 18, 341–8.

Waters, E. (1978) The reliability and stability of individual differences in infant–mother attachment. *Child Development*, 49, 483–94.

Waters, E., Wippman, J., and Sroufe, L. A. (1979) Attachment, positive affect, and competence in the peer group: two studies in construct validation. *Child Development*, 50, 821–9.

Watson, J. B. (1924) *Behaviorism*. New York: Norton.

Watson, J. B. (1928) *Psychological Care of Infant and Child*. New York: Norton.

Watson, J. S. (1972) Smiling, cooing, and "the game." *Merrill-Palmer Quarterly*, 18, 323–39.

Watson, J. S. (1985) Contingency perception in early social development. In T. M. Field and N. A. Fox (eds), *Social Perception in Infants*. Norwood, NJ: Ablex.

Weber, R. A., Levitt, M. J., and Clark, M. C. (1986) Individual variation in attachment security and strange situation behavior: the role of maternal and infant temperament. *Child Development*, 57, 56–65.

Webley, P. and Burke, M. (1984) Children's understanding of motives for deception. *European Journal of Social Psychology*, 14, 455–8.

Weiner, B. (1972) *Theories of Motivation: from mechanism to cognition*. Chicago: Rand McNally.

Weiner, B. (1979) A theory of motivation for some classroom experiences. *Journal of Educational Psychology*, 71, 3–25.

Weiner, B. (1985) "Spontaneous" causal thinking. *Psychological Bulletin*, 97, 74–84.

Weiner, B. (1986) *An Attributional Theory of Motivation and Emotion*. New York: Springer-Verlag.

Weiner, B., Frieze, I. H., Kukla, A., Reed, L., Rest, S., and Rosenbaum, R. M. (1971) *Perceiving the Causes of Success and Failure*. New York: General Learning Press.

Weiner, B., Russell, D., and Lerman, D. (1978)

Affective consequences of causal ascriptions. In J. H. Harvey, W. J. Ickes, and R. F. Kidd (eds), *New Directions in Attribution Research*, vol. 2. Hillsdale, NJ: Erlbaum.

Weiner, I. B. (1980) Psychopathology in adolescence. In J. Adelson (ed.), *Handbook of Adolescent Psychology*. New York: Wiley.

Weinraub, M. and Putney, E. (1978) The effects of height on infants' social responses to unfamiliar persons. *Child Development*, 49, 598–603.

Weinreich, P. (1983) Emerging from threatened identities. In G. Breakwell (ed.), *Threatened Identities*. Chichester: Wiley.

Weinreich-Haste, H. (1979) What sex is science? In O. Hartnett, G. Boden, and M. Fuller (eds), *Women: sex-role stereotyping*. London: Tavistock.

Weinreich-Haste, H. (1981) The image of science. In A. Kelly (ed.), *The Missing Half: girls and science education*. Manchester: Manchester University Press.

Weinreich-Haste, H. (1984) Cynical boys, determined girls? Success and failure anxiety in British adolescents. *British Journal of Social Psychology*, 23, 257–63.

Weisfeld, G. E. and Billings, R. L. (1988) Observations on adolescence. In K. B. MacDonald (ed.), *Sociobiological Perspectives on Human Development*. New York: Springer-Verlag.

Weisfeld, G. E., Muczenski, D. M., Weisfeld, C. C., and Omakr, D. R. (1987) Stability of boys' social success among peers over an eleven-year period. In J. A. Meacham (ed.), *Interpersonal Relations: family, peers, friends*. Basel: Karger.

Weisner, T. S. and Gallimore, R. (1977) My brother's keeper: child and sibling caregiving. *Current Anthropology*, 18, 169–90.

Weiss, B., Dodge, K. A., Bates, J. E., and Pettit, G. S. (1992) Some consequences of early harsh discipline: child aggression and a maladaptive social information processing style. *Child Development*, 63, 1321–35.

Weisz, J. R. (1980) Developmental change in perceived control: recognizing contingency in the laboratory and perceiving it in the world. *Developmental Psychology*, 16, 385–90.

Welch, R. L., Huston-Stein, A., Wright, J. C., and Plehal, R. (1979) Subtle sex-role cues in children's commercials. *Journal of Communication*, 29, 202–9.

Wellman, H. M. (1990) *The Child's Theory of Mind*. Cambridge, Mass.: MIT Press.

Wells, C. G. and Robinson, W. P. (1984) The role of adult speech in language development. In C. Fraser and K. R. Scherer (eds), *Advances in the Social Psychology of Language*. Cambridge: Cambridge University Press.

Wells, G. (1985) *Language Development in the Pre-school Years*. Cambridge: Cambridge University Press.

Wells, G. (1986) Variation in child language. In P. Fletcher and M. Garman (eds), *Language Acquisition*, 2nd edn. Cambridge: Cambridge University Press.

Werebe, M. J. G. and Baudonnière, P. M. (1988) Friendship among preschool children. *International Journal of Behavioral Development*, 11, 291–304.

van der Werff, J. J. (1985) Individual problems of self-definition: an overview, and a view. *International Journal of Behavioral Development*, 8, 445–71.

Werker, J. F., Pegg, J. E., and McLeod, P. J. (1994) A cross-language investigation of infant preference for infant-directed communication. *Infant Behavior and Development*, 17, 323–33.

Werner, E. (1991) Grandparent–grandchild relationships amongst US ethnic groups. In P. K. Smith (ed.), *The Psychology of Grandparenthood: an international perspective*. London: Routledge.

Werner, H. (1948) *Comparative Psychology of Mental Development*. New York: Science Editions.

Wertsch, J. V. (ed.) (1985) *Culture, Communication, and Cognition: Vygotskyan perspectives*. Cambridge: Cambridge University Press.

Wertsch, J. V. and Tulviste, P. (1992) L. S. Vygotsky and contemporary developmental psychology. *Developmental Psychology*, 28, 548–57.

Wertsch, J. V., McNamee, G. D., McLane, J. B., and Budwig, N. A. (1980) The adult–child dyad as a problem-solving system. *Child Development*, 51, 1215–21.

West, D. J. and Farrington, D. P. (1973) *Who Becomes Delinquent?* London: Heinemann.

West, D. J. and Farrington, D. P. (1977) *The Delinquent Way of Life*. London: Heinemann.

West, M. (1987) Student drug use in Bermuda. *European Journal of Psychology of Education*, 2, 327–36.

West, M. A. and Newton, P. (1984) Social interaction in adolescent development: schools, sex roles and entry to work. In W. Doise and A. Palmonari (eds), *Social Interaction in Individual Development*. Cambridge: Cambridge University Press.

Weston, D. and Turiel, E. (1980) Act–rule relations: children's concepts of social rules. *Developmental Psychology*, 16, 417–24.

Wetherell, M., Stiven, H., and Potter, J. (1987) Unequal egalitarianism: a preliminary study of discourses concerning gender and employment opportunities. *British Journal of Social Psychology*, 26, 59–71.

Wexler, K. (1982) A principle theory for language acquisition. In E. Wanner and L. R. Gleitman (eds), *Language Acquisition: the state of the art*. Cambridge: Cambridge University Press.

Wexley, K. N. and Pulakos, E. D. (1982) Sex effects on performance ratings in manager–subordinate dyads: a field study. *Journal of Applied Psychology*, 67, 433–9.

Wheeler, L. (1991) A brief history of social comparison theory. In J. Suls and T. A. Wills (eds), *Social Comparison: contemporary theory and research*. Hillsdale, NJ: Erlbaum.

White, J. L., Moffitt, T. E., Earls, F., Robins, L., and Silva, P. A. (1990) How early can we tell? Predictors of childhood conduct disorder and adolescent delinquency. *Criminology*, 28, 507–33.

White, P. A. (1988) Causal processing: origins and development. *Psychological Bulletin*, 104, 36–52.

Whitehurst, G. J. and DeBaryshe, B. D. (1989) Observational learning and language acquisition: principles of learning, systems, and tasks. In G. E. Speidel and K. E. Nelson (eds), *The Many Faces of Imitation in Language Learning*. New York: Springer-Verlag.

Whitehurst, G. J. and Sonnenschein, S. (1981) The development of informative messages in communication: knowing how. In W. P. Dickson (ed.), *Children's Oral Communication Skills*. New York: Academic Press.

Whitehurst, G. J., Arnold, D. S., Epstein, J. N., Angell, A. L., Smith, M., and Fischel, J. E. (1994) A picture book reading intervention in day care and home for children from low-income families. *Developmental Psychology*, 30, 679–89.

Whitehurst, G. J., Falco, F. L., Lonigan, C., Fischel, J. E., DeBaryshe, B. D., Valdez-Menchaca, M. C., and Caulfield, M. (1988) Accelerating language development through picture book reading. *Developmental Psychology*, 24, 552–8.

Whiting, B. B. and Edwards, C. P. (1973) A cross-cultural analysis of sex differences in the behavior of children aged three through eleven. *Journal of Social Psychology*, 91, 177–88.

Whiting, B. B. and Edwards, C. P. (1988) *Children of Different Worlds: the formation of social behavior*. Cambridge, Mass.: Harvard University Press.

Whiting, B. B. and Whiting, J. W. M. (1975) *Children of Six Cultures: a psycho-cultural analysis*. Cambridge, Mass.: Harvard University Press.

Whiting, J. W. M. (1941) *Becoming a Kwoma*. New Haven: Yale University Press.

Whiting, J. W. M. (1959) Sorcery, sin, and the superego: a cross-cultural study of some mechanisms of social control. In M. R. Jones (ed.), *Nebraska Symposium on Motivation*. Lincoln: University of Nebraska Press.

Whiting, J. W. M. (1990) Adolescent rituals and identity conflicts. In J. W. Stigler, R. A. Shweder,

and G. Herdt (eds), *Cultural Psychology: essays on comparative human development*. Cambridge: Cambridge University Press.

Whittaker, S. J. and Robinson, E. J. (1987) An investigation of the consequences of one feature of teacher–child talk for children's awareness of ambiguity in verbal messages. *International Journal of Behavioral Development*, 10, 425–38.

Whitten, P. L. (1987) Infants and adult males. In B. Smuts, D. Cheney, R. Seyfarth, R. Wrangham, and T. Struhsaker (eds), *Primate Societies*. Chicago: University of Chicago Press.

Wicklund, R. A. and Frey, D. (1980) Self-awareness theory: when the self makes a difference. In D. M. Wegner and R. R. Vallacher (eds), *The Self in Social Psychology*. New York: Oxford University Press.

Widdicombe, S. and Wooffitt, R. (1990) "Being" versus "doing" punk: on achieving authenticity as a member. *Journal of Language and Social Psychology*, 9, 257–77.

Widom, C. S. (1989) The cycle of violence. *Science*, 244, 160–6.

Wiemann, J. M. and Giles, H. (1988) Interpersonal communication. In M. Hewstone, W. Stroebe, J.-P. Codol, and G. M. Stephenson (eds), *Introduction to Social Psychology: a European perspective*. Oxford: Blackwell.

Wiersema, B. and van Oudenhoven, J. P. (1992) Effects of cooperation on spelling achievement at three age levels (Grades 2, 4, and 6). *European Journal of Psychology of Education*, 7, 95–108.

Wilke, H. and van Knippenberg, A. (1996) Group performance. In M. Hewstone, W. Stroche, and G. M. Stephenson (eds), *Introduction to Social Psychology*, 2nd edn. Oxford: Blackwell.

Wilkinson, L. C., Wilkinson, A. C., Spinelli, F. and Chiang, C. P. (1984) Metalinguistic knowledge of pragmatic rules in school-age children. *Child Development*, 55, 2130–40.

Will, J. A., Self, P. A., and Datan, N. (1976) Maternal behavior and perceived sex of infant. *American Journal of Orthopsychiatry*, 46, 135–9.

Willard, A. (1988) Cultural scripts for mothering. In C. Gilligan, J. V. Ward, J. M. Taylor, with B. Bardige (eds), *Mapping the Moral Domain: a contribution of women's thinking to psychological theory and education*. Cambridge, Mass.: Harvard University Press.

Willatts, P. (1989) Development of problem-solving in infancy. In A. Slater and G. Bremner (eds), *Infant Development*. Hillsdale, NJ: Erlbaum.

Willemsen, T. M. and van Schie, E. C. M. (1989) Sex stereotypes and responses to juvenile delinquency. *Sex Roles*, 20, 623–38.

Willes, M. (1983) *Children into Pupils: a study of language in early schooling.* London: Routledge and Kegan Paul.

Williams, F. (1976) *Explorations of the Linguistic Attitudes of Teachers.* Rowley, Mass.: Newbury.

Williams, F., LaRose, R., and Frost, F. (1981) *Children, Television and Sex-role Stereotyping.* New York: Praeger.

Williams, J. E. and Best, D. L. (1990) *Measuring Sex Stereotypes: a multination study.* Newbury Park, Calif.: Sage.

Williams, T. M., Joy, L. A., Travis, L., Gotowiec, A., Blum-Steele, M., Aiken, L. S., Painter, S. L., and Davidson, S. M. (1987) Transition to motherhood: a longitudinal study. *Infant Mental Health Journal,* 8, 251–65.

Wills, T. A. (1991) Similarity and self-esteem in downward comparison. In J. Suls and T. A. Wills (eds), *Social Comparison: contemporary theory and research.* Hillsdale, NJ: Erlbaum.

Wilson, E. O. (1975) *Sociobiology: the new synthesis.* Cambridge, Mass.: Harvard University Press.

Wilson, E. O. (1978) *On Human Nature.* Cambridge, Mass.: Harvard University Press.

Wilson, H. (1980) Parental supervision: a neglected aspect of delinquency. *The British Journal of Criminology,* 20, 203–35.

Wilson, M. (1989) Child development in the context of the black extended family. *American Psychologist,* 44, 380–5.

Wilson, T. D. and Linville, P. W. (1982) Improving the performance of college freshmen: attribution theory revisited. *Journal of Personality and Social Psychology,* 42, 367–76.

Wilson, T. D. and Linville, P. W. (1985) Improving the performance of college freshmen with attributional techniques. *Journal of Personality and Social Psychology,* 42, 287–93.

Wimmer, H., Hogrefe, J., and Perner, J. (1988) Children's understanding of information origins as a source of knowledge. *Child Development,* 59, 386–96.

Winefield, H. and Winefield, A. (1992) Psychological development in adolescence and youth: education, employment, and vocational identity. In P. C. L. Heaven (ed.), *Life Span Development.* Sydney and London: Harcourt Brace Jovanovich.

Winnykamen, F. (1990) *Apprendre en imitant?* Paris: Presses Universitaires de France.

Wintre, M., Hicks, R., McVey, G., and Fox, J. (1988) Age and sex differences in choice of consultant for various types of problems. *Child Development,* 59, 1046–55.

Wish, M., Deutsch, M., and Kaplan, S. J. (1976) Perceived dimensions of interpersonal relations. *Journal of Personality and Social Psychology,* 33, 409–20.

Wober, M. and Gunter, B. (1982) Impressions of old people on TV and in real life. *British Journal of Social Psychology,* 21, 335–6.

Wober, M. and Gunter, B. (1988) *Television and Social Control.* Aldershot: Avebury.

Wolfe, D. A., Katell, A., and Drabman, R. S. (1982) Parents' and preschool children's choices of disciplinary child-rearing methods. *Journal of Applied Developmental Psychology,* 3, 167–76.

Wolff, P. (1963) Observations on the early development of smiling. In B. M. Foss (ed.), *Determinants of Infant Behaviour,* vol. 2. London: Methuen.

Wolff, P. (1969) The natural history of crying and other vocalizations in early infancy. In B. M. Foss (ed.), *Determinants of Infant Behaviour,* vol. 4. London: Methuen.

Wolfgang, M. E., Thornberry, T. P., and Figlio, R. M. (1987) *From Boy to Man, from Delinquency to Crime.* Chicago: University of Chicago Press.

Wood, D. (1988) *How Children Think and Learn.* Oxford: Blackwell.

Wood, D. J., Bruner, J. S., and Ross, G. (1976) The role of tutoring in problem solving. *Journal of Child Psychology and Psychiatry,* 17, 89–100.

Wood, D. J., Wood, H. A., and Middleton, D. J. (1978) An experimental evaluation of four face-to-face teaching strategies. *International Journal of Behavioral Development,* 1, 131–47.

Wood, J. V. (1989) Theory and research concerning social comparison of personal attributes. *Psychological Bulletin,* 106, 231–48.

Wood, W., Rhodes, N., and Whelan, M. (1989) Sex differences in positive well-being: a consideration of emotional style and marital status. *Psychological Bulletin,* 106, 249–64.

Woodside, M. (1988) Research on children of alcoholics: past and future. *British Journal of Addiction,* 83, 785–92.

Woody, E. Z. and Costanzo, P. R. (1981) The socialization of obesity-prone behavior. In S. S. Brehm, S. M. Kassin, and F. X. Gibbons (eds), *Developmental Social Psychology: theory and research.* New York: Oxford University Press.

Wright, B. (1994) *Self-help among the Elderly.* New York: Garland.

Wright, E. O., Shire, K., Hwang, S.-L., Dolan, M., and Baxter, J. (1992) The non-effects of class in the gender division of labor in the home: a comparative study of Sweden and the United States. *Gender and Society,* 6, 252–282.

Wright, P. H. (1982) Men's friendships, women's

friendships and the alleged inferiority of the latter. *Sex Roles*, 8, 1–20.

Wundt, W. (1900–20) *Volkerpsychologie*, vols. 1–10. Leipzig: Engelmann.

Yaguchi, K., Otsuka, T., Fujita, T., and Hatano, S. (1987) The relationships between the emotional status and physical activities of the Japanese elderly. *Journal of Human Development*, 23, 42–7.

Yarrow, L. J., Rubenstein, J. L., and Pedersen, F. A. (1975) *Infant and Environment: early cognitive and motivational development*. New York: Wiley.

Yee, M. D. and Brown, R. (1992) Self-evaluations and intergroup attitudes in children aged three to nine. *Child Development*, 63, 619–29.

Yoder, P. J. and Munson, L. J. (in press) The social correlates of coordinated attention to adult and objects in mother–infant interaction, *First Language*.

Young, K. T. (1991) What parents and experts think about infants. In F. S. Kessel, M. H. Bornstein, and A. J. Sameroff (eds), *Contemporary Constructions of the Child: essays in honor of William Kessen*. Hillsdale, NJ: Erlbaum.

Young, W. C., Goy, R. W., and Phoenix, C. H. (1964) Hormones and sexual behavior. *Science*, 143, 212–19.

Youngblade, L. M. and Belsky, J. (1992) Parent–child antecedents of 5-year-olds' close friendships: a longitudinal study. *Developmental Psychology*, 28, 700–13.

Young-Browne, G., Rosenfeld, H. M., and Horowitz, F. D. (1977) Infant discrimination of facial expression. *Child Development*, 48, 555–62.

Younger, A. J., Schwartzman, A. E., and Ledingham, J. E. (1985) Age-related changes in children's perceptions of aggression and withdrawal in their peers. *Developmental Psychology*, 21, 70–5.

Youniss, J. (1989) Parent–adolescent relationships. In W. Damon (ed.), *Child Development Today and Tomorrow*. San Francisco: Jossey-Bass.

Youniss, J. (1992) Parent and peer relations in the emergence of cultural competence. In H. McGurk (ed.), *Childhood Social Development: contemporary perspectives*. Hove: Erlbaum.

Youniss, J. (1994) Children's friendships and peer culture: implications for theories of network and support. In F. Nestemann and K. Hurrelmann (eds), *Social Networks and Social Support in Childhood and Adolescence*. Berlin: de Gruyter.

Youniss, J. and Smollar, J. (1985) *Adolescent Relations with Mothers, Fathers, and Friends*. Chicago: University of Chicago Press.

Youniss, J. and Smollar, J. (1989) Adolescents' interpersonal relationships in social context. In T. J. Berndt and G. W. Ladd (eds), *Peer Relationships in Child Development*. New York: Wiley.

Youniss, J. and Volpe, J. (1978) A relational analysis of children's friendships. In W. Damon (ed.), *New Directions for Child Development*, vol. 1. San Francisco: Jossey-Bass.

Yuill, N. (1984) Young children's coordination of motive and outcome in judgements of satisfaction and morality. *British Journal of Developmental Psychology*, 2, 73–81.

Yuill, N. (1992) Children's production and comprehension of trait terms. *British Journal of Developmental Psychology*, 10, 131–42.

Yuill, N. (1993) Understanding of personality and dispositions. In M. Bennett (ed.), *The Child as Psychologist: an introduction to the development of social cognition*. New York: Harvester Wheatsheaf.

Yussen, S. R. and Levy, V. M. (1975) Developmental changes in predicting one's own span of short-term memory. *Journal of Experimental Child Psychology*, 19, 502–8.

Zahn-Waxler, C. and Kochanska, G. (1990) The origins of guilt. In R. A. Thompson (ed.), *Socioemotional Development: Nebraska symposium on motivation, 1988*. Lincoln: University of Nebraska Press.

Zahn-Waxler, C., Cole, P. M., and Barrett, K. C. (1991) Guilt and empathy: sex differences and implications for the development of depression. In J. Garber and K. A. Dodge (eds), *The Development of Emotion Regulation and Dysregulation*. Cambridge: Cambridge University Press.

Zahn-Waxler, C., Cole, P. M., Richardson, D. T., Friedman, R. J., Michel, M. K., and Belouad, F. (1994) Social problem solving in disruptive preschool children: reactions to hypothetical situations of conflict and distress. *Merrill-Palmer Quarterly*, 40, 98–119.

Zahn-Waxler, C., Iannotti, R. J., Cummings, E. M., and Denham, S. (1990) Antecedents of problem behaviors in children of depressed mothers. *Development and Psychopathology*, 2, 271–91.

Zahn-Waxler, C., Radke-Yarrow, M., and King, R. A. (1979) Child rearing and children's prosocial initiations toward victims of distress. *Child Development*, 50, 319–30.

Zahn-Waxler, C., Radke-Yarrow, M., Wagner, E., and Chapman, M. (1992) Development of concern for others. *Developmental Psychology*, 28, 126–36.

Zaitsev, S. V. (1992) What we wish to study in the child (or about adult "egocentrism"). *Journal of Russian and East European Psychology*, 30, 41–59.

Zajonc, R. B. (1965) Social facilitation. *Science*, 149, 269–74.

Zani, B. (1991) Male and female patterns in the discovery of sexuality during adolescence. *Journal of Adolescence*, 14, 163–78.

Zanna, M., Goethals, G., and Hill, J. (1975) Evaluating a sex-related ability: social comparison with similar others and standard setters. *Journal of Experimental Social Psychology*, 11, 86–93.

Zarbatany, L., Hartmann, D. P., and Rankin, D. B. (1990) The psychological functions of preadolescent peer activities. *Child Development*, 61, 1067–80.

Zayas, L. H. (1987) Toward an understanding of suicide risks in young Hispanic females. *Journal of Adolescent Research*, 2, 1–11.

Zebrowitz, L. A. (1990) *Social Perception*. Milton Keynes: Open University Press.

Zebrowitz, L., Olson, K., and Hoffman, K. (1993) Stability of babyfaceness and attractiveness across the lifespan. *Journal of Personality and Social Psychology*, 64, 453–66.

Zelnik, M. and Kantner, J. (1979) Reasons for nonuse of contraception by sexually active women aged 15–19. *Family Planning Perspectives*, 11, 289–96.

Zelnik, M., Kantner, J. F. and Ford, K. (1981) *Sex and Pregnancy in Adolescence*. Beverly Hills, Calif.: Sage.

Zeskind, P. S. (1980) Adult responses to cries of low and high risk infants. *Infant Behavior and Development*, 3, 167.

Zeskind, P. S. (1985) A developmental perspective of infant crying. In B. M. Lester and C. F. Z. Boukydis (eds), *Infant Crying: theoretical and research perspectives*. New York: Plenum Press.

Zeskind, P. S. (1987) Adult heart-rate responses to infant cry sounds. *British Journal of Developmental Psychology*, 5, 73–9.

Zeskind, P. S. and Collins, V. (1987) Pitch of infant crying and caregiver responses in a natural setting. *Infant Behavior and Development*, 10, 501–4.

Zeskind, P. S., Klein, L., and Marshall, T. R. (1992) Adults' perceptions of experimental modifications of durations of pauses and expiratory sounds in infant crying. *Developmental Psychology*, 28, 1153–62.

Zeskind, P. S., Sale, J., Maio, M. L., Huntington, L., and Weiseman, J. R. (1985) Adult perceptions of pain and hunger cries: a synchrony of arousal. *Child Development*, 56, 549–54.

Zinchenko, V. P. (1985) Vygotsky's ideas about units for the analysis of mind. In J. V. Wertsch (ed.), *Culture, Communication, and Cognition: Vygotskian perspectives*. Cambridge: Cambridge University Press.

Zinober, B. and Martlew, M. (1985) The development of communicative gestures. In M. D. Barrett (ed.), *Children's Single-word Speech*. Chichester: Wiley.

Zivin, G. S. (1982) Watching the sands shift: conceptualising development of nonverbal mastery. In R. S. Feldman (ed.), *Development of Nonverbal Behavior in Children*. New York: Springer-Verlag.

Zuckerman, D. M., Singer, D. G., and Singer, J. L. (1980) Children's television viewing, racial and sex-role attitudes. *Journal of Applied Social Psychology*, 10, 281–94.

Zukow, P. G. (1989) Siblings as effective socializing agents: evidence from Central Mexico. In P. G. Zukow (ed.), *Sibling Interaction across Cultures*. New York: Springer-Verlag.

Author Index

Subject Index